THE EPISTLES OF JOHN

VOLUME 30

The ANCHOR BIBLE is a fresh approach to the world's greatest classic. Its object is to make the Bible accessible to the modern reader; its method is to arrive at the meaning of biblical literature through exact translation and extended exposition, and to reconstruct the ancient setting of the biblical story, as well as the circumstances of its transcription and the characteristics of its transcribers.

THE ANCHOR BIBLE is a project of international and interfaith scope: Protestant, Catholic, and Jewish scholars from many countries contribute individual volumes. The project is not sponsored by any ecclesiastical organization and is not intended to reflect any particular theological doctrine. Prepared under our joint supervision, THE ANCHOR BIBLE is an effort to make available all the significant historical and linguistic knowledge which bears on the interpretation of the biblical record.

This project marks the beginning of a new era of co-operation among scholars in biblical research, thus forming a common body of knowledge to be shared by all.

William Foxwell Albright
David Noel Freedman
GENERAL EDITORS

THE ANCHOR BIBLE

The Epistles of John

TRANSLATED WITH

INTRODUCTION,

NOTES, AND COMMENTARY

BY

RAYMOND E. BROWN

THE ANCHOR BIBLE
DOUBLEDAY
NEW YORK   LONDON   TORONTO   SYDNEY   AUCKLAND

THE ANCHOR BIBLE
PUBLISHED BY DOUBLEDAY
a division of Bantam Doubleday Dell Publishing Group, Inc.
666 Fifth Avenue, New York, New York 10103

THE ANCHOR BIBLE, DOUBLEDAY and the portrayal of an anchor
with the letters AB are trademarks of Doubleday, a division of
Bantam Doubleday Dell Publishing Group, Inc.

NIHIL OBSTAT
Myles M. Bourke, S.S.L., S.T.D., *Censor Deputatus*

IMPRIMATUR
Joseph T. O'Keefe, *Vicar-General*
Archdiocese of New York
January 4, 1982

The *nihil obstat* and *imprimatur* are official declarations that a book or pamphlet is
free of doctrinal or moral error. No implication is contained therein that those who
have granted the *nihil obstat* and *imprimatur* agree with the content, opinions, or
statements expressed.

Library of Congress Cataloging in Publication Data
Bible. N.T. Epistles of John. English. Brown. 1982.
The Epistles of John.
(The Anchor Bible; v. 30)
Bibliography: p. 131.
Includes indexes.
1. Bible. N.T. Epistles of John—Commentaries.
I. Brown, Raymond Edward. II. Title. III. Series.
BS192.2.A1 1964.G3 vol. 30 [BS2803] 227′.94077
AACR2
Library of Congress Catalog Card Number 81–43380

ISBN 0–385–05686–9

With Personal Gratitude
To
Archbishop Jean Jadot
Apostolic Delegate in the United States (1973–1980)

In his role of representing the care of the preeminent
Presbyter of the Universal Church for the Church in the
United States, he illustrated so well the sentiments
uttered long ago by the Johannine Presbyter writing
about a church at a distance:

*Nothing gives me greater joy than to hear
that my children are walking in the truth*

(III John 4)

PREFACE

To explain my purpose and approach in this commentary, I need at once to say a few substantive words about the Johannine Epistles it discusses. II and III John are the shortest writings in the New Testament (henceforth NT). They are one-page letters written by a man who calls himself "the Presbyter." In II John, while he is associated with one church (v. 13), the Presbyter writes directions to another church which he addresses symbolically as "an Elect Lady and her children" (v. 1). He stresses the need for love within that church and insists on the exclusion of teachers who may arrive denying "Jesus Christ coming in the flesh" (v. 7). In III John, the Presbyter writes to Gaius praising him for the hospitality he has shown to itinerant missionaries and urging him to receive others who will come, especially Demetrius (v. 12). The reason for addressing the letter to Gaius is that the Presbyter's previous letter "to the church" (v. 9) had been ignored by Diotrephes who likes to be first in the church, and who refuses to welcome any missionaries and, indeed, expels from the church anyone who does (v. 10). In both letters the Presbyter expresses a hope to visit the addressees; but in III John he warns that, if he comes to Diotrephes' church, he will bring up the matter of that leader's hostility toward him.

The author of the much longer I John never identifies himself by a title; and while by analogy his work is classified as a letter in our Bible, nothing within it suggests that. The main concern of I John is to reinforce the belief and morality of the readers against a group that is doing the work of the devil and of the Antichrist (2:18; 4:1–6), a group that has seceded from the Community (2:19) but is still trying to win more adherents. Their errors are both christological and ethical. By not acknowledging Jesus Christ come in the flesh, they negate the importance of Jesus (4:2–3); and although they claim communion with God, they do not see any importance in keeping commandments and pretend to be free from the guilt of sin (1:6,8; 2:4). In particular, they do not show love for the brothers (2:9–11; 3:10–24; 4:7–21). Over and over again the author offers criteria for a right stance against such errors, so that a famous study of I John by Robert Law has been perceptively entitled *The Tests of Life.*

The three Epistles have sometimes been praised as a splendid recall to fundamentals, offering a sound basis for Christian doctrine. There is no doubt that occasionally the author of I John rises to eloquence, particularly in his description of love: "God is love. . . . In this, then, does love consist: not that we have loved God but that He loved us and sent His Son as an atonement for our sins" (4:8–10). No more practical test has ever been offered than that found in 4:20: "The person who has no love for his brother whom he has seen cannot love the God he has never seen." And there is perceptive conciseness in the author's summary of Christian obligation: "We are to believe the name of His Son, Jesus Christ; and we are to love one another just as He gave us the command" (3:23).

But despite these glorious moments, I cannot agree that the Epistles really *stand by themselves* as masterpieces of early Christian teaching. No other Epistle in the NT, with the possible exception of Hebrews, tells us less about its author than does I John. Indeed, it is a guess that the three Epistles are all by the same person, based chiefly on the fact that II John and I John seem to attack the same errors and use similar expressions. In I John it is virtually impossible to detect a structured sequence of thought, and the author repeats himself from chapter to chapter. Despite the almost elementary character of his Greek, the author's sentences are often infuriatingly obscure (1:1–4; 3:19–20), as is his symbolism, even when he is making a major point (5:5–8,15–17). It has been said with only moderate exaggeration that, because of grammatical impreciseness, every sentence in I John can be interpreted in three different ways. And this impreciseness seems to carry over into thought. For example, the author condemns those who boast, "We are free from the guilt of sin. . . . We have not sinned" (1:8,10), only himself to assert that everyone who abides in Christ does not commit sin and cannot be a sinner (3:6,9). The readers are told to live *just as* Christ did (2:6; 3:3,7), but there is no information at all on how Christ did live. Despite his vigorous condemnations of his opponents, we know little about their thought, so that scholars have to debate whether there were many groups or one, whether they were Jews or Christians, whether their condemned christology was too low (Jesus was not the Messiah or the Son of God) or too high (the Son of God has come but he was not truly human). Over against them, the author insists on the necessity of keeping the commandments; yet he never tells us what these commandments are, except the commandment to love one another (3:23; 4:21). And it is precisely on the issue of love that we encounter the great anomaly in the Johannine Epistles. The most eloquent NT author on the necessity of love is singularly unloving in dealing with those who disagree with him. He vilifies the opponents who had been members of his own Community as demonic Antichrists, false prophets, and liars (2:18–22; 4:1–6; II John 7) who should not be allowed through the door or even receive ordinary greetings (II John 10).

Indeed, their sin is so deadly that one should not even pray about it (I John 5:16–17).

After these somewhat unflattering remarks, how can I justify a long commentary on the Johannine Epistles? The key words in the opening sentence of the preceding paragraph were "stand by themselves." The author of the Epistles (if for the moment we accept that there was only one author) never dreamed that his encouragement to his readers against adversaries would be read in isolation from his Community's tradition which made his remarks intelligible. Not only did he presuppose this tradition, but he referred to it over and over again as what was "from the beginning" (I John 1:1; 2:13,14,24) and "the word you already heard" (2:7). Indeed (after the Prologue), the opening words of I John are: "This is the gospel that we have heard from Christ and declare to you" (1:5)—a gospel that, the author says, is "the gospel that you heard from the beginning" (3:11). Now, while we do not have preserved for us all the Community tradition that the author presupposed, we have a magnificent specimen of that tradition in *The Gospel According to John* (henceforth GJohn), a Gospel with a peculiar theology and style in which the epistolary author has immersed himself. (He has done this to the degree that only an expert can remember whether an isolated Johannine quotation, like "God is Spirit" or "God is light," is to be found in GJohn or in I John.) The Johannine Epistles must be understood, therefore, not by themselves but in relation to GJohn.

My understanding that it is important to relate the Epistles to GJohn goes beyond the obvious. I maintain that the struggle in I and II John between the author and his opponents is centered on two contrary interpretations of the Johannine Community's tradition as known to us in GJohn. Two groups of Johannine disciples are fighting each other over their ideas about Jesus, about the Christian life, about eschatology, and about the Spirit. Read thus, the Johannine Epistles acquire a value beyond their self-contained message. They tell us what happened to the Community that thought of itself as the heir to "the disciple whom Jesus loved" (John 21:24), the disciple who understood Jesus better than did even the most famous of the Twelve, Peter. This Community fought "the Jews" (John 9:22) and even other believers (8:31ff.) in the name of an exalted christology wherein Jesus could speak of having existed before the world began (17:5) and could claim, "Whoever has seen me has seen the Father" (14:9). But in the Epistles we find the polemic artillery turned around and aimed at former members of the Community who claimed an even more "progressive" evaluation of Jesus (II John 9). Thanks to the Epistles, we discover that the profound and innovative christology of GJohn also contained dangers, so that a drama of community history, religious sociology, and theological development unfolds before our eyes.

Indeed, it may be claimed that in some ways through the combination of
GJohn and the Epistles critically interpreted, we can discover more about
the internal history of the Johannine Community than we know about any
other NT churches, except the Pauline. It is a knowledge that stretches
from "the beginning" (I John 1:1) to "the last hour" (2:18). The attempt to have the Epistles make sense within such a history has made
writing this commentary exciting for me, and I hope I can bring my
readers to share some of the excitement.

                            *   *   *

No writer can hope to persuade many readers to approach his book exactly as he intends it to be read. But for students who are seriously working through the Johannine Epistles for the first time, let me recommend
that the INTRODUCTION be read twice, once before reading the commentary proper and once afterwards. In the INTRODUCTION I have to expound
the intricate problems that make these Epistles a battleground of scholarly
disagreement and to give reasons for my views about the community's life
situation. The comprehensive view presented therein is necessary in order
to understand the line-by-line commentary. On the other hand, only when
readers have plowed through the Epistles, attempting to understand every
line, can they come back to the INTRODUCTION and make intelligent personal judgments as to whether I saw the problems and dealt with them all.

After the INTRODUCTION I divide the Epistles into units. The detection
of what the author intended as a unit is no easy task, but stylistic devices
and cohesiveness of thought supply a guide. The discussion of each unit
begins with the translation made from a critically established Greek text.
My English rendering of the Greek is more concerned with fidelity to the
author's way of expression (and to his ambiguity) than with literary polish. (I am more literal than I was in my GJohn translation:[1] GJohn can
be reasonably called a literary masterpiece, but by no stretch of the imagination can that designation be justified for the Epistles.) If reviewers
choose to complain that occasionally the English translation could be
smoother, a partial response is, "So could the Greek original." The translation in each unit is followed by detailed NOTES, which serve as a vehicle
for factual and technical information, e.g., textual issues, problems of
translation, disputed interpretations. The basic meaning of the unit *as I
understand it* and how it fits into the author's overall outlook are the subject of the COMMENT, which follows the NOTES. Perhaps I should explain
why the NOTES in this volume, proportionately to the COMMENT, are
much longer than those in ABJ. There are two reasons. First, because of
the length of GJohn (15,416 words in Greek), even my 1,400-page com-

---

[1] In citing GJohn I shall generally use my own translation in the *Anchor Bible*,
vols. 29 and 29A (henceforth ABJ), although sometimes for the sake of comparison
I shall have to translate individual GJohn passages more literally.

mentary was not long enough to permit careful comparative studies of Johannine vocabulary and style. The much shorter Epistles (2,601 words; one-sixth the length) allow space in the NOTES for such studies; and indeed they are now necessary because of questions as to whether the epistolary author is the same as the evangelist and to what extent the thought of the Epistles differs from that of GJohn. A second reason for lengthy NOTES is the pervading obscurity of the grammar in these Epistles, as mentioned above. Since competent scholars are divided about the meaning of almost every verse,[2] interpretations need to be debated at length. There were far fewer of these detailed debates pertinent to GJohn, and they could be incorporated into the COMMENT. But to do that here would be to make the COMMENT unreadable and cause readers to come away with the impression of endless disagreements and no clear line of thought. Therefore I have chosen to put the debates in the NOTES and to base the COMMENT on the view that I think most reasonable. Obviously this decision has a disadvantage for those who choose to read only the COMMENT: They may not be aware of the wide diversity of interpretations. But this can be remedied by even a brief glance at the NOTES (and in footnotes in the COMMENT I shall call attention to important NOTES).[3] In my judgment, the gain of having the COMMENT mean something clear and sequential outweighs the disadvantages. By no means, then, do I invite the reader to skip the NOTES, for they represent the core of scholarship in this volume and contain its most significant material. My method is rather an attempt to protect the reader from losing sight of the forest because of the trees.

Read sequentially, then, the COMMENT alone offers an explanation of I, II, and III John of manageable length for the person who wishes an overall view. The commentary as a whole, on the other hand, with its lengthy NOTES offers resource material for those who need full and detailed information on individual passages. I have made a conscious effort to meet the needs of various kinds of readers.

In Appendix I there are charts comparing the Epistles to each other and to GJohn. (They are most pertinent to the INTRODUCTION; but since they are also called upon later in the commentary, they seemed better placed together where they can be found more easily.) Appendix II discusses Cerinthus, frequently proposed as the adversary attacked in I

[2] When I attach the names of a group of scholars to one or the other view about a problem, I do not pretend to list everyone who holds that view. The lists are meant only to give the reader a sense of the division and its importance. Because I shall inevitably make mistakes and because scholars sometimes phrase themselves ambiguously, I apologize in advance if I have misclassified a scholar on a particular issue.

[3] My attempt to be thorough in the NOTES by explaining various views in detail should mean that scholars and teachers who do not agree with my choice as expressed in the COMMENT have all they need in the NOTES to propose another theory.

John; and Appendixes III and IV deal with special questions arising from Latin additions to I John. Appendix V treats epistolary format as a background for the structure of II and III John. To encourage further reading there are ample bibliographies, both general (as the last unit of the INTRODUCTION) and sectional (following each unit). While I hope that my personal insights are of value, it is my goal to have summarized for the readers a broad range of scholarship. The bibliographies represent my tribute and my debt to all who have gone before. In this commentary, as in others I have written, I shall be gratified if I have covered previous work with enough thoroughness to have provided a convenient basis for subsequent reflection and a text presupposed in continuing study.

*   *   *

Part of the research for this volume was done in Jerusalem while I was on sabbatical leave from Union Theological Seminary (N.Y.), and I am indebted to the Albright Institute of Archaeological Research (the "American School" of yore) for having hosted me as its annual professor during that period, and to the Dominican *Ecole Biblique* for the gracious use of its library. Another half-year sabbatical, during which I did part of the first draft, was spent at St. Patrick's Seminary, Menlo Park, California, at the invitation of Archbishop John R. Quinn of San Francisco; and I wish to express my gratitude to him and to the seminary rector and faculty for a purely disinterested act of hospitality. Professor John Kselman of that seminary and now of the Catholic University of America, Washington, D.C., has helped me significantly on this volume, as in previous writings, by reading the typescript and catching mistakes. Stephenson Brooks, Marion Soards, Robert Van Voorst, and Robert Wollenburg, doctoral candidates at Union Seminary, graciously assisted by verifying biblical and bibliographical references in my typescript or by reading galley proofs.

Once again I am in the debt of the *Anchor Bible* personnel, in particular, Noel Freedman, Eve Roshevsky, Donald Hunt, and Cyrus Rogers— each a great help in a specific way through editing and encouragement. Perhaps Doubleday's greatest kindness has been its patience in allowing me, after I finished the two-volume ABJ commentary (1970), to turn to a commentary on the infancy narratives in Matthew and Luke, *The Birth of the Messiah* (1977), before completing the volume on the Epistles of John. The decade between my studies of the two parts of the Johannine corpus has been a godsend, for it has given me the necessary distance to see the whole history of the Johannine Community and to profit from dialogue with the very important work of my Union Seminary colleague, J. L. Martyn. If I had written the commentary on the Epistles right after that on GJohn, it would have been competent, I hope, but perhaps without excitement. My vision of these Epistles as the record of a theological life-and-death struggle within a Community at the end of the first century has made me want to make them more familiar to readers (and even to churches) at the end of the twentieth century. If I am right, the author of these Epistles wrestled in microcosm with problems that have tortured Christianity ever since and that are still with us today.

RAYMOND E. BROWN
Easter 1981

CONTENTS

THE FIRST EPISTLE OF JOHN

PRINCIPAL ABBREVIATIONS

Besides the standard abbreviations of books of the Bible used in the series:

Deuterocanonical Books of the OT:

Tob	Tobit
I & II Macc	I & II Maccabees
Sir	Sirach or Ecclesiasticus
Wis	Wisdom of Solomon
Bar	Baruch

Apocryphal Books related to the OT:

Jub.	*Jubilees*
En.	*Enoch* (Ethiopic) or *Henoch*
III, IV Macc.	*III, IV Maccabees*
II Bar.	*II Baruch* (Syriac)
Pss. Sol.	*Psalms of Solomon*
T. Levi etc.	*Testament of Levi,* and similarly for the testament of each patriarch contained in the *Testaments of the Twelve Patriarchs*

Early Christian and Patristic Writings:

Barn.	*Epistle of Barnabas*
I & II Clem.	*I & II Clement*
Did.	*Didache*
Hermas Man.	*Shepherd of Hermas, Mandate*
Hermas Sim.	*Shepherd of Hermas, Similitude*
Hermas Vis.	*Shepherd of Hermas, Vision*
Ign. *Eph.*	Ignatius, *Letter to the Ephesians*
Ign. *Magn.*	Ignatius, *Letter to the Magnesians*
Ign. *Phld.*	Ignatius, *Letter to the Philadelphians*
Ign. *Rom.*	Ignatius, *Letter to the Romans*
Ign. *Smyrn.*	Ignatius, *Letter to the Smyrnaeans*
Ign. *Trall.*	Ignatius, *Letter to the Trallians*
Pol. *Philip.*	Polycarp, *Letter to the Philippians*

Abbreviations of the Dead Sea (Qumran) Scrolls; Rabbinic Works:

CD	Cairo (Genizah text of) *Damascus Document*
1Q, 2Q	Numbered caves of Qumran
1QH	*Hôdāyôt* or *Thanksgiving Hymns* (of Cave 1)

1QpHab	*Pesher* (Commentary) on Habakkuk
1QM	*War Scroll*
1QS	*Manual of Discipline* or *Community Rule*
1QSa	Appendix A to the *Community Rule*
TalBab	Babylonian Talmud
TalJer	Jerusalem Talmud

Abbreviations of Publications, Versions, etc.:

AB	Anchor Bible
ABJ	*The Gospel According to John* by R. E. Brown (Anchor Bible 29 & 29A; Garden City, N.Y.: Doubleday, 1966, 1970)
AnBib	Analecta Biblica
ANF	The Ante-Nicene Fathers
AsSeign	Assemblées du Seigneur
ATR	Anglican Theological Review
ATRsupp.ser.	Anglican Theological Review, supplementary series
AUSS	Andrews University Seminary Studies
BAG	W. Bauer (as translated by W. F. Arndt and F. W. Gingrich), *A Greek-English Lexicon of the New Testament* (University of Chicago, 1957)
BAGD	W. Bauer (as translated by W. F. Arndt, F. W. Gingrich, and F. W. Danker), *A Greek-English Lexicon of the New Testament* (2d ed.; University of Chicago, 1979)
BDB	F. Brown, S. R. Driver, and C. A. Briggs, *Hebrew and English Lexicon of the Old Testament* (Oxford: Clarendon, 1907)
BDF	F. Blass and A. Debrunner (as translated by R. W. Funk), *A Greek Grammar of the New Testament and Other Early Christian Literature* (University of Chicago, 1961). References to sections.
BeO	Bibbia e Oriente
BETL	Bibliotheca Ephemeridum Theologicarum Lovaniensium
BFCT	Beiträge zur Förderung christlicher Theologie
BibLeb	Bibel und Leben
BibSac	Bibliotheca Sacra
BibS(F)	Biblische Studien (Freiburg)
BJRL	Bulletin of the John Rylands Library (Manchester)
BT	Bible Translator
BTB	Biblical Theology Bulletin
BU	Biblische Untersuchungen
BVC	Bible et Vie Chrétienne
BZ	Biblische Zeitschrift
BZNW	Beihefte zur Zeitschrift für die neutestamentliche Wissenschaft
CBQ	Catholic Biblical Quarterly
CC	Corpus Christianorum

CPL	*Clavis Patrum Latinorum* (CC, 2d ed., 1961)
CSCO	Corpus Scriptorum Christianorum Orientalium (Louvain)
CSEL	Corpus Scriptorum Ecclesiasticorum Latinorum (Vienna)
CTM	Concordia Theological Monthly
DBS	H. Denzinger and C. Bannwart, *Enchiridion Symbolorum,* rev. by A. Schönmetzer (32 ed.; Freiburg: Herder, 1963). References to sections.
DBSup	Dictionnaire de la Bible—Supplément
EB	Etudes Bibliques
EKK	Evangelisch-katholischer Kommentar zum Neuen Testament
EspVie	Esprit et Vie
EstBib	Estudios Bíblicos
EstEcl	Estudios Eclesiásticos
ETL	Ephemerides Theologicae Lovanienses
EvT	Evangelische Theologie
ExpT	Expository Times
FRLANT	Forschungen zur Religion und Literatur des Alten und Neuen Testaments
GCS	Die Griechischen Christlichen Schriftsteller (Berlin)
GPM	Göttinger Predigt-Meditationen
HNT	Handbuch zum Neuen Testament
HNTC	Harper's New Testament Commentaries
HSNT	Die Heilige Schrift des Neuen Testamentes
HSNTA	E. Hennecke and W. Schneemelcher, *New Testament Apocrypha* (2 vols.; Philadelphia: Westminster, 1963, 1965)
HTKNT	Herders theologischer Kommentar zum Neuen Testament
HTR	Harvard Theological Review
IBNTG	*An Idiom-Book of New Testament Greek* by C.F.D. Moule (Cambridge University, 1960)
ICC	International Critical Commentary
IEJ	Israel Exploration Journal
Int	Interpretation
ITQ	Irish Theological Quarterly
JAOS	Journal of the American Oriental Society
JB	Jerusalem Bible (Eng. transl. of SBJ)
JBC	*The Jerome Biblical Commentary,* ed. R. E. Brown *et al.* (Englewood Cliffs, N.J.: Prentice-Hall, 1968). References to articles and sections.
JBL	Journal of Biblical Literature
JEH	Journal of Ecclesiastical History
JR	Journal of Religion
JTS	Journal of Theological Studies
KD	Kerygma und Dogma
KJV	King James Version or Authorized Version
LavTheolPhil	Laval Théologique et Philosophique
LD	Lectio Divina

LFAE	*Light from the Ancient East* by A. Deissmann (rev. ed.; New York: Doran, 1927)
LJ	*The Legends of the Jews* by L. Ginzberg (7 vols.; Philadelphia: Jewish Publication Society, 1909–38)
LumVie	Lumière et Vie
LXX	Septuagint
MeyerK	(H.A.W. Meyer) Kritisch-exegetischer Kommentar über das Neue Testament
MGNTG	J. H. Moulton, *Grammar of New Testament Greek* (4 vols.; Edinburgh: Clark, 1908–76)
MNTC	Moffatt New Testament Commentary
MS.	Manuscript
MT	Masoretic Text
MTZ	Münchener theologische Zeitschrift
NAB	New American Bible
NEB	New English Bible
NHL	*The Nag Hammadi Library,* ed. J. M. Robinson (New York: Harper & Row, 1977)
NICNT	New International Commentary on the New Testament
NovT	Novum Testamentum
NovTSup	Novum Testamentum, Supplements
NRT	Nouvelle Revue Théologique
NT	New Testament
NTA	New Testament Abstracts
NTAbh	Neutestamentliche Abhandlungen
NTBD	*The New Testament Background: Selected Documents,* ed. C. K. Barrett (London: SPCK, 1956)
NTD	Neue Testament Deutsch
NTS	New Testament Studies
OL	Old Latin
OS	Old Syriac
OT	Old Testament
PG	Patrologia Graeca-Latina (Migne)
PL	Patrologia Latina (Migne)
RB	Revue Biblique
RechBib	Recherches Bibliques
RevExp	Review and Expositor
RevQ	Revue de Qumran
RevThom	Revue Thomiste
RGG	Religion in Geschichte und Gegenwart (3d ed., unless otherwise indicated)
RHE	Revue d'Histoire Ecclésiastique
RHPR	Revue d'Histoire et de Philosophie Religieuses
RNT	Regensburger Neues Testament
RSR	Recherches de Science Religieuse
RSV	Revised Standard Version
RV	Revised Version

SBFLA	Studii Biblici Franciscani Liber Annuus
SBJ	La Sainte Bible de Jérusalem
SBLASP	Society of Biblical Literature Abstracts and Seminar Papers
SBLDS	Society of Biblical Literature Dissertation Series
SBLMS	Society of Biblical Literature Monograph Series
SBLSBS	Society of Biblical Literature Sources for Biblical Study
SBS	Stuttgarter Bibelstudien
SBT	Studies in Biblical Theology
SC	Sources Chrétiennes
SNTSMS	Society for New Testament Studies Monograph Series
SP	*Sacra Pagina*, ed. J. Coppens *et al.* (Louvain, 1959)
SSNT	*Semitische Syntax im Neuen Testament* by K. Beyer (Göttingen: Vandenhoeck & Ruprecht, 1962)
St-B	H. L. Strack and P. Billerbeck, *Kommentar zum Neuen Testament aus Talmud und Midrasch* (5 vols.; Munich: Beck, 1922–55)
StEv	Studia Evangelica (Papers from the Oxford International Congresses of NT Studies; Berlin: Akademie Verlag)
TBC	Torch Bible Commentaries
TCGNT	*A Textual Commentary on the Greek New Testament* by B. M. Metzger (New York: United Bible Societies, 1971)
TCNT	Twentieth Century New Testament
TD	Theology Digest
TDNT	*Theological Dictionary of the New Testament,* ed. G. Kittel and G. Friedrich
TEV	Today's English Version
TG	Theologie und Glaube
TheolRund	Theologische Rundschau
THKNT	Theologischer Handkommentar zum Neuen Testament
THLJ	*A Translator's Handbook on the Letters of John* by C. Haas, M. de Jonge, and J. L. Swellengrebel (London: United Bible Societies, 1972)
TLZ	Theologische Literaturzeitung
TQ	Theologische Quartalschrift
TS	Theological Studies
TSK	Theologische Studien und Kritiken
TU	Texte und Untersuchungen
TZ	Theologische Zeitschrift
UBSGNT	United Bible Societies Greek New Testament
VC	Vigiliae Christianae
VD	Verbum Domini
WMANT	Wissenschaftliche Monographien zum Alten und Neuen Testament
WUNT	Wissenschaftliche Untersuchungen zum Neuen Testament
ZAGNT	M. Zerwick, *An Analysis of the Greek New Testament* (2 vols.; Rome: Biblical Institute, 1974, 1979)
ZAW	Zeitschrift für die alttestamentliche Wissenschaft

ZBG	M. Zerwick, *Biblical Greek* (Rome: Biblical Institute, 1963). References to sections.
ZKG	Zeitschrift für Kirchengeschichte
ZNW	Zeitschrift für die neutestamentliche Wissenschaft
ZTK	Zeitschrift für Theologie und Kirche
ZWT	Zeitschrift für wissenschaftliche Theologie

* * *

par.	Parallel verses, particularly in other Synoptic Gospels.
*	Indicates the original hand of a manuscript, as distinct from later correctors.
( )	In the OT, the KJV and RSV verse enumeration sometimes differs from the Hebrew enumeration followed by most other translations. I always follow the Hebrew, putting the RSV number in parentheses. Similarly, when the LXX enumeration of chapters differs from the Hebrew, I always give the Hebrew enumeration, even when I am discussing Greek words. Sometimes, as in Jeremiah, I give the LXX enumeration in parentheses; but I assume that the reader knows that in the Psalter the LXX enumeration is generally one psalm behind the Hebrew (MT Ps 130 = LXX Ps 129).
GJohn	In references to the Fourth Gospel that involve chapter and verse I shall use the designation John; but where no numbers are involved John can be ambiguous, for it covers both the (putative) author and the Gospel. In those instances I always use GJohn for the Gospel.
(?)	In a list of scholars who hold a particular view, a question mark behind a scholar's name generally means that the scholar has given tentative support to the view; occasionally it means that the scholar's mind is not clear to me.

For patristic works that are easily available I give book, chapter, and section (Apostolic Fathers; Justin; Irenaeus' *Adversus haereses* [*Adv. haer.*]; Origen's *Contra Celsum;* Eusebius' *Historia ecclesiastica* [*Hist.*]). For others, I give the edition (CC, CSEL, GCS, PG, PL), volume, and page number as well. The *Apostolic Constitutions* are cited according to the edition of F. X. Funk (2 vols.; Paderborn: Schoeningh, 1906); and the *Didascalia Apostolorum* according to the edition of R. H. Connolly (Oxford: Clarendon, 1929). The Mandaean works are cited according to the editions of the respective titles by M. Lidzbarski.

Introduction

I. Information from Tradition*

Of the 27 books of the NT, all but 6 are commonly classified as epistles or letters.[1] Among the 21 epistles, the 13 in the Pauline collection are entitled according to their named recipients (Romans, Timothy, etc.). The non-Pauline Epistle to the Hebrews is entitled according to the recipients as surmised from the contents. The remaining 7 epistles are entitled according to their authors who in the instances of James, I and II Peter, and Jude are named in the writings themselves, but surmised in the instances of I, II, and III John.

A. *Designation as Catholic Epistles and Epistles of John*

Already in the fourth century Eusebius (*Hist.* 2.23.25) records that the adjective *katholikos* ("universal") was being applied to these seven,[2] whence the frequent designation "Catholic Epistles" or "General Epistles." This adjective may have been used originally of I John[3] and then have spread to the other six. In the East the designation was generally understood to say something about the recipients: the seven were not letters addressed to a particular community, as were the Pauline Epistles to

* This chapter is the most technical in the INTRODUCTION. While logically the information it contains belongs first, the nonspecialist may prefer to treat it as a reference source and to begin reading with II.

[1] In footnote 191 below I shall discuss whether there is a difference between an epistle and a letter. The 6 exceptions are the 4 Gospels, Acts, and Revelation (Apocalypse); but even the last mentioned begins with letters to the seven churches.

[2] The history of how the non-Johannine epistles among the 7 were accepted into the canon does not concern us here. Symbolic significance may have governed the number 7, especially where (with the inclusion of Hebrews) the Pauline collection was counted at 14. The arrangement that has become common (James, I-II Peter, I-II-III John, Jude) was probably determined in part by the order of names in Gal 2:9. Some early codices and church writers (Alexandrinus, Athanasius, Jerome, Cyril of Alexandria) placed these epistles after the Acts of the Apostles, indicating the belief that the authors were of apostolic status.

[3] Apollonius, an anti-Montanist writer *ca.* A.D. 200, charged Themiso with composing a certain *katholikē epistolē* in imitation of the apostle (John?—see Eusebius, *Hist.* 5.18.5). Among the Johannine Epistles I John retained its status as *the* Catholic Epistle, as we see in the title supplied by the ninth-century Codex L: "Catholic Epistle of the Holy Apostle John."

Rome or Corinth, but encyclicals addressed to larger groups dispersed in various places, or even to Christians in general (the church catholic).[4] In fact, however, the designation is not then totally appropriate; for I Peter is addressed to specific churches, III John to an individual (Gaius), and II John to an individual church. In the West another interpretation appears whereby "universal, catholic," refers not to the general character of the audience but to the general acceptance of these epistles.[5] This is seen in the designation *epistulae canonicae,* e.g., Junilius (PL 68, 19C) may be interpreted to say that to the books that were called "canonical" (I Peter, I John) many added five more (James, II Peter, Jude, II and III John). Cassiodorus (*De institutione divinarum Litterarum* 8; PL 70, 1120B) understood "canonical" as an epithet for all seven epistles.

Whatever meaning one gives to the grouping of the seven as "Catholic Epistles," that grouping is not of particular importance for the interpretation of I, II, and III John. True, there are certain similarities if we compare I Peter or James with I John;[6] but these stem from the common problems and situations faced by the authors of such epistles, e.g., the passing of the apostolic era and of the great teachers, diversity within the same community, and the need to concentrate on the pastoral care of a flock in which Christianity is no longer a novelty. Otherwise, I, II, and III John are not any closer to the other "Catholic Epistles" than, for instance, to the Pauline Pastorals. This explains why in the *Anchor Bible* James, I-II Peter, and Jude have been treated in one volume (37), while the Johannine Epistles are discussed separately by another author who was responsible for the commentary on GJohn (29, 29A). The closest links of the Johannine Epistles are to the Fourth Gospel.

If the ancient designation "Catholic Epistles" is not particularly helpful, what about the value of the other ancient attempt to identify these epistles as "The First, Second, and Third Epistles of John"?[7] Such titles appear in

[4] Oecumenius attests to this interpretation of *katholikos* in the tenth (?) century (PG 119, 453A).

[5] This interpretation was not absent from the East; for Origen (see Eusebius, *Hist.* 6.25.5,8) speaks of Peter making a statement in his "catholic epistle," by which he means I Peter, an epistle commonly accepted as canonical, over against II Peter about which there was controversy.

[6] Comparative lists may be found in Holtzmann, "Problem (IV)" 478–79; Johnston, "Will" 238; Weiss, *Briefe* 8–9.

[7] These are the titles that appear in the most important Greek codices, but see the first NOTE on I John and Appendix III. The three epistles are contained in the fourth-century Codices Vaticanus and Sinaiticus, and the fifth-century Codex Alexandrinus. Codex Bezae (fifth century) has lost 67 leaves, part of which contained the Greek of I, II, and III John; but it preserves III John 11–15 in Latin. Codex Ephraemi Rescriptus (fifth century) contains I John up to 4:2 and III John 3–15. A third-century papyrus, P9, contains I John 4:11–12,14–17, while P74, a seventh-century Bodmer Papyrus (XVII), contains sections of I, II, and III John.

all modern Bibles, and readers instinctively tend to give them a greater authority than the facts warrant. The three Epistles under discussion originally bore no title. Only toward the end of the second century were there prefixed to NT books titles representing intelligent (but not necessarily correct) guesses about authorship made by Christian scholars of that period. Sometimes these guesses were based upon earlier traditions but often traditions that were oversimplified and confused. Sometimes the guesses were based on an analysis of the contents of the NT book. The scarcity of solid information about NT authorship becomes apparent when we realize that only in the letters of Paul, James, Peter, and Jude and in Revelation (1:1,4,9) does the book itself supply us with the author's name. And even in these instances caution is required, e.g., there is no reason to identify the prophet John of Revelation with any other "John" known to us in the NT (and specifically not with John son of Zebedee), and in the case of the letters a disciple may have used the name of a more important Christian figure (Paul, James, Peter) to indicate his dependency on that master's thought. To a modern reader it may be puzzling that a factor so important as authorship was not better defined in antiquity, but the authority behind the message was a far greater issue in Christian antiquity than the identity of the writer. For instance, what second-century title-givers dubbed "The Gospel according to Mark" presents itself simply as "The Gospel of Jesus Christ" (Mark 1:1). Granted these general limitations, we shall have to examine every facet of the claims implicit in the titles "The First, Second, and Third Epistles of John." Are all these works epistles? Are they all by one man? If so, was he the author of the Fourth Gospel? Again, if so, was he John son of Zebedee, or some other John (e.g., John the Presbyter mentioned by Papias—ABJ 29, xc–xci), or an unknown? In what order were these "Johannine" works written, and were they written about the same time? In answering these questions, let us begin with the limited information about these three "Epistles of John" supplied by antiquity.

B. *Attitudes toward These Epistles in the First Five Centuries*

There is no certain evidence among Christian writers of a knowledge of any of the Johannine Epistles before the middle of the second century. Of course, this does not mean that they were written so late; for, as we shall see, a date *ca.* 100 is most plausible for their composition. But the lack of early attestation makes us cautious about assuming that there was a solid tradition throughout the second century attributing them to a known figure named John. Let me begin with the proposed evidence for an early knowledge of the Epistles.[8]

1. Possible Echoes before A.D. 175

The following parallels, suggested by various scholars, are in my judgment quite *inadequate* to establish knowledge of the Johannine Epistles:

- The *First Epistle to the Corinthians,* attributed to Clement of Rome and dated to *ca.* 96, gives this instruction (49:1): "Let one who has love in Christ perform the commandments of Christ." I John 5:3 makes a connection between love and keeping the commandments, but the vocabulary of the two works is quite different. *I Clement* 49:5 and 50:3 describe God's people as "perfected in love," a phrase reminiscent of I John 2:5; 4:12,17–18; but the same form of the verb (*teleioun*) is not used by the two authors. Moreover, as I shall point out below in the NOTE on I John 2:5b (on "has reached perfection"), the complexus of ideas has its origin in Judaism and is attested elsewhere in the NT. A God who is faithful and righteous (*pistos, dikaios*) is hailed both in *I Clem.* 27:1; 60:1, and in I John 1:9; but this is too common an OT motif to establish an interdependence of two Christian works.

- The Epistles of Ignatius of Antioch are dated to *ca.* 110–15 and thus within about a decade of the composition of the Johannine Epistles and about two decades of the writing of GJohn. Ignatius, who came from Antioch, visited and wrote to churches in Asia Minor, not far from Ephesus, thus having contact with the two cities most often proposed as the center of Johannine Christianity. It is not surprising that scholars have debated whether such a chronological and geographical contemporary might have known GJohn[9] and/or I John. If we confine ourselves here to knowledge of I John, *Eph.* 11:1 mentions the last times, while I

---

[8] Although much of this evidence is not sufficiently convincing to establish dependence of the respective authors on the Johannine Epistles, it will prove useful in showing how many of the Johannine ideas could fit into common Christian thought patterns.

[9] A survey up to 1940 is offered by Burghardt, "Ignatius"; for later material, see ABJ 29, lxxxi. Those who hold for probable or certain Ignatian literary dependence on GJohn include: Battifol, Bernard, Burney, Calmes, Camerlynck, Knabenbauer, Lebreton, Lietzmann, Moffatt, Resch, and Streeter. Those who think that certainly or probably there was no such dependence include: Abbott, Bacon, Carpenter, Harnack, Réville, Schlier, and Schmiedel. Those who find it too difficult to decide include: Burghardt, Holtzmann, Lightfoot, C. Richardson, Sanday, Strachan, Tillmann, Westcott, and Zahn. The suggested points of similarity include the christological language (*Magn.* 8:2. "One God who manifested Himself through Jesus Christ His Son who is His Word" = John 17:3; 1:1), the eucharistic language ("flesh" and "blood" of Christ in *Phld.* 4:1, and "the medicine of immortality, the antidote that we should not die but live forever" in *Eph.* 20:2 = John 6:51–56), and the language pertaining to the Spirit (who "knows whence he comes and whither he goes" in *Phld.* 7:1 = John 3:8; 8:14). Seemingly Johannine are the terms "real life" (*alēthinos*) in *Trall.* 9:2, and "living water" within the Christian in *Rom.* 7:2.

John 2:18 mentions the last hour; *Eph.* 15:3 mentions that God will be revealed before us, as does I John 3:2. The parallels are far from verbatim, and once again we are dealing with common Jewish ideas. See below INTRODUCTION IV B3b for similarities between the opponents of Ignatius and those of I and II John, similarities that may arise from the common ambiance.

- The *Didache* was written somewhere between A.D. 90 and 120 (although more would favor the earlier date). In 10:5 it shares with I John (and *I Clement* above) the theme of perfecting the church in love. This parallel becomes somewhat more impressive when the very next verse (*Did.* 10:6) speaks of the world passing away, as does I John 2:17 (with slightly different vocabulary). The issue of testing those who speak in the Spirit appears affirmatively in I John 4:1 and negatively in *Did.* 11:7, but with different vocabulary. Since there are also parallels between *Didache* and GJohn (see ABJ 29, 248; 29A, 673, 746), it is not impossible that there were some contacts between Johannine thought and that of *Didache,* even if there is no proof of literary contact.

More adequate are the following suggested parallels, which I have arranged in ascending order of likelihood (so that only the last would I consider seriously as probative of knowledge of one or more of the Johannine Epistles):

- The *Epistle of Barnabas* (*ca.* 130?) has a passage about Jesus revealing himself "as the Son of God come in the flesh" (5:9–11; also 12:10) which is close to the wording of I John 4:2 and II John 7. Another passage (*Barn.* 14:5), ". . . that, when Jesus was revealed, he might redeem from darkness our hearts given over to the deception [*planē*] of lawlessness [*anomia*]," has parallels to themes in I John 3:4 (*anomia*), 3:7 (*planan*), and to 3:8, "The reason the Son of God revealed himself was to destroy the works of the devil."
- The *Second Epistle of Clement to the Corinthians* (*ca.* 150?) asks (6:9), "Who shall be our advocate [*paraklētos*], if we are not found having pious and righteous works?" I John 2:1 speaks of the righteous Christ as our *paraklētos*. Probably *paraklētos,* a Johannine word in the NT, was in wider Christian usage by mid-second century, and so its use is not sufficient to establish knowledge of I John by the author of *II Clement*.[10]

---

[10] Even if one were to argue for literary dependency based on the use of a term common to GJohn and I John (such as *paraklētos*), one would have to be careful in deciding which work was the source. For instance, I find quite unconvincing the thesis of Pheme Perkins that the (possibly) gnostic third-century (?) *Apocryphon of James* made use of I John (SBLASP [1979] §116). The argument centers upon I 11:5–6 (NHL 34) where Jesus says, "I intercede on your behalf with the Father, and he will forgive you much," as an echo of I John 2:1–2: "If anyone does sin, we

- The *Shepherd of Hermas* (before 150) has several interesting similarities to I John. In *Hermas Man.* 3.1 we find: "The Lord is truthful in every word and in Him there is no lie," resembling I John 2:27 where anointing from Christ is described as "true and free from any lie." The encouragement of *Hermas Man.* 12.3.5, "You will easily observe [the commandments], for they are not hard," resembles in thought I John 5:3: "We keep His commandments, and His commandments are not burdensome." The Christian is told in *Hermas Sim.* 9.24.4, "Of his [the Son of God's] Spirit you have received," even as I John 4:13 states, "He [God] has given us of His own Spirit."

- Both the *Apologies* and the *Dialogue* of Justin Martyr (*ca.* 150) contain similarities to the Johannine Epistles. The reference to Christ's blood purifying those who believe in him (*I Apol.* 32.7), which is similar to the affirmation of I John 1:7, would be too common a Christian idea to be at all persuasive were it not that the very next verse (*I Apol.* 32.8) speaks of the "seed of God, the Word," dwelling in the believer—themes found in I John 2:14 and 3:9. If one draws upon *Dialogue* 123.9, "We who observe the commandments of Christ are called genuine children of God—and that is what we really are," one finds a close parallel to I John's frequent theme of keeping the commandments (2:3; 3:22; 5:3) and more specifically to 3:1: "Enabling us to be called God's children—and that is what we really are."

- The *Epistle to Diognetus,* another apologetic work of uncertain date (guesses range from 125 to 225), states (10:2–3), "God loved human beings . . . to whom He sent His only Son. . . . How greatly will you love Him who first loved you?" This is very close to the wording of I John 4:9,19. In *Diogn.* 11:4 the Word is described as "the one who was from the beginning," a phraseology reminiscent of I John 1:1; 2:13–14.

- Polycarp's *Epistle to the Philippians,* which can scarcely be dated after 140, supplies the most important early parallel to the Johannine Epistles. Speaking of deceiving false brethren (6:3) who do not acknowledge the cross, Polycarp says in 7:1, "For everyone who does not confess Jesus Christ to have come [perf. infin.] in the flesh is Antichrist"; and this is uniquely close to two Johannine passages: "Many deceivers have gone out into the world, those who *do not confess Jesus Christ coming* [pres.

---

have a *paraklētos* [intercessor?] in the Father's presence, Jesus Christ, the one who is just; and he himself is an atonement for our sins." However, surrounding passages in the *Apocryphon* about Jesus' going away (I 10:22–23), about the "beloved" imploring the Father who will give to them (I 10:30–34), and about the tragedy of those who lack an advocate (I 11:11–12), all point to the Last Supper account in GJohn (14:12–16; 16:4b–10); and so the idea of Jesus' intercession with the Father and the forgiveness of sins may combine John 1:29 and 14:28. No *early* gnostic work makes clear use of I John, while GJohn is a favorite among the gnostics (footnote 148 in IV below).

ptcp.] *in the flesh. There is . . . the Antichrist"* (II John 7); "Every spirit who *confesses Jesus Christ come* [perf. ptcp.] *in the flesh. . . . Every spirit who does not confess Jesus . . . is of the Antichrist"* (I John 4:2–3).[11] The likelihood of a true echo of the Johannine Epistles is increased when we advert to the phrase "belong to the devil" in the next line of Polycarp 7:1 and in I John 3:8. Important too is the next verse in Polycarp (7:2): "Let us return to the word handed down to us from [*ex*] the beginning"; for the theme of what was known or heard "from [*apo*] the beginning" is found in I John 2:7,24; 3:11. Yet notice the difference of prepositions.

From the second set of suggested parallels it seems clear that by mid-second century ideas, themes, and even slogans of the Johannine Epistles (or, at least, of I John) were being cited in other Christian works. But no one of the proposed similarities consists of a verbatim citation, so that it is still very difficult to be certain that any of the mentioned authors had the text of a Johannine Epistle before him. Nevertheless, the likelihood that I John was available to Polycarp is increased by the information of Eusebius (*Hist.* 3.39.17) that Papias, who was a contemporary of Polycarp (3.36.1–2), "made use of testimonies from the First Epistle of John."[12]

2. From the Late Second Century to the Fifth Century

The first undeniable citations of the Johannine Epistles occur *ca.* A.D. 180 in the writing of Irenaeus of Lyons who is said, as a youth in Asia Minor, to have listened to Polycarp preach (Eusebius, *Hist.* 5.20.6). In three passages of the *Adversus haereses* there are direct citations[13] as part of Irenaeus' anti-gnostic polemic:

1.16.3 cites II John 11 (as coming from John, the Lord's disciple)
3.16.5 cites I John 2:18–19,21–22
3.16.8 cites II John 7–8; I John 4:1–2; 5:1

---

[11] Overall Polycarp is closer to II John, although the word order of the phrase "in the flesh" is closer to I John. He seems to have understood the ambiguous pres. ptcp. of II John as a past coming. For the disputed Greek text of I John 4:3, which is relevant to this question, see the NOTE below on that verse.

[12] The designation "First Epistle" or "Former Epistle" reflects Eusebius' fourth-century knowledge that there were other Johannine Epistles; it does not mean that Papias knew of them in the early second century. A proposed but dubious example of Papias' knowledge of one or more Johannine Epistles is his statement quoted by Eusebius (*Hist.* 3.39.3) that he took pleasure in "those who recall the commandments given by the Lord to faith and reaching (us) from truth himself (itself)." I John is insistent on the divine origin of the commandment of love (2:7; 4:21), and III John 12 speaks of testimony "from truth itself."

[13] There may be an implicit citation of I John 4:6 in 1.9.5 ("spirits of deceit"), and an implicit citation of I John 1:1–4 in 5.1.1 ("hearing with our own ear"; "we may have communion with Him").

Thus Irenaeus knew II John as well as I John, although perhaps not as a separate letter. When citing II John in 3.16.8, he refers to the citation as coming from the epistle he has already quoted, which has to be I John quoted in 3.16.5. Moreover, after citing II John he continues with other citations from "this epistle," namely I John 4:1–2 and 5:1.

A more obscure witness to I and II John is that of the Muratorian fragment or canon, a Latin list of books that were accepted as canonical. (The barbarous Latin probably represents a translation from Greek.) Customarily the fragment has been dated to the end of the second century (and thus roughly contemporaneous with Irenaeus) and associated with the church of Rome.[14] It describes how John wrote the Gospel and then refers to "his epistles" in which he claimed to write "what we have seen with our eyes, heard with our ears, and touched with our hands" (I John 1:1). Later the fragment makes another reference to the Johannine Epistles, which has usually been translated thus: "Certainly the Epistle of Jude and two of the aforementioned John are accepted in the catholic church."[15] If this translation is correct, surely the two are I and II John.

By the very end of the second century I John was being cited both in the West and in the East. For instance, Tertullian (d. 215) cites I John some forty or fifty times, referring to it as the work of John. Clement of Alexandria (d. *ca.* 220) not only cites I John[16] but speaks of it as "the greater epistle" (*Stromata* 2.15.66; GCS 15, 148), so that he knew at least one other Johannine Epistle. This is confirmed by the *Adumbrationes,* which contains Clement's commentary on II John.[17] When we join Clement to Irenaeus and the Muratorian fragment, we see that II John was receiving acceptance by A.D. 200, alongside I John.

---

[14] The usual date has been challenged by A. C. Sundberg, Jr., "Canon Muratori: A Fourth Century List," HTR 66 (1973) 1–41, who would attribute it to the East rather than to Rome. It is not yet apparent that Sundberg has much following in this thesis, and in my own judgment it raises more problems than it solves.

[15] "Epistola sane Jude et superscricti[o] Johannis duas in catholica habentur." Presumably *superscricti[o]* is a miswritten *suprascripti.* P. Katz, "The Johannine Epistles in the Muratorian Canon," JTS 8 (1957) 273–74, argues that *"catholica"* does not mean "catholic church" but "Catholic Epistle"; and so he interprets Muratori thus: "Certainly the Epistle of Jude and two of the aforementioned John, in addition to the Catholic Epistle [I John], are accepted." This would mean knowledge and acceptance of three Johannine Epistles. Holtzmann, "Problem (IV)" 484, argues that Muratori was referring to II and III John when it mentioned "two" because I John was placed with GJohn almost as part of that Gospel. He offers as evidence the custom of some later Western MSS. of placing I John (but II and III John as well) immediately after the Gospels and before Acts, e.g., Codex Bezae Cantabrigiensis.

[16] E.g., *Stromata* 3.5.44 and 3.6.45 (GCS 15, 216–17) cites I John 2:4,18–19, while *Quis dives salvetur* 37.6 (GCS 17, 184) cites I John 3:15.

[17] See GCS 17, 215. The *Adumbrationes* is a Latin translation (often attributed to Cassiodorus, *ca.* 540) of part of the lost Greek of Clement's *Hypotypōseis.* In referring to the latter, Eusebius, *Hist.* 6.14.1, makes a generalizing remark about its containing a commentary on Jude and "the other Catholic Epistles," but that is insufficient to prove that Clement also knew III John.

Before the middle of the third century we find in Alexandrian scholarship the first attestation of the existence of III John (but even then our evidence is secondhand). According to Eusebius (*Hist.* 6.25.10), the famous Origen (d. 253) knew of both II and III John but also that "all do not consider them genuine."[18] Origen's pupil Dionysius of Alexandria (d. 265) held that the apostle wrote both the Gospel and the "Catholic Epistle," but not Revelation; and he knew that there was a "reputed Second or Third Epistle of John" (Eusebius, *Hist.* 7.25.7–8,11). The *Sententiae Episcoporum* (※381) from the Seventh Council of Carthage (A.D. 256) shows that III John was known also in North Africa about this same time, alongside II John. (Harnack and Manson[19] have contended that the Latin translation of III John betrays a different hand from that of the translator of II John, an observation that probably implies a different and later history of acceptance in the West of III John.) Nevertheless, neither small Johannine Epistle was cited by Cyprian of Carthage (d. 258)[20] who quoted from I John.

In the early fourth century Eusebius of Caesarea placed I John among the "acknowledged books" of Scripture, while II and III John, although "well-known and acknowledged by most," were listed among the "disputed books" (*Hist.* 3.24.17 and 3.25.2–3). Evidently it was not clear to people whether the smaller Johannine Epistles were written by the evangelist or some other person.[21] Yet in Eusebius' own *Demonstratio evangelica* (3.5.88; GCS 23, 126–27), he says that the apostle who wrote the Gospel also wrote those Epistles wherein he calls himself a presbyter, a remark that would cover II and III John.

In mid-fourth century the North African Canon Mommsenianus (Cheltenham) listed three Epistles of John, but a marginal gloss corrected this to "only one." Toward the end of the century Jerome reported that many attributed II and III John to the Presbyter who was distinct from the Apostle John.[22] A later canon once attributed to Jerome's patron, Pope Damasus I (d. 384), spoke of only two Johannine Epistles, one of the

---

[18] In fact, however, while Origen makes frequent use of I John, he never cites II and III John. The only evidence of his knowledge of more than one Johannine Epistle in his extant works is in the Latin translation of the (lost Greek) *Homilies on Joshua* (7:1; GCS 30, 328) where he refers to the Johannine writer's "epistles"; yet in the same work (7:4; GCS 30, 331) he speaks of "his epistle."

[19] See the articles cited in footnotes 24 and 25 below.

[20] The fact that normally Cyprian speaks of "John in his epistle" (*in epistula sua*) has led to the false inference that he could have known of only one Johannine Epistle. P. Schepens, RSR 11 (1921) 87–89, has pointed out that Cyprian uses the same expression in reference to Paul, who was known to have written many epistles. It really means no more than "in an epistle of his." Cyprian was at the above-mentioned Council of Carthage and so had to know of more than one Johannine Epistle.

[21] See below in the INTRODUCTION, II A.

[22] *De viris illustribus* 9; PL 23, 655B. Yet in a letter to Paulinus (*Epistula* 53.8; PL 22, 548) without a sign of hesitation Jerome attributed them to John an Apostle.

Apostle John, the other of John the Presbyter. No use of II and III John was made by John Chrysostom (d. 407) or by Theodore of Mopsuestia (d. 428), influential figures in Eastern exegesis. Nevertheless, acceptance of three Johannine Epistles, with the assumption that they were written by the Apostle John, became the order of the day in the late fourth century, as can be seen from the Thirty-ninth Festal Letter of Athanasius (A.D. 367), the Synod of Hippo (393), and the Council of Carthage (397) at which Augustine was present.[23] The Alexandrian scholar Didymus the Blind (d. 398) wrote a commentary on all three, showing that they were now being considered a unit. The appearance of three Johannine Epistles in the great fourth- and fifth-century codices of the Bible was another sign of their ever wider acceptance in the Greek-speaking and Latin-speaking churches.

In the Syriac-speaking church to the East, possibly Aphraates (ca. 340) and surely Ephraem (d. 373) knew I John, and in the fifth century only that Johannine Epistle could be found in the Peshitta, the most commonly used Bible of the various Syriac-language Christians. Not until later and still not universally did II and III John make their appearance in Syriac Bibles, e.g., in the Philoxenian version at the beginning of the sixth century, while still not being accepted by the Nestorians.

How do we explain such a peculiar history of preservation with I John known and being accepted in mid-second century; with II John beginning to be accepted slightly later in that century; with III John not being mentioned till the third century;[24] and with doubts about the authorship and canonicity of II and III John lingering till much later? Even if the three Epistles were written by one man about the same time (which internal evidence favors), clearly they were not preserved side by side or evaluated on the same level. If the only problem were lack of citation by church writers, one could rightly argue that II and III John are the shortest works in the NT and that there would have been little occasion to cite them. But more is involved; for when II and III John are mentioned in the third and fourth centuries, there is marked doubt about them. Part of the answer surely lies in the fact that in the latter part of the second century I John, which supplies no direct information about its writer, won acceptance alongside GJohn as having the same apostolic author. However, II and III John describe their author as "the Presbyter," information which led many to judge that he was not the apostle to whom they attributed I John. This distinction was facilitated by reading the information of Papias (Eusebius, *Hist.* 3.39.4; ABJ 29, xc–xci) to mean that there were two

---

[23] Augustine's important commentary on I John (*In Epistolam Ioannis ad Parthos;* see SC 75), written in A.D. 415, is incomplete, stopping with 5:2.

[24] These three stages are carefully distinguished by T. W. Manson, "Entry into Membership of the Early Church," JTS 48 (1947) 25–33, esp. 32–33.

men named John, one a disciple of the Lord, the other "the Presbyter." Lack of apostolic authorship constituted a serious obstacle to the acceptance of the shorter Epistles as Scripture. When that was overcome by assuming that through modesty the Apostle John called himself simply "the Presbyter," even as the Apostle Peter called himself "the Co-presbyter" (I Pet 5:1), a distinction regarding canonicity could still have been made between II John addressed to a church and III John addressed to an individual—biblical books were God's word *to the Church*.[25]

---

[25] In discussing the Muratorian fragment, A. von Harnack, ZKG 3 (1879) 379–80, argues strongly that the two criteria for canonicity were apostolic authorship and destination to the church catholic.

II. Problems of Johannine Authorship

At the end of section A in the preceding unit I asked a number of important questions about the origin and authorship of the Johannine Epistles, questions not settled simply by repeating the titles given them in antiquity. Then in section B I surveyed the evidence of the first five centuries to see if an answer to those questions could be found in the early tradition. But in fact that tradition proved quite unable to tell us who wrote the Epistles, in what order, and how they are related to GJohn. Without neglecting that external tradition, confused as it is, we must now turn to the internal evidence of the Epistles themselves about authorship. We may concentrate on three issues: (A) Did the same author write all three Epistles?; (B) Did the same author write GJohn and the Epistles?; and (C) In what sequence were GJohn and the Epistles written?

A. *Did the Same Author Write All Three Epistles?*

A negative answer has been given to this question by many scholars ancient and modern.[26] The most common form of the negative answer attributes I John to one man (often the evangelist) and II and III John to another;[27] but some modern authors opt for three different writers for the three Epistles.[28] Doubts about common authorship arise from several factors. As we have seen, the Epistles were received as canonical Scripture separately and at widely different times, a fact that does not encourage a thesis of common authorship. We have also seen the difficulty caused by the fact that the author of I John never identifies himself by name or title, while the author of II John and of III John calls himself "the Pres-

[26] In antiquity: Origen, Dionysius of Alexandria, Eusebius, Ambrose, Jerome; more recently: Balz, Bergmeier, Bousset, Bultmann, Clemen, Ebrard, Harnack, Heinrici, Heise, Hirsch, Langbrandtner, Moffatt, Peake, Pfleiderer, Renan, Schleiermacher, Schwartz, Selwyn, von Dobschütz, von Soden, J. Weiss.

[27] Papias' seeming distinction between John the disciple of the Lord and John the Presbyter, mentioned at the end of the last unit, continues to contribute to this theory. J. Moffatt, *An Introduction to the New Testament* (New York: Scribners, 1922; reprinting 3d ed., 1918) 479–81, attributes not only II and III John to John the Presbyter, but also accepts the ancient theory (of Dionysius of Alexandria) that he wrote Revelation.

[28] A peculiar variant is that of Hirsch, *Studien* 177, who thinks that I John is composite, with the second writer of that composition being the author of II and III John.

byter."[29] Moreover, a clear epistolary format (Sender, Addressee, Message, Conclusion) sets off II and III John from I John, which is completely lacking in epistolary format.[30] Unfortunately II and III John are so short as to offer inadequate material for making a detailed comparison among the three Epistles, and so no certitude about their authorship is possible. All that one can hope to do is to establish probabilities. As Dodd, *Epistles* lxii, has recognized, the parallels between III John and I John are not striking. Consequently, the usual method of procedure in determining whether one author was involved is to make a comparison between III John and II John, and then to make a comparison between II John and I John. An affirmative judgment resulting from the two comparisons would logically establish the same author for all three Epistles.

1. Common Authorship for II John and III John?

These two letters are of almost identical length—in Greek respectively 245 words/1,126 letters and 219 words/1,105 letters, the length surely being dictated by the size of a sheet of papyrus.[30a] They have virtually the same Opening and Closing Formulas. In the first four verses of each letter a sender who designates himself as "the Presbyter" assures the addressee, "In truth I love you," and opens the Body of the letter with the words, "It gave me great joy," while praising the addressee for walking in truth. As for the closing of the Body of the letter and the Concluding Formula, a quotation illustrates the parallelism:

> *II John 12–13:* Though I have much more to write you, I cannot be bothered with paper and ink. Instead, I hope to come to you and have a heart-to-heart talk, so that our joy may be fulfilled. The children of your Elect Sister send you greetings.

> *III John 13–15:* I had much more that I should write you, but I do not wish to write it out with pen and ink. Rather, I hope to see you soon, and we can have a heart-to-heart talk. Peace to you. The beloved here send you greetings; greet the beloved there, each by name.

From these similarities, which set II and III John off from other NT letters, most scholars have concluded that they were composed by the same man. But in times past Clemen and Schleiermacher argued against that

---

[29] The argument that the author of I John cannot be an apostle because he does not identify himself as such has little value (even if I do not think the author was an apostle). It assumes that I John is a letter, which is probably not true (see below V C1). There may be *some* validity to the argument that the author of real letters like II and III John, which require an identification of the sender, would not identify himself as "the Presbyter" if he were an apostle.

[30] NT epistolary format will be discussed in detail in Appendix V.

[30a] The standard size seems to have been 8″ by 10″, or 20 cm. by 25 cm. Deissmann, LFAE 179–94, cites letters from Egypt (A.D. 150–200) which consist of 1,124 letters. Already Origen (Eusebius, *Hist.* 6.25.7) notes the brevity of the minor Johannine Epistles ("a few lines").

conclusion, and Bultmann and Heise attribute the similarity to a forger (with III John as the more original composition).

Clearly one must account for both similarities and differences. Neither similarity in length nor in epistolary format (especially in the Opening and Closing) proves much, since letters tend to have a set format, especially when they are written at roughly the same time. One might argue that the minor variations in the Opening and Closing of II and III John are more intelligible if they came from the one writer who would not have repeated himself with absolute consistency, while a forger would have been more inclined to copy exactly. (Notice the minor variations in Opening and Closing among the indisputably genuine Pauline Epistles.) As for the substance of the bodies of II and III John, often called "the Message," the two letters have little in common;[31] but that is not surprising granted the fact that they deal with quite different subjects—the Body is the area where one expects to find the most differences among letters.

From a stylistic comparison, then, there is nothing that makes common authorship either impossible or unlikely. While there is no way to disprove the possibility that one letter was copied from the other by a forger,[32] one may ask why a forger would choose as his model either of these two letters, which apparently enjoyed little fame in the ancient church and were among the last to be accepted as canonical Scripture. Why would a forger choose a letter whose author claimed only the modest title "the Presbyter"? In particular, the thesis that II John was a fiction copied from III John creates the paradox (not impossible, but amusing) that the fiction was known and accepted as canonical Scripture earlier than the original! In my judgment, probability favors common authorship and, as we shall see below, the same general period of composition.

2. Common Authorship for II John and I John?

If the same man did write II and III John, was this "Presbyter" also the author of I John?[33] Often statistics offered for answering this question on the basis of style are gleaned from comparing II and III John to I John and GJohn taken together (on the supposition that there is a common Johannine vocabulary and style shared by the latter two works). In such a comparison it has been observed that 70% of the significant words of III John are found in I John or GJohn, as are 86% of those in II John.[34] I

---

[31] If we compare II John 5–11 and III John 5–12, the verb *ergazein*, "to work for," occurs in v. 8 in II John and in v. 5 in III John.

[32] The uncontrollability of imaginative scholarly suggestions is best illustrated by the thesis of E. Hirsch that all three Johannine Epistles are fictional compositions!

[33] Or was he *one* of the authors of I John? Langbrandtner, *Weltferner Gott* 402, proposes that the Presbyter of II John was one of the "we" of I John 1:1–4.

[34] The lower percentage in III John is explained by the fact that the subject of that letter is quite different from the common subject shared by II John and I John (the correction of defective christology and ethical behavior).

have listed the most important of these similarities in Chart One of Appendix I, and a glance shows the closeness of II John to I John. By way of further analysis, the details supplied by Marty, "Contributions" 203–41, are interesting. He has found 74 points of minute similarity between II-III John and I John, and 54 points of similarity between II-III John and GJohn (and of the latter, 80% are to John 14–17, the Last Discourse). Thus he would judge that the two short Epistles are closest to I John and to a section of GJohn that many would attribute not to the evangelist but to a redactor.[35]

While such similarities, especially those between II John and I John, are impressive, once again some scholars would attribute them to copying by a forger. For instance, the thesis mentioned above that the forger of II John copied the Opening and Closing Formulas of III John goes on to propose that this forger copied the Body of his letter from I John (e.g., II John 7 from I John 4:1–2). There is no way to disprove such a thesis; but once again one may note that there are no verbatim quotations and always minor variants, a fact more consonant with the same author rephrasing himself rather than a forger. If, as most suppose, II John was written about the same time as I John and dealt with the same problem,[36] similarity of message would be expected. Moreover, the forgery thesis faces an objection as to why anyone would have done such a thing. Since II John does not report anything significant beyond what is already in I John, why did the proposed forger not send the original rather than create a spurious letter?

On the other hand, an objection against the common authorship of II John and I John has been raised because of minor dissimilarities[37] in thought and expression found in the two works. Let me mention the most notable:

- The sender identifies himself in II John but not in I John. One reply is that II John is a letter where identification is required, while I John is not (below, INTRODUCTION V C1).
- In II John 1 the audience is addressed as the *tekna* ("children") of a local church personified as a lady (see also vv. 4,13), while in I John the plural *tekna* refers to the children of God and of the devil, and other

[35] See ABJ 29, xxxvi–xxxviii (*Stage 5*) for the theory of a redactor of GJohn. The possibility that the author of the Epistles was not the evangelist but the redactor of GJohn will be discussed below, INTRODUCTION V D2b.

[36] Both deal with those who have "gone out" (seceded) and who deny Jesus Christ come/coming in the flesh and so are Antichrists and deceivers. Both stress the importance of loving one another. And the author of each manifests a sovereign confidence that his view of what is true in christology and ethics is conformable with what was from the beginning.

[37] It is interesting that Heise uses similarities to argue that II John was copied from I John, while Bergmeier and Moffatt use dissimilarities to prove difference of authorship.

plurals (*teknia, paidia*) are used for the audience as the author's "(little) children." However, as we shall see over and over again, the Johannine writers switch back and forth among synonyms, so that the variance among *tekna, teknia,* and *paidia* is not particularly significant. Moreover, the author of I John seemingly lives among those whom he addresses as his (little) children, while in II John he is addressing himself to a Johannine church at a distance which he hopes to visit; and so a shift of address from his children to the church's children is intelligible.

- The use of "Elect" (*eklektos*) in reference to ladies symbolizing churches in II John 1,13 has been deemed to be non-Johannine, for it is not found in I John or GJohn. However, neither of the latter works seems to be addressed to a community at a distance. Moreover, common terms of church address do appear in I John (e.g., "brothers"), and so we have no way of knowing that its author would not use "Elect Lady" which is a term for a church attested in I Peter 5:13 ("Co-elect"). Certainly in Johannine thought there is nothing against regarding Christians as the "elect" (*eklegesthai*) of Jesus (John 6:30; 13:18; 15:16,29).

- II John 2 speaks of "the truth that abides" in us, and no other Johannine work uses "truth" as the subject of the verb "abide in" (*menein en*). However, the Johannine writers make virtually equivalent realities the subject of this expression (NOTE on I John 2:6a), and the fact that "truth" happens to be a subject in II John but not elsewhere is surely accidental. Also *einai en,* "to be in," is often synonymous with *menein en;* and I John 1:8; 2:4 makes "truth" the subject of *einai en.*

- II John 3 speaks of "Jesus Christ, *the Son of the Father.*" While the italicized phrase is unique in the NT, it combines the very common Johannine theological concepts of "Father" and "Son"; and in fact the phrase under discussion is not much different from I John 5:20: "His Son, Jesus Christ."

- The expression "In truth and love" in II John 3 puts together two nouns not found *joined* elsewhere in the Johannine writings. However, these are very common Johannine nouns, and the governing grammar where the preposition *en* covers two anarthrous nouns is Johannine (NOTE on I John 3:18ab).

- The expression "walk in truth," which appears in II John 4 and III John 3, occurs nowhere else in the NT. However, "walk in light" occurs in I John 1:7 (see NOTE on 1:6b), and "light" and "truth" are almost interchangeable in Johannine theology, e.g., John 8:12 and 14:6.

- Bergmeier, "Verfasserproblem" 96–97, argues that the dualism which marks (with variations) both GJohn and I John is missing from II John. In the latter, for instance, although there are references to "truth," there is no counterposed "lie," as in I John 2:21,27. Yet there are references in II John 7 to "deceiver" (*planos*) and to "deceive, deceit" (*planan, planē*), the very terminology that constitutes a dualistic opposition to "truth" in I John 2:26 and 4:6, and which is a synonym for "lie."

▪Bergmeier maintains that "truth" in II John has become equivalent to "teaching" (II John 9), something that can abide and can belong to a community.[38] Actually his position has not won much acceptance. As Bultmann and Schnackenburg[39] both insist, one cannot so easily identify "truth" and "teaching" in II John; for example, "walk in truth" in II John 4 implies more than being faithful to teaching. On the other hand, as we shall see in the commentary, an element of "truth" as right teaching over against falsehood already appears in I John. Thus, it is far from clear that the Johannine Epistles differ notably among themselves on the concept of "truth."

Most of these differences[40] are really instances of the vagaries of Johannine style that one may find even within the same work and do not prove difference of authorship for I John and II-III John. In fact, if one examines I John 4:1-6 and 5:4b-8 (sections that taken together would be equivalent to II John in length), one would find more difference between these sections and the rest of I John than one finds between II John and I John. In my judgment, II John is too short and the evidence is too limited to build up a case for a significant difference of thought from I John. And so on all scores the theory that the same man wrote both works remains more plausible.

In this commentary, although I recognize that it cannot be proved, I shall work with the hypothesis that the same author wrote the three Johannine Epistles; and a perfectly coherent interpretation of the Epistles is possible upon the basis of that hypothesis.

B. *Did the Same Author Write the Fourth Gospel and the Epistles?*

We now move on to a more important question for understanding the Epistles and their place in the history of Johannine thought. That the an-

---

[38] In "Verfasserproblem" 100, he compares the theological development of II and III John over I John/GJohn to that of the Pastoral Epistles over the genuine Pauline Epistles in the matter of what "faith" means.

[39] See Bultmann, *Epistles* 108 and (in detail) Schnackenburg, "Begriff"; also Houlden, *Epistles* 143; Langbrandtner, *Weltferner Gott* 374; de la Potterie, *La vérité* 2, 548ff. However, Klein, "Licht" 307, is more favorable to Bergmeier's thesis. My objections to his thesis will appear in detail in the NOTES on II John.

[40] There are other minor differences, e.g., the use of "coming in the flesh" in II John 7 as contrasted with "come [past] in the flesh" in I John 4:2; the conditional particle *ei tis* ("if anyone") in II John 10 as contrasted with *ean tis* used some 15 times in GJohn; *koinōnein*, "to share," in II John 11 as contrasted with *koinōnian echein*, "to have a share," in I John 1:3,6,7. I shall explain in the respective NOTES that these are not meaningful differences.

swer will not be easy is suggested by the impressive number of scholars who have chosen opposite sides in the issue. Among those who opt for one author for GJohn and I John[41] are Abbott, Bacon, Baumgartner, Bernard, F.-M. Braun, Brooke, Burney, Chaine, Charles, Clemen, de Ambroggi, Feuillet, Findlay, Gaugler, Grimm, Harnack, Hauck, Headlam, Hilgenfeld, Howard, Jacquier, Jülicher, Law, Lepin, T. W. Manson, Marshall, W. Michaelis, Michl, Nunn, Percy, Schneider, Stott, Streeter, Turner, Vrede, B. Weiss, Wendland, Wernle, Westcott, Williams, and Wrede. Among those who hold that the author of I John was *not* the main author of GJohn (the evangelist)[42] are Matthew Arnold, Balz, Barrett, Bauer, Baur, Becker, Bornkamm, Bousset, Bretschneider, Brückner, Bultmann, S. Davidson, Dibelius, Dodd, Heitmüller, Hirsch, Hoekstra, Holtzmann, Horst, Houlden, Keim, G. Klein, Kreyenbühl, Lange, Léon-Dufour, McNeile, Marty, Moffatt, Pfleiderer, Réville, Richter, Riddle, Scaliger,[43] Schmiedel, Schnackenburg,[44] Schwartz, Scott, Soltau, Strauss, von Dobschütz, Weizsäcker, Wellhausen, Wendt, and Wilder.

On the pages that follow I shall discuss the arguments for each side. If I devote more pages to the arguments against common authorship, it is because B. H. Streeter[45] is correct: "The three Epistles and the Gospel of John are so closely allied in diction, style, and general outlook that the burden of proof lies with the person who would deny their common authorship."

1. The Argument for Common Authorship Based on Similarities in Style

The first recorded critical discussion of the question was by Dionysius of Alexandria (d. 265) who argued that, while Revelation was not written by the evangelist, I John clearly was (Eusebius, *Hist.* 7.25.18–23).[46]

---

[41] I have included here those who maintain that the author of GJohn gave over the physical writing of I John to a scribe who copied out basically what the author instructed (so F.-M. Braun, *Epîtres* 240–41). A particular variant is the thesis of C. F. Burney that, after GJohn was translated from Aramaic to Greek, the Epistles were dictated by the author of GJohn directly in Greek to the same amanuensis who had translated GJohn into Greek. Revelation, however, was written by the author of GJohn himself in his own imperfect Greek. See Burney's *The Aramaic Origin of the Fourth Gospel* (Oxford: Clarendon, 1922) 149.

[42] I have included here those who, thinking that there was both an evangelist and a redactor for GJohn, attribute I John to the redactor; see INTRODUCTION V D2b. J. Becker, "Abschiedsreden" 236, sees several different Johannine hands at work in chaps. 13–17 of GJohn and attributes I John to the writer of chaps. 15–16.

[43] According to Holtzmann, "Problem IV" 462, J. J. Scaliger was among the first modern scholars to deny the apostolic authorship (of GJohn) to the *three* Epistles.

[44] See the "Ergänzgungen" to the 5th ed. (1975) of Schnackenburg's *Johannesbriefe* 335, where he rejects his previously held position that the authors of the two works were identical.

[45] *The Four Gospels* (rev. ed.; London: Macmillan, 1930) 460.

[46] From Jerome to Robert Browning the romantic picture of the aged John at the end of his life has been influenced by the theory that he (the evangelist) also wrote

Dionysius' argument was centered on similarity in content and vocabulary. (One may add that there are also parallels in *structure* between GJohn and I John, especially in the beginning of the two works [the two Prologues are really unique in the NT] and in the ending [John 20:31 and I John 5:13 state the purpose of writing].) This remains the principal argument for assigning GJohn and I John to the same author. Many authors have drawn up extensive lists of parallels between the two works,[47] and Chart Two of Appendix I constitutes my attempt to draw together the most important similarities in phrase and idea. (One can make the case even more convincing by stressing the similarity in Greek grammatical constructions and by giving vocabulary lists.[48]) Even a brief effort to work through the chart with an English-language Bible should convince the reader that in the NT it is difficult to find two works more similar in expression than GJohn and I John. As many have observed, they are closer than Luke and Acts (which are attributed almost universally to one author), and no less close than I and II Thessalonians or Colossians and Ephesians. But in making that observation we encounter a problem; for many scholars today would argue that the same man did not write I and II Thessalonians and that the same man did not write Colossians and Ephesians, and that in each case the second work has been influenced by the first. Such imitation may have been partly unconscious if the two authors belonged to the same school. We must deal then with the question of deliberate copying or unconscious imitation within a school of writers by discussing the arguments of those who posit different authors for GJohn and I John.

2. The Argument against Common Authorship Based on Differences in Style

Already in his minute discussion of this issue Holtzmann ("Problem II" 138–39) listed 50 peculiarities of I John that distinguished it from

---

I John. This Epistle repeats the commandment to love one another, and that seems to have influenced the story told by Jerome (*In Galatas* 3.6 on v. 10; PL 26, 433): In old age John kept telling his assembled disciples, "Little children, love one another," with the explanation, "It is a commandment of the Lord. If only that is done, it is enough." In his poem "A Death in the Desert," Browning described the dying John speaking to his followers in an echo of I John 1:1: When my ashes scatter, says John,

> "there is left on earth
> No one alive who knew (consider this!)
> —Saw with his eyes and handled with his hands
> That which was from the first, the Word of Life.
> How will it be when none more saith, 'I saw'?"

47 Still very important is the work done a century ago by Holtzmann, "Problem I" 691–99. Among English works, see Westcott, *Epistles* xl–xli; Brooke, *Epistles* i–ix; Stott, *Epistles* 18–19; Painter, *John* 104–8; Johnston, "Spirit-Paraclete" 75–77.
48 See Holtzmann, "Problem II" 131–33.

GJohn, and so for a century it has been apparent that there are serious differences as well as similarities between the two works. The difficulty of evaluating this argument may be seen from a survey of how it has been used in scholarship. Thirty years after Holtzmann, Brooke (*Epistles* xiii–xvi) discussed one by one the peculiarities isolated by his predecessor and came to an opposite conclusion: "Thus on closer inspection a considerable number of the phrases which are actually peculiar to the Epistle remind us so strongly of similar phrases and thoughts in the Gospel that it is again the resemblance rather than the difference that is brought into prominence." Shortly afterward another detailed examination by R. H. Charles[49] seemed to settle the matter for the English-speaking world: "The body of evidence in favour of a common authorship of J and (1.) 2. 3. J carries with it absolute conviction." It was surprising, then, to find the issue reopened by C. H. Dodd[50] in 1937 with a long and detailed study arguing against common authorship. His views have not gone unchallenged, for writing in disagreement with him have been Howard ("Common Authorship") in 1947; Wilson ("Examination") in 1948; Salom ("Aspects") in 1955; Hering ("Aramaïsmes") in 1956; Higgins ("Words") in 1966–67; Turner ("Style") in 1976.

In these discussions the characteristics of "style" are sometimes very broadly understood. Dodd ("First Epistle" 155) thought he could detect in the more pedestrian I John "a mind inferior to that of the Evangelist in spiritual quality, in intellectual power and in literary artistry." Nunn ("First Epistle" 299), on the other hand, found that "the Epistle is the kind of book which we should expect to have from the last survivor of the Twelve, who was acquainted with the whole cycle of Christian doctrine, if not with all the writings which now make up the New Testament." Both statements are based on uncontrollable impressions. It is rather "style" understood in the sense of detailed grammatical features that interests us here.

In point of fact, Dodd ("First Epistle" 130–41) greatly refined the argument based on "peculiarities" proposed by Holtzmann a half-century before. He concentrated on the *minor* grammatical features that might unconsciously betray difference of authorship. For instance, he supplied statistics about the differences between GJohn and I John in their respective use of prepositions, particles, compound verbs, Aramaisms, etc. However, Dodd neglected to some extent the possibility that the difference of usage might be attributable to causes other than difference of

---

[49] *A Critical and Exegetical Commentary on the Revelation of John* (2 vols. ICC; Edinburgh: Clark, 1920) 1, xxxiv–xxxvii.

[50] He first published his views in the article "First Epistle" which he wrote as a preparation for his commentary on the Epistles, which appeared in 1946.

authorship,[51] e.g., different type of literature (gospel versus [putative] epistle), different length (GJohn is almost eight times longer than I John), different subject matter (narrative versus reflective comment), and the possible presence of different sources behind GJohn (so that I John might be similar to some parts of GJohn but not to others).

Let me give some examples of how Dodd's statistics are relativized if one takes other factors into account. At first blush, it is impressive that, while GJohn employs 23 prepositions, I John has only 14, until we realize that in the NT only the Gospels use more than 20 prepositions, and that 6 NT works of length comparable to I John employ between 14 and 17 prepositions. In other words, the numerical statistics for prepositions are normal, granted the respective lengths of GJohn and I John. Again the comparison of 64 uses of *gar*, "for," in GJohn over against 3 uses in I John is a striking difference. Yet if we compare two genuine Pauline letters (138 instances of *gar* in Romans over against 13 in Philippians), we are warned again that variations in frequency must be cautiously evaluated.[52] Dodd reports that I John is lacking many of the adverbial particles found in GJohn, but some of the missing particles are those of locale and time, which are needed in the narratives of GJohn but not appropriate to I John. The most impressive argument based on the statistics of particles centers upon *oun*, "therefore," which occurs 194 times in GJohn but never in I John, and indeed only once in the critically established Greek text of the Johannine Epistles (III John 8).[53] Can the same author who exhibited an idiosyncratic (and probably unconscious) overuse of *oun* in one work have written another work without using *oun* once? Yet BDF 451[1] points out that *oun* is most frequent in narrative, and I John is lacking in narrative. A more revealing statistic, then, is to compare the Johannine Epistles to the Last Discourse of Jesus (John 13:31–17:26), a section of Gospel similar in subject matter and length to the Epistles. If one omits the few connecting narrative verses, one finds in that section of GJohn only a single instance of *oun* (16:22),[54] quite comparable to the single *oun* in the Epistles!

Dodd notes that, except for dubious examples, I John is lacking in the Aramaisms that mark GJohn. Aramaisms are Greek expressions thought to betray an Aramaic background, but in evaluating them one should ac-

[51] This point is made strongly by Howard, "Common Authorship."

[52] Wilson, "Examination," is particularly effective against Dodd in pointing out that statistical differences among the Pauline Epistles are often more dramatic than those between GJohn and I John.

[53] See NOTE on I John 2:24ab.

[54] The connecting narrative verses are 13:31,37–38; 14:5,8–9,22–23; and 16:17–18, which altogether contain three instances of *oun*. The one *oun* in discourse (16:22) is slightly suspect, for the word order in that verse varies widely in the textual witnesses.

knowledge that the detection of Aramaisms is a very inexact science. First, the distinction between Aramaisms and more general Semitic features is not always precise; and, second, the significance of Semitisms in NT Greek is not agreed upon. For many, Semitisms are the sign of translation from a Semitic original: either the author had a Semitic source before him as he worked, or the author, though he spoke Greek, thought in a Semitic language and tended to preserve the Semitic coloration of a tradition he was preserving. But others[55] argue for the existence of a Semitized Greek dialect learned in the synagogues of the Diaspora, spoken by people many of whom knew no Aramaic or Hebrew. In the latter hypothesis, the presence of Aramaisms or Semitisms in a NT book may tell us little specific about the history of its tradition and author, e.g., whether or not they came from Palestine. Be that as it may, Hering[56] proposes for I John several examples of Aramaisms that Dodd neglected—examples, however, that would scarcely win universal agreement. Turner ("Style" 136) points to Aramaic style in the asyndeton that is seen in well over half the clauses in I John, and to an even higher percentage in II and III John. Higgins ("Words" 376) argues that of 69 phrases in GJohn that have a parallel in I John, 63 are found in sections of GJohn that have been thought to reflect an Aramaicizing trend. Beyer's table of Semitisms in the NT (SSNT 1, 298) shows that I and II John have the highest percentage of Semitisms per page in the NT, and that the percentage of Semitisms to Grecisms in I, II, and III John is very close to the percentage in GJohn (125% to 111%).

Overall, then, it seems that the variation of minute stylistic features between GJohn and I John is not much different from the variation that one can find if one compares one part of GJohn to another part. In particular, the Johannine Jesus *speaks* as the author of the Johannine Epistles writes.[57]

Though I do not think that the Holtzmann/Dodd method of comparing stylistic and grammatical features establishes a difference of authorship between GJohn and I John, I am persuaded that there is a marked difference between the two works in terms of clarity of expression. Having translated both GJohn and I John, I found the first relatively simple, while the obscurity of the second was infuriating. If one studies my NOTES

---

[55] See Turner, "Style" 136. For the complexity of NT Aramaisms, see J. A. Fitzmyer, *A Wandering Aramaean: Collected Aramaic Essays* (SBLMS 25; Missoula: Scholars Press, 1979) 12–17, 38–46.

[56] In the article "Aramaïsmes," Hering argues that the awkwardness of the Greek in I John 1:1; 2:8,12–14 indicates a problem in translating the Aramaic relative pronoun and conjunction (*de*).

[57] This presents a great dilemma for conservative scholars (who argue strongly that the same author wrote GJohn and I John), for one must wonder about the extent to which the Jesus of GJohn has become a spokesman for Johannine theology.

(following the units of text in the commentary) wherein I point out the number of scholars divided over the grammar and meaning of almost every verse in I John, one might well conclude that, simply from the viewpoint of translating correctly, there are more difficulties in any two chapters of I John than in the whole of the much longer GJohn. Earlier commentators theorized that, writing at a more advanced stage of life, John son of Zebedee (the putative author of GJohn) had become less mentally alert in expressing himself in I John. (Yet, with all its grammatical obscurity, I John is very vigorous.) Today, granted the fact that we know little about the identity or the age of the evangelist and/or the epistolary writer, the greater obscurity of the Epistles becomes an argument for difference of authorship.

3. The Argument against Common Authorship Based on Differences in Thought

Recently those who reject common authorship have shifted the main argument from style to thought and theology, contending that a critical analysis of the development of ideas within the Johannine tradition separates GJohn from I John (Conzelmann, G. Klein, Langbrandtner, Richter). Let me comment on the main points that have been brought up.

Some 35 key words that by frequency or emphasis are important in GJohn are absent from I John. Once again the statistic is relativized by a comparison among other NT works, e.g., in a list of 42 important Pauline words, only 7 are absent from Romans and from I Corinthians, but between 26 and 30 are absent from each of four other Epistles that are comparable to I John in length (I and II Thessalonians, Philippians, Colossians). If difference in length accounts for some differences in theological vocabulary, a difference in literary circumstances explains other vocabulary features. It is impressive that *kyrios,* "lord," which occurs 41 times in GJohn, does not occur in I John, until one notices how frequently *kyrios* is a vocative of address in GJohn ("O Lord"), a speech pattern not appropriate to the treatise we have here. The words *krinein/krisis,* "judge, judgment," appear 30 times in GJohn and never in I John; but in GJohn the usage is frequently in terms of a judgment upon "the Jews" who refuse to believe in Jesus, a situation that does not apply to I John. The fact that *zētein,* "to seek," occurs 34 times in GJohn but never in I John may be explained by GJohn's attention to conversion (in terms of seeking Jesus or being sought by him), while I John deals with the already converted. If *pempein,* "to send," occurs 32 times in GJohn but never in I John, it is noteworthy that 26 of the GJohn uses are in Jesus' phrase, "He who sent me," which would be inappropriate in I John.

Nevertheless, if we move from inconclusive vocabulary statistics, there

are differences in thought between GJohn and I John that are not so easily explained. I John is distinct[58] from GJohn in the following points:

■ Attribution of important features to God rather than to Christ.[59] In I
  John 1:5 God is light, while in John 1:4,9; 8:12; etc., Jesus is the light.
  Commandments are attributed to God in I John 2:3–4; 3:22–24; 5:2–3,
  specifically the commandment to love one another (4:21; II John 4–6),
  whereas GJohn speaks of *Jesus'* commandment(s) (13:34; 14:15,21;
  15:10,12).

■ I John stresses aspects of a lower christology in instances where GJohn
  stresses a higher christology.[60] The "word" in the Prologue to I John
  seems to refer to the gospel-message about life, whereas in the GJohn
  Prologue it is clearly personified. There is stress in the Epistles on the reality of the flesh of the Son of God (I John 4:2; II John 7), so that seeing him involves his tangibility (I John 1:1: "We felt with our own
  hands"), while GJohn calls attention to the glory that shines through the
  flesh ("The Word became flesh . . . and we have seen his glory"). Indeed, the glory of Jesus is never mentioned in the Epistles.[61]

■ The sacrificial and atoning character of the death of Jesus is much
  clearer in I John (1:7; 2:2; 3:16; 4:10) than in GJohn, where the death
  of Jesus is seen as his triumph and glorification (12:27–32; 13:1;
  14:30–31; 16:10–11,33; 17:1). An exception in GJohn is the enigmatic
  reference to "the Lamb of God who takes away the world's sin."[62]
  Richter ("Deutung") contends that in GJohn there are several strains of
  thought about the death of Jesus, and two of them are encountered in
  the narrative of the footwashing (13:1–20). Of these Richter attributes
  to the redactor rather than to the evangelist a theology whereby the
  death of Jesus was an act of love for his own and an example to be imitated (13:12–17), and so it is the redactor's theology on this point that
  finds echo in I John 3:16.

■ I John offers much less specific reference to the Spirit than does GJohn.
  Whereas "the Paraclete" (*paraklētos;* see ABJ 29A, 1135–44) is an im-

---

[58] Further development of the distinctive viewpoint of I John will be found in the
commentary. This list of points is not exhaustive.

[59] I am avoiding the oversimplification of saying that I John is theocentric while
GJohn is christocentric. Much of I John is highly christocentric, but there are
differences between the two works about what is attributed to God and what to
Jesus. Loisy, *Evangile-Epîtres* 73–74, exaggerates when he accuses I John of bordering upon Patripassionism in its attribution of salvation to the Father.

[60] Once again I am avoiding the simplification of saying that I John has a low
christology and GJohn a high christology. The two works share to a large extent the
same christology, even if there are differences of emphasis. See footnote 29 in unit
11 below.

[61] *Doxazein/doxa,* "glorify/glory," occur 39 times in GJohn and never in I, II,
and III John.

[62] For various interpretations of John 1:29, some of them implying atoning death,
see ABJ 29, 58–63.

portant and peculiarly GJohn designation of the Holy Spirit, that term is applied only to Jesus in I John (2:1). The treatment of the Spirit of Truth alongside the Spirit of Deceit in I John 4:1–6 is strangely vague about the personal quality of the Spirit. Nevertheless, there are relatively clear references to the Spirit in I John 3:24; 4:13; 5:6,8, even if the term "Holy Spirit" is never used (contrast John 1:33; 7:39; 14:26; 20:22). There may also be symbolic reference to the Spirit in the "unction/anointing" of I John 2:20,27 and in the "God's seed" of 3:9.[63]

- The final eschatology of I John differs from that of GJohn. A comparison is complicated by the Bultmannian thesis that the undeniable final eschatology of GJohn is to be attributed to the Ecclesiastical Redactor and that the evangelist held solely a realized eschatology (ABJ 29, cxvi–cxxi). Even if one does not accept such a hypothesis and acknowledges that the evangelist had both realized and final aspects in his eschatology, there is no doubt that the major emphasis in GJohn is on realized eschatology, e.g., the children of God already possess divine life, and both judgment and seeing God in Jesus are present privileges. Without denying the present reality of divine life, I John looks forward to a future judgment as the moment when we shall be like God and see Him as He is (2:28; 3:2). There are elements of apocalyptic vocabulary in I John (parousia, Antichrist, "the Iniquity" [*anomia*]) which are not found in GJohn. This focus on the future tends to give I John a greater sense of Christian history in which there is a sequence of time. Conzelmann, "Anfang," points out that, while in the GJohn Prologue "the beginning" involves the creation of the world, the I John Prologue speaks of "the beginning" of the Christian community or its tradition (1:1; also 1:5; 2:7; II John 5). A study by G. Klein ("Licht"[64]) is important on this point. The example that gives the article its title, "The true light is already shining" (I John 2:8), illustrates a difference between GJohn and I John. For GJohn the light has come into the world and the struggle with darkness is in the ministry of Jesus; for I John the darkness is gradually passing away and the effect of the light is gradually making it-

---

[63] Johnston, *Spirit-Paraclete* 78, argues that GJohn and I John are not so dissimilar on the issue of the Spirit as might first seem. See the parallels to I John 3:24; 4:13; 5:6–8 in Chart Two in Appendix I.

[64] Klein's article is difficult to evaluate, for he accepts without debate Bultmann's existential interpretation of GJohn. In my judgment Bultmann is right in the thesis that each person who faces the Johannine Jesus must choose between light and darkness. But the existential choice is not the only facet of the issue, for the light has definitively triumphed over the darkness in Jesus' victory over the Prince of this world. This means that the theology of GJohn on light is both existential and historical. While I do not agree fully with O. Cullmann, *Salvation in History* (New York: Harper & Row, 1967), who attributes to GJohn almost a Lucan view of salvation history, I think that Bultmann (and Klein) underestimate the Johannine sense of history as regards both past and future. See Brown, "Kerygma" 393–95.

self felt. In I John there has been a (greater) historicizing of eschatology. While GJohn speaks about "the hour" that covers the whole revelatory event embodied in Jesus (ABJ 29, 517–18), an hour that is already here to the believer, I John can speak about "the last hour" (2:18) as if there were a series of hours in which the "hour" of Jesus was preliminary to an hour involving the history of the Johannine Community. The Jesus of GJohn can speak of a "new" commandment in the sense of eschatological newness, while I John 2:7–8 can discuss the same commandment in terms of "old" and "new," thinking of it as having been given some time ago, even if it is still new in its impact.

■ There are no quotations from the OT in I John while there are many in GJohn.[65] On the one hand this fact should not be used to construct the thesis that I John is more Hellenistic than GJohn (Dodd, Wilder) if that means less influenced by Jewish thought. After all, a specific reference to an OT story (Cain) shapes a whole section of I John (3:12ff.), and the OT covenant theme had strong influence on its ethical outlook.[66] Key concepts of I John like "truth" are not modeled on Platonic lines but on apocalypticism and Jewish intertestamental thought,[67] and a close affinity has been detected between ideas in I John and those found in the Dead Sea Scrolls.[68] On the other hand, despite elements of Jewish background, there is no evidence in I John of the debate with "the Jews" of the synagogue that dominated GJohn—a fact that may explain the lack of direct references to the OT.

This last remark leads us into the next aspect of our discussion of the differences between GJohn and I John. The theological differences listed above cannot be denied (and I shall seek to make sense of them below in units IV and V of the INTRODUCTION, where I develop my theory of the relation of the epistolary author to his opponents). But do such differences necessarily demand different authors for GJohn and I John, or could the same author be stressing different themes because the situation he was facing when he wrote I John had changed from the situation prevalent when GJohn was written?

4. The Argument against Common Authorship Based on Differences in Life Situation

GJohn was written primarily to strengthen faith in Jesus as "the Messiah [Christ], the Son of God," so that through this faith believers might have life in his name (20:31). That there was a need for such

[65] It is noteworthy that few OT quotations are found in chaps. 13–17 of GJohn, the section that has the greatest affinity with I John. Only John 13:18 and 15:25 are specific OT citations; see 17:12.

[66] For detail, see Boismard, "La connaissance," and Malatesta, *Interiority*.

[67] Thus de la Potterie, *La vérité*, versus Bultmann and Dodd.

[68] For detail, see Brown, "Qumran Scrolls," and Boismard, "First Epistle."

strengthening becomes apparent when it is realized that the evangelist was writing on two levels, describing not only what Jesus did during his lifetime but also what had happened and was still happening to the Johannine Community. In my book *Community* I have detected in the pages of GJohn traces of a half-dozen groups of non-Christians and Christians with whom the Johannine Community had entered into debate about Jesus. They included "the Jews" of the synagogue who had expelled the Johannine Christians for confessing Jesus as the Messiah; crypto-Christians who remained hidden in the synagogues because they would not admit publicly their faith in Jesus; adherents of John the Baptist who claimed that he (not Jesus) was God's prime emissary; Jewish Christians who recognized Jesus as the Messiah but not as divine and who gave to the eucharistic flesh and blood of Jesus no sacramental import; and finally Christians of the "Apostolic Churches"—so entitled because in my judgment they regarded themselves as heirs of Peter and the Twelve—who recognized the divinity of Jesus but seemingly not his preexistence as the Word of God and who paid much attention to precise church structure.[69] It is not important for our purposes here whether or not my detection of these other groups is correct in every detail. What is important and, indeed, startling is that none of these outside groups is in view in the Epistles. The struggle is now with former insiders who have left the Community (I John 2:19)—with *secessionists,* to give them the name I shall most often employ in this commentary (see footnote 156 below).

If the adversary has changed, so has the point of the struggle. None of the opponents in GJohn seems to have had so high a christology (especially in terms of preexistence) as did the Johannine Community; and so, if the evangelist wrote to strengthen faith in Jesus as "the Messiah [Christ], the Son of God," he was emphasizing that the Father and the Son were one, existing together in glory before the world began (John 10:30; 17:5). The struggle in I John is still for a proper faith in Jesus as "the Christ" and "the Son of God" (5:1,5); but now the stress is on the human career of God's Son: a "Jesus Christ come in the flesh" (4:2; II John 7), a Jesus Christ who "came . . . in water and in blood" (I John 5:6). The struggle is against those who "negate the importance of Jesus" the man (4:3), against those who are too "progressive" (II John 9). Almost all scholars would agree that such ultraprogressives were not a main target in GJohn, although some would see them attacked in GJohn passages attributed to the final redactor (e.g., 1:14; 19:34–35).

[69] See Brown, *Community* 59–91, 166–67. See also Brown, "Other Sheep," and ABJ 29, lxvii–lxxix. I have resisted and continue to resist the theory that finds either in GJohn or its sources a major struggle with gnostics (in varying forms: Bultmann, Käsemann, Langbrandtner, Latte, Schotroff). I recognize that elements in GJohn could be interpreted to favor gnosticism, but the gnostic struggle came *after* the main composition of GJohn.

Granted the fact that the situation envisaged in GJohn is dramatically different from that envisaged in I John, what does this tell us about authorship? The least that it implies is that GJohn and I John were not written at the same time to the same group by the same man.[70] They could have been written at the same time by different men (and to different branches of the Johannine Community), or, and this is more probable, at a different time by either the same man (sadder and wiser as he faces a new battle, now from within the movement) or by different men. As will be seen below, I prefer the last alternative of a different author for the Johannine Epistles,[71] but I would insist that the differences thus far discussed cannot *prove* that. Such a decision depends on one's analysis of what happened in the history of the Johannine Community to bring about a secession, an analysis to be given in unit IV below. But before we turn to that, some other aspects of the interrelationship of the Johannine writings need to be considered.

C. *In What Sequence Were the Gospel and the Epistles Written?*

The overall issue of sequence involves, first, the inner epistolary sequence and, second, the sequence of GJohn and I John.

1. Sequence among the Epistles

As an introduction to the complexity of this first issue let me report the following views: F.-M. Braun posits the order III-II-I; Wendt and Langbrandtner opt for II-III-I, and Marshall, *Epistles,* comments on them in that order on the grounds that II-III can be read as an introduction to I; finally, Bultmann, *Epistles,* follows the order I-III-II. In this commentary I shall follow the traditional order (I-II-III) which, even if by accident, may have been the historical order of their composition.

(a) WAS II JOHN OR III JOHN COMPOSED FIRST? The similarity between the Opening and Closing Formulas of these two letters (II A1

---

[70] If II John was written at the same time as I John, as the similarity of content would suggest, the same comparative statement would be true of the shorter Epistle, and likewise for III John if the similarity of its Conclusion to that of II John indicates that the two Epistles were written and sent together.

[71] In my judgment all that we know of this Johannine author is that he identified himself as "the Presbyter" in II and III John. It is useless to press the case that he was John the Presbyter mentioned by Papias (p. 12 above), or the presbyter of Ephesus who converted Justin Martyr (*Dialogue* 3.1–8.1; thus Bacon). Indeed, I offer no names for the four Johannine figures I posit in the composition of GJohn and the Epistles, namely, the Beloved Disciple (the source of the tradition about Jesus), the evangelist, the Presbyter (author of the Epistles), and the final redactor of GJohn.

above) has led many to suggest that they were written at the same time, although the tendency of letter format to be stereotyped makes that quite impossible to demonstrate. Again, if the visit of the Presbyter (II John 12; III John 14) involved only one journey bringing him to several churches, the two letters would have been written in close proximity; but letter format makes it impossible to be sure that such a visit was more than a velleity. No likelihood can be given to the thesis that II John was the previous letter mentioned in III John 9 as having been written to the church (see NOTE there). Because I judge the emerging church structure implied by Diotrephes' actions in III John 9–10 to be a reaction to the secession discussed in I and II John, I shall discuss III John with the idea that *logically* it comes after the other two Epistles. But if all three Epistles were written in close proximity, there is no way to know whether III John was also chronologically last.

(b) WAS I JOHN OR II JOHN COMPOSED FIRST? Similarity of content (II A2 above) and of alarm about the same adversaries[72] make it logical to assume that these two Epistles were written about the same time. What most differentiates them is that the adversaries are rebutted at great length in I John and only briefly in II John. The false teachers have not arrived at the church addressed in II John 9–11 while they are a reality to be struggled with in I John: They have seceded from the author's Community, but their seductive propaganda makes them still a threat. Accordingly, it might seem more logical to guess that II John was written earlier when the danger was first making its appearance and before it had divided the Johannine Community, while I John was written after the warning of II John had not succeeded and secession was a fact.[73] One could even contend that the instruction in II John 10–11 to exclude the false teacher provoked the formal secession described in I John 2:19. However, the differences between I John and II John may stem more from geography than from chronological interval. The author of I John seems to live close to his addressees: There is no proof that it is a letter or that it has to be sent any distance. He can speak to the recipients as "we." On the other hand, II John is obviously a letter written to a church at a distance. Not only does the writer introduce and identify himself, but he addresses the

---

[72] Both works refer to them as Antichrists who had "gone out" (seceded), denying Jesus Christ come/coming in the flesh (I John 2:18,22; 4:1–3; II John 7); see II A2 above.

[73] That II John was written before I John is proposed by Wendt, "Zum zweiten" 18, who argues that this order explains why I John lacks any introduction: the author assumed II John as an introduction. However, that claim is not verified in any other pair of NT works written to the same audience; the second always has an introduction (I–II Thessalonians; I–II Corinthians; I–II Timothy; I–II Peter; Luke-Acts). See the NOTES on I John 2:12–14 and on 2:26a for the dubious contention that the *egrapsa* there ("I wrote") refers to II John.

church politely and formally ("To an Elect Lady and to her children"[74]) as if the relationship were more remote. The danger presented by the secessionist teachers may have already wracked the Community where the author of I John lived but may not have reached the outlying Johannine church addressed in II John. Indeed, one may well guess that the author of I John lived in the central locale of Johannine Christianity[75] with many house-churches and numerous adherents—the place where the secessionist movement had begun. That would also explain the fact that in III John the author seems to feel responsibility for the missionaries who were setting out: He had to be sure that the outlying house-churches would receive them and help them to continue on their journey. This support would have now become an urgent matter if he was using the missionaries (once the proclaimer of Christianity to the pagans) to warn and instruct the network of Johannine house-churches against the advent of the secessionist teachers who were themselves conducting a missionary campaign for their cause (II John 10–11). The author did not want the secessionists to have the success in the outlying churches that they already had in the central locale. It is perfectly possible, then, that the three Johannine Epistles were composed about the same time and dealt with ramifications of the same problem throughout the Johannine churches.

2. Sequence of GJohn and I John

A more important question will occupy our attention for the rest of this unit, a question that is essential in an analysis of the totality of Johannine thought and is meaningful whether or not we posit a common author. An answer in terms of the precise dating of GJohn and I John is not the crucial point, for I have argued that GJohn took shape over several decades of Community history, involving an accumulation of traditions about Jesus, the selection and rewriting of those traditions into a basic Gospel (perhaps in several editions), and final additions by a redactor after the evangelist's death.[76] In *Community* 22–23 I have suggested that the traceable period of pre-Gospel Johannine Community history stretched from the mid-50s to the 80s, with the body of the Gospel being written *ca.* 90, and the final redaction just after the turn of the century. Any such hypothesis makes it possible that I John was composed after some stages in the composition of GJohn and before other stages. Because of this complexity it will facilitate the discussion if for the moment we leave aside the question

---

[74] On pp. 17–18 I pointed out that the author of I John refers to the audience as *his* "Little Children," while in II John they are the "children" of the Elect Lady.

[75] See Schnackenburg, "Gemeinde" 281.

[76] See ABJ 29, xxxiv–xxxix. I remind the reader that I think of the Beloved Disciple as the source of the Johannine Community's traditions about Jesus and as the authority behind many of its theological insights, but not as the evangelist or writing author of GJohn. See footnote 71 above.

of the chronological relation of I John to the final *redaction* of GJohn (see below, V D2b) and concentrate on its relation to the basic composition of GJohn. It is to the work of the evangelist, then (as distinct from that of the redactor), that I refer when in the next pages I speak of GJohn.

That the question of whether GJohn or I John is prior will not be easily solved is once again suggested by the division of scholars. Although the majority opts for the priority of GJohn, the reverse is held by Bleek, Brückner, Büchsel, Feuillet,[77] Hilgenfeld, Howard, Huther, Pfleiderer, Scott, Vawter, B. Weiss, Wendt, and Zeller. The problem is epitomized in another way by statements of two British scholars. H.P.V. Nunn ("First Epistle" 296) asserts that if GJohn had been lost, it would have been impossible to understand I John in anything but a limited sense. But I. H. Marshall (*Epistles* 2) says, "It is probably easier in some ways to grasp John's message by beginning with the Epistles." Intelligibility is not necessarily the key to priority, as Marshall acknowledges; but it is a factor in our considerations of whether one work presupposes the other. Let us turn to the principal arguments on each side of the question.[78]

(a) ARGUMENTS FOR THE PRIORITY OF I JOHN (and often for an early absolute date for I John). Despite the many similarities between GJohn and I John listed in Appendix I, Chart Two, no passage in any of the Epistles is a direct or certain quotation from GJohn,[79] a surprising fact if I John was written after GJohn. A few passages in I John have been judged more "primitive" than the comparable passages in GJohn, e.g., the Prologue of I John is a much less finished product than the Prologue of GJohn.[80] The theology of I John has also been thought to be earlier or less developed (although chronological judgments about ideas are admittedly tenuous). For instance, I John's stress on the atoning death of Jesus and on final eschatology brings it into harmony with the earlier books of the NT, while GJohn's treatment of Jesus' death as his ascension, and its insistence on realized eschatology may be judged as more advanced theology. Terminology in I John reflective of Jewish apocalyptic (Antichrist, *anomia* or "Iniquity," false prophets) and the warning against idolatry in 5:21 have been cited for the thesis that I John is more "Jew-

---

[77] At least he judges that the I John Prologue is prior to the GJohn Prologue, a not uncommon view. See footnote 80 below.

[78] Brooke, *Epistles* xix–xxvii, gives arguments on both sides.

[79] The theme "that joy may be fulfilled" is shared by I John 1:4 and John 15:11. The commandment to love one another in I John 3:11,23 approximates a citation of John 13:34; 15:13,17. In the other direction much more problematic is the contention that John 19:34–35 is a later misunderstanding (by the redactor?) of I John 5:6.

[80] A chronological comparison of the two works based on the Prologues is complicated by the suggestion that the GJohn Prologue is a hymn that once circulated independently and thus antedated the evangelist's appropriation of it to preface GJohn (ABJ 29, 18–23).

ish" than GJohn (Robinson, "Destination" 132) and therefore composed at an earlier period in Community life, before major contact with Gentiles. The close parallels in terminology to the Dead Sea Scrolls (footnote 68 above) have also been invoked in this direction. Whatever position one takes in the debate about chronological priority, many of these "early" factors must be accounted for in one's theory of the composition of I John, and I shall attempt to do so in V C2d below where I comment on the author's frequent claim to present what was "from the beginning." The point here, however, is that early contents can *prove* no more than that the author knew old traditions, so that a date of writing (or at least of final editing) must be judged from the *latest* contents of a work.

(b) ARGUMENTS FOR THE PRIORITY OF GJOHN. If the presence of Jewish elements in I John shows that the author was aware of or dependent upon a period of Community life when there were close contacts with Judaism, the fact that the only Johannine Community members identified by name in the Epistles (Gaius, Diotrephes, and Demetrius in III John) all bear Greco-Roman names suggests that at the time of writing there were many Gentiles in the Johannine churches.[81]

The lateness of I John is also suggested by the different life situation it reflects when compared with GJohn, as discussed in II B4 above. A fierce struggle with outsiders, especially with "the Jews," dominates GJohn; there is no hint that the Johannine Community has already been divided and decimated by a secession. Could that Community, if it had already lost the larger part of its "progressive" members to the world (II John 7–9; I John 4:5), have then survived the traumatic expulsion from the synagogue (John 9:22; 16:2)? If there were already Johannine christological extremists (as attested in I John), would the evangelist have dared to present the prototype of the Community, the Beloved Disciple,[82] as superior even to Peter in his perception of Jesus? On the other hand, if I John came after GJohn, the situation is quite intelligible. The high christology attested in GJohn brought expulsion from the synagogue (Brown, *Community* 36–47). After a separation from a parent body, defensive concentration on live-or-die issues inevitably brings exaggeration, especially when a group feels alienated; for some will always push their understanding of the group's position beyond the stance that originally

---

[81] It is more likely that these three figures were Gentiles than Diaspora Jews who had adopted Hellenic names, for other NT figures who bear the names Gaius and Demetrius seem to have been Gentiles (see NOTES on III John 1a and 12a). Nevertheless, "Gaius" was the Greco-Roman name of many Jews, seemingly taken from admiration of Gaius Julius Caesar, considered a benefactor of Jews.

[82] See John 20:8; 21:7. In *Community,* 82–85, I argue that while the Beloved Disciple was as real a figure as any other follower of Jesus during the public ministry, he serves as the hero of the Johannine Community and personifies its theological development and self-understanding.

brought about the separation. While the silence of GJohn about inner-Johannine conflict is hard to explain if such a conflict had already occurred, the silence of I John about opposition by "the Jews" and other outsiders is not hard to explain: Internal struggle pushes aside worries about outsiders, for in religious polemics no enemy is so dangerous as the enemy within.

Certain features of theological difference between GJohn and I John also make better sense if the Epistle is later. Westcott (*Epistles* xxxi) makes a general observation: "It can only be said with confidence that the Epistle presupposes in those for whom it was composed a familiar acquaintance with the characteristic truths which are preserved for us in the Gospel." However, as we saw above in II B3, I John does more than presuppose ideas found in GJohn; the tone of those ideas is different, and that difference can be explained in every case if the thrust of GJohn has been exaggerated by those who accepted its message. If we go down the list on pp. 26–28, the thrust of I John is intelligible as a reaction to an *overemphasis* on high christology, on death as glorification, on the activity of the Paraclete-Spirit as teacher, and on final eschatology.[83] There is considerable truth to the comparison whereby the Johannine Epistles stand in relation to GJohn as the Pastoral Epistles stand in relation to the undisputed, earlier Pauline letters.[84] In each case there is a concretizing of insights, an appeal to tradition, a defensiveness against dangers from within, and a certain cautious retrenchment—the marks of the second generation of a community now more concerned with survival and preservation than with the conversion of Jews and Gentiles. As I explain my own theory of this development in V below, it will become apparent why I think it almost certain that I John was written after that tradition in GJohn took shape, and why I think it very likely but not certain that I John was written by one other than the evangelist.

[83] It would be very difficult, on the other hand, to explain GJohn as a reaction to ideas in I John, since in GJohn the main attack is against the ideas of outsiders.

[84] Although this idea has been popularized by Conzelmann, "Anfang" 198ff., I would not agree with the suggestion there that in the Johannine "Pastoral" Epistles "Early Catholicism" has triumphed. In I John there is none of the emphasis on structure and on authoritative teaching offices that one finds in I-II Timothy and Titus. I use the term "Pastorals" literally in relation to the Johannine Epistles: They are concerned with the care of the sheep of the Johannine fold, not with the sheep who are not of that fold (John 10:16) nor with the catch of fish. They represent the second stage of the fish and sheep images in John 21.

III. Source Theories for the Origin of I John

While the first two units of the INTRODUCTION have dealt with the three Johannine Epistles, the much longer I John is the main subject of this volume and is the key to an overall view of how the Johannine writings fit together coherently. Turning now to I John, we must first determine how the author composed his work, granted the fact that he criticizes or disagrees with many statements or maxims that he quotes throughout I John. Whence did he derive these statements? Explanations follow two main lines. The first is that he drew upon a source that had come down to him from an earlier period. The second is that he drew the maxims from adversaries who constituted a contemporary danger for the group addressed. In this unit (III) I shall discuss the first hypothesis, and in the next unit (IV) the second. A decision between them affects crucially one's theory of Johannine Community history and of the author's place in the range of early Christian thought.

One source theory has had a considerable following among German scholars, with a history of developments and modifications. I shall treat that first, and then turn to several other (somewhat idiosyncratic) source proposals.

A. *The German Theory of an Antithetical-Statement Source*

This theory has had a life-span of some sixty years from the original proposal in 1907 by E. von Dobschütz to Bultmann's commentary on the Epistles in 1967.

1. E. von Dobschütz

In a 1907 essay ("Studien" 4–5) this scholar made a close study of I John 2:28–3:12 and isolated a series of eight antithetical statements that could be grouped into four pairs. Three of the pairs (A, B, and D below) have the same beginning, and the first and the last are chiastically related:

> **A.** 2:29b Everyone who acts justly has been begotten by Him.
> 3:4a Everyone who acts sinfully is really doing iniquity.
>
> **B.** 3:6a Everyone who abides in him does not commit sin.
> 3:6b Everyone who does commit sin has never seen him.

C. 3:7b The person who acts justly is truly just.
    3:8a The person who acts sinfully belongs to the devil.

D. 3:9a Everyone who has been begotten by God does not act sinfully.
    3:10b Everyone who does not act justly does not belong to God.

No matter how one reacts to a source theory, one must somehow explain this pattern, which can scarcely be accidental.[85] Not only are the lines parallel, but there is parallelism between the pairs, e.g., between A and C.

Von Dobschütz theorized that the author of I John had derived these antithetical statements from a source and was commenting on them.[86] This hypothetical source was deemed to embody Hellenistic Semitic thought patterns, LXX style, and a moral dualism of doing good versus doing evil. The epistolary author's comments were distinguishable from the source material because of their rhetorical style, for he had abandoned the one-line affirmations in favor of periodic sentences. Moreover, by his theological modifications the author had moved the dualism of the source from the ethical to the metaphysical plane. For example, where the source offered a moral choice, "Everyone who has been begotten by God does not act sinfully," the author has added as an explanation, "because God's seed abides in him" (I John 3:9b), introducing a divine determinative factor that removes choice. Yet von Dobschütz considered the epistolary author to be only superficially gnostic, since the ethical origins showed through his metaphysical dualism.

Before we continue through the history of this source theory, it may be well at the very beginning to acknowledge some of the difficulties it presents.[87] Some of those are centered on the source itself: What was the original meaning of such a source and what would it have conveyed to its readers? What life situation accounted for its composition? If such a source existed, why did the epistolary author break up its statements, as in A and D; for he could have kept the lines together in pairs and added his comments after the pair? Further difficulties are related to the methodology employed in detecting the source. There are other statements in I John of the same style and ethical content as those von Dobschütz has attributed to the source; yet they were omitted from his reconstruction because they destroyed the neatness of the pattern he thought he detected. For instance, von Dobschütz has passed over 3:3: "Everyone who has this hope based on Him makes himself pure." The criterion for distinction

[85] Those who reject the source theory could maintain that the author himself created the pattern, perhaps under the influence of the slogans of his opponents which he was trying to counteract with slogans of his own.

[86] In "Studien" 6–8, he spoke respectively of *Grundschrift* and *Bearbeitung* and compared this process to Jewish midrashic reflection on a basic Scripture text. Such a reflective process is clearly at work. What is debatable is whether the object of reflection was a previously composed source-document.

[87] To their credit, proponents of the source theory have recognized difficulties, e.g., H. Braun, "Literar-Analyse" 211.

based on the stylistic difference between antithetical affirmations and rhetorical comment is dubious. Büchsel ("Zu den Johannesbriefen" 238–39) points out that in *Pirqe Aboth,* a Jewish work not far removed in its origins from the date of I John, antithetical and homiletic styles are found in close proximity. The criterion of theological difference (moral versus metaphysical dualism) is also hazy. How does one know that in von Dobschütz's last pair (D) acting or not acting justly is free from metaphysical dualism since it is related to being begotten by God? Does the introduction of "God's seed" in I John 3:9b do any more than make explicit what was implicit?

2. R. Bultmann

Twenty years later (1927) von Dobschütz's theory was rescued from obscurity by Bultmann who applied it to the whole of I John, reconstructing a source consisting of twenty-six antithetical couplets (or triplets) drawn from all five chapters, plus part of v. 9 of II John.[88] This source contained in whole or in part one-third of the verses of I John. In his commentary forty years later (1967) Bultmann gave a somewhat different arrangement; and since this final reconstruction is not printed in any one place in Bultmann's *Epistles,* I have gathered the dispersed verses in Chart Three of Appendix I.[89] For the moment let me call the reader's attention to the sections of that Chart to which I (not Bultmann) have assigned the letters A, B, and C, for they constitute convenient subsections of the proposed source. In (A), derived from 1:6–2:11,[90] there are a series of tristichs with one antithetical to the other; the style is apodictic. In (B), derived from 2:29–3:10, there are five distichs where the lines within the doublets are antithetical; this resembles the von Dobschütz source. In (C) scattered verses are culled from the remaining epistolary material; this is the area where Bultmann shows the most hesitation. That vagueness about what should be attributed to the source in (C) is related to Bultmann's claim (*Epistles* 2) that 1:5–2:27 was originally a rough draft and that what follows in I John was a haphazard collection of individual units which reflected on themes found in the rough draft. Some-

---

[88] The reconstructed source (in Greek) appears in Bultmann, "Analyse" 157–58.

[89] I do this with hesitancy, for it is not always easy to diagnose Bultmann's view. Sometimes his latest view has to be surmised from the confidence or hesitancy with which he discusses his earlier reconstruction. For instance, he admits that his thesis about the source background of 3:19 is problematical, and in reference to 4:12 he says that Schnackenburg's misgivings are justified. In reference to I John 1:5,9; 5:10; II John 9 he explains why and how he has changed his mind since the 1927 reconstruction; but I found no explanation of why in 1967 he omitted the following verses previously attributed to the source: 3:10; 4:5–6,16.

[90] Piper, "I John" 450, while not arguing for a general source theory, describes 1:6–10 as a hymn probably composed before the rest of I John.

times lines from the putative source provided the basis of such reflections, and so these have been scattered about in this subsequent section of I John.

Bultmann's source analysis of I John was influenced by his source analysis of GJohn, so that the reconstructed epistolary source resembles stylistically and ideologically the Revelatory Discourse Source that Bultmann has posited behind GJohn—a source thought to reflect Oriental non-Christian gnosticism.[91] (Later Bultmann recognized that the gnosticism would have had Jewish elements.) The author of I John, like the evangelist of GJohn, was thought to have corrected some of the gnostic tendencies of his source, leaving his mark in the homiletic and paraenetic passages with which he surrounded the selections he took from his source.[92]

About twenty-five years after his initial article on the source analysis of I John, Bultmann ("Redaktion") furthered his theory of composition and brought I John even closer to GJohn by positing an Ecclesiastical Redactor for I John. In the Bultmann GJohn theory[93] such a figure was deemed to have added a more traditional theology to the original evangelist's work; now he was thought to have done the same to I John. For example, the theme of final eschatology was added in I John 2:28; 3:2; 4:17; references to sacrificial death in 1:7; 2:2; 4:10; moral warning in 2:15–17; and an allusion to the sacraments in 5:7–9. The Redactor was also responsible for the Appendix that now appears as I John 5:14–21, even as he added the Epilogue (ch. 21) to GJohn.

Once more, before we continue through the history of the source theory, evaluative remarks are in order, although obviously some of the problems faced by von Dobschütz's theory apply here as well. If the reconstructed source was an artistic and intelligible piece of literature, why did the author break it up and scatter verses all over I John (even placing one in II John)? Why did he rewrite certain verses that made better sense as they were (cf. Bultmann's reconstruction of 5:1 and the canonical form)? D. Muñoz León ("El origen" 224) makes a valid point when he queries the legitimacy of confining the hypothetical source to antithetic formulas since there are in I John lapidary sentences of another type

[91] See ABJ 29, xxix. This source was claimed to have contained Aramaic poetry translated into Greek by the evangelist (or another). Bultmann thought that the later Mandaean literature offered a survival of the kind of antitheses found in the hypothetical GJohn source, e.g., "Whoever is enlightened and instructed by me rises and beholds the Place of Light; whoever is not enlightened and instructed by me is cut off (from the light)" (Mandaean *Book of John* 57 ⚭214; Lidzbarski pp. 204–5).

[92] Bultmann thinks he can detect the style of the epistolary author in the frequent "This is how" pattern (I John 2:3,5, etc.); in the sentences that have an explicative *kai,* "and"; and in the references to Jesus as *ekeinos,* "that one, he."

[93] See ABJ 29, xxx. I too posit a final redactor for GJohn but without the ideological bent given him by Bultmann (ABJ 29, xxxvi–xxxix: *Stage 5*).

(2:22; 3:23; 4:9,21; 5:1,5,13) that could just as well be attributed to a source. Büchsel's appeal to *Pirqe Aboth* for the coexistence in one work of antithetical pattern and homiletic exposition weakens the discernment between source and author posited by Bultmann, even as it weakened von Dobschütz's hypothesis. Moreover, the idea that the epistolary author corrected a source (non-Christian or Jewish gnostic) and that an Ecclesiastical Redactor subsequently corrected the author faces a serious objection that affects Bultmann's theory for both GJohn and I John: People generally preserve and comment upon works (sources), not because they disagree with them and wish to correct them, but because they agree with them and wish to clarify them. The thesis that the epistolary source resembled the Revelatory Discourse Source behind GJohn is not a confirmation, for it is exactly that part of Bultmann's GJohn analysis which has been most challenged.[94] The non-Christian and gnostic character of the posited epistolary source also offers difficulties. As reconstructed, the source appears non-Christian because Bultmann has systematically excluded Christian elements from I John verses, even from parts of sentences. For instance, in the 1927 source reconstruction Bultmann posited this antithesis underlying II John 9: "Anyone who does not remain in the Son does not possess the Father; anyone who does remain in the Son possesses the Father as well." Note what he has had to do to the existing text: "Anyone who is so 'progressive' that he does not remain in the teaching of Christ does not possess God, while anyone who does remain in the teaching possesses both the Father and the Son." Nevertheless, even with such systematic exclusion of Christian elements by Bultmann, the source he posits remains recognizably Christian to some who have commented on it (Beyer, H. Braun, Käsemann, Noack), as we shall see below.[95] Further, Bultmann's posited source contains both claims and corrections of those claims (see A in Chart Three), and it staggers the imagination to think that a gnostic made those corrections! Bultmann's wavering, although admirably honest, raises doubt about the possibility of detecting a source. Although, for instance, in 1927 he attributed 1:9 to the source, in 1967 he wrote (*Epistles* 21) that it was probably inserted in the source by the epistolary author (even though it completely accords with the source). In 1967 Bultmann removed 5:10 from his reconstructed source, for he now realized that there the epistolary author was not quoting the source but imitating its style (*Epistles* 82). And if once he thought that II John 9 belonged to the source, he

[94] See the painstaking critique by D. M. Smith, *The Composition and Order of the Fourth Gospel* (New Haven: Yale University, 1965).

[95] Eventually Bultmann removed from the reconstructed source some verses that seemed to have Christian themes, e.g., the forgiveness of sins in I John 1:9.

now attributed it to a later writer who copied I John (*Epistles* 113). The additions of the Ecclesiastical Redactor posited by Bultmann have also been challenged precisely because some of the theological emphases attributed to the Redactor are quite in harmony with the body of the Epistle, as we shall see when we discuss final eschatology and sacrificial death in the commentary.

3. After Bultmann

Within two years of its proposal (1927), Bultmann's source theory was the subject of lively discussion, being rejected by Büchsel and Lohmeyer and being accepted with variations by Beyer and Windisch.[96] Later (in the 1951 or 3rd ed. of the Windisch commentary) Preisker reconstructed a second source that underlay I John, a source in couplets dealing with eschatology and the parousia (2:28; 3:2,13–14,19–20,21; 4:17; 5:18,19). This source cut across material that Bultmann attributed both to the author of I John and to the Ecclesiastical Redactor. In the same year (1951) H. Braun subjected Bultmann's source theory to an intensive discussion wherein, while he agreed that the epistolary author's use of a source was absolutely certain, he disagreed about the character of the source. It was not gnostic, as Bultmann had judged, but Christian, replete with themes of forgiveness of sins and brotherly love (4:20).[97] Thus Braun attributed to the source antithetic *Christian* statements that Bultmann had been forced logically to exclude (4:2–3). Still in the same year Käsemann ("Ketzer") claimed to find the theology of *simul iustus et peccator*[98] in Bultmann's reconstructed source underlying 1:5–10, and accordingly Käsemann argued for the Christian character of the source. Also Käsemann found no sharp contrast between 1:8–9 and 2:1–2—one is the continuation of the other—and so he challenged the existence of the theological differences that Bultmann had detected between source and epistolary author.

Such modification of both the content and the theology of the hypothetical source, even by those who have favored the theory, has weakened the case for positing a source. After all, once one acknowledges the uncertainty of stylistic criteria separating source from author and once one

---

[96] Beyer, "Rezension" cols. 612–13, argued for the inclusion in the source of material from I John 3:19–20; he also insisted that the source was Christian, being an early non-Pauline treatment of justification. Windisch, *Briefe* (1930, 2nd ed.), expanded the contributions of the Redactor to include 1:2 and 4:13–16.

[97] H. Braun, "Literar-Analyse" 216, pointed out that, if the source had some of the Christianity that Bultmann had attributed to the author, the author had some of the dualistic outlook that Bultmann attributed to the source. The lines of distinction become much less sharp.

[98] This theology whereby one is justified and still a sinner is a famous Lutheran interpretation of Paul's thought.

allows that the source may have been Christian, inevitably one must ask the question posed by Käsemann himself:[99] Why posit a composer for this source other than the author himself? Indeed, as we shall see, Nauck did eventually posit a source written by the author of I John. More radically, Muñoz León[100] acknowledged that Bultmann was correct in holding that such rhythmic antithetic formulas must have preexisted I John but suggested that, since there were rhythmic dualistic antitheses in the words of Jesus in GJohn, those words inspired the epistolary author as he wrote to confute his opponents.

Nevertheless, Bultmann continued to maintain his source theory and composed his 1967 commentary on that basis.[101] Although he is virtually alone among modern writers of commentaries in holding such a position,[102] those who reject his theory are indebted to him and his predecessor, von Dobschütz, for having called attention to factors that must be dealt with in any theory:

▪ the presence of statements that can be interpreted in a gnostic way;
▪ the presence of lapidary statements that embody two different positions, often contrasted antithetically;
▪ a particular solemnity to such lapidary statements as if they had been shaped as slogans;
▪ the presence of homiletic and paraenetic comment on such statements.

In my commentary below I shall posit neither written source nor redactor;[103] but I shall seek to do justice to the above factors by contending that the author of I John took slogans from his adversaries (whence the *incipiently* gnostic tone) and opposed them with slogans of his own. (Both types of slogans echoed the themes and wording of the Johannine

---

[99] "Ketzer" 307. He does not think of I John as consisting of a source and an author's homiletic comment on it, but as a confrontation of two traditions, gnostic and Christian. For discussions and rejections of Bultmann's source thesis, see Schenke, "Determination" 204–5; Jones, "Structural Analysis" 436–39; Painter, *John* 110–12; Haenchen, "Literatur" 8–12, 15–20; Nauck, *Tradition* 1–14.

[100] "El origen" 241–42. Earlier in this article he examines each antithesis isolated by Bultmann and shows its background in GJohn. For example, as background for the first antithesis under A in Chart Three, Muñoz León studies John 3:20–21: "Everyone who practices wickedness hates the light. . . . He who acts in truth comes into the light." For the last antithesis under A, he studies John 11:9–10: "If a man goes walking by day, he does not stumble . . . but if he goes walking at night, he will stumble." Clearly I John is not thought to be quoting directly from GJohn; and so, although Muñoz León speaks of a source, this is not a source in the Bultmannian sense.

[101] Besides some minor modifications of content already noted, Bultmann, *Epistles* 2, now acknowledged (in dependence on O'Neill) that there was a Jewish coloring to the epistolary source material, something he had previously denied.

[102] An exception is Wilder, "Introduction" 212, who in 1957 posited a source in the manner of von Dobschütz and Bultmann.

[103] I shall not try to refute Bultmann's theory of composition in relation to every verse but discuss only a few crucial passages that according to Bultmann proved that different hands were involved (source, author, Redactor).

tradition found in GJohn, as Muñoz León has argued.) The author then commented on such contrasting slogans.

B. *Other Source Theories*

Let us turn now briefly to two more theories proposed respectively by W. Nauck and J. C. O'Neill. These are so idiosyncratic that they have no real following as whole theories, even though some of the insights, especially those of Nauck, are valuable.

1. W. Nauck

This writer rejected the source theory we have just discussed in favor of his own reconstruction. The source he envisaged in his book *Tradition* (1957) was made up of strophes drawn from three parts of I John: (A) Not unlike von Dobschütz, he discovered behind 2:29–3:10 four distichs with positive and negative sentences. These established ethical criteria for God's children versus the devil's children. (B) Not unlike Bultmann, he discovered behind 1:6–10 five strophes or tristichs, where the first line is a condition laying down a principle, the second line states the consequence of fulfilling the condition, and the third line (beginning with "and") expands the second line.[104] (C) He discovered behind 2:4–11 five more strophes or tristichs (vv. 4,5,9,10,11) in much the same style except that the first line is a participial or relative clause.[105] These features are not distinctive, however; for Nauck (*Tradition* 68–83) has found much the same style in the non-source sections of I John, a fact that has led him to conclude that source and final Epistle were written by the one man. (Thus Nauck really holds an earlier and later edition rather than a pure source theory.) The architectonic character of the reconstructed source is such that according to Nauck it must have existed independently; and since it is unlikely that someone would have composed a document and then immediately torn it apart to make it part of a larger document (I John), Nauck argued that the author must have composed the source sometime before I John. Not surprisingly, most reviewers of Nauck's thesis asked whether it was not equally illogical to claim that the author

---

[104] An example is 1:6:
1. If we boast, "We are in communion with Him," while continuing to walk in
2. we are liars;   ⌐darkness,
3. and we do not act in truth.

[105] An example is 2:4:
1. The person who claims, "I know Him," without keeping His commandments,
2. is a liar;
3. and there is no truth in such a person.

would have torn apart his architectonic source even after an interval. Some have asked whether it was not Nauck himself who created such a coherent source by separating from I John coherent sentences that were in fact attributable to the author (rather than to a source) as part of the debate he was engaged in.

Paradoxically, Nauck's arguments, made in defense of a source theory, have had influence among scholars who rejected a source altogether. Very important was Nauck's discussion (*Tradition* 26–66) of the character and background of the source. Although he recognized that the strophes of the posited source had analogies in the Mandaean literature (as Bultmann had argued), Nauck did not think that these analogies proved that the source consisted of non-Christian gnostic revelatory discourses. After all, the Mandaeans had older roots in Palestine and Mandaean-Johannine stylistic similarities may have stemmed from a pattern known there. Since the Mandaean discourses do not offer the intense stress on ethical behavior present in the Johannine epistolary antitheses, Nauck argued that there were closer parallels in different aspects of the Jewish writings of the pre-NT period. He argued that the absolute epistolary affirmations paralleled the proclamations of divine law (or moral demand) that A. Alt had isolated as the basis of the Pentateuchal law codes. These were most often phrased in participial style while the applications of them to local situations were phrased as conditions, so that a mixture of the participial and conditional could be found in the OT (Exod 22:18 and 13).[106] The demands imposed by OT legal proclamations were intimately related to God's covenant with Israel and with the covenant status of the Israelite as a member of God's people, even as the I John demands flow from the status of the Christian as a child of God, in communion (*koinōnia*) with Johannine brothers and sisters. The OT parallels, however, did not betray the dualism that marks the antitheses underlying I John, and so Nauck turned for that to the Qumran Community, which was contemporary with early Christianity and which produced the Dead Sea Scrolls. The OT proclamations of divine law had been kept alive through the centuries by covenant renewal ceremonies, which reminded each generation that it too was a part of God's people. The entrance ritual at Qumran was almost a parade example of such a covenant renewal, as members were challenged to accept the demands of the new covenant. Here, just as in I John, a dualistic choice was presented: "That they may love all that God has chosen and hate all that He has rejected, that they may abstain from all evil and hold fast to good" (1QS 1:3–5). There then followed demands (1QS 1:11–3:12) that stressed behavior, acknowledgment of sin, keeping the commandments, brotherly love within the community—

---

[106] For a brief treatment of these OT legal categories, see JBC, art. 77, ⅍⅍86ff.

marks for distinguishing the sons of light from the sons of darkness. Insisting that this sequence is extremely close in subject matter and outlook to I John (see also footnote 68 above), Nauck theorized that a similar covenant entrance ceremony may have accompanied Christian baptism, such as later attested in the *Apostolic Tradition* of Hippolytus (*ca.* 215). Along with other scholars[107] Nauck detected elements of primitive Christian baptismal ceremony or homily scattered in I Peter, James, and the Pauline Pastorals, and also in I John (e.g., purification, belonging to a community, the cleansing blood of Jesus, divine begetting, choice between two ways of light and darkness). This led Nauck to propose that the original life-setting of the hypothetical source behind I John was baptismal. Obviously there is much speculation and simplification in Nauck's theory, which brings together OT apodictic law, Qumran renewal ceremony, uncertain Christian baptismal practice, and later ceremony reported in Hippolytus. Nevertheless, there are points that Nauck has made which will be important in reading I John, e.g.,

- there are good OT and Jewish parallels for the form and tone of the lapidary statements that are so central in I John, relating salvific status and ethical demand;
- many of the themes in I John are quite at home in a covenant theology;
- the dualism of I John has good parallels in the dualism of intertestamental Judaism, as at Qumran;
- whether or not there are specific references to baptismal motifs, the demands of I John are related to the elementary requisites of belonging to a Christian community.

All of this is quite consistent with I John's claim that it is recalling what was proclaimed "from the beginning" and with the increasing consensus of scholars that the beginnings of the Johannine Community are to be found in Judaism.[108]

2. J. C. O'Neill

His theory is stated succinctly in *Puzzle 6*:

I wish to argue that the author of I John belonged to a Jewish sectarian movement, the bulk of whose members had become Christian by confessing that Jesus was the Messiah. The Epistle he wrote consists of twelve poetic admonitions belonging to the traditional writings of the Jewish movement; each of these he has enlarged in order to bring out the fact that it has reached its true fulfillment in the coming of

[107] See Boismard, *Quatres hymnes.* He developed the thesis of covenant influence on I John in "La connaissance," and he has been followed in this by de la Potterie and Malatesta.

[108] See Brown, *Community* 27–31, 171–78, citing Martyn, Richter, Cullmann, and Boismard.

Jesus. His opponents were members of the Jewish sect who had refused to follow their brethren into the Christian movement.

In addition (p. 66), O'Neill would posit a redactor or glossator who added further materials. Besides the difficult thesis that the Epistle (after the Prologue) consists of twelve self-contained paragraphs[109] that are, in turn, based on twelve separate pieces of Jewish poetry, this theory would ask us to believe that the references to the commandment of loving one another (I John 2:7,9–10 and 3:11) came from a Jewish source instead of from the Johannine tradition embodied in John 13:34–35; 15:12,17. The Jewish source reconstructed by O'Neill is filled with words that, from a study of GJohn, are surely Johannine. Moreover, O'Neill asks us to believe that the apologetic in I John was addressed to Jews, a view that (as we shall see in the next section) has little to recommend it, especially in light of I John 2:19: "It was from our ranks that they went out." In Johannine Community history it was GJohn, not I John, that refuted "the Jews." The judgment of Marshall (*Epistles* 30) on O'Neill's source-thesis is blunt but quite accurate: "It is completely speculative and has won no adherents."

---

[109] O'Neill writes these out in Greek, indicating which verses he considers more likely. They are: 1:5–10; 2:1–6; 2:7–11; 2:12–17; 2:18–27; 2:28–3:10; 3:10b–19; 3:19b–24; 4:1–6; 4:7–18; 4:19–5:13; 5:13b–21.

IV. Origin of I and II John in a Struggle with Adversaries

The various source theories have rightly called attention to the antithetical character of many statements in I and II John. Today, however, most scholars believe that these antitheses are best explained, not by positing a source that the author corrected, but by assuming that the author was reporting the views of contemporary adversaries and then contradicting or challenging them. In this approach there is no need to assume a past, written composition by the adversaries; rather, the author's urgency and his fears suggest that what he is criticizing is being actively proposed at the very moment he is writing. Much of what the author reports about the views of his adversaries is phrased in his own language. In part that may be because he and his adversaries have the same background; but in greater part it may mean that he has rephrased their slogans to make the thrust sharper—a technique in dialectic. Let me add here that a theory which gives prominence to the role of adversaries in the background does not automatically mean that I John should be classified as a polemical tract. (Literary genre will be discussed below under V C1.) The primary purpose of the work might well be to strengthen the author's own Community in a time when adversaries are causing trouble.[110]

Let us first discuss the problem of how to discern which views belong to the adversaries, and then attempt to describe the adversaries who plausibly could have held such views.

A. Which Views in I and II John Belong to the Adversaries?

A useful step in answering this question is to list the passages in which the author of I and II John corrects views or mentions them unfavorably, and in Appendix I, Chart Four, I have attempted to do that topically. Of course, there is always a problem when we have to study the views of a group seen only through a mirror supplied by someone who opposes them; for it is exceedingly rare that people think themselves represented fairly or accurately by hostile opponents. Even when the quotations are

[110] Heise, *Bleiben* 106: "The right understanding of faith is more important to him than a struggle against non-belief."

verbatim (and we have no way of knowing that for certain in I and II John), an opponent usually gives no context that might lead to understanding. We can be certain, then, that the adversaries would have presented their positions in a more sympathetic and convincing way than the author has done in the material assembled in Chart Four. It will be necessary for us to guess at the presuppositions that made such material intelligible, constituting a viable religious position.

Another difficulty is that we are not certain that all the ideas and attitudes opposed by the author were held by the adversaries. The author may have been using I John to correct such wrong ideas no matter who held them. For instance, in I John 4:18 we find, "Love has no room for fear; rather, perfect love drives out fear. . . . Love has not reached perfection in one who is still afraid." The context suggests the author is reassuring his readers against fears about judgment, rather than attacking opponents who say that love has room for fear. I have attempted to offset this difficulty, at least in part, by the topical grouping of the statements in Chart Four. Such a grouping shows that there are certain themes to which the author returns again and again and which, therefore, he particularly wishes to refute. It is a reasonable working hypothesis that such ideas were being proposed by the adversaries, especially if (as I hope to show) they can be woven together into a *consistent* body of thought.

Finally, let me remark that Chart Four does not do justice to ideas which the author presents only positively but which may implicitly constitute a refutation of the thought of the adversaries. For example, on several occasions the author of I John refers to the final revelation (coming) of Christ or God (2:28; 3:2; 4:17). Implicitly he may be hinting that his adversaries do not do justice to the parousia, even though the author does not cite unfavorably any statement that we might attribute to the adversaries as their slogan on this issue.

I have underlined these cautions to make clear that we have embarked on a complicated task in attempting to diagnose the Community situation of the author, his adherents, and his adversaries. Yet there is no need to yield to the implied skepticism of Pheme Perkins (*Epistles* xxi–xxiii); she dismisses broadly "scholars who are not sensitive to the language of oral cultures [and] often misinterpret statements about opponents in ancient writings" and who consequently think "the community was being ripped apart by the debates to which the author refers." She would count as rhetoric the hostile comments of the author—his clear references to those who have departed from the Community (I John 2:19) really refer to a minor family quarrel that does not destroy the fabric of the Community. Can one deal so blandly with the author's refusal to pray for the secessionists who have sinned unto death, to receive them into the Community house-churches, and even to greet them (see the discussion of I John 5:16 and II John 10–11)? If we must resist taking literally everything the author says about his adversaries, the solution need not lie in reducing it all to rhetoric with little foundation in reality.

B. *Reconstructed Portrait of the Adversaries*

Seeking a middle way based on what is actually said in these writings, let us now turn to Chart Four to see if we can draw a portrait of the adversaries that would make sense of the statements listed there. (In what follows references such as A1 are keyed to Chart Four.) Three general questions suggest themselves. Was there one well-defined group of adversaries? What was the general theological position of the adversaries? Are the adversaries identifiable with a group or groups known to have existed in the late first or early second century?

1. One Well-defined Group?

In his *Johannesbriefe* 4–5, Büchsel maintained that the author of I John was faced with an outbreak of Christian prophecy that had run amok. Although there are in I John references to putting Spirits to a test and to false prophets (A7), nothing there suggests uncontrolled behavior or speaking in tongues, in the manner of the enthusiasts at Corinth (I Cor 12 and 14). The false prophets who speak the language of the world (A7, 8) are faulted because of their christology, so that more than spiritual delusion is meant. Moreover, the tenor of I and II John suggests that the author is dealing with something organized rather than purely spontaneous.[111] There is reference to a refusal to listen to the author (A2); the adversaries are now distinct from the author's group since they have left it (A3); yet they constitute a threat through their propagandists, who seemingly claim to be teachers (C1,2; A1).[112] There is no real reason to doubt that the adversaries constitute a community of their own just as well organized as the author's. Indeed, they may be more numerous and successful than the author's group (A8), with more wealth (B12; A9).

Granted the seemingly organized opposition, is it possible that the author was facing several groups of opponents in I and II John? Chart Four lists statements of christological import (A4–7) and statements of moral import (B1–15). Did the same people err on the two scores, or does each error represent a different group? For instance, a number of older commentators (Bisping, Braune, Lücke, Luthardt, Mayer, Rothe) saw no

---

[111] K. Weiss, "Orthodoxie," questions the existence of a fixed heresy with recognizable characteristics. I would agree that the theological identity of the group is not so fixed as that of the heresies combated by Irenaeus in the latter part of the second century, but there is a middle position between that and unclassifiable pneumatics.

[112] The constant stress on the opponents as liars and deceivers (I John 1:6,10; 2:4,22; 3:7; 5:10; II John 7) makes it clear that the author thinks he is dealing not merely with people in error but with propagandists of error.

relationship between the christological discussion in I John 4:1–6 and the stress on loving one's brother that follows immediately in 4:7–13. Michl (*Briefe* 252–53) argues that the false teachers are mentioned only in the discussion of christology and that the paraenetic, ethical injunctions of I John 1:5–2:6 are directed not to secessionists but to lax Christians within the author's group. Weiss (*Briefe* 17–18) thinks that the moral abuses which the author condemns stemmed from those who misunderstood Paul —a group to which the christological errors could only with difficulty be attributed. One can go further in separating adversaries[113] and argue that even the christological corrections were not all aimed at the same adversaries, thus explaining the *"many* Antichrists" of A3. Painter (*John* 119) distinguishes two types of heretics, some dispensing with Christ altogether, others allowing a role to the *heavenly* Christ. Richter ("Blut" 127) and Smalley ("What") also distinguish two groups, one seeing in Jesus only the human, the other seeing only the divine. Today, however, the positing of more than one adversary group remains a minority opinion among scholars.

The text itself gives the impression that the christological and the moral (ethical) errors were closely related. For instance, I John 3:23 brings the two areas under the rubric of the one commandment: "Now this is God's commandment: we are to believe the name of His Son, Jesus Christ; and we are to love one another just as He gave us the command." II John 5–6 insists on the need to love one another and immediately afterward (7–8) attacks those who do not confess Jesus Christ coming in the flesh and warns against receiving those who come bringing an overly progressive teaching about Christ (9–10). The same language of lying and deceit is used of the christological error (A5,6) and of the moral error (B1–4,14). The propagators of the former belong to a Spirit of Deceit or to a Spirit that is not of God (A2,7), while the propagators of the latter are children of the devil rather than of God (B7,10). This impression of two closely allied errors is strengthened when it can be shown that there is a logical connection between them (see pp. 54–55, 80–81 below). None of this is firm proof; but one can state that I and II John give little reason to think of a variety of adversaries and can quite logically be explained if one well-defined group was being attacked. It seems an appropriate occasion to apply "Ockham's razor": Postulated entities should not be multiplied without necessity.

2. The Theological Positions of the Adversaries

Following the indications suggested in the divisions A and B in Chart Four, let us see if we can make sense of the mirror image of the adversaries given us in I and II John.

---

[113] Thus Düsterdieck, Lücke, Mangold, and Sander in the last century, and Brooke (*Epistles* xxxix–xli) and Goguel in this century.

(a) CHRISTOLOGY. The author makes the following affirmations or confessions:[114]

- Jesus is the Christ (*Christos*, "Messiah"; 5:1).
- Jesus is the Christ come/coming in the flesh (4:2; II John 7).
- Jesus is the Son (2:23; 3:23; 5:11–12).
- Jesus is the Son of God (1:3,7; 3:8,23; 4:9,10,15; 5:5,9,10,11,12, 13,20).[115]
- Jesus Christ is the one who came by water and blood (5:6).
- Jesus Christ is come in the flesh (4:2).

The author criticizes any who:
- deny that Jesus is the Christ (*Christos*, 2:22).[116]
- deny the Son (2:23).
- do not confess Jesus Christ coming in the flesh (II John 7).
- negate the importance of Jesus by not confessing Jesus Christ come in the flesh (4:2–3).

When the affirmations and the criticisms of the denials are put together, there emerges a picture of adversaries who deny that Jesus is the Christ, the Son of God, come in the flesh, and come by water and blood. What was their attitude, then, toward Jesus?

GJohn was written so that people might "believe that Jesus is the Christ (Messiah), the Son of God" (20:31). Clearly the major adversaries in GJohn were "the Jews" who questioned and denied that Jesus was the Messiah (7:25–27; 9:22; 10:24) and who claimed that he blasphemed when he said he was the Son of God (10:36; 19:7). And so it is not surprising that some should think that the adversaries of I and II John were, in whole or in part, Jews who denied that Jesus was the Messiah, the Son of God. This theory has had such proponents as Bardy, Belser, and Löffler; and it was massively defended at the beginning of this century by Wurm (*Irrlehrer*). It has been taken up again by O'Neill in his source theory (see III B2 above). However, if the adversaries were all one group, the thesis that they were Jews who rejected Jesus as the Messiah faces enormous difficulties. The statements in B6–9 suggest that the adversaries could be looked on as people who placed little emphasis on avoiding sin, keeping the commandments, and acting justly. Wurm attempted almost a tour de force to show that logically such people could be speaking from Judaism.[117] But even then one would have to explain

---

[114] All references are to I John unless otherwise indicated.

[115] Wurm, *Irrlehrer* 8–14, argues that the parallelism of the formulas stating that Jesus is the Christ and Jesus is the Son of God means that the two titles are interchangeable for the author (as they are also for his opponents). We remember John 20:31: "That you may believe that Jesus is the Christ, the Son of God."

[116] The designation of the adversaries as Antichrists (I John 2:18,22; 4:3; II John 7) is probably to be related to this.

[117] Wurm, *Irrlehrer* 128–29, is quite correct in my judgment in contending that there is no proof the adversaries were antinomians, as held by many older scholars

how the author's debate with the slogans of such adversaries did not have to center on the Scriptures (as it did in GJohn where the Johannine Jesus argued with his Jewish opponents about Moses, Abraham, and the Scriptures). The fact that there is not a single OT quotation in I and II John is an eloquent objection to the thesis that the adversaries were non-Christian Jews,[118] and an even more eloquent objection is the clear statement in I John 2:19 that they had gone out from the ranks of the author's Community.[119] (Some of the same objections apply to the theory that the adversaries were pagan nonbelievers, e.g., gnostics who did not accept Jesus but proposed another salvific figure[120]—they too could scarcely have been described as going "out from our ranks.")

One attempt to avoid these objections is the thesis that the adversaries were Jews who had converted to Christianity but had lapsed either totally or partially. The author would thus be continuing the polemic of GJohn against Jews who hesitated about Jesus, preferring the glory of men to that of God (8:31–59; 12:42–43). One may wonder, then, why there is no appeal in I John to that polemic. Granted the frequency of hostile references in GJohn to "the Jews," the lack of that designation in I John is a challenge even to "the lapsed Jew" hypothesis. Morever, would the recipients of I and II John really need to be admonished not to let lapsed Jews into their house as friends (C2) and not to pray for them (C3)? If these works were written after the expulsion from the synagogue (described in John 9:22; 12:42; 16:2),[121] the recipients would have been suspicious of Jews without any help from the author.

Most scholars take for granted that the adversaries were believing Christians whose faith was different from that professed by the author. Was this difference in the direction of low christology (overemphasizing the humanity of Jesus) or in the direction of high christology (overem-

---

(Bisping, Ebrard, Ewald, Hilgenfeld, Holtzmann, Mayer, Pflederer, Sander, Weizsäcker), often because they understood the *anomia* of I John 3:4 (see NOTE there) as "lawlessness" instead of as "iniquity."

[118] This does not mean that the adversaries were Gentiles but only that they were Christians (Jew or Gentile) whose differences from the author were not to be settled by an exegesis of the OT.

[119] This statement cannot be neutralized in a non-Christian direction by the lines that follow: "Not that they really belonged to us; for if they had belonged to us, they would have remained with us." By writing that about the adversaries, the author is not questioning the fact of their previous Johannine Christian existence but the depth of that adherence. We see this when we recall that 2:18–19 is part of a larger passage (2:18–27) where the verb *menein*, "to remain, abide," occurs six times. The author is afraid that some of his group will not remain but will follow the adversaries of the Community—a fear that tells us about the past history of the adversaries.

[120] Such a theory might be spun off from Bultmann's thesis that the author was correcting a non-Christian gnostic source.

[121] See Martyn, *History* 45–68 (64–81), and Brown, *Community* 40–43, 66–69.

phasizing the divinity of Jesus)? Some scholars (Eichhorn, Goguel, Haupt, Lange, Sander) have opted for low christology, speaking of Jewish Christians or Ebionites. The author's stress that Jesus was the Christ, the Son of God, would then have been directed against the propaganda of opponents who acknowledged Jesus as the *Christos,* but only in the sense that he was the expected Davidic king (Messiah), and that he was the son of God, but only in the sense in which every Davidic king was treated by God as His son or representative (II Sam 7:14; Ps 2:7). These adversaries would not have acknowledged Jesus as an *incarnate* ("become flesh") divine figure, whence the author's stress in A6,7 on the *coming* in the flesh. Statement A4 would then mean that Jesus had not been adopted as God's Son at the baptism ("came . . . not in water only"). Such a theory has the merit of identifying the adversaries with a type of Christianity that did exist at the end of the first century, but it faces many difficulties. For instance, it may explain the "not in water only" part of A4, but it does not explain the author's greater insistence on the coming "by blood"—an insistence that would stress the *humanity* of Jesus. Since the adversaries in this hypothesis stressed the humanity of Jesus, how would the author's attack on "everyone who negates the importance of *Jesus*" (A7) apply to them? Indications are that low christology at the end of the century was an arrested early understanding of Jesus held by those who regarded the increasingly popular high christology of incarnation and preexistence as a dangerous innovation leading to ditheism (two Gods). Could the author have described such adversaries as progressives who went too far from the traditional teaching (A1)? In GJohn Jewish Christians who deny that Jesus preexisted Abraham are bitterly attacked (8:31–58), but they are clearly outsiders regarded as no better than "the Jews" who sought to kill Jesus.[122] If the Epistles represent a post-GJohn stage, how could those so despised as outsiders in GJohn ever have become members of the Johannine Community, as the adversaries of I John had been (2:19)?

If the adversaries were once Johannine Christians, it is far more plausible that they held the high christology proclaimed by GJohn. The author would then be attacking them for going further and holding too high a christology, stressing the importance of preexistence to the point of neglecting the flesh or humanity of Jesus (A6,7). This would explain the charge (A1) that they were so progressive that they did not remain rooted in the teaching; it would also account for the author's self-defensive appeal to what was "from the beginning." The main objection to this hypothesis is the author's insistence that Jesus is the Christ, the Son of God—surely opponents with too high a christology would not have de-

---

[122] Cf. 8:59 with 10:31–33; and see Brown, *Community* 73–81.

nied such predicates! Possibly, however, the adversaries had trouble not with the predicate but with the subject in such confessions: *Jesus* is the Christ, the Son of God. The author would have been talking about the subject as a Jesus-come-in-the-flesh (A6,7) and thus insisting on the importance of the human career, including the death, of the Word become flesh (A4: "not in water only but in water and in blood").[123] I contend that the thesis that the adversaries held an overly high christology (exaggerating the christology of GJohn) can make intelligible all the author's statements, and I shall follow that approach in the Commentary. But let us leave till later (below, V B2) a complete delineation of the respective christologies and turn to the ethical or moral stance of the adversaries.

(b) ETHICAL BEHAVIOR AND ATTITUDES. Some, like Wendt, would maintain that moral error was a greater problem for the author than christological error.[124] The author warns of the danger of walking in darkness (B3), of not keeping the commandments (B4), of not behaving as Christ behaved (B5–7), of committing sin, and of not acknowledging sin (B1,2). If the adversaries were guilty of all this, were they libertines or radical antinomians (footnote 117 above) who lived an immoral life? Yet there are indications that the adversaries were not conscious of living in an ungodly manner; for they claimed to be in communion with God, to know and love Him, and to be begotten by Him (B3,4,5,9,14). Moreover, despite his disagreement with their ethical positions, the author never mentions any specific vices of his adversaries—and this at a time when catalogues of vices are well attested in Christian writings.[125] The author calls his adversaries "false prophets" (A7), the same charge leveled in II Pet 2:1 against the opponents of the Petrine author; but there is nothing in I John to resemble even remotely the oratory that II Pet 2:13–14 directs against the behavior of the opponents: "They are blots and blemishes, reveling in their dissipation, carousing with you. They have eyes full of adultery, insatiable for sin. . . . They have hearts trained in greed." The reticence of I and II John raises the strong possibility that the secessionists were at fault primarily in theory and were

---

[123] Since the author insists on the manner of "coming" (in flesh, in water, and in blood), the adversaries probably accepted a coming but interpreted it in a different way (Wengst, *Häresie* 18). Helpful in all this is Serafin de Ausejo, "El concepto" 420, who argues that I John is not stressing incarnation in itself but the soteriological significance of a complexus of deeds which constitute the terrestrial life of Jesus from the initial moment to the final moment. A weakness is that de Ausejo interprets the Johannine earthly life of Jesus as a *kenosis* or "emptying" in the light of Paul's statement in Philip 2:7, whereas John 1:14 and 2:11 speak of glory and not of lowliness.

[124] More nuanced is Stagg, "Orthodoxy" 429, who says that for the author orthopraxis was part of orthodoxy, since creedalism is not an end in itself in his thought.

[125] Gal 5:19–21; I Cor 6:9–11; II Cor 12:20; Rom 13:13; I Pet 4:3. See N. J. McEleney, "The Vice Lists of the Pastoral Epistles," CBQ 35 (1974) 203–19.

moral indifferentists rather than libertines (so Schneider, Wendt). Ultimately, of course, theory is likely to be translated into practice, and that danger may be why the author rails so strongly against the theory.

A theory that one's moral behavior has no great salvific importance could flow from a christology in which the earthly career of Jesus, the way he lived and died, had no great importance. The principle of "even as Christ" invoked by the author of I John (B5–7) may also have been congenial to the adversaries, but they would have had a different understanding of how Christ, the preexistent divine Word, was related to Jesus. For them an imitation of Christ would not be in terms of moral behavior but in terms of belonging to God and knowing Him.

The author's insistence on love of brethren (B9–15) also makes sense in light of a theory that the adversaries were (former) Johannine Christians of too high a christology. From the author's viewpoint (which would not be their self-interpretation), they had split the Community in *going out* (A3,6,7). If they had really loved the Johannine brethren, i.e., those loyal to the author,[126] they would not have gone out into the world. They had sinned against brotherly love by their attitude toward the author and the other witnesses to the Johannine tradition (A2) and by their attempts to seduce his followers (C1,2).

3. Comparison to Known Heresies

I have already indicated the difficulties of identifying the adversaries of I and II John with Jews, Jewish Christians, Ebionites, and libertines, but those have always been minority proposals in scholarship. Having joined the majority of scholars who identify the adversaries as Christians who held an exaggeratedly high christology, I now turn to attempts to identify them further with known heretics[127] in the century that stretches from the fall of Jerusalem (A.D. 70) to the writing of the great treatise against the heretics (*Adversus haereses*) by Irenaeus of Lyons (*ca.* 185).

---

[126] As we shall see (below, V B3c), this dispute was colored by the peculiar Johannine understanding of the commandment to love one's neighbor as referring to love of fellow (Johannine) Christians.

[127] Occasionally I shall use this term for various groups (docetists, Cerinthians, Valentinian gnostics, Montanists) who were finally judged heretical by late-second-century writers, like Irenaeus, whose views prevailed in the church. Obviously those so designated did not think of themselves as departing from orthodoxy; and when they began, it may not have been clear what was orthodox and what was not. Often orthodoxy had to be established in these second-century battles, even though the church fathers would write as if the matter were clear from apostolic times. While this point was made by W. Bauer (*Orthodoxy*), I do not think that he dealt sufficiently with a more important issue, namely, whether what won out as orthodoxy was not truer than its opposite to the *implications* of what was held at the beginning. See J. D. Dunn, *Unity and Diversity in the New Testament* (London: SCM, 1977); D. J. Hawkin, "A Reflective Look at the Recent Debate on Orthodoxy and Heresy in Earliest Christianity," *Eglise et Théologie* 7 (1976) 367–78.

(a) GROUPS CONDEMNED ELSEWHERE IN THE NT. The opponents of
the later Pauline letters have some similarities to the adversaries reconstructed from the evidence of I and II John. Colossians is aimed at a
christological deviation that involved worship of angels and calendrical
speculation (probably including the astrological control of human destiny).[128] The indication that this implies a pleroma with spiritual intermediaries has led many to characterize these deviates as gnostics. Less
specifically, the Pastoral Epistles refer to those who have wandered away
into vain discussions, desiring to be teachers, and to deceitful spirits who
lead others from the faith by their strange moral teachings and their
expositions of the Law.[129] The reference in I Tim 6:20 to the "contradictions of what is falsely called knowledge [*gnōsis*]" has caused these
opponents also to be identified as early gnostics. Neither of these sets of
Pauline opponents, which have clear Jewish components in their thought,
really matches the adversaries of I and II John; but from them we are reminded that in the late-first-century churches it was not unusual to find
internal conflict over strange speculation going beyond the community
tradition.

Searching closer to the Johannine sphere, some scholars (e.g., Büchsel)
have sought analogies in the groups condemned in the letters to the seven
churches in the Book of Revelation (Apocalypse). Those who think
(wrongly, in my judgment) that the epistolary adversaries were libertines point to the Nicolaitans of Ephesus and Pergamum (Rev 2:6,14-
15) who allowed the eating of food dedicated to idols and practiced immorality.[130] The mention at Thyatira of a wicked "prophetess" and "her
children" (Rev 2:20-23), seemingly as part of the same movement, has
been invoked in light of the "false prophets" of I John 4:1 and the
address to "an Elect Lady and her children" in II John 1. The persuasive-
ness of such parallels is somewhat diminished now that no critical scholar
attributes Revelation to the same author(s) who wrote GJohn and I, II,
and III John. Nevertheless, Revelation shows us problems in churches that
are at least related to the churches of the Epistles—perhaps proximately
in terms of geography and more distantly in terms of theology.[131] It is in-

---

[128] See Col 2:8-10,16-23. On the Colossian "heresy" see G. Bornkamm, TLZ 73
(1948) 11-20; A.R.C. Leaney, NTS 10 (1963-64) 470-79.

[129] See I Tim 1:6-7; 4:1-3; II Tim 3:1-9; Titus 1:10-11,14.

[130] The Nicolaitans were later deemed to have been gnostics; and Irenaeus, *Adv.
haer.* 3.11.1, says that John proclaimed the Gospel to remove the error disseminated
a long time before "by those termed Nicolaitans who are an offshoot of that *gnōsis*
falsely so-called" (also Hippolytus, *Refutatio* 7.36; PG 16³, 3343B). For an attempt
to fit the Nicolaitans into NT church history as extreme Hellenists, see Ehrhardt,
"Christianity" 164-67.

[131] The distance is pushed to an extreme by Elisabeth S. Fiorenza, "The Quest for
the Johannine School: The Apocalypse and the Fourth Gospel," NTS 23 (1976-77)
402-27, who argues that the author of Revelation "appears to have been more famil-

teresting, then, to see clearly delineated opponents within such churches.

Drawing still closer to the Johannine sphere, some have proposed that the adversaries of I John were the sectarians of John the Baptist who were implicitly a target in GJohn. Presumably these sectarians claimed that their master, not Jesus, was the light sent by God and that he outranked Jesus because he came first.[132] (The statement in I John 2:19 that the adversaries had gone out "from our ranks" would have to be seen as coming from converted disciples of the Baptist [John 1:35–37] and directed to their Baptist confreres who refused to believe [John 3:26].) However, since we know nothing of the soteriological and ethical teachings of the sectarians of the Baptist, it is a sheer guess that they held the views condemned in I and II John.

Our more specific knowledge about "heresies" comes from the post-NT literature; and so detailed attention must be paid to the opponents of Ignatius of Antioch, to the gnostics, and to Cerinthus.

(b) DOCETIC OPPONENTS OF IGNATIUS OF ANTIOCH. Under I B1 above I discussed whether GJohn and I John were known by Ignatius who was almost a contemporary geographically and chronologically of the Johannine writers. I am inclined to posit Ignatius' knowledge of the Johannine ambience but not of the Johannine writings; yet even that answer leads one to ask whether the adversaries of I and II John were closely related to Ignatius' opponents in the churches of Asia Minor[133] whom he criticizes on several scores. In *Phld.* 6:1; *Magn.* 8:1; 10:2–3 Ignatius warns against combining Judaism and Christianity. In *Smyrn.* 1–3; *Trall.* 9–10 he insists that Jesus was truly born of a virgin and baptized by John, truly made to suffer, and truly present after the resurrection. This insistence is directed against docetists who say that he only seemed to do such things (*Smyrn.* 4:2); for they "do not confess that he was clothed in the flesh" (5:2), and they "do not believe in the blood of Christ" (6:1).[134] This disdain for the humanity of Jesus is carried over into a disdain for love and into neglect toward the needy and afflicted (6:2). Are the Jewish Christians (attacked principally in *Philadelphians* and *Magnesians*) the same as the docetists (attacked principally in *Smyrnaeans* and *Trallians*)? Since the

---

iar with Pauline than with Johannine School traditions." I remain convinced that Revelation is somehow related to Johannine thought; but I acknowledge her criticism of my oversimplified agreement with Barrett in ABJ 29, cii, that Revelation came directly from John son of Zebedee. All that can be said is that the author was an unknown Christian prophet named John.

[132] See John 1:8,30; ABJ 29, lxvii–lxx, 46–47, and Brown, *Community* 69–71.

[133] How well did Ignatius know the churches of Asia Minor that he was visiting on his way to Rome? To what extent was he reading into their lives the situation he left behind at Antioch?

[134] Accordingly (7:1) "they do not confess that the Eucharist is the flesh of our Savior Jesus Christ *who suffered for our sins.*" The italicized expression may be compared to I John 2:1–2: "Jesus Christ . . . himself is an atonement for our sins."

time of J. B. Lightfoot, who spoke of a Judaism crossed with gnosticism, many scholars have answered affirmatively (Barrett, Bernard, Molland, Pfleiderer, J. Weiss, Zahn). However, there is a respectable number of the opposite persuasion (Bartsch, Corwin, Donohue, Hilgenfeld, Meinhold, Rathke, Škrinjar), arguing that different opponents were faced in the respective letters.[185] In my *Community* (79) I opted for the two-opponent theory, pointing out that GJohn attacks Jewish Christians very much like those described by Ignatius in *Philadelphians* and *Magnesians.* If the docetist opponents of *Smyrnaeans* and *Trallians* were not the same as the Jewish Christians, they have more resemblance to the adversaries of I John[186] in whose christology and ethics there are no overt traces of Judaism. In Asia Minor there could have been Christian extremists at both ends of the spectrum (Jewish Christians of a very low christology, and docetic Christians of a very high christology), and both the Johannine Community (at different stages in its history) and Ignatius may have had to combat them.

Be that as it may, there are differences between Ignatius and the Johannine writers. The docetists condemned by Ignatius seem to have denied reality to the humanity of Jesus,[137] and there is no suggestion of such a radical docetism in the adversary views criticized by I and II John. The epistolary author seems concerned with the salvific importance of the flesh and the death of Jesus, not with a defense of the reality of Jesus' human-

---

[185] Schnackenburg, *Johannesbriefe* 22, finds anti-docetism in *Magn.* 11 (the same letter that attacks the Jewish Christians), but such an interpretation depends on reading that chapter in the light of *Smyrnaeans.* Every reference to birth, passion, and resurrection need not be anti-docetist (see *Phld.* 8:2; 9:2).

[136] A close relationship (but not necessarily identity) is posited by Balz, Loisy, and Schnackenburg. A much larger group of scholars speaks of docetism in reference to the adversaries of I John without necessary stress on Ignatius, e.g., H. Braun, de Wette, Ewald, Gaugler, Haering, Holtzmann, Jülicher, Lücke, Polhill, Prunet, Reuss, Rothe, Schlatter, Schmiedel, Soltau, and Wilder. Since many writers mention several possible identifications for the epistolary adversaries, classification is extremely difficult here.

[137] I stress the "seem," for docetism came in many shades. Among the Nag Hammadi writings, the *Trimorphic Protenoia* (XIII 50:12–15; NHL 470), written *ca.* 200, shows a heavenly Word saying aloud, "I put on Jesus. I bore him from the cursed wood and established him in the dwelling places of his Father." In the third-century *Apocalypse of Peter* (VII 81:15–25; NHL 344) a living Jesus laughs at persecutors who torment the external Jesus. In the third-century *Acts of John* (88–93; HSNTA 2.225–27) the disciples whom Jesus loves can see that Jesus is able to appear indifferently as a child, as an old man, and as a young man. Yet we are not sure what the second-century (Valentinian) *Gospel of Truth* means (I 20:11–30; NHL 39) when it says about the Jesus who appeared and was nailed to a tree, that "he stripped himself of the perishable rags and put on imperishability." The *Letter of Peter to Philip* (VIII 136:20–22; 139:15–23; NHL 396–97), from the late second or early third century, states, "Our illuminator, Jesus, [came] down and was crucified"; but it also says that some did not recognize him because they thought he was a mortal man, whereas he is a stranger to suffering. Would either of these last two works affirm that Jesus was born of an earthly mother?

ity. Moreover, in Ignatius there is a massive emphasis on the importance of ecclesiastical structure, centered on one bishop, accompanied by presbyters and deacons. This structure is an essential mark of the church (*Trall.* 3:1) and a guarantee against heresy (*Eph.* 6). Such structural interest is completely lacking from I and II John and indeed opposed in III John 9. Thus it may be too simple to identify the docetic opponents of Ignatius with the adversaries of I and II John. Both nuance and church development may separate them.

(c) SECOND-CENTURY GNOSTICS. Most scholars, including those who speak of docetists and of Cerinthus, suspect that the adversaries of I and II John had gnostic leanings; and some are content to designate them as gnostics.[188] Gnosticism is notoriously hard to define;[139] the gnostics were marvelously varied; and orthodox Christians used the term *gnōsis,* "knowledge," almost as freely as did those whom they excluded as gnostics for proclaiming a "so-called *gnōsis.*" The complexity of the last issue as it pertains to Johannine thought is reflected by these statements: "Eternal life consists in this: that they *know* you, the one true God, and Jesus Christ, the one whom you sent" (John 17:3); and "Now this is how we can be sure that we *know* Him" (I John 2:3). All early Christians claimed to know God—how then did the claim of the Johannine authors differ from the claim of their adversaries?

Some nineteenth-century scholars thought that the adversaries of I and II John could be identified with gnostic groups named by Irenaeus and the other writers against heresy. For instance, Pfleiderer thought of them as followers of Basilides (*ca.* 120–145),[140] and Holtzmann referred to Satornil (Saturninus). Such associations often presupposed a very late dating for I John and have been abandoned today in favor of speaking of the adversaries as "proto-gnostics" who antedated the named gnostic systems of the mid-second century. (Indeed, it is possible in my judgment that the Johannine adversaries played a catalyzing role in the development of such later systems; see below, V D1). However, in speaking of "proto-gnostics" one has introduced the truly indefinable. How many and which features of

---

[188] With the understanding that the term is not exclusive of docetists, the following scholars seem to think of the epistolary adversaries as gnostic in some degree: Bultmann, Dodd, Filson, Haering, Hauck, Holtzmann, Michl, Pfleiderer, Rothe, Schlatter, Songer, and Wilder. Granted this (partial) list, it is all the more startling that at an earlier period Hilgenfeld found gnosticism in the author's own ideas, while Planck found elements of Montanism there.

[139] See the survey of attempts by E. Yamauchi, *Pre-Christian Gnosticism* (Grand Rapids: Eerdmans, 1973) 14–19.

[140] To some extent this identification depends on the interpretation of I John 1:5, "God is light and in Him there is no darkness at all." Were the adversaries holding the opposite, namely, that in the deity there was a mixture of light and darkness? That view was attributed to Basilides, even though no such internal divine dualism is found in the description of his thought by Irenaeus, *Adv. haer.* 1.24.3–4.

later gnosticism need have been present for a group to be so characterized? For instance, very important in later gnosticism were such features as a series of eons intermediary between the supreme God and human beings, an evaluation of the OT creator God as evil, and the preexistence of the souls of the *pneumatikoi*,[141] or spiritually elite. (Indeed, the latter element plays a role in U. Bianchi's famous effort at Messina in 1966 to have accepted a common definition of gnosticism.[142]) Yet no such features are apparent in the statements in Chart Four of Appendix I, which are the key to the thought of the adversaries of I and II John.

Perhaps the most helpful procedure here would be to cull from the situation envisaged in I and II John and from the views possibly held by the adversaries (Chart Four) those features that have a parallel in later gnosticism. This will provide the reader with a test for the thesis of K. Weiss ("Gnosis" 352) that, while the epistolary adversaries lacked many of the features characteristic of the great gnostic systems, they held positions that could grow into gnosticism. In the list that follows I shall generally give first the Johannine epistolary information and then cite by comparison either the gnostic works (chiefly those available to us from Nag Hammadi[143]) or the information in the anti-gnostic treatises of the church fathers (which remain our principal tool for understanding gnosticism[143a]). The reader is cautioned that, at most, similarity is suggested; and the gnostic citations are far from exhaustive.[144]

■ A dualism between light and darkness, between truth and falsehood (B15; A2). A seemingly non-Christian gnostic work, *The Paraphrase of Shem* (VII 1–49; NHL 308–28) is a whole treatise on the opposition between light and darkness. Opposition between truth and error is found in the *Gospel of Truth* (I 26:19–35; NHL 42) where we also hear that Christ "enlightened those who were in the darkness. Out of oblivion he enlightened them, he showed (them) a way. And the way is the truth

[141] The instruction in I John 4:1, "Do not believe every Spirit; rather, put these Spirits to a test," suggests that the adversaries claimed to be motivated by the Spirit (*pneuma*), which may be compared to the gnostics' designation of themselves as *pneumatikoi*. However, the comparison is muddled by the gratuitous assumption that either group is necessarily to be identified with the enthusiastic charismatics whom Paul cautions in I Cor 12–14. A special claim upon the Spirit need not involve external phenomena.

[142] G. W. MacRae, "Biblical News: Gnosis in Messina," CBQ 28 (1966) 322–33, esp. 331–32.

[143] This find of gnostic documents was described in ABJ 29, liii where I used the designation Chenoboskion, now replaced by Nag Hammadi. The works are conveniently available in English in NHL.

[143a] Against recent, exaggerated efforts to discredit the accuracy of Irenaeus, see J. F. McCue, "Conflicting Versions of Valentinianism?" in *The Rediscovery of Gnosticism*, ed. B. Layton (Leiden: Brill, 1980) 404–16.

[144] Wengst, *Häresie* 38–59, is extremely helpful as a guide to the gnostic similarities. The anti-gnostic patristic references may exaggerate or simplify.

which he taught them. For this reason error grew angry at him" (I 18:17–22; NHL 38).

- A claim to special union with God resulting in sinlessness (B3–5, 1–2). In the *Gospel of Mary* (BG 8502 7:13–8:4; NHL 471–72) we hear the Savior say, "There is no sin," for sin belongs to another nature in which one was once bound.
- A stress on the special privileges of the Christian. God is light (I John 1:5) and so the believer claims to be in light (2:9). Similarly 1:2 speaks of "eternal life which was in the Father's presence and was revealed to us." In the *Corpus Hermeticum* (I 21) we are told, "God the Father from whom the Man came is light and life. If then you learn that you consist of light and life and that you come from these, you will go back to life." In *Acts of Thomas* 34 (HSNTA 2.461–62) we hear of "him whose works are light and his deeds truth" who enables others to do good.
- The Christian is begotten by God (I John 2:29; 3:9; 4:7; 5:1,4,18). The overwhelming textual evidence in John 1:13 reads "those who were begotten by God"; but Tertullian, who thought the singular ("he who was begotten") referring to Jesus was original, blamed the plural on tampering by the Valentinians (*De carne Christi* 19.1; CC 2, 907). This means that he thought a theory of divine begetting to be characteristic of the gnostics. The *Discourse on the Eighth and Ninth* (VI 62:33–63:3; NHL 297) has the mystagogue, Hermes Trismegistus, instruct the initiate: "He who will not be begotten at the start by God comes to me by the general and guiding discourses," thus distinguishing two types of divine begetting.
- An unction received from Christ that teaches the Christian about everything is mentioned in I John 2:27. The *Hypostasis of the Archons* (II 96:35–97:4; NHL 159) speaks of "[the Spirit of] Truth which the Father has sent. Then he will teach them about everything. And he will anoint them with the unction of Life eternal." *Pistis Sophia* (chs. 86,112 or II 195; III 292) speaks of a spiritual anointing that the perfect will receive; and according to Hippolytus (*Refutatio* 5.9.22; PG 16³, 3159) the Naassenes spoke of being "anointed with ineffable ointment from the horn."
- God's seed remains in the one begotten by God, according to I John 3:9. The Valentinians believed that a spiritual seed was infused into human beings without the knowledge of the Demiurge who made the animal nature (Irenaeus, *Adv. haer.* 1.5.6). The *Gospel of Truth* (I 43:9–16; NHL 49) refers to "the ones who appear in truth since they exist in true and eternal life and speak of the light which is perfect and filled with the seed of the Father."

- A lack of emphasis on conduct is condemned in I John (B5–9). In a passage adjacent to the one cited above, Irenaeus (*Adv. haer.* 1.6.4) says that for the Valentinian gnostics, "It is not conduct of any kind which leads into the Pleroma, but the seed sent forth thence in a feeble, immature state, and here brought to perfection."
- Those who claim to be in the light but do not love their brethren are condemned in I John (B15,9–11). Irenaeus (*Adv. haer.* 1.6.4) describes the gnostics as despising those who guard against sinning even in thought or word as "utterly contemptible and ignorant persons, while they highly exalt themselves, and claim to be perfect, and the elect seed." In the *Second Treatise of the Great Seth* (VII 60:30–32; NHL 334) the "perfect and incorruptible" gnostics describe those Christians who think that Jesus really died as "small and ignorant since they do not contain the nobility of truth." The *Apocalypse of Peter* (VII 83:19–23; NHL 344–45) affirms, "There will be no honor in any man who is not immortal, but only in those who were chosen from an immortal substance."
- Those who love the world and its wealth but show no compassion for others in need are condemned (A9; B12), especially since "wealth breeds arrogance." Irenaeus (*Adv. haer.* 1.4.3) says that the gnostics were "not inclined to teach these things to all in public, but only to such as are able to pay a high price for an acquaintance with such profound mysteries."
- The *self*-image of the epistolary adversaries can be better understood through an analysis of the gnostic self-image. For instance, I John 2:19 speaks of a secession by the adversaries, while II John 10 urges their exclusion. From their own viewpoint the adversaries may have thought that they were unjustly excluded and that the author's group had seceded from union with them. Tertullian (*Adv. Valentinianos* 4.1; CC 2, 755) says that Valentinus rejected the authority of the Roman church and left to found a rival group; but Irenaeus (*Adv. haer.* 3.15.2) relates a complaint of the Valentinians as to why the orthodox were keeping aloof and calling them heretics, even though the Valentinians in their own judgment held doctrines similar to those held by the orthodox. The author of III John 7 praises the missionaries on his side who "set out for the sake of the Name," while the *Second Treatise of the Great Seth* (VII 59:22–26; NHL 333–34) protests, "We were hated and persecuted . . . by those who think that they are advancing the name of Christ." The author of I John 1:1–4 associates himself with a Johannine School of tradition-bearers and witnesses who can speak of "what we have heard" and "what we have seen"; he can say (4:6): "Anyone who has knowledge of God listens to us." The *Letter of Ptolemaeus to Flora* (Epiphanius, *Panarion* 33.3.8; PG 41, 560A) shows how a gnostic teacher

spoke: "It remains for us who have been counted worthy of the knowledge of both of these to provide you with an accurate and clear account. . . . We shall draw the proofs of what we say from the words of our Savior." A few units further on he says, "You will learn in the future about the origin and generation when you are counted worthy of the apostolic tradition which we have received by succession because we can prove all our statements from the teaching of the Savior" (33.7.10; PG 41, 568B). The author of I John characterizes his adversaries as moved by a Spirit of Deceit rather than by a Spirit of Truth (4:6) and uses the term "the devil's children" (3:10). The gnostics used the same language of their orthodox opponents. In the third-century *Apocalypse of Peter* (VII 73:23–26; 77:22–25; NHL 341–42) we hear, "Many will accept our teaching in the beginning. And they will turn from them again by the will of the Father of their error." Further, "Many others oppose the truth and are messengers of error." The *Authoritative Teaching* (VI 33:26; 34:28; NHL 282–83) characterizes the ignorant, nonspiritual as "sons of the devil" and speaks of "the demon of error." The author of I John says his purpose is "that you may be joined in communion with us" (1:3) and says, "Love has reached perfection with us" (4:17). II John 1–2 begins, "In truth I love you—and not only I but also those who have come to know the truth; this love is based on the truth." Such communion and love is stressed over against the secession of the adversaries. Similarly within gnostic circles the *Second Treatise of the Great Seth* (VII 67:15–19; 67:31–68:5; NHL 337) condemns division and breach of peace, while praising the "union and a mixture of love, all of which are perfected in the one who is." The writer says, "I was among those who are united in the friendship of friends forever, who neither know hostility at all, nor evil, but who are united by my Knowledge in word and peace which exists in perfection with everyone and in them all."

In evaluating the above similarities one faces many difficulties. Most of the gnostic material is to be dated from fifty to two hundred years later than the material in I and II John, and some of it has clearly been influenced by GJohn (see footnote 10 above). Similar ethical charges directed against both the epistolary adversaries and the gnostics tell us little about the relation of the two groups, for such charges (neglect of commandments, indifference about behavior, love of the world or money, lack of brotherly love) are standard polemic that one can find over and over again in Christian history. A more serious difficulty is that many gnostic similarities cited above apply as much to what the Johannine author affirms as to what he attacks. Here we touch upon a very curious aspect of the author's words in reference to his adversaries: He rarely rejects their claims outright; rather he criticizes the way they understand the implications of those claims (B3–5,8,9). The implication is that both he and his opponents claimed to know God, to be in union with Him, to be begotten by Him, and to be free of sin.[145] Indeed, one can surmise that both also claimed to have an anointing from Christ (I John 2:27), to have God's seed abiding in them (3:9), to possess the Spirit (4:1), and perhaps even to love their brothers, provided "brothers" were understood as Christians of the same persuasion. Therefore, to point out gnostic parallels to such claims does not greatly advance an investigation of the identity of the *adversaries*. The real issue is whether the adversaries understood such claims in a way that was closer to gnosticism than the way in which the Johannine author understood the claims. In all probability it was; but we face a charge of circular reasoning if, when the modality of the adversaries' claims is not specified in I and II John, we determine that modality on the basis of later gnostic views and then triumphantly use this to prove that they were gnostics.

Let me give an important example. I think it certain on the basis of B8,9 that the adversaries of I John claimed to be begotten by God; but I have no way of knowing how they understood that begetting. It has often been suggested that for the adversaries the status of being a divine child came from their own nature rather than from baptism, so that Christ would have revealed to believers their preexistent status rather than have conferred on them a status they did not have before. Certainly that was a very common gnostic view.[146] But I am dubious that the adversaries did hold such a gnostic interpretation since the epistolary author never criticizes the way his adversaries understood divine begetting, but only that they failed to draw the proper ethical conclusions from the status of divine childhood: "No one who has been begotten by God commits sin" (I John 5:18). In my judgment, then, the most one can argue from gnostic similarities is that many of the positions of the adversaries would have been at home in the gnostic circles which composed the Nag Hammadi documents and which were attacked by the church fathers.[147] But it may well be that the position of the epistolary adversaries had not yet jelled into a distinctively gnostic system of thought. In V D1 below I shall

[145] Although the author of I John challenges claims to sinlessness on the part of his adversaries (B1,2), he denies that the true Christian commits sin (B6–10). In the NOTE on 3:9cd I shall examine this apparent contradiction.

[146] Pagels, *Johannine Gospel* 88, explains the early gnostic Heracleon's exegesis of John 4 thus: the Samaritan woman is not a psychic who needs to be given life by Jesus (as is the centurion's son of John 5), but a pneumatic whose life has become weak: "She has no need of 'forgiveness of sins'; she needs only to call upon resources she already has without knowing it." The *Gospel of Truth* (I 21:4–22:35; NHL 40) is a lyrical description of how those who "were in the Father, not knowing Him" received from Jesus teaching about themselves.

[147] Despite its excellence (footnote 144 above), Wengst, *Häresie*, only establishes a list of *possible* gnostic features in the thought of the epistolary adversaries.

propose that the adversaries eventually *became* gnostics and, indeed, that their Johannine background may have catalyzed the development of the early gnostic systems.

On the other hand, while the second-century gnostics used GJohn (almost to the point of appropriating it), there is no clear evidence that they drew upon I John as a source for reflection.[148] Indeed, as I shall point out (V D2c), I John became a tool of the orthodox church writers in their arguments against the gnostic interpretations of GJohn. This would indicate that, whether or not he was combating proto-gnostics, the thought of the author of I John was oriented in a direction that gnostics could not find amenable.

(d) CERINTHIANS. Perhaps the most widely favored identification for the adversaries of I and II John is that they were followers of Cerinthus,[149] an early "gnostic" about whom relatively little is known with certainty. I shall reserve for Appendix II a survey of the information that can be gleaned from the church fathers about him, and I shall concentrate here on what might be relevant to the epistolary adversaries. Cerinthus is brought into the Johannine sphere by the tale attributed to Polycarp (Irenaeus, *Adv. haer.* 3.3.4) that John the disciple fled from a public bath at Ephesus, crying out, "Let us save ourselves; the bath house may fall down, for inside is Cerinthus, the enemy of truth." (In I John 2:21–22 there is an attack on the lie as "alien to the truth," and the adversaries are identified as "the Liar.") Moreover, Irenaeus (*Adv. haer.* 3.11.1) says that John proclaimed the Gospel "to remove the error which had been disseminated among men by Cerinthus." However, Irenaeus goes on to say that the same error had been disseminated "a long time before" by the Nicolaitans "who are an offshoot of the *gnōsis* falsely so-called." Since the Nicolaitans are mentioned in Revelation (above, IV B3a), one would be more inclined to date *them* as contemporary with I John (*ca.* 100), and therefore to date Cerinthus after I John in the first

---

148 See footnote 10 above for my rejection of Pheme Perkins's thesis that the *Apocryphon of James* draws upon I John. A.F.J. Klijn has challenged the designation of *Acts of Thomas* as gnostic (HSNTA 2.441–42); but if we accept the majority opinion, this third-century work may be the first gnostic citation of I John (143; HSNTA 2.518): "We beheld with the eyes of the body . . . we handled even with our hands." Although the transfiguration of Jesus is clearly in the writer's mind, he may also be citing I John 1:1. At least that is a more plausible citation of I John than is *Gospel of Truth* (I 30:27–32): "For when they had seen him and had heard him, he granted them to taste him and to smell him and to touch the beloved Son"—a reference to the risen Jesus!

149 For many scholars this is consonant with the claim that they were docetists or gnostics; but among those who call particular attention to Cerinthus are M. Barth, Bonsirven (?), Braune, Brooke, Camerlynck, Chaine, Chapman, de Ambroggi, del Álamo, Düsterdieck, Ebrard, Flemington, Hauck, Haupt, Hirsch, Holtzmann, Huther, Keppler, Lagrange, Nauck (?), Neander, Schneider, Seeberg, Stagg, Stott, Vrede, B. Weiss, Wengst, Westcott, Williams, R. McL. Wilson, Zahn.

quarter of the second century (a thesis I shall adopt below in V D1). At any rate one must be wary of the very approximate chronology supplied by Irenaeus' references.[150]

Those references, which primarily concern GJohn rather than I John, would have had little impact on the identification of the epistolary adversaries were it not that a view attributed to Cerinthus by Irenaeus (number 3 below) seems to cast light on one of I John's obscure attacks on the adversaries. Appendix II will show how difficult it is to know the thought of Cerinthus since each church writer attributed to him more errors, so that by the fourth century his doctrine had become an amalgam of heresies. The following list contains the principal views that the church fathers attributed to Cerinthus—the first or principal patristic witness for the attribution appears in parentheses:

1. The world was made by a deity inferior to the supreme God, i.e., by a type of demiurge (Irenaeus).
2. Jesus was not virginally conceived but was the natural son of Joseph and Mary (Irenaeus).
3. Jesus was at first a remarkably righteous, prudent, and wise man; then "after his baptism, Christ descended upon him in the form of a dove from the Supreme Ruler." Thus there began a career of preaching and working miracles; then at last Christ departed from Jesus. "Jesus suffered and rose again while Christ remained impassible, inasmuch as he was a spiritual being" (Irenaeus).
4. During the ministry Jesus proclaimed "an unknown God" (Irenaeus).
5. The world was created by angels who gave the law (Pseudo-Tertullian).
6. Eating and drinking of certain things was forbidden (Hippolytus?).
7. In the millennium the kingdom of Christ will be in this world and will be marked by passionate pleasures (Eusebius, citing Gaius).
8. Christ and the Holy Spirit were identical (Epiphanius).
9. Christ has not yet been raised (Epiphanius).

Some of these views are contradictory; and Appendix II will relate the controversy as to which views belonged to the real Cerinthus and whether he was primarily a Jewish Christian or a gnostic. (The antiquity of Irenaeus' witness gives his diagnosis a privileged place.) For the purpose

---

[150] Although in the passage under discussion Irenaeus puts Cerinthus after the Nicolaitans, in *Adv. haer.* I 23–28 he lists Cerinthus before them. Irenaeus had firsthand knowledge of the gnostic disciples of Ptolemaeus and Marcus but was dependent on an earlier catalog of heresies for the other groups he discussed; and his knowledge of the period before 150 was often jumbled and simplified. (See APPENDIX II, footnote 4.) In ABJ 29, lxxxviii we saw that his attribution of the writing of GJohn to the son of Zebedee, one of the Twelve, was oversimplified.

of judging the similarity of Cerinthus to the adversaries of I and II John, the question of which of the nine views above were truly Cerinthian is a bit academic; for a review of Chart Four will show that there is a plausible parallel only to number 3,[151] which we must now discuss in detail. The idea of "Christ" descending after the baptism and departing before the death has been thought to be the error attacked in I John 5:6: "Jesus Christ—this is the one who came by water and blood, not in water only, but in water and blood," with "water" meaning baptism and "blood" meaning death.[152] However, if the epistolary author was aiming directly at Cerinthus, would he not have spoken of the coming of Christ on Jesus, rather than the coming of Jesus Christ? Moreover, since Cerinthus held that Christ descended upon Jesus after the baptism, would the author not have been making a partial concession to Cerinthus when he said that there was a coming of Jesus Christ in water (at baptism)? If these difficulties (see also V B2b below) raise justified doubt about the identification of the epistolary adversaries as Cerinthians,[153] one may surmise at least that I John 5:6 was attacking a christological dualism which posited only a partial union between the divine and the human in Jesus Christ—a dualism less developed than that attributed to Cerinthus. (And indeed if there were already one dominant figure, such as Cerinthus, in the movement attacked by the epistolary author, his vague plurals such as "many Antichrists" and "false prophets" would be inexplicable.) Such a surmise is more plausible than attributing to the adversaries the full-scale docetism attacked by Ignatius or the precise gnostic ideas known to us from the Nag Hammadi literature.

This concludes the discussion of the identification of the adversaries with known "heretics" (those mentioned in the NT; the opponents of Ignatius, early gnostics, Cerinthians). While the Johannine adversaries have some points in common with all the proposed candidates, differences militate against a precise identification with any of these groups.[154] In any case, to have so identified the epistolary adversaries would not have been particularly enlightening; for granted the little we know about such groups, it would have been tantamount to explaining *ignotum per ignotius*. Yet it remains useful to know that the views attacked in I and II John

---

[151] One could argue that ##1,4 imply a dualism; yet the dualism attested in the thought of I John and of its adversaries never deals with evil creation or an unknown God (see 1:5; 2:4).

[152] Wengst, *Häresie*, would bring into the picture #8, so that the rest of I John 5:6, "The Spirit is the one who testifies," would be an attack against the Cerinthian confusion of the Spirit and Christ.

[153] Wengst, *Häresie* 21–34, argues against Schnackenburg's rejection (*Johannesbriefe* 20) of the Cerinthian identification of the adversaries; but even he does not fully identify the two, for he puts Cerinthus a stage beyond the epistolary adversaries.

[154] Clemen, "Beiträge" 272–75, issues wise cautions on this point.

were not without parallel in Asia Minor at the beginning of the second century. Having said that, I have not finished with the adversaries. Real light can be thrown upon them by asking how their thought and that of the author might be related to the theology of GJohn. That question enables me to propose the theory that makes the most sense of the exegetical conclusions I have reached in writing this commentary—a theory that is the subject of the next unit.

V. The Theory Adopted in this Commentary

Let me begin with a summary of my approach which, in the range of contemporary scholarship, is closest to the views of de Jonge and Houlden. I shall describe the overall life situation of the Epistles as I see it, and then in subsequent subdivisions of this unit work out the implications of this situation for interpreting the positions taken both by the epistolary author and his adversaries. A final subsection will consider III John as a key to further developments in the life of the Johannine Community.

A. *Brief Statement of the Theory*

In the decade after the main body of GJohn was written (*ca.* 90), the Johannine Community became increasingly divided over the implications and applications of Johannine thought. Before the writing of I John a schism had taken place. The resultant two groups, consisting of the epistolary author's adherents and his adversaries, both accepted the proclamation of Christianity known to us through GJohn, but they interpreted it differently. One can speculate whether outside influence played a role in the emergence of such different interpretations although there is no internal evidence of that; but almost surely the two groups justified their opposite positions on the basis of the Johannine tradition itself. One must be wary of arguing that GJohn led inevitably either to the position of the epistolary author or to that of his adversaries; nor is it clear that either position is a total distortion of GJohn.[155] Rather the Johannine tradition enshrined in GJohn, as it came to both the author and to his adversaries, was relatively "neutral" on some points that had now come into dispute. Either it did not contain direct answers for the divisive questions, or it contained texts that each side could draw upon for support.

[155] The subsequent church, by accepting I John into the canon of Scripture, showed that it approved the author's interpretation of the Johannine tradition rather than that of his adversaries. Technically, however, canonization does not make clear whether the approved teaching given us by the epistolary author resulted from preserving the correct interpretation of GJohn against distortion by the adversaries, or from the epistolary author's correcting tendencies found in GJohn itself. One thing is certain: The author of I John is not saying exactly what the author of GJohn said.

In the epistolary author's judgment, his adversaries were innovators or "progressives" who were distorting the tradition as it had come down from the beginning; and these innovators had seceded from the true Johannine Community (his adherents). Surely in their judgment these secessionists (as I shall henceforth call them[156]) thought that the author and his adherents had broken communion with them, and they may have thought that the author was reviving an outmoded christology instead of following the *implications* of the christology set forth in GJohn. In any case the author's admonitions did not stem the secessionists' success. In I John 4:5 he admits that they seem to be winning the world, and II John 10 shows that their missionary teachers were reaching even outlying communities.[156a] The author appealed to his adherents to "test the Spirits" (I John 4:1) as a safeguard against the secessionist claims, but there was not a sufficiently authoritative church structure to prevent secessionist inroads.

We have no certain knowledge of the outcome of the desperate situation portrayed in I and II John, but second-century history suggests that the two groups described in I and II John were swallowed up respectively by "the Great Church" (footnote 242 below) and by gnostic movements. Any amalgamation of the author's adherents with the apostolic Christians of the Great Church would have required on their part an acceptance of a much more authoritative church structure—an acceptance that would have caused friction. Such friction may explain III John where Diotrephes' exercise of authority in controlling who could visit (and presumably teach in) a local church is criticized by the author. How a need for structure and a reluctant Community tradition were ultimately reconciled may be

---

[156] Since I am commenting on I John (and not on any document written by the adversaries), I do not think it unscientific to use a term representing the author's evaluation (I John 2:19). The terminology secession/secessionists is preferable in every way to heresy/heretics, even though the canonical process mentioned in the previous footnote would make the heresy terminology appropriate from a later viewpoint. My belief that "heresy" is an anachronism for the I John situation stems from more than the truism that the adversaries did not think of themselves as heretics—few heretics ever do. I mean that only with hindsight was the subsequent church able to see where the movement of the adversaries had led. Non-Johannine Christians contemporary with the writing of I John may not have been able to appreciate the theological differences that separated the author from his adversaries and, indeed, may have thought that *both* held an extravagant christology and a deficient ecclesiology (Brown, *Community* 85–88). Moreover, the vocabulary of contemporary Christian writings casts light on attitudes at the end of the first century. Clement of Rome (*ca.* A.D. 96) never uses *hairēsis* (a word meaning "division, party," but moving toward "heresy, heretical sect"); rather he employs *schisma* ("schism") 5 times, and *stasis* ("rebellious dissension") 9 times. Ignatius (*ca.* 110) uses *hairēsis* twice, but *merismos* ("division") 6 times. During this period the schismatic, rather than the heretical, aspect of error was primary in the mind of those who wrote about inner-Christian disputes.

[156a] Just as the secessionists seem to have concentrated their missionary efforts upon the Johannine Christians, so the later gnostic missionaries concentrated more upon orthodox Christians than upon pagans (see Perkins, *Gnostic Dialogue* 123).

illustrated symbolically by John 21, which assigns to Peter, one of the Twelve, an authoritative pastoral care of Jesus' sheep, but still gives preference to the Beloved Disciple who received no such role. The amalgamation of the secessionists into the known gnostic movements of the second century would have required a heightening of the dualistic christology and perfectionist anthropology criticized in I and II John. If the secessionists constituted the larger part of the Johannine Community and if they brought GJohn with them into docetic, gnostic, and Cerinthian groups, we can understand why GJohn was better known among "heretics" than among orthodox church writers of the second century (ABJ 29, lxxxi–lxxxii), and why Irenaeus remembered a figure like Cerinthus when he discussed GJohn. The ultimate acceptance of GJohn into the church's canon, attested in the late second century, was in no small part due to the fact that I John offered an example of how GJohn could be read in a non-gnostic and even an anti-gnostic way.

Having summarily stated my theory, I shall now develop it in a systematic and detailed way.

B. *The Secessionists' Relation to the Fourth Gospel*

In Chart Four of Appendix I and in unit IV B2 above we saw the various christological and moral attitudes that the author of I and II John criticizes. Yet while he indicates that his adversaries are too progressive and that they have departed from what was held from the beginning, he never hints that their false views or "lies" have been derived or influenced from the outside. It seems incredible that, if there had been a major or discernible external influence upon the secessionists, the author would not have mentioned this in his polemic. Even the thesis (in itself not implausible) that an increasingly Gentile component in the Community made the Johannine Christians more susceptible to secessionist exaggerations[157] finds no support whatever in the wording of I and II John. The author's main appeal is to what was from the beginning—an appeal that makes it plausible that he and the secessionists were arguing over a common tradition. Since the author charges that his adversaries had seceded "from our ranks," i.e., from what he considers the Johannine Community, it is quite logical to assume that the Johannine tradition was the common

---

157 Bogart, *Orthodox* 134–35, posits that "the Johannine community suffered an influx of pre-gnostic gentiles who had never accepted the basic biblical doctrines of God and man." Painter, *John* 115, suggests that pagan converts accepted the teaching of GJohn enthusiastically, "perhaps . . . because the Judaism out of which the Gospel arose, represented by the Qumran texts, had some linguistic affinities with Gnosticism," but then they interpreted GJohn quite differently from the evangelist's intentions.

heritage. I shall try to show that *every idea of the secessionists (as recon-structed from the polemic of I and II John) can be plausibly explained as derivative from the Johannine tradition as preserved for us in GJohn.*

1. Methodological Cautions

At the outset let me remind the reader that we are dealing with seces-sionist views reconstructed from a polemic against them; and such a re-constructive process imposes severe limitations on the surety and quality of our conclusions, as explained at the beginning of IV A above. In seek-ing to relate these reconstructed views to GJohn, one must approach them sympathetically. It is not a matter of whether one likes such views or judges them as a tolerable Christian variant; the real issue is the inner logic of secessionist thought. The question is not whether the secessionist views were a correct interpretation of GJohn or even an inevitable deriva-tive from it, but only whether they represented a possible interpretation of GJohn or, at least, not a contradiction of it.[158] The last words in the pre-ceding sentence are important because of the above-mentioned possibility that GJohn may say nothing specific on a point that has now divided the author from the secessionists.

In the italicized sentence which immediately precedes these methodolog-ical cautions, I phrased my view very carefully: "from the Johannine tra-dition as preserved for us in GJohn." The evangelist himself (20:30) tells us that GJohn was only a selection from a wider body of material, namely, "the signs not preserved in this book." In addition to such extra-GJohn material, there may have been pre-GJohn written tradition that had a somewhat different focus and nuance from that of GJohn itself.[159] Nevertheless, GJohn is the only witness to the Johannine tradition that has been preserved for us and to which we can appeal with surety in discussing the Epistles. Consequently we have little choice about using GJohn as a guide in analyzing how Johannine Christians would have

---

[158] I find difficulty with the way Bogart, *Orthodox* 134–35, seeks to relate GJohn and the perfectionism of the secessionists (heretics): "Thus we must look at the per-fectionist *theology* found in the Gospel of John and ask, Is heretical perfectionism *inherent* here? Did it develop *naturally* out of it? No, because the theology (*i.e.*, the doctrine of God and creation), anthropology and soteriology underlying the Gospel of John are not gnostic." I agree with his negative answer to the two questions he has asked; but in my opinion he has not asked the right question and that is why he has reached the conclusion mentioned in the preceding footnote. The question I would ask is: Could the incipient perfectionism in GJohn be plausibly (even if wrongly) interpreted so as to produce the perfectionism of the secessionists? My an-swer to that question is yes.

[159] For instance, R. T. Fortna, "Christology in the Fourth Gospel: Redaction-Crit-ical Perspectives," NTS 21 (1974–75) 489–504, argues that, if there were any quasi-docetic tendencies in the Johannine tradition, it was on the pre-GJohn level rather than on the GJohn level. This raises the question of whether the secessionists were reviving older strains of thought.

thought and argued. Chart Two of Appendix I shows how much of I John's phraseology (covering views that the author accepts and criticizes) has echoes in GJohn. Below in V C1d and in VI A3b I shall propose that both the literary genre and structure of I John have been influenced by GJohn. The fact remains, however, that in neither the affirmations of the epistolary author nor in the reconstructed affirmations of the secessionists can one find a direct citation of GJohn (see footnote 79 above). Therefore, one cannot prove beyond doubt that either group reflected on the written GJohn as we now know it, and it is safer to speak of their knowing the proclamation of Christianity known to us through GJohn. *That is what I mean in all that follows when I speak of either side drawing upon GJohn or the Johannine tradition.*

In using GJohn as a guide to the Johannine tradition, I am aware of the possibility that parts of GJohn, especially those attributable to the redactor (ABJ 29, xxxvi-xxxviii: *Stage 5*), were added only after I and II John were written. In relating the secessionist views to GJohn, some would rule the redactional parts of GJohn out of the discussion; for the redactor is often thought to represent the same anti-secessionist theology that produced the Epistles and even to be the author of the Epistles. Obviously it would be easier to derive secessionist thought from GJohn if one could explain that every passage which does not favor the secessionist position had been added by a redactor in order to refute the secessionists. But then one is open to the charge of circular reasoning by establishing kinship between secessionist thought and a Gospel from which one has excluded all difficult passages. And so in this commentary as a basis of comparison for the Epistles I shall use the whole of GJohn.[160] Only when formally discussing the relation of the Epistles to the redaction of GJohn (below, V D2b) shall I indulge in the hypothesis that ch. 21, for instance, represents a situation posterior to the Epistles.

Thus the attempt to relate the thought of both the secessionists and the author to the tradition enshrined in GJohn is made under very definite limitations, and the hypothetical character of the results achieved are fully acknowledged. My claim is simply that this approach solves more problems than any other. Beginning with the reconstructed secessionist views, let me now test the approach in the two major areas of christology and ethics.

2. Christology—Secessionist and Fourth Gospel

The christology of GJohn may be the highest in the NT. Mark presents Jesus as the Son of God already at the baptism and so throughout the

---

[160] This is wise even if the redactor worked on GJohn after the Epistles were written, for he would have included in his additions some ancient material from the Johannine tradition (ABJ 29A, 1080–82), material that could well have been known to the epistolary author or to the secessionists.

whole public ministry.[161] Matthew and Luke picture Jesus conceived through the Holy Spirit without a human father, and so there is never a moment of his earthly life when he is not the Son of God. But no Synoptic Gospel proposes the incarnation of a being who came down from God, i.e., a preexistent Son of God.[162] Paul is often thought to have had a preexistence christology, although that is not certain.[163] However, even if Paul did refer to a type of preexistence, it was in highly poetic terms patterned on the OT hymnic portrait of divine Wisdom, with no clear indication of a preexistence *before creation*.[164] Hebrews 1:2 moves into a precreation sphere but still remains poetic.[165] GJohn too in the Prologue refers to preexistence before creation in a hymn patterned upon the OT Wisdom motif (ABJ 29, 521–23); but GJohn goes beyond the poetic hymn genre by introducing the preexistence motif into Jesus' own statements (8:58; 17:5).

Granted the uniquely high Johannine evaluation of Jesus, why did christology become the bone of contention between the secessionists and the epistolary author? The key to this question lies in the role christology played in Johannine history. The clear claim on behalf of Jesus' divinity led the Jews to frame a charge of ditheism, i.e., of believing in a second God (John 5:18; 10:33), which led in turn to the expulsion of the Johannine Christians from the synagogue (9:22), to persecution, and even to execution (16:2). The claim of preexistence was also rejected by Jews who believed in Jesus (8:31,37—probably representing the Jewish Christians of John's time); and indeed in GJohn famous disciples (representing perhaps those Christians who attached themselves to the memory of the apostles) failed to understand that whoever saw Jesus saw the Father (14:9). In many ways, then, high christology was an identity factor for the Johannine Community over against Jews and various Christian groups. Theologically, it was the cornerstone of Johannine soteriology: If Jesus had not come forth from God, he could not have brought eternal life, which was God's own life, and Christians would not be God's children (3:13,16; 6:57; 1:12–13). With such importance given to christol-

[161] I report what Mark presents; one cannot judge from his silence that he did not have a higher christology reaching back before the baptism.

[162] GJohn is the only one of the four Gospels to apply the term "God" to Jesus; see R. E. Brown, *Jesus God and Man* (Milwaukee: Bruce, 1967; or New York: Macmillan, 1972) 25–28.

[163] The most frequently cited passages are I Cor 8:6; II Cor 8:9; Phil 2:6–7; Col 1:15–16. For examples of hesitations, see J. Murphy-O'Connor, RB 83 (1976) 25–50, and 85 (1978) 253–67 and the literature he cites.

[164] Col 1:15–16 states that all things were created in the Son but still calls him "the firstborn of all creation," which on the analogy of 1:18, "the firstborn of the dead," could mean the first to be created. Moreover, Colossians may be post-Pauline.

[165] Heb 5:7–8 stresses the human limitations of Jesus to an extent that would be quite foreign to GJohn (cf. John 12:27).

ogy historically and theologically, it is not surprising, then, that if there was to be an internal dispute in the Johannine Community, it would be over this subject, and there would be little tolerance for deviation. The schism from Judaism over christology made less unthinkable a further inner-Johannine schism.

(a) NEGATING THE IMPORTANCE OF JESUS. But why did the secessionist christology take the direction it took? How is it possible that people who accepted the tradition known to us in GJohn could be charged with negating the importance of Jesus (I John 4:3) in a context that implies they did not confess adequately the significance of Jesus' life in the flesh (4:2)? We may begin to answer this question by recognizing that an incarnational christology based on preexistence bears within itself the possibility of relativizing the importance of Jesus' earthly life. If one relates divine sonship to Jesus' baptism (Mark) or to his conception (Matthew, Luke), then his ministry or his life becomes the arena in which the sonship expresses itself. But if God's Son existed before creation, what does an earthly career mean in reference to sonship? After all, GJohn insists that Jesus in his lifetime does and says nothing that he has not already seen and heard with the Father (5:19; 8:26,28,38). His message no longer concerns the kingdom of heaven come among men and women, as in the Synoptics, but is centered on a divine "I AM" (ABJ 29, cx, 535). In later discussions the question arose among Christian theologians whether Jesus had to die on the cross to accomplish salvation, since the incarnation itself brought eternal life into the world.[166] And GJohn lends itself to such an interpretation in the very sentence that is the most explicit profession of incarnational theology: "The Word became flesh and made his dwelling among us," for that sentence continues, "We have seen his glory, the glory of an only Son coming from the Father, filled with enduring love" (1:14). One might interpret this to mean that the real purpose of Jesus' earthly life was simply to reveal God's glory in human terms (7:18; 8:50; 11:40; 14:9; 17:5,24), but not to do anything new that changed the relationship between God and human beings. Käsemann has interpreted GJohn in much this way, calling it the vehicle of a naive docetism. His interpretation has been challenged;[167] but the very fact that he could propose such a thesis illustrates how the secessionists may have read GJohn.

The way in which the author discusses the christology of the secessionists helps to confirm their relationship to GJohn. He denies some positions that they hold, as we shall see below; but never does he resort to

---

[166] Such a theory focuses all soteriology on the beginning of Jesus' career, rather than on its end.

[167] See E. Käsemann, *The Testament of Jesus* (Philadelphia: Fortress, 1968) 26, and the response of G. Bornkamm, EvT 28 (1968) 8–25.

an attack on the basic incarnational or preexistence christology. Secessionist christology, which negated the importance of Jesus in his career in the flesh, could have been totally refuted if the author were free to declare that the earthly career of Jesus was his only career and that there was no career of God's Son before his conception. But if we theorize that the author was bound by the same Johannine christological tradition that fed the thought of his opponents, then it is not surprising to find him too speaking in the uniquely Johannine language of preexistence. He insists that "this eternal life which was in the Father's presence . . . was revealed to us" (I John 1:2); that "the Son of God was revealed" (3:8); that "God has sent His only Son into the world" (4:9,14);[168] and that Jesus is "the one who came" (5:6,20).[169] Thus, not the fact but only the manner of the coming is the subject of debate between the epistolary author and the secessionists.

(b) NOT ACKNOWLEDGING CHRIST COME IN THE FLESH AND IN BLOOD. If we reconstruct the secessionist position about the manner of the coming, I John 4:2 and II John 7 suggest that they did not acknowledge the coming of Jesus Christ *in the flesh*. Can such a position be derived from GJohn? The answer is no if the secessionists were similar to the docetists whom Ignatius of Antioch opposed (IV B3b above), i.e., those who denied the reality of Jesus' flesh and the reality of his actions. Texts like John 1:14; 19:34; 20:27 would not be favorable to such a docetism,[170] and there is nothing in the tone of GJohn to suggest that Jesus' earthly life was only an appearance. However, a more subtle secessionist position could be derived from GJohn, namely, if the secessionists admitted the reality of Jesus' humanity, but refused to acknowledge that his being in the flesh was essential to the picture of Jesus *as the Christ,* the Son of God.[171]

[168] "Sending" language is not necessarily indicative of a theology of preexistence, e.g., the prophets were *sent* to people (Isa 6:8; Jer 1:7; Ezek 2:3); John the Baptist was sent (Matt 11:10; John 1:6); and the Synoptic Jesus was sent (Mark 9:37; 12:6). But "sent into the world" by God is proper to GJohn (3:17; 10:36; 17:18) and I John.

[169] So also "coming" language is not necessarily indicative of a theology of preexistence. The idea of coming with a message from God is applied to the prophets (Jer 19:14), to John the Baptist (John 1:31), and to the Synoptic Jesus (Mark 1:7; 2:17; etc.). But John speaks of Jesus as "coming into the world" (John 3:19; 9:39; 12:46; 16:28; 18:37)—see also I Tim 1:15; Heb 10:5, works of two NT authors who call Jesus "God" (Titus 2:3; Heb 1:8).

[170] Some scholars would attribute such texts to the redactor who was attempting to refute the secessionists; but, for instance, there is nothing overtly polemic in 1:14. Indeed, when the whole of that verse is considered, if one wishes to attribute it to the redactor, such a redactor could be identified as the epistolary author only with difficulty; for the author of I John avoids the word "glory," which appears in 1:14.

[171] A sentence used by Pagels, *Johannine Gospel* 13, to describe the second-century Valentinians fits very well here: "Gnostic theologians do not necessarily *deny* that the events proclaimed of Jesus have occurred in history. What they deny is that the actuality of these events matters *theologically*."

For the secessionists Jesus would have been the Son of God who had always been at the Father's side and was sent into the world (John 1:18). That sending into the world would not only have revealed the preexistent Son of God, but also brought salvation to the world (3:17), in the sense that it now became possible to know God and possess eternal life (17:3). What the one who was sent did would be only confirmatory and not of salvific value.

If I am right in diagnosing the point of difference between the secessionists and the epistolary author to be the salvific value of Jesus' career in the flesh and the degree to which that career was part of his identity as the Christ, inevitably the attitude toward his death will be crucial. The author offers a formulation that, when negated, indicates the secessionist position: They were content with the notion that Jesus Christ came by/in water, whereas the author insists "not in water only, but in water and in blood" (I John 5:6).[172] In the commentary I shall argue that "water" is to be associated with Jesus' baptism, while "water and blood" means death by crucifixion, echoing the scene in John 19:34 where blood and water flowed out from the wound in Jesus' side.[173] If the secessionists were Cerinthians (above, IV B3d), holding that the Christ descended upon Jesus at the baptism but departed before the crucifixion, they could scarcely have derived their christology from GJohn. The presence of the Beloved Disciple at the cross (19:25–27) and the stress on the fulfillment of Scripture (19:24,28,36–37) would make little sense if the Christ had departed and the death of Jesus were a charade to deceive the material-minded. In GJohn the spiritual principle (which is what Cerinthus calls "the Christ") is clearly present until Jesus dies on the cross (19:30). However, if one does not think of the secessionist position in Cerinthian terms, "Christ came in water" could mean that the incarnation of the preexistent Christ took place in relation to the baptism of Jesus. Could such an interpretation have been derived from the kind of Johannine tradition known to us in GJohn? Readers of GJohn have usually interpreted "the Word became flesh" to mean that the incarnation took place *at the conception* of Jesus. However, while the conception is a theme of Matthew and Luke, it is never mentioned by GJohn. Before the statement that the light was coming into the world (1:9), the GJohn Prologue describes the role of John the Baptist (1:6–8). After the statement that the Word became flesh (1:14), the Prologue states that John the Baptist testified to the incarnate Word by proclaiming his preexistence (1:15).

[172] This passage fluctuates in its use of "in" and "by," reminding us that "come in the flesh" does not have the same force as "come in water." In the former, "in" means "into the sphere of"; in the latter, "in" means "by means of, through."

[173] In ABJ 29A, 945–46 I contended that 19:34 is not redactional, no matter what one may think about 19:35.

The Prologue is followed immediately by an opening scene centered on the testimony of the Baptist, which includes a repetition of his proclamation of Jesus' preexistence (1:31). The Baptist in GJohn has seen the Spirit descend on Jesus and has baptized with water so that Jesus might be revealed to Israel (1:31–32).[174] Independently of the question that concerns us here, R. H. Fuller[175] has used such GJohn evidence to argue that for the evangelist the shift from the *Logos asarkos* ("Word without flesh") to the *Logos ensarkos* ("Word enfleshed") came in relation *to the baptism*. Subsequently Fuller[176] modified his position, recognizing (rightly, in my opinion) that the "becoming flesh" of John 1:14 may have had a wider application than the baptism; but his earlier position shows how GJohn could have been read by the secessionists in terms of an incarnation at the baptism: "came by/in water." Or, if they did not press the formula that far, at least they could have related to the baptismal scene the primary gift of the Spirit and the primary revelation of Jesus as God's Son (John 1:33–34).

Against the secessionists the author (I John 5:6) insists: "not in water only, but in water and in blood." If this implies that an insistence on the death of Jesus corrects the secessionist error, we must ask whether the presumed secessionist lack of interest in the death of Jesus could have sprung from their interpretation of the tradition represented by GJohn. That Gospel speaks of the "hour" of Jesus (under which rubric it portrays the passion, death, and resurrection of Jesus) as his return to the Father and the manifestation of his glory (13:1; 17:1; 12:23–24).[177] Three times in GJohn (3:13; 8:28; 12:32) Jesus looks ahead to his death as a "lifting up"—an interesting contrast to the three predictions of passion and suffering in the Synoptic tradition (ABJ 29, 145–46). In the Johannine narrative of Jesus' arrest, trial, and crucifixion he is not a victim but one sovereignly in control: "I lay down my life in order to take it up again. No one has taken it away from me; rather, I lay it down of my own accord. I have power to lay it down, and I have power to take it up

---

[174] GJohn does not speak of John's having a baptism of repentance for the forgiveness of sins; his baptism has no purpose apart from testifying to Jesus.

[175] "Christmas, Epiphany, and the Johannine Prologue," in *Spirit and Light* (E. N. West Festschrift; ed. M. L'Engle and W. B. Green; New York: Seabury, 1976) 63–73.

[176] "New Testament Roots to the *Theotokos*," *Marian Studies* 29 (1978) 46–64.

[177] See R. E. Brown, "The Passion According to John," *Worship* 49 (1975) 126–34. U. B. Müller, "Die Bedeutung des Kreuzestodes Jesu im Johannesevangelium: Erwägungen zur Kreuzestheologie im Neuen Testament," KD 21 (1975) 49–71, compares the Johannine view to that of Paul's *opponents* at Corinth who did not share Paul's emphasis on the cross, since for GJohn the physical death of Jesus has no particular relevance except as a manifestation of *doxa*, "glory." Certainly the Johannine picture of Jesus' death differs from that of the hymn in Philip 2:8 where death on the cross is the lowest point in the humiliation of the servant. The Johannine Jesus is ascending on the cross.

again" (10:17–18). Such an affirmation may be contrasted to the view presented in Heb 5:8 where Jesus is said to have *learned obedience* through suffering. The Johannine Jesus never falls to the earth of Gethsemane in suffering and supplication as does the Synoptic Jesus; rather, Roman soldiers and Jewish police fall to the earth of the garden before him as he utters the majestic "I AM" (18:6). In the Roman trial scene the Johannine Jesus makes it clear that Pilate has no power over him except what comes from above (19:11), and indeed we are told that Pilate was afraid in encountering God's Son (19:8)! On the cross Jesus is not alone and rejected as he is in the other Gospels; he is surrounded by significant disciples who constitute his family (19:25–27), the beginnings of the church. He is in such control that only when he decides, "It is finished," does he bow his head and hand over his Spirit (19:30). This sovereign affirmation is far from the cry of the Marcan Jesus, "My God, my God, why have you forsaken me?" (15:34)—a cry that would be inconceivable on the lips of the Johannine Jesus who claimed in the face of desertion by his disciples, "I am never alone because the Father is with me" (16:32). T. Forestell[178] phrases well the peculiarity of the Johannine outlook on Jesus' death: "The cross of Christ in Jn is evaluated precisely in terms of revelation in harmony with the theology of the entire gospel, rather than in terms of vicarious and expiatory sacrifice for sin." Thus, clearly there are elements in the tradition of GJohn that might have led the secessionists to deemphasize the crucifixion as a salvific "coming" and to regard it simply as a continuation of that revelation of the glory of the preexistent which began through the Baptist's baptizing with water (1:14,31).

3. Ethics—Secessionist and Fourth Gospel

A glance at Chart Four in Appendix I shows that, while the author was solemn in his condemnation of secessionist christology, he devoted more attention to a criticism of their attitude toward moral behavior, sin, and the commandment to love.[179] In this area where he seems actually to have quoted secessionist slogans, the theory that the secessionists drew their ideas from the tradition found in GJohn could explain the strange way in which the author has argued against them. For instance, having cited (secessionist) claims to know God and to abide in God and in light (I

---

[178] *The Word of the Cross: Salvation as Revelation in the Fourth Gospel* (AnBib 57; Rome: Biblical Institute, 1974) 191. Also S. Talavero Tovar, *Pasión y Resurrección en el IV Evangelio* (Salamanca: Universidad, 1976), esp. 172–223: The passion is a revelation of Jesus as a king who came into this world but whose kingdom is not of this world.

[179] That is what I mean by "ethics." The propriety of using this term in discussing NT theology has been questioned on the grounds that there is nothing in the NT systematic enough to resemble what Aristotle called "ethics."

John 2:4,6,9), the author does *not* contradict these claims by saying that
no one knows God or that no one abides in God or in light. The secessionist claims were in themselves clearly defensible from Johannine theology (respectively in John 17:22,23,26; 14:7; 3:21; 8:12). The author's
disagreement with the secessionists is centered not on the claims but on
their failure to draw behavioral implications from the claimed relationship
to God, e.g., the claim to know God without an insistence on keeping the
commandments, or the claim to be in the light while hating one's brother.

(a) LACK OF EMPHASIS ON MORAL BEHAVIOR. I have argued above (IV
B2b) that the secessionists were not libertines notorious for scandalous
behavior but were indifferentists who attributed no salvific importance to
moral behavior by believers. Such an attitude would have been consistent
with their christology which put no salvific importance on Jesus' earthly
life. But could they have derived such an attitude from the tradition found
in GJohn? I would say yes in terms both of affirmations made in GJohn
and of its strange silence on ethical matters. By way of affirmations, some
statements of the Johannine Jesus seem to relativize earthly existence:
"You do not belong to the world, for I chose you out of the world"
(15:19), and "They do not belong to the world any more than I belong to
the world" (17:16). If eternal life consists in knowing God and the one
whom He sent, as GJohn affirms,[180] the secessionists may well have
claimed intimacy with God on the basis of their "knowing" Him without
emphasis on behavior. As for the ethical silence of GJohn, one is
reminded of Bultmann's famous axiom that the Johannine Jesus was a
revealer without a revelation.[181] The very fact that such a statement, however exaggerated, could be made indicates the extent to which christology
(in the sense of self-identification) dominated the Johannine proclamation. In his massive work on the Johannine concept of truth, I. de la
Potterie[182] shows that the Hebrew concept "to do truth" (OT, Qumran),
which meant to observe faithfully the prescriptions of the law, has been
interpreted in the Johannine literature as referring to adhesion to the truth
of Jesus. The early Christian struggle over the relation between faith and
works (Paul, James) has been resolved by John 6:28–29 in a way that
makes faith in Jesus the one "work of God." Such attitudes mean that
GJohn is deficient in precise moral teaching when compared with the
Synoptic Gospels. For instance, there is nothing in GJohn even remotely
resembling Matthew's Sermon on the Mount. If Matt 7:16 offers to the
follower of Jesus a criterion of behavior, "By their fruit you shall know

[180] For what John 17:3 means and whether it is a gnostic statement, see ABJ 29A,
752–53.
[181] *Theology of the New Testament* (2 vols.; New York: Scribners, 1955) 2, 66:
He "reveals nothing but that he is the Revealer." See the critique in Brown,
"Kerygma" 392–94.
[182] *La vérité* 2. 480–83,516.

them," in John 15:5 we find this language of fruit-bearing shifted over to adherence to Jesus: "He who remains in me and I in him is the one who bears much fruit."[188] In all three Synoptic Gospels discipleship is marked by *doing* the will or word of God (Mark 3:35; Matt 12:50; Luke 8:21); but for John 8:31, "If you *abide* in my word, you are truly my disciples." The appeal to repentance or reform (*metanoia/metanoein*), which is so much a part of the Synoptic proclamation of the kingdom (Mark 1:4,15; 6:12) and of the early Christian preaching in Acts (2:38; 3:19; 5:31; 8:22; etc.), is not found in GJohn.[184] Rather, the cleansing factor is the word spoken by Jesus (John 15:3). No specific sins of behavior are mentioned in GJohn, only the great sin which is to refuse to believe in Jesus (8:24; 9:41).[185] Especially interesting in relating ethics to christology is the Johannine Jesus' statement about the world (15:22): "If I had not come and spoken to them, they would not be guilty of sin." It is quite possible, then, that a secessionist lack of interest in moral behavior, in keeping the commandments, and in the dangers of sin may have been shaped by the dominance of christology in the Johannine tradition and by the lack of specific moral directives.

At first glance, this theory of a secessionist dependency on GJohn tradition may seem to be refuted by two of their positions that are not easily justified by GJohn, i.e., the claim to be free from sin, and the failure to love the brothers. Let us consider these positions in detail.

(b) PERFECTIONIST FREEDOM FROM SIN. In I John 1:8,10 two slogans are used to phrase a secessionist claim: "We are free from the guilt of sin" and "We have not sinned." While the author does not contradict other claims of the secessionists but conditions them (1:6; 2:4,6,9), he says outright that these two slogans are deceptive and make God a liar. Is that the author's way of stating that claims of sinlessness cannot be justified from the Johannine tradition? I think not, because ultimately the author makes his own claims of sinlessness (3:6,9; 5:18). Again the author is attacking *one* understanding of a perfectionist, sinless strain that comes from the Johannine tradition, while holding another himself. Let us test each of the two secessionist claims.

---

[188] GJohn too recognizes the importance of good deeds in one's *coming* to Jesus (3:19–21; 9:3), but the need for those deeds after one has become a believer is not so clear.

[184] However, the need for some change of life seems presupposed in John 5:14 ("Sin no more") and 8:34 ("Everyone who acts sinfully is a slave of sin").

[185] From Irenaeus (*Adv. haer.* 1.5.3–6) it would seem that for the gnostics there was an original ignorance rather than an original sin. His picture is fairly accurate if we may judge from the *Gospel of Truth* (I 17:10–17; NHL 38): "Ignorance of the Father brought about anguish and terror. . . . For this reason error became powerful; it fashioned its own matter foolishly, not having known the truth." The secessionists may have represented an early stage of such thought where ignorance of Jesus was the primary evil.

The first secessionist slogan, "We are free from the guilt of sin" (*hamartian ouk echein;* see NOTE on 1:8a), is easily related to GJohn when we remember that the terminology "guilty of sin" and "slaves of sin" is used there for nonbelievers. In John 8:31–34 Jesus addresses Jews who had (inadequately) believed in him thus: "Everyone who acts sinfully is a slave of sin," whereas, "If you abide in my word, you are truly my disciples; and you will know the truth, and the truth will set you free." Since, by contrast with the nonbeliever, the believer is freed from sin, the secessionists would really be rephrasing only slightly if they claimed to be free from the guilt of sin. Indeed, in the GJohn story of the blind man there occurs the very expression "guilty of sin" (*echein hamartian*). The man who was born blind (and therefore accused of being born in sin: 9:34) is enlightened. The Pharisees, on the other hand, are told that, if they recognized their blindness, they would not "be guilty of sin"; but because they claim to see, their sin remains (9:41). A logical assumption would be that the blind man who did recognize his blindness is not guilty of sin, and his sin does not remain.[186] The evangelist wished the reader to identify himself with the blind man, and the secessionists have done just that in regarding themselves as those who have been enlightened and thus not guilty of sin.

But could the secessionists have justified from GJohn the second perfectionist slogan: "We have not sinned" (1:10)? If this claim meant that they had never sinned in their lives because they had come into this world as God's children, then the secessionists probably should be classified as gnostics; but as I showed above (IV B3c), it is very dubious that the secessionists did claim that they were God's children by nature, instead of by baptism. And certainly such a view could not be derived from GJohn, which contrasts natural birth and a new status that comes through belief in Jesus' name (1:12–13) and through "water and Spirit" (3:3–6), which is almost surely a reference to baptism (ABJ 29, 141–44). True, there are passages in GJohn that point to an *orientation* or *predisposition* toward becoming a child of God, e.g., "No one can come to me unless it is granted to him by the Father" (6:65; 10:3). The evangelist probably meant them in terms of life-style before one encounters Jesus, namely, a sinfulness or a righteousness that turns one away from or toward Jesus when he comes: "The light has come into the world but some men have preferred darkness to light because their deeds were evil. . . . But he who acts in truth comes into the light, so that it may be shown that his deeds are done in God" (3:19–21). Thus, if the secessionists were in the

---

[186] See also John 8:24: "Unless you come to believe that I AM, you will surely die in your sins"; 15:22: "If I had not come and spoken to them, they would not be guilty of sin"; and 16:8–9: "The Paraclete will prove the world wrong . . . about sin —in that they refuse to believe in me." All these imply that believers will no longer be guilty of sin.

Johannine tradition, they thought of their status as children of God and the perfection it brought as something acquired through becoming Christians rather than as something with which they came into the world.

Suppose, then, that the secessionist claim "We have not sinned" referred to an inability to sin after becoming a Christian—could that slogan be justified from the tradition found in GJohn? One might argue that, since baptized believers have become God's children through divine begetting, they are like the Son of God who asked, "Can any one of you convict me of sin?" (8:46). Were not all Johannine Christians taught that they had received the Spirit which gives a power over sin (20:22–23; see ABJ 29A, 1041–45)? Were they not taught that whoever believed in the Son was not judged (3:18; 5:24)? After all, Jesus had told Simon Peter, "The person who has bathed has no need to wash . . . he is clean all over" (13:10). That the Johannine tradition lends itself to a thesis of the sinlessness of the believer in imitation of the sinlessness of God's Son is illustrated by the epistolary author's own affirmation in 3:5–6: "You know well that Christ was revealed to take away sins, and there is nothing sinful in him. Everyone who abides in him does not commit sin." He then goes on (3:9) to associate the challenge to sinlessness with being begotten by God: "Everyone who has been begotten by God does not act sinfully because God's seed abides in him; and so he cannot be a sinner because he has been begotten by God."

If both the secessionists and the author seem to advocate a perfectionism that leads to sinlessness, what is the difference between them? The epistolary author's theology in 3:6,9 and 5:18 is not easily diagnosed, and in the long NOTE on 3:9cd I shall have to discuss the many proposed interpretations. But even in this INTRODUCTION one clear difference may be brought out. No matter what he says about sinlessness, the author admits that in fact those who are already Christians *do* sin: "My Little Children, I am writing this to keep you from sin. But if anyone does sin, we have a Paraclete in the Father's presence, Jesus Christ, . . . and he himself is an atonement for our sins" (2:1–2). He criticizes the secessionists for a theory of sinlessness that puts no emphasis on continued forgiveness (1:7,9), evidently because they did not make the allowance, "If anyone does sin."

(c) LOVE OF THE BRETHREN.[187] Over and over again (Chart Four: B9–15) I John comes back to the theme of love of one's brother or the

---

[187] In modern usage one should think of "brothers and sisters"; for the female section of the Community is presupposed in the Epistles, even if never mentioned. However, in a translation to make its presence clearer by constantly adding "and sisters," especially in I John's criticisms of those who do not love their brothers, might suggest that there was an antifeminist issue involved in the schism; and there is no evidence of that. In GJohn women are highly significant; see R. E. Brown, "Roles of Women in the Fourth Gospel," TS 36 (1975) 688–99, reprinted in *Community* 183–98.

love of one another. Indeed, the author puts such love on the same level of importance as correct belief in Jesus Christ: "Now this is God's commandment: we are to believe the name of His Son, Jesus Christ; and we are to love one another just as He gave us the command" (I John 3:23). If he considered the secessionists defective on one score, almost surely he considered them defective on the other. His use of the term "commandment" in other passages dealing with such love (2:7–9; 4:21; 5:2–3; II John 4–6) suggests that, when elsewhere he hints that the secessionists did not keep the commandments (plural: I John 2:3–5; 3:22), this charge may narrow down to their not loving the brothers. Such a narrowing of ethical conflict to one issue would be intelligible against the background of GJohn where, when Jesus speaks about a commandment or commandments (plural) for his disciples, there is always mention of a demand to love (13:34–35; 14:15; 15:10,12,17), almost as if the commandment to love, especially "to love one another," subsumed all other commandments (ABJ 29, 504–5).

If the author's implication is true that the secessionists did not love their brethren, how could they have derived or justified their attitude from the tradition known to us in GJohn? Wengst (*Häresie* 53–59) thinks that they had shifted their love to God; for, since they regarded themselves as God's children, begotten by Him, they thought themselves capable of loving God connaturally and in a way different from those who were not God's children. He also thinks they were elitists and well-off, despising the less informed and impoverished ordinary Christians of the Johannine Community (I John 2:15–17; 3:17). That may be true, but I do not think it goes to the heart of the problem. Beyond the possibility that the secessionists may not have emphasized love of brethren or may have practiced it inadequately, did they affirm in their ethical theory that it was not necessary to love their brethren? That would be a direct contradiction of the Johannine Jesus: "This is my commandment, 'Love one another as I have loved you'" (15:12); "By this will all identify you as my disciples —by the love you have for one another" (13:35). In line with my theory that the secessionists did not contradict the GJohn tradition[188] but drew upon it, I propose that it was perfectly possible for the secessionists to affirm, "We love one another, as Jesus commanded," and still to earn the epistolary author's condemnation for not loving the brothers. The key to

[188] Other scholars think that the secessionists did contradict GJohn because they saw no connection between love of brethren and love of God, or because they so emphasized the individual's relation to God that they had no sense of community. However, the author treats them as a group or community, offering no indication that they were less communitarian among themselves than were the author's adherents. In some claims that he attacks, the protagonists speak as a "we" (I John 1:6,8,10), just as does the author in what he affirms (1:1–5).

this paradox lies in the definition of the "one another" or "brothers" who are to be loved. In the NOTE on 2:9b below I shall defend in detail the position that GJohn articulates no demand to love all human beings or to love one's enemies—only true believers in Jesus are the children of God and, therefore, brothers. When applied to the epistolary situation, this means that for the author "brothers" were those members of the Johannine Community who were in communion (*koinōnia*) with him and his fellow witnesses to the tradition, and who accepted his interpretation of the Johannine gospel (*angelia;* see I John 1:4–5). The secessionists had left and were no longer brothers; indeed, their very leaving was indicative of their lack of love. He did not regard himself as violating the commandment to love one another when he bitterly condemned the secessionists, characterizing them as demonic Antichrists and false prophets, and as the embodiment of eschatological iniquity (*anomia;* 2:18,22; 4:1–5; 3:4–5). Although he exhorted his own followers to love one another, the author of II John immediately afterward (vv. 5,10–11) told them to treat the secessionists in a way that was scarcely loving: "If anyone comes to you who does not bring this teaching, do not receive him into the house and greet him, for whoever greets him shares in his evil deeds."[189] If apostasy was the deadly sin of I John 5:15–17, as seems likely, the author advised against prayers for the secessionists.

May we not suppose that the secessionists would have had the same understanding of love of brothers, and would have regarded the author and his adherents exactly as he regarded them? In their own eyes, then, the commandment would have bound them to love their fellow secessionists but not the author's group. The failure to love the author's adherents in his eyes was a failure to love the only brethren or children of God he recognized: "Anyone who has knowledge of God listens to us, while anyone who does not belong to God refuses to listen to us" (4:6). If this is right, the limited understanding of brotherly love proclaimed by both the author and the secessionists is eloquent proof that they both adhered to GJohn tradition, for a wider concept of love was known to other Christian traditions (Matt 5:44; Luke 10:26–37). Even the refusal to pray for those who had left the brotherhood could be a transferal of the attitude of the Johannine Jesus who prayed for his own (17:6) and those whom they would convert (17:20), but refused to pray for the world (17:9). We saw above that Johannine incarnational christology could become heady

---

[189] There is little to be gained from the dubious observation that this was *loving* treatment since the author was doing this for the salvation of such false teachers. His intention does not change the character of his action, and the same Presbyter in III John 9–10 bitterly resents Diotrephes' doing to his emissaries exactly what in II John he had told his followers to do to the secessionists.

when worked out to an extreme; so also the dualistic tendencies present in the GJohn tradition could become dangerous when transferred into the inner-Christian debate.

C. *The Epistolary Author's Relation to the Fourth Gospel*

Having shown how reconstructed secessionist views may have been derived from the tradition in GJohn, let me turn to delineating precisely how the Johannine Epistles may have been related to GJohn—a somewhat less speculative task since the author has written down his views and we do not have to reconstruct them from an adversary document. I shall argue that the genre, polemic, argumentation, and even structure of I John depend essentially on GJohn,[190] as does the author's understanding of himself as a tradition-bearer in the Johannine "School."

1. Literary Genre of I John

If the same man wrote I, II, and III John (a thesis that, as we saw above in II A, offers the least number of difficulties), the latter two works show that he knew perfectly well the standard format for letters. Indeed, III John has sometimes been characterized as the most perfect example of epistolary format in the NT.[191] It is all the more startling, then, that all elements of epistolary format are lacking in I John.[192] This was noted concisely a century ago by Westcott (*Epistles* xxix): "No address, no subscription, no name is contained in it of person or place; there is no direct trace of the author, no indication of any special destination." Of the

[190] Although I could be content with showing that the author of I John knew the kind of tradition contained in GJohn, I think it more likely that he knew some form of GJohn itself, even if he wrote before the final redaction of GJohn (V D2b below).

[191] I use "epistle" and "letter" interchangeably in this volume, even though A. Deissmann made popular for a while a distinction between the two. In LFAE 228–29 he offered these definitions: "An epistle is an artistic literary form . . . just like the dialogue, the oration, or the drama. It has nothing in common with the letter except its form." On the other hand, "A letter is something non-literary, a means of communication between persons who are separated from each other . . . it is intended only for the person or persons to whom it is addressed, and not at all for the public or any kind of publicity." These precisions are too sharp for many NT works, including the main Pauline epistles/letters; and I John does not have the format required by either definition.

[192] Epistolary format will be discussed in Appendix V. I do not find impressive Bultmann's contention (*Epistles* 2) that the "I have written this to you" of I John 5:13 is the usual epistolary conclusion. It is true that III John, a letter, contains the words, "I did write something to the church" (v. 9), but this is not a conclusion. I John is probably echoing the conclusion of GJohn, "These things have been written" (20:31), and thus a nonletter form.

twenty-one NT works normally classified as epistles, I John is the least letterlike in format.[193] The question is appropriate, therefore, whether tradition has done justice to I John in calling it an epistle or letter, a question that I have seen traced as far back as Heidegger in 1681 (and Bengel in the 1750s). There is always the *prima facie* suspicion that such a work was classified as an epistle because there were so many epistles in the NT; and obviously it was not one of the known alternatives (a Gospel; a type of history like Acts; or an apocalypse like Revelation).

As one pursues the question of exact literary genre for I John, one should notice the few internal indicators, e.g., the 13 times that the author states he is *writing,* and the 22 addresses to a "you" (plural). Although these are sometimes cited as proofs of a letter genre,[194] they simply indicate that we are dealing with a literary form that is both written and addressed to an audience. May I add that one should avoid facile appeal to the category of the "Non-Real Letter" or "Letter Encyclical."[195] In the Hellenistic world the "epistle" or "letter" was a very inclusive mode of writing, so that disquisitions, essays, dialogues, biographies, and personal reflections were occasionally cast in a letter format, without such a "letter" or "epistle" ever being sent to a specific audience. But such a pattern does not describe I John, which precisely has *not* been cast in a letter format. Part of the complexity of the classifying task is caught by Lohmeyer's (overprecise) recognition of three styles in the one author: prophet, lawgiver, and homilist.[196] It is easier to recognize what the author is doing in his overall effort to counteract the secessionists than to classify the end product as a particular form of literature.

(a) UNIVERSAL RELIGIOUS TRACTATE. Windisch classified I John as a religious tractate that was apparently directed to a special group but really meant for the whole of Christianity.[197] Although other commentators use loosely the term "tractate," Windisch has had little following in taking "religious tractate" as a formal or technical classification for I John. The *Corpus Hermeticum* supplies us with examples of what would have been understood at the time as religious tractates, and neither the style nor the

---

[193] Hebrews has no Opening Formula (*Praescriptio*), but it has a Concluding Formula or customary greetings (13:22–25) which is lacking in I John. James and Jude have Opening Formulas (lacking in I John) but no epistolary Concluding Formula.

[194] Marshall, *Epistles* 99: "The author was writing for the benefit of a particular group or groups of readers, so that the writing is in effect a letter."

[195] For these literary forms, see Doty, *Letters* 6–8.

[196] "Aufbau" 258–60. I think he is right when he insists (258,262) that I John is not *Kleinliteratur* (a written work of minor or passing significance) but a literary work. He probably exaggerates when he claims that in this respect only Hebrews in the NT is comparable.

[197] *Briefe* 136. Jülicher combined this suggestion with the one in (b) below to propose identification of I John as a circular letter addressed to the universal church.

content is the same as I John.[198] Nor is there in I John the systematic development of a theme that we might expect in a tractate. Nevertheless,
one can find more support among scholars for the rest of the Windisch
thesis, namely that I John, whether tractate or letter, was directed to the
whole church or to all Christians. Kümmel (*Introduction* 437) tells us, "I
John is not to be understood as being in any way a writing intended for
specific readers," and "I John seems rather to be a tractate intended for
the whole of Christianity, a kind of manifesto." Much the same mentality
lay behind the designation of I John as a "Catholic Epistle" (above I A).
While I would agree that I John has a message *important* to all Christians
since they can learn from the struggles it reflects, I deny the thesis that it
was written for all (first-century or subsequent) Christians. A message to
Christianity at large from someone who does not identify himself would
have carried little weight. Furthermore, such a thesis does little justice to
the internal indications that the author is dealing with a specific tradition
possessed from the beginning, as well as a special way of interpreting that
tradition (the "we" of the Prologue). Also there is every reason to believe
that the author had in mind specific adversaries who had "gone out" from
his own community because they disagreed over issues of christology
(2:19,22). Finally, the thesis of a destination to all Christians does not fit
at all the history of Johannine Christianity that can be reconstructed from
GJohn. No community in the NT was less likely than the Johannine to
have such a universalist outlook, for GJohn treats various other Christians
as outsiders and even as nonbelievers.[199] Whatever the literary form, I
judge it certain that I John was addressed to a *Johannine* Community of
which the author was part, from which a major secession had taken place,
and where the faith of those who remained was endangered by the propaganda of the secessionists.

(b) CIRCULAR EPISTLE. An attempt to do justice both to the lack of an
epistolary address and to the presence of specific contents is seen in the
thesis that I John was an epistle addressed to the churches of a particular area (sometimes with the added suggestion that the appropriate address was supplied when the circular letter was read to a particular
church). The proposal of such a circular epistle (Neander and Gaugler
with different nuances) comes from the fact that often Christian churches
were in towns strung along a network of Roman roads, so that the same
letter carrier could visit more than one community. Yet when we study
the evidence for a messenger doing this, he seems to carry a different letter
to each community rather than one letter adaptable to every community,

[198] The Hermetic tractates have a dialogue or diatribe style and are not concerned
with specific pastoral problems (as is I John).

[199] Because of GJohn's hostility toward crypto-Christians in the synagogue and toward Jewish Christians of a low christology, the question has been asked whether
the Johannine Community was not a sect with a largely adversative identity (Brown,
Community 14–17, 88–91; also Segovia, "Love").

e.g., Tychicus carried Colossians *and* Philemon, and presumably the one messenger carried a separate letter to each of the seven churches in Rev 2–3. Really the concept of a circular letter as a literary form in NT Christianity rises and falls with one's approach to Ephesians, which is addressed simply "to the saints." Since some MSS. add "who are at Ephesus," a theory gained favor that this very general letter attributed to Paul was carried by Tychicus to various churches, that at each town the local name was supplied as it was read, and that the copy that has come down to us was the one preserved at Ephesus. Be that as it may, a comparison of Ephesians to I John does nothing to favor the classification of the latter as a "circular epistle," since it lacks the epistolary Opening Formula and Conclusion, which are quite clear in Ephesians.

In order to have plausibility, the suggestion that I John was addressed to several churches in an area would have to be modified so that only *Johannine* churches were envisioned. (The polemics in GJohn suggest that the Johannine Community lived in an area where there were also churches of Jewish Christians and churches of Apostolic Christians, as I have argued in my book *Community*.) But even with that modification, I doubt that I John was *meant* to be carried on the road to a number of Johannine churches, even though ultimately it may have been read in farflung Johannine churches that remained in *koinōnia* or "communion" with the author. The very existence of II John suggests that the secession had not taken place simultaneously in all the Johannine churches, and that a true letter might be sent to an outlying church when the secessionist missionaries approached. It is more plausible, then, to think of I John as addressed to Johannine Christians in one place,[200] presumably the "mother" Johannine group that spawned the Johannine churches in the outlying areas. For further discussion of the locale, see V C3 below.

(c) HOMILY; DIATRIBE; INFORMAL TRACTATE; PASTORAL ENCYCLICAL. One or several of these terms appear in many a modern commentary on I John.[201] There is a strong hortatory style in I John, and some of these designations give expression to that. However, the fact that no one of them fits perfectly and that each of them is quite general frustrates, in part, the search for a specific literary genre for I John. For instance, we do not really know much about the early Christian homily; but if P. Borgen[202] is right in judging that John 6:31–58 is a Christian

---

[200] These Christians may have met in many different house-churches in the one city.

[201] Chaine, *Epîtres* 120, speaks of a letter that contains a theological tractate, or a theological tractate that is at the same time a letter. Dodd, *Epistles* xxi, refers to an "informal tract or homily." Marshall, *Epistles* 14, evaluates I John as "a tract written to deal with a specific problem; it is a written sermon or pastoral address." Conzelmann, "Anfang" 201, compares I John to the Pauline Pastoral Epistles, since it treats of some of the same pastoral problems (albeit with quite different format).

[202] *Bread from Heaven* (NovTSup 10; Leiden: Brill, 1965); see ABJ 29, 277–78.

homily on an OT text dealing with manna, this genre throws little light on I John which is singularly lacking in OT citations. Others suggest a homily based on material supplied by standard Christian baptismal catechesis,[203] and to support this they point to the author's frequent appeal to what his audience has known "from the beginning" (2:12,13,24; etc.). Even if there is some truth in this suggestion and even if some of the material in I John was once orally proclaimed, the author's stress on *writing* throughout I John makes the ordinary meaning of "homily" somewhat inappropriate. Moreover, as one judges the genre, justice must be done to I John's attacks on christological and ethical positions advanced by adversaries.

My own position with regard to such designations (and to the designation "epistle"[204]) is that they do little to clarify the nature of I John. In what follows I shall offer no new name for the literary genre represented by I John but simply attempt to describe what the work basically does.

(d) COMMENT PATTERNED ON GJOHN. The peculiar format of I John may have been influenced by the author's attempt to refute the secessionists by commenting on GJohn to which they also appealed as a justification for their views.[205] His was not a commentary in a systematic or verse-by-verse style but an attempt to expound GJohn ideas misinterpreted by the secessionists. This exposition remained within the language and theological confines of the Johannine tradition[206] and at times appealed to older motifs that were only minor in GJohn. The author would not have been directing his exposition of GJohn immediately to his adversaries but to those Johannine Christians still in communion with him, in order to strengthen them and to prevent them from being confused by the plausible presentation of GJohn proclaimed by the adversaries.

In some ways this thesis, which posits an essential relationship of I John to GJohn, agrees with the most ancient patristic understanding of I John; for it was commonly held by the church fathers that I John was written to accompany GJohn as a kind of introduction to make GJohn more intelligible.[207] (However, I would maintain that for the post-Johan-

[203] See Nauck's views in III B1 above; also pp. 242–45 below.

[204] Although I do not think that I John should be classified as an epistle or letter, I shall from time to time employ without prejudice the traditional designation "First Epistle of John."

[205] My preference for this approach to the literary genre of I John explains why I have treated the question of genre in this section of the INTRODUCTION.

[206] Houlden, *Epistles* 31–32: "I John is then not a letter, it is a theological tract, modelled roughly on this congregation's existing production, GJohn, especially in structure and terminology, and in the use and contents of the prologue."

[207] Belser, Berger, Eichhorn, J. D. Michaelis, and Storr are among those who consider I John to constitute the practical or polemic part of GJohn. Ebrard, Hausrath, J.C.K. Hofmann, Lange, Lightfoot, and Meinertz are among those who consider I

nine reader it is GJohn that makes I John intelligible, and that an interval between the composition of the two works must be posited.) A modern variant of the patristic approach is found in Bakken, *Relationship,* who proposes that I John was written after GJohn to make that Gospel acceptable to other Christians (the Great Church) since already objections had been raised against the orthodoxy of GJohn. I suggest a different nuance: I John was written to preserve an interpretation (later recognized as orthodox) for insiders rather than to convince outsiders. It was only at a later time that I John was read by non-Johannine Christians, and then it helped them to see how GJohn could be read in a non-gnostic manner.

Let me illustrate how this analysis of the genre of I John as an exposition of GJohn may serve to answer some difficulties we have encountered. If the same man wrote the three Johannine Epistles, why has he not identified himself as "the Presbyter," as he did in II and III John? I would answer that II and III John are true letters in which the author identifies himself by his customary community title, whereas in I John he is deliberately wearing the mantle of the evangelist whose work he thinks he is authentically interpreting.[208] Thus the epistolary author chose to begin, not with the Opening Formula or *Praescriptio* that he uses when he is writing letters (II and III John), but with a Prologue written in imitation of the GJohn Prologue.[209] The same may be said of the ending of I John—no epistolary Concluding Formula as in II and III John, but an imitation of GJohn which has a final statement about the purpose of writing (20:31). This is seen in I John 5:13, a statement about the purpose of writing which is expanded in 5:14–21.[210] Below under Structure (VI A3b) I shall discuss the further possibility that I John has been divided into two

---

John to be a companion piece to GJohn. As late as 1918, Bacon, *Fourth Gospel* 185, spoke of I John as an "epistle of commendation" for GJohn. Loisy, *Evangile-Epîtres* 80, detects two editions of I John, the first meant to accompany the original edition of GJohn, the second to accompany the redacted form of GJohn.

[208] Wengst, *Häresie* 66, thinks that the author presents himself as speaking for the evangelist. One may cite I John 1:5: "Now this is the gospel that we have heard from Christ and declare to you."

[209] Conzelmann, "Anfang" 198–99.

[210] If one thinks that the epistolary author knew a written form of GJohn that already possessed ch. 21 (which was added as an Epilogue by a redactor), one may wish to speak of 5:14–21 as the I John Epilogue. Indeed, Bultmann thinks the same Ecclesiastical Redactor added both Epilogues. I think the relationship may be more complicated, namely, that the epistolary author knew GJohn with its original ending in 20:30–31, and that he imitated that ending in I John 5:13 but stretched out his reflections for a few more verses. If, as I think, the redactor worked on GJohn after I John was written, one may ask whether, in placing ch. 21 as an Epilogue to GJohn after the ending in 20:30–31, the redactor was not influenced structurally by the fact that comments followed a similar ending in I John. Parallels between John 21 and I John 5:14–21 are slight (knowing true testimony in 21:24 and the true God in I John 5:20).

parts in imitation of the two "Books" into which GJohn is divided (ABJ 29, cxxxviii–cxxxix).

2. Polemic and Argumentation Employed in I John

The patterning of I John on GJohn goes beyond structural aspects to the style of writing and the content of the argument. In Appendix I, Chart Two, I have listed the similarities between I John and GJohn. In V B3 above I mentioned that, instead of attacking the secessionists' principles of union with God, I John criticizes their failure to draw the right theological and ethical conclusions from the principles—a peculiarity that could be explained if both the author and the secessionists were deriving commonly accepted principles from GJohn. Let me now press the latter point to help show the dependency of I John on GJohn.

(a) REUSE OF GJOHN POLEMIC. I have argued (V B3c) that the author could attack his adversaries fiercely and still speak of the obligation to love the brothers, precisely because in Johannine thought the "brothers" were fellow children of God who constituted the Johannine Community (which the epistolary author identified with his adherents). This sense of close love within a community over against those outside is in complete harmony with GJohn, where strongly disliked adversaries appear in almost every scene of Jesus' public ministry (1:19–12:50, the Book of Signs); but there is a special period of tender affection for Jesus' own followers (13:1–20:31, the Book of Glory). The Prologue catches the two attitudes well: "To his own he came; yet his own people [the Jews] did not accept him; but all those who did accept him he empowered to become God's children" (1:11–12). The latter constitute a new "his own"; and GJohn is structured on an antagonism between "his own" born of the flesh who rejected Jesus and "his own" born of the Spirit whom he loved: "Having loved his own who were in the world, he now showed his love for them to the very end" (13:1).

It is not surprising, then, that once the focus of Johannine battle had shifted from outside adversaries in GJohn to schismatics from the Community in I John, the polemic attitude and language once applied to the GJohn adversaries were reused by the author of I and II John for the secessionists. It was a matter of turning the cannon around to face inward. The dualistic language in which GJohn had contrasted disciples of Jesus and "the Jews" (or those who constituted "the world") makes up the epistolary author's polemic arsenal.[211] In GJohn Jesus assured his followers that they were not walking in darkness (8:12; 12:46), for darkness was the realm of those who did not accept Jesus (1:5; 3:19–21;

---

[211] For instance, love/hate; light/darkness; truth/falsehood; from above/from below; of God/of the devil (or, in my translation, "belonging to God/to the devil"). One may guess that the secessionists were using the same dualistic arsenal against the author and his adherents.

12:35). In I John the secessionists, even though they claim to be followers of Christ, are said to walk in darkness (2:9–11). In GJohn one task of the Paraclete was to prove the *world* wrong about justice (16:8,10). In I John, although the adversaries claim to be just (3:7), the author offers a criterion of justice or righteousness with the clear implication that it will prove them wrong (3:7–8; 2:29). In a bitter passage in GJohn (8:44) Jesus attacked Jews who "believed" in him (Jewish Christians of inadequate faith from the evangelist's viewpoint) by telling them that they belonged to the devil their father, who was a murderer and liar. In I John 3:10–11, while speaking about the need for love of brothers, the author uses the same terminology for the secessionists: they are the devil's children; they are like Cain who belonged to the Evil One, a murderer from the beginning; they have the Spirit of Deceit and are the tellers of lies (3:8–15; 4:1–6; 2:22). GJohn (12:39–40) applied Isa 6:10 to "the Jews"—God had blinded their eyes—but I John 2:11 seems to apply it to the secessionists: "The darkness has blinded their eyes." One cannot prove that I John is quoting GJohn, but it is certainly using the same terminology.

(b) STYLE OF CORRECTING. If the epistolary author attacks his opponents verbally, he seems strangely unable to invoke any ruling authority in correcting them. In III John 9–10, although the Presbyter strongly disapproves of Diotrephes "who likes to be first," the most he does is threaten: "If I come, I shall bring up what he is doing."[212] In I John, although the author dubs the secessionists as antichrists who do the work of the devil, his only correction consists in appealing to the inner guidance of the Christians to whom he is writing, a guidance that stems from the knowledge of the truth and from having been anointed (with the Holy Spirit?): "Your anointing is from the Holy One, so all of you have knowledge" (2:20); "The anointing that you received from Christ abides in you; and so you have no need for anyone to teach you" (2:27). His does not seem to be the teaching or correcting power of the presbyter-bishops described in the Pauline Pastoral Epistles who were "to hold firm to the sure word as taught, in order to be able to give instruction in sound doctrine and also to refute those who oppose it" (Titus 1:9). I Timothy 5:17 gives double honor to those presbyters who labor in *teaching*—a function or office rendered otiose by I John. That there was a different understanding and style of authority in the Johannine Community is strongly suggested by GJohn. While other NT books show us that often the churches of apostolic foundation reacted to the death of their apostles

---

[212] Many commentators suggest that the Presbyter had authority to remove Diotrephes but refused to exercise it in deference to the ideals of Jesus and of the Community. Actually there is not a shred of evidence for that judgment, and behind it there often lies the assumption that the Presbyter was John, one of the Twelve Apostles.

by establishing a firm structure of presbyter-bishops to preserve the apostolic teaching and to protect the flock against innovations, GJohn handles the issue of ongoing teaching in a very different manner.[213] The Paraclete, the Holy Spirit, is the teacher who enabled the first Christian generation to bear witness (John 15:26–27); and this teacher, sent from heaven by God and Jesus, is not affected by the death of that generation, for he dwells forever in the heart of believers who love Jesus and keep his commandments (14:15–16). He guides the (Johannine) Christians "along the way of all truth" (16:13) and "teaches all things" (14:26)—a passage that seems to underlie I John 2:27: "His [Christ's] anointing teaches you about all things." Whether or not there were special ministries and even presbyters in the churches of the Johannine Community,[214] they could not have been assigned the teaching role that belonged to the Paraclete alone. This very lack of an ecclesiastical structure composed of teaching authorities rendered the Johannine Community vulnerable when the members differed over what the Spirit was teaching them. To counter the secessionists who claim the guidance of the Spirit, all the epistolary author can do is to urge his adherents: "Do not believe every Spirit; rather, put these Spirits to a test to see which belongs to God" (I John 4:1).

(c) THE "WE" OF THE JOHANNINE SCHOOL. There are some texts in I John that seem to contradict the GJohn indication that teaching is to be done by the indwelling Paraclete and, indeed, even to contradict the epistolary author's own statement that "You have no need for anyone to teach you" (I John 2:27). Among the texts that have been seen as favorable to the existence of authoritative human teachers is I John 4:6: "Anyone who has knowledge of God listens to us"; and this may be related to the "we" claim of the Epistle's Prologue: "This is what we proclaim to you: . . . what we have heard, what we have seen with our own eyes, what we looked at and felt with our own hands." This "we" is thought by some scholars to reflect the apostles, and the author is said to be claiming apostolic authority. (In the NOTE on I John 1:1 there will be a long, detailed discussion of various interpretations of the "we," so I summarize briefly here.) However, since no Johannine work mentions "apostles,"[215]

---

[213] See ABJ 29A, 1141–43; Brown, *Community* 86–88.

[214] I do not think there is real evidence for Schweizer's contention, *Church Order* 127 (12c): "Here [in the Johannine Epistles in continuity with GJohn] there is no longer any kind of special ministry, but only the direct union with God through the Spirit who comes to every individual; here there are neither offices nor even different charismata." The Spirit who comes to every individual does not necessarily rule out the ministries, the offices, or the charismata; it relativizes them. For a critical discussion of Schweizer's thesis, see Pastor, "Comunidad."

[215] *Apostolos* appears once in GJohn (13:16) in the nontechnical sense of "messenger." If one would argue that it should be translated "apostle" there, the verse becomes a "put-down" of apostles by Jesus: "No *apostolos* is more important than the

it is only loosely and by harmonization with non-Johannine literature that one can speak of the "apostolic we." In the I John Prologue the "we" is distinct from a "you" who are addressed: "What we have seen and heard we proclaim in turn to you" (1:3). This same phenomenon occurs in GJohn in passages that have much the same theme as the I John Prologue, namely, the theme of an eyewitness testimony to truth related by a "we" to "you."[216] Thus the "we" need not be a body of established church officers nor a group of authoritative teachers, but a group of witnesses. The Beloved Disciple was the Johannine witness *par excellence,* and so the whole Johannine Community can speak of itself as "we" because it shared his witness,[217] e.g., in the GJohn Prologue, "The Word became flesh . . . and we have seen his glory."[218] But in I John, because former members of the Community have seceded and have been propagating (what the author regards as) a wrong interpretation of the tradition derived from the Beloved Disciple, the author needs occasionally to distinguish among the faithful Johannine Christians a "we" that can reassure the "you." Now that the secessionists have left, if the "you" is the general group of disciples who constitute the Johannine Community, the "we" in this instance consists of the tradition-bearers and interpreters who stand in a special relationship to the Beloved Disciple in their attempt to preserve his witness.[219] Certainly part of that attempt involved writing; and so the "we," who were companions and disciples of the Beloved Disciple, include the Johannine writers. Foremost among them would have been the evangelist who was more responsible than any other for enshrining the testimony or witness of the Beloved Disciple as a gospel bringing life to all who believe (see the texts in footnote 216). Since the author of

---

one who sent him." The verb *apostellein,* "to send," is apparently interchangeable in GJohn with *pempein,* and those who are sent constitute a wider group than the apostles of other NT writings.

[216] For instance, 19:35: "This testimony has been given by an eyewitness and his testimony is true. He is telling what he knows to be true so that *you* too may have faith," when this passage is combined with the related passage in 21:24: "It is the disciple whom Jesus loved who is the witness for these things . . . and his testimony, *we* know, is true."

[217] Langbrandtner, *Weltferner Gott* 403, speaks of him as the *primus inter pares.*

[218] In ABJ 29, 13, I correctly but inadequately pointed out that the "we" in John 1:14 is not mankind but the (apostolic) eyewitnesses; I would now insist that it is the (Johannine) Christian community as heir to the eyewitness testimony. Barrett, *Gospel* 143, is right when he says it can only mean "we, the church," "we Christians," provided that he adds "Johannine" before "church, Christians." The fourth evangelist knows that there are other genuine Christians outside the Johannine Community (John 10:16: "Other sheep that do not belong to this fold"), but they are not the focus of his attention. The supposition is that ultimately they will be joined with the Johannine Community as one flock.

[219] Thyen, "Entwicklungen" 293, thinks that perhaps the Beloved Disciple's witness could be invoked against the secessionists because he died resisting the schism. Thyen sees him as an anti-docetist.

I John regards himself as writing in order to preserve the testimony of this gospel (1:5), he is part of the "we," as is also the redactor of GJohn.[220] This then is the Johannine *School* which has a special place in the Johannine Community.[221] Their authority is not as teachers but as witnesses who are vehicles of the Paraclete, the only teacher. The Beloved Disciple was for the Johannine Community the supreme example of a witness through whom the Paraclete bore witness and taught (John 19:35; 15:26–27). The closeness of the "we" of the Johannine School to the Beloved Disciple makes them also the spokesmen of the Paraclete, *the Spirit of Truth* (John 14:17; 15:26; 16:13). Finally, the presence of the Johannine School in the Johannine Community enables all the Christians of that Community, in *koinōnia* or communion with the School (I John 1:3), to bear witness to the true tradition about Jesus. I think that is the sense of the epistolary author's statement: "Anyone who has knowledge of God listens to us, while anyone who does not belong to God refuses to listen to us. That is how we can know the Spirit of Truth from the Spirit of Deceit" (I John 4:6).

Parenthetically, let me add that the special relation of the epistolary author to the Beloved Disciple may explain his self-designation as "the Presbyter" in II and III John where he is no longer wearing the mantle of the evangelist but writing a letter in his own name. In the NOTES on II John 1 it will be argued that the most plausible Johannine meaning of "Presbyter" is in harmony with the usage in Papias and Irenaeus, where it is used to designate a generation who had received the tradition from the eyewitnesses—people who had a certain authority because they had seen and heard others who had seen and heard Jesus. Refracted through the Johannine prism this chain of authority reaching to "the Presbyter" would be as follows: Only Jesus had seen and heard God and he could testify to this; of those who saw and heard Jesus the Beloved Disciple was the closest and his testimony was "true" in the fullest sense; the Johannine School, or the special "we," saw and were especially close to the Beloved Disciple and could therefore give surety to the other members of the Johannine Community (the "you") about the continuity of the gospel (I

---

[220] See the "we" of John 21:24. Footnote 71 above embodies my understanding of the main Johannine figures.

[221] In *Community* 101–2 I discuss R. A. Culpepper's excellent *School*, which has surveyed the use of the term "school" for other groups in antiquity (Pythagoreans, Plato's Academy, Aristotle's Lyceum, etc.) and has shown that the characteristics of a school are found in the Johannine situation. In fact, Culpepper wishes to extend the term "school" to the whole Johannine Community, even as I maintain that often "we" extends to the whole. Yet I would argue that a term like "school" is best kept for the "we" when that "we" is distinct from the "you" of the Community—in other words for the tradition-bearers and witnesses when they speak as a distinct group. Although the epistolary author speaks to the readers 15 times as "Brothers" in I John, he addresses them as "Little Children" 7 times, a usage which means that in some ways he is the same as all other Johannine Christians, but in other ways he has a distinct position (as a member of the Johannine School, in my terminology).

John 1:5; 3:11). Seemingly, this latter generation of witnesses was known as presbyters.

(d) "FROM THE BEGINNING"—OLDER JOHANNINE THEOLOGY. In I John it is because he speaks wearing the mantle of the evangelist who enshrined the witness of the Beloved Disciple in GJohn[222] that the author of I John can refer to "What was from the beginning, what we have heard, what we have seen with our own eyes, what we looked at and felt with our own hands" (1:1). The secessionists too are arguing from GJohn, but they are so progressive that they have lost their roots in the teaching of Christ (II John 9). They do not understand the "gospel" as it was "from the beginning" while the author does.[223] At times the author cannot deny the secessionist slogans taken from the tradition represented in GJohn (even though he will charge them with neglecting the implications of such affirmations); but he circumvents this difficulty by picking out more ancient Johannine themes that are somewhat submerged in GJohn and by showing that the secessionists' progressive interpretation of GJohn is a contradiction of such ancient tradition. This is not an unjustifiable circumvention since GJohn was written in a struggle with outsiders and therefore emphasizes only those parts of the Johannine tradition questioned by outsiders. In the author's view the whole of the Johannine tradition, including the presuppositions of GJohn, is what refutes the secessionist interpretations. This style of argumentation gives I John the air of being more archaic and less advanced than GJohn. If, for instance, there are many Jewish elements in I John (above II C2a), that is because the Johannine Community began as a Jewish Christian group,[224] and the author wishes to stress what was "from the beginning."

The epistolary author's attempt to go back to the presuppositions of GJohn is most apparent in his defense of the importance of Jesus' *human* career. GJohn did not have to defend the humanity of Jesus against "the Jews" or the Jewish Christians, and its silence on this score had been exploited by the secessionists who negated the importance of Jesus as the

[222] As I understand Johannine tradition, even as the Beloved Disciple reinterpreted the tradition about Jesus rather than simply repeating it, so also the evangelist gave new insights in reinterpreting the tradition that he received from the Beloved Disciple. Undergirding all this freedom is the notion of the Paraclete whom Jesus introduced thus: "I have much more to tell you, but you cannot bear it now. When he comes, however, being the Spirit of Truth, he will guide you along the way of all truth" (16:12–13)—a statement that implies insights going beyond those available in the ministry of Jesus (see also John 2:22).

[223] I John 1:1; 2:7,13,14,24; 3:11; II John 5–6. Piper, "I John" 437–40, detects 30 passages where the author refers to truths held by his audience. He is appealing to a common faith that his readers should acknowledge without doubt or qualification: a combination of creedal statements, theological axioms, and eschatological prophecies.

[224] Brown, *Community* 27–34, 172, 175, 178. I insist once again that such archaic Jewish features must not be misused to date the writing of I John very early or to determine the ethnic constituency of its recipients. They tell us about origins, not about composition.

Christ come in the flesh (I John 4:2–3). Writing his own form of the Prologue, the author in I John 1:1–4 corrects the secessionist interpretation of the GJohn Prologue, offering a more "primitive" christology. If we may suspect that the secessionists concentrated on lines like "In the [pre-creational] beginning was the Word" and "We have seen his glory" (John 1:1,14), the epistolary author treats "the beginning" of "the word of life" as a beginning of the self-revelation of Jesus to his disciples;[225] and there is no mention of glory, but only a sequence of increasing tangibility: "We have heard . . . seen . . . looked at . . . felt" (I John 1:1).

It may be true that the Jesus of GJohn gives little specific ethical teaching (because the Johannine Community and "the Jews" did not fight over morality); but the whole presupposition of Johannine anthropology is that believers are children of God in the image of Jesus, the Son of God, a Jesus who could claim to be without sin (John 8:46). And so the author of I John can propose a *kathōs* ("just as") ethic: "Walk just as Christ walked" (2:6); Make oneself "pure even as Christ is pure" (3:3); Act justly "even as Christ is just" (3:7).[226]

GJohn presents the death of Jesus as a glorification and ascension ("lifting up": John 3:14; 8:28; 12:32–34), but it contains minor indications that the sacrificial and vicarious character of Jesus' death was known and perhaps taken for granted, e.g., "The Lamb of God who takes away the world's sin" (1:29); "Jesus was to die for the nation, and not for the nation alone" (11:51–52): "For these sheep I lay down my life" (10:15). The secessionists may have had their own interpretation that discounted the import of such statements;[227] or they may have neglected them in light of the dominant theme of death as glorification. The epistolary author, however, exploits this vein of Johannine tradition, "The blood of Jesus, His Son, cleanses us from all sin" (I John 1:7); "For us Christ laid down his life" (3:16); "He himself is an atonement for our sins, and not only for our sins but also for the whole world" (2:2).

---

[225] See the NOTE on I John 1:1a for the evidence that this is the dominant meaning of "beginning" in I John.

[226] The fact that the epistolary author is not more precise in giving examples of virtuous actions by Jesus reflects the limitations of GJohn. The Synoptic Gospels could have supplied him with many examples; his failure to cite them indicates that either those Gospels were not known to him or they were not authoritative enough to be convincing in a debate with the secessionists. I find unconvincing the list of similarities between I John and Matthew supplied by Dodd, *Epistles* xxxix–xli; they are not close enough to show quotation or use of Matthew—similarly the warning "Let no one deceive you" shared by I John 3:7 and Mark 13:5, which reflects a common Christian fear of deceit in the last times. All that can be established is that the two authors would have emphasized some of the same points, ethical and eschatological, in their moral preaching.

[227] For example, by understanding the "Lamb of God" not as a victim atoning for the world's sin but as a destroyer of the world's sin (ABJ 29, 58–63) and by arguing that if Jesus laid down his life it was only to take it up again (10:17).

GJohn contained the saying of Jesus, "God loved the world so much that He gave the only Son" (John 3:16), but was noncommittal as to whether "gave" referred only to incarnation or also to expiatory death.[228] I John 4:10 leaves no doubt: "He loved us and sent His Son as an atonement for our sins."

Let me use eschatology as another example of how, against secessionist distortion, I John revived an earlier stratum of Johannine thought. While in the earliest works of the NT, e.g., the Pauline Epistles, there is a stress on the second coming of Jesus as the moment of judgment and divine reward (final eschatology), clearly GJohn has emphasized realized eschatology, with judgment and eternal life as part of the encounter with Jesus in this life (ABJ 29, cxv–cxxi). There are also in GJohn statements of final eschatology,[229] but in a debate with "the Jews" the evangelist scarcely needed to defend a theme like future judgment, which the Pharisees did not doubt. Rather "the Jews" would have challenged Johannine realized eschatology with its implicitly high christology. The secessionists, then, could plausibly claim to be loyal to GJohn in their perfectionist slogans about being in communion with God (I John 1:6), being free from the guilt of sin (1:8), and being in the light (2:9). Realized salvation would have been part of their theory that after a person believed and became a child of God, subsequent behavior had no salvific import. They could have taken literally John 11:26: "Everyone who has life and believes in me shall never die at all." In the secessionists' expectations their fate would be to pass from this world to which they never really belonged (17:14) to join Jesus in the mansions he had prepared for them (14:2–3) without further judgment (5:24). The author of I John challenges this approach, not by denying realized eschatology,[230] but by insisting that one must not neglect future judgment because that too is part of the gospel which was heard from the beginning. He admits that Christians already possess eternal life; yet that life is not a static possession and must manifest itself in the way one "walks" (I John 2:6). We are children of

---

[228] In ABJ 29, 134, on the analogy of Pauline texts, I argued that "gave" referred also to crucifixion. I would now be more cautious; see Schnackenburg, *Gospel* 1, 399, who does not deny a possible implication of expiatory death but argues rightly that the main force is incarnational.

[229] E.g., John 5:28–29; 6:39–40,44,54; 12:48. It is well known that Bultmann attributed affirmations of final eschatology in GJohn (especially those that echo the language of apocalyptic) to the Ecclesiastical Redactor. Here Bultmann failed to be faithful to one of his own principles, namely, that the *evangelist* might have included such sayings to demythologize them in favor of a realized eschatological *interpretation*—indeed they are often adjacent to statements of realized eschatology. See R. Kysar, "The Eschatology of the Fourth Gospel—A Correction of Bultmann's Redactional Hypothesis," *Perspective* 13 (1972) 23–33.

[230] The following statements in I John embody realized eschatology: the Evil One is already conquered (2:13–14); eternal life has been revealed (1:2); we already walk in the light (1:7; 2:9–10); divine love has reached perfection (2:5); we are truly God's children (3:1); God abides in the believer (4:15).

God, but a child of God is one who acts justly (3:10). Being in light must radiate forth in the way one treats one's brother (2:10). For the epistolary author the divine gifts acclaimed in Johannine realized eschatology are not an end in themselves but the source of confidence for the future: "Do abide in Christ so that, when he is revealed, we may have confidence and not draw back in shame from him at his coming" (2:28). The passage in 3:2-3 is a perfect example of the author's balance between realized and final eschatology, a balance that preserves the importance of human behavior in the plan of salvation: "Beloved, we are God's children right now; and what we shall be has not yet been revealed. But we know that at this revelation we shall be like Him, for we shall see Him as He is. Everyone who has this hope based on Him makes himself pure even as Christ is pure."

The negative side of this epistolary revival of Johannine final eschatology is the use of Jewish apocalyptic language to characterize the secessionists as Antichrists and false prophets (2:18,22; 4:1-3), the evil heralds of the last times.[231] The secessionist indifference to sin is judged as constituting the Iniquity (*anomia*) of the final struggle (3:4). In such imagery the epistolary author approaches Mark 13:22: "False christs and false prophets will arise"; and II Thess 2:1-12 which speaks of the mystery of Iniquity and the man of Iniquity.[232] These signs all constitute proof that "It is the last hour" (I John 2:18)—a phrase reinterpreting in terms of final eschatology the claim that the Johannine Jesus made in terms of realized eschatology: "An hour is coming and is now here" (John 4:23; 5:25; 16:32). The apocalyptic atmosphere serves as a warning to those who think little of commandments and who walk in darkness while claiming to be in light.

3. Date and Locale of the Epistles

If I John is so closely related to GJohn that the Gospel has influenced its literary form and argumentation, this relationship has implications for the dating and localization of the Johannine Epistles. (The value of these implications is relativized by the fact that, while I think that the epistolary

[231] There is no clearly attested pre-Christian Jewish expectation of the Antichrist or antimessiah, but the Christian expectation has Jewish components; see NOTE on 2:18b.

[232] Such warnings are absent from GJohn; and so the suggestion that the author is reaching back to the beginning of the *Johannine* tradition in reviving the language of Jewish apocalyptic is based in part on the assumption that the Johannine tradition had similarities to the early traditions attested in Mark and in Paul: "You *heard* that Antichrist is to come" (I John 2:18). This assumption receives some support from the presence of apocalyptic in the Book of Revelation, a distant cousin of the Johannine writings we are discussing here. (The dating of the apocalyptic in II Thessalonians is not absolutely sure, since some regard that Epistle as deutero-Pauline and contemporary with I John.)

author knew a written form of GJohn, albeit perhaps not the finally redacted form, the most that can be *shown* is dependence on the kind of tradition found in GJohn—a tradition that antedated the written Gospel.) Most probably I John was written not only after GJohn but after an interval long enough for a debate to have arisen about the implications of GJohn and for a schism to have taken place. Recognizing the approximations, if one dates the evangelist's final work (i.e., GJohn without the redactor's additions) to *ca.* A.D. 90,[233] I John may feasibly be dated to *ca.* 100.[234] This date would make sense of the fact that Ignatius' docetic opponents in Asia Minor (*ca.* 110) seem more advanced in their docetism than the secessionists described in I and II John (although sequence of ideas is a weak basis for chronological judgments). Above in II C1b we saw arguments for the proximity in time of I and II John, and below in V D2a we shall see how the schism that antedated I and II John may have catalyzed the emergence of authoritative church roles, such as that exercised by Diotrephes in III John 9. Consequently I would place III John between A.D. 100 and 110 and indeed in close proximity to the other two epistles—once again the church structure evident in Ignatius' letters is more developed than that discussed in III John.

As for locale, inevitably the places suggested for the composition of GJohn have entered the discussion. But before I mention specific places, it should be realized that the Johannine Epistles suggest a number of Johannine churches scattered over an area.[235] Since the author of I John never mentions distance from those whom he addresses, presumably he lived among the "Little Children" to whom he writes, while II and III John were written to churches of two locales at a distance from the Presbyter. Indeed, in the case of III John it is a serious likelihood that Gaius and Diotrephes belonged to two different Johannine house-churches in the same general locale, and that the Presbyter was trying to obtain hospitality for his emissaries in one house-church after having been turned down by the leader of another.[236] This brings us back to the thesis that

---

[233] ABJ 29 lxxx–lxxxvi. I remind the reader that I gave such a date to GJohn despite the fact that I recognized fully the presence in GJohn of earlier tradition about Jesus, some of it with an excellent claim to be considered historical. In my judgment the formation of the tradition written down in GJohn continued over decades before the evangelist gave it penultimate shape, perhaps from the late 40s to the late 80s.

[234] Other proposed datings range from one extreme of a 100-year spectrum to the other: 60–65 (J.A.T. Robinson); before 110 (Harnack, Wilder); 120 (Marty); 125–130 (Pfleiderer); 130–140 (Baumgarten, Brückner, Heitmüller, Hilgenfeld, Loisy, Weizsäcker); 155 (Kreyenbuhl, Loisy [for redaction]).

[235] "Churches" at this time consisted of a small group of people meeting in a house, usually that of a wealthy person who would have a house large enough to accommodate them. See below, pp. 728–32.

[236] The complicated situation implied in III John will be discussed in the COMMENT on that Epistle.

there was a metropolitan center with many house-churches of Johannine Christians (thus the mother community to which I John was addressed as an interpretation of GJohn), and that within reasonable traveling range there were provincial towns[237] with Johannine house-churches to which II and III John were addressed (above II C1b). The secession had begun in the center and was threatening to spread to the provincial churches.

Where was the center? If recent analyses of the GJohn milieu are correct,[238] before its internal schism took place the Johannine Community had been dealing with a very diverse group of outsiders, including Jewish synagogues (some of which still had crypto-Christian members), Jewish Christian churches, and churches of Christians who venerated the memory of the great apostles. A context of the diaspora among the Gentiles (John 7:35) and of persecution by the synagogues (16:2) is suggested. Among the places of composition suggested for GJohn (ABJ 29, ciii–civ) are Ephesus in Asia Minor, Antioch in Syria, and Alexandria in Egypt. (All three could match the internal GJohn evidence,[239] but Ephesus best matches the external evidence supplied by early tradition.) We know little about a network of Christian churches in the area surrounding Antioch and Alexandria but a good deal about churches in the towns around Ephesus. Revelation 2–3 contains letters to seven churches in the Ephesus region beginning with that city. Those churches are marked by false apostles and a false prophetess, and are divided by conflicting teachings (including that of the Nicolaitans—above IV B3a) and moral laxity. As we have seen, in the situation they envisage, the Johannine Epistles have many affinities to the letters of Ignatius of Antioch, most of which are also addressed to towns in the Ephesus area.[240] A late-second-century story localizes John's hostile encounter with Cerinthus at Ephesus, and we have seen (above, IV B3d) similarities between the Cerinthians and the secessionists. In addition, the secessionist appeal to the Spirit and prophecy may ultimately have influenced the

---

[237] Since in III John help is asked to enable the missionaries to continue their journey, at least several days' journey probably separated the various churches. I speak of "towns" because Christianity was an urban phenomenon until its spread into the countryside in the second century. See Malherbe, *Social Aspects* 63.

[238] In *Community*, 166–82, I present my own analysis and summarize five others.

[239] This is true in the sense that only a metropolis is likely to have had such a diversity of Jewish and Christian religious groups. However, even on this score what we know of the Ephesus region matches the GJohn situation very well. Revelation 2:9–10 tells us that in Smyrna near Ephesus there was opposition between the Christians and the "synagogue of Satan" and connects this with persecution of the Christians. Ignatius of Antioch in his letters to the *Philadelphians* and *Magnesians* (near Ephesus) attacks Jewish Christians not unlike those opposed by GJohn (Brown, *Community* 79–80). Yet see footnote 133 above.

[240] As we saw in IV B3b above, Ignatius has to struggle with proponents of even more advanced docetic tendencies; and he defends strongly the recently emerged single-bishop role to which the Diotrephes of III John 9 may be tending.

Montanist movement, also localized in Asia Minor. The great defender of GJohn in the West, who saved it for the church by interpreting it in the light of I John, was Irenaeus who came from Asia Minor. None of this is probative but it is more impressive than the evidence for other proposed locales.[241] Just as a move in Johannine history from Palestine to Ephesus might explain both the Jewish and Gentile factors in GJohn (Brown, *Community* 56–57), so also might it explain the schism that is the background for I John. Those converted in the new home of the Community might have been less familiar with Johannine Christianity as it was "from the beginning" and with its Jewish eschatological and ethical presuppositions. Such a lack of familiarity could explain the rise of the secessionist interpretation of GJohn and the epistolary author's need to emphasize these points.

D. *The Aftermath*

The author of I John proclaimed that the schism which confronted him marked "the last hour" (2:18), and he may well have been prophetic. The Gospel and I John were known in the second century, as were elements of Johannine thought; but after the Epistles there is no further trace of a distinct Johannine Community. One cannot deny the possibility that the author's adherents and/or the secessionists (or communities descended from both) did survive but left no traces in history; but it is far more likely that most of the author's adherents were swallowed up by the "Great Church,"[242] while the secessionists drifted off into various "heret-

---

[241] Syria could be argued for on the grounds that it was the spawning ground of many early gnostic groups and that Ignatius reflected his native Syria more than the Asia Minor to which he addressed his letters. Some see a direct connection between the secessionists and the gnosticism of Valentinus who came from Egypt. Gunther, "Alexandrian," 600–3, argues for Egypt on the basis of a very dubious reconstruction of Johannine church structure and the frequency in Egyptian circles of the personal names in III John—a statistic partially invalidated by the lack of papyri from the other candidate areas. On the basis of a Latin tradition that I John was addressed "to the Parthians" (see Appendix III below), Grotius and Paulus suggested Parthia as the place of composition, raising the possibility that the gnosis of the Persian magi shaped the adversaries.

[242] I use this term to describe the church of the second century that derived from those NT churches that claimed apostolic foundation and developed an authoritative ecclesiastical structure—from the churches described in the Pauline Pastorals, in Acts, Matthew, and I Peter. During the second century the pattern of a single bishop over a group of presbyters became dominant and served as an effective protection against dissenters, as the bishops developed a solidarity among themselves. Ignatius of Antioch foresaw that the episcopal pattern could be the web holding together a larger church: "Wherever the bishop appears, let the congregation be present, just as wherever Jesus Christ is, there is the church catholic" (*hē katholikē ekklēsia: Smyrn.* 8:2). That "church catholic" is the Great Church.

ical" movements (footnote 156 above), movements that finally were to be rejected by the Great Church. In each case there would have been necessary adjustments and concessions that would pull the descendants of the schism of I John farther apart. Let me sketch what may have happened.

1. The Secessionist Path toward Gnosticism

The epistolary author hoped to protect those whom he called his "Little Children" from secessionist inroads, but he would have been naive to think that his argumentation would convince his adversaries. Surely they would have hardened their position in face of his polemic; and while for the author their success meant that they really belonged to the world rather than to God (I John 4:5), for them success would have been a sign of divine approval. One does not need expertise in the sociology of religion to guess that once the epistolary author's adherents were forbidden to have anything to do with the secessionists (II John 10–11), the latter, cut off from all moderating influences, would have moved to even more "progressive" christology and ethics,[243] all the while claiming to be the true interpreters of the tradition enshrined in GJohn. For them it was the epistolary author who was retrogressively deviating.

In IV B3 above I discussed attempts to identify the secessionists with known heresies of the second century: in every instance these heresies seemed to go beyond what I and II John tell us of the secessionists. Nevertheless, the ancient and modern attempts to identify the Johannine secessionists in this manner constitute an implicit recognition of the plausibility of my thesis that eventually secessionists moved into exactly such heresies. After ostracism by the author of I John and his adherents, the secessionists, carrying GJohn with them, would have offered a marvelous catalyst to docetic and gnostic strains of Christian thought.

If the secessionists placed no salvific emphasis on the death of Christ, a further step in the same direction could have been taken by Cerinthus who denied that Christ really died. Adopting a Johannine theme like "I am leaving the world and going back to the Father" (John 16:28—spoken at the Last Supper), may he not have interpreted it as an affirmation that the divine principle returned to God before the death of Jesus, especially when in 17:11 the Son of God says, "I am no longer in this world"? Irenaeus' statement (above, IV B3d) that John was opposed to

---

[243] At the time of writing the secessionist teachers had not yet reached the outlying Johannine church of II John 10–11. The Presbyter's fear suggests that in such churches there were those who might be persuaded by secessionist theology. While the polemic approach of the Epistles was meant to stop this, it may actually have catalyzed the process of further schism and separation by forcing people to take sides. Note the somewhat similar situation in Rev 2:6,15: at the same period of time the Nicolaitans were a distinct group (to be hated) in the church at Ephesus, while in the church at Pergamum they were not visibly distinct. Similarly later on with the Valentinian gnostics (see above, p. 62).

Cerinthus may be a historicizing simplification of the fact that opponents of I John became Cerinthians.

We have no external proof that secessionists drifted into the type of docetism opposed by Ignatius of Antioch (above, IV B3b) wherein the humanity of Jesus was only apparent. Yet, sooner or later in the second century, the secessionist failure to see salvific importance in the human career of Jesus—his having "come in the flesh"—would have been exaggerated in a docetist direction, and the descendants of the secession would certainly have made common cause with docetists against church authorities who proclaimed the theology of a salvific humanity.

If the secessionists defended their insights as being inspired by the Spirit-Paraclete, a further step in the same direction could have been the claim of Montanus (ca. 160) to be the embodiment of the promised Paraclete (a NT term used only in the Johannine writings). The secessionists are called "false prophets" in I John 4:1, a designation which may mean that they called themselves "prophets"; and Montanism was the outpouring of prophecy *par excellence*. In particular, Montanus made use of two women prophets, Priscilla and Maximilla, who ecstatically revealed the words of the Lord. This would not be an inconceivable derivation from GJohn's picture of Jesus' ministry where women had an extraordinary position as proclaimers of the word.[244]

As for the relation of the secessionists to the later gnostic movements, we may begin with the gnostics' use of GJohn. According to Hippolytus (*Refutatio* 5.6.3ff. and 5.12.1ff.; PG 16^3, 3126ff., 3159Cff.) texts from GJohn played a role in both Naassene and Peratae theology. Among the Valentinian gnostics, Ptolemy interpreted the GJohn Prologue (Irenaeus, *Adv. haer.* 1.8.5) and Heracleon is responsible for the oldest known commentary on GJohn.[245] The early *Odes of Solomon* have affinities to GJohn, and many scholars think they are gnostic or semi-gnostic.[246] Above in IV B3c I culled from the gnostic writings of Nag Hammadi the many themes that show a similarity to secessionist thought. Another recent discovery, *The Secret Gospel of Mark*, which is somehow related to the Carpocratians, may reflect a knowledge of GJohn in mid-second century.[247] The popularity of GJohn in gnostic circles is all the more

[244] See John 4:39; 11:27; 20:18; and my *Community* 183–98. Obviously women proclaimers could be true or false, and Rev 2:20–23 shows the presence of a false prophetess in an early community related in a distant way to the Johannine Community.

[245] This Valentinian interpretation, as expounded by Pagels, *Johannine Gospel*, is considerably more "gnostic" than the secessionist position as I have reconstructed it.

[246] For a contrary interpretation, see J. H. Charlesworth, "The Odes of Solomon— Not Gnostic," CBQ 31 (1969) 357–69.

[247] R. E. Brown, "The Relation of 'The Secret Gospel of Mark' to the Fourth Gospel," CBQ 36 (1974) 466–85. It may draw indirectly on the written form of GJohn, or it may reflect oral Johannine tradition.

startling when we remember how little evidence there is for the knowledge and appreciation of GJohn among early-second-century writers whom the church subsequently judged orthodox.[248] A plausible explanation of this history is that the secessionist adversaries of I John were the bridge by which GJohn gained acceptance among the gnostics. Although the secessionists themselves may still have believed that the divine begetting of the Christian took place through a coming to faith, their downplaying of the salvific importance of the believer's subsequent life on earth could have led them to accept gnostic systems wherein the believers were the lost children of God trapped on earth till the coming of Christ—a preexistent begetting and a complete uselessness of earthly existence. Their ability to provide a theological work of the scope of GJohn may even have catalyzed the theological development of Christian gnosticism by supplying vocabulary and imagery in which to phrase the gnostic myth. The slogan of the gnostic initiate given us by Irenaeus (*Adv. haer.* 1.21.5), "I derive being from Him who is pre-existent and return to my own place from which I came forth," could conceivably have developed through applying to the Christian the words of the Johannine Jesus: "I have life because of the Father" (6:57); "I came forth from the Father . . . and I am going back to the Father" (16:28).

2. The Path from the Epistles to the Great Church

If the secessionist movement went down a path that in the second century led to (one or more varieties of) Cerinthianism, Montanism, docetism, and/or gnosticism, what was the fate of the author's adherents after the bitter reaction to the schism expressed in the pages of I and II John? The author himself seems pessimistic, although we must allow for rhetorical exaggeration: the schism was the sign of the last struggle before the parousia, a last hour marked by false prophets and Antichrists embodying the final Iniquity (I John 2:18–28; 4:1–6). And despite the somewhat tenuous testing of the Spirits, the secessionists were growing in numbers (4:5). Inevitably, as the author's adherents faced such a bleak prospect, they would have had to reflect upon other Christian churches that were more successfully surviving divisive movements because they had developed an authoritative church structure and official teachers to

---

[248] I have discussed the varying scholarly assessments in ABJ 29, lxxxi–lxxxiii. In summary, there is no specific citation of GJohn in Ignatius of Antioch although he seems to have known Johannine ideas (footnote 9 above). More curious is the absence of a citation of GJohn in Polycarp, *Philippians* (before A.D. 140) because he is said to have known John (ABJ 29, lxxxviii–xc) and because he seems to cite I and II John (above, pp. 8–9). While Justin Martyr in mid-second century certainly knew a *Logos* ("Word") christology, it is not clear that he knew or used GJohn itself. The earliest indisputable orthodox use of GJohn was by Theophilus of Antioch in his *Apology to Autolycus* in the last quarter of the second century.

correct error—the churches that would become the Great Church. Could the Johannine churches accept a similar structural development in order to survive, or was it indigestibly alien to their theological tradition, which emphasized the Paraclete as teacher and the believers as equal disciples (or branches on the vine)? There are two passages in the Johannine writings that may reflect the struggle over this issue, namely, III John 9–10 and John 21.

(a) III JOHN AND CHURCH ORDER. Summarizing here from the treatment to be given to III John in the body of the commentary, I contend that the hostility between the Presbyter and Diotrephes whom he criticizes was not over doctrine—Diotrephes was *not* a secessionist—but over the only issue the Presbyter mentions, namely, that Diotrephes claimed a certain primacy in a local church and used it to keep out the missionary emissaries friendly to the Presbyter. Since II John 10–11 portrays secessionist emissaries as propagandists for their teaching, there is a basis for the surmise that the Presbyter too was using emissaries as propagandists for his interpretation of the Johannine tradition. Why would Diotrephes be opposed to them if he was not a secessionist? The answer to this question may lie in seeking to place ourselves in the dilemma of a provincial Johannine church being visited by missionaries from the metropolis of the Johannine Community who were proclaiming contradictory interpretations of Johannine tradition. Should the missionaries be allowed to preach so that the local church members could determine which was the authentic interpretation? Would that not mean that half the time a platform was being provided for error, which was bound to win some adherents? One practical solution would be to refuse welcome to outside preachers of all persuasions and to depend on local advice about the way to interpret the tradition. Such a solution would be tantamount to ceding precedence to a local figure who would be virtually the teacher of the church. The situation I have just described is not purely speculative for we encounter it in the *Didache* (*ca.* A.D. 100) where a community is being visited regularly by teachers and prophets, some of whom are pernicious in the author's judgment. His solution (15:3) is to urge the local church to develop a ministry of bishops and deacons to take over the ministry of such teachers and prophets. The Diotrephes of III John may be the personification of such a step, with the further development that he has excluded visiting teachers and prophets.

The hostility of the Presbyter toward Diotrephes may have been based on the true judgment that such a step represented a radical departure from the Johannine tradition where the Paraclete was the teacher and there was an equality among disciples. But if the Presbyter was a Johannine purist, figures like Diotrephes may have been more perceptive about the only practical way in which the substance of the Johannine tradition could be preserved against secessionist inroads. If such a theory is correct, it was not the Presbyter-author of the Epistles but an emerging Johannine church leader like Diotrephes who was responsible for leading the Johannine remnant into the Great Church.

(b) THE EPISTLES AND THE REDACTION OF GJOHN. How did the redaction of GJohn fit into the Johannine movement toward the Great Church?[249] Was the redactor of GJohn the author of the Epistles? The thesis that one or more of the Epistles was written by the redactor is held by Becker, Bousset, Hirsch, Richter, and Schwartz, while distinct figures are posited by Bacon, Soltau, and others. The answer to the question presents formidable difficulties, not the least of which is uncertainty about what parts of GJohn are to be attributed to the redactor.[250] In ABJ 29, xxxvi–xxxviii, for instance, I found redactional elements in the GJohn Prologue, in 3:31–36; 6:51–58, and in chs. 11,12,15,16,17, and 21; but other scholars would assign the redactor a more modest role. Those who identify the author of I John with the redactor often propose these three arguments: (1) The redactor added chs. 15–17 to GJohn, and most of the clear parallels between I John and GJohn are in those chapters. (2) The redactor was responsible in whole or in part for the GJohn Prologue; and John 1:14, "The Word became flesh," is deemed to be anti-secessionist, equivalent to I John 4:2: "Jesus Christ come in the flesh." (3) The redactor added "ecclesiastical" touches to GJohn such as final eschatology and the portrait of Peter the shepherd; and the Epistles, sometimes called the "Johannine Pastorals," share the same churchly atmosphere. Let me examine these points one by one.

First, I John and the Last Discourse in chs. 15–17. Of some 115 similarities between I John and GJohn listed in Chart Two of Appendix I, about 35 involve John 15–17, or about one out of three. Did the redactor who added chs. 15–17 write I John? Footnote 250 has alerted us that we cannot simply assume a unified viewpoint and a single hand in chs. 15–17. Moreover the frequency of the parallelism of these chapters to I John is partially explained by the situation envisaged, for naturally the Epistle addressed to believers would have more similarity to the part of GJohn where Jesus speaks to his believing followers, namely the Book of Glory consisting of chs. 13–20, than it would have to the Book of Signs (chs. 1–12) where Jesus frequently addresses hostile nonbelievers. A more valid statistic of similarities than that gained from comparing I John first to John 15–17 and then to the rest of GJohn would be one gained from

[249] The reader is reminded that the designation "*Ecclesiastical* Redactor" is suggested by Bultmann.

[250] Even this glosses over the problem of whether there was only one redactor. While many attribute John 15–17 to *the* redactor, in several articles devoted to the Last Discourse J. Becker, ZNW 60 (1969) 56–83; 61 (1970) 215–46, finds evidence for three or more different theological views and writers in these chapters.

using 13:31–14:31 and 15–17 as the sections of GJohn to be compared
with I John—namely, the *evangelist's* form of Jesus' discourse to his followers and the *redactor's* form of the same discourse. Of the 115 similarities in Chart Two, about 27 involve John 13:31–14:31, or approximately
one out of four, which is a percentage not notably different from that involving John 15–17. Moreover, against identifying the redactor(s) behind
John 15–17 and the author of I John is the absence of polemic against
other Christians in the GJohn chapters, a polemic that runs throughout I
John. Also John 15–17 contains ideas that would have been most helpful
to the secessionists, and we can scarcely imagine the epistolary author
supplying arguments to his adversaries. For instance, the imagery of the
vine and branches in John 15 makes the direct adherence of the believers
to Jesus the only criterion of bearing fruit, whereas I John 1:3 makes
communion with the "we" of the tradition-bearers a necessary intermediary for communion with the Father and Christ. Would the author of I
John have wanted to stress the role of the Paraclete-Spirit as do John
15:26–27 and 16:7–15 when the secessionists were appealing to the
Spirit? That he might *not* want to do this is suggested by the paucity of
references to the Spirit in I John and by the absence of Paraclete terminology for the Spirit. Again, since the epistolary author stresses the career
of Jesus in the flesh and the need for ethical Christian living, he can
scarcely have been enamored of the saying in John 17:16 that could have
served as the slogan *par excellence* of the secessionist movement: "They
do not belong to the world any more than I belong to the world." The
least one may conclude is that, if chapters 15–17 and I John were written
by the same man, they were written at very different stages in his life, and
that the GJohn chapters were written before the secession had occurred.

Second, "The Word became flesh" (presumably redactional) as anti-
secessionist. G. Richter[251] has argued strongly that an anti-docetic redactor added John 1:14–18 to GJohn and composed I John as an apologetic
defense of the Son of God come in the flesh. But is John 1:14 really anti-
docetic? I would agree that if the secessionists denied incarnation and
postulated only an apparent life on earth (full docetism), John 1:14
would refute them.[252] But this is not my understanding of the secessionist
christology (above, V B2)—they could have accepted the *whole* of 1:14
as a slogan: "The Word became flesh . . . and we have *seen his glory.*" It
is no accident that Käsemann (above, footnote 167), who interprets

---

[251] For a summary of his theory, see A. J. Mattill, "Johannine Communities
behind the Fourth Gospel: Georg Richter's Analysis," TS 38 (1977) 294–315; also
Brown, *Community* 174–76. For this particular point, see Richter, "Fleischwerdung."

[252] Even this is not admitted by K. Berger, "Zu 'Das Wort ward Fleisch' Joh. I
14a," NovT 16 (1974) 161–66, who in opposition to Richter insists from second-
century evidence that such a phrase could easily be read to mean, "The Word appeared in the flesh"—a reading quite open to docetism.

GJohn as a vehicle of a naive docetism that approaches secessionist theology as I have reconstructed it, makes 1:14 the keystone of his thesis.

Third, an "ecclesiastical" attitude shared by the redactor and the Epistles. This vague argument for common authorship becomes very uncertain when one focuses on specifics. The redactor is thought by many to have added to GJohn the sacramental stress on baptism and eucharist in John 3:5 ("water") and 6:51-58 ("flesh and blood"), which might be compared to the stress on water and blood in I John 5:6-8. However, relatively few scholars think that baptism and the eucharist are the *primary* reference of "water" and "blood" in I John 5:6,[253] and there are no other hints of sacramental interest in the Epistles. Another "ecclesiastical" touch sometimes assigned to the redactor of GJohn is the addition of references to final eschatology, an eschatological outlook shared by I John. Yet, as pointed out in footnote 229 above, some of the final eschatology of GJohn surely came from the evangelist, and it is not provably a theme peculiar to the redactor.

A very frequent appeal in this "ecclesiastical" argument is to ch. 21, the section of GJohn most commonly assigned to the redactor. Certainly 21:24, which says of the Beloved Disciple, "His testimony, we know, is true," is very close to the Johannine School mentality of I John 1:2: "We have seen and testify, and we proclaim to you," and to the three "We know" affirmations of I John 5:18-20. But that similarity would remain if the redactor of John 21 were different from the author of I John, provided the two of them were members of the Johannine School (along with the evangelist—footnote 71 above). The best instance of distinct ecclesiastical atmosphere in John 21 is in vv. 15-17 where Jesus instructs Simon Peter, "Feed my lambs . . . tend [*poimainein*] my sheep," thus giving him an authority to rule.[254] Yet this authority is singularly lacking in I John. The shepherd image was popular for the presbyter-bishops in certain churches of Asia Minor in late NT times;[255] and Ignatius of Antioch (*Rom.* 9:1) compares his role as bishop in Syria to that of shepherd, for in his absence they must rely on God as the shepherd and Jesus Christ as the bishop. Thus, in having Jesus assign a shepherding role to Simon Peter, John 21 has moved notably closer to the ideals of church order

---

[253] In the COMMENT on I John 5:6-8 I shall argue that it is a reinterpretation of John 19:34 (a passage dubiously attributed to the redactor). If 19:35 comes from the redactor, then the epistolary author and the redactor have reacted to 19:34 in different ways.

[254] See ABJ 29A, 1105 for *poimainein* meaning both "to tend" and "to rule, govern."

[255] The Ephesian presbyters of Acts 20:17 were told to tend as shepherds (*poimainein*) the flock or church of God over which the Holy Spirit had made them bishops (20:28). The presbyters of Asia Minor were told in I Pet 5:2 to "tend as shepherds [*poimainein*] the flock of God, exercising an episcopate."

that would dominate the Great Church. In this vein E. Ruck-stuhl[256] has made some interesting suggestions that I would like to develop. The redactor in John 21 protects the memory and status of the Beloved Disciple and so there is no blatant betrayal of the Johannine heritage. (The destiny of the Beloved Disciple was planned by Jesus; and he is not of lesser dignity than Simon Peter, even if he did not die a martyr's death as Peter did—21:20–23.) But the chapter is designed to recommend Peter to the Johannine reader, underlining the acceptability of his pastoral role. The threefold question and affirmation of love (21:15–17) gives assurance that Peter is a genuine disciple, and it is on this basis that Jesus himself has given him pastoral authority. Since no similar pastoral role is given to the Beloved Disciple, we may be hearing a symbolic description of the structural difference between two different types of churches. The churches with shepherd-bishops are being told that they must recognize the legitimacy of the churches of the Beloved Disciple, which had no human shepherds, while the latter churches are told that the shepherding roles of the bishops are not contrary to the will of Christ. Why would there be such a need for mutual assurance? A need to reassure the bishops of the emerging Great Church that the followers of the Beloved Disciple were true disciples of Jesus could easily have arisen if (particularly in Asia Minor and Ephesus; footnote 255) they had encountered the Johannine secessionists. The need to reassure the Johannine Community about shepherd-bishops in neighboring churches could have arisen after a leading member of the Johannine School had opposed the appearance of a church supervisor such as Diotrephes in III John 9–10.[257] This reading of John 21 posits that the redactor-author of 21 and the epistolary author were different writers with a different opinion as to how the Johannine churches should proceed with regard to structure.[258] Certain similarities in their thought suggest that they were both anti-secessionists (although there is much less polemic in the redactor's work); but for the redactor it was not a betrayal of Johannine ideals to accept against

---

[256] "Zur Aussage und Botschaft von Johannes 21," in *Die Kirche des Anfangs* (H. Schürmann Festschrift; ed. R. Schnackenburg *et al.*; Leipzig: St. Benno, 1977) 339–62, esp. 360–61.

[257] Langbrandtner, *Weltferner Gott* 397, recognizes that Diotrephes and the redactor would have been close together in the Johannine spectrum. Both of them are innovators running against a tendency in GJohn to place only Christ over the disciples, e.g. John 13:12–17. In my judgment Thyen, "Johannes 13" 355, exaggerates this when he claims that such passages were written against Diotrephes, even as he does when he makes the redactor responsible for most of GJohn (and thus the real evangelist), a work written as part of a struggle between the redactor and Diotrephes.

[258] Although Bacon, *Fourth Gospel* 189–90, thought that the author of I John wrote most of GJohn, he recognized that the epistolary author would never have agreed with ch. 21. Despite the limitations of the category "early Catholicism," my thesis means that the redactor would have been closer to that concept of Christianity than was either the evangelist or the author of I John.

the schism the assistance of authoritative church structure with shepherd-bishops. His reasoning may have been that which Ignatius was developing almost simultaneously: "As children of the light of truth, flee from division and wrong doctrine and follow as sheep where the shepherd is" (*Phld.* 2:1).[259]

(c) EVIDENCE FROM THE CHURCH WRITERS. The above theory is a speculative reconstruction that makes good sense of the Johannine writings. There is no way of confirming it directly from the second-century church writers, but at least there is a negative check in seeing whether it explains the fate of GJohn in that century. In my reconstruction, high christology was the distinguishing mark of the Johannine Community from early in its existence until its "last hour." What first distinguished this Community from other Jewish Christian groups was its understanding of Jesus as the "I AM," the Son of Man who had already come down from heaven. This claim for the divinity of Jesus was regarded by some Jews as a denial of monotheism, and so members of the Community were expelled from the synagogue and persecuted. Finally the Community itself split over the implications of the Word-become-flesh for the importance of the earthly career of Jesus. The ultimate victory for the original Johannine Community was to have its preexistence christology accepted by the Great Church and become Christian orthodoxy. And so it may not be too romantic to think that, while some of the adherents of the author of the Epistles were accommodating themselves to the ecclesiology and structure of the Great Church (perhaps to the author's displeasure), that Church was accommodating itself to the christology of the Johannine Christians.[260] For example, although in an earlier period Matthew and Luke had attached christological affirmations to the virginal conception of Jesus without a hint of preexistence, Ignatius of Antioch, the proponent *par excellence* of "the church catholic," knew both of the Virgin Mary (*Eph.* 19:1) and of Jesus as God's Word. The latter reference in *Magn.* 8:2 is in a context that is

---

[259] I have given one example of how the epistolary author and the redactor (and implicitly the evangelist) differed; there are others. Klein, "Licht" 303, sees a progressive apocalypticizing. For the evangelist there is an absolute use of "the hour" of Jesus without temporal determination, i.e., a magnitude of divine presence that makes linear time categories meaningless and allows no other or future hours; for the epistolary author there is a series of hours and he is living in "the last hour"; for the redactor there is "the last day" in a positive sense as if the apocalyptic realities of the end-time had positive meaning. Of course, Klein achieves this distinction by the debatable (and unlikely) process of attributing all the apocalyptic in GJohn to the redactor.

[260] Two factors may have facilitated this acceptance: First, there were already strains of preexistence christology in other Christian communities like the Pauline (even if that christology was somewhat different from the Johannine christology). Second, one strain of the Johannine Community (the author's adherents) had shown that such a high christology did not have to result in docetism or gnosticism.

remarkably Johannine: "There is one God who manifested Himself through Jesus Christ His Son who is His Word proceeding from silence, who in all respects was well-pleasing to Him that sent him."[261] Ignatius was at the beginning of a long list of church writers who saw the Matthean-Lucan infancy christology and the Johannine preexistence christology not as contradictory but as sequential, so that one could claim that the Word became flesh in the womb of the Virgin Mary. Such a combination may be what Ignatius meant in his succinct description of Jesus as "both of Mary and of God" (*Eph.* 7:2). There are enough Ignatian references to Johannine ideas and terms (footnote 9 above) to suggest that, even if he did not use or have available GJohn, he had some contact with Johannine thought. A few decades later in the second century, Polycarp of Smyrna supplied eloquent proof as to where the sympathy of church writers would lie when they were choosing between the two communities that emerged from the schism of I John 2:19; for while he never cited GJohn, he had a passage very close to I John 4:2–3 and II John 7 condemning as Antichrist those who do not confess Jesus Christ to have come in the flesh (pp. 8–9 above). In mid-second century the *logos* christology of Justin Martyr was close to Johannine thought even if Justin never clearly cited GJohn. (For Justin's closeness to I John, see p. 8 above.)

The best explanation of this christological pattern in the "orthodox" church writers of the early second century is that they were not unfavorable to the Johannine christology brought into the ambience of the Great Church by the more restrained Johannine Christians; but they were not at ease with GJohn precisely because the secessionists, who constituted the larger part of the Johannine Community, had taken GJohn with them as they went down various paths to Cerinthianism, Montanism, docetism, and gnosticism. GJohn had proved too amenable to gnostic commentary and interpretation to suit many conservatives in the Great Church, and the ancient church historians supply us with some interesting examples of *anti*-heretical opposition to GJohn.[262] According to Epiphanius (*Panarion*

[261] In this quotation elements that are Johannine may be the references to the Word, to Jesus as the one sent, and to his having come forth from the Father (also *Magn.* 7:2); but non-Johannine is the image of God's Word proceeding from silence.

[262] The material about these early opponents of GJohn is scattered and confusing. For a brief guide, see H.P.V. Nunn, *The Authorship of the Fourth Gospel* (Oxford: Allen and Blackwell, 1952) 71–86; the most detailed treatment is Bludau, *Gegner*. There was opposition to GJohn on grounds other than heresy as well, e.g., Anicetus' mid-second-century opposition as presbyter of Rome to Polycarp, bishop of Smyrna, over the date to be assigned to Easter, even though Polycarp cited Johannine tradition (Eusebius, *Hist.* 5.24.16). There was also an uneasiness over GJohn's lack of agreement with the Synoptic Gospels, as attested in Tertullian, *Adv. Marcion* 4.2.2 (CC 1, 547) and Eusebius, *Hist.* 3.24.11–13.

51.3; PG 41, 892AB) the Alogoi, an obscure group, seemingly in Asia Minor, associated the works of John[263] with Cerinthus; yet despite his dislike for these Alogoi, Epiphanius makes clear that they were orthodox Christians who seemed "to believe the same things we do." Irenaeus (*Adv. haer.* 3.11.9) knew of a group who rejected "John's Gospel, in which the Lord promised that he would send the Paraclete," a statement that suggests an anti-Montanist opposition to the Johannine writtings.[264] Gaius (or Caius), a learned ecclesiastic of Rome at the end of the second century, is said by Eusebius (*Hist.* 2.25.6; 3.28.20; 6.20.3) to have attacked Cerinthus and to have accused the gnostics of manufacturing gospels; other information[265] suggests that he may have opposed GJohn as a Cerinthian gospel or perhaps on anti-Montanist grounds. With such opposition we can understand why both the Muratorian fragment and Irenaeus are somewhat defensive in appealing to GJohn as one of the Four Gospels.[266] Irenaeus (*Adv. haer.* 3.11) performed almost a tour de force by refuting the gnostics from GJohn, a work they had virtually monopolized, and indeed by claiming that GJohn had been written *against* Cerinthus and the Nicolaitan gnostics. And it was no accident that amid his citations of GJohn, Irenaeus (3.16.5,8) mixed in citations of I and II John, and that the Muratorian fragment (above, I B2) in its long defense of the peculiarities of GJohn (which was written with the approval of John's fellow bishops!) had also a quote from I John. The latter, thought to be by the same author as GJohn, was the undeniable proof that GJohn was not gnostic or Cerinthian. And so after his death the epistolary author may have made his ultimate contribution to Johannine history. In his lifetime he was able to save only a (smaller?) part of the Johannine Community from an ethereal christology and ethics by keeping them faithful to "the gospel that we have heard from Christ" (I John 1:5; 3:11). Those

---

[263] This means at least GJohn and Revelation. Elsewhere (*Panarion* 51.34; PG 41, 949C), Epiphanius betrays the fact that he is only guessing that the Alogoi rejected the Johannine Epistles. A distinction among the writings would confirm an early orthodox ability to tolerate I John more than GJohn.

[264] Bludau, *Gegner* 10–40, rejects the thesis of Harvey, Döllinger, Schanz, and others that this group was itself Montanist (a thesis assumed in ANF 1, 429, where the term "Montanists" is boldly introduced into the text). They are more intelligibly understood as attacking the outpouring of the Spirit and prophetism among the Montanists.

[265] Hippolytus (d. 235) wrote in defense of GJohn and of Revelation; he also composed a work against Gaius. Dionysius Bar Salibi (d. 1171) had available to him some of this lost material; and in a preface to his commentary on Revelation we are told that Gaius attributed GJohn to Cerinthus.

[266] Ehrhardt, "Gospels" 32–33, in discussing the Muratorian fragment, contends that the acceptance of GJohn by the Church of Rome was an olive branch extended to Eastern Christians (perhaps over the Easter controversy). The rise of Montanism forced Rome to make a benevolent decision that would not alienate the East. The tool the Roman authorities used in overcoming the objections of the Alogoi was I John.

adherents may have been able to hold on to the essentials of his interpretation of "the gospel" only by making ecclesiastical concessions that he
would not have approved and by melding into the Great Church. The
secessionists, perhaps the larger branch emerging from the schism, may
have seemed to triumph by taking GJohn with them down their paths to
even more *outré* christologies that would be rejected as heresies. In
those groups GJohn was treasured and became the basis of gnostic speculation. But eventually the comment patterned upon GJohn that the
epistolary author left behind (known to us as I John) accomplished the
purpose for which it was written—it saved the Johannine Gospel, no
longer for the elect of the Johannine Community but for the Great
Church and for the main body of Christians ever since.

VI. Structure and Text

There is no problem about the structure of II and III John, two letters
that follow closely the standard epistolary format (Appendix V). However, as we have seen (above, V C1), there is no real evidence that I John
is a letter. This fact creates problems, not only about the literary genre of
I John (which I have diagnosed in terms of comment patterned on
GJohn), but also about the structure or pattern according to which it was
arranged by the author. The other topic to be considered more briefly in
this unit is the original text of the Johannine Epistles, as reflected both in
the Greek textual witnesses and in the divergent Latin witnesses.

A. *The Structure of I John*

In the first of the great patristic commentaries to be written on I John,
Augustine (*Prologus in Epistolam Ioannis;* SC 75, 104) said that "in it
John speaks at length and almost the whole time about love," which is a
delicate way of approaching the apparent lack of sequence and of thought
development in this work. Calvin was more blunt in judging that there
was no continuous order in I John. In 1741 J. Operinus thought he could
detect a pattern of fundamental thoughts, even if he settled for the five-
chapter structure. At the beginning of the modern era, Westcott (*Epistles*
xlvi) summarized the problem: "No single arrangement is able to take account of the complex development of thought which it offers, and of the
many connections which exist between its different parts."[267] Almost a
century later Bruce (*Epistles* 29) found the situation little improved:
"Attempts to trace a consecutive argument thoughout I John have never
succeeded." With a certain wryness Wilder ("Introduction" 210) has
compared it to the River Meander winding through Asia Minor and virtually turning back on itself. With imagination Bogaert thinks of it as the

---

[267] This view was not shared by all, e.g., Law, *Tests* 2, claimed with an admission
of being venturesome: "The more closely one studies the Epistle the more one dis-
covers it to be, in its own unique way, one of the most closely articulated pieces of
writing in the New Testament." We shall see that, while some confirm Law's discovery, most would judge the articulated structure proposed by Law to be an invention
rather than a discovery.

Canticle of Canticles (Song of Songs) of the NT in the sense that love is the main subject, but we are not always certain whose views are being heard, and there seems to be little progress in the action. The author's logic is so obscure that one could move around units almost at will and still I John would read just as well as it does now. (In part, the absence of clear sequence is related to the source theories discussed above [III A,B]—scholars were forced to posit the joining of different compositions.) If at any of a half-dozen places in I John the rest of the work had been lost, no subsequent reader would have had the slightest suspicion that anything was missing. This is reflected in Bultmann's theory that the original composition stopped at 2:27 and that various loose Johannine pieces were tacked on to it, a theory rebutted by others for the paradoxical reason that they cannot explain why anyone would have added pieces that say little or nothing which was not already said in 1:5–2:27!

Faced with such lack of sequence, many scholars resort to positing free association of ideas (de Ambroggi), spirals of arguments or cyclic thinking (Houlden, Malatesta), or, more mysteriously, "Semitic thought patterns."[268] Finally, some have announced that it is useless to seek a pattern or structure (Brooke, Hauck, Holtzmann, Jülicher, Reuss, Rothe, to name a few). In fact, however, such brave announcements usually yield to the reality of having to divide I John into a rough structure of pericopes or sections, in order to write and arrange one's commentary. Moreover, both GJohn and the Book of Revelation have a definite structure, even though it is difficult to discern the exact lines dividing one pericope from another and sometimes the thought is repetitive. Such a realization suggests that there may be structure in I John as well; and, even if hesitantly, most commentators have proposed a division of the work that may correspond to the author's intent.

The number of distinct Parts in proposed divisions runs from two to twelve. Some of the proposals have been highly idiosyncratic or have fallen into desuetude; but divisions into two Parts, three Parts (the most popular), and seven Parts have a respectable following and raise the basic problems to be discussed below. Therefore, I give a rather long list of different examples of these divisions in Chart Five of Appendix I.[269] With

---

[268] Bogaert, "Structure" 33–34, in partial dependence upon de la Potterie, constructs a complicated series of inclusions. Since such a theory allows many exceptions and variations in the marvelous pattern(s) it detects, it disguises the brute fact that there is no discernibly regular pattern.

[269] A classification of divisions is complicated by the failure of some scholars to distinguish precisely between main divisions ("Parts") and subdivisions, or to indicate whether Prologue or Epilogue is counted as a Part. Other divisions than those found in Chart Five would have four Parts (Baumgarten, Büchsel [?], Davidson, Thompson, Wiesinger), five Parts (Belser, Ebrard, Gaechter, Hofmann, Operinus), six Parts (Michl), ten Parts (Lücke), and twelve Parts (O'Neill).

an eye on that chart, let us now discuss factors that contribute to making a decision about the structure of I John: How do we recognize units? Are there detectable patterns of thought? Do other works provide us with an analogy in detecting structure? In particular, how is the structure of I John related to the structure of GJohn?

1. Recognition of Units

Within I John there are a few clear units, set apart by their subject matter, that no proposed division breaks up, e.g., 2:12–14; 2:15–17; 4:1–6. Nevertheless, these units have little apparent direct connection with what has gone before and what comes after, and so their role in the plan of the letter is unclear. Less sharply defined (but still somewhat definable) are sections in which a particular writing pattern occurs with frequency. For example, in 1:6–2:2 three times an *ean eipomen* ("If we say [boast]") sentence is followed by a contrasting *ean* ("But if") sentence.[270] In 2:4–11 there are three *ho legōn* sentences ("The person who says [claims]"), each followed by a verse or two of development. One might mark as the framework of a unit 2:18, which is addressed to "Children" (*paidia*) and is concerned with the last hour, and 2:28, which is addressed to "Little Children" (*teknia*) and is concerned with the parousia, especially since between 2:18 and 2:28 there are three "As for you" appeals ([*kai*] *hymeis*). In the following unit, 2:29–3:10 there are seven clauses where *pas ho* ("Everyone who") is followed by a participle. At the end of I John three *oidamen* ("We know") sentences mark 5:18–20. Such patterns have given rise to the theory of different sources discussed above in III AB; but even if the majority of scholars thinks that these units with set patterns were composed by the author (rather than taken over by him), the division that one accepts must make sense of them.[271]

A look at Chart Five will show how units with set grammatical or stylistic patterns affect the various divisions proposed by scholars. In the most popular tripartite schema the two favorite places for bringing Part One of I John to a close are 2:17 and 2:27–29. One's choice between these options depends on whether one thinks the unit discussed in the preceding paragraph, 2:18–28 (or 2:18–27, or 2:18–29), goes with what follows (in which case 2:17 ends Part One), or with what precedes (in

---

[270] Some would truncate the unit as 1:6–10, not agreeing that the *ean* clause in 2:1b is part of the pattern, e.g., Bultmann.

[271] One scholar, Smit Sibinga ("Study" 196ff.), follows a principle of division based on a count of syllables (which he thinks is also verifiable in the paschal homily of Melito of Sardis, *ca.* 165), e.g., 1:1–2:26 has 1,450 syllables; 2:27–4:6 has 1,370 syllables; and 4:7–5:21 has 1,450 syllables. This division with its subdivisions often does not respect the unit structure suggested by logic or grammatical style.

which case 2:27[28,29] ends Part One). If we turn to another crucial spot in the tripartite schema, Hort and Westcott never agreed[272] whether Part Three should begin at 4:1 or 4:7 respectively; and this dispute has continued among scholars. All recognize 4:1–6 as a unit, but they differ on whether it goes with what follows (in which case 3:22[23,24] ends Part Two) or with what precedes (in which case 4:6 ends Part Two). Similarly 5:18–20 is recognized as a grouping that must be kept together, even if scholars are not agreed whether that grouping should be joined to 5:(12)13–17 or kept by itself as the terminus of I John.

If the reader is puzzled why in the preceding paragraph I discuss divisions that end Part One at 2:27, or 2:28, or 2:29, and Part Two at 3:22, or 3:23, or 3:24, or Part Three at 5:12 or 5:13, the answer lies in the existence of "hinge verses" in the Johannine writings, i.e., verses that end one section and begin another by having themes of both (ABJ 29, cxliii). Such verses facilitate transitions but make precise demarcations and divisions difficult. Indeed, one might even print a hinge verse like 2:28 twice, at the conclusion of one unit and again at the beginning of the next.

Thus far I have concentrated on how stylistic and grammatical patterns help scholars to diagnose units. Some are content to stop there and to think of I John as consisting of a series of independent units not closely interrelated by an overall schema (Houlden, *Epistles* 31). For practical purposes, that impression is given by the theories which speak of a large number of "Parts" in I John that are virtually coterminous with structural units, e.g., Houlden's seven-Part division, plus Prologue and Epilogue, or O'Neill's twelve-Part division. However, most scholars opt for a bipartite or tripartite schema wherein the units are organized into a larger sequence. Let us now discuss the two chief ways of interrelating units that underlie such divisions: first, the attempt to find a sequence among units on the basis of thought patterns; second, the detection of a pattern in I John on the basis of analogy with other writings.

2. Organization of Units through Thought Patterns

The idea that I John was an epistle has inevitably led to the suggestion that in some way the schema of arrangement is that of other NT epistles where a "doctrinal" section is followed by a "paraenetic" (hortatory, moral) section.[273] It is obvious that such a principle cannot be used to divide I John smoothly so that one half is doctrinal and the other half is paraenetic, but a case can be made for repeated doctrinal/paraenetic pat-

---

[272] In "Divisions" A. Westcott discusses the correspondence between his father, B. F. Westcott, and Hort over the structure of I John.

[273] In the Pauline Epistles this sequence is sometimes seen as an "indicative" section followed by an "imperative" section.

terns.[274] For instance, Michl's six-Part division is arranged so that Parts 1,3, and 5 (1:5–2:17; 2:28–3:24; 4:7–5:4) are paraenetic, while Parts 2,4, and 6 (2:18–27; 4:1–6; 5:5–12) are doctrinal. Häring finds an ethical and a doctrinal (christological) section in each Part of his tripartite division, while Belser attained a five-Part division by detecting two ethical sections, two doctrinal sections, and one mixed. Each of Giurisato's seven Parts (Chart Five) is claimed to contain a kerygmatic reference to primitive preaching, a paraenetic exhortation, and a casuistic application (usually in an "if" clause).[275] In my judgment, there is some truth in this general approach if for no other reason than that the secessionist adversaries are accused of christological and ethical errors, which inevitably become the object of doctrinal and paraenetic rebuttal. Yet, as a principle of division the pattern never works out logically. Most recognize, for instance, that a unit on the commandment of love (an ethical or paraenetic section) begins in 4:7 and terminates in 4:21 or 5:4. But in the heart of that unit (4:15) there is a statement about confessing Jesus as the Son of God which would go better with the "doctrinal" (christological) units that both precede and follow this unit on love. No proposed division I have seen explains adequately why that statement occurs where it does.[276]

The eye of many observers (e.g., Feuillet) has been caught by two bold affirmations in I John, "God is light" (1:5), and "God is love" (4:8). Could these be keys supplied by the author as a guide to his master plan? Could they be topic sentences for a bipartite division of I John? In light of the above discussion, the first statement might be seen as having a doctrinal stress, and the second a paraenetic stress. Yet, while 1:5 clearly begins a unit and even a whole section, it is very difficult to have 4:8 stand at the beginning of the second major Part of I John—it is sequential to 4:7.[277] Moreover, in both Parts the real emphasis is on *our* walking in light (1:6–7; 2:8–11) and *our* loving one another (4:11–12,19–21; 5:1)—the corollaries of God as light and love. An enlargement of the schema was suggested by de Wette in the last century and Nagl in this

[274] The Bultmann source theory (above, III A2) came close to this when it posited that the author added homilies (paraenetic) to collections of pithy affirmations (sometimes christological or theological) taken over from the source.

[275] His diagnosis of the topic in each of the seven Parts illustrates the fact that even authors who detect great regularity must cope with undecipherable logic in the sequence: 1. Commandments and sin; 2. Love; 3. Faith; 4. Justice and sin; 5. Love; 6. Commandments of faith and love; 7. Faith.

[276] A similar problem occurs in 5:1–4, which for the most part pertains to the theme of love, but in 5:1a demands faith in Jesus as the Christ. This is why, although some scholars join 5:1–4 to 4:7–21 where the theme of love dominates, other scholars join 5:1–4 to 5:5–12 where the theme of faith in Jesus as the Son of God dominates.

[277] Both the bipartite divisions I describe in Chart Five start the second Part a chapter earlier.

century, namely, the introduction of the theme of *God as just,* yielding the possibility of a tripartite division. (This would be facilitated if "he is just" in 2:29 were a reference to God rather than to Christ, but that is far from clear.[278]) Nagl, for instance, thinks that 1:5–2:28 deals with God as light, 2:29–4:6 with God as just, and 4:7–5:19 with God as love. Yet, while the theme of justice (whether God's, Christ's, or the believer's) is an important one in I John,[279] it is scarcely the third major theme next to faith and love. Moreover, Schwertschlager (*Aufbau*) has pointed out a significant weakness in any division based on the "God is . . ." statements: it is more appropriate to divide I John on the basis of what it says about Jesus rather than on the basis of what it says about God, for the issue on which the author wishes to reassure his followers is that Jesus is the Christ. If he speaks about God, it is in relation to christology, e.g., "God is love: This is how God's love was revealed to us: that God has sent His only Son into the world" (4:8–9). Hort[280] showed wisdom in being satisfied to argue that the themes of the three major Parts of I John are obedience, love, and faith, rather than seeking to hang his division on the "God is . . ." statements.

One of the most famous and influential divisions of I John in the English-speaking world has been that of R. Law (*Tests* 21–24) where the title of his book embodies his suggestion that each of the three Parts of I John offers three tests of the veracity of secessionist claims, a test by righteousness (justice), a test by love, and a test by faith. Obviously, the justice, love, and faith motifs are related to the analyses we discussed in the preceding paragraph; but now the motifs are wisely worked into a struggle against the secessionists who do not stress the salvific importance of *righteous* behavior, who do not *love* the brethren, and who do not acknowledge a *faith* in Jesus as the Christ come in the flesh (Appendix I, Chart Four). When one examines closely Law's division, one can find the three tests in the first two Parts (1:5–2:28; 2:29–4:6), albeit imperfectly, e.g., if 2:7–17 is supposed to be the test of love, that theme is absent from 12–14. However, it is commonly recognized that Law's thesis really falls apart in relation to the third Part (4:7–5:21) where it is very hard to find the test of righteousness. In an attempt to save Law's three tests, Oke ("Plan") would rearrange I John to put 2:13c–17 after 5:18–21 and

---

278 Since 2:28 insists, "Do abide in him so that, when he is revealed, we may have confidence and not draw back in shame from him at his coming [*parousia*]," and so gives reason to think that there the author is referring to the parousia of Christ, the "he" of "he is just" in 2:29 would more logically be Christ. It is also a bit romantic to put *dikaios estin* ("he is just"), which has not even a pronominal subject, on the same level as the "God is . . ." statements of 1:5 and 4:8.

279 "Justice, just" occurs seven times in 2:24–4:6.

280 He posited a ternary structure within each of his three large Parts: (a) Heresy is refuted, (b) Love is stressed, and (c) There is an attack on the world.

make that the test of righteousness in the third Part.[281] Tomoi ("Plan") proposes a different rearrangement with the same purpose: he divides I John into two Parts and finds the three tests (sin, love, faith) in each Part.[282] Such rearrangements are tantamount to a confession that, as I John now stands, especially in chs. 3–5, there is no perfectly logical order. Theories such as Law's come under the judgment that Painter (*John* 118–19) has passed on the various spiral structures suggested for I John: There is a connection of thought among the various units of the author's response to his adversaries; "but the connection does not provide a consistent development of argument."

3. Organization of Units through Analogy with Other Writings

Since it is not clear how suggested thought patterns provide organization for the various units in I John, some scholars have sought help externally by dividing I John on the analogy of other works. Let us survey the suggestions, keeping GJohn until last in the list of analogues.

(a) MISCELLANEOUS SUGGESTIONS. O'Neill's source theory (above III B2) implies that the structure of I John into twelve Parts was influenced by twelve poetic admonitions borrowed from a hypothetical Jewish sectarian document. Almost as adventurous is the thesis of Thompson that Psalm 119 supplied the author with the subject matter of the four Parts into which I John may be divided: The Way (1:1–2:21); Dangers (2:22–3:17); Safeguards (3:18–4:21); and the End (5:1–21). The underpinning of this thesis is a highly imaginative acrostic pattern that will convince few,[283] any more than will the claim that the use of "righteous (just)" in I John 1:9 and 2:1 reflects Ps 119:137.

Less implausible *prima facie* is the claim that the structure of I John may resemble a pattern found in a work distantly related to the Johannine writings, the Book of Revelation. Even here, however, some theses border on fantasy, e.g., that of A. Olivier[284] that Revelation, GJohn, and I John consist in their totality of a series of three-line ("sacred") strophes built around key words, with *kai* ("and"), *hina* ("in order that"), or *ho* (definite article) marking the beginning of lines. Nor do I consider really plausible the famous thesis of E. Lohmeyer that a pattern of sevens char-

---

[281] He also places 2:12–13b after 1:10 and thus removes the awkward 2:12–14 from the test of love in the first Part.

[282] He improves on the difficult last chapters of I John in this way: Love is the topic of 3:13–24 + 4:7–21, while 4:1–6 is placed with 5:1–12 as a section dealing with faith.

[283] Thompson, "Psalm 119," finds underlying the GJohn Prologue 22 lines in Hebrew parallelism, matching the 22 letters in an alphabetic acrostic! I John 2:12–14 has a set of six sentences (two groups of three) with a main verb in each; and if one uses this as a guide, one can find 22 such sets of six in I John. Psalm 119 has 22 stanzas of eight lines each, and this psalm is the only OT acrostic with the theme of the word of God as light (119:105).

[284] See the review of his book *La strophe* by P. Benoit, RB 48 (1939) 286–90, who points out that some of Olivier's posited lines are impossibly forced.

acterizes the three works.[285] The existence of sevens in Revelation is beyond question; and some would extend this to GJohn, albeit on dubious grounds.[286] But Lohmeyer ("Aufbau" 254–63; see Chart Five) detects seven Parts in I John, and seven subdivisions in each Part! (Minor confirmation is supplied by the seven uses of *teknia,* "Little Children," of "I write," and of "I wrote.") An elaborate pattern of inclusions enables Lohmeyer to match chiastically Parts 1,2, and 3 with Parts 7, 6, and 5 respectively, while Part 4 (2:18–3:24), dealing with Christ and the Antichrist, stands in the middle. Both structure and subject matter, then, convince Lohmeyer that I John stood close to the prophetic Book of Revelation and that it was truly a literary work.[287] The main internal objection to such a thesis is that, while Revelation goes out of its way to call attention to the seven pattern, there is not even a hint of this in either GJohn or I John, two works that have much in common with each other and relatively little in common with Revelation. Moreover, H. Braun ("Literar-Analyse" 218) is right in objecting to the widely varying lengths of the seven Parts posited by Lohmeyer, e.g., 4 verses in Part 1, and 35 verses in Part 4. His subdivisions break up clear epistolary units (3:2–6 separated from 3:7–10).

If one is fascinated by a numerical pattern for I John, three rather than seven would be the more plausible candidate. Although the numeral "three" is mentioned only once (5:7: "There are three who testify"), there are many patterns of three: three "If we boast" in 1:6–10; three "The person who claims" in 2:4–9; three groups of people and three "I write" in 2:12–13; three groups of people and three "I have been writing" in 2:14; three worldly offerings in 2:16; and three "We know" in 5:18–20. However, patterns of three are very common mnemonic devices, attested in parables, jokes, etc. ("the rule of the three"),[287a] so that such a numerical feature tells us little about the overall structure of I John.

   (b) GJOHN AS A STRUCTURAL MODEL. Chart Two in Appendix I shows

---

[285] In *The Lord's Prayer* (London: Collins, 1965; German orig. 1952) 25–31, Lohmeyer made a plausible case for a division into seven lines; but his other attempts at diagnosing sevens have not had much success, e.g., "Über Aufbau und Gliederung des vierten Evangeliums," ZNW 27 (1928) 11–36, esp. 30–32.

[286] A pattern of seven days has been detected by some in John 1:2–2:11; a pattern of seven signs throughout the Gospel; a pattern of a final week of seven days for the passion; seven vignettes in the Pilate scene—see ABJ 29, cxlii, 105–6, 525; 29A, 597, 803, 858–59.

[287] Part of Lohmeyer's goal ("Aufbau" 258–60) was to relativize the source analysis of von Dobschütz and Bultmann and to show that I John made sense as a unit. Unfortunately, it was part of Lohmeyer's contention that I John was addressed not to a particular group but to all—an aspect of his dubious contention that among the NT Epistles I John and Hebrews have the best claim to be considered as literature of a high level.

[287a] See A. Obrik, "Epic Laws of Folk Narrative," in *The Study of Folklore,* ed. A. Dundes (Englewood Cliffs, N.J.: Prentice-Hall, 1965; German orig. 1909) 129–41, esp. 132–34.

similarities of style and grammar between GJohn and I John; above (V C1d) we saw the possibility that the literary genre of I John might best be understood in terms of comment patterned on GJohn. If the epistolary author is drawing upon the theology and wording of the Johannine tradition embodied in GJohn and assumes the mantle of the evangelist as an interpreter of that tradition (the "we" of the Johannine School), *a priori* it is not inconceivable that he used GJohn as a model in *structuring* his comments in I John.[288] Let us see how that might be understood.

In ABJ 29, cxxxviii I detected this general structure in *GJohn*:[289]

I. The Prologue (1:1–18)
II. The Book of Signs (1:19–12:50): "To his own he came; yet his own people did not accept him." The public revelation of the light brought a judgment, which separated believers who came to the light from the world and "the Jews" who preferred darkness to light.
III. The Book of Glory (13:1–20:29): "But all those who did accept him he empowered to become God's children." The "hour" of Jesus' glorification where he speaks and acts on behalf of a new "his own"—the believers.
CONCLUSION (20:30–31): A statement of the author's purpose.
IV. The Epilogue (ch. 21)

The following structural plan may be detected in *I John* understood as an imitation of GJohn:

I. The Prologue (1:1–4)
II. Part One (1:5–3:10): The Gospel that God is light, and we must walk in the light as Jesus walked.
III. Part Two (3:11–5:12): The Gospel that we must love one another as God has loved us in Jesus Christ.
CONCLUSION (5:13–21): A statement of the author's purpose.

Let me now compare these two plans, moving from the more obvious to the more obscure: first, the Prologue; then, the Conclusion and Epilogue; finally, Part One and Part Two.

PROLOGUE. Similarity between the two Prologues was recognized already in mid-third century by Dionysius of Alexandria (Eusebius, *Hist.* 7.25.18) who observed, "The Gospel and Epistle agree with each other and *begin in the same manner*." Below in the COMMENT on I John 1:1–4 I shall have a special section on the relation of the two Prologues, and so I shall only summarize here. There are similarities in vocabulary: "the beginning, we have seen/looked [*theasthai*], word, life, in the Father's pres-

---

[288] Thus, Houlden, *Epistles* 31–32: I John "is a theological tract, modelled roughly on the congregation's existing production, GJ, especially in structure and terminology, and in the use and contents of the prologue." The most thorough exposition of this theory is given by Feuillet, "Structure"; I shall draw upon his contribution above even though I reject his thesis that the same man wrote GJohn and I John.

[289] The citations that begin II and III are from John 1:11–12. The crucial verses for the contents of my description of II and III are 3:19–21; 9:39–41; 12:35–41; 13:1.

ence." There are grammatical similarities: short clauses in parataxis; explanatory parenthetical interruptions. There are similar movements of thought: from a divine manifestation to our share in the result. In each case a clause that appears in the Prologue is picked up in the opening of the body of the writing that follows the Prologue. Thus, after speaking of how the Word became flesh, the GJohn Prologue tells us, "John testified to him" (1:15); and then the body of GJohn begins: "Now this is the testimony John gave" (1:19). After the I John Prologue states, "What we have seen and heard we proclaim [apangellein] in turn to you" (1:3), the body of I John begins, "Now this is the gospel [angelia] that we have heard from Christ and declare [anangellein] to you" (1:5).[290]

CONCLUSION AND EPILOGUE. Once again a full discussion of this will be found in the COMMENT on I John 5:13–21, and so I merely summarize here. In John 20:31 the evangelist states, "I have written these things to you so that you may believe that Jesus is the Christ, the Son of God, and that believing you may possess life in his name." In I John 5:13 the epistolary author states literally, "I have written these things to you so that you may know that you possess this eternal life—you, the ones believing in the name of the Son of God." Although each of these verses is a conclusion, there follows additional material. In GJohn that subsequent material (ch. 21) was probably added afterwards and by another hand, and in my judgment is rightly called an Epilogue (ABJ 29A, 1077–82). Although many authors speak of an Epilogue in I John, I shall argue in the COMMENT that there is inadequate evidence for this.[291] Consequently, in I John we should speak only of an expanded conclusion, wherein the epistolary author has reflected at length on the original conclusion of GJohn.[292] If there are some parallels between John 21 and I John 5:14–21, it may be because the redactor of GJohn knew I John.[293]

PARTS ONE AND TWO. Much more disputed is whether the structure of I John is bipartite in imitation of GJohn. In favor of this thesis one can point out that there is *more* frontal attack on the secessionist adversaries in the first chapters of I John, and *more* loving address to the author's ad-

---

[290] In Greek the parallelism between John 1:19 (*kai autē estin hē martyria*) and I John 1:5 (*kai estin autē hē angelia*) is apparent.

[291] I John 5:14–21 is closely connected to the rest of I John, and there is little reason to think it is from another hand. The deadly sin in 5:16–17 is probably the sin of the opponents who have been criticized throughout I John; and the three "We know" statements of 5:18–20 represent a typical triple pattern of the epistolary author.

[292] In the text above I indicated a parallelism between I John 5:13 and John 20:31; but I John 5:20 continues the parallelism: "We know, finally, that the Son of God has come and has given us the insight to know the One who is true, for we are in *His Son, Jesus Christ. He is the true God and eternal life.*"

[293] See footnote 210 above.

herents in the latter chapters[294]—a parallel to the outsiders/insiders pattern of the two Parts of GJohn. However, there is no clear break between two Parts of I John comparable to the clear break between the end of ch. 12 and the beginning of ch. 13 in GJohn. Most scholars who argue for a bipartite division of I John place the divider at the end of ch. 2, so that in both I John and GJohn the first half ends with a reference to final judgment (John 12:48; I John 2:28). If John 13:1 begins the second half of GJohn, "Having loved his own who were in this world, he now showed his love for them to the very end," one can point to 3:1 as the beginning of the second half of I John: "Look at what love the Father has bestowed on us in enabling us to be called God's children."[295]

Nevertheless, I think one can make a better case for the break between two Parts of I John after 3:10. Three arguments support this. First, such a division gives us reasonably proportionate parts. In my translation I break the verses of I John into quasi-poetic lines, and in Part One (1:5–3:10) there are 168 lines, while in Part Two (3:11–5:12) there are 142 lines. (In GJohn also Book One is longer than Book Two.) Second, each Part begins the same way, "This is the gospel," the only two times I John uses that expression. (In other words, the author may have told us where to break.) I shall discuss in the NOTE on 1:5a the possibility that *angelia*, "gospel," may be the Community's designation for GJohn. Third, the definition supplied by the author in his "This is the gospel" sentence, namely "light" in 1:5, and "love" in 3:11, sets the theme for the respective Part which that sentence introduces.[296] Let me illustrate that by tracing the theme through each Part.

In Part One the theme of God as light in whom there is no darkness is clearly echoed from 1:5 through 2:11 where there are warnings to walk in light and not in darkness. The choice between light and darkness is the language that GJohn used for a judgment which separated believing disciples from a disbelieving world (John 3:19–21), and so it is not surprising to find that also in I John walking in light and walking in darkness separate two groups. The first group consists of the author's adherents who are addressed as "Little Children" in 2:12–17 and warned away from the

---

[294] Notice the italicized "more"; each theme appears in the other Part as well.

[295] Feuillet, "Structure" 202, 210, would carry the parallelism based on this division even further. In the first half of each work he finds an A/B/A'/B' pattern of negative/positive/negative/positive, and in the second half of each an A/B/C/A'/B'/C' pattern. I fear that such systematic patterns are more in the eye of the beholder than in the detectable mind of the author.

[296] I am not covertly returning to the principle of division found inadequate above, namely, "God is light" and "God is love." In my judgment the two Parts are not concerned primarily with God but with the obligations of believers in reaction to the revelation of divine light and love in Jesus, respectively to walk in light and to love one another.

world and its pleasures. The second group consists of the hostile secessionists who are described in apocalyptic terminology in 2:18–3:10. The
last hour has come, the moment of judgment for those who have been
within the Community; and those who leave personify the expected Antichrist and the Liar and embody the Iniquity. The theme of a separating
judgment comes eloquently to a climax in 3:10, the last verse of Part
One: "That is how God's children and the devil's children are revealed."
That same language was used in GJohn for describing the believers and
the nonbelievers (particularly "the Jews"—above, V C2a); and both
works have Part One ending on the theme of the definitive separation of
the two groups.[297]

In Part Two of I John the opening sentence (3:11) defines the gospel
thus: "We should love one another," a commandment that is found in
Part Two of GJohn (13:34), which concentrates on the believing group
that has emerged from Part One. In I John, too, although the secessionists
are never out of mind, the intensity of direct address to the author's adherents becomes more pronounced, as the author interchanges
"Brothers," "Little Children," and "Beloved" in speaking to his readers.
And throughout Part Two the theme of love dominates,[298] a love for
which Jesus supplies the pattern. Part Two of GJohn (13:1) begins thus:
"Jesus was aware that the hour had come for him to pass from this world
to the Father. Having loved his own who were in this world, he showed
his love for them to the very end." Part Two of I John contains these
words at the beginning (3:14,16): "That we have passed from death to
life we know because we love the brothers. . . . For us Christ laid down
his life, so ought we in turn to lay down our lives for the brothers." If in
Part Two of GJohn (14:17; 16:7–14) Jesus speaks of the Paraclete/
Spirit of Truth who is the opponent of the (Prince of this) world, so
also in Part Two of I John (4:3–6) the author speaks of the Spirit of
Truth, which is opposed to the Spirit of Deceit operative in the secessionists who belong to the world. Near the end of Part Two of GJohn
(19:34) the evangelist describes blood and water flowing from the side of
the dead Jesus (with the water seemingly symbolic of the giving of the
Spirit now that Jesus had been glorified, as promised in 7:39)—a scene
that the evangelist or the redactor comments upon in terms of the Beloved
Disciple whose eyewitness testimony is true (19:35). Near the end of

[297] In John 12:46 that separation is expressed in terms of Jesus' having come as
light so that the believers no longer need remain in darkness.
[298] Of 7 uses of the noun *agapē*, "love," in GJohn, 6 are found in Part Two; of 18
uses of the noun in I John, 15 are found in Part Two. Of 36 uses of the verb
agapan, "to love," in GJohn, 25 are found in Part Two; of 28 uses of the verb in I
John, 25 are found in Part Two. Of the 6 uses of the adjective *agapētos*, "beloved,"
in I John, 4 are found in Part Two.

Part Two of I John (5:6–8) the author speaks of three who give testimony, the Spirit and the water and the blood, of whom the Spirit is the truth.

Granted these parallels, I find plausible the thesis that the body of I John can be divided into two Parts, influenced by the pattern of GJohn and following the same sweep of thought. (I do not imagine a meticulous study of GJohn by the epistolary author; I am speaking of a simple basic pattern that presumably shaped Johannine tradition—a pattern found summarized in the Community hymn, the Prologue [John 1:11–12], where one considers first and polemically those who do not believe, then second and lovingly those who do believe.) I think that just as the evangelist gave us the key to his division in 13:1, so the epistolary author may have provided a key to his division when he stopped twice (1:5; 3:11) to state that he was commenting on "the gospel." But I do not think that the author carefully structured the two Parts of his writing into the precise thought or numerical patterns mentioned above (VI A2 and A3a), patterns that reflect more the interpreter's genius than the author's intention. Within the two Parts, I shall designate *units* on such bases as repeated phrases (the three "If we boast" in 1:5–2:2), repeated forms of address (the double "Little Children" in 2:28–3:10), and inclusions (the "Spirits" in 4:1–6)—grammatical and stylistic features—rather than on the basis of detected themes that are irregular and provide no truly logical sequence.[299] These units, each of which will constitute a section for TRANSLATION, NOTES, and COMMENT, are listed in Appendix I, Chart Six, where I have offered an outline of I John, following a schema of Prologue, two Parts, and a Conclusion. I trust that the cautions and qualifications given above make it clear that I have no illusions about having diagnosed the author's mind exactly, and that at most I hope my outline does some justice to the author's intentions.

Since I think that the author is writing under the mantle of the evangelist, I find in I John the same quasi-poetry that was visible in the GJohn discourses of Jesus (ABJ 29, cxxxii–cxxxv). By this I mean no more than that one can divide his Greek into sense lines of relatively similar length which match each other in rough rhythm. As I have printed the English translation in poetic format, the reader should be warned that one Greek word does not always yield one English word, so that an appearance of balance between the English lines may not always be possible. But I resist doing what SBJ and JB have done in sacrificing the balance in the Greek to achieve balance in the translation; for me the Greek is the determining factor. Bultmann (above, III A2) thought that the antitheses in I John

---

[299] The acid test that favors my approach over any claim for logical sequence is that one can drop almost any unit (with perhaps the exception of the unit that contains the opening verse of each Part) without noticeably upsetting the sequence and without any loss of sense in I John.

came from a poetic source, and so in his commentary only the putative source material is presented as poetry. (Yet in dealing with GJohn Bultmann set up whole discourses in poetic format even though only a few lines contained strict parallelism!) In my judgment, while the antitheses may be a clearer type of poetry (and occasionally clearer poetry appears in certain lines of the GJohn discourses too), the rhythmic pattern of what I have dubbed quasi-poetry runs through most of I John.

B. *The Text of the Epistles*

To understand specific issues about the text of I, II, and III John, one needs to understand NT textual problems and methods in general, which I presuppose (see JBC 69 ##119–50).

THE GREEK TEXT. It has been customary to classify the Greek MSS. of the major NT books into four groups: *Alexandrian* (best represented by Codex Vaticanus[300]); *Western* (often a mixed group; represented by Codex Bezae and the text underlying the Old Syriac and the Old Latin); *Caesarean* (Ferrar and Lake group of minuscules; Codex Koridethianus); and *Byzantine* or Koinē (often represented by late minuscule MSS., and in the Gospels by Codex Alexandrinus). The Catholic Epistles are not the most frequently read section of the NT, either privately or in liturgical service; and so there is less textual evidence for them than for the Gospels and the Pauline Epistles. (For instance, Codex Bezae does not contain the Catholic Epistles.) Nor has there been accorded to the Catholic Epistles the same amount of scholarly attention given to the Gospels and the Pauline Epistles. For various reasons, then, it is not clear whether the above classification of four groups applies to the Johannine Epistles. For instance, Duplacy ("Texte") reports a division among scholars as to whether there was a Western text for them; and although Muriel Carder ("Text") argues for the existence of a Caesarean text, that theory has been sharply challenged by Aland ("Bemerkungen") and Richards ("Classification"). The latter scholar, using the Claremont Profile method, classifies 81 MSS. of the Johannine Epistles into three groups: Alexandrian (with three subgroups), Byzantine (seven subgroups), and Mixed (three subgroups). In the NOTES on various verses, where there is a disputed textual reading, I shall give a representative (not an exhaustive) list of the important textual witnesses.

THE LATIN TEXT. In those same NOTES generally I am interested in the Latin only as a witness to the underlying Greek. However, the Latin witnesses for I John offer support for a whole set of readings that have lit-

---

[300] Often too by Codex Sinaiticus, although this codex also has Western readings.

tle or no attestation in Greek.[301] One of these, the Latin of I John 5:7–8, called "the Johannine Comma," is so famous that it deserves an Appendix (IV) to itself. Another in 4:3, "Everyone who *negates the importance of Jesus*," which has some support among Greek writers, has won acceptance by leading scholars and will be discussed in the NOTE on that verse. But Harnack ("Textkritik") has called attention to less well-known Latin readings[302] as indicators that in the second century there may have been in circulation Greek textual witnesses for which we have no direct descendants. In most of these cases, however, other scholars have judged that the Latin readings come from translators who sought to clarify or expound the Greek text known to us. Brooke (*Epistles* 198) phrases it well: "The [inner Latin] evidence adduced also confirms the view that the tendency to add interpretative and explanatory glosses to the text of the Epistle is both widespread and dates back to early times."

[301] Brooke, *Epistles* 197–223, has an appendix on Old Latin readings. The title of I John as "The Epistle of John to the Parthians" (see Appendix III), which appears in late Vulgate MSS., deserves different treatment from other divergent Latin readings since almost certainly it entered the textual tradition upon the authority of St. Augustine rather than as a clear continuation of an early Latin MS. tradition.

[302] In particular, 2:5d,17e,20b,26c; 3:10b; 5:9e,16,18b,20a; II John 11b (see respective NOTES).The Latin additions to James (1:1; 2:16,25; 4:1) and I Peter (1:16,19; 2:23; 3:22), which are often cited as evidence of freedom in transmitting the Catholic Epistles, are generally longer than those in I John. Thiele, "Beobachtungen" 64–68, argues that the I John additions may have a Greek basis, for sometimes a plausible early chain can be constructed thus: Cyprian, Pseudo-Cyprian, Augustine, Pseudo-Augustine, Spanish Vulgate (especially Isidore of Seville and Theodolfus).

VII. General Bibliography for the Johannine Epistles

In this commentary, references contain the author's last name plus a key word from the title of the book or article, e.g., Harnack, "Textkritik." The reader should look up the author's name in the Bibliographic Index at the back of this commentary, which will indicate the page on which full bibliographic information may be found. Names containing the prepositions *de, du, van,* and *von* appear under "d" and "v" respectively. A list of the abbreviations of publications used in bibliographic entries may be found on p. xxiii above. There are two types of bibliographies. Works pertinent to individual verses or sections of the Epistles are listed in SECTIONAL BIBLIOGRAPHIES found at the end of the respective units in the commentary. Works pertinent to the Epistles in general or to sections of the INTRODUCTION are gathered in this GENERAL BIBLIOGRAPHY.[303]

A. *Bibliographies; Surveys*

Briggs, R. C., "Contemporary Study of the Johannine Epistles," RevExp 67 (1970) 411–22.

Bruce, F. F., "Johannine Studies since Westcott's Day," in B. F. Westcott, *The Epistles of St. John* (Grand Rapids: Eerdmans, 1966 ed.) lix–lxxvi.

Haenchen, E., "Neuere Literatur zu den Johannesbriefen," TheolRund 26 (1960) 1–43, 267–91.

Long bibliographies are found in Chmiel, *Lumière;* Malatesta, *Interiority.*

B. *Commentaries or General Analyses*

1. Earlier Commentaries

While I try to take cognizance of important views from all periods of scholarly research, with rare exception (Holtzmann, Plummer, Weiss, Westcott) the

---

[303] Notice the emphasis on works particularly *pertinent* to the Epistles. There are hundreds of translations, introductions to the NT, and commentaries on GJohn that make references to the Epistles. Occasionally in lists of names of those who support a particular opinion or translation I cite authors of such works (e.g., Heitmüller, Jülicher, Moffatt, Zahn). Giving bibliographical information for all such incidental material would result in an impossibly long bibliography that would be too cumbersome to be useful. Consultation of a basic NT introduction, such as that of Kümmel (which I do list), would enable an interested beginner to track down the authors thus cited.

works I have read and given as bibliography are from the twentieth century. Commentators or writers from the eighteenth and nineteenth centuries are occasionally mentioned, especially in lists of those who hold a particular view; and it may be useful to the reader to have the names and writing dates of the most important.

H. Alford (1871)	F. H. Kern (1830)
W. Beyschlag (1892)	S. G. Lange (1797)
A. Bisping (1871)	J. J. Lias (1887)
K. Braune (1865)	F. Lücke (1826)
B. Brückner (1853)	C. Luthardt (1888)
A. Calmet (1726)	G. K. Mayer (1851)
A. Camerlynck (1876)	J.A.W. Neander (1851)
W.M.L. de Wette (1837)	H.E.G. Paulus (1829)
F. Düsterdieck (1852–1856)	H. Poggel (1896)
J.H.A. Ebrard (1859)	E. Reuss (1878)
D. Erdmann (1855)	J. Rickli (1828)
H.G.A. Ewald (1861–1862)	J. Riemms (1869)
E. Haupt (1869–1870)	R. Rothe (1878)
J.C.K. (von) Hofmann (1875–1876)	J.E.F. Sander (1851)
J. E. Huther (1855)	J. Stockmeyer (1873)
C. R. Jachmann (1838)	G. C. Storr (1789)
W. A. Karl (1898)	C. A. Wolf (1881)

2. Recent Works

Alexander, N., *The Epistles of John* (TBC; London: SCM, 1962).

Asmussen, H., *Wahrheit und Liebe: Eine Einführung in die Johannesbriefe* (Die urchristliche Botschaft 22; Hamburg: Furche, 1957).

Auvray, D. P., *Saint Jean nous parle* (Thèmes Bibliques 10; Paris: Apostolat des Editions, 1972).

Balz, H., *Die Johannesbriefe*, in *Die Katholischen Briefe*, ed. W. Schrage and H. Balz (NTD 10; 11th ed.; Göttingen: Vandenhoeck & Ruprecht, 1973) 150–216.

Baumgarten, O., *Die Johannesbriefe* (Die Schriften des Neuen Testaments 4; 3d ed.; Göttingen: Vandenhoeck & Ruprecht, 1918) 185–228.

Belser, J. E., *Die Briefe des heiligen Johannes* (Freiburg: Herder, 1906).

Bonsirven, J., *Epîtres de Saint Jean* (Verbum Salutis 9; new ed.; Paris: Beauchesne, 1954).

Braun, F.-M., *Les Epîtres de Saint Jean*, in the vol. with D. Mollat, *L'Evangile de Saint Jean* (SBJ; 3d ed. rev.; Paris: Cerf, 1973) 231–77.

Brooke, A. E., *A Critical and Exegetical Commentary on the Johannine Epistles* (ICC; Edinburgh: Clark, 1912).

Bruce, F. F., *The Epistles of John* (Old Tappan, N.J.: Revell, 1970).

Büchsel, F., *Die Johannesbriefe* (THKNT 17; Leipzig: Deichert, 1933).

Bultmann, R. (with W. Werbeck), "Johannesbriefe," in RGG (3d ed.; Tübingen: Mohr, 1959) 3, 837–40.

————. *The Johannine Epistles* (Hermeneia; Philadelphia: Fortress, 1973; 2d German ed. 1967).

Calmes, T., *Epîtres Catholiques; Apocalypse* (Paris: Bloud, 1907) 68–100.

Carpenter, J. E., *The Johannine Writings* (Boston: Houghton Mifflin, 1927) esp. 456–72.

Chaine, J., *Les Epîtres Catholiques* (EB; 2d ed.; Paris: Gabalda, 1939) 97–260.

Charue, A., *Les Epîtres de S. Jean* (La Sainte Bible 13; Paris: Letouzey et Ané, 1938).

de Ambroggi, P., *Le Epistole Cattoliche* (Sacra Bibbia 14¹; 2d ed.; Turin: Marietti, 1949) 203–89.

de Jonge, M., *De Brieven van Johannes* (Nijkerk: Callenbach, 1968).

————. See Haas, THLJ.

Dibelius, M., "Johannesbriefe," in RGG (2d ed.; Tübingen: Mohr, 1929) 3, 346–49.

Dodd, C. H., *The Johannine Epistles* (MNTC; London: Hodder and Stoughton, 1946).

Eichholz, G., "Der 1. Johannesbrief als Trostbrief und die Einheit der Schrift," EvT 5 (1938) 73–83.

Filson, F. V., "First John: Purpose and Message," *Interpretation* 23 (1969) 259–76.

Findlay, G. G., *Fellowship in the Life Eternal: An Exposition of the Epistles of St. John* (London: Hodder and Stoughton, 1909).

Gärtner, B. E., *Johannesbreven*, in *De Katolska Breven*, ed. B. Reicke and B. E. Gärtner (Stockholm: Verbum, 1970) 113–223.

Gaugler, E., *Die Johannesbriefe* (Auslegung neutestamentlicher Schriften 1; Zurich: EVZ, 1964).

Gore, C., *The Epistles of St John* (London: Murray, 1920).

Haas, C., with M. de Jonge and J. L. Swellengrebel, *A Translator's Handbook on the Letters of John* (Helps for Translators 13; London: United Bible Societies, 1972).

Hauck, F., *Die Kirchenbriefe* (NTD 10; 5th ed.; Göttingen: Vandenhoeck & Ruprecht, 1949) 113–62.

Holtzmann, H. J., *Evangelium, Briefe, und Offenbarung des Johannes* (Handcommentar zum Neuen Testament 4; 2d ed.; Freiburg: Mohr, 1893).

Horn, F., *Der erste Brief des Johannes* (Munich: Kaiser, 1931).

Hoskyns, E., "The Johannine Epistles," in *A New Commentary on Holy Scripture*, ed. C. Gore et al. (New York: Macmillan, 1928) 2, 658–73.

Houlden, J. L., *A Commentary on the Johannine Epistles* (HNTC; New York: Harper & Row, 1973).

Kohler, M., *Le Coeur et les Mains: Commentaire de la Première Epître de Jean* (Neuchâtel: Delachaux & Niestlé, 1962).

Lauck, W., *Das Evangelium und die Briefe des hl. Johannes* (Die Heilige Schrift für das Leben erklärt; Freiburg: Herder, 1941).

Law, R., *The Tests of Life. A Study of the First Epistle of St. John* (Edinburgh: Clark, 1909).

Loisy, A. F., *Les Epîtres dites de Jean,* in *Le Quatrième Evangile* (2d ed.; Paris: Nourry, 1921) 71–85, 530–92.

Love, J. P., *The First, Second, and Third Letters of John* (Richmond: Knox, 1960).

Marshall, I. H., *The Epistles of John* (NICNT; Grand Rapids: Eerdmans, 1978).

Michl, J., *Die Katholischen Briefe* (RNT 8²; 2d ed.; Regensburg: Pustet, 1968) 190–272.

Moody, D., *The Letters of John* (Waco: Word, 1970).

Painter, J., *John: Witness and Theologian* (London: SPCK, 1975) 101–27.

Perkins, Pheme, *The Johannine Epistles* (New Testament Message 21; Wilmington: Glazier, 1979).

Plummer, A., *The Epistles of S. John* (Cambridge Greek Testament; Cambridge Univ., 1886).

Rennes, J., *La Première Epître de Jean* (Geneva: Labor et Fides, 1968).

Ross, A., *The Epistles of James and John* (NICNT; Grand Rapids: Eerdmans, 1958).

Schnackenburg, R., *Die Johannesbriefe* (HTKNT 13⁸; 3d ed.; Freiburg: Herder, 1965), plus the supplement for the 5th ed. (1975).

Schneider, J., *Die Kirchenbriefe* (NTD 10; 9th ed.; Göttingen: Vandenhoeck & Ruprecht, 1961) 137–98.

Shepherd, M. H., Jr., "The Letters of John," in *The Interpreter's One-Volume Commentary on the Bible,* ed. C. M. Laymon (Nashville: Abingdon, 1971) 935–41.

Stott, J.R.W., *The Epistles of John* (Tyndale NT 19; Grand Rapids: Eerdmans, 1964).

Thüsing, W., *The Three Epistles of St. John* (NT for Spiritual Reading 23; New York: Herder and Herder, 1971).

Vawter, B., "The Johannine Epistles," in JBC 62.

Vrede, W., *Die Johannesbriefe,* in *Die Katholischen Briefe,* ed. M. Meinertz and W. Vrede (HSNT 9; 4th ed.; Bonn: Hanstein, 1932) 143–92.

Weiss, B., *Die drei Briefe des Apostel Johannes* (MeyerK 14; 6th ed.; Göttingen: Vandenhoeck & Ruprecht, 1899).

Wendt, H. H., *Die Johannesbriefe und das johanneische Christentum* (Halle: Waisenhaus, 1925).

Westcott, B. F., *The Epistles of St. John* (New ed.; Grand Rapids: Eerdmans, 1966; orig. ed. 1883).

Wilder, A., "Introduction and Exegesis of the First, Second, and Third Epistles of John," in *The Interpreter's Bible* (Nashville: Abingdon, 1957) 12, 207–313.

Williams, R. R., *The Letters of John and James* (Cambridge Bible Commentary; Cambridge Univ., 1965).

Windisch, H., *Die Katholischen Briefe* (HNT 15; 3d ed., rev. H. Preisker; Tübingen: Mohr, 1951; orig. ed. 1911) 106–44, 164–72.

Wohlenberg, G., "Glossen zum ersten Johannesbrief," *Neue kirchliche Zeitschrift:* Art. I on 3:9 in 12 (1901) 581–83; Art. II on 3:15,16 in

12 (1901) 746–48; Art. III on 3:18–22 in 13 (1902) 632–45; Art. IV on 5:18 in 13 (1902) 233–40.

C. *Epistolary Theology*

1. General Works

Alfaro, J., "Cognitio Dei et Christi in I Jo.," VD 39 (1961) 82–91.

Boismard, M.-E., "La connaissance dans l'Alliance nouvelle d'après la Première Lettre de Saint Jean," RB 56 (1949) 365–91.

————. " 'Je ferai avec vous une alliance nouvelle' (Introduction à la Première Epître de Saint Jean)," LumVie 8 (1953) 94–109.

Bonsirven, J., "La théologie des Epîtres Johanniques," NRT 62 (1935) 920–44.

Braun, F.-M., "La réduction du pluriel au singulier dans l'Evangile et la Première Lettre de Jean," NTS 24 (1977–78) 40–67.

Cassem, N. H., "A Grammatical and Contextual Inventory of the Use of *kosmos* in the Johannine Corpus with some Implications for a Johannine Cosmic Theology," NTS 19 (1972–73) 81–91.

Coetzee, J. C., "Christ and the Prince of this World in the Gospel and Epistles of St. John," *Neotestamentica* 2 (1968) 104–21.

Davies, W. D., *The Setting of the Sermon on the Mount* (Cambridge Univ., 1964), esp. 408–12 on ethics in John and I John.

de Dinechin, O., "*KATHŌS*: La similitude dans l'Evangile selon Saint Jean," RSR 58 (1970) 195–236.

de Jonge, M., "The Use of the Word *Christos* in the Johannine Epistles," in *Studies in John* (J. N. Sevenster Festschrift; NovTSup 24; Leiden: Brill, 1970) 66–74.

de la Potterie, I., "La notion de 'commencement' dans les écrits johanniques," in *Die Kirche des Anfangs*, ed. R. Schnackenburg *et al.* (H. Schürmann Festschrift; Leipzig: St. Benno, 1977) 379–403.

Eichholz, G., "Erwählung und Eschatologie im 1. Johannesbrief," EvT 5 (1938) 1–28.

Feuillet, A., "La morale chrétienne d'après Saint Jean," EspVie 83 (1973) 665–70.

Gaugler, E., *Die Bedeutung der Kirche in den johanneischen Schriften* (Bern: Stämpfli, 1925). Also pub. in *Internationale kirchliche Zeitschrift* 14 (1924) 97–117, 181–219; 15 (1925) 25–42.

Johnston, G., "The Will of God: V. In I Peter and I John," ExpT 72 (1960–61) 237–40.

Kennedy, H.A.A., "The Covenant-conception in the First Epistle of John," ExpT 28 (1916–17) 23–26.

Lazure, N., *Les valeurs morales de la théologie johannique. Evangile et Epîtres* (EB; Paris: Gabalda, 1965).

Louw, J. P., "Verbal Aspect in the First Letter of John," *Neotestamentica* 9 (1975) 98–104.

Moule, C.F.D., "The Individualism of the Fourth Gospel," NovT 5 (1962) 171–90, esp. 180–82 on I John.

Mouroux, J., *L'Expérience chrétienne. Introduction à une Théologie* (Paris: Aubier, 1952), esp. 162–88 on I John. Earlier form in *La Vie Spirituelle* 78 (1948) 381–412.

Müller, U. B., *Die Geschichte der Christologie in der johanneischen Gemeinde* (SBS 77; Stuttgart: Katholisches Bibelwerk, 1975) esp. 69–72.

Percy, E., *Untersuchungen über den Ursprung der johanneischen Theologie* (Lund: Hakan Ohlssons, 1939).

Preiss, T., *Le témoignage intérieur du Saint-Esprit* (Cahiers théologiques de l'actualité protestante 13; Neuchâtel: Delachaux & Niestlé, 1946).

Prunet, O., *La Morale Chrétienne d'après les écrits Johanniques* (*Evangile et Epîtres*) (Paris: Presses Universitaires, 1957) esp. 71–81.

Rivera, A., *La redención en las Epistolas y en el Apocalipsis de S. Juan* (Rome: Gregorian Univ., 1939).

Rougé, P., *Dieu le père et l'oeuvre de notre salut d'après l'Evangile et la 1re Epître de S. Jean* (Carcassonne: Bonnafous, 1938).

Schenke, H.-M., "Determination und Ethik im ersten Johannesbrief," ZTK 60 (1963) 203–15.

Segalla, G., "L'esperienza cristiana in Giovanni," *Studia Patavina* 18 (1971) 299–342.

——. "Preesistenza, incarnazione e divinità di Cristo in Giovanni (Vg e 1 Gv)," *Rivista Biblica* 22 (1974) 155–81.

Škrinjar, A., "Prima Epistola Johannis in theologia aetatis suae," VD 46 (1968) 148–68.

——. "Theologia Epistolae I J comparatur cum philonismo et hermetismo," VD 46 (1968) 224–34.

——. "Theologia Primae Epistolae Joannis," VD 42 (1964) 3–16, 49–60; 43 (1965) 150–80.

Suitbertus a S. Joanne a Cruce, "Die Vollkommenheitslehre des ersten Johannesbriefes," *Biblica* 39 (1958) 319–33, 449–70.

Tarelli, C. C., "Johannine Synonyms," JTS 47 (1946) 175–77.

Vellanickal, M., *The Divine Sonship of Christians in the Johannine Writings* (AnBib 72; Rome: Biblical Institute, 1977).

2. Specific Theological Topics

(a) "ABIDING, REMAINING" (*menein*):

Heise, J., *Bleiben. Menein in den johanneischen Schriften* (Tübingen: Mohr, 1967).

Lammers, B., *Die MENEIN-Formeln der Johannesbrief* (typescript; Rome: Gregorian, 1954).

Malatesta, E., "Covenant and Indwelling," *The Way* 17 (1977) 23–32.

——. *Interiority and Covenant: A Study of* einai en *and* menein en *in the First Letter of Saint John* (AnBib 69; Rome: Biblical Institute, 1978).

Pecorara, G., "De verbo 'manere' apud Ioannem," *Divus Thomas* 40 (1937) 159–71.

(b) "LIFE" (*zōē*):

Coetzee, J. C., "Life (Eternal Life) in St. John's Writings and the Qumran Scrolls," *Neotestamentica* 6 (1972) 48–66.

Mussner, F., *ZŌĒ. Die Anschauung von "Leben" im vierten Evangelium unter Berücksichtigung des Johannesbriefe* (Theologische Studien 1[5]; Munich: Zink, 1952).

(c) "LOVE"(*agapan, agapē, agapētos*):

Barrosse, T., "The Relationship of Love to Faith in St. John," TS 18 (1957) 538–59.

Bowen, C. R., "Love in the Fourth Gospel," JR 13 (1933) 39–49.

Chmiel, J., *Lumière et charité d'après la Première Epître de Saint Jean* (Rome: Gregorian Univ., 1971).

Coppens, J., "'Agapè et 'agapân dans les Lettres johanniques," ETL 45 (1969) 125–27.

————. "La doctrine biblique sur l'amour de Dieu et du prochain," ETL 40 (1964) 252–99, esp. 289–99.

Dideberg, D., *Saint Augustin et la Première Epître de Saint Jean: une Théologie de l'Agapè* (Théologie historique 34; Paris: Beauchesne, 1975).

Eichholz, G., "Glaube und Liebe im I. Johannesbrief," EvT 4 (1937) 411–37.

Fensham, F. C., "Love in the Writings of Qumran and John," *Neotestamentica* 6 (1972) 67–77.

Feuillet, A., *Le mystère de l'amour divin dans la théologie johannique* (EB; Paris: Gabalda, 1972).

Menestrina, G., "*Agapē* nelle Lettere di Giovanni," BeO 19 (1977) 77–80.

Montefiore, H., "Thou Shalt Love the Neighbour as Thyself," NovT 5 (1962) 157–70.

Schlier, H., "Die Bruderliebe nach dem Evangelium und den Briefen des Johannes," in *Mélanges B. Rigaux*, ed. A. Descamps and A. de Halleux (Gembloux: Duculot, 1970) 235–45.

Segovia, F., "The Love and Hatred of Jesus and Johannine Sectarianism," CBQ 43 (1981) 258–72.

Sikes, W. W., "A Note on *Agape* in Johannine Literature," *The Shane Quarterly* 16 (1955) 139–43.

Spicq, C., *Agapē dans le Nouveau Testament* (3 vols.; EB; Paris: Gabalda, 1958–59) esp. 3, 111–351. Abbrev. in *Agape in the New Testament* (3 vols.; St. Louis: Herder, 1966) 3, 103–56.

(d) "SIN" (*hamartia*):

Braun, F.-M., "Le péché du monde selon Saint Jean," RevThom 65 (1965) 181–201.

Cook, W. R., "Hamartiological Problems in First John," BibSac 123 (1966) 249–60.

Cooper, E. J., "The Consciousness of Sin in I John," LavTheolPhil 28 (1972) 237–48.

McClendon, J. W., Jr., *The Doctrine of Sin in the First Epistle of John* (Princeton Dissertation, 1952).

Seeberg, R., "Die Sünden und die Sündenvergebung nach dem ersten Brief des Johannes," in *Das Erbe Martin Luthers und die gegenwärtige theologische Forschung*, ed. R. Jelke (L. Ihmels Festschrift; Leipzig: Dorffling & Franke, 1928) 19–31.

(e) "TRUTH" (*alētheia*):

Aalen, S., " 'Truth,' a Key Word in St. John's Gospel," StEv 2 (TU 87; Berlin: Akademie, 1964) 3–24.

de la Potterie, I., *La vérité dans Saint Jean* (2 vols.; AnBib 73–74; Rome: Biblical Institute, 1977).

Jackayya, B. H., "*Alētheia* in the Johannine Corpus," CTM 41 (1970) 171–75.

Mundle, W., "Das Wahrheitsverständnis des johanneischen Schrifttums," *Lutherischer Rundblick* 16 (1968) 82–94, 161–65.

Rüling, Dr., "Der Begriff *alētheia* in dem Evangelium und den Briefen des Johannes," *Neue kirchliche Zeitschrift* 6 (1895) 625–48.

Schnackenburg, R., "Wahrheit in Glaubenssätzen: Überlegungen nach dem ersten Johannesbrief," in *Zum Problem Unfehlbarkeit*; ed. K. Rahner (*Quaestiones disputatae* 54; Freiburg: Herder, 1971) 134–47.

D. *Authorship Issues*

Baur, F. C., "Die johanneischen Briefe. Ein Beitrag zur Geschichte des Kanons," *Theologische Jahrbücher* 7 (1848) 293–337.

———. "Das Verhältnis des ersten johanneischen Briefes zum johanneischen Evangelium," *Theologische Jahrbücher* 16 (1857) 315–31.

Becker, J., "Die Abschiedsreden Jesu im Johannesevangelium," ZNW 61 (1970) 215–46.

Bergmeier, R., "Zum Verfasserproblem des II. und III. Johannesbriefes," ZNW 57 (1966) 93–100.

Bonnard, P., "La Première Epître de Jean est-elle johannique?" in *L'Evangile de Jean*, ed. M. de Jonge (BETL 44; Gembloux: Duculot, 1977) 301–5.

Brooke, *Epistles* i–xix.

Burney, C. F., *The Aramaic Origins of the Fourth Gospel* (Oxford: Clarendon, 1922) esp. 150–59.

Dodd, C. H., "The First Epistle of John and the Fourth Gospel," BJRL 21 (1937) 129–56.

Freed, E. D., "Variations in the Language and Thought of John," ZNW 55 (1964) 167–97, esp. 194–96.

Goodenough, E. R., "John A Primitive Gospel," JBL 64 (1945) 145–82, esp. 160–65.

Hering, J., "Y a-t-il des Aramaïsmes dans la Première Epître Johannique?" RHPR 36 (1956) 113–21.

Higgins, A.J.B., "The Words of Jesus According to St. John," BJRL 49 (1966–67) 363–86, esp. 372–74 on Semitisms in I John.

Hirsch, E., *Studien zum vierten Evangelium* (Beiträge zur historischen Theologie 11; Tübingen: Mohr, 1936) esp. 170–79.

Holtzmann, H. J., "Das Problem des ersten johanneischen Briefes in seinem Verhältnis zum Evangelium," *Jahrbücher für protestantische Theologie:* Art. I in 7 (1881) 690–712; Art. II in 8 (1882) 128–52; Art. III in 8 (1882) 316–42; Art. IV in 8 (1882) 460–85.

Hoskyns, E., *The Fourth Gospel,* ed. F. N. Davey (2d ed.; London: Faber & Faber, 1947) esp. 48–57.

Howard, W. F., "The Common Authorship of the Johannine Gospel and Epistles," JTS 48 (1947) 12–25.

————. *The Fourth Gospel in Recent Criticism and Interpretation* (rev. ed.; London: Epworth, 1955) esp. 103–10, 276–96, part of which reprints the previous article.

Johnston, G., *The Spirit-Paraclete in the Gospel of John* (SNTSMS 12; Cambridge Univ., 1970) 75–79.

Klein, G., " 'Das wahre Licht scheint schon.' Beobachtungen zur Zeit- und Geschichtserfahrung einer urchristlichen Schule," ZTK 68 (1971) 261–326.

Nunn, H.P.V., "The First Epistle of St. John," *Evangelical Quarterly* 17 (1945) 296–303.

Salom, A. P., "Some Aspects of the Grammatical Style of I John," JBL 74 (1955) 96–102.

Skrinjar, A., "Differentiae theologicae I Jo. et Jo.," VD 41 (1963) 175–85.

Soltau, W., "Die eigenartige dogmatische Standpunkt der Johannisreden und seine Erklärung," ZWT 52 (1910) 341–59.

————. "Die Verwandtschaft zwischen Evangelium Johannis und dem I. Johannesbrief," TSK 89 (1916) 228–33.

Turner, N., "The Style of the Johannine Epistles," MGNTG 4, 132–38.

Valentin, A., "The Johannine Authorship of Apocalypse, Gospel, and Epistles," *Scripture* 6 (1953–54) 148–50.

Wilson, W. G., "An Examination of the Linguistic Evidence Adduced against the Unity of Authorship of the First Epistle of John and the Fourth Gospel," JTS 49 (1948) 147–56.

E. *Source Theories*

Beyer, H. W., "Rezension: *Festgabe für Adolf Jülicher zum 70. Geburtstag* (Tübingen: Mohr, 1927)," TLZ 54 (1929) 606–17—review of Bultmann, "Analyse" below.

Braun, H., "Literar-Analyse und theologische Schichtung im ersten Johannesbrief," ZTK 48 (1951) 262–92. Reprinted in his *Gesammelte Studien zum Neuen Testament* (2d ed.; Tübingen: Mohr, 1967) 210–42.

Büchsel, F., "Zu den Johannesbriefen," ZNW 28 (1929) 235–41.

Bultmann, R., "Analyse des ersten Johannesbriefes," in *Festgabe für Adolf Jülicher zum 70. Geburtstag* (Tübingen: Mohr, 1927) 138–58.

————. "Die kirchliche Redaktion des ersten Johannesbriefes," in *In Memoriam Ernst Lohmeyer*, ed. W. Schmauch (Stuttgart: Evangelisches Verlag, 1951) 189–201.

Lohmeyer, E., "Über Aufbau und Gliederung des ersten Johannesbriefes," ZNW 27 (1928) 225–63.

Muñoz León, D., "El origen de las fórmulas rítmicas antitéticas en la Primera Carta de San Juan," in *Miscelánea José Zunzunegui* (Vitoria: Editorial ESET, 1975) **5, 221–44.**

Nauck, W., *Die Tradition und der Charakter des ersten Johannesbriefes* (WUNT 3; Tübingen: Mohr, 1957).

O'Neill, J. C., *The Puzzle of 1 John: A New Examination of Origins* (London: SPCK, 1966).

Škrinjar, A., "De unitate epistolae 1J," VD 47 (1969) 83–95.

von Dobschütz, E., "Johanneische Studien, I," ZNW 8 (1907) 1–8.

F. *Life and Setting of the Community*

1. History

Bacon, B. W., *The Fourth Gospel in Research and Debate* (New Haven: Yale, 1918) esp. 184–209.

————. *The Gospel of the Hellenists* (New York: Holt, 1933) esp. 359–69.

Bakken, N. K., *The Gospel and Epistles of John: A Study of their Relationship in the Precanonical Period* (typescript; New York: Union Theological Seminary, 1963).

Bauer, W., *Orthodoxy and Heresy in Earliest Christianity*, ed. R. Kraft and G. Krodel (Philadelphia: Fortress, 1971; German orig. 1934) esp. 61–146.

Boismard, M.-E., "The First Epistle of John and the Writings of Qumran," in *John and Qumran*, ed. J. H. Charlesworth (London: Chapman, 1972) 156–65.

Brown, R. E., *The Community of the Beloved Disciple* (New York: Paulist, 1979).

————. "'Other Sheep Not of This Fold': The Johannine Perspective on Christian Diversity in the Late First Century," JBL 97 (1978) 5–22.

————. "The Qumran Scrolls and the Johannine Gospel and Epistles," CBQ 17 (1955) 403–19, 559–74. Reprinted in *The Scrolls and the New Testament*, ed. K. Stendahl (New York: Harper, 1957) 183–207; also in R. E. Brown, *New Testament Essays* (Garden City, N.Y.: Doubleday Image, 1968) 138–73.

Clemen, C., "Beiträge zum geschichtlichen Verständnis der Johannesbriefe," ZNW 6 (1905) 271–81.

Collins, Adela Y., "Crisis and Community in John's Gospel," TD 27 (1979) 313–21.

Conzelmann, H., "'Was von Anfang war,'" in *Neutestamentliche Studien für R. Bultmann* (Beihefte ZNW 21; Berlin: Töpelmann, 1954) 194–201.

Couture, P., *The Teaching Function in the Church of 1 John* (typescript; Rome: Gregorian Univ., 1967; printed excerpt, 1968).

Culpepper, R. A., *The Johannine School* (SBLDS 26; Missoula: Scholars Press, 1975).

de Jonge, M., "The Beloved Disciple and the Date of the Gospel of John," in *Text and Interpretation,* ed. E. Best and R. McL. Wilson (M. Black Festschrift; Cambridge Univ., 1979) 99–114.

———. "Variety and Development in Johannine Christology," in *Jesus: Stranger from Heaven and Son of God* (SBLSBS 11; Missoula: Scholars Press, 1977) 193–222. Pertinent also are items in pp. 169–91 of this book.

Ehrhardt, A., "The Gospels in the Muratorian Fragment," in *The Framework of the New Testament Stories* (Cambridge: Harvard Univ. [also Manchester Univ.], 1964) 11–36.

———. "Christianity before the Apostles' Creed," *Ibid.* 151–99. Orig. in HTR 55 (1962) 74–119.

Gunther, J. J., "The Alexandrian Gospel and Letters of John," CBQ 41 (1979) 581–603, esp. 600–3.

Hoffman, T. A., "I John and the Qumran Scrolls," BTB 8 (1978) 117–25.

Langbrandtner, W., *Weltferner Gott oder Gott der Liebe: Die Ketzerstreit in der johanneischen Kirche* (Beiträge zur biblischen Exegese und Theologie 6; Frankfurt: Lang, 1977).

Le Fort, P., *Les structures de l'Eglise militante selon Saint Jean* (Geneva: Labor et Fides, 1970).

Loisy, A., *Origins of the New Testament* (London: Allen and Unwin, 1950; French orig. 1936).

Manson, T. W., "Additional Note: The Johannine Epistles and the Canon of the New Testament," attached to "Entry into the Membership of the Early Church," JTS 48 (1947) 32–33.

Martyn, J. L., *The Gospel of John in Christian History* (New York: Paulist, 1978).

———. *History and Theology in the Fourth Gospel* (New York: Harper & Row, 1968; revised, Nashville: Abingdon, 1979). Refs. to orig. ed. (2d ed. in parentheses).

Matsunaga, K., "Is John's Gospel Anti-Sacramental?—A New Solution in the Light of the Evangelist's Milieu," NTS 27 (1980–81) 516–24.

Painter, J., "The Farewell Discourses and the History of Johannine Christianity," NTS 27 (1980–81) 525–43.

Pancaro, S., "'People of God' in St. John's Gospel?" NTS 16 (1969–70) 114–29.

Pastor, F.-A., "Comunidad y ministerio en las Epístolas Joaneas," EstEcl 52 (1977) 39–71.

Piper, O. A., "I John and the Didache of the Primitive Church," JBL 66 (1947) 437–51.

Richter, G., "Die Deutung des Kreuzestodes Jesu in der Leidensgeschichte des Johannesevangeliums (Joh 13–19)," *Bibel und Leben* 9 (1968) 21–36.

Reprinted in *Studien zum Johannesevangelium,* ed. J. Hainz (BU 13; Regensburg: Pustet, 1977) 58–73.

————. "Die Fleischwerdung des Logos im Johannesevangelium," NovT 13 (1971) 81–126; 14 (1972) 257–76. Reprinted in *Studien* 149–98.

————. "Präsentische und futurische Eschatologie im 4. Evangelium," in *Gegenwart und kommendes Reich,* ed. P. Fiedler and D. Zeller (A. Vögtle Schulergabe; Stuttgart: Katholisches Bibelwerk, 1975) 117–52. Reprinted in *Studien* 346–82. Analyzed and digested by A. J. Mattill, "Johannine Communities behind the Fourth Gospel: Georg Richter's Analysis," TS 38 (1977) 294–315.

Robinson, J.A.T., "The Destination and Purpose of the Johannine Epistles," in *Twelve New Testament Studies* (SBT 34; London: SCM, 1962) 126–38. Orig. in NTS 7 (1960–61) 56–65.

Sánchez Mielgo, G., "Perspectivas eclesiológicas en la primera carta de Juan," *Escritos del Vedat* 4 (1974) 9–64.

Sanders, J. N., "'Those whom Jesus Loved,'" NTS 1 (1954–55) 29–41.

Schlier, H., "Die Kirche nach den Johannesbriefen," in *Mysterium Salutis,* ed. J. Feiner *et al.* (5 vols.; Einsiedeln: Benziger, 1965–76) 4¹, 146–52.

Schnackenburg, R., "The Church in the Johannine Writings Including the Apocalypse," in *The Church in the New Testament* (New York: Herder and Herder, 1965) 103–17.

————. "Die johanneische Gemeinde und ihre Geisterfahrung," in *Die Kirche des Anfangs,* ed. R. Schnackenburg *et al.* (H. Schürmann Festschrift; Leipzig: St. Benno, 1977) 277–306.

Schweizer, E., *Church Order in the New Testament* (SBT 32; London: SCM, 1961) 117–30.

————. "The Concept of the Church in the Gospel and Epistles of St. John," in *New Testament Essays* ed. A.J.B. Higgins (T. W. Manson Memorial; Manchester Univ., 1959) 230–45.

Songer, H. S., "The Life Situation of the Johannine Epistles," RevExp 67 (1970) 399–409.

Streeter, B. H., "The Epistles of St. John," in *The Primitive Church* (New York: Macmillan, 1929) 86–101.

Thyen, H., "Entwicklungen innerhalb der johanneischen Theologie und Kirche im Spiegel von Joh. 21 und der Lieblingsjüngertexte des Evangeliums," in *L'Evangile de Jean,* ed. M. de Jonge (BETL 44; Gembloux: Duculot, 1977) 259–99.

————. "Johannes 13 und die 'Kirchliche Redaktion' des vierten Evangeliums," in *Tradition und Glaube,* ed. G. Jeremias *et al.* (K. G. Kuhn Festschrift; Göttingen: Vandenhoeck & Ruprecht, 1971) 343–56.

Wengst, K., *Bedrängte Gemeinde und verherrlichter Christus. Der historische Ort des Johannesevangeliums als Schlüssel zu seiner Interpretation* (Biblisch-Theologische Studien 5; Neukirchen, 1981).

Woll, D. B., *Johannine Christianity in Conflict* (SBLDS 60; Chico, CA: Scholars Press, 1981).

2. House-Churches

Filson, F. V., "The Significance of the Early House Churches," JBL 58 (1939) 105–12.

Klauck, H.-J., "Die Hausgemeinde als Lebensform in Urchristentum," MTZ 32 (1981) 1–15.

Malherbe, A., *Social Aspects of Early Christianity* (Baton Rouge: Louisiana State Univ., 1975) esp. 60–91.

Rordorf, W., "Was wissen wir über die christlichen Gottesdiensträume der vorkonstantinischen Zeit?" ZNW 55 (1964) 110–28.

Stuhlmacher, P., "Urchristliche Hausgemeinden," in *Der Briefe an Philemon* (EKK; Zurich: Benziger, 1975) 70–75.

3. Adversaries (in General)

Bludau, A., *Die ersten Gegner der Johannesschriften* (BibS[F] 22$^{1-2}$; 1925).

Bogart, J., *Orthodox and Heretical Perfectionism in the Johannine Community as Evident in the First Epistle of John* (SBLDS 33; Missoula: Scholars Press, 1977).

Brown, R. E., "The Relationship to the Fourth Gospel Shared by the Author of I John and by his Opponents," in *Text and Interpretation,* ed. E. Best and R. McL. Wilson (M. Black Festschrift; Cambridge Univ., 1979) 57–68.

Shepherd, M. H., Jr., "The Jews in the Gospel of John: Another Level of Meaning," ATRsupp.ser. 3 (1974) 95–112.

Škrinjar, A., "Errores in epistola I. Jo. impugnati," VD 41 (1963) 60–72.

Smalley, S. S., "What about 1 John?" *Studia Biblica 1978* (Journal for the Study of the New Testament Supplement Series 3; Sheffield 1980) 3, 337–43.

Stagg, F., "Orthodoxy and Orthopraxy in the Johannine Epistles," RevExp 67 (1970) 423–32.

Tuñí, O., "Motivacions ètiques de la 1Jn: La 1Jn i el Jesús històric," *Revista Catalana de Teologia* 4 (1979) 285–308.

Vorster, W. S., "Heterodoxy in 1 John," *Neotestamentica* 9 (1975) 87–97.

Weiss, K., "Orthodoxie und Heterodoxie im 1. Johannesbrief," ZNW 58 (1967) 247–55.

Wengst, K., *Häresie und Orthodoxie im Spiegel des ersten Johannesbriefes* (Gütersloh: Mohn, 1976).

Wurm, A., *Die Irrlehrer im ersten Johannesbrief* (BibS[F] 8^{1}; 1903).

4. Specific Adversaries

Bardy, G., "Cérinthe," RB 30 (1921) 344–73.

Barnard, L. W., "The Background of St. Ignatius of Antioch," VC 17 (1963) 193–206.

Barrett, C. K., "Jews and Judaizers in the Epistles of Ignatius," in *Jews, Greeks and Christians,* ed. R. Hamerton-Kelly and R. Scroggs (W. D. Davies Festschrift; Studies in Judaism and Late Antiquity 2; Leiden: Brill, 1976) 220–44.

Bartsch, H.-W., *Gnostisches Gut und Gemeindetradition bei Ignatius von Antiochen* (BFCT, 2 Reihe, 44; Gütersloh: Bertelsmann, 1940).

Burghardt, W. J., "Did Saint Ignatius of Antioch Know the Fourth Gospel?" TS 1 (1940) 1–26, 130–56.

Corwin, Virginia, *St. Ignatius and Christianity in Antioch* (New Haven: Yale Univ., 1960).

Dietze, P., "Die Briefe des Ignatius und das Johannesevangelium," TSK 78 (1905) 563–603.

Donahue, P. J., "Jewish Christianity in the Letters of Ignatius of Antioch," VC 32 (1978) 81–93.

Molland, E., "The Heretics Combatted by Ignatius of Antioch," JEH 5 (1954) 1–6.

Niven, W. D., "Cerinthus," *Dictionary of the Apostolic Church*, ed. J. Hastings (Edinburgh: Clark, 1915) 1, 172–73.

Pagels, Elaine H., *The Johannine Gospel in Gnostic Exegesis* (SBLMS 17; Nashville: Abingdon, 1973).

Richardson, C. C., *The Christianity of Ignatius of Antioch* (New York: Columbia Univ., 1935).

Rohde, J., "Häresie und Schisma im ersten Clemensbrief und in den Ignatius-Briefen," NovT 10 (1968) 217–33.

Schwartz, E., "Johannes und Kerinthos," ZNW 15 (1914) 210–19.

von Campenhausen, H., *Ecclesiastical Authority and Spiritual Power in the Church of the First Three Centuries* (Stanford Univ., 1969; German orig. 1953) esp. 121–23, 136–41.

Weiss, K., "Die 'Gnosis' im Hintergrund und im Spiegel der Johannesbriefe," in *Gnosis und Neues Testament*, ed. K.-W. Tröger (Berlin: Evangelische Verlagsanstalt, 1973) 341–56.

See also ABJ 29, lxv.

G. *Structure of I John*

Bogaert, M., "Structure et message de la Première Epître de Saint Jean," BVC 83 (1968) 33–45.

Feuillet, A., "The Structure of First John: Comparison with the 4th Gospel," BTB 3 (1973) 194–216.

Francis, F. O., "The Form and Function of the Opening and Closing Paragraphs of James and I John," ZNW 61 (1970) 110–26.

Giurisato, G., "Struttura della prima lettera di Giovanni," *Rivista Biblica* 21 (1973) 361–81.

Häring, T., "Gedankengang und Grundgedanke des ersten Johannesbriefs," in *Theologische Abhandlungen Carl von Weizäcker . . . gewidmet* (Freiburg: Mohr, 1892) 171–200.

Jones, P. R., "A Structural Analysis of I John," RevExp 67 (1970) 433–44.

Malatesta, E., *The Epistles of St. John: Greek Text and English Translation Schematically Arranged* (Rome: Gregorian Univ., 1973).

Nagl, E., "Die Gliederung des ersten Johannesbriefes," BZ 16 (1922–24) 77–92.

Oke, C. C., "The Plan of the First Epistle of John," ExpT 51 (1939–40) 347–50.

Olivier, A., *La strophe sacrée en St Jean* (Paris: Guenther, 1939).

Schwertschlager, R., *Der erste Johannesbrief in seinem Grundgedanken und Aufbau* (Coburg: Tageblatt-Haus, 1935).

Skrinjar, A., "De divisione Epistolae Primae Joannis," VD 47 (1969) 31–40.

Smit Sibinga, J., "A Study in I John," in *Studies in John* (J. N. Sevenster Festschrift; NovTSup 24; Leiden: Brill, 1970) 194–208.

Thompson, P. J., "Psalm 119: a Possible Clue to the Structure of the First Epistle of John," StEv 2 (TU 87; Berlin: Akademie, 1964) 487–92.

Tomoi, K., "The Plan of the First Epistle of John," ExpT 52 (1940–41) 117–19.

Westcott, A., "The Divisions of the First Epistle of St. John: A Correspondence between Drs. Westcott and Hort," *The Expositor* Series Seven, 3 (1907) 481–93.

Wiesinger, D., "Der Gedankengang des ersten Johannesbriefes," TSK 72 (1899) 575–81.

H. *Text*

Baird, J. A. *et al.*, *The Johannine Epistles—A Critical Concordance* (Computer Bible 3; Wooster, Ohio: Biblical Research Associates, 1971).

Carder, Muriel M., "A Caesarean Text in the Catholic Epistles?" NTS 16 (1969–70) 252–70.

Delaporte, L., "Fragments thébains du Nouveau Testament: I. Première Epître de Saint Jean," RB 14 (N.S. 2; 1905) 377–97, 557–60.

Duplacy, J., " 'Le Texte Occidentale' des Epîtres Catholiques," NTS 16 (1969–70) 397–99.

Harnack, A. (von), "Zur Textkritik und Christologie der Schriften des Johannes," *Sitzungsberichte der königlich Preussischen Akademie der Wissenschaften zu Berlin* (1915) 534–73.

Richards, W. L., *The Classification of the Greek Manuscripts of the Johannine Epistles* (SBLDS 35; Missoula: Scholars Press, 1977).

Thiele, W., *Wortschatzuntersuchungen zu den lateinischen Texten der Johannesbriefe. Vetus Latina* (Aus der Geschichte der lateinischen Bibel 2; Freiburg: Herder, 1958).

I. *Miscellaneous Works Cited in this Commentary*

Barrett, C. K., *The Gospel according to St. John* (2d ed.; Philadelphia: Westminster, 1978).

Bonsirven, J., *Le judaïsme palestinien au temps de Jésus Christ* (2 vols.; Paris: Beauchesne, 1934–35).

Brown, R. E., "The Kerygma of the Gospel according to John," Int 21 (1967) 387–400.

Kümmel, W. G., *Introduction to the New Testament* (Rev. ed.; Nashville: Abingdon, 1975).

Perkins, Pheme, *The Gnostic Dialogue* (Theological Inquiries; New York: Paulist, 1980).

Schnackenburg, R., *The Gospel according to St John* (3 vols.; New York: Herder and Herder, 1968, vol. 1; New York: Seabury, 1980, vol. 2 [vol. 3 scheduled for 1982]).

Scott, E. F., *The Fourth Gospel* (Edinburgh: Clark, 1906).

The First Epistle of John

A work consisting of comments on Johannine tradition as it is known to us in the Fourth Gospel. These comments were written to protect the author's adherents within the Johannine Community from further inroads by secessionist teachers whose slogans, christological and ethical, the author refutes.

The Prologue
(I John 1:1–4)

Reflections on the Prologue of the Fourth Gospel: "In the beginning was the Word . . . and the Word became flesh . . . and we have seen his glory" (John 1:1,14).

1. I John 1:1–4: *The Prologue*

	This is what we proclaim to you:
1a	**1** ¹What was from the beginning,
1b	what we have heard,
1c	what we have seen with our own eyes,
1d	what we looked at
1e	and felt with our own hands—
1f	our concern is about the word of life
2a	(²For this life was revealed
2b	as we have seen and testify,
2c	and we proclaim to you
2d	this eternal life
2e	which was in the Father's presence
2f	and was revealed to us.)—
3a	³what we have seen and heard
3b	we proclaim in turn to you,
3c	so that you may be joined in communion with us.
3d	Yes, for the communion we have is with the Father
3e	and with His Son, Jesus Christ.
4a	⁴Indeed, we are writing this
4b	so that our joy may be fulfilled.

NOTES

Title: "The First Epistle of John." The original work bore no title, although all ancient copies of the Greek text do. Codices Vaticanus, Sinaiticus, and Alexandrinus support this title, which has now become the standard designation. Sometimes the title lacks the Greek word for "Epistle," but that is implied since the enumeration "First" is by comparison with the other, smaller Johannine writings (II and III John) which are clearly Epistles. Other textual witnesses use a longer title that identifies John further as apostle and evangelist. For the designation "Catholic Epistle," which appears in some forms of the title, see INTRODUCTION I A; and for the title "The Epistle of John to the Parthians," see Appendix III.

A discussion of the debatable accuracy of the assignment of literary genre as "Epistle" is found in the INTRODUCTION V C. The attribution of authorship to "John" (son of Zebedee) represents an intelligent late-second-century scholarly guess and is intimately related to the similar guess that the author or authority behind the Fourth Gospel (ABJ 29, xcviii–cii) was John. In the INTRODUCTION (especially II and V D2b), I explain the greater plausibility of the thesis that *different* writers of the same School were responsible respectively for the body of GJohn, for I-II-III John, and for the redaction of GJohn, and that none of them was the son of Zebedee.

General note on the grammar of the Prologue. The initial four verses of I John have a good claim to being the most complicated Greek in the Johannine corpus, a passage "more remarkable for energy than for lucidity," as Loisy has acidly observed (*Evangile-Epîtres* 531). As the opening words of a literary work, "they can only be described as, formally at least, bordering upon incoherence"; and even in a work that does not aspire to literary heights, this Prologue is a "lapse into grammatical impossibilities" (Houlden, *Epistles* 45). The reaction of virtually all translators has been captured in the observation made by Dodd (*Epistles* 2): "The sentence is not good Greek, and it is only by paraphrase that it can be rendered into good English." Of course, the epistolary author may have had no interest in the coherence achieved by following classical rules, and his own style may have been more intelligible than "good Greek" to readers familiar with Johannine religious idiom and its facility in interchanging key words. Nevertheless, we who are not of the Johannine Community must seek as best we can to translate his composition into a logic we can grasp by working with the basic rules of "good Greek." Here I shall discuss grammar, leaving the flow of ideas to the COMMENT. Precisely because my translation does attempt to smooth out some of the difficulties (without, I hope, becoming a paraphrase), a literal rendering must be given in order to enable the reader to understand the somewhat technical NOTES that follow:

1a	What *was* from the beginning,	[imperf. *einai*]
1b	what we *have heard*,	[perf. *akouein*]
1c	what we *have seen* with our eyes,	[perf. *horan*]
1d	what we *looked at*,	[aorist *theasthai*]
1e	and what our hands *felt*	[aorist *psēlaphan*]
1f	about the word [*logos*] of life [*zōē*]	
2a	and the life *was revealed*	[aorist *phaneroun*]
2b	and we *have seen* and *testify*	[perf. *horan;* pres. *martyrein*]
2c	and we *proclaim* to you	[pres. *apangellein*]
2d	the eternal life	
2e	of the sort which [*hētis*] *was* toward [*pros*] the Father	[imperf. *einai*]
2f	and *was revealed* to us	[aorist *phaneroun*]
3a	what we *have seen* and *heard*	[perf. *horan, akouein*]
3b	we *proclaim* also to you	[pres. *apangellein*]
3c	so that you too may have communion [*koinōnia*] with us	
3d	and indeed our communion with the Father	
3e	and with His Son, Jesus Christ,	
4a	and we ourselves *write* these things	[pres. *graphein*]
4b	so that our joy may *be fulfilled*.	[perf. *plēroun*]

Overall there are three grammatical difficulties. *First,* the four verses constitute one long sentence, made all the more complicated by parenthetical remarks that seemingly interrupt, not once but twice. The line 1f above is the first interruption, while the other is the whole of v. 2, which is a parenthetical remark explaining the "life" mentioned in the first interruption. Thus, grammatically line 1e is followed by 3a in which after the long double interruption the author repeats himself, summarizing what he has said in lines 1b–e. *Second,* in this long, awkward sentence a main verb first makes its appearance in line *3b,* a postponement that leaves the "what" clauses of 1a–e in a most awkward position, especially since they are separated from that verb by the two interruptions just described. The reader does not discover until v. 3 whether these clauses are the object or the subject of what the author wishes to say! Some commentators seek to avoid this difficulty by supplying a copulative verb between the clauses of v. 1: "What was from the beginning *was* (or *is*) what we have heard, etc." However, this makes one of the clauses a subject when, in fact, all of them are objects. Others introduce the copula within the clause, treating the "what" freely: "It *was* there from the beginning; we have heard it, etc." (NEB). Still another stratagem is to anticipate, not the first main verb from 3b, but the second verb from 4a: *"We write* to you about the Word of life, which has existed from the very beginning" (TEV). However, thus to combine lines 4a and 1f and to place the combined line before 1a seems unnecessarily elaborate. It is simpler to anticipate the main verb from line 3b as I have done in the unnumbered line ("This is what we proclaim to you"), which precedes the text of the Prologue in my translation. *Third,* there is a puzzling alternation of tenses in the many "we" verbal forms, especially of the aorist and the perfect. Commentators debate whether it is a purely stylistic feature or connotes subtle distinctions of meaning. We shall have to discuss this question in relation to each verb.

Before moving on to a line-by-line discussion, let me mention a structural proposal made in comment upon the above by D. Noel Freedman, the editor of the AB series. It will help to make sense of many of the observations to follow. He suggests an alternating A/B/A′/B′ pattern in vv. 1,2,3,4, thus:

(A) 1a–e and (A′) 3a–e go together as indicated by the resumptive 3a. The "we proclaim" of v. 3 is the main verb governing the "what" clauses of v. 1.

(B) 1f + 2a–f and (B′) 4ab go together, with 1f serving as an indicator that a new pattern is beginning. The "we write" of v. 4 is the main verb governing the theme of life in 1f + 2a–f.

The "our communion" of A/A′ would be matched by the "our joy" of B/B′, even as the Father and His Son of A/A′ would be matched by the Father and eternal life of B/B′. It is difficult to be certain that all of this was in the author's mind, but it is a type of pattern that would not be strange to OT poetic oracles. Freedman's suggestion plus the chart of flow of ideas that I shall give below on p. 177 suggests that, while the author produced a Greek composition with many violations of "good grammar," he had his own sense of organization.

This is what we proclaim to you. As explained above, for easier reading I have anticipated here what is said in 1:3b; see NOTE there.

1a. *What.* The neuter relative pronoun (*ho*) introduces four clauses in lines 1a–d, and a fifth in 1:3ab. Although all these "what" clauses are the object of the verb "proclaim" in line 3b (which I have anticipated in the opening line of my translation), internally the "what" in this first clause is the subject of the verb "to be," while in the other four clauses the "whats" are the object of the various verbs of sensory perception. Among those verbs some ("see," "look at," "feel") suggest that a person is the object of attention; others ("hear," "proclaim") suggest that a message is the object. This ambivalence about the personal and impersonal characteristics of the "whats" continues when one considers the nouns governed directly or indirectly by those verbs, nouns that might be parallel to the "whats." For instance, the parenthetical v. 2 suggests that the object of seeing, testifying, and proclaiming was (eternal) life; but "life" (*zōē*) is a feminine noun, so that only awkwardly could the neuter "whats" refer to life. The parenthetical last line of v. 1 might give the impression that "the word of life" (personified or not?) was the object spoken about, but "word" is a masculine noun that could again only awkwardly be identified with the neuter "whats." If we look for help elsewhere in I John, outside the Prologue, the expression "him (who has been) from the beginning" in 2:13,14 shows that all personal reference can scarcely be excluded in 1:1a, "What was from the beginning." Overall, the explanation that bests fits the evidence is that the "what" is to be equated with no specific noun in the Prologue, but refers to the whole career of Jesus, with the neuter functioning *comprehensively to cover the person, the words, and the works.* See BDF 138[1] for the use of a neuter pronoun to describe persons of a particular kind or quality of life. There are comparable examples in John 3:6; 6:39; 17:2,7,24 and I John 5:4; note especially the use of *ho* in John 6:37: "What the Father gives to me will come to me." Such a comprehensive interpretation is preferable to all the theories that press the neuter for highly theological implications. For instance, Drumwright, "Problem Passages" 53–54, draws from it the hint that Jesus' life was a *fact* of history; Bonsirven, *Epîtres* 69, thinks it catches "Being-in-itself"; and THLJ 22 finds in it a suggestion "that the situation and qualities of the Word cannot clearly . . . be described in human language."

was. If "what" is comprehensive of the career of Jesus, just how comprehensive? Does it include a divine, preincarnational career, or only the earthly ministry of Jesus? Influenced by the GJohn Prologue, "In the beginning *was* the Word" (ABJ 29, 4), many assume that here the imperfect of *einai*, "to be," is timeless or of unlimited duration, arguing that in Johannine theology the incarnate or earthly career of God's Son requires not the verb *einai* but *ginesthai*, "to become," as in John 1:14, "The Word became flesh." The contrast between the two verbs in John 8:58 is often invoked: "Before Abraham even came into existence [*ginesthai*], I AM [*einai*]." However, the appeal to "I

AM" proves too much; for other examples of this sovereign Johannine use of the verb "to be" (ABJ 29, 532–38) show that "I AM" is not confined to the preincarnate period but covers the whole career of God's Son. In itself, then, the verbal form "was" does not tell us whether the "what" which begins v. 1a covers preincarnate existence. Caution is suggested by two facts. First, the "what was" of 1a is structurally parallel to the "what we have heard . . . seen . . . looked at . . . felt" of 1b–e, and those verbs can refer only to Jesus' earthly ministry. Second, the copula is not uniquely important to the epistolary author, for he omits it altogether in 2:13,14 when he speaks of Jesus as "him from the beginning." Thus, the copula in the first line of 1:1 may be supplied simply to create a parallelism with the verbs in the other lines.

from the beginning. This phrase, and not the copula "was," is the key to the comprehensiveness of the "what" in v. 1a. Of the 55 times *archē*, "beginning," appears in the NT, 3 instances are in Revelation, 8 in GJohn, and 10 in I and II John (always here governed by the preposition *apo*, "from"). The high proportion of Johannine usage suggests that *archē* may be a companion to other significant Johannine temporal words, e.g., "now," "already," "hour." The phrase discussed here occurs 4 times in GJohn, twice with *apo* (8:44; 15:27), twice with *ek*, "from, out of" (6:64; 16:4). Although de la Potterie would see a fine theological difference between the two "from" prepositions, a comparison of John 15:27 and 16:4 points to interchangeability and to the Johannine love for variation of vocabulary.

To what does "beginning" in v. 1a refer? Does it include preincarnate existence? First, let me make a general remark. In scholarly discussions of the Johannine *archē* one finds expressions like "absolute beginning," a "beginning before time" (de la Potterie), a "timeless beginning," and a beginning that is equivalent to eternity (de la Potterie, Marshall). In my judgment such terminology introduces non-Johannine categories into the discussion. The Council of Nicaea stated that there never was a time when the Son of God "was not" as part of its refutation of the Arians who were able to read "In the beginning was the Word" in the opposite sense. The very existence of the Arian interpretation suggests that Chaine, *Epîtres* 139, is perceptive in arguing that the Johannine *archē* is not easily equivalent to eternity. (If one protests that *aiōnios*, "eternal," is in common Johannine usage, the connotation of that word is closer to limitless than to timeless; for it can be used to modify *chronos*, "time," as in Rom 16:25 and II Tim 1:9.) There is no Johannine *archē* passage that itself raises the issue of "before time"—John 1:1–2 raises the issue of before creation, but that need not be the same as before time. Indeed, one can ask about the logic of a timeless beginning. In any case, leaving aside the issue of a beginning in eternity, I shall now summarize six interpretations of *archē* that lie within the framework of NT thought, asking which is/are the most plausible as the meaning intended in I John 1:1a. The first three given below allow "what was from the beginning" to include the preincarnational existence of God's Son; the last three confine the clause to the earthly existence of Jesus. I caution the reader that, while most commentators indicate which interpretation of *archē* they prefer for the verse under study, often they are not so precise about alternatives as I am here; and so it is with possible inexactness that I align names under one interpretation or another. Moreover, some authors (e.g., Bultmann) seem to support two different meanings of *archē* in their discussion of v. 1a.

(A) Belser, Bonsirven, Brooke, Chaine, de Ambroggi, de Jonge, Gaugler, Michl, Plummer, Schneider, Thüsing, Westcott, and Wilder are among those who relate the meaning of "from the beginning" in 1a to the phrase "In the beginning" of Gen 1:1 and/or John 1:1. (I say "and/or" for not all who make this connection clearly acknowledge the difference between Gen 1:1 in which creation is the beginning, and John 1:1 where the Genesis phrase has been reinterpreted to refer to a beginning before creation.) This interpretation of *archē* in I John 1:1a as a precreational beginning destroys the parallelism of "what was from the beginning" with the "what" clauses of seeing, hearing, and feeling that follow in 1b–e and that have to refer to the incarnate existence of Jesus. However, one can argue that even as the GJohn Prologue moves from preincarnation to incarnation (1:1 to 1:14), so the clauses in I John 1:1 must be understood sequentially. Not so easily dismissed is another objection that I John speaks of *"from* the beginning," which is quite different from the precreational "in the beginning" of the GJohn Prologue. (Arians would have been quite delighted with "From the beginning was the Word.") Although in Hab 1:12 and Sir 24:9 the LXX uses this "from" phrase for a precreational beginning, in none of the other 9 instances in I and II John does it have that meaning; see NOTES on the individual passages below (I John 2:7,13,14,24; 3:8,11; II John 5,6), and de la Potterie, "Commencement" 396–402.

(B) We read in John 8:44, "The devil . . . was a murderer from the beginning"; and there *archē* means the beginning of OT salvation history, whether the author is referring to Gen 2:17; 3:4,19 where the snake's lie brought death, or to the Cain and Abel story in Gen 4:8–9 (ABJ 29, 358). Clearly the latter is in mind in I John 3:8, "From the beginning the devil is the one who sins," since we find four verses later (3:12): "Not like Cain who belonged to the Evil One and killed his brother." However, only from such a specific context can one know that *archē* means the beginning of salvation history, and that context is not supplied here or for the other epistolary instances of "from the beginning." I see no reason to invoke this interpretation for the *archē* of v. 1a.

(C) Jesus himself can be identified as the *archē*, as we see in Rev 22:13 where Jesus (see 22:16) says, "I am the Alpha and the Omega, the first and the last, *the beginning* and the end." Since Rev 3:14 refers to him as "the Amen . . . the beginning of God's creation," there is no doubt that such a title covers the period before the earthly career of God's Son. Some would translate John 8:25 as "[I am] the beginning who speak to you" (but see ABJ 29, 347–48). Nevertheless, such a meaning of *archē* is never clearly encountered in the phrase "from the beginning," even though some argue for its equivalent in "him from the beginning" (I John 2:13–14).

(D) The real alternative to the preceding three interpretations of *archē*, all of which relate the beginning to the preincarnational career of God's Son, is that "the beginning" is related to Jesus' earthly career. The first possibility in this vein is to understand "from the beginning" as a reference to the *incarnation* of Jesus (Bultmann [?], Schnackenburg), generally understood to have taken place at his conception. However, there is no proof that *archē* ever refers to the conception of Jesus in the Johannine writings or elsewhere in the NT. (In contexts that would have allowed such a usage, Matt 1:18 uses *genesis*, "origin," and Heb 10:7 uses *kephalē*, "head.") Nor does GJohn show the slightest interest in the conception or even in the pre-ministry earthly career of Jesus (pp. 76–78).

(E) A well-attested NT use of *archē* is for the beginning of Jesus' ministry in terms of his *baptism* (Mark 1:1; the verb *archein* in Luke 3:23; Acts 1:22) or of his *early association with his disciples* (Luke 1:2; John 2:11; perhaps John 8:25; the verb *archein* in Acts 1:1). "From first association" is the meaning of the phrase "from the beginning" in John 6:64; 15:27; 16:4. In four epistolary instances (I John 2:7; 3:11; II John 5,6) the love commandment given by Jesus (at the Last Supper in John 13:34; 15:12,17) is referred to as a commandment that has been had or heard "from the beginning"; and so in these passages the "beginning" may very appropriately refer to Jesus' dealings with his disciples during the ministry. (True, in I John 2:7; 3:11; and II John 6 the commandment is what *you* [the readers] had [or heard] from the beginning, while II John 5 speaks of "a commandment *we* have had from the beginning"; but the readers are in continuity with the eyewitness tradition.) This is also a possible meaning of *archē* in I John 2:24, "What you heard from the beginning must abide in you." With difficulty it could also be the meaning in the twice repeated description of "him from the beginning" (I John 2:13,14) if the author is stressing that the earthly ministry of Jesus was an essential component of his being the Christ. There is only one epistolary text (I John 3:8, discussed under B above) where this meaning is not possible, whereas in the other epistolary texts it is the most fitting meaning. Balz, Bultmann, de la Potterie, Houlden, Tobac, and Wendt argue for this meaning in I John 1:1a.

(F) Another well-attested usage involves the *beginning of the Christian preaching* when those who had never seen Jesus first heard the Christian gospel. For instance, Acts 11:15 refers to the coming of the Spirit in Pentecost as "the beginning" (*archein*), while Luke 24:47 uses the same verb related to *archē* for "the beginning" of the preaching in Jerusalem. (In reference to I John 1:1a, Williams, *Letters* 17, speaks of "the earliest stage of the Christian church," but seems to mean by that the first contact of Jesus with his disciples, which would come under E above!) Presumably this use of "beginning" could be extended to the moment when the Johannine audience first heard the preaching or were baptized. In my judgment this is a *possible* meaning for seven of the epistolary uses of "from the beginning" (I John 2:7,24 [bis]; 3:11; II John 5,6). Nevertheless, such a meaning presents some awkwardness in 1:1a if we remember that the clause under discussion is the object of a proclamation (in 1:3b); for there is tautology in "We proclaim to you what was from the beginning (of our proclamation)." It may be wise to recognize that this meaning of *archē* does not stand independently of the meaning in E above.

As de la Potterie, "Commencement" 382, shrewdly observes, "The 'beginning' of the Christian mission is like a taking up again and actualization of the 'beginning' of the mission of Jesus."

Overall, if one judges from the various Johannine uses of *archē* and from the comparative structure of the "what" clauses in I John 1:1, the most plausible meaning is E above, so that "What was from the beginning" means the person, words, and deeds of Jesus as this complexus reflects his self-revelation (which is also the revelation of his Father) to his disciples after his baptism. Of course, the author assumes that a transcendent reality is involved (e.g., in 1:2 he speaks of "this eternal life which was in the Father's presence"); but he is concerned with the revelation of that reality during Jesus' public ministry. The following "what" clauses in 1b–e specify aspects of this.

1b. *we.* In lines 1b–e there are three verbs in the first person plural and two instances of the first person plural pronoun. This striking "we" motif continues in vv. 2–4 (7 verbs, 4 pronouns), and throughout I John a first person plural appears in 51 of 105 verses. (The first person singular is relatively rare [2:1,7,8,12–14,21,26; 5:13,16] and in all but one instance [5:16] is confined to the verb "write"—see Harnack, "Das Wir" 99–100.) Who are the "we"? Are they always the same group? Once again there are many scholarly answers, which may be divided, first, as to whether the "we" is a genuine plural or not.

(A) The "we" is *not a genuine plural* but is equivalent to "I," so that it designates the author (Chaine, Harnack, Michl; see IBNTG 119). This general view may be subdivided. **(1)** It is a plural of majesty or authority, so that the writer speaks as an authoritative figure in the early church or the Johannine Community (Harnack, "Das Wir" 104; compare the "I" of III John 9,10 with the "we" of III John 12). This interpretation is often championed by those who think the author was John, son of Zebedee, a member of the Twelve and an apostle. **(2)** It is an editorial "we." This differs from the plural of majesty in that it assumes no special status for the author but is simply a writing convention. Notice the "we are writing" of I John 1:4; the "we are talking about what we know" of John 3:11 when Jesus alone is speaking; and the "we know" of John 9:31 when the former blind man is speaking. But these are dubious examples of an editorial "we," for the person may be speaking on behalf of the larger Johannine Community or School. Since the epistolary author is perfectly capable of writing as "I" when he refers to himself (17 times in I, II, and III John versus 1 instance of "we write"), there is little reason to assume that either a plural of majesty or an editorial "we" was meant in 1:1.

(B) The "we" is a *genuine plural* involving more than one person. Here we may subdivide the interpretations according to whether the "we" has a distinctive or nondistinctive sense, i.e., whether the "we" think of themselves as distinct from another group or not. **(1)** In a *nondistinctive* interpretation the "we" represents the author and his associates but does not call attention to a group (a "you" or a "they") that is not included. Who then might be the author and his associates? The most frequent suggestion under the nondistinctive interpretation is that the "we" represents the writer and the readers. (This is the literary "we" of BDF 280, which is often hard to distinguish from the editorial "we" discussed above—cf. Heb 6:9 [editorial] and 6:1 [literary].) This would be equivalent to "we, the Johannine Community," as in John 1:14, "We have seen his glory" (footnote 218 above), in John 1:16, "We have all had a share," and in I John 4:13, "We abide in Him." *Aspects* of this interpretation are proposed by Dodd, Harnack, Wilder, and Williams. Other examples in the NT include Heb 1:2: "In these last days He has spoken to *us* by a Son"; and Luke 1:1: "The things that have been accomplished among *us*." Drawing upon these some would insist that the "we" of I John 1:1 goes beyond the Johannine Community to cover all Christians (*pluralis ecclesiasticus*), an interpretation that does not do justice to GJohn's exclusivity, which rejects very harshly some Christian groups (Crypto-Christians and Jews who believed in Jesus inadequately), and considers others as sheep who "do not belong to this fold" (10:16—see my *Community* 71–88). The same reasoning causes me to reject even more sharply the idea that the "we" joins the author and the whole of humanity. The dualistic Johannine mentality (visible in John 8:44 and I John 3:10) that treats unbelievers as children of the devil, whether they be "Jews" or former members of the Community, militates against such a wide-ranging inclusion. In summation, the only nondistinctive "we" that has any plausibility in I John 1:1–4 involves the whole Johannine Community, and even that interpretation faces serious difficulties from the mention of a distinct "you" in 1:3: "What we have seen and heard we proclaim in turn to *you*." Of course, one may argue that the "we" is nondistinctive in 1:1 and distinctive in 1:3 (a similar change can be posited for 4:12–13 and 4:14), but the fact that 1:3ab is a summary of 1:1 and uses some of the same verbs makes that unlikely.

(2) In a *distinctive* interpretation the author uses "we" as a genuine plural referring to a group that is distinct from the audience or the readers (the "you"). What group? One possibility is that they are the *eyewitnesses* of Jesus' lifetime who heard, saw, looked at, and felt him, and of which the author was one. (Many speak of this as a *pluralis apostolicus*, an unfortunate designation since the Johannine writings avoid the term "apostle"; moreover, the description reflects the theory that the author was John the apostle. In ABJ I myself was not always careful to avoid using the non-Johannine "apostle" and "apostolic" to describe the eyewitnesses of Jesus' ministry and the possible source of the Johannine tradition.) The eyewitness interpretation receives some support from John 20:29–31, which makes a clear distinction between eyewitnesses and non-eyewitnesses in the Johannine Community. The Beloved Disciple was the Johannine eyewitness *par excellence* (John 19:35; 21:24), and by the "we" he might be speaking on behalf of his confreres. Among the scholars who favor a form of this are Baumgarten, Belser, Bonsirven, Brooke, Büchsel, Camerlynck, Chaine, de Ambroggi, Gaugler, Häring, Holtzmann, Lee, Lohmeyer, Loisy (a fictitious pretense), Marshall, Schneider, Stott, Vrede, and Westcott. Plummer, *Epistles* 14, speaks of the author as "the last survivor of those who had heard and seen the Lord"; and in ABJ 29, xcix, there are samples of many ancient statements associating John with other disciples in the

composition of GJohn. However, in ABJ 29, xcviii–cii, I argued that the Beloved Disciple, an eyewitness of Jesus' ministry, was *not* the writer of GJohn; and above (INTRODUCTION V C2b–c) I argued that the epistolary author does not have the authority of the Beloved Disciple and was probably not an eyewitness of Jesus' ministry. Therefore, I do not accept the contention that the "we" of I John 1:1–4 designates a group of eyewitnesses.

A second possibility under the distinctive interpretation of the "we" is that it represents *the Johannine School* as I defined it on pp. 95–96: "The tradition-bearers and interpreters who stand in a special relationship to the Beloved Disciple in their attempt to preserve his witness." Most of them, including the epistolary writer, would not have been eyewitnesses of Jesus' ministry themselves, but rather the companions and disciples of the Beloved Disciple, who is their *primus inter pares* (Langbrandtner). In GJohn, in relation to (eyewitness) testimony, there is an occasional differentiating address to the readers as "you" (19:35; 20:31); and in the redactor's remarks in John 21:24 one finds in the same context a use of the "we" distinctively for the Johannine School: "It is this same disciple [whom Jesus loved] who is the witness for these things; . . . and his testimony, *we* know, is true." Such an interpretation of the "we" of I John 1:1–4 is suggested by Balz, F.-M. Braun, Bultmann, de Jonge, Dibelius, Haenchen, Harnack, Käsemann, Norden, and Windisch. See the brief debate between Lee, "I John 1, 1–3," and Guy, "I John 1, 1–3," for and against the "we" as eyewitnesses.

A standard objection to the "we" of 1:1 referring to a School of tradition-bearers rather than to eyewitnesses is the claim in 1e, "we felt with our own hands." Could non-eyewitnesses make such a claim? However, secular and religious literature offer many examples of verbs of sensation used by people who participated in the sensation only vicariously. Tacitus, *Agricola* 45, identified himself with a "we" of which he was not historically a part: "It was our hands which dragged Helvidius to the dungeon." In the NT, if one agrees with most scholars that II Peter is pseudonymous, it becomes noteworthy how the writer associates himself with Peter in the transfiguration, "We heard this voice coming from heaven when we were with him [Jesus] on the holy mountain" (1:18). The tendency of Christian authors to join their audiences to the NT witness is visible in Polycarp who writes many years after Paul's death (*Philip.* 9:1): "You also saw before your eyes . . . in Paul himself and the other disciples." Irenaeus (*Adv. haer.* 5.1.1) says of himself and of the Christians of his persuasion, "We could have learned in no other way than by seeing our Teacher, and hearing his voice with our own ears." Gregory Nazianzen (*Oration* 39.14; PG 36, 349C), even later in time, does the same thing: "We ran with the star, and we adored with the magi." Such association with the original participants reflects a covenant mentality where what happened at the origins of a community is a participated reality for the present generation, e.g., Amos (2:10) relays the word of the Lord to the Israelites of his time, "I brought you up out of the land of Egypt and led you forty years into the wilderness." As Bacon, *Hellenists* 57, observes, "So strong . . . is this feeling of solidarity with the past that in it the lines of demarcation between one era and the next are obscured."

The use of "we" referring to the Johannine School in the emphatic sensory expressions of I John 1:1 probably goes beyond a covenant identification with the first generation. It helps to authenticate the interpretation of the Johannine tradition that will be presented in I John. The writer will speak as part of a chain of tradition-bearers, and that is why he can tell his readers about "the gospel that we have heard from Christ" (1:5), "the gospel that you heard from the beginning" (3:11). The adversaries may be claiming an authentication by the Spirit for their interpretation of the tradition (4:1–6), but the same Paraclete-Spirit that enabled the Beloved Disciple to bear witness to what he had heard, seen, looked at, and felt is at work in the writer of I John (and his fellow disciples of the Beloved Disciple). Having "communion [koinōnia] with us" is one of the ways of testing the claim to the Spirit (1:3; 4:1,6). The writer of the GJohn Prologue spoke as part of a "we" (John 1:14); the I John Prologue is offered as the correct interpretation of the GJohn Prologue, and the epistolary author lays claim to that by also using "we." (See COMMENT.)

"We" will be used elsewhere in I John, but most often as the indistinctive plural for the author and his readers—the Johannine Community, in the sense discussed in B1 above. Are there any other uses of the distinctive "we" for the Johannine School, distinct from the "you" of the readers, besides those in 1:1–4? See the discussions in the NOTES on 1:5b; 2:25; 4:6a; 4:14a; 4:16a; III John 9b; 12c.

have heard. This is the first of four verbs of sensory action that govern the "what" pronouns in lines 1b through 1e: "heard," "seen," "looked at," "felt." It is implausible that in these verbs the author intended a salvation-history sequence beginning with precreation in 1a ("what *was* from the beginning") and moving through hearing (Law and the Prophets), seeing (ministry of Jesus), and feeling (postresurrection—John 20:25–26). Rather, the sequence and arrangement is stylistic. The first element of style may lie in the number of sensory verbs, for Drumwright, "Problem Passages" 54, contends that four was the number for rhetorical completeness among the Greeks. The second element of style is the alternation between simple verb and verb-plus-part-of-the-body: heard, seen with *our eyes,* looked at, *our hands* felt. The third element is the alternation of tenses: two perf. tenses followed by two aorist tenses (p. 152 above). Although scholars like Bonsirven, Brooke, Chaine, de Ambroggi, Plummer, Stott, Westcott, and Wilder see theological significance in the change of tense (aorist = the once-for-all character of Jesus), or emotional significance (aorist = the more concrete), it is more likely in my judgment that Bultmann, de Jonge, Marshall, and Schnackenburg are right in contending that the tense alternation is purely artistic and without the slightest significance. Louw, "Verbal Aspect," argues that overall there is no distinction between aorist and perf.; both cover a perfected past; see also BDF 343; MGNTG 1, 142–43; and the interchangeable aorist and perf. of *didonai,* "to give," in John 17:6–7, and of *apostellein,* "to send," in I John 4:9,10,14.

The verb *akouein,* "to hear," is used in GJohn indifferently in the aorist and the perf. for "ear-witness," e.g., 1:37 and 4:42 respectively. If in I John 1:1bc the perf. of *akouein* is combined with the perf. of *horan* in parallel lines, in John 3:32 the perf. of *horan* is followed by the aorist of *akouein;* and there is no discernible difference of meaning in the two passages. I have opted for the position that "what was from the beginning" in v. 1a and "what we have heard" in v. 1b are not in chronological sequence (preincarnation, incarnate ministry) but both refer to the ministry of Jesus—notice the combination "heard from the beginning" that occurs in I John 2:24; 3:11; II John 6; see I John 2:7. A comparison of I John 3:11, "the gospel that you heard [aorist] from the beginning," and 1:5, "the gospel that we have heard [perf.] from him [Christ]," shows both interchangeability of tenses and the identity of "the beginning" with the earthly career of Jesus.

1cd. *we have seen with our own eyes . . . we looked at.* The first verb of sight is the perf. tense of *horan;* the second is the aorist of *theasthai*—the two most frequently employed verbs (along with *idein*) for seeing in I John. That they have very distinct meanings is claimed by Bonsirven, Brooke, Chaine, de Ambroggi, Plummer, Stott, and Westcott, among others. In ABJ 29, 501–3, I discussed five different verbs of sight used in the Johannine writings, namely (with the respective GJohn and epistolary frequencies in parentheses) *blepein* (17 and 1), *theasthai* (6 and 3), *theōrein* (24 and 1), *idein* or *eidon* (36 and 3), and *horan* (31 and 8). I explained the subtle shades of meaning that some scholars would detect among them, but my own conclusion was: "There certainly are different types of sight in John. At most there may be a tendency to use one verb rather than another for a specific form of sight, but the consistency is not remarkable. Those scholars who think that the verbs are synonymous have almost as many texts to prove their point as do the scholars who would attribute specific meanings to the verbs." Tarelli, "Johannine Synonyms" 176, has argued plausibly that the Johannine diversity represents not a difference of meaning in the verbs but a preference for using one verb in one tense and another verb in another tense. For example, the Johannine writers never use *blepein, idein,* or *theōrein* in the perf. tense; and so if the epistolary author wanted a perf. tense in a verb "to see" to match the perf. of *akouein,* "to hear," it is not surprising that he chose *horan,* which in Johannine usage in the finite tenses is always future or perf. As for v. 1d and the second verb *theasthai,* the special meanings that scholars propose for it include: deliberate and perhaps pleasureful sight (Plummer); seeing with joy and admiration (Chaine); careful and deliberate vision that interprets its object (Brooke). It is not apparent how these meanings or even that of contemplation (which is most frequently proposed) would be appropriate, since in 1d the author seems interested in stressing physical sight. Freed, "Variations" 189, 195, has effectively challenged the whole special-meaning approach by pointing to passages identical in meaning where *theasthai* alternates with another verb, e.g., "No one has ever seen [*theasthai*] God" (1 John 4:12), compared with "No one has ever seen [*horan*] God" (John 1:18). What probably dictated the choice of the verb "to see" in v. 1d was the tense: Having used two perf. tenses in 1b and 1c, the author turned to two aorist tenses in 1d and 1e; and in Johannine usage the verbs of seeing usable in the finite aorist tense are *idein* and *theasthai.* Since the GJohn Prologue used the aorist of *theasthai* in 1:14 ("We have seen his glory"), imitation of that rather than shade of meaning is what dictated the choice in the I John Prologue.

1e. *felt with our own hands*. Literally, "our hands felt." The original meaning of *psēlaphan* was "to grope, feel after," as in the LXX of Gen 27:12 in the story of the blind Isaac feeling Esau and Jacob. The element of search often disappears, however, as it does here. Not very common in the NT, *psēlaphan* does appear in some passages where the realism of feeling touches upon the supernatural, e.g., in Luke 24:39 the risen Jesus challenges the disciples, "Feel me and see"; and in Heb 12:18 the mountain in the Sinai theophany is described as one "that may be felt." In a desire to show that the "we" of I John 1:1 does not refer to eyewitnesses, a few authors (including Harnack) have suggested that all four sensory verbs may refer to spiritual experiences rather than to historical ones; and to demonstrate that even "feel" may be spiritual they point to Acts 17:27, which speaks of feeling after God. However, the parallelism between "seen with our own eyes" in 1c and "felt with our own hands" in 1e makes a spiritualized interpretation farfetched. Clearly the author is claiming participation in a physical contact with Jesus. (As stated above, that need not mean he was an eyewitness; as a member of the Johannine School he would have had vicarious participation in the contact of the Beloved Disciple with Jesus.) Since Luke 24:39 uses *psēlaphan* of the risen Jesus, some would find here a reference to the Thomas scene in John 20:27; and Plummer, *Epistles* 15, suggests that the preceding verb, *theasthai*, may refer to a vision of the risen Jesus. This is unlikely, for neither *theasthai* nor *psēlaphan* is used in the postresurrectional scene in John 20, and there is no evidence that the epistolary author and his adversaries were quarreling over the reality of the risen Jesus. The "heard," "seen," "looked at," and "felt" of 1:1 are meant to underline the importance of witness to the realities of Jesus' preresurrectional ministry.

1f. *our concern is about the word of life*. Literally, "about [*peri*] the word of life"—my paraphrase is an attempt to smooth out the grammatical relationship between this prepositional phrase and the four substantive ("what") clauses that precede it. Some translations make them totally parallel as equal objects of the verb in 3b: "Our proclamation is of what existed from the beginning, of what we heard, of what we have seen . . . of what we looked at and felt . . . namely, of the word of life" (see Moffatt, Goodspeed, TCNT). However, the author would have been capable of saying that more grammatically as we see from 2:7, which deals with the "what" and the "about what" of writing: "I write to you . . . an old commandment which you have had from the beginning; this old commandment is the word which you already heard." Only slightly less violence is done to the Greek of v. 1f when the "about" phrase is made the objective complement of the verbs in the "what" clauses of v. 1b–e, as in Weymouth's translation: "What we once beheld and our hands handled concerning the Word of Life." Surely Bonsirven, *Epîtres* 67, is correct when he objects that, while one may *hear* about the word of life, it is more difficult to *see* about the word of life, and quite impossible to *feel* with one's hands about the word of life. I judge it more likely that the prepositional phrase is an ungrammatical interruption (indicated in my translation by a dash) introduced for clarification and is not the object of any verb, whether in 1:3b or 1:1b–e. This is all the more likely since a similar ungrammatical clarification interrupts the GJohn Prologue in 1:12c ("that is, those who believe in his name"). So understood, the phrase is resumptive and analytic of the "what" statements that precede it, as the author stops to reflect that he is really talking about the life-giving word.

This leads us to a discussion of the meaning of *logos*, "word," in the I John Prologue. (A) Many translators and commentators capitalize "Word" and contend that it has the same implication as *logos* in the GJohn Prologue, which describes a personal, precreation Word who was with God—thus many Church Fathers, Balz, Boismard, F.-M. Braun, Bultmann, Coetzee, de Ambroggi, Hauck, Michl, Moffatt, Plummer, Schnackenburg, Schneider, THLJ, Thüsing, Vrede; also KJV, JB, TEV. In a brief debate Weir, "Identity," advances arguments for the personal interpretation of *logos*, while Grayston, "Logos," refutes him on every point. Certainly, if one knew nothing of the GJohn Prologue, one would never take *logos* personally in the I John Prologue. No personal action is attributed to it in the latter, and the six other epistolary instances of *logos* (I John 1:10; 2:5,7,14; 3:18; III John 10) do not involve personification. And if one argues that the GJohn Prologue cannot be thus ignored (and that is true), one cannot simply assume that the epistolary author would necessarily want to use *logos* in the same way in which it is used in the GJohn Prologue. Indeed, he may be attempting to shift the emphasis to confute adversaries who are drawing their theology from a one-sided interpretation of the GJohn Prologue; and so without denying that Jesus embodied the preexistent Word of God, he may wish to remind his audience of the centrality of the proclamation of the gospel during Jesus' lifetime—the word proclaimed by the Word.

(B) Accordingly, other scholars hold for an impersonal meaning of *logos* as "word, message"—Barclay, Brooke, Bruce, Chapman, Dodd, Houlden, Johnston, Marshall (?), Stott, Tobac, and Wilder. In particular, Dodd, *Epistles* 3–5, and Tobac, "Christ-Logos" 233–34, are good exponents of this view; and in antiquity Tertullian at least opens up this possibility when in *De anima* 17.14 (CC 2, 806) he uses the translation *sermo vitae* (yet see *Adv. Praxean* 15; CC 2, 1179, for personification). In this interpretation, "the word" is equivalent to the "we proclaim" of v. 3b, so that the total career of Jesus (person, words, works), just as it was encountered in his ministry—the "what we have heard . . . seen . . . looked at . . . felt"—constitutes a word giving life to those who receive the proclamation. In a phrase such as "the word of life" there is as much stress on the second noun as on the first, and in what follows in v. 2 the theme of "life" and not the theme of "word" is developed. This already warns us that we cannot totally depend for guidance on the use of "word" in the GJohn Prologue where that is the main theme. The numerical use of *logos* in the Johannine writings overwhelmingly favors "message" (some 25 times), not a personified Word; and elsewhere in the NT the uses of "word" with genitival complement also support the message motif: "word of God" (John 10:35; Acts 6:7); "word of the kingdom" (Matt 13:19); "word of the cross" (I Cor 1:18). The I John expression, "word of life," occurs (without the def. article) in Philip 2:16 where it must refer to the gospel message; see also "gospel of life" in II Tim 1:1, and "words [*rēmata*] of eternal life" in John 6:68. That "word" as message need not be totally without personal reference (and therefore need not *contradict* the GJohn Prologue) may be seen from Heb 4:12: "The word of God is living and active, sharper than any two-edged sword, piercing to the division of soul and spirit . . . discerning the thoughts and intentions of the heart." Sometimes a counterargument claims that *peri*, "about," tends to govern persons in GJohn. That is true when the *peri* prepositional phrase is the object of *martyrein*, "to testify," or of *legein*, "to speak"; but otherwise there are instances of *peri* governing an impersonal object (John 3:25; 10:33; 15:22; 16:8; etc.). A final argument favoring the message motif is found in the fact that, when the author finishes the Prologue and moves on to the body of his work, he does so in terms of "the gospel [*angelia*] . . . that we declare to you"—the verb there in 1:5 is *anangellein*, related to the *apangellein* of 1:3b. An equation between *angelia* and *logos* in I John is supported by the parallelism in Col 1:5–6: "the word [*logos*] of the truth, the gospel [*euangelion*] which has come to you."

The second major problem in this line is the meaning of *zōē*, "life," suggested by its genitival relationship to *logos*. (For the theme of "life" in the Johannine tradition, see ABJ 29, 505–8; add to the bibliography there Coetzee, "Life.") There are three possibilities: (A) An epexegetical genitive (appositive: BDF 167): "about the word which is life"—thus Bonsirven, Chaine, de Ambroggi, Plummer. See this genitive in "the temple of his body" in John 2:21, and "the feast of Passover" in 13:1. This interpretation is sometimes favored by those who argue for a personified Word, since the GJohn Prologue (1:4) states: "That which had come to be in him was life." Bonsirven, *Epîtres* 76, contends that "the Word of Life" is Jesus' title, and indeed "Word of Life" is a title in the Mandaean literature. (B) A qualifying genitive, equivalent to the adjective "life-giving"—thus Brooke, Dodd, Michl, Thüsing, Tobac, Westcott. This type of genitive is found in the phrases "the bread of life" (John 6:35), "the light of life" (John 8:12), and "the water of life" (Rev 21:6). This understanding of the genitive is possible with both the personal and impersonal understandings of *logos;* and Thüsing, *Epistles* 9, virtually combines it with the epexegetical interpretation: "It is the 'Word' which can give life because it contains divine life within itself." If Bonsirven thought "Word of Life" could be a title for Jesus, Dodd, *Epistles* 5, thinks that it would not be a bad title for GJohn. (C) An objective genitive where "life" serves as the content of the message: "the word [revelation] about life"—thus Brooke, Stott, Westcott. This understanding is appropriate only if *logos* is understood impersonally. The chief argument for it is found in some of the *logos* ("word") phrases quoted in the preceding paragraph. They show that, when *logos* is followed by an impersonal genitive, that genitive ususally expresses the content of the message (Brooke, *Epistles* 5). Another argument is that a parallelism with 1:2cd, "we proclaim to you this eternal life," suggests that the "word" may be followed by an objective genitive. In judgment on these three meanings, perhaps we should avoid being too precise about the implications of the genitive: If the one case can express all three ideas, the author may never have thought out precisely what he meant by using the genitive. For instance, if *logos* means "message," the message that concerns life (objective genitive) may for that very reason be life-giving (qualitative genitive).

2a. *For this life was revealed.* Literally, "And the life . . ." The initial *kai,* "and," is typical Johannine Prologue style, and the article is used with demonstrative force referring to a previously mentioned noun (BDF 252[1]). In v. 2, then, we have a parenthetical explanation of "life" mentioned in the last phrase of 1:1, a phrase that, as we saw, was itself interruptive. If the GJohn Prologue featured the becoming flesh of the Word, the I John Prologue speaks of the revelation of life (*zōē*). Is it "life" rather than "word" that carries the personal thrust in this Prologue? Among those who argue for a personal rendering of *zōē* are Balz, de Ambroggi, Moffatt, Mussner, and Rivera. The insight is vividly caught by Stott, *Epistles* 68, when he says that "the word of life" is "the gospel of Christ." While in the GJohn Prologue *zōē* is not personal but something that comes to be and is communicated in the Word (1:14), later in John 11:25 and 14:6 Jesus says, "I am the life." In I John 5:20 Jesus will be identified as "the true God and eternal life"; in Rev 1:18 he says, "I am the living one"; and Ignatius, *Eph.* 7:2, calls Jesus "true life in death."

The possibility that *zōē* is personified in Jesus in I John 1:1–2 increases when we study the verb used in the passive here: *phaneroun,* "to reveal, manifest, show"; passive, "to be revealed, become visible, appear." Its span covers the making known of the unknown and the making visible of the invisible. (The related adverb, *phanerōs,* "openly," occurs in John 7:10 as opposed to "in secret.") Of the 18 Johannine uses of the verb (9 in GJohn, 9 in I John, out of a total of 49 NT uses), 11 are christological. *In GJohn's usage,* three times the risen Jesus is said to manifest himself to his disciples (21:1,14); the passive is used once for the revelation of Jesus to Israel at the beginning of the ministry (1:31), and once Jesus is challenged to manifest himself to the world by going to Jerusalem (7:4). The other four GJohn uses of *phaneroun* concern the manifestation of impersonal realities (glory, works, and the divine name). *In I John* the nonchristological uses involve the revelation of the love of God (4:9), of what we (believers) shall be (3:2), and of the secessionists as not belonging to the community (2:19). The one Johannine use of the related adjective *phaneros* occurs in I John 3:10 for the revelation of the children of God and of the devil. The clear christological uses of *phaneroun* in I John involve the parousia of Christ (2:28) and the manifestation of the Son of God in his earthly career to take away sins and destroy the works of the devil (3:5,8). The latter uses favor the thesis that the two revelation of life passages in I John 1:2 refer to the revelation of Jesus in his earthly career. If *zōē* is understood as personified, the first of these passages, "This life was revealed as we have seen and testify" (1:2ab), becomes a close parallel to the statement in the GJohn Prologue: "The Word became flesh . . . and we have seen his glory" (1:14). The second passage, "This eternal life which was in the Father's presence and was revealed to us" (I John 1:2def), echoes another GJohn Prologue statement: "The Word was in God's presence" (1:1). In the COMMENT I shall discuss why the author of the epistolary Prologue may have chosen to personify "life" rather than "word." It is difficult to know how far one should press the significance of the aorist tense of *phaneroun* in the affirmation, "This life was revealed." Some scholars (THLJ 25) think that the aorist reflects the historical character of the revelation which occurred at one specific time. An aorist appears in a similar statement, "He was revealed in the flesh" (I Tim 3:16), and an aorist participle in I Pet 1:20: "He was destined before the foundation of the world but was revealed at the end of time for your sake" (see also *Barn.* 14:5). Nevertheless, a perfect tense appears in Heb 9:26 which does not seem any less historical or punctiliar, "He has been revealed once for all at the end of the age to put away sin by the sacrifice of himself"; and we remind the reader again of Louw's contention ("Verbal Aspect") that there is really no distinction between aorist and perfect in representing the perfected past. We may note that these examples of *phaneroun* applied to Jesus' ministry by other NT writers reinforce the case for seeing a similar meaning in "This life was revealed."

2b. *as we have seen and testify.* Literally, "and we have . . ."; the first verb (*horan*) is in the perfect tense, the second (*martyrein*) is in the present. This same combination of tense and meaning occurs in I John 4:14: "We have seen [perf. *theasthai*] and testify"—note the interchangeability of *horan* and *theasthai* in these parallels, as discussed in 1:1cd. In lines 2b and 2c the movement from past to present connects the visible ministry of Jesus to the ongoing pastoral life of the Community, with the "we testify" intermediary between the "we have seen" of 2b and the "we proclaim" of 2c. Nevertheless, v. 2b illustrates once more the obscure grammar of the Prologue since here the verbs "to see" and "to testify" are used absolutely and without a clear object (either a *peri* ["about"] phrase or a dative; see ABJ 29, 152). The verbs may be related to line 2a (whence the "as" in my translation) or to lines 2cde ("and we proclaim . . ."). The choice really makes little difference in meaning; in both the action of the two verbs is related to the revelation of life. The verb *horan* was used in 1:1c, "What we have seen with our own eyes"—evidently the "what" of that line can be considered equivalent to the revelation of life in Jesus, which is the implicit object of the seeing in this line. This confirms my thesis that the "what" of 1:1 is a complexive term for the career of Jesus Christ on earth.

The verb *martyrein*, "to bear witness, testify," and the noun *martyria*, "witness, testimony," occur a total of 64 times in GJohn and the Epistles (verb 43 times; noun 21). The 33 uses of the verb in GJohn may be contrasted with a total of 2 uses in the three Synoptic Gospels, a contrast that indicates the extent to which the legal and trial atmosphere dominates Johannine thought (ABJ 29, 45,227–28).

2c. *and we proclaim to you.* The verb *apangellein* belongs to a family of verbs and nouns of which the most important for our purposes are:

- *angellein; angelia,* "announce; announcement." In the NT the verb occurs only in John 4:51?; 20:18; the noun only in I John 1:5; 3:11.
- *anangellein,* "report, announce." Of 13/14 NT uses, 5 are in GJohn (4:25; 5:15?; 16:13,14,15) and one is in I John 1:5.

▪ *apangellein*, "announce." Of 46 NT uses, one occurs in John 16:25, and two occur in I John (here and the next verse).

▪ *epangellesthai; epangelia*, "promise." Of 15 NT uses of the verb and 52 of the noun, there is one of each in I John 2:25.

▪ *euangelizein; euangelion*, "announce good news; gospel." Of 54 NT uses of the verb and 76 of the noun, none is in the Johannine writings.

The words in this family are often interchangeable in meaning, and clearly the Johannine writers have their preferences within the family. (It is very dubious, then, that one should press the *ap-* prefix of the verb used here as if the author wished to stress the origin ["from"] of his announcement.) These words express the public and beneficial character of the Christian message; and so it now becomes evident that the revealed life which has been seen and attested is "gospel, good news" for an audience, which is introduced for the first time in the "you," an audience that will be further specified as "My Little Children" in 2:1, and an audience that is distinct from the "we." In John 19:35 and 21:24, in reference to the Beloved Disciple, the theme of testifying is followed by a verb of dissemination ("tell," "write"), but the "announce" used here gives a clearer salvific tone to the dissemination.

2d. *this eternal life.* Of the 49 Johannine uses of *zōē*, "life" (one-third of the NT uses), 23 are characterized by the adjective *aiōnios*, "eternal" (17 in GJohn; 6 in I John). Indeed "life" is the only noun modified by that adjective in Johannine Greek (cf. Rev 14:6, "eternal gospel"). As I explained in ABJ 29, 507, for Johannine dualism eternal life is qualitatively different from natural life (*psychē*), for it is a life that death cannot destroy (John 11:26). Duration (everlasting, or even without beginning) is not the primary issue; it is a life from another eon (*aiōn*, whence *aiōnios*) or sphere. Indeed, it is the life of God Himself; and since only the Son has come down from that sphere and from God, he is the only one who can communicate that life. More simply, Jesus Christ is the eternal life (I John 5:20). The normal Johannine Greek is *zōē aiōnios* without any article, although John 17:3 has *hē aiōnios zōē*, and that expression is also found in I John 3:15; 5:11,13,20. Only here and in I John 2:25 does the full form with the two articles appear: *hē zōē hē aiōnios*. (In other expressions the double article is not unusual for Johannine Greek: I John 2:7,8; 4:9; II John 11,13.) Perhaps this lends a touch of solemnity and emphasis, but Plummer, *Epistles* 17, presses the distinction too far when he contends that the double article has the effect of presenting "life and eternity as two distinct ideas." With or without *aiōnios*, *zōē* for the Johannine writers is always eternal life.

2e. *which was in the Father's presence.* This is not the ordinary relative pronoun (*hos*) but the more def. relative *hostis*, "of the sort that," which can govern a relative clause expressing a specific quality. In the NT the masc. and fem. of *hostis* are virtually confined to the nominative case, being replaced by *hos* in other cases; and so the lines of distinction are blurred (BDF 64³, 293², a blurring contested by Brooke, *Epistles* 7). Nevertheless, in a parallel instance in GJohn (8:53; ABJ 29, 359) *hostis* is used with precision; and so it may be meant literally here where "life" is virtually personified, e.g., "such as it was in the Father's presence." The latter phrase is literally "toward [*pros*] the Father," a phrase I had to debate in discussing the GJohn Prologue (1:1b) where the Word was "toward God" (ABJ 29, 4–5). It may reflect Hebrew *lipnê*, "to the face of, before," which is often attitudinal and not simply spatial (see E. A. Speiser, *Genesis*, AB 1, 51). Although Greek *pros* can simply mean "with" (Mark 6:3; 9:19; 14:49; MGNTG 2, 467), here, besides presence with the Father, it has the added connotation of relationship toward the Father, for the Son's life came from the Father (John 6:57). In my judgment this is the first reference to preincarnational existence in the I John Prologue and explains the use of "eternal" in the preceding line. The same expression will be used in I John 2:1 to describe Jesus in the Father's presence as a Paraclete after his atoning death; and it will also be used of the Christian, the child of God, in the divine presence (3:21; 5:14).

Let us consider some significant statistics pertinent to the gospel use of *patēr*, "father," for God: Mark 5 times; Luke 17; Matthew 40; John 126. Some 23 times in GJohn Jesus speaks of God as "my Father," a usage that never occurs in Mark, and only 4 times in Luke. The other and more frequent use of the Johannine Jesus, occurring nearly 65 times, is to speak of God as "the Father," with an article but without the clarifying possessive pronoun—a usage that occurs 12 times in I John, and 3 times in II John, but only a total of 7 times in the three Synoptic Gospels (once in Mark [13:32]). See the discussion in Westcott, *Epistles* 27–34. The frequency of "the Father" in Johannine theology is explicable in terms of the very clear Johannine view of Jesus as "the Son" (ABJ 29, 408–9; 29A, 654–55). As Loisy, *Evangile-Epîtres* 533, points out, for John "God" is not simply a figure who acts paternally towards people; He is metaphysically the source of life, which the Son transmits to those who believe in him and who (alone) are God's children (John 1:12–13).

2f. *and was revealed to us.* This is the same aorist form of *phaneroun* that occurred in the first line of v. 2; there the subject was "life," while here it is "eternal life." The possible connotation of *hostis* discussed in the previous NOTE applies to this line as well. In 2c ("we proclaim to you") the "we" was clearly distinct from a "you"; and presumably the "us" here, like the "we" there, refers to the Johannine School of tradition-bearers, which was distinct from the rest of the Johannine Community. The whole Community shared in the revelation, of course, but the share came through the tradition-bearers and, in turn, through the Beloved Disciple. Such is the implication of "We proclaim in turn to you" (v. 3b below).

3a. *what we have seen and heard.* With this "what" clause the author returns to the train of thought he had been pursuing in 1a–e, before the interruptions of vv. 1f and 2 when he translated the "what" into "life." In fact, line 3a repeats the most characteristic verbs from v. 1, namely, the "what we have heard" of 1b and the "what we have seen" of 1c. How important is the fact that the author now switches the order of the two verbs? Westcott, *Epistles* 11, contends that "seen" came after "heard" in v. 1 because the author was leading up to incarnation; and "seen" comes first in 3a because the author is leading away from the incarnation—an interpretation that collapses if 1a refers to the incarnate Jesus (as I think it does). Brooke, *Epistles* 7, is cautious: "The difference in order, if it is not purely a matter of rhythm, may perhaps throw more emphasis on the earthly life of the Incarnate Logos, in which what was seen naturally takes precedence of what was heard." Bultmann, *Epistles* 8, says that the variation has no significance: "Nevertheless, one may say that 'we have heard' comes first in v. 1 because, with respect to revelation, 'the appropriate stance is above all hearing.'" The fact that Brooke and Bultmann have almost opposite interpretations of the order indicates that both should have followed their inclination to judge that the varied order has no significance, except perhaps as a chiasm meant to relate v. 3 to v. 1. A similar variation occurs in John 3:32 ("seen and heard") and 5:37 ("heard . . . seen"). The reason why "seen" comes first in 3a is purely stylistic: there was a reference to seeing in v. 2 (but not to hearing) which the author is resuming.

3b. *we proclaim in turn to you.* This is the main verb that governs all the substantive ("what") clauses in v. 1 (p. 153), as well as the clause in 3a. If 3a repeats 1bc, 3b repeats 2c with one change, namely, in 3b the better textual witnesses read a *kai*, "and, also," between "we proclaim" (*apangellein*) and "to you." It is missing in the Vulgate, important Coptic witnesses, a minor Syriac version, and in the Byzantine tradition; but its omission by scribes is explicable as an imitation of 2c, while its addition by scribes would be hard to explain. An implausible suggestion is that it means "also to you," i.e., after the proclamation had first been made to others who rejected it (to Gentiles after Jews). More likely it is an expression of sequence, moving from the tradition-bearers to those who received from them the testimony about Jesus. The reception of what the tradition-bearers saw and heard enabled the receivers to participate in the experience, e.g., "What *you* heard from the beginning" (2:24). The "you" are the "Those who have not seen and yet have believed" of John 20:29.

3c. *so that you may be joined in communion with us.* Literally, "have communion" (*koinōnian echein*), which may be stronger than the simple verb "be in communion" (*koinōnein*) used in II John 11. The noun *koinōnia*, which in the Johannine writings occurs only 4 times, all within the few verses of I John 1:3–7, is most important for appreciating the self-understanding of the early Christians, especially in the Pauline writings (which contain 13 of the 15 non-Johannine NT uses). Yet the word is difficult to translate, e.g., "communion, fellowship, partnership, community"; see J. Y. Campbell, "Koinōnia and its Cognates in the New Testament," JBL 51 (1932) 352–80; F. Hauck, *"koinos,"* TDNT 3, 789–809; S. Brown, "Koinonia as the Basis of New Testament Ecclesiology?" *One in Christ* 12 (1976) 157–67. It involves both the dynamic *esprit de corps* that brings people together and the togetherness that is produced by that spirit. (Campbell points out that the parties are in *koinōnia* because they have some reality *in common*). The equivalent of *koinōnia* in GJohn is the reference to being "one" in 17:11,21,22,23; and as I suggested in AB 29A, 776–77, both expressions, the epistolary "communion" (*koinōnia*) and the Gospel's "one" (*hen*), may be attempts to render into Greek a notion like the Hebrew *yaḥad*, "oneness, unity, community," which is the self-designation of the Qumran Community that produced the Dead Sea Scrolls. See also Boismard, "First Epistle" 160–61.

3d. *Yes, for the communion we have.* Literally, "and this communion of ours, indeed"—a *kai . . . de* construction in which one particle connects the clause to what precedes, while the other emphasizes the noun (see IBNTG 165). It occurs in John 6:51; 8:16,17; 15:27; and in III John 12. The possessive adjective form *hēmeteros*, "ours," used in classical Greek for emphasis, is rare in the NT (8 times, including here and I John 2:2); and its use both lends solemnity and helps to identify the kind of communion about which the author is speaking.

3de. *is with the Father and with His Son, Jesus Christ.* In Greek there is no copula "is," but simply a juxtaposition of two more *meta*, "with," phrases, continuing the *meta* phrase ("with us") of 3c. The Latin Vulgate mistakenly makes this a part of the preceding purpose clause: "and this communion of ours *may be* with the Father. . . ." However, normally a subjunctive copula would not have been omitted, and the *de* mentioned in the preceding NOTE indicates a shift from the subjunctive—the communion of the Johannine School with the Father and with Jesus already exists. The repetition of the preposition suggests that, although a *koinōnia* is spoken of, this communion does not produce a confusion of identities. In Johannine thought the Father has a certain priority, e.g., "The Father is greater than I" (John 14:28); "I have life because of the Father" (6:57). Nevertheless, the intermediary role of Jesus between the Father and the disciple (John 17:23: "I in them and you in me"; see 6:57) might have led us to expect Jesus to be mentioned first: "with Jesus Christ, the Son, and with the Father." Perhaps the sequence used here reflects a set Johannine phrase and word order, e.g., "the one true God and Jesus Christ" (17:3).

This is the first instance in the Epistles of two key designations of Jesus, "Son" (*huios*) and "Christ" (*Christos*), which we must discuss in order. There are 79 instances of *huios* in the Johannine literature. Of the 55 in GJohn, some have no theological significance, referring to ordinary human relationship. In relation to God, however, only Jesus is called *huios*, never the Christian (see NOTE below on 2:1a for the use of "child, children"). Some 10 times in GJohn Jesus is described as "the Son of God" or "His Son," 4 of which are in his own words (3:18; 5:25; 10:36; 11:4[?]). Another 17 times GJohn uses simply "the Son," an absolute designation with the article. This peculiar usage, which is found in only two Synoptic sayings (Mark 13:32, and the "Johannine *logion*" of Matt 11:27 and Luke 10:22), may have parable origins (see ABJ 29, 218–19). Of the 22 uses of *huios* in I John and the 2 uses in II John, the form "the Son of God" ("His Son") occurs 17 times, and the absolute form, "the Son," 7 times, a frequency that is the opposite of what is found in GJohn. For the theology of the relations between Father and Son, see ABJ 29, 407–8, and 29A, 654–55; a key statement is John 10:30: "The Father and I are one."

De Jonge, "Use," has made a significant study of the term "Christ" in the Johannine Epistles where it occurs 11 times, as compared with 19 times in GJohn. *Christos* means "anointed" and is a Greek translation of the Aramaic or Hebrew word for Messiah (with John 1:41; 4:25 being the only NT instances of the transliterated Greek *Messias*). The use of the term as a title would have hailed Jesus as *"the* Messiah" or *"the* Christ." Eventually, however, the frequency of that designation led to *Christos* becoming part of the combined name "Jesus Christ," which happens twice in GJohn (1:17; 17:3—the latter on Jesus' own lips!) and 7 times in the Epistles. In 4 of these epistolary instances "Jesus Christ" is combined with the designation as God's Son (here; I John 3:23; 5:20; II John 3). As background for this development we may remember that "Messiah" was an appropriate designation for the OT king who was *anointed* with oil, and it became the designation *par excellence* for the awaited anointed king who would be empowered by God to establish a perfect kingdom for Israel, an anticipation that Christians thought was realized in Jesus. Similarly the OT king could be thought of as God's *son* or representative (II Sam 7:14; Ps 2:7), and so Jesus as the Messiah, or anointed king, could bear the same designation. In Christian usage, however, both "Messiah" and "Son" took on a coloration from the insight that in Jesus, God had made Himself present on this earth, and so they became titles expressive of Jesus' divinity. (In the Johannine Community divinity carried with it an understanding of preexistence.) Thus, GJohn can express its whole purpose in terms of these two interchangeable titles: "I have written these things to you so that you may believe that Jesus is the Christ, the Son of God" (ABJ 29A, 1059–61). I and II John will insist that the divine title "Christ" is inextricably tied to the human figure, Jesus (I John 4:2–3).

4a. *Indeed, we are writing this.* Literally, "these things." This line contains the second main verb in the Prologue, and it is conjunctive to the first, which occurred in 3b: "we proclaim in turn to you . . . and (so) we write." The "we" is expressed by the pronoun *hēmeis* emphatically placed at the end of the clause. In its place "to you" (*hymin*) is read by the corrector of Codex Alexandrinus, the Byzantine tradition, the Vulgate, the Syriac, and the main Coptic versions. However, this alternative is probably a scribal improvement to harmonize 4a with 3b (where there is a "to you") and to alleviate the awkwardness of the unusual placing of the "we." Accepting the "we" as original, one must face the same problem encountered in v. 1b above, namely, whether it is a genuine plural and, if so, whether it is distinctive from a "you." I argued in 1b that it referred to the Johannine School of tradition-bearers as distinguished from the total Johannine Community. (Hitherto it has been customary for Christians to think of a generation of eyewitnesses who bore witness by oral proclamation and of a second generation of non-eyewitnesses who wrote excerpts from the oral proclamation of the first. In the symbiosis of the Johannine School such lines of division are blurred, for the "we" both proclaim and write.) The strong case for such a plural meaning in v. 4a as well is not weakened by the fact that in all 17 other epistolary instances of the verb "write," the author speaks as "I." At the beginning of I John, by using the emphatic *hēmeis* the author indicates that here he does not wish to speak simply in his own name, as he normally does. Physically, he and he alone is going to write; but at the start he wants to make it clear that what he writes bears more than personal authorization—it is Community tradition from the Community tradition-bearers. For that reason it is probable that the "these things" which are the object of his writing refer to more than the contents of the four verses of the Prologue (*pace* Stott and others); the term refers to what follows as well. I John is bracketed in 1:4 and 5:13 by statements of purpose for the writing of "these things," one statement pointing ahead, the other pointing back.

4b. *so that our joy may be fulfilled.* Just as there was disagreement among the textual witnesses in 4a as to whether "we" or "to you" should be read, so also here there is disagreement as to whether the original reading is "our" (*hēmōn*: Vaticanus, Sinaiticus, some Old Latin, Vulgate, Sahidic) or "your" (*hymōn*: Alexandrinus, Byzantine tradition, other Old Latin, Clementine Vulgate, Bohairic, Sahidic—defended by J. H. Dobson, *Bible Translator* 22 [1971] 58–60). Thus there are three possible readings for v. 4: (1) "We are writing these things to you [*hymin*] so that *your* [*hymōn*] joy may be fulfilled"; (2) "We [*hēmeis*] are writing these things so that *your* [*hymōn*] joy may be fulfilled"; and (3) "We [*hēmeis*] are writing these things so that *our* [*hēmōn*] joy may be fulfilled." (A similar expression occurs in II John 12, and there the textual evidence is again divided between "your" and "our.") Of the three the last is the most difficult in its logic and would be the one that the scribes would be most likely to change. The first and second may represent scribal improvements under the influence of John 15:11: "I have said this to you . . . that *your* joy may be fulfilled"; also 16:24: "that your joy may be full." Accepting the "our" of the third reading as original, one must still determine the extent of the pronoun's application. Although Plummer (*Epistles* 21) and others think it may mean "your joy as well as ours" and something along that line may have been understood by the scribes who introduced "your" into the Greek text, I think it more probable that the "our" is no wider than the "we" (see THLJ 25), i.e., it is distinctive and refers to the Johannine School. The distinction between "we" and "you" is too clear in vv. 3 and 5, for the "our" suddenly to become indistinct in v. 4. The author writes as part of that School which will have its joy fulfilled in and through *koinōnia* with those members of the Johannine Community who accept this writing. Grammatically "our" does not mean "ours and yours," but there is an implicit reference to a "you" in the idea of *koinōnia*.

The term *chara*, "joy," occurs 9 times in GJohn and once each in the three Epistles. (The related verb *chairein*, "to rejoice," occurs 9 times in GJohn, 3 times in II John, once in III John.) Of the total 12 Johannine uses, half involve the passive of *plēroun* in the sense of joy being fulfilled. This imagery is applied to John the Baptist (John 3:29), to Jesus (17:13), to the disciples (15:11; 16:24), and to the writer (I John 1:4; II John 12). Of those 6 instances, 4 involve the perfect passive participle *peplērōmenos;* and 3 of them have that participle in a periphrastic construction which may be a Semitism (MGNTG 4, 137)—the "so that our/your joy may be fulfilled" of John 16:24; I John 1:4; and II John 12. It is noteworthy that in GJohn all instances of "joy" but one are in the Last Discourse (15:17; 16:20–24; 17:13), where it is a future possibility opened up for Jesus' followers by his victorious death and return. This possibility is realized in the postresurrectional appearance of Jesus in John 20:20 where we are told, "At the sight of the Lord the disciples rejoiced." Such evidence suggests that "joy," like "peace" (see 14:27; 20:21),

designates an eschatological benefit received on becoming a believer and entering the Johannine Community. The fulfillment of joy, then, would be the
growth and flowering of the gift received earlier—a growth achieved through
living in *koinōnia* with God, Christ, and other Johannine believers.

COMMENT[1]

As exemplified in GJohn and I John, it seems to be a uniquely Johannine
feature in the NT to begin major writings with a theological Prologue.[2]
However if, as I shall suggest, the I John Prologue is a deliberate reflection on the GJohn Prologue, the uniqueness belongs to GJohn. Certainly
the GJohn Prologue, which may plausibly be regarded as a hymn of the
Johannine Community (ABJ 29, 20–23), is more poetic, more intelligible, and has been better appreciated than the I John Prologue. The term
"hymn" has also been applied to the latter (by Windisch), even though it
is not formally poetic and there is no reason to think it existed as a composition separate from I John. More realistically but also optimistically
the term "overture" has been used for the I John Prologue (Williams).
An overture is usually very carefully constructed since it anticipates the
main themes of the work to follow; and by classical standards the I John
Prologue is not well organized and is lacking such themes as keeping the
commandment(s) and practicing brotherly love, which are major concerns of I John. We saw in the initial NOTE that the one long sentence
that constitutes the I John Prologue is a grammatical obstacle course, and
in discussing the individual verses I rejected the theses of those who
would find fine theological subtleties and progressions of thought in the
numerous shifts of tenses and word order in the Prologue.[3]

Nevertheless, the I John Prologue has had a significant function in the
history of winning for the Johannine corpus of writings their authority as
an eyewitness production. In the late second century, if I John showed

[1] As a reminder let me summarize my explanation in the PREFACE (p. xiii) about
the relationship between the COMMENT and the NOTES. Difficulties and disagreements about the Greek text of the Epistles and how it should be interpreted, and
detailed information about the meanings of terms are found in the NOTES. In the
COMMENT I settle on the one interpretation that I regard as most reasonable and
seek to read I John concisely and intelligibly in light of that interpretation. Those
who read only the COMMENT and who wonder for what reason I am taking a position should go back to the NOTES for information.

[2] The only NT rival as a Prologue might be Heb 1:1-4, but that is more closely
integrated to what follows than is either Johannine Prologue.

[3] I would disagree strongly with de Ambroggi, *Epistole* 222, who traces the con-
torted grammar to "the contemplative spirit" of the author. I find little in I John to
suggest a contemplative spirit and consider that a myth deserving to be laid to rest.

against gnostic abuse that GJohn could be read in an orthodox way, the "we have heard . . . seen with our own eyes . . . looked at and felt with our own hands" became the hallmark of apostolic authorship.[4] While not sharing that conclusion, I would contend that the "what" clauses of the Prologue, though awkward grammatically, have a rough eloquence and successfully hammer home the point that the Christian proclamation involves intrinsically the ministry of Jesus on this earth. Those clauses do not constitute a dispassionate theological presentation but are rather an urgent manifesto called forth by struggle. The crescendo of references to sensory experience in 1:1 reflects defiant exasperation provoked by opposition over the thrust of the Johannine Gospel. And so, while not an overture, the Prologue sets the tone for I John in terms of a polemically exclusive claim, namely, that the proclamation about Jesus made by the author represents the authentic Gospel stemming from a true witness to Jesus, and those who refuse to accept it have communion with neither Father nor Son.

Let me illustrate this analysis by discussing three topics: (A) the Flow of Ideas in the Prologue; (B) the Prologue's Relation to the GJohn Prologue; (C) the Rationale or "Why" of the Prologue.

A. Flow of Ideas

In the NOTES I reached these conclusions: The "we" of v. 1 represent the Johannine School, i.e., the tradition-bearers and interpreters of the larger Johannine Community who preserved a witness of auditory, visual, and manual contact with Jesus, probably stemming from the Beloved Disciple. The "what" in the string of noun clauses in v. 1 is comprehensive of Jesus' person, words, and deeds "from the beginning" of his self-revelation to his disciples after being pointed out by John the Baptist until his victory over death. The proclamation of Jesus' person and ministry is a message of life (1:1f), for in Jesus an eternal life that had existed in and with God was revealed on this earth (v. 2). Speaking as a representative of the "we," the author addresses this proclamation of Jesus' ministry, this word of life, to an audience of Johannine Christians whom he wishes to bind in communion (*koinōnia*) with him; for he and the other tradition-bearers already have communion with the Father and the Son through the revelation of life they have received (v. 3). Communion among the

---

[4] See INTRODUCTION V C2c. In *De anima* 17.14 (CC 2, 806) and in *Adv. Praxean* 15.5 (CC 2, 1179) Tertullian relates I John 1:1 to the eyewitness of the apostles and in particular to John. As I have stressed, "apostle" is a term foreign to the Johannine writings, and the author's share in the "we" need not mean that he himself was an eyewitness.

Johannine Christians (which, as we shall see, is threatened) constitutes the author's goal in writing and will fill out his joy (v. 4).

In the adjacent chart I sketch the flow of ideas in the Prologue that make those points. Here I am indebted to de Jonge's article on the structural analysis of the Prologue, which I have refined and attempted to improve.[5] In the chart I combine structural features (consistent use of third, first, and second persons in A, C, and D respectively; and consistent use of durative tenses, past tenses, and present tenses also in A, C, and D) with a regular thought pattern (divine reality revealed, encountered, and communicated in B, C, and D). This analysis shows that behind the Prologue's grammatically awkward long sentence there is a patterned flow of ideas that carries over into 1:5, the opening sentence of the author's proclamation. Moreover it helps to confirm some disputed interpretations that I have chosen. As I explained in a NOTE on 1:1a, there are six possible meanings of "from the beginning," and one of the prominent suggestions involves a precreational beginning as in the GJohn Prologue. However, "from the beginning" would then have to go into the A column of my chart,[6] leaving no entry in the B column for v. 1. The meaning I have preferred (for other reasons), namely, from the beginning of Jesus' self-revelation in the ministry, matches perfectly the B entry for the other verses. Another example is my rejection of the proposal that in v. 1f "the word of life" refers to the preexistent Word of the GJohn Prologue—if it does, it would have to go into the A column and awkwardly duplicate "For this life" at the beginning of the next line (2a). If it means the *message* about life or *proclamation* of life, as I argue for other reasons, it matches perfectly the D entry of the other lines.

Why does the author stress this particular flow of ideas? Before discussing the rationale, let us look more closely at the origins of the I John Prologue.

B. *Relation of the I John Prologue to the GJohn Prologue*

Many commentators observe that a Prologue is an extraordinary beginning for an epistle since it violates all the standards of letter format. (I do not have that problem since I do not think that in any way I John is an

---

[5] I do not find that every section of I John lends itself to such an analysis. (The fact that the Prologue is an imitation of the GJohn Prologue has influenced its structure to some extent.) There is structure, of course, in every section and I have utilized that more than most commentators (INTRODUCTION VI A); but elsewhere the structure is less meticulous and of a different type.

[6] "What was from the beginning" in v. 1a becomes parallel to "this eternal life which was in the Father's presence" in 2de.

PATTERN OF THOUGHT AND STRUCTURE IN THE PROLOGUE TO 1 JOHN 1:1-4 + 1:5

A	B	C	D	E
A divine reality (person or attribute) described in the 3rd person singular, sometimes with the verb "to be" in a durative tense (impf.; pres.).	An indication, explicit or implicit, how the reality of A was made known to the group in C.	A 1st person nominative plural group ("we") encountered in the past (aorist or perf. tense) the reality of A in a sensory way.	To a 2nd person dative group ("to you"), mentioned explicitly or implicitly, the group in C communicates (pres. tense) the reality in A.	The goal of the action in D in relating the group in D to the group in C.
1a. What was	from the beginning (of the self-revelation of Jesus to his disciples in the ministry)	1b-e. (what) we have heard, seen, looked at, felt	1f. our concern is about-the word of life (directed to you)	
2a. For this life	was revealed	2b. as we have seen	2bc. and we testify and we proclaim to you	
2de. this eternal life which was in the Father's presence	2f. and was revealed to us	3a. (what) we have seen and heard	3b. we proclaim in turn to you	3c-e. so that you may be joined in communion with us . . . with the Father and with His Son, Jesus Christ.
			4a. We are writing this (to you)	4b. so that our joy may be fulfilled
5d. "God is light"	5a. is the gospel	5b. that we have heard from him (Christ)	5c. and declare to you	

epistle—INTRODUCTION V C1.) But some think they can find epistolary features (see Appendix V) in the Prologue. Bultmann (*Epistles* 2), for instance, who does not think I John is a letter, argues that the Prologue lends a fictional epistolary character to the work. In "Redaktion" 189–90 he singles out these features. First, the normal Opening Formula or *praescriptio* of an ancient letter identifies the sender and the addressee, while the Prologue identifies a "we" writing to a "you."[7] However, every written work has an author and an audience, and something so vague as "we" and "you" tells us nothing about literary genre. Second, in v. 4b the Prologue mentions "joy" (*chara*) which Bultmann regards as a variant of the standard NT epistolary Greeting or *salutatio,* "grace" (*charis*). However, II John, which is a true letter, uses *charis* as a Greeting (v. 3), and so there is no reason to think that *chara* would have become the Johannine Greeting.[8] Another scholar, F. O. Francis ("Form"), speaks of epistolary features in the Prologue that have not been recognized, drawing upon Hellenistic letters that have no Opening Formula or *praescriptio* and thus might offer a better parallel for I John. In these letters Francis points to an initial anticipatory exposition of themes, sometimes repeated more expansively, and terminating with a line transitional to the Body of the letter. In the Prologue Francis finds the initial exposition in v. 1, the expanded repetition in vv. 2–3, and a transitional line in v. 4. However, one must ask whether an introduction to most written works would not begin with an anticipatory exposition of the themes to be treated and conclude with a transition to the main part of the work where those themes are treated. In other words, the features that Francis highlights are not in themselves precise enough to distinguish a work as a letter, and the better comparisons he makes are not particularly helpful because they are to works that have a clear epistolary *praescriptio,* which tells us we are dealing with a letter[9]—a feature signally lacking in 1 John.

Dismissing, then, the purported epistolary character of the Prologue (and of I John), I suggest that it is a reinterpretation of the GJohn Prologue, done in order to refute adversaries who are distorting the meaning of the GJohn Prologue. In that way the Prologue is an essential part of I John, written to refute the same adversaries who are distorting the meaning of the Johannine tradition as a whole. For the moment let us concen-

---

[7] Bultmann's case ("Redaktion" 190) depended in part on his reading I John 1:4 as "We are writing this to you [*hymin*]," a reading that he later correctly rejected (*Epistles* 13, n. 27) in favor of "We [*hēmeis*] are writing this." See NOTE on 1:4a.

[8] In fact, moreover, the use of "joy" in I John 1:4 is not as a greeting: "We are writing this so that our *joy* may be fulfilled."

[9] He cites a letter in Josephus, *Ant.* 11.5.1 ※※123–24, but there we find, "The king, therefore, wrote the following letter to the satraps: 'Xerxes, king of kings, to Ezra, priest . . . greetings.'" He compares I John to James, but the latter opens, "James . . . to the twelve tribes in the diaspora, greetings." Although Marshall, *Epistles* 100, offers no reasons, his abrupt dismissal of Francis's thesis as "not convincing" is accurate.

trate on the formal relationships of the two Johannine Prologues, leaving the reinterpretation aspect till the next subsection (C below). In terms of vocabulary the following similarities are noteworthy:[10]

	John 1:1–18		I John 1:1–4(5)
1a	In the beginning was the Word	1a	What was from the beginning
1b	The Word was in God's presence	2de	Eternal life which was in the Father's presence
4a	In him (the Word) was life	1f	The word of life
4b	This life was the light of men	5d	God is light
5ab	The light shines on in the darkness, for the darkness did not overcome it	5e	and in Him there is no darkness at all
14a	The Word became flesh	2a	This life was revealed
14b	and made his dwelling among us	2f	and was revealed to us
14c	and we looked at his glory	1d	what we looked at
16ab	Of his fullness we have all received	3de	The communion we have is with
17a	through Jesus Christ		the Father and with His Son,
18b	God the only Son		Jesus Christ

Each Prologue begins with the theme of a divine reality which was in or from the beginning; partway through the two Prologues (John 1:4; I John 1:1e) the theme of life appears; in each there are double interruptions that break the grammatical connections;[11] in each the theme of witness or testifying (*martyrein*) appears only in the parenthetical interruption; each Prologue deals with the visual reaction of a "we" to the divine reality's manifestation; and lastly each Prologue refers to a participation with God brought about by the manifestation of the divine reality. The passages in the GJohn Prologue that the I John Prologue most closely echoes are 1:1 and 1:14.[12]

Precisely because there is so much similarity between the two Prologues, the differences are all the more startling. It is hardly conceivable that the author who wrote the GJohn Prologue with its careful staircase parallelism (ABJ 29, 19) and clear line of thought would later write the more awkward I John Prologue. Loisy (*Evangile-Epîtres* 532) has observed caustically that the GJohn Prologue has already said much better what the I John Prologue repeats. Consequently, if the I John Prologue

[10] On the I John side of the parallelism I have included v. 5, which is transitional from the Prologue to the body of the work.

[11] They are John 1:6–9,15 (dealing with the Baptist) and John 1:12c–13; I John 1:1f and I John 1:2. The sets of interruption in the GJohn Prologue may have diverse origins, with John 1:12c–13 (and 1:17–18) being an explanatory expansion, and the other (1:6–9,15) representing transposed verses about the Baptist. Possibly I John is imitative of John here.

[12] John 1:14, "The Word became flesh . . . and we have looked at his glory . . . filled with enduring love," while constituting a major Gospel theme, is partially phrased in a vocabulary that does not recur in GJohn. Similarly the key phrase in the I John Prologue, "the word of life," does not recur in I John. *Koinōnia*, "communion," does recur but only in 1:6–7.

came later,[13] it should be attributed to another author. Was he someone who did not understand the GJohn Prologue? Was his purpose a crude attempt to gain eyewitness authority for his work? These frequently made suggestions fail to do justice to the flow of ideas in the I John Prologue as diagnosed in the chart. Let me now discuss a theory that makes the I John Prologue with its awkwardness and its careful flow of ideas intelligible.

C. *The Rationale of the Prologue*

In ABJ 29, 20–22 I suggested that the GJohn Prologue was originally a hymn widely known in the Johannine tradition and that it was prefaced to GJohn because it summarized well the main lines of Johannine christology. Above (INTRODUCTION IV) the thesis was proposed that I John is a response to a struggle with Johannine adversaries who, although they believed that a divine preexistent Word had become flesh, attributed little importance to what he had done in the flesh. In their incarnational soteriology the very coming or sending of the Son of God, not his life or ministry or death, was what brought salvation. For such adversaries the GJohn Prologue could have been a perfect expression of their christology and their gospel: It stressed the divine origins of the Word and how he brought life and light into the world, but it said nothing about his earthly career and his death.[14] It offered a new status as children of God to all those who recognized and accepted the Word come into the world.[15] The secessionist adversaries I have posited for I John might well have made their slogan John 1:1,14,16 (the very verses that are closest in wording to the I John Prologue): "In the beginning was the Word; the Word was in God's presence . . . and the Word became flesh and made his dwelling among us. And we have looked at his glory . . . and of his fullness we have all had a share."[16]

---

[13] In the INTRODUCTION II C2 and V C1d, the thesis was defended that I John was written after GJohn, and I see no reason to exempt the Prologues from this sequence (although I acknowledge that, as a hymn, the GJohn Prologue once traveled separately in the tradition from the rest of GJohn). I shall try to show how the awkwardness of the I John Prologue can be explained in this sequence.

[14] Contrast the emphasis on these features in the hymns in Philip 2:8–9; Col 1:18b; and Eph 1:20.

[15] Later gnostics would contend that through faith people did not become God's children but recognized that they were already God's children (see INTRODUCTION V D1).

[16] It is often thought that the GJohn Prologue was anti-docetic and that the secessionists who were docetists could not have accepted it. In the INTRODUCTION above (V D2b and IV B3b) I have denied all aspects of that claim. If later the secessionists of I John *became* docetists, they would have reinterpreted the "became flesh" of John 1:14 as "was manifest in the flesh" (footnote 252 above). Ptolemaeus and the Valentinian gnostics had no problem about interpreting in a gnostic manner the GJohn Prologue in general and 1:14 in particular (Irenaeus, *Adv. haer.* 1.8.5).

If such was the case, how could the epistolary author correct his adversaries' (mis)use of the GJohn Prologue? He could not reject or attack that Prologue because it was a prominent item of Johannine tradition and, as a Johannine Christian, he himself accepted its christology. But he could comment on the GJohn Prologue so as to show that one can understand it properly only if one takes into account the thrust of GJohn itself. Beginning in 1:19, GJohn is the story of Jesus' self-revelation in word and deed from the time of his encounter with John the Baptist until the hour of his glorification in passion, death, and resurrection. In this process of self-revelation during an earthly career, it becomes clear that Jesus is the preexistent Son of God who has come down from heaven. Logically the GJohn Prologue placed that incarnation first, but such a highlighting of the incarnation makes sense only if it is seen as a preface to the life and death of Jesus which it presupposes—that is why the Prologue hymn was *prefaced* to the gospel story which now follows it. The adversaries of I John have ignored the presuppositions and thrust of the gospel story and thus (in the epistolary author's judgment) have distorted the import of the GJohn Prologue. To demonstrate this he reshapes some of the well-known and significant phrases of the GJohn Prologue to write his own Prologue reminding the reader of the presuppositions of the gospel story. The awkwardness of the I John Prologue, then, stems from an attempt to give familiar wording a different emphasis. Well has Houlden (*Epistles* 48) remarked, "The incoherence of the opening of I John is symbolic of the bewildering and perplexing nature of the challenge." Let us now see this line by line.

The GJohn Prologue started with "the beginning"; the epistolary author reuses that expression in another meaning that is just as authentically Johannine.[17] He would say that GJohn is correct: In the beginning before creation there was a divine Word who ultimately became flesh. But he would add that the only way this can be known is from another beginning when the Son began to reveal himself to disciples who could hear him, see him with their own eyes, and touch him with their own hands.[18] It is said that in the procedure of Greek courts an action had to be verified by two senses—I John supplies a third. But even without that background, in v. 1 there is clearly a crescendo of verbs to give emphasis to the reality of Jesus' earthly career. The GJohn Prologue reacted to the incarnation in v. 14 with the claim, "We have looked at his glory"; the I John Prologue

[17] John 2:11; 6:64; 15:27; 16:4.

[18] We may suspect that the secessionist adversaries would not have appreciated I John's stress on seeing and hearing in a sensory manner. In the Hermetic literature, *Poimandres* 5.2 says that the unbegotten one has no sensible image; he is not seen through the eyes of the body but the eyes of the mind. In A. J. Festugière, *La Révélation d'Hermès Trismégiste* (EB; 4 vols.; Paris: Gabalda, 1944–54) 4, 61–62, God is described as "unable to be heard or seen by eyes," but only by the mind of those who remain a stranger to the corporeal.

stresses that the glory was of one who lived a life so real that it can further be claimed, "We looked at (him) and felt with our own hands." The GJohn Prologue spoke of the experience of a "we" who were the whole Johannine Community (see INTRODUCTION, footnote 218). The epistolary author could concede that the whole Community does share an eschatological existential encounter with the Word become flesh. But this is possible only because there was a group who encountered Jesus historically, and so he would maintain that the "we" of the GJohn Prologue presupposed and included them. To stress this he reuses the "we" to bring out the eyewitness roots of the Community experience,[19] and the "looking at" of the I John Prologue becomes more sensory than the "looking at" of John 1:14. He reinterprets the "Word" from the GJohn Prologue to mean the message preached during his ministry by Jesus and afterward by the (Paraclete-inspired) witness-bearers of the Johannine School. The secessionists may rhapsodize about a preexistent Word, but such a Word can be known only because on this earth Jesus spoke an audible "word." The secessionists may rhapsodize about a life that the preexistent Word brought to believers (John 1:4,12–13), but that is possible only because God's Son lived out on this earth a career which revealed him to be the embodiment of the eternal life that was in the Father's presence. In a parenthetical interruption in the GJohn Prologue (1:6–8) John the Baptist bears witness or testifies to a light that was coming into the world. In v. 2, a parenthetical interruption in the I John Prologue, the "we" bears witness or testifies to an eternal life that has been revealed in the world. It is noteworthy that the epistolary author does not repeat the Word "*was* in the world" (as in John 1:10), nor describe the Word as having *come* or having been *sent* (typical GJohn terms)—although true, those images would not do justice to what happened after the incarnation.[20] Rather, I John states twice that the life was *revealed* (to us), using the verb *phaneroun* that was first employed in GJohn for the beginning of the public ministry. The Baptist revealed Jesus to Israel (John 1:31) and Jesus revealed his glory through the miraculous sign he performed at Cana (2:11; see also 7:4; 9:3).

Having seen how I John reinterprets key terms from the GJohn Prologue, let us now turn back to the chart where I described the thought pattern of the epistolary Prologue. The pattern shows what the epistolary author wanted to emphasize positively in his Prologue, as he wrote for Johannine Christians endangered by the secessionists. In that chart note

---

[19] See the discussion of the Johannine School in the INTRODUCTION V C2c. The experience stressed in the I John Prologue, while rooted in sensory contact (probably by the Beloved Disciple), is not purely physical, for the contact involves belief.

[20] The Mandaean literature can speak of the *coming* of Jokabar, "the word of life," to pious people, e.g. *Ginza Right* 3.86.21 (Lidzbarski ed., p. 88, line 19), and in the liturgies *Qolasta* 22 (Lidzbarski ed., p. 35, lines 6–7).

how brief the A factor is.[21] While half the GJohn Prologue was taken up with a description of the divine reality in itself, that reality is simply mentioned as a subject in the I John Prologue. (GJohn represented struggles with "the Jews" who denied that such a divine reality was involved, while the secessionist adversaries of I John presuppose it.) Nor does the B element in the chart receive much exposition;[22] for, once again, the revelation of the divine reality is not denied by the secessionists. It is the C factor that receives the most attention (nearly one-third of the I John Prologue),[23] for that factor had a double polemic thrust against the secessionist position in its emphasis on the "we" of the Johannine School of witness-bearers and on sensory experience.[24] The GJohn Prologue mentioned a "we" only toward the end (John 1:14,16) and never distinguished the "we" (representing the whole Johannine Community) from a "you." This is because at the time of the writing of GJohn the Johannine Community was not divided but stood together against "the Jews" and against other believers in Jesus whose faith was inadequate. Below we shall see that the "you" in the I John Prologue (the D factor) represents the author's audience and followers as implicitly distinct from the secessionists (the "they" of I John 2:19). Is the epistolary Prologue's "we" (representing the author and his fellow tradition-bearers) implicitly distinct from a chain of tradition and eyewitness support claimed by the secessionists for their interpretations of the Johannine gospel?[25] Had a prominent tradition-bearer of the Johannine School gone astray and given rise to the secession? We do not know; but it is clear that, by speaking in the first person plural, the author is contending that the secessionists are opposing not only him but others who shaped the tradition and passed it down,[26] i.e., vicariously the very people to whom Jesus made revelation

[21] In my translation there are 19 lines in the I John Prologue: the A column contains 2 full lines and parts of 2 others.

[22] The B column contains 1 full line and parts of 2 others. Together A and B take up 5 lines or one-quarter of the Prologue.

[23] It occupies 5½ lines—more than A and B together.

[24] Segalla, "L'esperienza," points out that GJohn tends to express experience by "see," "hear," and "know." The absence of the verb "to know" is noteworthy in the I John Prologue. Is it because the secessionists in their incipiently gnostic tendencies were overstressing *gnōsis*, "knowledge"? See the claim "I know God" in I John 2:4.

[25] The secessionists were on the road to gnosticism. Because Irenaeus refuted gnostics by citing a chain of tradition represented by bishops, e.g., at Rome (*Adv. haer.* 3.3.2), it has been assumed that the gnostically inclined were not interested in a chain of tradition. However, the gnostic gospels and apocrypha were attributed to famous NT witnesses (John, James, Philip, Thomas, Mary Magdalene); and the second-century Valentinian gnostic, Ptolemaeus, spoke in his *Letter to Flora* of "the apostolic tradition which we also have received by succession, because we can prove all our statements from the teaching of the Savior" (Epiphanius, *Panarion* 33.7.9; PG 41, 568B). See also Perkins, *Gnostic Dialogue* 144.

[26] He could scarcely have done this if his readers would have thought that his claim to speak thus was ludicrous, whence my contention that he may well have

from the beginning of his ministry. I John's distinction in the Prologue between a "we" and a "you" is not totally foreign to GJohn;[27] for 20:29 distinguishes between those who have seen and those who have not seen but still have believed, while 17:6,20 distinguishes between those to whom Jesus directly revealed (*phaneroun*) himself and those who would believe in him on the word (*logos*) of the first group. Thus, even in the Johannine Community where the role of the Paraclete was dominant as the teacher of all things (14:26), there is place for a human chain of tradition-bearers. In ABJ 29A, 1140, I argued that almost everything said about the Paraclete in GJohn had earlier been said about Jesus, so that the Paraclete is to Jesus as Jesus is to the Father. The epistolary author has the same mentality, but he emphasizes the "we" instead of the Paraclete. In John 3:31–32 Jesus was described as the one who had come from heaven: "What he has seen and heard (there), that is what he testifies to." It is no accident that I John 1:2–3 describes the "we" in the same language: "We have seen and testify . . . what we have seen and heard, we proclaim in turn to you." The shift is intelligible if the secessionists were claiming that the Paraclete-Spirit authenticated their teaching (as we may suspect from the order in I John 4:1,6 to test the Spirits to distinguish "the Spirit of Truth," which is another name for the Paraclete in John 14:17; 15:26; and 16:13). The epistolary author refutes such a claim by pointing out the lack of secessionist agreement with the human witnesses through whom the Paraclete speaks, as indicated in John 15:26 where the witness of the Paraclete is set side by side with the instruction: "You too should bear witness because you have been with me *from the beginning*." All of that Johannine background lies behind the author's statement, "What was from the beginning . . . what we have seen and heard, we proclaim in turn to you."

Turning again to the chart dealing with the pattern of thought in the

---

been a disciple of the Beloved Disciple. The thesis that he was *deceptively* claiming to be either the Beloved Disciple or the evangelist is implausible, for the use of "we" to express such a claim would be too subtle. There was no lack of Johannine precedent for mentioning the Beloved Disciple if the epistolary author wanted to assume his identity. Or if the author was deceptively pretending to be the evangelist, he had merely to refer to "what I previously wrote in the book of the signs which Jesus performed in the presence of his disciples," imitating John 20:30. Much more likely is the contention that the author followed a Johannine usage exemplified in 21:24 which distinguished the "we" from the Beloved Disciple and the Gospel composer, while at the same time associating the distinct parties—the Johannine School, in short.

[27] The distinction is not dominant, for the disciples in GJohn, especially at the Last Supper, can be surrogates for the Johannine Christians, so that when Jesus is addressing the disciples, he is speaking to the Johannine Community (ABJ 29A, 582). Neither is the distinction between "we" and "you" dominant in I John, for it is not kept up after the Prologue.

Prologue, we find that column D rivals C in importance.[28] The author was not simply a *laudator temporis acti* in stressing what was heard, seen, and felt in the past (C); he is interested in the present communication of that to a "you" consisting of the readers—a communication through witness, word, proclamation, and writing. Over against the secessionists who see salvific value only in the incarnation, the author is claiming a salvific role both for the earthly career of Jesus as he revealed himself to his disciples and for the continued proclamation of that revelation to the Johannine Community. The "community" element becomes explicit in the E column[29] where the present proclamation of the revelation that was seen, heard, and felt in the past brings about a communion (*koinōnia*) between the "we" and the "you." Thus the isolation of a "we" within the Johannine history was not a violation of the Johannine tradition in which none are called apostles and all are disciples, and it was not the introduction of a hierarchy. The joy of the "we" is fulfilled only when a communion with the "you" is brought about and the distinction between the two groups is removed.

Two suppositions by the author are noteworthy: the "we" is already in communion with the Father and with His Son, Jesus Christ,[30] and the "you" is yet to be joined in this communion. It is a clear teaching of GJohn that Jesus brought the Father's life to earth and made possible a union between the Father, the Son, and the believer. Like life, *koinōnia*, "communion," has been brought from heaven to earth, for there was a communion of the Father and the Son before the incarnation and it is into that communion that the believers are brought.[31] The author does not need to prove this in I John, for the secessionists claim such a communion for themselves (1:6; 2:6). The author challenges that claim by a distinction suggesting that not all who are in the Johannine perspective possess union with God. The "we" of the tradition-bearers possess it, and so do the more general "you" when they are united to the "we." This excludes the adversaries who "went out from us, not that they really belonged to us; for if they had belonged to us, they would have remained with us" (2:19).[32] The author's indication that his readers constitute a "you" that is yet to be brought in communion with the "we" and with the Father

[28] Of the 19 lines of the Prologue, 3 full lines and parts of 2 more are dedicated to the theme of D.

[29] Four lines of the Prologue are dedicated to the theme of E.

[30] In the NOTE on 3de I showed that the designation "Jesus Christ," attested in GJohn, is related to evaluating Jesus as the Son of God. The usage here may be antisecessionist, since the adversaries will be accused of denying that Jesus (in his human career) is the Christ (I John 5:1).

[31] In GJohn this is expressed in terms of "being in" (*einai en*) or "abiding in" (*menein en*). See John 14:23 and ABJ 29, 511–12; 29A, 602–3.

[32] In this passage the "us" refers to the united "we" and "you" of the Prologue.

and Son is an implicit admission that his readers are attracted by the secessionist version of Johannine thought. It is a warning that public adherence to the Johannine gospel is not sufficient unless it is to the gospel that the "we" heard from Jesus.[33] Since some "went out from us," complacency is a danger; and "communion with us" requires effort. In presenting the "we" of the Johannine School as intermediary between the "you" of the Johannine Community and the Father/Son, the author is leaving himself open to challenge. The secessionists could argue against him from the symbolism of the vine and branches in John 15 that indwelling is a two-way (not a triangular) affair: on one side Christ (and/or the Father); on the other side the believer.[34] Perhaps for his part the author could argue from a passage like John 17:20–21 where Jesus prays for those who believe in him though his disciples, "That they all may be one, just as you Father, in me and I in you, that they also may be one in us." There oneness seems to involve an older group of believers and a newer group being united with each other as well as with the Father and Son.[35]

This neuralgic difference between the author and the secessionists about union with God may be reflected in his choice of the term koinōnia, "communion," which never appears in GJohn. Schnackenburg (Johannesbriefe 64) is right when he says that koinōnia can serve as a nominal expression for what GJohn covers by verbs of indwelling (footnote 31 above). However, would the secessionists who gladly employed the verbs to express union with God have been happy with this noun which in NT usage was more frequently used for union among Christians[36] than for union with God?[37] As I pointed out in the NOTE on v. 3c, it is a word with a definite "ecclesiastical" tone that the author may wish to stress against the secessionists. While the secessionists had a certain sense of union among themselves, their theology of direct union with God proba-

[33] There is ambiguity here because those who are likely to read I John are (still) on the author's side and have not (yet) succumbed to secessionist propaganda. In a sense, then, they are already joined to the "we," and that is why through the rest of I John the author can use an inclusive "we" which embraces the readers, and why in 5:13 he says, "I have written this to you so that you may know that you *possess* this eternal life." Marshall, *Epistles* 105, remarks astutely, "Verse 3 is not necessarily prescribing the condition for entry to fellowship, but for continuance in fellowship."

[34] Or they could appeal to a passage like John 14:23: "If anyone loves me, he will keep my word. Then my Father will love him, and we shall come to him and make our dwelling place with him." See Balz, *Johannesbriefe* 164.

[35] De Jonge, "Who Are We" 153, understands the author's thought correctly: "What is essential is the trustworthy tradition from generation to generation in which the eyewitnesses from the past have a fundamentally different function from that of the believers in the present, and in which the believers in the present are referred, for their relation to God, to their relation to the eyewitnesses."

[36] See Acts 2:42; Philip 1:5; Gal 2:9; II Cor 8:4; 9:13; Rom 15:26; Philem 6; Heb 13:16.

[37] With the Holy Spirit in Philip 2:1; II Cor 13:13; with Christ in I Cor 1:9; 10:16; and with God in Philo, *Moses* 1.28 ⁂158.

bly meant that they could not give to a union among themselves the salvific value attributed to communion among believers in I John 1:3 where it becomes a *sine qua non* of being united to God.[38] Certainly they did not accept I John's interpretation of *koinōnia*, which involved adhesion to the interpretation of what was seen and heard as proclaimed by the Johannine School (of which the author was a part).

A further glance at the E column of the chart shows that the goal of the whole revelatory process described in the Prologue is not only communion but joy: "We are writing this so that our joy may be fulfilled." Just as the epistolary author has modified the GJohn tradition of a direct relation between the believers and the Father/Son (by the introduction of communion with "us" to form a triangular pattern), so he has modified the tradition about the joy that binds Jesus and the believers: "I have said this to you that *my* joy may be yours and *your* joy may be fulfilled."[39] The author has made this also triangular by speaking of *"our* joy," i.e., the joy of the Johannine School when, with and through them, the believers are joined in communion with the Father/Son.[40] Perhaps once again he could justify this by resorting to the kind of tradition found in John 17 where Jesus distinguishes between his immediate disciples and "those who believe in me through their word" (17:20) and where he prays "that they may share my joy to the full" (17:13). For the author that second generation of Johannine Christians could enter into this full joy, but they could not bypass those who had seen, heard, and felt.

[38] In later theology this condition would be made more formally ecclesiastic, e.g., Ignatius, *Magn.* 7:1: "As the Lord was united to the Father and did nothing without Him . . . so you do nothing without the bishop and presbyters"; Cyprian, *De ecclesiae catholicae unitate* 6.149–50; CC 3, 253: "One cannot have God for Father who has not the church for mother."

[39] John 15:11; see also 16:24. In the *Magnesians* passage cited in footnote 38 Ignatius says, "Let there be in common one prayer, one supplication, one mind, one hope in love, *in the joy* which is without fault, that is, Jesus Christ."

[40] Houlden, *Epistles* 47, recognizes that the meaning of GJohn has been altered but wonders whether the joy has not been trivialized since it now refers to the pleasure of the writer if he achieves his desired objective. Bultmann, *Epistles* 14, however, is right when he recognizes that the author is speaking of eschatological joy, which is the same as peace or life (ABJ 29A, 681). Compare John 10:10: "That they may have life and have it to the full." Moreover, since the joy comes from bringing the "you" into communion with the Father/Son (through communion with "us"), compare John 17:3: "Eternal life consists in this: that they know you the one true God, and Jesus Christ, the one whom you sent."

BIBLIOGRAPHY PERTINENT TO I JOHN 1:1–4

de Jonge, M., "An Analysis of I John 1. 1–4," BT 29 (1978) 322–30.

————. "Who Are 'We'?" in *Jesus: Inspiring and Disturbing Presence* (Nashville: Abingdon, 1974) 148–66.

Drumwright, H., "Problem Passages in the Johannine Epistles: A Hermeneutical Approach," *Southwestern Journal of Theology* 13 (1, Fall 1970) 53–64.

Feuillet, A., *Le prologue du quatrième évangile* (Paris: Desclée de Brouwer, 1968) 210–17.

Grayston, K., " 'Logos' in I John 1,1," ExpT 86 (1974–75) 279.

Gryglewicz, F., Polish article on the two Johannine Prologues, digested in NTA 3 (Fall 1958) ₦106.

Guy, H. A., "I John 1, 1–3," ExpT 62 (1950–51) 285.

Harnack, A. von, "Das 'Wir' in den Johanneischen Schriften," *Sitzungsberichte der Preussischen Akademie der Wissenschaften, Philosophisch-Historische Klasse* (1923) 96–113.

Lacan, M. F., "L'oeuvre du Verbe Incarné: le Don de la Vie (Jo., I, 4)," RSR 45 (1957) 61–78, esp. 74–75.

Lee, G. M., "I John 1, 1–3," ExpT 62 (1950–51) 125.

Tobac, E., "La notion du Christ-Logos dans la littérature johannique," RHE 25 (1929) 213–38, esp. 231–38.

Weir, J. E., "The Identity of the Logos in the First Epistle of John," ExpT 86 (1974–75) 118–20.

Wendt, H. H., "Der 'Anfang' am Beginne des I. Johannesbriefes," ZNW 21 (1922) 38–42.

See also de la Potterie, "Commencement"; Feuillet, "Structure"; Francis, "Form"; and VII C2 in the *General Bibliography*.

Part One
(I John 1:5–3:10)

The obligation of walking in light in response to the gospel of God as light. The response to this gospel divides the secessionist Antichrists from the author's Little Children.

2. I John 1:5–2:2: *The Gospel of God as Light;*
Three Boasts and Three Opposite Hypotheses

5a	**1**	⁵Now this is the gospel
5b		that we have heard from Christ
5c		and declare to you:
5d		*God is light*
5e		*and in Him there is no darkness at all.*

6a ⁶IF WE BOAST, "We are in communion with Him,"
6b   while continuing to walk in darkness,
6c   we are liars
6d   and we do not act in truth.
7a ⁷BUT IF we walk in the light
7b   as He Himself is in light,
7c   we are joined in communion with one another;
7d   and the blood of Jesus, His Son,
7e   cleanses us from all sin.

8a ⁸IF WE BOAST, "We are free from the guilt of sin,"
8b   we deceive ourselves;
8c   and the truth is not in us.
9a ⁹BUT IF we confess our sins,
9b   He who is reliable and just
9c   will forgive us our sins
9d   and cleanse us from all wrongdoing.

10a ¹⁰IF WE BOAST, "We have not sinned,"
10b   we make Him a liar;
10c   and His word is not in us.
1a **2**¹(My Little Children, I am writing this to keep you from sin.)
1b   BUT IF anyone does sin,
1c   we have a Paraclete in the Father's presence,
1d   Jesus Christ, the one who is just;
2a   ²and he himself is an atonement for our sins,
2b   and not only for our sins
2c   but also for the whole world.

NOTES

1:5a. *Now this is the gospel.* The formula, "And this is" (*kai houtos estin* with word-order variations), is common in the Johannine Epistles. Sometimes it has a personal predicate (NOTE on 5:6a below), more often an impersonal predicate noun, as in these instances:

> Now this is the promise which Christ himself made to us (I John 2:25)
> Now this is the commandment of God (3:23)
> Now this is the conquering power that has conquered the world (5:4)
> Now this is the testimony (5:11)
> Now this is the confidence we possess in the presence of God (5:14)
> Now this is love (II John 6)

Variations with this type of predicate are *hoti houtos estin* (I John 3:11: "For this is the gospel that you heard from the beginning"; 5:9: "For this is the testimony of God") and *houtos gar estin* (5:3: "For this is the love of God"). In GJohn the more frequent formula is *houtos [de] estin* (John 3:19; 6:29; 15:12; 17:3). Generally, but not always, the concept under discussion has been introduced in the verses that precede the "Now this is . . ." statement; and the "this" points ahead to a clause that will define or explain the predicate noun, almost as a summary of the whole discussion. (In the NOTE on 1:5d I shall discuss the types of clauses used as explanation.) Occasionally, however, the main force of the "this" points backward, so that the explanation has already been given and is simply being expanded. Ambiguity as to whether the primary direction of the "this" is to what precedes or to what follows is one of the more annoying grammatical peculiarities of the Epistles. The present instance, at least, is relatively clear. The notion of "proclaiming" (*apangellein*) appeared twice in the Prologue (1:2,3), preparing the way for the "Now this is the gospel [*angelia*]" statement; and the "this" points forward to a *hoti* ("that" of indirect discourse) clause in v. 5d: "Now this is the gospel . . . (that) God is light and in Him there is no darkness at all."

"Now" renders "and." In the minutely detailed discussions of Johannine logic in which commentators indulge, this "and" has been looked upon as inferential and translated "for," as if it supplied the basis for the *koinōnia* in 1:3 by telling the reader about the God who is the partner in that *koinōnia* (see Plummer, Westcott). However, *kai*, "and, now," is a set part of the formula and should not be pressed for great theological significance. Indeed, its occurrence here has been facilitated by the fact that in GJohn the first sentence after the Prologue read thus, *"And this is* the testimony of John" (John 1:19).

As for the copula "is," in the Greek of these formulas the verb normally follows the demonstrative; only here does it precede (*kai estin hautē*). Inevitably some scribes (e.g., Codex Alexandrinus) have shifted the order to the normal pattern. Although Westcott and others argue that the different word order here gives greater emphasis to the predicate noun, it is probably a meaningless variation.

The key word *angelia* occurs in the NT only twice, here and below in 3:11. (Codices Sinaiticus [corrector], Ephraemi Rescriptus, and Coptic versions would read the more familiar *epangelia*, "promise, announcement," which occurs 52 times in the NT and is the correct reading in 2:25 below.) Many commentators contrast *angelia*, "news," to *euangelion*, "good news," the word normally translated "gospel." (See the NOTE above on 1:2c for these interrelated words.) However, since *euangelion* never occurs in the Johannine writings, *angelia* may well be its technical Johannine equivalent. In the LXX the use of *anangellein angelian* in Isa 28:9 is not much different from the use of *euangelizein* in Isa 52:7; and the expression *agathē angelia*, "good news," is found in Prov 12:25; 25:25. Functionally *angelia* could appropriately serve as "gospel" in I John, for it is a proclamation by the tradition-bearers of the Community (the *anangellein* of 1:2–3 which *angelia* in 1:5 resumes); it is from Christ (1:5b); and it is salvific, since the purpose of the proclamation is communion (*koinōnia*) with God and fellow Christians. (It may be added that the corresponding verb *angellein* occurs twice in the NT, both times in GJohn: first in the Western textual tradition of John 4:51 where the royal official's servants met him "with the (good) news that his boy was going to live"; and second in John 20:18 where Mary Magdalene *announces*, "I have seen the Lord" —a resurrection message that is the heart of the Christian gospel.) As we shall see, the content of the I John *angelia* as expounded in 1:5 and 3:11 is intimately related to what is found in GJohn; and so there is reason to think that, when the Johannine believers spoke about the contents of what we call GJohn, they may have referred to it as the *angelia*.

5b. *that we have heard.* This is the same perfect tense of *akouein* used in the Prologue in vv. 1b and 3a; and the "we" is again the Johannine School of tradition-bearers speaking to the "you" of the Johannine Community.

from Christ. Literally, "from him"; but grammatically and theologically there can be little doubt that the reference is to Jesus Christ, the last third-person antecedent to be mentioned (3e). (Brooke, *Epistles* 11, is virtually alone among modern commentators in defending a reference to God.) Only a reference to Jesus makes sense granted the understanding of "what was from the beginning" chosen for v. 1a. And although in Johannine thought Jesus embodies and transmits a revelation from God, Hodges, "Fellowship," probably exaggerates when he suggests that I John deliberately chose the ambiguous "him" to cover God and Jesus. Bultmann, *Epistles* 15, finds the use of "him" instead of a proper designation surprising; but that is not so if the author presupposed that his audience knew he was writing in defense of his interpretation of the Jesus of GJohn. The "Christ" (implicit) and "God" (explicit) of 1:5 are matched inclusively by the explicit "Father" and "Jesus Christ" at the end of the unit (2:1).

The "from" is *apo* here, rather than the more normal Johannine *para* (which never appears in I John). Diverse commentators like Westcott and Bultmann have argued that *apo* refers to an ultimate but not necessarily immediate source or that it is used to indicate that the *angelia* did not necessarily come from the historical Jesus. I question such grammatical precision and regard *apo* as a meaningless variant for *para* following the verb *akouein* (BDF 210[3]; 173[1]), perhaps accounted for by alliteration since there are four instances of initial *alpha* (*a*) in five words. In particular *angelia apo* may echo the *apangellein* of 1:2–3. The author of I John would have understood this gospel as coming "from" Jesus to the same extent that any word spoken in GJohn was thought to come from Jesus. The fact that all such words came from the Paraclete/Spirit who taught everything (14:26) did not mean that they were not from Jesus, for the Paraclete did not speak on his own but only what he received from Jesus (16:13–15). Indeed, Jesus is also a Paraclete (I John 2:1).

5c. *and declare to you.* The verb is *anangellein* (NOTE on 1:2c), most often used in GJohn (16:13,14,15) for the Paraclete's "declaring" to the disciples what he had received from Jesus. Once again those who detect minute precision in Johannine grammar would argue that *anangellein* was used here rather than the *apangellein* of 1:2–3 because of concern with the direction of the message (*an*, "to," not *ap*, "from"). However, since a "to you" is involved in all three verses, there is no such delicate directional connotation. The GJohn Paraclete usage (where *anangellein* has a similar "from [*ek*] . . . to" pattern) was more determinative for I John than were such grammatical niceties. P. Joüon, "Le verb *anangello* dans Saint Jean," RSR 28 (1938) 234–36, stresses that the verb does not mean simply "to announce"; the classical and Johannine meaning is "to report," i.e., to declare to someone something said by someone else. (J. Schniewind, *"angelia. . . ,"* TDNT 1, 62, reports the frequent usage for a herald proclaiming a message.) In the Theodotion version of Daniel, *anangellein* has the connotation of revealing what has been hidden (2.2; 3:99; 5:12; etc.); and that implication may be present here, granted the context of secessionist confusion. But the translation "reveal" would be too strong, *pace* Giurisato, "Struttura," 364.

5d. *God is light.* A *hoti*, "that" (which I have not translated), introduces what is technically indirect discourse following *angelia*, "gospel," in v. 5a (BDF 397[3]). The demonstrative "this," discussed in the NOTE on 5a, is usually followed by an explanatory clause introduced either by *hoti* (here; 5:11,14) or by *hina* (3:11,23; II John 6; see I John 5:3ab). In 2:25 and 5:4 it is followed simply by another noun explaining the first. There are three Johannine descriptions of God:

God is Spirit (John 4:24)	*pneuma ho theos*
God is light (I John 1:5)	*ho theos phōs estin*
God is love (I John 4:8)	*ho theos agapē estin*

The copula "to be" (is/was), lacking in the GJohn formula, is the proper Johannine verb for God and the Word; human beings "become" or "have" or act. The predicate in all three formulas is anarthrous. There is a tendency of predicate nouns to be anarthrous with the possible exception of statements of identity (ABJ 29, 5), and so commentators have concluded that these are not statements of identity but at most descriptions of a quality of God (Plummer, Brooke), or existential statements about God's activity toward human beings, e.g., the God who is love shows that love by giving His own Son (I John 4:8–10). Nevertheless, these formulas also touch upon the mystery of God's own being. For instance, the Johannine Jesus speaks not only of God's love for human beings but (logically) first of all of God's love for him, the Son (John 3:35; 5:20; 10:17; 15:9), a love that is the model of God's love for Jesus' followers (17:23,26). In 17:24 Jesus makes it clear that he is speaking of a preincarnational love that existed before creation in the relationship between God and His Word. Thus, in such "God is" formulas, while there is emphasis on God's activity, that activity is internally related to what God is before creation. Dodd, *Epistles* 107–10, points out that the pagan Greek formulas about God have a different thrust. Among the philosophers the statements tend to speak of God's essence rather than of His activity. The Hermetic literature is less abstract and does stress activity (God is creative, life-giving), but God's personality is not always clear—He is a life force.

5e. *and in Him there is no darkness at all.* This antithetic pattern of a positive statement (5d) followed by a negative statement (5e) is biblical, e.g., "God is faithful, and there is no unrighteousness [in Him]" (Deut 32:4); "The Lord my God is righteous, and there is no unrighteousness in Him" (Ps 92:16 [15]). In this pattern the negative clause receives the emphasis, especially when, as here, one has a double negative: "In Him there is no darkness, none at all." In GJohn the closest verbal parallel is 19:11: "You would not have power over me, none at all." The two related nouns for "darkness," *skotos* and *skotia*, occur 47 times in the NT. *Skotia*, used here, is the Johannine preference, with GJohn and I John accounting for 14 of 17 NT uses, whereas only 2 of 30 NT uses of *skotos* are Johannine (John 3:19; I John 1:6). See ABJ 29, 515–16.

This is our first epistolary encounter with *einai en*, "to be in," one of the two frequent and revealing Johannine expressions for interiority; see Malatesta, *Interiority* 27–32. (The other is *menein en*, "to abide, dwell in"; it will be discussed in the NOTE on 2:6a, the first occurrence.) The expression *einai en* occurs in GJohn 13 times, and 14 more times with the verb "to be" clearly understood. In I John *einai en* occurs 18 times, with 4 more instances where the verb "to be" is clearly understood. The usage may be divided under three headings:

(A) INDWELLING PERTINENT TO GOD. *Einai en* is used to describe the presence of the Christian in God and Jesus and vice versa. (The more frequent formula for this, however, is *menein en;* and I shall postpone the general discussion of divine immanence until 2:6a; see also ABJ 29A, 602–3.) The 9 instances of this use in GJohn and the 3 in I John (one with verb implicit: 4:4) may be analyzed thus:

- for the Christian in God: I John 2:5
- for the Christian in Jesus: John 14:20; 15:2
- for the Christian in the Father and Jesus: John 17:21; I John 5:20
- for Jesus in the Christian: John 14:20,23; 17:23,26

▪ for Jesus in the Father: John 14:20
▪ for the Father in Jesus: John 17:23
▪ for both Jesus in the Father and the Father in Jesus: John 10:38; 14:10,11; 17:21
▪ for the Spirit of Truth in the Christian: John 14:17; I John 4:4

This use of *einai en* is not exclusively Johannine, e.g., Acts 17:28: "In Him we live and move and *are.*" In the Pauline Epistles there are 165 instances of the expression "in Christ" or its equivalent, and there are also instances of Christ in the Christian—the verb "to be" is often implied in these expressions (see JBC 79 ※138).

(B) INDWELLING OF OTHER REALITIES IN THE CHRISTIAN. The dualistic Johannine world view divided people according to their inmost being, so that various realities could be said to be in Christians and not in their opponents. There are some 5 instances of this usage of *einai en* in GJohn and 7 in I John. In the following instances realities related to God or Jesus are said to be in the Christian:

▪ light: John 12:35
▪ Jesus' joy: John 15:11
▪ the love the Father had for Jesus: John 17:26

But most often we learn of the divine realities in the Christian from a statement about their absence in opponents. The following *positive* things are said *not* to be in those of whom the Johannine authors disapprove (e.g., "the Jews," the secessionists, the devil):

▪ light: John 11:10
▪ love of the Father: I John 2:15
▪ truth: John 8:44; I John 1:8; 2:4 (cf. 2:8)
▪ word of God: I John 1:10 (cf. John 8:37)

By way of comparison we may note what Ignatius says in *Magn.* 5:2: (unless we choose to die to the world through Christ), "his life is not in us." Returning to the Johannine writings, we find that the following *negative* things are said *not* to be in Christ or in the true Christian:

▪ dishonesty (*adikia*): John 7:18
▪ sin (*hamartia*): I John 3:5
▪ stumbling block (*skandalon*): I John 2:10

(C) MISCELLANEOUS THEOLOGICAL USES. These are often corollaries of the dualism reflected in the preceding grouping but do not lend themselves easily to schematization. The following realities are the subject or object of *einai en:*

▪ light or darkness: God in light (I John 1:7); hater of one's brother not in light but in darkness (I John 2:9ac, 11); no darkness in God (I John 1:5)
▪ life: What came to be in the Word was life (John 1:4); eternal life in God's Son (I John 5:11)
▪ love: No fear in love (I John 4:18)
▪ in the world: Jesus (John 1:10; 9:5; 17:11); Christians (13:1; 17:11; I John 4:17); Spirit of the Antichrist or the Evil One (I John 4:3,4); evil things (I John 2:15–16)

6a. *If we boast.* This is the first of six *ean*, "if," clauses that run from 1:6 to

2:1 in three pairs (negative/positive apodoses), as indicated visually in my translation. These are not merely possible contingencies but reflect the language of jurisprudence. See my INTRODUCTION III B1 for Nauck's contention that the conditional pattern reflects the Pentateuchal law codes which flow from covenant demands and which specify the possibilities of observance and nonobservance. They are "expectational" (THLJ 33), equivalent to "whenever." The "we" is no longer the "we" of the tradition-bearers (the Johannine School) distinct from the "you" of the audience but is comprehensive of the two and represents the Johannine Community that remains after the secessionists have left (2:19). The substance of the "boast" (literally, "say") is a statement harmonious with secessionist theology and betrays the fact that, while the author addresses his own adherents, he is worried about the inroads of secessionist thought. Windisch, *Briefe* 111, unnecessarily posits that an erroneous group has remained after the false teachers left. Rather, anticipated error is the issue, whence the condition.

"We are in communion with Him." The Greek is in indirect discourse. The "Him" is clearly God (who is light), the last third-person antecedent. In this whole unit God is mentioned by name only in 1:5d but is referred to pronominally (*autos*) in vv. 6a, 7b, 10bc. The notion of having communion (*koinōnia*) resumes the theme of 1:3; and the author will return to it in v. 7c, which will be the last use of *koinōnia* in I John. As we have seen, GJohn phrases the theme of immanence in verbal forms, and perhaps the secessionists did as well. This may be the author's own formulation of their boast, done for the purposes of contrast with his idea of *koinōnia*.

6b. *while continuing to walk in darkness.* Literally, "and we walk," a subjunctive parallel to "we boast" and governed by "if." The initial *kai*, "and," has an adversative force (BDF 442[1]), while the present tense indicates the habitual character of the action. The error is not simply in the boasting but in the boasting combined with the contradictory walking in the darkness. Here "darkness" is by exception *skotos* rather than *skotia* (NOTE on 5e); but attempts to see a difference between the two nouns (e.g., abstract versus concrete) are unnecessary. At most the use of the feminine *skotia* in 1:5 and the masculine *skotos* in 1:6 may have been meant as a poetic technique to express collectivity. Nor is there any way to validate the suggestion of M.-E. Boismard, RB 68 (1961) 514, that I John may have been influenced here by Eph 5:6–8: "Let no one deceive you with empty words . . . for once you were darkness [*skotos*] but now you are light in the Lord—walk as children of the light."

The use of *peripatein*, "to walk," for pursuing a way of life and action is a Semitism. Hebrew examples of this idiom include: "Let us walk in the light of the Lord" (Isa 2:5); "I walk in the ways of justice" (Prov 8:20); "God created human beings to govern the world and appointed for them two spirits in which to walk until the time of His visitation: the spirits of truth and iniquity" (1QS 3:17–19). Sometimes the verb "to walk" is accompanied by the noun "way"; in other instances the noun alone carries the idea, as in 19 usages of "way" in Ps 119. This usage of "walk" is not overly frequent elsewhere in the NT outside Paul, but examples include: Mark 7:5: "Walk according to the tradition of the elders"; Acts 21:21: "Not to walk in the customs [of the Jews]"; Rom 14:15 and Eph 5:2; "Walking according to [or in] love"; Col 4:5: "Walk in wisdom"; and Eph 5:8: "Walk as children of the light." However, the idiom is quite Johannine; in the Epistles we find "to walk in truth" 3 times (II John 4; III John 3,4); "to walk in/according to commandments" 2 times (II John 6); and "to walk as Jesus walked" once (I John 2:6). The most frequent image of walking in light (day) or darkness (ABJ 29, 340) is not a strained symbolism and is the only metaphorical use of "walking" in GJohn (5 times: 8:12; 11:9,10; 12:35) and, with the exception of 2:6, the only use in I John (3 times: here, 1:7; 2:11). See also Rev 21:24: by the light of the heavenly Jerusalem shall all the nations walk. As background we may remember that the image of light in I John 1:5 was influenced by the GJohn Prologue where the creation of light was in mind, along with the story of the fall in Gen 3:8 when Adam could no longer *walk* with God (ABJ 29, 25–27). Besides the image of "walking," the Johannine writers speak of "being in light/darkness" and "abiding in light/darkness" (I John 1:7; 2:9–11; John 12:46).

At the root of the symbolism of light as a context for a good way of life and that of darkness as a context for an evil way of life is the fact that night with its lack of light offers opportunity and protection for criminals. Job 24:13–17 describes how the adulterer and the thief work at night; and in Sir 23:18–19 the adulterer asks, "Who sees me? I am surrounded with darkness." Eloquent is Isa 29:15: "Woe to them . . . whose works are in darkness and say, 'Who has seen us?'" For John, of course, darkness is more than a context for evildoing; it is a symbol for a principle from which evil comes.

6c. *we are liars.* Literally, "we lie" (verb *pseudesthai*). The themes of light and truth go together in John as we shall see in the next line of this verse; and so do their opposites, darkness and falsehood. In Johannine dualism, as part of the opposition to truth, there are such terms as *phaulos,* "wickedness" (John 3:20–21); *adikia,* "dishonesty" (John 7:18; cf. II Thess 2:12); *hamartia,* "sin" (John 8:32–34,45–46; see I John 1:8). But the principal opposition is expressed by two sets of falsehood terms: those from the root *pseud-* translated by words related to "lie," and those from the root *plan-* translated by words related to "deceit." I list the Johannine uses of the first set of terms here (and the second set under 1:8b below):

▪ *pseudesthai,* "to lie," only here
▪ *pseudos,* "lie," John 8:44; I John 2:21,27
▪ *pseustēs,* "liar," John 8:44,55; I John 1:10; 2:4,22; 4:20; 5:10
▪ *pseudoprophētēs,* "false or lying prophet," I John 4:11

In the Pauline corpus, truth is dualistically opposed to *pseudos,* "lie," in Rom 1:25 and Eph 4:25; and God is radically opposed to the lie in Titus 1:2, for He is "the never lying" (*apseudēs*). In Hellenistic thought influenced by Platonic categories, where there is another world of perfect truth and beauty, the earthly is a lie because it is illusory. In some forms of gnostic thought the world with its lies was the creation of an errant eon or demiurge, e.g., in the gnostic *Gospel of Truth* (I 17:14–29; NHL 38) a creature is made by error, a substitute for truth; and this "creature of lying" is contrasted with the supreme truth "immutable, imperturbable, perfect in beauty." As for Hebrew thought we find in the OT that the lie (*šeqer*) is a perverse wickedness equivalent to violence (Hos 12:1); and those who tell lies constitute a group opposed to God (Jer 9:2[3]), as exemplified above all by the false or lying prophets. In the Dead Sea Scrolls "lie" (*kāzāb* or *šeqer*) is used to describe the specific enemies of the sect, e.g., "the man of the lie" (1QpHab 2:1–2; 5:11); "the prophets of the lie" (1QH 4:16); "a congregation pregnant with lying deeds" (1QpHab 10:11–12). Such titles befit all those who have distorted the Law (1QH 4:10; CD 5:21–6:2) by interpreting it in a way different from the Qumran Community or who did not keep the Law. However, in Qumran dualism the spirit of truth is opposed not by the spirit of the lie but by the spirit of "iniquity" (*ʾāwel*), e.g., in 1QS 3:18–19; 4:23; 5:10.

Against this Hebrew background it is not surprising that the Johannine writers do not regard the position of their opponents as ignorance but as a lie; and not a lie of self-deception but a lie involving active hostility to the truth: "Every lie is alien to the truth" (I John 2:21). The devil, the great opponent of Jesus, is a liar (John 8:44; see ABJ 29, 365); the secessionist teachers or Antichrists are false or lying prophets (I John 4:1); and the christology of the secessionists and their cavalier attitude toward commandments is nothing but the telling of lies (2:22; 2:4; 4:20).

6d. *and we do not act in truth.* Literally, "we do not do [*poiein*] truth"—another Semitism. In I John there is reference to *doing* the following: the will of God (2:17), what is pleasing before Him (3:22), justice (2:29; 3:7,10); sin (3:4,8–9); and lawlessness (3:4). The expression "doing a lie" occurs in Rev 21:27; 22:15; and it involves acting falsely (see 1QpHab 10:11–12 in the preceding NOTE). The idiom of "doing" applied to divine realities suggests that they can be concretized in human behavior.

The expression "to do the truth" brings the first epistolary occurrence of *alē-theia*. Of 109 NT instances of this term, almost half are Johannine, with 25 in GJohn and 20 in the Epistles. (For the related adjectives *alēthēs*, "true," and *alēthinos*, "true, real," see the NOTE on 2:8ab below.) The greater proportional frequency in the Epistles is explained by the fact that Johannine thought tends to identify "truth" with the revelation in and by Jesus, and in the author's judgment that revelation is now under attack by the secessionists. In ABJ 29, 499–501, I discussed the two main schools of thought about the background of the Johannine notion of truth: the Dodd-Bultmann thesis of a Greek background whereby for John truth is a quasi-Platonic heavenly reality; the de la Potterie thesis of an OT and intertestamental background whereby for John truth is predicated of God's mysterious plan of salvation, which is revealed to human beings. Since that time de la Potterie has published his massive study, *La vérité*, making his case even more convincing; and Aalen, "Truth," and Mundle, "Wahrheitsverständnis," think in a similar manner. The Hebrew word for "truth" (*ʾĕmet*) is related to a root (*ʾmn*) that conveys the notion of firmness or solidity as a basis for trustworthy acceptance. When the truth of God's revelation is accepted by the believer, it becomes the basis from which that person lives; and if one acts in truth (does truth), one is not simply following an outside model of what is right (which would be Platonic) but is acting from an interior principle. This becomes apparent in the Dead Sea Scrolls where identity is expressed in terms of an interior relation to truth, so that the Community's members are the "sons of truth" (1QS 4:5–6), or "men of truth" (1QH 14:2), "generations of truth" (1QS 3:19), "witnesses of truth" (1QS 8:6). The Community itself is a "community [*yaḥad*] of truth" (1QS 2:24,26) and a "house of truth" (1QS 8:9).

The phrase "to do truth" (*'aśāh 'ĕmet*) occurs twice in the Hebrew Bible: in Neh 9:33 in reference to God's fidelity in action, and in II Chr 31:20 in reference to King Hezekiah's doing the prescripts of the Law. The literal Greek expression (*alētheian poiein*) is more frequent in the LXX but has about the same span of reference, e.g., Gen 32:10 in reference to God's action; Gen 47:29; Isa 26:10; Tob 4:6; 13:6 in reference to a range of human actions (being faithful, doing right). "To do truth" is quite frequent in the Hebrew of Qumran and in the intertestamental works preserved in Greek, often colored by the view that what is found in the Law (or in the interpretation of it) is truth. This is implied in 1QpHab 7:10–11: "The men of truth, those who do the Law"; and it is explicit in 1QS 8:1–2, which speaks of the community officers as "perfectly knowledgeable in all that is revealed of the Law in order to do truth." In *T. Benj* 10:3 there is the instruction "to do the truth, each one to his neighbor, and to keep the Law of the Lord and His commandments"—a combination of commandments and love of neighbor attested in John (see also *T. Reuben* 6:9). For the Johannine Christians Christ has replaced the Law as the basis of operation, and so "truth" as an interiorized principle is more personal in John than at Qumran—it is close to OT Wisdom and the Qumran spirit of truth. De la Potterie insists that to do the truth is not the same as to walk in light: it involves belief, intermediary between truth, the interiorized principle, and the exterior action which corresponds to one's faith. Personally I find the distinction oversubtle. For more detail, see Zerwick, "Veritatem facere"; de la Potterie, *La vérité* 2, 479–535; and ABJ 29, 134–35, 148–49.

7a. *But if we walk in the light*. The three sentences that express a secessionist position distorting the Johannine tradition are begun by the author with "If we boast" clauses (*ean eipōmen* in 1:6,8,10). Correspondingly the three sentences that express the author's understanding of the tradition also begin with an "If" clause (*ean* in 1:7,9; 2:1). The adversative "but" may be expressed clearly as here (*de*) or implied as in 1:7 (no particle) and in 2:1 (adversative *kai*). This "if" clause takes its theme from the negative description of the secessionist position in 1:6b ("while continuing to walk in darkness"); see the NOTE there on the idiom of walking.

7b. *as He Himself is in light*. For "He" (*autos*) as God, see NOTE on v. 6a ("communion with *Him*"). For the expression *einai en*, "to be in," see NOTE on v. 5e ("in Him there is no darkness"). The image of God's being *in* light represents a change from "God *is* light" (5d); and the new image has better biblical parallels: Ps 104:2: "You cover yourself with light as a garment"; Dan 2:22: "He knows what is in the darkness, and light is with Him"; Isa 2:5: "Walk in the light of the Lord"; I Tim 6:15–16: "The Lord of Lords . . .

whose home is in unapproachable light." Klein, "Licht" 284, maintains that the change is serious, but Bultmann, *Epistles* 20, says that the meaning of the two formulas is the same. Certainly one must take into account the author's love for varying his formulas. (See, for example, the variation within two verses in 4:7–8, which is closely parallel to the present variation: "God is love" [4:8]; "Love is from [belongs to] God" [4:7].) Nevertheless, the two formulas have slightly different functions: One portrays God's being as the basis for Christian experience; the other portrays Him as the model for Christian behavior. The choice of the image, "God is in light," here may have been determined by the idiom "walk *in* light" used in v. 7a—the two "in" prepositions helped the "[just] as" comparison. Compare Matt 5:48: "You must be perfect as your heavenly Father is perfect."

7c. *we are joined in communion with one another.* This is the fourth and last occurrence of *koinōnia* in I John. An alternative reading is "with Him," supported by the original hand of Codex Alexandrinus (?); an OL MS.; the Harclean Syriac; and early church fathers like Tertullian and Clement of Alexandria. O'Neill, *Puzzle* 8, 10, prefers this poorly attested variant on the grounds that "with one another" imports a new idea into the contrast with 1:6a, which speaks of "communion with Him." However, the imitation of 6a was precisely what caused a later scribe to change 7c to "communion with Him." In genuine Johannine style such contrasts almost always add a new element. The author is going back to the idea he proposed in the Prologue by insisting that the secessionist boast, "We are in communion with Him," must be wrong precisely because they do not have communion with the other Johannine Christians who are adherents of the author and the tradition-bearers. I find totally unacceptable the thesis of Bultmann, *Epistles* 20, that "communion with one another" refers to a communion among all humanity and not only among believers; indeed, I would go in the opposite direction by insisting that the communion is not even among all Christians but only among true Johannine believers. The author is not excluding non-Johannine Christians; he is simply not thinking of them and is not pastorally concerned about them in this writing.

7d. *and the blood of Jesus, His Son.* Codex Alexandrinus and some versions add "Christ" in imitation of "His Son, Jesus Christ" in 1:3e. With or without that addition the *koinōnia* statement in v. 7bcd has the same three dramatis personae (He Himself, one another, Jesus) as had the *koinōnia* passage in v. 3cde (us, the Father, Jesus). The next line (7e: "cleanses us from all sin") is part of this clause that begins in 7d. While one can break the clause into two "poetic" lines, as I have done, the whole clause fits only awkwardly into the linear format that illustrates the quasi-poetic style of I John (p. 128); and for that reason and because of its theology Bultmann attributes it to the Ecclesiastical Redactor (INTRODUCTION III A2). However, it provides an almost necessary connective to 1:8 where the notion of "sin" appears in a secessionist boast. (Bultmann, *Epistles* 20, would argue that 7de is a back-formation from v. 8 with its notion of "sin"; however, that implies that the putative source had a string of unrelated statements which a later Johannine writer connected.)

Some of the difference in tone between 7de and what precedes can be explained by the theory that up to now the author has been answering the secessionist boast by appealing to Johannine antitheses of light and darkness (familiar to us in GJohn; see INTRODUCTION, footnote 100), but now he broadens the attack by developing a theme that is only obscure or minor in GJohn, namely, the sacrificial quality of the death of Jesus.

Before discussing the details of that theme, let me ask about the force of the "and" that begins 7d. Since it incorporates 7de into the apodosis of the "if" clause that begins in 7a, is the author saying that the power of the blood of Jesus depends on our walking in light? ("If we walk in the light . . . the blood of Jesus, His Son, cleanses us.") Such a theology would seem to be a negation of the Pauline stress that works do not bring about initial justification. One (unsatisfactory) explanation is that the author is speaking only of cleansing minor sins, not serious ones—an explanation appealing to a (wrong) interpretation of the distinction between sins in I John 5:16–17, which is not even suggested by the context here. Another explanation (Alford, Ebrard, Westcott) is that there are two salvific steps described in v. 7, namely, justification and sanctification. One form of this thesis is that "walk in the light" in 7a is the same as "come to the light" in John 3:20–21 and refers to an initially favorable response to the divine offer of salvation, so that the author is putting the condition that there be an openness or obedience to faith before salvation can become operative for the individual (see Gaugler, *Johannesbriefe* 69). However, "walk in the light" almost certainly refers to one's behavior *after* one has come to the light. Perhaps the best explanation (Hoskyns, Schneider, B. Weiss, Wilder) is to stress that the author of I John is not worried about *initial* justification but about the forgiveness of sins committed as a Christian. When people first believe and come to the light, their sins are forgiven. They may sin again; yet if they try to walk in the light, the blood of Jesus, which cleanses from all sin, cleanses from these sins as well.

Moving on from the grammatical logic of the clauses in 7cd, let us discuss "the blood of Jesus." Of the 362 uses of "blood" in the Hebrew Bible, 103 refer to sacrificial blood (Morris, *Apostolic Preaching* 109). The distinctive note in sacrifices for sin was not the death of the animal but the use made of the blood in sprinkling the Temple veil or in anointing the horns of the altar, a task confined to the priests. It was demanded, of course, that the blood have been obtained by the violent death (slaughter) of the victim; and this presupposition affects the NT understanding of the sacrificial quality of Christ's blood as well. J. Behm, *"haima,"* TDNT 1, 175, wrongly underplays this when he says, "The early Christian representation of the blood of Christ as sacrificial blood is simply the metaphorical garment clothing the thought of the self-offering, the obedience to God, which Christ demonstrated in the crucifixion." It has those notions, of course; but the *shedding* of blood was important as well (see John 19:34; ABJ 29A, 951). In the NT the term "blood" occurs 97 times; of those, 6 are in GJohn and 4 in I John, a statistic which means that proportionately "blood" is far more important in I John. Of the six usages in GJohn, four (6:53–56) refer to Jesus' (eucharistic) blood to be drunk, and only one (19:34) refers to the blood shed on the cross. In concentrating on the latter, then, the epistolary author is capitalizing on a minor theme of GJohn. Yet, if the Book of Revelation is an offshoot of Johannine thought, the frequency of the blood theme there suggests that GJohn may not have done justice to its overall importance in Johannine thought, e.g., "To him who loves us and has freed us from our sins by his blood" (Rev 1:5); "For you were slain and by your blood you ransomed men for God" (5:9); "They have washed their robes and made them white in the blood of the Lamb" (7:14; see 12:11). Certainly the theme of the redemptive blood of Christ is common in the NT for initial justification (Col 1:20; Acts 20:28; I Pet 1:18–19), combined with ongoing forgiveness and reconciliation (Eph 1:7; 2:13; Rom 5:9; I Pet 1:2; Heb 9:14).

For information on blood and sacrifices, see R. de Vaux, *Ancient Israel: Its Life and Institutions* (2ed.; London: Darton, Longman & Todd, 1965); D. J. McCarthy, "The Symbolism of Blood and Sacrifice," JBL 88 (1969) 166–76; L. Morris, "The Biblical Use of the Term Blood," JTS 3 (1952) 216–27; Westcott, *Epistles* 34–37; S. Lyonnet, "The Sacrificial Function of Blood," in S. Lyonnet and S. Sabourin, *Sin, Redemption, and Sacrifice* (AnBib 48; Rome: Biblical Institute, 1970) 167–84; also the bibliography there (306–8).

7e. *cleanses us from all sin.* The Johannine redemptive language contains many words to describe what has been done to sin (see Rivera, *La redención* 20–26), including:

- "forgive" (*aphienai*): John 20:23; I John 1:9; 2:12
- "take away" (*airein*): John 1:29; I John 3:5
- "destroy" (*lyein*): I John 3:8
- "atonement, expiation" (*hilasmos*): I John 2:2; 4:10
- "cleanse" (*katharizein*): here; I John 1:9
- "clean" (*katharos*): John 13:10–11

The idea of cleansing or being clean from sin is well attested in the OT, e.g., Ps 19:13(12); Prov 20:9. I John 1:9d will use the synonymous expression, "cleanse us from all wrongdoing" (*adikia*); and that is found in Jer 33(40):8: "I will cleanse them from all their wrongdoings whereby they have sinned against me." Although in the OT such cleansing can refer to either making clean or simply declaring clean, the fact that I John speaks also of destroying and taking away sin makes it clear that a real cleansing is meant here. In John 13:10–11 the disciples are said to be cleansed with the *word* of Jesus (although the context there describes an action of Jesus that is symbolic of his death); but here the author uses the imagery of cleansing with blood reflecting sacrificial terminology from the levitical practices of Israel, as discussed in the preceding NOTE. The outlook is eloquently summarized in the words of the Lord in Lev 17:11: "I have given it [blood] to you that you may make atonement with it upon the altar for your souls," and in Heb 9:22: "According to the Law almost everything is cleansed with blood, and without the shedding of blood there is no forgiveness." Probably the author of I John had a particular OT sacrifice in mind when he described the shedding of Jesus' blood, i.e., the sacrifice on the Day of Atonement; but we shall discuss that under "atonement" in 2:2a below. The present passage never specifies the circumstances under which the cleansing takes place, but I do not find plausible the suggestion of Houlden, *Epistles* 56, "The sense of 1:7 may be that the sacrifice of Jesus serves to obliterate a Christian's sins as soon as they are done." An interval is required between the sin and the forgiveness; for v. 9 casts light on v. 7, and from that verse we learn that a confession of sin was desired. The power over sin given in John 20:23 was probably invoked in the cleansing from sin.

Let us turn now to a discussion of "sin." Inman, "Vocabulary," reports that some 48 NT words are related to this concept, of which only 13 are found in the Johannine literature. And within that 13, four basic words account for 90% of the usage: *hamartia*, "sin"; *hamartanein*, "to sin"; *planan*, "to deceive"; and *poneros*, "evil." The noun used here is *hamartia*, of which there are 17 instances in GJohn (compared to 6 in Mark, 7 in Matthew, and 11 in Luke). Despite the relatively high frequency in GJohn, the fact that there are also 17 uses of *hamartia* in I John (none in II and III John) means that proportionately more attention is given to "sin" here because of the struggle with the secessionists over this question. (The verb *hamartanein* occurs only 3 times in GJohn but 10 times in I John; yet the noun *hamartōlos*, "sinner," occurs 4 times in GJohn and not at all in I John.) Of the 34 Johannine instances of *hamartia*, only 10 are in the plural—this reflects an outlook more concerned with the fundamental reality of sin or the root of sinfulness than with species of sins. The fact that 6 of the 10 plurals are in I John raises the possibility, however, that the author's concern about moral living causes him to think of individual sins somewhat more frequently. (See F.-M. Braun, "La réduction" 51–56.) Some would make a great deal of this variance between the singular and the plural, e.g., H. Braun, "Literar-Analyse" 265, regards the use of the plural in I John as a sign of editorial addition to the putative source, which used the singular. In particular, a comparison between the phrase in the singular in 1:7e "cleanses us from all sin," and the phrase in the plural in 1:9c, "forgive us our sins," has led many to posit a theological difference, e.g., pre-Christian sinfulness in 7e versus sins committed after becoming a Christian in 9c, or justification versus sanctification. Such theories neglect the fact that "all sin" is certainly as inclusive as "our sins." Let me comment on the peculiar form of theological difference posited by Cook, "Problems" 251. For him v. 7 deals "with the defilement caused by the sin nature," while v. 9 deals with defilement caused by sinful acts. Such a distinction imports into the first century later (largely post-Reformation) theological concepts. More seriously, it supposes, first, that there is a Johannine theory of a sinful human *nature*, and, second, that this human nature is not totally changed by belief but needs to go on being controlled. In my judgment, the Augustinian theology of "original sin" goes beyond anything in the NT, and even then it is closer to Pauline than to Johannine thought. According to John 3:3–6, by natural begetting one is of the flesh, which is a mark of incapacity and mortality but not of sin or evil. By being begotten of the Spirit one is dramatically changed, becoming a child of God living by His life. The rule of evil exercised by the Prince of this world is external to human nature, and only by their personal sins do human beings belong to the devil. There is no proof that "sin" for John is an antigodly determination of human nature (*pace* Cooper, "Consciousness" 240), for perduring in sin is the result of personal choice (John 9:41; 15:22,24; 19:11). Personal sins create an orientation toward darkness and away from light; then the orientation leads to more sin. I remain very dubious, then, about profound distinctions found between the singular "sin" in v. 7 and the plural "sins" in v. 9.

8a. *If we boast.* This is exactly the same wording as in 1:6a, followed again in Greek by indirect discourse.

"We are free from the guilt of sin." Literally, "We do not have sin." The "we" again represents Johannine Christians who might make this boast under the influence of secessionist theology. In v. 6a the boast, "We are in communion with Him," was wrong only when those who made it continued to walk in darkness. Here the boast about having no sin seems to be wrong under any circumstance. Why? Some have understood it as a perfectionist claim: We are so perfect that we never have had the slightest lapse into evil. But it has also been understood in a libertine sense: For us who are illumined nothing, however seemingly evil, is sinful. The contrast between the two interpretations is sharp: a perfectionist boast, "We are not guilty, for we have never sinned," over against a libertine, "We are not guilty although we have sinned" (see Kubo, "I John 3:9," 53; he favors the former). This dispute is but the tip of the iceberg, for the implications of this statement have been the subject of theological discussion for centuries. The XV(I) Council of Carthage in 418 took up this text in relation to the Pelagians, denying that the demanded admission of sin was a matter of humility (DBS 228). Over 1100 years later the sixth session of the Council of Trent rejected any claim "that a person once justified cannot sin again . . . that one can avoid all sins, even venial, in one's whole life without a special privilege of God" (DBS 1573). Such later theological discussions have sometimes been read anachronistically back into the texts. Let me list a few suggestions from them that should be firmly rejected (see Bonsirven, *Epîtres* 92–93). The statement, "We do not have sin," cannot be reduced to: "We do not have concupiscence, or an affection for sin." There is no indication that we should confine this "sin" to original sin, or to sexual sin, or to minor sin, or to forgiven past sin, despite early church fathers who have understood it in one of these ways (Tertullian, Cyprian, Cyril of Jerusalem). Even granted the Hebrew distinction between conscious and unconscious sin, there is no evidence that the author is talking about only unconscious sin (*pace* Hodges, "Fellowship" 55).

The key to what the author means is to be sought in the exact connotation of the peculiar Johannine expression, "have sin" (*hamartian echein*), which I have translated as "be guilty of sin." The analogy of the many Johannine phrases in which "have" (*echein*) governs an abstract noun suggests that the expression refers to a state, e.g., to have communion (*koinōnia:* I John 1:3,6,7), confidence (2:28; 3:21; 4:17), hope (3:3), life (3:15; 5:12–13), love (John 5:42; 13:35; 15:13; I John 4:16), joy (John 17:13; III John 4), and peace (John 16:33). The expression "have sin" occurs four times in GJohn (9:41; 15:22,24; 19:11), always in a situation in which a wrong action has already been committed or there is a wrong attitude already existing, and in which something further has occurred to underline the evil of that action. In John 9:41 the Pharisees have not been able to "see" Jesus with the eyes of faith: If they were physically blind, they might not *have sin;* but because they claim to see, their sin remains. In 15:22,24 Jesus says, "If I had not come and spoken to them, they would not *have sin;* but as it is, they have no excuse for their sin." In 19:11 the one who handed Jesus over to Pilate *has* a greater sin than Pilate who will sentence Jesus. In I John 1:8, which is the only instance of "have sin" in the Epistles, the meaning seems to be the same. The author is warning people who have sinned that they cannot claim, "We are free from the guilt of sin." Theirs need not have been an extreme libertinism that said there were no wrong actions for the enlightened and urged wicked deeds with impunity as a way of showing one's freedom from the powers that rule the world (a view attributed to Carpocrates, a second-century heretic, in Irenaeus, *Adv. haer.* 1.25.4, and Eusebius, *Hist.* 4.7.9). Rather, their claim may have reflected the thesis that actions committed by the believer were not important enough to be sins that could challenge the intimacy with God acquired through belief. The author sees such a putative freedom from guilt as a deception.

8b. *we deceive ourselves.* The verb is *planan,* "to lead into error, deceive." The frequency of the verb and related nouns in the Johannine writings may be listed thus:

- *planan,* "to deceive": John 7:12,47 (of Jesus' deceiving people); I John 1:8; 2:26; 3:7 (of people deceiving themselves or others). It may be worth adding that this verb is used eight times in Revelation for the deception practiced by the forces of evil against the servants of God or the nations.
- *planē,* "deceit": I John 4:6: "the Spirit of Deceit"
- *planos,* "deceiver": two times in II John 7

In itself the present usage, "we deceive ourselves," could refer simply to self-deception arising from confusion; but all the other usages of the verb and nouns in the Johannine Epistles refer to the secession that is affecting the Johannine Community. In I John 2:26 "those who deceive you" are the Antichrists who have gone out of the Community denying that Jesus is the Christ (2:18,19,22), even as are the deceivers in II John 7. In I John 3:7 the direction, "Let no one deceive you," is in the context of warning against opponents who are the children of the devil (3:8-10); and the Spirit of Deceit in I John is opposed to the Spirit of God (and of Truth) and is allied to the Antichrist who negates the importance of Jesus (4:1-6). The constant association of deceit with the Antichrist and secession makes it likely that there too the author is thinking of self-deception under the influence of secessionist propaganda. Like the terms for "lie" (the *pseud-* stem words discussed in the NOTE on 1:6c), the terms for "deceit" are the language of Johannine dualism where they appear in opposition to truth. (In the verb "to deceive" there may be greater emphasis on corruption than that found in the verb "to lie.")

The roots of this opposition between deceit and truth are ultimately in the OT, as de la Potterie, *La vérité* 2, 955-56, has pointed out. The noun *planē* occurs in the LXX 6 times, but the verb *planan* 121 times, particularly with the implication of going astray and thus being deceived. The truly heinous danger is the false prophet who "spoke in order to *lead* you *astray* from the Lord your God" (Deut 13:6[5]). In a passage that combines several of the terms that appear in I John 1:5–2:2, the wicked confess in Wis 5:6, "We went astray from the way of truth, and the light of justice did not shine upon us." The intertestamental Jewish material, which offers the best parallelism for dualism, shows awareness of a term besides "lie, falsehood" (*kāzāb, šeqer = pseudos*) as an opposite to "truth," namely, "error, deceit" (*tā'ût*, from the verb root *t'h*, "to err," hiphil "to deceive" = *planē, planan*, as we see from the LXX). The various Hebrew words are virtually interchangeable in the Dead Sea Scrolls for describing wicked enemies. In 4QpNahum 2:8 the deceivers (root *t'h*) are spoken of in terms of lying (*šqr*) and falsehood (*kzb*), while in 1QH 4:16, "the lying [*kzb*] prophets" are said to be "deceived by error [*t'yt*]." In 1QH 2:14–15,31 we find interchangeably "deceiving interpreters" and "lying interpreters." The term *planē* appears opposite "truth" frequently in the Greek *Testaments of the Patriarchs*, e.g., *T. Issachar* 4:6 speaks of "the error of this world" that can make eyes evil; *T. Judah* 20:1 claims, "Two spirits wait upon humanity: the spirit of truth and the spirit of deceit"; *T. Reuben* 2:1; 3:1–6 speaks of seven spirits of deceit. In the NT *planē* as "deceit" becomes a feature of the last times, e.g., I Tim 4:1: "In later times some will depart from the faith by giving heed to deceitful spirits"; Matt 24:24: "The false christs and the false prophets will . . . deceive, if possible, even the elect" (also 24:11); in Rev 12:9 the devil is called "the deceiver of the whole earth" (a description picked up in *Didache* 16:4). Even in a passage without eschatological stress, Eph 4:14 warns against false doctrine shaped by men with cunning and "craftiness in the wiles of deceit." In the gnostic *Gospel of Truth* (I 17:10–18:24; NHL 38) we find a whole myth built around personified Error (*Planē*). Not having known the truth, she fashioned a creature who was a substitute for the truth. When Jesus Christ came and enlightened those who were in darkness, Error grew angry and crucified him but was annihilated by him. For this gnostic use see J.-E. Ménard, "La planè dans l'Evangile de Vérité," *Studia Montis Regis* 7 (1964) 3–36.

8c. *and the truth is not in us*. This is an example of the B classification of the formula of *einai en* discussed in the NOTE on 1:5e. A smoother English translation would be "in our hearts," but the literal Johannine expression catches the note that in Johannine theology people are identified by their inmost being. The logic of the relation between 8c and 8ab is that if the truth were part of one's inner being, it would be efficacious. That is why there can be no truth in the devil (John 8:44).

9a. *But if we confess our sins*. This is an *ean* condition with the present subjunctive as in v. 7a, but with the adversative idea expressed by asyndeton rather than by a *de* particle as there. ZGB 327 says that in this instance the classical grammatical distinction has broken down between a condition that expresses what is possible (usually future in tone) and a condition that expresses a general truth (an atemporal present). The verb *homologein*, "to confess, acknowledge," occurs 4 times in GJohn, 5 times in I John and once in

II John 7, so that the Johannine literature accounts for 40% of the total NT usage (26 times). All the other 9 Johannine uses refer in one way or another to confessing Christ; this is the only instance of confessing sin. Indeed, the expression "confess sins" with *homologein* occurs only here in the NT, although the same expression with the related verb *exomologein* is well attested, both in connection with baptism and for people who have already been Christians for a while. Consult Mark 1:5 and Matt 3:6 for the confessing of sins as or after people were baptized by John the Baptist; Acts 19:18 for believers confessing past evil practices; Jas 5:16 for believers confessing sins to one another in the Christian community; and *Didache* 4:14: "In the church you will confess your transgressions," as part of the instruction before receiving baptism. As for the need to make one's sins known, Prov 28:13 (Heb) gives the principle: "He who conceals his transgressions will not prosper, but the one who confesses them and forsakes them will obtain mercy." Sirach 4:25–26 instructs, "Never speak against the truth, but be mindful of your ignorance. Do not be ashamed to confess your sins." Often this was done in a liturgical context, e.g., Lev 5:5–6: "When someone is guilty of such things, he shall confess the sin he has committed and shall bring his guilt offering to the Lord"; and Dan 9:20: "While I was yet speaking, and praying, and confessing my sin . . ."

All the parallels and background given thus far suggest that the Johannine expression refers to a public confession rather than a private confession by the individual to God (although the latter view was held by Augustine, Oecumenius, Bede, and Theophylact). The fact that in the rest of I John 1:9 God alone is the agent of forgiveness does not prove that the confession is to God rather than to the Community (*pace* Schnackenburg, *Johannesbriefe* 86), for both 1:7 (the previous "But if" condition) and 1:3 show that relations to God are in a Community context. The passage in I John 5:16 suggests some public knowledge of sin in the Johannine Community (though not necessarily public confession). The idea of public confession also receives support from the four uses of *homologein* in GJohn (1:20; 9:22; 12:42) which involve public professions in relation to Jesus. The four christological uses of *homologein* in I John 2:23; 4:2,15 and II John 7 are also most likely public. Michl, *Briefe* 207, argues that the confession in 1:9a has to be public in order to end the self-deception; and he thinks in terms of the Sunday service, as in *Didache* 14:1 where the eucharist on the Lord's Day follows the confession of transgressions. Others, as we shall see, think baptismal practice is being recalled; but there is no way of knowing whether in the Johannine Community the public acknowledgment of sin would have been in a liturgical or worship context. What is probable is that the confession would have been seen as related to Jesus' promise, "If you forgive men's sins, their sins are forgiven; if you hold them, they are held fast" (John 20:23). It is not surprising, then, to find that the Council of Trent (Session XIV, chap. 5; DBS 1679) saw in I John 1:9 a reference to sacramental confession, a view upheld by Bellarmine, Belser, Camerlynck, and Vrede but abandoned by most Roman Catholics today. In the Roman understanding a church usage of Scripture shows how a passage is relevant to church life, but is not necessarily indicative of what the original author meant when he wrote the passage.

9b. *He who is reliable and just.* The two adjectives are *pistos*, "faithful, believing," and *dikaios*, "just, righteous, honest, saintly." The third person is supplied by the verb and refers to the same "He" as in vv. 6 and 7, namely, God (although, as we shall see, Jesus is also "just" in Johannine thought). There are two other Johannine instances of *pistos:* in John 20:27 Jesus addressed Thomas, "Do not persist in your disbelief [*apistos*] but become a believer [*pistos*]"; and in III John 5, "You demonstrate *fidelity* by all the work that you do for the brothers." It is related to *pistis*, "faith, belief" (I John 5:4), and the very frequent Johannine *pisteuein*, "to believe" (ABJ 29, 512–13). The adjective covers the quality of God to which human beings correspond by faith, a characteristic summed up as His fidelity. Deuteronomy 7:9 admonishes, "Know that the Lord your God . . . is the *faithful* God who keeps the covenant and covenant mercy with those who love Him and keep His commandments." This is carried over into the New Covenant, for I Cor 1:9 states, "God is *faithful* by whom you were called into communion [*koinōnia*] with His Son, Jesus Christ," and II Tim 2:13 gives the reassurance, "Even if we are unfaithful, He remains *faithful;* for He cannot deny Himself."

The adjective *dikaios* occurs three times in GJohn: in 5:30 Jesus says, "I judge as I hear, and my judgment is *honest* because I am not seeking my own will but the will of Him who sent me"; in 7:24 he appeals to "the Jews" not to judge by appearances but to give an *honest* judgment; and in 17:25 he addresses as "Father most just" the God whom the world has not known. Thus in GJohn there is no evidence of "just" as a title for Jesus, such as one finds in Acts 3:14; 7:52; and 22:14 (see also *Enoch* 38:2; 53:6). As for I John, besides the present passage, which joins GJohn in calling God "just," there are four occurrences of *dikaios* in 2:1,29; and 3:7. Three of them describe Jesus as "just" while the fourth asks Christians to be just in imitation of him. (Piper, "I John" 442, contends that the epistolary author's tendency to use this title of Jesus reflects primitive Semitic strains in the Johannine tradition [see INTRODUCTION II C2a and V C2d]). In the 3:7 passage the statement that Christ is just is prefaced in 3:5–6 by the idea that he revealed himself to take away sins and "there is nothing sinful [*hamartia*] in him." Indeed, *adikia*, "wrongdoing," or what is not *dikaios*, is another Johannine word for sin; and I John 5:17 states, "All wrongdoing is sin" (cf. 1:9). Similarly John 7:18 states that in Jesus, who seeks the glory of the One who sent him, "there is no wrongdoing." This opposition to sin is usually thought to imply a negative, punitive aspect of the just God or the just Christ, making justice equivalent to condemnation; but in I John the just God is related to the forgiveness of sins, as we see in the next line (1:9c). This is true in the OT as well, where *dikaiosynē*, "justice" (to be discussed in the next paragraph), can be used in the LXX to translate Hebrew *ḥesed*, "God's covenant mercy" (Exod 15:13; 34:7). In Isa 45:21 we hear of "a just God and therefore a Savior," and in Isa 50:8 the verb *dikaioun* is used for God's vindication of the afflicted Servant of the Lord. In Ps 88:12–13(11–12) God's justice is placed in parallelism to His mercy. Lyonnet, "Noun *hilasmos*" 152, concludes, "God is called 'just,' not inasmuch as He punishes sinners, but for the very same reason that He is called 'faithful,' namely insofar as He spares them." Thus, the joining of *pistos* and *dikaios* reflects a covenant attitude toward God, echoing the OT description of a God who is *"faithful* and without injustice, *just* and holy" (Deut 32:4), a God "just and faithful" who could be invoked by His people as a covenant witness (Jer 42[49]:5). Evidently the combination had a certain currency among Christians; for, writing about the same time as the author of I John, Clement of Rome urged: "Let our souls be bound to Him who is faithful in His promises and just in His judgments" (*I Clem.* 27:1; also 60:1).

The related noun *dikaiosynē,* "justification, righteousness," so popular with Paul, occurs only two times in GJohn (16:8,10), both in reference to Jesus' death. The idea is that, despite appearances of sinfulness, he is justified by his return to the Father. Scholars debate whether primarily this means juridical innocence (his cause is shown to have been just) or moral righteousness (involving sanctity by which he has conquered sin); but surely in Johannine thought the first would have to be based on the second, so that both are meant (see Vellanickal, *Sonship* 248–49). As for I John, *dikaiosynē* occurs three times, always in the phrase *poiein (tēn) dikaiosynēn,* "to do justice, act justly." This is a Greek OT phrase, often occurring in passages that combine judgment (*krima, krisis*) with doing justice. For instance, in II Sam 8:15 David exercises his rule over the people by "doing judgment and justice." In Ps 106:3 there is a macarism for those who "keep judgment" (observe what has been decreed) and "do justice" (act rightly); and a similar combination is found in Isa 56:1 and 58:2. In a first-century B.C. work, *PsSol* 9:5, we find doing justice and doing wrong in antithetic parallelism. In the NT outside I John, the Greek phrase "to do justice" occurs only three times (Matt 6:1; Rom 10:5; Rev 22:11; see Titus 3:5); but similar expressions include "to work [*ergazesthai*] justice" (Acts 10:35, etc.; see Ps 15:2) and "to fulfill justice" (Matt 3:15). A study of the three I John passages shows that, as in GJohn, the approach to justice or righteousness is not merely juridical. The author is putting the demand to act justly in the OT sense of doing what is right; only now it is in imitation of Christ who is just (2:29; 3:7), and this broadens the concept. (Thus Bonsirven, *Epîtres* 162, claims that for John *dikaiosynē* has become the ensemble of all virtues.) In the context of 3:7,10 the author, like *PsSol* 9:5, contrasts doing justice with doing sin, and the two ways of acting become revelatory of whether one belongs to God or to the devil.

One can put together the Johannine occurrences of *dikaios,* "just," and *dikaiosynē,* "justice," to construct a typically Johannine chain of relationship. God the Father is just; Jesus the Son who does God's will and does not commit sin is just; this is manifested particularly in his death where what appeared to the world to be a conviction because of Jesus' sinfulness is really a victory because of his justice; Jesus manifests his justice by judging justly, separating those who believe in him from those who reject him unjustly because they do not know God; the believers must imitate him, in turn, by acting justly.

9c. *will forgive us our sins.* Literally, "so that He forgives us sins": a *hina* clause dependent on two adjectives; see the similar construction in John 1:27. Although *hina* usually introduces an intended result rather than an actual one (which should be expressed by an infinitive: BDF 391[5]), Johannine grammar is not precise enough for us to decide whether such a clause is final (purpose) or consecutive (result). Moule, IBNTG 142, comments on the Semitic lack of feeling for such a distinction. In any case, I have used the future to indicate both intention and assured result. The assurance comes not only from a divine decree but also from the divine being, since God is reliable and just.

In the NOTE on 1:7e, in listing the various Johannine words for removing sin, I mentioned that *aphienai*, "to forgive," is used three times. The verb literally means "to let go, release" and reflects a legal background, being used of debt and trespass as well. In the LXX it appears in a cultic setting as well: "The priest will make atonement for sin, and the sin will be forgiven" (Lev 4:20; 19:22). A covenant setting is apparent in Num 14:19: "Forgive the sin of your people according to the abundance of your covenant mercy." In the present Johannine passage "sins" is a plural, as contrasted with the singular in 1:7e (see NOTE there). There is no "our" in the Greek, for the "us" makes the meaning clear; but some MSS. introduced it for smoothness (Sinaiticus, Ephraemi Rescriptus), as I have done in my translation.

9d. *and cleanse us from all wrongdoing*. I discussed the verb *katharizein*, "cleanse," in the NOTE on the parallel expression in 1:7e, "cleanses us from all sin." The term *adikia*, "wrongdoing," which is the opposite of *dikaios*, "just," was chosen by the author here (instead of "sin") by way of antithesis to the "just" God of v. 9b (see NOTE there). In I John 5:17, the only other epistolary use of *adikia*, "sin" and "wrongdoing" are identified. (The only GJohn use of *adikia* is 7:18 where it is opposed to truthfulness.) This makes it clear that v. 9c, "forgive us our sins," and 9d, "cleanse us from all wrongdoing," are in parallelism and there is no progression (*pace* Plummer), as if forgiveness concerned individual sins or legal guilt, while cleansing concerned original sin or internal purification. In both these ways of saying the same thing, more than the removing of a legal barrier is involved—the human being is cleansed. Brooke, *Epistles* 20–21, says, "God cannot treat it [sin] as non-existent, unless it has been actually or potentially removed or destroyed."

10a. *If we boast, "We have not sinned."* This is the same "If [*ean*] we say that" condition, followed by indirect discourse, that we saw in 1:6a and 8a. For many scholars, "We have not sinned" (perf. tense of *hamartein*) is a repetition of 1:8a, "We do not have sin" (pres. of *hamartian echein*)—thus Kirbo, Marshall, Schnackenburg, Schneider. Others find a sharp difference, based either on grammar (different tenses) or on factors introduced from later theology (e.g., a sinful principle or nature in 1:8a versus actual sin here)—thus Cook, Westcott. In the NOTE on 8a I argued from the Johannine usage of *hamartian echein* that the earlier boast involved a denial of the guilt of sin; here I think a denial of sins or bad actions is involved. But could secessionist theology really have urged people to say that they never had committed sins? There would have been enormous OT weight to the contrary of such a position, e.g., Prov 20:9, "Who can possibly brag that he is clean [*katharos*] from sin?"; and I Kings 8:46: "There is not a man who will not sin" (see also Gen 8:21; Ps 14:3; 53:2; Job 4:17; 15:14–16; Eccl 7:20[21]). And in intertestamental Judaism the consciousness of sinfulness was accentuated. At Qumran those who entered the community had to confess, "We have sinned and our fathers before us in walking counter to the commandments of truth and justice" (1QS 1:25–26). Philo, *Allegorical Interpretation* (1.13 ⅔35), explains that someone may try vainly to escape the charge of having sinned either by claiming that, not having known what was good, he did not know what was evil, or by claiming that what happened was involuntary. As for Christians, the demand for *metanoia*, "repentance," was remembered as part of Jesus' preaching of the kingdom (Mark 1:5) and as part of the apostles' demand before baptism (Acts 2:38). The fundamental Christian prayer contained the words, "Forgive us our sins/debts" (Luke 11:4; Matt 6:12). And in GJohn there is a supposition that Jesus came down from heaven to encounter a human race afflicted by sin: the Lamb of God takes away the sin of the world (John 1:29) and those who refuse to believe die in their sins (8:24). These texts make the secessionist-inspired claim quoted in I John 1:10, "We have not sinned," difficult to understand, unless it refers to *sins committed after becoming a Christian*. Such a limitation would make sense in the context, for the four preceding verses all concern the behavior of Christians and how they walk after they have seen the light. In the COMMENT I shall try to show how the secessionists might have deduced from GJohn that, having been begotten as children of God (the believers), they could not be convicted of sin.

10b. *we make Him a liar*. For the "Him" as God, see the NOTE on 1:6a, "communion with Him." If I am correct in arguing that 1:10a claims more than 1:8a, so also 1:10b is stronger than 1:8b, "We deceive ourselves." It is one thing to deceive oneself; it is far more serious to make a liar out of God. (The same expression occurs in I John 5:10: "The person who does not believe God has made Him a liar.") The expression "making" a person what he is not occurs in GJohn in various charges against Jesus: making himself a king (19:12); making himself greater than Abraham (8:53); making himself God's equal or God's Son (5:18; 10:33; 19:7). The devil "is a liar and the father of lying" (8:44), so to make God a liar is to reduce Him to the level of a devil. The charge that a secessionist-inspired claim would make God a liar is not surprising granted the fact that in I John 2:4,22 and 4:20 those who hold secessionist theology are branded as liars. There is Johannine logic to the charge that the denial of sins makes God a liar because God claimed to have sent Jesus as the Lamb who takes away the world's sin.

10c. *and His word is not in us*. Like the parallel statement in 1:8c, "the truth is not in us," this is an example of the B classification of the formula *einai en* discussed in the NOTE on 1:5e. Malatesta, *Interiority* 114, contends that there is a progression from "truth" to "word" in that the word, as an interior principle within the soul, communicates the truth. Such precisions may go beyond the author's intentions, however, for John 17:17 says, "Your word is truth." In any case, it is clear that "word" (*logos*) here is not personified as in the GJohn Prologue. It is the divine revelation spoken by Jesus—a word that remains God's word: "The word that you hear is not my own but comes from the Father who sent me" (John 14:24). People are given this divine word by Jesus (17:14); they hear the word (5:24); they believe the word (4:50) or believe in Jesus through God's word (17:20); they keep the word (8:51–52; 14:23; 15:20; 17:6); they remember the word (15:20); they remain in the word (8:31) and the word remains in them (5:38; I John 2:14); and they are cleansed by the word (15:3). On the other hand, the Johannine opponents cannot hear the word (8:43); they are divided over it (10:19); they find it hard (6:60); they question its meaning (7:36); it finds no place in them (8:37); they do not keep it (14:24); and they are judged by it (12:48). Some of these ideas can be found elsewhere in the NT, e.g., Col 3:16, "Let the word of Christ dwell in you"; Jas 1:21: "Receive the implanted word which is able to save your souls." (These are all references involving *logos;* much the same is said of the synonym *rēma,* "word.") Such passages attributing activity to the divine word have a background in the OT: Isa 55:11, "So shall my word be that goes forth from my mouth; it shall . . . accomplish that which I intend"; Wis 16:26, "Your word preserves those who trust in you."

2:1a. Every commentator recognizes that this line breaks the pattern of the unit under discussion. As the author suddenly begins to write in the first person singular, he also shifts to direct address in the second person plural, a "you" rather than a "we." However, these changes, which are not continued in the rest of the verse, probably do not mark the beginning of a new unit. Rather a third *ean* ("But if") clause, expressing the author's own view, appears in 2:1b. It challenges the third *ean* ("If we boast") secessionist statement of 1:10a, even as the "But if" clause of 1:9a challenged the "If we boast" statement of 1:8a, and the "But if" clause of 1:7a challenged the "If we boast" statement of 1:6a. The best way to explain 2:1a is as a parenthesis called forth by pastoral need: Although insisting that Christians do sin, the author does not wish to encourage sin.

1a. *My Little Children.* The Greek is the pl. of *teknion.* In his use of "we" in vv. 6–10 the author has been speaking as part of the Johannine Community; but, as was apparent in vv. 1–5, there is a sense in which he is part of a "we" (the Johannine School of tradition-bearers) that is distinct from a "you" (those in the Johannine Community who receive the tradition from the tradition-bearers). He now interrupts the unit parenthetically to resume the first-person-to-second-person relationship and speaks to the "you" as to his children. (When he speaks as part of the "we" of the Johannine Community, he can use "Brothers" as direct address; see NOTE on 3:13.) There are three words for "children," always plural, employed in the Johannine Epistles, distinct from *huios,* "son," which is confined to Jesus when it is used religiously (12 times in the Johannine literature, of which 9 are in the Epistles). Helpful here is Culpepper, *School* 301–2.

- *Teknon,* "child," is used a total of 9 times in the Epistles. In I John it is used 4 times (3:1,2,10; 5:2) for the children of God, and once (3:10) for the children of the devil. In II John it is used 3 times (1,4,13) for members of local churches which are personified as women; in III John 4 such church members are spoken of as the author's own children. In 3 GJohn uses, it is twice used for children of God (1:12; 11:52) and once for children (descendants) of Abraham (8:39).

■ *Teknion*, "little child," is a diminutive of *teknon*, whence my (overly) literal translation. The two words were probably interchangeable in common speech, but their use is quite distinct in the Johannine writings. If *teknon* refers to God's children and is not an address, the 7 uses of *teknion* in I John (2:1,12,28; 3:7,18; 4:4; 5:21) are direct addresses by the author to those whom he considers his (spiritual) children. *Teknion* has a caritative or endearing force, setting up an affectionate relationship between the speaker and his audience. The one use in GJohn (13:33) is at the beginning of the Last Discourse, as Jesus addresses his disciples, "his own." (Compare Mark 10:24: "My children" [*teknon*].)

■ *Paidion*, "child," is a diminutive of *pais*, "boy, son." (In the one use of *pais* in GJohn [4:51] it is interchangeable with *paidion* [4:49].) In GJohn there is one instance of *paidion* in the plural as an address by Jesus to his disciples in 21:5. The two uses in I John (2:14,18) are plural addresses to the author's audience, interchangeable with the plural of *teknion* as a comparison of 2:12a and 2:14a shows.

In summary, then, in the Epistles *teknon* is used in the plural for the children of God or the church, while the plurals of *teknion* and *paidion* are used as direct address for the readers who are clearly Christians of the author's own Community. (The latter usage is peculiar in the NT; it is *teknon* that Paul uses in the plural as an address in Gal 4:19.) Such a paternal address need not imply that the author had converted or baptized the Christians to whom he is writing (along the lines of I Cor 4:15: "You do not have a plurality of fathers, for in Christ Jesus I begot you through the gospel"). Wisdom teachers were accustomed to address those whom they instructed as "child" or "children" (*teknon* in Sir 2:1; 3:1; Ps 34:12 [11]; *pais* in Prov 4:1; *huios* in Prov 5:1; 7:24; 8:32; *paidion* in Tobit 4:3,12,13—note that *teknion* does not occur in the LXX). This pattern was influenced by the fact the genre of wisdom admonitions had its origins in a father's instructions to his sons. More widely Deut 11:19 instructs the Israelites to teach God's words "to your children" (*teknon*); and Isa 54:13 (cited in John 6:45) promises, "All your sons [*huios*] shall be taught by the Lord." In 1QH 7:20–21 the Qumran psalmist (the Righteous Teacher?) says, "You made me a father to the sons of grace . . . they have opened their mouths like children at the breast." See St-B 1, 198–99, for the rabbinic pattern of addressing "sons" or "children." Elsewhere in the NT, I Pet 2:2 compares Christians to "newborn babes." In light of this background the use of the address in the Johannine Epistles means that the author speaks as a member of the Johannine School preserving a tradition "from the beginning," imitating Jesus' affectionate address for his disciples at the Last Supper as he gave them the commandment to love (John 13:33). In this father-to-children pattern the implicit authority is that of a tradition-bearer; the implicit age is that of an elder in Christianity ("the Presbyter" of II and III John).

It need not mean that the author was an old man, although the "children" address has contributed to the picture of the aged John as the author of the Epistles. In the famous story of the apostle John told by Clement of Alexandria (*Quis dives salvetur* 42.1–15; GCS 17, 188–90) and by Eusebius

(*Hist.* 3.23.6–19), John seeks out a robber chief (who had been entrusted to a bishop for upbringing but who had gone astray) and addresses him, "Why, my child [*teknon*], do you flee from me, your own father, who is unarmed and aged?" In the story of John in "extreme old age" told by Jerome (INTRODUCTION, footnote 46), he addresses his disciples over and over as "Little Children" (pl. of *filiolus* which represents *teknion* in the OL).

I am writing this. Contrasted with "we are writing this" in the Prologue (4a) when the author spoke in the name of the whole Johannine School, the present formula reflects a more personal stance. In the Epistles the first person singular of "write" appears 12 times (6 present tense, 6 aorist). In II Corinthians there is a similar phenomenon; for, after Paul says "we write" in 1:13, he shifts to the first person singular (5 times: once in the present [13:10], 4 times in the aorist). To what does the "this" (literally, "these things") refer? In the Prologue (4a) the "this" was most probably a reference to the whole of I John, and Brooke, Büchsel, Stott, and Westcott opt for the same reference here. However, the purpose clause that follows ("to keep you from sin") is too narrow a goal for the whole Epistle; and so Bultmann, Plummer, Schnackenburg, THLJ, and others are more likely correct in arguing that the reference is to 1:8–10 where the author has been talking about the certainty of sin.

to keep you from sin. Literally, "in order that you may not sin"; the aorist tense of the verb may suggest that the author is thinking of sinful actions. MGNTG 3, 72 and ZGB 251 contend that the pres. tense of this verb means "to be a sinner," while the aorist means "to commit a sin." Yet Stagg, "Orthodoxy" 428, sharply rejects this; for he contends that the pres. tense is progressive while the aorist looks at a situation nondescriptively from a momentary viewpoint and tells us nothing about the nature of the action itself. In any case, Gaugler, *Johannesbriefe* 85–86, is right in arguing that more is meant here than an urging not to be a habitual sinner (so that occasional sins would be tolerable)—the author is placing upon the Johannine Christian the same absolute eschatological demand that Jesus placed on the healed paralytic: "Sin no more" (John 5:14). A somewhat similar sentiment is found in Rom 6:1: "Are we to go on sinning so that grace may abound? By no means."

1b. *But if anyone does sin.* An *ean*, "if," condition (preceded by a *kai* adversative) is counterposed to the secessionist-inspired *ean* condition of 1:10a. In the two previous examples of this construction (1:7a and 9a), the subject was "we"; here it is "anyone" (*tis*), perhaps stylistic, perhaps because the contents of this condition are more negative than in the previous examples and so he prefers a hypothetic subject.

1c. *we have a Paraclete.* The "we," absent from the protasis, appears in the apodosis with its positive message. In ABJ 29A, 1135–1144 I discussed the term *paraklētos* which in the NT is peculiar to the Johannine writings. "Advocate, intercessor, consoler, exhorter" are possible meanings; but none of them fully captures the GJohn picture of the Spirit as *paraklētos*, which accordingly I left simply transliterated as "Paraclete." In this passage, the sole use of the term in I John, it is often translated as "intercessor, spokesman"; but again it may be just as well to leave the term untranslated for reasons to be explained under 1d below. Two details from GJohn partially prepare us for the fact that *Jesus* is called a Paraclete in I John. First, the Spirit/Paraclete of GJohn is closely modeled on Jesus, to the point that the Spirit functions as another Jesus (ABJ 29A, 1141). Second, in John 14:16–17 Jesus speaks of the Spirit as "another Paraclete," implying that he himself had been a Paraclete. Yet the problem of Jesus as the Paraclete in I John 2:1c is not solved, for in GJohn Jesus would have been a Paraclete in his earthly ministry, while in I John Jesus is a Paraclete in heaven before the Father. Moreover, in I John the relative silence about the Spirit is puzzling—the fact that Jesus is a Paraclete does not explain why the term is never applied to the Spirit (which is not even called "Holy Spirit").

in the Father's presence. Literally, "toward [*pros*] the Father," the same Greek as in 1:2e where eternal life "was in the Father's presence," and in John 1:1b where "the Word was in God's presence." The expression connotes both presence with and relationship toward; it can be used to describe both a preincarnational and a postresurrectional relationship between Jesus the Word and God the Father. Such a relationship makes Jesus effective as a Paraclete.

1d. *Jesus Christ, the one who is just.* The full personal name occurring near the end of this unit matches the usage of "Jesus Christ" near the end of the Prologue (1:3e) and lends solemnity. The appositive is literally, "the just one [*dikaios*]," but Westcott, *Epistles* 43, rightly insists on predicative force. In discussing *dikaios* as a description of God in 1:9b, we saw that it need not imply a punitive attitude but more often is salvific; certainly it is salvific here where the just Jesus serves as a Paraclete for sinners. As Stott, *Epistles* 81, has recognized, it is not a case of the loving Jesus pleading with the just God, but the just Jesus in the presence of the God who is love (I John 4:8,16). *Dikaios* here has also the connotation of innocence and righteousness (Spicq, *L'origine* 263–64): before the Father, Jesus is one in whom there is no *adikia*, "wrongdoing," from which all others need to be cleansed (1:9d). Note that the mention of Christ as "just" in I John 3:7 follows 3:5: "There is nothing sinful in him."

Granted both the salvific and innocent implications of Jesus as *dikaios*, what precisely does the just one do as a Paraclete for sinners in the Father's presence? Is he an *advocate* seeking justice in defending the sinner or an innocent *intercessor* pleading for those who are not—both are translations of *paraklētos*. The latter is the more usual interpretation and has good OT background. In Gen 18:20–33 Abraham intercedes for Sodom, and in Exod 8:28–29 Moses for Pharaoh. Closer to Jesus' time, Wis 18:21 describes Aaron's ability to intercede because he was a blameless man; and Philo, *On the Migration of Abraham* 21 ⚹⚹121–22, comments on how God gives His gifts in answer to the supplications of the just man (*dikaios*). In the NT, Heb 9:14 asks rhetorically, "How much more shall the blood of Christ, who through the eternal Spirit offered himself without blemish to God, purify your conscience from dead works to serve the living God?"; Rom 8:34 speaks of Christ "who is at the right hand of God, who indeed intercedes for us"; and I Pet 3:18 affirms, "Christ died for sins once for all, the just for [*hyper*] the unjust." Nevertheless, against the intercession interpretation of I John 2:1, Lyonnet, "Noun *hilasmos*" 152–53, points out that in John 16:26–27 the believer needs no intercessor: "On that day you will ask in my name; and I do not say that I shall have to petition the Father for you, for the Father loves you Himself." To this objection one may counter that the Johannine Jesus is talking about believers who are themselves "just," while I John is talking about believers who have sinned and thus lost the direct line to God. In John 9:31 we hear "that God pays no attention to sinners"; and *II Clem.* 6:9 asks, "Who will be our Paraclete if we are not found to have holy and just works?" Still the point made by Lyonnet has force in turning us toward the possibility that in I John 2:1 the author may be thinking of Jesus not primarily (or only) as intercessor but as advocate or attorney, depriving Satan of his ancient legal role in relation to sinners before the judgment seat of God (Job 1:6–2:7; Zech 3:1–3). I John 3:8 says, "The reason the Son of God revealed himself was to destroy the works of the devil"; and John 16:8–11 shows that there is a forensic aspect in the role of the Spirit/Paraclete. But in the Johannine substitution of the Paraclete(s) for Satan there is a reversal: Those prosecuted are those who refuse to believe in Jesus (John 16:9), while those defended successfully are Jesus and the believers. On earth the Spirit/Paraclete defends Jesus after death—in ABJ 29A, 1138, I raised the possibility that the very idea of *paraklētos* was derived from the OT picture of the angelic spokesman (*mēlīṣ*) who defends the just man, even after death, against Satan. At the same time that the Spirit/Paraclete is active on earth, Jesus the Paraclete has gone victoriously to the Father, casting down Satan (John 16:7,10–11; 12:31; Rev 12:10). This means that believers now have someone who defends them before God instead of accusing them. As we shall see, the next verse in I John makes implicit reference to the Day of Atonement, and a talmudic tradition (TalBab *Yoma* 20a) is interesting, if it was known in the first century: "On the Day of Atonement Satan is deprived of every power to accuse Israel." Perhaps the best solution is to recognize that in I John 2:1–2 Jesus stands before the Father both as intercessor and defending advocate: Not only does he plead for sinners, but he points out that as believers in the Son they are children of God who have a right to be forgiven by a God who is their Father. Jesus had promised such believers that they would not come under condemnation (John 5:24); and God's relation to them was to be one of communion (I John 1:3: *koinōnia*). Here then we would not be too far from Matt 10:32, "Everyone who acknowledges me before men, I also will acknowledge before my Father who is in heaven."

2a. *and he himself is an atonement for our sins.* As Balz, *Johannesbriefe* 169, has recognized, we move now from the setting of an advocate before a heavenly court to that of a high priest in a heavenly temple; and Westcott, *Epistles* 44, is correct in insisting that the manner in which Jesus is a *paraklētos* in 2:1 must be interpreted through the reference to him as a *hilasmos*, "atonement," in 2:2. Bultmann, *Epistles* 23, exaggerates when he sees a contradiction between forgiveness of sins through intercession (2:1 from the epistolary author) and atonement for sins through blood (2:2 from the Ecclesiastical Redactor). Those ideas were already joined in intertestamental Judaism where the martyrs made intercession at the moment they were shedding their blood, e.g. *IV Macc.* 6:28–29 in which Eleazar says as he faces martyrdom, "Be merciful [adj. related to *hilasmos*] to Your people and let our punishment suffice for them; make my blood serve as a *cleansing* for them and take my life for theirs." (See E. Lohse, *Märtyren und Gottesknechte* [FRLANT NF 48; Göttingen: Vandenhoeck & Ruprecht, 1955] 64–110.) And if *parakletos* has a more forensic background, the introduction of *hilasmos* into such a setting is not unattested, e.g., Ps 130:3–4: "If you, O Lord, mark iniquities, Lord, who could stand? But with you there is mercy [*hilasmos*] for the sake of your name."

Let me begin with reflection on the word *hilasmos* itself and then turn to the Johannine context. Since the author was describing Jesus, a person, one might have expected him to use the concrete term *hilaster* (one who offers atonement) rather than the abstract *hilasmos* (atonement/atoning action). The answer to this may lie in the fact that like the neuter "what" in 1:1, the abstract noun is more complexive (Clavier, "Notes" 295–97; THLJ 41) and catches the fact that Jesus is victim as well as priest. A glance at the Bibliography for this unit will suggest that *hilasmos* is not a term easily understood. English translations for it include: atonement, atoning sacrifice, expiation, propitiation, remedy for defilement, sacrifice for sin; and in antiquity the Latin translations reflected a similar range of meaning: *deprecatio, exoratio, placatio, propitiatio*. A series of Greek words from the same root must be considered:

- *hilaskesthai*, a verb used 11 times in the LXX and twice in the NT (never in the Johannine writings): Luke 18:13: "God, *be merciful* to me a sinner"; and Heb 2:17: Jesus became "a merciful and faithful high priest in the service of God to *make expiation* for the sins of the people."

- *exilaskesthai*, which with over 100 uses in the LXX is ten times more frequent than *hilaskesthai*. It is never used in the NT but appears in the Apostolic Fathers: *I Clem.* 7:7: "The people of Nineveh . . . when they repented, they *propitiated* God and gained salvation"; *Hermas, Vis.* 1.2.1: "How shall I *propitiate* God for the sins I have committed?"

- *hilasterion*, a noun used 27 times in the LXX (22 of which refer to the mercy seat or cover of the Ark of the Covenant) and twice in the NT (never in the Johannine writings): Rom 3:24–25: "The redemption which is in Christ Jesus whom God put forward as an *expiation* (propitiation) by his blood, to be received by faith"; Heb 9:5: "Above the Ark were the cherubim of glory overshadowing the mercy seat."

- *hilasmos*, a noun used 10 times in the LXX and twice in the NT, both in I John: the present passage, and 4:10: "God loved us and sent His Son as an *atonement* for our sins."

- *hileos*, an adjective used some 35 times in the LXX, particularly to describe God as He turns His anger from His people. It is used twice in the NT (never in the Johannine writings): Matt 16:22, "[May God] be merciful to you, Lord"; Heb 8:12 (citing Jer 31[48]34): "I will be merciful toward their wrongdoings [*adikia*]."

The root of the Greek word is related to *hilaros* and *hilaroun* (English "hilarity") and so has something to do with rendering pleasant. However, a sharp debate has developed among scholars about the imagery involved in the biblical religious usage of the terms above. Is there an angry God who is placated by having sacrifices offered to Him by the offender (propitiation), or is the offender made pleasing in God's eyes by the wiping away of the sin and impurity that had made him offensive (expiation)? Even though the same action might be involved, propitiation is primarily directed toward the offended person, while expiation is directed toward removing what has caused the breakdown (Hill, *Greek Words* 23). In classical Greek and in the common pagan religion usage of NT times, words related to *hilasmos* had the meaning of placating or propitiating. In the LXX of Zech 7:2 and Mal 1:9 *hilaskesthai* is used with God as an object to express the pagan idea of placating God, an idea of which the author disapproves. However, as Dodd and Lyonnet have observed, this is not the dominant usage of *hilasmos*-related words in the LXX, for *hilaskesthai* and *exilaskesthai* normally do not have God as an object. Rather God is the subject and the verb takes on the sense of forgiving; or there is a human subject (a priest) who cleanses something from sin and impurity, thus making it pleasing to God. Most frequently these Greek words render a Hebrew word from the stem *kpr* which has as one meaning "cover over," and indeed can be translated into Greek by words other than the *hilasmos* group, e.g., words meaning "sanctify, cleanse." On the basis of the Hebrew background and the LXX usage there has been a growing tendency to translate NT *hilaskesthai*, *hilastērion*, and *hilasmos* in terms of "expiate, expiation," i.e., "an activity which is essentially intended to remove sin by cleansing and therefore reconcile man to God" (Lyonnet, *Sin* 146).

Other scholars, however, like Hill, Morris, and Thornton, object that there is a strong sense of propitiation in the words related to *hilasmos*. First, Hill (*Greek Words* 33) points out that in cultic passages it is often impossible to distinguish propitiation from expiation. Second, Thornton, "Propitiation," points out biblical passages where *hilaskesthai* probably does refer to propitiating God without any pagan or pejorative connotation, e.g., Ps 106:30; Sir 45:23. Indeed, Zech 8:22 envisions many people coming to Jerusalem "to propitiate the face of the Lord." Third, Morris, *Apostolic Preaching* 138-40, argues that those who opt for expiation have neglected the context in the LXX use of *hilasmos*-related words where the wrath of God appears frequently. Indeed, the rationale for the possibility of atonement is supplied by Micah 7:18-19: "God does not retain His anger forever because He delights in mercy." (Note John 3:36: "Whoever disobeys the Son . . . must endure God's wrath.") Fourth, the imagery that sacrifices have a pleasing smell to God cannot be separated from propitiation. Fifth, early church writers accepted the notion of propitiation in both OT and Christian contexts, as the citations of the Apostolic Fathers under *exilaskesthai* above show. None of this need imply crudely buying off an angry deity with sacrifices; rather God has appointed for His people means of removing evil and of turning away wrath. God is not manipulated by rites; He instituted the rites and always takes the initiative in pardoning. The sin sacrifices please Him because of the obedience to His will shown by those who offer them, an obedience expressive of sorrow. And in the case of Jesus, as Hoskyns, "Epistles" 661–62, observes, God's love is apparent not only in accepting the sacrifice after it was offered but even more in providing the priest and victim (see I John 4:10).

Overall, then, it seems that there are connotations both of expiation and of propitiation in the *hilasmos*-related words. Which dominates in I John 2:2 where Jesus is designated as a *"hilasmos* for our sins"? If one considers the other I John passage where *hilasmos* is employed (4:10), it favors expiation: "God loved us and sent His Son as a *hilasmos* for our sins." There is no mention of wrath in the context, and the Son is sent from God—if he was propitiating God, the action would be in the other direction. If we consider the context of 2:2a, that line is parallel to 1:7de, "The blood of Jesus, His Son, cleanses us from all sin"; and that parallelism favors expiation since human beings are cleansed. (As mentioned above, *katharizein*, "to cleanse," is sometimes used to translate *kippēr*, the Hebrew verb most often rendered by *hilaskesthai*, e.g., Exod 29:37; 30:10). Nevertheless, the preposition in the expression *"hilasmos* for our sins" leaves open the possibility of a victim propitiating God, even if Stott, *Epistles* 87, makes too much of the preposition. It is *peri*, "with respect to," and not *hyper*, "on behalf of," and reflects the LXX translation of Hebrew *'al* after *kippēr* (Lev 5:6 and *passim*), an idiom that is noncommittal on the expiation/propitiation issue.

Still more light is cast on 2:1–2 when we consider a special OT background. Already in the third century Origen (*Homilies on Leviticus* 9.5; GCS 29, 427) recognized that the passage was written in light of the Jewish ritual for the Day of the Atonement, called in the LXX of Lev 25:9 *hē hēmera tou hilasmou*, reflecting Hebrew *yôm hakkippurîm* (Yom Kippur), a holy day celebrated on the tenth day of the seventh month. According to Lev 16, the high priest offered a bull and a goat as a sacrifice in respect to (*peri*) the sins of the priesthood (including his own) and those of the people. He then took this blood into the Holy of Holies (the only time in the year he entered there) and sprinkled it on the *hilastērion* (*kappōret*), i.e., the gold lid or "mercy seat" or "propitiatory" covering the Ark of the Covenant—a term rendered into Aramaic as "covering" in 4QTLevi 1:6. This was the locus of God's presence in the Tabernacle and the Temple. As described, this rite of *hilasmos* points toward expiation rather than propitiation. In the key sentence (Lev 16:16), "Thus he shall___[form of *exilaskesthai* in Greek and of *kippēr* in Hebrew] the Holy Place from the impurities of the Israelites and from their wickednesses [*adikēma*] in respect to [*peri*] all their sins," the only plausible translation of the verb is "cleanse, sanctify." The blood has removed the sins of the people. In Hebrews 9–10 this ritual of the Day of the Atonement is applied to Jesus. As a high priest he passes through a celestial outer court into the heavenly Holy of Holies where God is present (9:11,24); he does not do this once a year but once for all (9:7,12); he does not bring the blood of bulls (he has no sin of his own: 7:26–27) or the blood of goats but his own blood—he is the spotless victim who has offered himself at the end of the ages (9:12–14), and his sacrifice is consummated in heaven (see JBC 61 ⚹⚹52–53) where he is now seated at the right hand of God (10:12). Indeed, his blood continues to purify (9:14), offering encouragement: "Let us then with confidence draw near to the throne of grace that we may receive mercy and find grace to help us in time of need" (4:16); "We have confidence to enter the sanctuary by the blood of Jesus" (10:19). Since according to the Law things are cleaned with blood "and without the shedding of blood there is no forgiveness of sins" (9:22), believers are sanctified and purified through this sacrifice of Christ (10:10), and sin is annulled (10:17–18). There is no doubt that the sacrifice of Christ on the once-for-all Christian Day of Atonement described in Hebrews is more an expiation than a propitiation.

There is good reason to think that I John reflects this background when we find in quick succession: "The blood of Jesus, His Son, cleanses us from all sin" (1:7), and "We have a Paraclete in the Father's presence, Jesus Christ, the one who is just, and he himself is an atonement (*hilasmos*) for our sins" (2:1–2). Hebrews' Day of Atonement description and I John share the concepts of *hilasmos*, blood, cleansing, the innocent victim, and the idea that the one who atones is himself in heaven continuing to cleanse, thus offering a basis of confidence for sinners. (Overall C. Spicq, *L'Epître aux Hébreux* [2 vols.; Paris: Gabalda, 1952] 1, 109–38, lists 16 parallels between Hebrews and the Johannine writings; for parallels to the Prologue of Hebrews, see ABJ 29, 21,521,522.) It is worth adding that GJohn and Hebrews share the view of Jesus as priest-victim. In John 10:36 on the feast of the Dedication of the Temple-altar (Hanukkah), Jesus speaks of himself as "the one whom the Father consecrated and sent into the world" (cf. Heb 5:5–6; 10:5–9). The "high priestly" prayer of John 17 is uttered when Jesus is no longer in the world (17:11) and is on the way back to the glory that he shares with God (17:5)—this prayer exemplifies the Paraclete function of Jesus in I John 2:1 as he prays for those whom he has left behind. The statement in John 17:19, "It is for [*hyper*] them that I consecrate myself, in order that they too may be consecrated in truth," is very close to Heb 9:14: "Christ . . . through the eternal Spirit offered himself without blemish to God" and to Heb 10:14: "By a single offering he has perfected for all time those who are consecrated" (also 10:10). The Johannine notion of the crucifixion as the lifting up of Jesus (ABJ 29A, 541–42) blurs the dividing line between death and ascension, and resembles Hebrews' picture of Jesus going with his own blood into the heavenly Holy of Holies. The priestly imagery that GJohn uses for Jesus may have influenced I John's description of Jesus as a *paraklētos* and a *hilasmos* for sins; for when Philo (*Moses* 2.26 ※134) describes the high priest and the Father's Son (the world), he speaks of a *paraklētos* so that sins might be remembered no more; and the relatively early *Midrash Sifra* (*Metzora, Negaʿim*, end of Parsha 3) says that the sin offering is like a Paraclete before God, making appeasement.

For the above reasons I think that *hilasmos* in I John 2:2 is better translated as "atonement" rather than as "expiation" (and, *a fortiori*, than as "propitiation"). Certainly it is preferable to the bland modernizing of *hilasmos* by NEB as "remedy," a translation that loses "a whole universe of discourse familiar in the everyday life of the ancient world but which is no longer our world of thought. Indeed the idea [of propitiation] is one that is repellent to the modern mind; yet it is central to the beliefs of the primitive Church" (M. Black, "Modern English Versions of the Scriptures," in *The New Testament in Historical and Contemporary Perspectives*, eds. H. Anderson and W. Barclay [G.H.C. Macgregor Memorial; Oxford: Blackwell, 1965] 83–98, esp. 97.) Those who find the idea so strange may rejoice in the accident that the literal English meaning ("at-one-ment") catches the thought of the epistolary author who saw the *hilasmos* by Jesus in the Father's presence as making possible "the communion (*koinōnia*) we have with the Father and with His Son, Jesus Christ" (1:3).

2bc. *and not only for our sins but also for the whole world.* These are two more *peri* ("for, in respect to") phrases continuing the *peri* phrase in 2a, "for our sins." Westcott, *Epistles* 44, gives an emphasis to the *de* in the first of the two phrases (e.g., "not only for our sins, *however*"), since he thinks the author is guarding against an error that overly restricts the efficacy of the atonement. In my judgment any attack on secessionist error here is in the very idea of atonement rather than in the extent of the forgiveness. Moreover, Johannine style does not favor overtranslating the *de;* for the same construction (*ou . . . de monon alla*) followed by *peri* phrases appears in John 17:20, "I pray *not only* for these *but also* for those who believe in me through their word," where there is no sharp contrast. If there is a grammatical irregularity in these two *peri* phrases of 2:2, it is that the object of the first is "our sins," while the object of the second is "the whole world"—a seeming mixture of things and people. The Old Latin translations and many modern scholars (Houlden, Marshall, Schneider, RSV, TEV) assume an ellipsis: "for (the sins of) the whole world." On the one hand, ellipsis is known in Johannine style: "I have testimony even greater than (that of) John" (John 5:36). On the other, it is possible to mix objects in such prepositional phrases, e.g., "The high priest . . . taking blood which he offers for *himself* and the *errors* of his people" (Heb 9:7). Thus, authors like Bonsirven, Plummer, and Westcott deny that an ellipsis is involved. In that case "for the whole world" is quite inclusive, covering not only sins but all the evil effects of sin in the world. It covers sins (ours, and of the whole world) and people (us, and the whole world). Bengel quotes the Latin epigram: *quam late peccatum, tam late propitiatio:* "The propitiation is as broad as the sin." Certainly the tendency in the protasis of the three *ean* phrases in 1:7; 1:9; and 2:2 is toward the more universal: "from *all* sin"; "from *all* wrongdoing"; "for the whole world."

2c. *world.* In the NT, 185 passages employ the Greek word *kosmos,* usually translated "world"; but see ABJ 29, 508–10, for the broad range of meaning. Most germane to our interests here is the world as the sphere of human beings and of human experience, for in that aspect the world is related to the salvific action of God and Christ. Elsewhere in the NT we find *kosmos* as the object of redemption in passages like Mark 16:15; Rom 11:15; II Cor 5:19; I Tim 1:15; and Rev 11:15. But there are other passages where, even after Christ's coming, the world is regarded as unfriendly, hostile, and destined for damnation, e.g., Matt 18:7; I Cor 2:12; 7:31; 11:32; Gal 4:3–4; 6:14; Col 2:8; and Jas 4:4. Such a hostile view of the world is not derived from the OT but is close to the dualism of Jewish intertestamental literature where an evil spirit has been set loose to dominate the world (whether that is considered a place or the conglomeration of human beings). Works like *Jubilees* and *Enoch* (*passim*) portray the sons of God who committed sins with the daughters of men (Gen 6:1–4) as unleashing corruption in the world, while *IV Ezra* 7:12 attributes this worldly corruption to the sin of Adam. The result of such ideas is that *II Baruch* 40:3 can speak of the world in its present era as "the world of corruption." Similarly, the pejorative outlook on the world, which is foreign to classical pagan thought, becomes prominent in Hellenistic mysticism, so that *Corpus Hermeticum* 6.4 states, "The *kosmos* is the totality of evil, and God the totality of good."

If we turn to the Johannine writings, *kosmos* occurs 78 times in GJohn, 23 times in I John, and once in II John—in sum, 55% of the total NT usage (only 3 times in Revelation!). About half the time the Johannine writers speak of "*the* world," which is often personified as the subject of verbs (20 different ones, but most prominently "know, receive, see, hate, love") in which cases it is clearly a world of human beings. Cassem, "Inventory," has carefully studied the positive and negative uses of *kosmos* and found that in John 1–12 (which covers the public ministry) the positive uses dominate two to one, while in John 13–18 and in I John the negative uses dominate four or five to one. To be specific, the passages in GJohn and I John that show a salvific attitude toward the world include: "God loved the world so much that He gave the only Son. . . . For God did not send the Son into the world to condemn the world, but that the world might be saved through him" (John 3:16–17); "This is really the Savior of the world" (4:42); "God's bread comes down from heaven and gives life to the world" (6:33,51); "As light have I come into the world . . . for I did not come to condemn the world but to save the world" (12:46–47); "The Father has sent the Son as Savior of the world" (I John 4:14). However, there are more passages that show hostility to a world which is evil and unredeemable. These include: "The world did not recognize him" (John 1:10; 17:25); "The world hates me because of the evidence that I bring against it that what it does is evil" (7:7; 15:18); Jesus and his kingdom do not belong to the world (8:23; 18:36); "Now is the judgment of this world; now will the Prince of this world be driven out" (12:31; 9:39); "The reason why the world hates you is that you do not belong to the world, for I chose you out of the world" (15:19; 17:14,16; I John 3:13); "I have conquered the world" (John 16:33; I John 5:4–5); "I do not pray for the world" (John 17:9); "Have no love for the world . . . the world is passing away" (I John 2:15,17); the Spirit that does not belong to God is described as "in the world" and the secessionists are "people who belong to the world" (I John 4:3–5; II John 7); "The whole world lies in the grasp of the Evil One" (I John 5:19).

Despite scholarly distinctions about different senses of *kosmos* in these opposing statements, there is clearly a conflict that goes beyond semantics. Houlden, *Epistles* 63, doubts that the Johannine author could offer a completely logical explanation of his attitudes toward the world. In part the conflict may reflect the history of the Johannine Community, e.g., a first enthusiasm for the wider world after hostility developed against "the Jews," and then disillusionment as the Christian message proved no more palatable to non-Jews than to Jews (see Brown, *Community* 55–56, 63–66). However, the overall effect of such contradictory statements within the same works is to create a theological sequence wherein the divine intent is initially salvific toward the world, but people prefer darkness to light (John 3:19); and so "the world" becomes the name of those who refuse Jesus and choose Satan as their father, "the Prince of this world" (cf. I John 3:1,10). The present passage in 2:2, if read as "atonement . . . for the whole world," speaks of the divine intent in its broadest extension. In Hebrew thought about the Day of Atonement, Lev 16:17 portrays the high priest as atoning "for himself, for his house, and for all the assembly of Israel"; but Philo, *On the Special Laws* 1.17 ※97, points wider: "Among other nations the priests are accustomed to offer sacrifices for their kinsmen and friends and fellow countrymen only, but the high priest of the Jews makes prayers and gives thanks not only on behalf of the whole human race but also for the elementary parts of nature." And certainly universalism came to dominate in the Christian picture of Christ's sacrifice, e.g., *I Clem.* 7:4, "The blood of Christ . . . was poured out for our salvation, and brought the grace of repentance to the whole world."

COMMENT

In discussing the structure of I John (INTRODUCTION VI A3b), I admitted that one could not be precise; nevertheless, there was reason for designating 1:5–3:10 as Part One, wherein the author expounded the gospel of God as light against false claims. Within Part One there are units that are structurally discrete, even though I can detect no real development of thought from one to the other. The first of these structural units begins with 1:5 and ends with 2:2.[1] Within this unit 1:5 serves as a transition from the Prologue to Part One by proclaiming the basic gospel message the author wishes to defend; and 1:6–7; 1:8–9; and 1:10–2:2 offer three pairs of claims and counterclaims ("If we boast. . . . But if") that specify the implications of the message.

Some scholars (Brooke, Gaugler, O'Neill, Plummer, Westcott, Wilder) would end the unit at 1:10, because they regard 2:1a ("My Little Children, I am writing this to keep you from sin") as a break in the pattern of claims and counterclaims.[2] I think that line is only parenthetical, and 2:1b supplies the "But if" counterclaim to the "If we boast" claim of

[1] Similarly Alexander, Bonsirven, Bultmann, Chaine, de la Potterie, Jones, Malatesta, Marshall, Schnackenburg, Schneider(?), Stott, and THLJ.
[2] A glance at Chart Three in Appendix I will show that Bultmann thought that the source consisted of 1:6,7,8,10, while 2:1–2 was the epistolary author's paraenetic comment and the Ecclesiastical Redactor's expansion.

1:10. Others would extend the unit to 2:5 (Williams), to 2:6 (Dodd), or to 2:11 (Balz, Houlden, Thüsing). I would agree that the basic process of rejecting false claims continues in 2:3–11, but those verses have a different structural pattern centered on the formula, "The person who claims," in 2:4,6,9 (*ho legōn*). Also in favor of ending the unit at 2:2 is the existence of an inclusion between the first pair of claim/counterclaim (1:6–7) and the third (1:10–2:2), an inclusion that "packages" this first unit. For instance, the "we are liars" response to the claim of 1:6 matches the "we make Him a liar" response to the claim of 1:10. The "blood of Jesus, His Son, cleanses us from all sin" in the counterclaim of 1:7 matches the "Jesus Christ . . . himself is an atonement for our sins" in the counterclaim of 2:1–2.

A. *God is Light without Darkness* (1:5)

The key passage for the meaning of this unit and, indeed, for the whole of Part One is the sentence in 1:5 that the author himself presents so solemnly. On p. 177 I gave a chart that shows the pattern of thought and structure in the I John Prologue, and I took the liberty of including in that chart not only the Prologue itself (1:1–4) but also this verse in order to show the extent to which it continues the thought flow of the Prologue. Following that chart we find once again a divine reality in the third person ("God is light") that implicitly is made known ("is the gospel") to a first-person plural group who claim sensory experience ("that we have heard from Christ") and who communicate this divine reality to a second-person plural group ("and declare to you"). Even the vocabulary of the Prologue is echoed in 1:5abc ("gospel,"[3] "we have heard," and "we declare"[4]), so that we may say that the relation of the I John Prologue to the beginning of Part One of I John is closer than that of the GJohn Prologue to the beginning of Part One of GJohn. This comparison is apt because the beginnings of Part One of the two works seem to have been made deliberately parallel, with the "Now this is the gospel" of I John 1:5 matching the "Now this is the testimony" of John 1:19.[5]

If 1:5, especially in its first three lines, continues the theme of the Prologue, the actual substance of the proclaimed gospel, expressed in 1:5de, "God is light and in Him there is no darkness at all," leads into the claims and counterclaims that follow in the unit. Those claims ("If we boast . . ." in 1:6,8,10) probably represent secessionist thought, and so logi-

---

[3] "Gospel" is *angelia* echoing the verb *apangellein* in the "we proclaim" of 1:2,3.

[4] This verb is *anangellein*.

[5] Just as the vocabulary of I John 1:5 echoes the vocabulary of the I John Prologue, so John 1:19 echoes John 1:6.

cally one must ask if 1:5de also is secessionist in origin. Among those who think so, it is often assumed that only the first part, "God is light," was a secessionist slogan,[6] and that the second part, denying the presence of darkness in God, was added by the epistolary author as a correction. Was such a correction necessary because the secessionists claimed there was darkness in God? In the OT Isa 45:7 has God saying, "I am the One who prepared light and made darkness," and in the view of some gnostic systems the divine sphere contained a mixture of light and darkness.[7] On the general analogy of gnosticism, however, it is more likely that the secessionists, like the author, would have held that there was no darkness in God.[8] In this case the author would have been attacking not the slogan itself but the secessionist moral attitudes that belied the true antagonism between light and darkness—they were claiming to know a God who is light but were walking in darkness (1:6). The latter suggestion raises doubt about the whole theory that the author is quoting a secessionist slogan in 1:5de. First, in this unit the author marks off claims of a secessionist hue very clearly ("If we boast. . . ."); and he gives no such indication here. Second, the statement that God is light is identified as "the gospel that we have heard *from Christ*." Granted that the secessionists were Christians who contended that their positions came from the Johannine Christ, the author would scarcely have condoned that by describing one of their slogans as coming from Christ. Third, the affirmation, "God is light and in Him there is no darkness at all," can be derived from Johannine tradition, as known to us in GJohn, without any hint of error.

Let me explain this third point, for this is our first opportunity to see how the author may be drawing on the Johannine Jesus for his "gospel" (*angelia*).[9] In GJohn Jesus is the one who comes from God, declaring

---

[6] That the secessionists would be happy with such a slogan has been deduced from the popularity of "light" terminology among the later gnostics, e.g., the Hermetic tract *Poimandres* 1.21 reports, "The Father of all things consists of light and life." The Mandaean *Ginza Right* 1.3.2 (Lidzbarski, p. 6) calls God "the sublime king of light." See ABJ 29, liv.

[7] Irenaeus, *Adv. haer.* 2.4.2–3, mentions the gnostic thesis that the Pleroma contains both shadow and light. Stott, *Epistles* 70, thinks that the secessionists claimed that God was light only for the illuminated and darkness for the rest. See also Windisch, *Briefe* 111.

[8] Bultmann, *Epistles* 16: "In ordinary Gnosis, light and darkness are mutually exclusive antitheses." The Mandaean *Ginza Right* 1.3.8 (Lidzbarski, p. 6) describes the world of the king of light as one "in which there is no darkness." In such thought darkness was often a lower and aberrant eon, of which creation was a manifestation (and hence not attributable to the supreme God). There is no evidence that the secessionists of I John held such a view.

[9] Windisch, *Briefe* 111, contends that 1:5de is a word of the Lord; Schneider, *Briefe* 144, denies it; but often such a debate does not take into account the freedom involved in the Paraclete-inspired transmission of what has been received from Jesus (John 16:15).

(*anangellein*) all things just as he heard them from the Father (John 4:25; cf. 12:49–50). The Paraclete declares all things just as he heard them from Jesus (16:13–15). The "we" of the Johannine School declare (*anangellein*) to the members of the Johannine Community "the gospel . . . heard from him" (I John 1:5). In this chain of Father, Jesus, Paraclete, and "we," the "from him" of 1:5b is from Jesus, but Jesus as interpreted by the Paraclete. The discourses of GJohn, while rooted in a Johannine tradition of the sayings of Jesus, are not a literal quotation of the historical Jesus; and neither is "God is light and in Him there is no darkness at all" a literal quotation either of the historical Jesus or of the Jesus of GJohn.[10] The reworking of the Jesus tradition through the Paraclete which produced GJohn did not stop with that document; and I John's tradition "from Christ" may represent a (Paraclete-inspired) reworking of sayings similar to those in GJohn about light and darkness, e.g., "The light has come into the world, but men have preferred darkness to light because their deeds were evil" (John 3:19); "I am the light of the world; no follower of mine shall ever walk in darkness" (8:12); "The light is among you only a little while longer; walk while you have the light or the darkness will come over you" (12:35); and "As light have I come into the world, so that no one who believes in me need remain in darkness" (12:46).

Even more precisely, from the continuity we have found between I John 1:5 and the I John Prologue, and from the relationship that exists between the latter and the GJohn Prologue, the source for the epistolary author's statement about light and darkness is plausibly to be found in John 1:4,5,9: "This life was the light of men. The light shines on in the darkness, for the darkness did not overcome it. . . . The real light which gives light to every human being was coming into the world."[11] For the epistolary author the GJohn Prologue was a hymn distilled from the teaching of the Johannine Jesus,[12] so that he could say, "We have heard from him," when he was drawing upon that hymn. We shall see that in 4:8 the epistolary author will draw upon a saying of the Johannine Jesus, "God loved the world so much that He gave the only Son" (John 3:16) and recast it as "God is love." Here he has drawn upon GJohn Prologue statements about Jesus as the light come from God into the world and recast them as "God is light." As a partial model for such an affirmation

[10] The suggestion that the author is quoting a saying of the Johannine Jesus that was not incorporated into GJohn is unprovable and unnecessary.

[11] I John 1:1–4 picked up and rewrote most of the main themes of the GJohn Prologue ("beginning, we, word, life, the Father's presence, Jesus Christ," incarnation) except that of light and darkness; that neglect is repaired in 1:5.

[12] For example, from the passages I have quoted at the end of the preceding paragraph, esp. 12:35.

he had the saying of Jesus in John 4:24, "God is Spirit" (see NOTE on 1:5d).[13]

What does I John mean by the light/darkness affirmation in 1:5de, and how does the suggestion that it is a recasting of statements from the GJohn Prologue affect the meaning? Johannine symbolism was enriched by ideas from biblical and intertestamental sources. In OT passages God is associated with light (Ps 4:7[6]; Hab 3:4); God's wisdom is a reflection of His light (Wis 7:26); the creative action of God is phrased, "Let there be light" (Gen 1:3; Isa 45:7); God's salvific action in the world is light (Isa 9:1[2]; 60:1–3); God enlightens minds through His teaching and virtue (Isa 51:4; Ps 36:10[9]; 119:105; Prov 6:23); in particular, God is "the light of Israel" (Isa 10:17) and is the light of the individual Israelite (Ps 27:1; Isa 60:19–20). In the intertestamental literature, especially in the Dead Sea Scrolls and the *Testaments of the Twelve Patriarchs,* there is a dualism of light and darkness[14] far sharper than any OT contrast between the two. There are angelic princes of light and darkness who govern human beings (1QS 3:20–21); consequently people can be divided into "sons of light" and "sons of darkness" (1QM 1:1) as they choose between light and darkness (*T. Levi* 19:1). In the thought of GJohn which is also dualistic, Jesus is the light who has come into the world and caused people to decide to come to the light or to prefer darkness; his opponent is the Prince of this world whose realm is night.[15]

The epistolary author assumes all this, but in his affirmation that "God is light" there is an interesting shift in Johannine predication. Of the 23 times that "light" (*phōs*) occurs in GJohn, it refers 19 times to Jesus directly or indirectly. In seeking to explain why "light" is predicated of God in I John 1:5,[16] some are satisfied to comment that the Epistle is theological in emphasis, while GJohn is christological.[17] However, if I am right in arguing that the primary background for this verse is the GJohn Prologue, the key to the problem may lie in the claim in John 1:4,5,9 that a preexistent light has come into the world. The epistolary author is

[13] The epistolary author has no need to emphasize that "God is Spirit," since his adversaries already devalue the earthly and corporeal.

[14] See ABJ 29, lxii–lxiii, 340; and Brown, "Scrolls."

[15] See ABJ 29, 515–16, adding to the bibliography given there: J. C. Bott, "De notione lucis in scriptis S. Ioannis Apostoli," VD 19 (1939) 81–90, 117–22; P. Gutierrez, "Conceptus 'Lucis' apud Iohannem Evangelistam in relatione ad conceptum 'Veritatis,'" VD 29 (1951) 3–19.

[16] That the Johannine writers call both God and Jesus "light" helps to explain the Nicene formula, "Light from light," even as the designation of the Word as "God" helps to explain the formula "God from God." The formula, "True God from true God," should be seen in light of the designation of Jesus as "true God" in I John 5:20.

[17] Klein, "Licht" 284–88, uses this shift as an argument that different men wrote GJohn and I John. He is right, but his treatment of 1:5 needs to be integrated into an analysis of how the epistolary author modified other concepts in the GJohn Prologue.

convinced that the divine light is not known simply in and through the light's entrance into the world but also in and through the career of the light in the world. By way of developing this point, let me mention Schaeffer's refutation ("Gott" 467–69) of the thesis that "God is light" refers to His sanctity, glory, or perfection: "In no passage does Scripture show knowledge of light as a way of depicting God's glory." Rather "light" refers to the knowability of God.[18] The secessionists, drawing upon the GJohn Prologue, could argue that because the light has come into the world, God is known by those who have come to the light.[19] But for the epistolary author, "God is light" is a *gospel* that was experienced in Jesus' revelation to his disciples during the ministry. The authentic tradition about that revelation is passed on through the Johannine School ("We have heard from him and declare to you"). Thus for I John divine light has shone in the life of Jesus on earth and continues to shine in the lives of those who truly follow him. The Jewish philosopher Philo could also say, "God is light"; but he meant by this that God is the archetype of light in the universe, and that as one descends from the heavens there is a greater admixture of darkness.[20] For I John, however, the gospel means that through the life of Jesus we have come to know even below on this earth that God is light without darkness.

Like the other Johannine "God is . . ." formulas (NOTE on 1:5d), "God is light" is not an abstract definition but portrays God's identity revealed in terms of function.[21] This is equally true of the more emphatic

[18] See Brooke, *Epistles* 11–12, who insists that the primary connotation is illumination. The later gnostics would speak of God in terms of obscurity, e.g., as "the abyss" or "unspoken silence" (Irenaeus, *Adv. haer.* 1.11.1); but the Johannine God is one of self-revelation.

[19] Painter, *John* 119, thinks that the secessionists claimed a mystical enlightenment that did away with historical revelation and supplied direct entrée to God. I find no reason in I John for assuming this and little in GJohn that would give rise to it. One need posit only that the secessionists stressed the incarnation as the coming of the light, which in itself was *the* revelation.

[20] Philo, *On Dreams* 1.13 ❊75: "God is light [*ho theos phōs esti*] . . . and not only light but the archetype of every other light, or rather more ancient and higher than every other archetype." *On Abraham* 36 ❊205: "Light in heaven is pure from any mixture of darkness, but clearly in regions below the moon is mixed with dusky air." James 1:17, which describes God as "the Father of lights," has a certain resemblance to Philo. F. N. Klein, *Die Lichtterminologie bei Philo von Alexandrien und in den Hermetischen Schriften* (Leiden: Brill, 1962) brings out the intellectual aspect of light in Philo.

[21] See ABJ 29, 172. Among Roman Catholic scholars, Chmiel, *Lumière* 88, stresses the functional: God is light inasmuch as He is a revealer. Malatesta, *Interiority* 98, however, says, "In the oikonomia [of His self-revelation] we learn not only what He does for us, but also what He is in Himself." (That is true; but granted the history of Roman Catholic thought, it is the functional that may well need the emphasis.) Wilder, "Introduction" 222, is right when he says that such a description of God is not mythological, nor metaphysical, and is not a mere figure of speech.

part of the formula: "In Him there is no darkness at all." When divine light was revealed in Jesus' ministry, he *removed* darkness from those who came to the light by forgiving sin, the principal manifestation of darkness. That is why those who preferred to continue their sinful lives turned away from the light, so that Jesus' very presence constituted their judgment (John 3:19–21). That judgment imposes a demand on those who have come to the light to go on preferring light to darkness.[22] The secessionists might well argue that for one who has emerged from the initial encounter with Jesus as a son of light there is no judgment: The believer has passed from death to life (John 5:24).[23] But in the mind of the epistolary author the opposition to darkness goes on because of the very nature of light. As we shall see again and again, his is a convenant mentality where the people of God must reflect in their lives the God to whom they adhere ("You must be holy for I am holy": Lev 11:45). However, in Johannine thought this reflection of God is no longer a matter of purely volitional adherence; it is based on being begotten from above as God's children with His life (John 3:3,5). In the Johannine chain of thought, if God is light without darkness, and if Jesus as incarnate light opposed darkness and sin, so must the children of God live as sons of light without admixture of darkness. When the Johannine Jesus said, "God is Spirit," he himself drew a practical inference from that formula: "Those who worship Him must worship in Spirit" (John 4:24). When I John says, "God is love," the author draws the practical inference that we must love one another (4:8,11). So too, if God is light, there is a practical inference that we must walk in light and not in darkness. The failure to live out that practical inference really means that one has a different notion of God. These are exactly the points that the author will insist upon in what follows; at the beginning of I John he has given us a principle from which he will draw much of the refutation of his opponents, as he develops the themes of light and darkness through a series of claims and counterclaims.

B. *Ethical Implications of God as Light* (1:6–2:2)

As we move from 1:5 to 1:6–2:2, it is surprising that the first overt attack on dangerous ideas is in the moral sphere. One might have expected

---

[22] Bultmann, *Epistles* 16, "It is characteristic for I John (as for John) that the eschatological salvation which is given to faith as a gift is not a possession, but rather includes the demand that the believer is never a finished man (of faith) but rather is always on the way."

[23] It is interesting to see the Johannine influence on the *Odes of Solomon* (11:18–19), which many think is incipiently gnostic: "Blessed, O Lord, are they who are planted in your land . . . and have passed from darkness into light."

the author to begin with the christological errors that are so much on his mind throughout I John.[24] Did he fear that if the secessionists won over his followers to their moral outlook which placed little emphasis on behavior and commandments, there would be little chance to defeat them on the more abstract christological issues? In any case, his first polemic salvo is phrased in six conditional sentences, neatly paired off in three sets of two. In each set the first condition expresses a view of which the author disapproves, and the second condition, the view of which he approves. But one cannot see the development of ideas in this unit if one concentrates solely on the internal contrast within each pair of conditions, for there is a sequence from one pair to the next. Moreover, the three disapproved conditions have a consistency among themselves, as do the three approved conditions. Let me then begin my treatment with the three disapproved conditional sentences and turn afterwards to the three approved conditions.

1. The Disapproved Conditions

In each pair the first conditions may be arranged thus:

(a) PROTASES
6ab: If we boast, "We are in communion with Him," while continuing to walk in darkness,
8a: If we boast, "We are free from the guilt of sin,"
10a: If we boast, "We have not sinned,"

(b) COMPOUND APODOSES
6cd: we are liars and we do not act in truth.
8bc: we deceive ourselves and the truth is not in us.
10bc: we make Him a liar and His word is not in us.

The apodoses help us to understand the protases. First, they are so clearly similar that they encourage us to think that the protases are also similar despite their difference in wording. Second, the apodoses show an increasing intensity: It is one thing knowingly to tell an untruth or lie; it is worse to deceive oneself to the point where there is no truth; it is still worse to make God a liar. Such a progression in the apodoses makes one suspect that the same phenomenon exists in the protases. Let us test these suspicions drawn from formal structure.

(a) PROTASES. In 2:19 the author explicitly mentions adversaries who were former members of the Johannine Community: "From our ranks they went out." It is significant that the subject of these boasts in 1:6,8,10 is not a "they" but a "we." He thinks of those who remain within and

---

[24] I pointed out above (pp. 119–20) that some think of I John as consisting of alternating moral (ethical) and christological units. The moral units involve a positive stress on love and commandments and a negative stress on the evil of sin.

form a "we" with him.[25] But the use of conditions indicates the strong possibility that even those who are now with him may make such objectionable boasts. One might theorize that these boasts arose totally independently of the secessionists who are attacked elsewhere in I John, but it is more likely that the author fears contamination by secessionist propaganda.[26] Such contamination phrased in a "we boast" would be more serious than a simple "they boast," because if "we" are allowed to say it without challenge, the boast will pass as *the* Johannine position.[27] Also, since he does not use a "they," it is possible that the boasts are not verbatim quotations of secessionist thought or slogans but are recast in a way that might be better comprehended and accepted by his own adherents whom he is addressing—in other words, he is offering for rejection statements that have a realistic chance of being made by his "brothers."

First Protasis. Verse 1:6a, "We are in communion with him," employs the term *koinōnia;* and above (p. 186) I expressed doubt that this term with its ecclesiastical connotations was used by the secessionists. If they followed the language of GJohn, they would probably have spoken in terms of "being in" God or "abiding in" God (*einai en; menein en:* John 14:23; 17:21; I John 4:15–16). By his phrasing of the boast the author reminds the reader that *koinōnia* with God involves *koinōnia* with the Johannine School of tradition-bearers (1:3), and that is conspicuously lacking from the boast in 1:6a.

More is lacking, for what disturbs the author most is the failure to see that a communion with the God who is light requires one to live a life that reflects light. In the INTRODUCTION (V B3a) I diagnosed the ethical or moral position of the secessionists: They were probably not libertines notorious for scandalous behavior; yet they gave no salvific import to ethical behavior by believers. I showed that there are many passages in GJohn that might lead to such a position. Here I shall not repeat the argument but simply show how that general position might have been reflected in terms of light and darkness. In 3:19–21 the Johannine Jesus says, "The light has come into the world, but people have preferred darkness to the light. For everyone who practices wickedness hates the light

---

[25] In 1:1–5 "we" referred to the Johannine School of tradition-bearers who were addressing a "you" consisting of the ordinary members of the Johannine Community. In 1:6 the "we" represents the whole Johannine Community—the previous "we" and the "you"—in which those addressed have achieved a *koinōnia* with those who have seen and proclaimed.

[26] The secessionists have been relatively successful (I John 4:5) and are conducting an active missionary campaign (II John 10–11). Moreover, the secessionists derive their theology from the Johannine tradition, and so the ideas they propose might mistakenly be accepted by the author's adherents. See the INTRODUCTION (IV B1) for my contention that only one major group is attacked in I and II John.

[27] A claim made as "we" challenges Johannine Christians to decide whether this is really "our" position and whether it is true to the Johannine tradition.

and does not come near the light for fear his deeds will be exposed. But he who acts in truth comes into the light." Clearly this means that deeds are important in one's orientation toward light or darkness; but from it one might gain the impression that, once having chosen for the light, darkness is no more an issue. This might be confirmed by reading other GJohn passages which use darkness of that portion of humanity that never accepted Jesus: "The light shines on in the darkness, for the darkness did not overcome (receive) it" (John 1:5). "The Jews" are the ones who have to be told that the light is among them only a little while longer; and if they do not choose to walk in the light, the darkness will come over them (12:34–35). They are the ones who have not seen the revelation and have been blinded (12:38–40). For the believer the message is quite different: "I am the light of the world. No follower of mine shall ever walk in darkness; no, he will possess the light of life" (8:12). Presumably the secessionists would have regarded that message as a promise dispensing them from worrying about darkness, while the epistolary author would have understood it as a command not to walk in darkness. Part of the problem is that the GJohn affirmations were phrased in polemic struggles with "the Jews," wherein the debate centered on the salvific importance or uselessness of *coming* to the light. The evangelist and "the Jews" argued about what constituted one a member of God's people: whether one was a child of God through begetting by the flesh (of Jewish parents) or through begetting from above (John 3:3–6). They did not quarrel over the necessity of walking as a child of God once one had been begotten (i.e., covenant morality); both would have taken that for granted. Now the epistolary author has the problematic task of emphasizing against secessionist propaganda what was taken for granted but not spelled out in GJohn—hence his proclaimed intention of passing on what was heard "from the beginning" (I John 1:1). It is no accident, then, that his insistence on walking in light rather than in darkness (a Semitism; see NOTE on 1:6b) reflects the mentality and language of intertestamental Judaism and/or Jewish Christianity. *Enoch* 92:4–5 promises, "God will be gracious to the just man . . . and he shall walk in light, while sin shall perish in darkness forever" (see also *Enoch* 58). Noteworthy is *T. Levi* 14:3–4: "As the heaven is purer in the Lord's sight than the earth, so also should you, the lights of Israel, be purer than the Gentiles. But if you be darkened through sin, what will the Gentiles do, living in blindness?" And *T. Naphtali* 2:10: "Neither while you are in darkness can you do the works of light."

Second Protasis. The author also disapproves of the boast in 1:8a: "We are free from the guilt of sin." The connection between darkness and sin (the themes of the first and second protases) is apparent in the story of the man born blind: while he is enlightened through faith in Jesus, the Pharisees who refuse to believe, even though they claim to see, are "guilty of sin" (John 9:41). In the INTRODUCTION (V B3b) I showed how the claim to be free from the guilt of sin[28] might be justified by reading passages in GJohn that identify nonbelievers as those guilty of sin. Therefore, the problem raised by the boast of I John 1:8a may have been that, in the author's opinion, it was correct to think that upon becoming a believer the Johannine Christian was rendered free from the guilt of sin, but it was wrong to think that this condition automatically remained after belief no matter what one did.

That such a wrong view existed in early Christianity is attested by Justin Martyr who has to argue against it in *Trypho* 141.2. He contends that Ps 32:2 ("Fortunate is the one to whom God does not impute sin") does not mean that if sinners know God, no sin will be imputed to them. And Irenaeus, *Adv. haer.* 1.6.2, criticizes the gnostic theory that, while ordinary Christians need works to be saved, the pneumatic who is spiritual by nature is certainly saved, independently of conduct.[29] The author of I John is upset by the secessionist-inspired boast because he considers sins committed after coming to faith in Jesus to be all the more guilty since they are contrary to the believer's status as a child of God. The dispute is not primarily about psychological culpability but about a theological issue: For the author sin comes from darkness, and any attempt to reconcile light with sin is a form of lying.

Third Protasis. Secessionist leanings are also reflected in the boast in 1:10a: "We have not sinned." In the NOTE I suggested that the boast probably entailed a denial of having sinned since becoming a believer; and in the INTRODUCTION (V B3b) I tried to show how such a denial might be based on an understanding of GJohn whereby the Christians as children of God were so conformed to Jesus the Son of God that they could say, even as did Jesus, "Can any one of you convict me of sin?" (John 8:46). Thus all three boasts flow from an exaggeration of the same principle, i.e., that at the time of becoming a disciple the believers received enormous privileges—a perfectionist principle thoroughly at home in GJohn. Yet the three boasts show a mounting exaggeration of the implications drawn from the perfectionist principle. The claim to have *koinōnia* with a God of light while walking in darkness shows an insensitivity toward right and wrong. The claim to have no guilt from sin recognizes

---

[28] For this translation of the Greek, which says literally, "We do not have sin," see NOTE on 1:8a.

[29] There is no proof that the Johannine secessionists would have traced their security to such a metaphysical source as a spiritual nature different from the nature of other Christians, or even to a special revelation granted to initiates. In my theory the secessionists would have contended that all (Johannine) Christians had the same privilege. I add "Johannine," not because they would necessarily have denied the privilege to non-Johannine Christians, but simply because they were concerned only with Christians of their own tradition.

that the deeds are wrong but contends that they have no effect. The claim not to have sinned denies the possibility of wrongdoing. Let us see now how the three apodoses match the mounting exaggeration in the three protases.

(b) COMPOUND APODOSES. The three statements (p. 231) that describe the bad results coming from the erroneous boasts are phrased in terms of lying and truth. The shift from light/darkness to truth/falsehood is not surprising on several grounds. *First,* the same mixture of symbolism is found also in the intertestamental literature of a dualistic bent. In *T. Asher* 5:3 we hear, "It may not be said that truth is a lie . . . all truth is under the light." In the Dead Sea Scrolls, 1QS 3:17–21 is particularly detailed: "God has appointed for human beings two spirits in which to walk until the time of His visitation: the spirits of truth and iniquity. The generations of truth spring from a fountain of light, but the generations of iniquity from a source of darkness. All the sons of righteousness are under the rule of the prince of light and walk in the ways of light, but all the sons of iniquity are under the rule of the angel of darkness and walk in the ways of darkness." In the strongly Hellenistic Philo we hear, "Truth is light" (*On Joseph* 14 #68). And in the *Mandaean Liturgy, Oxford Collection* 28 (Lidzbarski, p. 198): "Your eyes are eyes of lying; my eyes are eyes of truth. The eyes of lying darken and do not show the truth." *Second,* light/darkness and truth/falsehood are virtually interchangeable in GJohn, e.g., Jesus who is the light of the world is also the truth (8:12; 14:6).[30] The devil is a liar and the father of lying (8:44); and when Satan enters Judas, the betrayer goes out into the night (13:27,30). If Christians are challenged to walk in light (I John 1:7a), so must they walk in truth (II John 4). *Third,* and most important, the Johannine understanding of revelation makes walking in darkness truly a betrayal of truth. One misses the thrust of Johannine thought if one thinks of revelation simply as the intellectual communication of a truth that is received mentally. Rather, in the act of revelation Jesus brings a divine reality, a divine life and presence, which radically changes believers from flesh to spirit. His communication of the Holy Spirit, like the divine breath in Gen 2:7, is creative of a new human being (John 20:22; ABJ

---

[30] De la Potterie, *La vérité* 2, 514, argues that "light" is revelation from the viewpoint of its origin, while "truth" is revelation from the viewpoint of its entrance into the sphere of human activity. Thus, he theorizes (2, 1010) that Johannine theology could affirm that "God is light" but not that "God is truth," for truth involves the coming of Jesus. In my judgment, such a distinction is overly subtle, and one cannot prove that the absence of the formula "God is truth" in preserved Johannine texts is significant or intentional. One may think of John 17:17, "Your word is truth," joined to 1:1, "The Word was God." While I think that de la Potterie's analysis of the Johannine concept of truth is far more profound than Bultmann's, I think Bultmann is right on this point: "Just as God is 'light' (v. 5), so is he also 'truth,' and just as 'light' is (is intended to be) the mode of human existence, so also is 'truth'" (*Epistles* 19).

29A, 1022–23; 1037–38). To be children of the light and to continue to walk in darkness is, therefore, truly a lie because the behavior does not match the reality (and *alētheia* is both "truth" and "reality").

Thus, in his own way, the epistolary author is operating from a perfectionist principle, even as his opponents are. From the exalted status of the Christian, the secessionists deduce a position of indifference toward what the Christian does. From the exalted status of the Christian the author deduces a position emphasizing the importance of what the Christian does. Theirs is a static view of the perfection that God has given to the Christian; his is a dynamic view. We see this if we examine the two elements in each of the compound apodoses in 1:6,8,10. The first clause of each concerns lying ("we are liars"; "we deceive ourselves"; "we make Him a liar"). The second clause of each concerns the lack of truth ("we do not act in truth"; "the truth is not in us"; "His word is not in us"). The dynamic attitude is apparent in the fact that the first derives from the second—divine truth, like divine life, is a reality that inheres in us and must be active. "If you abide in my word, you are truly my disciples; and you will know the truth, and truth will set you free" (8:31–32). Thus understood, the charge of lying becomes more than a charge of *telling* an untruth. A lie indicates what one is: a child of darkness rather than a child of light—one whose father is the devil, a liar. (In the NOTES on 1:6c and on 1:8b we saw that the respective terms for lying and deceit appear in the dualistic Judaism of the intertestamental period as descriptions of the forces opposed to God.) Just as there was a progression in the boasts (the protases) from bad to worse, so there is a progression in the apodoses in the clause that deals with lying, but not in the clause dealing with truth. The truth clause supplies the basis of the action (lying), and the basis remains the same.

In summary, to pretend to have communion with the light while walking in the darkness (1:6ab) and thus to say that one's action makes no essential difference shows that one is a liar (1:6c); for if one walks in darkness, one must be living in darkness. To recognize that one's actions are wrong but to say that wrong action creates no guilt in a child of God (1:8a) is worse than being a liar; it is to choose to deceive oneself (1:8b) and thus voluntarily to be on the side of the Spirit of Deceit. Worse still is to deny that one's wrong actions are really wrong (1:10a); this is to make light darkness, to make falsehood truth, to make God the devil who is a liar (1:10b).

2. The Approved Conditions

If the epistolary author were interested solely in refuting bad secessionist theology that could pervert his adherents, he might have been satisfied with the three conditional sentences expressing his disapproval. But he is also interested in communicating to his adherents the positive thrust of the Johannine tradition on these issues made obscure by secessionist propaganda. And so the author has matched every conditional sentence of disapproval with a conditional sentence of approval. The three approved conditions may be arranged thus:

(a) PROTASES

7ab:	But if we walk in the light as He Himself is in light
9a:	But if we confess our sins
2:1b:	But if anyone does sin

(b) COMPOUND APODOSES

7c:	we are joined in communion with one another
7de:	and the blood of Jesus, His Son, cleanses us from all sin
9bc:	He who is reliable and just will forgive us our sins
9d:	and cleanse us from all wrongdoing
2:1cd:	we have a Paraclete in the Father's presence, Jesus Christ, the one who is just,
2:2abc:	and he himself is an atonement for our sins, and not only for our sins but also for the whole world

Following the same pattern I used for the disapproved conditions, let me now consider each of these parts of the approved conditions.

(a) PROTASES. Looked at in themselves, the three protases form an interesting contrast. The first insists on walking in light; the other two, recognizing that some walking in darkness will occur, tell what to do about it. But, of course, these protases of the approved conditions are not meant simply to be taken by themselves, for they are the opposite of the protases of the disapproved conditions.[31] The secessionist-inspired boast to be in communion with God who is light while walking in darkness (1:6ab) is matched with the idea of walking in light corresponding to the divine light (1:7ab).[32] The secessionist-inspired boast to be free from the guilt of sin (1:8a) is matched with the idea of publicly confessing sins (1:9a). The secessionist-inspired boast denying the fact of having sinned (1:10a) is matched by a statement suggesting the likelihood of sin (2:1b). The term "matched" is not precise, for in the second condition the approved protasis does more than negate the disapproved protasis. In response to the boast, "We are free from the guilt of sin," the author does not simply say, "We are not free from the guilt of sin," but proposes a public confession of sin.[33]

[31] It is interesting to note that the protases (disapproved and approved) in the first conditional pair are longer than those in the second and third pairs—the author was interested in patterns.

[32] See the NOTE on 1:7b for the shift from "God is light" (1:5d) to "He is in light," a shift from God as the basis of Christian activity to God as a model.

[33] I have argued in the NOTE on 1:9a that this means confession before the Johannine Community, reflecting the author's theology that koinōnia with one another is essential to having koinōnia with God (1:3). Sin is harmful to both forms of koinōnia.

(b) COMPOUND APODOSES. In this set of approved conditions, the apodoses bear the weight of the epistolary author's theology. Like the apodoses of the disapproved conditions, these are compound. There is less regularity in the first clause of the compound sentence, but the second clause always deals with a remedy for sin (cleansing or atoning). In the disapproved conditions we found a pattern: The first clause stated that wrong or sinful behavior was a lie or deceit because (second clause) it could not be based on truth. In other words, in the disapproved conditions the apodosis stressed that God's gift was dynamic and could not produce sinful deceit. Now, however, having shown in reaction to the secessionist-inspired boasts that he disapproves of indifference toward walking in darkness and sin, the author comes to grips with the fact that sometimes the behavior of Christians is not worthy of the light. The secessionists were facing the same problem but solved it by claiming that wrong behavior was not important, or should not cause guilt, or was not really sinful. The author avoids such lies and wants Christians publicly to recognize and confess wrong behavior as darkness and sin, which cannot come from God's life and light and truth inhering in them. Do these acknowledged sins then deprive believers of that life and light and truth? No! Precisely because the divine gift inhering in them is dynamic, it not only enables believers to walk in light and truth but also brings forgiveness and cleansing when the believer fails. The true gospel is not that by initiation into Christianity believers are impervious to sin, but that they have been initiated into a dispensation that has effective power against sin. Sins do not destroy Christian existence; and this is not because sins are blameless or insignificant, but because the God who is light is also reliable and just. He thus possesses the attributes of a covenant God who seeks the salvation of His people and does not abandon them when they are unfaithful (see NOTE on 1:9b for justice as salvific).

Granted what we know of the penitential practices of early Christianity, the Johannine attitude is liberal toward sins committed after becoming a believer.[34] In Heb 10:26–27 we have a theology of atonement similar to that of I John but a much stricter attitude toward sin: "If we sin deliberately after receiving knowledge of the truth, there no longer remains a sacrifice for sins but a fearful prospect of judgment."[35] Later *Hermas* (*Man.* 4.3.6) instructs: "After the great and holy calling if a person be tempted by the devil and commit sin, he has one repentance; but if he sin and repent repeatedly, it is unprofitable for such a person. He shall with difficulty attain eternal life." And in the first centuries it was ecclesiastical discipline not to forgive the sins of adultery and apostasy. But I John envisions a cleansing "from all sin" and "from all wrongdoing," and an

[34] In the NOTES on 1:7e and 8a I have rejected the suggestions that I John is speaking of original sin or is concerned only with initial justification.
[35] The author may refer specifically to apostasy, which is the subject of 10:32–36.

atonement "not only for our sins but also for the whole world." Curiously, then, at the same time the author is both rigorous and understanding: He will not tolerate sin except as an evil that can be forgiven.[36]

Into his theology of forgiveness enter two factors that constitute an implicit attack on secessionist thought. In the first apodosis (1:7cde) he relates "communion with one another" to cleansing from sin (as he does implicitly in the second protasis [1:9a] when he speaks of confessing sins publicly). The new life given by God makes the believer a child of God, but among other children of God —there is no Christian life outside the Christian communion of believers, a communion (koinōnia) that in the author's judgment his opponents have left.[37] Possibly the author found GJohn support for this in the washing of the feet by Jesus at the Last Supper, an action symbolic of the cleansing power of Jesus' death (13:8,10; ABJ 29A, 562) which has been interpreted on a secondary level as referring to the effects of baptism.[38] There Jesus instructs his disciples that, if he has washed their feet, they must wash *one another's* feet (13:14). Thus, communion with one another is a context for cleansing by Christ. A second antisecessionist factor in the epistolary author's theology of the forgiveness of sins may be the stress on the bloody death of Christ, especially if the secessionists thought that salvation was accomplished simply through the coming of the light into the world.[39] In the first apodosis (1:7de) we hear that "the blood of Jesus . . . cleanses us from all sin";[40]

---

[36] Käsemann, "Ketzer" 182, sees I John as anticipating the theology of *simul justus et peccator*. Less anachronistically, the author is not far from Wisdom 15:1–2: "But you, our God, are good and true, slow to anger and governing all with mercy. But even if we sin, we are yours and we know your might; but we shall not sin, knowing that we belong to you."

[37] See Michl, *Briefe* 204. Some scholars have proposed that it would be more logical to read 7de before 7c, so that Jesus' cleansing us from sin could lead into the idea of our communion with one another. Besides assuming that verbal sequence signifies historical sequence, this suggestion reflects a twofold misinterpretation. First, it assumes that cleansing from sin means initial justification. But I John is talking about *our* being cleansed, which means the cleansing of those who are already Christians from sins they have committed after conversion. Second, the suggestion does not do justice to the sequence in 1:3 where communion "with us" precedes communion with God.

[38] Many MSS. read 13:10 with a phrase I have italicized: "The man who has bathed has no need to wash *except for his feet;* he is clean all over"; and this was understood to mean that the baptized person needs no further bath (baptism) but only a lesser washing (penance for later sins). A few scholars think this was the original meaning; see ABJ 29A, 567–68.

[39] From I John 5:6 one surmises that the secessionists would have denied that Jesus Christ "came in blood," affirming only that he "came in water." Presumably this means they accepted the salvific importance of Jesus' first appearance symbolized by John's baptism with water (John 1:31) but not of his death when blood and water flowed from his body (19:34).

[40] In the second apodosis it is God who cleanses from all wrongdoing; but in Johannine thought Jesus and the Father are one (John 10:30), and Jesus' passion and death is part of the work the Father gave him to do (17:4).

and in the third apodosis (2:2) we hear that the just (*dikaios*) Jesus, a Paraclete in the Father's presence, is "himself an atonement for our sins," a reference to the OT ritual of the Day of Atonement when the high priest brought the blood of a spotless animal into the Holy of Holies to expiate the sins of the people.[41] We do not know how the secessionists would have interpreted John 1:29, "Here is the Lamb of God who takes away the world's sin," if that was part of the Johannine tradition known to them. Perhaps, since it was uttered by John the Baptist when Jesus first made his appearance, they understood the removal of sin to have occurred then (above, pp. 77–78). But the epistolary author would have understood Jesus as a sacrificial lamb by whose bloody death sin was taken away, combining 1:29 with hints of sacrificial symbolism in the Johannine passion narrative.[42] The reference in I John 2:2 to "an atonement . . . for the whole world" may have been an echo of the theology of salvific death inherent in the Johannine eucharistic formula, "The bread that I shall give is my own flesh for the life of the world" (John 6:51). As I pointed out in the NOTE on "blood" in 1:7d, while the theme of salvific death may be a minor motif in GJohn, the redeeming blood of the lamb is an important motif in Revelation (5:9; 7:14; 12:11); and so the epistolary author may once more be reaching back to the early stages of Johannine tradition ("from the beginning") to refute his opponents' reading of the tradition. Plausibly the early Johannine tradition would have had much in common with other early Christian tradition, e.g., Rom 3:24–25: "Through the redemption which is in Christ Jesus whom God put forward as an atonement [*hilastērion*] by his blood to be received by faith—this was to show God's justice [*dikaiosynē*] in remitting past sins."

The reference to Jesus as "a Paraclete in the Father's presence" in the third apodosis (2:1c) may also be an attack on secessionist thought, although this is less clear. The secessionists certainly claimed the authority of the Spirit for their positions (I John 4:1–6), and presumably they invoked the Spirit under the title "Paraclete" so prominent in John 14–16: a Paraclete-Spirit whose ability to teach could justify them in ignoring the tradition-bearers of the Johannine Community (like the author). If the author cannot deny such a role to the Spirit (for he too is bound by the

---

[41] For this OT background see the NOTE on 2:2a. The fact that the third apodosis fits with the others challenges Bultmann's thesis which separates 2:1–2 from 1:5–10 (1:5–10 from the source; 2:1 from the epistolary author; 2:2 from the Ecclesiastical Redactor). Moreover, it is not exact that 2:1–2 are paraenetic, as distinct from the apologetic tone of 1:5–10. The parenthesis in 2:1a may be paraenetic, but the rest of 2:1–2 has the same anti-secessionist tone as 1:5–10.

[42] John 19:14 has Jesus sentenced at noon on Passover Eve (when priests began to slaughter lambs in the Temple); John 19:29 mentions hyssop which was used for sprinkling the blood of animals and of the paschal lamb; John 19:36 compares Jesus to the paschal lamb of which not a bone was to be broken. See ABJ 29, 61–63; 29A, 883, 930, 937.

GJohn tradition), he never mentions it and never gives to the Spirit the title "Paraclete." (That silence may be accidental, however.) Moreover, he reinterprets GJohn's implicit reference to Jesus as a (first) Paraclete (14:16) to mean that he remains a Paraclete when he has left the earth and is in the Father's heavenly presence. This Paraclete exercises his role of intercession or of advocacy (NOTE on 2:1d) as an atonement for sins, in other words as a blameless ("just") self-sacrifice that continues to cleanse sin from the children of light who seek to walk in light.[48] By this usage the epistolary author may be challenging the claim of the secessionists to speak for the Paraclete(-Spirit) when they tell people that Jesus' death was of no salvific importance and that he did not "come by blood" (I John 5:6).

3. Summary

I have analyzed the disapproved and approved conditional sentences of 1:6–2:2 in their separate protases and apodoses in order to show both the carefully balanced structure given to them by the author and the fact that they make sense when read against the background of a refutation of secessionist theology as I have reconstructed it in the INTRODUCTION (IV B2; V B). Let me now sum up the whole treatment (NOTES and COMMENT) by a brief running commentary on the passage read consecutively. In 1:6 the author is fearful that his own adherents in the Johannine Community will be misled by the secessionist interpretation of GJohn perfectionism whereby the privilege of divine indwelling makes subsequent behavior, even wicked behavior, irrelevant toward salvation. The author says that those who take such a position belong to the Satanic forces of falsehood. Action follows one's real constitution: If one is of the truth, one cannot lie; if one is in communion with God who is in light, one walks in light (1:7). Walking in light or virtuous living is an aspect of being joined to a whole community of God's children. Then wrongdoings are put in proper perspective: They are not a matter of indifference, as the secessionists claim, but are sins. Yet, precisely within this community of God's children the power to cleanse that comes from the death of Jesus is effective.

Those influenced by secessionist propaganda may object that there is no guilt of sin for the believer (1:8), since Jesus found guilty of sin only those who refused to believe in him. But in the author's judgment such an approach reflects the deception of the Antichrist, the great Deceiver (see II John 7). It is true that in his ministry, which was a judgment between believers and nonbelievers, Jesus described the latter as "guilty of sin" be-

---

[48] The idea is not exactly that Christ continues to offer an atoning sacrifice, but that he is eternally present to God as one who took away sin by shedding his blood. We are not far from Rev 5:6 where he stands before God as a slain lamb.

cause they preferred darkness to light. But now if "believers" walk in darkness, are they not also preferring darkness to light? The answer to wrongdoing by believers lies not in refusing the guilt of sin but (1:9) in confessing it within the Johannine Community of the children of God; for the God who begot such children is reliable and just, faithful and merciful, and He forgives.

Those influenced by the secessionists may claim (1:10) even more radically that for the believer there is no sin. Did not Jesus say (John 3:18; 5:24) that whoever believed in him would not be judged? Why should not the child of God be able to say with the Son of God, "Can any one of you convict me of sin?" (8:46). For the author such a mindset is an even more serious perversion, for it makes a liar of the God who through Jesus entrusted the power of forgiveness to his followers (20:23). Parenthetically (2:1a) the author stops to reassure his readers that, if he is insisting on the reality of sin, it is not to encourage them to sin. He simply wants them to face the fact of sin by believers (2:1b–2) and to reassure them that the Lamb of God who takes away the sin of the world continues to do so in heaven. He is their Paraclete, serving as advocate in the Father's presence against a Satan who would claim sinners for his own. Jesus remains an atoning sacrifice for the acknowledged sins of believers and indeed for the whole world.

C. The Life-Setting of the Material in 1:5–2:2

Granted that the author may be trying to defend his adherents from the seduction of secessionist theological propaganda, is there a precise setting that brought to the fore this particular set of antitheses dealing with moral alternatives? The author proclaims a gospel "that we have heard" from the beginning of Christ's self-revelation in his preaching. Is it likely that this is also the gospel that the audience heard from the beginning when they first came to Christ? That can only be a guess unless a study of conversion exhortation[44] elsewhere in the NT shows parallels to the ideas in this unit of I John.

Even before turning to the NT, we should consider the known ritual of admission to the Dead Sea Scroll community at Qumran,[44a] a community with many theological and structural parallels to the early Christian community. After a covenantal liturgy containing a public confession of sins,

---

[44] I do not wish to decide whether the NT passages I shall discuss represent an instruction before baptism, or a baptismal liturgy, or a homily at baptism, or a homily about baptism.

[44a] See INTRODUCTION III B1. Also Barbara Thiering, "Inner and Outer Cleansing at Qumran as a Background to New Testament Baptism," NTS 26 (1979–80) 266–77.

accompanied by blessings and curses (1QS 1:18–2:25), there was a strong warning that no one could enter the community who did not walk in the ways of God: "If seeking the ways of light, he turns toward darkness" (3:3). Such a person could not be purified by atonement or cleansed by purifying waters (3:4). Only the person who walked in the ways of God would receive the true teachings, be cleansed of sin, be accepted because of a pleasing atonement before God, and become part of the covenant of eternal communion (3:11–12 with Hebrew *yaḥad* = *koinōnia*). Then there followed an instruction to all the sons of light about the difference of the spirit that they possess from the spirit that dwells in outsiders. The opening words of that instruction were as follows:

> God has created mankind to govern the world and has appointed for human beings two spirits in which to walk until the time of His visitation: the spirits of truth and iniquity. The generations of truth spring from a fountain of light, but the generations of iniquity from a source of darkness. All the sons of righteousness are under the rule of the prince of light and walk in the ways of light; but all the sons of iniquity are under the rule of the angel of darkness and walk in the ways of darkness. The angel of darkness deceives all the sons of righteousness; all their sins are caused . . . by his dominion (1QS 3:17–22).

This whole scene shares a remarkable number of themes with I John 1:5–2:2: a dualism of light and darkness, of truth and perversion; walking in light and not in darkness; a prince of light who enables the sons of righteousness (justice) to walk in light; the relation of truth to light; the ability of darkness to deceive; cleansing of sin; atonement; *koinōnia*. The overall Qumran theology is that people act according to an internal principle (light/truth versus darkness/iniquity/deceit), and for those who walk in light there is atonement, cleansing, and a place in the covenanted community.

Alas the NT does not describe a similar Christian initiation ceremony, and from scattered passages we have to piece together the themes that people heard when they became Christians. In Acts 26:18 the newly converted Paul is sent to the Gentiles: "To open their eyes that they may turn from darkness to light and from the power of Satan to God, that they may receive forgiveness of sins and a place among those who have been sanctified by faith."[45] Colossians 1:13–14 gives thanks to God who "has delivered us from the power of darkness and transferred us to the kingdom of His beloved Son, in whom we have redemption and the for-

---

[45] This is Luke's understanding of Paul's mission; it should at least reflect the language associated with making converts in Luke's own time.

giveness of sins." The author of Eph 5:6–11 reminds Gentile converts of what they were: "Let no one mislead you with empty words . . . do not associate with them [the sons of disobedience]; for once you were darkness but now you are light in the Lord. Walk as children of the light, for the fruit of light consists in all goodness and justice and truth. . . . Have no communion [*synkoinōnein*] with fruitless works of darkness." Hebrews 10:19–21 speaks of the new and living way to heaven that has been opened by the blood of Jesus, the great priest over the house of God, and then exhorts (10:22–23): "Let us approach with a true heart in full assurance of faith, our hearts sprinkled clean from an evil conscience and our bodies washed with clean water. Let us hold fast the confession of our hope."[46] The first two chapters of I Peter are often thought to be related to baptism since in 1:23 the author addresses his audience as if they had just been born anew. There is a strong covenantal demand by God, "You shall be holy, for I am holy" (I Pet 1:16, from Lev 11:44–45). The Christians are told, "You were ransomed from the futile ways inherited from your fathers . . . with the precious blood of Christ like that of a lamb without blemish or spot" (1:18–19). A glance over such passages will show that one could make a NT mosaic containing most of the features and terminology found in the Dead Sea Scroll community's initiation of new members.

At the turn of the first Christian century, *Didache* 7 gives instruction on how to baptize; but first (chs. 1–5) there is an instruction on two ways (life and death) and a warning: "Let no one deceive you from this way of teaching" (6:1). The expression "two ways" must have been standard dualistic language but with a certain flexibility, for *Barnabas* 18 speaks of ways of light and darkness over which there are light-bearing angels of God and the angels of Satan. In both *Didache* (4:14) and *Barnabas* (19:12) there is a confession of sins before the congregation as part of the right way.

The similarities between the ideas common to these various forms of conversion/initiation/baptism and the ideas in I John 1:5–2:2 are striking. I do not suggest that I John gives us in whole or part a homily for an initiation ceremony or for baptism. I do not believe that the author used a written source along the lines of Nauck's thesis of fixed antitheses prepared for a Johannine baptismal or entrance-to-the-covenant ceremony

---

[46] A "confession" seems to have been part of the conversion/initiation/baptism process, at least in terms of confessing Jesus: "Confess with your lips that Jesus is Lord" (Rom 10:9; Philip 2:11); "Confess me before men" (Matt 10:32); "Confess him as the Messiah/Christ or Son of God" (John 9:22; 12:42; I John 4:2,15; II John 7). As for confession of sins (I John 1:9), this is mentioned as part of the baptismal initiation proclaimed by John the Baptist (Mark 1:5; Matt 3:6) and in the *Didache* and *Barnabas* passages to be discussed in the text above. See Seeberg, "Die Sünden" 22–23.

(see INTRODUCTION III B1). But I do think that in this unit of I John the association of ideas is not accidentally similar to that found elsewhere in contemporary Jewish and Christian initiation practice. I John begins with a demand for walking in light because the Johannine Christians had heard about the ways of light and darkness, truth and falsehood, and about sin and forgiveness "from the beginning" of the proclamation of the gospel to them. These ideas were part of the Johannine conversion paraenesis.[47] Inevitably, some of these ideas featured in secessionist theology; but it is the author, not the secessionists, who brought them into the sequence found in 1:5–2:2, as he deliberately echoed themes his audience would have heard at the time they were converted. The conditional sentences (not unlike the casuistic examples of the OT law codes) and the antitheses (not unlike the two ways) represent Christian initiation style adopted by the author to remind his readers of their first commitments. This was all part of his campaign to show that his interpretation of the Johannine gospel was the traditional one, and that his opponents were innovators changing what was originally taught. The theological reworking of the GJohn Prologue with which the epistolary author has prefaced his work in 1:1–4, and spilling over into 1:5, may reflect the same conversion/initiation/baptism background if, as most scholars suspect, the GJohn Prologue was originally the basic Johannine hymn. It may have been the hymn people learned and sang when they entered the Johannine Community.

BIBLIOGRAPHY PERTINENT TO I JOHN 1:5–2:2

Clavier, H., "Notes sur un mot-clef du johannisme et de la sotériologie biblique: *hilasmos*," NovT 10 (1968) 287–304.

Dodd, C. H., "*Hilaskesthai*, Its Cognates, Derivatives and Synonyms in the Septuagint," JTS 32 (1931) 352–60.

———. "Atonement," in *The Bible and the Greeks* (London: Hodder & Stoughton, 1935) 82–95.

Hill, D., "The Interpretation of *hilaskesthai* and Related Words in the Septuagint and in the New Testament," in *Greek Words and Hebrew Meanings* (SNTSMS 5; Cambridge Univ., 1967) 23–48, esp. 36–37 on I John 2:2; 4:10.

[47] Hebrews, which is close to Johannine thought, speaks of conversion as being "enlightened" (10:32). In John 9 the story of the man born blind who regains his sight has many baptismal innuendoes (ABJ 29, 380–82). We can be reasonably sure that the language of conversion and baptism in the Johannine tradition involved a passing from darkness to light.

Hodges, Z. C., "Fellowship and Confession in I John 1:5–10," BibSac 129 (1972) 48–60.

Lazure, N., "Les voies de la connaissance de Dieu (1 Jn 2, 1–5a)," AsSeign, 2d series, 24 (1970) 21–28.

Lyonnet, S., "The Noun *hilasmos* in the Greek Old Testament and 1 John," in S. Lyonnet and L. Sabourin, *Sin, Redemption, and Sacrifice* (AnBib 48; Rome: Biblical Institute, 1970) 148–55. This is a translation of S. Lyonnet, *De Peccato et Redemptione* (2 vols.; Rome: Biblical Institute, 1957, 1960) 2, 99–105.

Martino, C., "La riconciliazione in 1 Gv. 1,9," *Antonianum* 54 (1979) 162–224.

Morris, L., *The Apostolic Preaching of the Cross* (London: Tyndale, 1955) esp. 125–85 on "Propitiation" (against Dodd); 177–80 treats I John.

Schaeffer, O., " 'Gott ist Licht', 1 Joh. 1,5," TSK 105 (1933) 467–76.

Spicq, C., "L'origine johannique de la conception du Christ-prêtre dans l'Epître aux Hébreux," in *Aux Sources de la tradition Chrétienne*, ed. O. Cullmann and P. H. Menoud (Mélanges M. Goguel; Neuchâtel: Delachaux & Niestlé, 1950) 258–69, esp. 263–64.

Thornton, T.C.G., "Propitiation or Expiation? *Hilastērion* and *Hilasmos* in Romans and 1 John," ExpT 80 (1968–69) 53–55.

Zerwick, M., " 'Veritatem facere' Ioh. 3, 21; 1 Ioh. 1, 6," VD 18 (1938) 338–42, 373–77.

See also "Sin" in VII C2 in the *General Bibliography*.

3. I John 2:3–11: *Three Claims of Intimate Knowledge of God to be Tested by Behavior*

3a	³Now this is how we can be sure that we know Him:
3b	by keeping His commandments.
4a	⁴THE PERSON WHO CLAIMS, "I know Him,"
4b	without keeping His commandments,
4c	is a liar;
4d	and there is no truth in such a person.
5a	⁵But whoever keeps His word—
5b	truly in this person the love of God has reached perfection.
5c	This is how we can be sure that we are in Him.
6a	⁶THE PERSON WHO CLAIMS to abide in Him
6b	ought himself to walk
6c	just as Christ walked.
7a	⁷Beloved, this is no new commandment that I write you,
7b	but an old commandment that you had from the beginning—
7c	an old commandment which is "the word" you already heard.
8a	⁸On second thought, the commandment I write you is new
8b	as it is made true both in Christ and in you,
8c	since the darkness is passing away
8d	and the true light is already shining.
9a	⁹THE PERSON WHO CLAIMS to be in the light,
9b	all the while hating his brother,
9c	is still in the darkness even now.
10a	¹⁰The person who loves his brother abides in the light
10b	and in him there is no cause for stumbling.
11a	¹¹But the person who hates his brother is in the darkness.
11b	He walks in the dark
11c	with no idea where he is going,
11d	for the darkness has blinded his eyes.

NOTES

2:3a. *Now.* The initial *kai* ("and") here is not a simple connective, as THLJ rightly observes. A similar initial *kai*, plus a somewhat different form of the demonstrative "this," was also found in 1:5, where the author stated, "Now this is the gospel . . . God is light." After three pairs of conditional sentences, he is going on "now" to tell the readers how we know the God who is light.

this is how. The Greek is *en toutō*, "in this," with the *en* as instrumental, equivalent to "by means of" (Moule, IBNTG 77). This is a frequent and most troublesome Johannine idiom, occurring 5 times in GJohn (4:37; 9:30; 13:35; 15:8; 16:30) and 12 times in I John (2:3,5c; 3:10,16,19,24; 4:2,9,10,13,17; 5:2), without counting 2:4b and 2:5b where *en toutō* means "in this person." While the pedagogic thrust of the phrase is to make a "this" perfectly clear, the intent fails woefully; for there is no point more disputed than whether in I John the "this" refers (always or normally) to what precedes or to what follows. To avoid repetition each time *en toutō* occurs, let me list here the statistics of usage and how they affect the interpretation of the "this":

(A) Passages where the *en toutō* statement is followed by a subordinate clause or a prepositional phrase. In Johannine usage clauses or phrases following the *en toutō* statement (whether or not they are related to the *toutō*—see below for an explanation of the underlined and italicized numerals) are introduced by the following words:

- *ean*, "if": John 13:35; I John 2:3
- *hina*, "(in order) that": John 15:8; *I John 4:17*
- *hotan*, "whenever": I John 5:2
- *hoti*, "that": John 4:37; 9:30; 16:30; I John 2:5c; 3:16,19; 4:9,10,13,17
- *ek*, "from" (prepositional phrase): I John 3:24.

(B) Passages where the *en toutō* statement is *not* followed by a subordinate clause or prepositional phrase. In I John 3:10 and 4:2 it is followed by another main clause.

The above division seems disproportionate in terms of the passages included under (A) and (B) unless one observes the hint I gave under (A) that even if there is a following subordinate clause or phrase, one must decide whether it is related to *toutō*. For instance, 9 of the *en toutō* statements are a variation of this pattern: "This is how we/you know [can be sure] . . ." (John 13:35; I John 2:3,5c; 3:16,19,24; 4:2,13; 5:12). If the verb "to know" governs a *hoti* ("that") clause telling what we/you know, that *hoti* clause tells us nothing about how we know—it is not related to the *toutō*. Or the following *hoti* may introduce a "because" clause which again does not interpret the *en toutō*, e.g., "In this has love reached perfection . . . because we are just the same as Christ is" (4:17). In such cases, if there is not a second subordinate clause or phrase that can be related to the *toutō*, we are really dealing with instances of

(B). For that reason I have underlined under (A) those passages that indisputably belong under (B), and I have italicized passages that are debatable but probably belong under (B). Thus (B) is a larger group than would first appear (7 out of 17 uses) and includes: John 4:37; 16:30; I John 2:5c; 3:10,19; 4:2,17.

The reason I am being so precise is that, where there are true (A) passages, I would contend that the *en toutō* statement must have its primary thrust forward to the subordinate clause or prepositional phrase; otherwise, that clause or phrase has no grammatical function. Sometimes in these instances there is a tone of continuing what precedes, sometimes not; but this tone is always minor. On the other hand, in the (B) group of statements grammar supplies no help in determining the thrust of the *en toutō* statement; for that statement has an independent sentence preceding it and another following, and it could refer to either. Each case under (B) has to be decided on its own merits. In I John 4:2 I judge that the *en toutō* refers to what follows; in John 16:30; I John 3:10,19; 4:17 I judge that it refers to what precedes; and in John 4:37 and I John 2:5c it refers to both what precedes and what follows. I disagree, then, with the sweeping statements in many commentaries about the direction in which *en toutō* "always" points (usually forward).

If we apply these rules to the present passage, since there is an *ean* clause in 3b which follows the *en toutō*, the passage comes under (A); and there is no doubt that "by keeping His commandments" (literally, "if we keep") explains the "this." (In fact, this is a rare passage about which all commentators seem to agree!) The statement points forward, and there is very little relationship to what immediately precedes. As I suggested, the initial *kai* really points back to 1:5 rather than to 2:2.

we can be sure that we know Him. That observation is important in understanding why the *auton*, "him," does not refer to the last mentioned person (2:1d), Jesus Christ, as many scholars hold (Asmussen, Bengel, Büchsel, Calmes, Erdmann, Gaugler, Häring, Heise, Karl, Rothe). Like the *autos* forms in 1:6a,7b,10bc, it refers to God, last mentioned as "God" in 1:5 (Belser, Bonsirven, Bultmann, Chaine, de Ambroggi, Haas, Holtzmann, Houlden, Lazure, Loisy, Malatesta, Marshall, Michl, Schnackenburg, Schneider, Stott, Vrede, B. Weiss). It is true that sometimes in I John there is "no sharp distinction between God and Christ" (THLJ 44); but that principle should not be invoked here as is done by Dodd (?), Hauck, THLJ, Thüsing, Westcott, and Windisch. Nor is there need to resort to a putative source in which 2:3 followed 1:10 and so clearly referred to God; but now that 2:1–2 has been inserted, the *auton* is Christ (Wilder). The problem that the author is dealing with is how to know the God who is light, not how to know Christ. All the secessionist-inspired claims in 1:5–2:11 concern God.

Literally, the clause reads, "we know that we have known Him," with a present tense of *ginōskein* ("to know") followed by a perfect tense. As for the first verb, 8 of the 12 uses of *en toutō* in I John are followed by the verb *ginōskein*, more often in the present tense (here; 2:5c; 3:24), but by the future in 3:19, and by the perfect in 3:16. As for the second verb, some commentators

(Marshall, Westcott) see significance in the shift of tense and insist that the perfect here stresses the result of past action still realized in the present; but many simply translate the perfect as if it were another present tense—see the reference to Louw in the NOTE on "have heard" in 1:1b. Variety of tense is, in part, a stylistic device.

Ginōskein appears 25 times in I John (once in II John; 56 times in GJohn), and it covers a wide range of knowledge as illustrated here by its use in two slightly different senses in the same line ("be certain," "know"). Proponents of a Johannine "grammatical theology" (Abbott, de la Potterie, Stott, Westcott) would see *ginōskein* as sharply distinct from the other favorite Johannine verb "to know," *oida* (i.e., *eidenai*—15 times in I John, once in III John, 85 times in GJohn). The former is supposed to cover the experiential knowledge that one has gained through effort; the latter to cover immediate certitude possessed with assurance. Let me quote the conclusion I came to in ABJ 29, 514: "The proponents of distinction have elaborate explanations for the instances when either verb is used in a way that seems to violate the meaning proposed for it. However, there are so many exceptions that it is probably best to come to the same decision here that we reached about the attempts to distinguish the various verbs 'to love' and 'to see.' John may tend to use one verb in one way and another verb in another way, but it is really a question of emphasis and not of sharp distinction."

The theme of knowing God or knowing Christ (under various titles) occurs in I John 11 times, always with *ginōskein* (2:3,4,13; 3:1,6; 4:6,7,8; 5:20). In GJohn the first use of *ginōskein* for knowing God or knowing Christ is in the Prologue (1:10); and then it is used in 8:55; 10:15; 14:7; 16:3; 17:3,25, while *eidenai* (*oida*) is used in 1:26,31,33; 7:28,29; 8:19,55; 14:7; 15:21. The impossibility of a sharp distinction is illustrated by two GJohn statements: "You do not know [*eidenai*] me or my Father; if you knew [*eidenai*] me, you would know [*eidenai*] my Father too" (8:19); "If you knew [*ginōskein*] me, you would know [*eidenai* or *ginōskein*—witnesses divided] my Father too; from now on you do know [*ginōskein*] Him" (14:7). See also examples of interchangeability in ABJ 29, 514. Far more important than which verb is used is what is meant by knowing God, and that will be discussed in the COMMENT.

3b. *by keeping His commandments.* Literally, "if we keep His commandments." As explained in 2:3a above, the "if" (*ean*) is epexegetical of the "this" (*en toutō*) in the first line; BDF 394 explains that *hoti* should play this role if actual fact is involved, while *ean* may be used if there is an assumption (also MGNTG 3, 139). This is the first epistolary occurrence of *entolē*, "commandment," which is used 18 times in the Epistles (14 in I John; 4 in II John), 10 times in the singular, 8 in the plural. In reference to Jesus *entolē* occurs 10 times in GJohn (6 times in the singular, 4 in the plural), covering something that the Father has given to Jesus, and that Jesus has given to his disciples. Jesus speaks of a commandment from the Father telling him what to say and to do, and especially to lay down his life and to take it up again (in the singular in 10:18; 12:49,50; 14:31; once in the plural in 15:10). In 13:34 and 15:12 Jesus speaks in the singular of the commandment to love one another, which he is giving to his disciples, while in 14:15,21 and 15:10 he speaks of "my commandments," which he gives to his disciples. In ABJ 29A, 638 and 641, I showed that the variation between singular and plural is not of clear theological significance; see also F.-M. Braun, "La réduction" 47–51. Chmiel, *Lumière* 133, follows G. Schrenk in attributing significance to the fact that in I John a plural usage is followed by a singular (e.g., 2:3–4 followed by 2:7–8); but then he makes the telltale admission that discounts this: the singular in 4:21 is followed by the plural in 5:2–3 (cf. also the alternation pl./sg./pl. in 3:22,23,24). Alternation of number (like variety of tense) is, in part, a stylistic device.

One may put the GJohn information about commandment(s) together thus: Jesus has received as a command from his Father a total direction of life, covering his words, deeds, and death; it is not imposed from the outside but flows from the fact that he is the Son who acts spontaneously after the pattern of his Father. This "commandment" is, in turn, the prototype for Jesus' commandment(s) to his disciples. Specifically he commands them to love one another "as I have loved you," and his love for them reflects the Father's love in sending His only Son (3:16). The use of a plural does not mean that Jesus gives to his disciples a number of specific commandments (not recorded in GJohn); rather the plural gives a comprehensive force to the commandment to love. That commandment involves a whole way of life that relates Christians to one another and to Jesus. Such a way of life would include keeping the Ten Commandments, but that is never made specific in GJohn.

I and II John also know of a commandment in the singular; and in I John 2:7–8 (implicitly) and in 4:21 and II John 5–6 it is a commandment to love one another (one's brother) just as in GJohn. The "commandment" (sg. and pl.) is described 8 times in I John as "his," and once as "from him" (4:21). There are scholars who contend that in some of these instances the his/him reference is to Christ, especially on the grounds that "it is a commandment we have had from the beginning" (II John 5), i.e., from the beginning of Jesus' self-revelation during his ministry. Consistently, however, I have interpreted the "his" as a reference to God. Sometimes the context makes this lucidly clear (I John 4:21). I John 3:23 not only implicitly ascribes the commandment to God but makes it twofold: "Now this is His commandment: we are to believe the name of His Son, Jesus Christ; and we are to love one another just as He gave us the commandment." Similarly interesting is II John 4, which describes "walking in truth" as "a commandment we have received from the Father"; for these passages show the tendency to move beyond brotherly love to general behavior and faith. See the COMMENT for the significance of the shifts in usage from GJohn to I John.

"*Keeping* commandments" is an idiom employing the verb *tērein* with the plural, 4 times in GJohn (including 15:10, the one time where Jesus speaks of having commandments [plural] from his Father) and 5 times in I John. In GJohn the reference is to keeping the commandments of Jesus; in I John to keeping the commandments of God (2:3,4; 3:22,24; 5:3). Parallel expressions are "to do the commandments" of God in I John 5:2, and "to walk according to His commandments" in II John 6. The variety of the expression indicates the comprehensiveness of the idea. As Lazure, *Valeurs* 128, recognizes, the implication of the idiom is that of *realizing* in one's life what those commandments ask. The verb "keep" with its durational atmosphere enables the epistolary author to indicate an abiding realization. For "keeping" commandments the LXX employs the verb *phylassein*, translating Hebrew *šāmar;* yet *tērein* appears in one instance (Sir 29:1; see also "keep the Law" in Tob 14:9, and Acts 15:5; Jas 2:10). Westcott, *Epistles* 47, contends that while *phylassein* means to guard an unchangeable deposit, *tērein* means to observe watchfully; but the usage is scarcely so precise. (The Vulgate recognized the difficulty of catching the exact nuance of *tērein*, translating the three occurrences in I John 2:3–5 by three different verbs: *observare, custodire, servare.*) In Prov 19:16 we hear: "The person who keeps [*phylassein*] the commandments keeps [*tērein*] his own soul"; and Jesus says in John 17:12: "I kept them safe [*tērein*] with your name . . . I kept watch [*phylassein*] and not one of them perished." Elsewhere in the NT "keeping [*tērein*] the commandments" occurs in Rev 12:17; 14:12; Matt 19:17; cf. I Cor 7:19; Mark 7:9.

For the sake of comparison it is useful at this time to discuss also *logos,* "word," which is virtually interchangeable with *entolē*, "commandment," in some of the usage just discussed. (I find meaningless the distinction made by Chmiel, *Lumière* 134: "It is necessary to obey the divine word in order to keep the commandments.") In GJohn *tērein* is used with *logos* 8 times (7 in the sg.—thus, as regards the sg./pl. issue, the opposite of the usage with *entolē*, which is always pl.; the one LXX usage of "keep the word" [I Sam 15:11] is pl.). Once again we have a chain of thought: Jesus keeps the Father's word (8:55); and the disciples keep Jesus' word (8:51; 14:23; 15:20; and 14:24 [pl.]). However, the disciples also keep God's word (17:6), and other people are challenged to keep the disciples' word (15:20). Interesting in this regard is 14:21–24: "Whoever keeps the commandments that he has from me is the person who loves me. . . . If anyone loves me, he will keep my word. . . . Whoever does not love me does not keep my words; yet the word that you hear is not my own but comes from the Father." Turning to I John, we find "keeping His word" (sg.) only in 2:5 where it follows a double reference to "keeping His commandments" in 2:3–4. In 2:7 the author speaks of "an old commandment which is 'the word' you already heard." Such predication, confirming the interchangeability of the terms, makes sense if we remember that in the OT (Hebrew and Greek) the technical name for the Ten Commandments was the "Ten Words" (Deca*logue*): Exod 20:1; 34:28; Deut 4:13; 10:4. Whereas the Hebrew of Deut 17:19 refers to a whole law code as "all the words of this Law," the LXX reads "all these commandments"; and in both languages Ezra's law code is called "the words of the commandments of the Lord" (Ezra 7:11).

4a. *The person who claims, "I know Him."* Literally, "the one saying that I have known Him." This is the first of three masc. sg. pres. participles of the verb "to say" (2:4a,6a,9a) that introduce claims that the author rejects. Brooke and Westcott are among those who think that the three participles in ch. 2 indicate that the threat is more real than expressed by the three "If we say [boast]" conditions of ch. 1. However, the Greek participle can be translated conditionally; and the participle in 2:4a is opposed by a semiconditional sentence in 2:5a, just as the conditions in ch. 1 were opposed by contrary conditions. If there is any difference in tone between the two sets of three disapproved theses in chs. 1 and 2, it lies in the use of the first person in ch. 1 ("we") and the third person ("one, person") in ch. 2. The false statements here may approach being exact quotations from the secessionists, while those in ch. 1 may have been secessionist-inspired but rephrased in the author's wording.

In the present passage the *hoti* (or untranslated "that" of indirect discourse) is omitted by the scribes of the Byzantine textual tradition in imitation of 2:6a,9a, where it is genuinely absent. The boast that the author rejects is "I have known Him"—the same verb (*ginōskein*) and the same tense (perf., equivalent to pres.) used in 2:3a where the author *approved* the possibility of knowing God! Clearly then the author's rejection of the boast hangs on the clause in 4b: "without keeping His commandments." The parallelism with 2:3a where most likely the "Him" is God, and with 2:6a ("The person who claims to abide in Him") where the "Him" must be God, and the fact that in I John "commandments" (pl. in 2:4b) are always referred to God make a reference to Christ in 2:4a hard to defend, although that idea is found elsewhere in I John (2:13b,14d: "You have known him who has been from the beginning").

4b. *without keeping His commandments.* Literally, "and not keeping His commandments," continuing the participial construction from 4a. The negative is *mē*, as usual with participles in the NT and almost without exception in the Johannine writings (BDF 430[1]).

4c. *is a liar.* For the relation of *pseustēs* to other *pseud*-words, see the NOTE on 1:6c, "We are liars." The claim of Westcott and Brooke that the noun "liar" may be more revelatory of the character of the person who makes the false claim than is the verb "to lie" employed in 1:6c is another example of the tendency of the older commentators to lend significance to what are only stylistic variations.

4d. *and there is no truth in such a person.* Literally, "in this one," a phrase that Codex Sinaiticus omits, reading rather, "and there is no truth of God" in scribal imitation of the phrase "love of God" in the next verse. The initial "and" is omitted by Codex Alexandrinus. As with 1:8 ("If we boast . . . the truth is not in us") and 1:10 ("If we boast . . . His word is not in us"), this is an example of the B classification of the formula *einai en* discussed in the NOTE on 1:5e above.

5a. *But whoever keeps His word.* This sentence illustrates the nominative absolute construction (or *casus pendens* of Semitic grammar: BDF 466[2]) whereby in order to focus attention on "this person" in 5b, the identification of that person is placed in a clause that comes first in the sentence, standing in a loose grammatical connection to what follows. It is more dramatic and emphatic than if the author had used a simple relative clause: "Truly in the person who has kept His word . . ." The indefinite relative *hos d'an* ("But whoever") has a force not unlike the *ean de* used in the adversative condition of 1:7a ("But if") as once again, after attacking a claim reflecting his opponents' theology, the author counterposes a (semi)conditional sentence that shows how to approach the issue correctly. As for "His word," Westcott, *Epistles* 48, contends that the position of the pronoun "His" is emphatic; however, there is no reason to think that the author is counterposing God's word to his opponents' word. As I indicated at the end of the NOTE on 2:3b, I find no difference between "His word" and "His commandments" of 2:3b,4b. Westcott would argue that the commandments are definite instructions, while the word is the "principle which is ever taking a new embodiment in the very process of life" (p. 47); and for Brooke, Marshall, Plummer, and Wilder "word" is a wider term, covering the whole of revelation or the gospel or God's promises. While "word" can have such a meaning, in this context it makes perfect sense if "word" means God's ethical demands, i.e., His commandments. As indicated previously, a comparison of John 14:21 and 14:23 shows this.

5b. *truly in this person.* A few scholars would read "truly" with line 5a; but it is read better with 5b, for just as 2:5a ("whoever keeps His word") is antithetically parallel to 2:4ab ("The person who claims . . . without keeping His commandments"), so 2:5b is antithetically parallel to 2:4cd ("is a liar . . . no *truth* in such a person"). The adverb *alēthōs* in Johannine usage has a deeper connotation than the English "truly," for it describes something that corresponds to *alētheia*, "truth," which inheres in the believer. Keeping the word of God stems from the truth that is in a person, just as not keeping God's commandments shows that there is no truth in a person.

the love of God. This is the first mention of "love" (*agapē*) in the Johannine Epistles. Let me discuss *agapē* in general, and then the peculiar problems of the phrase "love of God."

LOVE, AGAPĒ. In treating this concept in ABJ 29, 497–99, I had to devote much time to the thesis, massively defended by Spicq and held by many, that there is a distinction between the two verbs "to love" used by GJohn, *agapan* and *philein,* a thesis that I rejected. (To the bibliography there should be added R. Joly, *Le vocabulaire chrétien de l'amour est-il originel?* [Brussels: Université Libre, 1968], who offers detailed historical and philological arguments against Spicq's thesis.) That problem need not concern us here, for the Johannine Epistles never use *philein,* and *philos* occurs only in III John 15. They use *agapan* 31 times (28 in I John) and *agapē* 21 times (18 in I John)— thus one-fifth of the usage of these words in the NT are in Epistles that constitute in length only one-fiftieth of the NT! To this may be added 10 uses of *agapētos,* "beloved" (NOTE on 2:7a below). In classical Greek *agapē* is scarcely found, and the verb is used colorlessly, "to like, prefer, be content with." Even if there is some increase of its usage in the common secular Greek of the NT period, Christians gave a new intensity and specific meaning to *agapē/agapan/agapētos.* The basic picture that A. Nygren painted in his classic *Agape and Eros* (2 vols.; London: SPCK, 1932–37) was true of the usage in GJohn and remains true of the Epistles as well. *Agapē* is not a love originating in the human heart and reaching out to possess noble goods needed for perfection; it is a spontaneous, unmerited, creative love flowing from God to the Christian, and from the Christian to a fellow Christian. There is an admirable summary in I John 4:10–11: "In this, then, does love consist: not that we have loved God, but that He loved us and sent His Son as an atonement for our sins. Beloved, if He so loved us, we in turn ought to love one another." Indeed, *agapē* is so totally divine in origin that twice the author claims, "God is love" (I John 4:8,16).

Nygren insisted that the proper response to God's love for us consisted in our love for others and our faith in God, but not in our love for God. To love God, for Nygren, would be to seek to possess Him, and such motivated love would not be *agapē*. Here I disagree on several scores. *First,* it is true that in the Pauline writings the normal response to God's love (shown in justification) is to believe in Him. But as T. Barrosse, "Relationship" 541–43, has shown, "faith" for Paul is a dynamic reality that grows throughout a Christian's life, while John does not speak of such a growth in faith. "To believe," for John, means to perform the initial but definitive act of totally accepting Christ (speculatively and practically). In Johannine thought the ongoing growth comes in the mutual love that binds together Father, Son, and Christian. *Second,* Prunet, *La Morale* 113, points out that the Johannine model for Christian love is in part the eternal mutual love of the Father for the Son and of the Son for the Father, the one conferring good, the other responding to the good received. And so Johannine love is not totally unmotivated in Nygren's sense. (Indeed, one should modify Nygren's terminology by distinguishing between love as a response to goodness conferred and love as seeking a good not yet possessed, confining "motivated" to the latter.) It is not surprising then that in I John 4:20–5:2 the desirability of loving God is made very clear. Here the author stands close to the OT (Judg 5:31; Ps 31:24[23]; Sir 7:30; Wis 3:9) and to intertestamental Judaism as illustrated in the Dead Sea Scrolls wherein "those who love God" is virtually a self-designation for the Qumran community (CD 19:2; 20:21; 1QH 15:9; 16:13). See also *T. Dan* 5:3; *T. Issachar* 5:2; 7:6; and Philo, *On the Special Laws* 2.15 ⚹63, for the joining of the commands to love God and to love neighbor, as in the Synoptic tradition (Mark 12:29–31 and par.). In Nygren's theory this OT and intertestamental background would help to prove that such love for God is not pure *agapē*, for he maintained that there was no real concept of *agapē* before Christianity. However, his judgment on that score represents a significant failure to understand the *ḥesed* of the covenant God of Israel. *Third,* as we shall see in the NOTE on 2:9b below, the love of brother or of one another in Johannine literature is love within the (Johannine) Christian community, which Sikes, "Note" 141, describes as "the exclusive fellowship of those who believe, know and love Christ as the Son of God come in the flesh. Loving one's enemy or any one outside this circle of believers is quite unknown in this literature." Such an attitude qualifies the disinterested character of *agapē*.

THE LOVE OF GOD. I have treated the range of love in the Johannine tradition and its extension to God precisely to offer a context for discussing the phrase "the love of God [or of the Father or of Him]." Such a genitival phrase occurs with *agapē* 8 times in Johannine usage: twice in GJohn (5:42; 15:10) and 6 times in I John (2:5,15; 3:17; 4:9,12; 5:3). Scholars are utterly divided as to what this phrase means or, indeed, as to whether it always means the same thing. The possibilities are five: (a) love for God, i.e., an objectival genitive; (b) love from God or God's love for us, i.e., a subjective genitive; (c) both the preceding, e.g., ZBG 36–39, stresses a wider grammatical scope than either the objective or the subjective genitive; (d) divine love, i.e., a qualitative genitive; see BDF 165; (e) love of God, i.e., a noncommittal translation, either because it is impossible to decide among the other possibilities, or because one suspects that the author was innocent of such genitival precisions. In every instance that the phrase occurs I do *not* intend to enter into a full discussion for each position; but this first time such an exercise is worthwhile, for it may throw light on the fundamental Johannine understanding of love.

(a) Human love for God. In relation to 2:5b the objective genitive is defended by Alexander, Chaine, Charue, Coppens, Dodd, Hauck, Marshall, Moffatt, Plummer, Stott, B. Weiss, Wilder, RSV, and TEV. The paragraph above in criticism of Nygren was written to show that this interpretation cannot be dismissed as unworthy or unJohannine. Bultmann, *Epistles* 25, is too cavalier when he speaks of "the fact that man's love cannot be directly oriented toward God." In favor of the objective genitive are OT passages that deal with the same topic as the present verse: Exod 20:6 has God speaking in parallelism of "those that love me" and "those that keep my precepts," while Jer 2:2 has God speaking of the "perfection" (*teleiōsis*) of Israel's love for Him. Indeed, since I John 2:5b speaks of the love of God reaching perfection, it is human love for God that is most easily conceived as perfectible.

(b) God's love for human beings. In relation to 2:5b the subjective genitive is defended by Bengel, Bonsirven, Bultmann, Calvin, Gaugler, Heise, Houlden, Lazure, Schlier, Westcott, JB, and THLJ(?). The best argument is that this is John's primary understanding of *agapē*, as seen above. (Indeed, it may be the dominant meaning in the whole Bible if one judges from BDB 13.) It is the only possible meaning in some of the eight Johannine instances of the genitival phrase, e.g., the parallel with "my love," employing an adjective in John 15:9, shows that the genitival phrase in 15:10 has to be read subjectively. The objection that God's love is already perfect and cannot "reach perfection" (I John 2:5b) is not convincing: In the Johannine sense it is perfectible (*teleioun*) in that it has to be lived out in our lives. John 13:1 uses a related word when it says that Jesus, "having loved his own who were in this world, now showed his love for them to the very end [*telos*]." A passage very close to the one under discussion is I John 4:12: "If we love one another, God abides in us and *hē agapē autou* has reached perfection in us." Because of the context that has just preceded that verse where "the love of God" (4:9) must mean God's love for us, the Greek phrase in 4:12 should be translated subjectively: "His love" rather than "the love of Him." The fact that both 4:12 and the present passage speak of the love of God reaching perfection in the person who keeps God's word suggests by parallelism that a subjective genitive is meant here.

(c,d,e) When we turn to the last three possibilities in relation to 2:5b, (c) is held by Brooke, de Ambroggi (?), Hoskyns, Schneider, and Windisch; (d) is held by Schnackenburg and NEB; while (e) is suggested by THLJ. All three reflect an unease about deciding between (a) and (b). One may wonder whether even implicitly the epistolary author ever stopped to ask himself which type of genitive he meant; or did he simply use a set phrase with a whole complexus of meaning which he did not refine further? Here I think it impossible to be sure what the author meant, although he would certainly have included meaning (b). I shall use the noncommittal "love of God," which has the dubious advantage of ruling out nothing.

has reached perfection. The predicate of 2:5b employs the perfect passive tense of *teleioun,* "to complete, perfect." THLJ 47 stresses that the perfect tense here is equivalent to a present; similarly BDF 344 sees this as a rare instance of the classic Greek use of the perfect tense in general assertions. *Teleioun* (23 times in the NT) is used a total of 5 times in GJohn: for Jesus' completion of the work the Father gave him to do (4:34; 5:36; 17:4); for the complete fulfillment of Scripture (19:28); and for bringing those who believe in Jesus to completion as one (17:23). In I John it is used 4 times, always for the completion or perfection of love (here; 4:12,17,18); and the related adjective *teleios* appears (only Johannine use) as a description of love in 4:18: "Perfect love drives out fear." Since keeping the commandments (or God's word) certainly involves living out the commandment to love one another, the love of God shown us in Jesus Christ reaches its perfection when the same love is shown to "one another" and to the God who abides in the Christian. We saw that the idea of loving God is strong both in the OT and in intertestamental Judaism; similarly we find there that love and perfection are related to keeping the commandments. The love of Wisdom is identified with keeping her laws in Wis 6:18. Just as "those who love God" is a self-identification of the Qumran community, so also is "those who walk perfectly in all God's ways, keeping His precepts" (1QS 2:2; 4:22; 8:20–21; 1QM 14:7; 1QSa 1:17,28). This was very clearly part of the covenant concept of the Qumran community which believed that God had constituted it as a "house of perfection and truth" to establish a covenant according to eternal precepts (1QS 8:9–10).

In the NT "being perfect" (*teleioun, teleios,* etc.) is a frequently stated goal (I Cor 2:6; 14:20; Col 1:28; Eph 4:13), most clearly held up as a covenant ideal by Matt 5:48: "You must be perfect as your heavenly Father is perfect." For Matt 19:21 perfection is brought about by good works done for the poor; Jas 1:25 sees the doer of good deeds as living according to "the perfect law of liberty." For Paul (1 Cor 13:8,10) *agapē* is what will remain when all else passes away—"the perfect" that outlasts the imperfect. Particularly strong in Hebrews is the theme that the perfection which was not possible through the Law and through the works and sacrifices it commanded (7:11,19; 9:9; 10:1) has been brought about through Jesus, the perfecter (12:2), the high priest who made atonement through his blood (10:14; 12:23–24). (See P. J. Du Plessis, *TELEIOS. The Idea of Perfection in the New Testament* [Kampen: Kok, *ca.* 1960]; A. Wikgren, "Patterns of Perfection in the Epistle to the Hebrews," NTS 6 [1959–60] 159–66.) Thus in the NT there are survivals of a Jewish ideal whereby perfection comes about by doing what God has commanded; but this is modified by the belief that only God's accomplishment in Jesus enables us to do what God really wants. Close to I John in relating the perfection of love to keeping the commandments is *I Clement* (p. 6 above), and *Didache* 10:5 which prays, "Remember, Lord, your church . . . to make it perfect in your love." At the end of the first century, then, in such documents church life was being seen as the arena for perfection in love. Bultmann, *Epistles* 26, points to similar connections between perfection and love in the Mandaean writings: "Love one another in faithfulness and bring your love to perfection" (*Ginza Right* 1.20.8; Lidzbarski, p. 22). Perfection and "the perfect" constitute a strong theme in gnosticism as well; see W. Schmithals, *Paul and the Gnostics* (Nashville: Abingdon, 1972) 99–104 for possible NT roots of later gnostic usage. However, gnostics would normally relate perfection more to knowledge than to love and keeping commandments.

5c. *This is how we can be sure.* The same expression (*en toutō* followed by *ginōskein*) was used in 2:3a. Here, however, the *en toutō* is not followed by a subordinate clause that modifies the *toutō;* it belongs to the (B) rather than to the (A) classification discussed in the NOTE on 2:3a; and so grammatically the "This is how" can refer either to what precedes or to what follows or to both. If it relates to what precedes, it forms an inclusion with 2:3a, packaging this subunit (Chaine). Or, since 2:3a led into the first "The person who claims" statement in 2:4–5, so could 2:5c lead into what follows, i.e., the second "The person who claims" statement in 2:6 (Williams starts here a new unit: 2:5c–11). A problem with such reasoning is that 2:3 introduces the whole unit, not just vv. 4–5; and so there is no structural need for 2:5c to serve as an introduction to 2:6. Favoring a relationship to what precedes are Bonsirven, Bultmann, de Ambroggi, de la Potterie, Haas, Nestle, THLJ, Schnackenburg, Schneider, and the KJV. Favoring a relationship to what follows are Balz, Brooke, Bruce, Dodd, Ewald, Heise, Holtzmann, Stott, Westcott, Williams, and the NEB, RSV, and TEV. That it refers to both is suggested by Chaine and Wilder. The difference in meaning among these views is not significant. I would judge that primarily it refers to what precedes, summing it up; but at the same time it is a transition to what follows—"are in Him" at the end of v. 5c leads into the claim "to abide in Him" in 6a.

we are in Him. The expression of relationship is so abrupt that many translators paraphrase, e.g., "in union with Him"; but that obscures the fact that this is an instance (the first) of *einai en*, "to be in," used as a formula of divine immanence or indwelling (God or Christ and the Christian). This belongs to the (A) grouping of *einai en* discussed in the NOTE on 1:5e. The more frequent formula for immanence is *menein en*, "to remain in," which occurs in the next line (v. 6a), and I shall postpone the general discussion of indwelling until then. In the present line the identity of the "him" is determined by one's decision about the "him" in 3a, where I opted for "God." Some scholars think that the reference here is to Christ (Dodd, Heise, Stott, Williams); but virtually the same expression in the next line (2:6a "abide in Him") has to refer to God.

5d. We find here the first of the Latin readings (INTRODUCTION VI B) that have little or no attestation in Greek: *si in ipso perfecti fuerimus* (or *consummati inveniemur*), "if we have been made perfect in Him." This is found in Augustine's commentary (*In Epistolam* 1.9; SC 75, 134), but also in Pseudo-Augustine, Bede, and the Spanish Vulgate, as well as in an eighth-century Greek MS. (*psi*—Thiele, "Beobachtungen" 68, argues for a Greek original). Grammatically this would change 2:5c radically, for the *en toutō* would now have a continuation and would have to point forward (class [A] in the NOTE on 2:3a): "This is how we can be sure that we are in Him, namely, if we are made perfect in Him." The pattern of an "if" clause continuing *en toutō* was established in 2:3 and may have influenced scribes in making an addition here.

6a. *The person who claims to abide in Him.* Literally, "the one saying," as in 2:4a but here followed by an infinitive rather than by a *hoti* clause of indirect discourse. The distinguishing use of *ekeinos* for Christ in 2:6c makes clear the identity of the *autos* ("Him") here as God, although Büchsel, Heise, and others argue for a reference to Christ.

Menein, a favorite Johannine verb (55% of the total NT usage; 40 times in GJohn), makes its first epistolary appearance (24 times in I John, 3 in II John). It has a wide range of meaning; and Pecorara, "De verbo" 164, lists 7 meanings for John: "remain, dwell, rest, live, persist, persevere, be intimately united to." Nevertheless, for our purposes "remain" and "abide/dwell" offer an adequate range of translation. Particularly among German scholars even that range is disputed as regards the formula *menein en* which most concerns us. Heise, *Bleiben* 172, rejects the translation *wohnen,* "dwell, abide," in favor of *bleiben,* "remain," while Schenke, "Determination" 209–10, rejects *bleiben* on the grounds that *menein* implies much more than duration. Lammers, *Menein* 166–69, insists that in Johannine usage the verb is more eschatological than temporal, involving a participation in God's fullness and perfection. In most instances in GJohn and I John I have favored "abide" in order to catch the vital relationship intended; nevertheless, the symbolism of the vine and the branches in John 15 made "remain" more intelligible there, for a branch does not abide on a vine.

The expressions *einai en,* "to be in," and *menein en,* "to abide in," are almost interchangeable. In the NOTE on 1:5e I divided the theological uses of *einai en* under three headings that may be used as well for *menein en,* an even more frequent Johannine expression (19 times explicitly or implicitly in GJohn, 22 times in I John, 3 in II John):

(A) INDWELLING PERTINENT TO GOD. *Menein en* is used to describe the abiding presence of the Christian in God and Jesus, and vice versa. (A discussion of immanence will follow this grouping of usages.) The 10 instances of this use of *menein en* in GJohn and the 14 instances in I John may be analyzed thus:

- for the Christian in God: I John 2:6; 3:24; 4:13,15,16
- for the Christian in Jesus: John 6:56; 15:4,5,6,7; I John 2:27,28; 3:6
- for the Christian in Jesus and the Father: I John 2:24
- for God in the Christian: I John 3:24; 4:12,13,15,16

▪ for Jesus in the Christian: John 6:56; 15:4,5

▪ for the Father in Jesus: John 14:10

▪ *menein para* is used for the Spirit of Truth abiding *with* the Christian in John 14:17 (see I John 3:24; 4:13)

(B) INDWELLING OF OTHER REALITIES IN THE CHRISTIAN. There are 2 instances of this usage of *menein en* in GJohn and 7 in I-II John. The frequencies for *einai en* were respectively 5 and 7; but the phrasing with *einai en* was almost always negative, while *menein en* is often positive, e.g., the following realities are said to abide in the Christian:

▪ the word: John 15:7 (of Jesus); I John 2:14 (of God)

▪ truth: II John 2

▪ what the Christian heard from the beginning: I John 2:24

▪ the anointing received from Christ: I John 2:27

▪ God's seed: I John 3:9

The following positive realities are said *not* to remain or abide in those of whom the Johannine authors disapprove (e.g., "the Jews," the secessionists):

▪ word of God: John 5:38

▪ eternal life: I John 3:15

▪ love of God: I John 3:17

It is to be noted that the "word of God," "truth," and the "love of God" are realities in both the *einai en* and *menein en* lists under (B).

(C) MISCELLANEOUS THEOLOGICAL USES. Once again these are often corollaries of the dualism reflected in the preceding grouping but do not lend themselves easily to schematization. The first three items below can be found also in the *einai en* list under (C). One can abide or remain in:

▪ light or darkness: lover of one's brother in light (I John 2:10); no believer in darkness (John 12:46)

▪ life or death: man without love in death (I John 3:14)

▪ love: Christian in love (John 15:9,10; I John 4:16); Jesus in the love of the Father (John 15:10)

▪ word: Christian in word of Jesus (John 8:31)

▪ teaching: Christian (but not the overly progressive secessionist) in the teaching of Christ (II John 9)

Having thus classified the Johannine uses of *menein en*, I shall now concentrate on the (A) grouping of which the present passage is the first epistolary instance. The fact that this grouping for both *einai en* (NOTE on 1:5e) and *menein en* has virtually the same range of relationships indicates that the two expressions are not greatly different. Indeed, in certain passages they are almost interchangeable, e.g., "The Father is in me . . . the Father abiding in me" (John 14:10). It is true of both verbs that indwelling in Christ is more common in GJohn, while indwelling in God is more common in I John. *Einai en* is more frequent for the internal divine relationships (Father in Jesus and vice versa). *Menein en*, which is proportionately more frequent in I John than in GJohn, communicates the two important points: first, that the Christian's relationship to God is not just a series of encounters but a stable way of life; second, that the stability does not imply inertia but a vitality visible in the way one walks.

In seeking background we must distinguish between the vocabulary of immanence and the concept. If we start with vocabulary, there is little to help us by way of exact parallelism in the Bible or in the Hellenistic world. Biblically, *menein en* is almost exclusively a Johannine expression for *divine* indwelling. God is said "to remain forever" in OT passages (Greek of Ps 9:8 [7]; 102:13 [12]; Dan 6:27[26]) but is not said "to remain *in*" individuals. (Similarly divine realities are said "to remain forever"; see NOTE on 2:17d, and Heise, *Bleiben* 171–72.) In the NT, although Paul speaks frequently of being in Christ, he does not use *menein en* in this sense. As for Hellenistic religious thought, Dodd, *Epistles* 32, comments that, among the many formulas for mystical union with God, the formula *menein en* has no place. Nor is it current in Philo or the Stoics. (Lammers, *Menein* 166, points to *menein syn*, "to remain with," in the Mithraic cult to describe divine relationship.) Indeed, John's use of *menein en* may have served to keep the Johannine view of divine immanence distinctive; for F. Hauck, *"menein,"* TDNT 4, 576, contends that this formula avoids that identification with divinity that marked many Hellenistic systems, citing *Corpus Hermeticum* 5.11: "For all that You are I am . . . for You are all and nothing exists besides You." When we move beyond vocabulary to the concept of divine indwelling, there is important background for the Johannine idea in the OT and intertestamental Jewish writing, as I shall explain in the COMMENT on 2:5.

6bc. *ought himself to walk just as Christ walked.* Literally, "ought, just as that one [*ekeinos*] walked, also this person thus to walk"—a clumsy comparison that places the emphasis on "this person," a reference back to the subject of v. 6a: "The person who claims to abide in Him [*autos*]." The *autos* at the end of 6a and the *ekeinos* of 6b can scarcely be the same. It is logical that the *autos* refers to God (as it has done in the objectionable claims of 1:6a and 2:4a) while the *ekeinos* refers to Christ since "walking" better fits a human career. Some would make it a universal rule throughout I John that *ekeinos* refers to Christ (Brooke, Chaine, Plummer, Schnackenburg, THLJ, Vellanickal, Westcott, Williams—Bultmann, *Epistles* 24–25, has been converted to this view). Marshall, *Epistles* 128, thinks that "Christians were so used to talking about Jesus that 'that One' was a self-evident term." The rule is not implausible, for most of the six uses of *ekeinos* in I John (here; 3:3,5,7,16; 4:17) are in comparisons quite like the present one. Nevertheless, let us study each case as it occurs, since in GJohn, depending on circumstances, *ekeinos* can refer to God (5:19,37,38; 6:29; 8:42), to Jesus (1:18; 2:21; 3:28,30; 9:37), or even to the Paraclete (14:26; 15:26; 16:8,13,14). Brooke, *Epistles* iv, argues that only in John 19:35 is there an exact GJohn parallel to the *ekeinos* usage of I John, and that there was a growing tendency in Johannine circles to use *ekeinos* almost as a name for Jesus. Nevertheless, because of the frequency of *autos* and *ekeinos* in ordinary speech, Painter, *John* 120, questions whether readers would have caught the subtlety of a convention whereby one pronoun always referred to God and the other to Christ. In any case, it is noteworthy that *ekeinos* could be used both honorifically, as when the Pythagoreans referred to their dead master as *ekeinos* (Iamblichus, *De vita Pythagorica* 35.255), and disparagingly, as when the Jewish authorities referred to Jesus as "that fellow" without ever using his name (John 7:11; 9:28; 19:21)—a practice that continued later in Judaism when Jesus was regularly *'ôtî hā'îš,* "that man."

The "ought" is not *dei,* "must," the divine imperative (John 3:7,30; 12:34; ABJ 29, 146), but a form of *opheilein,* describing an obligation that comes from the very nature of the realities dealt with. The two uses in GJohn supply an interesting contrast: "The Jews" say that according to the Law Jesus ought to die because he has made himself God (John 19:7); Jesus says that he has given to his disciples an example according to which they ought to wash one another's feet (13:14)—the Law is the source of Jewish obligation, while the example of Jesus is the source of Christian obligation. That example as the basis of obligations to one another is in mind in I John not only here but also in the three other epistolary uses of *opheilein:* "For us Christ laid down his life; so ought we in turn to lay down our lives for the brothers" (I John 3:16); "If God so loved us [in sending His Son], we in turn ought to love one another" (4:11); since the missionaries set out for the sake of "the Name," for our part "we ought to support such men" (III John 7–8).

The example in the present passage is expressed by the adverb *kathōs,* "just as," followed in the next line by the adverb *houtōs,* "thus, so." Although this is a normal comparative construction, it is rendered a bit awkward by the *kai,* "and, also," which introduces the line (6c) that contains the *houtōs.* As Westcott, *Epistles* 159, points out, such a *kai* can replace the *houtōs,* as it does following *kathōs* in I John 2:18; 4:17; and that may partially explain the scribal omission of *houtōs* from 2:6c in Codices Vaticanus and Alexandrinus, the Vulgate, and the Syriac Peshitta. (Or the omission may stem from homoeoteleuton, since *houtōs* follows the look-alike word *autos.*)

The word *kathōs* occurs 31 times in GJohn and 13 times in the Epistles, and is the key to a set of comparisons that reflect the Johannine chain of revelation. (Plummer, *Epistles* 39, sees it as different from the more general comparative adverb *hōs,* for *kathōs* demands an exact imitation.) In his article, "KATHŌS," de Dinechin analyzes four separate Johannine comparisons expressed through this word. I adapt them as follows:

(I) *"Just as it is written"* or *"Just as I said"*—comparisons based on the Scripture (John 1:23; 3:14; 6:31; etc.) or on Jesus' own words (13:33). The present reality is similar to what was written or said by these unquestioned authorities.

(II) *Just as the Father to the Son, so Jesus to the disciples*—comparisons based on the relationship between Jesus and his Father (see IV below also). Thus, in John 17:18, "Just as you sent me into the world, so I sent them into the world" (see 20:21). Other examples include actions of hearing (5:30), teaching (8:28), speaking (12:50), commanding (14:31; 15:10), loving (15:9; 17:23), giving life (6:57–58), and giving power (17:2).

(III) *Just as Jesus was or did, so must the disciples be or do*—comparisons based on Jesus and his behavior. This comparison is succinctly phrased in John 13:15: "You are to do exactly as I have done for you." The GJohn examples involve love (13:34; 15:12) and not belonging to the world (17:16). There are modified forms of this *kathōs* relationship in I John 2:6,27; 3:3,7; 4:17

where the basis of comparison is not only what Jesus was in the past but Jesus as he is now. Probably to be included here are I John 3:23 and II John 4 ("just as God gave us the command"); for the author is thinking of the commandment of love given by God through Jesus during his ministry (II John 6). In I John 2:27e, "just as his anointing teaches you," the anointing is from Christ (2:27a).

(IV) *Just as the Father to the Son, so the disciples to others*—another group of comparisons based on the relationship between Jesus and his Father, a group that combines an aspect of the first half of II with the last half of III. Examples are John 17:11,21,22: "That they may be one just as we are one." The unity of the Father and the Son is a fact; the unity of the disciples is a wish; and the second is brought about by the first.

Outside the Johannine writings there are frequent examples of I, but the other three comparisons are relatively rare. (Pauline instances of III are Rom 15:2–3,7; I Cor 11:1; Eph 5:1–2.) Johannine theology has given to the Son the exemplary authority that in the *kathōs* language of the rest of the NT is attributed to the Jewish Scriptures. (Of course, other NT works urge Christians to do what Jesus did, but not in *kathōs* language; see Rom 15:5; Heb 12:2. Although in such other NT comparisons Jesus' earthly life serves as the analogue only occasionally, e.g., his lack of sin [Heb 4:15; I Pet 2:21–23], implicitly the Synoptic Gospels offer Jesus as a basis for comparison.) There is little that is Platonic in the Johannine view of how the heavenly is a model for the earthly. Only in IV is the whole basis of comparison otherworldly, and even then there is an element of causality that requires a divine intervention in this world. Comparisons II and III involve the earthly ministry of Jesus which is the author's main concern in I and II John. Heise, *Bleiben*, an important study of *menein*, is marred by the uncritical acceptance of Bultmann's source approach to the Epistles and by the presupposition that the epistolary author knew and accepted a gnostic redeemer myth wherein both the redeemer and the souls of the believers preexisted. We see the effects of these presuppositions when Heise (124–25) argues that "walking" here does not mean Jesus' behavior during his life but his "walking" back and forth to the Father, his descent and ascent. This may well be the way the opponents understood the imitation of Christ, but it is certainly not the analogue in the author's comparison, as the passages listed under II and III above show.

7a. *Beloved. Agapētos* occurs 61 times in the NT, 10 of which are in the Johannine Epistles (never in GJohn or Revelation). "Beloved" is a pl. address in I John 2:7; 3:2,21; 4:1,7,11. The Latin translations vary between the literal *dilectissimi* and the *carissimi*, "Most dear ones," of the Vulgate; the latter may explain the common English rendition, "Dearly beloved." Although here the Byzantine tradition reads *adelphoi*, "Brothers/brethren," that is a scribal correction under the influence of lectionaries where "Brethren" was used to introduce pericopes from the NT writings attributed to apostles. (For the one use in I John of "Brothers" as a vocative, see 3:13.) In the Greek OT *agapetos* is sometimes used to translate *yāḥîd*, "uniquely beloved," a designation that can be applied to a special son (e.g., Isaac) and which can be translated also as *monogenēs* (see NOTE on 4:9b below). This background is reflected in the Synoptic use of *agapētos* for Jesus as God's "beloved Son" (Mark 1:11; 9:7). Another usage of *agapētos* in the Greek OT is as an adjective to describe God's beloved people (Jer 6:26; 31[38]:20; Ps 60:7[5]; 108:7[6]; 127:2). This covenant designation is carried over to the NT epistles where Christians are "God's beloved who are called saints" (Rom 1:7). On the basis of the general NT usage of *agapētos* as an address especially associated with "Brothers," Spicq (*Agapē* 1, 188–89) argues that it is a title of honor in religion, equivalent to "Reverend or esteemed brothers." However, granted the emphasis in I John on *agapē*, "love" (NOTE on 2:5b), the author surely intends the title to have a theological connotation for a community whose model figure was "the disciple whom Jesus loved." Christians are "beloved" because God has loved them; what follows the address in 2:7 concerns their obligation to love one another. The author's logic is implicit here; it is explicit in the use of *agapētos* in 4:11: "Beloved, if God so loved us, we in turn ought to love one another." Some scholars regard the vocative at the beginning of 2:7 as a sign that a new subunit is beginning (Hauck, Plummer, Westcott, Williams); but like "My Little Children" in 2:1a this is a hortatory device, as the author brings to bear on the lives of his readers the theoretical discussion that has preceded.

this is no new commandment that I write you. As he continues in 2:7a the author slips into an "I" and "you" posture which explicates the "we" that was used in 2:3–5—he did the same in the parenthetical 2:1a. The concept of *entolē*, "commandment," was discussed in the NOTE on 2:3b where we saw that, when it is used in the singular in John 13:34; 15:12; I John 3:23; 4:21; II John 5–6, it refers to the commandment to love one another. This is surely what is meant here as well: it makes sense of the "Beloved" address, and it prepares for the discussion of loving one's brother in 2:9–11. However, because of the denial that it is a new commandment, some scholars have doubted that the author is referring to the commandment of love, which is specifically called a "new commandment" in John 13:34. One alternative proposal is that vv. 7a and 8a ought to be read thus: "It is not the new commandment [of loving one another] that I write to you. . . . On second thought I am going to write to you about the new commandment [of love]." Yet I find it unlikely that the epistolary author, who puts so much emphasis on love, would ever say that he did not intend to write about love. Moreover, when we compare the narrowing down from "keeping His commandments" in 2:3–5 to a single commandment in 2:7, we are reminded of a similar narrowing in John 15:10–12: "You will remain in my love if you keep my commandments. . . . This is my commandment: Love one another as I have loved you."

If the author is writing about the commandment to love in 2:7a, why does he deny the newness? Possibly he is protecting himself against a charge by his opponents that he is imposing on his adherents new commands beyond those found in the tradition. In the author's view his opponents are the "progressives" (II John 9), and it is important for him to justify his gospel as one held from the beginning (I John 3:11), whence the rejection of novelty. But on what basis might his opponents have charged him with writing a "new [novel] commandment"? To answer this, one must recognize that the word "commandment" is doing double duty in 2:7a. The author refers not only to the commandment of love but also to what he just said in v. 6: "The person who claims to abide in God *ought* himself to walk just as Christ walked." This *opheilein*, "ought," is a commandment aimed at the secessionists, and they are sure to object to his imposing this new obligation. The author denies any novelty; for his *kathōs* model, "just as Christ walked," is inherent in the great commandment that all Johannine Christians must acknowledge: "Love one another as [*kathōs*] I have loved you."

7b. *but an old commandment that you had from the beginning.* The imperfect tense of the verb "to have" is durative. Another suggestion is that it is also an imperfect of incomplete or unaccomplished action sometimes employed with verbs of commanding (BDF 328), implying that while "you had it from the beginning," it has not been fully activated. Although in John 13:34; 15:12 the commandment to love is given *by Jesus* to his disciples, that commandment is described in I John 3:23; 4:21 as coming *from God.* Nevertheless, the description here of "an old commandment that you had from the beginning" (also II John 5) constitutes proof that for the epistolary author also the commandment came from Christ, since (NOTE on 1:1a) "from the beginning" refers to Jesus' self-revelation to his disciples during his ministry. (Also compare I John 1:5, "the gospel that we have heard from him [Christ]," and 3:11, "the gospel that you heard from the beginning.") There may be a secondary meaning to "from the beginning," namely, that the commandment (the only specific one in GJohn) was taught to the Johannine Christians as part of the conversion/ baptismal catechesis. On both scores the commandment to do as Christ did and love as he loved would be "old," not novel.

7c. *an old commandment which is "the word" you already heard.* Literally, "the old commandment is the word which you heard"—not only the restrictive clause but also the use of the article (BDF 273[1]) indicates a definite and well-known "word." The aorist of the verb "to hear" is used, in contrast with the perfect tense used in 1:1,3,5. Nevertheless, the similarity of 1:1ab ("What was from the beginning, what we have heard") to 2:7 ("An old commandment that you had from the beginning . . . which is 'the word' you already heard") shows that the distinction between two past tenses should not be overdone. The Byzantine textual tradition adds "from the beginning" to the end of this line, but the addition is a scribal imitation of that phrase in the preceding line. B. Weiss, *Briefe* 48, uses the broader connotation of "word" to argue that the commandment is not simply to love, for love is not the whole word. Such a distinction neglects the fact that after Jesus gave the commandment to love in John 15:12,17, he said, "Remember the word that I have spoken to you" (15:20). See also the NOTE on 2:3b above where I argued for the interchangeability of "word" and "commandment" in John, reflecting a Semitic background where the Ten Commandments were the "words" of God. Here the epistolary author is implicitly equating the commandment of Jesus with the Decalogue, the covenant demand of the OT (Exod 34:28: "Moses wrote upon the stone tablets the words of the covenant, the Ten Words").

8ab. *On second thought, the commandment I write you is new as it is made true both in Christ and in you.* Literally, "Again I write to you a new commandment (that) which is true [*alēthēs*] both in him [*autos*] and in you." Christ was mentioned as *ekeinos* in 2:6c, and this is the first personal reference since then; so the *autos* refers to him. (In 1:5b we saw an *autos* referring to Christ mentioned by name in 1:3e.) Codex Alexandrinus reads "to us" instead of "to you." A few scholars (Bengel; cf. Haupt) propose that v. 8 refers to a different commandment from the one described in v. 7. However, the force of *palin*, "again, a second time," is to point back: the issue is not another commandment, but a further thought about the same one. Within this sentence there is a grammatical difficulty about the relation of the two clauses: "commandment" in 8a is feminine, while the pronoun *ho* that begins 8b is neuter (see Westcott, *Epistles* 53). One solution is to regard *ho* as introducing an objective, substantive clause in apposition to "commandment," e.g., "I write a new commandment, namely, that which is true etc." (Law, Plummer). However, this tends to make the commandment in 8a different from what has gone before. Most scholars think *ho* introduces a relative clause and struggle to explain the gender. Häring, "Aramaismes" 115–16, suggests that the neuter reflects the Aramaic *dᵉ* which has no gender. Moule, IBNTG 130–31, suggests that the neuter relative modifies the whole idea rather than simply the noun "commandment." Accordingly one might translate v. 8b thus: "which thing (i.e., that it is new) is true both in him and in you," although, as Malatesta, *Interiority* 138, points out, 8b then modifies the idea of newness, not "the whole idea."

This question of *newness* needs to be discussed as it runs through vv. 7–8. The adjective involved is not *neos* ("young" versus "aged") but *kainos*, "fresh, novel," as opposed to "old, worn out." It is a newness of kind as well as of time. (In Mark 2:22 the recent-vintage wine [*neos*] should go into new [*kainos*] wineskins.) There are two uses of *kainos* in GJohn: for a new tomb that has not been used before (19:41), and for the commandment, "Love one another: as I have loved you, so must you love one another" (13:34). The epistolary uses are here (twice) and in II John 5: "It is not as if I were writing you some new commandment; rather it is a commandment we have had from the beginning: *Let us love one another.*" Thus four of the five Johannine instances of *kainos* pertain to the commandment to love. In v. 7 the author denied that the commandment was new in the sense of being novel or that he was asking more than Jesus asked. But since Jesus himself designated the love commandment as "new" in John 13:34, the author now comes back to agreeing that after all the commandment is new. The *kainos* here, then, is simply a term borrowed from the tradition; I see no reason to give it the meaning "unheard of, marvelous," as does THLJ 49. What did it mean on the lips of the Johannine Jesus? (For a full discussion see Muñoz León, "La novedad.") In ABJ 29A, 613–14, I rejected the notion that Jesus meant his commandment was new over against the commandments of the Hebrew Scriptures that were a matter of Law but not of love. The Johannine writers did not share the (incorrect) view of Nygren that there was no *agapē* in the OT, for I John 3:11–12 assumes that the commandment to love was binding in OT times. Nor for Jesus was the newness simply that of a new cultural or moral ideal. Rather it was related to the theme of the New Covenant which appears at the Last Supper in Luke 22:20 and I Cor 11:25—the same context in which John places the new commandment to love. (See Heb 8:8 for the New Covenant attached to the context of Jesus the high priest bringing his blood into the heavenly sphere.) All these authors are reflecting Jer 31(38):31–34 where it was promised that in the days to come God would make a New Covenant with the house of Israel, a Covenant involving intimacy between God and His people. Thus for Jesus the commandment to love, which he exemplified in laying down his life, was new because of the intimacy with God made possible by the gift of divine life—an intimacy that now enables his disciples to love one another with God's love. The newness of the commandment is eschatological; it is part of the realization of God's promises in the last times. In this way it resembles the realities that Revelation calls "new" (*kainos*): a new heaven and a new earth (Rev 21:1), a new Jerusalem (3:12; 21:2), a new name for each Christian (2:17; 3:12), a new song (5:9; 14:3); in short, "all things new" (21:5).

Granted that by speaking of a new commandment I John is repeating Jesus' designation, something more than that seems to be demanded by the specification in v. 8b: it is new "as it is made *true* both in Christ and in you." The key word is *alēthēs*, an adjective related to *alētheia*, "truth," discussed above in the NOTE on 1:6d. If proportionately the word for "truth" is quite Johannine in the NT, even more so are the adjectives related to it, *alēthēs*, "true," and *alēthinos*, "true, real." Of 26 NT uses of *alēthēs*, 17 are Johannine (14 in GJohn, 2 in I John, one in II John); and of the 28 NT uses of *alēthinos*, 13 are Johannine (9 in GJohn, 4 in I John). Both adjectives occur in this verse, *alēthēs* in this line, *alēthinos* in the next. Kilpatrick, "Idioms," points out that the three epistolary uses of *alēthēs* are predicative, while the four epistolary uses of *alēthinos* are attributive; and he asks whether in the Epistles the difference between the two adjectives is not mostly syntactical. Yet there is no such regular syntactical pattern in GJohn, for *alēthinos* is predicative in John 4:37; 7:28; 19:35. As I pointed out in ABJ 29, 500–1, in GJohn *alēthinos* means "the only real," as contrasted with the reputed or would-be, chiefly in contrasts between the heavenly and earthly. *Alēthēs* means "true" in the sense of corresponding to inner reality or the inner basis of stability, without an implied contrast with the putative. In Johannine thought, since truth for human beings is God's revelation (specifically in Jesus) and since this truth is given to believers, *alēthēs* can be applied to actions that correspond to the revealed truth abiding in the Christian, e.g., "true witness" in John 5:31,32; 8:13,14,17; 21:24; III John 12. In the only other use of *alēthēs* in I John (2:27) the unction or anointing that teaches the Christian is guaranteed to be "true" since it works from within as a teacher. In the present verse, then, *alēthēs* means "verified, realized, made true," rather than "right, correct"; and Wengst, *Häresie* 76–77, rightly stresses that the "in" is instrumental: "made real both through him and through you." The newness of the commandment, therefore, involves its being operative on an ongoing basis.

8c. *since the darkness is passing away*. The compound clause that constitutes
8cd is introduced by *hoti*. Grammatically it is possible for *hoti* to mean "that"
and for the clause to be epexegetical of the commandment: "The commandment I write you is new . . . namely, that the darkness is passing away" (thus
Bisping, Windisch). However, it is difficult to find a commandment in the
statement about light and darkness, and so most scholars agree that *hoti* should
be translated "because, since." But that still does not decide the issue of
whether the *hoti* clause offers a reason for the newness of the commandment
(8a—Chaine, Wilder) or a reason for the way in which it is true in Christ and
the Christian (8b—THLJ, B. Weiss). I agree with Malatesta (*Interiority* 151)
that it offers a reason for both, since in part the newness is found in the making true (realization) of the commandment in Christ and the Christian; and as
love becomes real the eschatological victory over darkness becomes apparent.

The verb *paragein*, "to go by, pass away," could be translated here in terms
of darkness "lifting"; but since the verb reappears in 2:17 in relation to the
world, it seems best to use "passing away" in both places. Vicent Cernuda,
"Engañan" 158–59, argues for the meaning "to lead away, mislead, deceive,"
thus, "since darkness deceives." He contends that the following verses
(2:9–11) do not suppose that darkness has passed away, but one can respond
that those verses make no better sense if v. 8c has described darkness as deceptive. Indeed, v. 9c, which states that the opponents are in darkness even now,
makes excellent sense if 8c states that darkness is passing away for the author's
adherents. A similar sentiment is found in *Enoch* 58:5: "It has become bright
as the sun upon earth, and the darkness is past"; also Rom 13:12: "The night
is far gone; the day is at hand."

8d. *and the true light is already shining*. Vicent Cernuda, "Engañan," argues
that *alēthinos* here is not an adjective describing "light" but is used as a substantive, the object of the verb: "and the light is manifesting the truth." This
would be the only nonattributive use of *alēthinos* in I John. He finds precedent
in John 1:9, which he also translates nonattributively (not "The true light" but
"The light was the truth"). However, with most commentators I see no need
for such an unusual translation. In the NOTE on 2:8b above, I discussed the
basic meaning of *alēthinos*, meaning "real" as opposed to reputed. Here, as
usual in the NT (I Thess 5:5; Eph 5:8), the opposite to light is darkness, not
false light. It is unlikely then that the author thinks of the secessionists as a
false light over against the true or genuine light; they are rather still in darkness (2:9–11). "Darkness" is the realm of evil, deprived of God's presence and
ruled by Satan. The contrast implicit in the *alēthinos* is between the secessionist
reading of the Johannine tradition about light and the reading had "from the
beginning." For the author "light" is not only Jesus himself but also his salvific
accomplishment. Scholars like Bonsirven and Chaine would argue that the
newness of the command to love (v. 8ab) involves the fact that the Gentiles
are hearing it for the first time, and in relation to v. 8cd they point out that
Christ is described as the light to the Gentiles (Luke 2:32; Acts 26:23), even
as the conversion of the Gentiles is compared to passing from darkness into
light (Rom 2:19; Col 1:12; Eph 5:8; I Pet 2:9). But that is scarcely the issue

in the Johannine Epistles, which are concerned with the relationship to light/ darkness of those who are already Christians.

What are the exact implications of "already" in v. 8d? Because the "light" is not simply Jesus (as in GJohn) but is a whole salvific complex involving the believers' walking in light, I John is making a proclamation concerning the end-time. Later (2:18) he will announce that it is the last hour and the Antichrist has appeared; here he describes the positive side of the picture. What is not clear is the relation between the already present light and the future self-revelation of Jesus at the parousia (2:28). Presumably that will be the final defeat and disappearance of darkness.

9a. *The person who claims to be in the light.* Literally, "the one saying," i.e., the same participial construction as in 2:4a and 2:6a; and like the latter it is followed by an infinitive. While the three participles of *legein,* "to say, claim," mark the subdivisions within this unit (2:3–11), it is noteworthy that the third subunit (2:9–11) is also marked by three participles: "the one saying" in v. 9; "the one loving" in v. 10, and "the one hating" in v. 11. The infinitive "to be in" in v. 9a represents a usage of *einai en* classified under (C) in the NOTE on 1:5e.

9b. *all the while hating his brother.* (Codex Sinaiticus adds "is a liar and," a scribal imitation of 2:4cd.) In Johannine usage the opposite of loving is not the lack of love or indifference, but the hate of one's brother (I John 2:11; 3:15; 4:20). Undoubtedly this mentality has been shaped by the experiences of the Johannine Community wherein relations with "the Jews" and the secessionists moved quickly to hostility. The verb *misein,* "to hate," occurs 12 times in GJohn and 5 times in I John, a usage that is 40% of the NT frequency (39 times). Most instances in GJohn (and I John 3:13) involve the world's hatred for Jesus, his Father, and his disciples; but in John 3:19–20 there is reference to loving darkness and hating light (also 12:25). In part such a love/hate choice reflects the lack of highly differentiated verbs in the Hebrew background (see "love/hate" in Deut 21:15; Prov 13:24; Mal 1:2–3; Matt 6:24); in part it reflects Johannine dualism.

This is the first occurrence of *adelphos,* "brother," which is used 16 times in the Epistles for spiritual relatives (presumably female as well as male—see INTRODUCTION, footnote 187). In GJohn *adelphos* is used for physical relatives (also I John 3:12) with only two exceptions, 20:17 and 21:23, both situated in the postresurrectional period. In the Epistles "brother" appears 6 times with *agapan,* "to love," 4 times with *misein,* "to hate," and once in the expression "to lay down one's life for" (I John 3:16)—two-thirds of the significant uses concern love or hate for one's brother.

The Christian use of "brother" for coreligionists is common in the NT (over 200 times), being found in every work except Titus and Jude. (Only I Cor 7:15 and Jas 2:15 take the trouble to distinguish "brother or sister," although individual women are called "sister" in Rom 16:1; Philem 2; cf. I Cor 9:5.) Several factors explain this development. Already in the OT a fellow Israelite could be addressed as "brother" (Jer 22:18)—a usage explicable from the tribal origins of Israel which involved physical relationship. The close-knit community of the New Covenant at Qumran employed "brother" as a quasi-technical term for one who had gone through the period of probation and had been admitted to membership (1QS 6:10,22; CD 7:1,2; 20:18—see B. Lifshitz, "The Greek Documents from Naḥal Seelim and Naḥal Mishmar," IEJ 11 [1961] 53–62, esp. 60–61). This is confirmed by Josephus, *War* 2.8.3 ✠122, who comments on the fraternal attitude among the Essenes: "Like brothers they enjoy a single patrimony." Outside Judaism *adelphos* was widely used in the Greek fraternities; see H. F. von Soden, "*adelphos*," TDNT 1, 146. When we turn to Jesus, in a common Synoptic passage (Mark 31:35 and par.) he says that his (true) mother and brothers are those who do the will of God or hear the word of God. In other words he distinguishes between relatives by birth and an eschatological family called into being by his proclamation of God's will and word. The notion of a common Father shared by Jesus and his disciples is inherent in the "Our Father" that Jesus teaches to his disciples (Matt 6:9). In John 20:17 Jesus tells Mary Magdalene, "Go to my brothers and tell them, 'I am going to my Father and your Father'" (see Matt 28:10). God is the Father of believers because He begets them through His Spirit (John 3:3–6); and that Spirit is given through the death and resurrection of Jesus (7:39; 19:30,34; 20:22). Thus the words of Jesus to Magdalene mean that his Father is now the Father of those who believe in him and who therefore are his brothers (ABJ 29A, 1016–17).

We should note, however, that in Johannine thought the spiritual term "brothers" must be confined to "those who believe in his [Jesus'] name—those who were begotten not by blood, nor by carnal desire, nor by man's desire, but by God" (John 1:12–13). And indeed that belief involves an acceptance of Johannine christology, for I John 5:1 is precise: "Everyone who believes that *Jesus* is the Christ has been begotten by God." The secessionists who did not share the author's standard of belief would not have been children of God by his standards. What about other Christians outside the Johannine Community, not by choice (or secession) but by historical origins? In my book *Community* I showed that the evangelist rejected both crypto-Christians in the synagogues who hid their belief, and Jewish Christians of inadequate christology who may have claimed the "brothers of the Lord" as their prototypes. As for the large number of non-Johannine Christians descended from the missionary endeavors of the apostles (the Twelve, Paul, etc.), while GJohn shows a more favorable attitude toward them as "other sheep, not of this fold" (10:16), it is not clear whether "brother," a term of inner-Johannine affection, would have been applied to them.

All of this seems so obvious that it is astounding to find scholars like Balz and Bultmann stating that "brother" in the present passage means fellow human being, e.g., Bultmann, *Epistles* 28 (without advancing proof), "'Brother' means . . . not especially the Christian comrade in faith, but one's fellowman, the 'neighbor.'" Westcott, *Epistles* 55, was far closer to the biblical evidence a century ago when he stated, "There is, as far as it appears, no case where a fellow-man, as man, is called 'a brother' in the N.T." (He specifically included Matt 5:22 and Luke 6:41, which are not clear on this point.) The reference to "the neighbor" shows that the basis of Bultmann's claim is not the Johannine notion of God's children through faith and the Spirit but the Synoptic command to love the neighbor as oneself (Matt 19:19; 22:39 and par.; see Rom 13:9; Gal 5:14). It is true that the Hebrew word *rēa'*, normally translated in Greek by *plēsion*, "neighbor," can also be translated by *adelphos*, "brother" (Gen 43:33; Jer 31[38]:34); nevertheless, in the NT the two terms are not the same. The Synoptic command to love the neighbor reaches to outsiders as well; for the Lucan Parable of the Good Samaritan interprets the confines of the term "neighbor" (Luke 10:27–29). Indeed, Matt 5:44 demands love of enemies. But we cannot assume that the Synoptic command to love the neighbor and the Johannine command to love the brother or one another have the same extent. There are contrary indications elsewhere in the NT, e.g., in I Thess 3:12; 5:15 Paul mentions loving or doing good for "one another" and "for all," an implicit indication that "one another" means Christians. Similarly I Pet 2:17 distinguishes, "Honor all; love the brotherhood," keeping the latter term for Christians. The context of the reference to *philadelphia*, "brotherly love," in Heb 13:1 indicates that fellow Christians are in mind. Moving from the NT in general to GJohn, we remember that the command to love one another was given at the Last Supper where Jesus was addressing "his own" (13:1). (Houlden, *Epistles* 121, speaks correctly, albeit sharply, of "the enclosed community of the redeemed.") Immediately after the command in 13:34, the Johannine Jesus says, "By this will all identify you as my disciples— by the love you have for one another." Could it be any clearer that this is a command to love within the Christian fellowship? And the repetition of the command in 15:12,17 is in the context of the symbolic description of the vine and the branches, wherein certain branches (Christian "believers") that do not bear fruit are cast off, so that the love of one another concerns only the fruitful branches: "I appointed you to go and bear fruit. . . . This I command you: Love one another" (15:16–17). This passage reinforces my contention above that "brother" means fellow *Johannine* Christian—the command to love is narrower than the extent of Christianity, for it is primarily within the Johannine fellowship.

Some modern readers may be scandalized by this suggestion. Besides Bultmann, scholars like F.-M. Braun, Dodd, Feuillet, Hoskyns, and Prunet argue for a broad extent of the Johannine command to love, while Bowen, Fensham, and Montefiore have underlined the narrowness of the Johannine outlook. F.-M. Braun, "La réduction" 50, thinks that John *presupposes* the disinterested love of neighbor which was the basic catechism lesson and goes beyond it; in my judgment, however, love of one another was rather the basic Johannine catechism lesson as contrasted with the Synoptic catechism demand. Feuillet, *Le mystère* 109–13, would qualify the air of exclusivity at the Last Supper on the grounds that in fact only the disciples are present and so naturally Jesus speaks only to that audience whom he loves. But there is a deeper question: Why is the Johannine Last Supper so exclusively to "his own"? The account in GJohn is not simply historical; it is the reflection of the self-understanding of the Johannine Community that thinks of itself precisely as Jesus' own. Dodd and

Hoskyns would modify the impression of an inward Johannine concentration by pointing to outgoing statements in GJohn, which insist on bearing witness to others. Yet a desire to make converts does little to change the impression of a brotherhood confined to fellow Johannine Christians. When outsiders come to the light and believe, they become children of God and can be loved as "brothers." Indeed, while the God of Matt 5:44–45 loves both just and unjust, the Johannine Jesus is more restrictive: "The man who loves me will be loved by my Father" (14:21,23). If one objects on the basis of John 3:16 that the Johannine God loves the whole world, it may be noted that such a statement of love antedates the choice made by those who prefer darkness to light (3:19). It is not clear that the Johannine God loves the sons of darkness.

A narrower, inner-communitarian concept of love is not without antecedents. The command of Lev 19:18, "You shall love your neighbor as yourself," seemingly referred to fellow Israelites (Montefiore, "Neighbour" 158); but the Dead Sea Scroll community changed it to "love one's brother as oneself" (CD 6:20–21), narrowing its extent to just the community. This narrowing was accompanied by a stress on hating outsiders, for one of the goals of the Qumran community given to it by the Righteous Teacher and placed at the head of its Manual of Discipline was "to love all that God has chosen and to hate all that He rejected" and "to love all the sons of light and hate all the sons of darkness" (1QS 1:3–4,9–10; CD 2:15; 1QH 14:9–11). This is exactly the picture of the Essenes painted by Josephus, War 2.8.7 §139, who tells us that the newly initiated members had to swear to "hate the unjust," and by Philo, Every Good Man is Free 12 §83, "They are trained . . . how to choose what they should and avoid the opposite." Since the Johannine Community similarly narrowed the scope of love to its own members, did it also develop an attitude of hate toward outsiders? On the one hand, while the verb "to hate" is frequent in Johannine writings, the Community is the *object* of others' hate and is never told to hate anyone. The only passage favorable to hating is John 12:25, "The man who hates his life in this world preserves it to live eternally." And so Bowen ("Love" 40) exaggerates when, albeit hesitantly, he calls John the Apostle of Hatred. On the other hand, there are many passages in GJohn reflecting extreme prejudice, even if they do not use the word "hate." Unlike the Matthean Jesus who tells the disciples, "Pray for those who persecute you" (Matt 5:44), the Johannine Jesus, knowing that the world hates him (7:7; 15:18,23–25), says, "I do not pray for the world" (17:9). He says that he is laying down his life *for his sheep* (10:11,15) and invites his followers to lay down their lives *for their friends* (i.e., for those whom they love—there is no greater love than that! 15:13). This is somewhat distant from the sentiment of Paul toward his unbelieving Jewish brothers: "I could wish that I myself were accursed from Christ for my brothers, my kinsmen according to the flesh" (Rom 9:3; see also Acts 28:21). The Johannine Jesus speaks to unbelieving Jews as to children of the devil (John 8:44). A passage such as I John 2:15, "Have no love for the world," is tantamount to "Hate the world." There are alleviating factors, of course, and the overall view of outsiders is broader than that found in the Dead Sea Scrolls. At the same time the attitude is narrower than that found elsewhere in the NT. Montefiore, "Neighbour" 169, exaggerates but only partly: "What was distinctive about Jesus' teaching about neighbourly love came to be altered [in John] until it was similar to the best Jewish teaching on love, except that mutual love was demanded in a religious rather than a natural group, and became grounded on different theological doctrines."

With all its limitations the Johannine theme of loving one another has real strengths also. The attitude toward the outsider is most often by implication; the primary concern is love for the insider. That explains why in 2:9b the author regards hating one's *brother* as an insuperable contradiction to the light (also 2:11a). It is a heinous offense by the secessionists who are misleading some of the author's adherents on this score. In what way did the secessionists hate their brothers? My treatment of this in the INTRODUCTION (V B3c) suggests that the secessionists did not say they hated their brothers and did not urge others to do so. Rather they too spoke of loving one another even though, since they put little salvific emphasis on human actions, they may not have given this commandment much centrality. In my judgment the issue in the controversy was not primarily theoretical but practical and pastoral. From the author's viewpoint, the secessionists hated the true brotherhood, for they hated him and his adherents. They would not support the needy among the author's adherents (I John 3:17); and they had withdrawn from fellowship (2:19) and were persuading others to do so (II John 10). Such secession would have been the supreme example of hatred of one's brothers, for it destroyed fraternal relations. From the secessionist viewpoint, they loved their brothers who were defined as fellow secessionists. Their dislike for the author and his adherents was not a violation of love since the latter were not brothers.

9c. *is still in the darkness even now.* As in v. 9a, this is a usage of *einai en* classified under (C) in the NOTE on 1:5e. The English idiom is smoother if one does not translate the article before "darkness," but the author has a definite realm of darkness in mind. The phrase *heōs arti,* "until now," occurs three times in GJohn (2:10; 5:17; 16:24) but nowhere else in the Epistles. Bultmann, *Epistles* 28, suggests that the author added it to the antithesis he found in the source; but without resorting to a source hypothesis, I shall show in the COMMENT how this phrase has a role in the conflict between the author and the secessionists.

10a. *The person who loves his brother abides in the light.* In 2:5a the antithesis to the first secessionist claim (4a) was expressed by an indefinite relative ("But whoever keeps His word"); here the antithesis, like the secessionist claim itself, is expressed by a participle (the second of three in 2:9a,10a,11a). The person who loves his brother (and sister) is a faithful member of the Johannine Community, as explained above, and has *koinōnia* with the Johannine School of tradition-bearers represented by the author. Therefore, according to 1:3, this person has *koinōnia* with the God who is light (1:5). As with *einai en* in 2:9ac, the usage of *menein en* here ("abides in light") belongs to the (C) classification in the NOTE on 2:6a. While we have seen the general interchangeability of the two verbal expressions, a differentiation in shade of meaning may be implied here. In 2:9 the opponents cannot even *be* in the light because they are outside the brotherhood of the author's adherents. Those within the brotherhood not only *are* in the light but also remain or *abide* in the light by sustaining the brotherhood in love. This is the first positive phrasing of the commandment to love which the author has been discussing since v. 7; but even this phrasing is not without a negative implication, for it can also be translated, "The person who loves his brother is the one who abides in the light."

10b. *and in him there is no cause for stumbling.* The Greek *en autō* is ambiguous, meaning "in him" or "in it" (the light); and perhaps that ambiguity explains the scribal tendency to move it from before the verb "is" (Codex Vaticanus, Byzantine tradition, Vulgate) to after the verb (Codices Sinaiticus, Alexandrinus, Ephraemi Rescriptus, Sahidic, Peshitta). "Light" is the closer antecedent; and the translation "in it" is favored by the general symbolism whereby light enables one to see something over which one might otherwise stumble. (The "in it" translation is favored by Hering, Kohler, Michl, O'Neill, Schnackenburg, Spicq, Williams, and the RSV.) However, in favor of the "in him" reading (Brooke [?], Bultmann, de la Potterie, Malatesta, Marshall, Plummer, THLJ, B. Weiss, and SBJ) one may argue that the *einai en* formula (of which this might be an example of the [B] classification in the Note on 1:5e) almost always has a personal subject or object. That has been true in the antitheses seen thus far, e.g., 1:8: "the truth is not *in us*"; 1:10: "His word is not *in us*"; 2:4: "no truth in *such a person.*" Unfortunately the next verse (2:11), which is meant as a contrast with 2:10, does not help us to decide the ambiguity. The first line (2:11a), "The person who hates his brother is *in the darkness,*" would favor the "in it [the light]" translation, while the fourth line (2:11d), which has darkness operative on a person, would favor the "in him" translation. The difference of meaning is not enormous.

The Greek of 10b speaks of a *skandalon* (which I have translated as "cause for stumbling"), the only Johannine instance of this noun. Not a classical word, it is found in the LXX, the NT, and the papyri; and the original meaning seems to have been "snare, bait in a trap." Vicent Cernuda, "Engañan" 172, would press that meaning here as part of his thesis that in 2:8c *paragein* means mislead—darkness deceives but in the person who is in the light there is nothing that can deceive. Bultmann, *Epistles* 28, defends the meaning "blemish" for *skandalon*. However, the traditional meaning "stumbling block" makes good sense here, especially if one finds a hint in 2:11 that the person who walks in the dark is going to stumble. One is reminded of Lev 19:14: "You shall not put a *skandalon* in the way of the blind." The other NT uses of *skandalon* refer to an obstacle whether by way of temptation (Matt 16:23; 18:7; Rev 2:14) or of offense (I Cor 1:23; Gal 5:11)—the latter is also the meaning of the two uses of the verb *skandalizein* in GJohn (6:61; 16:1). What can "no cause for stumbling" mean in the present passage? Does it mean nothing destined to cause *the person* to stumble or nothing destined to cause *others* to stumble? (B. Weiss, *Briefe* 52, thinks the author does not mean to specify.) Usually a *skandalon* is a stumbling block for others, as it is in the two Johannine instances of *skandalizein;* and one might conjecture that the Johannine Christian who loves his brother will not drive others out of the Community into the embrace of the secessionists. (That is more plausible than the suggestion that the author is thinking of a scandal to pagans.) But it is simpler to think that love for one's brothers will prevent the person himself from leaving the Community or will save him from sins against the *koinōnia,* the spirit of communion that binds one to God. Brooke, Hoskyns, Malatesta, Plummer, and THLJ are among those who agree that the author is talking about a *skandalon* for the person himself. Good OT parallels are Ps 119:165: "Those who love your Law have great peace; there is nothing in them that causes them to stumble"; Hos 4:17 (LXX): "By having become entangled with idols, Ephraim has placed a stumbling block for himself." Judith 5:20 equates sin committed by people with "a stumbling block in them"; and in *Jubilees* 1:21 Moses prays to God for the people whom He is going to covenant with as His own: "Create in them a clean heart and a holy spirit, and let them not be ensnared in their sins." Nauck, *Tradition* 39–40, calls attention to the covenant ceremony at Qumran: "Cursed be the person who enters this covenant . . . setting up before himself the stumbling block of iniquity so that he may backslide" (1QS 2:11–12). The epistolary author in 2:10 is interested in the exclusion of such a stumbling block.

11a. *But the person who hates his brother is in the darkness.* This participial expression is the perfect antithesis to that in 10a, shifting only from the *menein en,* "abide in," used with love to the *einai en,* "is in," used with hating (9c). This *einai en* represents the (C) classification discussed in the NOTE on 1:5e. Again the opposite of love is hate; as Bultmann, *Epistles* 28, remarks, "A third possibility, a neutral relationship to one's brother, is excluded. *Tertium non datur.*"

11bc. *He walks in the dark with no idea where he is going.* Literally, two co-ordinated main clauses: "and he walks . . . and he does not know." This is the first epistolary use of *oida* (*eidenai,* "to know"); in the NOTE on 2:3a I compared it with *ginōskein* and stressed the impracticality of positing clear distinctions between the two. The verb "to walk" is resumed from 2:6, and the idiom of walking in light/darkness from 1:6–7. The opponents are not only in the darkness; they walk in darkness. In 1:6 walking in darkness was opposed to being in communion with God; here it is opposed to being in light (see COMMENT). The use of "walk" here, while still primarily symbolic (= moral behavior), verges on the realistic (needing light to walk physically), so that we are dealing with a type of parable drawn from ordinary experience. The author shifts from stumbling to not knowing one's direction in order to hint at the loss that has affected those who left the Community. But beyond aimlessness, walking in the dark involves evil.

11d. *for the darkness has blinded his eyes.* This is the third mention of darkness in one verse. Klein, "Licht" 279–80, finds the repetitions in vv. 9–11 cumbersome, and certainly there is some tautology. However, a new note of malice is introduced by "blinding." Darkness is not a neutral absence of light; it is a force that causes lack of sight. The aorist is complexive (BDF 332) describing the results of a long process, and once again the author may be drawing upon ordinary experience that someone who has been in utter darkness for a long time may emerge blind. In the NT culpable blindness is often associated with the failure to believe; for instance, a series of passages (Matt 13:13–15 and par.; Acts 28:25–27; John 12:39–40; Rom 11:9) applies to disbelief such OT statements as "They have shut their eyes lest they see with their own eyes" (Isa 6:10) and "Let their eyes be darkened so they cannot see" (Ps 69:24[23]). In II Cor 4:4 we hear that "the god of this world has blinded the minds of the unbelievers"; and while no Satanic force is mentioned in I John in these lines, "the Evil One" will appear in the next unit (2:13–14) and the Antichrist in the following unit (2:18,22).

COMMENT

The critique of false claims stemming from secessionist theology, which began in the previous unit (1:5–2:2), continues in this unit (2:3–11).[1] Although some scholars see subtle developments of thought as one moves from one unit to the other (Malatesta, *Interiority* 120), my chief reason for distinguishing two units is that the false claims are expressed in different grammatical patterns, respectively three conditional boasts in 1:6,8,10, and three participial affirmations in 2:4,6,9. However, the pattern of antitheses is not so neat in the present unit as it was in the previous, and so there is no unanimity in the detection of substructure.

The opening sentence in 2:3 has certain similarities to the previous unit's opening in 1:5, although that was more comprehensive. Verse 3 continues the "we" language which dominated in 1:5–2:2, but which will be significantly lacking in the rest of the present unit, occurring only in 2:5c, a sentence that is very like the first line of 2:3. It is not surprising then that some scholars extend the unit from 1:5–2:2 to include 2:3–5, and start a new unit only with 2:6. Their argument is strengthened by the fact that only in 2:4–5 does one find a false claim in one verse immediately corrected by a true claim in the next verse—the set pattern that recurred three times in 1:5–2:2.

There are counterarguments, however, for connecting 2:3–5 with what follows. The first verse (2:3) can be looked upon as a topical sentence introducing a unit, even as 1:5 introduced the previous unit.[2] That unit commented upon "God is light and in Him there is no darkness at all" by

---

[1] Dodd, *Epistles* 32: "In this passage our author is not only rebutting dangerous tendencies in the Church of his time, but discussing a problem of perennial importance, that of the validity of religious experience." I would rather say that the author's goal was limited to the dangerous tendencies of his time, which he thought to be "the last hour" (2:18), but what he said is of perennial importance.

[2] But 1:5 also introduced the whole Part One of I John.

ruling out any walking in darkness through sin—a somewhat negative approach. The present unit comments more positively by a stress on keeping the commandments, especially the commandment of love. The topic of commandment, never mentioned in the previous unit, runs through 2:3–11, binding it together,[3] as does also the thrice repeated participial pattern, "The person who claims . . ." And so common structural patterns make it logical to treat these verses as a unit. In the last verses (9–11), however, the theme of light and darkness, which opened the previous unit recurs, establishing an inclusion. This similarity between 1:5–7 and 2:9–11 gives us a long tractate consisting of six boasts or claims (phrased in three conditions and three participles) that the author rejects —a tractate divisible into two units.

Within this second unit, the following substructure is detectable, aligned according to verses:[4]

3:     General theme: We can be sure we know God by keeping the commandments.
4–5:   The first wrong claim picks up from 3 the theme of knowing God:
    4: The opponents claim to know God without keeping the commandments; they are liars.
    5ab: Antithesis: Whoever keep's God's word is perfected in the love of God.
    5c: Summary statement (matching v. 3): We can thus be sure we are in God.
6–8:   The second wrong claim picks up from 5c the theme of being in God:
    6: The opponents claim to abide in God; they ought to walk as Christ walked.
    7–8: New or old? The commandment is not new in the sense of novel; from the beginning it was part of the command to love as Christ loved. It is new in the sense that it must be lived out in this last hour when the darkness is passing away and the light is shining.
9–11: The third wrong claim picks up from 8d the theme of light:
    9: The opponents claim to be in light while hating their brothers; they are still in darkness.
    10–11: Pair of antitheses: The person who loves his brother abides in light; the person who hates his brother is in darkness which blinds him.

A. Knowing God by Keeping the Commandments (2:3)

The second unit of Part One begins with the theme of knowing God, an almost universal religious ideal in antiquity. Dodd (*Epistles* 29–30) shows how in the Greek classical period there was unbounded confidence in human reason, so that Plato could posit a knowledge of eternal realities

[3] Even Dodd (*Epistles* 29), who thinks that the unit runs from 1:5–2:6, recognizes that a new point is made in 2:3.

[4] In the structure proposed by Law (above, p. 121), the stylistic similarity of the three claims (2:4,6,9) is ignored, and 2:3–5 is part of the test of obedience (moral test) that runs from 1:8 to 2:6, while 2:7–11 is part of the test of love (social test) that runs from 2:7 to 2:17. In Stott's refinement, 2:3–6 serves as the whole moral test, and 2:7–11 serves as the whole social test. Malatesta, *Interiority* 119–21, finds a complicated design of concentric patterns (under the influence of de la Potterie) giving the structure 2:3–6,7–8,9–11, which also ignores the much more obvious three participial claims.

in heaven to be contemplated by pure reason. In the Hellenistic period confidence faltered, and the possibility of knowing God moved from philosophy to mystery religions with their special revelations. Israel, of course, always posited a special revelation to God's people: "Let him who glories glory in this: that he understands and knows me, that I am the Lord" (Jer 9:23[24]). The fulfillment of that challenge would be facilitated in the last days: "The earth will be filled with the knowledge of the glory of God" (Hab 2:14). The Qumran hymn that expresses the members' sentiments proclaims, "My justification is with God . . . my light has sprung from the source of His knowledge" (1QS 11:2–3). Matthew 11:27 and Luke 10:22 speak of knowing the Father as a special privilege given here and now to those to whom the Son chooses to reveal Him, while Paul distinguishes, "Now I know in part; then I shall know fully" (I Cor 13:12). John 17:3 identifies eternal life (which is given to believers by Jesus) with knowing the Father and the Son (see ABJ 29A, 752–53). Philo, *On the Decalogue* 16 #81, considers it a supreme goal to have "knowledge of Him who truly is"; and the second-century A.D. *Midrash Sifre* 49(85a) on Deut 11:22 says, "Study the *haggada;* then you will know God and be attached to His way." In Greek Oriental mysticism the *Corpus Hermeticum* 10.9 affirms, "He who has attained knowledge [*gnōsis*] . . . is already divine."

Why has the epistolary author chosen to introduce this concept of the knowledge of God *here?* We saw that the I John Prologue followed the GJohn Prologue closely, and that the light/darkness motif of the previous unit (1:5–2:2) probably also came from the GJohn Prologue. There, after the reference to the light coming into the world (John 1:9), we are told that "the world did not *know* him" (1:10). Then the GJohn Prologue turns positively to those who did accept him and become God's children (1:12–13) with the obvious implication that they did know him. That sequence may have led the epistolary author to turn to knowledge after discussing light/darkness. Secessionist theology misinterpreted the implication of the Johannine tradition on God as light; it also misinterpreted that tradition on the knowledge of God.

Against that misinterpretation the author argues that one cannot know God without keeping His commandments. His logic here stems in part from the previous unit where, in relation to the theme of God as light, he argued that there is no darkness in God and so believers should not be walking in darkness or in sin. (The state of not being in sin, however, was to be achieved not by denying sin but by asking forgiveness.) From that sequence one might get the impression that human behavior can be deduced from a knowledge of God. But the opposite is also true: One gains a knowledge of God through behavior, when that behavior is governed by God's commandments. Keeping the commandments is more than an external way of verifying a claim to know God; rather it is a criterion that has an essential relationship to the claim made.[5] In the Semitic understanding, knowledge is more than intellectual, for it involves an experience of the whole person—that is why "knowledge" can be used for sexual intimacy. To know God means to share His life, as can be seen from the parallelism between "know Him" in 2:4a and "abide in Him" in 2:6a. Sharing God's life means living according to His will, and so by keeping His commandments one comes to know Him intimately.[6] The sequence from action to knowledge is apparent as well in I John 4:7, "Everyone who loves has been begotten by God and knows God,"[7] and in the equation in Rev 3:8,12 between those who have kept Christ's word and those who will receive God's name.

The connection between way of life and knowledge of God reflects, in particular, the New Covenant atmosphere of Johannine thought.[8] In the covenant associated with the Exodus, God made Himself known through the actions He performed in delivering Israel from Egypt (Exod 7:5,17); and it was promised that His cultic dwelling in the midst of the people in the Tabernacle would enable Israel to know the Lord their God (Exod 29:45–46). The prophets looked upon God's continuing historical action in crushing the enemies of Israel as a way of knowing the Lordship of Yahweh (Ezek 25:5,11,17). On the other side of the coin, when Israel was unfaithful, God's punishing action also supplied a way of knowing His Lordship (Ezek 6:7,10,13). Hosea (4:1–2) associates the failure to keep the Ten Commandments with "no knowledge of God in the land." Job 36:10–12 says that those who do not hearken to the Lord's commands die without knowledge. The sons of Eli who broke the commandments were characterized as "those who did not know the Lord" (I Sam 2:12; see also Isa 1:3–4). To correct such situations a more intimate knowledge of God was promised when God would renew His covenant with Israel. In the New Covenant God would put His Law within the hearts of the Israelites; and they would no longer need people to teach

[5] There is a problem with R. Law's thesis that I John supplies the "tests" by which one can detect the presence of divine life (previous footnote), as exemplified by the many "This is how we can be sure" sentences (see NOTE on *en toutō* in 2:3a). The idea of external criteria is common, e.g., Matt 7:20, "By their fruits you will know them"; or Aristotle, *Nicomachean Ethics* 1.3.16, "Not *gnōsis*, but *praxis*." But for the Johannine writer what is offered is more than a test; it is a means.

[6] Bultmann, *Epistles* 25: "It is doubtless more nearly correct to say that 'keeping the commandments' (like 'fellowship with one another,' 1:7) is not the condition, but rather the characteristic of the knowledge of God."

[7] The connection with 2:3 is apparent when we realize that the primary commandment is the one to love. Chmiel, *Lumière* 137, finds background for this Johannine feature in Deut 30:16 where hearing the commandments of God and loving Him are side by side.

[8] For Christians as for Jews the original meaning of "new" in New Covenant was not "new in place of old" but "renewed." By the end of the NT period, especially in John and Hebrews, the replacement motif had set in. For John the Old Covenant has been replaced by a new one, as one can judge from the changing of the water for Jewish purifications to the "best wine" at Cana.

them to know the Lord, "for they shall all know me from the least to the greatest" (Jer 31:33–34). "I shall give them a heart to know that I am the Lord" (24:7). "A new heart I will give you and a new spirit I will put within you . . . and cause you to walk in my statutes and be careful to observe my ordinances" (Ezek 36:26–27). The Qumran sectarians, thinking of themselves as the community of the New (renewed) Covenant, maintained that God had put a spirit of truth[9] within human beings as enlightenment for their hearts to show them how to keep God's ordinances (1QS 4:2–3; 5:20–22). The composer of the *Hymns* at Qumran can thank God for having allowed the covenant to illumine him (1QH 4:5) and for having hidden the divine Law within him (5:11).[10] It is precisely this internal principle of knowledge, promised in the New Covenant, that makes sense of the epistolary author's attitude toward commandments. Those who "keep"[11] God's commandments are acting according to the Spirit that God has put into their hearts, indeed according to the new hearts (or natures) that God gave them when He begot them from above as His children. And those new hearts and the life according to the commandments enable the children to know the Father connaturally.

Both GJohn and I John use the plural and singular of commandment interchangeably.[12] Against a Jewish background the plural would normally mean the commandments enjoined by God on Israel through the covenant, especially the Ten Commandments. This is true of the one common Synoptic instance of the plural (Mark 10:19 and par.; see also Luke 1:6). Now, that meaning is not excluded from GJohn, but there the body of commandments is seen under the aspect of the commandment of loving one another as Jesus has loved. As we saw in the INTRODUCTION (V B3ac), while this may be a magnificent concept, it means that little by way of specific commandments is supplied in GJohn. Since the epistolary author is commenting on GJohn tradition[13] to strengthen his followers

---

[9] This spirit is sometimes personified as an angel, but other times it has an impersonal role within the human heart. See NOTE on 4:1a below.

[10] See J. de Caevel, "La connaissance religieuse dans les Hymnes d'action de grâces de Qumrân," ETL 38 (1962) 435–60.

[11] Often this Johannine idiom means no more than "observe" (NOTE on 2:3b). Nevertheless, here it may catch the continuity of behavior that the epistolary author wishes to inculcate. The fact that the opponents have seceded (2:19) makes verbs of continuation ("abide," "keep") very important emotionally in I John.

[12] For the statistics and texts pertinent to the Johannine use of "commandment(s)," see the detailed NOTE on 2:3b; also ABJ 29A, 638.

[13] Indeed, the whole passage in I John 2:3–5 makes limited sense without the background supplied by GJohn, e.g., "If you love me and keep my commandments," (14:15); "Whoever keeps the commandments he has from me is the one who loves me" (14:21); and "Whoever does not love me does not keep my words" (14:24). Muñoz León, "El origen" 230–31, uses this as an example of his thesis that the antitheses of I John arise from those of GJohn.

against the inroads of the secessionists who also claim the support of GJohn, he is not free to introduce entirely new vocabulary. While he cannot and would not avoid the GJohn equation of commandments with the commandment to love, by speaking twice as frequently of commandment(s) and by always referring them to God and never explicitly to Jesus (the opposite of the GJohn practice), he implicitly reminds his readers more vividly of the Ten Commandments. When he does turn to Jesus (e.g., v. 6), he capitalizes upon the idea that in GJohn Jesus walked in obedience to a commandment or commandments. He not only appeals for obedience to God's commandments on the part of the Christian, but he also stresses the interiorization of the commandments so that moral action follows what one really is.

B. *The First Wrong Claim and Its Antithesis* (2:4–5)

The author's difficulty is not simply with admitted sinners who do not keep the commandments; it is with would-be saints who do not think that keeping the commandments is related to the knowledge of God. His opponents think of themselves as those who know (*ginōskein*) God. What kind of knowledge did they think that they possessed? Balz and Hauck are among those who think of the secessionists as worthy of the name gnostic (INTRODUCTION IV B3c), i.e., claiming *gnōsis*.[14] Certainly the "I know God" of 2:4a may be a verbatim secessionist claim, but there need be no pejoratively gnostic ring to it since the author made exactly the same claim in 2:3a. The respective claims in 2:3a and 2:4a support my thesis that the secessionists were Christians of the Johannine tradition who shared many ideals with the author (INTRODUCTION V A). The claim of both the author and the secessionists to know God is simply a reflection of GJohn, which uses that language some dozen times (NOTE on 2:3a). There is no proof that they differed because the secessionists claimed all knowledge,[15] or a special revelation, or a mystical knowledge

---

[14] How significant is it that the author does not use this Greek term in his anti-secessionist polemic? At the end of the first century it would have been a less emotionally charged word than at the end of the second century when Irenaeus had written his five-volume work against the "*gnōsis* falsely so-called" (*Adv. haer.* 2.1.1). Yet we must remember that this pejorative characterization of *gnōsis* came from I Tim 6:20, a work roughly contemporary with I John. Consequently, the author of I John may not have thought his opponents were guilty of the same false *gnōsis* that plagued the adversaries of the Pastoral Epistles, if the term had acquired any such set value.

[15] The gnostics condemned by Irenaeus, *Adv. haer.* 2.28.9, claimed "a universal knowledge of all that exists, being such as Valentinus, or Ptolemaeus, or Basilides, or any other of those who maintain that they have searched out the deep things of

of God, or a knowledge through myths. The reason they differed is given by the author: The secessionists combine the Johannine claim to know God with an indifference about the way a moral life enters into that claim. While claiming the intimacy with God implied in "knowing" Him, they see no need to live God's way of life as expressed in the commandments. This makes liars of them, not only in the sense that they teach a false interpretation of the tradition, but more importantly in the sense that they embody a contradiction between a claimed internal principle (divine life, intimacy, knowledge) and the manifestation of the principle (a life indifferent to divine commandments). The author means 2:4d literally: There is no truth *in* such a person. By comparing 2:4 with 1:6 one realizes how the author repeats thematically and stylistically his objection to the secessionists:

1:6:   If we boast, "We are in communion with Him,"
        while continuing to walk in darkness,
        we are liars
        and we do not act in truth.
2:4:   The person who claims, "I know Him,"
        without keeping His commandments,
        is a liar
        and there is no truth in such a person.

In 2:5, having corrected the opponents' claim, the author offers by way of antithesis his own claim.[16] Since he has just denied truth to the person who does not keep the commandments, one might have expected him to say that in whoever keeps the commandments (word) the *truth* of God has reached perfection.[17] Rather he speaks about the love of God reaching perfection. On the one hand, this reminds us of the interchangeability of such Johannine terms as truth and love—Westcott (*Epistles* 48) remarks, "Love is the Truth realised in a personal relation." On the other hand, we should recognize that the choice of "love" is not haphazard, for that is the commandment of Jesus *par excellence*. I have devoted a long NOTE on 2:5b to what "the love of God" means. In its origin it is a love that comes from God to the Christian and is embodied in God's giving His only Son (I John 4:7–10). This love was not motivated by any value that human beings possess; rather it creates their value by

---

God." They also had a superiority complex: "They have sublime knowledge on account of which they are superior to others" (2.10.3). The Johannine secessionists may also have had a superiority complex, but indeed so did the whole Johannine Community modeled upon the Disciple whom Jesus especially loved (see Brown, *Community* 84–85).

[16] If the claim of 2:4 and the boast of 1:6 resemble each other, the antithesis in 2:5 does not closely resemble the antithesis in 1:7. The failure of the author to carry through his patterns in a way *that would make sense to a modern reader* is what makes a discussion of the author's structural intention so complicated for us.

[17] Or even the *life* of God, as in John 8:51: "If a man keeps my word, he shall never see death."

making them children of God. Keeping the commandments, and especially keeping the commandment to love one another as Christ loved us, involves the perfection of the love of God, for it means that the love God had for us is being extended to others and allowed to re-create them as children of God. The perfection may also have involved loving God in response to His love for us,[18] and thus establishing a mutuality between God and the Christian upon the pattern of the mutuality of love between God and Jesus. This is the dream the author dared to voice in 1:3: "That you may be joined in communion with us, for the communion we have is with the Father and with His Son, Jesus Christ." Divine love as creative of God's children is what brought the Johannine Community into being, and the dynamism of such love exhibits itself in keeping commandments that bind the Christians to God and to each other. In Johannine theology keeping the commandments is not the first step to a higher love in which there will be no commandments;[19] it is the perfection of love, for commandments are simply an expression of God's will and of His very being.

All of this makes logical the summary in 2:5c: "This is how we can be sure that we are in Him." We have here an instance of the Johannine theology of immanence (the Christian in God/Jesus; God/Jesus in the Christian; God and Jesus in each other) which is vocalized some 35 times in GJohn and the Epistles in the formulas *einai en,* "to be in," and *menein en,* "to remain/abide in" (NOTES on 1:5e; 2:6a).[20] Since the commandments, including that of love, stem from God's inner being, keeping them exemplifies union with that being. In the question of the precise Johannine meaning of immanence or indwelling, some scholars speak of mysticism (an experience usually thought to be the privilege of the few). But the OT background of the concept points in other directions.[21] First, there is a cultic indwelling of God among His people. When Solomon built the Temple, he wondered if God would dwell with human beings upon earth (II Chron 6:18), but Ezek 48:35 predicted that this would be so much a part of the future that the name of the New Jerusalem would be "The Lord is there." In Zech 2:14-15(10-11) the

---

[18] Some scholars have suggested that the author's opponents spoke of the love of God exclusively in the sense of a love for God, ignoring the command to love one another. In the INTRODUCTION (V B3c) I maintained that the secessionists probably did say they loved one another; but whether they put more stress on love for God than did the author is impossible to say. They may also have spoken of the love of God reaching perfection—an idea attested in *Did.* 10:5; *I Clem.* 49:5; 50:1,3—but presumably perfection in a way different from that intended by the author.

[19] In Johannine thought God gave the Son a commandment that predated his entry into the world (John 10:18; 12:49), and so there never will be a "time" in which there are no commandments.

[20] As with the commandments so also with the indwelling, when I John is compared to GJohn, the relationship to God is more prominent in I John than is the relationship with Jesus.

[21] See Feuillet, *Le mystère* 99–103, for the general background; also the full-scale work on the subject by Malatesta (*Interiority*), and ABJ 29, 510–12; 29A, 602–3.

Lord promises in the last day, "I will dwell in the midst of you." This is continued in the intertestamental period in *Jubilees* 1:17,26: "I will build my sanctuary in their midst and I will dwell with them. . . . I will descend and dwell with them throughout eternity." Moving beyond the cultic, we find God sending to dwell in Israel divine Wisdom which had come forth from His mouth (Sir 24:3,8). In Wis 7:25,27 Wisdom, which is a pure emanation of the glory of the Almighty, passes into holy souls, making them friends of God.

Much of this background stems from the mentality of the covenant relationship, both Old Covenant and New (renewed). Certainly the cultic indwelling of God was a fundamental corollary of Israel's being chosen as God's people. The question of Israel in the desert was, "Is the Lord in [among] us or not?" (LXX Exod 17:7). When Israel violated the covenant, it could ask, "Have not these evils come upon us because our God is not in [among] us?" (Deut 31:16–17). The Wisdom passages cited above are a reflection of the claim that the divine Law had been placed in the midst of Israel (as symbolized by the decalogue tablets in the Jerusalem Temple). In the prophetic reflections on the New Covenant, this divine presence was to be interiorized in individual Israelites. The passages cited above (pp. 279–80) promising an intimate knowledge of God as part of the New Covenant (Jer 24; 31; Ezek 36) connect such knowledge with an immanence of the divine spirit and the Law in those who accept the covenant. In Johannine theology Jesus is the divine Word who has come down from heaven to dwell among God's people (to "tent" or "tabernacle": John 1:14), and so represents both the cultic presence of God and the indwelling Law and Wisdom. Beyond that, in the person of the Paraclete/Spirit Jesus makes possible a divine presence abiding *within* those who keep the commandments (14:16–17). This immanence goes beyond the OT expectations of the New Covenant, for it has a mutuality: not only God in His children, but His children in God.[22] The reason for this development is that the model for the immanence is the intimate relationship between Father and Son revealed by Jesus. The immanence of the Christian New Covenant is new because of Jesus' ideal, "That they all may be one, *just as you Father in me and I in you,* that they may also be in us" (17:21).[23] This is not a mysticism for the few but a new spiritual status for all who truly believe in Jesus.[24]

[22] In the covenant blessing upon Benjamin in Deut 33:12 there is a rare hint of mutual indwelling: the Lord shelters Benjamin who dwells by Him, while the Lord makes His dwelling between Benjamin's shoulders. (Perhaps this is a reference to the location of the ark before the building of the Shiloh tabernacle.)
[23] To be in God is not just a matter of existing in a place (as being in a room) or of passive presence (as being in the glow of a light by which one is warmed); it is a communion that produces oneness.
[24] Schenke, "Determination" 209–10, suggests that abiding in God is a synonym for being begotten by God.

C. *The Second Wrong Claim and the New Commandment* (2:6–8)

The second (implicitly objectionable) claim involves abiding in God without walking as Christ walked. It picks up the theme of immanence from the preceding verse (2:5c) even as the first wrong claim in 2:4 picked up the theme of knowing God from 2:3. I speak of an *implicit* objectionable claim. In this unit the first claim (2:4: to know God without keeping His commandments) and the third claim (2:9: to be in the light while hating one's brother) are clearly wrong claims, for the author describes the claimant respectively as a liar or as one who is in the darkness. That there is a wrong claim behind 2:5 is by implication: when the author says that the person who claims to abide in God *ought* to walk as Christ walked. Presumably the reason the author chooses to handle the second claim in this unusual way is that the "ought" leads into the theme of commandment which he wants to develop.

The author's objection to the claim is not over the possibility of abiding in God, which is legitimate Johannine theology that both he and his opponents would share.[25] The objection is to abiding or indwelling when it is divorced from the way one lives one's life (walks). By insisting that the person who claims indwelling ought to walk just as Christ walked, the author shows that the struggle with the secessionists over moral principles is really rooted in a struggle over christology (see INTRODUCTION V B2,3). In my theory, the secessionists attach the salvific gift of eternal life primarily to the incarnation of Jesus, not to his life and death.[26] Since they attribute no importance to the way he "walked," they attribute no importance to the way Christians walk. The author insists on both and sees the obligation to walk just as he walked as an obvious specification of the Johannine commandment, "Love one another *as* I have loved you" (John

[25] John 17:21 is the only GJohn passage that posits the indwelling (*einai en*) of the Christian in God; but John 14:20; 15:2 (*einai en*) and John 6:56; 15:4,5,6,7 (*menein en*) posit the indwelling of the Christian in Jesus, who is one with the Father (10:30). And so I cannot agree that the claim to abide in God has to be the author's rephrasing of an opponent's claim (Heise, *Bleiben* 123) or was added by him to a source (Bultmann, *Epistles* 25–26). If the opponents were former Johannine Christians, as we are told in I John 2:19, this is precisely the way they would have phrased their claim of mutual indwelling with God. I disagree also with Westcott and Hauck who see a deliberate progression in the claims "know Him," "be in Him," and "abide in Him" in 2:4a,5c,6a. These are alternative ways of describing the same intimacy with God.

[26] I John 4:7–11 shows that the commandment to love one another as Christ loved us was combined in Johannine tradition with John 3:16, "God loved the world so much that He gave the only Son." In the INTRODUCTION (V C2d) I pointed out that the ambiguous verb "gave" in that axiom may have been understood differently by the secessionists ("gave" in incarnation) and by the author ("gave" in death).

13:34; 15:12). That is why he can insist that his demand is nothing new (novel) but a commandment that was had "from the beginning" since it was taught to his disciples by Jesus at the Last Supper and taught to the Johannine Christians at their entrance into the Johannine Community. (Once again, as we saw at the end of the COMMENT on the previous unit, the life-setting from which the author draws his arguments may have been the conversion/initiation/baptism paraenesis.) His demand reflects the commandment that in Johannine circles is known simply as "the word" of the New Covenant (I John 2:7c; see NOTE), even as the Ten Commandments or stipulations of the Exodus covenant were known as "the words" of the Lord in the OT.

In a NOTE on 2:6c I discussed at length the use of *kathōs,* "just as," in Johannine writing. In I John it is used to place demands patterned on Christ's past actions (just as he walked, loved, died) and on his present state (just as he is pure, just, or even just as he is). The comparisons are not very specific as to what moral action is to be done or what immoral action is to be avoided.[27] In part, as I have argued in the INTRODUCTION (V B3a), that is because GJohn offers virtually no specific moral instruction either by word or deed. In greater part, however, the lack of specificity reminds us that the "just as Christ" comparison involves more than the imitation of a model. Christians have the same eternal life that Jesus had and has;[28] this life, as an internal principle, must express itself in the same way as it did and does in him. The author's point of difference with the secessionists is that he conceives this life (also truth, knowledge, light, love) to be a dynamic element expressing itself in behavior rather than a static possession.

Having denied that he is imposing a novel demand, on second thought (2:8ab) the author admits that his specification of the commandment to act just as Jesus acted is new. In the NOTE I explained that even though the author may have used the term "new" because it was fixed for this commandment in the tradition (John 13:34), he has his own tonality. For Jesus the newness of his commandment was eschatological, proclaimed in "the hour" when human beings were being given an inner power (God's own life) enabling them to love as God loved. The epistolary author draws on this idea when he says the commandment is new "as it is made true [*alēthēs*]" both in Christ and the Christian. "True" implies a correspondence with one's inner reality, and so the commandment to love is made true in Christians when the eternal life that Christ gave to believers expresses itself in loving deeds. It is made true anew in Christ

---

[27] The argument with the secessionists, in my view, was not over specific sins but over a whole outlook on the importance of behavior.

[28] If the author were interested only in Jesus on earth as a model, he would have confined his *kathōs* comparisons to the past.

because he not only died for others in the past as an atonement for sins but because he continues the cleansing effect of that atonement as a Paraclete in the Father's presence (2:1–2).

Let me pause to consider the author's claim that he is not really writing anything new and yet, on second thought, he is—this admission is a crucial qualification of his insistence that he proclaims a gospel that was had "from the beginning." It is no accident that the Johannine description of the Paraclete's relationship to Jesus also involves the ideas of nothing new and yet an ability to declare the things to come (John 14:26; 16:13–15). The Fourth Evangelist must have regarded himself an an instrument of the Paraclete when in GJohn he reported what Jesus said and did but at the same time completely reinterpreted it. The epistolary author is playing the same Paraclete role in relation to GJohn (see INTRODUCTION V C2c). His understanding of a tradition had "from the beginning" is no more static than his understanding of eternal life.

As we return now to 2:8, the sudden introduction of darkness and light in the last lines of the verse reminds us that the author is still struggling to interpret the GJohn Prologue against the secessionists. The relationship of 2:8b ("made true [alēthēs] both in Christ and in you") to 2:8cd ("since the darkness is passing away and the true [alēthinos] light is already shining") is somewhat clarified when we remember themes of the GJohn Prologue: "The light shines in the darkness, for the darkness did not overcome it" (John 1:5)[29] followed by "The true [alēthinos] light was coming into the world" (1:9). For GJohn with the incarnation of Jesus a true light shone forth on the earth offering people a choice between light and darkness (3:19–21). Darkness could overcome neither the light nor those who came to the light, but it did overcome those who did not walk in the light of Jesus (12:35). I John is right then when it speaks of a newness made true both in Christ and the Christian in relation to the idea that the darkness is *passing away*. As Bultmann, Klein,[30] and others have pointed out, the epistolary author has historicized the eschatological struggle between light and darkness. But one exaggerates the difference unless one recognizes an incipient historicization in GJohn as well in the sense that it leaves room for the future working out of the victory won by Jesus. In Jesus' "hour" the Prince of this world is driven out (12:31) as part of a judgment in which the world is conquered (16:33). Nevertheless, the

[29] This is the only other Johannine use of "shine" (*phainein*) in the context of light/darkness.

[30] Klein, "Licht" 270–91, 308–19, uses the difference from GJohn as proof that the epistolary author was not the evangelist. I do not object to that, but I do object to any implied value judgment preferring the eschatological GJohn to the historicized I John. Rather I John wrestles intelligently with the problem caused by the overly punctiliar outlook of GJohn. I John is not without eschatological urgency: "It is the last hour" (2:18).

Spirit of Truth must come and prove that the world was defeated in that judgment and its Prince condemned (16:8–11). While the Paraclete is doing that, Jesus' followers have to remain in the world which hates them and have to be kept safe from the Evil One (17:14–16). In having Jesus look to a future continuation of the struggle, GJohn agrees with other NT works that recognize the continued presence of "the world rulers of the present darkness" (Eph 6:12) who are "doomed to be wiped out" (I Cor 2:6)—a picture that is not purely eschatological but offers a faint sketch of continued salvation history.

Having said that, I acknowledge that the historical pattern is stronger in I John than in GJohn and understandably so. When salvation is pictured, not primarily as a punctiliar divine shining of light into the world, but as the continued shining of that light gradually overcoming darkness, it becomes possible to give attention both to the career of Jesus and to the career of Christians as part of that salvific process. The secessionists probably concentrated exclusively upon the GJohn portrait of the incarnation as the coming of the true light into the darkness (John 1:9), and upon their own choice to become Christians as the disappearance of darkness for them (3:21).[31] But the epistolary author insists that, as the commandment of love is made true in ongoing forgiveness by Jesus and in ongoing deeds by Christians on behalf of their brothers and sisters, the darkness is being pushed back and the true light is shining. For the author the choice of light over darkness must be made and manifested daily—one must walk in light. There is always a newness in the way one's behavior shows one to be true to the new life of being a child of God.

D. The Third Wrong Claim and the New Commandment (2:9–11)

Just as the first and second wrong claims drew upon an immediately preceding theme (2:4a drawing upon 2:3; 2:6a drawing upon 2:5), so the third wrong claim in 2:9a about being in the light draws upon the previous theme of light in 2:8. Indeed, it draws also on the theme of the new commandment in 2:7–8, which (implicitly) is the command to love one another, for the wrongness of the claim involves not the possibility of being in the light but the thought of being in light while hating one's brother. In such a claimant the commandment of love has not been

---

[31] "Enlightenment" was an early Christian designation for the experience of conversion and baptism (Heb 6:4; 10:32; Justin, I Apology 61.13); and that may have been true in the Johannine tradition as well, as suggested by the baptismal implications of the story in John 9 of how a man gained sight by washing in the pool designated as "the one sent" (ABJ 29, 381–82).

"made true" (2:8b), and for him the darkness has not passed away (2:8c)—he "is still in the darkness even now" (2:9c).

A comparison of the substance of the three wrong claims, "I know Him," "I abide in Him," and "I am in the light" (2:4a,6a,9a), implies that the last is a claim of closeness with God. That is confirmed by 1:7, which states that God is in light. Some commentators posit a special gnostic background for this claim. For instance, Painter (*John* 121) thinks that the "heretics" may have claimed to be illumined by supernatural knowledge, either through mystical experience or because they thought that their nature partook of the essence of light. Once more I see no need for positing such a developed gnostic background to the secessionist claim which is perfectly justifiable in word and idea from GJohn. It is true that there we do not find the expression "to be in" (*einai en*) with light or darkness as an object;[82] but in GJohn the closely parallel expression "to abide/remain in" (*menein en*) occurs: "No one who believes in me need remain in darkness" (John 12:46). That passage implies that those who believe in Jesus abide in light—a claim any Johannine Christian might make.

Once more the author's refutation involves not the claim but the understanding of the claim.[83] Being in light is not a static but a dynamic condition that must find expression in keeping the commandments, especially the commandment to love one another (or one's brother[34]) as Christ loved us. (As usual, the Johannine way of thinking is the opposite of what we might spontaneously have expected: not that loving enables one to be in the light, but that being in the light given by Christ enables one to love—because love is from God and is not a purely human action.) Notice the qualification of the claim in 2:9b: not "The person who claims to be in the light *without loving his brother,*" but "all the while hating his brother." As I have indicated in the NOTE, since love is commanded, there is no room for an antithesis consisting of indifference or neutrality; the antithesis involves malice and hate and blindness. That is why the failure to love has such a power to nullify spiritual claims, as attested also by

---

[82] John 11:10; 12:35 have "light" as a subject "being in" people.

[83] Already with his reference to "true light" in 2:8d the author has prepared us to distinguish between a genuine and a false understanding of light.

[34] Just as the three claims of knowing God, abiding in Him, and being in the light (2:4,6,9) amount to substantially the same thing, so also the three conditions of keeping the commandments, walking as Christ walked, and loving one another amount to the same thing. In I John 3:11,23; 4:7,11,12; II John 5 the author speaks of the commandment in terms of loving *one another,* which is GJohn terminology; but here and in 2:10,11; 3:10,14,15; 4:20,21 it is a question of loving or hating the *"brother,"* a more common ecclesiastical term. In 5:1,2 the author speaks of loving the one begotten by God or *God's children.* All these terms describe the same reality, namely, one's fellow Johannine Christian—not all people or even all who claim to be Christian (see NOTE on 2:9b).

Paul: "If I can prophesy and know all mysteries and have all knowledge . . . but have no love, I am nothing" (I Cor 13:2).

In 2:5 the author stated that "the love of God" is perfected in whoever keeps God's commandments or word; in 2:9–11 he makes clear that keeping the commandments or word of God involves the love of brother. Thus the love of God and the love of brother are joined in Johannine thought even though GJohn does not have the famous double commandment (love of God and of neighbor) found in the Synoptics, Paul, and intertestamental Judaism (p. 255 above). In the NOTE on 2:5b I mentioned the reluctance of some NT scholars to admit any connotation of love *for* God in the Johannine understanding of *agapē,* and to avoid this some speak of loving God *in* the brother. Coppens ("La doctrine" 297), however, is surely correct when he says that in no NT work is there ever a reference to loving God in one's brother. John in particular is clear that love for God is illusory if it is not reflected in love for brother, but the two loves are not confused. If there is any confusion, it springs from the ambiguity of the expression "love of God" which, as I pointed out in the NOTE, means primarily love from God exhibited in Christ, a love that the Johannine believers must extend to their brothers and sisters who are also children of God. Often, however, the author thinks also of a mutual love between the children and God their Father. In exercising that love the Johannine Christians did not have to search for God in their brothers, for as children of God they had His presence in themselves.

The author's judgment on the first wrong claim in this unit was: "There is no truth in such a person" (2:4d). The judgment on the third wrong claim is similar: the person "is still in darkness even now" (2:9c). Darkness and falsehood (and hate), light and truth (and love) are virtually interchangeable; and a wrong claim means that one is operating out of falsehood/darkness rather than out of truth/light. To be in darkness before the light came into the world was bad enough (John 3:19), but it is truly tragic to be in darkness "even now" when the darkness is passing away and the true light is already shining. Once again there is a certain historicization in I John when we consider the use of the phrase "even now," employed by GJohn (2:10; 5:17; 16:24) to describe the eschatological moment of Jesus' ministry. The epistolary author, who sees the shining of the light not simply as the incarnation but as the continued loving action of Jesus and the Christian, uses "even now" to describe the continued action. For the GJohn tradition those who never believed are in the darkness "even now"; for the epistolary author those who claimed to believe but have seceded (thus hating their brothers) are in the darkness "even now."

In 2:10–11 the author emphasizes this point by a compound antithesis. The positive half of the antithesis (2:10: "The person who loves his brother abides in the light") takes up from 2:9a the secessionist claim to be in light and shows how it may be justified through love. The negative half of the antithesis (2:11: "The person who hates his brother is in the darkness") takes up from 2:9b the wrong feature in the secessionist claim, namely, that they made the claim while hating their brothers, and stresses its disastrous results. The new features in 2:10–11 are the reference in v. 10b to a "cause for stumbling"[35] and the themes of loss of direction and of blindness in v. 11cd. Here one sees the plausibility of the thesis of Muñoz León (INTRODUCTION III A3) that the source of the sharp antitheses in I John is the antithesis pattern in GJohn. Behind 2:10–11 may be a saying like John 11:9–10: "If a man goes walking by day, he does not fall . . . but if goes walking by night, he will fall."[36] Also John 8:12, "No follower of mine shall ever walk in darkness"; and 12:35, "The man who walks in the dark does not know where he is going." In the NOTE on 2:10b I suggested that the most probable interpretation of "in him there is no cause for stumbling" is that in the person who abides in light and manifests this by loving his Johannine brother there is nothing that will cause him to sin by leaving the Community. On the other hand, the person who manifests his hate for his Johannine brother by seceding has cut himself off from koinōnia with God and Christ (1:3)[37] and is plunged into the realm of darkness.

This choice of darkness amounts to deliberate self-blinding (2:11d). As I indicated in the NOTE, the NT uses the image of deliberate blindness, borrowed from Isa 6:10, to explain the fact that some Jews refused to believe in Jesus. For instance, John 12:39–40 comes at the end of the public ministry as a judgment on "the Jews" who have resisted Jesus' challenge in 12:35–36 to walk in the light and become sons of light: "The reason they could not believe was, as Isaiah said, 'God has blinded their eyes . . . for fear they might see.'" Perhaps in imitation of this GJohn pattern, after having given six boasts or claims reflecting secessionist theology (in two units), the epistolary author concludes the second unit with the judgment that "darkness has blinded the eyes" of anyone who holds such theology. GJohn's polemic language, hitherto used against outsiders like "the Jews," is now being applied to former confreres who have be-

[35] In the text above I mentioned the parallelism between 2:4d, "There is no truth in such a person," and 2:9c, where such a person "is still in the darkness even now." In the positive antitheses that follow those respective judgments there is a parallelism between 2:5b, "Truly in this person the love of God has reached perfection," and 2:10b, "In him there is no cause for stumbling."

[36] In turn, the symbolism in GJohn has OT background, e.g., Prov 4:18–19: "The paths of the just shine as with light . . . the paths of the wicked lie in darkness; they do not know over what they fall."

[37] That the author connects these ideas is not a guess if we remember 1:6: "If we boast, 'We are in koinōnia with Him,' while continuing to walk in darkness, we are liars."

come the most dangerous "sons of darkness" (see INTRODUCTION V
C2a). At the beginning of the first unit (and of Part One of I John) the
author had summarized the Johannine gospel as "God is light and in Him
there is no darkness at all"; and now to his own satisfaction he has shown
that the secessionists and any seduced by them belong to the darkness. It is
clear, then, that they do not know God or abide in Him or have communion with Him as they have boasted and claimed. Having consigned the
secessionists to outer darkness, the author will turn his attention in the
next unit to those who are Jesus' own, i.e., the sons of light who constitute
the Johannine Community, which is *koinōnia* with himself.

BIBLIOGRAPHY PERTINENT TO I JOHN 2:3–11

Kilpatrick, G. D., "Two Johannine Idioms in the Johannine Epistles," JTS 12
　　(1961) 272–73, on 2:8.
Muñoz León, D., "La novedad del mandamiento del amor en los escritos de S.
　　Juan: Intentos modernos de solución," *XXIX Semana Biblica Española*
　　(1969, pub. 1971) 193–231.
Vicent Cernuda, A., "Engañan la oscuridad y el mondo; la luz era y manifiesta
　　lo verdadero," EstBib 27 (1968) 153–75, 215–32, esp. 166–73 on 2:8,
　　and 215–26 on 2:17.
See also G. Klein, "Licht"; and "Abiding, remaining" and "Love" in VII C2 in
　　the *General Bibliography*.

4. I John 2:12–17: *Admonitions to Believers: Having Conquered the Evil One, They Must Resist the World*

12a	12LITTLE CHILDREN, I write to you:
12b	your sins have been forgiven because of Christ's name.
13a	13FATHERS, I write to you:
13b	you have known him who has been from the beginning.
13c	YOUNG PEOPLE, I write to you:
13d	you have conquered the Evil One.
14a	14Yes, CHILDREN, I have been writing to you:
14b	you have known the Father.
14c	Yes, FATHERS, I have been writing to you:
14d	you have known him who has been from the beginning.
14e	Yes, YOUNG PEOPLE, I have been writing to you:
14f	you are strong,
14g	for the word of God abides in you,
14h	and you have conquered the Evil One.
15a	15Have no love for the world,
15b	nor for the things that are in the world.
15c	If anyone loves the world,
15d	there is in him no love of the Father.
16a	16For all that is in the world—
16b	human nature full of desire,
16c	eyes hungry for all they see,
16d	material life that inflates self-assurance—
16e	does not belong to the Father;
16f	all that belongs to the world.
17a	17And the world is passing away
17b	with all its desires;
17c	but the person who does the will of God
17d	remains forever.

NOTES

General note on 2:12–14. These verses consist of six main clauses, the beginnings of which may be schematized thus:

12a *graphō hymin teknia hoti*
13a *graphō hymin pateres hoti*
13c *graphō hymin neaniskoi hoti*
14a *egrapsa hymin paidia hoti*
14c *egrapsa hymin pateres hoti*
14e *egrapsa hymin neaniskoi hoti*

Some of the problems to be discussed below have been troublesome to versifiers of the NT; for while one might have expected two verses dividing the six clauses on a 3 + 3 pattern, or even four verses dividing the clauses on a 1 + 2 + 1 + 2 pattern, the arrangement in the critical Greek editions and most translations gives three verses and a 1 + 2 + 3 pattern, resulting in a v. 14 that is longer than vv. 12 and 13 taken together! The question of versification is even more complicated for readers of the English-language Bible, since the KJV, RSV, and NEB (following an inferior Greek *Textus Receptus* tradition) place as part of v. 13 the first main clause of Greek v. 14 (14ab), giving three verses with 1 + 3 + 2 pattern, and leaving v. 13 with a mixture of tenses: *graphō-graphō-egrapsa.*

The problems to be discussed also bothered the ancient scribes, who changed the text in order to smooth out difficulties. A few minor Greek witnesses read *paidia* instead of *teknia* in v. 12a, so that the two sets of titles become identical. Some minor Greek MSS. (Codex K), the OL, and the Vulgate read only one tense of the Greek verb throughout the six clauses (*graphō-scribo*), and the Clementine Vulgate omits the fifth clause (14cd) altogether, presumably because it repeats the second clause (13ab). Despite such "improvements" one aspect of the author's intention emerges clearly: He intended two groups of three clauses. The author had a predilection for threes as seen in the three boasts of 1:5–2:2, and the three claims of 2:3–11, and soon to be seen in the three things the world has to offer in 2:16. The real problems of vv. 12–14 are also three. First, why the alternation of tenses between *graphō* and *egrapsa?* Second, how many groups of people are included under *teknia/paidia, pateres,* and *neaniskoi?* Third, how should the *hoti* be understood?

First, the alternation of tenses. In the first three clauses the verb is present in tense (*graphō,* "I write"); in the second three the same verb is aorist (*egrapsa,* "I wrote"). Explanations for this change tend to fall into two large divisions (each with subdivisions), centered on the issue of whether the two tenses refer to different writings or both refer to the same writing.

(A) TWO WRITINGS. The present tense refers to what is being written in I John; the past (aorist) tense to what was written by the author on a previous occasion. One may subdivide this view on whether the previous writing was (1) GJohn—thus Belser, Braune, Ebrard, Holtzmann, Loisy (?), Mangold, Plummer, Rothe, Vrede; (2) II John, presumed to have been written before I John—Hauck (?), Wendt; (3) a lost letter—Schneider, Windisch (?); (4) the putative source which underlies I John—Nauck. These positions offer the simplest explanation of the past tense, and one can point to III John 9 where *egrapsa* clearly refers to a previous writing. However, there are considerable difficulties. Why would the author refer to his previous writing *after* he refers to his present writing? Since the substance of the "I wrote" clauses is virtually the same as the substance of the "I write" clauses, if the author literally means that he wrote these things before, why does he think it necessary to write them again to the same audience? Moreover, each of the proposed candidates for the previous writing is open to objection. The appeal to a lost letter is a desperate hypothesis that is quite unverifiable. Wendt, "Beziehung," has argued eloquently for II John as a candidate, but his effort on pp. 142–44 to find the substance of the "I wrote" clauses in II John is not convincing, as we see when we make the most sympathetic comparison:

a) The addresses to the audience in 2:14 as Children (*paidia*), Fathers, and Young People. None of these terms occurs in II John.
b) The affirmation in 2:14b that what he wrote was: "You have known the Father." The closest one can come to this is II John 9 where the believer is said to possess (have) the Father.
c) The affirmation in 2:14d that what he wrote was: "You have known him who has been from the beginning." The closest is II John 5: "A commandment we have had *from the beginning*," combined with II John 1, "Those who *have come to know* the truth."
d) The affirmation in 2:14f that what he wrote was, "You are strong." Nothing corresponds to this in II John.
e) The affirmation in 2:14g that what he wrote was, "The word of God abides in you." The closest is II John 2: "The truth that abides in us."
f) The affirmation in 2:14h that what he wrote was: "You have conquered the Evil One." Nothing corresponds to this in II John.

Thus there is not a single close parallel in II John to what the author of I John says he wrote.

The hypothesis of GJohn as the previous writing had more currency when it was widely held that the same author wrote both GJohn and I John; today the theory has to face the objections raised in the INTRODUCTION II B2–4. Perhaps the theory could be advanced more subtly if one proposed that in 2:14 the epistolary author is referring to GJohn not because he physically wrote it but because he is interpreting it so closely that he speaks as if he and the evangelist are one (pp. 95–96, 160 above). Using the same features listed above for comparison with II John, we find the following possible background in GJohn:

a) *Teknia* as an address in John 13:33; *paidia* in 21:5.
b) "They know you the one true God" (17:3); "If you knew me, you would know my Father too" (8:19; 14:7; 16:3).

c) "In the beginning was the Word" (1:1); "(I am) what I have been telling you from the beginning" (8:25).

d) "Do not let your hearts be troubled and do not be fearful" (14:27); "I have said this to you to prevent your faith from being shaken" (16:1).

e) "If my words abide in you" (15:7); "You [Jews] do not have God's word abiding in your hearts because you do not believe the one He sent" (5:38).

f) "I have conquered the world" (16:33); "Now will the Prince of this world be driven out" (12:31); "Keep them safe from the Evil One" (17:15).

These similarities are not close enough to give us any certainty that, when the epistolary author wrote *egrapsa*, he was referring to GJohn.

(B) THE SAME WRITING. I John employs *egrapsa* elsewhere (2:21,26; 5:13) when the author is referring to what he has been writing in I John; and most scholars think that is what is involved in 2:14 as well. Once again one may subdivide this approach on the basis of variations in interpreting the verb tenses. (1) The past tense (*egrapsa*) refers to the part of I John already written (1:1–2:11), while the present tense (*graphō*) refers to what he is now writing—thus Brooke, Charue, de Wette, Law, Wilder. (Sometimes the change of tense is made more intelligible by the guess that the author was interrupted between 2:13 and 2:14, so that time had elapsed when he picked up his pen in 2:14.) To support this theory it is argued that some of what the author says he wrote (2:14) can be found in 1:1–2:11. Using again the features listed above for comparison with II John, we find:

a) *Teknia* in 2:1.

b) The claim "I know Him" in 2:4.

c) "What was from the beginning" in 1:1.

d) Nothing corresponds to this in 1:1–2:11.

e) "Whoever keeps His word" (2:5).

f) Nothing corresponds to this in 1:1–2:11.

De la Potterie ("La connaissance" 80–81) has a special form of this theory, for he thinks that in 2:14 the author refers to statements just made in 2:12–13. Even then, one cannot find (d), (e), and (f) in 2:12–13. Thus there is little to recommend this approach where *egrapsa* refers to the part of I John already written.

(2) The past tense (*egrapsa*) refers to the whole of I John even as does the present tense. We are dealing with a stylistic variant where the aorist of 2:14 is slightly more emphatic than the present of 2:12–13, chiefly because the author is repeating himself—whence my "*Yes, I have been writing.*" (Other translators use: "What I have just written, *I repeat.*") Sometimes the idea of an epistolary aorist is invoked here (BDF 334; MGNTG 3, 73), namely, that while from the viewpoint of the author the present tense is appropriate ("I am writing"), from the anticipated viewpoint of those who will later have the written work read to them the aorist is appropriate ("I have written"). For in-

stance, Paul uses the present tense in I Cor 14:37, "What I am writing is a command of the Lord," but the aorist in I Cor 9:15, "I have not written these things so that they should be done for me." Other instances where *egrapsa* is an epistolary aorist referring to the work that is being written include Gal 6:11; Rom 15:15; Philem 19,21 (although when it occurs at the end of a letter, it may simply be a reference to the work "I have just finished writing"). For secular examples, see n. 13 on line 9 of Letter 14 in LFAE 187–89, and lines 28–29 of Letters 15–16 in LFAE 194–95. A persuasive argument for the theory that in I John 2:12–14 *graphō* and *egrapsa* are variants with no significant difference of meaning is that hitherto the author has always used *graphein* in the present tense (1:4; 2:1,7,8) and henceforth he will always use it in the aorist tense (2:21,26; 5:13) with no apparent difference! The following scholars accept the stylistic variant approach for 2:12–14: Balz, Bultmann, Chaine, de Ambroggi, Gaugler, Houlden, Michl, Noack, Schnackenburg, Spicq, Stott, THLJ, Westcott, and Williams. It seems to me the most plausible theory. (In this NOTE I have mentioned the most important proposals; there are others, e.g., that 2:12–13 and 2:14 represent two different drafts of the same statement, which for some reason were included side by side—Bruce thinks that 2:12–13ab represents the earlier draft, while O'Neill opts for 2:14 as earlier.) I would add only that the use of the aorist fits in well with the author's style where in 1:1–5 he joins himself to a Johannine School of tradition-bearers and can say, "We have heard, we have seen, etc." The idea that what he writes in I John is something that he has been writing reinforces his claim that "This is the gospel that you heard from the beginning" (3:11).

Second, the different groups of people. In the six main clauses of 2:12–14 the author uses the following sequence in addressing his audience:

2:12a *teknia* ("Little Children")	2:14a *paidia* ("Children")
2:13a *pateres* ("Fathers")	2:14c *pateres*
2:13c *neaniskoi* ("Young" [masc.])	2:14e *neaniskoi*

The verbal forms *graphō* and *egrapsa* divide the six clauses into two groups of three; and so almost all recognize that, even though four different words of address are involved, *teknia* and *paidia* (both meaning "children") are alternative and complementary ways of referring to the same group, and so we should speak of *three* terms of address. Granted that, how many groups of people were meant to be covered by the three terms of address: three, one, or two?

(A) THREE GROUPS (differing in physical age or spiritual maturity). Obviously the simplest interpretation, this has been held by older interpreters like Clement of Alexandria, Origen, Oecumenius, and by some modern exegetes like Bruce, Gaugler, and Stott. Thus understood, the titles Children, Young People, and Fathers could refer to neophytes, to those making progress, and to the mature—a progression covering either stages of structural seniority after baptism or stages of spiritual development. (Theoretically these could be the Johannine titles for the three church offices that Ignatius of Antioch designates deacons, presbyters, and bishop; but there is no clear evidence in the NT that such a three-stage ministry was already a fact.) However, the progression theory ill befits the actual order of titles in I John which is neither ascending or descending.

(B) ONE GROUP (designated by three different names). This was the view of Augustine (*In Epistolam* 2.4–8; SC 75, 162–66): all Christians are "Children" because they are born anew and sinless through baptism; all Christians are "Fathers" because they believe in Christ who was from the beginning; and all Christians are "Young" because they are strong and brave in Christ over against the devil. One could then explain the Johannine order of titles as determined by the fact of baptism, by the faith expressed at baptism, and by the way in which the baptized live. Among modern scholars a form of this theory is held by Dodd, de la Potterie, and Marshall. For instance, Dodd, *Epistles* 38, contends, "The threefold arrangement is probably not much more than a rhetorical figure. All the privileges mentioned belong to all Christians, but emphasis and variety of expression are secured by distributing them into groups." By way of argument for this position, one may point to the *Corpus Hermeticum* 11.20 and 13.11, which indicates that the mystic can experience different stages of existence at once. Within I John, if one regards the alternation between *graphō* and *egrapsa* as merely stylistic, one should be open to seeing simply a stylistic distinction among the three forms of address. Dodd argues that virtually the same thing is said to the "Children" in 14ab ("You have known the Father") as is said to the "Fathers" in 14cd ("You have known him who has been from the beginning"). However, it should be noted that the second statement probably refers to Christ rather than to the Father, so the argument is dubious. De la Potterie ("La connaissance" 89) argues for the theory of stylistic variation on the basis of the New Covenant text in Jer 31:34, "They shall *all* know me from the least to the greatest," and Acts 2:17, "I will pour out my spirit upon *all* flesh . . . and your young men [*neōteroi*] shall see visions and your old men shall dream dreams." However, one may debate the import of such texts: Are not the least/greatest and the young/old two groups within the "all"? This leads us to a final interpretation.

(C) TWO GROUPS AS PART OF THE WHOLE. The first address in each group of three, "Children" (*teknia, paidia*), may refer to the whole Johannine Community that is in *koinōnia* with the author, while the second and third addresses, "Fathers" and "Young People," refer to distinct subdivisions of the Community. This is the most popular view among modern scholars: Balz, Belser, F.-M. Braun, Brooke, Büchsel, Bultmann, Calmes, Chaine, Charue, de Ambroggi, Hauck, Houlden, Loisy, Malatesta, Michl, Plummer, Schnackenburg, Schneider, Spicq, THLJ, Vrede, B. Weiss, Westcott, Williams. It makes the best sense of the order of the titles: first, a general address to all as the author's children; and then seniority within the subdivisions with the "Fathers" being addressed before the "Young People." This interpretation finds backing in Johannine usage. *Teknia* and *paidia* as "(Little) Children" are employed by Jesus in GJohn to address his disciples, and by the author elsewhere in I John to address his whole audience. (Indeed, it is almost impossible that suddenly here, and here alone, *teknia* and *paidia* could refer only to one group constituting one-third of the audience.) Some scholars would see a difference of nuance between the two terms, e.g., B. Weiss, *Briefe* 54–56, thinks that *teknia* does not connote age while *paidia* does; Westcott and Stott think that *teknia* expresses the common nature shared by the audience as God's children, while *paidia* portrays the audience as under the author's discipline. More probably there is no distinction, and both terms place all the audience in a Christian family relationship to the author because he is a member of the Johannine School of tradition-bearers.

As for the other two titles, *pateres* and *neaniskoi* are appropriate for addressing subdivisions, for nowhere in the NT is either term used to address the whole community. That the people of God can be divided into two groups on the basis of dignity and/or age is not strange. The Greek of Gen 19:11 and of I Sam 5:9 confirms that the New Covenant text of Jer 31(38):34 envisions two groups when it divides the "all" into the "least" (*mikroi*) and the "greatest" (*megaloi*). In passages like Exod 10:9; Josh 6:21; Isa 20:4; and Ezek 9:6 the constituents of the whole people are described as young (*neaniskoi*) and old (*presbyteroi, presbytai*). In the community of the New Covenant at Qumran there is a distinction of this sort that goes beyond dignity and age and extends to the less instructed and the more instructed (see Dupont, "Les simples"). For instance, 1QpHab 12:4–5 distinguishes between the "simple of Judah" who do the Law and the fully initiated who are in the council of the community. Rules are given in 1QS 6:13–24 and CD 13:11–13 for stages of advancement from partial adherence to full adherence, and 1QSa 1:6–19 shows a ranking based on age. Jesus is portrayed as turning the established order upside down since through him God's revelation has been given to the *nēpioi* rather than to the wise (Matt 11:25; Luke 10:21)—the term *nēpios*, "babe," refers to both innocence and youth. Nevertheless, as Grundmann, "Die *nēpioi*," has shown, early preaching assumed that the *nēpioi* within the Christian community were underage spiritually, beginning to learn but still open to perversion by false teaching, and thus distinct from the mature (*teleioi*). This distinction arose from an imagery depicting the recently baptized as newborn babies (I Pet 2:2) and from the natural assumption that over the years there would be growth from that stage. In I Cor 3:1 Paul writes as chastisement to those who should have been mature: "I could not address you, brothers, as spiritual men but as men of the flesh, as babes [*nēpioi*] in Christ."

The OT terminology dividing people into young (*neaniskoi*) and old (*presbyteroi*) was taken over by Christians both in a broad sense to include age groups (Acts 2:17) and then in a stratified sense to designate roles in the community. It is well known that in some works of the NT *presbyteros* serves as a designation for senior church officers, for all practical purposes equivalent with *episkopos*. It is less well known that *neōteros* (*neaniskos*) serves as a designation for junior church officers, equivalent to *diakonos*. (See R. E. Brown, TS 41 [1980] 333, in dependence upon Elliott, "Ministry.") Just as the *episkopoi* eventually became separate from and superior to the *presbyteroi* (Ignatius' writings), so the *diakonoi* seemingly became separate from and superior to the *neōteroi* (who in Polycarp, *Philip.* 5:3, are urged to be subject to the presbyters and deacons).

I have gone into this detail to show that it is perfectly plausible that there were two groups in the Johannine Community called *pateres*, "Fathers," and *neaniskoi*, "Young People." True, one might have expected *presbyteroi* and *neōteroi*. But Acts 5:6,10 shows that *neōteroi* and *neaniskoi* were interchangeable; and Johannine usage may have preferred to keep *presbyteroi* as a designation for members of the Johannine School who were disciples of the Beloved Disciple (Note below on II John 1). In Judg 17:10; 18:19; and II Kings 2:12; 13:14 we see the use of "Father" as a reverential designation respectively for priest and prophet. *Midrash Sifre* 34 (74a) on Deut 6:7 shows the second-century use of the title "Father" for rabbis: "If the pupils are called 'sons,' so will the teachers be called 'fathers.'" Some Christian communities rejected such reverential titles, e.g., Matt 23:8–9 rejects both "Rabbi" and "Father." Other communities gave the titles new nuances, e.g., I Cor 4:15 makes a distinction between those who are "pedagogues" to Christians and those who are preachers of the Gospel, with the latter called "Fathers" (so that Paul has been a "Father" to the Christians at Corinth). It is impossible to determine the exact connotation that the title "Fathers" had for the Johannine Community. Clearly it refers to more than heads of families (the meaning in the *Haustafel* or list of household offices in Eph 6:4). The fact that in both 2:13ab and 14cd the "Fathers" are said to "have known him who is from the beginning" gives the impression that they have been Christians a long time, and in that sense are both senior to and more mature than the *neaniskoi*. However, one would have to characterize as a pure guess the tendency of Houlden, *Epistles* 70–71, to regard the *pateres* and *neaniskoi* as Johannine church officials comparable to the *presbyteroi/episkopoi* and the *neōteroi/diakonoi* of the churches of the Pauline Pastorals. I disagree with his further surmise that since I John has no comparable feminine forms of address, the Johannine Community accorded women no prominence, unlike the Pauline churches where they played an important part! The grammatical argument is weak because frequently in NT Greek a plural masculine noun covers subjects of both genders (MGNTG 3, 22); and from an analysis of GJohn I would conclude that women had a role of extraordinary importance in the Johannine tradition, outranking their role in the Pauline tradition (see Brown, *Community* 183–98).

Third, the interpretation of hoti. In all six main clauses of 2:12–14 the verb form (*graphō/egrapsa*) is followed by a *hoti* introducing a subordinate clause. This conjunction may be translated causatively, "because, since," or declaratively, "that." (Hering, "Aramaïsmes" 116–19, would introduce a further complication by suggesting that *hoti* is a literal translation of the Aramaic *dᵉ* which means both "that" and "who," and so originally this may have been a relative clause modifying the "Children," the "Fathers," and the "Young People.") The following scholars support a causal translation: Belser, Brooke, Bultmann, Charue, de Ambroggi, Dodd, Gaugler, Holtzmann, Marshall, Plummer, Schneider, Spicq, B. Weiss, Westcott, and Windisch. It appears in the Vulgate (*quoniam;* Augustine has *quia*), RSV, and TEV. Despite the fact that Westcott, *Epistles* 58, states vigorously, "There can be no doubt that the particle is causal and not declarative," the following scholars support the declarative: Balz, Bengel, Boismard, Bonsirven, Lindeskog, Malatesta, Noack, Rivera,

Rothe, Schnackenburg, and THLJ. The issue cannot be settled on grammatical grounds alone. *Graphō* is followed by *hoti* in only one other instance in the Epistles (I John 2:21) and that instance is as obscure as 2:12–14. Otherwise, however, *graphō* is followed by a direct object (noun or pronoun), a fact favoring a declarative meaning for *hoti*. But the proponents of the causal meaning can answer that in 2:12–14 *graphō/egrapsa* governs the Epistle as an implicit direct object ("I write/wrote this 'Epistle' to you"), so that *hoti* is free to mean "since."

Marshall, *Epistles* 136, contends that the choice does not make much difference in meaning; yet it does affect the relationship of this section to what precedes and what follows. The author has now shifted from refuting objectionable claims and boasts inspired or phrased by his adversaries, and he is addressing his "Children" affectionately. What meaning does *hoti* causative give? He would be writing because they have had their sins forgiven, because they know the Father and Jesus, and because they are strong. This would imply a confidence that they are firmly on his side, even though subtly he would be making it embarrassing for them to be otherwise. One is then surprised by the warning that follows in 2:15–17—if the author writes to the "Young People" in 2:14e–h because they are strong and have conquered the Evil One, why does he need to warn them, "Have no love for the world" (2:15)? On the other hand, if *hoti* is declarative, the author would be writing because he felt a need to tell his "Children" that their sins are forgiven, that they know the Father and Jesus, and that they are strong. This would imply a demoralized audience unsure of themselves and their status. This picture corresponds with the "we" boasts of 1:6,8,10 where the author seemed afraid that his own adherents might mouth secessionist theology and where his antitheses (1:7,9; 2:1–2) were intended to strengthen them on such subjects as the forgiveness of sins and the role of Jesus Christ, and (2:3) the knowledge of God. The declarative sense of *hoti* also explains what follows in 2:15–17: Because he has felt the need to reassure them, it is no contradiction to warn them.

The logic, then, of the total sequence of thought makes me agree with the strong appeal for the declarative translation made by Noack, "On I John." He is right that if 2:12 stood by itself, almost everyone would instinctively translate *hoti* as "that." (Indeed, some early translations did that, even though they shifted to "because" in the other clauses.) Nevertheless, Marshall, *Epistles* 136–37, has a point when he observes that Greek readers might not have made a sharp distinction between the two senses of *hoti* that grammarians have detected. For that reason, I have chosen not to translate the *hoti* but to use a colon, which orients the reader toward a declarative meaning, but does not exclude a causal undertone.

Having now treated the three general problems basic to the overall interpretation of 2:12–14, let me turn to some individual points in 2:12–17.

2:12a. *I write.* As in 2:1a (see NOTE there) the author now prefers the first person singular to the "we are writing" in 1:4a.

12b. *your sins have been forgiven.* This is the same perfect passive form of *aphienai* which is found in the best MSS. of John 20:23 ("If you forgive men's sins, *their sins are forgiven"*) and which has been the subject of much sacramental discussion (ABJ 29A, 1023–24). There it was part of a conditional sentence and the present tense was an appropriate translation: when you forgive men's sins, at that moment God forgives those sins and they remain forgiven. The Vulgate uses a present tense here in I John, and that would not be foreign to the idea of ongoing forgiveness through Christ mentioned in 2:1–2. Nevertheless, since the verbs in the other clauses governed by *graphō* in 2:13 are perfect in tense ("have known," "have conquered"), the context suggests that in 2:12 the author is thinking primarily of a past forgiveness that remains effective (Westcott, Plummer). De la Potterie ("La connaissance" 91) speaks of the eschatological state of the Christian in which forgiveness is a permanent reality.

because of Christ's name. Literally, "the name of him," raising once more the question whether "him" is God or Christ. The last mentioned "him" (2:8b) was surely Christ; but even without that syntactical assistance, BDF 282³ is correct in describing this as a set phrase where the "his" is easily understood from common Christian usage. "Because of my name" is associated with Jesus in John 15:21 and widely elsewhere (Matt 10:22; 24:9; Mark 13:13; Luke 21:17; Rev 2:3), even as would be the phrase "because of his name" (see Acts 4:30; I Cor 1:10). The preposition is *dia* with the accusative, which normally supplies the grounds for the sake of which something is accomplished, while *dia* with the genitive means "through." Thus the idea is not so much that sins are forgiven through or by means of Jesus' name, but are forgiven by God because of Jesus' name.

This is the first epistolary instance of *to onoma* which will occur thrice more with special theological nuance: 3:23 and 5:13 speak of believing in "the name of the Son," and III John 7 speaks of missionaries setting out "for the sake of the name." GJohn refers 8 times to the *name of God:* in that name Jesus has come (5:43; 12:13) and performs works (10:25); he reveals it to his followers (17:6,26), so that they may be kept safe by it (17:11,12)—thus does God glorify His name (12:28). GJohn makes reference 12 times to the *name of Jesus* (the Son) in which people believe (1:12; 2:23; 3:18), make and receive requests (14:13,14; 15:16; 16:23,24,26) and are given life (20:31) as well as the Paraclete/Spirit. Leaving aside the word *onoma,* Westcott, *Epistles* 136–38, has a list of all the titles or names of Jesus that are confessed in the Epistles (chiefly "Christ" or "Son" in different combinations). We are dealing here with a Semitic outlook where "name" stands for the very identity of the person and to know a person's name gives the knower access to the power of the person (whence the urgency of Moses' knowing God's name in Exod 3:13–14). Ezekiel 20:8–9 portrays God as showing forgiveness to His people because of His name, i.e., lest His punishing them would cause the Gentiles to despise His name and His power. The fact that Jesus comes bearing God's name enables him to act with God's power to the point where he can say, "The Father and I are one" (John 10:30). (In my view a good case can be made for the thesis that John means specifically the divine name "I AM"; see ABJ 29, 537; 29A, 754–56.)

This power and name are passed on to those who believe in Jesus' name as God's Son, and they become God's children. The idea of being forgiven because of Christ's name (which is God's name), along with the address "Children," may indicate a baptismal background for I John 2:12. The idiom of being baptized in the name of Jesus Christ (Acts 2:38; 8:16; see I Cor 1:13,15) probably involved a confession by the one baptized of Jesus as Messiah (Christ), Son of God, or Son of Man. In particular, "Lord" was the name bestowed upon Jesus that was above every other name (Philip 2:9–10). In turn, the one baptized came to be known by Jesus Christ's name, i.e., as Christian. Acts 3:6,16; 4:30 show Peter healing in the name of Jesus Christ, "for there is no other name under heaven given among men by which we must be saved" (Acts 4:12). Ignatius, *Magn.* 10:1, states, "Whoever is called by any name other than this is not of God."

13b. *you have known.* This is the same perfect tense of *ginōskein* used in the author's statement in 2:3a ("we know Him"; see NOTE there) and in the boast of the opponents in 2:4a ("I know Him") made false by their failure to keep God's commandments. As with the verb "forgiven" in 2:12b, this could be translated by a present tense; but the appearance of "from the beginning" in the predicate suggests that the Greek perfect should be rendered here by a past tense that is still true in the present. The author does not mean that the "Fathers" whom he is addressing were eyewitnesses of Jesus' ministry, but clearly he is appealing to a long-standing knowledge. Schnackenburg, *Johannesbriefe* 124, thinks of a knowing made perfect by being lived out in the Community as distinct from an initial moment of knowledge. This insight might be rendered, "You have come to know."

him who has been from the beginning. One is reminded of "What was from the beginning" in 1:1a, which employed the neuter and the imperfect tense, but here there is no copulative verb. The literal Greek "the one [masc.] from the beginning" allows the reader to supply the verb "has been," "is," or "was." The reference both in 1:1a and here is probably to Christ (with the neuter in 1:1a as more comprehensive, including his career). Stott, *Epistles* 97, is almost alone in arguing for a reference here to God, which is not an inconceivable position granted that the previous object of "knowing" in 2:3a,4a was God. A weak argument for that position is that 2:14e will soon state, "You have known the *Father*." That I John might describe knowledge of the Father and of the Son sequentially is suggested by John 17:3, ". . . that they know you the one true God, and Jesus Christ, the one whom you sent." Granted that the reference here is to Christ, quite surprising is the assurance of Marshall, *Epistles* 139, that the reference must be "to the beginning of time and not to the beginning of the Christian era or the readers' Christian experience." I find quite convincing the insistence of de la Potterie, "Commencement" 397, that "from the beginning" here means what it means generally in the Epistles, i.e., the beginning of Jesus' self-revelation to his disciples in the ministry. The author is reassuring his audience about their knowledge of the importance of Jesus' earthly life—that is what he is writing and has been writing to them (see 2:14cd). The absence of the copula gives the clause this tone: "You have known him inasmuch as he is from the beginning." The emphasis is not on enduring existence from before creation, but on a quality of Jesus as manifested during the ministry.

13d. *you have conquered*. This is the perfect tense of *nikan*, "to conquer," a verb that occurs only once in GJohn but 6 times in I John (almost one-quarter of the NT usage). Also, I John 5:4 offers the only NT instance of the noun *nikē*, "victory." These passages speak of Jesus or of the Christian conquering the world (John 16:33; I John 5:4–5), the Evil One (I John 2:13,14), and the secessionist Antichrists (I John 4:4). Since the Evil One is the Prince of this world whose language the Antichrists speak (4:5), the Johannine writers are consistent about the Satanic nature of the object to be conquered. This warlike language is at home in a dualism where the forces of darkness seek to overcome or to kill the forces of light. Similarly Luke 11:22 uses "conquer" (the one Synoptic instance) for the stronger one (Jesus) overcoming the strong (Beelzebul), while Rom 12:21 exhorts, "Do not be conquered by evil, but conquer evil by good." It is no accident that there are 17 instances of "conquer" in Revelation, which concentrates on the final battle between Christ and Satan, and where Christians are "those who conquer."

As with "forgiven" and "known" in 12b, and 13b, the perfect tense here refers to the past with an enduring effect, for the Johannine "Young People" are sharing in the victory that Jesus won in his life and death: "I have conquered the world" (John 16:33). The Johannine Community could have addressed to Christ the praise addressed to God in the Qumran *Scroll of the War between the Sons of Light and the Sons of Darkness* (1QM 11:4–5): "The battle is yours and the power comes from you, not from us. Our strength and the power of our hands accomplish no mighty deeds except by your power and the might of your valor."

the Evil One. Although the Geneva Bible understood this masc. adjectival substantive *ponēros* as "the wicked [man?]" (while Codex Sinaiticus read a neuter "evil"), clearly this is I John's first reference to the devil. Coetzee, "Christ" 104, gives a survey of the Johannine terminology for the diabolic. In GJohn the evangelist uses "Satan" once (13:27—only Johannine usage), while the Johannine Jesus speaks 3 times of "the Prince of this world" (12:31; 14:30; 16:11); and 6 times the Jewish charge that Jesus has a "demon" (*daimonion*) is suggested or debated. None of these terms appears in the Epistles. *Diabolos*, "devil," which occurs 3 times in GJohn (6:70; 8:44; 13:2), appears 4 times in I John (3:8,10); and *ho Ponēros*, "the Evil One," used in John 17:15, appears 5 times in I John (2:13,14; 3:12; 5:18,19). The wicked "Spirit of Deceit" that does not belong to God is the subject of I John 4:3,6. The idea of a devil or groups of devils is common in post-exilic Judaism, and in part is traceable to the OT figure at the heavenly court ("the Satan") who seeks out evil in the world. However, there is no clear pre-Christian evidence of the title "the Evil One" for the devil. It is not frequent in rabbinic literature (Spicq, "La place" 525), but it occurs in the Mandaean writings and in the *Odes of Solomon* (14:5).

The Johannine writers do not speak of demonic possession but concentrate on a cosmic power of evil whose human minions resist God's plan revealed in Jesus (John 6:70; 8:44; 13:2,27) since the goal of that revelation was to destroy the devil's works (I John 3:8). In Jesus' hour of return to the Father, the Prince of this world was driven out (John 12:31) and condemned (16:11). Nevertheless, the whole world still lies in the grasp of the Evil One (I John 5:19), and the children of the devil commit sin and even murder (I John 3:8–10,12). The secessionists belong to this nefarious group; but since the Johannine Christians in *koinōnia* with the author belong to God, he can say to them: "You have conquered these people, for he who is in you is greater than he who is in the world" (4:4). And again in 5:18: "The one begotten by God is protected, and so the Evil One cannot touch him." This view is not distant from that found in the Dead Sea Scrolls: "God has appointed for human beings two spirits in which to walk until the time of His visitation, the spirits of truth and iniquity. . . . All the sons of righteousness are under the rule of the prince of light, but all the sons of iniquity are under the rule of the angel of darkness" (1QS 3:17–21). "For God has established the spirits in equal measure until the final age and has set everlasting strife between their divisions" (4:16–17). The other NT references to "the Evil One" agree that his activity continues and is dangerous for the Christian. Matthew 13:19 pictures the Evil One snatching away the good seed of the word before it takes root, while 13:38–39 shows the devil sowing weeds that are "the sons of the Evil One." The Lord's Prayer in Matt 6:13 teaches Christians to pray, "Deliver us from the Evil One." In Eph 6:16 the Pauline writer urges his readers, "Take the shield of faith with which you can quench all the flaming darts of the Evil One," while in II Thess 3:3 he assures them, "The Lord is faithful: he will strengthen you and guard you from the Evil One."

14a. *Children.* This is the first epistolary use of *paidion,* diminutive of *pais* and a synonym of *teknion,* "little child," discussed in the NOTE on 2:1a.

14b. *the Father.* See the NOTE on 1:2e for the Johannine predilection for "Father" as a title for God.

14d. *him who has been from the beginning.* Codex Vaticanus reads a neuter, "that which." In 2:12–14, only in vv. 13b and 14d is a clause in the first group of three exactly the same as a clause in the second group, and so a scribe may have decided to create a contrast by changing 14d in the direction of 1:1a, "*What* was from the beginning."

14f. *you are strong.* This address to the "Young People" contains the only Johannine use of *ischyros* (9 times in Revelation). Strength and youth obviously go together: "Judas Maccabeus has been strong in might from his youth" (I Macc 2:66). Yet the biblical concept of strength is not purely physical: "Even youth shall faint and be weary . . . but they who wait for the Lord shall renew their strength" (Isa 40:30–31). Hebrews 6:18 speaks of a "*strong* encouragement [*paraklēsis*]" given to Christians"; also Eph 6:10: "Be powerful in the Lord and in the force of His strength."

14g. *for the word of God abides in you.* Literally, "and"; the three clauses in 14fgh are coordinate; yet they are interrelated in the sense that 14g and 14h explain the strength of the Young People (14f). This is an example of the (B) classification of *menein en* usage discussed in the NOTE on 2:6a; and in the GJohn instances cited there the word (*logos*) of God was said not to abide in "the Jews" (5:38), while the words (*rēma*) of Jesus were said to abide in his followers (15:7). In the only similar use of the closely parallel *einai en* (I John 1:10) it was said that God's word (*logos*) was not in those who made a secessionist-inspired boast. The "word" here is not the personified *Logos* of the GJohn Prologue but "the word of life" or divine message revealed by and in Jesus (I John 1:1) or, even more precisely, the word (or commandment) of loving one's brother, stressed in 2:5–11 (see COMMENT). The connection of the "Young" to commandments was already made in the OT: "How can a young man [*neōteros*] keep his way pure? By guarding it according to Your words [*logos*]" (Ps 119:9).

15a. *Have no love for the world.* Literally, "Do not love"; the meaning here of "to love" (*agapan*) and of "world" (*kosmos*) will be discussed in the COMMENT, but see the NOTES on 2:5b and 2:2c respectively.

15b. *nor for the things that are in the world.* The verb *einai* is not expressed but understood, as indicated in the parallel line in 15d: "No love for the Father *is* in him." The implicit use of *einai en* in 15b exemplifies a species of classification (C) discussed in the NOTE on 1:5e where various persons and realities are to be or not to be in the world, according to their place in the Johannine dualistic outlook.

15d. *there is in him no love of the Father.* Of the 8 Johannine instances of the genitival phrase describing the love of the deity, this is the only one that speaks of Him as "Father," whence the tendency of scribes (Alexandrinus, Ephraemi Rescriptus) to substitute "God." In the NOTE on 2:5b I discussed 5 different ways of understanding "love of God/Father." Of those, the objective genitive, "love for the Father," is proposed here by Barrosse (?), Brooke, Chaine, Coppens, Loisy, Marshall, and Schnackenburg. It has in its favor the fact that the contrast, "Have no love for the world," is clearly objective. The subjective genitive, "love from the Father," is favored by Bonsirven, Houlden, Malatesta, Schlier, and Wengst. It has in its favor that this class (B) of *einai en* expressions (NOTE on 1:5e) usually involves a divine reality which is said not to be in an adversary. That there are good arguments on both sides of the issue is reflected by the number of scholars who believe with various nuances that both types of love are involved: Balz, Bultmann, de Ambroggi, Gaugler (?), THLJ, and Westcott. Balz, *Johannesbriefe* 174, phrases it well: "Love for the Father is only a reflection of the love which comes from the Father."

16a. *all that is in the world.* As in v. 15b the verb *einai*, "to be," is not expressed but understood: the Latin Fathers in citing the text supply a copula even as I have done. While 15b spoke in the plural of "the things (that are) in the world," the singular here tends to unify the three factors that follow. (Nevertheless, to give emphasis to the distinction between sing. and pl. is not true to Johannine style where nouns like "commandment" and "word" can be used interchangeably in either number.) After characterizing the following three factors as *in* the world, the author will speak of them in 16f as *of* the world. He does not state that these three factors are all that is in the world; they are examples of what is in the world.

16bcd. Before I treat the factors separately, let me discuss them together, listing the Greek phrases with a literal translation:

hē epithymia tēs sarkos	the desire of the flesh
hē epithymia tōn ophthalmōn	the desire of the eyes
hē alazoneia tou biou	the pride of life

Like most I John groupings, it lacks perfect balance: One would have expected three different governing nouns, or the same noun used thrice, but why two the same and one different? Most scholars understand the first two genitives to be subjective (the flesh and the eyes initiate the desire) and the third to be objective (the life/livelihood is the object of the pride). While I shall challenge that analysis below, such difficulties have led some scholars to detect a subordination among the three phrases. For Houlden, the first is the general category under which the second and third are species; for Findlay, the first and second go together describing the evil that arises from desire, while the third concerns the evil that arises from possession. Also, in relation to the opening clause in 16a ("all that is in the world"), does the author mean that the two desires and the pride (and therefore, the *actions*) are in the world? Or is he somewhat carelessly indicating that the flesh, the eyes, and the life (the *subjects*) are in the world? More often scholars assume that the unmentioned *objects* of the two desires and the mentioned object of the pride are in the world, so that one may translate freely: "What the flesh desires, what eyes desire, the life that one is proud of—all that is in the world." Perhaps we should not press the author's grammar too exactly, for in his generalization he may have allowed logic to yield to dramatic effect.

The tendency to list *three* sources or species of evil is widespread and may exemplify the rule of three characters exemplified in storytelling (e.g., a Scotsman, an Irishman, and an Englishman in a joke). Rather romantically, scholars have counterposed the three Johannine components of love of the world with the three Synoptic factors in loving God (Matt 22:37: "with all your heart, with all your soul, with all your mind"; but see the fourth, "with all your strength," in Mark 12:30; Luke 10:27). Others, including Augustine, have related the Johannine triad to the three temptations of Jesus in Matt 4:3–11; Luke 4:3–13: the temptation to turn stones to bread being related to "the desire of the flesh"; the showing of all the kingdoms of the world, to "the desire of the eyes"; and the throwing of oneself from the pinnacle of the Temple, to "the pride of life" (note the Lucan order of the temptations). Of course, the three temptations are not narrated in GJohn (but see ABJ 29, 308), and the points selected for this comparison are scarcely the main thrust of the Matthean/Lucan accounts. Philo, *On the Decalogue* 28 ≉153, traces all wars to desire, "the desire for money, or glory, or pleasure," a triad that appears also in Lucian (*Hermotimus* 7.22). *Jubilees* 7:20–24 traces the flood to "three things": fornication, uncleanness, and all iniquity. CD 4:15–18 describes "the three nets of Belial" by which he catches Israel since he gives them the appearance of righteousness: impurity, wealth, and the profanation of the sanctuary. *Pirqe Aboth* 4.21 states: "Envy, desire, and ambition bring man out of the world"; and about the same time Justin (*Dialogue* 82.4) mentions the triad: "love of money, love of glory, love of pleasure." This appears in the Middle Ages as the triad "pleasure, avarice, and pride"; and Thomas Aquinas (*Summa Theologica* I–IIae, q. 108, a.3–4) uses I John 2:16 to reduce worldly goods to three (honors, riches, and pleasures) and to suggest that the three religious vows of obedience, poverty, and chastity were designed to offset them. A triad better known in modern times is "the world, the flesh, and the devil." The possibility of turning the Johannine passage into a clever triad is caught by the translation: "sensuality, superficiality, and showmanship." But when one begins to study in detail the worldly factors mentioned by I John 2:16, one realizes that such comparisons and interpretations are too facile.

16b. *human nature full of desire.* In the phrase *hē epithymia tēs sarkos,* "the desire of the flesh," the genitive is subjective (desire arising from the flesh; Moule, IBNTG 40) or at least qualitative (the kind of desire associated with the flesh; MGNTG 3, 213[?]). This can be determined not only from the parallelism supplied by the next line ("the desire of the eyes") where the genitive cannot be objective, but also from other NT usage, e.g., "the desires of their hearts" (Rom 1:24), "the desire of the soul" (Rev 18:14). It is difficult to decide what each noun would have meant for the Johannine author. Theoretically *epithymia,* "desire, wish," is a neutral word that can be directed toward bad things (more frequently in the NT) or good things (Philip 1:23, "My desire is . . . to be with Christ"; also Luke 22:15; I Thess 2:17). The only other Johannine use outside the threefold occurrence here is John 8:44: "The devil is the father you belong to, and you willingly carry out your father's desires." The classical Greek usage is discussed by Lazure, "La convoitise," and Schweizer, "Komponente": when desires are criticized, it is because they are opposed to control by reason. However, in LXX Greek, "desires" tend to be opposed to the will of God expressed in the Law. Two of the Ten Commandments are warnings against covetousness, which is expressed in the LXX by the verb *epithymein:* "You shall not desire your neighbor's wife; you shall not desire your neighbor's house" (Exod 20:17; Deut 5:21). In post-exilic Judaism there appears the concept of two inclinations in human beings, one good, the other bad. It is tempting to equate this concept of *yeṣer,* "inclination, tendency," with *epithymia,* although the Greek Sirach, which uses *epithymia* frequently, does not use it in 15:14: "God created man in the beginning and left him in the power of his own inclination [Hebrew: *yeṣer*]." For Philo, *Allegorical Interpretation* 3:47–51 ※※139–49, *epithymia* is one of the four passions (Stoic thought) and must be suppressed, for it is the root of evil in human beings.

The second noun, *sarx,* "flesh," in classical Greek describes the most physical aspect of human corporality, i.e., what is involved in eating, drinking, and sex. For Platonic writers "flesh" can serve as a substitute for "body" when one is emphasizing the imprisonment of the soul. As an equivalent for the Platonic "desires according to the flesh" (*epithymiai kata sarka*) Epicurean philosophers would tend to speak of "*pleasures* according to the flesh"; and so in the Hellenistic world the desires of the flesh were increasingly considered to be crudely carnal and irreconcilable with piety. In Hebrew thought "flesh" had a wider domain, covering the whole man with all his weaknesses—not primarily the sensual or the carnal, but the human, as distinguished from the "spirit," which was the element associated with God. This still appears in the NT where "flesh and blood" are used to describe a human source of knowledge, as distinct from divine revelation (Matt 16:17; Gal 1:16). Much attention has been devoted by scholars to the special connotation of "flesh" in the Dead Sea Scrolls (see Huppenbauer, Kuhn, Murphy, Pryke in the *Sectional Bibliography*). While sometimes at Qumran "flesh" has the same connotation as in the OT, at other times it is associated closely with sin, evil, and deception. One group of humanity constitutes "wicked flesh" opposed by God (1QS 11:9; 1QM 4:3); but the Qumran psalmist cries out, "If I stumble because of the wickedness of my flesh, my justification will be the justice of God which endures forever" (1QS 11:12). Upon this strain of Jewish thought Paul tends to concentrate when he describes flesh as a power that moves toward sin and struggles against the Spirit (Rom 7:5), so that one puts off the body of the flesh in the circumcision of Christ (Col 2:11). In Gal 5:13 Paul contrasts using freedom as "an opportunity for the flesh" and "through love being servants of one another."

The expression we encounter in I John 2:16b, "desire of the flesh," which does not occur as such in the OT or at Qumran, appears several times in Paul's writings. In Rom 13:14, after having spoken of revels, drunkenness, debauchery, and jealousy, Paul says, "Put on the Lord Jesus Christ, and do not make provision for the desires of the flesh." In Gal 5:16–17 he says, "Walk in the Spirit and do not fulfill the desire of the flesh, for the flesh desires against the Spirit"; then in 5:19 he lists the works of the flesh, including impurity, uncleanness, and lewdness; and he concludes in 5:24: "Those who belong to Christ Jesus have crucified the flesh with its passions and desires." Elsewhere in the NT, I Peter 4:2–3 contrasts the desires of human beings living in the flesh with the will of God, and then goes on to list the vices associated with the former. II Peter 2:10 speaks of those who follow "after the flesh in defiling desire."

Against such a background what does I John mean by "the desire of the flesh"? Lazure, "La convoitise," divides scholars according to whether they stress the Greek background and understand it as the desire for pleasure that rises from the carnal side of human nature (Chaine, Charue, Dodd, Malatesta, Selwyn, Schnackenburg), or stress the Hebrew background and understand it as the tendency that rises from human nature bereft of divine help (Asmussen, Bonsirven, Huby, Kuhn, Schweizer). The two lists of scholars I have given are approximate, for it is difficult to classify them exactly on this topic. Another group can be distinguished consisting of those who interpret I John in a Pauline sense to refer to the general bad tendencies of sinful people (Bultmann, Lazure, Nauck). Two cautions are in order: as Michl, *Briefe* 213, warns, one should not jump to the conclusion that "flesh" means sex and "the desire of the flesh" is concupiscence; and as Wengst, *Häresie* 69, insists, one should not too quickly read the Johannine writings through Pauline spectacles, even when both writings use the same phrase. For John "flesh" is not an evil or

sinful principle; after all, "the Word became flesh" (John 1:14). That statement shows also that it refers to more than a body and, *a fortiori*, to more than
the physical aspects of the body—an equivalent might be "man" or "human."
As in the OT, so also in John, "flesh" is the human as distinct from the divine.
"Flesh begets flesh, and Spirit begets spirit" (John 3:6), and so without being
begotten by Spirit one cannot enter the kingdom of God (3:5). To judge according to the flesh is to judge by human standards (8:15). Lazure, "La convoitise" 202, is correct when he insists that "the will of the flesh" in John 1:13
has no moral meaning, but when joined to "blood" (the noun that precedes it),
it covers the span of human begetting. Thus it is likely that in I John 2:16b
"the desire of the flesh" is directed toward all that satisfies the needs and wants
of human beings taken as such. The implicit opposite is not the noble desire of
the human spirit, but the desire of the children of God begotten from above.
Certainly some desires of the flesh would be crass and sinful, but others would
be neutral and even noble by secular standards. My translation, "human nature
full of desire," is faithful to the Johannine thought world.

16c. *eyes hungry for all they see*. In the phrase *hē epithymia tōn ophthal-
mōn*, "the desire of the eyes," again the genitive is subjective (desires arising
from the eyes). It is tempting to relate the repetition of *epithymia* to the fact
mentioned above that two of the Ten Commandments begin, "You shall not
desire [*epithymein*]," since the reference to "word of God" in 2:14g suggests
that the author had commandments (words) in mind, especially the Decalogue
(Ten Words). This phrase does not occur in the OT, at Qumran, or elsewhere
in the NT. It differs from "the desire of the flesh" by calling attention to those
desires that come out of the conscious part of human nature. Once more, they
need not be wicked desires, for Ezek 24:16 uses "the desired things [*epithy-
mēma*] of the eyes" for the vision of the sanctuary of God. The *Testament of
Reuben* mentions seven spirits given to human beings at their creation to make
them active; and the second, immediately after the spirit of life itself, is the
spirit of "sight which arouses desire" (2:4–5). Nevertheless, in the OT to follow one's eyes toward where one is inclined is more often equivalent to resisting God's will. In the Genesis story (3:6) the forbidden tree was seen by Eve
"to be pleasant to the eyes and desirable." Numbers 15:39 warns: "You shall
remember all the commandments of the Lord and do them, and you shall not
turn back toward the wantonness of your own heart and your eyes." The
Qumran member was given the warning: "Let no one walk in the obstinacy of
his heart going astray after his heart and his eyes and the desire of his inclination [*yeṣer*]" (1QS 5:4–5). The eye thus becomes an occasion of sin (Mark
9:47). In *T. Issachar* praised is he who shuns "eyes (made) evil through the
error of the world, lest he should see the perversion of any commandment of
the Lord."

Toward what is "the desire of the eyes" likely to be attracted? The OT indicates at least three possible attitudes: (a) Pride. "Haughty eyes" or the "eyes
of the haughty" is a common expression (Isa 5:15; Prov 6:17; 21:4; Ps
101:5), which can be combined with a "proud heart." However, this meaning
is less appropriate in an idiom where "eyes" is combined with "desire." (b)

Avarice or cupidity, when eyes are directed toward wealth. In Qoh 4:8 the person is criticized "whose eyes are never satisfied with riches" (also Sir 14:10[9]), while Qoh 5:10(11) says that great riches are not much use except to feast one's eyes upon them. Some attribute this meaning to I John, combining "the desire of the eyes" with the third factor, "the pride of livelihood." I John 3:17 criticizes someone who has enough of this world's livelihood but no compassion. (c) Sensual desire, especially sexual lust. Houlden, *Epistles* 74, who takes "the desire of the flesh" in a Pauline sense of sinful human tendencies, understands "the desire of the eyes" to include both greed and lust. Genesis 39:7 associates casting eyes upon someone with an urge toward intercourse; and that thought is frequently repeated (Job 31:1; Sir 9:5,8; *Jub.* 20:4; 1QS 1:6; Matt 5:28; II Pet 2:14), even in the extended sense where adultery means false worship and the eyes are turned toward idols (Ezek 6:9). Sirach 23:4–6 pleads to God, "Do not give me restless eyes and remove from me desire [*epithymia*]; let neither sensual attraction nor carnal [*sarx*] union overcome me." Those scholars who understand "the desire of the flesh" to be concupiscense often take "the desire of the eyes" to be lust. Augustine (*In Epistolam* 2:13; SC 176) interpreted the latter as "every species of curiosity," especially that of attending the pagan shows (which earlier Tertullian, *De spectaculis* 8:10; CC 1, 235, decried as participating in idolatry).

While one cannot exclude these meanings from the intention of I John, I find little in Johannine thought to support them. Dodd, *Epistles* 41, is closer to the mark when he interprets the phrase as "the tendency to be captivated by the outward show of things without enquiring into their real values." Just as flesh and Spirit express Johannine dualism, so also does the ability to see only the earthly (flesh) versus the ability to see beyond to the heavenly (Spirit). In John 4:35 Jesus invites his disciples to open their eyes and look for the significance of the harvest of the Samaritans. Twelve times John uses "eyes" in relation to the blind man of ch. 9 where the real significance is not that Jesus opened the man's eyes to physical sight but to the spiritual sight of Jesus as the one sent by God, to which the Pharisees were blind (although they could see physically). I John criticizes "the desire of the flesh" not primarily because it is sinful in itself but because it is not of the realm of the Spirit. And so it is not unlikely that in the next phrase I John criticizes the tendency of the eyes to be caught by the visible and not by what comes from above and is physically invisible. A literal translation might be "the desire for what the eye sees physically," which I have rendered less prosaically as "eyes hungry for all they see."

16d. *material life that inflates self-assurance.* A literal translation of *hē alazoneia tou biou* is complicated by a double uncertainty: the exact Johannine meaning of the nouns, and the type of genitive involved. *Alazoneia* covers a whole range of pride, arrogance, and boastfulness. In classical Greek "pretentiousness" was the most frequent connotation, whereas in Hellenistic Greek "ostentation" is more often the exact nuance. In the LXX *alazoneia* appears only in the late compositions, e.g., for a boastful display of power and success (II Macc 9:8; 15:6), of wisdom (Wis 17:7; *IV Macc.* 8:19), and of wealth (Wis 5:8). A relationship between the "desire" of the previous epistolary phrases and the boastful assurance of *alazoneia* is suggested by Hab 2:5: "The boastful [*alazōn*] man . . . who like the grave has enlarged his appetite and like death is never satisified." The two NT occurrences of this adjective *alazōn* (Rom 1:30; II Tim 3:2) are not precise enough to be helpful here, nor are the several uses of the noun in *I Clement* (although 16:2 and 21:5 seem to mean "boastfulness"). The only other NT use of the noun, "You boast in your arrogance" (Jas 4:16), has the tone of "presumption, overconfidence," which is the meaning that Joüon, "I Jean" 479-80, suggests for I John.

The noun *bios* appears 10 times in the NT, of which two are in I John. One basic meaning is "the means of life, livelihood"; and that is the clear meaning in I John 3:17 (and in Mark 12:44 where the widow contributes her whole *bios* to the Temple treasury). Another meaning is "life, duration of life," as in I Tim 2:2, "a quiet and peaceful *bios*." In the latter meaning *bios* as the life of the flesh would be the Johannine opposite to *zōē* which always means eternal life come from God above.

What then does the combination of *alazoneia* and *bios* mean? Most take the genitive as objective so *bios* is the object about which one has *alazoneia*. Possible connotations would then be: (a) Pride about one's means of livelihood, boasting about wealth, displaying possessions, and conspicuously expending them. With variations this is an interpretation suggested by Brook, Calmes, Hoskyns, Plummer, Schneider, and Wilder (partially). Presumption based on wealth is Joüon's nuance (subjective genitive—see below). (b) Pride about one's life-style and boasting about social status. This meaning, which takes *bios* as "life," is vigorously defended by Chaine. However, it is also possible to understand the genitive as subjective (Joüon, Michl, Plummer, Schnackenburg) or even as qualitative (Büchsel), and that leaves open another interpretation where the *bios* gives rise to the *alazoneia*. (c) Overconfidence stemming from the security of one's life. In this vein Wilder, "Introduction" 240-41, thinks that part of the range of the phrase is a presumptuous trust in outer securities; and Schnackenburg, *Johannesbriefe* 130, refers to a pretentiousness that makes man forget his dependence on God. It is the overconfidence of those begotten of the flesh who feel no need to be begotten from above. If Jesus came so that those who believe in him "might have *zōē* and have it to the full" (John 10:10), these are people who have *bios* to the full and are content with that. Such a dualistic interpretation of the third phrase is harmonious grammatically (subjective genitive) and theologically with the other two phrases. All three describe a world into which the light of God's Son has not yet penetrated.

16ef. *does not belong to the Father; all that belongs to the world.* Literally, "is not from [*ek*] the Father." The subject is "All that is in the world" of 16a. Since the three phrases just discussed (16bcd) are only examples of all that is in the world, the author's condemnation is more wide-ranging than if he said those three factors are not from the Father. He is saying that nothing in the world is from the Father. John is interested in the basic origins of things; perhaps that is why *ek*, "from," appears so often: some 200 times in the Johannine writings, almost one-fourth of the the total NT usage.

The expression *einai ek*, "to be from," occurs 55 times in the Johannine writings: 28 times in GJohn (plus 7 times where the verb *einai* is understood); 19 times in I John, and once in III John. It occurs some 28 times in the rest of the NT. The phrase covers both origin and appurtenance, i.e., not only coming from but also still belonging to. In the second aspect of its meaning it describes the very being of that to which it is applied (Bultmann, *Epistles* 34). De la Potterie (*La vérité* 2, 614ff.) relates *einai ek* to the perfect tense of *gennan*, "to have been begotten," i.e., not only the beginning but what results and endures. We catch the double meaning of *einai ek* in John 3:31 where the phrase is repeated: "The one who is from the earth [origin] is from the earth [appurtenance]." Indeed, that meaning can be seen in the few nontheological uses, e.g., Philip is from the same town as Peter and Andrew (John 1:44); Nicodemus is from the Pharisees (3:1); the Messiah is from David's seed (7:42); circumcision is from the patriarchs (7:22—with the implication that it still has their authority).

The main theological usage of *einai ek* is in the Johannine dualistic worldview to indicate origin from and/or adherence to one side or the other. The *good side* is described 15 times explicitly or implicitly in terms of being "from God (the Father)," 2 times as being "from heaven" (John 6:32), once as being "from above" (8:23), and 3 times as being "from the truth" (18:37; I John 2:21; 3:19). It is worth noting that "to be from God" is very infrequent in the NT outside John, e.g., in Acts 5:39 and (with *einai* understood) I Cor 11:12. Returning to John, we may remember for future reference that 6 times there is a reference to being from the followers of Jesus (John 10:16,26 [this fold of my sheep]; 18:17,25 [his disciples]; I John 2:19 ["us"—the author's adherents]). The *bad side* is described 3 times in terms of being "from the devil (Evil One)" (John 8:44; I John 3:8,12), 12 times as being "from the world (earth)" (John 3:31; 8:23; 15:19; 17:14; 18:36; I John 2:16; 4:5), and once as being "from below" (John 8:23). The equivalence of these evil derivations and appurtenances is important for evaluating the force of Johannine dualism.

The present passage is an instance of the typical Johannine dualistic employment of *einai ek:* one side "is of" (belongs to) the world; the other, of God. (Only here and in John 10:32 does *einai ek* govern "the Father" instead of "God.") More frequently *people* are said to be from God, the devil, or the world; but among the *things* that are said to be from God (or not) are Jesus' doctrine (John 7:17) and his good works (10:32), the Spirit (I John 4:1–3), and love (1 John 4:7)—besides what is mentioned here.

17ab. *the world is passing away with all its desires.* Literally, "and the desire [*epithymia*] of it"; presumably the genitive is subjective on the analogy of the two "desire" phrases in 16bc, and of the phrase "the will of God" in 17c. Codex Alexandrinus and some Old Latin and Sahidic MSS. omit "of it," presumably as a scribal attempt to broaden the scope of what the author condemns. Bultmann, *Epistles* 34, thinks this is a traditional aphorism but not derived from the putative source, even though it is in antithetical parallelism to 17cd: "The person who does the will of God remains forever." The verb *paragein* was used in 2:8c, "the darkness is passing away"; but Bultmann and others (Balz, Schnackenburg) argue that the meaning is different here. There the meaning was eschatological: the darkness was passing away because the light was already shining; here, they argue, the world is passing away because it is by nature transitory. The transitoriness of the world, however, is by contrast with the heavenly or eternal; it is not clear that in Johannine thought the world would have an in-built time limit if God did not act. The author of the contemporary *II Baruch* is convinced of the transitoriness and corruptibility of the world; but he has to ask, "How long will that which is corruptible remain?" because only when the Messiah establishes his kingdom will the world of corruption be brought to an end (40:3; 74:2). In the next verse (2:18) I John will say, "It is the last hour," and cite the presence of the Antichrist(s) as a sign thereof; 2:28 will speak of the coming of Christ—is not the author thinking eschatologically in 2:17 as well, so that the passing away of the world and of the darkness belong together? (Thus, Westcott, Windisch.) Certainly elsewhere in the NT the idea is eschatological: "The appointed time has grown very short . . . the form of this world is passing away" (I Cor 7:29,31); "Heaven and earth will pass away [*parerchesthai*], but my words will not pass away" (Mark 13:31); "Let grace come, and let this world pass away [*parerchesthai*]" (*Did.* 10:6). We saw that in 2:16 I John described "desires" as belonging to the world, which is equivalent to belonging to the devil; surely then the passing away of "the desire" of the world in 2:17ab, like anything that belongs to the devil, requires God's eschatological action. As the *Assumption of Moses* 10:1 phrases it, "When His kingdom shall appear throughout all creation, then Satan shall be no more." Neither the world nor the devil are gifted with "eternal life" and in that sense they are transitory; but the coming of Jesus makes it clear that the transitoriness has run its appointed course.

Once more (NOTE on 2:8c) Vicent Cernuda, "Engañan," argues that *paragein* here means "deceive" rather than "pass away." (He also defends that translation for I Cor 7:31, cited above, despite 7:29!) His struggle is more uphill than ever because of the contrast in 17cd with "remains forever," but he tries to translate that expression as "remains firm."

17c. *the person who does the will of God*. This use of "do" is a Semitism meaning "to act according to." Although 2:15d and 16e have mentioned "the Father" and although "the will of my Father" is a Johannine phrase (John 6:40; also Matt 7:21; 12:50), the author ends this strophe or subunit talking about "the will of *God*," even as he ended the previous strophe (2:14g) talking about "the word of God." *Thelēma*, "will," occurs 11 times in GJohn (7 times of God); the only other epistolary instance is I John 5:14 (of God). Since the author wrote in 17a, "the world is passing away," we might have expected as a contrast, "the will of God remains forever" (see 17e below); he chooses rather to speak of the person who does that will, thus returning to the participial pattern (literally, "the one doing the will") that appeared five times in 2:3–11. He is about to describe the Antichrists who went out from the Community (2:18–19), and so a reference to a person at the end of 2:17 serves as a transition (Johnston, "Will" 239). In Mark 3:35 Jesus uses similar language to describe an eschatological family that replaces his natural family:

"Whoever does the will of God is my brother, and sister, and mother"; and so once again we have evidence for an eschatological tone in the Johannine contrast. In GJohn Jesus insists that he has come not to do his own will but the will of God who sent him (4:34; 5:30; 6:38); that will involves eternal life for those who believe in Jesus as God's Son (6:39–40); and those who do God's will shall be able to recognize that Jesus' doctrine comes from God (7:17) and can be sure that God hears them (9:31 and I John 5:14). Granted the usage of GJohn, it is clear that here "the person who does the will of God" is doing what Jesus did; and, as we have seen, "to walk just as Christ walked" is one of I John's strongest appeals in refuting adversaries.

17d. *remains forever.* The Greek *eis ton aiōna*, "unto the aeon," is a LXX rendition of Hebrew *lᵉʿôlām.* In the NT it occurs 26 times, of which 12 are in GJohn, one here (with *menein*, "to remain/abide"), and one in II John 2 (with *einai*, "to be"). While it can mean an unforeseeably long period within the framework of time in this world (Ps 102:29[28]; Sir 44:13), the fact that here the author says the world is passing away and his use of the verb *menein* suggests a qualitatively different duration proper to God. In the Greek Bible the phrase occurs 12 times with *menein*, most frequently for the divine: God remains forever (Ps 9:8[7]; 102:13[12]; Dan 6:26 [Theodotion]), as does His justice (Ps 111:3), His truth (Ps 117:2; cf. *I Esdras* 4:38), His word (Isa 40:8), and His will (Prov 19:21). The statement that "David's offspring remains forever" (Ps 89:37[36]) may be the background for the GJohn affirmations that the Son and the Messiah remains forever (8:35; 12:34—only GJohn instances with *menein*). Since, as indicated at the end of the last NOTE, the person who does the will of God is imitating Jesus, that person receives the privileged endurance proper to the Son. (See Lammers, *Menein* 152–58.) A close parallel in GJohn is 8:51, "If a person keeps my word, he will not taste death forever." The Mandaean *Ginza Right* 7.218 (Lidzbarski p. 219) states: "The person who does not do the Master's will is closer to death than to life."

17e. At the end of v. 17 there is Latin evidence for an additional line (IN-TRODUCTION VI B): *sicut et ipse [Deus] manet in aeternum* (Augustine, *In Epistolam* 2.14; SC 148, 180) or *quomodo et Deus manet in aeternum,* "just as God Himself remains forever." Harnack, "Textkritik" 561–62, thinks that the evidence for this reading in Cyprian, Lucifer of Cagliari, and Augustine points to an African Old Latin reading, ultimately finding its way into the Latin Bible tradition of Spain (Toledo). Because there is also Sahidic evidence for the reading, Harnack posits a Greek original that may have fallen out through homoeoteleuton, since the line would have had the same ending as 17cd. However, I pointed out in the NOTE on 17c how scribes may have improved the contrast with "the world is passing away" by adding "God remains forever." Moreover, the underlying Greek *kathōs* clause posited by Harnack breaks the pattern of the other *kathōs* clauses in I John which hold up Christ, not God, as the example (see comparison III in the NOTE on 2:6bc).

COMMENT

Verses 12–14 and 15–17 constitute two subunits, each with a structure centered on patterns of three. *Within 2:12–14* there are three sets of three: (a) 2:12–13: three times "I write to you," addressed to "Little Children, Fathers, Young People," respectively; (b) 2:14a–e: three times "I have been writing to you," addressed to "Children, Fathers, Young People," respectively; (c) 2:14fgh: the last "I have been writing to you" is followed by three coordinated clauses.[1] *Within 2:15–17* there are two sets of three: (a) Each verse contains an antithesis: v. 15 has love for the world versus love of the Father; v. 16 has what belongs to the world versus what belongs to the Father; v. 17 has the world passing away versus the doer of God's will remaining forever; (b) 2:16bcd lists three things that are in the world.

This internal structure has caused a few scholars to regard 2:12–14 and 2:15–17 as self-contained units that have little to do with each other and little to do with their context. They thus become digressions or redactional additions.[2] O'Neill and Oke are among the very few who break up the internal unity of either set of verses, with O'Neill regarding 2:14–17b as one of the twelve units that came from the author's source (leaving 2:12–13 as an editor's addition and 2:17cd as a pious gloss), and Oke contending that 2:12–13 originally came after 1:10, while 2:14–17 came after 5:21 as the ending of the Epistle.[3]

In various ways the majority of scholars relate 2:12–17 to the context. Erdmann puts 2:12–14 with what precedes, and 2:15–17 with what follows, thus bringing the first main Part of I John to a conclusion with 2:14. Many scholars[4] put the whole of 2:12–17 with what precedes, thus

---

[1] The other five verbs of writing govern only one clause each.

[2] Stott speaks of two successive digressions. For Bultmann the author added 2:12–14 to the source, while the redactor added 2:15–17 to the author's work. Loisy (*Evangile-Epîtres* 72) thinks that 2:12–13 may have come from the author and the repetitive 2:14 from a redactor who sought to identify the author as having written GJohn. Williams thinks of 2:12–14 as a parenthesis consisting of two different drafts of the same statement.

[3] Oke, "Plan" 348–50, argues that this explains why the author used a past tense in 2:14: "I have written"—the letter was finished. The last papyrus leaf containing 2:14–17 broke loose, and the person who found these detached verses placed them erroneously in their present location. On the opposite extreme, Smit Sibinga, "Study" 197, felt so secure that 2:15–17 was a unit that he made it the basis of his syllable count according to which he then divided the rest of I John into units (above, INTRODUCTION, footnote 271).

[4] De Jonge, Ewald, Gaugler, Hauck, Hort, Nestle, Prat, Schnackenburg, Schneider, Thüsing, Vogel, Westcott, Wilder (Part II), NEB.

concluding the first main Part with 2:17. More scholars[5] would relate 2:12–17 also to what follows, thus postponing the conclusion of the first main Part to 2:27/28/29. However, within this group some would emphasize more the relationship of 2:12–17 to what precedes (Brooke, Dodd); and others, the relationship to what follows (Balz, de la Potterie, Malatesta). There is also a debate on the relationship of 2:12–14 to 2:15–17, e.g., whether 2:12–14 is introductory giving the grounds for the appeal in 2:15–17 (Westcott), or whether the two are of equal stance (THLJ).

I shall explain my own views below, but as a preliminary let me state that I see a very close relationship between 2:12–17 and the context in both directions, so that a chain of ideas runs through from 2:3–11 to 2:12–17 to 2:18–27.

A. Reminders to Those Who Abide in Light (2:12–14)

Scholars who dissociate 2:12–14 from what precedes argue from these factors: Abruptly the list of boasts and claims begun in 1:6 ends; the references to light/darkness begun in 1:5 end; and a directly hortatory address begins. However, the author already let the hortatory purpose of his writing break through in 2:1a in his parenthetical address to "My Little Children"; and so now he may be turning full attention to what has been implicit all along. After all, in 1:5–2:11 he was not listing those boasts and claims simply as a theological disquisition. At the end of that section he answered the last secessionist boast (2:9) with an antithesis that distinguished between those who abide in light (2:10) and those who walk in darkness (2:11). Hitherto he has been concerned with showing that those who make secessionist-inspired boasts are walking in darkness without knowledge of the God who is light. Now he turns directly to exhort the sons of light.

1. Basic Questions of Interpretation

The meaning of 2:12–14 depends greatly upon the answers to three basic questions to which I dedicated the long first NOTE in this unit. There the reader may find discussed a wide diversity of opinions; here I shall work with the conclusions I reached.

First, although he alternates the tense of the verb from "I write" to "I have been writing" (each three times), the author is in all instances referring to the present work (I John). The alternation is a stylistic stratagem to give emphasis that what he is saying is nothing new (as in 2:7). His "I

---

[5] Balz, Bonsirven, F.-M. Braun, Brooke, Chaine, de Ambroggi, de la Potterie, Feuillet, Francis, Häring, Huther, Jones, Law, Luthardt, Malatesta, Nagl, Schwertschlager, Smit Sibinga, Škrinjar, Tomoi, Vrede.

have been writing" makes a connection between his present writing and all that has been previously written by the Johannine School as part of the tradition—not because he wrote all that himself but because I John is part of what was "from the beginning."

Second, the three forms of address he uses also reflect his position as a tradition-bearer. In addressing the *whole* Johannine Community of his adherents as "(Little) Children" (2:12a,14a) he is following the model of the wisdom teachers of the OT who themselves adopted the convention of a parent addressing children.[6] The precise issue is not one of authority or the right to correct; rather he is speaking from the aggregate experience of a School of tradition and speaking with family affection, whence the diminutive forms from "child."[7] After first addressing the whole body, he then recognizes two existing groups within the Johannine Community, known respectively as "Fathers" and "Young People." On the basis of OT and Christian parallels, one may assume that length of time as Christians underlies the distinction. From the vantage point of the Johannine School with its closeness to the Beloved Disciple and to the beginnings, all other Community members are "Children" to the author; but at the same time he tactfully recognizes that some have been Christian as long as he,[8] and he counts upon the support of these "Fathers" who know the true tradition about Christ and his earthly ministry. If proportionately he devotes more time to the "Young People," it may be that he fears their vulnerability to secessionist propaganda. They would not be so aware of what was "from the beginning" as are the "Fathers," but at least he can stress their basic victory won through conversion.

Third, he is writing to his adherents to tell them *that* they have been forgiven, that they have known, and that they have conquered, not *because* of these things (problem of translating *hoti*). To translate "I am writing because you have known, etc." would give a picture of the Community as living in peaceful self-assurance, whereas in fact it is in danger of being confused and divided over the interpretation of "the gospel" because of seductive secessionist propaganda. The author is reminding his readers that the positive side of the antitheses he has been presenting in 1:5–2:11 is applicable to them as sons of light. Thus I would consider 2:12–14 as exhortatory kerygma. The verses are not pure exhortation (as a "because" translation might indicate) but are urgently informative. Yet

---

[6] NOTE on 2:1a. The pattern of threes here probably also stems from Wisdom Literature, which indulges in numerical devices (often mnemonic); see Prov 30:15–31; 6:16–19; Sir 25:7; 26:5,19[28]; Job 5:19; 40:5.

[7] Note his preference here over against the more egalitarian address forms "Beloved" (6 times in I John) and "Brothers" (I John 3:13).

[8] Length of status as believers would not necessarily make them members of the Johannine School of tradition-bearers; relationship to the Beloved Disciple would enter in.

they are repeated kerygma rather than simple *didachē* (instruction), for the author is enunciating the essentials of the Johannine proclamation of Christianity. In the author's view, if the clauses of 2:12–14 are not affirmed, one is not a (Johannine) Christian. Hitherto he has led off his discussion with false claims, but these are true claims.

Granted my answers to the three basic questions of interpretation raised by 2:12–14, other problems remain. If "Fathers" and "Young People" are two groups within the Community (even though logic requires that they must be fairly comprehensive, to the point of constituting a merism), they are not necessarily the only divisions. Why did the author choose them? Also, among the many things he might have written to the three addressees, why has he chosen the particular affirmations of 2:12–14? The answer to such problems may lie in the literary genre of the verses and in the particular life-setting that gave rise to them.

2. The Life-Setting of the Material in 2:12–14

I have already mentioned that the address to "Children" and the numerical pattern of threes are reminiscent of OT Wisdom Literature. More specifically many commentators call attention to the wisdom genre of *Haustafeln*, i.e., NT catalogues of moral admonitions directed to various members of Christian households (husbands, wives, children, slaves, masters) and occasionally to the functionaries of the house-churches.[9] Yet, while not unrelated to that genre, the I John clauses are not primarily moral admonitions and the grouping is not clearly domestic.

Others propose that the author is drawing upon the conversion/ initiation/baptismal experience of the Johannine Community,[10] and, in particular, upon the self-estimation of that Community as representing the New Covenant between God and His people. Johannine converts must have thought of themselves as coming from the darkness to the light (John 3:19–21), and the author has composed 2:12–14 in sequence to the antitheses in 2:9–11 contrasting those who are in darkness and those who abide in light. By belief in Jesus, converts became children of God begotten with new life from above (John 1:12–13; 3:3–7); and the author twice addresses his adherents as "Children."[11] The two groupings of "Fathers" and "Young Men" remind the respective groups how long ago

[9] Col 3:18–4:1; Eph 5:21–6:9; I Pet 2:18–3:7; I Tim 2:8–15; Titus 2:1–10.

[10] Nauck, Windisch, and others support a baptismal background, but that thesis is rejected by such scholars as Balz, Schneider, and Schnackenburg. As I explained at the end of the COMMENT on 1:5–2:2, I wish to make the suggestion broader by mentioning conversion and initiation because we know so little of Johannine baptismal practice. In previous units I have already called attention to the New Covenant theme, especially pp. 267, 279.

[11] For the variations of vocabulary for "Children," see the NOTE on 2:1a.

or how recently they entered the Community.[12] Beyond making sense of the sequence and the titles of address, this proposed background for 2:12–14 renders intelligible the clauses that the author "writes" to each group of addressees, clauses that I shall now consider in detail.

FIRST, to the "Children" (the whole Community) two affirmations are made: "Your sins have been forgiven because of Christ's name" and "You have known the Father." It is scarcely accidental that forgiveness of sins and knowledge of God constitute the basic promises of the New Covenant in Jer 31(38):34: "They shall all know me from the least to the greatest, for I will forgive their iniquity and remember their sin no more" —a passage that refers to a whole ("all") and then to two groups within it, even as does I John 2:12–14. In the Qumran group that used New Covenant language of itself, those who were admitted had to accept the special knowledge of God given through the Qumran interpretation of the Law and had to have their sins forgiven so that they could approach the "purity" (sacred meal?) of the community (1QS 2:25–3:12). At the end of the rule book (1QS 11:14–16) the author sings the praise of God who cleanses him of sin and opens his heart to knowledge. It is likely that knowledge of God and forgiveness of sins were also part of the initiation of Johannine Christians whereby they became children of God. Begetting from above through water and Spirit gives entry to the kingdom and eternal life (John 3:3,5,15), and "Eternal life consists in this: that they know you the one true God, and Jesus Christ whom you sent" (17:3). At the moment that Jesus breathes the Holy Spirit upon his disciples making them God's children, he says, "If you forgive men's sins, their sins are forgiven" (20:22–23).[13] The secessionists, as former members of the Johannine Community (I John 2:19), must have had the same initiation instruction as that to which the author appeals for those whom he calls "Children." We see this echoed in the secessionist-inspired boasts about being free from the guilt of sin and not having sinned since becoming Christian (1:8,10) and in the claim to know God (2:4). Precisely because he rejects the secessionist interpretation of forgiveness and knowledge as static gifts that free Christians from subsequent responsibility, the author reminds his adherents of these gifts so that they will ask for the forgiveness of subsequent sins (1:9; 2:1–2) and will deepen their knowledge of God by keeping the commandments (2:3–5), especially that of brotherly love.

It is noteworthy that the author speaks of the forgiveness of sins "be-

[12] There is no evidence that any of the vocabulary in 2:12–14 reflects the practice of infant baptism in the Johannine Community. One does not write to infants; all the classifications refer to adults.

[13] The Greek of this GJohn passage is echoed in I John 2:12b (see NOTE). The author may also be thinking of the Baptist's initial proclamation of Jesus as "The Lamb of God who takes away the world's sin" (1:29)—probably an initial proclamation for Johannine converts as well.

cause of Christ's name." In the NOTE on 2:12b I discussed the NT baptismal theology of confessing the name of Jesus. But here let me call attention to the first demands on would-be converts in the Pentecost scene in Acts 2:38: "Be baptized every one of you in the name of Jesus Christ for the forgiveness of your sins." Later on the occasion of the baptism of Cornelius, Peter says, "Everyone who believes in him [Jesus] receives forgiveness of sins through his name" (10:43; see 22:16). The phrasing of these kerygmatic formulas in Acts is so close to that of I John 2:12b that we may suspect that both authors were drawing upon traditional Christian baptismal language. Within the Johannine tradition the place of Christ's name in conversion kerygma is suggested by III John where missionaries "set out for the sake of the name." Revelation of the name of God (which Jesus bears) is the fundamental revelation in John 17:6. Any Johannine Christian familiar with GJohn would know the stated purpose for writing that Gospel (20:31): "That you may believe that Jesus is the Christ, the Son of God, and that believing you may possess life *in his name*," which is also the stated purpose of I John (5:13). Indeed, in Johannine terminology conversion may have been referred to as coming to believe in the divine name borne by Jesus: "Those who believe in his name—those who were begotten . . . by God" (John 1:12–13; 3:18).

SECOND, to the "Fathers" (presumably those who have been Christians longer) the same affirmation is made twice (13b,14d): "You have known him who has been from the beginning," with the repetition perhaps reflecting the unchangeability of "the gospel heard from the beginning" (3:11).[14] The message is appropriate for those who came to believe in the name many years before. "From the beginning" applied to Jesus means from the beginning of his self-revelation to his disciples: hence, the Jesus of the earthly ministry. "From the beginning" applied to Christians' knowledge means from the beginning of their (eternal) life as believers (NOTE on 1:1a). The author is reinforcing his adherents against the novelty of the secessionist position which concentrated exclusively on the preexistence involved in the GJohn Prologue, "In the beginning was the Word," neglecting "the beginning" marked by Jesus' deeds on earth (John 2:11). It was the latter beginning to which the tradition-bearers of the Johannine School could testify "because you have been with me from the beginning" (15:27).

THIRD, to the "Young People" (presumably more recent members of the Johannine Community)[15] the same affirmation is made twice (13d,14h): "You have conquered the Evil One"; but in the repetition it

[14] The sequence of the objective clauses in 2:14bd (knowledge of the Father; knowledge of him who has been from the beginning) echoes John 17:3: "That they know you the one true God and Jesus Christ."

[15] While *neaniskoi* is masculine in form, probably it included young women as well (p. 300 above).

is prefaced with "You are strong" (14f) and "The word of God abides in you" (14g). Once again reminiscences of conversion/initiation may explain the choice of the three points for emphasis. They are interrelated. The strength of the Christian "Young" comes from their faith, and that is what enables them to conquer the Evil One: "Now this is the conquering power that has conquered the world: this faith of ours" (I John 5:4bc). In a Synoptic parable describing the struggle between Jesus and Beelzebul, we read, "When a strong man [Beelzebul/Satan], fully armed, guards his own palace, his possessions are safe; but when a stronger one [Jesus] assails and overcomes him, he takes away the armor in which the man trusted and divides the spoil" (Luke 11:21 and par.). The recent believer in Jesus' name[16] has put on Jesus' strength and overcome the Evil One. As for the other reminder given to the "Young" ("The word of God abides in you"), it is a reference to the commandment had from the beginning, "the word" of brotherly love already heard (2:7). Surely new converts to the Community were taught the one explicit commandment/ word in the Johannine tradition, "Love one another as I have loved you." This is invoked in the context of conquering the Evil One because "That is how God's children and the devil's children are revealed: everyone does not belong to God . . . who does not love his brother" (3:10). Hating and killing one's brother is the mark of the Evil One (3:12,15).

Thus, a good case can be made that the reminders given to the three addressees in 2:12–14 are a distillation of the gospel preached to prospective converts and inculcated as part of their entrance into the Johannine Community. (The author has selected from the general kerygma points best suited to the respective groups addressed; but the fact that "Fathers" and "Young People" constitute a merism means that what is said to one group is also an ideal for the whole.) That this complexus of proclamation had a rather fixed substance is suggested by the fact that the three solemn "We know" statements at the end of I John (5:18–20) repeat the same topics of knowing God and Christ and of struggle with the Evil One (with 5:16–17 dealing with the forgiveness of sins).[17] I have argued that the author's decision to remind his adherents of such an elementary proclamation shows not only his contention that he is proclaiming what was from the beginning but also his fear that secessionist inroads may erode the fundamentals of Johannine Christianity. It is not

---

[16] Obviously all Johannine believers would have conquered the Evil One through faith, e.g., I John 4:4: "Little Children, you belong to God and so you have conquered." But recent converts would be more aware that they had just been freed from the dominion of Satan. Luke 10:17–18 connects missionary activity with the submission of demons and the fall of Satan.

[17] In the NOTES I have called attention to parallels between I John 2:12–14 and other NT passages associated with baptism. Prebaptismal proclamation and training may have been one of the standard features among the Christian churches in the last third of the first century.

surprising, then, that he turns next from exhortatory reminders to warnings;[18] for, although the Evil One has been conquered, he remains the Prince of this world.

B. *Warning against Love for the World* (2:15–17)

The sequence between the end of 2:14 ("You have conquered the Evil One") and the beginning of 2:15 ("Have no love for the world") makes perfect sense in Johannine theology. In John 17:15–16 Jesus prayed to his Father: "I am not asking you to take them out of the world but to keep them safe from the Evil One; they do not belong to the world any more than I belong to the world." Being kept safe from the Evil One is being kept safe from the world, for "the whole world lies in the grasp of the Evil One" (I John 5:19). The cohesion of these ideas, which seems patent to me, has been called into question by scholars who think that 2:15–17 differs from the rest of Johannine thought because it contains a different concept of love and a different concept of the world. Let me examine each of these two points.

1. Love for the World

Since the author warns, "Have no love for the world," most interpreters assume that the secessionists were saying, "Love the world." This assumption makes sense in the light of II John 7, "Many deceivers have gone out into the world," and I John 4:5, "Those people belong to the world . . . the world listens to them." But confusion arises when some scholars interpret the secessionist love for the world in terms of worldliness: concupiscence, lust, and vanity (a possible exegesis of 16bcd). Thus understood, the *agapan* of 2:15a differs markedly from the unmotivated, disinterested *agapē* of Johannine tradition.[19] Since very shortly (2:19) we shall hear that the secessionists had been Johannine Christians, I deem it unlikely that they would have a concept of love so different from the standard

[18] The remarks in 2:15–17 are probably meant for the whole Johannine Community of the author's adherents (the "Children") and not just the "Young People" of 2:14. But footnote 16 above helps to explain the absence of a new title of address in 2:15—what was said to the "Young People" (or to the "Fathers") was applicable to all.

[19] For this see the NOTE on 2:5b. Bultmann, *Epistles* 33, is confident: "Naturally *agapan* does not mean love in the sense of Christian *agapē* but, in accordance with common Greek usage, 'Appetitus,' to take a fancy to." Bultmann does not explain how an author who has stressed love of God (2:5: *agapē*) and love of brother (2:10: *agapan*) can in 2:15, without warning, give to love (*agapan*) a totally different sense that he never uses elsewhere. Dodd, *Epistles* 43, wonders whether the secessionist teachers had a conscious intention of lowering ethical standards or (more likely) had lowered them unconsciously through accommodation to the world. I doubt that this is the issue at all in 2:15–17; not the world as morally corrupting but the world as darkness opposed to light is the issue.

Johannine concept.[20] Let me then try to make sense of their position by presuming that they took the Johannine gospel seriously.

If the secessionists said, "Love the world" in a Johannine sense, they would not be seeking their own carnal satisfaction from the world but generously offering to it their version of the gospel. This would explain the charge mentioned above that they "have gone out to the world" and "speak the language of the world." They could justify their attitude upon the basis of John 3:16: "God loved the world so much that He gave the only Son." But why then would the author warn, "Have no love for the world"? First, he would be insisting that for the Johannine Christian the primary object of love commanded by God and Christ was one's fellow Johannine Christian (NOTE on 2:9b). Jesus said, "Love one another"; he did not say, "Love the world." With all their outreach to the world, the secessionists had failed to love their Johannine brethren as shown by the very act of secession. Second, the author would contend that a loving attitude toward the world betrayed a failure to evaluate correctly God's relation to the world in Johannine tradition.[21] Yes, God loved the world and sent His only Son, but the world did not recognize that Son and hated him. The world, which preferred darkness to light, aligned itself under the Satanic Prince of this world against Jesus; and so ultimately Jesus refused to pray for the world. He told his followers that they had been chosen out of the world and did not belong to the world. The author would not deny a continued divine offer of salvation and forgiveness (I John 2:2; 4:14); but that is precisely for those who are converted out of the world. Those who remain in the world are under the Evil One and do not belong to God (5:19). Barrosse ("Relationship" 550–51) is perfectly correct when he says that love for the world is another phrasing of what GJohn condemns as a love for darkness (3:19), a love for oneself (12:25: *psychē*), and a love for praise or glory (12:43).[22]

[20] The secessionists are accused of distorting "the gospel had from the beginning" but never of importing totally foreign ideas.

[21] I summarize above the detailed treatment of the "world" in the NOTE on 2:2bc; see corroborating GJohn references there. I think many scholars compound confusion by explaining Johannine thought in terms of different senses of *kosmos*, "world," as if there were no change of attitude as GJohn unfolds. If God loves the world in John 3:16 and Jesus refuses to pray for the world in 17:9, it is not simply because *kosmos* has different meanings. It is because the majority of people preferred darkness to light and have come to constitute the world over against Jesus' followers who no longer belong to the world. I find Dodd, *Epistles* 44, misleading here when he hints that God's love for the world resolves the dualistic attitude toward the world! The act of God's love toward the world was the *occasion* of a division that calls for a dualistic attitude.

[22] Commentators from Augustine to the present have felt a pastoral need to qualify the author's "Have no love for the world." Augustine (*In Epistolam* 2.11; SC 75, 172) asks, "Why should I not love what God has made?" He answers his own question, "God does not forbid one to love these things but to love them to the point of

Understood thus, love for the world is a corollary of the basic secessionist christological error. The secessionists concentrate on the incarnation when God showed His love for the world by sending His only Son, but they pay no attention to the salvific import of what happened afterward during Jesus' ministry when he turned from the world to his own.

2. The Things that Are in the World

The contention that there is a different concept of love in 2:15–17 (which I have just rejected) coincides with the contention that there is a different concept of the world in those verses. This is supported by reading the three examples of things that are in the world (16bcd: desire of the flesh; desire of the eyes; pride of life) as a catalogue of sexual attraction, of sensory pleasure, and of vanity based on material possessions.[23] Thus there emerges a "world" characterized by worldly temptations rather than by dualistic opposition to Jesus. The author's "Have no love for the world" becomes the Johannine form of "You cannot serve God and mammon . . . do not be anxious about your life, what you shall eat . . . nor about your body, what you shall put on" (Matt 6:24–25). Schnackenburg (*Johannesbriefe* 134) argues that the world here is not the world of people but the material world and all that fills it. *A priori,* such a view of the world and antipathy toward it would be quite intelligible on the NT scene. Pagan authors like Tacitus, Suetonius, Juvenal, and Seneca portrayed the licentiousness and extravagance of the Greco-Roman world and often decried it.[24] The seductions of sex and money were the objects of warning in pious Judaism (*T. Judah* 17:1: "not to love money, nor to gaze upon the beauty of women"); and the philosopher Philo (*On the Posterity of Cain* 40 #135) portrayed unfavorably passions aroused by pleasures. The NT has long catalogues of vices, one of which lists them as "works of the flesh" (Gal 5:19–20). Polycarp, *Philip.* 5:3, decries "the desires in the world."

Nevertheless, in the NOTES on 2:16bcd I tried to show that it is possible to interpret the three worldly factors in a totally different way that

---

finding one's beatitude in them." Williams, *Letters* 29, says, "We have to love what is good in it [the world] and hate what is bad." All that is true, but it is not what the epistolary author says or means. If one wishes to qualify his intensity, one should do so by admitting that he is one-sided and by citing other NT authors who were more open to a mission to the world. But, to be fair, I John is not alone in its view of the world: "Religion that is pure is . . . to keep oneself undefiled by the world" (Jas 1:27); "Love [*philia*] for the world is enmity with God" (Jas 4:4).

[23] J. E. Bruns, CBQ 25 (1963) 414, makes a passing reference to I John 2:15–17 as "the Johannine epitome of Qoheleth," a book that describes all things as vanity. Others evaluate this subunit as Johannine ethics. It consists rather of reflections drawn from Johannine soteriology.

[24] See W. Barclay, "Hellenistic Thought in New Testament Times: The New Emphasis," ExpT 71 (1959–60) 280–84.

would find echoes in Johannine thought, as an attack upon vices would not.[25] "Flesh" (16b) is not a sinful principle in John or a synonym for sex; rather, as described in John 3:5–6 it is human nature incapable of attaining to God unless it is re-created by His Spirit. "The desire of the flesh" would then be the needs of nature on the level of what is below, as distinct from the desire of the Spirit. "Eyes," mentioned in 16c, play a role in the GJohn dualism between physical sight and spiritual sight (ch. 9), so that those who see only physically are blind to the light come into the world. "The desire of the eyes" means seeing only the visible and missing the invisible that is from above. "Life" (*bios*), mentioned in 16d, is biological life, as distinct from *zōē*, the (eternal) life brought to human beings by Jesus. "The pride of life" is contentment with material life and not reaching out for God's own life (*zōē*). Not the sinful but an absence of the otherworldly is what characterizes the three factors, all of which are on one side of Johannine spatial dualism: They belong to what is below, not to what is above.

In themselves, before the coming of the light, these factors "that are in the world"[26] were like the world itself, having a self-sufficiency to survive but completely incapable of moving toward heaven and God. The coming of the light offered to human nature a new life from above and to human beings the possibility of becoming God's children. But after the offer has been lovingly made by God, in "the world" where it has been refused the all-consuming preoccupation with what is below takes on a hostile character. Flesh and natural life become the tools of the Prince of this world,[27] and their self-interest constitutes an obstacle to any need for salvation from above. To people occupied by such factors may be applied the words of Jesus in John 15:22,24: "If I had not come and spoken to them, they would not be guilty of sin; but as it is, they have no excuse for their sin." The world, the flesh, and natural life (*bios*) had always been marked by temporality and corruptibility; but the coming of the light signals their end and their judgment. Now the world is passing away (2:17), not just because it is composed of impermanent matter, but because it has hated Jesus and aligned itself with Satan against him, so that Jesus' victory over him is the conquest of the world (John 16:33). That is why

[25] Wurm, *Irrlehrer* 116–21, recognized this as part of his thesis that the adversaries of I John were not libertines.

[26] Since the many patterns of three in 2:12–17 are a stylistic device, there is no reason to think that the three factors in 2:16bcd are an exhaustive list of all that is in the world or even a profound analysis of its attractions. An element of oratory governed the author's choice.

[27] This outlook is shared by other NT passages wherein the desires of the flesh are carnal, e.g., "You walked according to the course of this world, according to the Prince of the power of the air who is the spirit now at work in the sons of disobedience; among these latter we all lived in times past doing the wishes of the flesh" (Eph 2:2–3).

the secessionist love for and openness to the world represents a misunderstanding of christology.

Above I suggested that the conversion/initiation/baptismal experience of the Johannine Community provided the basic issues about which the author reminded the addressees of 2:12–14. In any Johannine initiation ceremony one may suspect that the discourse of Jesus to Nicodemus in John 3:1–21 would have played a part, especially since it precedes a scene where Jesus baptizes (3:22–26). Nicodemus would then represent a convert coming to Jesus and being instructed about the kingdom of God and about how a person can be begotten from above or born again. The instruction is centered on the incapacity of the flesh, the need for eternal life over natural life, and the need to turn one's eyes to see the light from above. It is not surprising to find the author in 2:15–17 warning his followers not to backslide on these points. In other NT conversion/baptismal passages that warn against backsliding, the fear is often centered upon the sensuality and carnality of the converts' former lives as pagans, e.g., "the desires of your former existence" (I Pet 1:14). Faithful to Johannine dualism, the author of I John does not see the Evil One at work in paganism but in a world deprived of the Spirit.

At the end of this subunit the author contrasts the world that is passing away with the person who does the will of God and hence *remains* forever. At the end of the preceding subunit (2:14g) he stressed that the word of God (His commandment of love) *abides* in the Christian. By implication, doing the will of God involves keeping the commandments/words of God. Once again he is inviting his adherents to walk as Jesus walked, for Jesus did not do his own will but the will of God who sent him (John 4:34; 6:38). The importance of remaining forever will become intelligible in the next unit, which opens by proclaiming that the last hour is at hand.

Bibliography Pertinent to I John 2:12–17

Bruns, J. E., "A Note on John 16:33 and I John 2:13–14," JBL 86 (1967) 451–53.

de Giacinto, S., "'. . . a voi, giovani, che siete forti' (1 Giov. 2,14)" BeO 2 (1960) 81–85.

de la Potterie, I., "La connaissance de Dieu dans le dualisme eschatologique d'après I Jn, ii, 12–14," in *Au Service de la Parole de Dieu* (Mélanges A.-M. Charue; Gembloux: Duculot, 1969) 77–99.

Dupont, J., "Les 'simples' (*petâyim*) dans la Bible et à Qumrân: A propos des *nēpioi* de Mt. 11,25; Lc 10,21," in *Studi sull' Oriente et la Bibbia,* ed. G. Buccellati (G. Rinaldi Festschrift; Genoa: Studio e Vita, 1967) 329–36. Cf. "Young" in 2:13–14.

Elliott, J. H., "Ministry and Church Order in the NT: A Traditio-Historical Analysis (I Pt 5, 1–5 and parallels)," CBQ 32 (1970) 367–91. Cf. "Fathers, Young" in 2:13–14.

Grundmann, W., "Die *Nēpioi* in der urchristlichen Paränese," NTS 5 (1958–59) 188–205. Cf. "Young" in 2:14.

Huppenbauer, H. "*Bśr* 'Fleisch' in den Texten von Qumran (Höhle I)," TZ 13 (1957) 298–300. Cf. 2:16b.

Joüon, P., "I Jean ii, 16: *hē alazoneia tou biou.* 'La présomption des richesses,'" RSR 28 (1938) 479–81.

Kuhn, K. G., "New Light on Temptation, Sin and Flesh in the New Testament," in *The Scrolls and the New Testament,* ed. K. Stendahl (New York: Harper, 1957) 94–113, esp. 101–8. Cf. 2:16b.

Lazure, N., "La convoitise de la chair en I Jean, ii, 16," RB 76 (1969) 161–205.

Murphy, R. E., "*Bśr* in the Qumrân Literature and *Sarks* in the Epistle to the Romans," SP 2, 60–76. Cf. 2:16b.

Noack, B., "On I John ii. 12–14," NTS 6 (1959–60) 236–41.

Pryke, J., "'Spirit' and 'Flesh' in the Qumran Documents and Some New Testament Texts," RevQ 5 (1964–66) 345–60, with bibliography. Cf. 2:16b.

Schweizer, E., "Die hellenistische Komponente im neutestamentlichen *Sarx*-Begriff," ZNW 48 (1957) 237–53. Cf. 2:16b.

Spicq, C., "La place ou le rôle des jeunes dans certaines communautés néotestamentaires," RB 76 (1969) 508–27, esp. 523–26 on 2:12–14.

Wendt, H. H., "Die Beziehung unseres ersten Johannesbriefes auf den zweiten," ZNW 21 (1922) 140–46. On *egrapsa* in 2:14 as a reference to II John.

5. I John 2:18–27: *Warning against the Secessionists as Antichrists who Deny the Son and the Father*

18a   18CHILDREN, it is the last hour.
18b   You heard that Antichrist is to come:
18c   well, now many Antichrists have made their appearance,
18d   and this makes us certain that it really is the last hour.
19a   19It was from our ranks that they went out—
19b   not that they really belonged to us;
19c   for if they had belonged to us,
19d   they would have remained with us.
19e   Rather, this helped to reveal them
19f   in that none of them belongs to us.

20a   20As FOR YOU, your anointing is from the Holy One,
20b   so all of you have knowledge.
21a   21I have not been writing, then, to tell you
21b   that you do not know the truth,
21c   but that you do know it,
21d   and that every lie is alien to the truth.
22a   22Who, then, is the Liar?
22b   None other than the person who denies that *Jesus* is the Christ.
22c   Such is the Antichrist:
22d   the person who denies the Father and the Son.
23a   23No person who denies the Son
23b   possesses the Father either,
23c   while the person who confesses the Son
23d   possesses the Father as well.

24a   24As FOR YOU, what you heard from the beginning
24b   must abide in you.
24c   If you have abiding in you
24d   what you heard from the beginning,
24e   then will you yourselves abide in the Son and in the Father.
25a   25Now this is the promise
25b   which he himself made to us,
25c   and it amounts to eternal life.
26a   26I have been writing this to you
26b   about those who deceive you.

27a **27**As for you, the anointing that you received from him
27b   abides in you;
27c   and so you have no need
27d   for anyone to teach you.
27e   Rather, inasmuch as his anointing teaches you about all things,
27f   it is true and free from any lie;
27g   and just as it taught you,
27h   so you are to abide in him.

NOTES

2:18a. *Children.* The address is *paidia* as in 2:14a; see the NOTE on 2:1a. There is very slight textual evidence for reading *adelphoi,* "Brothers," a form of address found in 3:13.

it is the last hour. The Greek has no article. Under the rule given by BDF 273, while predicate nouns are usually anarthrous, a definite article may be inserted to indicate that the predicate noun is "that which alone merits the designation." Following that rule, some would argue that the author is saying "*a* last hour" (Westcott). Following the rule that abstract nouns are often anarthrous (BDF 258), others contend that the author is speaking generically (Bonsirven, Schnackenburg, B. Weiss). More plausibly the absence of the article flows from the author's treating "last" as if it were an ordinal number—GJohn never uses an article with "hour" modified by an ordinal (BDF 256; John 1:39; 4:6; 19:14). "The last hour" is a translation that some would avoid in order to preserve the (inspired) author from a mistake, for 1900 years have passed since he made this announcement. Chaine, *Epîtres* 167–68, admits a mistaken opinion but says it was not a teaching. Augustine (*In Epistolam* 3.3; SC 75, 188) took another tack: "The last hour has a long duration, but it is the *last* hour." The way toward such a solution was already shown by II Pet 3:8; and many commentators adopt it, pointing to Acts 2:17 as an indication that the whole of the Christian period is "in the last days" (see Marshall, *Epistles* 148–49). However, the epistolary author would scarcely need to make an urgent announcement of such a general truth. Since he has just said that the world is passing away, since the presence of the Antichrists is cited as a sign of the end, and since the coming of Christ is mentioned in 2:28, there can be little doubt that the author thought the end was coming soon. In his time he was not alone in that view (Rev 22:20; I Cor 7:29,31; Philip 4:5; I Pet 4:7; Jas 5:8; Heb 10:25,37; *I Clem.* 23:5; *Barn.* 4:3; 21:3); but like every other Christian who stated it then or since, he was wrong. It is not certain whether he thought it was coming in his lifetime (Brooke) or whether he had worked out a precise chronology. He is proclaiming the last hour, not speculating about it (Balz).

In the OT the expression *bĕ'aḥărît hayyāmîm,* "in the end of days," translated in the LXX as "in the last of days," was used to designate the final period of history (from the speaker's perspective and often in relation to a desired happening). Thus, Jacob told his sons what was going to happen "in the last days" when they came into the Promised Land (Gen 49:1); and Balaam told what would happen to Israel "in the last days," i.e., seemingly when the Davidic dynasty would arise (Num 24:14; see Isa 2:2; Micah 4:1). At Qumran "in the last days" was used for still-future events of which the signs were already present in the history of the Community (1QpHab 2:5–6; 9:6; 1QSa 1:1; CD 4:4). In the NT the expression occurs 5 times, twice to describe what has already happened in Jesus Christ (Acts 2:17; Heb 1:2), thrice for the period of final distress and judgment (II Tim 3:1; II Pet 3:3; Jas 5:3). Only GJohn uses the singular ("the last day"); it refers to the day of judgment (12:48) and of the resurrection of the dead (6:39,40,44,54; 11:24). A comparable NT expression is "the last time(s)" (*kairos* or *chronos*), which once describes what has already happened in Jesus Christ (I Pet 1:20) and twice describes the period of final revelation (I Pet 1:5) and judgment (Jude 18 = II Pet 3:3 which uses "last days"). Ignatius, *Eph.* 11:1, uses it to describe the times in which he is living. (A variant is the *hapax legomenon* "latter times" used in I Tim 4:1 in the context of an apostasy from faith caused by deceiving spirits and the teaching of demons.) This phrase may be related to the Hebrew expression "end-time" (*qēṣ* with or without *'ēt*), which appears for the time of final judgment in OT apocalyptic (Ezek 35:5; Dan 8:17) and at Qumran (1QpHab 5:7; 1QS 4:16).

With such a diversity of chronological words attached to "last," it is noteworthy that nowhere else in the Bible does "last hour" occur. Yet an eschatological "hour" is known. Sirach 18:19(20) advises: "Before you are judged, seek merit for yourself; and at the *hour* of visitation you will find forgiveness." The LXX of Dan 8:17,19 describes the final vision as being appointed "for an hour of time." The Synoptic tradition designates as at "that hour" the future persecution (Mark 13:11), the coming of the Son of Man (Matt 24:44; 25:13), and the passing away of heaven and earth (Mark 13:31–32). Revelation speaks of "the hour" of trial (3:10), of Jesus' coming (3:3), and of God's judgment (14:7,15). It is not impossible that I John's use of the "last hour" is to be considered a specification of GJohn's "last day," as if this were the last hour in the last day (*pace* Stott). However, the last hour may be simply the equivalent of the last day, for a comparison of the dating of the resurrection of the dead in John 6:40 and 5:25 shows the equivalence of the last day with an "hour" that "is coming." The coming hour is mentioned 7 times by Jesus in GJohn, and 3 times he adds "and is now here [or already come]." In some instances he seems to be talking of events that took place in his own ministry, e.g., the scattering of disciples at his arrest (16:32). In other examples he is talking about things that began to be true in his ministry but were also future from that standpoint, e.g., when he says "an hour is coming" for worshiping God not on Gerizim or in Jerusalem but in Spirit and truth (4:21,23), for the resurrection of the dead (5:25,28–29), and for him to speak plainly instead of figuratively (16:25). In one instance he clearly refers to what will happen after his lifetime: "An hour is coming when anyone who puts you to death will think he is paying homage to God" (16:2).

In ABJ 29, 517–18 I discussed the relationship of these "coming hour" passages to another use of "hour," namely, "my hour" or "the hour," i.e., the hour of Jesus' return to the Father in passion, elevation on the cross, and resurrection/ascension. Klein, "Licht," cites I John 2:18 as part of his thesis that the Epistle historicizes the eschatology of GJohn. He notes that, whereas GJohn speaks of "the hour" of Jesus without qualification and the evangelist thinks of no other or future hour, I John has to specify "the last hour" as if there were a series. While recognizing a greater historicization in I John, I think one must distinguish, as I have just done, two viewpoints about "hour" in GJohn itself. When Jesus speaks of an hour that is coming, he is applying the effects of his own hour to the disciples (and to the Johannine Community); and I John is in continuity with the "coming hour" phrase. If GJohn were written overtly from the viewpoint of the later Community rather than prima facie from the viewpoint of Jesus' lifetime (where the Community is necessarily future), I am not sure the evangelist would have resisted the expression "the last hour." Klein's affirmation ("Licht" 294) that there is no concept of chronological sequence in GJohn because the post-Easter period is not different from the pre-Easter period is refuted by 16:12–13. (Klein recognizes that GJohn speaks of "the last day," but he consigns that expression to the redactor.) The epistolary author shares with other NT authors cited above the idea of an eschatological hour; it is the appearance of the Antichrists that causes him to stress finality. In calling it "the last hour" rather than "the last day," he may wish to connect the present and crucial moment of Community life with the hour of Jesus' victory. This hour is the final manifestation of the victory won in that hour.

18bc. *You heard . . . well, now.* Literally, "And just as [*kathōs*] you heard . . . so [*kai*] now." The *kathōs . . . kai* construction (BDF 453[1]), occurring here for the first time in I John, was used in GJohn in comparing what the Father did for Jesus and what Jesus does for the disciples (II of de Dinechin's *kathōs* patterns discussed in the NOTE on 2:6bc), e.g., "Just as the Father loved me, so have I loved you" (15:9); "Just as the Father has sent me, so do I send you" (20:21). But in I John the basis of comparison has shifted to III in de Dinechin's classification: Just as Jesus was or did for the disciples, so must his disciples be or do (I John 2:6; 3:3,7; 4:17). There is a commandment to love that comes from the Father through Jesus (I John 3:23; II John 4); of that II John 6 says, "As [*kathōs*] you heard it from the beginning, so must you walk in it." That passage makes it plausible that when here the author says, *"As you heard,"* he means a teaching about the Antichrist that came from or through Jesus. (See also I John 2:7: "An old commandment which is 'the word' you already heard.") Certainly he is appealing to Johannine tradition.

18b. *Antichrist.* Codex Alexandrinus and the Byzantine tradition insert a definite article, probably under the influence of v. 22 where it is textually correct. Westcott, Plummer, and others are right in arguing for capitalization, for the author is thinking of a specific expectation, even if, as we shall see, that expectation takes different forms. (Here one may invoke the anarthrous character of abstract nouns; BDF 258.) In the Bible the term occurs only in I John 2:18,22; 4:3; II John 7. Neither it nor Antimessiah is found in the intertestamental literature, the Midrashim, or the Talmud. D. Flusser, *Immanuel* 10 (1980) 31–37, would find the concept of the Antimessiah in the Qumran fragment 4QPsDan A[a]; however, this is a very uncertain interpretation (see J. A. Fitzmyer, NTS 20 [1973–74] 391–94). In the Apostolic Fathers it is found only in Polycarp, *Philip.* 7:1 ("Everyone who does not confess Jesus Christ to have come in the flesh is Antichrist"), a passage that seems to depend upon II John 7 and I John 4:2–3 (pp. 8–9 above). Thus the Johannine School may have coined the term "Antichrist" for a concept designated less vividly elsewhere. If we examine the term, the Greek preposition *anti*, "in place of," is used for substitution; and sometimes nouns compounded with it imply only that, e.g., *antibasileus*, "viceroy, the substitute for the king." Other times, however, substitution involves a false thing taking the place of the real; and so a term like *antichristos* need not be far from the *pseudochristos*, "false Christ," of the Synoptic warnings (Mark 13:32; Matt 24:24). Finally, there can be antagonism between the substitute and the real, giving Greek *anti-* compounds the force of English *anti-* compounds, e.g., *antitheos* as what is opposed to God (Philo, *On Flight* 25 ※140); *antidikos* (related to *dikē*, "justice") as the opponent in a lawsuit (Luke 18:3) and applied to the devil (I Pet 5:8). Thus *antichristos* acquires the meaning of "opponent to Christ." See F.-M. Braun, "La réduction" 58–59.

The term "Antichrist," peculiar to the Johannine Epistles in the NT, represents a convergence of various background factors in Judaism: (A) THE SEA MONSTER. The pagan myth of the struggle between the "creator" god (Babylonian Marduk or Canaanite Baal) and the ancient sea monster (Tiamat or Yamm) was taken over into Israel as the victory of Yahweh over the dragon Rahab or the sea beast Leviathan (Isa 51:9; Ps 74:13–14; 89:11[10]; Job 26:12). Although sometimes the Bible describes the monster as destroyed, at other times he is alive as a serpent at the bottom of the sea (Amos 9:3), watched over by guards (Job 7:12), and still dangerous if aroused (Job 3:8). Job 40:25–41:26 gives an awesome description of this monster, still alive and fierce, ending with the note that he is "king over all the sons of pride." The latter reflects the tendency to demythologize the monster to a political power; and so for Isa 30:7 Egypt is "Rahab quelled," while Ezek 29:3 compares the Pharaoh to "the great dragon that lies in the midst of the streams." Isaiah 27:1 envisions a climactic struggle: "In that day the Lord with His cruel, great, and strong sword will punish Leviathan . . . the coiled serpent, and he will slay the dragon that is in the sea." This background for the Antichrist has been developed by Bousset, *Der Antichrist*, whose contributions are conveniently summarized in Brooke, *Epistles* 69–75; see also T. Jacobsen, "The Battle between Marduk and Tiamat," JAOS 88 (1968) 104–8.

(B) THE SATAN OR ANGELIC ADVERSARY. In Job 1:6 and Zech 3:1 we find the Satan ("Adversary") as a "son of God" or angel of the Lord in the heavenly court playing a role as the accuser of human beings. Eventually he was identified as the devil and the serpent of Gen 3:1–15 through whose temptation evil entered the world (Wis 2:24)and whose antihuman hostility continues (Gen 3:15). He (with angelic cohorts) became the patron angel of the forces opposed to Israel, e.g., as the angel prince of Persia fighting Michael the angel prince of Israel (Dan 10:13; 12:1). Indeed, he gains power over all human beings as Beliar (*Jubilees* 1:20) who has a dominion or empire (1QS 1:18,23–24; 2:4–5), or as an angel of darkness (3:20–21), which is a spirit of iniquity leading people astray and away from God's paths. In the Synoptic Gospels he is the "strong one" whose kingdom Jesus has come to destroy and with whom Jesus does battle daily by driving out demons; in GJohn he is the Prince of this world (cf. Eph 2:2) who is cast down in the victory of Jesus. But Belial (= Beliar) remains opposed to Christ (II Cor 6:15); and Satan continues his activity on earth hindering the work of the apostles (I Thess 2:18), so that the Pauline writer can exclaim, "We are not contending against flesh and blood, but against the principalities, against the powers, against the world rulers of the present darkness, against the spiritual hosts of wickedness in the heavenly places" (Eph 6:12). According to *Enoch* 6–16, the evil angel Azazel led the sons of God in their sins with women (Gen 6:1–2) that unleashed evil on the earth; but he has been bound up in a pit until the final time when he will be released in one last struggle before being destroyed. The Qumran War Scroll describes in anticipation the great battle to be fought between the sons of light and "the sons of darkness, the army of Belial," a collection from every Gentile power (1QM 1:1–2). In the *Sibylline Oracles* 3. 63–74 the eschatological adversary is Beliar.

(C) THE HUMAN RULER EMBODYING EVIL. The destruction of Israel by Assyria and the conquest of Judah by Nebuchadnezzar of Babylon introduced a period in the last millennium B.C. when the Jews were increasingly at the mercy of world rulers. This came to a head in the Hellenistic king of Syria, Antiochus IV Epiphanes (reigned 175–164), who tried to integrate Judea into his empire by persuading the Jews to see the religion of Yahweh as a form of the worship of Zeus Olympios whose statue he erected in the Jerusalem Temple (I Macc 1:54; the "Abominating Desolation" of Dan 8:13; 11:31; 12:11). This arrogance was looked upon as an action against God Himself, "the Prince of princes" (Dan 8:25); and Antiochus was deemed a man who had made himself equal to God (II Macc 9:12). The Book of Daniel fictionally cast its account of Antiochus into the future so that his abomination would mark the last of the seventy weeks of years prophesied by the angel Gabriel before the restoration of God's people (Dan 9). It is not surprising that subsequently the erection of the abomination of desolation became a way of signifying the final evil (Matt 24:15). An expectation arose that the pagan nations would gather their forces for one last thrust against God's people to be led by a king described symbolically after the image of Nebuchadnezzar and/or Antiochus Epiphanes (the two kings who had raised their hand against the Temple). Ezekiel 38:1; 39:1,6 describes the exotic Gog, chief prince of Magog, of Meshech and Tubal, who comes up like a sudden storm with his assembled hordes but whom

God destroys. Zechariah 14:2–3 describes the gathering of all the nations against Jerusalem, with God doing battle against them. *Enoch* 90:13–18 pictures the gathering Gentile forces like evil vultures and ravens; *IV Ezra* 5:6–13 portrays a sovereign who lets loose evil on earth in the end-time. *Assumption of Moses* 8:1 depicts in the manner of Antiochus Epiphanes "the king of kings" who brings wrath such as has not been seen since the beginning of time, until the Most High appears to punish the Gentiles (10:7). Where a belief in a Messiah developed, i.e., an anointed king of David's line to rule in Jerusalem, this Messiah was often expected to lead the armies of God against the assembled forces of evil. Some LXX MSS. of Num 24:17 have the Davidic king ruling over the nations and exalted over Gog; *II Baruch* 40:1–2 describes how the pagan hosts will be put to the sword and the last leader brought before the Messiah who will convict him; *IV Ezra* 11–12 has the monstrous Roman eagle rebuked and judged by the Davidic Messiah in the end of days; *Psalms of Solomon* 17:23–27 portrays the Davidic king destroying the godless nations with the word of his mouth.

(D) THE FALSE PROPHET. Deuteronomy 13:2–6(1–5) and 18:20 describe a prophet who may arise and do signs and wonders leading the people to serve other and strange gods; such a prophet must be purged from Israel. The description is generic, even as is the description of the opposite kind of prophet, the prophet like Moses, who shall speak the words of God and must be obeyed (18:15–19). But the Prophet-like-Moses was personified as a specific future expectation, e.g., in the Qumran hope for a prophet who would precede the Messiahs (1QS 9:11; see JBC 68, ※103), and in the NT identification of Jesus with *the* prophet (ABJ 29, 34 [also 234, 491–92]). So also the false prophet was personified in the singular or plural as a characteristic of the last times, a figure who would lead astray by signs and wonders. *Didache* 16:3–4 says, "In the last days the false prophets and corrupters shall be multiplied . . . and then shall appear the deceiver of the world as son of God and shall do signs and wonders. The earth shall be given over into his hands, and he shall commit forbidden deeds such as have not occurred since time began." Since Rev 12:9 describes the devil as "the deceiver of the earth," we may have in *Didache* the diabolic embodied in one false prophet. The *Sibylline Oracles* 3. 63–74 describes Beliar himself performing signs and deceiving mortals (including faithful Hebrews) till the vengeance of Almighty God burns him up. Sánchez Mielgo, "Perspectivos" 15–17, argues for the false prophet as an important background for the Antichrist.

These expectations were combined in different ways in Christian expectations of future evil. The most comprehensive combination is found in the Book of Revelation. The great dragon of Rev 12 who tries to destroy the Messiah is Satan the ancient serpent, a combination of (A) and (B) above. Its first cohort is the beast from the sea (13:1–10), which gets men to worship the dragon. Making war on the saints and blaspheming against God, this beast with ten horns is clearly modeled upon the description of Antiochus Epiphanes in Dan 7 and thus echoes (C) above. The second cohort is the beast from the land (Rev 13:11–18); specifically called the false prophet (16:13; 19:20; 20:10), it works signs to deceive and thus echoes (D) above. The first of these beasts was mortally wounded but healed; the second beast has horns like a lamb; they are, then, a blasphemous parody of Christ the Lamb that was slain but lives. Afterward Jesus comes from heaven as a warrior and destroys the two beasts and the kings whom they have gathered to make war (19:11–21); he binds the ancient serpent for one thousand years; but when finally loosed, Satan gathers Gog and Magog against Jerusalem, only to be defeated and thrown into hell (20:1–10). Almost every piece in the Jewish picture of future evil has been put into this mosaic.

Somewhat less ambitious is the sketch of what precedes Jesus' coming in II Thess 2:1–12 (either written in the 50s by Paul, or after 70 if deutero-Pauline). The day of the Lord cannot come until first there come the apostasy and "the Iniquitous One" (*ho anomos*), who is also called the son of perdition. This figure who exalts himself, taking a place in the Temple of God, proclaiming himself to be God (2:4), is clearly patterned on Antiochus Epiphanes in (C) above. At the same time he is a tool of Satan, working signs and wonders and deceiving many (2:9–10), and so he is the false prophet of (D). Ultimately he will be slain by the Lord Jesus (2:8). While much of the description is mythological, there is historicizing in terms of a failure of faith as part of the signs of the last times. Irenaeus, *Adv. haer.* 5.25.1, identifies the "Iniquitous One" of II Thessalonians as the "Antichrist" without citation of I and II John. Tertullian, *De resurrectione carnis* 24. 18–20; CC 2, 952, does the same.

The "Marcan Apocalypse" predicts wars and movements of nations (13:7–8), the persecution of the saints before kings (9), and the desolating abomination (14—a neuter modified by a masc. participle, which probably means that Mark was interpreting the Danielic symbol as a person, not unlike II Thess 2). All of these echo (C) above, and the echoes are more specific in Matt 24:15; Luke 21:24. But there is also an expectation of false christs and false prophets (Mark 13:22) who will lead astray with signs and wonders, echoing (D) above. (Luke 18:8 hints at apostasy before the end.) Ultimately the Son of Man will come with his angels to rescue the elect (Mark 13:26–27), but no great battle is described.

At least some of this must have been what the author of I John meant when he told his readers that they had heard that Antichrist was coming. He probably meant "heard" not only from Jewish tradition but also from Jesus tradition. It is true that no such prediction exists in GJohn; but I have contended throughout that at times the epistolary author goes back to "the beginning," beyond GJohn to the pre-Gospel tradition upon which the evangelist also drew. Both the Synoptic Apocalypse and Revelation (a work distantly related to GJohn) point to a strong apocalyptic tradition in early Christianity about personified future evil. If II Thessalonians is genuinely Pauline, that tradition can be dated to the early 50s at least. If Jesus spoke of the kingdom of God echoing Dan 7:26, might not some of the symbolism of the supreme evil figure so prominent elsewhere in Dan 7 also go back to Jesus? Certainly the nonapocalyptic Jesus is a modern creation.

Antichrist is to come. Literally, "comes" (from *erchesthai*), which in indirect discourse could yield "was coming." However, it is better not to obscure a possible wordplay. Three times (1:15,27; 12:13—see 3:31; 6:14) GJohn uses the participle of *erchesthai* (*erchomenos*) and once the present tense (*erchetai,* as here) to describe Jesus as "the one who is to come." All NT expectations of a future evil opponent of Jesus describe him with some of Jesus' own features and thus as a pseudomessiah. Might not he also have been the perversion of the one who is to come? In Mark 13:5 Jesus predicts, "Many will come [*erchesthai*] in my name, saying, 'I AM.' "

18c. *well, now many Antichrists have made their appearance.* The Greek *kai nyn* ("and [well] now"), which occurs twice in GJohn (11:22; 17:5) and 4 times in the Epistles (I John 2:18,28; 4:3; II John 5), relates what follows it to the statement that precedes, usually as a specification of what has been said in general. Probably all the temporal force of the *nyn* has not been lost here, since the author is referring to the moment of crisis in which he is living. This is the only use of the verb *ginesthai* in I John. In the GJohn Prologue *einai,* "to be," is used absolutely of the Word in 1:1, while *ginesthai,* "to become, make one's appearance," is used absolutely of the Baptist in 1:6. The being of humans has resulted from a becoming. In the I John Prologue *einai* is used in relation to Jesus in 1:1 ("What was from the beginning"), while here *ginesthai* is used of the Antichrists.

It has been suggested that these Antichrists are meant by the author as the precursors of the great Antichrist still to come (Allo, Belser, Camerlynck, de Ambroggi[?], Plummer, Stott, Vrede). That idea is refuted by the use of the Antichrists as a sign of the *last* hour, for that means he is not thinking of them as *precursors.* Others, who recognize them as the actual manifestation of the Antichrist, would contend that the author has not committed himself about the future Antichrist (Brooke, Westcott). In part, such suggestions are designed to protect the inerrancy of II Thess 2:1–12 which describes a single evil figure, "the man of iniquity." Some scholars cannot allow one NT author to disagree with another since all are inspired by the same Spirit. (With others, I would question whether an inspiring Spirit need have produced uniformity. This is just another aspect of the problem of whether the author could have made a mistake about its being the last hour.) It is more likely that although the epistolary author knew mythological expectations of the final opposition (e.g., Revelation with its beasts), as well as quasi-historicized expectations of a single evil person, he is reinterpreting all such tradition as part of his polemic against the secessionists, in order to associate them with ultimate evil. (Eschatological expectations were plastic and inconsistent, offering individual thinkers the possibility of shaping them according to need.) Opposition to false teachers arising from within a community is attested in Acts 20:30; I Tim 1:3; II Pet 2:1; but Johannine dualism catalyzed the identification of false teaching with the ultimate and diabolic opposition to Christ expected at the end time.

18d. *and this makes us certain.* Literally, "from which [*hothen*] we know." This Greek adverb is used in the NT as "whence" to refer to motion from places, and also, less literally, to mean "from which fact." Surprisingly this is the only Johannine use, for it would have been clearer than the frequent *en toutō*, "in [by] this," which gives no certainty that the reference is to what precedes (NOTE on 2:3a).

that it really is the last hour. The emphasis ("really") comes not from a special word but from the exact repetition of the phrase used in v. 18a, "It is the last hour." Notice the inclusion (envelope pattern) whereby the verse ends with the same words with which it began.

19a. *It was from our ranks that they went out.* Literally, "From us they went out." *Hēmōn*, the genitive of *hēmeis*, "we," is used 5 times in the 6 lines of this verse, 4 times in the phrase "from [ex] us." The position of the phrase moves around in the Greek to obtain emphasis: It comes first in 19a and last in 19b, offering a chiasm: "From us they went out, but not that they were from us." The "we" does not include all good Christians (*pace* Plummer), for the author is concerned only with the Johannine Community. "From us" means from the Johannine Christian adherents of the author. Notice Acts 20:30: "From you [*ex hymōn*] there will arise men speaking perverse things." The verb *exerchesthai*, "to go out," reappears in II John 7: "Many deceivers have gone out into the world." The use of the aorist both there and here suggests a specific action. There may have been a constant leakage of apostates to the secessionists; but there had been a major rift that brought the secessionist group into existence.

Although the statement seems perfectly clear, preconceptions about the Community situation have raised questions. First, B. Weiss, *Briefe* 65, argues that all may not have gone out and so some could still be among the author's adherents (despite 19d which indicates that they did not "remain with us"). Bultmann, *Epistles* 36, assumes that the secessionists still claim to belong to the congregation, and the author refutes that claim in the next line (19b). However, that line does not say, "They *are* not from us," but, "They *were* not from us." There is no reason to think that secessionists still consider themselves part of the author's group; more likely they consider themselves the one true Johannine Community. The author fears losses if his adherents are won over to secessionist tenets; but presumably such converts (whom he would consider apostates) would "go out" to join the secessionists who constitute a recognizable group distinct from his own. Bultmann, *Epistles* 36, assures us that 2:19 does not mean that the opponents organized themselves independently as a sect. If they thought of themselves as the true Johannine Community, however, they probably had no less (or more) organization than the group they left (about which we know little). They probably looked on the author's group as a sect.

Second, Carpenter, *Writings* 470, contends that it is not clear whether they went forth of their own accord or were expelled; and Chaine argues for excommunication. It is true that *exerchesthai* can be used when there has been coercion, e.g., in Mark 1:26 the evil spirit is said to have gone out of a man after it had been ordered out by Jesus. But such coercion has to be made explicit in the context; the verb itself carries no tone of expulsion. One may theorize that the author says that they went out in order not to create sympathy for them, but surely his readers would know the facts of a split that must have been fairly recent and affected all deeply (whence the urgency of the present communication). The attitude of the author of III John 10 toward Diotrephes, "If I come, I shall bring up what he is doing in spreading evil nonsense about us," suggests that even prestigious individuals like "the Presbyter" did not have the power themselves to correct. That was up to the congregation. In any case, the real point in I John 2:19a is the opposite of expulsion: *"From us they went out"*; we did not go out from them. The author is refuting the secessionist propaganda that he is an innovator who has abandoned true Johannine teaching while they are preserving the true Johannine Community. In this bitter split (see the language of war in 4:4) each group probably said it could no longer live with the other; but the author and his adherents were not so sovereign that they could have expelled the secessionists as a small band of troublemakers.

19b. *not that they really belonged to us.* Literally, "but not that they were *from us.*" There are three instances of *einai ek,* "to be from," in this verse; and the present example shows it means appurtenance ("belong to") more than origin (NOTE on 2:16ef), which was mentioned in the previous line. They destroyed their origins by the act of secession (aorist); and in this case their origin was deceiving, for they did not belong (imperf. tense). The author is saying that their visible enrollment did not correspond to their real being. He says of his own adherents, "We are called God's children and that is what we really are" (3:1), whereas despite appearances the secessionists were and are the devil's children (3:10). In harshly condemning apostasy ("It is impossible to restore again to repentance those who have been enlightened") Heb 6:4–8 at least admits that apostates were once enlightened. The author of I John would have to say, "They were never really enlightened." He is closer to the remarks of Ignatius (*Trall.* 11:1–2) against the docetists: "Flee from these wicked offshoots . . . for these are not the planting of the Father. If they were [*ei gar ēsan*], they would appear as branches of the cross."

19c. *for if they had belonged to us.* The Greek is *ei gar ex hēmōn ēsan* (the same words used by Ignatius with "from us" in the center). Codices Sinaiticus and Alexandrinus place the phrase "from us" after the verb, but that is probably by scribal imitation of the word order in the preceding line. *Gar,* "for," used 64 times in GJohn, occurs only 6 times in the Epistles (p. 23 above). For the indicative imperfect used in an unreal condition, see MGNTG 3, 91.

19d. *they would have remained with us.* This is the only epistolary example of *menein* followed by *meta* (plus genitive, meaning "with")—once also in GJohn (11:54) which has 3 instances of the equivalent *menein para* (plus dative). All have a personal subject. To catch the tone of the Greek unreal or contrary-to-fact condition, the Latin inserted *utique,* "certainly"; and Tyndale and KJV have "no doubt." The pluperfect, here without augment (MGNTG 2, 190), is rare in the NT especially in conditions; it stresses the duration of time up to the present. The sentence illustrates well the author's concept of the relationship between *einai* ("to be" in previous line) and *menein* ("to remain/abide"): what one is shows up in what one remains. To remain is to be like Christ: "While no slave remains in the family [*oikia*], the Son remains there forever" (John 8:35). Against deception by sin and apostasy Heb 3:12–14 urges, "We share in Christ only if we hold our first confidence firm to the end." Tertullian says, "People are not Christians unless they persevere to the end" (*De praescriptione haereticorum* 3.6; CC 1, 188).

19e. *Rather, this helped to reveal them.* Literally, "But in order that [*alla hina*] they might be revealed." Although MGNTG 4, 66, points to examples of this breathless and somewhat obscure *alla hina* in Sophocles and Epictetus, it is characteristically Johannine in the NT. In GJohn sometimes it pertains to the fulfillment of Scripture (where it might be translated as an imperative; ABJ 29A, 553–54, 688; MGNTG 3, 95); more often it pertains to a general aspect of God's plan (John 1:8,31; 9:3; 14:31; 15:25). In all cases it is an elliptic expression (BDF 448[7]) where one must fill in something after the "But" like "this was" or "this happened." The form of the Greek verb *phaneroun*, "to reveal," used here appears in GJohn in 1:31 on the Baptist's lips, "Rather (it was) in order that Jesus might be revealed to Israel," and in 9:3, "Rather (it was) in order that the works of God might be revealed in the man." Although I John 2:19 was appealed to in later theological debates about predestination, that is not the Johannine issue. The inevitability of *krisis* ("judgment") is the point—as the light shines forth, nothing remains obscure. The author does not deny free choice (and he implicitly appeals to his audience to make a right choice), but the choice will show up what one really is. A similar outlook is found in I Cor 11:19: "For there must be [*dei*] factions among you in order that those who are genuine among you may be recognized." Klein, "Licht" 314–16, sees here another proof that I John has a different outlook from GJohn where the instances of revealing (*phaneroun*) are all christological (except 3:21), whereas in I John 2:19 and 3:2 there is a revealing of Christian identities in church history. Although Klein dismisses as not comparable John 3:21, "He who acts in truth comes into the light so that his deeds may be revealed," it is in continuity with the *krisis* in that text that the epistolary author sees the self-revelation of the Antichrists as they withdrew from the light. Clearly the evangelist envisioned a continued *krisis* as the Paraclete and Jesus' disciples bore witness to the light before the world (15:26–27; 16:8–11).

19f. *in that none of them belongs to us.* Literally, preserving the Greek word order, "that not are all from us." Here the (fourth) *ex hēmōn* phrase of the verse comes at the end of the line, and the third *einai ek* again means "belong to." The verb is present in tense, and one should resist the temptation to translate it as if the author were talking about the past history of the secessionists. The grammatical problem that has led to different renditions of this line is whether the negative (*ou*) modifies (a) the "all" or (b) the verb. (a) "Not all belong to us," with the "all" understood broadly and not simply as all the Antichrists (Balz, Bultmann, Camerlynck, Hauck, Schneider, Vrede, Windisch). The implication of this is caught by the NEB: "Not all in our company truly belong to it"; or Bultmann, *Epistles* 37, "Not all (who so claim) belong to us." This is used to support the theory (rejected above) that there are still secessionists within the author's section of the Johannine Community. Unconvincing is the grammatical example cited on behalf of such a translation, i.e., "Not all the ones from Israel belong to Israel" (Rom 9:6), precisely because in that example the negative is placed before the "all," and the meaning "all from Israel" is specified—in other words Paul did exactly what the author of I John would have done if he wanted to say, "Not all from us belong to us." But here the author has placed his negative immediately before the verb; and Brooke, *Epistles* 54, argues that such a word order in "the usage of the New Testament in general, and of the author in particular, is decisive against" taking the negative as modifying the "all." **(b)** "All do not belong to us," with the negative modifying the verb and the "all" referring to the Antichrists of whom he has been speaking (Bonsirven, Brooke, Calmes, Chaine, Charue, Loisy, Westcott). But then one should not mistakenly argue that such a statement logically implies that some do belong to us. The grammatical phenomenon involved is cited as a Semitism by Brooke, Plummer, and Windisch (Hebrew *lō' kōl*); but Law, *Tests* 379, questions this, and MGNTG 2, 433 and 3, 196 points to its occurrence in vernacular Greek. "All" is to be taken in a collective, not a distributive, sense, so that "all are not" means "none are [is]." Let me give some LXX examples with the crucial words in literal word order: "Every servile work you will not do on these days" (Exod 12:16: no servile work will you do); "Every foreigner will not eat of the Passover" (Exod 12:43: no foreigner will eat); "All those who hope in Him will not be weak" (I Macc 2:61: none who hopes will be weak). Elsewhere in I John we find: "Every lie is not from the truth" (2:21d: no lie is from the truth); "Everyone denying the Son does not have the Father" (2:23ab: no one denying the Son has); "Every murderer does not have eternal life" (3:15b: no murderer has); "Everyone begotten by God does not commit sin" (5:18a: no one begotten by God commits sin). Similarly II Pet 1:20, "Every prophecy of Scripture is not a matter of one's own interpretation," means that no prophecy is that.

20a. *As for you.* Three times in this unit the author begins a sentence by a second person pl. address: *kai hymeis* here; *hymeis* in 2:24; *kai hymeis* in 2:27. (The *kai hymeis* in 2:24e does not begin a sentence, but only the protasis of a condition begun in 2:24c.) The Vulgate translates *kai* as "but," as if he were contradicting or making an exception to what had been just said. On the other hand, Dodd, *Epistles* 60, would translate *kai hymeis* here as "You too," with the implication that the Antichrists were claiming an anointing and so the author is assuring his adherents that they have one also. (Dodd's influence on the NEB is clear: "You, no less than they.") However, there has been no hint of such a secessionist claim; and because of the pattern of three "You" (pl.) addresses in this unit, I have opted for seeing this as an instance of *kai* in simple contrast (BDF 442[1]). Having spoken about the Antichrists in the third person, the author is turning directly to his own adherents.

your anointing is from the Holy One. The word *chrisma*, which I translated "anointing," occurs only 3 times in the NT, all in this unit of I John. (The related verb *chriein*, "to anoint," occurs in 5 passages, 4 of them referring to the anointing of Jesus [Luke 4:18; Acts 4:27; 10:38; Heb 1:9], and one to the anointing of the Christian [II Cor 1:21]; the verb *epichriein* occurs only in John 9:6,11 for the anointing of the blind man.) To help with the discussion that follows, I give a literal translation of the three passages:

2:20ab   You have a *chrisma* from the Holy One and you all know
2:27ab   The *chrisma* that you received from him remains in you
2:27e   His *chrisma* teaches you about all things

Granted the rarity of *chrisma,* scribes substituted in these verses more familiar or clearer terms: *charisma,* "charism," is read by a minuscule MS. (116) in 2:20a, by Vaticanus in 2:27a, and by 33 and a few other minuscules in 2:27e; *pneuma,* "spirit," in Codex Sinaiticus* of 2:27e.

Four basic questions need to be answered. First, should *chrisma* be translated "ointment" or "anointing"? Second, either way, did the action involve a ritual, physical use of oil or only a figurative anointing? Third, was the anointing through the reception of the Holy Spirit or of the word of God? Fourth, is "the Holy One" God or Jesus?

First, "ointment" or "anointing"? The *unctio* of the Old Latin and Vulgate favors the second; but *unguentum* appears in several Jerome references to I John 2:20 (CC 73A, 664; 76A, 639) and in the Latin translation of Didymus the Blind (PG 39, 1784C). The early English translations (Tyndale, Cranmer, Geneva Bible) favored "ointment," while most recent translations favor "anointing." (Variants include: "initiation, consecration, having been anointed/ initiated"; the C. K. Williams translation reads "appointment"!) One can sidestep the issue by using an English word with both meanings, e.g., "chrism" or "unction"; but a debate about the meaning casts light on deeper problems.

"Ointment" or "oil" is accepted by Bultmann, de la Potterie, Marshall, Michl, Schnackenburg, B. Weiss, and Westcott. Perhaps the strongest argument for this view is the Greek noun form, since neuters ending in -*ma* tend to be things rather than actions. Marshall, *Epistles* 153, states boldly, "The noun does not mean 'act of anointing,'" and he dismisses Brooke's claim (*Epistles* 55) that "words ending in -*ma* can certainly denote the action of a verb." In fact the picture is complicated: Nouns ending in -*ma* generally indicate the result of a verbal action (BDF 109²), e.g., *rēma* is a thing said and therefore a saying; *pragma* is a thing done and therefore a deed or doing. But one cannot be sure on the basis of noun-formation that *chrisma* could not be anointing, even as *baptisma* is baptizing or baptism. If we move from morphology to the argument from usage, in the Hebrew OT the phrase *šemen hammišḥâ* can mean both "oil of ointment," an epexegetical construct meaning the oil that is ointment, and "oil for anointing," a construct of purpose, as the Syriac understood it. (That means it is not clear whether *mišḥâ* in this phrase means "ointment" or "anointing.") This phrase is rendered in the LXX by *to elaion tou chrismatos,* "the oil of *chrisma*" (cf. MT and LXX of Exod 29:7; 35:14[12]; 35:19[15]; 40:9), an equally ambiguous phrase. On behalf of the "ointment" translation is the description by Josephus (*Ant.* 3.8.2; ※※197–98) of the mixing of oils and perfumes into a "sweet-smelling *chrisma*" for the anointing of priests. But several other factors suggest that, no matter how the Greek or Hebrew phrases were originally meant, they came to be understood as referring to an oil for anointing. An alternative LXX expression is *to elaion tēs chriseōs* (cf. MT and LXX of Exod 29:21; 31:11; 35:28) of which the second noun is a -*sis* formation, usually a noun of action and here meaning "anointing." Similarly in Hebrew the noun of action *měšîḥâ* (which will become standard in rabbinic Hebrew) appears at Qumran as an alternative for *mišḥâ* in an unambiguous context where the meaning "anointing" is required: "They shall not profane with blood the oil for anointing their priesthood" (1QM 9:8). Finally, in other LXX usages where *chrisma* is used, it cannot mean oil, e.g., Sir 38:30, "anointing, glazing"; Dan 9:26, "anointed person or place." Thus, it seems to me that Jewish usage contemporary with the NT favors "anointing" in I John. (Of course, one may always wonder would the author have been precise: Might he not have meant "anointing with oil," indistinguishably?)

Second, what kind of anointing? (This question has meaning even if chrisma means "ointment, oil," for I John 2:20,27 makes sense only if that ointment was used in an action that has had effects.) The two possibilities are: (a) a ritual action in which the Johannine Christian was physically anointed; (b) a figurative anointing or illumination. In either case the aorist in 2:27a ("The *chrisma* that you received from him") suggests a specific experience rather than an ongoing series. I have spoken frequently of a conversion/initiation/baptismal background for the author's ideas, but that background could fit either type of anointing.

(a) Initiatory ritual anointing. Myrrh with nard was poured over Jesus' head or feet (Mark 14:3–9 = Matt 26:6–13; Luke 7:36–50; John 12:1–8; see ABJ 29, 449–52), and this action symbolized his preparation for death. His followers might have ritually imitated such an anointing as, at conversion, they died to what they had been and received new life. Ignatius, *Eph.* 17:1, says, "The Lord received myrrh on his head in order that he might breathe immortality on the church." However, it should be noted that in none of these passages does *chrisma* or a word related to it appear. Water baptism is the most obvious occasion on which Johannine Christians might have been physically anointed with oil. Such a view was known in antiquity (Cyril of Jerusalem) and is held by Asmussen, Chaine, and Reitzenstein. (Some Roman Catholic scholars think of confirmation [Belser, Camerlynck, Vrede]; but there is no real evidence for a separate postbaptismal sacrament of confirmation in the first century.) In terms of evidence, the first clear reference to the practice of using oil at baptism is *ca.* A.D. 200 from Tertullian, *De baptismo* 7.1–2; CC 1, 282: "Afterwards, having come up from the washing, we are anointed with the blessed unction, according to the ancient practice by which they used to be anointed for the priesthood by oil from a horn, by which Aaron was anointed by Moses. . . . In our case the unction flows on the flesh but gives spiritual profit." In the story of the blind man in John 9 (which is generally acknowledged to have baptismal significance), it is stated twice that Jesus anointed (*epichriein:* 9:6,11) the man's eyes (but with mud, not oil); and so it is not impossible that physical anointing developed early in the Johannine initiation tradition.

Another suggestion is a special prebaptismal ceremony of anointing with oil, symbolizing the gift of the Spirit, which had developed in the second century in the Syriac-speaking churches of the East, as attested in the *Didascalia,* the

Pseudo-Clementines, and the *Acts of Judas Thomas.* We shall have to discuss this in more detail in relation to I John 5:6–8 because scholars (de la Potterie, Manson, Nauck) think that "the Spirit, the water, and the blood" of 5:8a (see NOTE there), in that order, represent three liturgical actions of prebaptismal anointing, baptism with water, and the eucharist. It is noteworthy that in John 9 the anointing of the man's eyes precedes his washing in the pool; on the other hand, John 3:5, "begotten of water and Spirit," mentions water before Spirit.

Somewhat related is the attempt to determine the anointing practice of the Johannine Community through the practices of the adversaries and their gnostic descendants. *Chrisma,* it is suggested, was a word that the author of I John borrowed from the secessionists. One dubious argument for that comes from reading 2:20a as "You too have an anointing"—a reading rejected above. A better argument is the popularity of *chrisma* among later gnostics. (Alexander, *Epistles* 69, thinks that heretics used the noun *chrisma,* while orthodox Christians preferred the verb *chriein.*) The *Gospel of Philip* (II 67:27–30; NHL 140) speaks of five sacramental mysteries done by Jesus, with "chrism" second, between baptism and the eucharist. While the anointing of Jesus at his baptism was figurative in the NT, eventually it may have been understood literally, especially by the gnostics as a basis for their own ceremonial. In the Pseudo-Clementine *Recognitions* 1.45.5 (GCS 51, 34) the Son is called Christ because "the Father first anointed him with oil which was taken from the tree of life." Such a statement may explain Celsus' charge that among some Christians the initiate was called the Son; and so he answered "the Father" who initiated him, "I have been anointed with white *chrisma* from the tree of life" (Origen, *Contra Celsum* 6.27); yet Origen does not know of the practice. Hippolytus (*Refutatio* 5.9.22; PG 16[3], 3159–60) tells us of the second-century Naassenes who claimed, "Out of all we are the only true Christians who complete the mystery at the third gate [of regeneration] and there are anointed with an unutterable [*alalos*] *chrisma* from a horn as was David." Irenaeus, *Adv. haer.* 1.21.3–5, says that some gnostic initiates were anointed with oil and water mixed. Of course, a century separates Irenaeus' contemporaries from the Johannine secessionists, and rituals would have developed during that time. It is noteworthy, however, that the epistolary author never tells his own adherents that they are the only ones who have been anointed. If he were speaking of a purely figurative anointing, he could have denied that to the secessionists. But if all Johannine Christians were physically anointed when they entered the Community, the secessionists would have received such an anointing upon entrance; and the author could not have denied that they were anointed.

(b) Figurative anointing. This is favored by more scholars: Bonsirven, de Ambroggi, de la Potterie, Malatesta, Michl, and Schnackenburg. Some suggest the occasion was baptism by analogy with Jesus who was the Anointed (*Christos*—I John 2:22b); and Acts 10:38 implies that the occasion of God's anointing Jesus was his baptism (*chriein;* also Acts 4:27; Heb 1:9). In Luke 4:18, shortly after his baptism, Jesus himself quotes Isa 61:1 to the effect that the Spirit of the Lord had anointed him. Thus, believers may well

have looked upon the moment of their baptism, when they became acknowledged followers of the *Christos,* as a *chrisma;* certainly that seems to be the
idea behind II Cor 1:21–22: "God . . . has anointed us; He has put His seal
upon us and given us His Spirit in our hearts as a guarantee." (Yet, Bultmann,
Epistles 37, points out that the first certain designation of baptism as *chrisma*
was by Gregory of Nazianzus, d. 390.) If the idea of baptism as a figurative
anointing was common Johannine parlance, after the secession those who
moved toward gnosticism may have developed the physical anointings described above among the gnostics. De la Potterie, "Anointing" 80–81, points
out that, while Christian gnostics speak of *chrisma,* the term is absent in the
pagan mysticism of the *Hermetica.*

Third, the Holy Spirit or the word (gospel) of God? Physical or spiritual,
the anointing received by the Johannine Christians abides in them and teaches
them all things. What spiritual factor does that anointing involve?

(a) The Holy Spirit. Held in antiquity by Augustine, Cyril of Jerusalem, and
Bede, this is the majority view today: Balz, Bonsirven, F.-M. Braun, Bultmann,
Chaine, de Ambroggi, Hauck, Hunter, Jackayya, Marshall, Michl, Mouroux,
Schnackenburg, Schneider, Stott, B. Weiss, Wengst, Westcott, and Windisch.
The "holy spirit" is associated with initiation in the Qumran rule (1QS
3:6–10): The candidate "shall be cleansed from all his sins by the holy spirit
uniting him to God's truth. . . . And when his flesh is sprinkled with purifying
water and sanctified by cleansing water, it shall be made clean by humility and
obedience to all the commandments of God . . . to walk perfectly in all the
ways of God." Also 1QS 4:21–22: "God will . . . cleanse human beings from
all godless deeds through a holy spirit and will sprinkle a spirit of truth as purifying water." It is not surprising that the baptism brought by Christ was described as "in the Holy Spirit" (Mark 1:8 and par.; Acts 1:5). Since in the OT
the coming of the spirit of the Lord was connected to the anointing of the
Davidic king (I Sam 16:13) and to the anointing of a prophet (Isa 61:1),
Jesus can say after he was baptized, "The Spirit of the Lord is upon me because he anointed me" (Luke 4:18). The Holy Spirit is mentioned explicitly in
NT texts connecting anointing with baptism (of Jesus, in Acts 10:37–38;
implicitly of the Christian, in II Cor 1:21–22). The classic Christian understanding of baptism as anointing with the Holy Spirit is enunciated *ca.* 350 by
Cyril of Jerusalem (*Mystagogical Catecheses* 3.1; SC 126, 120–22) in comment upon the *chrisma* of I John: "You are properly called 'Christs' by receiving the mark [*antitypos*] of the Holy Spirit. . . . After you came up from the
pool of the sacred streams, there was given to you the *chrisma,* the mark of
that with which Christ was anointed; and this is the Holy Spirit." At the same
period in the West, Augustine (*In Epistolam* 3.13; SC 75, 208) says, "The
spiritual anointing is the Holy Spirit of which the sacramental sign is the visible
anointing" (which takes place at baptism; see *Sermo* 227.1; PL 38, 1100). In
the East the *Apostolic Constitutions* (7.22.2; Funk 1, 406), in reference to the
anointing with holy oil before water baptism, says, "The *chrisma* is a sharing in
the Holy Spirit."

The functions of the *chrisma* in I John may be related to the Holy Spirit. In

2:27a the Johannine Christians are told "you received" the *chrisma,* while John 14:17 contrasts the disciples with the world that cannot "receive" the Paraclete/Spirit. I John 2:27b says that the *chrisma* abides in Christians (*menein en hymin*); John 14:17 is addressed to the disciples: the Paraclete "abides [*menein*] with you and is in you [*en hymin*]." (John 1:32, alone among the canonical Gospels, speaks of the Spirit *remaining* on Jesus in the setting of his baptism; cf. *Gospel of the Hebrews* ≹2 in HSNTA 1, 164.) I John 2:27e says that the *chrisma* teaches Christians about all things (*disdaskein hymas peri pantōn*); John 14:26 says that "the Paraclete will teach you everything" (*hymas didaskein panta*). I John 2:20b and John 14:17 attribute knowledge to the *chrisma* and the Paraclete respectively. Thus I John uses the same language of the *chrisma* that GJohn uses of the Paraclete/Spirit. Within I John itself there is little explicit teaching about the Spirit to which one might compare the *chrisma* statements, but both 3:24 and 4:13 relate to the Spirit a *knowledge* of God's *abiding.* Finally, if the knowledge given by the *chrisma* (2:20) enables one to say that Jesus is the Christ (2:22), it is important that such professions of christological faith elsewhere in the NT are attributed to the Spirit: "No one can say 'Jesus is Lord' except by the Holy Spirit" (I Cor 12:3).

(b) The word of God. (The notion of "spirit" and "word" may not have been so sharply distinct for Christians with a background in OT where spirit is breath: in Ps 33:6 we find in parallelism "word of the Lord" and "the breath [spirit] of His mouth" to express the creative factor.) There are many variations of this proposal that the anointing is through a word/gospel/teaching preached and heard (de la Potterie, Dodd, Galtier, Houlden, Lazure, Malatesta, Reitzenstein), and sometimes a baptismal setting is urged. De la Potterie would relate this thesis to the previous suggestion: The anointing is the word assimilated by faith under the action of the Holy Spirit (also Marshall). Lazure connects "the *chrisma* received from Christ" of 2:27 with the affirmation in 5:20 that the Son of God "has given us insight [*dianoia*] to know the One who is true." Houlden, *Epistles* 79, says "to be anointed is to have received a doctrine." Dodd, *Epistles* 63, contends that the anointing "is the Word of God, that is, the Gospel, or the revelation of God in Christ, as communicated in the rule of faith to catechumens, and confessed in Baptism." Certainly the NT speaks of the preached word of God or the gospel in passages frequently associated with baptism and conversion (Acts 2:41; 6:7; Eph 1:13; Col 1:5–6; Mark 16:15–16); and Jas 1:18 and I Pet 1:23 associate the divine begetting of the Christian with the word.

The most impressive positive argument for this proposal comes from the structure of the unit. If one examines the three sentences addressed to "you" (I John 2:20,24,27), the first and the last speak of an anointing from the Holy One or "from him," while the middle one speaks of "what you heard from the beginning." Both "what you heard" and the anointing *abide* in the Christian (but so also does the Paraclete/Spirit). Helpful too for this proposal is the difficulty of having the anointing refer to the Spirit because of the absence of the verb "anoint" in the (few) I John passages dealing with the Holy Spirit. However, the infrequency of those passages and the indirectness of anointing language (if anointing refers to the Spirit) could be explained if the secessionists were stressing the Spirit as their authority. Moreover, no NT passage predicates the verb *chriein* of "word" or "teaching," and so the negative argument is inconclusive.

As for external evidence, de la Potterie ("Anointing" 114–38) points to patristic teaching about an anointing by faith, e.g., Clement of Alexandria, *Adumbrationes, In Joh.* 2:20; GCS 17, 213, comments on I John 2:20 in terms of "an anointing from the Holy One which is done according to faith." De la Potterie seeks to combine this with the second-century prebaptismal anointing (mentioned above, p. 343), which he interprets as the reception of truth and belief and the gift of baptismal faith. Sometimes the evidence of gnostic anointing is invoked, for not illogically it is claimed that such an anointing would have involved the gift of knowledge (while among orthodox Christians anointing might have been considered the gift of the true gospel or teaching). The Hippolytus passage about the Naassenes cited above speaks of "an unutterable *chrisma*" (which I do not find probative in either direction). However, the *Hypostasis of the Archons* seems to relate the Holy Spirit to gnostic anointing: "When the True Man . . . reveals the existence of [the Spirit of] Truth which the Father has sent. Then he will teach them about everything, and he will anoint them with the unction of life eternal" (II 96:35–97:3; NHL 159). Overall the evidence favoring the thesis that the anointing is by the word is weaker than that for an anointing by the Spirit.

Fourth, is "the Holy One" God or Jesus? (Even though this title is never used in the NT for the Spirit, Houlden [*Epistles* 131] and Morris mention that as another possible identification.) The phrase anointing "from the Holy One" in 2:20a is parallel to anointing "received from him" in 2:27a, and there the "him" (*autos*) is probably Christ even as the *autos* ("he himself") in 2:25b is probably Christ. Nevertheless, if in one passage (v. 27a) the anointing, which involves the Spirit, is from Christ, theoretically in another passage (v. 20a) it could be from God. After all, in John 15:26; 16:7 Jesus sends the Paraclete, while in 14:16,26 the Father gives or sends the Paraclete. De la Potterie, "Anointing" 1045, complicates the issue by arguing that the *apo*, "from," of the two phrases in vv. 20a and 27a, unlike *para*, "from," allows intermediaries. As elsewhere, de la Potterie attributes to the Johannine use of prepositions too much precision; for I John 4:21 and II John 4 speak of a commandment *from* God, using *apo* and *para* respectively without difference of meaning. Leaving aside the question of intermediaries, let us see the evidence for identifying the Holy One of 20a.

(a) The Holy One is God. Thus, Alexander, Bauer, Büchsel, de Ambroggi, Dodd, Houlden (*Epistles* 79, cf. however, 131), Nauck, B. Weiss. Besides OT passages referring to "God the holy" (Isa 5:16; Hos 11:9; II Macc 14:36) or to God as "the Holy One of Israel" (Isa 1:4; Ps 71:22), there are clear instances in the LXX where "the Holy One," with a definite article, is a title for God (Hab 3:3; Bar 4:22,37; Sir 23:9; Vaticanus of Tob 12:12,15). This title becomes very frequent in rabbinic Hebrew. In the NT God is adjectivally described as "holy" in passages like John 17:11; Rev 6:10; I Pet 1:16; but nowhere is the title "the Holy One" applied to Him. If the anointing of I John 2:20,27 is through the Holy Spirit, in I John 3:24; 4:13 it is God who gives the Spirit. The one NT passage that describes the anointing of Christians (II Cor 1:21) has God as agent. In the two Paraclete passages of GJohn (14:16,17,26) which most resemble I John 2:20,27, the Father, not Jesus, is the one who gives/sends the Spirit.

(b) The Holy One is Jesus. This is held by the majority of scholars: Balz, Belser, F.-M. Braun, Brooke (?), Bultmann, Camerlynck, Chaine, de la Potterie, Loisy, Malatesta, Marshall, Michl, Procksch, Schnackenburg, Schneider, Vrede. It would be quite appropriate to have the *chrisma* coming from the *Christos*. In the NT, besides passages where Jesus is called "the Holy One of God" (Mark 1:24; Luke 4:34; John 6:69), he is twice called by the title "the Holy One" (Acts 3:14; Rev 3:7), a title continued in *I Clem.* 23:5; *Diognetus* 9:2. If the anointing of I John 2:20,27 is through the Spirit, Jesus sends the Paraclete in John 15:26; 16:7; and Acts 2:33 has Jesus pouring out the Holy Spirit. Thus, even without appeal to the parallelism of the phrase "from him [Christ]" in 2:27a, there are persuasive arguments for considering "from the Holy One" of 2:20a as a reference to Christ. Yet one can sympathize with those who think the passage too obscure to permit decision (Bonsirven, Windisch), leaving open the possibility that the author of I John did not want to make the distinction.

In summary response to the four questions discussed in this NOTE, it is likely that the author was referring to an *anointing with the Holy Spirit*, the gift *from Christ* which constituted one a Christian. This anointing, whether figurative or *physical* (which I think more likely), was probably connected with entry to the Community.

20b. *so all of you have knowledge.* Literally, "and you all [*pantes*] know," or "and you [pl.] know all things [*panta*]." The verb *oida* occurs once here and twice in the next verse; see NOTE on 2:3a, "we can be sure that we know Him." Codex Vaticanus and the Sahidic omit the initial "and," a reading that Westcott favors. The consequential character of the second clause remains, but the syntax then becomes unduly abrupt. Much more serious is the division of the textual witnesses as to whether "all" is masculine nominative (*pantes*) or neuter accusative (*panta*). The *pantes* reading (which I adopt) is supported by Codices Vaticanus and Sinaiticus, the Sahidic and Jerome, and is accepted by Aland, Alexander, Balz, Bonsirven, F.-M. Braun, Brooke, Bultmann, Chaine, de Ambroggi, Dodd, Haas, Holtzmann, Malatesta, Marshall, Michl, Schnackenburg, Stott, THLJ, B. Weiss, Westcott, Wilder, JB, RSV. The *panta* reading ("you have all knowledge") is supported by Codices Alexandrinus, Ephraemi Rescriptus, the Byzantine tradition, the Old Latin, Vulgate, Syriac Peshitta, Bohairic, and Ethiopian versions; it is accepted by Belser, Büchsel, Grundmann, Harnack, Hauck, Kohler, Manson, Nauck, and Windisch. (See Harnack, "Textkritik" 563–64.)

The textual evidence is so divided that it cannot decide the issue. The context indicates that the author wants to give confidence to his adherents in face of secessionist claims to knowledge. It would seem logical for him to derive from the *chrisma* received by his adherents the fact that therefore all of

them have knowledge, so that they need not feel ashamed in face of the Antichrists' claims. In other words, the fact of their knowledge (*pantes*), not the
extent of its object (*panta*), seems best to fit the reassurance. In v. 22 the author will specify as necessary a certain object of knowledge ("that *Jesus* is the
Christ")—this seems curious if he has just said that they know all things. The
strongest argument for the accusative (*panta*) is that the verb "to know"
(*oida*) is not used absolutely in the Gospels and Epistles, i.e., without an object. Yet that argument cuts two ways; for it may explain why scribes might
change the original nominative (*pantes*) to an accusative, namely, to make the
difficult construction more normal, especially in imitation of John 16:30
(addressed to Jesus), "You know all things [*oidas panta*]." Moreover, the parallel anointing passage in 2:27e ("His *chrisma* teaches you about all things")
and the parallel Paraclete passage in John 14:26 ("will teach you all things")
would also influence scribes in favor of the accusative. If we return to the author himself, the New Covenant motif from Jeremiah, which is very much in
his mind, favors the nominative, "They shall all [*pantes*] know me, from the
least to the greatest" (Jer 31[38]:34).

Interpreted either way, the statement in I John 2:20b is quite intelligible
against a biblical background. The idea that God's people, sharing the fear of
the Lord, gained special wisdom is a frequent motif in OT Wisdom Literature.
Proverbs 28:5 states, "Evil men do not understand justice, but those who seek
the Lord understand it in all things." In Mark 4:11; Matt 11:25; 13:16 Jesus'
followers are said to receive a special knowledge not given to others. Paul disclaims what the world calls wisdom, proclaiming "Christ Jesus whom God has
made our wisdom" (I Cor 1:18–31). Colossians 1:28 portrays Paul as teaching "every man in *all* wisdom, that we may present everyone mature in Christ."
Similar confidence continues in Ignatius, *Eph.* 14:1, "Nothing remains hidden
from you if you possess perfect faith in Jesus Christ and love," and in
Polycarp, *Philip.* 12:1, "I am confident that . . . nothing remains hidden from
you."

The statement in I John 2:20 creates a pastoral problem: How does a writer
further instruct people all of whom got the necessary knowledge initially? He
can rebuke them for forgetting what they once knew (Gal 4:9), or he can
remind them of what they already know (Jude 5: "I want to remind you,
though once you knew all things [*panta*]"; also II Pet 1:12). Moreover, the
idea of having knowledge can cause arrogance: "Now we know that we all
[*pantes*] have knowledge, but knowledge puffs up while love builds up" (I
Cor 8:1). In the COMMENT I shall treat the specific problems of I John, but
this background warns against thinking that the I John claims and problems
are unique.

21a. *I have not been writing, then, to tell you.* Literally, "I did not write
[*egrapsa*] to you." On pp. 296–97, I discussed at length the author's use of
this aorist tense as a reference to the whole of I John which he is now writing.
The author is afraid that his warnings here against secessionist claims to knowledge will be interpreted as an overall denial of the possibility of such knowledge of divine truth and will discourage the readers.

21bcd. *that . . . but that . . . and that.* Three clauses, each introduced by *hoti,* "that, because," form the three lines following *ouk egrapsa,* "I have not been writing." Literally,

21b   *hoti* you do not know the truth
21c   but *hoti* you know it
21d   and *hoti* every lie is not from the truth

In 2:12–14 the three instances of *graphō* and the three instances of *egrapsa* were all followed by *hoti* clauses; and on pp. 300–1, I discussed why I thought that there *hoti* should be translated "that" and not "because," although I warned that the Greek reader (and even writer) of I John might not make so sharp a distinction as do scholarly grammarians. Not surprisingly the same problem arises here, and I have once more favored the declarative (recitative) translation; but let me expound the three interpretations that have been proposed. (a) All three should be translated as "because": Brooke, Schneider, Westcott (?), RV, NEB. From the viewpoint of grammar this translation leaves *egrapsa* awkwardly without an object; for if the author intended the clauses causally, a better phrasing would have been, "I have not been writing *these things* to you, because . . ." From the viewpoint of meaning, "because" makes good sense for the first clause, but offers problems for the second and third clauses. Why would he write his readers *because* they know the truth or *because* every lie is not from the truth? (b) The first two should be translated as "because" and the third as "that": Büchsel, Chaine, Dodd, Hauck, B. Weiss, Tyndale, Cranmer, KJV, RSV, TEV. This means that the first two clauses are governed by *egrapsa,* while the third clause is governed by the "you know" in the second clause: either, "I have been writing . . . because you know it [the truth], and that every lie is not from the truth," or, "because you know it, namely, that every lie is not from the truth." (Michl insists strongly that there is no double object of "you know," and indeed the first rendition implies a harsh construction.) This is better than (a), but it is still awkward to have the author writing because they know that every lie is not of the truth. (c) All three should be translated as "that": Balz, Bonsirven, Bultmann, de la Potterie, Marshall, Schnackenburg, THLJ. Normally the three clauses would be governed by *egrapsa,* but it is not impossible that the third might be the object of "you know" in the second (Bultmann). Grammatically this is the easiest and makes good sense. The author is writing to reassure them that he recognizes that they know the truth and to remind them of the incompatibility of the Antichrists' lie with the truth. In its affirmation "that you know the truth," 2:21c agrees with the statement in II John (v. 1) that it is written to "all those who have come to know the truth."

21bc. *that you do not know the truth, but that you do know it.* These two lines offer the only NT examples of *oida* (*eidenai*) with "truth" as an object. Although de la Potterie, *La vérité* 2, 575–92, tries valiantly to prove that it has a different meaning from *ginōskein,* "to know" (NOTE on 2:3a above), reflecting a possessed certitude based on *internal* experience or faith, I find it impossible to think that anything else was meant by *ginōskein* in Jesus' promise in John 8:32, "You will know the truth," or in II John 1, which speaks of Johannine Christians as "those who have come to know the truth."

21d. *and that every lie is alien to the truth.* Literally, "not from the truth." In the NOTE on 2:19f we saw that "all, every" as the subject of a negated verb must be understood collectively, not distributively—not "every is not" (= some are) but "none is." *Einai ek,* "to be from," expresses both origin and appurtenance (NOTE 2:16ef): he is not saying only that no lie takes its origin from the truth, but also that no lie belongs to the truth. "To be from the truth" has two other Johannine occurrences (John 18:37; I John 3:19), and it has the same dualistic impact as the more frequent "to be from God," since truth involves a revelation of and by Jesus, Son of God (v. 22b), which has been interiorized through the Spirit. The "lie" represents the dualistic opposite to truth (NOTE on 1:6c).

22a. *Who, then, is the Liar?* Of the seven Johannine instances of *pseustēs,* "liar," this is the only one with the definite article, which is usually a sign that the author is speaking of the known or the particular (BDF 252[1]). Nevertheless, most think that here the author is simply passing from the abstract ("lie" in 21d) to the concrete: "Who is really the one telling lies?" (a rhetorical question shaped by the claim of the opponents to know the truth). Schnackenburg, *Johannesbriefe* 155, says that "the liar" is not a set expression like "the Antichrist." However, John 8:44,55 apply *pseustēs* to the devil; and just as there was a diabolic component in the background of the Antichrist, may not the devil as a liar have been a component in an apocalyptic expectation of *the Liar?* The figure thus entitled would be a divine opponent like the Antichrist, a title that appears in parallelism with the Liar in this same verse. This would make comprehensible the horrendous nature of the charge about making God a liar (I John 5:10), for God is "free from lying" (*apseudēs*), as Titus 1:2 calls Him. If "the Liar" is an apocalyptic expectation like "the Antichrist," v. 22 becomes an excellent parallel to v. 20 as in each verse the author shows how the apocalyptic expectation is fulfilled in the secessionists of his own time. Possibly the origin of *ho pseudēs* as a title is related to the expectation of the false prophet (NOTE on 2:18b, esp. [D]), the *pseudoprophētēs.* In II Thess 2:8–9 we hear, "Then there will be revealed the Iniquitous One [*ho anomos*] . . . whose appearance [*parousia*] is according to the power of Satan with all the miraculous power and signs and wonders of the lie [*pseudos*]." Particularly important is the title "the Man of the Lie" at Qumran to describe the chief adversary. If I John identifies "the Liar" with the Antichrists who "went out" from the Community, CD 20:14–15 speaks about "the men of war who deserted to the Man of the Lie." 4QpPs 37 IV 13–14 applies Ps 37:35–36 to "the Man of the Lie who . . . against the chosen of God," while I 17–19 applies Ps 37:7 to "the Man of the Lie who misled many with his lying words, since such people opted for worthless things and did not listen to the interpreter [*mēlîṣ*] of knowledge"—the word *mēlîṣ* is a plausible Hebrew antecedent for the term *paraklētos* (ABJ 29A, 1138). Thus it is perfectly possible that "the Antichrist," "the Liar," and "the Iniquitous One" were current titles for the anticipated opponent of the last times. In II John 7 "the Deceiver" (*ho planos*) is in parallelism with "the Antichrist"; and in II Thess 2:11 God sends a great *"deceit* [*planē*] so that they will believe the lie" upon the followers of "the Iniquitous One," while in Matt 24:4–5 the false Christs "deceive" many.

22b. *None other than*. Literally *ei mē* means "unless" or "if not." An exact parallel of the rhetorical question followed by *ei mē* is I John 5:5: "Who then is the conqueror of the world? None other than . . ." See also I Cor 2:11; II Cor 2:2.

the person who denies that Jesus *is the Christ*. The literal Greek construction, "the one who denies that Jesus is not the Christ," involving a negative particle after a verb containing a negation, is classical (BDF 429), albeit redundant in English. The same participial expression, "the person who denies [*arneisthai*]," appears in the last line of this verse as a definition of the Antichrist—a good argument for seeing the Liar and the Antichrist as equivalent. *Arneisthai*, used in I John only in 2:22–23, appears four times in GJohn, three of which involve Peter's denial of Jesus during the passion, while the other is in the expression "he confessed and did not deny" (1:20). Here the secessionist adversaries not only fail to confess the truth proclaimed by the author; they actually deny it.

That truth is that Jesus is *ho Christos* (see end of NOTE on 1:3de). That Jesus is the Messiah (*ho Christos*) is preached against Jewish adversaries in Acts 5:42; 9:22; 17:3; 18:28; but that can scarcely be the issue here where the secessionists had been members of the Johannine Christian Community. Can the secessionists have denied that Jesus is the Christ in the divine sense of being the Son of God (Bonsirven, Chaine)? Certainly *Christos* and Son of God are virtually interchangeable in Johannine terminology; but for that very reason how could the secessionists have been Johannine Christians if they did not believe the main theme of GJohn, "that Jesus is the Christ, the Son of God" (20:31)? Could one have been admitted to the Community without that faith? Indeed, the author may be quoting a Johannine initiation/baptismal formula when he insists that Jesus is the Christ or that Jesus is the Son of God (2:22,23; 3:23; 4:15; 5:1,5,13). I propose that the secessionists accepted such formulas (learned when they were Johannine Christians) but understood them in a way that weakened the human content of the formulas, not the divine. (This is suggested by the author's addendum which the secessionists would not have accepted: Jesus is the Christ *come in the flesh* [I John 4:2; II John 7—see INTRODUCTION IV B2a].)

The issue, then, may not center on the predicate "the Christ," but on the subject "Jesus." Not, of course, that the secessionists thought someone else was the Christ (e.g., the false christs of Matt 24:5); but, as proposed by THLJ 68, the debate "was whether the man Jesus could be the same person as the divine Christ." To be precise, the secessionists may have confessed that the Divine Word (who became flesh but was not really changed by the incarnation) was the Christ. For them to stress that *Jesus* was the Christ would mean that his humanity and the way he lived were essential for understanding his role as the Christ, the Son of God. Such a christology could have arisen from a (one-sided) reading of GJohn and/or the Johannine tradition.

22c. *Such is the Antichrist*. Literally, "this is," pointing back to "the Liar" in

v. 22a; but the "this" receives further definition in v. 22d. The definite article, present here but missing in the best textual tradition of 2:18b, shows a set expectation. One might have expected 22c and 22d to be reversed, "The person who denies the Father and the Son is the Antichrist"; but by starting out, "Such is the Antichrist" (22c), the author keeps that line close to 22b, ". . . denies that Jesus is the Christ," and makes a wordplay. That wordplay may explain why he uses the Antichrist in the singular, although he has spoken of Antichrists in 2:18c.

22d. *the person who denies the Father and the Son.* For the peculiar Johannine tendency to use "the Father" and "the Son" absolutely, without modifier, see the NOTES above on 1:2e and 1:3de. Presumably "the Father" is put first to underline the heinousness of the denial; in fact, however, the secessionists are never accused of denying the Father separately from their christology. There is no evidence that they separated the Father from the Creator, regarding the latter as a demiurge (a view that Irenaeus, *Adv. haer.* 1.26.1, attributes to Cerinthus). The author shifts here from a denial of doctrine (22b) to a denial of persons, and shifts from "the Christ" to "the Son" (indicating the interchangeability of the two titles). The desire for a term correlative to "the Father" influenced him, and the shift of order in vv. 22–24 from Father/Son to Son/Father (three times) also suggests correlativity.

23ab. *No person who denies the Son possesses the Father either.* Again *pas*, "all, every," with a negated verb: "everyone denying . . . does not have," meaning "no denier has." This is the first instance of *pas* followed by an articular participle, usually present tense (BDF 413[2]), a construction that Howard, *Fourth Gospel* 278, classifies as a Johannine idiom. It occurs 13 times in GJohn, 13 times in I John, and once in II John 9. The ability to make sweeping classifications is part of a dualistic outlook where all are divided into two sides.

This is our first encounter with the absolute expression "to have [possess] the Father." (I John 2:2, "We have a Paraclete in the Father's presence" is not an absolute statement but is modified by the indication of locale. Not absolute either is a statement describing a role: "We have God as . . .") *Echein* with a divine object occurs twice more in the Epistles: "The person who possesses the Son possesses life" (I John 5:12); "Anyone who is so 'progressive' that he does not remain rooted in the teaching of Christ does not possess God, while anyone who remains rooted in the teaching possesses both the Father and the Son" (II John 9). Although Paul can speak of having the Spirit (I Cor 7:40), this absolute expression "to have God/Father/Son" occurs nowhere else in the NT, not even in GJohn. ("We have but one Father, God Himself" in 8:41 is not comparable.) Hanse's important monograph, *Gott Haben*, points out that in the OT there is no Hebrew verb that expresses the idea exactly. Approximations include: "I will be your God, and you shall be my people" (Lev 26:12 = You will have me as your God); "You shall not have other gods besides me" (Exod 20:3); the Lord is the portion of Levi (Num 18:20; Deut 12:12; Sir 45:22). In Greek religious philosophy people were said to have the divine in them in the sense of having a divine element (soul, *logos*), or in the sense of having unity with the deity, which in ecstasy amounts to possessing the deity and being possessed. It is in Epictetus (*ca.* A.D. 100) that "to have God" expresses an ontological relationship: One has God as creator, father, leader. In Jewish documents preserved in Greek from a period close to the NT the expression "to have God" appears: "They possessed God even unto death" (*III Macc.* 7:16); "You shall be in peace, possessing the God of peace" (*T. Dan* 5:2); "You (shall) have with you the God of heaven and earth" (*T. Issachar* 7:7). Josephus (*Ant.* 9.2.1; ∦20) and Philo (*On Sobriety* 11 ∦58) speak of the Israelites having God as their own heritage.

The background, then, is not particularly helpful for the use of "to have [possess] God" in the Johannine Epistles, except that we may be encountering here a Johannine adaptation of the covenant motif: we have God as Father through Jesus Christ. Suggestions that the expression is the same as "to know God" (Bultmann, B. Weiss) or as "to have *koinōnia* with God" are of limited utility, for more is involved. Hanse, *Gott* 106, points to statements in GJohn about having/possessing divine realities through Christ: life (3:16,36 etc.), word of God (5:38), love of God (5:42), light (8:12; 12:35–36), peace (16:33), and joy (17:13). Since these realities are from God, we have God in the realities. Did the author borrow the expression (absent in GJohn) from the secessionists? More likely it was part of the common Johannine vocabulary of entering the New Covenant, and the author is showing how it may be used properly, in contrast to the secessionists who have their own interpretation (see COMMENT). It continued to be used by both orthodox and heterodox in the second century. On the orthodox side: "You possess Jesus Christ in yourselves" (Ignatius, *Magn.* 12:1); "If anyone possesses God in himself, let him understand what I wish" (*Rom.* 6:3); "The man who possesses the Lord in his heart is master of all things and all these commandments" (*Hermas Man.* 12.4.3; cf. *Hermas Sim.* 1.7); "We who have believed have become more numerous than those who seemed to possess God" (*II Clem.* 2:3). On the heterodox side, Hanse, *Gott* 112–13, discusses the expression in popular gnosticism and the magical papyri. Irenaeus (*Adv. haer.* 1.15.3) tells us of Marcus' view: Upon Jesus, a man specially formed in the womb of Mary, there descended the Being who had formerly ascended on high, the power that was the seed which had in itself the Father and the Son. "After he had received that Aeon, He possessed Anthropos himself, and Logos himself, and Pater [Father]. . . ."

23cd. *while the person who confesses the Son possesses the Father as well.* The statements in 23ab and 23cd are set in asyndetic contrast between the person who denies and the person who confesses. The Byzantine tradition omits these last two lines by homoeoteleuton, i.e., since lines 23b and 23d end with the same Greek words, the scribe's eye skipped down from one to the other. In 1:9 (see NOTE above) the verb *homologein* was used for the confession of sins, the only one of its 10 uses in the Johannine Literature that is not directly or indirectly christological in content. GJohn opens (1:20) with the Baptist confessing and not denying (note the two verbs) that he is not the Messiah, in preparation for his pointing to Jesus as the Lamb of God, the chosen one, and the Messiah. And twice in GJohn (9:22; 12:42) a confession of belief in Jesus (as the Messiah) is said to lead to expulsion from the synagogue. The Johannine Christians developed a confession of Jesus as Son (of Man in 9:35–38, or of God in 20:31), presumably used in admission to the Community. In the epistolary author's view the secessionist interpretation of this confession is tantamount to a denial.

The reciprocal relationship between belief in the Son and belief in the Father echoes GJohn: "The Father and I are one" (10:30); "No one comes to the Father except through me" (14:6); "If you really knew me, you would recognize my Father too" (14:7); "He who refuses to honor the Son refuses to honor the Father who sent him" (5:23); "To hate me is to hate my Father too" (15:23). However, the GJohn statements, when condemnatory, were directed against outsiders who refused to believe in Jesus, whereas I John employs them for an inner-Community struggle in which both parties claim to believe in and honor Jesus. The correlative principle appears also in Matt 10:32–33, "Everyone who confesses me before men, I will confess before my Father who is in heaven; whoever denies me before men, I also will deny before my Father who is in heaven" (note the confess/deny pattern), and in Matt 11:27, "No one knows the Son except the Father, and no one knows the Father except the Son and anyone to whom the Son chooses to reveal him." II Peter 2:1 shows how such ideas were being used in other Christian communities for intramural debate: "False prophets also arose among the people, just as there will be false teachers among you, who will bring in destructive sectarian ideas [*hairesis*], denying the Master who purchased them." The words of II Tim 2:12 are also directed to Christians: "If we deny Christ, he will deny us."

24ab. *As for you, what you heard from the beginning must abide in you.* The sentence begins with *hymeis*, "You"; see NOTE on 2:20a. (The Byzantine tradition, which omits 23cd, inserts here *oun*, "then, therefore"; but this is a scribal imitation of GJohn style where *oun* occurs 194 times in GJohn but only once in the Epistles [p. 23 above].) This *hymeis* indicates a shift of thought from what has preceded, for it stands in a *casus pendens* construction—a Johannine favorite, occurring 28 times in GJohn as compared with a total of 21 times in the three Synoptic Gospels. In this construction a word (often a pronoun) is anticipated from the sentence that follows (here the "you" of "in you") and highlighted by putting it first in the nominative case (a case different from the one it has in the sentence; see ABJ 29, 10 on John 1:12; BDF 466²; MGNTG 4, 71). One might have expected the emphasized "you" to be the agent in what follows; but the real agency is divine, for "what you have heard" implies divine revelation. The "you" are being asked to let the revelation be active in them. For that revelation (expressed comprehensively by a neuter) the author reaches back to "the beginning" of Jesus' self-revelation to his disciples, and also to the repetition of that revelation at "the beginning" of the audience's experience as Johannine Christians (NOTE on 1:1a). "Heard" is aorist as in 2:7c, interchangeable with the perfect tense used in 1:1a. *Menein en,* "to abide in," occurs three times in this verse (lines b,c,e). The first two uses, applying to "what you heard" abiding in Christians, exemplify the (B) category discussed in the NOTE on 2:6a; the closest parallel is "the word" abiding in Christians (John 15:7; I John 2:14) or "the truth" (II John 2). None of these abiding factors is necessarily the same as the anointing that abides (NOTE on 2:27ab).

24cd. *If you have abiding in you what you heard from the beginning.* This repeats words from the first two lines of the verse in a slightly different order within the "heard" clause (Codex Sinaiticus smooths this out), a variation not reflecting a change of emphasis (*pace* Westcott) but Johannine stylistic preference for variety. More importantly, 24ab and 24cd form a chiasm (24a matches 24d; 24b matches 24c). GJohn has chiasms stretching over verses (ABJ 29, cxxxv, 276; 29A, 667, 728) as well as brief chiasms of four lines as here (16:28).

24e. *then will you yourselves abide in the Son and in the Father.* The initial *kai hymeis* means "you in turn." The second "in" (*en*) is omitted by Codex Vaticanus and the Vulgate, followed by B. Weiss. In speaking of the Antichrist denial in 2:22d, the order was "the Father and the Son" (imitated here by Sinaiticus); but now the Son is put first, probably because it is through the Son that the Christian abides in the Father (5:20). Unlike the previous two instances of *menein en,* "to abide in," in this verse, this one represents classification (A) in the NOTE on 2:6a, covering divine indwelling. While many Johannine passages have the Christian abiding in God or in Jesus, only this one has the Christian abiding in the Son and the Father mentioned together. However, two passages use the interchangeable *einai en,* "to be in," in the same circumstance (John 17:21; I John 5:20).

25. *Now this is the promise which he himself made to us, and it amounts to eternal life.* Literally the last part (lines bc) reads, "which he [*autos*] promised to us, eternal life." This construction, "the promise which he promised," is a cognate accusative or accusative of content (BDF 153; cf. "the love with which you loved me" [John 17:26]). The noun *epangelia,* "promise," which occurs 52 times in the NT, is used only here by John (although some scribes substitute it for *angelia* in I John 1:5; 3:11). It is a word related to *epangellein* discussed in the NOTE on 1:2c. Here it means not so much the action of making a promise (covered by the verb) but the content promised.

Codex Vaticanus, some minuscules, and some Vulgate MSS. read "to you" instead of "to us," a scribal change to make the verse conform with the surrounding verses that refer to the second person. The shift to the first person plural (only instance in 2:20–27) raises the question of whether the author is speaking as a member of the Johannine School (the "we" of 1:1–5) or as a fellow member of the Johannine Community (the "we" elsewhere). Since the promise involves eternal life, which is possessed by all true believers, he probably means the latter; but the way in which the Johannine School appropriates *koinōnia* with God in 1:3 demands caution in judging the author's mind—the "us" always includes the Johannine School as a presupposition.

There are two major problems of translation. (a) We have here another "And this is" sentence (*kai houtos estin*), discussed in the NOTES on 1:5a and 1:5d. *A priori,* in such a construction it is not certain whether the reference of the "this" is to what precedes (here the "abiding" and indwelling of v. 24) or to what follows ("eternal life" in 25c). Without some reference to what precedes (for which B. Weiss argues) the thought is very abrupt. But does it seem likely that the content of v. 24 was a promise that Christ himself made? One does not find verbatim in GJohn among the sayings of Jesus the words of 24cde: "If you have abiding in you what you heard from the beginning, then will you yourselves abide in the Son and in the Father." Yet passages resembling that include: "Abide in me as I abide in you. . . . If you abide in me and my words abide in you . . ." (John 15:4,7); ". . . that they may be one just as we are one, I in them and you in me" (17:22–23). Nevertheless, "This is the promise" in 2:25a cannot refer only to what precedes in v. 24, since the last words of v. 25, "eternal life," are in the accusative and stand in apposition to "which" as the object of the verb "he promised" (see BDF 295). That grammatical fact leads some like Schnackenburg to exclude all reference in the promise to the preceding verse; but I would argue along with Wilder that the reference is both backward and forward. Primarily the promise concerns the abiding in 24cde, but that abiding in Son and Father leads to and is a form of eternal life, which then becomes part of the promise. If one searches the sayings of Jesus in GJohn, again one does not find verbatim a promise of eternal life; but eternal life is frequently offered to those who believe (3:16,36; 5:24; 6:40,47; etc.).

The epistolary author may mean that such an offer can be looked upon as a promise *now* fulfilled in those who have abiding in them what they heard from the beginning, i.e., in those who have continued to profess their belief in Jesus (Bultmann, Marshall). However, others (Bonsirven, Chaine, Mussner, Schnackenburg, Thüsing) think that I John itself is referring to future fulfillment, so that eternal life is still a future promise. Houlden and Malatesta argue that for the author the promise is both present and future. Since this is the only Johannine use of the verb and noun for "promise," vocabulary itself does not solve the question. Nor do other NT references to the futurity of promised salvific gifts, e.g., Jas 1:12: "Blessed is the man who endures trial, for when he has stood the test, he will receive the crown of *life* which God has promised to those who love Him" (also I Tim 4:8). In the area of eschatology Johannine thought is in many ways *sui generis* and has to be diagnosed from within. That there is futurity in I John's outlook on God's gifts cannot be denied; for I John 3:2 says, "What we shall be has not yet been revealed." And there are several GJohn passages that make a future promise in terms of life, e.g., John 5:28–29: "An hour is coming in which all those in the tombs will hear his voice and will come forth. Those who have done what is right will rise to live"; 12:25: "The man who hates his life in this world preserves it to eternal life." This future attitude toward life exists also in Revelation (a distant Johannine "cousin"), e.g., "Be faithful to death, and I shall give you the crown of life" (2:10). However, despite the greater emphasis on futurity in I John, there is not a single epistolary passage that clearly relegates eternal life to the future. I John 3:14 states, "That we have passed from death to life we know"; and 5:12 assures, "The person who possesses the Son possesses life." The latter passage makes it most likely that here in 2:25 the author means a promise fulfilled in the present life of the believers, i.e., in those who have abiding in them the word that has come down from Jesus and who abide in the Son and in the Father (2:24). The author may be thinking of John 17:3 as the promise: "Now this is eternal life: that they know you, the one true God, and Jesus Christ, the one whom you sent."

(b) Does the "he" (autos) who makes the promise refer to God or to Christ, or even (by intentional vagueness) to both? (The Coptic versions omit the pronoun.) In a previous instance of ambiguity (2:3a) I opted for God, but each case must be decided on its own merits. The fact that a promise in GJohn would have had to be made by Jesus does not solve the problem; for Jesus gave the commandment to love one another in GJohn, but the epistolary author always attributes the commandment to God. That God is meant here (Büchsel, B. Weiss) is favored by the fact that closest antecedent for the pronoun is "Father" in v. 24e. Certainly the NT knows of promises of life by God (Titus 1:2; Jas 1:12). That both God and Christ are meant (Houlden) is favored by the fact that both are mentioned in v. 24e. Nevertheless, more scholars (Balz, Bonsirven, Chaine, de la Potterie, Schnackenburg) contend that *autos* is Christ. I accept this last position because the *autos* has some emphatic force ("he himself"), and the dispute in the previous verses has centered on denying that Jesus is the Christ (v. 22b) and on denying the Son (23)—it is Jesus, not the Father, whom the author needs to underline.

26a. *I have been writing this to you.* The author shifts back from the "us" of v. 25 to the "you" of v. 24. Accordingly Westcott starts a new subunit here; but the "As for you" in 27 marks a greater refocusing than does 26. The verb is *egrapsa* as in 2:21a and three times in 2:14. Each usage makes it more difficult to think that a past writing is envisaged—it would have been remarkably unsuccessful since he is writing all over again. Among the proposed candidates for such a past writing, GJohn was scarcely written "about those [secessionists] who deceive you" (26b); however, II John might fit that description. But surely the present writing fits the description best of all.

26b. *about those who deceive you.* The participle of *planan* may be a conative present (BDF 319): "those who would deceive you"; but even that would be a polite way of indicating what the author and his readers know to be a fact, namely, that the deception is in progress (1:8; 3:7). There is Coptic and Armenian evidence for reading the participle as a singular, and this scribal modification hints at a correct theological insight. The secessionists are Antichrists embodying the apocalyptic expectation of the Antichrist; they are liars embodying the apocalyptic expectation of the Liar; even so they embody the great deception of the last times. In the NOTE on 1:8b I showed the range of "deceive/deceit" in Johannine dualism. In I John 4:6 opposed to the "the Spirit of Truth" is "the Spirit of Deceit," and deceit is characteristic at Qumran for the spirit promoting evil on earth. Further references in that NOTE show that elsewhere in the NT deceit is connected with the last times and the false prophets, culminating with the description of the devil as "the deceiver of the whole earth" (Rev 12:9). The last days are described thus in *Didache* 16:4: "As iniquity [*anomia*] increases, they shall hate, persecute, and betray one another; then shall appear the deceiver of the world as God's Son." To describe the secessionists as "those who deceive" is to reinforce their connection with the Antichrist.

26c. Augustine (*In Epistolam* 3.12; SC 75, 208) and some Spanish and Montpellier Latin MSS. have at the end of v. 26 a Latin reading with little or no Greek support (see INTRODUCTION VI B): "so that you may know that you have an anointing (and that you know all things)." The first part of this additional line is clearly transitional to v. 27 which continues in Augustine's Latin: "and the anointing which we have received from him abides in us." The second part (in parentheses because it is not found in Augustine) echoes 2:20b, translating *panta* (accusative, common in the Latin textual witnesses) rather than *pantes* (nominative).

27a. *As for you. Kai hymeis* as in 2:20a (NOTE there); here, however, it is not the subject of the sentence but a *casus pendens* as was the *hymeis* of 2:24a (NOTE there). It anticipates the pronoun from the phrase "in you" of 27b, and sets up a strong contrast with "those who deceive you" of the preceding verse.

27ab. *the anointing that you received from him abides in you.* The Greek for the last three words is *menei en hymin;* in 2:24b it was *en hymin menetō* ("must abide in you"). Scribes of some codices in the Byzantine tradition imitate that word order here, but the reversed order is a typical intentional stylistic variant. Some Greek minuscules and the Vulgate also imitate the imperative of 2:24b, but here the author is arguing from a fact ("abides"), not exhorting ("must abide"). In a long NOTE on "anointing" in 2:20a I discussed most of the issues of this verse, arguing that the author was probably speaking of an anointing (perhaps physical) with the Holy Spirit, the gift from Christ that makes one a Christian. *Charisma,* "grace, charism," read here in place of *chrisma,* "anointing," by Codex Vaticanus, if not merely a scribal slip, may be an attempt to identify the factor involved as baptismal grace. The *autos* in "from him" probably refers to the same person as the *autos* in 2:25b ("he himself") and as "the Holy One" in 2:20a—in both cases Christ was the most plausible possibility. The use here of *menein en,* "to abide in," reflects the (B) classification in the NOTE on 2:6a, although it overlaps the (A) classification; for here the reality which abides (anointing) is really a divine presence (the Paraclete/Spirit). John 14:17 says that the Paraclete abides with (*menein para*) the Christian and is within (*einai en*) the Christian, while I John 3:24 makes the Spirit the sign of God's abiding in us. Indeed, if we remember the present sequence where abiding in the Son and in the Father (v. 24e) is part of the promise of v. 25, the meaning of the anointing may be clarified by 4:13: "This is how we can know that we abide in Him and He abides in us: in that He has given us of His own Spirit."

27cd. *and so you have no need for anyone to teach you.* The exact Greek form of this expression denying need (and using *hina*) is peculiar to the Johannine writings in the Bible (John 2:25; 16:30), although the positive form expressing need occurs in the Sinaiticus of Tob 5:7. The range of teaching words in the Johannine literature is as follows:

▪ *didaskein,* "to teach": a total of 9 times in GJohn (6 times for Jesus' teaching; once [8:28] for the Father's teaching Jesus; once [14:26] for the Paraclete's teaching the disciples), and 2 times in I John (both in this verse).

- *didachē,* "teaching": thrice in GJohn for Jesus' teaching; thrice in II John 9–10.
- *didaskalos,* "teacher": 7 times in GJohn (6 referring to Jesus).
- *didaskalia,* "act of teaching": not used.

27e–h. To make intelligible the problems of the last four lines of v. 27, let me supply a literal translation:

27e But as [hōs] his anointing teaches you about all things
27f and is true and is not a lie
27g and as [kathōs] it/he taught you
27h [you] abide in it/him [autos]

There are a few textual variants, mostly sparked by the grammatical obscurity of the passage. In 27e Codex Vaticanus omits the "as," but that is probably a scribal attempt to soften the construction, since the sentence makes better sense without it. Codex Alexandrinus and the Byzantine tradition read "the same anointing" for "his anointing," perhaps a scribal attempt to avoid both the ambiguity of the "his" and the awkward way the author has written the possessive. ("The same anointing," however, would represent a construction nowhere else attested in John.) The Sinaiticus reading of "Spirit" for "anointing" is clearly interpretive. In 27g Codex Alexandrinus and the Sahidic omit the initial "and"—a scribal attempt (in the right direction!) to straighten out the hopelessly complicated grammar. In 27h the Byzantine tradition reads a future (*meneite,* "you shall remain"), and this appears in early English versions, including the KJV. It is a scribal attempt to avoid the problem of whether the original *menete* is indicative or imperative, and echoes the future of *menein* in 24e. The basic problem throughout these variants is not corrupt copying but the author's propensity for writing obscure sentences. Three difficult points need to be discussed.

First, should this all be read as one sentence? This seems to be the view of Bonsirven, Brooke (?), Chaine, de la Potterie, Dodd, Malatesta, Marshall, Schneider, Westcott, and Windisch. A possible way of translating it as one sentence is: "Rather, inasmuch as his anointing teaches you about all things, and is true and free from any lie, and even as it/he taught you, so also do you abide in it/him." Thus the first three clauses constitute the protasis of the comparison, and the fourth clause constitutes the apodosis. However, the third line (27g) becomes very awkward and must almost be considered parenthetical. Why does the author shift from "teaches" in 27e to "taught" in 27g, if there is only one comparison involved? Why is the "as" repeated in 27g if that line is already covered by the "as" of line 27e? Because of these objections, another group of scholars prefers to think of two sentences (or, at least, of a compound sentence) where there are two comparisons, with 27ef containing one protasis and apodosis, and 27gh containing the other. This view is supported by Belser, Büchsel, Bultmann, Haas, Hauck, Schnackenburg, and B. Weiss (and is implied by the textual correction in Alexandrinus mentioned above). A possible way of translating this understanding of the lines is: "Rather, as his teaching teaches you about all things, so it is true and free from any lie; and just as it taught you, so you are to abide in him." Thus understood, the presence of a second comparative ("just as") in line 27g becomes intelligible, as does the shift from "teaches" (27e) to "taught" (27g)—he is drawing one comparison from the present and another from the past. The weakness of this approach is that the *kai,* "and," beginning line 27f, must be understood as "so," introducing an apodosis. Grammarians agree this is possible (BDF 442[7]), but Marshall, *Epistles* 163, stresses that it is hard to find an example truly parallel to this. Nevertheless, I have opted for this interpretation where 27e–h consists of a compound sentence with two comparisons; it fits better the rhythm of 27a–d which is also a compound sentence.

SECOND, the reference of some of the pronouns, implied or explicit, is unclear. Is the implicit subject of "taught" in 27g the "he" from whom the anointing was received (27a), or the anointing itself? In the one-sentence rendition of the four lines, "he" might be better in order to explain why there is a line 27g—if "anointing" is the subject of 27g, that line virtually repeats 27e. In the two-sentence (or compound-sentence) interpretation of the four lines, the parallelism between the two protases (27e and 27g) suggests that the subject in each should be the same, i.e., the anointing. Another question is whether the form of *autos* that is the object of the preposition "in" in the last line of v. 27 is to be read as "it" (the anointing) or as "him" (the Christ of 27a)? The "it" reading is favored by Büchsel, Bultmann, Thüsing, and some Latin MSS. that read *in ipsa* (feminine, agreeing with *unctio,* "anointing"). The "him" (Christ) reading is favored by Balz, Brooke, Haas, Malatesta, Marshall, Michl, Plummer, Schnackenburg, and THLJ. (B. Weiss would argue that the "him" of 27a and 27h is God; Westcott thinks the "him" refers to God-in-Christ; but these views have little following.) I have opted for the "him" on the grounds that if the author referred to an abiding in the *chrisma,* he would normally have written *en toutō,* "in this," rather than *en autō.* Moreover, in the repetition of this same *en autō* phrase in the line beginning the next verse (2:28a), the reference is more plausibly to a person.

THIRD, is the verb form (*menete*) in the last line (27h) to be read as an imperative or an indicative? Brooke, Chaine, de la Potterie, Kohler, Loisy, Malatesta, and Westcott argue for an indicative, pointing to the parallelism with 27ab: "the anointing . . . abides in you." On the other hand, Bultmann, Heise, Marshall, Schnackenburg, Schneider, Thüsing, and Windisch argue for an imperative, pointing to the parallelism with 24b: "must abide in you." The fact that the same form (*menete*) is imperative in the next verse (28a) may favor an indicative here, so that the author is not simply repeating himself. In any case there is little difference of meaning, for even the indicative would stress the necessity of continuing to abide in him. With that understanding I have opted for the indicative.

COMMENT

Because the previous unit (2:12–17) consists of clear subunits (2:12–14; 2:15–17), each with easily detectable internal structure, most scholars posit a new unit or subunit beginning with 2:18. The real problem for the structure of the present unit, then, is not the beginning but the end. Scholars are almost evenly divided as to whether this unit should end with 2:27 or 2:28.[1] Those who extend the unit from 2:18 to 2:28 often point to an inclusion between those two verses, e.g., both have an address to "(Little) Children"; and while one mentions the coming of the Antichrist, the other mentions the parousia, or coming of Christ. However, those similarities still have validity if 2:18 is meant to introduce one unit, while 2:28 introduces the next unit—the beginning verses of the two units are then parallel. Part of the difficulty arises from the Johannine love of hinge verses that end one section and begin another (p. 119 above) and have the themes of both.

As for the internal structure of 2:18–27 (or 2:18–28), there are different approaches. One is chiastic (ABJ 29, cxxxv), and the main features of the proposed chiasm may be sketched thus:

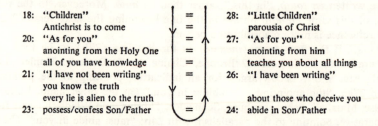

18:	"Children"	=	28:	"Little Children"
	Antichrist is to come	=		parousia of Christ
20:	"As for you"	=	27:	"As for you"
	anointing from the Holy One	=		anointing from him
	all of you have knowledge	=		teaches you about all things
21:	"I have not been writing"	=	26:	"I have been writing"
	you know the truth			
	every lie is alien to the truth	=		about those who deceive you
23:	possess/confess Son/Father	=	24:	abide in Son/Father

As impressive as the sketch is, a perusal of the verses involved will show that many features which do not fit the chiasm have been left out. Moreover, other sets of parallels would hopelessly complicate the proposed chiasm, e.g., 2:27 is closer in some themes to 2:24 than to 2:20.[2]

Malatesta, *Interiority* 163, speaks of an introduction in v. 18 and a paraenetic conclusion in v. 28, with a triple set of antitheses in between:

[1] Balz, Brooke, de Jonge, Häring, Hauck, Houlden, Jones, Marshall, Schnackenburg, Schneider, Schwertschlager, Stott, B. Weiss, Wilder, Williams, and Windisch (also NEB, TEV) end a main division or unit with 2:27. Alexander, Chaine, de la Potterie, Dodd, Huther, Law, Malatesta, and Nagl end it with 2:28. Bonsirven, F.-M. Braun, THLJ, Westcott, and JB end it with 2:29.

[2] Both 2:24 and 2:27 address a "You," mention something from the past that should abide in the Christian, and speak of the Christian abiding in Christ.

v. 19: nonbeliever   vv. 22–23ab: nonbeliever   v. 26: nonbeliever
vv. 20–21: faithful   vv. 23cd–25: faithful   v. 27: faithful

However, these "antitheses" are quite unlike the antitheses of the units in 1:5–2:2 and 2:3–11, where there is a similarity of structure between the two parts of the antithesis. Moreover, Malatesta himself (*Interiority* 193–95) seems implicitly to see the inequities of structures in the three antitheses, for he speaks of seven strophes as a principle of division (18, 19, 20–21, 22–23, 24, 25, 27—with v. 26 seemingly a summary).

I have adopted another arrangement of 2:18–27 based on a pattern of direct initial addresses to the audience as markers of subunits. The opening address for the whole unit is "Children," comparable to the opening address "Little Children" in the preceding and following units (2:12a; 2:28a). Then, within the unit the author turns three times to address a "You" (plural) by placing the personal pronoun *hymeis* at the beginning of a sentence (2:20,24,27—NOTE on 2:20a). Each of these is accompanied by a reference to an anointing or a message received from Christ. These addresses and references serve well as the opening lines of subunits. The idea that the author might use addresses to mark off subunits has been tested favorably in 2:12 and 2:14; and without arguing that the author was working consciously to form subunits, one may claim that a sudden turn by the author to his audience as an addressed "You" represents his way of grouping thoughts.

Nevertheless, this unit is held together by more than a series of addresses: there is a common thought pattern. Verse 18 serves as a topical sentence: "It is the last hour." The prophets and Jesus had spoken of the last days (or "that hour") and the signs that would accompany that period. The author thinks the signs have come to pass in his own time in the secession. In the first subunit (2:18b–19) he speaks of the coming of the Antichrist; in the second subunit (2:20–23), of the Liar and the Antichrist; in the third subunit (2:24–26), of those who deceive; with a final appeal in v. 27 to his readers to abide in Christ and not to be like the secessionists who went out from the Community and did not abide. The readers are capable of abiding in Christ because the anointing (through the Spirit) they received from Christ abides in them and enables them to distinguish Christian truth from the lying of the Antichrists.

A. The Secessionists as the Antichrist of the Last Hour (2:18–19)

This unit opens with a lapidary sentence: "Children, it is the last hour." Schnackenburg (*Johannesbriefe* 141), recognizing this, argues for beginning Part Two of I John here; but I would contend that the connection to what precedes is too strong for that. We saw (pp. 291–92) that the unit 2:3–11 ended with the Johannine division of all people into those who abide in the light and do not stumble and those who walk in the dark while claiming to be in the light. In the next unit (2:12–17) the author turned his attention to the first group, the children of light who are his "Children," reassuring them that they have known Christ, have had their sins forgiven, and have conquered the Evil One. He warned them not to compromise by loving the world, which was under the power of the Evil One. In the present unit (2:18–27) the author turns his attention to the other group, the children of darkness. Hitherto he has referred to their claims and boasts; but now, just as he identified the children of light as his "Children," so he identifies the children of darkness as secessionists or schismatics who have left his adherents.[3] GJohn used the language of "darkness" and of "going out" for opponents of Jesus;[4] it has been reapplied to an inner Johannine struggle.

Going further, the epistolary author draws upon the figurative language of Jewish and Christian apocalyptic to describe the adversaries. In the NOTE on 2:18b I discussed at length the background in the OT and intertestamental Judaism that led Christians to expect a great adversary in the last days, an adversary known to the recipients of I John as the Antichrist. One does not find such an apocalyptic expectation in GJohn (although GJohn speaks of the Prince of this world who orchestrates hatred of Jesus during his lifetime and afterward), but its presence in the Book of Revelation suggests that at one time it may well have been part of the Johannine heritage.[5] The epistolary author, interested in what has been from the beginning, reminds his readers that they had heard the language of final eschatology (INTRODUCTION V C2d);[6] and he uses this language alongside that of GJohn ("darkness") in his struggle.

The Johannine Jesus spoke of his salvific work as taking place in "the

[3] I remind the reader that in speaking of "secessionists" I am using the author's own terminology (2:19: "It was from our ranks that they went out"). The adversaries may have used the same terminology of the author and his adherents, at least by charging them with having departed from the Johannine truth. Whichever group moved physically from the other undoubtedly justified the move as a separation from corruption.

[4] Blindness, darkness, and turning away from light constitute charges against nonbelievers, especially Jews, in John 3:19; 9:39–41; 12:35,37–40. The language of "going out" (aperchesthai, exerchesthai, hypagein) is applied to former disciples who do not believe in Jesus any longer and to Judas (6:66,67; 13:30–31).

[5] The stress in GJohn on realized eschatology (ABJ 29, cxvi–cxxi) is seen by some as the evangelist's attempt systematically to remove final eschatology. I do not think the evangelist worked so dialectically; rather he emphasized what was necessary in the struggle with the synagogue. There was no fight with "the Jews" over future judgment, but there was need to emphasize that the coming of Jesus was a present judgment.

[6] Hoskyns, "Espistles" 663: "This passage [2:18] clearly disproves the theory that in the Johannine writings primitive Christian eschatology had been entirely displaced by the mystical union with God and with His Son."

hour," an hour that was also a moment of judgment for those who opposed him and for the Prince of this world (John 12:23, 31–32). In some passages, including one where he predicted the persecution of his followers (16:2—NOTE on 2:18a above), Jesus spoke not only as if the hour had come but also as if it were still coming. In other words, he indicated that the effect of his own hour and its struggle had yet to be shared with his disciples. The author of I John, influenced by the standard apocalyptic expressions "the last days" and "the last time," speaks of the fulfillment of that coming hour as "the last hour." He knows it is present because the great adversary of the final time, the Antichrist,[7] has made his presence felt. Jews and Christians expected Satan to be let loose, false prophets and false messiahs to appear, along with a deception of God's people and a loss of faith. The author finds this fulfilled in the secession by former brethren who had now become false prophets (I John 4:1) and who were busy trying to deceive his adherents (2:26; 3:7). By treating them as the manifestation of the Antichrist, he shows that he does not regard their action simply as human wrongdoing; rather they reflect the power of the Evil One in whose grasp the whole world lies (5:19).[8] In this historicizing of the apocalyptic struggle,[9] the epistolary author made an important theological step, pressing common Christian oratory to new conclusions. For instance, James 4:4 asks, "Do you not know that one who is a lover of the world becomes an enemy of God?" In the previous unit I John 2:15 advised, "Have no love for the world"; now the author identifies the supreme enemy of God, the Antichrist.

It is interesting to survey how commentators react to this bold use of apocalyptic imagery in I John. As I mentioned in the NOTE on 2:18a, some try to explain away the author's mistake in thinking that his time was "the last hour" of the world. Others cannot believe that the author had given up the expectation of a further, personal Antichrist (such as predicted by II Thess 2:1–12). Houlden, *Epistles* 76, finds a lower level of sophistication in the author's resort to Jewish eschatological and apocalyptic language, which GJohn had relegated to minor importance. I disagree with such a value judgment. It is true that apocalyptic imagery may

[7] In the NOTE on 2:18b I showed that while the term is attested only in I John before the second century, the components of the idea were known on a wide scale. Other titles may have been used: the Iniquitous One, the Adversary, the Liar, the Deceiver.

[8] In discussing the relation between the singular "Antichrist" of 2:18b and the plural "Antichrists" of 2:18c, F.-M. Braun, "La réduction" 59, is right in seeing the assimilation of the plural to the singular as the subordination of individuals to a higher power.

[9] Historicizing is at work in Revelation as well; for behind the mythological beasts of ch. 13, the visionary is referring to Rome and to such emperors as Nero and Domitian. On a regional level, Rev 2:20 uses the biblical image of Jezebel and the apocalyptic image of the false prophet(ess) to condemn a woman (sibyl?) opponent in the Thyatira area.

arise from a primitive world view; but its perdurance means that, in dealing with the unseen and the future, apocalyptic preserves a sense of mystery which more rational and logical descriptions cannot encompass. Yes, the author was wrong, as were his NT contemporaries, in thinking that the end of time was at hand; and theological platitudes about the whole Christian era being the final period (even if that is true) will not disguise his error which has been made many times since. But an exaggerated sense of the end-time may be a lesser theological error than the naive assumption that God's plan of salvation must be worked out in an ever-continuing ordinary time, such as experienced in our own lives. After all, even a too hasty identification of the end-time is an act of faith that God does have a purpose and a goal. Dodd, *Epistles* 49–51, hints that identifying a supreme evil figure, like the Antichrist, with historical contemporaries reflects a vision of the power of evil in the world which is less erroneous than the banal attribution of all that goes wrong to human error and ignorance. Nevertheless, the author of I John has begun a chain of identifications of the Antichrist that would have enormous repercussions in Christian history. While he saw his adversaries as the Antichrist, a century later Tertullian would see his adversaries as the Antichrist;[10] and many centuries later the Reformers would see their enemy (the Pope) as the Antichrist. Often such identifications of the Antichrist with contemporary adversaries were made with the supposition that the biblical writer had seen the future and had predicted the appearance of the adversaries now being encountered. But if the epistolary author demythologized the Antichrist by seeing an apocalyptic expectation of evil fulfilled in a schism that had wracked the Johannine Community, perhaps the time has come to demythologize further his insight by recognizing what he really teaches —not the advisability of continuing to identify one's Christian opponents as the Antichrist, but the evil of schism and of doctrinal division in the Christian community.

The few lines of 2:19 constitute most of our historical knowledge about the Johannine schism. Seemingly the secession took place at a particular time[11] and resulted in the emergence of a distinct group who now can be spoken of as "they." The author's adherents already know of the secession, and he does not have to explain it to them; rather he interprets it as the manifestation of the Antichrist. If we analyze the statement, "It was

---

[10] *De praescriptione haereticorum* 33.11; CC 1, 214: "In his epistle [John] designates as the chief Antichrists those who deny Christ to have come in the flesh and those who think that Jesus was not the Son of God. Marcion proved to be an example of the former, Ebion of the latter."

[11] The author may worry about continuing secessionist inroads, but already the secessionists and the author's adherents are distinct groups hostilely facing each other. This is indicated by I John 4:4: "You have conquered those people," a saying scarcely referring to hidden adversaries still among the author's adherents.

from our ranks [from us] that they went out," it is interesting that he does not say that they broke *koinōnia* with *me*,[12] even though they may have been more opposed to him than to his adherents whom they are still trying to win over (I John 2:26; 3:7; II John 10–11). It was part of the author's polemic technique to make his readers feel betrayed by the secessionist action. Moreover, he places the blame for hostility on the adversaries: They went out from us; we did not go out from them. Consequently he can accuse them of hating their brethren (as already in 2:9, 11). Here he is echoing the OT description of the most dangerous rebels against God, the false prophets: "If you hear that . . . the iniquitous [*paranomoi*] have *gone out from your ranks* and have drawn away the inhabitants of your city, saying, 'Let us go and serve other gods,' . . ." (Deut 13:2–6, 13–14 [RSV 13:1–5, 12–13]). No matter how a third party might have apportioned blame in the schism, for the author his adversaries are apostates, and apostasy is a sign of the last times.[13] By leaving, the secessionists were not making a mistake but were acting consistently according to their internal principle of darkness: "If they had belonged to us, they would have remained with us; rather, this helped to reveal them in that none of them belongs to us" (2:19c–f).[14] Thus the author turns the schism from a disastrous defeat into a triumph of God's light. The coming of the Johannine Jesus, who was God's Son, as light into the world identified those who preferred darkness because of their evil life-orientation as manifested in their deeds (John 3:16–21). That same *krisis* or judgment is continued by the proclamation of the truth about Jesus as the Christ, the Son of God (I John 2:22–23): it forces some who were within the Community to show their preference for darkness; and that is far better than if they remained hidden. Houlden, *Epistles* 78, is right in insisting that nowhere else in the NT is there evidence of a schism such as that described here, not even in the Pauline Pastorals (1 Tim 1:3–7) despite their oratory.

[12] The "us" in 2:19a is not the "we/us" of I John 1:1–5 where it stood for the Johannine tradition-bearers (the Johannine School) distinct from the general Johannine Community (the "you" being addressed). Here 2:18d makes it clear that the "us" includes the author and his adherents.

[13] Some have argued, wrongly in my judgment (NOTE on 2:19a), that the dissidents were excommunicated—I do not think the Johannine tradition-bearers had sufficient authority for that. A judgment on them by authority, no matter how justified, would always be external and could be dismissed as failing to see the truth. By stressing that they went out, the author is underlining their judgment on themselves.

[14] The archetype of the secessionist movement in GJohn was Judas who, although he was nominally one of the Twelve and thus appeared to be one of those given by the Father to Jesus, was really a "son of perdition" and a devil (John 17:12; 6:70–71). The hour of Jesus brought out his real identity, for Satan entered into him (13:2,27) and he "went out" into the night to which he belonged (13:30).

B. *Anointing as a Reassurance against Secessionist Lies* (2:20–23)

Hitherto the author's attacks on boasts and claims (implicitly against the secessionists) have concerned walking in darkness, not keeping the commandments, not loving one's brother, and pretending to be sinless— ethical issues that gave the lie to perfectionist attitudes of knowing God, being in communion with and abiding in Him (1:5–2:11). Only in this subunit does it at last become clear that a christological issue sparked the secession, something that we might have guessed from GJohn which is so single-mindedly christological. Since only one group of secessionists is involved (INTRODUCTION IV B1), the ethical indifference to commandments, to how one walks, and to sin must somehow be related to the denial "that *Jesus* is the Christ." In the NOTE on 2:22b I have argued that in this confession "Jesus" means for the author the *incarnate* Word in his life and death, while the secessionists would acknowledge primarily the preexistent Word as the Christ, the Son of God, with the incarnation adding nothing essential.[15] Their failure to appreciate the life of the incarnate Word or, in the language of I John, their failure to appreciate the way he walked, leads to their failure to appreciate the importance of the way in which Christians must walk—that is how their christological and ethical errors are connected.[16] Even more disastrously, their failure to appreciate the death of Jesus on the cross (his blood) makes them misunderstand how we have become God's children—not through the incarnation alone but through the crucifixion. And so their denial of Jesus (the incarnate Word) as the Christ or the Son is tantamount to a denial of the fatherhood of God (2:22c–23).[17]

In reference to the preexistent Word who is in the world (but without any emphasis on his career or death) the GJohn Prologue says that those

[15] I suspect that, being Johannine Christians, the secessionists could say "Jesus is the *Christ*" but with different emphasis—the Christ became Jesus. This is still not Cerinthianism (INTRODUCTION IV B3d), where the Christ descended on a full human being named Jesus. The secessionist view, as I have constructed it, is not absurd. Orthodox theology of the Trinity has struggled how to reconcile the unchangeability of the divine Second Person with the incarnation. A Scholastic answer is that the incarnation did not change the divine Son but gave him a new relationship.

[16] Walking as Christ walked helped to make the author's adherents "Christian"; the failure to do so helped make the secessionists "Antichrists."

[17] For the author denying the Son as equivalent to denying the Father is not an intellectual matter but one relative to Christian life itself. In 2:23 he equates correct confession of Jesus as the Son with possessing (having) the Father. In a NOTE on this strange Johannine expression in 2:23ab, I followed the thesis that it may be related to "having" divine realities (God's life, light, love, word, etc.) so that through them the believers "have" God within themselves.

who believe in his name are those begotten by God (John 1:10–12). It is not obvious, then, from GJohn that the secessionist position is unfaithful to Johannine tradition, and understandably the epistolary author fears that the secessionists may deceive his adherents (I John 2:26). His first and main support against them is that his adherents have been anointed with the Holy Spirit, a gift from Christ, when they began their Christian life (2:20a, 27a,e).[18] The Paraclete/Spirit who guides along the way of all truth (John 16:13) gives all of them knowledge about Christ. The author never denies that his adversaries were once anointed. If that argument were possible, his silence is most curious since it would have been an excellent polemic point. Rather, if anointing was received when one became a Christian, the secessionists as former members of the Community necessarily would have been anointed. This is consonant with their obvious claim to possess the Spirit (I John 4:1). In that case how does anointing (with the Spirit) guarantee a correct knowledge of Christ for the author's adherents if anointing did not protect the secessionists from diabolic deceit? Hidden beneath the oratory in 2:20,27 about the effectiveness of the anointing as a teacher of the Christian is the author's presupposition that the Spirit will confirm the Johannine School's interpretation of the Gospel because the Spirit inspired that interpretation. In other words the author assumes the criterion that he will make explicit in 4:6: "Anyone who has knowledge of God listens to us. . . . That is how we can know the Spirit of Truth from the Spirit of Deceit." Dodd, *Epistles* 54, phrases this well: "He writes with authority just because he is confident that he expresses the corporate convictions of the Church, which will be recognized as such by all humble and sincere believers."[19] But more of this in the next subunit (2:24–26).

In 2:20b the author says to his adherents, "All of you have knowledge."[20] He is clearly contrasting his adherents (the "you") with the secessionists of whom he has just said, "None of them belongs to us"; and

[18] In the long NOTE on 2:20a, in discussing four disputed points about "the *chrisma* from the Holy One," I concluded that the *chrisma* probably means anointing and not simply ointment, that the anointing *may* have been physical and was probably associated with entrance into the Community, that the anointing was symbolic of the gift of the Spirit, and that the Holy One who was the source of the anointing was Christ.

[19] Dodd continues, "It is to him and to others like him that we owe it that the faith emerged from the stage of fluidity with new forms of thought and expression adapted to its wider environment, but with its Gospel intact."

[20] De la Potterie, *La vérité* 2, 589–90, discusses various interpretations of this verse. For some (Brooke, Büchsel, Charue, Dodd, Michl, Schnackenburg) it means: You have true gnosis over against the false gnosis of the opponents. For others (Belser, Bonsirven, Chaine, Westcott) it means: You have the internal ability to discern truth from error. De la Potterie himself thinks it means: You have the certitude that Jesus is the Christ and you dwell in him. In substance I agree that this last view is intended, but I cannot see that it is much different from what the other scholars are saying. De la Potterie tends to be overrefined in his precisions.

his stress on knowledge contradicts their claims to know God (2:4). Probably the secessionists maintained that they were the only ones to have such knowledge, charging that those who did not join them were ignorant and immature. If such propaganda was making the author's adherents uncertain of themselves, he is now assuring them that they know the truth (2:21) and possess the Father and the Son (2:23). This is a common possession of Johannine Christians. In the OT only a few (kings, prophets, priests) were anointed and given the spirit of wisdom; but this is the time of the New Covenant when the words of Jeremiah (31[38]:34) are fulfilled: "They shall all know me from the least to the greatest." Once again then the author seems to be invoking the memories of the conversion/initiation/baptismal experience of his readers.[21] Anointing with the Holy Spirit was surely associated with the "anointing" of Jesus by the Spirit at his baptism (Acts 10:38). In the Johannine tradition "anointing" may have been understood as a consecration based on OT models, e.g., as indicated by Jesus in his "high priestly" prayer in John 17:19: "It is for them that I consecrate myself, in order that they too may be consecrated in truth"—a consecration that made them children of God in imitation of "the one whom the Father consecrated and sent into the world" and who for that reason could call himself God's Son (10:36).

If the anointing/consecration was in imitation of Jesus, so also the knowledge. Over and over again GJohn stresses Jesus' knowledge (7:29; 8:14), often with the word "all, everything" in the context (13:3; 18:4; 19:28: all using *oida* [*eidenai*], "to know," as here). In 16:30 the disciples say to Jesus, "Now we know that you know all things"; and in 8:32 Jesus promises to those who believe in him, "You shall know the truth." Because of the anointing in I John 2:20,27e the author can say, "All of you have knowledge" and it "teaches you all things," so that "you do know it [the truth]" (2:21c). In other words, the Christians who have been anointed or consecrated in truth have the privileges of God's consecrated Son because their anointing was through his Spirit.

The covenant setting of the author's language, if it goes back to Johannine Community patterns of conversion, initiation, or baptism (or all three), helps to explain the wording of the christological confessions in 2:22–23. If the author and the secessionists disagree about the meaning of "Jesus" (incarnate Word or preexistent Word) in the confession, "Jesus is the Christ" (2:22c), why does he not phrase the christological

[21] Dodd and Stott argue for an initiation interpretation, and Dodd's influence may be seen on the NEB translation of 2:20: "You, no less than they, are among the initiated; this is the gift of the Holy One." However, there is no evidence that the Johannine Christians were initiated in the manner of a Greek mystery religion. It is not impossible that if the secessionists continued the practice of anointing as they moved along the road to gnosticism. something like the Naassene sacrament of anointing ultimately emerged (p. 344 above).

statement more exactly in order to exclude the secessionist interpretation, e.g., "The Word-become-flesh is the Christ"? The answer is that, since he and the secessionists are arguing about the right interpretation of the Johannine tradition and since he is claiming to represent what was from the beginning, he has to remain faithful to confessions that his readers would remember from their conversion/initiation/baptism. From John 20:31 one may guess that at entrance to the Community, Johannine Christians confessed, "Jesus is the Christ, the Son of God"; and so his references in 2:22–23 concern those who deny the Jesus is the Christ or deny the Son. Since his readers were anointed (with the Spirit) when they first made that confession,[22] such anointing should keep them faithful to the true christology implicit in the Johannine understanding of the confession. This is particularly necessary in "the last hour." If the secessionists are the fulfillment of the apocalyptic expectation of the great apostasy and deceit of the last times,[23] the continuance of those who make a true christological confession fulfills the tradition that connects a confession of or by Jesus with the last judgment (Matt 10:32–33; Rev 3:5; Rom 10:9–10).

C. *Tradition as a Reassurance against Secessionist Deception* (2:24–26)

In 2:24 the author advances the criterion of "what you heard from the beginning" as a bulwark against those who deceive (2:26). How is this related to the reassuring criterion given by "the anointing from the Holy One" (2:20,27)? On pp. 345–47 I discussed the theory of those scholars who would identify the two, thinking of an anointing by word/gospel/teaching. I rejected that in favor of anointing with the Holy Spirit; and so I contend that in this unit the author brings forward as reassurance

---

[22] In I Cor 12:3 Paul attributes a true christological confession to the power of the Spirit: "No one can say 'Jesus is Lord' except by the Holy Spirit." GJohn would look upon such confessions as part of the Paraclete's role of glorifying Jesus (16:14), for the refusal to confess Jesus as the Christ is the same as the refusal to glorify God (cf. 9:22 with 12:42–43). The GJohn Prologue (1:14) combines glory with correct christological perception: "We have seen his glory, the glory of an only Son coming from the Father."

[23] In 2:22 the author identifies the secessionist Antichrists as the embodiment of the Liar; in 2:21 he insists that their lie "does not belong to the truth" (even as in 3:19 he will tell his adherents: "We belong to the truth"). Throughout I have insisted that surely the secessionists were using similar opprobrious language of him. According to Irenaeus, *Adv. haer.* 1.6.4, the gnostic Ptolemaeus thought of ordinary Christians as not belonging to the truth; and the Nag Hammadi *Apocalypse of Peter* (VII 75:9–14; NHL 342) denies that all souls belong to the truth and are destined for immortality.

against the secessionists two great criteria: anointing with the Spirit and the tradition of Jesus' words ("what you heard from the beginning"), both of which must abide in the Christian. In GJohn passages Jesus speaks of "abiding" in relation to his words: "If you abide in my word, you are truly my disciples" (8:31);[24] and "If you abide in me and my words abide in you, ask for whatever you want and it will be done for you. My Father has been glorified in this: in your bearing much fruit and becoming my disciples" (15:7–8). Jesus also speaks of "abiding" in relation to the Spirit: "The Father will give you another Paraclete to be with you forever. He is the Spirit of Truth . . . he abides with you and is within you" (14:16–17).

Presumably both the secessionists and the author spoke of an abiding tradition (word) and an abiding Spirit, since both groups (in my hypothesis) accepted the Johannine gospel. How would they have differed in relating tradition and the Spirit in reaching their respective ethical and christological positions? Later Christians who reached different positions would all claim that they accepted an apostolic tradition handed down from the beginning, but would differ on how the Spirit functions—does the Spirit function within each Christian (as a type of inner light or guide), or within an official body of teachers (a magisterium), or both? But that is not the precise issue between the epistolary author and the secessionists, for in 2:27 he is clear that no body of teachers is needed. Nor does he mean by "the word" or "what you have heard from the beginning" an apostolic tradition in the sense of an absolutely fixed body of teaching. A comparison between GJohn and the Synoptic Gospels shows the extent to which the traditional words of Jesus have been reinterpreted in the light of a profound christological insight. In speaking of an "abiding" word the author is not thinking statically. Rather, because of the life experience of Christians, the word lives on and takes new meaning and needs to be phrased differently—all of which has happened in GJohn. It is here that the Paraclete/Spirit plays his role since he ensures that in this developmental process the word of Jesus is not falsified or distorted. Notice the subtlety in the statement of Jesus, "I have much more to tell you but you cannot bear it now. When he comes, however, being the Spirit of Truth, he will guide you along the way of all truth. For he will not speak on his own but will speak only what he hears and will declare the things to come" (16:12–13). Such a statement is not unambiguous concerning the question: Does the Spirit say anything new that Jesus did not say? The last line in the statement indicates a negative answer; the first line indicates a positive answer. A yes-and-no is not contradictory because in

---

[24] The next verse in GJohn (8:32), "You shall know the truth," joins the abiding word and knowledge just as in I John 2:20–24. Similarly after mentioning the abiding Spirit in 14:16–17 (cited above), GJohn says that that Spirit "will teach you all things" (14:26).

the Johannine outlook a correct new interpretation of Jesus' words cannot be new, for Jesus knew all things and the Paraclete is merely leading Christians to understand what Jesus always intended.[25] Thus, the two criteria offered by the author in 2:20,27 and 2:24, the anointing (with the Spirit) and "what you heard from the beginning," are not separate but in a symbiotic relationship: the Spirit that abides in the Christian interprets the word the Christian has abiding from the beginning. In GJohn Jesus connects both his revelation and the Spirit to eternal life (6:35,63). That is why the epistolary author can say in 2:25 in comment upon the abiding word: "Now this is the promise which he himself made to us and it amounts to eternal life."

How would the secessionists differ on these points, since this is being written in face of their attempt to deceive (2:26)? It would be simpler if one could posit that the secessionists totally denied either criterion (what was heard from the beginning or anointing with the Spirit) or both. I have argued above that they too claimed an anointing with the Spirit (p. 369), but now we must discuss their attitude toward the tradition. Since they are "progressives" (II John 9), it is not likely that they argued for an unchangeable tradition or that they overly emphasized tradition against the Spirit. It has more often been suggested that they were Spirit-led enthusiasts who acted with total freedom in regard to what was heard from the beginning.[26] However, I have consistently argued that their theology can be so reconstructed as to have a basis in the Johannine tradition known to us in GJohn. The available evidence, then, makes it likely that, like the author, the secessionists too paid homage to both the Johannine tradition and the role of the Paraclete/Spirit, but combined them in a different balance. The designation of the secessionists as progressive, the intensity of the author's stress on what was from the beginning, and the infrequency of explicit references to the Spirit in I John—all these factors combine to suggest that the secessionists gave a greater role to the Spirit's ability to interpret the tradition in a new way. Indeed, in the author's judgment they exaggerated to the point that "what was heard from the beginning" no longer abided in them.[27] On the other side, in the judgment of

[25] In the language of I John 2:27, the anointing received in the past both *taught* you to abide in Christ (27gh) and *teaches* you about all things truly and free from any lie (27ef).

[26] Sometimes this reflects a prejudice that the gnostically inclined always reject tradition because it refutes them. However, see footnote 25, p. 183 above.

[27] Because of that they would have lost the promise that amounts to eternal life (2:25), and so he can say that "we have passed from death to life" but they remain "in the abode of death" (3:14). The realization of a promise shows the continuity of God's plan. For that reason, most NT authors are concerned to show that Jesus fulfilled the "promises" of the OT (Acts 13:32–33; II Cor 1:20; Eph 3:6; Heb 6:12). Johannine christology is so high that, in the Community debate, not the fulfillment of OT promises, but the fulfillment of Jesus' promises shows the continuity of God's plan.

the secessionists the author was probably despised as one who did not take seriously enough the promise of Jesus that he had much more to tell his disciples than he told them during the ministry and that the Paraclete would declare the things to come (16:12–13).[28] The author refutes them by insisting that not only the anointing with the Spirit must abide in the Christian but also the word that Jesus spoke from the beginning.

D. *Rejection of Teachers as a Reassurance against Secessionists* (2:27)

In II John 10 the writer will exhort a Johannine church: "If anyone comes to you who does not bring this teaching, do not receive him into the house and greet him; for whoever greets him shares in his evil deeds." The ultimate weapon against the secessionists and their attempts to deceive is to keep them away from the faithful; and the author of I John moves toward that attitude in 2:27 when he tells his adherents that, because they have the anointing received from Christ abiding in them, there is no need for anyone to teach them. False prophets were a traditional sign of the last times,[29] and in 4:1 the author dubs those who had "gone out [from his adherents] into the world" as false prophets. False teachers were also a traditional sign of the last times (II Pet 2:1; II Tim 4:3; Eph 4:14), and the implication in I John 2:27 is that the author considers the secessionists as false teachers.

Nevertheless, in his opposition to false teaching the author goes to the extreme of denying the need of any teacher. Other NT works inculcate the need for authoritative teachers (I Tim 4:11: "Command and teach these things"), and indeed "prophets and teachers" were a regular feature in many churches (I Cor 12:28; Eph 4:11; Acts 13:1). Matthew 23:8 allows only Christ to be called a teacher, but I John's objection goes beyond the title.[30] Since it is the anointing of the Christian that dispenses

[28] One of the standard gnostic defenses against the orthodox church was an appeal to gospels and apocalypses where the risen Jesus gave to a chosen individual revelation that he had not given in the ministry. (See Perkins, *Diaglogue* 144.) Presumably in the Johannine line of development that tendency would be manifested through a greater role assigned to the Paraclete. In the *Apocryphon of James* (INTRODUCTION, footnote 10) one group, presumably gnostics, using Johannine language, look on their opponents as lacking a Paraclete (advocate), at the same time as they deplore dependence on the flesh (I 11:11–12 and 11:35–12:13; NHL 34). The Valentinian gnostics looked upon themselves as spiritual and their orthodox opponents as psychics (Pagels, *Johannine Gospel* 60–65).

[29] In the NOTES on 2:18b and 2:22a I showed that the appearance of "false prophets" was a component of the expectations of the Antichrist and of the Liar.

[30] Matthew dislikes the title because it is in Pharisee usage, and that attitude may also underlie the sarcastic application of "Teacher" to Nicodemus in John 3:10. John 13:13–14 would seem to preclude "Lord" or "Teacher" being used for Johannine Christians. II John 9–10 suggests that, if one can speak of Community "teaching," it is because that teaching is considered to be the teaching of Christ.

with the need for a teacher, the author is most likely basing himself on the promise of Jesus that the Paraclete would teach all things and guide the Johannine Christians along the way of all truth (John 14:26; 16:13).[31] Behind that is the mentality that this is "the last hour" when direct divine guidance replaces human intermediaries. In Jeremiah's description of the New Covenant (31[38]:34), which I have invoked as background several times, we hear, "No longer shall each man teach his neighbor and each his brother, saying, 'Know the Lord.' "[32] And in John 6:45, the Johannine Jesus says, "It is written in the prophets, 'And they shall all be taught by God' [Isa 54:13]. Everyone who has heard the Father and learned from Him comes to me." In the NOTE on 2:27cd I surveyed the range of teaching words in the Johannine literature, and by far the dominant usage pertains to Jesus. If the Paraclete teaches, it is because he takes over Jesus' role once Jesus leaves.

Despite the author's clear statement against the need for human teachers, some scholars persist in referring to the "we" of I John 1:1–5 and 4:6 as if a group of apostolic teachers were involved. I have argued that more likely the Johannine School (including the author) thought of themselves as "witnesses," a title that would offer no rivalry to an anointing by the Spirit. (In John 15:26–27, after Jesus speaks of the witness of the Paraclete, he says, "You too should bear witness because you have been with me from the beginning.") Indeed, in the INTRODUCTION V D2a, I have suggested that the lack of organized teaching authority in the author's branch of the Johannine Community was what made the propaganda of the secessionists such a threat, and that eventually some churches in that Community had to develop local authority with the power to teach. Even if I am correct in judging that the author's vision of a Christianity without human teachers ultimately failed, subsequent Christianity, which had a fully developed magisterium of human teachers, still accepted into its canonical Scripture his dictum, "You have no need for anyone to teach you."[33] Already Augustine, a teaching bishop himself,

[31] J.D.G. Dunn, "The Washing of the Disciples' Feet in John 13:1–20," ZNW 61 (1970) 247–52, esp. 252, invokes in this matter John 13:10: "The man who has bathed has no need to wash [except for his feet], he is clean all over." He regards this as a polemic against gnostic claims to special spiritual experiences (whether cleansings from sin or anointings with knowledge). Similarly the epistolary author seems to be saying that the Christian *chrisma*, received once, suffices.

[32] This Jeremiah passage is cited in Heb 8:11. Similarly in I Thess 4:8–9, after mentioning God's gift of the Holy Spirit, Paul says, "You yourselves have no need for anyone to write to you about love of brother, for you yourselves have been taught by God to love one another." Speaking of the Lord dwelling in the Christian, *Hermas, Man.* 3:1, says, "The Lord is true [*alēthinos*], and with Him there is no lie"—language very close to I John 2:27f.

[33] Some churches have sought to avoid the conflict by not classifying church officials as authoritative teachers; but usually a deviation from church positions brings authoritative action, and it becomes apparent that "by any other name" some are teachers.

wrestled with this problem (*In Epistolam* 3.13; SC 75, 210): "There is here, my brothers, a great mystery on which to meditate: the sound of my voice strikes your ears, but the real Teacher is within. Do not think that one learns anything from another human being. We can draw your attention by the sound of our voice; but if within there is not the One who instructs, the noise of our words is in vain. . . . The internal Master who teaches is Christ the teacher; his inspiration teaches. Where his inspiration and anointing are not found, the external words are in vain." Church writers picked this comment up and pointed to I Cor 3:6, "I planted, Apollos watered, but God made it grow," as an indication of how God could teach from within. Among the many commentators who have opted for an interior teaching by the Spirit corresponding to an exterior teaching are Belser, Bonsirven, Chaine, de Ambroggi. A particular variant is expounded by Paulinus of Nola (*Epistola* 23.36; CSEL 29, 193) who died *ca.* 431. He points out that since the Spirit dwells in each faithful Christian, the faithful as a whole have a guide to the truth. This has resulted in the thesis that the universal and constant belief of the Christian community guarantees Christian truth. Still another interpretation is that the anointing of a Christian by the Spirit guarantees the private exegesis of the Scripture. Obviously these interpretations go beyond what the author had in mind, but all of them reflect a continuation of the line of thought he represented. In the long run, his position has meant that the Church has to live with a tension between authoritative teachers and the Spirit enlightening individual Christians, both of which are attested in the NT.

BIBLIOGRAPHY PERTINENT TO I JOHN 2:18–27

Bousset, W., *Der Antichrist in der Überlieferung des Judentums, des Neuen Testaments und der alten Kirche* (Göttingen: Vandenhoeck & Ruprecht, 1895).

Couture, P., "The Teaching Function in the Church of I John (I John 2,20.27)," excerpt from dissertation mentioned in *General Bibliography* VII F1.

de la Potterie, I., "Anointing of the Christian by Faith," in *The Christian Lives by the Spirit,* by I. de la Potterie and S. Lyonnet (Staten Island: Alba, 1971) 79–143, esp. 99–117 on I John 2:20,27. French orig. in *Biblica* 40 (1959) 12–69.

Hanse, H., *"Gott Haben" in der antike und im frühen Christentum* (Religionsgeschichtliche Versuche und Vorarbeiten 27; Berlin: Töpelmann, 1939), esp. 104–8 on I John 2:23.

Michl, J., "Der Geist als Garant des rechten Glaubens," in *Vom Wort des*

Lebens, ed. N. Adler (M. Meinertz Festschrift; NTAbh 1 Ergänzungs-band; Münster: Aschendorf, 1951) 142–51.

Rigaux, B., *L'Antéchrist et l'opposition au royaume messianique dans l'Ancien et le Nouveau Testament* (Gembloux: Duculot, 1932).

Schlier, H., "Vom Antichrist—Zum 13. Kapitel der Offenbarung Johannes," in *Die Zeit der Kirche* (Freiburg: Herder, 1956) 16–29.

Yates, R., "The Antichrist," *Evangelical Quarterly* 46 (1974) 42–50.

6. I John 2:28–3:10: *God's Children vs. the Devil's Children*

28a **2**²⁸And now, LITTLE CHILDREN, do abide in Christ
28b   so that, when he is revealed, we may have confidence
28c   and not draw back in shame from him at his coming.
29a ²⁹Once you realize that he is just, you know this as well:
29b   Everyone who acts justly has been begotten by God.
 1a **3**   (¹Look at what love the Father has bestowed on us
 1b   in enabling us to be called God's children—
 1c   and that is what we really are!
 1d   The reason that the world does not recognize us
 1e   is that it never recognized Him.
 2a   ²Yes, beloved, we are God's children right now;
 2b   and what we shall be has not yet been revealed.
 2c   But we know that at this revelation
 2d   we shall be like Him,
 2e   for we shall see Him as He is.
 3a   ³Everyone who has this hope based on Him
 3b   makes himself pure even as Christ is pure.)
 4a   ⁴Everyone who acts sinfully is really doing iniquity,
 4b   for sin is the Iniquity.
 5a   ⁵And you know well that Christ was revealed
 5b   to take away sins,
 5c   and there is nothing sinful in him.
 6a   ⁶Everyone who abides in him does not commit sin.
 6b   Everyone who does commit sin has never seen him
 6c   nor come to know him.

 7a   ⁷LITTLE CHILDREN, let no one deceive you:
 7b   The person who acts justly is truly just
 7c   even as Christ is just.
 8a   ⁸The person who acts sinfully belongs to the devil,
 8b   because from the very beginning the devil is the one who sins.
 8c   The reason the Son of God was revealed
 8d   was to destroy the works of the devil.
 9a   ⁹Everyone who has been begotten by God does not act sinfully
 9b   because God's seed abides in him;

9c   and so he cannot be a sinner
9d   because he has been begotten by God.
10a   10That is how God's children and the devil's children are
        revealed.
10b   Everyone who does not act justly does not belong to God,
10c   nor does anyone who does not love his brother.

NOTES

2:28a. *And now.* This is the Greek *kai nyn,* also used at the beginning of the previous unit in 2:18c. Again it is transitional, connecting what follows to what precedes by way of specification; yet all its temporal value is not lost. It picks up the eschatological reference to "the last hour" of 2:18a (as it did in 2:18c) which has been somewhat muted since 2:23. Houlden, *Epistles* 85, suggests, "At this crucial time." The usage in John 17:5 ("And now, glorify me, Father") is quite similar, specifying an urgent moment in "the hour" of Jesus.

Little Children. A few minuscule MSS., the Coptic, and the Ethiopic read "My Little Children" in imitation of 2:1a. In 2:12a and 2:14a the author varied artistically the synonymous plurals of *teknion* ("Little Children") and of *paidion* ("Children"). The first unit after that passage began (2:18a) with "Children"; the next unit begins here with "Little Children," a title that will be repeated in the opening line of the second half of this unit (3:7a).

do abide in Christ. The Greek *menete en autō* is exactly the same wording as in the last line of the previous verse where it was not clear whether *menete* should be translated as an indicative or as an imperative. Here it is more clearly an imperative since it is followed by a purpose clause in the next line. The *autos* ("he/him") is plausibly a reference to Christ since the next two lines mention the parousia. Indeed, the three uses of *autos* in this verse are referred to God by only a few exegetes (Loisy, B. Weiss). Because of the urgency he gives to the "now," Houlden, *Epistles* 87, thinks that *menein* here may almost mean "to persevere," along the lines of the related noun *hypomonē* in Luke 8:15; 21:19. However, the previous use in 2:27 militates against that.

28b. *so that, when he is revealed.* Literally, "so that if [*ean*]." The Byzantine textual tradition reads *hotan,* "whenever," for *ean;* but that is a scribal effort to remove any uncertainty that *ean* might create about the final coming of Christ. Actually in this period of Greek *ean* often means "whenever, when" (BAG 210 [BAGD 211], 1d). As in Tobit 4:3 ("when I die"), the use of *ean,* "if," does not indicate uncertainty about eventuality but about the exact time. The verb *phaneroun,* "to reveal," will be used in the passive 5 times in this unit (here; 3:2,5,8). Of 17 other Johannine uses of *phaneroun,* as we saw in the NOTE on 1:2a, 10 refer to Jesus, none to God—a statistic that favors the reference of *autos* in the preceding line (28a) to Christ. In I John 1:2a *phaneroun* referred to the manifestation of Christ in his earthly career, as it will again below in 3:5,8. Its use here and in 3:2 for the parousia causes Bultmann to attribute this verse to the Ecclesiastical Redactor. However, the Johannine christological usage of the verb is flexible, e.g., in John 1:31 it is used for the manifestation of Jesus at the beginning of his career, and in 21:1,14 for his postresurrectional appearances. It is possible, then, that for the epistolary author *phaneroun* covers the revelation of the Word on earth from incarnation through ministry and resurrection to parousia, constituting one supreme divine manifestation (Schnackenburg, *Johannesbriefe* 164). In any case, this whole section is too marked by final eschatology to attribute an individual line with apocalyptic characteristics to an epistolary redactor (whose very existence is dubious). In 2:19 the author wrote about the revelation of the Antichrists in the last hour; here he writes about the revelation of Christ. The form is passive but can be translated reflexively ("reveals himself"); yet it is better to remain literal and to leave open the possibility that God was thought of as the agent of the revelation. (See the NOTE on John 2:22 in ABJ 29, 116 for a similar problem of whether to translate the passive form *egerthē* as "had risen" [Jesus' own agency] or "was raised" [God's agency].)

we may have confidence. Although Codex Sinaiticus* and the Byzantine tradition read a present subjunctive of "to have," the aorist subjunctive, more punctiliar in implication, is better attested. Although the author has been addressing a "you" with the imperative in 2:28a, he now underlines his *koinōnia* with his "Little Children" by joining himself to them as "we." This is the first instance of *parrēsia*, a word that occurs 9 times in GJohn and 4 times in I John, constituting 40% of total NT usage (31 times). Etymologically it comes from *pan-rēsia*, "saying all"; and its range of meaning includes: speaking openly rather than secretly; speaking truth rather than falsehood; speaking courageously rather than keeping quiet out of fear or respect; speaking plainly rather than obscurely. Peterson, "Parrēsia," and Van Unnik, "Freedom," give useful surveys of the development of the idea. While not frequent in the Greek poets or dramatists, *parrēsia* was an important concept in Attic democracy, being more aggressive than "freedom" (*eleutherostomia*) in expressing the right to speak against the tyrant. Among friends it covered the right to correct moral faults, and it was used that way especially by the Cynics and Isocrates. Although relatively infrequent in the LXX, this noun in Judeo-Hellenistic literature (Philo, Josephus) took on a meaning not found elsewhere: the right to speak openly to God, e.g., of Moses as a friend of God. The NT usage seems to draw upon both backgrounds. Paul (10 times) links it with the open preaching of the Gospel, the mystery and victory of which is being made clear. In Acts (5 times) it applies to unhindered preaching and to the confident interpretation of prophecy. The solitary Synoptic use (Mark 8:32) refers to Jesus' plain speaking about his suffering. Five of the GJohn passages refer to Jesus' speaking in public, openly, or without fear; four refer to his speaking plainly, without figures of speech, and without obfuscation. In all 4 uses in I John it refers to one's having confidence before God or His Son as one makes petitions (5:14) or faces judgment (2:28; 4:17), or both (3:21–22). This is the same meaning *parrēsia* has in Heb 4:16; 10:19. In the early church, martyrs are said to have *parrēsia* both on earth against their opponents and in heaven toward God (for they are His friends). This view is carried over to "confidence" in the intercession of the saints. In the liturgies of both East and West the recitation of the Lord's Prayer, daring to call God "Father," was looked upon as an act of *parrēsia* or "boldness." The author of I John makes clear that the source of "confidence" at the revelation of Christ is that Christians have abided in him, and so he comes as a loving friend and not as a judge.

28c. *and not draw back in shame from him at his coming.* The "him" and "his" are both forms of *autos*, which has the same reference as the *autos* in 28a (probably Christ). The NT verbs "to be ashamed" *aischynesthai* and *epaischynesthai* occur a total of 16 times, but this is the only Johannine use. The form of *aischynesthai* here may be read as a middle, "turn away with shame from him," or as a passive, "be ashamed." The passive reflects a legal situation where one is disgraced, while the middle has more the psychological aspect of the individual's feeling shame. Bultmann and Schnackenburg favor the passive, but the use of the preposition "from" favors the middle. (Usually the verbs would take an accusative; and MGNTG 2, 460, suggests that *apo*, "from," reflects a Semitism, while Schnackenburg would treat it almost as if it were *hypo*, "by [him]," a possibility recognized by BDF 210[2].) The passive would make two steps out of 2:28b and 28c, namely, having confidence (before the verdict) and not being put to shame (by the verdict). It is preferable to posit chiastic parallelism where both lines say the same thing in different order:

so that (A) when he is revealed, (B) we may have confidence
and (B') not draw back in shame from him (A') at his coming.

Such a parallelism between *parrēsia* and not being ashamed occurs in an opposite way in Prov 13:5: "An ungodly man is ashamed and does not have *parrēsia*." The idea of shame at the final revelation before the divine judge is common: in Isa 1:24,29, when the Lord comes with wrath to execute judgment upon transgressors, the people are told, "You shall be ashamed of the oaks in which you delighted, and made ashamed of the gardens which you chose" (also Jer 2:35–36). Revelation 6:15–17 has the kings hiding their faces before the Enthroned One while they ask, "The great day of wrath has come, and who can stand before it?"

The word I translated here as "coming" is *parousia*, used 24 times in the NT but only here in the Johannine literature. Its choice may be dictated by the sound-alike *parrēsia* in the preceding line. (Other NT terms for the [second] coming of Christ, beside the passive of the verb *phaneroun* discussed under 2:28b, include *epiphaneia*, "epiphany," and *apokalypsis*, "revelation," neither of which is used in the Johannine literature.) The fact that the author does not have to explain this technical term suggests again a Johannine apocalyptic tradition (not represented in GJohn). In the ancient world *parousia* has a pertinent twofold sense: (1) the coming of a hidden divinity who makes his presence felt by his power or miracles; (2) the visit of a king or emperor to a province (Latin: *adventus*). Christians took over the second aspect in their picture of how Christ would come back.

29a. *Once you realize that he is just*. Literally, "If [*ean*] you know [*eidenai*]." The condition expressing reality is usually *ei* with the indicative (BDF 372) rather than *ean* with the subjunctive. The latter construction here is not meant to question the certainty that "he is just," but to turn the audience toward self-interrogation: Have they realized that he is just? (The THLJ suggestion of "Since" or "As it is a fact that" loses this nuance.) Again we are faced with the problem of the author's "he" (expressed in the verbal form)—God or Christ? As we saw there were three instances of *autos* (which is missing here) in v. 28, two of them in the last line; and they probably referred to Christ. There is also an *autos* in the next line (29b), probably referring to God. (An occasional use of a proper name by the author would have been very helpful! One wonders whether the author reflects a Jewish reluctance to employ divine names.) That the "he" here refers to God is favored by Bonsirven, Bruce, Büchsel, Camerlynck, Chaine, Loisy, Plummer, Stott, Vrede, B. Weiss, Wilder, and Windisch (?) for these reasons: (a) God is described as "just" in I John 1:9; John 17:25; (b) a reference to God here avoids a harsh transition to the next line where *autos* means God. That the "he" here refers to Christ is favored by Balz, Brooke (?), Häring, Hauck, Marshall, Schnackenburg, Schneider, THLJ, Vicent Cernuda, and Westcott for these reasons: (a) the author called Christ "just" in 2:1; (b) since not even a pronoun has appeared to signal a change of reference from the preceding line, the "he" is the same as the *autos* there, i.e., Christ; (c) the whole point of v. 29 is that everyone who acts justly has been begotten by God because that person resembles the one who is just—who, therefore, has to be God's Son; (d) v. 29 strongly resembles 3:7 where there is no doubt that it is Christ (*ekeinos*) who is just. The fact that the very next line (29b) will speak of an *autos* who is probably God is no serious argument for understanding the "he" of 29a as God, precisely because the introduction of the pronoun *autos* there may signal a change of reference. In 5:1, which has parallels to 2:29, there is a similar movement from Christ in one clause to God in the next: "Everyone who believes that *Jesus* is the Christ has been begotten by God." The arguments favoring a reference to Christ here are clearly stronger.

For the Johannine use of *dikaios*, "just," see the NOTE on 1:9b. I stressed there that while justice involves opposition to sin, aspects of this opposition are mercy, forgiveness, and taking sin away. In 2:1 "just" was applied to Jesus Christ serving as Paraclete in the Father's presence, atoning for our sins and thus winning the case for us. Here it is applied to Christ who will return in judgment, not as an enemy but as a friend who gives confidence because he is forgiving.

you know. The form of *ginōskein* here can be indicative or imperative. The imperative reading is favored by the Vulgate, early English versions, and by de Wette, Dodd, Hauck, Vellanickal, Vicent Cernuda, Westcott, and Windisch who point to the imperatives in the surrounding verses ("abide" in 2:28a; "look at" in 3:1a). The indicative reading is favored by the KJV, RSV, and by

Balz, Büchsel, Bultmann, Chaine, Plummer, Schnackenburg, Schneider, THLJ, and B. Weiss who point to the indicative "you know" (*eidenai*) statements in 2:20,21. I have opted for the latter because in I John knowledge is described as an already existing fact flowing from the reader's being a Christian (2:3,5,20,21; 3:16,19,24; 4:2,13; 5:2). Some scholars would see a difference of meaning in the author's shift from *eidenai*, "to know, realize," at the beginning of 29a to *ginōskein* here at the end of 29a, e.g., from intuitive knowledge to experiential knowledge (Plummer), or from absolute knowledge to observation (Westcott, de la Potterie). I see only Johannine artistic variation (see ABJ 29, 514; NOTE above on 2:3a); one finds the *eidenai/ginōskein* pattern in John 13:7; 21:17; and vice versa in 14:7 (even as the Hebrew Bible occasionally changes the Jacob/Israel pattern to Israel/Jacob).

this as well: Everyone who. This *hoti* clause is governed by *ginōskein* discussed in the previous NOTE. A *kai*, "and, also," is read between the *hoti* and the "everyone" in such textual witnesses as Sinaiticus, Alexandrinus, Ephraemi Rescriptus, the Sahidic, the Syriac Peshitta, and the Vulgate; but it is omitted by Vaticanus, the Byzantine tradition, and some Latin witnesses—a strong combination, which Westcott accepts. The presence of the *kai* constitutes a difficult reading that scribes would more likely have avoided (by omission) than created. How to translate the *kai* is a problem discussed by Vicent Cernuda, "La filiación," who rejects any purely intensive meaning in favor of "in a certain manner" (also in 3:1c; he defends this attenuated *kai* in EstBib 32 [1973] 57–76). Most scholars (Chaine, Malatesta, Nestle, Schnackenburg, THLJ, B. Weiss) understand the *kai* to mean "as well." This agrees with taking the *ginōskein* form as indicative and with giving the two verbs of knowing the same meaning: If you know this, you know this as well.

29b. *Everyone who acts justly.* Literally, "Everyone doing justice [*dikaiosynē*]." I remarked in the NOTE on 2:23ab on the Johannine idiom of employing *pas*, "all, every," with a (present) participle to make a sweeping dualistic classification: All those consistently engaged in or affected by a particular action belong to a certain group, good or bad. This unit has seven such clauses (2:29b; 3:3a,4a,6ab,9a,10b) covering everyone who does what is right opposed to everyone who commits sin; and everyone who has been begotten by God opposed to everyone who does not belong to God. As explained in the INTRODUCTION (III A1), these antithetical statements were the backbone of von Dobschütz's source theory, which Bultmann took over (attributing 29b to the source: Appendix I, Chart Three).

The phrase "to do justice" occurs thrice in I John, all in this unit. Although contrasted with doing sin (3:7–8; cf. 3:4), it means more than not sinning; for justice (NOTE on 1:9b) involves holiness. (Rev 22:11 puts doing justice in parallelism with being holy, and contrasts this with acting unjustly and being unclean.) One can do justice only if one is acting according to a holiness that dwells within, even as "to do truth" (NOTE on 1:6d) means to act according to the truth internal to the Christian, for whom Jesus is the truth. Christ is just by his very nature as the Son of God, and automatically he does God's will because he and the Father are one. If human beings do what is just, it is because they are children of God begotten in Christ's likeness. (Plummer, *Epistles* 70, wonders whether the definite article used before *dikaiosynē* here should not be translated as "his," since such an article indicates something familiar, and the author has just said, "he is just"—the translation is too strong but the instinct is right.) Westcott, *Epistles* 83, correctly affirms that for John *dikaiosynē* is not the condition but the consequence of being God's child. In Matt 6:1 the disciples are warned against "doing justice" before men to be seen by them; but John probably could not allow that possibility, for the action would be "just" only if it came from a holy principle. In Rom 10:5–6 Paul contrasts "doing justice" based on what the Law commands and a justice based on faith in Christ.

has been begotten by God. This is the perfect passive tense of *gennan*, "to beget, give birth to," or "[passive] to be begotten/born," followed by the prepositional phrase "from him [*autos*]." Grammatically there is no way to know whether *autos* refers to Christ as did the three uses of *autos* in 2:28, or is being used after the preceding reference to Christ (2:29a—in the verbal form "he is") to change the agency to God. A third possibility is that *autos* refers imprecisely to both Christ and God the Father (Vicent Cernuda). Because grammar offers little help, the decision may be based on the customary usage with *gennan* which occurs 18 times in GJohn and 10 times in I John. (In the active, only in John 16:21; I John 5:1.) The passive is often used with a phrase indicating origin, governed by the preposition *ek*, "from/of," e.g., "from God" (John 1:13; I John 3:9; 4:7; 5:1,4,18); "from (water and) Spirit" (John 3:5,6,8); "from flesh" (John 3:6). Since there is never an instance of *gennan* (passive) with the *ek* governing Christ and there are 8 instances with *ek* governing God, almost all scholars take *autos* here to be God (except Westcott). Difficult too is the decision whether to translate the passive as "to be born" (as from a female) or "to be begotten" (as by a male). Although some make no distinction, paraphrasing in terms of "child," the KJV, RSV, Catholic translations from the Latin, Alexander, Hauck, and Houlden favor "born," while JB, RV, Plummer, and Wilder favor "begotten." Since the next usage of this phrase (3:9) contains a reference to the "seed" of God, it seems more likely that the writer is imagining a divine begetting. Other NT writers share the idea of Christians as the children (sons) of God and receiving life from God, but only the Johannine writers speak of the Christian as begotten by God, employing *gennan*. Close approximations to Johannine usage include: I Peter's use of *anagennan*, "to regenerate, beget anew," for God's having begotten us to an imperishable hope (1:3), and for our having been begotten with an imperishable seed (1:23); I Peter's use of *artigennētos* (2:2) in describing Christians as "newborn babes"; the reference in Titus 3:5 to God our Savior having saved us through the water of regeneration (*palingenesia*) and the renewal of the Holy Spirit; and James' use of *apokyein*, "to give birth, bring forth" (1:18), in saying that God brought us into being through the word of truth.

What are the roots of the idea of the divine begetting of human beings? (The wider idea of being children of God will be discussed in the next verse; that includes the possibility of adoption.) Bultmann, *Epistles* 45–46, is confident: "Although the expression 'born of God' is not attested in the same form in the mystery religions and Gnosticism, nevertheless there can be no doubt that this manner of speaking, i.e., the notion, born of God, derives from this sphere." Vellanickal has devoted a whole book (*Sonship*) patiently working through all the pertinent texts to show that there is serious doubt about such a claim. When Bultmann goes on to say that the Johannine writer and the gnostic share a belief that without divine assistance human beings cannot attain to salvation but require a renewal of being, he is right. That view is held in one form or another by many biblical writers, including those of the OT who insist that God's choice of Israel as His people was a creative act giving a salvific status to which the people could never have attained on their own. The issue, then, is not belief in the need for divine intervention but the description of the manner of the intervention. In the OT, despite the references in general or in particular to Israelites as God's children, the language of divine begetting is rare. Poetically the Hebrew of Deut 32:18 reminds Israel of "the Rock that begot you . . . the God who gave you birth," which in the LXX becomes "the God who begot you . . . the God who feeds you." More prominently it is said that God begot the Davidic king as His Son on the day of the king's coronation (Ps 2:7; LXX Ps 110[109]:3). See G. Cooke, ZAW 73 (1961) 202–6. Similarly at Qumran in 1QSa 2:11–12 there is left open a future possibility that God will beget the Messiah. Philo, *Allegorical Interpretation* 3.77 ❧219, speaks of creation as a divine begetting, but does not use this idea of begetting to explain the status of Israel as God's children. It is very dubious that he thinks the patriarchs were begotten by God as some have claimed (see R. E. Brown, *The Birth of the Messiah* [Garden City, N. Y.: Doubleday, 1977] 521). In the *Migration of Abraham* 7 ❧35, Philo speaks of ideas being *sown* in man from above, an image he may have borrowed from the mystery religions. In fact, however, in what we know of the ceremonial of the mystery religions there is little to show that they used for initiates the language of being begotten by God (see F. Büchsel, TDNT 1, 669–70). Epictetus, *Discourse* 4.10.16, has God begetting a human being as his child. In rabbinic Judaism, but perhaps after NT times, the language of new birth was applied to converts, e.g., "A proselyte just converted is like a child just born" TalBab *Yebamoth* 22a). However, God's role in this seems primarily to be one of creation and formation (K. H. Rengstorf, TDNT 1, 666–68).

In the NT the imagery in Ps 2:7 about the begetting of the king as God's son is applied *to Jesus* in various ways: in Heb 1:5; 5:5 it is applied to him in his lifetime; in Acts 13:33 it is applied to him in his resurrection; the Western text of Luke 3:22 looks on Jesus' baptism as his begetting; and Luke 1:35; Matt 1:20 regard his conception as his begetting. It is tempting to think that the idea of the Messiah (Christ) being begotten by God spread to the Christian being begotten by God; but that is unlikely since the NT works that refer to the begetting of the Messiah do not refer to the divine begetting of the Christian, and the Johannine literature that refers to the Christian being begotten by God never says that Jesus was begotten by God. (See ABJ 29, 11–12,13 for the rejection of the reading "he was begotten" in John 1:13, and of the translation "only begotten" in 1:14; also see NOTE below on 5:18b.) Rather the idea of the divine begetting of the Christian probably developed through an analogy based on eternal life. From intertestamental Judaism, which expressed the idea that God would give and (at times) had already given his select followers the life of the age to come (ABJ 29, 506–7), Johannine Christians developed the notion that the followers of Jesus already possessed this (eternal) life. This led to a comparison wherein, just as ordinary life is given by human begetting, eternal life is given by divine begetting. This is explicit in John 3:3–7 and is implied in I John 3:9, which speaks of God's seed. (Bultmann, *Epistles* 46, rejects strongly any idea in I John of God's *physis*, "nature" [II Pet 1:4] being in the Christian. Even if technically he is right, God's life as a principle is in the Christian; and that is not too far from what some later theologians mean by "nature.") Begetting reflects the creative power of God (most visibly shared by human beings in their power to give life), whence the appeal in John 3:5 to the Spirit as the agent in begetting—the Spirit that functioned in creation (Ps 104:30). For John the time of begetting by God is the moment of belief (John 1:12–13), which is accompanied by water baptism (3:5; see ABJ 29, 141–44). A baptismal setting seems also to be envisioned by the regeneration passages in I Pet 1:3,23; 2:2, and Titus 3:5.

Nevertheless, since the Johannine "begetting from above" (*anōthen*) could be understood as "born again" (ABJ 29, 130–31), the regeneration motif was open to a gnostic interpretation wherein those who were already children of God before their natural birth were reborn as they discovered this fact through special knowledge (*gnōsis*) of their origins and destiny. In the *Excerpts from Theodotus* preserved by Clement of Alexandria we hear, "The Valentinians say that when the psychic body had been formed, a male seed was implanted by the Logos in the elect soul while it slept" (2:1). The role of the Savior is to waken the impregnated soul (3:1), and this is the second birth (80:1—GCS 17, 105–6,131). In Hippolytus' account (*Refutatio* 5.7.40; PG 16³, 3139A) the second-century Naassene gnostics held that "All earthly birth is mortal, but that which originates in heaven is immortal; for from water alone and the Spirit, the spiritual man is born, not the man of the flesh." The third-century A.D. *Corpus Hermeticum* 13 is a tractate on "rebirth" (*palingenesis*), seen as a gift of God coming through knowledge that alienates from the world: "He that is born by that birth is another person: he is a God and a child [*pais*] of God" (13.2).

The attention that the epistolary author gives to the phrase "begotten by God" makes it reasonably certain that the secessionists were using it, but the suggestion that he borrowed it from them is quite unnecessary. John 3:5 makes it more likely that divine begetting was part of the language of admission to the Johannine Community and thus a heritage common to both the author's adherents and the secessionists. What secessionist *interpretation* of divine begetting is the author refuting? Since he never attacks a claim that the Christians are children of God before birth, I deem it unlikely that the secessionists had yet moved into the full gnostic myth. What the author does criticize is the failure to draw the proper implications of being begotten by God. This becomes apparent when we put together the statements of I John on divine begetting:

2:29: Everyone who acts justly has been begotten by God
3:9: Everyone who has been begotten by God does not act sinfully
He cannot be a sinner because he has been begotten by God
4:7: Everyone who loves has been begotten by God
5:1: Everyone who believes that *Jesus* is the Christ has been begotten by God
5:5: All that is begotten by God conquers the world
5:18: No one who has been begotten by God commits sin
The one begotten by God is protected . . . the Evil One cannot touch him

The statement in 5:1 indicates that right belief is a necessary condition for being begotten by God; so presumably the author would deny that the secessionists are thus begotten. The rest of the statements show that divine begetting not only brings the gift of life but manifests itself in a way of life, especially in acting justly (and not sinfully) and in manifesting love. (Bultmann points out that *Corpus Hermeticum* 13, with all its concentration on rebirth, never mentions love.) If one judges a person's humanity not simply on his having been begotten by human parents but on his living in a human manner, the same may be said of a person's relationship to God. De la Potterie, *La vérité* 2, 604ff., makes this valid point; but with his usual predilection for the theory of exact Johannine theological grammar, he would argue that the 6 Johannine uses of *gennan* in the aorist tense refer to receiving the divine word which begets, while the 11 uses in the perfect tense indicate continuance and express the idea of belonging to God as His child.

3:1a. *Look at what love.* "Look at" is the pl. form of the imperative *ide* which is used at least 6 times in GJohn in a revelatory formula (1:29,36,47; 19:14,26,27) where a speaker reveals the mystery of the mission of the person whom he is pointing out (ABJ 29, 58). Westcott, *Epistles* 95, comments on the remarkable usage here, for normally the object of the *ide* would be visible. (The Vulgate renders it as *videte*, "See," rather than *ecce*, "Behold.") However, visibility may be the nuance intended. While not yet here, the parousia of Christ (2:28) is near; and the love that one can already see bestowed in the first coming guarantees the loving quality of the second coming. The "what" modifying "love" is *potapos*, a Hellenistic interrogative used where classical Greek would employ *poios*, to express both quantity and quality, thus, how much love and what amazing love. For the Johannine concept of *agapē*, "love," see the NOTE on 2:5b above.

the Father has bestowed on us. Codex Vaticanus reads "to you [pl.]," probably under the influence of three second pl. verb forms in 2:29 and 3:1a. The author uses "the Father" rather than "God," as befitting the mention of children in the next line; see NOTE on 1:2e above. The position of "us" is somewhat emphatic in harmony with the author's exaltation of his adherents in this unit; it may have the nuance of "to such as us." Some commentators would see in the perf. tense of *didonai*, "to give," here a stress on the permanent and lasting results of the divine action. However, as pointed out on p. 161 above, the perf. and aorist (read here by Codex Alexandrinus) seem to be used almost interchangeably, e.g., the aorist of *didonai* is employed in 3:23,24; 5:11 for God's having given us the command to love, the Spirit, and eternal life (all quite enduring), while in 4:13; 5:20 the perf. is employed for God's having given us the Spirit and insight.

More important than the tense is the verb *didonai* itself, which the Johannine writers tend to use for heavenly realities. In GJohn (a) *God gives to Jesus:* the divine name (17:11,12), eternal life (5:26), glory (17:22,24), power over all flesh (17:2), power to judge (5:22,27), what to say (12:49; 17:8), the works he was to do (5:36; 17:4), the commandment about his death (14:31; cf. 18:11), his disciples (6:37,39,65; 17:6,7,9,24; 18:9), in short, all things (3:27,35; 10:29; 11:22; 13:3). (b) *God gives to human beings:* His only Son (3:16), the Paraclete (14:16), the bread of life (6:32), and whatever is asked in Jesus' name (15:16; 16:23). (c) *Jesus gives to those who believe in him:* power to become children of God (1:12), the Spirit (3:34), eternal life (10:28), water springing up to life (4:14–15), the bread of life (6:27,51), glory (17:22), peace (14:27), his Father's words (17:8,14), a new commandment to love (13:34), and an example of service (13:15). Such frequent usage conveys the concreteness and reality of the divine gifts. In the instance of love, God does not simply exhibit it but gives it to dwell in the Christian.

1b. *in enabling us to be called God's children.* Literally, "that [*hina*] we should be called." The *hina* is epexegetical, explaining what the love consists in; but all sense of purpose in the *hina* is not lost since this is also the goal of love. "To be called" is often the same as "to be" (see A. Vicent Cernuda, *Augustinianum* 15 [1975] 445–55). For instance, the two expressions are parallel in the LXX of Hos 2:1 (RSV 1:10): "The number of the sons of Israel shall be like the sand of the sea . . . and they shall be called the sons of the living God"; and in Luke 1:32: "He will be great and will be called the Son of the Most High." Also one may compare Matt 5:9, "They shall be called sons of God," and Luke 6:35, "You will be sons of the Most High." Here the "to be called" has the added innuendo that the status will be known publicly. Through God's love Christians are given a new (eternal) life and a new identity, and so they have a new name.

This is the first use of *teknon* (pl. *tekna*), "child." In the NOTE ON 2:1a, while discussing the words for "children" used by the author in addressing his audience (*teknion, paidion*), I discussed *teknon* which is never used by the author in that way. It is used in John 8:39 for the believing children of Abraham, and in II and III John for the children of the church. Its most frequent use, however (6 of 12 times), is for the children of God (John 1:12; 11:52; I John 3:1,2,10; 5:2). *Teknon* is the technical Johannine term covering divine sonship/daughterhood, since *huios*, "son," is reserved for Jesus in relationship to God. Other NT authors are not so precise. Paul, for instance, calls Christians the *tekna* of God in Rom 8:16,17,21; 9:8, and the *huioi* of God in Rom 8:14,19 (although he never calls the individual Christian "the son of God"). One might have expected Paul to distinguish the terms, for he distinguishes between the Christians as the adopted children/sons of God (Rom 8:15; 9:4) and Jesus who is constituted Son of God in power (Rom 1:4). John's language of begetting by God makes more realistic the imagery of "children of God" than if he spoke of adoption; it also brings the status of the Christian children close to that of Jesus, God's Son. Both Paul and John, despite the adoption/begetting difference, relate the Christians' status to baptism and the Spirit (see Gal 3:26–27; 4:6; Rom 8:15–16; John 3:5). For "children of God" in Paul, I John, and GJohn, see R. A. Culpepper, NTS 27 (1980–81) 24–31.

In ABJ 29, 139–41, I outlined the use of children/sons of God in the OT and intertestamental literature, where first it is used for the whole people of Israel and then, in the postexilic period, for individual Israelites. Because of their piety such individuals are already God's children (Wis 2:13) or will join the sons of God after death (Wis 5:5). Philo, *On the Confusion of Tongues* 28 ≹147, catches the ambiguity of the last situation: "For if we have not yet become fit to be thought sons of God, yet we may be the sons of His invisible image, the most Holy Word." Two things stand out in this history of the term. *First*, the status of Israel as God's son or child is a covenantal relationship. God established Israel as His Son through the saving act of the deliverance from Egypt (Exod 4:22–23) that was an act of love: "When Israel was a child, I loved him; and out of Egypt I called my Son" (MT of Hos 11:1—the LXX is slightly different but uses *agapan* and *tekna*, the vocabulary of I John 3:1). This theme continues into rabbinic Judaism: "Beloved [of God] are the Israelites, for they are named 'sons' of the Omnipresent; by a special love was it made known to them in the Scripture: 'You are the sons of the Lord your God'" (Mishnah *Aboth* 3:14). The passage cited is Deut 14:1, which tells the Israelites of their filial dignity while giving them the commandments that they had to live by. This leads to the *second* aspect of Israel's divine sonship: since it is a covenant relationship, the people must *live* as God's sons. The Hosea passage cited above begins a prophetic reproach to God's children who, despite His loving parental care, have turned away from Him and His Law. The same theme appears in Deut 32:18, the one OT passage that speaks of the divine begetting of Israel, "You were unmindful of the Rock that begot you, and you forgot the God who gave you birth." Jeremiah 31:9 has God saying, "I will make them walk . . . in a straight path in which they shall not stumble; for I am a father to Israel, and Ephraim is my first-born." D. J. McCarthy, CBQ 27 (1965) 144–47, shows the importance of love in this "walking." This stress on living as God's children brought about the understanding that not all Israelites were worthy of that name but only those who were pious and observant. Sirach 4:10 puts a moral condition: "To the orphans be a father and help their mother as a husband would; then you will be like a son to the Most High." *Jubilees* 1:24–25 takes the covenant promise that God made to Israel (Lev 26:12: "I will be your God, and you shall be my people") and that God remade to David about Solomon (II Sam 7:14: "I will be his Father, and he shall be my son") and rephrases it: "Their souls shall cleave to me and all my commandments . . . and I will be their Father, and they shall be my children." One of the tasks of the Messiah will be to distinguish the true children of Israel; for *Ps. Sol.* 17:28–30 says of the Son of David: "He shall gather together a holy people whom he shall lead in justice. . . . He shall know them, that they are all sons of God."

Both these aspects of divine sonship/childhood (the covenantal basis and the requisite that one live by the commandments) come to a focus in the community of the renewed covenant at Qumran. "Sons of God" is not a Qumran term for human beings (a concordance confines the phrase to a Qumran hymnic fragment). Even the angels whom the OT freely calls "sons of God" are called "sons of heaven" in Qumran literature, while the sectarians are the "sons of God's pleasure" (1QH 4:32–33; 11:9). Over and over again the new status of the sectarians as "sons" is repeated in the entrance ceremony, which is called "admission into the covenant of grace [ḥesed]" (1QS 1:8). We hear of "sons of light" (1:9; 2:16; 3:13,24,25); "sons of justice" (3:20,22); "sons of truth" (4:5,6); and elsewhere of the "sons of His truth" (1QM 17:8; 1QH 6:29). Admission to the congregation brings to sectarians the wisdom of the "sons of heaven" (1QS 4:22); and indeed they come to share the company of the "sons of heaven" (1QSa 2:8–9; 1QH 3:22), thus gaining the filial status of angels. (The same outlook is found in Luke 20:36.) All of this, of course, is dependent upon their remaining faithful to the Community's interpretation of the Law.

Although the Johannine writers developed the language of divine begetting to explain the origin of divine sonship/childhood (a language virtually absent from the Jewish background except for the king/Messiah), they hewed closely to the Jewish tradition in reference to the covenant atmosphere of sonship and to the demand to *live* as God's children. In this verse the epistolary author states that it was an act of God's love that made us His children, and surely he thinks that such a status came about through entrance into the Johannine Community of those who believe in Jesus (John 1:12), with the begetting motif closely associated with baptism (3:5). Divine childhood is part of the New Covenant. (A related work, Rev 21:7, uses the OT covenant formula for the Christian child of God: "He who conquers . . . I will be God to him, and he shall be to me a son.") The implication of the combined statements in 2:29b; 3:1ab that God has made us His children and that everyone who acts justly shows this status is one that authors like Sirach and the Qumran Righteous Teacher could have accepted cheerfully. Presumably the secessionists would not have shared the old (Jewish) ethical presuppositions behind the children language. In stressing that the children of God cannot be sinners (I John 3:9; 5:18) but must obey the commandments (5:1–2), especially that of love (4:7), the author stands close to a common Christian outlook illustrated in the Synoptics. In Matt 5:9 the peacemakers are the ones who "shall be called sons of God"; and in Matt 5:44–48 we hear a strong echo of the OT covenant attitude: "Love your enemies . . . so that you may become sons of your Father in heaven, for He makes His sun rise on the evil and the good. . . . You must be perfect as your heavenly Father is perfect." The theme is continued in the second century, as we see in Justin, *Trypho* 123.9: "By virtue of Christ's begetting us unto God . . . we who observe [*phylassein*] the commandments of Christ are called genuine [*alēthinos*] children of God—and that is what we really are" (see p. 8 above).

Before we leave the topic of the children of God, we should consider some helpful observations from Pancaro, "People" 114–24. Besides 1:12–13, which says that the Word who came into the world has empowered those who believe in him to become God's children through divine begetting, the only other GJohn passage that speaks of "children of God" is 11:48–52 where Caiaphas says that it is better to have one man die for the people than to have the whole nation destroyed. Obviously Caiaphas identifies the people (*laos*) of God with the Jewish nation (*ethnos*), which would be imperiled if the Romans came and took away "our holy place and our nation." (It may seem odd to have Caiaphas speaking of the Jews as *ethnos* which in the LXX usually refers to the Gentiles. However, this may be Johannine irony: the Jews are behaving not as the people of God but as a Gentile nation that has not known Him.) John finds in this a prophecy: Jesus was going to die for the (Jewish) nation—"yet not for the nation alone, but to gather together the dispersed children of God and make them one." In other words, the people of God is no longer the Jewish nation alone, but the children of God, i.e., the believers. Like *Jubilees* 1:24–25 cited above, John has rephrased the covenant saying, "I will be your God, and you shall be my people," into "I will be your God, and you shall be my children." Similarly he has redefined Israel, so that the genuine Israelite is one who confesses Jesus to be God's Son and King of Israel (John 1:47–49).

1c. *and that is what we really are!* The *hina* clause of 3:1b took the subjunctive; and were that clause continued here, one would have expected another subjunctive (as in the Vulgate): "in order that we may be called God's children and really be God's children." The use of the indicative involves an interruption. (The total omission of this line in the Byzantine tradition may reflect scribal puzzlement at the abruptness of the construction, or may stem from homoeoteleuton involving *klēthōmen*, "we are called," and *kai esmen*, "and we are.") Vicent Cernuda, "La filiación," argues here as he did in 2:29a (last NOTE there) for an attenuated *kai*, meaning not "and" but "in a certain manner," so that both verses describe the limited filial status of Christians, as compared with the full filial status of Jesus. Most scholars, however, see this interruption in the indicative as underlining the reality of the filiation. And despite its grammatical awkwardness, it has an oratorical flair; compare Epictetus, *Discourse* 2.16.44: "Because of this he [Heracles] was believed to be a son of God, and he was." (Also the Justin citation in the preceding NOTE.) "To be called God's children" in 3:1b really means to be God's children, and this clause reiterates that against a world which does not recognize such dignity.

1de. *The reason that the world does not recognize us is that it never recognized Him.* Codex Sinaiticus* and the Byzantine tradition read "you" for "us" (even as did Codex Vaticanus in 3:1a). Were scribes trying to avoid the implication that the author (thought to be John the Apostle) was not recognized? The verb used twice in this sentence is *ginōskein*, "to know," used to confirm the knowledge of the Christian in the main clause of 2:29a. Even if the secessionists are headed toward gnosticism (a term related to *ginōskein*), the author writes with an appreciation of the importance of *knowledge* of divine truth. In the nonrecognition by the world some would find a hint of persecution, but the expression is not strong enough for that.

This is the first instance of the phrase *dia touto*, "for this reason," which gives rise to the same debate as the phrase *en toutō* discussed in the NOTE on 2:3a, namely, does the "this" refer to what precedes, to what follows, or to both? Here Bultmann, Marshall, and THLJ favor a reference to what has preceded, i.e., the world does not recognize us because we are children of God. Brooke, Schnackenburg, and the RSV favor a reference to what follows, i.e., the world does not recognize us because it never recognized him. Plummer and B. Weiss favor a reference in both directions. However, a study of the 15 times the phrase appears in GJohn shows that it is used with remarkable regularity. Six times it clearly refers to what follows (5:16,18; 8:47; 10:17; 12:18,39), and in all those cases it is followed by an epexegetical *hoti* clause. Nine times it clearly refers to what precedes (1:31; 6:65; 7:21–22; 9:23; 12:27; 13:11; 15:19; 16:15; 19:11), and in none of those cases is it followed by such a *hoti* clause. The latter is the case in the two other instances of *dia touto* in the Johannine Epistles (I John 4:5; III John 10). In the present instance it is followed by an epexegetical *hoti* clause; and so, unless it is the one exception in the Johannine corpus, *dia touto* here should point forward.

The reason, then, why the world does not recognize us is that it did not recognize him (*autos*). Among those who take the *autos* to refer to God (or at least God in Christ) are: Balz, Brooke, Bruce, Chaine, Houlden, Schnackenburg, Schneider, THLJ, and Windisch. Taking it as a reference to Christ are: Bultmann, Dodd, Häring, Hauck, and Stott, while a reference to either or both is favored by Wilder. The sentence makes sense either way: Failure to recognize the children could stem from failure to recognize the Father or to recognize the unique and model Son. During the ministry of Jesus (the past tense "never recognized" is aorist) both failures occurred: "They never knew [aorist *ginōskein*] the Father or me" (John 16:3; 8:19). The exact expression, "the world never knew," is applied to Christ in John 1:10, and to the Father in John 17:25; and in I John the author will refer to a failure to know Christ in 3:6 and to know God in 4:8. Since the usage is not decisive, my opting for God ("Him") rests upon the fact that God is mentioned by name in the lines on either side of this sentence.

2a. *Yes, beloved, we are God's children right now.* There is strong emphasis in this affirmation, which repeats the "we are God's children" of 3:1bc, and the "now" of 2:28a (In the NOTE on the latter I pointed out that the *nyn* of *kai nyn* had not lost all temporal value, and that is borne out by the *nyn* here.) The *agapētoi*, "beloved" (NOTE on 2:7a), picks up the "love [*agapē*] the Father has bestowed on us" of 3:1a; but since that is a frequent Synoptic designation of Jesus, its use here may also imply our likeness as God's children to God's beloved Son.

2b. *and what we shall be has not yet been revealed.* Literally, "and not yet has it been revealed [*phaneroun*] what we shall be." The initial "and" gives the impression of wonder upon wonder. *Oupō*, "not yet," is part of the apocalyptic atmosphere that has permeated I John since 2:18 and agrees with the future reference of "when he is revealed" in 2:28b. An *oupō* is used by Jesus in the Synoptic eschatological discourse to distinguish between the introductory signs of the last times and the end (*telos*): "When you hear of wars and rumors of wars, the end is *not yet*" (Mark 13:7; Matt 24:6). It is also used in Rev 17:10,12 to speak of the final manifestation of evil in the last kings who have not yet come. Its presence in 3:2b, counterposed to the "now" of 3:2a, is proof again for Klein, "Licht" 312–13, that I John has lost the "once-for-all" character of the time words in GJohn and has introduced a chronological, salvation-history schema. He says that for GJohn everything was "now" for the believer, and "not yet" for those who refused to believe in Christ, whereas for I John the "now" and the "not yet" are two chronological steps that affect all, with the second containing a revelation that has not happened in the first. As I pointed out in the NOTE on the "last hour" of 2:18a, I do not think Klein does justice to a vein of chronological eschatology in GJohn itself where there is still an "hour" to come.

Along with most commentators I have taken the "what we shall be" as the subject of the third person singular aorist passive form of *phaneroun*. Synge, "I John 3,2," proposes a different division of the verse and a different understanding of the subject. His first line (adapted to my translation) would be: "Beloved, now we are God's children, and He has not yet been revealed." His chief argument is that otherwise this is a peculiar use of *phaneroun*. However, the usage of this verb is complicated (NOTE on 1:2a). In 5 of the 9 GJohn uses Jesus is revealed; but in 4, realities are revealed (2:11; 3:21; 9:3; 17:6)—2 of them employing the same passive form as here. In I John there are 7 other uses of *phaneroun* (besides the 2 here); 3 have Jesus revealed (2:28; 3:5,8) and 2 have realities revealed (2:19; 4:9—the latter with the passive form), while the revelation of "life" in 1:2 falls in between. Thus it is perfectly possible in Johannine usage to have an impersonal subject for one or both of the aorist passives of *phaneroun* in the present verse. Against Synge, I would argue that in 2:19 the author spoke of the revelation of the presence and nature of the Antichrists, and so it is appropriate now that he speak of the (future) revelation of the Christians. In Col 3:4 the passive of *phaneroun* is used of the future revelation of the Christians in glory (cf. I Pet 5:4), and the unveiling (*apokalypsis*) of the sons of God is expected in Rom 8:19; thus we may be dealing with a common eschatological image. The use of the neuter, "*what* we shall be," puts less stress on identity and more on quality (BDF 299[2]), since our identity as God's children is already established. When shall this revelation take place? In John 14:3; 17:24 the victorious Jesus is to return to take his own out of the world to be with him in heaven, and that could easily have been understood as taking place at the death of individual Christians. In John 5:27–29 there is foreseen a general resurrection of the dead when those who have done what is right will rise to live. Bultmann, *Epistles* 48, thinks that it is an open question as to which view is in mind here, but the apocalyptic context certainly favors the latter.

2c. *But we know that at this revelation.* Literally, "we know that if [*ean*] it/he is revealed." The Byzantine textual tradition, the Coptic, and the Peshitta supply an adversative particle (*de*), which is probably not original but represents a correct scribal feeling for the adversative character of this clause. In Synge's theory (preceding NOTE) the "we know" should not be read with this line but with the preceding: "What we shall be we know [*eidenai*]." The *hoti* that follows becomes causal rather than declarative: "because when he is revealed, we shall be like him." This is an unlikely grammatical construction. Of the 16 uses of *eidenai* (*oida*) in I John, in no other does the object of the knowledge precede the verb as Synge demands; and the construction of *eidenai* with a declarative *hoti* following is quite common. (It is also unlikely that *hoti* should be divided into *ho ti*, which with *ean* would mean: "whatever may be revealed.") The *ean* is to be interpreted in the same way as the *ean* in 2:28b (also used with a passive subj. form of *phaneroun*), i.e., as "when(ever)" allowing certainty about the happening but uncertainty about the time.

Is the passive of *phaneroun* to be translated as "he is revealed" (as in 2:28b) or as "it is revealed"? The subject is taken as "he" (presumably Christ) by Alexander, Balz, Bonsirven, Brooke, Bruce, Bultmann, Dodd, Häring, Law, Marshall, Vellanickal, Westcott, Windisch, the RV and RSV. The subject is taken as "it" (the "what we shall be" from the preceding line) by H. Braun, Chaine, Haupt, Holtzmann (?), Klein, Plummer, Schnackenburg, THLJ, and the NEB. In my judgment the grammatical arguments favor the latter position. In the preceding NOTE we saw that the passive of *phaneroun* has both personal and impersonal subjects. The argument that *phaneroun* must have the same meaning here as it had (same form) in 2:28b where it refers to Christ being revealed backfires on two scores. First, in 2:28b a personal subject (*autos*, Christ) had just been mentioned at the end of the preceding line, and so it was natural to take this person as the subject of "is revealed." Here there is no such personal reference in the preceding line (2b) that can serve as subject. Indeed, the closest personal subject is God in v. 2a, for Christ has not been mentioned by title or pronominally since 2:28c. Second, if one seeks an analogy in a previous use of *phaneroun*, the obvious one is the preceding line where "what we shall be" is the subject of the passive of *phaneroun*. The sequence makes perfect sense: what we shall be has not yet been revealed; but we know that when it is revealed, etc. The revelation of "what we shall be" will take place only when Christ is revealed, but Christ is probably not the subject of the verb "revealed" in either instance in 3:2. I find no contradiction, as Synge does, between the fact that what we shall be has not yet been revealed, and the fact that we know that we shall be like Him—that is the minimum that we know.

2d. *we shall be like Him.* Once more we face the problem of whether the *autos* ("him") is God or Christ. A reference to God is favored by Alexander (?), Chaine, Plummer, Schnackenburg, Schneider, THLJ, B. Weiss, Westcott (God in Christ), while a reference to Christ is favored by Balz, Bonsirven, Brooke (?), Bultmann, Dodd, Holtzmann, Houlden, and Marshall. Naturally, if one takes Christ as the subject of "is revealed" in the previous line, the resemblance has to be to Christ. But if the previous line deals with the revelation of what we shall be, and we are already God's children, then more likely we children are being assured that at the final revelation we shall be like God the Father, a God whom the world has never known or recognized (3:1e). Grammatically, a reference to God is easier to defend. In the next verse, where Christ is meant, the author uses *ekeinos* to identify him; this pronoun is hard to explain if Christ has already been discussed in this verse. Also theologically, a reference to God is more acceptable. True, elsewhere in the NT it is attested that we shall be like Christ, e.g., "The Lord Jesus Christ . . . will change our lowly body to be like his glorious body" (Philip 3:20–21; also I Cor 15:49; Col 3:4). However, Johannine theology emphasizes that we are already like Christ, possessing his life, his Spirit, his truth, and his love. One must bring into the discussion the promise in the next line (2e) to "see him [*autos*] as he is." Would the author say that the believers shall see Christ as he is, with the implication that they have not already seen him thus? John 17:24 promises a future seeing of Jesus' glory, but seeing him "as he is" seems too broad a concept to refer to seeing his glory. At the Last Supper in 14:19 and 16:16 the Johannine Jesus assured his disciples that in a little while they would see him and receive life from him. This was fulfilled when Magdalene could say, "I have seen the Lord" (20:18) and when the risen Jesus breathed the Spirit upon his disciples (20:22). In light of this the epistolary author could speak in the past tense of seeing Jesus: "This life was revealed as we have seen" (I John 1:2). Any implication that the Christ who was seen in the ministry was not Christ "as he is," or that the vision of Christ remains for the future would seem to be a damaging admission on the author's part in his struggle with the secessionists. On the other hand, it would be perfectly good Johannine theology to say that we have not seen God as He is. Johannine thought emphasizes that no one, save Jesus, has ever seen God in Himself (John 1:18; 6:46; I John 4:20). Through faith it is possible to see God in Jesus (John 14:9) but seeing God as He is in Himself is the ultimate revelation.

2e. *for we shall see Him as He is.* I have just argued that the *autos* here is God as it was in the previous line. (Matt 5:8 and I Cor 13:12 promise a future vision of God, but other passages speak of an end-time vision of Christ: Matt 26:64; Mark 13:26; I Pet 1:7–8; Rev 1:7.) This accords with the view common among the Greek Fathers, while the Latins understood it as a reference to Christ. There is OT background to such a promise of seeing God. In some biblical traditions, for his own good Moses was not allowed to see God's face (Exod 33:20,23). Nevertheless, the Psalms (11:7, 17:15) promise that the just will see the face of God. In particular, this became an idiom for visiting the Temple where God dwelt (Ps 42:3[2]; see Exod 23:17). In cultic terms I John 2:1–2 describes Jesus as making atonement in the presence of the Father (almost as if, like Hebrews, the author was thinking of God's presence as a heavenly Temple; see Rev 21:22); and so now the author may be using cultic terminology to describe the entrance of believers into God's presence in the last hour.

It is difficult to understand the precise implication of the *hoti* that begins this clause. By translating it as "for," I have rejected the opinion of the very few (THLJ) that it is the second declarative (recitative) *hoti*, "that," in a row and thus the second object of "we know" in 3:2c: "We know that at this revelation we shall be like Him, [yes,] *that* we shall see Him as He is." Were that the case one would have expected a reversed order of clauses and a connective *kai*, "and," to avoid the abruptness of the juxtaposition. I also reject as unprovable and unnecessary the suggestion of an underlying Aramaic *dᵉ*, meaning "that" (*hoti*) and "when" (*hote*), with the implication that the wrong Greek translation (*hoti*) was chosen here. The author did mean, "We shall be like Him *when* we shall see Him as He is"; but he meant more than that, and so he used *hoti*, "because."

Even when one accepts a causal *hoti*, does the clause offer the reason why we know (Schnackenburg) or the reason why we shall be like Him (Bultmann)? If our seeing God as He is is *the basis of our knowledge*, the logic is this: we are like God as His children now, and so we shall still be like Him at the revelation; and therefore we shall be able to see Him as He is, for like knows like. Grammatically this is quite defensible, for in 3:14 the author uses a similar sequence: "We know that . . . because," and there many think that "because" is the reason for knowing. The principle of like knowing like is well attested in the thought of the time. Philo, *On the Giants* 2 ⁂9, cites it as the basis for the mind's ability to see the spiritual. If, on the other hand, our seeing God as He is is *the basis for our being like Him*, the logic may be (a) that we shall become more like Him than we already are (ontological change) and do this through sight; or (b) that we shall recognize that we are like Him (noetic change). Most commentators assume that (a) is meant: it is common Greek philosophy that knowledge of an object brings about conformity to that object; and it is the basic principle of the mystery religions and of gnosticism that mystical vision or gnosis deifies. Dodd, *Epistles* 71 says, "Our author is assuming principles which he held in common, not only with the 'Gnostic' teachers whom he is combating, but with the higher thought of the Hellenistic world in general." However, such an evaluation may be too subtle, for the author may have meant his statement in sense (b). Perhaps all we can be certain of is that the author made two future claims without being clear on the relationship between them: We shall see God as He is, and we shall be like Him. Both claims are common in NT thought and in early Judaism (see COMMENT). The real question is how much separates the future expected state from the present situation of believing Christians. A strong emphasis on realized eschatology would imply little change from one to the other. I John 3:2ab indicates continuity between the two states but some change.

3a. *Everyone who has this hope based on Him.* This is the only instance in Johannine literature of the noun *elpis*, "hope," which occurs 53 times in the NT (but is absent from Revelation as well). The verb *elpizein* occurs 31 times in the NT, once in GJohn (5:45: "Moses on whom you have set your hopes"), and once each in II and III John ("I hope to come to [see] you soon")—notice no Johannine use in a Christian theological sense. Only the Johannine stress on realized eschatology can explain the absence of such an important Christian theological theme. But in the current passage where the parousia has been mentioned, the theme of hope is quite appropriate. Indeed, Alexander, *Epistles* 81, argues that the expression here "to have hope" is stronger than the simple verb "to hope." The preposition *epi*, "on, upon," used with a personal object, offers the basis for the hope and the source from which fulfillment is expected (BDF 235²; 187⁶). There is the usual debate about the reference of the "him" (*autos*). Those who see a reference to God include Chaine, Schackenburg, B. Weiss, Westcott (God in Christ), while those who see a reference to Christ include, Alexander, Balz, Brooke, Bruce, Bultmann, Cook, Houlden, Marshall, and Stott. Bonsirven leaves the question undecided; and certainly there are NT texts mentioning hope in God (Acts 24:15; I Tim 4:10 [*epi*]) and hope in Christ (Rom 15:12 [*epi*]). In my judgment three arguments strongly favor a reference to God in the *autos* here: (1) in the next line, where the author clearly wishes to speak about Christ, he uses *ekeinos;* and it would be strange within the same verse to have Jesus referred to as *autos* and as *ekeinos;* (2) in the immediate context (3:1,2) *autos* seemingly refers to God; (3) this verse in its "hope based on *him*" probably refers back to the affirmation in 3:1, "Look at what love the Father has bestowed on us"—our hope for the future is based on what He has done in the past.

3b. *makes himself pure even as Christ is pure.* "Christ" in my translation represents an interpretation of *ekeinos,* "that one"; but an interpretation on which almost all agree (see NOTE on 2:6bc). The argument here is not based simply on the demonstrative, but on the theology of the *kathōs* ("just as") construction that belongs to class III in the de Dinechin analysis (same NOTE). It is part of the author's apologetic emphasis on the moral behavior of Jesus as the model for the Christian. Yet here there are several puzzling factors. In the *kathōs* example in 2:6bd the Christian was told to walk as Christ *walked,* with the past (aorist) tense clearly referring to the earthly ministry of Jesus. But here the model is the present state: "as Christ is pure." While all these examples have a certain vagueness (INTRODUCTION, footnote 226), the author is very vague here; for *hagnos,* "pure," is never used in any Gospel to describe Jesus. The adjective *hagnos,* the noun *hagnismos* ("purification"), and the verb *hagnizein* ("to purify") are relatively rare in the NT, occurring a total of 16 times. In the only other Johannine use, John 11:55, the verb describes Jewish purifications for Passover, a cultic context found also in Acts 21:24,26; 24:18. Moral admonitions about purity in Titus 2:5 and in I Pet 3:2 refer to sexual matters. But there is no indication of a christological use that the readers would be familiar with, and one wonders why the author did not choose a more familiar word like *hagios,* "holy" (*sanctus* is the Vulgate rendition in this verse, perhaps by free translation, or perhaps by reading *hagios* in place of *hagnos*).

A possible explanation lies in the Greek OT use of *hagnizein* for ritual purification, especially in Exod 19:10–11 where God tells Moses: "Go down and solemnly charge the people, and *make them pure* today and tomorrow . . . for on the third day the Lord will descend on Mount Sinai before all the people." In other words a purification was demanded before encountering the appearance of God. Similarly the Levites had to purify themselves before going into the presence of the Lord in the Sanctuary (Num 8:21). I John 2:1–2 gave a picture of Jesus the just one in the Father's presence making priestly atonement for our sins; and according to GJohn before he went to heaven Jesus said, "It is for them that I consecrate [*hagiazein*] myself, in order that they too may be consecrated in truth" (John 17:19). Thus one may have the image (as in the Exodus scene) of Jesus making himself holy and pure and then going into the divine presence. If Christians wish to encounter the divine presence at the revelation in the last hour, they must similarly purify themselves, or in the terminology of John 17:19, be consecrated, i.e., made holy. (The beatitude in Matt 5:8 uses still another language, but seemingly without cultic tones: "Happy the *clean* of heart, for they shall see God.") If "seeing God" reflects the cultic terminology of the Israelite Temple, so also may the statement about making oneself pure. Replacement of Israelite cult is a strong motif in GJohn (ABJ 29 cxliii); and we may have it here again, transferred to final eschatology. James 4:8, as part of an invitation to draw near to God, demands, "Purify your hearts"; and I Pet 1:22–23 speaks in sequence of "having purified your souls by your obedience to truth" and having "been begotten anew." These last two NT uses of *hagnizein* raise the possibility that the Greek words for "purify, pure, purification" were part of the Christian initiation/baptismal ceremony (see COMMENT). If so, I John is reiterating a demand for purity that his adherents heard when they came to know God in Jesus and became God's children, and he is assuring them that the best preparation for seeing God as He is and for being like Him is still reflected in that demand. Although the author speaks of the Christian making himself pure, this has to be understood in terms of taking advantage of the cleansing from sin through the blood of Christ (which was mentioned in 1:7,9; 2:2), as the contrast with the next verse makes clear.

4a. *Everyone who acts sinfully.* The Greek phrase is *poiein tēn hamartian,* literally, "to make/do the sin"; and some commentators contend that this is more forceful than the simple verb "to sin." Similarly, Westcott, *Epistles* 102, thinks the presence of the definite article lends emphasis and scope: "sin in its completeness." (In reference to this same expression in 3:8a, Vellanickal, *Sonship* 257, thinks a specific sin is meant, namely, the refusal to believe in Jesus that John 16:9 calls simply "sin.") However, this verse is in contrast with 2:29b, "Everyone who acts justly" (*poiein tēn dikaiosynēn*), and both the idiom "to make/do" and the article are called for by that contrast. The antithesis is so perfect that the von Dobschütz and Bultmann source theories (INTRODUCTION III A) place 2:29b and 3:4a next to each other in the reconstructed source. In the NOTE on 2:23ab I called attention to the author's tendency to use the "everyone who" construction (*pas* + article + participle) which reflects dualism—here a dualism between "justice" and "sin." A rebuke to those who "act sinfully" was addressed in John 8:34 to Jews who believed inadequately in Jesus. Here in my judgment (against Schnackenburg and Schneider) it is not a general observation but refers to the secessionists, corresponding to the secessionist-inspired boasts of 1:8,10, "We are free from the guilt of sin . . . we have not sinned." This is confirmed by 3:4b which identifies with the apocalyptic Iniquity the sin of those who act sinfully, just as the secessionists were identified with the Antichrist in 2:18–19.

is really doing iniquity. Literally, "also iniquity [*anomia*] does." The arrangement of the two Greek phrases in 4a is artistically chiastic: doing sin = iniquity doing. For *hamartia,* "sin," see the NOTE on 1:7e. Frequently *anomia,* "without law, transgression of the Law, iniquity" (14 times in the NT; only here in Johannine literature), is a synonym for "sin" in the LXX, since in Jewish thought sin is a violation of the revealed Law of God and so is an act of lawlessness. For instance, Ps 51:5(3): "For I know my *anomia*, and my *hamartia* is continually before me." The same phenomenon is found in Rom 4:7 (citing Ps 32:1): "Happy are they whose iniquities [*anomia*] were forgiven and whose sins [*hamartia*] were covered over" (also Heb 10:17).

4b. *for sin is the Iniquity*. Despite the usage just cited, this solemn statement shows that *hamartia* and *anomia* are not simply synonyms for the author. There are two basic lines of scholarly interpretation. FIRST, those who take *anomia* in its root meaning of "lawlessness" include Belser, Boismard, Bonsirven, Brooke, Bruce, Büchsel, Calmes, Chaine, Dodd, Galtier, Hauck, Houlden, Loisy, Meinertz, Plummer, Vrede, B. Weiss, Westcott, and Windisch. The statement is then a definition: Sin is lawlessness; and it is sometimes supposed that the opponents were antinomians who thought that the Law had no significance and who lived lives of licentiousness. Against them the author, with his Jewish tendencies, would be reasserting the obligation to keep God's Law. The opponents would have learned their attitude either from Paul's opposition to the Law or from the attitude of the Johannine Jesus that the Law pertained to the Jews (and implicitly not to his followers: "your Law" in 8:17; 10:34; "their Law" in 15:25). Houlden, *Epistles* 92, thinks that for the author "sin is not so much a cosmic force of evil . . . as a matter of rule-breaking, a matter for regulation by the discipline of the community." However, nowhere in I and II John does the author ever accuse his adversaries of statements against the Law. Nor is there evidence of libertine behavior by the secessionists (INTRODUCTION IV B2b). If the opponents were permissive about lawlessness, one would have expected the author to say, "Lawlessness is sin," not "Sin is lawlessness." (Indeed, one finds an example of this type of statement in the Pseudo-Clementine *Recognitions* 7.37.2; GCS 51, 215: "To break any commandment is sin.") Moreover, can we seriously suppose that the author hoped to have a stress on the Law accepted as true Johannine tradition? Jesus said that Moses gave the Law to the Jews (John 7:19), but for his followers, "You will know the truth, and the truth will set you free" (8:32). An attempt to meet this objection is the variation of the lawlessness approach offered by Lyonnet, "Notion" 43, who suggests that such a term might mean rejection of the one Johannine "law," i.e., the commandment to love one another. But then one would have expected at least one reference to that commandment as "law," a word that never occurs in the Johannine Epistles.

SECOND, those who take *anomia* to mean apocalyptic iniquity include F.-M. Braun, Charue, de la Potterie, Lyonnet, and Schnackenburg. The statement in the present verse then ceases to be a definition, and the article before *anomia* is given full force so that it indicates a definite and well-known predicate (BDF 273¹, as above in 2:7c). Sin is being identified as *the* Iniquity which is the expected state of hostility at the end of the world. In 2:18 the secessionists were identified as the manifestation of the expected Antichrist; now their sins (toward which they are indifferent) are identified as manifestations of the expected Iniquity. What evidence do we have for such a meaning of *anomia?* The root meaning of "rejection of the Law" would involve in the Jewish outlook rebelliousness against God the giver of the Law, and *anomia* would therefore be appropriate to the final manifestation of evil as anti-God (and, for Christians, anti-Christ). In the LXX, *anomia* can translate Hebrew *'āwel* or *'awlâ,* frequent Dead Sea Scroll terminology to describe the realm of iniquity opposed to the realm of God's truth and justice. (See passage cited on p. 235 above.) If the author of I John had such an apocalyptic view of the end-time, one could understand why he would counterpose doing justice (2:29) and doing sin, which is the Iniquity (3:4). *Anomia* is also used in the LXX to translate *bᵉlîya'al,* "worthlessness," which Ps 18:5 associates with the nether world, and which becomes at Qumran and in the NT a technical name for the devil, "Belial," or (by dissimilation of labials) "Beliar." In a dualistic NT passage (II Cor 6:14–15) that closely resembles Qumran theology we read, "What partnership has justice [*dikaiosynē*] with iniquity [*anomia*]? What community [*koinōnia*] has light with darkness? What in common has Christ with Belial?" The *Testament of Dan* 6:1–6 speaks of the final period in which the angel of peace and Satan struggle as "the time of the iniquity of Israel." In the ending of Mark found in the Freer Gospels (Washington) and in some MSS. known to Jerome, Jesus speaks of the present age that is coming to an end as "the age of *anomia*" under Satan, dominated by unclean spirits who resist the truth of God. The *Epistle of Barnabas* 4:1–4 associates the "works of *anomia*" with the "error of the present time" as constituting the last kingdom foretold by Daniel, while *Barn.* 18:1, speaking of the two ways, associates the way of light with the Lord, and the way of darkness with "the ruler of the present time of *anomia*" (see also 14:5). In Matthew's form of the eschatological discourse (24:11–12), Jesus speaks of the time when false prophets will arise (p. 335 above) as a time when *anomia* will be multiplied, while in Matt 7:22–23 Jesus castigates those who will prophesy (unwarrantedly) in his name: "Depart from me, you who work *anomia.*" Indeed, in Matt 13:41 Jesus says that when the Son of Man sends out his angels, they will gather out of his kingdom all those who do (*poiein*) *anomia.* These associations continue in *Didache* 16:3–4: "For in the last days the false prophets shall multiply . . . as *anomia* increases . . . and then shall appear the deceiver of the world as a son of God." In light of our discussion of the Antichrist (p. 336 above), the most important text is II Thess 2:3–8 which speaks of the final evil in terms of the revelation of "the man of *anomia,* the son of perdition," also called "the Iniquitous One [*ho anomos*]." All of this constitutes the "mystery of *anomia*" which is already at work. Against this background, it seems to me that when I John 3:4 says that everyone who acts sinfully is making manifest the Iniquity, and when 3:8 says that everyone who acts sinfully belongs to the devil, the author is again appropriating the apocalyptic expectations of the final time to describe his opponents. Not only in their belief about the Christ but also in their ethical stance of ignoring sin are they manifestations of the Antichrist and sons of the diabolic Iniquity.

5ab. *And you know well that Christ was revealed to take away sins.* Codex

Sinaiticus and some Sahidic MSS. read "we know," while the same Codex and the Byzantine tradition add an "our" before "sins." The fluctuation between "we" and "you" is unpredictable (see 2:28–29), for "we" dominated in 3:1–2, but "you" will appear in 3:7. With either pronoun the author is reiterating implicitly here that his audience needs no teacher (2:27) and is appealing to the Johannine tradition. The subject of the subordinate clause is *ekeinos*, which was used previously in 3:3b for Christ. One may wonder why *autos* is not used since there has been no change of divine subject since that verse, even as in the next line (5c) *autos* will be used to continue the reference to Christ (*ekeinos*) in this line. The author's grammar is a bit mysterious, but there can be little doubt that *ekeinos* is Christ, if we consider the unambiguous parallel in 3:8: "The Son of God . . . was revealed to destroy the works of the devil." Since the Iniquity of the preceding verse, represented by sin, is part of the context of the Antichrist, it is only fitting in Johannine dualism that the author counterpose the figure of Christ who takes away sins.

The aorist passive of *phaneroun*, "to reveal" (NOTE on 1:2a above), could be translated as "revealed himself." If the reference here is to the incarnation as most writers assume, "revealed himself" would underline the preexistent aspect of Christ. However, if my analysis is correct, such an emphasis would be close to the thought of the secessionists, while the epistolary author is thinking of the *incarnate* divine Word as the Christ being revealed during his public ministry. In the GJohn Prologue *phaneroun* is not used for the incarnation; its first use is for the Baptist's revelation of Jesus to Israel (John 1:31), a revelation that designated Jesus as "the Lamb of God who takes away the world's sin" (1:29)—precisely the role of Christ that is at issue here. Since I John 1:7 spoke of the blood of Jesus cleansing us from all sin, and 2:1–2 presented Jesus as the atoning sacrifice for sins, the author obviously would include the death of Jesus as part of the revelation "to take away sins" (reflecting his interpretation of the Lamb of God passage; see ABJ 29, 60–63). If the revelation of Jesus in his ministry and death took away sin, it is understandable that his future revelation will not be a matter of shame to those who act justly (I John 2:28–29).

In the NOTE on 1:7e I discussed various verbs for the action that counteracts sin ("forgive," "destroy," "atone," "cleanse"), but this is the only epistolary use of the verb *airein*, "to take away." Used 26 times in GJohn (mostly of physically removing), *airein* is of import for our purposes as it appears in John 1:29, just cited above, and in 15:2. There God takes away from the vine any branches that do not bear fruit. That passage cautions us against the interpretation of *airein* offered by W. Grundmann, TDNT 1, 305, who in connection with John 1:29 argues that the Lamb of God *takes to himself* the sin of the world. Although some argue for that from the imagery of the scapegoat (Lev 16:8–10,20–22) or the imagery of the Suffering Servant (Isa 53:4–7—a passage that Argyle, "I John," argues is the background for I John 3:5), it is difficult to see how the author in the very next line (3:5c) could then say, "There is nothing sinful in him." It is safer to understand "take away sins" in light of 1:7e ("his blood cleanses us from all sin") and of 2:2a ("an atonement for our sins"). Jesus died as a sacrificial lamb, and his blood was an expiation cleansing us from sin. Hebrews uses the sacrificial context of the Day of Atonement when it speaks of "Christ offered one time for the taking away [*anapherein*] of the sins of many" (9:28). The background may be the New Covenant context that has been so strong in I John; for in Exod 34:9–10 Moses begs the Lord, "Take away our sins and our iniquities [*anomia*], and we will be yours," to which God responds, "Behold, I make a covenant for you." Surely the author's readers would have understood their entrance into the Christian covenant as the moment when their sins were taken away through Christ, and that is why the author can say, "You know well" this (v. 5a). I Peter 2:24, in what many consider to be a baptismal context, speaks of Christ "bearing our sins."

Let us reflect on I John's use of the plural in "take away sins," where John 1:29 uses the singular, "takes away the world's sin." As I remarked in the NOTE on 1:7e, by using the plural I John may be stressing that the ordinary sins of life are a manifestation of evil and opposed to Christ. Bultmann, *Epistles* 50, argues that "take away sins" in I John does not mean the cleansing of past sins but the possibility of freedom from sinning, a point also made by Boismard. Yet I would think that more likely if the author has used the singular (which in GJohn is the root sin of disbelief), and if we did not have other statements in I John about cleansing from all sin (1:7) and atonement for sins (2:2). If anything, the plural usage extends the cleansing from past sins to present sins.

5c. *and there is nothing sinful in him.* Literally, "and sin in him is not." The "him" is *autos*, continuing the *ekeinos* (Christ) of v. 5a. Almost the same thing was said by Jesus in oblique reference to himself in John 7:18: "And unrighteousness [*adikia*] in him is not." In I John 2:1–2, in relation to atonement for sins, the author called Christ "the one who is just"; he is making the same point in another way here. It is not clear whether this clause stands by itself as a co-ordinate with 5ab, or is subordinated as the second object of "you know well" in 5a. Certainly the author could have supposed knowledge of the sinlessness of Jesus, which is a common NT theme (Heb 4:15; I Pet 2:22; II Cor 5:21) and is found in GJohn as well: "Can any one of you convict me of sin?" (8:46), and "The Prince of this world . . . has no hold on me" (14:30). For the epistolary author the sinlessness of Christ is more than a fact; it verges on ontological necessity, since it flows from his oneness with the Father. The thought is not too far from Philo's in *On Flight* 21 ⌗117: "As long as this holiest Word is alive and is still present in the soul, it is out of the question that an unintentional offense should come back into it, for this holy Word is by nature incapable . . . of admitting to itself any sin whatsoever." The secessionists may have used the sinlessness of Christ as the basis of the type of boast recorded in I John 1:10: "We have not sinned." The author objected to that boast, but now he will say almost the same thing himself.

6a. *Everyone who abides in him does not commit sin.* This is another example of *pas* ("all") + article + pres. ptcp., a construction used by the author to divide the human race into two all-inclusive groups (NOTE on 2:23ab). This line refers to the good group; in the next line the same construction will refer to the bad group. Curiously, Bultmann, who posits a source consisting of antithetical statements, is dubious now (*Epistles* 45, n. 5) whether this antithesis belonged to it, because of the presence of Johannine vocabulary (which in his theory belongs to the author, not to the source). Precisely to show the antithesis, I have translated the *pas* construction in line 6a literally even though, as explained in the NOTE on 2:19f, when such a construction is negated, a better translation would be: "No one who abides in him commits sin." "Abides in" is a *menein en* construction of the type (A) discussed in the NOTE on 2:6a where divine indwelling is involved: here the Christian abides in Jesus as already in I John 2:27,28. "Commit sin" is the verb *hamartanein* discussed in the NOTE on 1:7e where I treated *hamartia,* "sin."

The logic of this statement flows from the preceding verse: there is no sin in Christ, and so those who abide in him should have no sin in them. Most Christians would recognize the incompatibility of sinning with the new operative principle of life received through belief in Jesus. However, more explanation is needed because of a seeming contradiction with the author's previous condemnation of Christian boasts of sinlessness in 1:8,10. The author will virtually repeat this line (6a) in 3:9a ("Everyone who has been begotten by God does not act sinfully") and will heighten it to impeccability in 3:9c ("and so he cannot be a sinner"); therefore, I shall postpone a full discussion of the question to the NOTE ON 3:9cd.

6b. *Everyone who does commit sin has never seen him.* The verb "to see" is the perfect of *horan,* previously used in 1:1c ("what we have seen with our own eyes"). It is difficult to anticipate the author's mind. After "Everyone who abides in him does not commit sin" one might have expected a perfect chiastic antithesis: "Everyone who does commit sin does not abide in him," reflecting a world where there is no middle ground. However, the author is harsher: the sinner not only does not abide in Christ; he has not even seen Christ! Perhaps neither the author nor his secessionist opponents had physically seen Jesus of Nazareth, but that is not the point of his attack. The secessionists, by their indifference to the malice of sin, are not heirs to the Beloved Disciple, "the one who saw" these things (John 19:35; perf. of *horan*). In III John 11 the author will state: "Whoever does what is bad has never seen [perf. *horan*] God." The interchangeability of "see Christ" and "see God" is partially explained by John 14:9: "Whoever has seen [perf. *horan*] me has seen the Father." Notice that here the author does not speak of "Everyone who *did* commit sin" but uses the present tense, because he is not concerned with past sins that may have been forgiven. His objection is to a continued life-style and outlook on sin that is incompatible with being a Johannine Christian.

6c. *nor come to know him.* Literally, "and has not known him." Since knowledge implies intimacy, this denial may be even more biting than the denial of sight in the previous line.

7a. *Little Children.* The use of *teknion* (NOTE on 2:1a) echoes the usage at the beginning of this unit in 2:28a. Codex Alexandrinus and some minuscules read the pl. of *paidion* ("child"), presumably because a scribe thought the author would alternate as in the past (*teknion* in 2:12; *paidion* in 2:14; *paidion* in 2:18; *teknion* in 2:28).

let no one deceive you. This is the only instance in the Johannine literature of *mēdeis*, the proper word for "no one," and it may be emphatic: this warning is true no matter how plausible the person appears. I discussed words pertaining to deceit in the NOTE on 1:8b.

7b. *The person who acts justly is truly just.* Literally, "The one *doing justice* is just"—the same idiom as in 2:29b (half of which Bultmann combines with the present line for the original of 3:7 in his reconstructed source; see Appendix I, Chart Three). Apparently the author wishes to specify clearly who is just, whence my addition of "truly." Probably this is meant to refute a secessionist claim equating "being just" with knowing God. For I John, as Plummer, *Epistles* 77, states by way of paraphrasing James 2:17,20: "Knowledge without works is dead." Or perhaps better: "Knowledge without works is not knowledge." Since the author contrasts "to do justice" here with "to do sin" in the next verse, no one who does sin can be just.

7c. *even as Christ is just.* This is a *kathōs* construction belonging to de Dinechin's type III, as discussed in the NOTE on 2:6bc above. The analogue of the comparison is *ekeinos*, "that one," used for Christ as in 3:3b, so that Christ dominates the thought from 3:3 to 3:8. This is the third time that Christ has been called "just" (2:1,29) as part of the author's campaign to put emphasis on the way Jesus lived and died.

8a. *The person who acts sinfully belongs to the devil.* Literally, "The one who does sin is from the devil." See the NOTE on 3:4a where the same Greek expression (*poiein harmartian*) occurs: "Everyone who does sin is doing iniquity [*anomia*]." When we join the two statements, we realize that the great *anomia* of the last times is a diabolic manifestation, but it takes place within the sphere of Christian history. The statement in 8a is counterposed both to 7b, "The person who acts justly is truly just," and to 9a, "Everyone who has been begotten by God does not act sinfully." The phrase "to be from the devil" is an instance of the *einai ek* formula discussed in the NOTE on 2:16ef—an expression employed in Johannine dualism for describing not only origin but also (and even primarily) appurtenance to the good side or to the bad side. "To be from the devil or Evil One" occurs 3 times in Johannine literature, as contrasted with "to be from God or the Father," which occurs 15 times. It describes a life under diabolic influence. The phrase is found in Polycarp, *Philip.* 7:1: "Whoever does not confess the witness of the cross belongs to the devil," a passage immediately following the one cited on p. 8 above.

This is the first instance of *diabolos*, "devil," used in the Epistles along with "Evil One" (GJohn uses as well: "Satan," "Prince of this world," "demon"). All the uses of "devil" are concentrated in 3:8 (3 uses) and 3:10 (1 use). In GJohn (8:44) the Jews were said to be "from the devil your father," while Judas was a devil or devil-inspired (6:70; 13:2). The antithetic parallelism between God and the devil is noteworthy since the antithesis seems to be confined *to this title of the diabolic leader.* God has children and is called their father; the devil has children (I John 3:10) and is called their father (John 8:44).

Einai ek is used in each case to describe the children as from God or from the devil (I John 3:8a). God's children are said to be begotten by (from) Him in I John 3:9a (NOTE on 2:29b); but nowhere in the Johannine literature are the devil's children said to be begotten by him. The author will mention Cain in 3:12; and some have surmised that the author knew the Jewish legend (attested only later) that the devil had intercourse with Eve in begetting Cain, but we have no way of proving that. Most commentators think the absence of a reference to diabolic begetting is deliberate, for the Johannine opposite to being begotten by God is to remain begotten of the flesh, not to be begotten by the devil. The basic argument is that it takes a positive, life-giving, creative action by God to make children out of those who believe in Him, but the devil is not creative. He does not give life but takes it away. People become children of the devil not by an action of his but by an action of theirs. They refuse to believe in Jesus because their lives are evil, and so by imitation they become like the devil whose other name is "the Evil One." Vellanickal, *Sonship* 102, says that to be a child of the devil is a moral (immoral) relationship, while to be a child of God is more than moral. While such observations are common among the church fathers (e.g., Augustine, *In Epistolam* 4.10; SC 75, 238), Origen does not hesitate to say, "Everyone who acts sinfully is *born* [*natus*, reflecting Greek 'begotten'?] of the devil" (*Homily on Ezekiel* 9.1; GCS 33, 407). As for possible Jewish background, one obscure Dead Sea Hymn (1QH 3:7–12) seemingly contrasts a woman bearing a child who has the royal (messianic) titles of Isa 9:5 with a woman made pregnant through a viper; yet that is not clearly diabolic begetting. The issue has importance because a division of human beings into those begotten of God and those begotten of the devil would be a giant step toward a gnostic myth in which human beings have a preexistent status. What did the secessionists think of the devil? In forms of the gnostic myth the creator, who is the lawgiver of Israel and therefore the God of the OT, becomes a demonic figure. The GJohn statement that the father of the Jews is the devil (8:44) could easily have moved Johannine Christians in that direction, but there is no way to tell how far along that road the secessionists were. The author never challenges them on their view of OT salvation history, and so presumably that was not a matter of active dispute between him and them.

8b. *because from the very beginning the devil is the one who sins.* Literally, the last part is "the devil sins," an awkward present tense clashing with "the beginning" which necessarily is past. It implies that with the devil sin is not just an occasional occurrence but his very *raison d'être*. In the NOTE on 1:1a I discussed six different interpretations of "from the beginning" as it applied to the revelation about Jesus, and almost as many have been offered for the devil as a sinner "from the beginning" (a phrase placed first for emphasis). Bultmann, *Epistles* 52, thinks of a "primordial beginning" since the nature of the devil is being characterized; THLJ thinks of the beginning of the world; Schnackenburg thinks of the beginning of human history and the sin under the serpent's tempting in Gen 2–3 (a passage perhaps in mind in John 8:44 where the devil is characterized as a liar); de la Potterie argues for the beginning of human hatred when Cain murdered Abel. In support of the last possibility there is the statement in John 8:44 that the devil "was a murderer from the beginning." Indeed, the only overt OT reference in I John (3:12) says that Cain "belonged to the Evil One and killed his brother." That this can be considered a "beginning" we see from Philo, *On Rewards and Punishments* 12 #68: "At the very beginning . . . there was a fratricide." Since in Jewish thought the evil in Gen 4 was the continuation and cursed result of the evil in Gen 2–3, and since the epistolary author must have shared such an idea in order to associate Cain with the Evil One, it is most likely that by using "from the beginning" the author is thinking of sin inspired by the devil in the whole complex of Gen 1–4, a section which starts with "In the beginning" when God created all things good, but in which the diabolic serpent persuaded Adam and Eve to sin. That sin led to further sin among two "brothers" who should have loved one another. From the devil's appearance on the scene at the beginning of human history he has been active, and the author is worried that now the devil is active in "the last hour."

8c. *The reason the Son of God was revealed.* Literally, "Unto this [*eis touto*] was revealed the Son of God." The initial phrase offers the usual difficulty of *en toutō* discussed in the NOTE on 2:3a, namely, whether it points to what follows, what precedes, or both. Observing the principle given there, I judge that it points forward because it is followed in the next line by an epexegetical *hina* clause that would be inexplicable unless it were interpreting *eis touto*. Once more the passive of *phaneroun* (NOTE on 1:2a) could be translated as "revealed himself" as in the incarnation; but presumably, as in 3:5, the author means the revelation that took place during the ministry, beginning with the revelation by the Baptist (John 1:31). (Here, however, a reference to the incarnation would be less awkward than it was in 3:5; for "Son of God" would be an appropriate name for the preexistent Word, whereas in the author's view "Christ" would not.) As we saw under 3:8a, Origen read a form of the verb *gennan*, "was begotten/born," instead of "was revealed"—possibly indicative of his interpretation of the "when" of revelation.

8d. *was to destroy the works of the devil.* The verb *lyein* can mean "to loose," as in John 1:27, or "to destroy, dissolve, nullify," as in John 2:19. Wilder, "Introduction" 259, favors the latter meaning here in the sense of depriving the devil's works of the supernatural power to harm human beings. *Ergon,* "work," is used frequently in GJohn to describe the works of Jesus that the Father gave him to do, and that therefore were "the works of God"; but there is no explicit reference in GJohn to "the works of the devil." (The closest the NT comes is in Rom 13:12 and Eph 5:11: "the works of darkness.") However, in the dialogue of John 8:39–44 Jesus says to "the Jews who had believed in him" but were seeking to kill him, "You are indeed doing the works of your father" (8:41) and "The devil is the father to whom you belong" (8:44). This agrees with the GJohn principle that a son cannot do anything by himself but only what he sees his father doing (5:19). In other GJohn passages where the devil is not mentioned, the works of disbelievers are called "evil works" (3:18–19), as are the works of the world (7:7). Similarly in the Johannine Epistles (where *ergon* occurs 5 times) we are told that Cain "who belonged to the Evil One" killed his brother "because his works were evil" (I John 3:12); and the works of the secessionist missionaries are called evil in II John 11, as are the works of Diotrephes who speaks against the Presbyter (III John 10). Thus "works" are manifestations of the two spheres of Johannine dualism. If one asks more specifically what are the works of the devil which the Son of God was revealed to destroy, there can be no doubt that they are sins. This is clear from the first line of this verse, "The person who 'does sins' belongs to the devil," and from the parallel statement in 3:5, "Christ was revealed to take away sins." Presumably the secessionists would agree that the Son of God was revealed to destroy the works of the devil but would differ on what constituted the revelation (the incarnation alone, for them). Later gnostic groups would also understand the devil differently (identifying him with the creator god) and "the works" differently. For example, Clement of Alexandria (*Stromata* 3.9.63; GCS 15, 225) reports a passage in the Encratite *Gospel of the Egyptians* where Jesus says, "I have come to destroy [*katalyein*] the works of the female"; and Clement comments that by "female" they mean lust, and by "works" they mean birth and decay. In such thought, natural life has become an evil work.

While one can understand the statement, "The Son of God was revealed to destroy the works of the devil," by combining scattered passages in GJohn, that statement is not representative of the main thrust of GJohn; for the public ministry of the Johannine Jesus is singularly free of confrontation with the demonic. (The references to "the Prince of this world" all come when the public ministry is over.) On the other hand, in Matt 4:1–11 and Luke 4:1–13, after the baptism has revealed Jesus to be the Son of God, the devil confronts him with temptations based on this revelation ("If you are the Son of God. . . ."). And Jesus' ministry is taken up with driving out demons who recognize that he is the Son of God and has come to annihilate them (Mark 1:24; 3:11). In Matt 12:38 Jesus says, "If it is by the Spirit of God that I cast out demons, then the kingdom of God has come upon you"; and in Luke 10:18 he says that, when the disciples were on their mission, he saw Satan fall like lightning from heaven. Hebrews 2:14 phrases the impact of the death of Jesus thus: ". . . that he might destroy him who holds the power of death, that is, the devil." Outside the NT, the diabolic component in the background of the Antichrist expectation (p. 334 above) indicates that some Jewish circles anticipated a fierce struggle between Satan and the Messiah. The *Test. Levi* imagines that Beliar will be bound by the Anointed Priest of the final period, in whose priesthood sin shall come to an end (18:9,12). Thus, I John's statement in 3:8cd (as elsewhere in I John's apocalyptic) may be drawing on older Johannine tradition, not represented well in GJohn but with parallels in wider Christian thought. This tradition continues in Ignatius of Antioch (*Eph.* 13:1): "When you gather together frequently [for the Eucharist], the powers [*dynamis*] of Satan are overcome, and his destructiveness is nullified [*lyein*]."

9a. *Everyone who has been begotten by God does not act sinfully*. This statement combines phrases from two previous lines in the unit, namely, 2:29b,

"Everyone who acts justly *has been begotten by God"*; and 3:4, "Everyone who acts sinfully [*poeien tēn hamartian*]." A similar idea is found with different vocabulary in 3:6: "Everyone who abides in him [Christ] does not commit sin." I have kept the "everyone who" translation pattern so that the reader may see the similarity to all the other statements in this unit employing *pas* + article + participle, even though a better translation when the statement is negative would be, "No one . . . does," rather than "Everyone . . . does not" (NOTE on 2:19f). In 5:18 below, where the context does not require me to be literal, I shall translate: "No one who has been begotten by God commits sin." In 3:6, 3:9, and 5:18, then, one has three sweeping denials of sin for those who have been begotten by God and who remain in Christ. This sinlessness will be discussed under 3:9c below.

9b. *because God's seed abides in him.* Literally, "his *sperma* abides in him," with no article before *sperma,* and two uses of the pronoun *autos.* The reference of the first *autos* ("his") is generally conceded to be God; the reference of the second ("him") depends on the meaning accorded to *sperma.* That noun covers both male agency for begetting life ("generative seed, sperm") and the result of the begetting ("descendant, offspring"). Let me discuss the possibilities here.

(A) **Sperma means offspring.** In John 8:33,37 there is a debate whether the Jews are the *sperma* of Abraham, while in 7:42 the tradition is cited that the Messiah is supposed to be from the *sperma* of David. Thus in three of the four Johannine uses *sperma* means "offspring." The suggestion that this is also the meaning in I John 3:9b has to be subdivided according to whether "God's offspring" is understood to be Christ who is the Son of God, or the Christians who are the children of God. (1) *Christ:* "because God's offspring [Christ] abides in him [the Christian begotten by God]." A translation similar to this is given in the JB and was defended in the last century by Karl. There is no problem in Johannine theology about Christ abiding in (*menein en*) the Christian (John 6:56; 15:4,5). And certainly elsewhere in the NT Christ is designated as "offspring," e.g., the *sperma* of David (Rom 1:3; II Tim 2:8; John 7:42), and the *sperma* of Abraham (Gal 3:16). But he is never called the *sperma* of God; and granted the failure of the Johannine writers ever to speak of Jesus as "begotten," one may well wonder whether "the *sperma* of God" would be for them a tolerable christological title. Moreover, suddenly to introduce Christ under this title in 3:9b when the Christian has just been spoken of as "one who has been begotten by God" in the preceding line (9a) would really require a definite article before *sperma,* and there is none. And so I judge that this suggestion has little to recommend it. (2) *the Christian:* "because God's offspring [the Christian believer] abides in Him [God]." This interpretation is held by Alexander, Argyle, Bengel, Lange, Moffatt, Sander, and Wohlenberg. *Sperma* is anarthrous, it may be argued, because, being parallel to and synonymous with the subject of the previous line, it is generic. Argyle, "I John," who has argued for the influence of Isa 53 on the whole unit, points out that *sperma* in 53:10 means offspring (of the Servant). The notion of *sperma,* "offspring," remaining forever is found in the OT (Ps 89:37[36]; Sir 44:13). Once again in Johannine theology this translation offers no difficulty, for Christians are said to abide in God in I John 2:6; 3:24; 4:13,15,16. Elsewhere in the NT Christians are designated as "offspring," e.g., in Matt 13:38 the good *sperma* sown by the Son of Man is identified as "the sons of the kingdom"; Heb 2:16 speaks of the *sperma* of Abraham as the object of Christ's deliverance; Rev 12:17 designates Christians as the *sperma* of the woman who gave birth to the Messiah (presumably a reference to Israel that has become the Church). But Christians are never called the *sperma* of God, even though in the argument in Rom 9:6–9 they are called both the promised *sperma* (offspring) of Abraham and "the children [pl. *teknon*] of God." Since the Johannine writers think of Christians as those begotten by God, there would be less objection than there was in the instance of Christ to their being considered God's offspring. But would the term *sperma* be used for that idea, since *sperma* as "offspring" always seems to mean physical descendants for John (7:42; 8:33,37)? The pl. of *teknon* would be the more normal Johannine terminology for God's offspring. The most, then, that one can say for this interpretation of 3:9b is that it does not lack all possibility.

(B) **Sperma means male generating seed.** In this case "his seed" would surely be God's seed. (Theoretically "his" might refer to the one begotten by God, but even then he would have received the seed from God.) The "in him" would refer to the Christian. Some balk at the crude anthropomorphism involved in speaking of God's sperm; but the imagery is no more difficult than that of God's begetting Christians. What spiritual reality is symbolized by "God's seed"? There is no agreement among the commentators. Du Preez, "Sperma" 106–7, lists de Wette, Johnston, Plummer, Stott, Vincent, Williams, and Wuest as holding that *sperma* is new life from God (either the power of new life or the germ of new life), while he himself favors interpreting it as a new nature. (The RSV renders "his seed" as "God's nature.") Undoubtedly, in Johannine thought the one begotten by God has both a new life and a new nature in the sense of now being from above rather than from below. However, would not the basic meaning of *sperma* suggest that we think of the agent of life rather than life itself, and correspondingly of that which causes us to be from above? Some of the Greek Fathers (Severus of Antioch, Didymus the Blind, Maximus the Confessor) spoke of the *sperma* as an interior force by which the soul ceases to be oriented toward sin, and it is a form of this interpretation that Bonsirven and Charue share. The medieval theologians thought the author meant grace, and they enunciated the principle that grace and sin cannot be in the soul at the same time. In this they are articulating a NT insight in the language of later theology. Closer to the mentality of the NT period are the theories that *sperma* represents God's word or the Holy Spirit. Commentators usually decide for one or the other; but de Jonge, Marshall, Ross, and S. Schultz see the possibility of a reference to both. Du Preez, "Sperma" 107, has a formula that covers almost every theory: The *sperma* is "that new life born of God, given in Christ, communicated by the Spirit, and realized in practice by the proclaimed word." Cautioned that we should not be too narrow in our interpretation, I think it nevertheless useful to examine the arguments for giving it a more precise meaning.

(1) *God's word:* "because God's seed [word] abides in him [the Christian

begotten by God]." This view (as the primary interpretation) has been held in times past by Clement of Alexandria, Augustine, Bede, and Luther, and in modern times by Alford, Barclay, F.-M. Braun, Couture, de Jonge, de la Potterie, Dodd, and Malatesta. Certainly the word of God or of Christ is an active force in Johannine thought, making the disciples clean (John 15:3) and abiding in the Christian (15:7; I John 2:14,24). And since opposition to the devil is in the context here, it may be noted that the GJohn passage on the devil (8:44) stresses the role of truth and is preceded by an appeal to abide in Jesus' word (8:31–32). However, nothing in Johannine literature associates the word with the begetting of the Christian, even though that is found elsewhere in the NT, e.g., "He brought us forth by the word of truth" (Jas 1:18); "You have been born anew, not of perishable seed [*spora*] but of imperishable, through the living and abiding word of God" (I Pet 1:23). In the NT the word of God is called *spora* (or *sporos* in Luke 8:11) but never *sperma;* that comes in Justin, *I Apology* 32.8: "Those who believe in him are people in whom there dwells the *sperma* of God, the Word." The oft-cited passage in I Cor 4:15, "I have begotten you through the gospel," is not apropos, since Paul, not God, is the begetting agent. Certainly there is ample biblical evidence for wisdom, revelation, or truth as a principle fortifying people against sin, e.g., Ps 119:11; or as *Enoch* 5:8 phrases it, "There shall be bestowed upon the elect wisdom, and they shall all live and never again sin." Overall, however, the evidence is not very strong that the epistolary author thought of the word of God as a seed that both begets the Christians and abides in them so that they cannot be sinners.

(2) *Holy Spirit:* "because God's seed [Spirit] abides in him [the Christian begotten by God]." This view (as the primary interpretation) has been held in Reformation times by Calvin and Beza, and in modern times by Balz, Braune, Brooke, Büchsel, Chaine, Feuillet, Hauck, Haupt, Holtzmann, Loisy, Luthardt, Schnackenburg, Schneider, Škrinjar, and Vawter. Since I have frequently stressed the New Covenant setting of I John, the promise of the New Covenant passage in Ezekiel (36:26–27) is worth remembering: "A new heart will I give you, a new spirit will I put within you . . . and I will put my spirit within you." The Spirit is clearly a factor in begetting in John 3:5—the kind of passage the epistolary author may be presuming when, without explanation, he relates divine begetting with God's abiding seed in I John 3:9. The risen Jesus breathing forth the Spirit upon his disciples who are now his brothers in John 20:17,22 (see ABJ 29A, 1015–16) could also be invoked. As for the element of abiding, the Spirit/Paraclete was given by Jesus "to be with you forever" (14:16); and if in I John 2:27 the anointing is with the Spirit, that anointing abides in the Christian. Also in I John 3:24 and 4:13 divine abiding is associated with the Spirit. If we are told here that because of God's abiding seed the Christian cannot be a sinner, the Spirit/Paraclete is presented as the great opponent of sin, convicting the world on this subject (John 16:8–9). On this point *T. Benjamin* 8:2 is interesting when it says of the pious: "He has no defilement in his heart because the Spirit of God rests upon him." As for evidence in the rest of the NT, one may combine references to baptism with the

Holy Spirit (Mark 1:8 and par.; Acts 1:5; 19:5–6; I Cor 12:13) with references to baptism as rebirth or regeneration (p. 384 above). There is also an association of the Spirit with sonship, "For those who are led by the Spirit of God are sons of God" (Rom 8:14; cf. Gal 4:6), although in Paul this is through adoption, not through begetting (Rom 8:15). None of this constitutes proof, and there is still the objection that begetting or giving life through the Spirit (breath) and through seed are different images. Yet overall I think the evidence favors identifying God's seed with the Spirit rather than with His word. But in the long run the exact identification is not so important, so long as we recognize that the author is talking about a divine agency for begetting God's children, which not only brings us into being but also remains and keeps us His children.

Before we close the discussion, it is worth noting how this thought of begetting by divine seed appears elsewhere. Philo, *Moses* 1.50 ⁂279, says that the Israelites' "bodies were molded from human seeds, but their souls from divine seed." In *On the Cherubim* 13 ⁂⁂43–44 he expresses his theory that God plants His seed of generation in the virtuous: "Virtues . . . if they do not receive the seed of generation from Another, will never of themselves conceive. Who then is he who sows in them the good seed save the Father of all." This is especially true in the case of the patriarchs where the conceptions symbolize the generation of virtues in the human soul. Abraham says, "I could not exercise [virtue] if you did not send down from heaven the seeds to cause Sarah to be pregnant and were she not to give birth to Isaac" (*That the Worse* 17 ⁂60). The idea of begetting by divine seed does not seem to have found its way into the Apostolic Fathers of the second century (but see the citation from Justin above). However, it is a popular concept among the gnostics. The Nag Hammadi *Gospel of Truth* I 43:9–14; NHL 49, speaks of "the light which is perfect and filled with the seed of the Father." This seems to mean preexistent seed that would enter life. Irenaeus, *Adv. haer.* 1.1.1, describes a gnostic theory wherein at the very beginning of being Bythos (the primary Abyss) puts seed in the womb of Sigē (Silence) who becomes pregnant and gives birth to Nous (Mind). In descent from the first pairing we find (1.15.3) that the Being that came down upon Christ at the baptism was the seed of the Father "in whom there existed the seed of those who were produced contemporaneously with Himself." In the gnostic *Excerpt from Theodotion* reported by Clement of Alexandria (53.2; GCS 17, 124) we hear that Wisdom sowed spiritual seed in Adam, and that one of the tasks of salvation is the assembling of the scattered seeds of God (49.1; GCS 17, 123). We do not know how far along this path the secessionists had already gone, but we may suspect that they would have had no difficulty with the notion of the seed of God begetting Christians as His children, presumably at the time of conversion. (There is no evidence from the author's polemic that they thought of Christians as preexistent children.) But probably they would not have thought that the seed needed to remain an active force changing the earthly life of the Christian so that by fidelity to the commandments it mirrored divine life.

9cd. *and so he cannot be a sinner because he has been begotten by God.* Literally, "he cannot sin." We have in v. 9 two statements (9a, 9c), each followed by a *hoti,* "because," clause (9b, 9d). Taken together, they say that the person begotten by God not only does not sin but cannot be a sinner, because God's seed remains in him. It is now time to discuss the sinlessness and impeccability of the Christian. There are four basic statements of this theme in I John; literally they read:

3:6a: No one who abides in him [Christ] commits sin [*hamartanein*].
3:9a: No one begotten by God acts sinfully [*hamartian poiein*].
3:9c: He [everyone begotten by God] cannot commit sin [*hamartanein*].
5:18a: No one begotten by God commits sin [*hamartanein*].

Clearly these statements posit an exalted status traceable to a divine begetting which has brought Christians into being and which is looked upon as an abiding force (e.g., the perf. tense of "begotten," and the affirmation in 3:9b that "God's seed abides" in the Christian). Of the four statements, three concern sinlessness: A person thus begotten does not commit sin or act sinfully. (Galtier, Inman, and Stott are among those who argue that *poiein hamartian,* "to do sin," refers to a practice of sin and therefore means more than *hamartanein,* "to sin," so that one has a mounting series of claims in 3:6a,9a,9c—this is quite dubious.) The other statement (3:9c) concerns impeccability: The person who has God's seed abiding in him not only does not sin; he cannot sin. The verb "to be able, can," is *dynasthai,* used again in the Epistles only in I John 4:20, but 36 times in GJohn. Most often it describes a religious ability, e.g., to do signs or wonderful things (3:2,9; 5:19,30), to see or enter the kingdom (3:3,5), to believe (5:44; 12:39), to come to or with Jesus (6:44; 7:34, 36; 8:21,22), or to hear the word (8:43).

In themselves such claims are not so extraordinary as might first seem. La Rondelle, *Perfection* 236, contends that the Johannine attitude toward sin is in continuity with the OT. The psalmist (119:11) exclaims, "Within my heart I treasure your promise that I may not sin against you." In Gal 5:16 Paul challenges, "Walk in the Spirit, and you will not fulfill the lusts of the flesh." Jude 24 hails "God who is able to keep you from stumbling." Ignatius, *Eph.* 8:2, writes, "Spiritual people cannot do carnal things." In pagan religion a classical author like Seneca states, "A wise man cannot fall" (*Epistula* 72, ℀6), and "A good man cannot help but do the [good] things he does" (*De beneficiis* 6.21, ℀2). Yet in this picture there is a dark side, for claims of perfection and impeccability can lead to licentiousness. Irenaeus (*Adv. haer.* 1.6.4) attacks a group of "spiritual and perfect" Valentinian gnostics (he may be wrong in identifying them) who misbehave sexually on the grounds: "It is not special conduct that brings man into the pleroma, but the seed which was sent out from its infancy and is made perfect in this world." The issue of impeccability was raised in the Augustinian-Pelagian controversy in the fifth century, and after the Reformation in debates with the Antinomians.

Beyond the general issue of the place of sinlessness and impeccability in Christian theology, there is a special problem in I John about the consistency of the author's thought; and it is to that issue that most commentators have devoted their attention. In 1:8a the author condemned a (secessionist-inspired) statement, "If we boast, 'We do not have sin [*hamartian echein*],' we deceive ourselves." In 1:10 there was another condemnation: "If we boast, 'We have not sinned [perf. *hamartanein*],' we make God a liar." Is not the epistolary author now making the same boast himself, and presenting it as a necessary corollary of being a Christian? Furthermore, in 1:9 the author said, "If we confess our sins, He . . . will forgive us our sins." In 2:1-2, although he insisted that he was writing to keep his audience from sin, he assured them, "If anyone does sin, we have a Paraclete in the Father's presence, Jesus Christ, . . . and he himself is an atonement for our sins." In 5:16 he will urge intercessory prayers, "if anyone sees his brother sinning." How can the author who says such things state in 3:9c that the Christian cannot sin? How is it possible for Christians to confess sins and pray for sinning brothers when, the author says in 3:6a,9a and 5:18a, no Christian commits sin? No other NT author contradicts himself so sharply within such a short span of writing, and inevitably much scholarly energy has been devoted to proving that no contradiction exists. Sometimes this effort stems from a theory of inspiration that forbids contradictions between passages of Scripture; but it may also stem from a very practical rule of exegesis: We should never assume that ancient authors were stupid or illogical and could not see difficulties, especially within the same brief piece of writing. Other commentaries (e.g., Stott, *Epistles* 130–36) list solutions to this problem. I would prefer to group the solutions according to their main thrust, and I detect seven general approaches.

(1) Two different writers are involved. Windisch, *Briefe* 136, asserts, "The contradiction involved between the advice to confess sin (1:5ff.) and to intercede for the sinner (5:14ff.) on the one hand, and the profession of sinlessness (3:9f.; 5:18) on the other can be clarified through the thesis that the latter was added later [by a redactor]." Bultmann would attribute at least some of 5:16 to the Ecclesiastical Redactor.

(2) The author's statements are directed to two different groups of adversaries. In 1:8–2:2 where he insists that Christians do sin and need forgiveness, he is fighting those who think that the possession of gnosis makes them so perfect that they never sin. In chs. 3 and 5 where he says that Christians do not or cannot sin, he is fighting indifferentists who think they are above moral demand, so that their commission of sins has no importance. Scholars like Dodd, Stagg, and Stott have offered a form of this suggestion.

(3) The author is thinking of specific kinds of sin when he says that the Christian does not or cannot sin. Augustine, Bede, and Luther thought of *sins against love* because of the frequent emphasis on love in I and II John. Belser suggests *impurity*, while Galtier thinks of the basic evil of *refusing to believe* in Jesus as the Christ. Because of the OT distinction between deliberate sins (those done with a high hand) and indeliberate sins, some have thought that the author is referring only to *deliberate sins*. Because of the distinction in I John 5:16–17 between deadly sin and sin that is not deadly, *deadly sin* (secession?) has been suggested. Some Roman Catholic scholars have developed this to mean that *mortal* (serious) *sins* are involved.

(4) The author is thinking only of special or elite Christians when he says that those begotten by God do not or cannot sin. He is talking about those who live up to their status by abiding in Christ (3:6), and he would recognize that most Christians do not meet this demand. Galtier, "Le chrétien" 140, attributes this view to Maximus the Confessor; but it is also reflected in many modern interpretations that take for granted that 3:6,9 do not give a factual description of the average Christian. Bonsirven, for instance, after arguing (correctly) that the real point at issue here is the contradiction between sin and the principle that underlies Christian life, goes on to insist that there are different categories of Christians distinguished according to their moral dispositions, and that few meet the ideal of not committing sins.

(5) The author means that Christians do not or cannot sin habitually even though there are occasional lapses. Plummer, *Epistles* 77, says, "Although the believer sometimes sins, yet not sin, but opposition to sin, is the ruling principle of his life." Some, like Stott and Zerwick, would establish this distinction upon a grammatical basis. ZBG 251 (also MGNTG 3, 72) points out that in 2:1, "I am writing this to keep you from sin," the aorist tense is used (= commit a sin), while in 3:6 the pres. tense is used (= does not continue a sinful life) and in 3:9 a pres. infin. (= cannot continue a sinful life). Note however that in 1:10 the author condemns a perfectionist boast that is expressed in the perf. tense ("we have not sinned"), a tense that is supposed to continue true in the present. Alexander, Dodd, and Prunet question whether the author would let such an important distinction rest on so fragile a grammatical subtlety. Would the readers perceive such subtlety?

(6) The author is thinking on two different levels. When he demands that Christians acknowledge sins and petition for forgiveness (1:8; 2:1–2), he is speaking on a real or pastoral level. When he says that Christians do not or cannot sin (3:6,9; 5:18), he is speaking on an ideal level. This is the view of Alford and Düsterdieck. Close to it are Belser and Clemen who contend that really the author is exhorting Christians not to sin. Houlden, *Epistles* 94, thinks of an aspiration stated in the form of an attainment. Chaine, *Epîtres* 185, suggests an exaggerated way of speaking in imitation of stoic philosophy. Brooke, *Epistles* 90, mentions "the absolute language of the prophet," while Bultmann, *Epistles* 51, 53, refers to an imperatival demand placed by the author, who is talking about a possibility to be realized. Another form of this explanation is the contention that when the author acknowledges that Christians sin, he is speaking on an individual or empirical level, while the statements about sinlessness and impeccability describe the state of the whole group—the sons of light over against the sons of darkness. In face of the devil who has been mentioned in the context, the Christians have the power to resist sin: "The word of God abides in you, and you have conquered the Evil One" (2:14). Still another suggestion (de la Potterie, "Impeccability" 190) makes a distinction in the sinlessness statements between the divine point of view (from which the statements are unconditional) and the human point of view (from which they are conditionally true, i.e., if we place no obstacle to God's help).

(7) The author is speaking in two different literary contexts. A form of this

view is held by de la Potterie and Vellanickal. In 1:8 and 1:10–2:2 he is exhorting in a kerygmatic passage, reminding the readers of the proclamation of forgiveness that they heard when they were converted ("from the beginning"). In 3:6,9 and 5:18 he is speaking in an apocalyptic context where the last hour has come (2:18), involving a struggle with evil (the Antichrist, those who would deceive, the Liar, the Iniquity). In Jewish apocalyptic expectation the final period would be without sin on the part of those who were close to God. As part of the New Covenant, Ezekiel (36:29) records a promise that the Lord will deliver from all uncleanness. *Enoch* 5:8–9 predicts, "Then, too, will wisdom be bestowed upon the elect; and they will all live and never again sin, either through heedlessness or pride." In a *Jubilees* passage (5:12), which may be future in its idealism, we hear about God making "for all His works a new and just nature, so that they should not sin in their whole nature forever, but should be just, each in his own kind always." *Testament Levi* 18:9 promises, "In the time of the priesthood [of the Anointed] sin will disappear." The one who enters the Qumran Community is assured: "God will cleanse him from all wicked deeds with the spirit of holiness . . . that he may teach the wisdom of the sons of heaven [the angels] to the perfect of way [fellow sectarians]. . . . There shall be no more iniquity, and all the works of falsehood shall be put to shame" (1QS 4:21–23). The result is that the sectarians designated themselves "the men of perfect sanctity" (CD 20:2,5,7). In such apocalyptic works there is usually a sense that these expectations of sinlessness have not yet been realized; but in I John the signs of the last hour have led the author to conclude that impeccability is realizable because of the intimacy of God's indwelling.

One may debate whether any of the above suggestions really removes the seeming contradiction; and some of them, while ingenious, are scarcely diagnoses of the texts. Against (1) is the fact that the theory of author and redactor has little following in I John scholarship today; moreover that theory is a confession to the irreconcilability of the I John statements. Against (2) I have argued that there is only one detectable set of adversaries (INTRODUCTION IV B1). There is nothing in the context of 3:6,9 to encourage acceptance of (3) or (5), both of which confine the statements to particular sins or ways of sinning; and (4), which limits the statements to specific Christians, is excluded by the Johannine "Everyone who" idiom that is meant to include the whole good side of a dualistically divided world. To some extent, suggestions (6) and (7) overlap, with (7) closer to the mentality of the author. But even under (7) one may wonder how the author could have phrased his kerygmatic and eschatological/apocalyptic statements with so little nuance that they emerge as almost contradictory. The Christians to whom he addresses the kerygmatic exhortation to acknowledge and confess sins—are they not living in the last hour? And why are the eschatological/apocalyptic statements in 3:6,9 left without the distinction made in 3:2—a distinction (even in the last hour) between what we are and what we shall be? Undoubtedly there is truth in suggestions (6) and (7) but serious difficulty remains.

No matter how one modifies or relativizes the I John claims to sinlessness and impeccability, the truth in those claims comes from the divine principle that begot Christians and that remains active in them. Observations on how secessionists and the author might differ on the activity of this principle will be made in the COMMENT.

10a. *That is how God's children and the devil's children are revealed.* This is an *en toutō* construction, classifiable as B (NOTE on 2:3a) since it is not followed by a subordinate clause and therefore can point either to what precedes or what follows. Those who think that it refers to what precedes include Belser, Camerlynck, Plummer, and B. Weiss; those who think it refers to what follows include Bruce, Büchsel, Bultmann, Calmes, Chaine, and Loisy; and those who think it refers in both directions include Marshall, Schnackenburg, and Windisch. A reference to what follows would imply that acting justly and loving one's brother is the point of distinction between God's children and those of the devil, while a reference to what precedes would imply that sinning is the point of distinction. Since sinning would certainly include acting unjustly and hating one's brother, the issue is not crucial. Structurally it seems to make better sense if *en toutō* refers to what precedes, while what follows (3:10bc) is seen as transitional to the next unit. The *en toutō* statement in 3:10a then becomes the conclusion of the whole apocalyptic theme that began with the mention of "the last hour" in 2:18. "Revealed" here is not the passive of *phaneroun* (used 5 times in this unit: 2:28; 3:2,5,8) but is the related adjective *phaneros* (used only here in the Johannine literature). Its use with the verb "to be" gives a stative tone to the affirmation: There are two groups that already exist when the author writes, namely, the author's adherents and the secessionists (whose revelation was mentioned in 2:19). This is the only instance in the NT of people being called "children of the devil," although that title could be derived from John 8:44 which speaks of the devil as "the father" of some. Elymas the magician is called a "son of the devil" in Acts 13:10; and Matt 13:38 speaks of the weeds among the wheat as "sons of the Evil One." An OT description of the worthless receives a dualistic sense in the Dead Sea Scrolls (4QFlorilegium 1:8): "the sons of Belial." According to Irenaeus, *Adv. haer.* 3.3.4, Polycarp addressed Marcion as "the first-born of Satan." Many other epithets substitute a form of evil for the diabolic: son of hell (Matt 23:15); sons of disobedience (Eph 2:2); children of wrath (Eph 2:3); children of destruction (*Jub.* 15:26); sons of wickedness and wrongdoing (1QH 6:29–30); sons of darkness (1QS 1:10, etc.).

10b. *Everyone who does not act justly does not belong to God.* Literally, "do justice [*poiein dikaiosynēn*]," the phrase the author has been counterposing to "do sin [*poiein hamartian*]" (3:4,9). There is versional (Vulgate, Syriac) and patristic (Tertullian, Origen, Cyprian, Augustine) evidence for reading "Everyone who is not just," a reading attested in an eighth/ninth-century Greek MS. preserved on Athos (*Psi*) and accepted by Lachmann and Harnack. However, it is probably a scribal modification influenced by 3:7b ("The one who acts justly *is* just"—if that is so, a scribe may have substituted "Everyone who is not just" for "Everyone who does not act justly"). The phrase "belong to God" involves the *einai ek* formula discussed in the NOTE on 2:16ef. Near the beginning of this unit we heard the statement, "Everyone who acts justly has been begotten by God" (2:29b). By inclusion the author closes the unit by saying the same thing in a negative way here. Westcott, *Epistles* 84 and 109, detects a difference of meaning between the two statements because an article was used before *dikaiosynē*, "justice," in 2:29 but is not used here. Once again, I would insist that there are many insignificant variations in Johannine style, and one must beware of overexegesis.

10c. *nor does anyone who does not love his brother.* Literally, "and the one who does not . . ." This verse is transitional to the theme of love that will dominate Part Two of I John, beginning in the next verse. If acting justly is a criterion for detecting who belongs to God, the most important example of acting justly is love of brother. (As explained in the NOTE on 2:9b, "brother" means fellow Johannine Community member, male or female.) Matthew 5:44–45 relates love of others and being God's children, but in an order opposite to that of I John: "Love your enemies . . . so that you may be sons of your Father"—for I John love stems *from* being God's children. Bultmann, Chaine, Law, Plummer, and Sisti are among the many who rightly insist that in 3:10b and 3:10c we are not dealing with *two* criteria for detecting who belongs to God. It is exaggerated, however, to argue that the initial "and" in 10c should be translated as "namely," for love is a distinctive specification of justice. In the NOTE on 1:9b above, I insisted that one should not contrast God's justice and His love, since the "justice" of God is manifested in His saving covenant. Augustine (*De natura et gratia* 42.49; CSEL 60, 270) is perceptive: "Love is the most true, most full, and most perfect justice."

COMMENT

It is a matter of dispute among scholars as to where this unit begins and ends. The beginning, tied in with the problem of where the previous unit ends (p. 362 above), is placed at 2:28, at 2:29, or at 3:1.[1] Because of internal structure to be discussed below, I have opted for 2:28, which means that three units in a row begin with the address "[Little] Children" (2:12,18,28). As for the ending, popular suggestions include 3:3 (de

---

[1] In the tripartite divisions of I John listed in Chart Five of Appendix I, almost half begin their Part Two with 2:28 or 2:29. However, that sharp a break between what follows 2:28/29 and what precedes overlooks the fact that the strong apocalyptic element which began in 2:18 continues in the description of the final struggle with "the Iniquity" and the devil in 2:28–3:10, and the fact that no major new theme is introduced in those verses. The struggle about sin is a continuance of a theme introduced in 1:8–2:2. It is true that divine begetting and God's children are mentioned for the first time here, but that is reason for positing a new unit, not a whole new Part of I John.

Jonge, Marshall, Schnackenburg, Windisch),[2] and 3:12 (du Preez, Hauck, Plummer, Schneider, Westcott).[3] However, I would argue for an ending at 3:10, as do most scholars (Alexander, Bruce, Dodd, du Toit, Malatesta, Schlatter, Stott, Škrinjar). A strong factor in this decision is the clear inclusion that exists between 2:28–29 and 3:9–10, which share the themes of revelation (*phaneroun/phaneros*), abiding (*menein en*), begotten by God, and "Everyone who acts [does not act] justly."

Within the unit 2:28–3:10 a remarkable stylistic feature is the number of sentences that have as their subject a participle preceded by a definite article and (many times) by "every" (*pas*). In all there are nine such statements:

A. 29b Everyone who acts justly   has been begotten by God
    3a *Everyone who has this hope based on Him* *makes himself pure*
    4a Everyone who acts sinfully   is really doing iniquity
B. 6a Everyone who abides in him   does not commit sin
    6b Everyone who does commit sin   has never seen him
C. 7b The person who acts justly   is truly just
    8a The person who acts sinfully   belongs to the devil
D. 9a Everyone who has been begotten by God   does not act sinfully
   10b Everyone who does not act justly   does not belong to God

If one omits for the moment the statement (3a) I have italicized, the eight statements yield four antithetical pairs (marked A, B, C, D). In A (29b, 4a) and C the contrast is between acting justly and acting sinfully. In B and D the contrast is achieved by having the second statement pick up and reverse the conclusion of the first statement, i.e., the "does not commit sin" that concludes 6a is reversed at the beginning of 6b, "Everyone who does commit sin"; and the "does not act sinfully" that concludes 9a is reversed at the beginning of 10b in terms of acting unjustly. The neatness of these pairs gave von Dobschütz (INTRODUCTION III A1) the inspiration for positing a source composed of antithetical statements. Without resorting to that theory, one should at least pay tribute to these statements in analyzing the structure of the unit. A and D form an inclusion marking off the limits of the unit (2:28–3:10). The author, who begins the unit with the address, "Little Children," in 2:28a, repeats that address in 3:7a; and since A and B follow the first address, while C and D follow the sec-

---

[2] Against such a division, which would separate 2:28–3:3 from 3:4–10, is the fact that "Everyone who acts justly" in 2:29 has its antithesis in "Everyone who acts sinfully" in 3:4a. See also the list of chiastic parallels I shall give in the text above. Even Schnackenburg, who favors this break, acknowledges (*Johannesbriefe* 163) that there is a unity of theme in 2:29–3:10. See footnote 6 below.

[3] A new address to "Brothers" begins 3:13, but I shall argue that this is a mark of subdivision within the unit 3:11–24, rather than a divider between units. What follows 3:13 about murdering one's brother should be kept together with the reference to Cain in 3:12.

ond address, we should probably think of a subdivision into two strophes: 2:28–3:6 and 3:7–10.[4] Indeed there is an inclusion between the beginning and end of each of these strophes, i.e., 2:28 and 3:6 both refer to abiding in Christ, and 3:7 and 3:10 both refer to acting justly.

Coming back to the one statement (3a) that I have italicized because it does not fit the four pairs of antitheses,[5] I propose that the whole of 3:1–3 is a type of exclamatory interruption by the author.[6] He mentions "begotten by God" at the end of 2:29; and in an aside he stops to exclaim about the wonder of being God's children, only to resume his main thought in 3:4. If one does not count this parenthesis, the first strophe in the unit (2:28–29 + 3:4–6) is about the same length as the second strophe (13 sense lines in my translation compared to 14).

Some would see a chiastic relationship between the two strophes or subdivisions of this unit as I have delineated them:

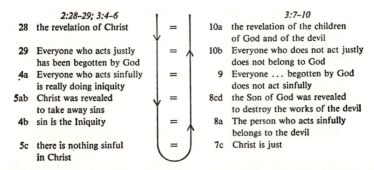

2:28–29; 3:4–6		3:7–10
28 the revelation of Christ	=	10a the revelation of the children of God and of the devil
29 Everyone who acts justly has been begotten by God	=	10b Everyone who does not act justly does not belong to God
4a Everyone who acts sinfully is really doing iniquity	=	9 Everyone … begotten by God does not act sinfully
5ab Christ was revealed to take away sins	=	8cd the Son of God was revealed to destroy the works of the devil
4b sin is the Iniquity	=	8a The person who acts sinfully belongs to the devil
5c there is nothing sinful in Christ	=	7c Christ is just

There is certainly parallelism between the two strophes, but the contention this is chiastic involves difficulty: Notice the shifting of lines in vv. 4,10 above to achieve a chiasm. There are just as many parallels if one proceeds sequentially rather than chiastically: e.g., "Little Children" in 2:28a and 3:7a; Christ is just in 2:29a and 3:7c; one who acts sinfully does iniquity and belongs to the devil in 3:4a and 3:8a; Christ or the Son of God was revealed in 3:5a and 3:8c; this was to take away sins and to destroy the works of the devil in 3:5b and 3:8d; everyone does not commit sin or act sinfully in 3:6a and 3:9a. That there are parallels between

---

[4] I do not imply that the author carefully planned such subdivisions but simply that his repetitive style lends itself to subdivision into patterns of thought and expression.

[5] Malatesta, *Interiority* 238, tries to make an antithesis of 3:3 and 3:4; but 2:29 is a better antithesis to 3:4: Both concern acting (literally, doing justice and doing sin) and the root of that action.

[6] This is implicitly acknowledged by those who wish to start a new unit with 3:4: they are right in seeing a break between 3:3 and 3:4, but do not do justice to the sequence between 2:29 and 3:4.

the two strophes shows planning; that the parallels are both chiastic and sequential warns us how difficult it is for modern interpreters to understand how the author worked.

As for overall theme, since 2:9–11 the author has been dealing with a world divided between those who abide in light and those who are in darkness. The unit in 2:12–17 contained encouragement and warning for the author's adherents, i.e., those whom he would classify as belonging to the light. The unit in 2:18–27 described the secessionists, the Antichrists whom the author would classify as belonging to the darkness. In the present unit he describes two groups, God's children and the devil's children, who are distinguished by the way they act (justly or sinfully)—a criterion to be added to the christological norm offered in the preceding unit.

Before passing on to a detailed analysis of the unit, let me say a final word about the structure, centered upon 3:10. I have argued that 3:10ab forms an inclusion with the beginning of the unit, and so 3:10 is the ending of the unit. But 3:10c shifts the theme from acting justly (three times within the unit) to loving one's brother, the theme that will dominate the next unit.[7] In other words the beginning of v. 10 belongs to the present unit, while the end of v. 10 pertains to the next unit. Once again (see p. 119) we are dealing with a Johannine hinge verse that closes one section and opens another.

A. *The Revelation of Christ at the Parousia* (2:28–29)

In the last unit we heard that it was the last hour and that the Antichrist/Liar was at hand in the person of secessionists who denied that Jesus is the Christ, thus failing to confess the Son (in his earthly life). But the author had previously expressed concern about another, moral issue centered in the earthly life of Christians, namely, that they not sin but act justly. It is to that parallel issue the author now turns. If the last hour has brought the revelation of the Antichrist, it will soon bring the revelation of Christ (2:28b); for traditionally the supreme embodiment of evil is to be destroyed by God acting definitively through His Messiah: "Then will be unveiled the Man of Iniquity whom the Lord [Jesus] . . . will destroy by the manifestation of his parousia" (II Thess 2:8).[8] The Johannine author wants his adherents to face this parousia with confidence based upon their abiding in Christ. The language of *not being ashamed* reflects old

---

[7] It is recognition of this that has led Häring to the expedient of closing the present unit with 3:10b and opening the next with 3:10c.

[8] II Thessalonians uses *parousia* to describe the coming both of the Man of Iniquity (*anomos, anomia*) and of Christ, even as I John uses *phaneroun* of both comings. The identical vocabulary reflects the idea that the Antichrist will be a parody of Christ. (See NOTE on 2:18b above.)

Christian tradition about the second coming (a tradition not well represented in GJohn). If we remember that in the preceding unit in relation to
the coming of the Antichrist the author insisted on the necessity of
confessing and not denying the Son, these parallel Synoptic passages are
informative: "Everyone who will confess me before men, I shall also confess before my Father in heaven; but whoever will deny me before men, I
shall also deny before my Father in heaven" (Matt 10:32–33); "Whoever
is ashamed of me and my words . . . the Son of Man will also be
ashamed of when he comes in the glory of the Father" (Mark 8:38).

In his pastoral concern about how his adherents face the coming of
Christ, the author encounters two difficulties, the first of which is peculiarly Johannine. First, how could Johannine Christians have any real
concern about the parousia as judgment, since they had already been
judged? "The person who hears my word and has faith in me possesses
eternal life. He does not come under judgment; no, he has passed from
death to life" (John 5:24). The secessionists, capitalizing on such texts,
may have argued that the condemnation involved in the second coming
would affect only nonbelievers.[9] In that case the author would be contending that in the parousia there is an element of judgment for Christians
as well. According to John 3:17–21 judgment has taken place when Jesus
appeared as the light come into the world and people preferred darkness
or light according to their deeds. But the epistolary author is arguing that
at the parousia the same principle will be in effect; and if people's deeds
are good, they will continue without shame toward the light they have already chosen. The second difficulty encountered by the author involves
the danger of destroying confidence once he has begun to warn about the
parousia as judgment. This would be a common Christian problem, but
perhaps more acute in Johannine Christianity, granted its fundamental
conviction that Christians already possess eternal life. Faithful to such realized eschatology, the author appeals for confidence on the basis of abiding in what has already been received from God. Since believers are already in Christ (John 14:20), they will not meet a stranger at the
parousia. Believers have already been begotten by God (John 1:13); if
they allow the life they have received to manifest itself in acting justly,
they will come as faithful children to meet their Father. The author is applying to the parousia the basic insight of John 15:1–6: It is not enough
for the branch to be on the vine; it must bear fruit; and it does that by
abiding in Christ. "He who abides in me and I in him is the one who
bears much fruit" (John 15:5).

In the NOTE on 2:29b I discussed the peculiar Johannine theological

[9] I presume that the secessionists believed in the second coming. Not only are
there references to it in GJohn; but also the epistolary author makes no effort to
argue for it, as he would have were it denied.

idiom of God's "begetting" the believer, a figure distinct from Paul's image of adoption, or from that of the emanation of God's children (Acts 17:28?). In my view the imagery of begetting was the corollary of the Johannine emphasis on the Christian's possessing God's eternal life, an image carried to the point of speaking of God's seed. Presumably the secessionists capitalized on the idea of begetting,[10] even as they capitalized on the realized eschatology of judgment: If believers are truly begotten as God's children and possess His life, what more can or need be done? Against them the author insists with his own logic that if eternal life is truly life, it must be lived out, even as natural life is lived out. Therefore the way in which eternal life is manifested in the earthly career of believers is important for salvation. Behind this reasoning is the strong conviction that the divine childhood of believers is based on the divine sonship of Jesus; he is just and so we must be just (I John 2:29). Being just (righteous) as Christ is just is the Johannine form of the OT covenant demand of being holy as God is holy (Lev 19:2; I Pet 1:16—see under E below).

B. *Confidence in What We Are; Revelation of What We Shall Be* (3:1–3)

In what appears to be an emotional aside, the author interrupts his chain of thought (to be resumed in 3:4) in order to express amazement over what God has already given to believers and how that offers hope in face of what is yet to come. In this aside he does not seem to be aiming so directly at secessionist ideas as is his wont, although one may wonder whether his obvious emotion has not been provoked by the fact that secessionists are downplaying the status of those who were left behind as the author's adherents. If the struggle involved in the secession was fought in part over the author's insistence on the salvific relevance of the way Christians live, the logical secessionist retort would have been that such a theology degrades the value of the status received at entrance into Christianity. They may have been contending that the author is not taking seriously enough the fact that Christians are already God's children, existing in Him, knowing Him, and being like Him. And so the author exclaims emotionally that his theology in no way underplays the love of

[10] At the end of the NOTE on 2:29b I contended that the struggle between the author and the secessionists over begetting probably did not involve the gnostic myth of the preexistence of God's children, since the author does not have to defend the idea that begetting was a specific past action (presumably at the moment of faith). What has to be defended is the importance of action or deed after one has received God's life.

God or the dignity of His children—two items that were part of the Christian baptismal catechesis (see E below). He acknowledges that the world (i.e., the secessionists[11]) may not recognize the exalted status of his adherents as God's children, but that is no reason to be discouraged. Rather it is a proof that his adherents are truly God's children: since the world never recognized the Father (John 17:25),[12] naturally it does not recognize His children. The world knows its own who are the secessionists (I John 4:5). As I have shown in the NOTE on 3:1b, in the OT Israel was looked upon as God's son or child; but John 11:50–52 regards as children of God those for whom Christ died—a group wider than "the nation" of Israel. The covenant-God has manifested His love by calling to Himself this people who constitute His children, and the readers are reminded that they are part of that people. Surely this is an echo of language used when they entered the Johannine Community.

How does this present status as God's children relate to the revelation of Christ yet to come? Here the author is remarkably subtle in combining Johannine realized eschatology with a future eschatology that he wants to hold out to his adherents as an incentive. He insists that if, as commonly believed, God's Son is yet to be revealed in the last hour, then it is possible for a future aspect of God's children yet to be revealed. The parousia of Christ in 2:28 is counterposed to the appearance of the Antichrist; so also the revelation of the Johannine Christians is counterposed to the revelation of the secessionists as not belonging to the Community (2:19ef). But the revelation of the Antichrists brought nothing new, for it simply showed up what they always were—evil is not creative. The revelation of the Johannine Christians will not concern their identity as God's children since that does not have to be revealed anew (3:2a); but it will bring a new manifestation of that creative love by which God made Christians His children. Later (4:8,16c) the author will explain that God is love, and such a God can no more be static than can His children: His love did not terminate when He bestowed upon Christians the status of being His children. Since the new manifestation of love will come from the same God who manifested love in sending His Son, there will be a continuity between the present and future status of God's children. Christians are already like God as He showed Himself in His Son; the final revelation will

---

[11] For the epistolary author "the world" consists of those who do not believe in Christ. To this world the secessionists have gone out (II John 7), attracted to it precisely because they really belong to it and speak its language (I John 4:5). Because the secessionists do not confess Christ come in the flesh (I John 4:2; II John 7), they are no better than nonbelievers.

[12] In the NOTE on 3:1de I gave my reasons for preferring to identify the "him" of "it never recognized him" as God rather than Jesus. In the somewhat inverted Johannine thought pattern it can be claimed that outsiders do not know God and therefore they do not know Jesus, His Son (John 8:47,54–55).

make it possible for Christians to be like God seen as He is Himself. In speaking of this the author very carefully refers to *"what* we *shall* be," not to "what we *are"* or *"who* we shall be." Those other formulations would call into question respectively the Christian's present identity and the continuity of a future identity with a present identity. Nor does the author say "what we shall become"; for that might raise the possibility of Christians becoming something totally other. His whole idea is that "what we shall be," even if it has not yet been revealed, will be another aspect of "what we really are"; and that is why he phrases the recommended preparation for the future in terms of "abiding."

The author says "we *know* . . . we shall be like Him," not "we shall know" (3:2c). Even though there may be a future revelation, this does not contradict the previous claim that "his anointing teaches you about all things" (2:27e). By saying "we know" the author is assuming that what he states about future revelation is part of the knowledge his adherents already possess.[13] Although the author gives us no apocalyptic details about the benefits of the future revelation, commentators speculate about what "shall be." THLJ (78) mentions the view that the author cannot mean to say that Christians will become like God, while Westcott (*Epistles* 100) doubts that one can see the Father as He is. This may be a modern difficulty; for Athanasius (*De incarnatione Verbi* 54.3; SC 199, 458) did not hesitate to speak of a future deification (*theopoieisthai*), and medieval theologians like Thomas Aquinas anticipated a beatific vision that would see God in His essence. Nor do such ideas lack a biblical background. Men and women were created with a certain likeness to God.[14] The temptation of the serpent in Gen 3:5 was, "You will all be as gods"; and it is never clear whether that destiny was totally beyond God's plans, or only temporarily so while Adam and Eve were in a trial period. In the hymn in Philip 2:6, which was probably meant to contrast Jesus and Adam, Jesus is described as being "in the form [*morphē*] of God" but not grasping at being "equal [*isos*] to God."[15] Yet because of his humility, especially in crucifixion, Jesus is exalted and given what was refused to Adam, namely, a divine status as one who has "the name which is above every other name" (Philip 2:9). GJohn thought is somewhat different: Jesus already possesses the divine name on earth (17:11,12), for he has come in that name (5:43; 12:13). As for equality with God, Jesus does

---

[13] "We know" (*oidamen*) may have been customary Community terminology in relation to the truths of the Johannine tradition. In John 21:24 it is said of the Beloved Disciple, "We know that his testimony is true"; in 3:11 Jesus, speaking for his followers, says, "We are talking about what we know." In I John 3:5 the epistolary author begins his appeal to tradition with, "You know."

[14] The phrase in Gen 1:26 is "according to the *eikōn* and the *homoiōsis* of God."

[15] Possibly the hymnist thinks that all human beings are "in the form of God," if *morphē* is equivalent to *eikōn*, but Jesus is not trying to be equal to God—that was Adam's sin.

not "make himself equal [*isos*] to God,"[16] as "the Jews" charge (5:18); for he never *makes* anything of himself—God has *given* him everything, including the divine name. Granted the Johannine penchant for patterning the divine childhood of Christians upon the divine sonship of Jesus, a corresponding status of the Christians ("like God") offers no difficulty. After all, they are the ones who have believed in Jesus' divine name (John 1:12; 3:18); he has revealed God's name to them (17:6,26); they have received life and protection through the name (17:11,12; 20:31); and they have suffered for the name (15:21). By being called children of God, they are identified with the Son of God and, in a sense, bear his name.

As for the second promise, "We shall see Him as He is" (I John 3:2e), no other Johannine passage promises this, although Rev 22:4 puts in parallelism the future privilege of seeing "the face of him [God/the Lamb]" and bearing his name.[17] In the epistolary context it is dubious that this is a greater privilege than that contained in the first promise, "We shall be like Him." That these may be alternative ways of describing the same future is suggested by comparing I Cor 13:12, "Now we see through a mirror in an enigma," with II Cor 3:18, "We all, with unveiled face beholding the glory of the Lord, are being changed into His likeness from one degree of glory to another." Nor does Jewish tradition balk at such an exalted future. Philo, *On Abraham* 12 ⁂57–59, indicates that the vision of the Father of all things is a human being's greatest blessing. *Pesiqta Rabbati* 11.7 (46b) states, "In this world Israelites cleave to the Holy One . . . but in the time to come they will become like Him." In the *Midrash* (⁂1 270a) *on Ps 149* we find, "When the children of Israel see God in the world-to-come, they will become saints."

If the epistolary author really did mean that his adherents would become like God and see Him as He is, how much change would this imply? Klein, "Licht" 313–14, contends that the author is thinking of an ontic change and thus betrays a difference from GJohn where no ontic change was envisioned for the Christian future. It does seem to be more than a noetic change, i.e., finding out what Christians already are. (Smyth-Florentin, "Voyez" 37, judges the author to mean that the future will reveal the real nature of our present state as God's children.) But since the author himself says that what we shall be has not yet been revealed, there is no way of knowing whether the change will be from a lower to a higher degree of the same reality, e.g., becoming more like God than we already

---

[16] Did the evangelist think that Jesus was "equal to God" (even though he had not made himself so)? John 10:30 and 14:28 give contrary indications.

[17] Notice the parallelism in Matt 5:8–9, "Happy are the pure in heart for they shall *see God;* happy are the peacemakers for they shall *be called sons of God.*" In Johannine thought believers are already called children of God, while seeing God remains a future possibility.

are. Schnackenburg, *Johannesbriefe* 171, insists there is no reason to think that the author predicted a radical abolition of all distinction between the creature and God, as found in some gnostic works, e.g., the *theoun,* "deify," of *Corpus Hermeticum* 1.26. What would the secessionists have said about the change to be effected at the parousia (if they believed in a parousia)? The Pseudo-Clementine *Homily* 17.16 (GCS 42, 238) states that in this life "the eyes of mortals cannot see the incorporeal form of the Father or Son," but in the resurrection of the dead the just will be able to see God because they will have no more hindrance from the flesh, which will be changed into light. We can only guess that secessionist thought might have been similar. Smyth-Florentin has made a comparison between the author's position and that of later gnosticism on four points: (a) The author thinks that what we are now (children of God) was determined by a past act of God's love; he does not posit a complicated process of initiation or magic formulas such as marked the mystery religions. (b) We can verify the authenticity of what we are by the fact that the world treats us as it did the Son; seemingly no such despair of success with the world marked secessionist thought or some forms of gnosticism. (c) What we now are is the promise of a still invisible future —a stress that would be troublesome to those who regarded themselves as liberated by a gnosis already possessed. (d) We are going to encounter Him whom we already know, and we shall be transformed; but if for the author God has not yet been seen as He is, God is still not described as the Great Unknown who stands at the beginning of many gnostic tables of emanations—we have seen God in Christ.

In 3:3 the author sums up all this as "hope," the only occurrence of the term in the whole of the Johannine literature. The presence of this theme in passages of I Peter and Titus to be studied below under E strengthens the case that the author is reaching back to language characteristic of Christian conversion/initiation/baptism, a language that in the Johannine Community had lost much of its importance (as did final eschatology) in the period when GJohn was stressing realized eschatology against Jewish opponents. As the author closes the parenthesis of 3:1–3, he again makes clear that patterning upon Christ affects not only our present status as children begotten by God (2:29) but also our hope of what we shall be. The patterning here is based on Christ's life which is described as "pure," also the only time this term (with its strong cultic overtones) appears in the Johannine literature. In the NOTE on 3:3b I showed why it too may have been drawn from the language of admittance into the Johannine Community. Presumably the secessionists would make little of hope since in their theology the believer was already perfect; for them purity would have been brought about through initial contact with Christ, so that the

Christian had no need to "make himself pure." They might well cite against the author John 13:10: "The man who has bathed has no need to wash; he is clean all over." But the author might remind them that while Jesus said, "You are clean already" (15:3), he surrounded that statement with others insisting upon the need of abiding in him and bearing fruit, and with the reminder that the Father cleans even the fruit-bearing branches to make them more fruitful (15:2,4).

C. Sin as the Iniquity Opposed by the Revelation of Christ (3:4–6)

With 3:4 the author returns to his main theme, which is not the revelation of what *we* shall be but our preparation for the revelation of Christ. The greatest obstacle to being able to meet him with confidence (2:28) is a life of sin, which the secessionists dismiss as irrelevant (1:8,10). Even as the author historicized the expected Antichrist by finding that expectation fulfilled in the secessionists, so does he historicize the great Iniquity expected for the end-time (see the discussion of *anomia* in the NOTE on 3:4b) by finding it already present in the sins of professed Christians. The secessionists are Antichrists because, while professing to believe in Christ, they nullify the importance of Jesus' earthly life. Their attitude toward sin constitutes the Iniquity because by finding sin inconsequential they are supposing that God (who dwells in the Christian) can be manifested publicly in evil actions. The characteristic of the Antichrist as the distorted mirror-image of Christ is to make evil seem good, and that is a function of the Iniquity as well. Sin as the Iniquity is opposed to Jesus who was revealed to Israel as the Lamb of God who takes away the sin of the world (John 1:29). In GJohn the singular noun referred to the basic sin of refusing to believe in the light, but the plural noun of I John 3:5 ("Christ was revealed to take away sins") directs the opposition to all types of evil that turn people away from the light (see John 3:20). There was nothing sinful in Christ, and there can be nothing sinful in the Christian (I John 3:6).

The author is saying in 3:6 that the person who commits sin is not a Christian, but he phrases this in terms of never having seen Christ. He has been talking about a future in which Christians will see God as He is, but in Johannine thought true believers have already seen God in Christ. "Whoever has seen me has seen the Father," says Jesus (John 14:9). Thus the judgment that the epistolary author passes here is tantamount to denying his adversaries the true Christian experience of God. This writing began with the author's laying claim to the Johannine tradition about

Jesus, "What we have *seen* with our own eyes" (1:1c); and now he is excluding the secessionists[18] from all share in such tradition.

The second hostile judgment (3:6c) adds "nor come to know him" to the charge of never having seen him. In John 16:3 Jesus judged "the Jews" in the same way, "They never knew the Father nor me." In I John 2:5 the author denied a (secessionist) claim to know *God* which was not based on keeping the commandments; here he denies knowledge of *Christ* to those who sin. Clearly there is no halfway house between the Johannine Community who know both Christ and the Father (I John 2:14bd) and the secessionists who know neither. The failure to know is not ignorance but is culpable, reflecting a decision to turn away from the light, a decision embodied in going out from the Community (2:19). Part of the expectation of the New Covenant was that all God's people would know the Lord from the least to the greatest and that God would forgive their sins (Jer 31 [38]:34). The secessionists are excluded on both scores.

As we look back on the ideas found in the first subdivision of this unit (2:28–29; 3:4–6, leaving aside the parenthesis of 3:1–3), they seem scattered despite a certain inner logic. If one asks why the author has fixed on certain ideas, in part the explanation may lie in the conjunction of these ideas in the Johannine conversion/initiation/baptism tradition. But also one must look to the association of ideas in GJohn upon which the author may be informally commenting (INTRODUCTION VI A3b). For instance, in John 16:8 the task of the Paraclete is to prove the world wrong about sin, justice (*dikaiosynē*), and judgment. The theme of judgment is implied in I John 2:28, and the themes of acting justly (doing *dikaiosynē*) and acting sinfully (doing sins) are explicit in 2:29 and 3:4. The epistolary author is playing the role of the Paraclete in proving the secessionists wrong about sin, justice, and judgment. What was originally a task of defending the Johannine Community against outsiders ("the Jews") has now become a task of defending the author's adherents against their former brethren.

D. *Revelation of God's Children and the Devil's Children* (3:7–10b)[19]

We move here into the second subdivision or strophe of this unit; many of the ideas from the first strophe are continued, but the apocalyptic hos-

---

[18] It may be objected that others besides the secessionists commit sin, but the author is not uttering abstract moral principles. The references to the Iniquity and to children of the devil in the context make it clear that he is still talking about the Antichrists whom he attacked in 2:18–19.

[19] Since 3:10c becomes transitional to the next unit by introducing the theme of love of brother, I shall comment on it in the next unit.

tility is heightened. The author has criticized *"everyone* who acts sinfully" (3:4) and *"everyone* who commits sin" (3:6); but when he says, "Little Children, let no one deceive you" (3:7a), it becomes clear that he is worrying about the inroads of propagandists and not just about some weak Christians. In 2:26b he spoke of the secessionists as "those who deceive you" in a context where their attempted deception concerned christology; here their deceit concerns morality.[20] It may be surmised that secessionist propagandists were telling the author's adherents that one did not believe sufficiently in the cleansing power of divine begetting if one worried about sins. Hitherto the author has identified the secessionists and their activity with the expected Antichrist, the Liar, the instruments of Deceit, and the Iniquity. But now for the first time since he introduced the theme of the last hour (2:18) he unmasks the motivating force behind them as the other great player in the apocalyptic drama of evil, the devil. (In the NOTE [2:18b] on the background of the Antichrist, I pointed out that often the evil human figure was seen as the tool of the devil who would be the last enemy to be destroyed by God.) The attitude of the adversaries toward sin shows that they belong to the devil who is the one who sins from the beginning (3:8b), as illustrated in the stories of Adam and Eve and of Cain. The devil[21] deceived Adam and Eve promising that they would be as gods, and he brought death; now he has deceived the secessionists into thinking that sins are of no import and has thus deprived them of eternal life—they will never be like God as will the true believers (3:2d). The devil deceived Cain into killing his brother Abel and then into pretending to be innocent; he has deceived the secessionists into leaving behind in hate their brothers of the Johannine Community and then into pretending that it is the author who is really at fault. If in Johannine tradition Christ was revealed to take away sins (John 1:29,31), he was thereby revealed to destroy the works of the devil (I John 3:5,8cd); and so Christ is opposed to the secessionists not only on the level of what they are doing but also on the level of what they are. This whole unit has been concerned with revelation: the *future* revelation of Christ (2:28), which involves the revelation of what the Johannine Christians shall be (3:2); and the *past* revelation of Christ against sin and against the works of the devil (3:5,8), which involves the revelation of what the Johannine Christians and the secessionists are: respectively, God's children and the devil's children (3:10). In attacking this realm of diabolic influence, the author is continuing the work of the Paraclete. In the above-mentioned passage where the Paraclete proves the world wrong about sin, justice, and judgment, we hear, "About judgment—in that the Prince of this world has

[20] The christological error is to deny the salvific import of Jesus' earthly life; the moral error is to deny the salvific import of the Christian's earthly life.

[21] It is doubtful that the author of Genesis understood the serpent as the devil, but that was the understanding in NT times (Wis 2:24; Rev 12:9).

been condemned" (John 16:11). The author thinks the secessionists have already been condemned.

Over against the devil who has been a sinner from the very beginning and against the devil's children who act unjustly and sinfully, the author proposes the image of God's children who have the power not to sin. Sinlessness and impeccability become the distinguishing signs of those begotten by God (3:9). In the long NOTE on 3:9cd I discussed seven different ways in which commentators have tried to reconcile the author's claims about sinlessness in 3:6,9; 5:18 with his previous condemnation of secessionist claims of sinlessness in 1:8,10. None of them is really satisfactory; but certainly a partial explanation is that here the author is speaking in the eschatological context of the last hour when in Jewish apocalyptic it was believed that God would prepare a sinless generation in the great struggle with evil. In the INTRODUCTION (V B3b) I suggested that both the secessionists and the author held a perfectionism based upon GJohn statements which seemed to confine sin to disbelief by outsiders, so that Johannine believers could model themselves on Jesus who was without sin. Thus both sides of the Johannine schism would have been contending that Christians do not commit sin. If in fact Christians do evil things, the secessionists would argue that these are not "sins" that can destroy one's salvific state because by faith Christians are irrevocably outside the realm of sin. The author, however, would acknowledge wrongdoing as sin (5:17) and affirm, "If anyone does sin, we have a Paraclete, Jesus Christ . . . and he himself is an atonement for our sins" (2:1–12). Logically the secessionists may be more consistent with the Johannine principle that the Christian does not and cannot sin; but the author is dealing with pastoral reality. Even if this is the last hour, there is a "not yet" (2:18; 3:2).

No matter what the author thought, the wording of his affirmations about sinlessness and impeccability is not sufficiently nuanced. In struggling to understand this, Augustine (*In Epistolam* 4.8; SC 75, 234) perceptively stressed the relationship of the divine principle (3:6: abiding in Christ; 3:9a: being begotten by God; 3:9b: having God's seed abiding in one) and the claimed power against sin: "To the extent that the Christian remains in Christ, to that extent he does not sin." Others have phrased the idea less succinctly, but this approach runs through commentators of various times and places.[22] The Greek church fathers[23] thought of the seed of God as an interior force by which the soul, no longer oriented toward sin, allows itself to be led by a dynamism that makes it incapable of choos-

[22] See Bonsirven, de la Potterie, Lyonnet, Vellanickal, and B. Weiss.
[23] De la Potterie, "Impeccability" 176, digests Severus of Antioch, Didymus the Blind, and Maximus the Confessor.

ing evil. A modern writer (La Rondelle, *Perfection* 232) states, "John bases the impossibility of sinning not in the Christian as such, but in the transforming and keeping presence of God's Seed, i.e., in the *Christus praesens* who is 'greater than he who is in the world' (4,4)." According to Prunet, *Morale* 92, the author believes that the new nature given by divine begetting produces a new humanity incapable of sin. To the extent that the principle of life is active, but only to that extent, sin is impossible. One may debate about the precise way in which GJohn has portrayed divine begetting as operative, but for I John "having been begotten" means more than a terminated divine creative activity of the past. Whether the seed is the word of God or His Holy Spirit (NOTE on 2:9b), it remains active after it has brought the child of God into being. In John 6:44 Jesus says, "No one can come to me unless the Father who sent me draws him"; the drawing toward Jesus continues after one has first come to him.

One is forced, then, to understand the claims to sinlessness and impeccability in I John 3:6,9 in light of the statements on status in 3:1,2. We are God's children already, and there is a freedom from sin attached to that state. Jesus had issued the challenge, "If you really are Abraham's children, you would do works worthy of Abraham" (John 8:39). The epistolary author has his own variation on that theme, "You really are God's children, and so you must do works worthy of God, and not sin which is the work of the devil." But in this last hour he recognizes that we are not yet all that we shall be, and so there is a growth in God's children. The divine seed abides and continues to transform the child of God into the image of God's Son which is the image of God Himself, until at the final revelation we are like God Himself. The more that this divine seed transforms the Christian, the more impossible it is for the Christian to sin. I have insisted throughout that the author is attacking a static understanding of divine begetting that is held by the secessionists, for whom divine childhood is a once-for-all gift and not a life that has to express itself in the behavior of the Christian. A further corollary for the author is that this life not only expresses itself in action but also grows, and increasing sinlessness is a mark of that growth. At the beginning of their Christian existence believers choose to come to the light rather than to the darkness (John 3:19–21). But walking toward the light and away from darkness is an ongoing movement, until finally we come to the God who is light and in whom there is no darkness at all (I John 1:5). I find an inclusion, then, in the beginning and end of Part One of I John (as I have diagnosed the limits of Part One), namely, between "God is light. . . . If we boast, 'We are in communion with Him,' while continuing to walk in darkness, we are liars and we do not act in truth" (1:5–6) and "That is how God's children and the devil's children are revealed; everyone who does not act justly does not belong to God" (3:10).

E. *The Covenant/Initiation/Baptism Background of this Unit*

In the INTRODUCTION (III B1) I discussed the theory of Nauck whereby 2:29–3:10 contains elements from a source composed (by the author himself) in the context of a baptismal ceremony or homily. In formulating the thesis that baptismal hymns influenced I Peter, Boismard compared in detail this unit of I John with I Peter 1 and Titus 2–3. In an accompanying chart I have supplied the pertinent passages. From that chart one may detect the following ideas held in common by I John and one or both of the others (arranged in I John order):

- revelation/unveiling/appearance of Christ (several times): all 3
- begotten anew or regeneration by God: all 3
- love/mercy of God for us: all 3
- a future yet to be revealed/unveiled: I John and I Peter
- hope: all 3
- Christian is to be pure/purified: all 3
- being pure/holy as Christ/God is: I John and I Peter
- "You know" assurance: I John and I Peter
- taking away sins; ransoming from futility; renouncing worldly desires: all 3
- nothing sinful in Christ; a lamb without blemish: I John and I Peter
- iniquity (*anomia*): I John and Titus 2
- revelation/appearance of Christ/Son of God for salvific purpose: all 3
- love of brother and love of one another: I John and I Peter
- begotten by seed which abides: I John and I Peter

Clearly there is a remarkable number of similarities. Although the three NT works share half the similarities, I Peter has the middle role in having similarities with I John and with Titus[24] that they do not have with each other. Boismard[25] thinks that I John drew directly from I Peter and not from the sources underlying I Peter. However, the similarities are more of ideas than of wording. For example, even in the remarkable idea of begetting through divine seed shared by I John and I Peter, two different words for seed (*sperma, spora*) are used. A less demanding hypothesis would recognize that the similarities between the two works are neither

---

[24] Similarities shared by I Peter and Titus (but not by I John) include mercy, heir/heritage, ransom, people of His own, word of God.

[25] *Quatre hymnes*, 130–31. He finds parallels between I John and most of I Peter 2 as well, e.g., I Pet 2:22, "He committed no sin" (= I John 3:5); I Pet 2:24, "bore our sins" (= I John 3:5); I Pet 2:24, "that we might die to sins and live for justice" (= I John 3:7–8: acting justly not sinfully).

SIMILARITIES* BETWEEN I JOHN, I PETER, AND TITUS

I John 2–3

2:28: when *Christ is revealed*
2:29: Everyone who acts justly has been *begotten by God* (*gennan*).
3:1 Look at what *love* the Father has bestowed on us in enabling us to be called God's children.
2 What we shall be has *not yet been revealed*; at this revelation we shall be like Him, for we shall see Him as He is.
3 Everyone who has this *hope* based on Him makes himself *pure even as Christ is pure.* 5 *You know* well that Christ was revealed to *take away sins,* and there is *nothing sinful in him.* 4 Sin is the Iniquity.
8 The Son of God was *revealed to destroy the works of the devil.*
10 Everyone who does not act justly does not belong to God, nor anyone who does not *love his brother.* 11 We should *love one another.* 9 Everyone *begotten by God* does not act sinfully because God's seed (*sperma*) abides in him.

I Peter 1–2

1:3: the God and Father of Jesus Christ by His great mercy has begotten us anew (*anagennan*) to a living hope, 4 to a heritage kept in heaven for you, 5 to a salvation ready to be unveiled in the last times.
18 Set your hope completely on the grace to be brought you at the unveiling of Jesus Christ; 14 as obedient children do not conform yourselves to the passions of your former ignorance, 15 but be holy yourselves in all conduct as He who called you is holy. 18 You know that you were ransomed from the futile ways inherited from your fathers 19 with the precious blood of Christ like that of a lamb without blemish. 20 He was revealed at the end of time for your sake.
22 Having purified your souls by your obedience to the truth for a sincere love of the brothers, love one another earnestly. 23 You have been begotten anew, not of perishable seed (*spora*), but of imperishable through the living and abiding word of God. 2:9: a people of His own possession.

Titus 3

3:4: when the goodness of God appeared, 5 he saved us in virtue of his own mercy by the washing of regeneration and renewal by the Holy Spirit, 7 so that we might become heirs with the hope of eternal life.

Titus 2

2:11: The grace of God has appeared 12 teaching us to deny impiety and worldly desires 13 awaiting our blessed hope, the appearance of the glory of Jesus Christ 14 who gave himself for us to ransom us from all iniquity, to cleanse for himself a people of his own.

3:8 The word is sure.

* These texts are abbreviated by omitting words not useful for the comparison.

accidental nor the result of direct copying but are best explained if these works (and Titus as well) represent exhortations drawn from a common body of ideas. The most plausible locus for such a body of ideas would be the process of entrance into the Christian community. In such an entrance one might well wish to emphasize: God's love and mercy in begetting us as His children; that this was accomplished through the appearance of Jesus Christ; that there is still a future to be unveiled for which we should hope; that Christ who was sinless took away sin; that we are challenged to be holy and pure as he was; and that love of brother was his basic demand.

The evidence adduced by Boismard's comparisons strengthens the case I have been making throughout the commentary that the author is reminding his readers of the Johannine theology proclaimed to them and accepted by them when they became Christians. When the author speaks of "the beginning," he means the beginning of the revelation of Jesus to his followers during the ministry, but for his readers this means the beginning of their contact with the tradition that came with conversion/initiation/baptism.[26] While the Johannine theological proclamation had its peculiarities, it shared many features with other Christian baptismal proclamations, whence the parallels just discussed. The secessionists also had heard the Johannine conversion/initiation/baptismal proclamation; but, in the author's judgment, their subsequent stance distorted it. They had shown that despite their baptism they were children of the devil and not children of God.

BIBLIOGRAPHY PERTINENT TO I JOHN 2:28–3:10

Argyle, A. W., "1 John iii 4f.," ExpT 65 (1953–54) 62–63.

Boismard, M.-E., "Une liturgie baptismale dans la Prima Petri," RB 63 (1956) 182–208; 64 (1957) 161–83, esp. 200–4 (1956 article) on I John 3:1–10.

———. *Quatre hymnes baptismales dans la Première Epître de Pierre* (LD 30; Paris: Cerf, 1961), esp. 129–32 on I John 3:1–10.

de la Potterie, I., "The Impeccability of the Christian According to I Jn 3,6–9," in *The Christian Lives by the Spirit,* by I. de la Potterie and S. Lyonnet (Staten Island, N.Y.: Alba, 1971) 175–96. French orig. in *L'Evangile de Jean: Etudes et problèmes* (RechBib 3; Bruges: Desclée de Brouwer, 1958) 161–77.

[26] I remind the reader that I use this complex expression because we know so little about the exact procedure of entering the Johannine Community and because I think that the validity of tracing ideas to such a "beginning" does not depend on the exact procedure.

————. " 'Sin is Iniquity' (I Jn 3,4)," *Ibid.* (*The Christian*) 37–55. French orig. in NRT 78 (1956) 785–97.

du Preez, J., " 'Sperma autou' in 1 John 3:9," *Neotestamentica* 9 (1975) 105–12.

Galtier, P., "Le chrétien impeccable (1 Jean 3,6 et 9)," *Mélanges de Science Religieuse* 4 (1947) 137–54.

Inman, V. K., "Distinctive Johannine Vocabulary and the Interpretation of I John 3:9," *Westminster Theological Journal* 40 (1977) 136–44.

Kubo, S., "I John 3:9: Absolute or Habitual?" AUSS 7 (1969) 47–56.

La Rondelle, H. K., *Perfection and Perfectionism* (2d ed.; Andrews Univ. Monographs: Studies in Religion 3; Berrien Springs, MI: Andrews, 1975), esp. 227–36 on 3:9.

Lyonnet, S., "The Notion of Sin in the Johannine Writings," in *Sin, Redemption, and Sacrifice,* by S. Lyonnet and L. Sabourin (AnBib 48; Rome: Pontifical Biblical Institute, 1970) 38–45, esp. 42–45 on I John 3:4–9; 5:16. Latin orig. in S. Lyonnet, *De Peccato et Redemptione* (2 vols; Rome: Pontifical Biblical Institute, 1957, 1960) 1, 71–76. See earlier version, "De natura peccati quid doceat Novum Testamentum: V—De scriptis Ioanneis," VD 35 (1957) 271–78.

Peterson, E., "Zur Bedeutungsgeschichte von *parrēsia,*" in *Reinhold-Seeburg-Festschrift,* ed. W. Koepp (2 vols.; Leipzig: Deichert, 1929) 1, 283–97, on 2:28.

Schrage, W., "Meditation zu I. Johannes 2,28–3,3 (3,1–6)," GPM 20 (1965–66) 33–41.

Segalla, G., "Il Dio inaccessibile de Giovanni," in *Dio nella Bibbia e nelle culture ad essa contemporaneo* (Turin: 1980) 84–123, esp. 114–18 on 3:2.

Smyth-Florentin, Françoise, " 'Voyez quel grand amour le Père nous a donné' (1 Jn 3,1–2)," AsSeign (2d ser.) 25 (1969) 32–38.

Synge, F. C., "I John 3,2," JTS 3 (1952) 79.

van Unnik, W. C., "The Christian's Freedom of Speech in the New Testament," BJRL 44 (1961–62) 466–88, esp. 485–86 on *parrēsia* in I John (2:28).

Vicent Cernuda, A., "La filiación divina según *kai* en 1 Jn 2,29 y 31," EstBib 36 (1977) 85–90.

See also von Dobschütz, "Johanneische Studien."

Part Two
(I John 3:11–5:12)

The gospel that we must love one another as God has loved us in Jesus Christ; only then can we love God and believe in Jesus as His Son.

7. I John 3:11–24: *The Gospel of Loving One Another*

11a	11For this is the gospel
11b	that you heard from the beginning:
11c	*We should love one another.*

12a	12Not like Cain who belonged to the Evil One
12b	and killed his brother.
12c	And why did he kill him?
12d	Because his own deeds were evil,
12e	while his brother's were just.

13	13BROTHERS, do not be surprised [then] when the world hates
14a	14That we have passed from death to life we know |you.
14b	because we love the brothers.
14c	The person who does not love remains in the abode of death.
15a	15Everyone who hates his brother is a murderer;
15b	and, as you know, no murderer has eternal life abiding in him.
16a	16This is how we have come to know what love means:
16b	for us Christ laid down his life;
16c	so ought we in turn to lay down our lives for the brothers.
17a	17Indeed, when someone has enough of this world's livelihood
17b	and perceives his brother to have need,
17c	yet shuts out any compassion towards him—
17d	how can the love of God abide in such a person?

18a	18LITTLE CHILDREN, let us not give lip service to our love with
18b	but show its truth in deeds— |words
19a	19that is how we shall know that we belong to the truth.
19b	Indeed, before God we shall convince our hearts,
20a	20even if the heart knows something prejudicial to us,
20b	that God is greater than our heart,
20c	for He knows everything.
21a	21And, Beloved, if the heart knows nothing prejudicial,
21b	we can have confidence in the presence of God

22a 22and can receive from Him whatever we ask,
22b   because we are keeping His commandments
22c   and doing what is pleasing in His sight.

23a 23Now this is God's commandment:
23b   we are to believe the name of His Son, Jesus Christ;
23c   and we are to love one another just as He gave us the
               command.
24a 24And the person who keeps God's commandments
24b   abides in God and God in him.
24c   Now this is how we can know that He abides in us:
24d   from the Spirit that He gave us.

NOTES

3:11ab. *For this is the gospel that you heard from the beginning*. The line begins with *hoti*, "because," and so grammatically is subordinate to the end of 3:10: "Nor does anyone [belong to God] who does not love his brother." However, the subordination is minimal; for as BDF 456¹ and BAG 594 (BAGD 589) 3b point out, in the Greek of this period connection by *hoti* is often very loose. One may translate it as "for" at the beginning of a new sentence, since the consequence that it draws is from all that has gone before. The clause itself is virtually a copy of 1:5, "Now this is the gospel that we have heard from Christ." Almost the same group of textual witnesses that substituted *epangelia*, "promise, announcement," for *angelia*, "gospel," there (NOTE on 1:5a) do so again here. In 1:5 the perfect tense of the verb "to hear" was used; here the tense is aorist. This is a real challenge to those who would see a precise theological implication in such variations; for certainly the author, despite his use of the aorist here, means a past hearing that lasts into the present (the meaning a perfect should have). The "from Christ" in 1:5 was the same as the "from the beginning" that the author had used a few verses before (1:1). The author was speaking there as a Johannine tradition-bearer and associating himself with those who had heard Jesus during the ministry. Now he is addressing a community of believers whose hearing "from the beginning" was their first encounter with the Johannine message proclaimed by the tradition-bearers. There is a continuity in the two "from the beginning" concepts, for what Jesus proclaimed during the ministry was what the tradition-bearers proclaimed to those who believed in Jesus through their word (John 17:20): The one commandment Jesus gave was the commandment heard from the beginning by the Johannine Christians (I John 2:7).

11c. *We should love one another*. There is minor versional evidence

(Bohairic) for "you should love" in obvious sequence to "you heard"; but the author too considers himself bound by the gospel. This clause is introduced by *hina*, "that, in order that," which is epexegetical of "the gospel." Although many deny any telic force to the *hina* (e.g., Brooke versus Westcott) and, in fact, it is equivalent to *hoti* of 1:5d, one may wonder whether the gospel that consists of the command to love does not also bring love about. While we heard the author speak about "one another" (*allēlos*) before in 1:7 ("We are joined in communion [*koinōnia*] with one another"), the other six epistolary uses make it the object of the verb *agapan*, "to love." When we compare "to love one another" with "to love one's brother" (which occurs 5 times in I John), they are equivalent, as illustrated by the use of "love his brother" in the last line of the preceding verse. (The same interchangeability is found in *T. Gad* 6:1: "Now, my children, you should love each one his brother . . . loving one another.") However, the author gives preference to "love one another" when he is quoting the commandment from Jesus (John 13:34; 15:12,17) as he is here. Indeed, the form of this verse, "This is the gospel . . . [*hina*] we should love one another," besides being shaped by I John 1:5d, "This is the gospel . . . [*hoti*] God is light," is shaped by John 15:12: "This is my commandment that [*hina*] you should love one another." Both the "one another" and the "brother" refer to members of the Johannine Community; the former is Jesus' terminology, and the latter is Community terminology (NOTE on 2:9b above).

12ab. *Not like Cain who belonged to the Evil One and killed his brother.* Literally, "not as [*kathōs*] Cain was of the Evil One and he killed . . . ," a construction that Westcott, *Epistles* 110, calls "irregular and elliptical." It would read better without the negated *kathōs*, "like, as"; nevertheless, elliptical negative *kathōs* constructions may be a feature of Johannine style, e.g., John 6:58 reads literally, "Not as [*kathōs*] the ancestors ate and died" (also 14:27). The two GJohn examples contrast others with Jesus; the I John example contrasts Cain with the Christian. Elsewhere in the NT the negated *kathōs* is found only in II Cor 8:5, although there is a good parallel in the LXX in Judith 8:26–27. De Kruijf, "Nicht wie" 50, challenges Schlatter's view that this construction is a Semitism. ZGB 452 suggests that the comparative conjunction really governs the verbal idea in the sentence with subordination of the words in between: "not belonging to the Evil One as Cain did." The author is indulging in litotes, a figure of speech where an affirmative is expressed by the negative of the contrary. He wants his adherents not only not to do as Cain did but to do just the opposite. "Belonged to" translates the *einai ek* phrase (NOTE on 2:16ef) used in Johannine vocabulary for origin and appurtenance: Not only this particular action but the whole sphere of Cain's life was evil. John 8:44 charges that "the Jews" belong to the devil, and I John 3:8 charges that the person who acts sinfully belongs to the devil. "Evil One" (*ponēros*, last used in 2:13–14) is preferred to "devil" here because the author will go on in 3:12d to speak of Cain's actions as "evil." The verb "to kill," *sphazein*, occurs elsewhere in the NT only in Revelation (8 times); it implies violent death. Frequently in the LXX it describes animal sacrifice, "to slaughter, butcher, cut the throat"; in Gen 22:10

it is the verb used for Abraham's sacrificing his son Isaac. However, it also covers murders that have no ritual setting, e.g., in the killing of the princes in II Kings 10:7. In Revelation it is used for the Lamb who was slain (5:6,9,12; 13:8) and for the martyrs (6:9; 18:24), but also for the beast (13:3) and for people killing each other (6:4). In the present passage the verb has no necessary cultic significance; it catches the brutality of one brother's action toward the other.

Scholars are agreed that the Cain/Abel imagery (which is the only direct OT reference in the Epistles) affects more than this verse, with some authors extending the influence to v. 15, or even (Lohmeyer, Schlier) to v. 21. In fact, Lohmeyer, "Aufbau" 242, would find it anticipated in the previous unit in 2:28 in the theme of facing the parousia with confidence and not shame, and in "Everyone who acts justly has been begotten by God" in 2:29. (See also de Kruijf, "Nicht wie" 55.) A brief sketch of Jewish and Christian thought about Cain may be useful. (Note that the author does not develop the Abel side of the imagery; in Mandaean thought Abel is one sent from heaven, and the author might have debated that point were it known to him.) Two Johannine features seem to go beyond the ordinary understanding of the story in Gen 4:1–16, namely, that Cain belonged to the Evil One, and that he killed his brother because his own deeds were evil. However, Bauer, "Misfatto," would draw even these two points from Genesis without resorting to extrabiblical traditions about Cain (of which there are many, as we shall see). In Gen 4:4–5 we read that God favored Abel and his sacrifice, but "for Cain and his offering He had no respect," an attitude that angered Cain. Already then, even before Cain killed Abel, there was something wrong with Cain in God's eyes. The key to the issue is the word of God to Cain in Gen 4:7 after He has asked why Cain is angry: "If you do good, will you not be acceptable? And if you do not do good, sin is crouching at the door; and its desire is directed towards you, and you will have to master it." Since Cain went on to kill Abel, obviously he chose the second alternative of not doing good. (The import of such a choice can be illustrated from Ps 36:2–5[1–4]: "Sin speaks to the wicked man in his heart . . . he has ceased to act wisely and do good; he plots wickedness.") From these texts it becomes intelligible why I John says that Cain killed Abel "because his own deeds were evil," and further that Cain "belonged to the Evil One." Genesis personifies sin as a force crouching at the door seeking to control him (see J. Coppens, ETL 14 [1937] 132–40); and when Cain lets it have its desire, it causes him to murder. The epistolary writer, who has said that "from the very beginning the devil is the one who *sins*" (3:8b), seems to have combined the serpent-tempter story of Gen 3:1–4 with the story of personified sin crouching at the door and desiring to master Cain in Gen 4:7, so that murder becomes the external manifestation of Cain's belonging to the Evil One. Cain illustrates two principles: "The person who acts sinfully belongs to the devil" (3:8a), and "The devil . . . was a murderer from the beginning" (John 8:44).

Although one can trace such motifs to Genesis, the author probably had at his disposal more than the brief biblical account of Cain; for both Jewish and

Christian writings attest to imaginative developments of the Cain motif. Philo wrote four works on Cain (Loeb vol. 2); and in *On the Posterity and Exile of Cain* 11 ※38, he charges people with taking Cain as a "master and instructor." (Later a group of second-century gnostics were called Cainites, and some scholars have associated the adversaries of I John with them because of the author's attack on Cain.) In *On the Migration of Abraham* 13 ※74, Philo says that Cain prevailed over Abel by skill rather than by strength. Josephus, *Ant.* 1.2.1 ※53, says that Abel had respect for justice (*dikaiosynē*), while Cain was thoroughly evil (*ponēros*)—note the vocabulary in light of I John 3:12 which contrasts Cain's deeds as *ponēros* and Abel's deeds as *dikaios*. In *Ant.* 1.2.2 ※60 we are told by Josephus that Cain's depravity increased after his punishment. Later the *Targum Pseudo-Jonathan* on Gen 4:7 makes Cain an unbeliever, and the *Apocalypse of Abraham* 24:5 says, "Cain acted lawlessly under the influence of the Adversary [Satan]," who had deceived Adam and Eve. In the medieval *Pesiqta de Rab Kahana* 16.5 (126a) Jews are told to behave toward their brothers "not like Cain toward Abel; Cain slew Abel." Indeed, there is a rabbinic tradition that Eve had intercourse with the devil; and Cain was the son of the tempter, while Abel was the son of Adam (Ginzberg, *LJ* 5, 133–34). It is tempting to invoke this idea as background for I John's contention that Cain "was from" the devil (3:12a); but it is not clear that the legend was known in the first century A.D. (See the NOTE on 3:8a above as to whether the Johannine writers thought that the devil begot children.) As for Christian tradition, Heb 11:4 states, "By faith Abel offered to God a more acceptable sacrifice than did Cain"; and Jude 10–11 says that those who revile what they do not understand "have gone on the path of Cain." The shedding of the innocent blood of Abel figured large in Christian imagery as foreshadowing the death of Jesus and the persecution of Christians (Heb 12:24; Matt 23:35–36). In summary, the tendency in both Jewish and Christian works to make Cain a model for disbelievers may explain I John's use of Cain as a model for the secessionists (since 3:12 must be related to 3:17). Close to our author's mindset would be *T. Benjamin* 7:5, which envisages the punishment of "those who are like Cain in the envy and hatred of brothers." The Jewish-Christian Pseudo-Clementine *Homilies* 3.25 (GCS 42, 65) calls Cain "a murderer and liar," a designation which approaches the language used for the devil in John 8:44.

12c. *And why did he kill him?* There is a similar dramatic use of a question in John 9:36. The "why" is literally "for the sake of what," employing *charin* as an improper preposition (BDF 216¹). The usage is classical, but in the NT not frequent and never in the word order found here where the preposition precedes the word it governs.

12de. *Because his own deeds were evil, while his brother's were just.* We saw above that these adjectives, "evil, just," resemble Josephus' language for Cain and Abel. This is not a psychological analysis but a reflection of Johannine dualism. The psychological motivation for a killer is most often his dislike or fear of what his adversary is doing; but in dualism evil hates good because it is good, and evil does evil because like does like. Thus Cain's hatred for Abel stems from the fact that Cain was inclined to act evilly (Bultmann, *Epistles* 54). The attitude echoes John 3:19, "The light has come into the world, but men have preferred darkness to light because their deeds were evil," as well as John 8:41 where Jesus castigates Jews who "believe" in him for seeking to kill him: "You are indeed doing your father's [the devil's] works." As for "evil" and "just," they reflect origin, since the devil is "the Evil One" (I John 3:12a) and Christ is "the Just One" (2:1,29); and the dualistic approach to "deeds" continues the theme of two types of behavior in the previous unit, reflecting God (2:29b; 3:7) and the devil (3:4,8). Clearly then, Cain and his brother stand respectively for the secessionists (children of the devil) and the author's adherents (children of God who are like Christ), two groups of whom the author wrote in much the same way in the last unit. This is the last appearance of "just/justice" words in I John; henceforth the author will concern himself with that specification of justice which is love (a specification made clear in the relationship between 3:10b and 3:10c).

13. *Brothers, do not be surprised [then] when the world hates you.* Codices Sinaiticus and Ephraemi Rescriptus*, and the Peshitta, Armenian, and Ethiopic versions support a *kai* ("and, then") before this verse, a reading Aland accepts with hesitation. If original, it could have fallen out by homoeoteleuton in relation to the last word of the preceding verse, *diKAIa*. A number of scholars, including Plummer and Westcott, would start a new unit here, but the *kai* connective and the continued reference to Cain (3:15) do not favor that. This is the only Johannine instance of "Brothers" as an address to fellow Christians (NOTE on 2:9b above); but it is found frequently in the NT (Acts, James, Hebrews, II Peter, and Paul). In some instances it appears with the possessive as "My Brothers" (Philip 4:1; James 2:1), a reading that the Byzantine and Syriac traditions imitate here. The normal Johannine epistolary greetings are "Little Children," when the author is speaking as a tradition-bearer, and "Beloved," when he is seeking to approach his audience on a more egalitarian plane. (In James 1:16,19; 2:5; Philip 4:1 the combination "Beloved Brothers" appears, and in I John 2:7a the Byzantine tradition substitutes "Brothers" for "Beloved.") The address "Brothers" is especially appropriate here where the author has just described how Cain killed his brother; it is part of the author's appeal to his adherents not to imitate Cain who killed his brother. (Because of that reference the archaic ecclesiastical plural "Brethren" is not helpful here —indeed, elsewhere it may obscure the belief that Jesus established a new, eschatological family that is more real than the physical family [Mark 3:33–35].) The use of family terms (also "Fathers," "Children") underlines an affectionate relationship among Johannine Christians over against a hostile world. This affection helps to soften the admonitions that usually follow such an address.

In the NT the negative imperative of *thaumazein*, "Do not be surprised," is peculiar to the Johannine writings (John 3:7; 5:28). Just as English "surprise," the Greek *thaumazein* can be followed by "that" (*hoti*) or by "if" (*ei*), depending on whether one is describing fact or possibility. While Attic Greek prefers *ei*, both GJohn instances take *hoti;* and so the appearance of *ei* here is unexpected, especially since the hatred by the world is a fact. While BDF 454[1] explains that sometimes *ei* is used for *hoti*, perhaps one should not neglect all "if" connotation: Although the hatred is a fact, Christians do not always encounter it; and so it may be encountered as a surprise. My "when" is an attempt to cover the various implications. Brooke, *Epistles* 93, would press the significance of the present imperative as responding to the continuing character of the hatred. In the previous unit (3:1) we heard "the world does not recognize [know] us"; but now a lack of affection has moved from implicit to explicit, for the word order in the present line emphasizes the hate. The author is drawing on formulas from the Johannine tradition where Jesus said, "If the world hates you, bear in mind that it has hated me before you" (John 15:18) and "the world has hated them [his disciples]" (17:14). Ignatius, *Romans* 3:3, seems to echo this language when he exclaims, "Christianity is truly great when it is hated by the world."

14a. *That we have passed from death to life we know.* The pronoun "we" is expressed, and so there is emphasis—no matter what the world may think, *we know*. (I have reversed the Greek word order to express that emphasis.) The verb "know" is *eidenai* (*oida*), and there is the usual speculation that it is used rather than *ginōskein* because the knowledge here is more emphatic or experiential (to the contrary, see ABJ 29, 513–15). But any emphasis here comes from the pronoun; and *oidamen*, "we know," may simply be the Community's set formulation for reliable tradition (footnote 13 in the preceding unit). The object of the "we know" is a "that" clause (the first *hoti* clause in this verse). The assurance with which the author joins his readers in this knowledge is part of his technique of subtly reminding them of what they should know as Community members. He is less diplomatic in 5:13: "I have written this so that *you* may know that *you* possess eternal life."

The verb of motion, *metabainein*, "to pass," sharpens the sense of a dualistic division between death and life. Comparable is John 5:24: "The man who hears my word and has faith in him who sent me . . . has passed from death to life." (In John 13:1 *metabainein* is used for Jesus' passing from this world to the Father.) Of the 6 uses of "death" in I John, 2 occur here, and the other 4 in the discussion of "the deadly sin" in 5:16–17. Perhaps the author still has Abel in mind and would consider that Abel too has passed from death to life. (Hebrews 11:4 states that "Abel died but through his faith he is still speaking.") Passing from death to life is another way of phrasing what John 3:5 refers to as "entering the kingdom of God" (which is also Synoptic imagery), or what both GJohn (3:19–21; 8:12; 12:35,46) and I John (2:9–11) refer to as coming from darkness and walking in light. The imagery of change from death to life is common in the Pauline tradition, e.g., "Christ Jesus destroyed death and brought life to light" (II Tim 1:10); "When you were dead in your trespasses . . . God made you alive with Christ" (Col 2:13; Eph 2:1,5). This imagery appears in Jewish thought as well, e.g., Philo, *On Flight* 11 ※58, "What is good and virtuous constitutes life; what is bad and wicked constitutes death." But in a general discussion on Abel, Philo, *That the Worse* 14 ※48, warns of motion in the opposite direction: "The soul that has extirpated from itself the principle of the love [a *philein*-related word] of virtue and the love of God has died to the life of virtue." Granted I John's reference to just/justice, the comment in the *Letter of Aristeas* is interesting: "Injustice is equivalent to the deprivation of life [*zōē*]" (212).

14b. *because we love the brothers.* Codex Sinaiticus and some versional evidence read "our brothers," a correct but unnecessary clarification. This second *hoti* clause in v. 14 is causal, but does it offer the reason for our knowing or the reason for our passing from death to life? (In other words is love the sign of life or cause of life?) The same problem occurred with a second *hoti* clause following a verb "to know" in 3:2e (see NOTE there). The author's habit of using *hoti* twice in quick succession, first meaning "that" and then meaning "because, for," is neither elegant nor illuminating. Bruce, Marshall, Schnackenburg, and Westcott are among the majority who relate it to "we know," so that love of brothers becomes the exterior sign of the presence of divine life and love within us. As support one may cite John 13:35, "By this will all know you as my disciples—by the love you have for one another." Some object to the alternative explanation (that we have passed from death to life because we love) as giving a meritorious role to our action. (Since the Reformation, suggestions of merit in the NT are quite suspect!) More precisely, however, in Johannine thought our love for our brothers is a form of God's love for us (I John 4:7–11); and so it would be divine love that caused us to pass from death to life. In support of this approach Wengst, *Häresie* 67, points perceptively to the next line of 3:14: "The person who does not love remains in the abode of death." If hate is more than a *sign* of death (also v. 15), love is more than a sign of life. (Similarly *T. Gad* 4:6, "For as love [*agapē*] would give life even to the dead . . . so hatred would slay even the living.") One might argue that the author has phrased himself ambiguously to cover both interpretations: love both as sign and cause of life. More realistically, he may have phrased his sentence ambiguously because he never asked himself this kind of question. Of the five statements in I John about loving one's brother, this is the only instance in which "brother" is plural, a usage probably influenced by the use of "Brothers" as an address in v. 13.

14c. *The person who does not love remains in the abode of death.* Codex Ephraemi Rescriptus, the Byzantine tradition, and some versional evidence add "the brother" after "love" and Papyrus 69 adds "his brother"—an imitation of the standard Johannine phrase. Without this added object the absolute statement is very strong. Love comes from God and is correlative with life. "The person who" translates the definite present participle as in 2:4,6,9,10,11; 3:7,8; and here too it is part of the anti-secessionist dualism. "Remains in the abode of" is a more elaborate translation of *menein en* discussed in the NOTE on 2:6a. In Johannine usage there are only two instances of "remaining in" something negative, namely, the nonlover remaining in death (here) and the nonbeliever remaining in darkness in John 12:46. The closely parallel *einai en* is used with a negative only in I John 2:9 where the person who hates his brother "*is in* the darkness." Clearly "darkness" and "death" are names for the same abode or realm; and as John 3:36 shows, this abode is marked not only by the privation of light and life, but also by God's wrath.

15a. *Everyone who hates his brother is a murderer.* Codex Vaticanus reads the intensive pronoun "his own brother," with no significant difference of meaning. This is another instance of *pas,* "all, every," before the definite present participle, a dualistic feature first discussed in 2:23ab and very frequent in the last unit (NOTE on 2:29b). This generalization, based on the example of Cain, shows that the hater not only remains in the abode of death but causes death. The word for "murderer" (*anthrōpoktonos*) is rare in classical Greek (Euripides uses it) and occurs only twice in the Greek Bible, here and John 8:44: "The devil . . . was a murderer from the beginning," a reference to Gen 3–4 also. The devil's drive to destroy life is what leads the hater to kill and thereby to betray that he is a child of the devil (I John 3:10). (In the NOTE on 3:14b I cited *T. Gad* 4:6, the next verse of which reads, "The spirit of hatred works together with Satan . . . in all things to men's death, but the spirit of love works together with the law of God in long-suffering unto the salvation of men.") Although one might theorize that the secessionists had aligned themselves with the forces who were killing Johannine Christians (John 16:2), it is more probable that the reference to murder is hyperbole for maltreatment, a hyperbole nourished by the legal mentality reflected in Deut 19:11 which anticipates that hatred of neighbor may lead to murder. In comment on the commandment, "You shall not kill," the Matthean Jesus (5:21–22) says, "I say to you that everyone who is angry with his brother will be liable to judgment." A late Jewish work, *Derek Ereṣ Rabba* 11.13 (57b), attributes to Rabbi Eliezer ben Hyrcanus, a contemporary of the Johannine writers, the maxim, "He who hates his neighbor is among the shedders of blood."

15b. *and, as you know, no murderer has eternal life abiding in him.* Literally, "and you know [*eidenai*] that every murderer does not have. . . ." The problem of translating the negated "every" sentence was discussed in the NOTE on 2:19f. "Eternal life" is anarthrous here, the most frequent Johannine usage (NOTE on 1:2d). Codices Sinaiticus, Alexandrinus, Ephraemi Rescriptus, and the Byzantine tradition read the final phrase with the intensive pronoun "in himself." The "as you know" is an appeal to a common tradition which may be a Johannine variant of the principle in Gen 9:6 that every murderer shall be deprived of life, a principle that has now been applied to eternal life. (Did such an application occur in the conversion/initiation/baptism process when the commandments, including the commandment not to kill, were taught and explained?) In Rev 21:8 murderers are specifically mentioned as destined for the place of "second death" whence there is no resurrection. Wohlenberg, "Glossen II," argues that the last phrase ("abiding in him") should be read not with this line (15b) but with the next (16a). But the "abiding" phrase would be awkward with 16a, and such a division neglects a Johannine idiom, e.g., John 5:38, "You do not have His word *abiding in you.*" Just as "abode" was part of the parallel line in I John 3:14c, so "abiding" is part of 15b. For the various realities that abide or remain in the Christian, see the B grouping of *menein en* formulas in the NOTE on 2:6a. The statement here implies that the secessionists were never real believers and never received eternal life (see COMMENT).

16a. *This is how we have come to know what love means.* Literally, "In this we have known [*ginōskein*] love." Some codices of the Vulgate and the Latin

Clementine version read "the love of God," and this influenced Wycliffe and the KJV. But as in v. 14c above, the absoluteness of the original reading ("love" without specifications) is more effective than scribal clarifications. This is another *en toutō* construction. As explained in the NOTE on 2:3a, when it is followed by an explanatory *hoti* clause as here (16b), "in this" points forward to the contents of that clause. And in fact, that is the general view of scholars here, but Westcott thinks it refers "both backwards and forwards." Translators from Tyndale and Cranmer to Bonsirven have rendered the perfect tense of *ginōskein* as a present ("we know"), but the author implies that the knowledge we now have comes from a past encounter. There is a definite article before "love," and so the question concerns the very meaning of the term. Noting that *agapē*, "love," is a term virtually unknown in classical Greek, some have suggested that for outsiders *agapē* did need a definition. Here, however, the author is surely reminding his adherents of the meaning of a term used almost thoughtlessly but whose original connotation they had learned when they became Christians because it reflected basic Johannine christology.

16b. *for us Christ laid down his life.* In Greek this is introduced by *hoti,* "that," which is epexegetical of the *en toutō* phrase in the preceding line. (BDF 394 contends that *hoti* is used rather than *ean,* "if," when the explanation is factual.) "Christ" translates *ekeinos,* "that one" (NOTE on 2:6bc), for here the context points to Christ rather than to God as the reference. "To lay down life" employs the verb *tithenai,* "to put, put off," with *psychē,* "soul, life." (The latter in GJohn [10 times], along with *bios,* refers to earthly life, as distinct from *zōē,* "eternal life"; it occurs twice in I John [both in this verse] and once in III John 2.) Although Bonsirven, *Epîtres* 168, understands the idiom as "deliver oneself," the imagery is probably that of putting off one's life as if it were a garment (see *tithenai* in John 13:4). In secular Greek this expression is rare; in the NT it is peculiar to GJohn (8 times: 10:11,15,17,18; 13:37,38; 15:13) and to I John (twice in this verse)—the more normal expression is "to give one's life" (Mark 10:45; Western textual tradition of John 10:11). Five of the 8 uses in GJohn refer to Jesus laying down his life (as in this line); 2 to Peter laying down his life for Jesus; and 1 to someone laying down his life for those he loves (as in the next line here). Thus the explanation of love in I John 3:16 is in language well known to the Community.

The Greek word order in 16b puts emphasis on "for us," whence my moving it first in the translation. The preposition used 5 times in GJohn in the phrase "to lay down life" is *hyper,* "for," employed both here and in the next line (the only uses of this preposition in I John). If we think of John 10:15, *"For* these sheep I lay down my life"; Rom 5:8, "Christ died *for* us"; Mark 14:24, "This is my blood of the covenant which is poured out *for* many," all of which employ *hyper,* we realize that this preposition had become standard in Christian descriptions of Christ's death on behalf of others. (As we saw in the NOTE on 2:2a above, "He himself is an atonement for our sins" uses *peri* under the influence of OT sacrificial texts.)

16c. *so ought we in turn to lay down our lives for the brothers.* The "we," expressed by a pronoun (as in 3:14a), is emphatic, whence my translation "in turn." I discussed *opheilein,* "ought," in the NOTE above on 2:6bc; it is primarily used by the Johannine writers for an obligation based on the example of Jesus, as also here. The Byzantine textual tradition uses a present infinitive of *tithenai,* "to lay down," but the majority of ancient textual witnesses are right in preferring the aorist. The image involves a single action of giving up one's life (aorist), along with a continuous willingness (present) to do so out of love. Bonsirven, *Epîtres* 169, wonders why the plural "lives" was used. Perhaps it also reflects the problem of the single and the continuous, for the next verse interprets "laying down our lives" in terms of actions that can be repeated. The sequence of Christ's laying down his life for us and our laying down our lives for the brothers is the same as in John 15:12–13: "Love one another as I have loved you. No man can have greater love than this: to lay down his life for those he loves." The suffering and death of Christ is a frequent motive offered for imitation, chiefly in the form of being willing to suffer, be brave, be generous (I Pet 2:21–24; Heb 13:12–13; II Cor 5:15; Philip 2:5ff.; I Tim 6:12–13). The idea of Christians dying for other Christians is not tied explicitly into this imitation, although it occurs in other contexts, e.g., Prisca and Aquila risked their lives for Paul's life (Rom 16:3–4). In particular, it becomes a frequent motif in martyrdom contexts (a context known in GJohn whether or not it was known in I John), e.g., in Ignatius' feeling that he was giving his life as a ransom for the churches he addressed (*Eph.* 21:1; *Smyrn.* 10:2). In the story that Clement of Alexandria tells about John, the apostle as an old man encounters again a youth who had lapsed from Christianity to become a bloodthirsty bandit; and he says to the robber, "I will willingly endure death for you as the Lord did for us" (Eusebius, *Hist.* 3.23.17)—an echo of the motif in I John 3:16.

17a. *Indeed, when someone has enough of this world's livelihood.* Literally, "But whoever has the livelihood of this world," a clause opening with an indefinite relative, *hos d'an,* discussed in the NOTE on 2:5a where the grammar is the same. The first three lines of v. 17, which are governed by this relative, consist of three coordinated clauses; together they constitute one long nominative absolute (or *casus pendens:* BDF 466²; see NOTE on 2:24ab) anticipating and explaining "such a person" of 17d. This construction is more dramatic than if the author had written, "Such a person who has enough. . . ." In 2:16d the author has already expressed his contempt for *bios,* "livelihood, material life," as one of the things that belong to the world. While "world" could be neutral here, the contrast made in 2:16 between what belongs to the world and what belongs to the Father suggests that the term never lacks a pejorative tone. (We are not far from Luke 16:9, "mammon of iniquity [injustice, *adikia*].") Since *bios* covers both life and livelihood, it is not illogical for the author to move from being willing to lay down one's life (*psychē* in v. 16) to being willing to give of one's *bios.*

17b. *and perceives his brother to have need.* This is the only Johannine epistolary use of *theōrein,* a verb for seeing used 26 times in GJohn. In the NOTE on 1:1cd and in ABJ 29, 501–3 there is a rejection of the attempt to find consistent subtle shades of meaning among the five Johannine verbs "to see."

(Chaine, *Epîtres* 190, for instance, would argue from *theōrein* here that the person described had not only seen physically but considered consciously the needy brother.) "Have need" is a deliberate contrast with "has this world's livelihood" in the preceding line; see the beginning of the NOTE on 2:27cd. "Brother" refers to a member of the Johannine Community, presumably either male or female.

17c. *yet shuts out any compassion towards him.* Literally, "and shuts his inner parts from him." Although *splanchna* (pl. of *splanchnon,* "entrails") appears in the LXX mostly in passages that have no MT counterpart, once this word translates Hebrew *beṭen,* "belly," and another time *reḥem,* "womb [sg.], compassion [pl.]." (Traditionally it has been rendered as "bowels of mercy/ love," an expression not very meaningful today.) Since *splanchna* also covers the upper inner parts of the body, e.g., the heart or lungs that were thought to control emotion, it is tempting to render the expression as "closes his heart"; but the literal word for "heart" occurs two verses later. Luke 1:78 refers to "God's *splanchna* of mercy," while Paul cherishes all Christians "in the *splanchna* of Jesus Christ"; and so the best rendering may be "compassion." The author is envisioning a situation where a person not only does not help his brother in need, but actually shuts off a feeling of compassion that the needy would instinctively arouse.

17d. *how can the love of God abide in such a person?* As explained in the NOTE on 3:17a, all of v. 17 up to this line has been an anticipated description of the "person" herein condemned. In the NOTE on "the love of God" in 2:5b we saw that this phrase (6 times in I John) is subject to five different interpretations. Here Alexander, Brooke, Haupt, Plummer, and B. Weiss think it means love for God, i.e., an objective genitive. Bonsirven, Büchsel, Bultmann, Haas, Houlden, Marshall, Schlier, Stott, and Wengst think that it means love that comes from God, i.e., a subjective genitive. Chaine and Westcott think that the author meant both those types of love, while Schnackenburg opts for "divine love," a qualitative genitive. Bruce and THLJ indicate the difficulty of deciding and seem to favor leaving the meaning ambiguous. Although in 2:5 I chose that last option, now I am influenced by the parallel between the statement here that the love of God does not abide in one who neglects his brother's needs and the statement in 3:15b that eternal life does not abide in a murderer. I would judge that love, like eternal life, has to refer to what comes from God, a love the author has just defined in the preceding verse (3:16). The person described in 17abc is blocking the movement of divine love, which would lead him to treat his brother as Christ treated us, so divine love does not function in such a person. Notice the antithesis in *T. Gad* 5:2, "My children, you may drive out hatred [which is of the devil] and cleave to the love of God." The use of "abide in" here represents the B classification of *menein en* formulas described in the NOTE on 2:6a, whereby divine realities dwell in the Christian. The identification of the form of *menein* in 17d is disputed: Chaine, Nestle, B. Weiss, and Westcott identify it as a present indicative, whereas J. B. Bauer and Windisch opt for a future subjunctive—a division also apparent among the ancient copyists. BDF 366[4] argues that an indicative is rare in a deliberative sentence, but MGNTG 3, 98 seems to dispute that. J. B. Bauer, *"Pōs in der griechischen Bibel,"* NovT 2 (1957–58) 81–91, maintains that the present tense gives a "How" question the connotation of something unbefitting or not permitted, while the future implies the impossible or unthinkable. He favors the future here because the line means, "How is it possible . . . ?"

18a. *Little Children.* The Byzantine tradition adds "My," a frequent scribal "improvement," but authentic in only the first of seven epistolary uses of *teknion* (NOTE on 2:1a).

18ab. *let us not give lip service to our love with words but show its truth in deeds.* Literally, "let us go on loving" (pres. subjunctive, indicating duration) followed by four nouns in parallel pairs:

> not by word nor the tongue
> but in deed and truth

Scribes have tried in various ways to make the parallelism perfect: Some have inserted an "in" before "word" to match the preposition in the second line; Codex Sinaiticus and some other textual witnesses change the "nor" to "and"; they also drop the "the" before "tongue," the only arthrous noun of the four. But Johannine parallelism is never perfect.

Most scholars assume that within each line-pair of nouns there is the same internal relationship. One possibility is a synonymous relationship whereby "word" means the same as "tongue," while "deed" means the same as "truth." Thus, "Let us love, not by words, eloquently, but by deeds, factually." Bultmann, *Epistles* 56, speaks of a hendiadys and points to John 4:23 where the two anarthrous nouns "Spirit" and "truth" really mean "Spirit of truth" (ABJ 29, 180). Thus, "Let us love, not by word of mouth but by real deeds." Some think of a complementary relationship whereby the second noun lends a tone to the first, i.e., "the tongue" adding the tone of insincerity, and "truth" the opposite. Thus, "let us love, not by words with lip service only, but by deeds with sincerity." THLJ 92–93 distinguishes the relationship in the parallel lines, with the first line-pair of nouns related synonymously, and the second line-pair related complementarily, e.g., "Let us not love with spoken words but by deeds with sincerity." There are two difficulties with all such translations. *First,* the assumption is that the fundamental contrast between the two lines is based on the first noun in each phrase: "by word" versus "in deed." Yet, as de la Potterie, *La vérité* 2, 665, shows, the contrast between "word" and "deed" in classical Greek does not employ the preposition *en,* "in." As for the second noun in each line, contrasts between "tongue" and "truth" are not easy to find; for to have "tongue" mean "insincerity, untruth," it needs to be accompanied by a specifying adjective, e.g., Prov 26:28, "A lying tongue hates truth." *Second,* such translations assume that I John is giving us a general wisdom maxim to which there are many parallels. For example, in Matt 23:3 Jesus condemns the Pharisees because there is a discrepancy between what they say and what they do. In II Cor 10:11 Paul warns that what he writes by *word* when absent he will effect by *deed* when present. James 1:22 urges, "Be doers of the word, and not hearers only, deceiving yourselves." Philo, *On the Posterity of Cain* 24 ⳥⳥86–87, asks rhetorically, "For what good is it to say the best things but to plan and carry out the most shameful things? . . . And what good is it to have right intentions and yet resort to unfitting deeds and words?" (We may leave aside the occasional but implausible suggestion that the contrast in I John is the same as that found in I Cor 12–14 between acting in love and speaking in tongues.) Despite all these wisdom parallels, it would be strange in the impassioned flow of I John, largely directed against a specific erroneous group, to have the author stop to underline a general maxim of behavior.

There is another possible understanding, eloquently defended by de la Potterie, *La vérité* 2, 663–73, who cites supporting scholars, ancient and modern (Bernard of Clairvaux, Luther, Bonsirven, Windisch), namely, that full emphasis must be given to the second noun in the second line, i.e., to "truth" which as elsewhere in I John refers to a divine reality. Reflecting upon the phrase "in deed [*ergon*] and truth," we discover that *alētheia*, "truth," is governed by *en*, "in," 11 times in the Johannine writings (4 in GJohn, here in I John, 3 in II John, 3 in III John). Of those instances, it is employed by itself in simple *en* phrases (mostly anarthrous) 7 times, while it is compounded 4 times with another noun (the two governed anarthrously by the same preposition): "in Spirit and truth" (John 4:23–24); "in truth and love" (II John 3); and "in deed and truth" (here). Leaving a full discussion of the linguistic history of *en alētheia*, "in truth," until the first time we encounter the simple phrase (II John 1b), let us concentrate here on these compound phrases. The necessity of doing justice to the other noun, plus the fact that the order is not so fixed that "truth" always comes second, means that it is somewhat arbitrary in the present passage to reduce "in truth" to an adverb, as do most scholars who render it as equivalent to "truly" (Bonnard, Bultmann, de Ambroggi, Preisker, Schneider) or as "with sincerity" (Venerable Bede, Belser, Brooke, Büchsel, Chaine, Plummer, Vrede, B. Weiss). Rather in the phrase "in deed and truth" the two nouns can be of equal value in constituting a sphere of activity, so that one is speaking of deeds that have truth as the principle from which they flow, i.e., "truth" as God's revelation dwelling within the Christian which expresses itself in the way the Christian lives. This understanding, whereby the second noun in the second phrase (3:18b) is the source of the first noun (truth source of deeds), receives confirmation if we analyze the first phrase, "not by word nor the tongue." The "tongue" is not equivalent to "word," nor is it an oratorical appendage to "word"; rather it is the source of words. We may compare Jas 3:5–10, where the *tongue* is described poetically as one of the most powerful forces in the world with the power to bless, to curse, and to effect great changes, with *I Esdras* 4:35–41, where *truth* is described as greater and mightier than all, living and conquering forever, and doing all things that are just.

In my judgment, then, de la Potterie is quite correct in arguing that I John is not referring to sincere deeds or even real deeds, but to "the deeds of truth" (deeds produced by truth), which is precisely the idiom in the Dead Sea Scrolls: "Blessed be the God of Israel in His entire holy plan and the deeds of His truth" (1QM 13:2; also 1QS 1:19; 1QH 1:30). *Enoch* 10:16 compares truth to a plan that produces blessed deeds. For the author of I John, God's love is an active force; it must express itself in deeds and not only be talked about. The Christ whom God gave for us by an act of love is the truth; and, as the next sentence makes clear, our acts of love show that we belong to the truth. Indeed, a Sahidic MS. anticipates the connection between the two verses by borrowing a clause from 3:19 and adding it at the end of 3:18: Let us show our love in deed and truth "because we are of the truth."

19–21. We have already seen that the epistolary author is singularly inept in constructing clear sentences, but in these verses he is at his worst. Most commentators kindly call the passage a *crux interpretum;* less charitably, Loisy, *Evangile-Epîtres* 559, dubs it "gibberish" (*un galimatias*). At the least, it offers the Prologue competition for the prize in grammatical obscurity. Let me first supply a literal translation (which is no mean feat) and then discuss the nine most disputed points of interpretation. (I shall move through those consecutively line by line, taking the occasion to note any other factors that need mention; and so the disputed points will serve as the backbone for the NOTES on these verses.)

> 19a In this we (shall) know that we are from [*einai ek*] the truth,
> 19b and before Him we shall convince/calm [*peithein*] our heart [*kardia*]
> 20a that/because if [*hoti ean*] { our heart accuses [*kataginōskein*]
>   { the heart accuses us
> 20b that/because [*hoti*] God is greater than our heart
> 20c and He knows all things [*panta*].
> 21a Beloved, if [*ean*] the heart does not accuse
> 21b we have confidence towards [*pros*] God.

SCRIBAL TEXT "IMPROVEMENTS." Inevitably scribes have tried to clarify the obscurity of the Greek text. Codices Sinaiticus and Ephraemi Rescriptus, the Byzantine tradition, and the Peshitta read at the beginning of **19a** a *kai*, "and" (accepted by the UBSGNT in brackets), presumably in order to tie this verse closer to 3:18 and thus to encourage one to interpret the "In this" as a reference to what precedes. Also in 19a most of the major Greek codices, including Vaticanus, read a future ("we shall know"), while the Byzantine tradition, Augustine, the Vulgate, and the Syriac read a present tense ("we know"). It is often argued that the future tense was original and that scribes changed it to the present because *en toutō,* "in this," is normally followed by the present. However, it could be argued (less persuasively) that the present was original and that scribes changed it to the future to agree with the future tense of *peithein* in the next line. This difference has little import for the meaning of the line, especially since the future may be gnomic (BDF 349[1]) and equivalent to a present. In **19b** Codex Vaticanus and the Peshitta Syriac read a singular "heart," while Codex Sinaiticus, the Byzantine tradition, the Latin, and the Harclean Syriac read a plural. The singular is probably original if the underlying thought is influenced by Hebrew where the distributive singular is expected for a part of the body; and all 10 other Johannine uses of *kardia* are singular (including 20b and 21a). A scribe may have changed it to the plural because of the plural pronoun "our." The English idiom requires a plural even if the Greek is singular. In **20b** the initial *hoti* is omitted by Codex Alexandrinus and Family 13 of Greek minuscules (and some versional evidence that is hard to interpret); but this omission is surely an attempt to free the passage from the redundancy of two *hoti* clauses in a row. In **21a** Codex Sinaiticus reads "Brothers" instead of "Beloved," a scribal imitation of 3:13. In the same line there are 11 different variants of wording and order as scribes attempted to make the condition in 21a parallel to the condition in 22a (Metzger, TCGNT 713). Most text critics, however, accept the "leanest" reading found in Codex Vaticanus and Origen. In **21b** Codex Vaticanus reads "it has" for "we have" and thus makes "heart" from the preceding line the subject that has confidence.

SCHOLARLY EMENDATION. In modern times Windisch suggests that a negative had been left out before "we shall convince" in 19b. Moreover, he thinks that all of 20a should be deleted as a scribal corruption introduced in imitation of 21a. Bultmann, *Epistles* 57, is tempted to speculate that the source used by the author made better sense since it did not have a *hoti* at the beginning of 20a ("Before Him we shall calm our heart if our heart condemns us"). Carpenter, *Writings* 469, thinks that the author forgot to tell us the criterion he began to give in 19a (namely, what the "In this" consists in). J. E. Frame thinks that the lines 19b and 20a were inadvertently switched and that the sequence 19a, 20a, 19b, 20b makes better sense: In this we shall know that we are from the truth, namely, that if our heart is prejudiced (against the truth), even before Him we shall convince our heart (of it) because God is greater than our heart. The parentheses indicate that more than rearrangement is necessary for him to make sense of the verse.

PRINCIPAL PROBLEMS. If we refuse to take the route of emendation, nine problems face us in the text accepted by most scholars:

(1) *En toutō,* "In this," in 19a. In the NOTE on 2:3a I argued that "in this" always points forward when it is followed by a *hoti* clause that interprets it. There are *hoti* clauses both in 20a and 20b; however, it is perfectly possible that one or both of these may be governed by the verb *peithein* (19b) and thus have nothing to do with explaining the "In this" of 19a. Actually most scholars have argued that the reference of *en toutō* is back toward v. 18—even some of the scholars who separate 18 and 19 into different paragraphs. They include Alexander, Bruce, Bultmann, Chaine, Dodd, Hauck, Houlden, Plummer, Schnackenburg, Schneider, Spicq, Stott, THLJ, B. Weiss, Westcott, Wilder, and Wurm (also KJV, RSV, JB). A reference forward to what follows is supported by Bonsirven, Brooke (?), and Holtzmann, while others do not commit themselves on the issue (Marshall). In my opinion the evidence is strong for a reference to what precedes, especially if v. 18 is understood in terms of truth expressing itself in deeds of love; for then deeds of love are "how we know that we belong to the truth"—the exterior deed shows the interior reality. Other Johannine passages that offer criteria for our status of belonging to God (*einai ek;* see NOTE on 2:16ef) do so in terms of action, e.g., hearing God's words (John 8:47); acting justly (I John 3:10); confessing Jesus Christ (4:2); listening "to us" (4:6). It would be anomalous to claim that we know we belong to God by means of the contents of either of the two *hoti* clauses that follow 3:19a, namely, that our heart accuses us (20a), or that God is greater than our heart (20b).

(2) *Emprosthen*, "before," in 19b. The initial "and" of this line probably builds upon the knowledge mentioned in 19a and so has the connotation "and so." In other words, the author is not saying, "In this [by the fact that truth has manifested itself in loving deeds] we shall convince/calm," but "We shall know and [by that knowledge] we shall convince/calm." We act toward our hearts with the knowledge that we belong to God. The Johannine literature expresses the idea of "before, in the presence of" 6 times with *emprosthen* and 3 times with *enōpion*. Each governs "Him" (God) once, *emprosthen* here and *enōpion* in 3:22c. Those commentators who base their understanding of Johannine thought on minute precision in verb tense and word choice try to find a difference between the two phrases that occur so closely together. For instance, Plummer thinks that the *emprosthen* phrase in 3:19 is more from the human side, while *enōpion* in 3:22 is more from God's side. Rather, these two (improper) prepositions (along with a third, *enantion*, that John does not use) render Hebrew expressions meaning "in the eyes of" or "to the mouth of" (BDF 214⁶); and the variation is purely stylistic. Whether there is a forensic sense to *emprosthen*, as Bultmann maintains against Schnackenburg, depends not on the preposition but on the context. ("Before God" with *emprosthen* is forensic in a context of judgment [Matt 10:32; 25:32; I Thess 2:19], but not elsewhere, e.g., Matt 11:26.) There is a general context of judgment in I John, set up by 2:28–3:3.

(3) *Peithein* in 3:19b. The basic meaning of this verb is "to convince, persuade, win over," usually with the implication of persuading people to do something toward which they would not naturally be inclined, or of convincing them of the truth of something that is not obvious. For instance, it is used in I Sam 24:8 where David persuades his men not to attack Saul, and in II Macc 7:26 for the mother who (deceptively) promises that she will persuade her son against his resolve to die. The "convince" meaning is accepted for the present verse by Beyer, Bruce, Büchsel, Camerlynck, Findlay, Hoskyns, Plummer, Richardson, B. Weiss, and Wohlenberg. But among such scholars there is no unanimity as to what we shall convince our hearts about—is it that we belong to the truth (19a), or is it that God is greater than our heart (20b)? The problem is complicated because there is another, derived meaning of *peithein*, "to calm, reassure, satisfy," in reference to people who would be inclined to be angry or disturbed. For instance, it is used in II Macc 4:45 for bribery designed to pacify the king who is angry toward the donor, and in Matt 28:14 for the Jewish authorities promising to calm Pilate if he hears that the guards fell asleep at the tomb. The "calm" meaning is accepted for the present verse by Belser, Bonsirven, F.-M. Braun, Brooke (?), Charue, Marshall, Schneider, Spicq, THLJ, Westcott, and Wilder, and by JB and RSV. Since the immediate object of *peithein*, whether it means "convince" or "calm," is *kardia*, "heart," that leads us to the next problem.

(4) *Kardia* in 3:19b. The word means "heart," which is for us the seat of physical life, but in antiquity had other connotations that affect our interpretation here. *Kardia* is the place where moral decisions are made and hence is close to what we call conscience. (There is a Greek word *syneidēsis* that

more technically describes conscience, but Johannine usage is closer to Hebrew anthropology.) In I Sam 24:6 David's *kardia* smote him because he had committed *lèse majesté* against Saul. In Acts 2:37, when Peter has spoken to the people of Jerusalem about having crucified Jesus, they are stung or cut to the heart, i.e., their consciences are troubled. *Testament of Gad* 5:3 explains that the just man is ashamed to do what is unjust, not because he will be reproved by others, but because of his own "heart" which the Lord sees. Probably the majority of scholars understand "heart" to mean conscience in 3:19b (Bonsirven, F.-M. Braun, Brooke, Chaine, Marshall, Spicq, Stott, Westcott). Nevertheless, *kardia* also covers the emotional element in human life and can refer to the affections, feelings, and impulses. For instance, in II Cor 7:3 and Philip 1:7 Paul keeps people in his heart, i.e., in his affections. Among the relatively few scholars who think that I John 3:19b refers to feelings or impulses, Hoskyns interprets *kardia* as the base, natural inclinations (to hate the secessionists?) and thinks that the author's idea is that before God we shall overcome them. Finally, *kardia* is equivalent to the mind or seat of intellectual perception. In the Bible to know people's hearts is to know their thoughts, and in Acts 1:24 a prayer is addressed to the Lord "who knows the hearts of all human beings." Since *kardia* is both object of the verb *peithein* in 19b and the subject of the verb *kataginōskein* ("accuse") in 20a, it is important to know whether the author is thinking about conscience, feelings, or mind.

(5) *Hoti ean* in 3:20a. There are two obvious translations: "that if" and "because if." In two other instances of this expression in I John (3:2; 5:14) it means "that if/when"; and that seems to be the favored alternative here. However, it is also possible to redivide these words as *ho ti ean*, where the first word is read as an indefinite relative (form of *hostis*), meaning "whatever" (BDF 300[1]). In that case *ean* is no longer "if" but a form of *an*, a particle used after relative particles to give a conditional flavoring to the clause (BDF 107). Accordingly, a third possible translation would be "(as to) whatever," with the indefinite relative serving as an accusative of respect. This is supported by Bengel, Brooke, Chaine, Charue, Dodd, Haupt, Karl, Law, Schnackenburg, Spicq, Stott, Westcott, Windisch (?), and Wohlenberg; but there are serious difficulties. The posited form *ho ti ean* never occurs clearly in the NT (although there are three Johannine instances of *ho ti an:* "Do whatever he tells you" [John 2:5]; "The Father will give you whatever you ask in my name" [15:16; 14:13]). A few verses later (I John 3:22), when the epistolary author wants to express an indefinite relative, he does not use *ho ti ean* but *ho ean:* "receive . . . whatever we ask." Moreover, the parallelism between 20a and 21a makes it very likely that in both cases *ean* means "if." Finally, as awkward as it may be to have two *hoti* clauses in a row (20a, 20b), this awkwardness is typical of the author; for it has already occurred (confusingly) in 3:2,14, in both of which the translation "that . . . because" seemed preferable. I shall favor that here as well. (See, however, 4:13ab below where "that . . . that" may be better.) All of this means that, from the point of usage, "that if" emerges as the most plausible of the three translations of *hoti ean.*

(6) *Kataginōskein* in 3:20a. The verb, which means literally "to know

against [*ginōskein kata*]," is used with forensic or legal connotations, "to reproach, accuse, judge against, declare guilty." It appears only 3 times in the NT (twice here) and 4 times in the LXX (with Sir 14:2 using it for condemnation by one's conscience). The epistolary author may have chosen it as a counterpoise to *ginōskein*, "to know," since these verses give a pattern of *ginōskein* (19a), *kataginōskein* (20a), *ginōskein* (20c), *kataginōskein* (21a). Beyer, "Rezension" 612–13, argues that such a pattern of antithesis is a sign that the section should be attributed to Bultmann's proposed source. The subject of this verb in 20a is *kardia*, a noun accompanied by the genitive pronoun *hēmōn*. This may be translated as an emphatic possessive, *"our* heart" (Bonsirven, Richardson, Wendt); or since the verb can take an object in the genitive, it may be the object of the verb: "the heart accuses *us*" (Chaine, Hauck, Spicq). The word order somewhat favors the latter; and that is the way Clement of Alexandria in the East, and Tertullian and the Vulgate in the West understood the passage. In either translation one must still ask about the material object of the verb. About what is the accusation leveled by the heart? Does the accusation concern past conduct in general or, more specifically, the failure to do acts reflecting love? Medieval theologians thought that it might concern venial sins, which God could forgive even after death. Of course, if one has opted for the *ho ti an* reading discussed in the preceding paragraph, then one has the material object expressed: "as to whatever the heart accuses [us] of."

(7) *Hoti* in 3:20b. The first two lines of v. 20 begin with *hoti*, "that, because"—see (5) above. How does one translate this awkward sequence? If one accepts the unlikely thesis that the "In this" of 19a points forward, one could argue that 19b and 20a are a parenthesis, and that the *hoti* clause of 20b continues 19a: "In this we shall know that we are from the truth . . . that God is greater than our heart." However, the arguments given under (1) above against this interpretation are strong; and while grammatically possible, it does not make much sense. In the more likely thesis that the "In this" of 19a points to what precedes and does not affect these clauses, both the *hoti* clauses of v. 20 have to continue 19b (*"Before Him we shall convince/calm our heart"*). That statement, with the appropriate choice of "convince" or "calm," should precede all the italicized translations I supply below. Let me list the more likely possibilities of how the two *hoti* clauses may be translated. First, if the *peithein* of 19b means "convince": (a) The two *hoti* conjunctions may be translated as "that," with the second "that" resumptive. This is a technical way of suggesting that the author has repeated himself ungrammatically; and so for all practical purposes the second "that" is not translated (or is translated "that, I repeat"): *"that if our heart condemns (us), (that) God is greater than our heart."* Bonsirven, Hauck, Houlden, and Wurm are among those who speak of a resumptive *hoti*. Some ancient scribes, as we saw, tended to omit it. Tantamount to this is Bultmann's suggestion (*Epistles* 57) that the verb "we know" dropped out of the text before the second *hoti* clause; or the suggestion that "it is" should be supplied before that clause. (b) The two *hoti* conjunctions may be translated as "because," again with the suggestion that the second *hoti* is resumptive: *"because if our heart condemns (us), because, I repeat, God is*

greater than our heart." With either of these suggestions (a and b) a resumptive is hard to justify after such a short interval, but it is even harsher in the second ("because") explanation. B. Weiss, however, argues that the author may have felt the need to repeat the conjunction lest his statement, "God is greater than our heart" (20b), seem to depend for its truth on the condition in 20a. (c) The first *hoti* can be looked upon as awkwardly introducing a parenthetical condition and translated as "namely," while the second *hoti* means "because": *"namely, if our heart condemns (us), because God is greater than our heart."* (d) The first *hoti* (*ean*) can be read as *ho ti an* and translated "whatever," while the second *hoti* means "because": *"as to whatever our heart condemns, because God is greater than our heart."* This reads well, but in (5) above I mentioned the difficulties of thus rewriting *hoti ean*. **Second,** if the *peithein* of 19b means "calm," the last three translations (b,c,d) are possible but the first (a) may be eliminated. Personally I am inclined to accept the more normal "convince" translation of *peithein*. In this instance, however, since it is a question of convincing the heart about a truth that may console it, "convince" is not too far from "calm." Of the four possible translations that accompany the meaning "convince," the first ("that . . . that") is the least objectionable. Frankly, though, there is not a great difference in real meaning among the four, and one may be asking for more precision than the author was capable of or interested in supplying.

(8) *Panta*, "all things," in 20c. The *kai*, "and," that introduces this line is epexegetical of the preceding line: God is greater in that He knows (*ginōskein*) all things. But difficulty arises about the implication of His omniscience. Is it that, knowing all, God mercifully forgives all? The context, which mentions our acting in love as a sign that we are children of God, has inclined many scholars in this direction: Luther, Brooke, Spicq, Stott, Wendt, Westcott. Or is it that, knowing all, God is more demanding and strict in judgment? The author has spoken of the heart accusing (*kataginōskein*, "to know against") — may not God more effectively accuse or "know against" since He knows all? In many biblical passages God's ability to search the heart and see all things is the reason why His judgment is to be feared or respected (Ps 7:10[9]; Prov 15:3). Among the scholars who interpret 3:20 as a reference to severity are Calvin, Alford, Ebrard, Richardson, and Wohlenberg. Or finally is the idea simply that, knowing all, God will be more objective than human beings, no matter which way the evidence points? He will be merciful toward those who have shown love, and severe toward those who have shown hate. In I Cor 4:5 Paul urges Christians to refrain from judgment until the Lord comes precisely for such a reason: God will shed light on hidden things and manifest the counsels of hearts, and treat each one fairly. Hauck (also B. Weiss) argues strongly for this interpretation. In two passages in GJohn (2:24; 21:17) where Jesus is said to know all things, his reaction is negative in one and positive in the other; and this flexibility could confirm the last-mentioned view.

(9) *Mē kataginōskein*, "does not accuse," in 3:21a. The address that opens this line, "Beloved" (NOTE on 2:7a), shows that the theme of love which prefaced these difficult verses (3:18) is still on the author's mind. I mentioned

that many textual variants betray scribal attempts to make the wording of 21a ("if the heart does not accuse") match that of 20a ("if our heart accuses" or "if the heart accuses us"). Some modern scholars join in this by reading "our heart" in 21a (Bonsirven, UBSGNT), or "accuse us" (Bonsirven, Haupt). Behind such suggestions is the deeper problem of how 21a is related to 20a. Are alternatives being offered (if the heart accuses, and if the heart does not accuse) or is one sequential to the other with the second condition meaning: if the heart that once accused now ceases to accuse (Bultmann, Plummer)? And if, as most think, alternatives are involved, are the results different? If the heart accuses, is God more severe than if the heart does not accuse? (Some commentators think that the author would judge it more normal that the heart of a Christian not accuse [Brooke, THLJ].) Or is the idea that, whether the heart does or does not accuse, God's attitude is positive and merciful (Schnackenburg)? Verse 21 ends with the theme of *parrēsia*, "confidence," a theme associated with the revelation of Christ at the parousia in 2:28 and 4:17. Therefore, although the "confidence" here is related to asking things of God (a theme repeated in the next verse, 3:22), it may also be related to the way Christians will be judged "in the presence of God." That last phrase in 3:21 (*pros ton theon*) was used in 2:1 in terms of having Christ the Paraclete "in the Father's presence" (a judgment context) and will reappear in 5:14–17 in the context of asking for things. Acts 24:16 speaks of "a blameless conscience before God [*pros ton theon*] and before human beings."

SUMMARY. I have led the reader through nine infuriatingly complicated problems in three enigmatic verses. Now let me summarize by saying that in real meaning, no matter what one decides on the minor problems, there is only one major issue, namely, do the verses speak of the severity or the mercy of God? A view that goes back to the early church fathers (Greek, Syriac, and Latin) and runs from Augustine through the *Glossa Ordinaria* of the Middle Ages to Calvin and the Catholic Counter-Reform renders the verse in terms of severity. Using the literal translation supplied at the beginning of this NOTE, we may render the severe interpretation of vv. 19–20 thus: "In this [by showing the truth of our love in deeds] we shall know that we are from the truth, *and before Him we shall convince our heart [about the importance of such deeds]. Because if our heart condemns us [for not doing such deeds], God is greater than our heart and knows all things [and will thus condemn us all the more]*." As Augustine (*In Epistolam* 6.3; SC 75, 282) exclaims, "You hide your heart from human beings; try to hide it from God if you can." But another interpretation in terms of mercy was given popularity by Luther in his 1527 lectures on I John; and although at first resisted by Calvinists and Catholics alike, it has won the day among most Christians today. For the italicized portion above, it may be rendered thus: *"and before Him we shall calm our heart as to whatever our heart might condemn us for, because God is greater [in forgiving] than our heart and knows all things."* The translation of the next verse (21—"Beloved, if the heart does not condemn us, we can have confidence in the presence of God") offers no problem for either interpretation. With the severe interpretation, v. 21 would present the other side of the human picture: if our own heart condemns us, God will condemn us even more; while if our own heart does not condemn us, we can have confidence in the presence of God. With the merciful interpretation, v. 21 continues in the same line: if our own heart condemns us, God will use His greater knowledge to forgive us; while if our own heart does not condemn us, we can have even greater confidence in the presence of God.

One cannot decide the interpretation through grammar alone; it is a question of which rendering best fits the general outlook of the epistolary author. Those who argue for the severe view contend that the author is insisting on the importance of deeds of love as a sign of belonging to the truth, and he is using the fear of God as a motive for changing some of his adherents who are weak on this score (whose heart condemns them). In my judgment that is not the precise situation of the author. He is worried that some of his adherents may be seduced to the secessionist position, and so he tries to show the fallacy and evil of secessionist views; but there is little by way of pastoral correction for Community members that is not related to the secession. In other words, when he says, "Let us not give lip service to our love with words but show its truth in deeds," he is not directly correcting inadequate behavior on the part of some of his adherents; he is attacking the secessionist position that the way one behaves (walks) is of no import. Elsewhere when the epistolary author speaks of God's ultimate judgment upon his adherents, he does so in terms of encouragement. If they sin, they have a Paraclete (2:1–2); on the other hand, they should abide in Christ so that they may have confidence when he is revealed in the parousia (2:28). In the merciful interpretation of 3:19–21, these are precisely the imports of the two "if" clauses: the one deals with the heart that knows something damaging (sin); the other deals with the heart that is not ashamed. In 4:17–18, when the author speaks of Judgment Day, he describes a love that casts out fear and gives confidence; and that seems to be the theme here as well. Thus, I think that the evidence favors the merciful rather than the severe interpretation.

22a. *and can receive from Him whatever we ask.* Plummer (*Epistles* 89) and others argue that the initial *kai* is epexegetical, explaining the reference in the preceding line (21b) to having confidence. However, I think it more likely that "have confidence in the presence of God" in 21b is a wider concept involving God's estimation of us, and that the ability to receive what is asked for in 22a is a *specification* of the wider confidence. The "whatever" is *ho ean* (also John 15:17; III John 5), which in the NT frequently replaces the more classical *ho an* (to which it is corrected here by Codex Vaticanus). See above on the reconstruction *ho ti ean* under problem (5) in the preceding NOTE.

This is the first epistolary instance of the Johannine theme of making requests of God that shall be answered. The verbs here are *aitein,* "to ask," and *lambanein,* "to receive." In the GJohn Last Discourse, on several occasions Jesus says there will be *done* or *given* whatever the disciples ask in his name (14:14–16; 15:7,16; 16:23–26); and once (16:24) he uses exactly the same vocabulary as here: "Ask and you shall receive." The verb *aitein* is the dominant verb for asking in these passages (8 times); only in one possible GJohn instance (16:23; see ABJ 29A, 722–23) is *erōtan*, "to question, ask, request," used for such a request *by the disciples*. In I John 5:14–16, which is the second epistolary passage on this theme, *aitein* will be used 4 times, and *erōtan* once; and I shall argue in the NOTE on 5:16d (under "petitions") against attempts to find subtle differences between these synonyms. This theme of asking/receiving is not peculiar in the NT to John, e.g., "Ask [*aitein*] and it will be given to you" (Matt 7:7); "All things that you pray and ask for [*aitein*], believe that you have received [*lambanein*] and it will be yours" (Mark 11:24; also Jas 1:5–6). What is significant here is that I John has related the receiving to a confidence based on a heart that knows nothing prejudicial to the asker (v. 21) and to keeping the commandments (22b). Protestant Reformation issues cast their shadow on some discussions of the passage, e.g., criticism of this as a reversion to legalist piety with the presupposition that true Christianity eschews merit. Leaving that aside and heeding the warning of B. Weiss, *Briefe* 108, against reading Pauline issues into a Johannine text, we may situate the issue in the relationship of a covenanted people to its God. Part of the covenant is that the people of God live up to His commandments (words), not because they are an imposition or a test, but because they give expression to God's very nature as a just and loving God. In turn the people who live according to the commandments are brought close to the God whose justice and love they mirror in their lives, and the unity of wills brings the granting of their requests. Job 22:23–27 states as a principle: "If you remove injustice from your tents . . . you will make your prayer to God and He will hear you." Philo, *On Rewards* 14 ≉84, says that a great nation "has God to listen to its prayers inspired by true religion, and to draw nigh to them when they call upon Him with a clean conscience." Brooke, *Epistles* 102, cites an unidentified Jewish saying, "Do His will as if it were yours, and He may do your will as if it were His." In the NT John 9:31 recalls as a well-known principle, "We know that God pays no attention to sinners, but He does listen to someone who is devout and obeys His will." James 5:16 states, "The prayer of a righteous man is strong in its effectiveness." In the post-NT era *II Clem.* 15:3 urges, "Let us remain just and holy in our faith that we may make our requests [*aitein*] with confidence [*parrēsia*] to God"; *Hermas, Man.* 9.1–2, warns against asking, "How can I make any requests [*aitein*] from the Lord and receive [*lambanein*] them after having sinned so greatly against Him; . . . rather turn to the Lord with all your heart and make your request of Him without doubting, and you shall know His great compassion [*eusplanchnia*]"; *Hermas, Sim.* 6.3.6, assures those who serve the Lord with a pure heart that "they will receive [*lambanein*] from the Lord whatever they ask [*aitein*]."

22b. *because we are keeping His commandments*. The NOTE on 2:3b discussed both the Johannine usage of *entolē*, "commandment," and the expression "to keep [*tērein*] the commandments." As always in I John, the commandments here are of God (not of Jesus, as in GJohn occasionally). In Johannine literature keeping the commandments or divine word leads to many good things (besides having one's requests granted), e.g., never seeing death (John 8:51); being given the Paraclete (14:15–16); being loved by the Father

(14:21); having the Father and the Son indwell (14:23); remaining in Jesus' love (15:10). In other words keeping the commandments is an essential part of the covenant (preceding NOTE), and the benefits of being God's people and God's children are intimately related to it. The failure to appreciate the importance of living according to God's commandments was used by the author in I John 2:3–5 as a criterion against secessionist claims, and in 5:18 it will be used to discern who is the true Christian, begotten by God.

22c. *and doing what is pleasing in His sight.* The last phrase is "before [*enōpion*] Him"; see the discussion of *emprosthen* in this phrase in the NOTE on 3:19b. *Arestos*, "pleasing," occurs only 4 times in the NT, one of which is here and another is in John 8:29, where Jesus says that he always does what is pleasing to the One who sent Him. Some commentators (Brooke, Plummer, Westcott) would argue that, despite the parallelism between 3:22b and 22c, there is a distinction between keeping God's commandments and doing what is pleasing in His sight. However, other usage supports equivalency (as defended by Chaine, Schnackenburg), e.g., Sir 48:22 comments that "Hezekiah did what was pleasing to the Lord . . . as the prophet Isaiah commanded"; Eph 5:3–10 lists things forbidden by the commandments and urges people "to try to learn what is well pleasing [*euarestos*] to the Lord."

23a. *Now this is God's commandment.* Literally, "His commandment," with the "his" identified by the usage in the next line, *"His* Son." The word order is similar to that of John 15:12, "This is my commandment," and to I John 3:11, "This is the gospel."

23b. *we are to believe the name of His Son, Jesus Christ.* This line and the next ("and we are to love one another . . .") are governed by an epexegetical *hina*, which interprets the commandment in terms of believing and loving. However, the subjunctive of the verb "to believe" is aorist, while that of "to love" is present. Codices Sinaiticus, Alexandrinus, and the Byzantine tradition have removed the difficulty by changing the aorist subjunctive of "believe" to a present that would convey the idea of a continuous faith, parallel to continuous love. Some have wondered whether a punctiliar aorist refers to the initial basic act of faith (THLF, Westcott). Brooke, *Epistles* 104, thinks of a complexive aorist (BDF 332) that covers the whole process of faith as a unity. (Westcott, *Epistles* 120, surveys the Johannine usage of the tenses of *pisteuein* to support the thesis that they are used with "significant exactness.") Here *pisteuein* takes the dative of "name" (see BDF 187[6]), and this creates a problem for some who think that John has regular prepositional patterns in which *eis*, "in," following *pisteuein*, describes a higher form of faith. The scribes seem to have anticipated this problem: a few minuscules and the Vulgate read "in" before "the name," while other minuscules omit "the name of."

Such difficulties require a full discussion of *pisteuein*, which appears 98 times in GJohn and 9 times in I John, a Johannine usage constituting almost half the NT usage (241 times). See ABJ 29, 512–15, and to that bibliography add A. Vanhoye, "Notre foi, oeuvre divine, d'après le quatrième évangile," NRT 86 (1964) 337–54. It is startling that the noun *pistis*, "belief, faith," which occurs 243 times in the NT, appears only once in the Johannine writings (I John

5:4)—graphic proof of the Johannine preference for the dynamic over the static. As for the object of belief, I John is highly christological: 5 uses of *pisteuein* involve believing in (the name of) Jesus as the Christ, the Son of God (3:23; 5:1,5,10a,13—echoing John 20:31), while 3 deal with believing God as He expresses His love in sending His Son (4:16) or testifies to Jesus as His Son (5:10cd); one involves belief in that Spirit which confesses Jesus Christ come in the flesh (4:1–2). As for the grammar of *pisteuein* in I John, the usage with objects reflects varieties encountered in GJohn:

- the accusative (I John 4:16)
- the dative (3:23; 4:1; 5:10b—18 times in GJohn)
- *eis,* "in, into," with the accusative (5:10ac,13—36 times in GJohn)
- *hoti* objective clause (5:1,5—13 times in GJohn, which also uses an objective *hina* clause)

Is there a distinction of meaning in these different grammatical uses? Some maintain that *pisteuein* with the dative involves acceptance, but not necessarily personal commitment, while *pisteuein* with *eis* is a total engagement of one's being. De la Potterie, *La vérité* 1, 296, has constructed Johannine theology on the basis of exact Johannine usage of prepositions; see his article on Johannine *eis* in *Biblica* 43 (1962) 366–87. Others (Bruce, Bultmann, Chaine, Schnackenburg) would argue that, while there may be some patterns of frequency, there is no difference among the Greek usages that reflect an underlying Semitic idiom, *he'ĕmîn* followed by *bĕ* ("in") or *lĕ* (dative). Certainly, despite claims of total engagement related to *eis,* that idiom in John 4:39 can describe a faith which is to be improved upon (4:41). Interchangeability between *eis* and the dative is seen in John 3:36 and 5:24. In I John 5:10 the verb appears 3 times, twice with *eis* and once with the dative; and it takes extraordinary ingenuity to distinguish different kinds of faith in that verse. Although the author uses the dative in the present verse, it is unbelievable that he means anything other than total commitment since he is dealing with the basic commandment that sums up the gospel. It certainly means more than Wilder's suggestion ("Introduction" 270–71) of belief "in the gospel message associated with his name." Alexander, *Epistles* 99, is truer to the mark when he speaks of accepting "as true all that Jesus Christ is and has done and stands for." Even Marshall, *Epistles* 201, who argues for distinctions in *pisteuein* usage, has to admit that "The present verse is an exception to the rule"—another way of saying that such "rules" do not correspond to Johannine reality.

The NOTE on 2:12b described the Semitic and Johannine use of "the name." As God's Son, Jesus bears God's name; belief in the Son makes people children of God, under the protection of the divine name (John 17:11,12), enabled to ask things in Jesus' name (14:13–14). We saw in that NOTE also the motif of baptism in the name of Jesus, and the author's formula here may be the Johannine reworking of that motif. "His Son, Jesus Christ" surely has anti-secessionist intent, for in 2:22–23 the author attacked those who would deny that Jesus is the Christ and thus deny the Son. The secessionists might be able to use such a baptismal formula but not with the author's emphasis on "Jesus" as the subject.

23c. *and we are to love one another just as He gave us the command.* The Byzantine tradition omits the "us," perhaps because the scribes were thinking of Christ giving the command to his disciples. *Kathōs,* "just as," is not used here in the normal christological comparison ("do just as he did"; NOTE on 2:6bc above), but with a slightly causal tone: "inasmuch as" (BDF 453²). Who is the "he" contained in verbal form, "he gave"? (Bultmann and THLJ opt for God, while Chaine, Schnackenburg, and B. Weiss opt for Christ.) The three surrounding lines (23ab,24a) contain the genitive pronoun "his" (*autou*) referring to God, so that one would need a strong reason to posit a reference to Christ here. Even though Jesus gave the commandment to love one another (John 13:34; 15:10,17), we have seen that regularly I John attributes commandments to God (NOTE on 2:3b); and II John 4–5 uses a *kathōs* clause (as here) to refer to a commandment to love one another that we have received "from the Father." In referring to love as God's commandment, I John may not be far from common early Christian teaching: "Concerning brotherly love you have no need for anyone to write you, for you yourselves have been taught by God to love one another" (I Thess 4:9). Although the expression "to give commandment(s)" occurs in a classical author like Demosthenes, in the NT it is peculiar to the Johannine writings, 4 times in GJohn (11:57; 12:49; 13:34; 14:31[?]) and once in I John (here). We saw in the NOTE on 3:1a that the verb "to give" is a Johannine favorite for the communication of heavenly realities to human beings, and so there is nothing strange in the idea of God giving a commandment or a "word."

24a. *And the person who keeps God's commandments.* Literally, "And the one keeping His commandments." Throughout I John the author has used the present participle, prefaced by the definite article, to personify the secessionist and the true Johannine spokesman (see 2:10,11). In the NOTE on 2:3b we saw that the verb *tērein,* "to keep," is always used with the plural of "commandment," whence the shift from the singular in 3:23 to the plural here (see the plural in 2:3–4, where *tērein* occurs, and the sing. in 2:7–8, where that verb does not occur). Almost all scholars (even those who think the last line of 3:23 refers to Christ) understand the "his" before "commandments" in 24a to refer to God—Balz, Brooke, Bultmann, Chaine, Marshall, Plummer, B. Weiss, Westcott, and Wilder. That was the reference in 2:22b and will be again clearly in 5:3.

24b. *abides in God and God in him.* In both instances "God" translates *autos,* "he, him." Although a literal translation is inelegant ("abides in Him, and He in him"), this use of *autos* 4 times in 8 words has been deemed an example of paronomasia (BDF 488¹—see NOTE on 4:7a below). I John 4:13,15,16 are other examples of mutual abiding between God and the Christian. A previous one-way example (the Christian in God) in 2:6–8 also brought in commandment as a criterion, for the claim to abide in God was being made by someone of secessionist mentality who saw no obligation to walk as Christ walked.

24c. *Now this is how we can know that He abides in us.* This is an *en toutō* construction, followed in the next line by a subordinate construction. According to the rule I gave in the NOTE on 2:3a, the "in this" points forward to that next line, which defines the "this" as the gift of the Spirit. (Thus Bonsirven, F.-M. Braun, Brooke, Bruce, Büchsel, Bultmann, Chaine, de Ambroggi, Haupt, Law, Marshall, Plummer, THLJ, B. Weiss.) However, because here the subordinate construction consists of a prepositional phrase and introduces an idea not hitherto mentioned in the unit (the Spirit), some scholars think *en toutō* refers both to what precedes (keeping the commandments) and to what follows. (Thus Belser, de la Potterie, Lauck, Lias, Lücke, Michl, Painter.) I question a reference to what precedes; for the author has already said that keeping God's commandments results in a person's abiding in God (24ab), and there is no need to repeat that. His goal now is to take the theme of abiding in God and use it to introduce the Spirit, which will be the theme of the next unit. It is true that elsewhere love is a sign that God abides in the Christian (4:12–13); but several different divine realities or related actions serve as a criterion for divine abiding (2:5,27; 4:15), and so one cannot use this argument as proof for a necessary reference of *en toutō* in 24c to love in 23c. In the present instance *en toutō* is followed by *ginōskein*, as it was also in 3:16a, 19a. Thus there are three tests of knowledge in this unit. In 3:16a *ginōskein* is aorist ("have come to know"); in 3:19a it is future ("shall know"); in 3:24c it is present ("can know"). Since the three tests stem from the very nature of the Christian life (Christ laid down his life for us; that we show the truth of love in our deeds; from the Spirit He gave us), the time factor is not really important—the criteria stem from God's past action in Christ and are present in the continuing effects of Christ's action in the life of his followers.

24d. *from the Spirit that He gave us.* Below in 4:13b one finds almost the same expression, "He has given us of [*ek*, 'from'] His own Spirit"; and there from the context (4:12) we can see that the subject is clearly God. Analogously, most scholars accept God as the subject here, although Windisch thinks it could be either God or Christ. (A comparison of John 14:16 and 16:7 shows that either figure can give/send the Spirit.) The verb here is aorist in tense, while the verb in 4:13 is perfect; see the NOTE on "we have heard" in 1:1b for the interchangeability of these two tenses. The "giving" is past and it does have an enduring effect, but no undue emphasis should be placed on either aspect. Chaine, *Epîtres* 195, sees the "to us" as emphatic against the secessionists, and certainly in what follows (4:1–6) the secessionists are depicted as not possessing the Spirit of Truth that is of God.

Since this line begins with *ek*, "from," de la Potterie, *La vérité* 1, 292, faithful to his theological interpretation of prepositions, argues that it cannot offer the direct interpretation of *en toutō*. He contends that the Spirit may serve as the origin of our communion with God but not as the criterion by which we know that communion. However, the giving of the Spirit is clearly a criterion in 4:13 where a *hoti* epexegetical clause involving the giving of the Spirit interprets the *en toutō*. Moreover, in the matter of prepositions the author is not so sensitive as are some of his interpreters, for in 4:6 he uses *ek toutō* with the same meaning that *en toutō* sometimes has. If there is no persuasive objection, then, to 3:24d interpreting the *en toutō* of 3:24c, the use of *ek* governing "the

Spirit" may be significant in another way. In 4:13b cited above, *ek* gives a partitive sense to God's giving *of* the Spirit, and one may wonder whether that is anticipated here. Some explain the *ek* in 24d on the basis of the verb "know" ("we can know . . . *from* the Spirit"), but there is also a partitive *ek* phrase that is equivalent to a partitive genitive (BDF 164[2]—the genitive of "Spirit" is underlined here since the relative it governs, "*that* He gave us," is also in the genitive by attraction [BDF 294]). A partitive aspect may be traditional in reference to the Spirit in Johannine thought, for John 3:34 reads literally, "He does not give the Spirit by [*ek*] measure." (Compare Heb 6:4, "Having tasted of the heavenly gift and become partakers of the Holy Spirit.") Of course, the Johannine writings also speak of giving the Spirit as a direct object (John 14:16); but since the Spirit is the Spirit of Jesus, there is theological precision in referring to God's giving *of* the Spirit that remains the Spirit of Jesus. As Williams, *Letters* 49, stresses, no individual has the whole Holy Spirit.

But perhaps we are ahead of ourselves in assuming what "the Spirit" in 3:24d means, for scholars are not agreed (see de la Potterie, *La vérité* 1, 289–91, for a summary). Augustine, Bede, and Theophylact were among the ancients who thought of the Spirit inasmuch as it arouses love, thus relating 24d to 23c. Belser and Chaine, following some medieval interpreters, think of charisms (while Dodd thinks specifically of the spirit of prophecy), a theory which may imply that 4:1 is asking for a test of charisms. Other scholars, including Bonsirven, de Ambroggi, Schnackenburg, and Spicq, think of an interior witness borne by the Spirit speaking within us to our own spirit. Still others, including Boismard, de la Potterie, Häring, and Oke, think of the Spirit that inspires a confession of faith, such as that to be mentioned in I John 4:2. This is the view I shall discuss in the COMMENT. Looking at the other explanations, I doubt that the author wishes to use as a criterion an inner experience of the Spirit, since the opponents could claim that too, and he is about to deny that they have the Spirit of Truth. There is no evidence whatever in I John of anything remotely resembling the Pauline picture of charisms in I Cor 12:27–31, nor a concern about how gifts of the Spirit relate to one another. The Johannine passages on the Spirit or the Paraclete speak of begetting, forgiving sins, teaching, and proving the world wrong; but there is no Johannine statement about the Spirit as the source of love. Some of the above interpretations of 3:24d assume that various NT Christians shared a common pneumatology, whereas pneumatology was probably as diverse in the first century as was christology. It is better then to interpret I John through the Johannine passages about the Spirit. Both in terms of opposition to the world (4:1,5) and in positive descriptions (given by God; a sign of abiding), the Spirit portrayed in I John 3:24–4:6 is closest to the GJohn descriptions of the Paraclete (16:8–13; 14:16–17). This was also true of the description of anointing (with the Spirit) in I John 2:20,27 (pp. 345–47 above).

COMMENT

In the INTRODUCTION (VI A3b) I explained in detail why a theory that divides I John into two Parts[1] might well choose 3:11 as the beginning of Part Two. Briefly: (a) Part One (1:5–3:10) and Part Two (3:11–5:12) would then be of proportionate length; (b) Each Part would begin with the announcement, "This is the gospel" (1:5; 3:11), the only two times this expression occurs in I John; and (c) The theme of loving one another, which is proclaimed in 3:11 as "the gospel," dominates what follows, even as the theme of love is strong in the second Part of GJohn, which is also bipartite.

If Part Two begins with 3:11, *a fortiori,* the present unit starts with that verse. That the unit terminates in 3:24[2] is suggested by the fact that the following verses in 4:1–6 constitute one of the most easily recognized units in I John, so that one cannot attach them to 3:11–24. Internally as well, these confines make sense. If the unit starts in 3:11 with "This is the gospel," followed by an interpretative *hina* clause that identifies the gospel with love, by inclusion the unit approaches an end in 3:23 with "This is the commandment," followed by a compound interpretative *hina* clause, the second part of which identifies the commandment with love. And in this unit, as in previous units, the very last verse (3:24) is a hinge concluding the theme of commandment and introducing the theme of the Spirit, which will be the subject of the next unit (see p. 119 above).

The subdivision of the unit is less clear. Many scholars, including Bonsirven, Bruce, Bultmann, Dodd, Jones, Marshall, THLJ, Thüsing, Wilder, and Windisch, make a break between 3:18 and 3:19 on the grounds that v. 19 leads into 20–22. Others, like Balz, de la Potterie, Gaugler, Hauck, Schneider, and B. Weiss, place the break between 3:17 and 3:18.[3] I favor this because in the previous two units of I John subdivision has been marked by titles of address, and a title of address occurs in 3:18. Indeed, in this unit one can recognize two strophes of equal length: 3:13–17, introduced by "Brothers"; and 3:18–22, introduced by "Little Children."

[1] Preceded by a Prologue (1:1–5) and followed by a Conclusion (5:13–21).

[2] That the unit is constituted by 3:11–24 is held by F.-M. Braun, Chaine, de la Potterie, Malatesta, Thüsing, etc.

[3] Among this group of scholars and among the preceding group there are some who think the break is sharp enough to warrant positing two units in vv. 11–24, e.g., 3:11–17 and 3:18–24; or 3:11–18 and 3:19–24. The inclusion I detect between 3:11 and 3:23 militates against that.

On either side of these strophes there is the inclusion already mentioned between 3:11 and 3:23.

A. *The Gospel of Loving One Another* (3:11–12)

In suggesting that Part Two of I John begins here, I do not mean that there is a sharp break with what precedes, any more than Part Two of GJohn is a sharp break with what precedes there. In GJohn the group of disciples who were with Jesus during the ministry (Part One) constitute the audience for the Last Supper at the beginning of Part Two (13:1). The enemies ("the Jews") are still in mind but less frequently, and they are spoken about rather than directly addressed. So also in I John, the author's "Little Children" mentioned in Part One along with the secessionists move to the fore, and their life-style becomes the main concern. The secessionists are still much in mind, but now one hears less directly of their boasts and claims. The secession has rent the life of the Johannine Community, and the author is taking pains to rebuild that life. He does this by giving full stress to the gospel of loving one another.

If one reads v. 12 with reference to the Community situation, one understands the urgency of the author's insistence on love. He has terminated Part One by speaking of the revelation of God's children and the devil's children. As he continues speaking more directly to God's children, he is aware of the harm that has been done to them by the devil's children. When the author evokes Cain, who belonged to the Evil One and so killed his brother (Abel), he is using the violent image of fratricide and of diabolic machinations to express his view of the secessionists. They had been members of the Johannine Community (at least on the surface); they had once called the author's adherents "Brothers," an address the author uses in 3:13 by way of reminder. But the secessionists had gone out of the Community, and now they were attacking the author and his adherents. Along with the Cain image the author is implicitly recalling two passages of GJohn where the devil worked in a similar murderous manner. One is John 8:39–44 where Jesus' fellow Jews (indeed, "Jews who had believed in him" [8:31]) seek to kill him, protesting that they are children of Abraham and children of God, whereas really they are children of the devil who was a liar and murderer from the beginning.[4] The other passage is John 13:2,27 which describes Judas who is handing Jesus over: Judas is one into whom the devil or Satan has entered and induced to act thus. This is an action that reveals the truth of what Jesus had said long before: "One of you [Twelve] is a devil"

---

[4] This is illustrated in the Adam/Eve and Cain stories in the biblical book (Genesis) called by Jews "In the beginning," from its opening words.

(6:70–71). In the Johannine view, just as Cain killed his own brother, and just as "the Jews" who were once "his own" (John 1:11) sought to and eventually did kill Jesus (5:18; 11:53–54), and just as Judas who was a candidate to be one of the new "his own" betrayed him to those who would kill him—all of these being children of the devil, belonging to the Evil One—so the secessionists have dealt with the Johannine Community.

Because of the strength of the epistolary language, one may wonder whether there was not factual truth in the charge of killing leveled against the secessionists. GJohn accused "the Jews" of killing Johannine Christians (16:2), and scholars like J. L. Martyn have thought that the synagogue authorities actually put some Christians to death.[5] Were the secessionists engaged in similar hostile acts? I see no way of answering that question with any surety. Common hatreds make strange alliances, but the secessionists from the Johannine Community should have been no more acceptable either to the Jews or to the Romans than were the author's adherents. The language of killing by opponents probably stems from the Johannine Jesus' own predictions;[6] and the epistolary author is finding that prediction fulfilled in his own times, just as he previously declared fulfilled the expectation of the Antichrist (2:18). For the author there is no need to look for some apocalyptic event—all the expectations are realized in and through the secessionists. The charge of killing need not have had a literal reference to the secessionists, any more than the charge of being the Antichrist. If the secessionists were charging that the author's adherents did not know God and hence were not children of God (the same charge the author made against the secessionists), they would be striking at the identity and eternal life of the Johannine Christians. The seriousness of this attack in the author's view may have made "murder" an appropriate term for the adversaries, even though they had not acted physically against the author's adherents or even denounced them to the civil authorities. (Matthew 5:21–28 shows how in Christian eyes hatred was equivalent to killing, and lust to adultery.) Or if the secessionists constituted the wealthier branch of the Johannine Community and their departure had left the common funds bankrupt, their failure to take care of their former brothers and sisters who were in dire need (I John 3:17) may have been equivalent to murder in the author's mind (see below). Nevertheless, the examples cited at the end of the preceding paragraph

[5] In my *Community* 42–43, I have made the contrary suggestion that the synagogue authorities expelled the Johannine Christians and then denounced them as non-Jews to Roman inquisitors, thus taking away from the Johannine Christians the umbrella of belonging to a permitted religion. If they were considered Jews, Christians could have explained why they were not taking part in pagan worship sanctioned by Rome, since Jews were exempted by the Caesars.

[6] See also Matt 24:9; 5:11–12.

constitute an argument for a more literal interpretation of "murderer" in I John 3:15.

Be that as it may, the author's main purpose here is not to address himself by accusations to the secessionists but to prevent his adherents from following them in their hatred of the brothers.[7] His adherents are urged in 3:12a not to act just as (*kathōs*) Cain acted. Throughout I John the author uses *kathōs*, "just as," language (NOTE on 2:6bc) to describe the resemblance that should exist between the lives of his adherents and the life of Christ. It is significant that now he says, "Not just as Cain." The secessionists are Antichrists (2:18–19; 4:3), and they have their diabolic model, even as Christians have their God-given model. The special reason why the author's followers should not be just as Cain is that from the beginning of their lives as Christians they have heard as part of the gospel: "We should love one another."[8] The author phrases his digest of the gospel in words virtually identical with those used by Jesus when he spoke at the Last Supper of his commandment (15:12,17; 13:34); and, in fact, the epistolary author at the end of this unit will (by way of inclusion) refer to love as part of God's commandment. The association of ideas makes one think that the author is once more appealing to his adherents on the basis of what they heard when they entered the New Covenant (their "beginning"). The Ten Commandments were the basic stipulations of the covenant God made with His people, and the love commandment plays the same role in the New Covenant. For the Synoptic tradition, to love one's neighbor as oneself is one of the two great commandments (Mark 12:28–31; Matt 22:34–40), or one of the two things written in the Law as necessary to inherit eternal life (Luke 10:25–28). For Paul, love of neighbor fulfills the Law and sums up all the other commandments.[9] For the Johannine tradition, to love is the only commandment explicitly mentioned, the "new commandment." This was hinted in 3:10bc where loving one's brother was the final specification of acting justly. That the commandment to love must have been part of the entrance instruction of every would-be Christian finds added proof in the

---

[7] In part this means that, while living in the Johannine Community, they should help those in need. In part it means that they should not join the schism, for that will inevitably lead them to hate their former brethren. In Johannine dualism there is no possibility of a nostalgic departure from the Community without recriminations against former comrades. One is going over to the children of the devil, and one will begin to act evilly.

[8] In 3:11 the author is again implicitly contending that his opponents have departed from the tradition as it was at the beginning. They do not meet the demand he places on his adherents: "As for you, what you heard from the beginning must abide in you" (2:24).

[9] In Rom 13:8–10 it is worth noting that, after Paul explains positively, "You shall love your neighbor as yourself," he looks at the negative side: "Love does no wrong to a neighbor." This is exactly the pattern of I John 3:11–12.

chart given at the end of the last unit (p. 433), which shows parallels among passages that Boismard would argue are baptismal. I Peter 1:22-23 gives as a positive instruction to those who have been begotten anew, "Love one another earnestly," even as I John 3:11 says, "We should love one another," to those just described as "begotten by God" (3:9). It is interesting that, in what is plausibly a baptismal setting, I Peter speaks of loving *one another*. I have explained above (NOTE on 2:9b) that the Johannine tradition speaks only of love of fellow Community members ("brothers, one another"); but even the other Christians who spoke in terms of the wider love of neighbor must have had their moments when they concentrated on love within their group. And what more appropriate moment for that than when people entered the group? Certainly that was the case in the Qumran Community of the renewed covenant where "an abundance of covenant love [*ḥesed*] toward all the sons of truth" was inculcated as part of the basic instruction (1QS 3:13; 4:5).

B. *Laying Down Our Lives for Our Brothers* (3:13-17)

This next subdivision contrasts the Johannine Community and the world (mentioned in vv. 13 and 17). It may seem at first that the author has jumped from an implicit attack upon the secessionists to a wider enemy;[10] but in I John the world and the secessionists are united: "Those people belong to the world; that is why they speak the language of the world and why the world listens to them" (4:5). In the struggle with the secessionists the author is historicizing the apocalyptic expectation of persecution. At the Last Supper Jesus had spoken of hatred of his disciples by the world (John 15:18; 17:14) in a context that mentions future synagogue persecution "when the[ir] hour comes" (16:2-4). The reason for foretelling such persecution is so that faith may not be shaken when the events transpire (16:1,4). Similarly, but in even more apocalyptic language, I Pet 4:12 states: "Beloved, do not be astounded at the fiery ordeal which comes upon you to prove you, as though an astounding thing were happening to you." The epistolary author's "Brothers, do not be surprised" (3:13), introducing his statement about the world's hate, may simply be part of the customary prediction of hatred (which has now been realized). However, the surprise may be literal in recognition of the fact that the anticipated hatred by the world (predicted by the Johannine

---

10 Some, like Schnackenburg, *Johannesbriefe* 196, have found in "the world hates you" a possible reference to the Roman persecution of Christians under Domitian, as in Revelation. But Bultmann, *Epistles* 54, points out that the quasi-technical word for persecution (*diōkein*) is not used here.

Jesus) has appeared primarily from within rather than from without, since it is embodied in former Community members.[11] There was a hint of surprise in 2:18 where the author identified these people as Antichrists.

The Cain imagery from 3:12 continues in this subdivision, identifying the world that hates the author's adherents with the secessionists who have gone out from them. It helps to explain the equation of hatred by the world with hatred of *brothers*. As murderers in the image of Cain, those who do not love their brothers "remain in the abode of death" (3:14c), while "we know that we have passed from death to life" (14a). Among the parallels between I Peter and this unit of I John (p. 432), we find in I Pet 2:9 that Christians have been "called out of darkness into God's marvelous light." Since "world," "death," "darkness," and "hatred" cover virtually the same realm, it was probably part of the common Christian baptismal teaching that Christians had passed into a realm of life, light, and love in Christ.[12] The fulfillment of the basic commandment or word[13] to love was an excellent criterion of whether one had truly made such a passage, because that commandment was so stressed at one's entrance from the world into the New Covenant. Notice the contrast in Jesus' prayer to his Father in John 14:14: "I have given to them your *word*, and the world has hated them because they do not belong to the world" (also 15:18-19). In the epistolary author's mind may be Jesus' saying (5:24), "The man who hears my *word* and has faith in Him who sent me . . . has passed from death to life"; for in I John 3:23 the author will interpret the commandment (or word) as both faith and love.

But does not the charge, "The person who does not love remains in the abode of death" (3:14c), challenge my contention that the author is referring to the secessionists? Should he not have said that they (the secessionists) have committed the sin that is unto death (to be mentioned below in 5:16-17) and so have passed *from life to death*? This objection overlooks two aspects of the author's thought. First, it is not clear that in Johannine theology one can lose eternal life ($z\bar{o}\bar{e}$),[14] for by its very nature "life" abides. This means that the sin unto death may not be a sin which has the power to take away life, but a sin of unbelief which reveals

[11] Of course, from the viewpoint of psychology the author should not have been surprised about a lack of love on the part of the secessionists for him and his adherents, since he scarcely loves them and has told his adherents, "Have no love for the world" (2:15). When I discussed the last-cited passage, I mentioned that some scholars thought that "world" there had a different meaning from its usual Johannine sense. That is oversubtle: 2:15 and 3:13 are two sides of the same coin.

[12] While I John 3:14a speaks of our passing from death to life, John 13:1 speaks of Jesus' passing from this world to the Father.

[13] For the interchangeability of "word" and "commandment," see the end of the NOTE on 2:3b.

[14] The Johannine writings use *psych\bar{e}*, "soul, life," 13 times in the context of losing or giving up one's life, but never *z\bar{o}\bar{e}*. Jesus says in John 11:26: "Everyone who is alive [verb related to *z\bar{o}\bar{e}*] . . . shall never die at all."

that one never had life.[15] Second, in the author's thought, the secessionists (despite appearances) never really belonged to the Community (2:19b) and so never had received life. They turned away from the light because their deeds were evil (John 3:20), just as Cain's deeds were evil (I John 3:12d); and their failure to love, exhibited in murderous hate of their brothers, illustrates that they do not have life abiding in them (3:15).

In v. 16 the author turns from the negative example of Cain, who killed his brother, to the positive example of Christ, who laid down his life for his brothers (i.e., those made children of God and thus brothers of Jesus by his passion, death, and resurrection; see John 20:17). Just as hatred leads to murder, love confers life. In 3:16b the author emphasizes Christ's death as an act of love "for [*hyper*] us." In the NOTE on this verse I pointed out that this was a set phrase in early Christian descriptions of Christ's death on behalf of others. The "us" in such phrases[16] is often a general reference to human beings, and is equivalent to the "many" in Mark 14:24 and Matt 26:28; both speak of the blood of the covenant "poured out for many." In the NOTE on I John 2:2c, a verse where Jesus Christ is designated as "an atonement for our sins, and not only for our sins but also for the whole world," I explained that the Johannine situation was probably more complicated. The divine intent toward non-believers is initially salvific, but their choice to remain (or to go) outside the community of believers represents a preference for darkness over light. Effectively, then, Jesus lays down his life for the sheep who hear his voice and belong to him (John 10:4,11), not for the sheep who belong to another. The sheep who belong to Jesus are the Johannine Christians, along with those Christians who are of another fold (10:16);[17] counterposed to them are those who belong to the world for whom Jesus did not lay down his life.[18] "For us" is opposed then to a "for them."

The sense of privilege in belonging to this "us" constitutes the basis of obligation. If Jesus had a commandment from the Father to lay down his life for his sheep (10:18), so Christians have a commandment to lay

---

[15] One is not to pray for someone who has committed the sin unto death (5:16), and the Johannine Jesus prays only for believers (John 17:9,20).

[16] Sometimes this is without *hyper*, e.g., "To him who loves us and has freed us from our sins by his blood" (Rev 1:5). Sometimes the individual is used for the totality: "I live by faith in the Son of God who loved me and gave himself for me" (Gal 2:20).

[17] See my *Community* 81–88, where I have suggested that the "other sheep who do not belong to this fold" were the Christians of the Apostolic Churches, who thought of figures like Peter and the Twelve as their progenitors in the faith, and who held a high enough christology to warrant being characterized as "true" by Johannine standards.

[18] For this other group see John 17:16; I John 2:16; 4:5; 5:19. That Jesus did not lay down his life for "the world" in this sense is an *a fortiori* assumption from his refusal to pray for the world (John 17:9).

down their lives for their brothers (I John 3:16c).[19] Christians received their life from an act of love, and the life that abides in them must express itself in love. In 3:16c the epistolary author is simply rephrasing John 15:12–13: "Love one another as I have loved you; no man can have greater love than this: to lay down his life for those he loves."[20] Where the epistolary author makes an original contribution to the tradition known to us from GJohn is in 3:17 where he relates laying down one's life to sharing one's livelihood. Generally this is seen as an *a maiore ad minus* argument: If one is obliged to give up one's life for one's brother, one is obliged to the lesser gift of the means of livelihood. That may not be the author's mind, however.[21] If he equates the secessionists with the Antichrist and hatred with murder, he may *equate* giving one's livelihood with laying down one's life. In other words, he may have historicized not only apocalyptic evils but also apocalyptic ideals. The reason for his historicizing the expected cosmic evil was his belief that the last hour was at hand (2:18). Perhaps in this last hour he is no longer expecting many martyrs—after all, the Beloved Disciple had died, and he was not a martyr (ABJ 29A, 1120–22). But he still sees the crucial need for people who have compassion for the brothers and sisters in want.

In being specific about the need to show love by helping the poor, the author is not holding up a new moral demand; rather he is reaching into the heart of Christianity's Jewish heritage. Deuteronomy 15:7 warned, "Do not harden your heart or close your hand against your brother who is poor." In the community of the renewed covenant at Qumran the equivalent of two days' wages had to be set aside for the poor and needy (CD 14:14–16). In Mark 10:21 Jesus tells the person who keeps all the commandments that he lacks one thing: "Go, sell what you have and give to the poor . . . and come, follow me." The Lucan Jesus (10:25–37) interprets the commandment of loving the neighbor in terms of loving a Samaritan in need.[22] James 2:15–16 asks, "If a brother or sister is naked and in lack of daily food, and one of you says to them, 'Go in peace; be

---

[19] The idea of a commandment to do this is a specification of the general commandment to love one another (John 13:34; 15:12,17); it is also a vocalization of the "ought" in I John 3:16c. In any case, modern readers who assume that there is a contradiction between doing things from love and doing things because of a commandment will find it difficult to claim John as a support.

[20] See ABJ 29A, 664, for the reasons why *philos* in the last phrase should not be translated simply as "for his friends." Since the epistolary author interpreted these *philoi* as "the brothers" (3:16c), he saw them as fellow Johannine Christians, whom he calls "Beloved."

[21] Nor do I think it catches the author's mind to cite the danger of loving everybody in general but not loving anybody in particular. The author is not issuing a statement of general wisdom but speaking to a particular situation in history.

[22] Luke is close to John not only in this specification but also in the picture of the priest and the levite whose actions were tantamount to shutting out compassion to the neighbor in need (I John 3:17b).

warmed and filled,' without giving them the things needed for the body, what good is that?" Ignatius, *Smyrn.* 6:2, attacks those "who have no care for love, nor for the widow, nor for the orphan, nor for the distressed . . . nor for the hungry or thirsty." Even the Mandaean literature (gnostic in tendency but with Jewish roots) warns that no one can ascend to the place of light who has driven the poor away from the door (*Ginza Right* 5.187.4; Lidzbarski, p. 188).

The author of I John gives his own tonality to showing love for the poor by criticizing those "who shut out any compassion" to the brother in need (3:17bc). This insistence makes sense if the secession has created a problem of need so urgent that the author may well think it reflects the last hour. The passage raises the *possibility* that the members of the Johannine Community with "enough of this world's livelihood" (3:17a) had joined the secession, leaving the author's adherents in dire need.[23] The reference in III John 5–7 to testifying to love by helping the brothers as they go from one church to another for the sake of "the Name" gives an impression of relatively poor communities where basic necessities are supplied by charity. The secession in the main Johannine church may have upset this pattern of charity. Reacting as bitterly toward those they left behind as the author has acted toward them, the secessionists may have allowed those whom they once called brothers to suffer need. (One can only wonder whether, were the shoe on the other foot and were the secessionist "children of the devil" in need, the epistolary author would have helped them—let us hope that he would not have forbidden his adherents to give them food and clothing even as he forbids his adherents to greet them in II John 10.) The author's rhetorical question, "How can the love of God abide in such a person?", challenges again the fact that the secessionists are Christians (since Christians are constituted by God's loving them) and expresses amazement that his adherents would find such people attractive. That implicit disgust is understandable if the secessionists maliciously hoped that poverty and need would ultimately lead the author's adherents to come out and join them. If the reader thinks all of this is fantasy that could not have happened in idealistic early Christianity, let attention be focused on Acts 6:1–6 (surely historical in its kernel) which describes how Christians who were arguing with one another[24] shut off food from the widows of their opponents! Alas, making others

[23] II John 7 says that the secessionists went out into the world, and I John 4:5 says that they belong to the world—a world that I John 2:16–17 characterizes as marked by desires and self-assured material livelihood. The attack in 3:17 on those who have the *bios* ("livelihood") of this world must be related to the only other epistolary reference to *bios* in the condemnation of the world in 2:16.

[24] The argument was probably over a theological issue since the Hellenist view in Acts 7:48–49 would scarcely have pleased those Hebrew Christians who went to the Temple daily (Acts 2:46).

suffer so that they will see the truth about God's love is a practice as old as Christianity itself![25] To a Jewish Christian mind such behavior might be a sign that the ultimate evil of the last hour has come if we may judge from *T. Zebulun* 7:3; 8:2: "And if you do not have the wherewithal to give something to the needy person, have compassion and mercy for him. . . . Because in the last days God will send His compassion on the earth, and where compassion and mercy are found, He will dwell in that person."[26]

C. *The Assurance before God of Those Who Belong to the Truth* (3:18–22)

Although he has just been addressing his brothers on the importance of love and of giving one's life and livelihood for a fellow Christian, the author has been doing this through condemnation of the bad example offered by the secessionists. He now turns more positively to the way love functions in their own lives. For various reasons (thought, background, and grammar) v. 18 and vv. 19–21 are much disputed among scholars, as I have spelled out in the NOTES. Here I shall work with the translation that seems to me the most defensible. When the author says, "Let us not give lip service to our love with words but show its truth in deeds," he is once more close to the *Testaments of the Patriarchs;* for *T. Gad* 6:1 states, "My children, let each one love his brother and put away hatred from your hearts, loving one another in deed and word." The epistolary author is not simply pleading for sincerity over against hypocrisy. As I understand them, the secessionists were not hypocrites: they did not preach one course of procedure and follow another. Rather they taught that actions or deeds were not salvifically important since one already possessed eternal life through faith in Christ. That is the position the author is attacking when he insists that love must manifest itself in deeds.[27] For him, love, truth, and light are all ways of describing what has been

[25] See also Matt 23:4 if more than hypocrisy is being condemned there.
[26] Both sentences use the noun *splanchna*, "bowels (of mercy)," found in I John 3:17c (see NOTE).
[27] Is he also attacking the fact that the secessionists are actually manifesting deeds of hate instead of deeds of love? Yes, but evaluating that attack is complicated by the author's failure to see a conflict between insisting that love must show its truth in deeds and his own attitude toward the secessionists as children of the devil whom one should not even greet (II John 10–11). Despite their theoretic stance about the nonimportance of deeds, one may well suspect that the secessionists showed love to *their* brothers and sisters. But the narrow definition of the object of love (*our* "brothers") on both sides of the Johannine dispute made it hard for the one side to see love on the other side. The author can see only that the secessionists do not love *his* adherents.

revealed in Jesus Christ and been appropriated through faith by those who have become children of God. They are all vital principles that must continue to manifest themselves in life. In 2:9–11 the author insisted that a person cannot claim to be in the light and hate his brother; such hate is a sign that he is in the darkness. So now he says that a person cannot claim to belong to the truth (3:19a) and hate his brother—truth manifests itself in deeds of love, not in hate.[28]

In 3:19 the knowledge of belonging to the truth is related to convincing or assuring one's heart in face of two possibilities, spelled out in 3:20a and 3:21a. Previously, in 3:6,9 the author made statements about impeccability and perfection, namely, that the Christian does not sin and cannot sin. But in 1:8–2:2 he insisted that Christians must acknowledge that they have sinned and are not free from the guilt of sin. While these ideas seem contradictory, apparently the author has reconciled them, probably in terms both of an internal principle of sanctity that produces sinlessness as it permeates Christian life, and of a factual failure to live that life perfectly. The two conditional sentences in 3:20a and 3:21a set side by side these two aspects. The first concerns the reality of sinning: "If the heart knows something prejudicial to us" (3:20a). In 1:8–2:2 the sinner was assured that God forgives through the atonement of Christ, and that same assurance is repeated here. God knows everything and knows our faults better than our heart knows them,[29] and still He forgives for He is greater than our heart (3:20bc). In 2:1–2 it was stated that Christ is just; yet, contrary to expectations, the just one is forgiving, for God's justice is salvific. The same logic is at work here: God's greater knowledge of the faults of those who belong to the truth leads to forgiveness. None of this is meant to lead to laxness (see also 2:1a), as we learn from the second condition: "If the heart knows nothing prejudicial" (3:21a). The author has not forgotten his goal of perfection and sinlessness; and where that goal is realized, Christians can have confidence before God (3:21b).[30] The theme of confidence was introduced in reference to the parousia of Christ in 2:28, and that theme will return in 4:17. Obviously Christians who abide in Christ should have confidence about the last judgment because they have been begotten by God and live as His children. But the author is saying more than that. If Christians live so much as God's chil-

---

[28] The intimate connection between 3:18b (showing the truth of love in deeds) and 3:19a (belonging to the truth) is another reason why I have contended that the subdivisional break between strophes comes best before v. 18 and not after it (p. 467).

[29] I have translated *kataginōskein* in 3:20a and 21a as "to know something prejudicial," so that the reader will not miss the play the author intended between that verb and *ginōskein*, "to know," in 3:19a and 20c.

[30] One is reminded of the axiom of Philo, *Who is the Heir* 2 §6: "When is it that the servant speaks confidently to his master? Surely it is when his conscience tells him that he has in no way wronged his owner."

dren that their heart knows nothing by way of a sin that could mar that relationship, they can be totally confident before God right *now*.[31] Indeed, they can make claims on Him as His children, as we shall see in 3:22.[32]

The message of 3:20–21 is that, whether they have sinned and repented or have not been conscious of sin, the author's "Little Children" can have confidence. Presumably the author needs to reassure them on this score because of the polemics of secessionist theology. Emissaries may be seeking to persuade the author's adherents that, if they have to pay attention to their deeds as a sign that they belong to the truth (as the author claims), then they are not really confident of their status. The secessionist principle of certitude may well have been more attractive: One is begotten by God through faith in Jesus, and deeds cannot change that. But the author refuses to concede that the need of showing the truth of love in deeds must lead to a lack of confidence about one's status before God. He is thus wrestling with a well-known difficulty in religious psychology: People who are earnest about the way they live often cannot believe that God is truly forgiving.[33] In affirming that the God who knows everything is greater than a heart which recognizes wrong and accuses us, I John is applying the insight that the God who judges His sinful children is the God who loved sinners enough to call them to be His children (3:1; 4:9–10). This insight was surely shared with Christians when they entered the New Covenant as God's children. While there is novelty in its embodiment in Jesus, the insight was already vocalized in Hosea's description of a God who knew in detail the unfaithfulness of His covenant partner and threatened reckoning, but ultimately said to Israel, "How can I give you up? How can I destroy you? . . . My heart recoils from that; my compassion grows warm and tender" (Hos 11:8—yet see a different interpretation in AB 24, 588–89). An eloquent writer (the Righteous Teacher?) of the community of the renewed covenant at Qumran cries out: "I remembered my sins. . . . I said in my sinfulness, 'I have been abandoned outside your covenant.' But when I remembered the strength of your hand and the multitude of your mercies, I rose and stood up, and my spirit was strengthened in face of the trial" (1QH 4:34–36). After describing what happened through Jesus as the fulfillment of Jeremiah's

---

[31] Although it is the last hour (2:18), the author still distinguishes between what we are now and a parousia that is yet to come (2:28–3:2). Writers like Houlden and Spicq are probably correct that here he is thinking primarily of "in God's presence" rather than of the parousia.

[32] Some see the confidence as purely forensic, in face of God's judgment; others see it as purely imprecatory, in terms of having requests answered. From what precedes and what follows in this unit, the confidence is surely both.

[33] If I may offer an example, parents who from love will receive back into the home youngsters who are leading a wayward life may still be anguished at the thought that these children are going to hell. What this means is that they believe that God, because He is just, will not be so forgiving as they are.

words about a New Covenant, Heb 10:16–19 issues the invitation to Christians to "have confidence to enter the Holy Place by the blood of Jesus," using the same word for "confidence" (*parrēsia*) that I John employs. After insisting on the obligation to help the needy, James 2:1–6,13 stresses that, while judgment may go hard on those who show no mercy, ultimately mercy triumphs over judgment. Thus it is no new doctrine of divine graciousness that the author of I John proclaims, but the gospel of the God of the Covenant, Old and New.

In 3:22 the author gives another indication of the graciousness by which God responds to Christians who have struggled so victoriously with sin that their hearts can detect nothing prejudicial to them; he asserts that they receive from God whatever they ask.[84] He then goes on to specify what he means by the heart knowing "nothing prejudicial"; that is verified when one keeps the commandments and does what is pleasing to God (22bc). The idea that such a life gives one confidence before God in the matter of requests made to Him will reappear in 5:14: "Now this is the confidence which we possess in the presence of God, namely, that whenever we ask anything according to His will, He hears us." The phrases "His will," "His commandments," and "what is pleasing in His sight" all refer to the same thing: God's covenantal demand upon His people. As I explained in the NOTE on 3:22b, it is not a question of our behavior meriting an answer to our prayers. Rather, living as God's people constitutes a condition in which God can act toward us as the covenant partner who is faithful to His promises. In other words, there is a correspondence of love whereby we do what is pleasing to God and God does what is pleasing to us. Beyond the general covenant love between God and His people, there is a special Christian family relationship as the Father responds in love to His children who live "just as" His Son. (One may recall the saying of Jesus in the "Q" tradition: "If you who are evil know how to give good gifts to your children, how much more will the Father in heaven give good things to those who ask Him?" [Matt 7:11; cf. Luke 11:13].) The comparison with the Johannine Jesus is important here. In GJohn Jesus described his obedience to what the Father had commanded him as covering every phase of his life, but especially giving his life for others in love (John 10:18; 12:49,50; 14:31; 15:10). He said also, "I always do what pleases him" (8:29). Thus in his lifetime the Johannine Jesus met the demand phrased in the parallel lines of I John 3:22bc: "Keeping His commandments and doing what is pleasing in His sight."[85]

[84] Presumably they would not be petitioning about their own sins, but 5:14–16 envisions Christians praying for life for brothers who sin.

[85] Jesus did this out of love, and that is the context that I John assumes for the Christian: "You will remain in my love if you keep my commandments, just as I have kept my Father's commandments and remain in His love" (John 15:10; also 14:31).

Because of this obedience, which was a union of wills, Jesus could say to the Father in relation to his prayers, "Father, I thank you because you heard me; of course, I knew that you always hear me" (John 11:41–42). I John is applying this to Christians who show a similar obedience to their Father; they can be sure that "we can receive from Him whatever we ask" (3:22a). This fulfills Jesus' promise, "On that day you will ask in my name, and I do not say that I shall have to petition the Father for you. For the Father loves you Himself because you have loved me and have believed that I came forth from the Father" (John 16:26–27).[36]

D. *The Commandment to Believe and Love* (3:23–24)

As I have indicated in discussing the structure of the unit, the "Now this is the commandment" of 3:23a is an inclusion with "This is the gospel" of 3:11. Yet most commentators are surprised that in defining the commandment in 3:23bc the author puts "believe the name of His Son" alongside "love one another." The surprise disappears if one accepts my thesis that the epistolary author is commenting on the Johannine tradition known to us in GJohn, for the GJohn passage cited above has the same combination: "You have *loved* me and have *believed* that I came forth from the Father." The present unit of I John has discussed love of brothers for one another; the unit we are about to begin (4:1–6) will discuss confessing Jesus Christ. One cannot understand how a fellow Christian is a "brother" to be loved without understanding Jesus as God's Son, for his sonship makes those who believe in him brothers and sisters.

We have already seen that the commandment to love one another was surely learned by the Johannine Christians at "the beginning," i.e., during the process of conversion/initiation/baptism, even as the Ten Commandments were the stipulations of the Israelite Covenant. As indicated in the NOTE on 2:12b, Christians spoke of baptism *in the name* of Jesus; and so the commandment "to believe the name of His Son, Jesus Christ" was probably also learned by Johannine Christians at "the beginning." The stated purpose for writing GJohn, "so that you may *believe that Jesus is the Christ, the Son of God,* and that believing you may have life *in his name*," confirms that. We shall see in the next unit how the author's understanding of this belief (confessing "Jesus Christ come in the flesh": 4:2) refutes the secessionists, even as in this unit he has used the love commandment to refute them.

---

[36] In John 14:13–16 Jesus speaks of his own role in granting requests, a role that involves his petitioning the Father. That thought may have influenced I John 2:1–2 where the epistolary author presents Jesus as a Paraclete in the Father's presence upon our behalf. The "in my name" in John 16:26 cited above suggests that the Christian is praying as a child of God in the image of His Son.

As admirably as "the commandment" of 3:23 fits the author's purpose, it has made modern commentators uneasy. Beyond a dislike of the category of commandment (footnote 19 above), some who would read the NT through Pauline glasses find a commandment to believe dangerously close to making faith a work. Whether or not Paul would approve, the epistolary author is faithful to the GJohn tradition where Jesus says, "This is the work of God: have faith in him whom He sent" (6:29).[37] For John 3:19–21, the ability to come to the light and believe is intimately related to the character of one's works. Part of the reason the Johannine tradition thinks of faith or belief as something "to do" is because this theology has been shaped in controversy that required public confessions of faith.[38] The Johannine forebears proclaimed publicly that Jesus was the Messiah and were cast out of the synagogue because of that (John 9:22; 12:42–43; 16:2). The schism in the Johannine Community is being fought over what one is willing to confess about Jesus—is it salvifically important that he lived in the flesh? If one believes, one has to be willing to confess that belief in formulas which may prove costly to one's welfare and one's life! Some scholars would deprecate this Johannine "dogmatic" faith in favor of the "purer" Pauline concept of faith as trust in Jesus and obedience to God.[39] Even laying aside the fact that Paul did not hesitate to formulate the gospel in creedal language (Rom 1:3–4), one may wonder how long Christians could go on trusting in Jesus without having to formulate their evaluation of the one in whom they trusted. In any case, faith is scarcely univocal; and in the Johannine Community a faith that refused to take a christological stand would not have been worthy of a disciple.

Another query, less oriented by outside prejudices, may be directed to the twofold definition of God's commandment in 3:23. Granted the inclusion with 3:11, how good a summary of "the gospel" is this commandment? The double commandment of the Synoptic tradition (Mark 12:28–31, and par.) offers a parallel attempt to say what is crucial: love of God and love of neighbor as yourself. I John offers instead[40] belief in Jesus and love of one another, and the differences are not accidental. As for the first of the two elements, belief in Jesus (as God's Son) is a Johannine interpretation of the love of God: "This is how the love of

[37] I find curiously prejudiced the remark in Bultmann, *Epistles* 59: "When faith is called an *entolē* ('commandment'), it is not thereby understood to be an *ergon* ('work') in the sense of the Pauline antithesis to *pistis* ('faith'). Paradoxically, faith is designated as an *ergon* in Jn 6:29." It is a paradox only if one thinks Paul is the center of the NT.

[38] For I John the verb "to confess" (*homologein*: 2:23; 4:2,3,15) is as important christologically as the verb "to believe" (*pisteuein*: 3:23; 5:1,5,10,13).

[39] Thus Scott, *Fourth Gospel* 267.

[40] One cannot tell how original the Johannine combination is; after all, Gal 5:6 speaks of "faith working through love."

God was revealed in us: that God has sent His only Son into the world
. . . as an atonement for our sins" (I John 4:9–10). And for the second
of the elements, the Johannine Community history of persecution has led
to a stress on the love of one's "brother" or fellow Community member,
rather than a wider love of neighbor. Mussner, "Kurzformel," has
suggested that I John 3:23 might serve very well as the NT sentence that
best expresses the essence of Christianity. The theology that underlies it
makes clear that faith in Jesus is really a faith in God whose Son he is;
that Christian life begins with a vertical action by this God in sending His
Son; that what we do comes after what God has done; and that our love is
a horizontal but essential continuation of the vertical love that God has
shown. In its own way it refutes a dogmatic conservatism which makes
creedal orthodoxy the only criterion, a fideism in which giving of oneself
to Jesus is all that matters, and a liberalism which defines Christianity
simply as a way to live. And it does all this in a pedagogical order
whereby through faith we learn about love.

The last verse of this unit (3:24) shows how far the author is from a
legalistic understanding of keeping the twofold commandment he has
enunciated, for he relates it to abiding in God, the closest type of intimate
union. The two statements he makes about abiding in God supply an interesting contrast. On our part the abiding is conditioned upon keeping
the commandments given by God;[41] but on God's part our abiding stems
from His giving the Spirit, which is not conditioned. The same God who
gave the commandment (3:23c) *gave* the Spirit that enables us to live out
the commandment. The author introduces the notion of the Spirit here in
preparation for the unit on testing the Spirits, which is to follow (4:1–6).
But the sequence from commandment to Spirit, which seems strange to
some commentators,[42] is perfectly understandable if the author is commenting upon the Last Discourse—a comment that in turn is more understandable if Part Two of I John has in mind Part Two of GJohn. The
commandment he has spoken of, "Love one another," is first proclaimed
in John 13:34; and the first Paraclete passages come in 14:15–17,25–26.
The commandment to love is reiterated in 15:12,17; and the next
Paraclete passages come in 15:26–27 and 16:7–13.[43] Besides being associated in the Last Discourse, commandment and Spirit would have been
associated in the catechesis related to conversion/initiation/baptism. If

[41] The logic is that keeping the commandments constitutes a union of the Christian's will with God's will and thus removes any obstacle to mutual love.

[42] Windisch, *Briefe* 126, thinks that the saying about the Spirit may be secondary.

[43] The language of God giving the Spirit employed in I John 3:24d echoes the language of the Father giving the Paraclete in John 14:16. The title "Spirit of Truth"
that the author will use in the next unit (I John 4:6) reflects the alternative title for
the Paraclete in John 14:17; 15:26; 16:13—a title that in the NT only John uses for
the Holy Spirit.

the basic commandment enunciated in 3:23 would have been the stipulation of the New Covenant, Ezekiel (36:27) had made an essential part of the newness-to-come: "I will put my Spirit in your midst." At Qumran (1QS 4:21-22) it is promised that God will pour out the spirit of truth upon those whom he has chosen for an everlasting covenant. And I John 2:27 has already spoken of an anointing (with the Holy Spirit) received by the Johannine Christians, almost certainly when they entered the Community. The reference to baptizing with the Spirit in John 1:33 and to begetting with water and Spirit in John 3:5 makes it very plausible that the notion of God giving the Spirit was associated with the baptismal part of the entrance ceremony.[44] Indeed, the frequency with which the NT uses the verb "to give" in relation to the Spirit may mean that this is a set Christian description for the baptismal conferring of the Spirit.[45]

In NT thought it is not unusual to find the Spirit as a type of criterion or pledge. For instance, Rom 8:14 states, "As many as are led by the Spirit of God are sons of God," while II Cor 1:22 speaks of God "having given the pledge of the Spirit in our hearts." But what precisely does the author of I John mean when he contends that we know that God abides in us "from the Spirit that He gave us" (3:24d)? How does an invisible Spirit that the world cannot see or recognize (John 14:17) show that God abides in us? In the NOTE on 3:24d I mentioned some proposals that are not convincing in my judgment. The answer may be found in the next unit in I John 4:2: "Now this is how you can know the Spirit of God: Everyone who confesses Jesus Christ come in the flesh reflects the Spirit which belongs to God." One may know that God abides in Christians from the fact that they profess a true faith about His Son, and they can do that only if the Paraclete has taught them.[46] This is in perfect harmony with I John 2:27 where no human teacher is needed because the anointing (with the Holy Spirit) teaches the Christians about all things. In the next unit of I John the function of the Spirit/Paraclete as teacher (reflecting John 14:26; 16:13-14) will be combined with the function of the Spirit/Paraclete who bears witness against the world (John 16:8-11); for

---

[44] Bultmann, *Epistles* 60, rejects this, partly because of his theory that sacramental thinking is foreign to the Johannine mainstream (see ABJ 29, cxi-cxiv). Since the secessionist teachers were also baptized (as former members of the Johannine Community), they too claimed the Spirit; and the author handles that objection in the next unit by asking that the Spirits be put to a test.

[45] See Schnackenburg, *Johannesbriefe* 209-15; specifically I Thess 4:8; Rom 5:5; Eph 1:17; II Tim 1:7; Acts 11:16-17; 15:8.

[46] It is implied in Rom 8:15 and Gal 4:6 that the gift of the Spirit makes us (by adoption) God's sons. In Johannine theology the gift of the Spirit brings eternal life that makes us God's children; but the fact that we are God's children and that God abides in us is shown when the Spirit bears witness through us (John 15:26-27). A closer Pauline parallel to this idea would be I Cor 12:3: "No one can say, 'Jesus is Lord,' except in the Holy Spirit."

according to I John 4:2–6 the true faith confessed by those who have the Spirit that belongs to God will unmask the secessionists, who belong to the world. The author's argument against the secessionists in 3:23–24 is by way of reminding his adherents of the time when they left the world to join the Johannine Community, when they were baptized with water and Spirit, when they accepted as part of the New Covenant the commandment to love one another, as through the Spirit they professed Jesus as the Christ, the Son of God, receiving life in his name.

BIBLIOGRAPHY PERTINENT TO I JOHN 3:11–24

Bauer, J. B., "Il misfatto di Caino nel giudizio di S. Giovanni," *Rivista Biblica* 2 (1954) 325–28.

de Kruijf, T. C., "'Nicht wie Kain (der) vom Bösen war . . .' (1 Joh. 3,12)," *Bijdragen* 41 (1980) 47–63.

de la Potterie, I., "Aimer ses frères et croire en Jésus Christ (1 Jn 3, 18–24)," AsSeign 2d series, 26 (1973) 39–45.

Dupont, J., "Comment aimer ses frères (1 Jn 3,13–18)," AsSeign 1st series, 55 (1962) 24–31.

Mussner, F., "Eine neutestamentliche Kurzformel für das Christentum," *Trier Theologische Zeitschrift* 79 (1970) 49–52.

Richardson, C. C., "The Exegesis of I John 3. 19–20. An Ecumenical Misinterpretation?" An unpublished but exhaustive article, which he kindly allowed me to see before his death; I refrained from quoting it, for he was still changing his mind on points.

Sisti, P. A., "La carità dei figli di Dio (1 *Giov.* 3,10–18)," BeO 9 (1967) 77–87.

Spicq, C., "La Justification du Charitable (1 Jo 3,19–21)," *Biblica* 40 (1959) 915–27.

Thyen, H., "'. . . denn wir lieben die Brüder' (1 Joh 3,14)," in *Rechtfertigung: Festschrift für Ernst Käsemann*, ed. J. Friedrich (Tübingen: Mohr, 1976) 527–42.

Wendt, H. H., "Zum ersten Johannesbrief," ZNW 22 (1923) 57–79, esp. 60–63 on 3:19–21.

Wohlenberg, G., "Glossen II" on 3:15,16; and "Glossen III" on 3:18–22.

8. I John 4:1–6: *The Spirits of Truth and of Deceit, and Their Respective Adherents*

1a	**4** ¹BELOVED, do not believe every Spirit;
1b	rather, put these Spirits to a test
1c	to see which belongs to God,
1d	because many false prophets have gone out into the world.
2a	²Now this is how you can know the Spirit of God:
2b	Everyone who confesses Jesus Christ come in the flesh
2c	reflects the Spirit which belongs to God,
3a	³while everyone who negates the importance of Jesus
3b	reflects a Spirit which does not belong to God.
3c	It is rather of the Antichrist,
3d	something which, as you have heard, is to come—
3e	well now, here it is in the world already!
4a	⁴As for you, LITTLE CHILDREN, you belong to God,
4b	and so you have conquered those people;
4c	for he who is in you is greater
4d	than he who is in the world.
5a	⁵Those people belong to the world;
5b	that is why they speak the language of the world
5c	and why the world listens to them.
6a	⁶We belong to God
6b	and anyone who has knowledge of God listens to us,
6c	while anyone who does not belong to God refuses to listen
6d	That is how we can know the Spirit of Truth	to us.
6e	from the Spirit of Deceit.

NOTES

4:1a. *Beloved, do not believe every Spirit.* For the use of *agapētos,* "Beloved," see the NOTE on 2:7a. The three Greek words that come at the end of the line (*panti pneumati pisteuete*) may be a deliberate alliteration, for the author has certain oratorical skills, as we saw in 2:15–17. It is difficult to decide whether his use of the present imperative of *pisteuein* is meant to have iterative force (MGNTG 1, 125): "Do not go on believing," with the implication that there was already a tendency to accept the secessionist teachers as the vehicle of the Spirit. Some would translate *pisteuein* with the dative as "trust"; however, the use of the same construction two verses before (NOTE on 3:23b) with the clear sense of "believe" and even "commit oneself to" requires a strong translation here.

Besides meaning "air, wind" (John 3:8), *pneuma* means "spirit." For precision we may distinguish different NT meanings of "spirit" (cf. THLJ 99–100): (1) the breath or life-principle that God places in human beings (Zech 12:1), so that God is the "Father of spirits" (Heb 12:9); (2) the higher faculty of human nature, the seat of insight, feeling, and will, even as we speak of someone of "noble spirit" or as "lacking in spirit"; (3) the human soul after it has left the body and gone to "the spirit world"; (4) other incorporeal beings who rank above mankind, i.e., the good spirits or angels, and the evil spirits or demons; (5) God's Spirit, the Holy Spirit, which is poured forth on Jesus and given by him to his followers. As for the meaning of *pneuma* in I John 4:1–6, THLJ opts for meaning (2) in the present verse, while Schneider, *Briefe* 171, argues that the author is talking about human spirits under supernatural influence. As I shall explain, I think that we have here primarily a combination of (5) and (4), the Holy Spirit and the Evil Spirit.

This difficulty of interpretation underlies the tendency of translations to paraphrase this line as "Do not believe every *person*, that he has the Spirit (of God)," and the next line as "Test every *manifestation* of the Spirit." But the author is literal about the necessity of believing and testing Spirits, for he is interested in what lies at the root of a person's action. He means here, "Do not believe every Spirit to be the Spirit that God gave us," i.e., the Spirit that he has just mentioned in the preceding verse. He is thinking of two Spirits, divine and diabolic, that manifest themselves in human behavior, and specifically manifest themselves in true and false confessions of faith, as he will make clear in vv. 2–3. A true confession comes from the Spirit of God; an erroneous confession indicates not only the absence of the Spirit of God, but also the presence of the wicked Spirit of Deceit (4:6e). We have here an instance of the opposition described in John 16:11 between the Paraclete (Spirit of Truth) and the Prince of this world, two spiritual forces who exercise their leadership and influence on the children of God and the children of the devil respectively. It is not surprising that a Johannine writer conceives of the Spirit of Truth as dwelling within human beings; for John 14:17 said of him, "He remains with you and is within you." But to find Johannine evidence for the Evil Spirit dwelling within people one must equate the Prince of this world with the devil and Satan. In John 8:44 it is said that people belong to the devil and carry out their "father's" wishes; and in 13:27 Satan is described as entering into Judas. Texts from Ignatius of Antioch indicate how the Prince of this world was conceived as motivating human behavior: "Be not anointed with the evil odor of the teaching of the Prince of this world, lest he lead you away captive from the life which is set before you" (*Eph.* 17:1); "Flee from the wicked arts and snares of the Prince of this world lest . . . you grow weak in love" (*Phld.* 6:2).

We are close here to the thought of the Dead Sea Scrolls. (See the *Bibliography* at the end of this section for significant literature.) In CD 2:11–12,18 we hear how God has made known His holy spirit to those called by name, while the fallen "heavenly watchers" are related to those who walk in stubbornness of heart. But in 1QS 3:17–21 these heavenly forces seem to act within human beings: "God has appointed for human beings two spirits in which to walk until the time of His visitation: the spirits of truth and iniquity. . . . All the sons of righteousness are under the rule of the prince of light and walk in the ways of light, but all the sons of iniquity are under the rule of the angel of darkness and walk in the ways of darkness." The two angelic principles involved (Michael and Beliar) are interiorized, and people walk according to them. As Martini, "Il discernimento" 407, states, "The doctrine of the *Manual* [1QS] presupposes at root ontological objective elements (angelology, fall of angels, and the temptation of man); then almost without notice it changes into a subjective, psychological, ethical, and ascetic plane." If we apply this to I John 4:1a, among the meanings of *pneuma* given above, (5) and (4) have become intermingled with (2) because the Holy Spirit and the Evil Spirit influence and direct each human spirit. The Jewish or Jewish-Christian *T. Judah* 20:1–2 captures this in another way: "Two spirits concern themselves with human beings: the spirit of truth and the spirit of deceit. And in the middle is that (spirit) of understanding of the mind to which it belongs to turn whichever way it will. And what pertains to truth and to deceit is written in the human heart." Sometimes in the *Testaments* the bad spirit is plural, while the good spirit is always singular. When the bad spirit is singular, as in the passage cited, it may be equated with the "Spirit of deceit of Beliar," mentioned in *T. Levi* 3:3 (pl.); *T. Judah* 19:4; *T. Simeon* 2:7. In the NT the good spirit is the Holy Spirit, but again the Evil Spirit can be singular or plural. It is singular here in I John, as also in Eph 2:2–3, which describes "the Prince of the power of the air" as "that spirit which is now at work in the sons of disobedience," while I Tim 4:1 employs a plural: "In later times some will depart from the faith by giving heed to deceitful spirits and to the teachings of demons." A Christian survival of the older two-spirit idea where the good spirit is still an angel is found in the *Shepherd of Hermas* (*Man.* 6.2.1): "There are two angels with human beings: one of righteousness [*dikaiosynē*], one of wickedness [*ponēria*]." Those angels are described as coming into the heart, so that people act accordingly with righteous or wicked deeds. (See de la Potterie, *La vérité* 1, 284–85, for the scholarly debate as to whether in *Hermas* there is the concept of a personal Holy Spirit and how that Spirit might be related to the angelic spirit.)

1bc. *rather, put these Spirits to a test to see which belongs to God.* The present imperative here (more than in the preceding line) may convey continuous action ("keep on testing") because of the number of false prophets involved (the "many" of 4:1d) and their implied success in making converts. This is the only Johannine use of *dokimazein* (22 times in the NT), meaning "to test,

tempt, experiment with." Another verb for "try, attempt," is *peirazein*, occurring in John 6:6 where Jesus tests Philip's reaction. (*Peirazein* often has the
notion of "tempt," while *dokimazein* can cover friendly or neutral tests, as in
testing metals.) Still another verb useful for our discussion is *diakrinein*, "to
judge [*krinein*] between," with the related noun *diakrisis*, "discernment." By
relating the testing of the Spirits to the presence of false prophets, I John reveals that the idea stems from the OT notion of testing prophets. Deuteronomy
13:2-6(1-5) and 18:15-22 make a distinction between the prophet-like-
Moses who speaks the true word of God and so must be heeded, and the
prophet who speaks a word that God has not commanded and so must be
purged from the midst of the people. The author of I John has just these two
types of prophet in mind when, on the one hand, he says, "Listen to us" (4:6b
= heeding the true prophet), while on the other hand he speaks of the "many
false prophets" who "have gone out into the world" (4:1d = the purge of the
false prophets). Already in Deuteronomy the key to whether a prophet is true
or false is what he says about God; in I John 4:2-3 it is what he says about
Jesus. Above we have seen parallels between Qumran and I John on the question of the two Spirits, and so it is not surprising to find a Qumran reference to
a test. When new members entered the Qumran community, they were to be
examined with respect to the practice of the Law, namely, "their spirits" as illustrated by their deeds (1QS 3:13-14). This test was to be repeated every
year thereafter (5:20-21,24), since a correct understanding of the Law according to the interpretation of the Righteous Teacher was as crucial for
Qumran as a correct understanding of Jesus was for Christianity. In these
thought patterns no incorrect presentation of God, the Law, or Jesus is attributed to honest misunderstanding. If the result is evil, the cause must have
been evil; if the result deceives people, the cause must have been the Spirit of
Deceit.

The epistolary author is drawing upon a widely accepted relationship between the spirit and prophecy. The OT notion that the Spirit of the Lord came
upon the prophet (II Chron 15:1; Ezek 2:2; Micah 3:8; Zech 7:12) is carried
over into the NT when John the Baptist, who is to have the role of Elijah, is
filled with the Holy Spirit from his mother's womb, even as his father
Zechariah is filled with the Spirit and prophesies (Luke 1:15,67). Acts 2:17
cites Joel: "I will pour out my Spirit upon all flesh, and your sons and your
daughters shall prophesy" (see also Acts 11:27-28; 21:10-11). A principle is
enunciated by II Pet 1:21: "No prophecy ever originated from the will of man;
but moved by the Holy Spirit, human beings have spoken from God." Ignatius
of Antioch, *Phld.* 7:1-2, claims that when he preached about church order, he
did not speak from humanly gained knowledge but with God's own voice:
"The Spirit was preaching and saying these things." Thus the working of the
Spirit in the prophetic teacher need not imply his making extraordinary statements, but covers even his basic affirmations of ecclesiology and, *a fortiori*, of
christology. There is less material for discussing the relation of false prophecy
to the Evil Spirit, for often these "prophets" were charlatans who were refuted
simply as not having been sent by the Lord (Jer 23:21). However, I Kings

22:22–24 traces false prophecy to a "lying spirit." In apocalyptic literature, where the appearance of false prophets is a diabolic evil of the last times, there is an occasional affirmation that such prophets are moved by the Evil Spirit (p. 335 above). In Rev 13:11–18; 16:13 the Satanic dragon uses as a tool the beast from the earth, which is the false prophet.

Seeking parallels for the testing of the Spirits of prophets, many scholars point to I Cor 12:10 where, after Paul has indicated that prophecy is a gift of the Spirit (also 14:1), he speaks of the "discernments [*diakrisis*] of spirits." However, Paul is clearly talking about a distinction among charisms (for which "spirits" are another designation in 14:12) that would all come from the one, good Spirit, and his words have nothing to do with distinguishing between the Spirit of God and the Evil Spirit. Also, when Paul says, "Let two or three prophets speak, and let the others discern," and "The spirits of prophets are subject to prophets" (I Cor 14:29,32), he is dealing with the problem of the order in which prophets should speak and be heard, so that they should learn from one another. Balz, *Johannesbriefe* 189, correctly argues that the testing of the Spirits in I John 4:1 has nothing to do with the Pauline problem of misunderstood charisms of the one (good) Spirit at Corinth. In I Thess 5:19–22 we hear Paul again, "Do not quench the Spirit; do not despise prophecies; but test [*dokimazein*] everything; hold fast to what is good; and abstain from every kind of evil." This may be somewhat closer to I John in vocabulary, but still is without any suggestion of the involvement of the Evil Spirit. Other Pauline and NT texts that have direct relevance to I John's testing of the Spirits will be treated in the COMMENT.

1d. *because many false prophets have gone out into the world.* There are many biblical varieties of false prophets. Frequently in the OT there were charlatans who pretended to speak God's message about what would happen but actually told kings what they wanted to hear (I Kings 22:6,13). In the NT Bar-Jesus is a false prophet and a magician (Acts 13:6). Matthew 24:24 predicts that in the last times there will be false Christs (messiahs) and false prophets who will show great signs and wonders; and in Rev 19:20 the beast from the earth, which is the false prophet, works deceptive signs. Dodd, *Epistles* 97, thinks that at the time of I John, "The Church still has experience, as in the time of Paul, of inspired prophetic utterance by its members." However, I do not think that the false prophets of I John can be identified with any of these understandings. There is no suggestion that they foretell the future, or are magicians, or work miraculous signs. Nor are they charlatans, nor (*pace* Dodd) is there any indication they have special charisms. (See my objections to proposed I Corinthian parallels in the preceding NOTE.) *All* the author's adherents and *all* the secessionists possess a Spirit; the secessionists are false prophets because the Spirit that moves them is the Spirit of Deceit. Although the author is especially angry against secessionist *teachers* (who may claim for themselves the title of "prophet"), by "false prophets" in 4:1d he means everyone who negates the importance of Jesus (4:3). This negation, which embodies secessionist christology, reflects the Spirit of the Antichrist. The author is identifying the secessionists collectively with the predicted false prophets of the last times who "will deceive many" (Matt 24:11). Their success is their "sign," for they continue to seduce the author's adherents and (seemingly) to win over non-Christians. (Of course, in their own estimation they possess God's Spirit; they speak truly about Christ; and their success is the sign that they are true prophets.) In this usage "prophet" is close to the OT image of one who speaks God's word; and both sides in the Johannine schism share the NT assumption that the Spirit has been poured out on all, who can now speak God's revelation as the Spirit teaches them (Acts 2:17; John 14:15,16,26). Prophet and teacher are closely joined throughout the NT (Acts 13:1; I Cor 12:28), and at times they are virtually indistinguishable (II Pet 2:1; *Didache* 11:3ff.). In the mid-second century the *Apocalypse of Peter* (Achmimic Greek fragment, 1–2; HSNTA 2, 680) lamented: "Many of them shall be false prophets and shall teach ways and diverse doctrines of perdition; and they shall become *sons of perdition*," thus identifying the false prophets and teachers with the apocalyptic figure in II Thess 2:3. In 2:27 the author of I John hinted that there are secessionist false teachers; here he speaks explicitly of the secessionists as false prophets. (Cf. II Peter 2:1, "Just as there arose false prophets among the people, so also there will be false teachers among you"—in I John the false teachers have seceded, while in II Peter they are scattered within the group.) The statement that "*many* false prophets have gone out" does not mean that some have remained but echoes apocalyptic expectations of the volume of evil: "Many false prophets will arise" (Matt 24:11).

Plummer, *Epistles* 95, sees little or no connection between the "many false prophets have gone out into the world" of this verse and the "many Antichrists . . . went out from us" of 2:18–19, since the false prophets may "never have been Christian." However, II John 7 clearly identifies the group by combining words from both references: "Many deceivers have gone out into the world. . . . There is the Antichrist." So did Tertullian, *Adv. Marcion* 5.16.4; CC 1, 711, who states, "Antichrists have gone out into the world." The fact that a perfect tense is used for "gone out" in I John 4:1, as compared with an aorist in 2:19 and II John 7, has been seen by some commentators as a sign that here the author is stressing the permanence of their departure ("have gone out and remain out"). Rather, it reflects the frequent Johannine alternation between the two tenses (NOTE ON 1:1b). Although *Didache* 11:6 designates as a false prophet one who "goes forth" as an apostle and asks for money, the going forth in I and II John is not concerned with an apostle's mission but with secession from the Community. (Nor do we have any evidence that a geographical movement of the secessionists is meant, e.g., from the original Johannine homeland in Palestine to Asia Minor [Belser].) Undoubtedly the secessionists who "have gone out into the world" are making some converts outside the Johannine Community; but the author phrases their departure thus because he wishes to underline their choice of the world, theologically understood as the enemy of Christ. Bultmann, Chaine, Schnackenburg, THLJ, and B. Weiss constitute a formidable group of scholars who would contend that the "world" here is neutral, and that the author is saying no more than that they appeared on earth. I find this interpretation virtually impossible in the light of 4:5 where the author makes it clear that, in going out to the world, the secessionists were going where they belonged. In the dualism of GJohn the enemies of Jesus, including "the Jews," could be lumped together with the world; the epistolary author has taken this language over for his enemies. These false prophets are a parody of Jesus who is the truth: he "went out from the Father and came into the world" (John 16:28; cf. 8:42; 13:3). They are also a parody of true disciples who were "sent into the world" by Jesus (17:18) but did not "belong to the world" (17:14).

2a. *Now this is how you can know the Spirit of God.* Literally, "In this [*en toutō*] you know [*ginōskete*]*.*" According to the classification of *en toutō* passages in 2:3a, this belongs to the (B) category where it is *not* followed by a subordinate clause to which it must refer. Consequently, from sheer grammar "In this" can refer either to what precedes or to what follows. However, in terms of its making good sense almost all scholars agree that here it refers to what follows. (The only way knowledge of the Spirit of God in 4:1b can be related to what precedes is by this unlikely chain of thought: the false prophets have gone out into the world; John 15:18 reports that the world hates Jesus; their affinity for the world shows that they do not have the Spirit of Jesus, which is the Spirit of God.) There is considerable textual confusion about which form of *ginōskein* is to be read. Codices Vaticanus, Alexandrinus, and the corrected Sinaiticus support *ginōskete*, the form I have translated. The Byzantine tradition, the Syriac Peshitta, and the Latin Vulgate favor *ginōsketai*, which appears to be a passive form, "it is known." However, the Johannine writers do not tend to use such an indirect expression in this construction; and in fact, the *ginōsketai* form may be simply an itacism (writing *ai* for *e*). The original hand of Sinaiticus, followed by the Armenian, reads *ginōskomen*, "we know"; but that is almost certainly a scribal attempt to make this passage agree with all other Johannine instances of the verb *ginōskein* following *en toutō*, for they are all in the first plural (in the surrounding units, see 3:16,19,24; 4:13). However, if *ginōskete* is favored both by the textual evidence and by the rule that the more difficult reading was probably original, we still have to ask whether that form is imperative or indicative. An imperative (accepted by KJV and B. Weiss) is favored by the fact that the explanation which follows is not connected to *ginōskete* by *hoti*, "that," as one might expect with the indicative ("you know that"). Yet, nowhere else is the Johannine *en toutō* followed by an imperative, and the genius of this phrase seems to demand that a way of knowing be offered, not commanded. A command to know might imply that the audience did not already have knowledge through anointing by the Spirit (2:27). Note too that the variant readings are indicative. In general, therefore, scholars favor the indicative (Alexander, Brooke, Bultmann, Chaine, Malatesta, Marshall, Plummer, Schnackenburg, Stott, THLJ, and the RSV). This is the only example in the Johannine writings of the expression "the Spirit of God"; the Epistles never speak of "the Holy Spirit."

2bc. *Everyone who confesses Jesus Christ come in the flesh reflects the Spirit which belongs to God.* Literally, "Every Spirit that confesses Jesus Christ come in flesh is from God," a translation that might give the wrong impression of as many Spirits of God as there are true confessors. My use of "everyone" here (and in the antithetic parallel in 4:3), which introduces human beings as those who make the confession, does no violence to the author's thought; for he is offering an external criterion for which Spirit is at the root of the actions of two groups of people (Chaine, *Epîtres* 197). He shows this in vv. 4b,5a where he suddenly shifts over to "you (people)" and "those people," despite his previous reference to Spirits in vv. 2,3.

Here and in II John 7 we find Jesus Christ described as come/coming *in (the) flesh*. In the NOTE on 2:16b we saw that "flesh" covers the human within men and women, as distinct from the divine. The author's warning there against "the desire of the flesh" has not led him to undervalue the importance of the flesh of Jesus. He may be reflecting a widespread Christian phraseology, for I Tim 3:16 speaks of the "confessedly great" mystery of him who "was revealed [*phaneroun*] in the flesh." The epistolary author speaks of the Spirit being "from God," using the *einai ek* construction, which I translate "belong to" (see NOTE on 2:16ef). Each of the three "belong to God" phrases in this unit (4:2c,4a,6a) has a counterposed "belong to" phrase, namely, "not belong to God" (4:3b), "belong to the world" (4:5a), and "not belong to God" (4:6c). If here it is the Spirit that belongs to God, in v. 4a it will be "you" (the true Johannine Community) who belong to God; and in v. 6a it will be "we" (the general Johannine Community or the special Johannine School of 1:1–5) who belong to God.

In the expression "come in the flesh" Codices Sinaiticus, Alexandrinus, and Ephraemi Rescriptus read a perfect participle of the verb *erchesthai*, "to come," while Vaticanus reads a perfect infinitive. The latter is better Greek and is probably a scribal "improvement" of the somewhat awkward participle. (The use of an infinitive in set christological formulas, e.g., Acts 8:37, also may have influenced the scribe.) When Polycarp, *Philip.* 7:1, quoted this passage (pp. 8–9 above), apparently he made the same correction: "Everyone who does not confess Jesus Christ to have come [perf. infin.] in the flesh is the Antichrist." (The last part of Polycarp reflects II John 7, which is literally, "Many deceivers went out into the world not confessing Jesus Christ coming [pres. ptcp.] in flesh. This is . . . the Antichrist.") Accepting the perf. ptcp. reading in the present verse, one is faced with three possible ways to translate it. In discussing these below, I shall pay attention to what the author may have meant. (Too often scholars have been distracted by speculating that there was a somewhat similar *secessionist* slogan which the author corrected in order to achieve the present wording.) (a) *"Confesses Jesus Christ come in the flesh,"* a translation where the verb "confesses" has only one object, namely, the phrase "Jesus Christ come in the flesh" taken as a unit. Bonsirven, Brooke, Sánchez Mielgo, THLJ, and Westcott opt for this possibility. It is favored by the parallel in II John 7 and by one of the two possible textual readings of the parallel in the next verse: "Everyone who does not confess Jesus"—such a reading of 4:3a (which I do not accept as original) understood the verb "to confess" to have a single object. (b) *"Confesses Jesus Christ as come in the flesh,"* a translation where the verb "confesses" has a double object (BDF 416³). Chaine and

B. Weiss opt for this possibility. Evidently Codex Vaticanus (and Polycarp) understood the passage in this way, as indicated by the substitution of the infinitive for the participle—a more grammatical way of expressing the basic idea. A difficulty faced by this translation (which puts more emphasis on the manner of coming rather than the status after coming) is that "Jesus Christ" becomes the name of the preexistent or preincarnate, who is not so designated elsewhere in John. If I am right, the author's theology is that only in the incarnate (namely, Jesus of the flesh) does one find "the Christ," a designation for the salvific aspect of the Word's career. (c) *"Confesses Jesus as the Christ come in the flesh,"* a translation where again the verb "confesses" has a double object. Alexander, Houlden, Serafín de Ausejo, and Stott opt for this possibility. Often cited in support is John 9:22, "Anyone who confesses him [Jesus] as Christ"; there, however, the verb is placed between the two objects, rather than coming at the beginning as here. A better parallel is Rom 10:9, literally, "If you confess with your mouth Lord Jesus," which is best understood to mean "confess Jesus as Lord." In I John 4:15 one finds a parallel idea, "Whenever anyone confesses that Jesus is the Son of God"; but there the author inserts the verb "to be" between the two nouns, as he does also in 2:22. The absence of a copula that might relate such a long second object to the first object is a grammatical objection to this translation of 4:2b. Another objection is the absence of a Greek article before the second object ("*the* Christ") or, alternatively, before the postpositive ptcp. that modifies that object ("Christ, the one who has come in the flesh" (BDF 412[3]; also 272—cf. Ignatius, *Magn.* 7:2, "Hasten . . . to one Jesus Christ, *the* one who has come forth from the one Father"). At least, however, this translation does not face the theological objection raised by (b) above, namely that "Christ" becomes the name of the preincarnate (although some have unwarrantedly assumed that 4:2b is meant to refute the position of Cerinthus that "Christ" descended upon Jesus at baptism—see Appendix II).

When all factors are taken into account, translation (a) seems best. The import of that translation is to put emphasis on the person modally understood: there is no separation between "Jesus" and "Christ," and the individual involved must be understood in terms of his career in the flesh. It must be noted that the author says "come in the flesh," not "come into the flesh," and so the act of incarnation is not the point. (*A fortiori,* Johannine thought does not imagine a preformed flesh or body into which the Word came; rather "the Word became flesh": John 1:14.) Houlden, *Epistles* 107, finds the epistolary author inconsistent in being antiworld but pro-flesh. I would not agree since "world" does not mean "earth" but refers to a realm and people with a set attitude of disbelief toward Jesus; it offers little parallelism to "flesh," which is simply earthly human nature. In I John 4:2b one is tempted to press the value of the perf. tense of the ptcp. as emphasizing the enduring result of a past coming: he came and remained in the flesh. However, such tense value is probably foreign to the Epistles, since II John 7 uses the pres. ptcp. in this formula, while I John 5:6 has an aorist finite verb: "Jesus Christ—he is the one who came by water and blood." At least one can argue that there is no stress on a punctiliar view of the coming. This text gives little support to those scholars who have assumed that the secessionists denied that there was a real incarnation.

3ab. *while everyone who negates the importance of Jesus reflects a Spirit which does not belong to God.* Literally, "and every Spirit that *does not confess* Jesus is not from God," or "and every Spirit that *annuls* Jesus is not from God." The initial *kai,* "and," is adversative (= "but": BDF 442[1]). Obviously this is in antithetical parallelism to the preceding statement, and scribes have been busy making the conformity more exact. After "Jesus" the Byzantine tradition adds the same words found in 4:2b: "Christ come in the flesh." Codex Sinaiticus adds "Lord come in the flesh," seemingly combining I John 4:2b with Rom 10:9: "If you confess . . . Jesus as Lord."

A much greater textual problem is whether scribal imitation of the preceding statement in 4:2b has affected the choice of the main verb in 4:3a. There are two candidates as indicated by the alternative literal readings italicized above. The translation "does not confess" renders *mē homologei,* which is simply the negative of *homologei* in 4:2b. This is the reading in the body of the text of all extant Greek MSS. and of all versions except the Latin. Normally such textual support would be more than adequate to establish it as the original text. The translation "annuls" renders *lyei* from the verb *lyein,* "to loosen, dissolve, destroy, make nothing of." This reading is supported by Greek patristic evidence and by Latin evidence. By way of *Greek evidence* for "annuls," von der Goltz, "Arbeit," describes Mount Athos Codex 1739 in Laura Athanasius 184 (B. 64), copied in the tenth century in Caesarea of Cappadocia from a sixth-century predecessor. While this codex reads *mē homologei* in the body of the page, it reads *lyei* in the margin with the following comment in Greek: "Thus Irenaeus in Book 3 of *Adversus haereses;* Origen clearly in Book 8 of his *Commentary on Romans;* and Clement the Stromateus [of Alexandria] in his *About the Pasch.*" That annotation agrees partially with the information supplied by the Greek historian Socrates (*ca.* A.D. 440) that the reading "annuls" was found in old copies of the Scriptures but had been tampered with in favor of "does not confess" by the Nestorians (*Ecclesiastical History* 7.32; PG 67, 812A). Of the Greek Fathers mentioned in the Mount Athos marginal comment, while we do not have the Greek original of Irenaeus, *Adv. haer.* 3.16.8, the Latin reads *solvit,* "dissolves," from *solvere,* reflecting the Greek *lyein.* We do not have preserved in either Greek or Latin a citation of I John 4:3 in Origen's *Commentary on Romans,* but the Latin of his *Commentary on Matthew* 65; GCS 38, 152, uses *solvit.* In the Greek of his *Commentary on Matthew* 16.8; GCS 40, 500, he writes, "I do not loosen [*lyein*] Jesus from Christ," which seems to be a reuse of I John 4:3. We do not have Clement of Alexandria's work *About the Pasch;* but *Adumbrationes* (GCS 17, 215; the Latin summary of Clement's lost *Hypotyposeis,* which contains his commentary on II John) has these words, probably echoing II John 7, which is very close to I John 4:2–3: ". . . so that no person divides [*dividere,* another way of rendering *lyein*] Jesus Christ but rather believes that the one Jesus Christ came in the flesh." Thus it seems certain that Clement knew the reading "annuls."

By way of *Latin evidence* for "annuls," *solvere*, besides being used in the fourth-century Vulgate, appears in all the Old Latin MSS. (except Codex r or 64, a seventh-century Munich MS.); this means it was known in the second century. In A.D. 210 Tertullian, *Adv. Marcion* 5.16.4; CC 1, 711, attacks "spirits who are precursors of the Antichrist who deny Christ to have come in the flesh and so dissolve [*solvere*] Jesus." In the next century Lucifer of Cagliari, Priscillian, and Augustine show knowledge of the "annuls" reading.

Besides the Greek patristic and Latin textual evidence, we must consider the logical arguments that support the "annuls" reading against the overwhelming Greek textual evidence for "does not confess." If the latter (*mē homologei*) were the original reading in 4:3a, why would a later scribe have destroyed the parallelism to *homologei* in 4:2b? He would be doing this by introducing *lyei* ("annuls") governing a personal object, a construction found nowhere else in the Johannine writings. In the opposite direction, *mē homologei* could easily have arisen from scribal imitation of "confesses" (*homologei*) in 4:2b, especially under the influence of the closely parallel statement in II John 7 (*mē homologountes*). We see evidence of this process of harmonization at work already in Polycarp, *Philip.* 7:1, which seems to combine I John 4:2 with II John 7 to give an echo of I John 4:3 (pp. 8–9 above). A. Rahlfs, TLZ 40 (1915) 525, correctly observes that the "does not confess" reading, with its use of *mē* before a finite verb form, is dubious grammar (also BDF 428[4] versus Law, *Tests* 396); it may have arisen from a slavish imitation of II John 7 where *mē* is appropriate before a participle (BDF 430).

Harnack, "Textkritik" 559–60, asks, if the epistolary author had written "does not confess Jesus" in I John 4:3a, would his formula have been truly effective against his secessionist opponents? Elsewhere in his attempts to formulate christological formulas against them he always adds a designation of Jesus, namely, that he is the Christ or the Son of God (an addition made here by later scribes who accepted the "do not confess" reading). THLJ 103 argues that "does not confess Jesus" can make sense in 4:3 because it means "does not declare publicly belief in the man Jesus"; but more likely this reading means that the person who does not confess Jesus Christ come in the flesh (4:2b) does not confess Jesus in any real sense. Be that as it may, would not "annuls Jesus" have been a more effective anti-secessionist formula?

Many scholars who reject the *lyei* reading (Brooke, Hoskyns, Metzger, B. Weiss, Windisch, Wurm) suggest that it was introduced into the text of I John by scribes defending an orthodox christology against second-century heretics, e.g., Cerinthus, docetists, or gnostics, who made a distinction between a spiritual Christ and a Jesus of the flesh. However, this argument is dubious on two scores. First, in the works of the orthodox church fathers writing against forms of docetism, we do not find the verb *lyein* playing a significant part. Second, the validity of positing such an antidocetic origin for *lyein* depends on rendering it as "divides" (the Latin understanding reflected in the choice of *solvere* and *dividere*). Piper, "I John," and Wilder, "Introduction" 275–76, reject that, for *lyein* also means "annuls" or "destroys" (BAG 485 and BAGD 483, under section 4). The only other Johannine epistolary use of *lyein* is in I John

3:8 for *destroying* the works of the devil; and indeed *lyein,* meaning "render ineffective, nullify," seems to have been standard in formulas for *destroying* the power of evil (Piper, "I John" 443–44). We find in Ignatius, *Eph.* 13:1: "When you gather together frequently [for eucharist], the powers of Satan are wrecked and his mischief is annulled [*lyein*] by the concord of your faith." In *Eph.* 19:3 Ignatius says that at the nativity of Jesus "all magic was annulled." This would match the mind of the author of I John for whom the secessionist refusal to confess Jesus Christ come in the flesh (4:2) amounts to depriving Jesus of all meaning, thus annulling him and allowing the Evil Spirit to triumph. It fits the author's attribution of the condemned christological attitude to the Antichrist. Evaluating all these arguments, I join BDF, Büchsel, Bultmann, Chaine, Harnack, Haupt, Piper, Preisker, Rahlfs, Schnackenburg, Vawter, Wengst, Wilder, and Zahn in preferring *lyei*, "annuls," as the original reading.

3c. *It is rather of the Antichrist.* Literally, "And this is . . . ," wherein a neuter demonstrative pronoun refers back to 3a: "Every Spirit that negates the importance [*lyei*] of Jesus." The subject, then, would be "Spirit," but in its dimension of annulling Jesus, a dimension that is a specific aspect of the Evil "Spirit which does not belong to God" (3b). The predicate, "is of the Antichrist" (*einai*, "to be," plus the genitive), is not an exact grammatical parallel to the predicate of the statements in 4:2c and 3b ("belong to God" and "does not belong to God," which used *einai* plus *ek*). The *einai ek* clause, as we saw in the NOTE on 2:16ef, includes both origin and appurtenance, for the Holy Spirit comes from God. The Evil Spirit, however, does not come from the Antichrist; rather it produces him. The Vulgate understands *einai* in the present line to be accompanied by an epexegetical genitive: "is the Antichrist." Such a translation creates a seeming conflict with 2:18. There the secessionists themselves are the Antichrist, while here the Spirit that motivates them is the Antichrist. This conflict is removed if we recognize the genitive as qualitative: an Evil Spirit that is characteristic of eschatological opposition to Christ is manifesting itself in Antichrists who negate the importance of Jesus. Chaine, *Epîtres* 198, is not exact when he describes the Antichrist as a being of reason who lives within the false teachers; rather the Evil Spirit dwells within them and makes them play the role of the Antichrist. The secessionists are not only a manifestation of evil; they manifest *eschatological* evil.

3d. *something which, as you have heard, is to come.* Literally, "which you have heard that it is coming," with the perf. tense indicating that the author is speaking of a traditional expectation. The neuter suggests that the author prefers to continue speaking of "the Spirit of the Antichrist," rather than shifting to "the Antichrist who. . . ." This makes it easier for him to historicize in terms of the secessionists ("Those people" of 4:5) the expected monstrous opponent of Christ. We are close to I John 2:18b, "You heard that Antichrist is to come"; and as I indicated at the end of the NOTE on that line, there is probably a play on the designation of Jesus as "the one who is to come."

3e. *well now, here it is in the world already!* This resembles 2:18c, "Well, now many Antichrists have made their appearance," which also begins with a *kai nyn*, "and now" (see NOTE there). Here *ēdē*, "already," comes last in the sentence for emphasis, as in John 9:27 (but not John 4:35, since there it should be read with 4:36; see ABJ 29, 174). As I indicated in discussing 4:1d above, "in the world" means more than "on the earth"; and so the author says more here than in 2:18c, just cited. He is referring to the realm of "the Prince of this world" and indicating that the eschatological moment of evil activity in that realm has now arrived.

4a. *As for you, Little Children, you belong to God.* The use of *hymeis*, "you," by way of emphasis and contrast in order to start a new strophe was seen in 2:20,24,27, the last unit that dealt specifically with the Antichrist. "Little Children" (*teknion*; see NOTE on 2:1a) began a new strophe in the previous unit (3:18a). Here it emphasizes that the author is shifting from talking about the Spirits to talking about the people who live by those Spirits. In 4:2a (the first of three *einai ek* clauses in this unit governing "God") we heard of "the Spirit which belongs to God"; now we hear about a "you" (the author's adherents) who "belong to God"; and they will be contrasted in the next verse with those who "belong to the world."

4b. *and so you have conquered those people.* Literally, "conquered them." As I explained in the NOTE on 4:2bc above, although in 4:2–3 the author was contrasting two Spirits, he was really contrasting people who live by the respective Spirits and who now suddenly appear as "you" and "them." The "them" is a reference to the secessionist false prophets of 4:1d. "Conquer" is the verb *nikan*, the objects of which in Johannine usage include the Evil One, the Antichrists, and the world (NOTE on 2:13d). In 2:13 one section of the author's Little Children were singled out as having conquered the Evil One, namely, the "Young People" (*neaniskoi*); here all the Little Children are assured of victory.

4cd. *for he who is in you is greater than he who is in the world.* In 3:20b the author has *meizōn*, "greater," governing the classical genitive of comparison; here he uses the comparative particle *ē*, "than," which is not unusual for Johannine style (John 3:19; 4:1; see BDF 185[2]). Having contrasted the Johannine Christians ("you") with the secessionists ("those people"), the author returns to comparing the personal, superhuman forces who "are in" the respective human antagonists. (The "is in" construction is *einai en* discussed in the NOTE on 1:5e.) The idea of invisible heavenly spirits who are stronger than earthly opponents (who have their own resources) is not foreign to the OT: when Elisha saw the Syrian armies and chariots drawn up, he said, "Fear not, for those who are with us [God and his heavenly armies] are more than those who are with them" (II Kings 6:16).

In I John whom does the author mean by "he who is in you"? Bonsirven, Brooke, Bultmann, Chaine, Hauck, Houlden, Marshall, Schneider, THLJ, B. Weiss, and Wilder think of God the Father, pointing out that victory is attributed to God in I Cor 15:57; see also the reference to the strength of the Lord in Eph 6:10. However, the Father is never said "to be in" (*einai en*) the Christian in the Johannine writings, even though He is said "to abide in" (*menein en*) the Christian (I John 3:24; 4:12,13,15,16). Erdmann and Westcott (?) think that "he who is in you" is Christ; and, in fact, *einai en* is used for Christ in the Christian in John 14:20,23; 17:23,26. However, nowhere in the immediate context of I John 4:4 is Jesus described as a personal agent. I agree with Alexander (?), Bruce, and Stott that the contrast between "he who is in you" and "he who is in the world" continues the contrast between "the Spirit which belongs to God" and "the Spirit of the Antichrist which does not belong to God" (4:2–3), and anticipates the contrast between the Spirit of Truth and the Spirit of Deceit in 4:6de. "He who is in you" echoes the description of the Paraclete/Spirit of Truth in John 14:16–17, where Jesus says that this Spirit is to "be with you" and "be in you" (*einai en*). The antagonism of the Paraclete/Spirit toward the world is the subject of John 14:17; 16:8–11. The power to conquer is attributed to the Spirit of God in Zech 4:6, while at Qumran the angelic Spirit of Truth is destined ultimately to conquer the angel of darkness (1QS 3:17–25).

There is no doubt that "he who is in the world" is the figure whom John calls "the Prince of this world" (12:31; 14:30; 16:11), and whom the epistolary author designates as the Spirit of the Antichrist, which does not belong to God (I John 4:3), and as the Spirit of Deceit (4:6). (Ephesians 2:2 equates "the Prince of the power of the air" with "the Spirit that is now at work in the sons of disobedience.") In 2:13–14 the author told a group of Johannine Christians, "You have conquered the Evil One"; now he explains that this victory was won by the Holy Spirit which is greater than the Evil Spirit, and that it has been won in terms of a victory over the secessionists. Bultmann, *Epistles* 63, who argued that "world" in 4:3 means simply the perceptible world, is forced to admit that in 4:4–5 it means a realm of hostility to God. I would argue that the latter is the meaning throughout.

5a. *Those people belong to the world.* Literally, "They are from [*einai ek*; NOTE 2:16ef] the world." This is not surprising because their Spirit is the Prince of this world. The author's Johannine Christians were told in 4:4a, "You belong to God," and in 2:19 that those who went out "did not really belong to us." In this unit "world" is used 4 times in 4 lines; cf. 3 times each in John 1:10; 3:17; 17:14; and 5 times in 15:19.

5b. *that is why they speak the language of the world.* Literally, "For this reason [*dia touto*] from the world they speak." In the NOTE on 3:1de I pointed out that where there is no following epexegetical *hoti* clause, *dia touto* points to what precedes. Clearly that is the case here: it is because "those people belong to [*einai ek*] the world" (4:5a) that "they speak the language of [*lalein ek*] the world." In John 3:31 we have affirmed the relationship of speech to the origin of the speaker: "The one from the earth belongs to [*einai ek*] the earth and speaks the language of [*lalein ek*] the earth."

5c. *and why the world listens to them.* Besides affirming connaturality (the world recognizes its own), this statement hints at the success of the secessionists. Paradoxically, the Pharisees complained about the success of Jesus in somewhat similar terms: "Look, the world has run off after him" (John 12:19). The Greek here (*akouein*, "to hear," with the genitive) implies audition with acceptance. The author has shifted from speaking to listening, and that theme will dominate the next verse.

6a. *We belong to God.* As I explained in the NOTE on 1:1b above, there are two uses of "we" as a genuine plural in I John: (1) a nondistinctive use where the author joins himself with his "brothers" in the Johannine Community *with-*

out calling attention to another intra-Community group ("you") which is not included; and (2) a distinctive use where the "we" of the Johannine tradition-bearers or Johannine School addresses the other members of the Community as "you." The latter "we" was last encountered in I John 1:1–5; and since then the author has spoken as "I" when he wished to give advice or instruction to the "you" of the Johannine Community whom he considers his "Little Children." What "we" is involved here? Because the author has already said in 4:4a, "Little Children, *you* belong to God," Bonsirven, Chaine, Houlden, Plummer, Stott, and B. Weiss are among the scholars who assume that the distinctive "we" of the Johannine tradition-bearers is meant here. This interpretation receives support from the next line (4:6b): "Anyone who has knowledge of God listens to us," a claim with a touch of authority not unlike that which runs through 1:1–5. The three "belong to God" statements in the present unit would then give a neat progression: in v. 2 the Spirit belongs to God; in v. 4 the "you" of the author's Little Children belong to God (because the Spirit confesses through the Johannine Christians); and in v. 6 the "we" of the Johannine School of tradition-bearers belong to God (and serve as the "mouthpiece" of the Spirit of Truth: John 15:26–27). However, a solid group of scholars (Bultmann, Harnack, Schnackenburg, Schneider, THLJ, Windisch) argues here for the nondistinctive "we," referring to the whole Johannine Community (including the tradition-bearers), a "we" not really distinct from the "you" of v. 4. Elsewhere, it is argued, the author shifts back and forth between a plural "you" and a nondistinctive "we," both meaning the Johannine Community, e.g., 2:19–20,24–26,28; 3:13–14; 5:13–14. However, in many such cases he also speaks as "I" in addressing the "you" of the Community (2:20–21,25–6; 5:13–14); and so they offer precedent for the first and second person being used to distinguish between tradition-bearer and Community. A more impressive argument for the nondistinctive "we" in 4:6a is the clearly nondistinctive "we" in 4:6de: "We can know the Spirit of Truth from the Spirit of Deceit"—the whole purpose of the unit has been to get the *Community members* to distinguish between the two Spirits.

A decision between the distinctive and nondistinctive use of "we" is difficult here, but overall I am inclined toward the latter. In 4:1d the author has referred to the secessionists as a whole as "false prophets," even though such a description implicitly underlines their leaders. In 4:5 he has referred to the secessionists as a whole when he said that "those people" speak the language of the world, even though, once again, he may be thinking especially of their spokesmen and "theologians." It would seem his style here to be thinking of the Johannine Community as a whole when he emphasizes that "We belong to God" and that there is a necessity of listening "to us," even though he is implicitly underlining his own role and that of the other Johannine tradition-bearers as spokesmen for the Community's christology. Throughout 4:4–6, then, there would be only two groups involved: the "you" or "we" of the Johannine Community, and "those people" who are the secessionists.

6bc. *anyone who has knowledge of God listens to us, while anyone who does not belong to God refuses to listen to us.* Codex Alexandrinus omits the whole second clause ("while . . ."). Grammatically the two clauses are not exactly parallel; for the first is a present ptcp. (literally, "the one knowing God"), while the second is introduced by a relative pronoun (literally, "he who is not from God"). To some this may sound like a statement of predestination, involving a world in the grasp of the Evil One (I John 5:19), incapable of hearing a message of salvation, and on the other hand people who are by nature disposed toward God (the *anima naturaliter christiana*). Dodd, *Epistles* 100–1, points to John 10:3–5 where the sheep that (are destined to) belong to the Good Shepherd recognize his voice when he calls their names. However, as Dodd recognizes, one cannot divorce either statement from the history of the Johannine Community by making it an ontological affirmation. In GJohn the evangelist is assuring persecuted Johannine Christians who have been expelled from the synagogue that by divine providence they are Jesus' own sheep whom he will lead and feed. In I John the author is reassuring his adherents that they belong to God, as they confront the large, successful secessionist movement. Missionary success is a criterion by which people judge God to be on their side, and undoubtedly the secessionists invoked that. Where such success is lacking, a group will often fall back on the opposite criterion of God's special providence for the few. (See the two opposing criteria in Luke 24:47 and 6:26, respectively.) The Johannine Jesus envisions some missionary success for the disciples in John 17:20, but prepares for failure before the world in 15:19. Thus, no profound issue of predestination is involved here, but the dualism of decision that is a constant in Johannine literature. In GJohn the dualism centered on the decision whether or not to listen to Jesus; in I John it is centered on the decision whether or not to listen to the Johannine proclamation as it is presented among the author's adherents.

6de. *That is how we can know the Spirit of Truth from the Spirit of Deceit.* Literally, *"From this* we know . . . ," the only epistolary use of *ek toutou,* which occurs twice in GJohn (6:66; 19:12) to introduce something that takes place because of and after what has preceded. MGNTG 3, 260 recognizes this connotation by pointing out the causal sense of *ek.* Inevitably scholars have compared *ek toutou* to the more frequent *en toutō* (NOTE on 2:3a). Westcott, *Epistles* 146, argues, as always, for Johannine exactness: *en toutō* refers to a fact that is in itself a direct indication of what is perceived, while *ek toutou* implies a further process by which the conclusion is reached. Brooke, *Epistles* 116, thinks *ek toutou* may offer a less obvious criterion. Rejecting such distinctions as overprecision, I find little difference between the two phrases, except that *ek toutou* refers unambiguously to what has preceded (while *en toutō* can point in either direction). But to how much of what has preceded does 4:6d refer? Is it to the whole of 4:1–6 (Alexander, Dodd, Wilder), to 4:4–6 (Marshall?), or to 4:6abc (Brooke, Schnackenburg?, Schneider, THLJ?)? I suggest that *ek toutou* catches up the *en toutō* of 3:24c, which leads into this unit: "Now *this is how* we can know that He abides in us: from the Spirit that He gave us." Moreover, the reference in 4:6de to knowing the Spirit of Truth from the Spirit of Deceit resumes the theme of 4:1b: "Put these Spirits to a test." Thus we have an inclusion indicating that *ek toutou* refers to the whole unit (4:1–6, introduced by 3:24cd). The counterargument that 4:2–3 offers a criterion of confessing while 4:6 offers a different criterion of listening is confusing: The confession is what must be listened to, and so there is only one criterion. The "we" of "we can know" has to refer to the whole Johannine Community since the purpose of this unit has been to offer the author's adherents a way of knowing "the Spirit that God gave *us*" (3:24d; cf. 4:1).

As with 4:1a (see NOTE there), scholars argue whether the spirits of truth and deceit are superhuman Spirits (the Holy Spirit and the Evil Spirit) or are primarily human spirits. Yet I would judge that 4:6 clarifies the obscure reference to spirits in 4:1, indicating that both passages refer to superhuman Spirits exercising influence over human spirits. As in John 14:17; 15:26, 16:13, "the Spirit of Truth" is another name for the Paraclete or Holy Spirit. In I John 5:6 the author says, "The Spirit is the truth"; and so he means more than that the Spirit leads to truth—it is a Spirit whose essential quality is truth, for it is the Spirit of Jesus who is the truth (John 14:6). The contrasting title, "the Spirit of Deceit," occurs nowhere else in the NT as a designation for the Prince of this world or the devil/Satan. However, in the NOTE on *planan*, "to deceive," in 1:8b, I pointed to Rev 12:9 (*Did.* 16:4) where the devil is called "the deceiver of the whole earth," while I Tim 4:1 speaks of "deceitful spirits." Both there and in the first NOTE of the present unit, I discussed the dualistic distinction between the spirit of truth and the spirit of deceit in the Dead Sea Scrolls and the *Testaments of the Patriarchs,* namely, two angels who establish a dominion in and over respective human spirits. The title "The Spirit of Deceit" for Satan is appropriate in the present context of the last hour and the Antichrist, as II John 7 recognizes when it equates the Deceiver and the Antichrist. Matthew 24:11 expects the false prophets of the end-time to "deceive many"; and II Thess 2:11, in its description of the lawless one through whom Satan will work miracles as a parody of Christ, mentions "a powerful deception so that they will believe the lie." The present passage makes clear that for the author the Antichrist(s) is/are not the primary actor, for the deceit comes from an Evil Spirit. Like the Spirit of Truth, the Spirit of Deceit is so named, not only because he promotes deceit, but because he is deceptive by his nature. "When he tells a lie, he speaks his native language, for he is a liar and the father of lying" (John 8:44).

COMMENT

There is little doubt among scholars that 4:1–6 constitutes a unit.[1] There is a discrete subject,[2] namely, the theme of the two Spirits that are in human beings and how to distinguish between them. Stylistically there is

[1] B. Weiss is an exception in positing 4:1–13 as a unit, with 1–6 and 7–13 as subunits.
[2] The first epistolary instance of "Spirit" is in 3:24d; it does not occur again (except for a passing reference in 4:13) until 5:6–8.

an inclusion between the beginning (3:24cd + 4:1) and the end (4:6), which may be combined thus: "Now this is how we can know that He abides in us: from the Spirit that He gave us. Beloved, do not believe every Spirit; rather put the Spirits to a test. . . . That is how we can know the Spirit of Truth from the Spirit of Deceit." If one takes into account the larger structure of I John, it must be noted that the end of the last unit (3:23) enunciated a twofold commandment: *to believe* in the name of Jesus Christ, and *to love* one another as God commanded. The present unit (4:1–6) concentrates on the Spirit-given ability to confess Jesus Christ truly as one come in the flesh; the next unit (4:7–5:4a) will concentrate on the implications of loving one another; and so we have a unit on each aspect of the twofold commandment. Many scholars have correctly observed that 4:1–6 has many themes in common with an earlier unit (2:18–27)[3] in Part One of I John. However, I find unconvincing the claim that these two units have parallel positions in the schema of their respective Parts. Certainly Part Two of I John picks up and continues the theme of "the last hour" from Part One (2:18), chiefly in terms of comforting and reassuring the author's adherents, but there is no neat parallel sequence of units in the respective Parts.

Within the unit there is a clear subdivision between vv. 1–3 and 4–6. The addresses "Beloved" in v. 1 and "Little Children" in v. 4 mark the subdivision (as sometimes in previous units: 2:28; 3:7,18; see 4:7,11). The two subunits are of equal length (twelve lines in my translation). The first subunit describes how to recognize the two Spirits that manifest themselves in human behavior, while the second assures the author's adherents that they possess the Spirit of Truth, which is more powerful than the Spirit of Deceit so active in the secessionists. Within the first subunit some would detect a chiastic arrangement (abc/c'b'a'):

a.   1d: false prophets have gone out into the world
b.   2a: the Spirit of God
c.   2bc: Everyone who confesses Jesus . . . reflects the Spirit which belongs to God
c'. 3ab: Everyone who negates Jesus reflects a Spirit which does not belong to God
b'. 3c: the Spirit of the Antichrist
a'. 3e: Antichrist . . . in the world already

---

[3] Besides the common themes of the going out of the Antichrists, lying/deceit, and a true christological confession, one may include the Spirit if the anointing from the Holy One (2:20,27) is a reference to the Spirit. In 2:20–22 that anointing makes a christological confession possible, even as in 4:2 such a confession reflects the Spirit that belongs to God.

A. *Distinguishing the Spirit of God from that of the Antichrist* (4:1–3)

At the end of the preceding unit the author spoke of the twofold commandment to believe and to love; and so, while he concentrates on belief and its true confession here, he addresses those who make that confession as "Beloved." (Implicit in his thought is the thesis that a false confession leads to secession and thus to a sin against brotherly love.) Although some scholars see the key statement, "Many false prophets have gone out into the world," as no more than a general affirmation that there are people, Christian and non-Christian, controlled by the passions of this world,[4] I have argued in the NOTES that the false prophets are the secessionist deceivers who went out from the Community and aligned themselves with the hostile world (I John 2:18–19; II John 7). In so doing they found their spiritual home: It was the Evil Spirit that led them to distort Jesus to the point of negation, and the world to which they have gone is the realm of which that Spirit is "the Prince." In GJohn "the world" became a designation for all those who rejected Jesus, preferring darkness to light (3:19; 7:7; 16:33); in I John it comes to include those who once appeared to be Jesus' followers but whose christology is tantamount to a denial of him. If the secessionists are the false prophets who have gone out into the world, they are already known and visible. Why then is a criterion needed for putting their Spirit to the test? The criterion is for the sake of the author's adherents to help them against the secessionists' seductive claim to have the Spirit of God and to speak the truth. He wants his "Beloved" to realize that, instead of coming to know God better, those who "go out" acknowledge the supremacy of the Spirit that does not belong to God.

Testing the Spirits, then, has nothing to do with Paul's idea of discerning the (good) spirits or charisms among the Corinthian Christians (I Cor 12:4ff.). The Pauline charisms are all manifestations of the same Holy Spirit, and I John is talking about the manifestation of the Holy Spirit versus the manifestation of the Evil Spirit. The ability to discern the spirits is a special charism given only to some according to Paul (I Cor

---

[4] Hoskyns, *Epistles* 666. See also those mentioned in the NOTE on 4:1d who think that "world" here means little more than earth. Dodd, *Epistles* 98, understands the symbolic importance of "the world" but puts too much emphasis on its being the *pagan* world. In my judgment the author of I John pays little heed to outsiders, whether non-Christians or non-Johannine Christians. The world for him is marked by a failure to believe in Jesus, and he makes no distinction among nonbelievers (Jews, pagans, secessionists).

12:10); every Johannine Christian can test the difference between the two Spirits because of the anointing that all have received and that enables them to know everything (I John 2:20,27). The Pauline charism of true prophecy is given only to some (I Cor 12:10,29; 14:5), while the author of I John would characterize all the secessionists as false prophets.[5]

All of this makes sense if we remember the eschatological, and even apocalyptic, context previously announced: the last hour, with the secessionists as the manifestation of the expected Antichrist, the great Liar (2:18–19,22). In that previous treatment the author had contrasted the secessionists with his own followers who were taught by an anointing they had received from Christ (2:20,24–27). In the present treatment the author concentrates on the two Spirits that are at work in the respective groups. The Spirit that does not belong to God, the Spirit of the Antichrist, is Satan; for in apocalyptic expectations he was to be let loose in the last times to "go out to deceive" (Rev 20:7–8; see p. 334 above). The Spirit that belongs to God, the Spirit confessing Jesus Christ (come in the flesh), is the Holy Spirit, the very outpouring of which marks the last days (Acts 2:17). The connection between "the Spirit that God gave us" and the true confession of Jesus Christ[6] was probably fortified by a background of conversion/initiation/baptism in which Christians received the Spirit (p. 482) and made a confession of Jesus.[7] This Spirit remains an active force, testifying and bearing witness to Christ (I John 5:6; John 15:26–27).

The secessionists had been Johannine Christians; and to all appearances they would have received the Holy Spirit at baptism when they confessed Jesus Christ.[8] The specification of the confession that the au-

---

[5] The author would think emphatically of the secessionist *leaders* and *propagandists* as false prophets, and they may have claimed the title of "prophets." (Some later gnostics developed the paraphernalia of prophecy [vision, oracles, ecstasy] and spoke of prophets in their groups [Irenaeus, *Adv. haer.* 1.7.3]; others claimed the Spirit but eschewed prophecy [*Apocryphon of James* I 6:20–38; NHL 32].) But in the author's view those who follow the secessionist teachers share in the false prophecy, i.e., false interpretation of revelation. Such terminology came to the author from apocalyptic expectation, and so we do not know whether he would consider his adherents who make a correct confession as "true prophets." In 2:27 he saw no need for teachers, and so he may see no need for prophets.

[6] Notice the stylistic parallel between 3:24 ("Now this is how we can know that He abides in us: from the Spirit that He gave us") and 4:2 ("Now this is how you can know the Spirit of God: Everyone who confesses Jesus Christ come in the flesh reflects the Spirit which belongs to God").

[7] Such a confession is presupposed by John 9:22: "The Jews had already agreed that anyone who confessed Jesus as the Christ would be put out of the synagogue." See also John 20:31.

[8] While christological affirmations were demanded of early Christians, it was known that even the demons could recognize Jesus as the Holy One or Son of God (Mark 1:24; 3:11; 5:7–8); and Acts 19:2–6 describes Christians who could confess the Lord Jesus without receiving the Holy Spirit when they were baptized.

thor gives in 4:2 is what will separate the secessionists from his own adherents and thus constitute a criterion of the Spirits: "Jesus Christ *come in the flesh*." As I explained in the INTRODUCTION (IV B2a; V B2a), the issue is not that the secessionists are denying the incarnation or the physical reality of Jesus' humanity; they are denying that what Jesus was or did in the flesh was related to his being the Christ, i.e., was salvific.[9] The opponents of Ignatius of Antioch (INTRODUCTION IV B3b) may have been more advanced toward docetism than the adversaries of I John, but it is interesting that Ignatius uses language not unlike that of I John in refuting them. In *Smyrn.* 5:2 he equates "not confessing that he was clothed in flesh" with "blaspheming my Lord"; and in *Eph.* 7:2 he insists that "Jesus Christ our Lord" is both flesh and Spirit. The author of I John sees his adversaries' refusal to confess "Christ come in the flesh" as annulling or negating the importance of Jesus,[10] and thus accomplishing the work of the Antichrist which is to destroy Christ. In 3:8 the author used the verb "to annul, destroy" (*lyein*) in the statement: "The Son of God was revealed to destroy the works of the devil." Since by their christology they are annulling or destroying Jesus, the secessionists are diabolically reversing the purpose of the coming of God's Son. The real Pauline parallel is not the list of charisms of the one (Holy) Spirit in I Cor 12:11, but the contrast Paul makes before he gives that list, a contrast which separates the Holy Spirit of God from consummate evil: "No one speaking in the Spirit of God says, 'Jesus is anathema [cursed]'; and no one can say 'Jesus is Lord' except in the Holy Spirit" (I Cor 12:3). The source of a blasphemous christological confession is made clear elsewhere by Paul when he condemns those who preach "another Jesus" as having received "a different Spirit" from the one his followers received (II Cor 11:4). In the Pauline tradition I Tim 4:1 predicts: "In later times some will depart from the faith by giving heed to deceitful spirits." Thus, for the Pauline corpus as for I John there are only two christological possibilities: to confess Jesus correctly (as Christ or as Lord) or to curse and annul him. One course of action reflects the Spirit of God; the other, the Spirit of Deceit.

I Timothy mentions "later times"; and I have mentioned Synoptic texts pointing to the coming of false prophets in the last times, i.e., those who

[9] Minear, "Idea" 300-1, is brilliantly persuasive that "come in the flesh" is not the brute fact of incarnation or equal to "in human form." It refers to a mode of existence that is ultimately shared with other children of God, and that is why I John can relate christology to ethical demand. But Minear (292) goes so far as to argue that "Christ come in the flesh" in 4:2 is the same as "he who is in you" in 4:4; but in Johannine thought the divine indweller is scarcely Christ *in the flesh*.

[10] In the NOTE on 4:3ab I have argued for the reading "annuls Jesus" as more original than "does not confess Jesus" and have pointed to formulas about annulling or destroying Satan.

would deceive many by prophesying in Jesus' name, saying, "Lord, Lord," without living a life that matches such a confession.[11] In the Dead Sea Scrolls we find that the time of the false prophets has already arrived: "False prophets have led your people astray . . . but you, O God, despise all the designs of Belial" (1QH 4:7,12–13). Both the authors of the Qumran hymns and of I John have historicized the apocalyptic expectation in terms of the enemies of their respective groups.

In Christian communities the difficulty of testing those who confess the Lord was increased by the memory of Jesus' lifetime where his enemies attributed to the Prince of demons the good works done by God's Son— this was the sin against the Holy Spirit (Mark 2:22,29). The danger of attributing to the Evil Spirit a true prophecy that comes from the Holy Spirit has left its mark on *Didache* 11:7–8 where, although the community is afflicted by the presence of false prophets/teachers, the author cautions, "Do not put to trial [*peirazein*] or judge [*diakrinein*] any prophet who is speaking in a spirit; for 'every sin shall be forgiven, but this sin shall not be forgiven.' But not everyone who speaks in a spirit is a prophet—only the one who has the behavior of the Lord. From behavior then will the false prophet and the true prophet be known." While *Didache* and I John seem to differ on the matter of testing, *Didache* agrees with I John in making behavior a criterion. And even on the issue of testing, *Didache* may be warning simply against a formal procedure; for *Didache* 12:1 uses the verb found in I John to insist: "Receive everyone who comes in the name of the Lord; then by testing [*dokimazein*] you will come to know him, for you will have the wisdom to distinguish between right and left." The same problem remained in the second century,[12] as we see from *Hermas* (*Man.* 11:7): "You shall test [*dokimazein*] the prophet and the false prophet: test by his way of life the man who has the divine Spirit." The bishops of the church tried to examine (*peirazein*) the spirit that was in Maximilla, the Montanist prophetess, but were prevented by her accomplices from doing so (Eusebius, *Hist.* 5.16.16–17). In the Pseudo-Clementine writings there is a test of prophets who were largely understood as foretelling the future. In *Recognitions* 4.21.5–6 (GCS 51, 157) demoniac spirits are said to operate behind oracles to deceive people, sometimes admixing truth with falsehood to deceive all the more. In *Homilies* 1.19.8; 2.6–11 (GCS 42, 33–39) it is affirmed that one must test the true prophet both by his knowledge and correct foreknowledge. Then, once he has been tested, he is to be listened

---

[11] Matt 7:21–23; 24:11,24; Mark 13:32; also *T. Judah* 21:9: "There shall be false prophets"; see p. 335 above.

[12] See also Polycarp, *Philip.* 7, where I John 4:2–3 and II John 7 are quoted in a combined form as a test of heresy: "For everyone who does not confess Jesus Christ to have come in the flesh is Antichrist."

to without question, "because without him it is impossible that any certainty can come to people."

B. *Distinguishing Those who Belong to God and to the World* (4:4–6)

Having discussed the two Spirits (of God and of the Antichrist),[13] the author now turns less abstractly to the two groups of people who manifest those Spirits. He speaks directly to his "Little Children" as "You," just as he did in a previous unit when he was discussing the Antichrist (2:20,24,27). Against the background of that horrible figure of the last hour, he wants in both units to assure his adherents that they are on God's side, not on that of God's opponent. The very need to assure his audience that they have knowledge, that they have the anointing with the Spirit, and that they are conquering is an indication that the author's tests are not really working, and that the secessionists are having outward success as far as numbers are concerned. What then does the author's claim mean: "You have conquered those people"? It is a corollary of saying they are on God's side; for in Johannine tradition, despite appearances, it is that side which is victorious in the struggle with the world (to which the secessionists have gone out). "Have courage, I have conquered the world," announces Jesus (John 16:33). The Paraclete, the Spirit which the Father and Jesus send/give,[14] proves the world wrong by showing that the Prince of this world has been condemned (16:8–11). One may wonder whether I John's claim to conquering also has a historical note. We have seen (p. 475) the *possibility* that the secessionists were wealthy and numerous. They may have thought that their departure would have caused the demise of the Johannine Community faithful to the author, and he may be proclaiming that he and his adherents have won the battle of survival. In any case the war is being fought on two levels: the level of the Spirits locked in combat, and the level of their human hosts. As I pointed out in the NOTE on 4:1a, this world view is close to that of the Dead Sea Scrolls, where the two angelic spirits of truth and deceit are locked in struggle, as are the sons of righteousness and the sons of iniquity who walk according to these spirits.

The author is most insistent that these secessionist opponents "belong to the world," "speak the language of the world," and are listened to by the world (4:5). Besides echoing apocalyptic language where the kings of

---

[13] The "everyone" of 4:2b,3a is literally "every Spirit"; see NOTE on 4:2bc.

[14] In the NOTE on 4:4cd I argued that "he who is in you" is not God or Christ but the Paraclete/Holy Spirit ("the Spirit of God" of 4:2a), even as "he who is in the world" is the devil ("the Spirit of the Antichrist" of 4:3c).

the world are allied with the anti-God forces (Ezek 38:1–6; Rev 20:7–9), the charge that the secessionists "belong to the world" reflects polemically the language of the Johannine Jesus, who assured his followers that they did not belong to the world any more than he belonged to the world (John 15:19; 17:14,16).[15] Clearly, for the author, the secessionists are not followers of Jesus, but are like "the Jews" to whom Jesus said, "You belong to what is below; I belong to what is above. You belong to the world—the world to which I do not belong" (8:23). The secessionist christological formulations[16] which negate the importance of Jesus are like the christological views of the world (including "the Jews"), a world that did not recognize him (John 1:10), a world that hated him (15:19). That is why the world is attracted by and listens to (I John 4:5c) the secessionist preaching, which is an evisceration of all that is scandalous in the earthly career of Jesus ("in the flesh") through its emphasis solely on the fact of incarnation.[17] (The world may also have found attractive the moral perfectionism of the secessionists, which removed all need to think about sin, but in 4:1–6 christology is primarily in mind.) As I indicated in the NOTES on 4:5bc and 6bc, assigning the secessionists to the world and the world to the secessionists involves a pessimism on the author's part about further missionary successes of his own Community. Of the two religious options (success proves that we are right; smallness proves we are God's elect), he has chosen the second and has made rejection by outsiders an index of truth.

At the end of v. 5 the author shifts from the theme of speaking to the theme of listening.[18] In GJohn the ability to listen to Jesus was a criterion for discerning who belongs to God and who belongs to the devil, e.g., "Why do you not understand what I say?—because you are incapable of listening to my word. The devil is the father you belong to" (John 8:43–44). Or again, "The person who belongs to God listens to the words of God" (8:47; also 10:26–27). This attitude is summed up in the sweeping claim of Jesus, "Everyone who belongs to the truth listens to my voice" (18:37). It is not surprising, then, that the epistolary author makes listening "to us" the criterion of who belongs to God (4:6ab). The

---

[15] See also I John 2:15–17, which describes desires that belong to the world and, by that fact, do not belong to God.

[16] I John almost anticipates the modern philosophical insight that identity or nature comes to expression in the "speech event" (*Wortereignis*).

[17] Schneider, *Briefe* 172, thinks that the world could accept secessionist Christianity more easily because it contained no such incomprehensible truths as the incarnation and redemptive death. I would contend that there is evidence that the secessionists rejected the implications of the incarnation (the importance of what Jesus did in the flesh) rather than the fact of the entry of the Word into human life.

[18] Although the author says that the secessionists ("those people") belong to the world and speak the language of the world, when by contrast he says, "We belong to God," he shifts to listening; for he does not say, "We do not speak the language of the world" or "We speak the language of God."

Johannine Community has received the Spirit from Jesus and bears witness to Jesus. If listening to Jesus was the criterion for who belonged to God, listening to the Community that bears witness to Jesus is the continuing criterion,[19] especially since the object of the listening is the confession of "Jesus Christ come in the flesh." This listening is a criterion not only of belonging to God but also of knowing God. In Johannine theology, knowledge of God is not the goal of Christian existence but its presupposition. Every Johannine Christian possesses eternal life through faith in Jesus (John 3:15), and "Eternal life consists in this: that they know you, the one true God, and Jesus Christ, the one whom you sent" (17:3). Accordingly, both the secessionists (I John 2:4) and the author's adherents (2:13b,14b; 5:20) are sure that they know God. Hitherto the author has offered the criterion of keeping commandments as a way of being sure who knows God (2:3); now he offers the criterion of listening to the christology espoused by the Johannine Community.

This passage has often been cited as justifying magisterial teaching authority in hierarchically organized churches. Bonsirven, *Epîtres* 189–90, for instance, claims that the need to test the Spirits shows the necessity for a magisterium of Pope and councils, since setting up the criteria can scarcely be left to individuals: "The only part left to the faithful is the application of the criterion under the inspiration of the Holy Spirit which they have received." In the opposite direction Plummer, *Epistles* 94, thinks that the demand to test *every* Spirit means that the Pope cannot be infallible, for then his Spirit would be exempt from the test.[20] If this debate about the impact of I John 4:1–6 for the papal magisterium is clearly beyond the epistolary author's intent, Dodd, *Epistles* 100, would argue that in his demand for listening "to us" the author refers to a "we" which "stands for the Church as a whole, speaking through its responsible teachers, who embody the authentic apostolic tradition."[21] I find this quite unlikely on many scores. First, I John is concerned with the Johannine Community and not with "the Church as a whole"—a concept that is not attestedly Johannine. John 10:16 mentions that there are "other sheep" of Jesus but they are not part of "this fold," and so there is no evidence that a Johannine writer would have thought of his Community being in the same "church" as other Christians. Second, the author would scarcely

[19] In the NOTE on 4:6a, in discussing whether the "we" of this verse referred to the Johannine tradition-bearers (the Johannine School) or the whole Johannine Community, I found the arguments for the latter somewhat stronger.

[20] Actually in Roman Catholic thought there is foreseen the possibility of a heretical Pope. Infallibility is invoked only when he is officially teaching the faith of the Church.

[21] Dodd (103–6) goes on to find here the subordination of the prophetic stream to the apostolic stream, but that interpretation is somewhat dependent on the Pauline list of charisms in which apostles and prophets are listed first and second (I Cor 12:28; Eph 2:20; 4:11). See footnote 5 above.

speak of "responsible teachers" since in 2:27 he has denied the need for teachers! As far as we know, the one contemporary teacher for the Johannine Community was the Paraclete who replaced Jesus (John 14:26). Third, the idea of apostolic tradition is foreign to a body of writing that never uses the term "apostle." The Community had the idea of a true witness borne to Jesus by a disciple whom Jesus loved,[22] but that witness was itself the work of the Paraclete (15:26–27).

When one lays aside presuppositions derived from other NT works, the criterion to which the author appeals as authoritative is a christology that he thinks of as traditional in the Johannine Community.[23] It was shaped under the guidance of the Paraclete; it has been passed down by the tradition-bearers of the Community (I John 1:1–5); and those who agree with it (by listening "to us") reflect the Spirit of Truth. (Thus the criterion is not substantially different from "His anointing teaches you about all things" [2:27].) In other words, the author is warning his adherents who waver: If you agree with us, you are on our side, and our side is God's side. Obviously the secessionists would reject the need to agree with the author and his adherents, but within their own circles the secessionists would probably make the same demand to be listened to. In my judgment the criterion had little practical chance of success, and ultimately some of the author's adherents may have sought out the clearer criterion of hierarchical teachers who claimed apostolic authentication (see INTRODUCTION V D2)—the very office that Dodd thought was involved here but was really found in other Christian churches, e.g., the churches of the Pauline Pastorals and of I Peter. Such human teaching authority would have been an intrusive novelty on the Johannine scene but may have been the only way to refute secessionists who were also insisting, "Anyone who has knowledge of God listens to us." It may have seemed the only alternative to obliteration by further divisions.

[22] Although he is never identified as an apostle, some have argued that the Beloved Disciple was John son of Zebedee, one of the Twelve Apostles. (I am less inclined toward that identification now than I was in AB 29, lxxxviii–cii, although even there I contended the evidence was not probative.) Even were that true, the failure of the Johannine writers to call him an apostle would indicate that esteem for him was on another basis.

[23] "Traditional interpretation" is not the same as Dodd's "apostolic tradition." It requires no statement of an apostle to which one could refer but simply a long-continuing way of understanding Jesus. The author of I John 1:3 stresses *koinōnia*, "communion," with a School of tradition-bearers, not obedience to church officials.

BIBLIOGRAPHY PERTINENT TO I JOHN 4:1–6

de la Potterie, I., *La vérité* 1, 282–310, on the Spirit of Truth and the Spirit of Deceit.

Minear, P., "The Idea of Incarnation in First John," Int 24 (1970) 291–302.

Serafín de Ausejo, "El concepto de 'carne' aplicado a Cristo en el IV Evangelio," EstBib 17 (1958) 411–27, esp. 416–20 on I John 4:2 and II John 7.

von der Goltz, E. F., "Eine textkritische Arbeit des zehnten bzw. sechsten Jahrhunderts," TU 17 (Heft 4, 1899), esp. 48–50 on 4:3.

The Dead Sea Scroll Doctrine of the Two Spirits

Daniélou, J., "Une source de la spiritualité chrétienne dans les manuscrits de la Mer Morte: la doctrine des deux esprits," *Dieu Vivant* 25 (1953) 127–36.

Holstein, H., "Les 'deux esprits' dans la Règle de la communauté essénienne du Désert de Juda," *Revue d'ascétique et de mystique* 31 (1955) 297–303.

Martini, C., "Il discernimento degli spiriti in un testo antico del deserto di Giuda," *La Civiltà Cattolica* 107 (IV: Nov. 17, 1956) 395–410.

Treves, M., "The Two Spirits of the Rule of the Community," RevQ 3 (1961) 449–52.

Wernberg-Møller, P., "A Reconsideration of the Two Spirits in the Rule of the Community," RevQ 3 (1961) 413–41.

9. I John 4:7–5:4a: *Loving One Another as a Way of Abiding in and Loving God*

7a	7BELOVED, let us love one another
7b	since love is from God.
7c	Everyone who loves has been begotten by God
7d	and knows God.
8a	8One who does not love has known nothing of God,
8b	for God is love.
9a	9This is how God's love was revealed in us:
9b	that God has sent His only Son into the world
9c	so that we have life through him.
10a	10In this, then, does love consist:
10b	not that we have loved God
10c	but that He loved us
10d	and sent His Son as an atonement for our sins.
11a	11BELOVED, if God so loved us,
11b	we in turn ought to love one another.
12a	12No one has ever seen God.
12b	Yet if we love one another,
12c	God abides in us;
12d	and His love has reached perfection in us.
13a	13This is how we can know that we abide in Him and He abides
13b	in that He has given us of His own Spirit. | in us:
14a	14As for us, we have seen and can testify
14b	that the Father has sent the Son as Savior of the world.
15a	15Whenever anyone confesses that *Jesus* is the Son of God,
15b	then God abides in him and he abides in God.
16a	16As for us, we have come to know and believe
16b	the love that God has in us.
16c	16cGod is love,
16d	and the person who abides in love
16e	abides in God and God abides in him.
17a	17In this has love reached perfection with us,
17b	with the result that we may have confidence on Judgment Day

17c   because already in this world we are just the same as Christ is.

18a   18Love has no room for fear;

18b   rather, perfect love drives out fear,

18c   for fear carries with it punishment.

18d   Love has not reached perfection in one who is still afraid.

19   19As for us, we love because He loved us first.

20a   20If anyone boasts, "I love God,"

20b   while continuing to hate his brother,

20c   he is a liar.

20d   For the person who has no love for his brother whom he has

20e   cannot love the God he has never seen. | seen

21a   21And the commandment we have had from Him is this:

21b   the person who loves God must love his brother as well.

1a   5 1Everyone who believes that *Jesus* is the Christ has been
          begotten by God,

1b   and everyone who loves the parent loves the child begotten
          by him.

2a   2This is how we can be sure that we do love God's children,

2b   whenever we love God and obey His commandments.

3a   3For the love of God consists in this:

3b   that we keep His commandments.

3c   And His commandments are not burdensome,

4a   4because all that is begotten by God conquers the world.

NOTES

4:7a. *Beloved, let us love one another.* For "Beloved," see the NOTE on 2:7a. The clause echoes the second part of the commandment in 3:23: "We are to love one another [*agapōmen allēlous*] just as He gave us the command"; and the result here is an alliteration: *agapētoi agapōmen allēlous*. It is possible to give a durative or iterative meaning to the Greek here: "Let us go on loving each other" (BDF 318²·³). For the theme and vocabulary of love, see the NOTE on 2:5b.

7b. *since love is from God.* This is the *einai ek* phrase that elsewhere I have translated "belongs to," since it indicates appurtenance as well as origin (NOTE on 2:16ef). Here, however, origin is primary, as indicated in the sentences that follow and develop this statement.

7c. *Everyone who loves has been begotten by God.* Although there is an introductory *kai*, "and," in the Greek, the clause is not governed by the "since" of the previous sentence. Codex Alexandrinus adds "God" after "loves," reflecting a scribal tendency to specify the object of love. Schnackenburg, *Johannesbriefe* 227, observes that the author is speaking about "love" without specification. Charlier, "L'amour" 59, phrases it forcefully: "It is not fraternal love, nor love for God, nor the love of God for men, but love in itself. The Semitic world to which John belongs ignores our distinctions of object and subject." However, if there is an implicit specification, it would be in terms of love of one's Johannine "brother" rather than of love of God, as some of the Latin church writers recognized. (Bultmann, *Epistles* 65, argues against Schnackenburg that love for the author is always fraternal love—even though I allow as possible an implicit reference here to fraternal love, I find Bultmann's generalization inaccurate; see p. 255 above). I pointed out in the NOTE on 2:23ab the author's tendency to use *pas*, "all, every," with the present, articular participle in generalizations reflecting his dualistic outlook that neatly categorizes people. The perf. tense of the verb ("has been [and remains] begotten") makes unlikely the inference that by loving one *is being* begotten by God; a Christian's love does not cause divine begetting but flows from it. In 3:1 we heard, "Look at what love the Father has bestowed on us in enabling us to be called God's children." Now we are told that God's children manifest themselves in love; it is an essential aspect of their connaturality. Verse 11 will give priority to God's action, which in turn imposes love of one another. Arguing wrongly from that, Plummer, *Epistles* 100, interprets I John to mean: "If a Socrates or a Marcus Aurelius loves his fellow-men, it is by the grace of God that he does so." The Johannine authors are talking about the love of fellow (Johannine) Christians and are not concerned with how pagans love one another.

7d. *and knows God.* We saw that an alliteration begins this verse, and consonance continues in the sequence of the verbs *gennan*, "to beget," and *ginōskein*, "to know." The contrast, however, between the perf. tense in the first verb and the pres. tense in the second verb catches attention (see the next line with the Greek aorist tense: "has known nothing of God"). A few scholars explain the perf.-pres. tense sequence in terms of an underlying Hebrew *wayyiqtol* construction where the second verb in the indefinite tense has the value of the first verb in the definite tense. Still others would translate the second verb as "and goes on knowing God," with the implication that, although before loving the Christian knows God, love increases knowledge. Such theories are unnecessary. In Johannine thought it is not simply that knowledge of God flows from our past acts of love, nor that our love leads to a future knowledge of God. The relationship is synchronized: by loving (one's brother), one comes to know God (who is love). Charlier, "L'amour" 61, states that for I John: "Love is not only a type of divine incarnation; it is a human divinization."

Bultmann thinks that this line (7d) did not belong to the hypothetical source, and that 7c was originally followed by 8a. Yet in the COMMENT I shall show that there is antithetical parallelism and chiasm between the existing text of 4:7cd and 4:8ab.

8a. *One who does not love has known nothing of God.* The negative participial subject is the antithesis of the positive participial subject in v. 7cd: "Everyone who loves." (Although elsewhere I have translated the participial constructions as "The person who" [2:4,6,9; 3:7,8,24], I use "The one who" here to illustrate visibly the antithesis.) The predicate is the antithesis of the second part of the predicate of 7cd: "and knows God." Codex Alexandrinus and some minuscules make the contrast more exact by reading a pres. tense here ("does not know God"), while the corrector of Sinaiticus reads a perf. tense of "know" to match the perf. "has been begotten" in 7c. The aorist tense, however, is supported by most textual witnesses and is correct. It is not a gnomic aorist with a present force (BDF 333) but negates absolutely. (The sequence of pres. and aorist tenses of *ginōskein,* "to know," in 4:7d,8a was previously encountered in 3:1: "The reason that the world does not recognize [know] us is that it never recognized [knew] Him"; and there too the aorist involved an absolute negative.) The author's vigorous negation may be aimed at a secessionist claim to know God. Wilder, "Introduction" 279, would make the aorist even stronger by taking it as inceptive (BDF 331): "has not even begun to know God." It is interesting to compare I Cor 8:2–3: "If one thinks he knows, he has not yet known [aorist] as he ought to know; but if one loves God, one is known by Him."

8b. *for God is love.* As in the other two Johannine descriptions, "God is Spirit" (John 4:24) and "God is light" (I John 1:5; see NOTE there for the "God is" formula), the predicate is anarthrous. The author does not say simply, "God loves" (a style he uses of the Johannine Christian, e.g., "Everyone who loves" in v. 7c), for loving is not just another action of God, like ruling. Rather, all God's activity is loving activity (Dodd, *Epistles* 110; THLJ 107). Nor does the author say, "Love is God"; for he is interested in the loving activity of a person, not in abstract definitions (Feuillet, *Le mystère* 194). As Wilder, "Introduction" 280, says of the Johannine formula, "The present verse requires a personal view of God."

9a. *This is how.* In this unit there are 5 instances of the *en toutō* construction (4:9,10,13,17; 5:2). The first 3 are followed by a *hoti,* "that," clause and come under the A classification of *en toutō* constructions discussed in the NOTE on 2:3a above, i.e., instances where the "this" is explained by a following clause. In the present instance, at least, most scholars agree that the reference is to what follows.

God's love. The phrase "the love of God" was discussed in the NOTE on 2:5b above where 5 different suggestions about meaning were offered. My translation here reflects the conviction that in this instance no debate is possible: the genitive is subjective, and what follows in vv. 9–11 shows that the author is thinking of God's love for us.

was revealed. This is the aorist passive of *phaneroun,* discussed in the NOTE on 1:2a. Its dominant Johannine use is directly christological: the revelation of Jesus in his earthly career or after the resurrection. But in other instances impersonal divine realities are revealed, and it is to this latter category that the only Johannine reference to the revelation of the love of God belongs. Indirectly, as we shall see, this revelation is christological, for God manifests His love in sending His Son.

in us. The phrase *en hēmin* occurs again in 4:12d ("His love has reached perfection in us") and in 4:16b ("the love that God has in us"), while in 4:17a we find *meth hēmōn* ("love has reached perfection with us"). To what extent are such phrases interchangeable? Does *en hēmin* mean more than "to us"? One must discuss several grammatical alternatives. The phrase can be read with the noun "love," rather than with the verb "revealed," e.g., "God's love for us was revealed" (Balz, Houlden [?], JB). This would agree with the theme in 4:10c, 11a that God loved us; also with 4:16b, "the love that God has in [= for] us." Certainly this rendition is favored by the Greek word order of 4:9a, which is literally, "In this was revealed the love of God in us." However, John 9:3 has exactly the same word order ("in order that there might be revealed the works of God in him"), and there the "in him" phrase cannot be rendered "for him" and must be taken with the verb "revealed."

The majority of scholars read the phrase *en hēmin* in 4:9a with the verb "revealed"; but that still leaves two possibilities. (a) *En hēmin* is equivalent to a dative ("to us, for us, in our case") since sometimes, albeit rarely, *en* with the dative has that meaning (ZBG 120; BDF 220[1]), e.g., II Cor 5:11: "We have been revealed to God [dative] and also, I hope, to your consciences [*en* with dative]." There would be nothing unJohannine about the idea that by the Son God's love was revealed *to us,* as indicated in I John 3:16: "This is how we have come to know what love means: for us Christ laid down his life." Nevertheless, the preposition *eis* would be more appropriate than *en* for such a meaning, as in Rom 5:8, "God's love for [*eis*] us"; and even more appropriate would be the simple dative, as in I John 1:2: "This eternal life . . . was revealed to us." (b) *En hēmin* is to be taken more literally as the locale of the manifestation of love ("in us, among us, in our midst"). This is precisely the meaning of the identical construction in John 9:3 cited at the end of the preceding paragraph. This understanding, supported by Brooke and Schnackenburg, is phrased concisely by Plummer, *Epistles* 102: "Rather *in us* than 'toward us': we are the sphere in which God's love is exhibited." It finds support in John 1:14, "The Word became flesh and made his dwelling among [*en*] us," and in I John 4:12, "If we love one another, God abides *in* us." However, on closer examination these last quotations point to an ambiguity. If *en hēmin* is taken locally, does it mean "among us," with the "us" referring to human beings; or does it mean "in us," with the "us" referring to (Johannine) Christians? If the former, the love is manifested in the incarnation; if the latter, the love is manifested in the incarnation plus indwelling. The rest of v. 9 points to the latter, for 9b describes the incarnation ("God has sent His only Son into the world"), while 9c describes the effects of divine indwelling ("that we may have life through him"), which becomes explicit in v. 12.

9b. *that God has sent His only Son.* The word order stresses the object. *Monogenēs,* "one of a kind," occurs 5 times in NT reference to Jesus, always in the Johannine literature (John 1:14,18; 3:16,18; here in I John). Although in these passages Jerome rendered it by *unigenitus,* "only begotten," the more correct Latin translation was *unicus,* "only," as in the nonchristological passages in the Vulgate (Luke 7:12; 8:42; 9:38; see ABJ 29, 13–14). The underlying Hebrew word is *yāḥîd,* "uniquely beloved," a meaning reflected in the two LXX terms that rendered it: *monogenēs,* "only, unique," and *agapētos,* "beloved." *Yāḥîd/agapētos* was used for Isaac, Abraham's specially loved son (Gen 22:2,12,16), as was *monogenēs* (Heb 11:17). Isaac was connected with God's promise that through Abraham's offspring/seed all the nations of the earth would bless themselves or be blessed (Gen 22:18; Sir 44:21; *Jub.* 18:15), a promise that Christians saw fulfilled in Jesus. And so the Isaac language was shifted to Jesus, with John using *monogenēs* and Mark using *agapētos* (1:11; 9:7 [12:6]), to describe him as God's unique and beloved Son. (The use of *monogenēs* for Wisdom [Wis 7:22] may also have contributed to this terminology.) Seemingly the Johannine writers made a distinction: all the Johannine Christians deserve the designation *agapētos,* "beloved" (NOTE on 2:7a), as God's children (*teknon*), but only Jesus is *monogenēs* as God's Son (*huios*). There is, of course, a hint of God's love for His Son in *monogenēs,* a theme made explicit in John 17:26.

This is the first epistolary reference to the "sending" of Jesus by the Father, a common notion in GJohn. For "send" GJohn uses both *pempein* and *apostellein* without difference of meaning (except to those who consistently find in interchangeable Johannine words subtle refinements of significance). The only verifiable difference between the verbs is one of tense and mood (Kilpatrick, "Idioms" 27). *Pempein* in reference to Jesus always occurs in GJohn (23 times) as an aorist active ptcp. describing the Father as the one who has sent him; it never appears in the Epistles. *Apostellein* in reference to Jesus occurs 17 times in GJohn in the finite tenses (15 times aorist; 2 times perf. [5:36; 20:21]) in statements about God's sending the Son. It occurs 3 times in the Epistles, namely, in I John 4:9 (perf.), 4:10 (aorist), and 4:14 (perf.). While some scholars, like Lightfoot, would insist that the perf. of *apostellein* is more durative than the aorist, Bultmann, Schnackenburg, and others are correct in arguing against this distinction (Moule, IBNTG 14; MGNTG 3, 69–70). Both tenses refer to the act of sending, which constitutes revelation; the enduring results "for us" of that act are contained, not in the verb, but in the context. The sending itself involved a fixed time and place.

into the world. For the positive and negative uses of *kosmos,* see the NOTE on 2:2c above. B. Weiss, *Briefe* 120, stresses the negative, for he speaks of the Son's being sent to a fallen world, opposed to God. However, in these incarnational formulas "world" is positive, as confirmed in 4:14 below.

9c. *so that we have life through him.* Bultmann thinks that the "us" of 9a and the "we" of 9c may refer to all human beings; but I would agree with most scholars that in both lines the reference is to Johannine Christians. ("Life" is eternal life which could be given only to those who believe in Jesus.) Luise Schotroff, *Der Glaubende und die feindliche Welt* (WMANT 37; Neukirchener Verlag, 1970) 287, goes in the other direction from Bultmann when she denies any universal outreach in the reference to the world in 9b; for the world is not the object of God's love, only its showplace. That the world has to be more than a showplace we see from 4:14 where I John speaks of Jesus as the "Savior of the world." My contention is that the difference between "the world" of 4:9b and the "we" of 9c reflects salvation history. God had a real love for the world; but some preferred darkness and rejected God's love, and so only the Christian "we" received life. For that reason I would take this line as a result clause rather than a purpose clause (the latter is favored by THLJ). The purpose of the sending of the Son was to save the world and that every believer might have eternal life (John 3:16–17); but in fact the Christian "we" are selected from the world for eternal life. This is the only epistolary instance of *zēn*, "to live" (corresponding to the noun *zōē*, "life"; NOTE on 1:2a), which occurs 17 times in GJohn. In passages like John 5:25; 6:57; 11:25; 14:19, Jesus promises his disciples (those who believe in him and eat the bread of life) that they shall live. In I John we see the promise realized.

"Through him" is *dia* with the genitive. See in ABJ 29, 283 the discussion of *dia* with the accusative in reference to Jesus' claim, "Just as the Father who is living sent me and I am living because of [*dia*] the Father, so the one who feeds on me will live because of [*dia*] me" (John 6:57). Such a use with the accusative does not normally mean source, but that is the meaning both there and here.

10a. *In this, then, does love consist.* Literally, "In this is love," an *en toutō* construction followed by *hoti* ("that") clauses, which interpret the "this" (NOTE on 2:3a)—in this instance virtually all commentators agree. In v. 9 the author said that God's love was revealed; now he tells us in what this love consists. Not surprisingly scribes (Sinaiticus, Sahidic) added "of God" after "love" in imitation of v. 9a. No such specification is needed; the author is speaking of a comprehensive love.

10bc. *not that we have loved God but that He loved us.* Pronouns are used for "we" (*hēmeis*) and "He" (*autos*, although Alexandrinus has *ekeinos*) to increase the contrast. The construction "not . . . but" is found elsewhere in the Johannine writings, e.g., John 15:16: "It was not you who chose me, but I who chose you" (also 6:38; 12:6; II John 5). An interesting parallel is Titus 3:4–5: "When the goodness and loving kindness of God our Savior appeared, He saved us, not because of deeds done by us in righteousness, but according to His own mercy."

The second verb "loved" in this statement is clearly aorist; and most textual witnesses have an aorist for the first verb too, but Codex Vaticanus and some minuscules have the perf. tense, which is the more difficult reading and probably to be preferred. (Scribes would have tended to conform the two verbs.) Curiously Schnackenburg, *Johannesbriefe* 230–31, who finds no distinction of meaning between the perf. of "send" in v. 9b and the aorist in v. 10d, would distinguish between the perf. of "love" in 10b (durative) and the aorist in 10c (single act). Since the perf. in 10b is negated, the durative ("have gone on loving") seems unlikely. But clearly the "He loved us" of 10c refers to a specific action on God's part in sending His Son (10d). More important is the issue of whether "not that we have loved God" is a denial of a secessionist affirmation. Many think that the secessionists, who did not love their brothers, claimed to love God, a claim that the author is denying. (In part this may reflect Nygren's thesis, discussed in the NOTE on 2:5b, that human love for God was not a pure Christian ideal.) Others think that the secessionists, who did not love their brothers, made no claim to love God. I would argue that both the author and the secessionists claimed to love God and brother. The author is arguing with the secessionists not about a priority that they attribute to love for God but about whether the atoning death of Jesus (v. 10d) was a necessary part of God's salvific love.

10d. *and sent His Son.* The tense of *apostellein* is aorist, although Codex Alexandrinus reads a perf. to make this line agree in tense with the perfects in 9b (see NOTE) and 14b.

as an atonement for our sins. In a NOTE on 2:2a dealing with *hilasmos* as "atonement," I argued from the context there (1:7: "The blood of Jesus, His Son, cleanses us from all sins") that the author thought of Jesus as an expiatory sacrifice removing sin, in his role of a heavenly Paraclete standing in the Father's presence making intercession. Here the author is thinking of Jesus' death and not simply of the incarnation when he mentions the sending of the Son as an atonement. In 2:2 the author specified the breadth of the atonement: "for our sins . . . but also for the whole world." In the preceding verse here (4:9) the author mentioned a salvific sending of the Son "into the world," and now he mentions "for our sins." The preposition "for" is *peri* as it was in 2:2a (see NOTE there), probably under the influence of LXX vocabulary used in describing the effects of OT sacrifice. In the nonsacrificial descriptions of Christ's laying down his life *for* people, *hyper* is the more usual preposition (NOTE on 3:16b: "for us Christ laid down his life").

11a. *Beloved.* This is the last of the 6 uses of this address in I John (NOTE on 2:7a). Indeed, after this verse the author abandons until the very end of I John (5:21) his custom of frequent titles of address.

if God so loved us. The condition is *ei* with the indicative, which normally indicates the reality of the assumption (BDF 371[1]). The tense of *agapan*, "to love," is aorist as in 10c ("He loved us"). The "so" is *houtōs*, used previously in I John 2:6bc (see NOTE there) in connection with *kathōs*: "The person who claims to abide in Him ought himself to walk just as [*kathōs* . . . *houtōs*] Christ walked." The usage here was surely influenced by the use of *houtōs* in John 3:16 ("God so loved the world that He gave the only Son"), a passage upon which this whole section is a commentary. All these factors join to make it clear that "so loved" involves the historical career ("walking") and death of Jesus, interpreted as the giving of God's only Son in order that we might have life and forgiveness of sins. In other words, the *houtōs* in this first line of a new subdivision resumes the whole previous subdivision (vv. 7–10). Spicq, "Notes" 368, stresses that *houtōs* puts an accent on the vertical character of God's love, and he points to this use of "so" in the LXX of Isa 54:10 ("So shall My mercy not fail you"; see also I Macc 3:60). Spicq would translate *houtōs:* "in a manner so excessive [intensely]," making it a "so" that demands response or imitation.

11b. *we in turn ought to love one another.* The same Greek is found in I

John 3:16: "This is how we have come to know what love means: for us Christ laid down his life; *so we in turn ought to* lay down our lives for the brothers." See also John 13:14: "If I washed your feet . . . so ought you in turn to wash one another's feet." The initial *kai* is strongly sequential; hence the translation "in turn." The position of the pronoun "we" is emphatic, establishing a contrast with "God" in the preceding line. In discussing the verb *opheilein* in the NOTE on 2:6bc, we saw that this "ought" does not flow from law but from the very nature of the realities involved. In 2:6, cited in the previous NOTE, the Christian obligation was based on the example of Jesus as God's Son; here the presence of God's Son is implied from 4:10d. (The same verb occurs in Rom 13:8: *"Owe* no one anything except to love one another.") In I John 3:23c and 4:7a the phrase "to love one another" was *agapan allēlous;* here the Greek order is inverted to stress "one another."

12a. *No one has ever seen God.* Literally, "God [anarthrous] no one has ever seen." Westcott, *Epistles* 172–74, argues that the anarthrous usage stresses the general conception of divinity, i.e., "God as God." However, the author may be imitating the GJohn Prologue, "No one has ever seen God" (1:18) where the object is also anarthrous. In four other instances where the Johannine writers deny that anyone has seen God, the verb *horan* is employed (John 1:18; 5:37; 6:46; I John 4:20); here the verb is *theasthai.* Although Plummer, *Epistles* 103, would find a special nuance of gazing upon and contemplating God, I agree with W. Michaelis, TDNT 5, 345 (see ABJ 29, 503) in rejecting a distinction. Exhibiting his predilection for alternating vocabulary, here the author may simply have opted for *theon . . . theasthai* to match the alliteration of *agapan allēlous* in the immediate context. Also plausible is the thesis of van der Horst, "Wordplay," that *theasthai* here involves a play on the etymology of *theos,* "God" (a connection already attested in the second century B.C.). This play would be appropriate in a section drawing corollaries from the statement "God is love."

In a way this denial is surprising; for in John 14:9 Jesus told his disciples, "Whoever has seen me has seen the Father." This was scarcely meant to be a unique privilege of those first disciples who saw Jesus physically during the ministry, since in 16:16 Jesus promised the disciples that they would see him again "in a little while," i.e., after his death and return—a sight that presumably the Johannine Christians would share as second-generation disciples. Nevertheless, we would have to conclude that the sight of the Father in Jesus is not the same as seeing God, for in I John 3:2 the author promises that as a future reward: "We shall see Him as He is." In GJohn the statement that no one has ever seen God (3 times) was used to defend the uniqueness of Jesus against Jewish claims (actual or possible) about the superiority of Moses or Elijah. (For the inner-Jewish debate about whether Moses saw God on Sinai or through an assumption into heaven after death, see ABJ 29, 36 and 225; also Josephus *Ant.* 3.5.3; ✗88; Deut 34:7,10.) Once again the author has taken over anti-Jewish polemic from GJohn and used it in his war with secessionists; see COMMENT below.

12b. *Yet if we love one another.* (The adversative is implied by the context.) Unlike 11a, this condition is expressed by *ean* with the subjunctive, a construction which supplies no certitude about the reality of what is described but which can express an expectation (BDF 371[4]). Here the author returns to the word order *agapan allēlous* (NOTE on 4:11b).

12c. *God abides in us.* For the *menein en* formula used for divine indwelling, see the NOTE on 2:6a. It is peculiar to I John (as distinct from GJohn) to use it for the indwelling of God in the Christian. The first instance of that theme was in 3:24, and it will be repeated in 4:13,15,16. Here it continues the emphasis on the divine initiative toward human beings.

12d. *and His love has reached perfection in us.* There are attested three different Greek word orders for the last four words. Perhaps scribes were confused by finding the phrase "in us" in two consecutive lines: If the phrase were omitted from the present line (as it is in a minuscule), there would have been confusion about where to place it when it was restored. In I John *teleioun* is used 4 times in the perf. passive form to describe the perfection or completion of love (NOTE on 2:5b), but this is the only instance where the construction is periphrastic (a ptcp. plus the verb "to be," as in John 17:23). This is merely a stylistic variation (MGNTG 3, 88), but it may have contributed to scribal confusion about the word order. In three of the epistolary passages (2:5ff.; 4:17; and here) it is clear that the perfection of love involves the love of Christians for each another. Literally the Greek here reads "the love of Him," a construction that is open to the five possible interpretations of "the love of God" discussed in the NOTE on 2:5b. Since the love reaches perfection "in us," many argue that this must be an objective genitive covering our love for God (Belser, Camerlynck, Chaine, Dodd, Hauck, Holtzmann, Luther, Moffatt, Plummer, Vrede, Windisch). Since the author has been talking about God's love for us (11a), and since he has talked about that love being revealed "in us," an even better case can be made for the subjective genitive, meaning His love for us (Bonsirven, Brooke, Bruce, Büchsel, Bultmann, Charue, Schlier, Schütz, Stott, THLJ, B. Weiss, Wengst). Hoskyns argues for both a subjective and objective meaning, while Schnackenburg, Vellanickal, and Westcott argue for a qualitative genitive that is neither subjective nor objective (divine love); and Marshall opts for a combination of subjective and qualitative. My translation reflects a choice for the subjective genitive on the grounds that 12d continues 12c: God abides in us and the love that comes from Him reaches perfection in our love for others (see Schütz, *Vorgeschichte* 4–5).

13a. *This is how we can know.* Literally, "In this we know [*ginōskein*]." In the *en toutō* varieties classified in the NOTE on 2:3a, this falls under (A), i.e., a passage where there is a following *hoti* subordinate clause to which "in this" points. In fact, there are two following *hoti* clauses, the first of which (rest of 13a) explains what "we know," the second of which (13b) is epexegetical of "in this" by explaining how we know. (Cf. the *hoti . . . ean* in 2:3, and the *hoti . . . ean* in 5:2, where the first and second clauses have the same role as the *hoti . . . hoti* here.) Most scholars (e.g., Brooke, Dodd, Marshall, Stott, Westcott, Wilder) attribute a forward thrust to *en toutō*, although B. Weiss argues for a reference to what has preceded, and Painter for a reference in both directions.

that we abide in Him and He abides in us. The second "abides" is understood, not expressed, in the Greek. In the NOTE on 2:6a covering the use of *menein en* for divine indwelling, we saw that within the Johannine corpus only I John 3:24; 4:13,15,16 describe a mutual indwelling of God and the Christian. In the preceding verse only God's abiding in us was mentioned.

13b. *in that He has given us of His own Spirit.* Although Bultmann, *Epistles* 70, prefers translating *hoti* as "because," there is little difference between that connotation and understanding it as a "that" epexegetical of "In this" of 13a. Some commentators are surprised to find the Spirit suddenly introduced as a criterion of divine indwelling (see COMMENT), although the author prepared for this idea in 3:24cd: "Now this is how we can know that He abides in us: from the Spirit that He gave us." There the verb was aorist without an introductory *hoti;* here the verb is perfect with an introductory *hoti.* (Codex Alexandrinus and minuscule 33 harmonize by reading the aorist of "gave" here.) Although Westcott and de la Potterie would stress the durative aspect of the perf. (cf. John 14:16 where the Paraclete is "to be with you forever"), the criterion offered here is a *definite* action of God's having given the Spirit, similar to God's having sent His Son (perf. in v. 9b, aorist in 10d, perf. in 14b). If the tense difference, then, is meaningless, I have also suggested that the "of [*ek,* 'from'] the Spirit" in both sentences has the same partitive meaning.

14a. *As for us, we have seen and can testify.* The initial, emphatic *kai hēmeis,* "And we," is similar to the "As for you" ([*kai*] *hymeis*) used to mark plausible subdivisions in 2:20,24,27; 4:4. However, a subdivision here seems unlikely since the theme of divine abiding and mutual indwelling in vv. 12–13 returns in v. 15. The perf. tense of *theasthai,* "to see," and the pres. of *martyrein,* "to testify," seem to echo previous statements in the I John Prologue (1:1,2): "What we have seen [aorist *theasthai*] with our own eyes . . . as we have seen [perf. *horan*] and testify [pres. *martyrein*]." (As usual, scribes have harmonized, e.g., aorist of *theasthai* here in Codex Alexandrinus.) GJohn twice uses the phrase "to have seen [perf. *horan*] and testify" (1:34; 19:35). Probably the use of *theasthai* here was dictated by its previous use in 4:12a: "No one has ever seen [perf. tense] God." If God has not been seen, His Son has.

Is the author returning to the distinctive "we/us" of 1:1–5, referring to the Johannine School of tradition-bearers who inherited and continued the testimony of the Beloved Disciple who was an actual eyewitness? (The thesis of the special "we" is supported by Balz, Bonsirven, Brooke, Chaine, Dodd, Hauck, Holtzmann, Schnackenburg, Schneider, Stott, B. Weiss, and Westcott.) The use of "see and testify" in reference to the Beloved Disciple in John 19:35 makes this a serious possibility. The argument that *theasthai* must refer to physical sight is too dubious to reinforce that possibility (ABJ 29, 503), however; and the eyewitness motif is called into question by the reference in 14b to seeing that God has sent His Son *as Savior,* a sight that must be other than physical. Moreover, v. 16 ("As for us, we have come to know and believe"), which echoes 14a, seems to refer to a whole Community experience. (The nondistinctive "we" is supported by Bruce, de Jonge, Hoskyns [?], and Marshall, sometimes phrased [unhappily] as "the Church as a whole.") I take it in this latter sense: the "we" that has seen and can testify is not the Johannine School alone but the members of the Johannine Community faithful to the author, who are being reminded of their special privilege in light of the general affirmation, "No one has ever seen God" (4:12a).

14b. *that the Father has sent the Son as Savior of the world.* For the Johannine use of "send" and the alternation between the perf. tense (4:9 and here) and aorist (4:10), see the NOTE on 4:9b above. Both 4:9 and John 3:17 mention "the world" positively in the context of God's sending the Son; and the further theme of salvation is shared by John 3:17 and the present verse. That Gospel passage uses the verb *sōzein* (6 times in GJohn, plus 1 usage of the abstract noun *sōteria*); only here do the Epistles use a word from the same root: *sōtēr,* "Savior," which appears in the Samaritan confession of faith in John 4:42: "We have heard for ourselves, and we know that this really is the Savior of the world." (Note the interchangeability of hearing and seeing that Jesus is Savior.)

In the OT Yahweh is the salvation of Israel and of the individual Israelite (Deut 32:15; Ps 24:5; Isa 12:2), passages that are rendered in the LXX as "Savior." The Messiah king is not called a savior; yet see Zech 9:9 where the LXX has "saving" for "victorious." *Enoch* 48:7 speaks of the Son of Man as saving the righteous, but that section of *Enoch* may be of Christian origin. In the NT "Savior" is a more common title in the later works, e.g., in the uncontested Pauline works it occurs only in Philip 3:20, but 10 times in the Pastorals (both for God and for Jesus; see Titus 1:3–4), 4 times in Luke/Acts, and 5 times in I and II Peter. The fact that GJohn places it on the lips of Samaritans has suggested to some that it came into Johannine Christianity from that group usually considered to be highly Hellenized. In classical paganism the title was given to many deities, especially to Zeus, to the gods of the mystery religions, and to the healing god Aesclepius (Aesculapius); and ultimately it was taken over into the cult of the Roman emperor. (Cicero, *In Verrem* 2.2.63, ℣154, comments that there is no Latin word to express its richness and defines *sōtēr* as one who gives salvation.) The title "Savior of the world" was borne by the Emperor Hadrian (reigned A.D. 117–38). Is there a polemic aspect to the Johannine use of the title? The struggle against emperor worship is clear in Revelation (seemingly over the imperial use of the titles "Lord" and "God"), but not in I John or GJohn, although the atmosphere of Domitian's persecution has been detected in the latter by F. Vouga, *Le cadre historique et l'intention théologique de Jean* (Paris: Beauchesne, 1977) 97–111; see my *Community* 65. The idea that there is an epistolary polemic against a title used in the mystery religions depends for validity on whether or not the secessionists were devotees of such cults, a view for which I find little evidence.

15a. *Whenever anyone confesses that Jesus is the Son of God.* Literally, "Whoever [*hos ean*] confesses"; the more elegant form *hos an* was seen in 2:5a above, but BDF 107 points out that *ean* is becoming interchangeable for *an* in NT Greek. The literal construction ("Whoever confesses . . . God abides in him") makes the whole first line a *casus pendens* (BDF 466²), where a noun or pronoun that is part of the main clause is brought forward and mentioned by anticipation in order to highlight it. To render it as a conditional sentence makes smoother grammar; see BDF 377 for the Greek equivalence between "whoever" and "whenever anyone." The verb *homologein* is in the aorist subjunctive here, as contrasted with the pres. subjunctive in 1:9a ("If we confess our sins") where a continued acknowledgment was appropriate. Although Codex Alexandrinus would read the pres. here, the author is now talking about the (single) basic public confession of faith that makes one a Christian. Obviously he assumes that the person who makes the confession continues to believe in it, but he is not envisaging a constant oral repetition of the confession as a basis of divine abiding. In the NOTE on 1:9a we saw that 9 of 10 uses of *homologein* in the Johannine writings are christological. In I John 2:23 the confession concerned the Son; in 4:2 (and II John 7) it concerned Jesus Christ come in the flesh; here it concerns *"Jesus* is the Son of God." (By harmonization Codex Vaticanus and some versional evidence have "Jesus Christ is the Son of God.") The predicate has the article, which implies that "the Son of God" is a definite and well-known designation (MGNTG 3, 183; BDF 273). Thus the issue is not who Jesus is, but whether the well-known Son of God is Jesus.

15b. *then God abides in him and he abides in God.* As in 4:13a, the second "abides" is understood rather than expressed in Greek. The previous two references to mutual indwelling between God and the Christian (3:24b; 4:13a) placed first the Christian's abiding in God; the reversed order here suggests that there is no set priority. For the *menein en* formula, see the NOTE on 2:6a.

16a. *As for us.* A *kai hēmeis* as in 14a above. There is less reason here for arguing that the "we" is distinctive (the Johannine School of tradition-bearers), since understanding and believing are clearly attributable to the whole Johannine Community. (Schnackenburg, who opts for the distinctive "we" in 14a, thinks that the author has returned to the general Johannine "we" here!)

we have come to know and believe. As in 14a two verbs follow the "as for us," literally, "we have known and have believed," the perf. tenses respectively of *ginōskein* (NOTE on 2:3a) and of *pisteuein* (NOTE on 3:23b). The author is again talking about the basic knowledge and act of faith involved in Christian conversion/initiation/baptism. Scribes (Codex Alexandrinus, minuscule 33) have changed the second verb to the pres. tense ("and continued to believe"); but that is not the point being made. These two verbs are most often combined in the same tense, but also in perf./aorist with future/pres. combinations:

- John 6:69: "We have come to believe [perf.] and know [perf.] that you are God's Holy One."
- John 8:31–32: To the Jews who believed [perf.] in him, "You will know [future] the truth."
- John 10:38: "Believe [pres.] in these works that you may come to know [aorist] and do know [pres.]."
- John 14:7–10: "If you really knew [perf.] me, then you would know [future] my Father too, and from now on you do know [pres.] Him. . . . Do you not believe [pres.] that I am in the Father, and the Father is in me?"
- John 17:8: "They knew [aorist] in truth that I came forth from you, and they believed [aorist] that you sent me."

■ I John 4:1–2: "Do not believe [pres.] every Spirit. . . . Now this is how you can know [future] the Spirit of God."

A quick glance at these texts should convince the uncommitted that there is little difference between the aorist and perfect tense usages of "to know," and that there is no set sequence of priority between knowing and believing. Chaine, *Epîtres* 206, is convinced that there is a significant difference between the "We have come to believe and know" of John 6:69, and the "We have come to know and believe" of the present verse, since Chaine finds a sequence of knowledge leading to faith, which in turn leads to more perfect knowledge. De la Potterie, *La vérité* 1, 302, insists that in GJohn belief is always prior to knowledge and is annoyed with Schnackenburg's "pretending" that there is no difference in the word order. In my judgment it is no pretense: The word order makes no difference whatever for a reason that de la Potterie himself has recognized: in these combinations "knowing" and "believing" are two ways of describing one composite action. For that reason I reject also Westcott's contention (*Epistles* 155) that in the present verse knowledge is more prominent than belief: "We must have a true if limited knowledge of the object of faith before true faith can exist."

16b. *the love that God has in us.* This accusative object is governed by the composite action of the two verbs of the preceding line, not simply by the verb "to believe," which in Johannine usage would take either a dative (18 times) or *eis*, "into," with the accusative. The expression "to have love" (which may reflect Semitic usage) covers a wide range for the Johannine writers. John 5:42 speaks of people having the love of God in themselves (see the NOTE on 2:23ab for the theme of "having" God and "having" divine realities); John 13:35; 15:13 speak of Christians' having love for one another; and now we hear of God's having love for Christians. Among 28 uses of *echein*, "to have," in I John, this is the only instance of God as subject. (The anomaly may have been noticed by scribes; for J. H. Greenlee, HTR 51 [1958] 187, points to a variant reading in P⁹ which makes Christ the subject.) Some want to stress the durative value of the present (God goes on having love for us); however, without excluding duration, the whole context points to a unique act of love by which God loved us in sending His Son and giving us life (4:9). The duration comes, not from the verb, but from the fact that we go on living by the life that God gave us.

The notion that the divine love includes the gift of life leads to my rendering *en hēmin* literally as "in us," as I have elsewhere throughout this unit (a view shared by Bonsirven, Büchsel, Chaine, de Ambroggi, de la Potterie, Dodd, Malatesta, Marshall, Ross, B. Weiss, Westcott, and Zerwick). The phrase is capable of other meanings, as we saw in the NOTE on 4:9a, e.g., "to/for/toward us," with *en* serving for *eis* (BDF 206³, 218); thus Schnackenburg, but to the contrary ZBG 105. Certainly that is the meaning in John 13:35: "the love that you have for [*en*] one another." "For/to us" is a common rendering here in English translations (KJV, RSV, NEB, NAB). Or else the phrase can mean "among us, in our midst," i.e., in the Community (Bruce?, Spicq). However, as Malatesta, *"tēn agapēn,"* points out, in only 2 other instances of the verb "to have" in I John does it govern the preposition *en;* and in both cases (3:15;

5:10) it is taken literally. Outside this unit the noun "love" is constructed with *en* in 2:5,15; 3:17, and in those cases it means "in." The emphatic position that the phrase has at the end of the treatment also makes better sense if it means "in us."

16c. *God is love.* The Greek is identical with 4:8b.

16d. *and the person who abides in love.* The initial *kai*, "and," has a consecutive force here. In the discussion of the *menein en* formulas in the NOTE on 2:6a, I classified this under (C), the miscellaneous group. The only other use of "abiding in love" is John 15:9–10: "Abide in my love. And you will abide in my love if you keep my commandments, just as I have kept my Father's commandments and abide in His love." The very similar *einai en* ("to be in") formula occurs in relation to love in 4:18a below.

16e. *abides in God and God abides in him.* The second "abides," which is the last word in the Greek order of the verse, is omitted by Codex Alexandrinus, minuscule 33, and the Vulgate. While this may reflect a scribal attempt at elegance (avoiding a third use of the verb within a dozen words), more likely it is imitation of the two other mutual indwelling statements in 4:13a,15b where the second verb is not expressed.

17a. *In this.* This *en toutō* construction is particularly complex; for there is a *hina* clause in 17b and a *hoti* clause in 17c; and according to the rule I gave in the NOTE on 2:3a, either of these subordinate clauses could plausibly explain the "In this," which would then point forward. However, it is also possible that these clauses have a different function not directly related to *en toutō*, which could then point backward to the preceding verse. Let us discuss three possibilities.

(a) The *en toutō* is explained by the *hina* clause of 17b: "In this has love reached perfection with us, that we have confidence on Judgment Day" (Bonsirven, Brooke, Bruce, Bultmann, Chaine, Haas, Hauck, Hoskyns, Schnackenburg, Schneider, THLJ, Wilder). An epexegetical *hina* interpreting *en toutō* is attested in John 15:8. The main difficulty centers on the awkward logic: love has reached perfection in something that has not yet happened. Even the counterargument that for the author "it is the last hour" (2:18) does not solve the difficulty, for 2:28 makes clear that the coming of Christ (in judgment) is still future. Translators attempt with subtle shifts (italics mine) to get around the difficulty: "Love is complete with us when we have absolute confidence *about* the day of judgment" (Moffatt); "Love *will come* to perfection in us when we can face the day of Judgment without fear" (JB).

(b) The *en toutō* is explained by the *hoti* clause of 17c: "In this has love reached perfection with us . . . that already in this world we are just the same as Christ is" (see Romaniuk, "Liebe" 82). This makes better sense than the preceding interpretation, and a *hoti* clause most frequently interprets *en toutō*. However, 17b would have to be parenthetical, a harsh construction (and even "unnatural" according to Westcott, *Epistles* 157). If the author meant to say this, he should have reversed the order of 17b and 17c.

(c) The *en toutō* is explained by what precedes in 16de: "The person who abides in love abides in God and God in him; in this has love reached perfection with us" (Alexander, de Ambroggi, Marshall, Plummer, Vellanickal, B. Weiss, Westcott). The sense is excellent and agrees precisely with what the author has said previously in 4:12: "If we love one another, God abides in us; and His love has reached perfection in us." Excellent sense can be found in the clauses that follow, provided that the *hina* of 17b is seen as introducing a result clause, and *hoti* means "because" (see my translation). Some would reject this interpretation on the incorrect grounds that *en toutō* always refers to what follows; but a reference to what precedes is quite defensible in John 16:30; I John 3:10,19.

has love reached perfection with us. The Clementine Vulgate makes "love" more specific by adding "of God." There is the usual dispute as to whether this means God's love for us (THLJ), or our love for God (Dodd, Romaniuk, Stott), or our love for others, or combinations. The verb "make perfect" (*teleioun*) was used previously of love in 2:5 and 4:12. The topic was discussed in the NOTE on 2:5b, along with the contention (wrong) that God's love could not be perfected (see also the NOTE on 4:12d). Since 16c has said that God is love, and that has to imply a love that is outgoing (toward the Son and toward Christians), it is relatively clear that this outgoing love from God reaches perfection, from one aspect, when it produces children in whom God dwells. (There can be no love in the Christian that does not involve love of one's brother Christians, as the author will insist in 4:20ff.; but that is not the issue at the moment, *pace* Chaine.)

How is *meth' hēmōn*, "with us," to be understood? In the Greek it stands closest to "love"; and so it can be read with the noun, "love toward us," which Bultmann argues would be equivalent to "He loved us" in 4:11, and "the love that God has in us" in 4:16b. However, the simple noun "love" often means God's love for us, and so there would be no need to attach awkwardly the prepositional phrase to the noun. I say "awkwardly" because in Greek a prepositional phrase modifying a definite noun would normally be preceded by the definite article, which is lacking here. It is more likely that the ancient versions, Westcott, B. Weiss, and others are right in taking the phrase *with the verb* "reached perfection." Even then many translations have been suggested: (a) "With regard to us" (Chaine). In this interpretation the prepositional phrase is equivalent to a dative (IBNTG 183), or the Greek *meta*, "with," is taken to represent Hebrew *'īm* with a verb of acting toward another (cf. Ps 78:37 with Josh 2:12). (b) "In us" (Bonsirven, Romaniuk). It becomes equivalent to *en hēmin* of 4:9a,12d,16b, meaning not merely "among us" (BDF 227[1]) but "within us." Sometimes II John 3 has been invoked for this interpretation ("With [= in] us there will be grace, mercy, and peace from God the Father"). (c) "Together with us," i.e., a "with" of cooperation (Westcott, and Schnackenburg who points to Hebrew *'et*), as in Acts 15:4: "They declared publicly the things that God had done together with them." Interpreters who are scandalized at the thought that God's love can be brought to perfection are even more scandalized at the suggestion that this might be through human cooperation; but the Johannine sensibilities are not necessarily those of later theology. The author seems to have gone beyond what he said in 4:12, "God abides in us, and His love has reached perfection in us"; for he now says, "The person who abides in love abides in God and God abides in him; in this has love reached perfection with us." Since he now mentions first the Christian's abiding in God, he may well mean "with us" literally in terms of our action.

17b. *with the result that we may have confidence on Judgment Day.* I explained in the NOTE on "in this" of 17a why the *hina*, "that," here is best taken as introducing a consecutive clause (ZBG 352) pointing to the result that the perfection of love will bring about, rather than as epexegetical of the "In this." (The failure to recognize that may have led scribes to introduce an indicative form of the verb here [Codex Sinaiticus] in place of the subjunctive.) The word *parrēsia*, "confidence, boldness," was discussed in the NOTE on 2:28b, where we saw that its epistolary use is in terms of having confidence before God or His Son, especially while facing judgment (I John 2:28; 3:21). This confidence stems from a friendship already established, so that *parrēsia* as a result of divine indwelling makes perfect sense. I John here is not far from Heb 10:35: "Do not throw away your confidence which will be richly rewarded."

As for "on Judgment Day" those who take this line as epexegetical of "in this" of 17a would often like to translate the *en* here, not as "on" but as if it were *eis*, "into, in relation to" (Bonsirven). Yet while in the NT *eis* is used for *en*, the reverse use of *en* for *eis* is rare (BDF 218). "Judgment Day" is literally "the Day of the Judgment," the only NT example where both nouns in the phrase have the definite article (cf. "the hour of the Judgment" in Rev 14:7). Both nouns are anarthrous in the 6 other NT instances in Matthew and II Peter, while Jude (v. 6) has "judgment of Great Day." Jewish literature of the two centuries before and after Christ has various expressions for Judgment Day:

> (the day of) the great judgment: *Enoch* 10:6; 16:1
> the day of the great condemnation: *Jub.* 5:10
> the day of judgment: *IV Ezra* 7:113
> the day of the wrath of judgment: *Jub.* 24:30
> the day of the Lord's judgment: *Ps. Sol.* 15:13

There can be little doubt that the expression in I John refers to the same climactic moment that GJohn calls "the last day" and I John calls "the last hour" (NOTE on 2:18a above), the moment when Christ will be "revealed . . . at his coming" (2:28) and "we shall see God as He is" (3:2). The verb *krinein*, "to judge," occurs 19 times in GJohn but not at all in the Epistles; the noun *krisis*, "judgment," occurs 11 times in GJohn but only here in the Epistles. The theme of judging is part of the realized eschatology of GJohn; the very presence of Jesus as the light come into the world is the judgment (John 3:19–21). The author of I John, however, is interested in future judgment. Bultmann, who attributes future eschatology in GJohn to the Ecclesiastical Redactor, also attributes to him this phrase "on Judgment Day." In the INTRODUCTION (III A2) I questioned the need for positing such a Redactor for I John, and I think it a serious mistake to overlook the importance of future judgment to the main theme of I John (see COMMENT).

17c. *because already in this world we are just the same as Christ is.* Literally, "because [or that: *hoti*] just as [*kathōs*] that one [*ekeinos*] is, so are we in this world." This is an example of group III of the *kathōs* comparisons discussed in the NOTE on 2:6bc, namely comparisons based on how Jesus was or is. The *kathōs* . . . *kai*, "just as . . . so," construction was mentioned in the NOTE on 2:18bc. Hauck and Schneider are among those who think that this line is corrupt and untranslatable. Bultmann, *Epistles* 72–73, who has exercised surgery on the preceding line, thinks that this line can be saved only by an addition: "because as that one is *in the love of the Father*, so are we *in love*." The obscurity is not centered primarily on the identity of "that one"; for, since 3:2 states that we shall be like God only in the future, that one to whom we are already alike ("just the same") must be Christ. Some who take the phrase "in this world" to modify "Christ" are puzzled by the present tense, for it sounds to them as if the author were stating that Christ is still in the world; they insist that the author should have said, "Just as that one *was* in the world, so are we." Independent of the grammatical relationship of the phrase, there is a question as to what aspect of Christ's terrestrial life was in mind, e.g., his incarnate, human status (Spicq); his moral life (Büchsel, Vrede, Westcott—see I John 2:6); his love for others (Bonsirven, Chaine, de Ambroggi, Dodd, Holtzmann, Schlatter, B. Weiss—see I John 3:16,23). Evidently ancient scribes felt some of the same difficulty, e.g., after "on Judgment Day" at the end of the preceding line, the minuscule MSS. 876, 1611, and 2138 add the words: "Before the one who took on human form," making Christ the judge the object of comparison. Then, after "as that one" in this line, MSS. 876 and 2138 change the wording to read: "was blameless and clean in this world, so shall we be." The future tense of the last words is supported also by Codex Sinaiticus.

In this commentary I have not hesitated to point out the author's grammatical ineptness, but in 17c I would argue that he is not obscure at all and that none of these changes should be made. The author is offering a reason why we should have confidence on Judgment Day, a judgment to be rendered by Christ, as the author previously indicated when he said, ". . . that we may have confidence and not draw back in shame from him at his coming" (2:28). The reason for the confidence is that already in this world we have a resemblance to Christ, for we are in mutual union and indwelling with God, just as Christ *is* (Erdmann, Holtzmann, Romaniuk, Schneider, B. Weiss). Already we are children of God, just as Christ is (Vellanickal). In other words the author is repeating the reason he gave for confidence when he first spoke about the parousia: "We are God's children right now" (3:2). As Plummer long ago insisted, the "in this world" phrase describes us, not Christ (just as the literal word order indicates); and the author is writing about the present status of Christ, not about his past terrestrial life. (The attempt to substitute a past tense in relation to Christ is refuted by the pres. usage in the "just as Christ is" statements of 3:3,7.) The logic of the statement is that since we are already like Christ, we shall not be judged harshly. Our likeness to Christ is based on his status as Son of God, without any hint that he has been changed through the resurrection. Indeed "as Christ is" has a tone of changelessness that is vocalized by means of the verb "to be" in GJohn, e.g., "Before Abraham even came into existence, I am" (John 8:58); "In the beginning was the Word" (1:1). Balz, Harrison ("Key"), Houlden, and Vellanickal are among those who hold a view of this verse more or less similar to mine.

18ab. *Love has no room for fear; rather, perfect love drives out fear.* The first part is literally, "Fear is not in love," which some editions of Nestle's Greek text and some commentaries (Bultmann, Schnackenburg) treat as the last part of v. 17. (Verse divisions were first introduced by Robert Estienne [Stephanus] in his 1551 Greek NT and in his 1555 Latin Vulgate NT. Subsequently T. Beza changed some verse numbers, and in this he was followed by the Elsevirs who produced the *Textus Receptus* or standard Greek NT in 1633. Here most versions and commentaries follow the *Textus Receptus* division allotting the clause to v. 18.) Among scholars there is the usual debate as to whether the author means God's love for us (Bultmann), our love for God (Dodd, B. Weiss), our love for one another, divine love, etc. (NOTE on 2:5b). There is probably continuity with the theme of love that has run through the unit: an outgoing love that comes from God, is manifested in Jesus, gives us life, and remains in us actively manifesting itself in love of others and of God. The word for "perfect" (*teleios*) appears only here in the Johannine writings but has the same meaning as "made perfect" (*teleioun*) in 4:12d,17a, and in the last line of the present verse. As we have heard, the perfection of love comes from divine indwelling: when God comes and abides in love, there is no room left for fear. The use of the term "to drive out" (*exō ballein*) hints at the type of fear (*phobos*) involved; for in passages like Matt 8:12; 22:13; 25:30 the verb *ekballein* is employed in scenes of final judgment where the evil are cast out into the darkness. *Ekballein exō*, "to drive out outside," appears in John 6:37 where Jesus promises, "Anyone who comes to me I will never drive out." In a way, then, the epistolary author is saying that, for those in whom love is perfected through God's indwelling, judgment has already taken place and the evil of fear has been cast out. The fear concerns being condemned by God on Judgment Day, a fear well attested in OT and NT. Eloquently Isaiah (2:19) writes, "Men shall burrow into caves in the rock and holes in the earth from the fear of the Lord and before the glory of His majesty, when He rises to terrify the earth." For those who commit deliberate sins, Heb 10:27,31 holds out: "a fearful prospect of judgment and a fury of fire that will consume adversaries. . . . It is a fearful thing to fall into the hands of a living God."

Despite the clarity given by the context to the author's mention of fear, some commentators think it necessary to speculate on the relation of love to different kinds of fear, e.g., that love is consonant with the fear of hurting another and with the fear of affronting the love of God (Alexander, Dodd). Tertullian (*Scorpiace* 12.4; CC 2, 1092) used this text to prove that one need not fear martyrdom. Other scholars discuss whether there is a contradiction between I John's rejection of fear and the biblical stress on fearing God, e.g., "You shall fear the Lord your God" (Deut 6:13; also Isa 11:1; Prov 1:7), and "Fear Him who can destroy both body and soul in hell" (Matt 10:28). However, besides such passages that regard fear (reverence, respect) in reference to God as necessary and praiseworthy, there are passages that present fear as a less worthy attitude toward God, e.g., Paul can write passages of opposite import:

"Do not become proud but stand in fear" (Rom 11:20), and in the same letter (8:15): "You did not receive a spirit of slavery to fall back into fear; rather you received the spirit of sonship." Ignatius of Antioch offered a choice: "Let us either fear the wrath to come or love the grace which is present—one of the two" (*Eph.* 11:1). In Judaism Philo affirmed, "To love God is most suitable for those into whose understanding of the Existing One . . . no passion enters; . . . to fear is most suitable for others" (*On the Unchangeableness of God* 14 ✠69); also "To love God as a benefactor, or failing that, to fear Him at least as ruler and Lord" (*On the Special Laws* 1.55 ✠300). One may ask whether "fear" as a good category had not completely disappeared from the Johannine scene with its realized eschatology. (Bonsirven, *Judaïsme* 2, 43–47, points out that this was happening in contemporary Judaism; and in Greco-Roman moral thought Seneca insisted, "Love cannot be mingled with fear" [*Epistulae Morales* 47 ✠18].) In John 6:19–20 Jesus tells his disciples not to be afraid; and when Jesus enters Jerusalem, the Scripture is fulfilled: "Do not be afraid, O daughter of Zion" (12:15). While there is fear of "the Jews" who are a menacing force (7:13; 9:22; 19:38; 20:19), and Pilate is afraid of Jesus whom he hears to be the Son of God (19:8), no GJohn passage advises salutary fear for the disciples. This sole mention of fear in the Epistles may mean that the Johannine writers regarded every kind of fear, including fear of God, as something that has no place among God's children.

18c. *for fear carries with it punishment.* Literally, "fear has punishment" (*kolasin echein*). Windisch does not do justice to this phrase when he suggests that it means "Fear has punishment in view." Yet it is not clear whether the author means "Fear has to do with [includes] punishment" (Bonsirven, Westcott) or "Fear has [is] its own punishment" (Brooke, Law). Nevertheless, the difference of meaning is not enormous. It now becomes clear that for the author fear involves not only the absence of love but also the presence of the punishment it anticipates. By detracting from love, which involves God's presence, fear is anticipating final punishment, which consists of the absence of God. The Greek *kolasis* seems originally not to have meant "torment" but "pruning, correcting, chastising for one's own good." Thus, Philo (*On the Confusion of Tongues* 34 ✠171) comments, "*Kolasis* is not something harmfully punitive, but a preventive and a correction of sin." In Hellenistic Greek increasingly *kolasis* did come to mean "punishment," e.g., "eternal punishment" is a set expression employing *kolasis* in the *Testaments* (*Reuben* 5:5; *Gad* 7:5). When Andronicus, a murderer, is put to death, II Macc 4:38 describes it in terms of the Lord according to him the *kolasis* he deserved; and Wisdom 19:4 sees the destruction of the firstborn of the Egyptians amid the slaughter of them in the Red Sea as fulfilling their *kolasis*. The only other NT occurrence is in Matt 25:46: "They shall go away into eternal punishment." In light of I John's contrast between the attitudes of confidence and fear on Judgment Day, the author is surely relating fear to eternal punishment which is already making itself felt. *Hermas* (*Sim.* 9.18.1) has a somewhat similar outlook: "He who does not know God and acts wickedly has punishment [*echein kolasin*] for his wickedness."

18d. *Love has not reached perfection in one who is still afraid.* Literally, "the fearer is not perfected in love." The author means this as a contrast to 17a where he has spoken about love reaching perfection (same verbal form of *teleioun*) when one abides in love and God abides in him. Some scholars have speculated that we have here a parallel to the Pauline idea of gradation among Christians so that only some are perfect or mature (*teleios*), e.g., I Cor 2:6; 14:20; Philip 3:15; Col 1:28; 4:12. This is dubious, however, for in Johannine dualism the opposite to perfect love may not be imperfect love but hate. To hold on to fear is to be on the wrong side of judgment.

19. *As for us, we love because He loved us first.* The personal pronoun *hēmeis* placed first for emphasis echoes the technique used in 4:14a,16a (but here it is without initial *kai*). Bultmann, *Epistles* 75, denies that the position lends emphasis when there is no accompanying particle (*oun, de*); but the same pattern has occurred before (*kai hymeis* in 2:20; *hymeis* in 2:24; *kai hymeis* in 2:27) where the presence or absence of a *kai* made no difference in the emphasis. (Here some scribes supply an *oun*, "accordingly" after *hēmeis*, e.g., Codex Alexandrinus and the Vulgate; but although *oun* is used 194 times in GJohn, its only epistolary use is in III John 8 [BDF 451¹].) After "we love" some scribal traditions supply an object (perhaps reflecting a feeling that the verb is subjunctive) e.g., the Byzantine tradition supplies "Him"; Codex Sinaiticus, the minuscule 33, the Syriac, Bohairic, and Clementine Vulgate versions supply "God"; and a few minor witnesses supply "each other." The absence of an object in Codices Vaticanus and Alexandrinus, and in the Sahidic and Jerome's Vulgate is original (TCGNT 714). Scribes have also tended to clarify the "He" that is the subject of "loved," for Codex Alexandrinus and the Vulgate read "God." All such "improvements" testify to the almost epigrammatic character of the Johannine statement.

Grammatically, the use of *prōtos*, "first of all," for the comparative *prōteros*, "before, earlier, first of two," is common in the NT (BDF 62); see John 2:10; 20:4,8. It is difficult to determine whether *agapōmen* should be read as a hortatory subjunctive, "let us love" (Latin, Peshitta, Balz, Bonsirven, Bultmann [?], Hauck, Schnackenburg), or as an indicative, "we love" (Brooke, Bruce, Houlden, Marshall, Metzger, Plummer, Schneider, Stott, B. Weiss, Westcott, Windisch). The scribal attempts to supply *oun* and a direct object reflect a sense for what would be more normal in a subjunctive construction. The subjunctive is favored by the parallelism with 4:7a, "Beloved, let us love one another." The indicative is favored by the parallelism with 4:14a,16a where there is an introductory *hēmeis*, "we." There is really no way to decide, but the tone of confidence throughout this subsection favors the indicative, for "we love" has the implication "we are able to love."

Not only scribes but also modern commentators have debated about the object implied in "we love." Bonsirven, Houlden, and B. Weiss argue that it means (primarily) "we love God," while Bultmann and Schnackenburg see a reference to brotherly love. Probably the author is thinking of all love that deserves the designation *agapē* without reflecting whether that love is directed to a Christian brother or to God. Only in the next verse does he draw the implication for fraternal love.

20abc. *If anyone boasts, "I love God," while continuing to hate his brother, he is a liar.* The word for "liar" is the noun *pseustēs*. The author has reverted to the style of adversary statements used at the beginning of I John, namely, the three "If we boast" statements of 1:6,8,10, and the three "The person who claims" statements of 2:4,6,9. (This parallelism shows that here the author is thinking of the secessionists and not simply enunciating a general maxim, *pace* Alexander.) In particular, the present statement resembles 1:6: "If we boast, 'We are in communion with Him,' while continuing to walk in darkness, we are liars [*pseudesthai*]," although there is also a similarity to 2:4: "The person who claims, 'I know Him,' without keeping His commandments, is a liar [*pseustēs*]." In all these instances there is a claim about a relationship to God that *can* be made good within the sphere of Johannine expectation but is negated by the behavior of the claimant. Therefore, in this verse the author is not rejecting the ideal of loving God (see NOTE on 2:5b). One might have expected him to contrast the claim to love God with indifference toward one's brother. However, in Johannine dualism neither indifference nor insufficient love is the opposite to loving—that opposite is described as not loving at all (4:20d) or hating (4:20b), as we saw in the NOTE on 2:9b. Again one might have expected the author to charge any person who claims to love God and still hates his brother to be guilty of misunderstanding or incompleteness, but Johannine dualism is harsher. Just as hate is opposed to love (and God is love), so lying is opposed to truth (and Jesus is the truth). As I stressed in the survey of Johannine vocabulary for lying (NOTE on 1:6c), the author is hereby accusing such a person of belonging to the realm of Satan for whom the lie is native language (John 8:44). If God is present in love, "the father of the lie" is present in hate.

20de. *For the person who has no love for his brother whom he has seen cannot love the God he has never seen.* Literally, this involves an artistic chiasm of the A,B,B′,A′ type: "[A] The one not loving [B] the brother whom he has seen, [B′] the God whom he has not seen, [A′] he is not able to love." Over against Codices Vaticanus and Sinaiticus, which support the text I have translated, many traditions thought that a rhetorical question ("how can he love the God . . . ?") would be stronger or stylistically more elegant (Codex Alexandrinus, and the Latin, Peshitta, Bohairic, Armenian, and Ethiopic versions). However, they were conforming the style of 4:20 to that of 3:17, a passage where there is a similarity of thought: "When someone has enough of this world's livelihood and perceives his brother to have need, yet shuts out any compassion towards him—how can the love of God abide in such a person?" In both verses the author is talking about a brother who is physically seen (respectively *theōrein* and *horan*, without difference of meaning). In the earlier text the rhetorical question *implied* that the love of God could not abide in a person who neglected his brother; here he is more explicit that such a person cannot (*dynasthai;* see p. 412) love God. Does 4:20de represent the Christianization of a secular aphorism? That may well be true in 5:1b below, as we shall see; but here I doubt it for several reasons. Would a secular (pagan) aphorism speak of a "god never seen"? That is the author's language in 4:12a. Moreover, the parallel in 3:17 was surely the author's composition, and so there is good reason to think this may be as well. If one does attribute the statement to the author, how does he understand the inability he describes? (See Dodd, *Epistles* 124.) Is it simply factual or practical inability since one love is a necessary step to the other? (An example of this inability is that a person who does not know how to read cannot receive education from reading books—the easier must precede the more difficult.) Or is there a more radical inability stemming from the nature of love? (A person who is mentally retarded may be taught basic reading but still be unable to receive education from books.) I would argue for the latter stemming from the Johannine notion that all *agapē* comes from God and *has to express itself* in love of brother (as well as love of God). And so a person who does not love his brother cannot love God, not simply because he has not taken the first, easier step, but because he has no love (from God) with which to love (see COMMENT).

21ab. *And the commandment we have had from Him is this: the person who loves God must love his brother as well.* Literally, "And this commandment we have from Him that [*hina*] the person. . . ." The "and" tightly connects v. 21 to the preceding verse, upon which it is a commentary. Although the twofold commandment of 3:23 has dominated this whole unit, this is the first explicit mention of a commandment since that verse and the only mention in chap. 4. "Commandment" will be a strong motif in the following verses. The *hina* clause is epexegetical of "this commandment" (MGNTG 3, 139), but there may remain a tonality of purpose: love is the substance and goal of the commandment. Some scribes have interpolated "God" in place of "him" for clarity (Codex Alexandrinus; Clementine Vulgate); the textual reading may be wrong, but the interpretation of the "Him" is correct, as most modern commentators agree (Brooke, Chaine, Plummer, Schnackenburg, Schneider, B. Weiss, West-cott) on the basis of the context. The attempt of Hauck, Houlden, and the NEB to interpret the "him" as Christ is implausible—were he suddenly invok-ing Christ, the author would probably have used *ekeinos* as in 4:17. Despite the fact that in GJohn Jesus himself gave the commandment, we have seen in 2:3–4 and 3:22–24 that more plausibly the epistolary author consistently attrib-utes the commandment to God; and II John 4 speaks unambiguously of hav-ing "received a commandment from the Father." In the five other Johannine statements of the love commandment (John 13:34; 15:12,17; I John 3:23; II John 5), the phraseology is loving "one another"; this is the only instance of its being phrased as one "must love his brother." This equation supports the thesis I have been defending, that the commandment always refers to love of one's fellow (Johannine) Christian and is narrower than the Synoptic commandment to love one's neighbor (NOTE on 2:9b). In the next verse the author will confirm this by speaking of God's believing children.

5:1a. *Everyone who believes that* Jesus *is the Christ has been begotten by God.* We have seen that all the uses of *pisteuein*, "to believe," in I John (NOTE on 3:23b) are christological, either directly (as here) or indirectly (as in 4:16a, the only other use in this unit). In 5:5b, the next instance of *pisteuein*, the au-thor will speak of the person who "believes that *Jesus* is the Son of God." Thus

5:1 and 5:5 together invoke the full Johannine confession: "Jesus is the Christ, the Son of God" (John 20:31). It has been fashionable to affirm that what is demanded is not belief in an intellectual truth about Jesus but belief in a person with whom one enters a relationship. While not denying the latter, I would insist that there is an intellectual content in the Johannine demand for belief, and that one must understand Jesus correctly in order to have a salvific relationship with him. Brooke, *Epistles* 128, perceptively affirms that the author "would have regarded the belief that Jesus is the Christ as inseparable from faith in Jesus *as* Christ." Klein, "Quasimodogeniti" 207, is right in his observation that for the author the issue is not the christological legitimacy of the title "Christ" (or "Son of God") but the unique and unreserved applicability of that title to Jesus in his earthly career.

One might have expected a reverse order whereby belief would precede divine begetting, as in John 20:31 belief leads to the gift of divine life. Yet John 1:12–13 agrees with the present passage since it describes believers as those who were begotten (aorist) by God. Scholars disagree: Chaine, *Epîtres* 210, followed by Vellanickal, sees love as a consequence but faith as a cause of filiation; yet Stott, *Epistles* 172, would make believing the consequence of the new birth; and Brooke, *Epistles* 128, holds that the author is not clear on the cause or result issue. (One may find similar ambiguity in Paul by comparing Gal 3:26, "Through faith you are all sons of God," with I Cor 12:3, "No one can say, 'Jesus is Lord,' except by the Holy Spirit.") Probably the Johannine writers think of believing and begetting as belonging together and simultaneous, even though confessed belief may serve as a sign of having been begotten. Second-century gnostics who had a theory of the preexistence of the saved could interpret a formula such as this in their favor: the true believer is one who has been begotten by God (before life in this world).

The perf. tense of *gennan*, used here for "begotten by God," is employed by the Johannine writers 9 times for the divine origin of the Christian. (See the NOTE on 2:29b for why "begotten" is preferable to "born.") All the other I John statements (2:29; 3:9; 4:7; 5:18) relate the divine begetting to the Christian's behavior (acting justly, not sinning, and loving)—an indication that belief and behavior are two aspects of the same struggle in I John, for the author is defining the status of God's children in terms that exclude the secessionists.

1b. *and everyone who loves the parent loves the child begotten by him.* Literally, ". . . loves the one [masc.] who begot [aorist] loves the one begotten [perf.] by him." Stott, *Epistles* 172, insists that the idea is not simply static, for begetting and being begotten establish an affinity and affection that explain why love for the one demands love for the other. A likeness has been communicated, and the author is not asking for love for the individuals independently of their inherited character. An impressive group of textual witnesses (Codices Sinaiticus and Alexandrinus, and the Peshitta, Clementine Vulgate, Armenian, and Ethiopic versions) reads a *kai*, "as well," after the main verb (the second "loves"); but both this *kai* and the jussive interpretation ("must love") are probably a scribal imitation of 4:21 where both are correct: "The person who loves God must love his brother as well." Augustine and a few modern scholars (e.g., Windisch) have suggested that "the one who is begotten by him" is Jesus; but this is surely wrong on several counts: "begotten" is unattested in the Johannine language for Jesus (see NOTE on 5:18b below); the phrase echoes "has been begotten by God" in the previous line, which cannot refer to Jesus; and the next line interprets the phrase in terms of "God's children." If the phrase does not refer to Jesus, how is this line to be understood? At least three possibilities have been suggested: (a) It is a general statement applicable to any parent; (b) It is a statement in reference to one's own parent, namely, that everyone who loves his own parent loves the other children begotten by him, i.e., one's brothers and sisters; and (c) It is a statement applied to God, drawing upon 5:1a, namely, that everyone who loves the God who begot loves the (Christian) child begotten by Him. Brooke, Haas, and Westcott (?) opt for (b), while Bultmann, Chaine, and de la Potterie opt for (c). However, while the epistolary author ultimately intends (b) and (c) as applications of his statement, it is not clear that either is the meaning of the statement itself. Most scholars, then, take it as an aphorism in sense (a). An aphorism on father and child/son probably underlies John 5:19–20a, e.g., "A son cannot do a thing by himself—only what he sees the father doing" (see ABJ 29, 218); also Matt 11:27: "No one knows a son the way a father does; no one knows a father the way a son does." Plutarch, *Moralia* (*On Brotherly Love* 6 ※480DEF), says, "Excellent and pious [*dikaios*] children will not only love each other the more because of their parents, but will also love their parents more because of each other. . . . To love one's brother is a more immediate proof of love for both father and mother."

2a. *This is how we can be sure.* This the last of eight epistolary instances of the *en toutō ginōskein* expression ("in this we/you know") and perhaps the most obscure (Bultmann, *Epistles* 77: "almost incomprehensible"). Literally the Greek reads:

> 2a. In this we know that [*hoti*] we love the children of God
> 2b. whenever [*hotan*] we love God and [*kai*] do His commandments

Among those who think that the primary reference of *en toutō* is backward to 5:1 are Alexander, Dodd, Haas, Kittler, Marshall, Schnackenburg, THLJ, B. Weiss, and Wilder. Among those who think the reference is forward to the *hotan*, "whenever," clause are Balz, BDF, Bonsirven, Brooke, Bultmann, Chaine, Hauck, Moffatt, Schneider, Stott, Vellanickel, Windisch, and NEB. A third possibility is proposed by Painter (*John* 124), who argues that this is one of the instances in I John (along with 3:24 and 4:13) where *en toutō* points in both directions.

In the NOTE on 2:3a I gave as a grammatical rule the principle that *en toutō* points forward when it is followed by a subordinate clause which is related to the *toutō*. Here there are two subordinate clauses, one introduced by *hoti* and the other by *hotan;* but does either explain the *toutō*? Almost all scholars think that the *hoti* clause does not and is rather the object of "we know." (However, a desperate solution makes the *hoti* epexegetical of *en toutō* thus: "Of this we can be sure: we should love God's children if we are to love God and keep His commandments." Not only does this implausibly make *en toutō* the object of "we know"; it also posits a cohortative translation of the first verb "to love.") And so the discussion centers on the role of the *hotan* clause. It can introduce an independent sentence: "Whenever we love God, we do His commandments as well [= *kai*]," in which case the *en toutō* would surely refer backward to 5:1. Or it can introduce a subordinate clause (as I have translated it literally above), a role that would establish this as an *en toutō* construction (type A) pointing forward to the subordinate clause. As support for the independent sentence rendition, one finds in GJohn several sentences introduced by *hotan*, e.g., "Whenever he tells a lie, he speaks his native language" (John 8:44); "As long as I am in the world, I am the light of the world" (9:5; also 7:27; 16:21). Although Wilder and B. Weiss defend the possibility of the independent sentence here in 5:2b, the presence of *kai*, to be rendered "as well," is awkward. The meaning would be more smoothly expressed without it, and one is left with the question of what "we do" first, since "we do His commandments as well." As support for the subordinate clause in 5:2b, one must remember that *hotan* is an abbreviation of *hoti + an (ean)* and that both *hoti* and *ean* are well attested as introducing epexegetical subordinate clauses following "In this we know." (See BAG 592 or BAGD 587–88 for the relative interchangeability of *hotan* and *ean*, and BDF 394 for epexegetical *hotan*.) The subordinate clause allows a natural translation of *kai*, and is the more plausible of the two renditions.

Then, however, we face a major difficulty of meaning: love for God becomes the criterion for knowing that we love God's children, whereas a few verses earlier (4:20) the reverse was true: Love of one's brother was the criterion for genuinely loving God. Bultmann, *Epistles* 77, acknowledging that *en toutō* points forward to the *hotan* clause, recognizes that the normal interpretation would then produce a circular paradox comprehensible only to the Johannine insider: "Because brotherly love is proof of love of God, so also love of God is proof of brotherly love." But how can the love for God, which cannot be measured, become the criterion for knowing the much more measurable love for brother? There are various attempts to avoid the obvious implication. For instance, one can treat the *hotan* clause of 5:2b as subordinate but not epexegetical of 5:2a, so that *en toutō* refers to what precedes (5:1). Usually this treatment involves adding an element to 5:2a that is not clear in the Greek. Schnackenburg suggests: "That is how we can be sure that we love God's children *too* when we love God and obey His commandments." Suggestions in THLJ would lead to this translation: That is how we can be sure that we *should* love God's children at the same time as (*hotan*) we love God and obey His commandments. Another possibility is to rearrange 5:2a and 5:2b (Ethiopic versions, Grotius): "This is how we can be sure that *we love God:* whenever we love God's children and obey His commandments." Dodd suggests: "By this we know that, when we love God, we love the children of God." Such interpretations are really commentators' proposals for what the author should have said—"improvements" rather than translations.

Many scholars (Balz, Bonsirven, Hauck, Klein, Schneider, Spicq, Stott, Vellanickal, Williams, Windisch, and TEV) acknowledge that *en toutō* points forward to an epexegetical *hotan* clause which is to be interpreted at face value: "This is how we can be sure that we do love God's children: whenever we love God and obey His commandments." They differ in diagnosing why the author would make such a statement. Hauck and Spicq see a warning against a purely humanitarian love, a danger that could come from the subject or the object. By way of subject, the author could be insisting that *agapē* is not philanthropy originating in human kindness—somewhat along the lines of I Cor 13:3, where Paul states that a person can distribute his goods to the poor and still not have *agapē*. One must recognize God as the origin for *agapē*, and this is done by loving God. Or the humanitarianism could come from the object, for in Johannine theology to love all human beings is not *agapē*. This is the love of one's fellow Christians, the children of God; and so one must love God as a control that true *agapē* is involved. (Sometimes cited as a parallel is Philo, *Questions on Genesis* 3, 42, "A lover of God is by the same token usually a lover of mankind"; in fact, however, that is quite contrary to the author's principle.) Above all, *agapē* is not a love of the world (Balz). While such points may be true, we do not find a struggle with humanitarianism in I John, although the last point (against love of the world) could be related to 2:15–17. Schneider argues that in using the love of brothers as a criterion for the love of God the author is speaking against his opponents, while in using the love for God as a criterion for the love of brothers the author is speaking to his own adherents. Yet it is more likely that the key to both statements lies in the debate with the secessionists who, if I am right, claimed to love their brothers, i.e., their fellow secessionists. In other words, the author may still be concerned with defining love for one's brother (thus, with different nuances, Büchsel, Kittler, Vellanickal). How does one child of God recognize and love another? In 5:1a the author made clear that for the object of one's love to be a brother, he has to be a believer with a true christology (the secessionists have a wrong christology). In 5:1b he stated the principle that to love God is to love those begotten by Him, i.e., His genuine Christian children. (Schnackenburg, Vellanickal, and others observe that 5:2a is related to 5:1b; the fact that the *en toutō* of 5:2a points forward to 5:2b does not mean that what follows it cannot repeat in another way what precedes.) From 5:1b the author proceeds in 5:2 to make an observation about the subject who does the loving: This subject must be one who loves God and obeys His commandments. (The secessionists regard the latter as unimportant.) Only a loving and obedient child is capable of a love that is divine (Vellanickal, *Sonship* 330, drawing upon Spicq, *Agapē* 3, 307). Thus, in secessionist love neither the subject nor the object meets the criterion for true *agapē*. The Arabic translation seems to have come near to this interpretation of the passage, for it reads, "This is how we can be sure that they are pure children of God, whenever. . . ."

2b. *whenever we love God and obey His commandments*. The "whenever" is *hotan*, the only epistolary use of this conjunction. As we saw in the preceding NOTE, a more normal Johannine usage would be *ean*, "if, when." Bonsirven and Westcott suggest that *hotan* was used to give greater attention to the repeated aspect of the verbs (MGNTG 3, 112); indeed, Westcott speaks of each act of love, each act of obedience, but that is overprecise. What *hotan* does catch is simultaneity. The idea is not that only after (or if) we love God and obey His commandments, do we then love God's children, but that the two actions go together and are simultaneous. In the Greek word order the object precedes the verb in both parts of this line and so may receive a certain emphasis.

Codex Sinaiticus and the Byzantine tradition read "keep [*tērein*] His commandments," a scribal harmonization with the next verse that illustrates normal Johannine usage ("keep" 9 times, as compared with "do [*poiein*]" only here—see NOTE on 2:3b above). While doing (obeying) commandments may offer a more energetic image than keeping commandments, there is no difference of meaning, as we see from the parallelism in I John 3:22: "We are *keeping* His commandments and *doing* what is pleasing in His sight." In 2:17 the author uses *poiein* for doing the will of God, which is the same as doing His commandments. It may be wondered whether in 5:2 the author speaks of commandments (plural) because he is thinking of both love and faith. However, when he did refer to the twofold idea in 3:23, he used "commandment" in the singular. More likely he is thinking of commandments as covering the whole moral life, subsumed in the commandment to love one another (or one's brother), last mentioned in the singular two verses before (4:21). In the NOTE on 2:3b we saw the Johannine tendency to alternate singular and plural without difference of meaning, e.g., "commandments" (3:22), "commandment" (3:23), "commandments" (3:24). *Pace* Bonsirven, the author is not subtly stressing a number of specific actions, but a totality of behavior that expresses love. This raises the question of whether the second part of the line is interpretative of the first, as a type of hendiadys (Bultmann; also Bonsirven, Chaine): "Whenever we love God by obeying His commandments." This would fit in with my thesis that the ability to love comes from God, and indeed as His commandment. Nevertheless, Bultmann urges this interpretation because he does not think that in Johannine theology we can love God in any other way than by loving one another. That is too narrow, and so I prefer to retain the coordination ("and obey His commandments"), understanding the second phrase as a necessary but not exhaustive specification of the first ("love God"). We are loving God in return for and by means of His love for us, and a necessary aspect of that is to share His love by loving one another as He commanded. This interpretation is not refuted by the next verse, which is scarcely meant as an exhaustive definition of the love of God.

3ab. *For the love of God consists in this: that we keep His commandments.* The opening formula is *houtos gar* ["for"] *estin*, a variant of the normal I John definition formula *kai houtos estin*, "Now this is" (NOTE on 1:5a—it will occur in the next verse and twice more in this chapter [5:11,14]). The *gar*, used in place of *kai*, draws an inference from what precedes and does nothing to aid Schnackenburg's proposal that a new subdivision begins here. The existence of other Johannine definitions of love shows that this one is not exhaustive, e.g., "In this, then, does love consist: . . . that He loved us and sent His Son as an atonement for our sins" (I John 4:10), and "Now this is love: that we walk according to His commandments" (II John 6). In the latter, "walking according to commandments" is still a third variant on "keeping" them (here) and "obeying" them (5:2), so that Brooke, *Epistles* 130, exaggerates when he finds in the use of "keep" a hint that the commandments are the expression of an underlying principle. In the Greek of this verse the "this" is defined by a *hina* ("that") epexegetical clause, as in I John 3:11,23; II John 6. Some would argue that the *hina* has not lost all its sense of purpose ("in order that"): Love not only consists in keeping commandments but enables such action.

Instead of the usual debate about one or the other of the five possible meanings of "love of God" (NOTE on 2:5b), most scholars assume that it means our love for God on the analogy of the previous line ("we love God"). An objective interpretation of the genitive is reinforced by parallels in GJohn where Jesus repeats the demand to "love me and keep my commandments" (14:15,21,23) and says of his own relationship to God, "I love the Father and I do exactly as the Father has commanded me." While accepting this, I would suggest that the subjective interpretation (God's love for us) is never absent from the epistolary author's use of this phrase. If one resorts to parallels in GJohn, then 15:10 should not be forgotten: "And you will remain in my love if you keep my commandments, just as I have kept my Father's commandments and remain in His love," a passage where "love" in relation to commandments has an element of the subject who loves. And within I John the present verse resembles strongly 2:5: "Whoever keeps His word—truly in this person the love of God has reached perfection," a passage where God's love for us is involved. The main idea here may be that our love for God must find expression in keeping the commandment to love one another, but only because God loves us are we able to love one another.

3c. *And His commandments are not burdensome.* In the traditional verse division the subordinate clause that follows and explains this line is marked as the beginning of v. 4, but to solve that awkwardness SBJ and JB begin v. 4 here. Brooke, *Epistles* 130, makes the point that the author does not say "difficult"; but the distinction between "burdensome" and "difficult" is not established by Jewish sources. In Deut 30:11 God says, "This commandment which I command you this day is not too excessive for you"; and in commentary on this passage Philo (*On the Special Laws* 1.55 ✕299) states, "God asks nothing from you that is burdensome or complicated or difficult, but only something quite simple and easy." This reassurance may have been all the more necessary in the Judaism of the Roman period where Schnackenburg, *Johannesbriefe* 253, detects a spirit of mistrusting one's own religious abilities and strengths. In Matt 11:30 we hear Jesus claim, "My yoke is easy, and my load is light"; and in Matt 23:4 similar language is used to reproach the scribes and Pharisees, "They bind heavy burdens which are hard to bear and lay them on people's shoulders." A rabbinic distinction between "light" commandments and "difficult" (*hămûrôt*) ones is not in mind here.

In discussing why the commandments are not burdensome, commentators draw upon the whole Bible. Among the reasons suggested (see Plummer, *Epistles* 111) are the following: (a) God never demands what is truly hard. Some of the texts in the preceding paragraph might point in that direction; see also I Cor 10:13 on God's not allowing us to be tempted beyond what we can bear. The Council of Trent (Session VI, cap. 11; DBS 1536) cited this passage as proof that God does not demand the impossible. However, for I John the question here may be not whether the commandments of God are light or heavy in themselves, but whether they are heavy for a child of God (Chaine, *Epîtres* 211). (b) The burden is to be compared to the greatness of the reward. In Rom 8:18 Paul says, "I consider that the sufferings of the present time are not worth comparing with the glory that will be revealed to us." (c) Our love for God makes the burdens light. In Gen 29:20 we hear, "Jacob served seven years for Rachel, and they seemed to him but a few days because of his love for her." (d) God gives the strength to obey the commandments. Granted the reference in the next verse to conquering, one might invoke the maxim that the Qumran *War Scroll* (1QM 11:4–5) addresses to God: "Yours is the struggle and yours is the strength, not ours." In Philip 4:13 Paul says, "I can do all things in Him who strengthens me." *Hermas* (*Man.* 12.4.3–5) affirms, "The man who has the Lord in his heart is able to master all things and all these commandments; but those who have the Lord on their lips while their heart is hardened . . . for them these commandments are hard and difficult to walk in. . . . Put the Lord into your heart, and you shall know that nothing is easier or sweeter or more gentle than these commandments." Perhaps this is what *I Clement* 49:1 means, "Let him who has love in Christ perform the things ordered by Christ." The Johannine way of expressing this would be that God's love for us makes possible the keeping of the commandment to love one another. The specific reason that the author offers in the next line for the commandments not being burdensome is not precisely the same as any of the above but is closest to (d).

4a. *because all that is begotten by God conquers the world.* In 5:1b the author spoke of "the one begotten by him" and in 5:18a he will speak of "everyone who has been begotten by God"—both masculine. In 4:4 he spoke to his "Little Children" in the masculine plural: "You belong to God, and so you have conquered" (see also 2:13). Yet here the author uses the neuter to describe those who were begotten and who conquer. A somewhat similar use of the neuter where we would expect the masculine was the "what" of 1:1a (see NOTE there); and the neuter is frequent in GJohn, e.g., "what" or "all that" the Father has given to Jesus, referring to people in John 6:37,39; 17:2,7,24, and "what is begotten of the flesh" in 3:6. BDF 138[1] offers this explanation: "The neuter is sometimes used with reference to persons if it is not the individuals but a generic quality that is to be emphasized" (also MGNTG 3, 21). Here that would mean: "All those begotten by God inasmuch as thus begotten"; it would underline the power of divine begetting. MGNTG 2, 437 sees a stress on the collective aspect: As a group, those begotten by God conquer. ZAGNT 305 (on John 6:37) suggests the influence of Aramaic *kol d^e*, which means indifferently "everyone who, everything which." There is truth in one or more of these suggestions, but none of them explains why within a few verses the author shifts back and forth between masculine and neuter, a shift that may more simply reflect his liking for variety. If a reason needs to be offered for a neuter here (but not in 5:1b and 5:18a), it may be the author's desire to set up a category of what God has begotten over against another category, "the world."

Unexpectedly we are told that *the conquest of the world* by those begotten by God stops the commandments from being burdensome. In puzzling about an obstacle placed by the world that would make burdensome God's commandments (i.e., presumably the commandment to love one another), one should remember that elsewhere I John uses *nikan*, "to conquer" (NOTE on 2:13d), against the Evil One (2:13,14) and the secessionist Antichrists (4:4). Does the world tempt Christians to love it rather than one another (2:15–17), so that the author is thinking of a battle against pagan standards (Dodd)? Does the world or its Evil Prince tempt Christians to hate, an action characteristic of the world (3:12–17)? Or do the secessionists, who belong to the world and speak the language of the world (4:5), seek to confuse the author's followers about who are the brothers whom they should love? The last suggestion is closest to the general theme of this section, but the author does nothing to make his meaning clear. Indeed, one wonders if he is not just lending pastoral encouragement by using a Johannine aphorism without thinking out in detail the questions just discussed. Nor is it clear how far one should press the pres. tense ("conquers," "is conquering") to call attention to an ongoing battle between God's children and the world, especially since 5:4b will use an aorist to refer to the conquest of the world as a past and completed action. What is clear is that the victory of Jesus (John 16:33: "Have courage, I have conquered the world") has been extended to the Community of those who believe in him.

COMMENT

After the unit on the testing of the Spirits, the statement, "Beloved, let us love one another," may seem abrupt and disconnected. Indeed, the abruptness has led a number of scholars to regard 4:7 as opening a major new division of I John (usually Part Three).[1] However, the sharpness of the change of idea is greatly reduced if we remember the twofold commandment of 3:23 which the author presumably intended as a guide for

[1] Brooke, de la Potterie, de Wette, Ewald, Häring, Jones, Law, Malatesta, Nagl, Schwertschlager, Smit Sibinga, and Westcott.

what would follow: "Now this is God's commandment: we are to believe the name of His Son, Jesus Christ, and we are to love one another just as He gave us the command." The unit 4:1–6, which began with "Beloved," was related to the first part of that commandment; for the test of the Spirits centered on "Everyone who confesses Jesus Christ come in the flesh" (4:2). The present unit, which begins with "Beloved," is related to the second part of that commandment; for it praises "Everyone who loves" (4:7), a praise that is specified later in the unit: "The commandment we have had from Him is this: the person who loves God must love his brother as well" (4:21). If each of the two units develops respectively a part of the twofold commandment, there is also a thought sequence from one to the other.[2] The first unit sharply divides those who "belong to the world" from those (us) who "belong to God." Since the latter group is hated by the former, there is urgent need for those who "belong to God" (4:6) to hold together by loving one another, especially since "love belongs to [is from] God" (4:7). The Spirit of God, prominent in the previous unit, returns here (4:13), as does the theme of correctly confessing Jesus (4:15).

There is very little agreement among scholars as to where the unit that begins with 4:7[3] comes to an end. Various suggestions for the perimeters are 4:7–12, 4:7–21, and 4:7–5:4.[4] Let us discuss each of those suggestions. (a) *The unit as 4:7–12* (Balz, Dodd, Häring, Marshall, Stott, Wilder, Williams). The chief argument is that love is the dominant theme of those verses, while 4:13–16a shifts the focus to christology and believing. However, the theme of love reappears in 4:16b and continues strongly to 5:4. Moreover, if one begins a new unit with 4:13, one should begin another unit with 4:16c, for 4:13–16b is no closer in theme to what follows it than it is to what precedes.[5] Thus, it seems better to evaluate 4:13–16a as a minor diversion relating the whole to 4:1–6, rather than as

[2] Wurm, *Irrlehrer* 142–43, criticized nineteenth-century scholars who saw no connection between 4:1–6 and 4:7–15, e.g., Bisping, Braune, Lücke, Luthardt, Mayer, and Rothe. Those who did see a connection included Düsterdieck, Ebrard, and Haupt. Later, Bonsirven, *Epîtres* 198, could still think it impossible to find a connection. For Dodd, *Epistles* 107, the unit 4:1–6 is a parenthesis, with 4:7ff. returning to the main theme.

[3] Since almost all interpreters recognize 4:1–6 as a unit, there is little debate about where the current unit begins.

[4] A few would press farther, e.g., Wilder to 5:5. Some who see 4:7–12 as a unit would see 4:13–21 or 4:13–5:4 as another unit. Klein, "Quasimodogeniti," argues for 5:1–5 as a self-contained unit marked off by chiasm (5:1aa = 5:4b–5; 5:1ab = 5:4a; 5:1ba = 5:2b–3; 5:1bb = 5:2a—note that 1aa refers to the first half of line 1a, and 1ab to the second half).

[5] Dodd thinks that Part Three, "The Certainty of Faith," runs from 4:13 to 5:13. Häring sees an alternation between love and faith thus: love (4:7–12); faith (4:13–16); love (4:17–21); faith (5:1a); love (5:1b–4); faith (5:5–12).

a new unit in itself. (b) *The unit as 4:7–21* (Brooke, Bruce, Feuillet, Hort, Hoskyns, Jones, Malatesta, Schneider, Westcott, Windisch). The chief argument again is that after 4:21 the theme shifts in 5:1a to belief and christology. However, only 5:1a mentions belief, and the theme of love returns in 5:1b for a few verses more. (c) *The unit as 4:7–5:4* (Alexander, Schnackenburg, THLJ). To be more precise, I would end the unit with 5:4a, as does Alexander; for once the theme of belief and christology begins in 5:4b, the theme of love does not return. One can have no certainty, but this understanding of the perimeters of the unit has two advantages. First, it keeps together a major treatment of love (with short interruptions pertaining to belief in 4:13–16a and 5:1a). Second, it ends the unit on the theme of love and commandments (5:2–3) that was introduced in 3:23, a passage that has served as a guide in determining the two units we have been discussing in ch. 4. Thus, a type of inclusion is involved.

There is even less agreement among scholars in discerning subdivisions within the unit. On the one hand, Hoskyns does not indicate any break within 4:7–21; on the other hand, other scholars have suggested breaks in a total of over ten places, as exemplified below:[6]

10/11:	Dideberg, Häring, Malatesta, Schnackenburg, Schneider, Westcott
11/12:	de Ambroggi, Moody
12/13:	Alexander, Balz, Brooke, Bruce, Bultmann, Dodd, Häring, Hort, Law, Marshall, Michl, Stott, Wilder, Williams, NEB, RSV, TEV
13/14:	Malatesta, B. Weiss
14/15:	de Ambroggi
15/16:	Hort
16b/16c:	Balz, Brooke, Haas, Hauck, Schneider, Westcott, Williams, Windisch, NEB, TEV
16/17:	Bonsirven, Bultmann, de Ambroggi, Gaugler, Häring, Law, Malatesta, Michl, Moody, Schnackenburg, THLJ
18/19:	Balz, Bonsirven, Bultmann, de Ambroggi, Dodd, Hort, Malatesta, Michl, Moody, Schnackenburg, Wilder, TEV
19/20:	Alexander
21/5:1:	Balz, Brooke, Bruce, Chaine, de la Potterie, Feuillet, Häring, Hauck, Hort, Hoskyns, G. Klein, Jones, Malatesta, Michl, Schneider, Stott, B. Weiss, Westcott, Williams, Windisch, NEB, RSV, TEV

[6] The list above should be read thus: The scholars mentioned after 10/11 propose a break between 4:10 and 4:11, so that 4:11 begins a new subdivision. It supposes that those who want to start a new unit with a verse (e.g., 4:13 or 5:1) would, *a fortiori,* favor at least a subdivision there.

My own inclination once more is, where possible, to use the author's apostrophes or terms of address as a guide. This helps with the first two subdivisions, for he addresses the Community as "Beloved" in 4:7 and 4:11. After that, the signs of subdivision are less clear; and so in the four subdivisions I list below I am far from certain that I have discerned the author's intent:

4:7–10, consisting of 13 lines.[7] It begins with "Beloved" and treats the origin of love. In 4:7 the author states, "Love is from God"; in 4:10, "He loved us [first]"—a type of inclusion.

4:11–16b, consisting of 14 lines. Its opening in 4:11 ("Beloved, if God so loved us, we in turn ought to love one another") matches the opening of the previous subunit in 4:7 ("Beloved, let us love one another since love is from God"). Dideberg, "Esprit" 97, observes that the first subunit deals with the origin of love in God, while the second deals with its terminus in believers. A type of inclusion marks off this subunit; for in 4:11 the author states, "God so loved us," while in 4:16b he speaks of "the love that God has in us." The theme of God's abiding occurs in 4:12 and 4:15 (the second and the penultimate verses).

4:16c–19, consisting of 11 lines. This is the least definable subdivision and seems to be a parenthetical reflection on themes of the preceding subunits. The theme of God abiding in us and of love reaching perfection, which occurred near the beginning of the second subunit, occurs near the beginning of this subunit as well. And both these second and third subdivisions close by stressing what *we* do (we know and believe; we love) in response to God's love for us. Most of the third subdivision is concerned with the opposition between perfected love and fear.

4:20–5:4a, consisting of 15 lines. The author returns to the theme of love of brothers (i.e., God's children), not mentioned specifically since 4:12, which spoke of loving one another. He sees this as a necessary component of loving God. The notion of commandment comes to the fore, matching the introduction (to the two units of ch. 4) in 3:23: "This is God's commandment . . . we are to love one another just as he gave us the command [ment]." There are also inclusions between this fourth subunit and the first subunit: "Everyone who loves has been begotten by God" (4:7) matches "Everyone who believes . . . has been begotten by God" (5:1); and "In this, then, does love consist" (4:10) matches "The love of God consists in this" (5:3). These inclusions support the thesis that the respective subunits constitute the beginning and end of the large unit.

Looking over these proposed subunits, one finds that the first three are similar in that they both begin and end with an emphasis on God's love. Let me list the three beginnings and the three endings:

---

[7] I shall report the length of each subdivision according to the number of lines in my translation, so that the reader can get an idea of the approximate length.

4:7:   Beloved, let us love one another since *love is from God*

4:11:   Beloved, if *God so loved us,* we in turn ought to love one another

4:16c: *God is love,* and the person who abides in love abides in God

4:10:   Not that we have loved God but that *He loved us*

4:16b: As for us, we have come to know and believe the *love that God has in us*

4:19:   As for us, we love because *He loved us first*

There remains one general problem about this unit. Why has the author thought it necessary to give such a long treatment of love when he has already treated this subject at least twice before? In 2:7–11 the love of brother was presented in relation to keeping the commandments and walking in light; in 3:10c–18 love was presented as the gospel heard from the beginning and was contrasted with the world's hatred. The return to the theme of love in the present unit is often regarded as an instance of the spiral technique whereby an author comes back again and again to a subject, each time adding ideas.[8] In any case, this is the most intensive treatment of love in I John; for of I John's 28 uses of *agapan,* "to love," 18 occur in this unit; and of I John's 18 uses of the noun *agapē,* 13 occur in this unit—thus two-thirds of the "love" vocabulary occurs here, at times making more precise the statements of a previous unit. In discussing 2:5b I had to devote a long NOTE to show that the ambiguous phrase, "the love of God," more often means God's love for us, rather than our love for God. In 4:7 at the beginning of this unit the author says less obscurely, "Love is from God," putting emphasis on God as the source rather than the object of our love. In 3:1 the author spoke of "the love the Father has bestowed on us in enabling us to be called God's children"; here it is made explicit that begetting by God makes love possible (4:7b). In 3:10bc the author stated that anyone who does not love his brother "does not belong to God"; here he specifies that such a lack of love indicates that a person has known nothing of God (4:8). In 3:16 the author defined love in terms of Christ's having laid down his life for us; here he specifies that this death was an atonement for our sins (4:10). Such specifications and clarifications are useful but scarcely warrant the composition of a whole new unit.

---

[8] Scholars tend to detect neat patterns in these three love units, e.g., light implies love in 2:3–11; life implies love in 3:11–19a; and love itself is treated in 4:7ff. (Alexander). While there are lines that could contribute to such an analysis, the author's thought is scarcely so neat. Less pretentious is Dideberg's analysis of the progression ("Esprit" 97): in 2:3–11 fraternal love represents the observance of a commandment; in 3:10c–24 fraternal love is the imitation of a Christ who gave his life; in 4:7–21 fraternal love is related to its source in the God who is love.

But there are some developments in this unit worthy of being called "new."[9] One of them is the admixture of affirmations about christology and faith in the treatment of love (4:14-15; 5:1a). Brooke, *Epistles* 116-17, thinks that this third treatment of love in I John is most helpful in making it clear that faith and love (the christological and the ethical) are inseparable.[10] As for new developments about *agapē* itself, here the author twice makes the lapidary statement "God is love" (4:8b,16c). Also he describes the antithesis between love and fear (4:18). Finally, he dramatizes as effectively as has ever been done in any literature the contradiction between love for God and hate for a fellow human being: "The person who has no love for his brother whom he has seen cannot love the God he has never seen" (4:20de). The result is that this third treatment of love in I John is the one that has been the most cited in Christian reflection and literature on the subject.

A. *Love Is from the God Who Is Love* (4:7-10)

The author begins with his customary "Beloved," which as an introduction to a unit concerned with love is even more appropriate here than it was in 4:1. Echoing the twofold commandment of 3:23, his exhortation in 4:7a is so strong that his words are tantamount to a commandment, "Let us love one another."[11] He wants those who "belong to God" (4:6) to love one another "since love is from God" (4:7b). By inculcating this love, the author hopes to keep his followers from falling under the influence of the Spirit of Deceit and going out into the world (4:1d,6), a world where hate of the brothers is characteristic (3:13).

The idea that love is from (or belongs to) God who is love dominates this subdivision. Like truth, light, and life, *agapē*, "love," is a reality from above, even as is divine begetting and, indeed, Jesus himself (John

---

[9] Others are more pessimistic. Bultmann, *Epistles* 75, denies that there are any "new and developing thoughts" in most of this unit, so that "what we have here is not an original, coherent composition." Vellanickal, *Sonship* 303, thinks that what is new in 4:7-21 is that love is no longer presented as a commandment. I disagree, for in 3:23 the unit is introduced with the statement that love is a commandment, an idea repeated in 4:21 and 5:2-3—there is no "progression" on this score in I John. If *entolē*, "commandment," occurs 6 times in 2:3-11, it occurs 4 times in 4:7-5:4a (plus 3 times in 3:23-24, which introduces this unit). De la Potterie, *La vérité* 1, 313, thinks that the "heretics" virtually drop from view in this unit. Again I disagree: The secessionists are in the background throughout, and specifically so in 4:8,20; 5:1.

[10] This means that Bultmann's treatment of 4:7ff. as homiletic does not do justice to this passage.

[11] The author avoids the more direct second plural form of *agapan*, "You love one another," and prefers to join himself to his audience in the obligation.

3:3,31). The logic is that those who belong to God, or are begotten by God, or know God will therefore love. Two interchangeable sets of expressions, one relating love to God, the other relating love to the God-given status of the Christian, explain the chiastic arrangement that marks 4:7cd and 4:8ab:

4:7c *Everyone who loves*   4:8a *One who does not love·*
    has been begotten by God   has known nothing of God
7d and knows God   8b for God is love

The connection of ideas is this: God is love; the offspring He begets must be marked by love;[12] by loving, the children come to know their Father. This is an application of the general principle that human beings are in the likeness of God, but now that likeness is not through creation but through faith and love.

A few commentators note that, while the author says, "Everyone who loves has been begotten by God," he does not say, "Everyone begotten by God loves." They speculate that for the author to have made the latter statement would have been too dangerous because the secessionists, who as former Johannine Christians were "begotten by God," did not love, and so the statement would not have been true. I question this, for I think the author could have said, "Everyone begotten by God loves." To him, a lack of love would prove that, despite their claims, the secessionists had not been begotten by God,[13] even as their departure from the Community proved that they had never really belonged to the Community (2:19). Since in Johannine thought it is through divine begetting that one becomes part of God's people (John 3:3–7), the claim that love serves as a criterion of divine begetting[14] may be related to the OT idea that love (*ḥesed*) was a criterion for being God's people (Hos 6:4–6; Mic 6:8).

I John also presents love as a criterion for the knowledge of God (4:7d), a claim made intelligible by the parallel role of faith and love in this work; for faith is related to knowledge in Johannine thought (ABJ 29, 512–15). The author says, "Everyone who loves . . . knows God."

---

[12] If the chiasm were perfect, one would have expected 4:8b to read "and has not been begotten by God." One may derive that implication, however, from the logic of the author's remarks: The God of love cannot beget children who do not love.

[13] Vellanickal, *Sonship* 357, argues that in Johannine thought divine sonship can be lost, and he draws this conclusion from the observation that sonship is dynamic and must grow. While I agree with the latter point (but always with the insistence that for John we are children of God, not sons), I suspect that in the instance of apparent loss the author would deny that the parties had ever been children of God. Jesus never loses those who are really given to him by the Father. The apparent exception is Judas, but he belonged to the Evil One (John 17:12; 6:64–70).

[14] Other criteria of divine begetting are faith (John 1:12–13; I John 5:1) and freedom from sin (I John 3:9; 5:18). See pp. 386–87 above.

Arguing just as I did above, I would insist that he could also have said, "Everyone who knows God loves."[15] The secessionists claim to know God; but since they do not love, their claim is false. If we compare this to 2:4 ("The person who claims, 'I know Him,' without keeping His commandments, is a liar"), we see the interchangeability between loving and keeping the commandments as an index of knowing God.[16] Indeed, it is not simply a question of an index or *external* criterion—existentially, only through keeping the commandment to love one another does one gain knowledge of the God who is love.[17] Once again this is true to the OT picture where *ḥesed* or covenant love is characteristic of God, and the absence of this love on earth is equated with an absence of the knowledge of God (Hos 4:1). The author's negative statement (4:8a), "One who does not love has known nothing of God," places the secessionists (against whom it is aimed) on the same level as "the Jews" of John 16:3 who "never knew the Father" and as the world which "never knew [recognized] God" (I John 3:1e).

At the end of v. 8 we find that the author has moved from his previous affirmation, "Love is from God," to the claim "God is love." The ability to shift formulations was already seen in 1:5, "God is light," when compared with 1:6, "God is in light." It warns us that we are not dealing with precise definitions of God but with descriptions of Him in relation to human beings. The description is not purely functional, however; for if God is love toward us, it is because He is love in Himself.[18] If He manifests love toward human beings by giving His Son, He loved His Son before the world began (John 17:24).

"God is love" (4:8b,16c) may be the most famous saying in the NT.[19] St. Augustine writes glowingly, "If nothing else in praise of love was said in the rest of the Epistle, nay in the rest of Scripture, and we had heard

---

[15] This is confirmed by the negative counterparts: In 3:10 he states that everyone who does not love his brother does *not belong to God* (a status equivalent to being begotten by God); and in 4:8a he states, "One who does not love has *known nothing of God.*"

[16] In 4:6 the author offered another criterion: "We belong to God, and anyone who has knowledge of God listens to us." He has now said, "Love belongs to [is from] God . . . one who does not love has known nothing of God." These two statements make clear that if the Community (the "we/us") serves as a criterion, it is because its members remain faithful to the divine commandment to love one another.

[17] For the noetic function of love and its ability to assimilate one to God, see Mouroux, "L'Expérience" 183.

[18] See the Note on "God is light" in 1:5d for the nuance of the "God is" formula. Spicq, "Notes" 363–65, argues that *agapē*, even in relation to God, is always love that has been made manifest or revealed, but from the manifestations one comes to know the Source.

[19] Less eloquent but close in thought is Paul's "God of love" in II Cor 13:11.

from the mouth of the Spirit of God only that one statement, 'God is love,' we would not have to look for anything else."[20] It is a shame, then, that by overuse and misunderstanding this saying has often become trite and misleading. That it has complexity was already recognized in patristic exegesis, as we see from Dideberg's study of its interpretation by Augustine who cited it some 58 times.[21] In three different periods of his life Augustine interpreted the love of God in three different ways. In an earlier period, *ca.* 393, he saw the Holy Spirit as the love of the Father and the Son, an interpretation that has some justification in the association of 4:10 and 4:13 (God loved us; God has given us of His own Spirit). By his middle period, *ca.* 407, Augustine was speaking of fraternal love (charity) as a way of union with God or, as I John would say, of knowing God. Before 418 and the Council of Carthage against the Pelagians, Augustine was interpreting charity as God's gift to human beings, indeed the presence of God Himself among us, an interpretation that can be related to I John's "Love is from God."

Despite the abstract character of Augustine's interpretations, they are often closer to the intent of I John than some recent reflections on "God is love." Some would see a contrast between an OT concept of the justice of God and a NT concept of God as love. This outlook both misunderstands the biblical concept of justice as primarily punitive[22] and ignores OT passages that make *hesed,* "covenant love and mercy," characteristic of God.[23] The real Johannine contrast involved in "God is love" is to a world that hates (John 15:18; 17:14; I John 3:13). I would also judge negatively Holtzmann's contention (*Evangelium* 232) that, while gnostic adversaries might come to realize that God is Spirit (John 4:24) and God is light (I John 1:5), they could not know that God is love, for that goes beyond natural religion. In fact, however, all three "God is" formulas go beyond natural religion, for all are christological. We know that God is Spirit because Jesus communicates the Spirit (see ABJ 29, 328–29, and John 7:39: "There was as yet no Spirit, since Jesus had not been glorified"). We know that God is light through Jesus the light of the

---

[20] *In Epistolam* 7, 4; SC 75, 320.

[21] Dideberg, "Esprit" 99. In his earlier writings Augustine translated *agapē* by *dilectio,* "love"; later he switched to *caritas,* "love, charity." In *Sermo* 53.10.11 (PL 38, 369) he says, *"Caritas is nothing other than dilectio."*

[22] See the NOTE above on 1:9b. Schütz, *Vorgeschichte* 12–15, points out similarities between I John's "the love of God" and Paul's "the justice [*dikaiosynē*] of God" (e.g., Rom 1:17), which is a property of God that comes to human beings (Philip 3:9). Within I John one may compare "Everyone who loves has been begotten by God" (4:7) and "Everyone who acts justly [*dikaiosynē*] has been begotten by God" (2:29).

[23] E.g., Ps 130:7, "With the Lord is steadfast love." Note also the use of the related adjective *hasîd:* "'I am loving,' says the Lord" (Jer 3:12; Ps 145:8).

world (John 8:12; see above, pp. 228–30).[24] We know that God is love through God's sending His only Son into the world. If the adversaries of I John could say that God is Spirit and light, they could also say God is love (despite the contrary position of Feuillet, Holtzmann, Plummer, and Wilder). They were not simply proponents of natural religion or gnostics; they had been Johannine Christians, and love would have been part of their vocabulary.[25] Probably the disagreement between the author and the secessionists in this area would concern the extent of the christological element in the "God is" formulas. Did Jesus reveal what God is simply by coming into the world, or were his life and death of importance? Another disagreement would have concerned the salvific importance of having Christians live out the implications of these formulas in their own lives.

Such disagreements come closer to the surface in 4:9–10 as the author explains how God's love was revealed[26] and in what it consists. It was revealed in and through God's Son. As I have already insisted, this does not mean that there was no divine love before the coming of God's Son into the world. God *is* love; He did not become love at the incarnation but only revealed what He already was. As the Prologue of GJohn indicates (1:16–17; see ABJ 29, 15–16), the loving grace (*charis*) revealed in the incarnation was in place of a love already shown in Moses. The Word that became flesh was the same Word that was with God before creation, the same Word through whom God created, and the same Word that was the source of life and light to human beings before the darkness attempted to overcome it.[27] But now, in a context where he will speak about the perfection of love (I John 4:17–18), the epistolary author is concerned with the definitive revelation of God's love. What is new in this revelation of God as love is that He has given His unique and beloved Son, even as Abraham was willing to give Isaac.[28] The reference in v. 10d to this giving or sending "as an atonement for sins" shows that the author

[24] Feuillet, *Le mystère* 202, comments that, while "God is light" seems to stress the transcendence of God and His distance from us, "God is love" has the opposite effect. Rather both imply the incarnation, for the sending of God's Son manifests God as light and as love.

[25] When I suggest that the secessionists claimed to love one another, I am joining two Johannine statements, namely, that the secessionists belong to the world (I John 4:5) and that the world loves [*philein*] its own (John 15:19). When I suggest that the secessionists claimed to love God, I am basing myself on I John 4:20a, "If anyone boasts, 'I love God'. . . ."

[26] Balz, *Johannesbriefe* 192, calls attention to the sequence of three statements, each with its own contribution: "Love is from God" (4:7); "God is love" (4:8); "God's love was revealed" (4:9). The logical sequence of these statements would be two, one, three.

[27] In ABJ 29, 25–27 it is proposed that John 1:3–5 refers to the Genesis story of the fall.

[28] See the NOTE on 4:9b for the OT background of the Johannine use of *monogenēs*, "only."

is thinking not only of the incarnation but also of the death of Jesus, even as previously in 3:16: "This is how we have come to know what love means: for us Christ laid down his life." The element of voluntary death matches Jesus' own standards: "No one can have greater love than this: to lay down one's life for those one loves" (John 15:13). We may speak of a triple revelation: first, that God has an only beloved Son; second, that He is willing to send or give this Son, even to death; third, that He is willing to do this for us, "for our sins," and "that we may have life through him." As the author of the *Odes of Solomon* (3:3–4) exclaims, "I should not have known how to love the Lord if He had not continuously loved me. Who is able to discern love except one who is loved?"

In this passage the epistolary author may be commenting on the theme that appears in John 3:16–17: "God so loved the world that He gave the only Son, that everyone who believes in him may not perish but may have eternal life. For God did not send the Son into the world to condemn the world, but that the world might be saved through him."[29] From parallel NT christological uses of "give" (Rom 8:32; Gal 1:4; 2:20), I argued in ABJ 29, 134 that that GJohn passage referred to the death of Jesus as well as to the incarnation; but other scholars disagree (e.g., Schnackenburg, *John* 1, 399). This division among modern interpreters of GJohn makes it far from implausible that the epistolary author and the secessionists disagreed precisely on this point. The secessionists may have interpreted the standard Johannine theology of the giving and sending of God's Son only in terms of his entry into the world or incarnation. The author (rightly in my judgment) interpreted the giving and sending to include the whole career of Jesus, including his atoning death for sins. Here he was joining a common Christian catechesis, e.g., "Our Lord Jesus Christ who gave himself for our sins" (Gal 1:4); "God did not spare His own Son but gave him up for us all" (Rom 8:32). Was this catechesis part of the entrance into Christianity by conversion/initiation/baptism?[30] That would help to explain I John's connection of this christological formulation of love with being begotten by God (4:7), with our having life through the Son (4:9), and with his being an atonement for our sins (4:10). The frequency with which the ideas of I John 4:7–10 are found joined contributes to the conversion/initiation/baptism theory, e.g., Eph 2:4–5: "The great love with which God loves us, and even when we were

---

[29] The language of God's sending the son was common Christian terminology but did not have a univocal meaning. In the Synoptic tradition it is found in the parable of the wicked tenants (Mark 12:1–9 and par.), probably to be understood in terms of the sending of a prophet. Many would take as a reference to the incarnation Rom 8:3 ("God sending His Son in the likeness of sinful flesh") and Gal 4:4 ("When the fullness of time had come, God sent forth His Son, born of a woman"), but that is not clear (see my *Community* 45–46). See E. Schweizer, "Sendungsformel," and his article in TDNT 8, 375–76.

[30] Wilder, "Introduction" 283: "The elder invokes various current formulas of confession understood as typical of the church from the beginning."

dead through our trespasses, made us alive together with Christ"; and II Tim 1:9–10: "God saved us . . . not in virtue of our works, but in virtue of His own purpose and the grace given us in Christ Jesus . . . which has now been revealed through the appearance of our Savior Jesus Christ who abolished death and brought life . . . to light."[31] This theory also helps to explain the strongly collective use of "we" and "us" throughout this epistolary unit—God as love is presented not as "my personal Savior" but as the Savior of a people. On the other hand, the author is not interested in the universalism of God's design of salvation although he speaks of God's sending His Son "into the world" (John 3:17; I John 4:9; see 2:2), as "Savior of the world" (John 4:42; I John 4:14). The epistolary author is interested in the Johannine "we" who have life through the Son (I John 4:9bc).[32]

In the NOTE on 4:9a I sided with those scholars who argue that "revealed in us" is meant literally and not simply as a synonym for "revealed to us." In speaking of the revelation of God's Son as an act of love, the epistolary author wants to say more than John 1:14: "The Word became flesh and made his dwelling *among* [in] *us.*" When he says, "God sent His Son . . . that *we may have life through him*" (4:9), he shows that part of the revelation is what happens within Christians. In the Johannine chain of life-giving, the Son has life from the Father; and the believer gets this life from the Son (John 5:26; 6:57; I John 5:11). Therefore, the way in which Christian believers live is part of God's loving, salvific plan. The secessionists could agree that God's love had been revealed "to us"; they could agree that it had been revealed by the Word's dwelling "among us"; but (if I have understood them correctly) they could never agree to a revelation "in us" in the sense just explained, for that would give a salvific value to the way Christians live.

B. *The God of Love Abides in Us* (4:11–16b)

The preceding subdivision began, "Beloved, let us love one another" (4:7). Having laid a foundation for this by enunciating the principle that

[31] This reference in the Pastorals (see also Titus 3:4–5) is all the more important because of Boismard's theory that baptismal catechesis is a common basis underlying I Peter, the Pastorals, and parts of I John (pp. 432–34 above). Since the "atonement" of I John 4:10d has the notion of a blood sacrifice for sins (see 1:7; 2:2), it is worth noting that I Pet 1:19 speaks of ransom with the precious blood of Christ, like that of a lamb, and 1:22 demands, "Love one another."

[32] I agree then with Preisker versus Bultmann (*Epistles* 66), who opts for a wider "we" from which only those who refuse to believe would be excluded. I John is concerned with "us" and "those who went out from us" (2:19). Certainly there are non-Johannine believers, but they are of no visible concern here. I would not agree, however, with Schotroff who thinks that the author would *deny* the universality of God's salvific intention.

love is from God who is love, the author returns at the beginning of this subdivision to the same theme: "Beloved, if God so loved us, we in turn ought to *love one another*" (4:11).[33] The love of God incarnate in Jesus must become incarnate in Christians; and love, which is received in and with divine life, must, like that life, be active. One might have expected the author to say, "If God so loved us, we in turn ought to love God." But while divine love has an element of reciprocity (which the author may be assuming), it is primarily outgoing to others, in imitation of God Himself. This is part of the revelation "in us" just discussed.

Some commentators characterize this subunit as the noblest treatment of love in I John because the obligation to love is based on what God is and has done rather than on a commandment. Yet the fact that the author returns to the language of commandment in 4:21 and 5:2–3 without the slightest sign of contradiction shows that this is a false distinction.[34] God's commandments are His words coming from His inner being; it would be meaningless for the author to distinguish between an obligation based on commandment and an obligation based on the fact that God is love and acts lovingly—He gives the commandment to love because He is love. The Word that became flesh and the word that says we should love one another are intertwined in Johannine thought. The giving or sending of the Son to die an atoning death was both an act of God's love (I John 4:9–10) and a commandment from the Father (John 10:18; 14:31). Whether he mentions commandment or not, the epistolary author is commenting on a tradition that does: "You will abide in my love if you keep my commandments, just as I have kept my Father's commandments and abide in His love. . . . This is my commandment: love one another" (15:10–11). It is that tradition that explains why now suddenly in 4:12 the author introduces the idea of God's abiding in us if we love one another.

The author prefaces his affirmation of divine indwelling with the maxim, "No one has ever seen God." As I explained in the NOTE on 4:12a, this maxim came into the Johannine tradition from the struggle with the synagogue reflected in GJohn that exalted Jesus as the only one who had ever seen God, over against possible Jewish claims for Moses and Elijah. In the context of I John, where the author has affirmed that

---

[33] The second subunit is a practical application flowing from the theological analysis of love in the first subunit. In Bultmann's theory the author was adding homiletic reflections to material borrowed from the source, but I would contend that both theological statement and homiletic application come from the author. He is basing his argument not upon a written source but upon common Johannine theology and catechesis taught at entrance into the Community and enshrined for us in GJohn.

[34] The impossibility of the distinction is illustrated by comparing I John 2:5 and 4:12, which speak of the love of God reaching perfection respectively in the person who keeps God's word or commandments and in the persons who love others on the basis of God's having loved them.

the God of love who has never been seen has been revealed "in us," does the maxim have an anti-secessionist thrust? An affirmative answer is given by some scholars who think that the secessionists, influenced by Greek mystery religions, were claiming a direct intuition or vision of God that made them better than other Christians (Alexander, Bourgin, Dodd).[35] There is no way to prove or disprove that; but my general principle that the secessionists were loyal to the clear affirmations of the tradition found in GJohn makes it likely that they too would affirm that no one has ever seen God. Thus I would see 4:12a not as anti-secessionist but as a general Johannine principle[36] that makes divine indwelling all the more wondrous.

The anti-secessionist thrust begins in 4:12b where the author dares to make divine indwelling (in some ways a greater intimacy with God than seeing Him) dependent on and expressed by our loving one another.[37] If God is love, His presence must be marked by love. Indeed, the love that God revealed in sending His Son to die for us and to give us life reaches perfection (passive of *teleioun*) when we love one another by that same love (4:12d). The objection that God's love, since it comes from Him, must already be perfect independently of human beings is based on a philosophical conception of God quite foreign to Johannine thought. The fact that the Word was with God already before creation implies a God who is outward-looking, for a word needs an audience. This God is who He is when He is speaking and acting; and He is love when He is loving. His love is not *perfectly* what it should be until it begets children in His image who themselves love. In John 17:23 Jesus prays to his Father for those who believe in him, "that they may be brought to perfection as one; thus the world may come to know that you sent me and that you loved them even as you loved me." Well does Westcott, *Epistles* 152, perceive that love is brought to perfection in the believer when the believer is brought to perfection in love. Jesus himself, the embodiment of divine love, showed his love for his own to the very end (*telos:* John 13:1) by laying

[35] The idea of seeing God in the mystery religions is treated by W. Michaelis, TDNT 5, 322–24. While gnosticism might affirm that the highest God is invisible, the gnostic who was deified through knowledge could see God. Gnosis makes possible the vision of God; indeed it is the vision of God.

[36] Indeed, God as invisible or unseen is a general Christian principle (Col 1:15; I Tim 1:17; 6:16). An equivalent in the Q tradition is Matt 11:27 and Luke 10:22: "No one knows the Father except the Son and anyone to whom the Son chooses to reveal Him." Dodd, *Epistles* 112–13, points out that the inability to see God would not seem a terrible deprivation to Jews, for Hebrew thought gave primacy to hearing God.

[37] He does not mean that when we begin to love one another, then God comes to dwell in us; rather our love is the evidence of God's indwelling. In speaking of God's *abiding* in those who love one another after he has spoken of their receiving *life* from the God who loves (4:9c), the author is rephrasing the theme of 3:15: Eternal life does not abide in the one who hates his brother.

down his life for them. This was the perfection of divine love in Jesus.[38] A previous passage in I John (3:16) has already called for an imitation of that example: "For us Christ laid down his life; so ought we in turn to lay down our lives for the brothers."

Having introduced the theme of God's abiding in us (4:12), the author in 4:13 offers a criterion for the mutual indwelling of God and the Christian.[39] Both the theme and the criterion, which is the Spirit, must seem abrupt to all those who begin Part Three of I John with 4:7 (p. 542). They are not abrupt to those of us who think of 3:23–24 as a transition to the two units 4:1–6 and 4:7–5:4a and as a guide to their contents. I have already insisted that the twofold commandment (3:23), to *believe* in Jesus Christ and to *love* one another, supplies the respective main themes of the two units. In 3:24cd the author said, "Now this is how we can know that God abides in us: from the Spirit that he gave us." In the preceding unit (4:1–6) the author identified God's Spirit as the motivating force for *belief* in Jesus Christ: "Everyone who confesses Jesus Christ come in the flesh reflects the Spirit which belongs to God." It is not surprising, then, to find a reference to the Spirit in this unit on *love* as well.

Many scholars relate the mention of the Spirit in 4:13 directly to love;[40] and there is precedent for this in Paul: "The love of God has been poured into our hearts through the Holy Spirit which has been given to us" (Rom 5:5). Yet, since 4:13 does not mention love and since the next verse says "that the Father has sent the Son as Savior of the world," a few scholars would relate the Spirit to faith instead (Law, Michl, Nauck). Others (de la Potterie, Häring, Lauck) think the Spirit is related both to love and faith, while Büchsel and Chaine speak of charisms.[41] Some would invoke the mention of testifying in the next verse to explain how

[38] Wilder, "Introduction" 281–82, observes that the Johannine idea of love's being perfected involves its being realized or brought into activity.

[39] The intensity of the theme of abiding in the next few verses causes some to speak of a parenthesis or digression (Schnackenburg). Loisy, *Evangile-Epîtres* 566, finds 4:13–16a so repetitious that he dubs it the afterthought of a redactor, while Windisch, *Briefe* 129, thinks that it was added to have the Spirit complete a trinitarian picture! Dodd opens a totally new Part (Three) of I John with 4:13, while B. Weiss argues that obviously 4:13 closes the preceding unit, for the "In this" points to what precedes and the verse is an inclusion with 3:24.

[40] Bonsirven, Bultmann, Camerlynck, Charlier, Charue, Kohler, and Plummer, to name a few. A trinitarian theology whereby the Spirit is the love between the Father and the Son is scarcely in the author's mind. The Johannine writers speak of "the Spirit of truth"; I am not certain whether they would be comfortable with Westcott's "the spirit of love" (*Epistles* 152). Paul can say in Gal 5:22, "The fruit of the Spirit is love, joy, peace. . . ."

[41] De la Potterie, *La vérité* 1, 297–306, helpfully surveys views. A few scholars avoid the problem by relating 4:13a to what precedes (indwelling is related to love), so that the reference to Spirit in 4:13b stands by itself (see NOTE on 4:13a).

the Spirit is the criterion of divine indwelling. Dodd[42] appeals to the interior testimony or witness of the Spirit, and secondly to an exterior testimony in a public confession of faith. While there is no way to refute such suggestions (even though the idea of charism and of interior witness is not clearly attested in Johannine theology), it is important to remember that in 4:13 the criterion of divine indwelling offered by the author is not the Spirit directly but the fact that God has given us of the Spirit.[43] When he spoke in 4:9 of the revelation of God's love in us, he referred to God's having *sent His only Son* into the world and our having life through him. May he not be thinking of the giving of the Holy Spirit as a second and continuous step? It is the Spirit of Jesus and continues his sending (being sent in his name: John 14:26; 16:7); it is a Spirit that begets divine life (3:3,5) and indeed can be called "the giver of life" (6:63) and symbolized by living water (7:39).

Precisely because the gift of the Spirit has begotten them as God's children, the Johannine Christians can speak in 4:14 as a people with a special privilege. Despite the fact that "no one has ever seen God," they can say, "As for us, we have seen"[44]—seen not God in Himself but God in Jesus, seen the Father in the Son. The ability to see Jesus in his ministry as the Son of God and the Savior of the world is part of the work of the Paraclete/Spirit. Jesus has gone to the Father and the world can see him no longer; but the Paraclete proves the world wrong about him (John 16:10). Jesus came into this world for judgment, "that those who do not see may be able to see, and those who see may become blind" (9:39), and the Spirit continues his role. Alongside seeing, I John 4:14 mentions testifying or bearing witness. This second function is also the work of the Paraclete/Spirit in the Community: "When the Paraclete comes, the Spirit of Truth . . . he will bear witness on my behalf. You too should bear witness because you have been with me from the beginning" (John

---

[42] *Epistles* 114–16. He insists that Christianity does not depend on external testimony alone, for it is confirmed by an inward conviction wrought by the Spirit of God. One can show this from Rom 8:15,16,26. But where is the evidence that this is Johannine thought? Others like Schneider (*Briefe* 176) reject internal witness here since the author is thought to be talking about an observable possession of the Spirit. Yet in Johannine thought the world cannot see or know the Paraclete (John 14:17). Neither interior awareness of the Spirit nor observable presence may be intended by the author in this verse—he knows God has given of the Spirit because the Johannine Jesus said so!

[43] B. Weiss, *Briefe* 125, brings out this point well. The partitive in 4:13b ("of His own Spirit") indicates that our knowledge has not come directly from the Spirit but from God's sharing of His Spirit with us. Love is reflected in the boundless gift of the Spirit spoken of in John 3:34.

[44] In the NOTE on 4:14a I argued that the "we" here is not the distinctive Johannine School of tradition-bearers but the "we" of the whole Community (which includes the tradition-bearers).

15:26–27).[45] In seeing and testifying that the Father has sent the Son as Savior of the world, the Johannine Christians are continuing the work of the Beloved Disciple who stood at the foot of the cross and "saw and testified" (John 19:35) as the salvific gifts of blood and water (symbolizing the Spirit—see ABJ 29A, 949–50) flowed from the pierced side of Jesus.[46]

How does this strong emphasis in 4:14 on seeing and testifying fit into the author's struggle with the secessionists who are Christian believers of some sort? Is the "As for us" by contrast with them? Opposite theories are encountered. For some, the secessionists would have had no problem with Jesus as the Savior of the world, for they were attracted by higher paganism and the mystery religions, and had "gone out into the world" (I John 4:1). For others, the secessionists were docetists or gnostics who rejected the material world and would have been more interested in a Jesus who is a Savior *from* the world.[47] If one leaves aside such guesses and works with the information that the secessionists had been Johannine Christians, they should have had no trouble with the title "Savior of the world," which was used approvingly of Jesus in John 4:42. Any contention between them and the author would more likely have been over the sense in which "the Father *has sent* the Son as Savior of the world." In 4:10 the author made clear that he interpreted the sending in terms of an atoning death for sins, and presumably the secessionists would have rejected that interpretation.

The confession in the next verse (4:15), which vocalizes the testimony of 4:14, is another attempt to underline the christological dispute between the author and the secessionists. Originally such formulas, which presumably took shape in the tradition surrounding conversion/initiation/baptism, were meant to identify Jesus, e.g., that he is "the Son of God."[48] But as Christians of Johannine descent, both the author and the secessionists would have agreed upon the Son of God as the saving divine

[45] See below the discussion of I John 5:9, which stresses God's testimony. A combination of human and divine witness/testimony is found in Acts 5:32: "We are witnesses of these things, and so is the Holy Spirit whom God has given to those who obey Him"; and in Acts 15:28: "It seemed good to the Holy Spirit and to us."

[46] Even if 19:35 was an addition to GJohn by the redactor who wrote *after* the composition of I John, he was scarcely an inventor of this picture of the Beloved Disciple; and often he introduced old traditions into GJohn.

[47] In fact, the gnostic picture is complicated. W. Foerster, TDNT 7, 1019–20, points out that "Savior" as a title probably came into gnosticism under Christian influence, and in Valentinian gnosticism is preferred over "Lord" as a title for Jesus. It is frequent in the Nag Hammadi collection. In *Acts of Thomas* 10 (Syrian gnosticism of the third century), Jesus is described as "the Savior of all creation, the one who gives life to the world."

[48] This was the intent of GJohn over against "the Jews" and against inadequate believers among the Jewish Christians: "Jesus is the Christ, the Son of God" (John 20:31).

emissary. Their disagreement would have been centered on the author's interpretation of the traditional confession, namely, that the Son of God *is Jesus* as he walked among us and died on the cross (see INTRO-DUCTION V B2). Presumably all Johannine Christians believed that "the Word became flesh" (John 1:14), but the author is writing to emphasize an aspect of the incarnation: "What we have seen with our own eyes . . . and felt with our own hands" (I John 1:1). The first part of the double commandment of 3:23 was: "We are to believe the name of His Son, Jesus Christ"; and those who kept this commandment could know that God abides in them from the Spirit that He gave them (3:24). In the preceding unit, which was the author's first step in interpreting that dou-ble commandment, we heard: "Everyone who confesses Jesus Christ come in the flesh reflects the Spirit which belongs to God" (4:2). In the present unit, which is the author's second step in interpreting the double commandment, we hear that God has given us of His own Spirit (4:13) and so "Whenever anyone confesses that Jesus is the Son of God, then God abides in him" (4:15). Obviously the two Spirit-guided confessions are harmonious: The Jesus who is the Son of God is "Jesus Christ come in the flesh."

But the main theme of the present unit (and subunit) has been the other half of the double or twofold commandment of 3:23: "We are to love one another just as He gave us the command" (see 4:11–12), and it is to the theme of love that the author returns in 4:16ab. Having begun the subdivision in 4:11a, "Beloved, if God so loved us," he ends it in 4:16b by speaking of "the love that God has in us." His "As for us" (4:16a) refers to his adherents (as distinct from the secessionists) who have a correct christology based on the ministry and salvific death of Jesus.[49] Through this christology *we* have come to know and believe the extent and depth of God's love—a love to the very end (John 13:1) in self-giving for others (15:13). And this is not merely an intellectual knowledge, for the love that God has is "in us" (I John 4:16b) in the sense that it has conformed us to His Son by making us His children,[50] and the way we live is a manifestation of God's love. Experience of that love makes the Johannine Christian grow in knowledge and belief.[51] Herein is fulfilled Jesus' prayer for future believers in John 17:26: "And

---

[49] The NOTE on 4:16a contends that the "us/we" in this verse is not the distinctive "we" of the Johannine School of tradition-bearers but the "we" of the author's Com-munity.

[50] Chaine, *Epîtres* 206, is not precise when he claims that the Spirit and faith are principles of filiation, but love is the consequence. The author is speaking of God's love that begets children.

[51] Compare John 8:32 and 8:45–46 for knowing and believing the truth—knowledge and belief, love and truth are closely related in Johannine thought.

to them I made known Your name; and I will continue to make it known, so that the love You had for me may be *in them,* and I may be in them."[52]

C. *Love Has Reached Perfection in Us, Driving Out Fear* (4:16c–19)

Many scholars recognize that v. 16 is significant for a new subdivision in this long treatment of love; but they are divided as to whether all of v. 16 belongs to the preceding subdivision or only part of it, in the sense that v. 16c starts the next subdivision. I have opted for the latter possibility for two reasons. First, the "in this" of v. 17 probably refers to what precedes, and therefore cannot begin a new subdivision. Second, if v. 16c is taken as the opening of a subdivision, then there is parallelism among the openings of three subunits, 4:7, 4:11, and 4:16c respectively, as shown on p. 546. In particular, the combined themes of love, divine abiding, and reaching perfection began the preceding subunit (see 4:11–12) and begin this subunit as well (4:16c–17).

Indeed, we are led to wonder why all this repetition, since "God is love" of 4:16c repeats 4:8b, and "the person who abides in love abides in God and God abides in him" of 4:16de repeats 4:12bc. Beyond a certain rhythm achieved by repetition, a partial answer is nuance, e.g., the first "God is love" statement found its principal verification in the sending of the Son, while the second stresses the result (divine abiding) in the Christian. Similarly, the first divine indwelling (abiding) statement stressed the wondrous result of love, while the second will stress the implications for the Christian. A Christian's abiding in love is a condition making possible divine indwelling. Previous conditions were keeping the commandments (3:24) and loving one another (4:12), and confessing that Jesus is the Son of God. These are various ways of phrasing the basic covenant demands that Christians have known since they entered the following of Jesus. The Ten Commandments or basic covenant demands of the OT involved acceptance of the God of Israel and a peculiar relationship to Him and to each other in loving behavior. The covenant demands of the NT involve acceptance of Jesus as God's Son and a peculiar relationship of love toward each other because of him. What is important in 4:16cde is the reminder that this love is not something that we can do of ourselves, for it comes from the God who is love. Abiding in love, then, is more than a condition for divine indwelling—by loving we experience God's

---

[52] Note Philo, *On the Posterity of Cain* 20 ⚹69: "Moses defines living in accordance with God as loving Him; for he says, 'Your life is to love Him who is.'"

indwelling.[53] The opposite of "abiding" is "going out," the very thing the secessionists have done.[54]

Love reaches its perfection in the abiding in each other that binds God and the Christians (4:17a).[55] Love that is truly expressive of the God who sent His only Son must be effective in us in terms of loving others;[56] then "we are just the same as Christ is" (4:17c), a Christ who loved us enough to die for us and who continues as a Paraclete in the Father's presence as an atonement for our sins (2:1–2). This similarity enables the Johannine Christians to approach Judgment Day with confidence (4:17b).[57] In 2:28–3:1 that confidence was related to the "love the Father has bestowed in enabling us to be called God's children"; here it is related to a love that has reached perfection in a divine indwelling that makes us "just the same as Christ is." These are two different ways of expressing the same result of love.

In 4:18 the author develops the theme of Christian confidence by speaking eloquently of how love excludes fear.[58] I Peter 2:17 can urge, "Love the brotherhood and fear God," but I John assures the readers that there is no need for fear at all. (In the NOTE on 4:18ab I mentioned the views of those who think that I John is excluding only servile fear, but *no* fear is presented positively in the Johannine writings.[59]) If the secessionists thought they were already saved and that there would be no further judgment, there would have been no reason for them to fear. But the author's adherents, hearing him underline the theme of final judgment as

---

[53] We have seen that "to abide" (*menein;* see NOTE on 2:6a) is an active, not a stative or passive concept.

[54] Dodd, *Epistles* 118, is right in warning against the sentimental reading of 4:16cde, for it is a theological summary of 4:7–15.

[55] In the NOTES on 4:17a (a very disputed line) I explain why I think "In this" refers to what precedes, and why "with us" is to be taken literally and not simply as "in our regard." In the NOTE on the equally disputed 4:17c I have argued that the author made no mistake in not saying "as Christ *was*," for "in this world" refers to us, not to Christ.

[56] Presumably the secessionists based perfection on knowing the mystery of Christ's origin and believing in him rather than on loving one another.

[57] It is plausible that in secessionist theology the only judgment was that brought by Jesus (and passed successfully by those who believe in him—p. 421 above), whereas the author revives the theme of final judgment, which was Christian tradition from the beginning (INTRODUCTION V C2d).

[58] Plummer, *Epistles* 107, argues that 18bc are parenthetical, so that 18a ("Love has no room for fear") connects directly to 18d ("Love has not reached perfection in one who is still afraid"). I prefer a more poetic analysis where the first line (18a) matches the third (18c): "Love has no room for fear . . . for fear carries with it punishment"; and the second line (18b) matches the fourth (18d): "Rather, perfect love drives out fear . . . love has not reached perfection in one who is still afraid."

[59] Bengel speaks of four stages of human reaction: a stage in which there is neither fear nor love of God; one where there is fear but not yet love; still another where there is both fear and love; and the culmination where there is love without fear. Perhaps the epistolary author would consider only the last stage truly Christian.

a correction of secessionist moral theology, could regard it as fear-provoking. This is not the author's intention at all. When love has been perfected in divine indwelling, how can one be afraid of the God who already abides in one's heart? To be afraid of God is already to be suffering the punishment of a negative judgment. Neither in this world nor on Judgment Day can a Christian be judged negatively by a God who dwells lovingly within. When the author says encouragingly, "Love has not reached perfection in one who is still afraid" (4:18d), he is not implicitly admitting the existence of imperfect love. All true *agapē* comes from God and moves toward perfect expression. When frustrated, it is aborted; and the person involved becomes one who does not have God's love abiding in him.

In 4:18, however, the author is not discussing such negative possibilities but emphasizing the positive. The fact that several times in I John he has to foresee that his admonitions may produce fear and shake confidence casts light on the delicate relationship that he has with his followers. Constantly he needs to protect his message against possible secessionist counterattacks, for they will exploit opportunities opened by misinterpretations. They must not be allowed to win over his frightened adherents by their comforting gospel of no future judgment, no sins, and no worry about relationship to God once one has believed.

In 4:19 the author implicitly continues his theme of confidence: "As for us, *we* love"[60]—we do not fear. Here the "we" is opposed, not so much to actual opponents, but to the theoretical possibility that "we" (Johannine Christians) might be fearful. His earlier statements of assurance (4:14a; 4:16a) were phrased similarly: "As for us, we have seen and can testify," and "As for us, we have come to know and believe." Warnings are for others; we are God's children. This is not arrogance, since our status and way of life comes from God ("We love because He loved us first"). This affirmation (4:19) ends the present subunit on the same theme with which the author ended the preceding subunits (4:10c: "He loved us"; 4:16b: "The love that God has in us"). It also constitutes an inclusion with the line that opened this whole unit: "Love is from God" (4:7b). If all these verses agree in giving primacy to God as the origin of love, it becomes clear that there is no contradiction between the author's urging "us" to love and his affirmation that we already love. The love that comes from God is not static and requires our cooperation (the "with us" of 17a), and so there is room for urging that a love that is already possessed should not be blocked.[61]

---

[60] See the NOTE on 4:19 for the probability that this is an indicative rather than a cohortative ("let us love").

[61] Bourgin, "L'amour" 36: God's love is not simply an *élan* that carries us along automatically; *we* must abide in love, and abiding is a free act.

D. *Loving One's Brother as Commanded by God* (4:20–5:4a)

In the previous subdivisions of this unit the secessionists have been in mind but only as background, for the author has been primarily concerned with the self-reflective "we" of the Johannine Community. In 4:20ff. the tone changes[62] as he turns directly against the false theology of his adversaries in a style reminiscent of the polemics of 1:5–2:2 and 2:3–11, for he again quotes the secessionist position to show what is wrong with it. He dubs his opponents as liars. He is no longer simply urging love of one another upon those who need some encouragement; he is theologically defending love of brother.[63] On p. 546 I pointed out that the three previous subdivisions of this unit open and end in the same way; the fourth subdivision is an exception, standing by itself as the conclusion of the final treatment of love in I John.

The basic theme is set in 4:20–21: love for God and love for brother are two facets of the same love ("The person who loves God must love his brother as well"), so that where one is missing, the other is missing. The underlying idea has been expounded in the earlier subdivisions of this unit: all *agapē* comes from God; if it is to abide in the Christian, it must actively express itself in love for one's brother (along with love for God[64]). The reason, as will become clear in 5:1–2, is that one's "brother" is a child of the God from whom love comes, and God the Father expresses concern for His children by having each child love the other. As I indicated in the NOTE on 4:20de, the affirmation, "The person who has no love for his brother whom he has seen cannot love the God he has never seen," is not simply an argument *a minori ad maius*[65] but expresses a necessity that arises from the very nature of a love that comes from God.[66] But why does the author express this argument in terms of

---

[62] Although some would attach v. 19 as a beginning to this new subdivision, I explained on p. 546 that parallelism with the endings of the first and second subdivisions favors treating v. 19 as the conclusion of the last subdivision.

[63] Schnackenburg, *Johannesbriefe* 249, notes the change to a much stronger hortatory style here, but he thinks the change begins with v. 19, where he reads a cohortative subjunctive (footnote 60 above). Dodd, *Epistles* 122–24, recognizes that 4:19–21 is related to 5:1–5.

[64] Throughout I have argued against Bultmann and others that love for God is both possible and necessary in Johannine thought and is not identical with love for brother. The author does not mean that one can love God only *in* one's brother; rather love for brother and love for God coexist.

[65] For this argument, called by the rabbis *qal wāḥômer*, see St-B 3, 223–26. It is invoked here by Baumgarten, Büchsel, Rothe, Schnackenburg, and B. Weiss.

[66] See Wengst, *Häresie* 71. Sometimes attention is called to Pascal's famous epigram: We must know human beings in order to love them, but we must love God in order to know Him. However, the epistolary author would say: We must love people in order to love God.

the visible and the invisible? That no one has ever seen God is a datum that came to him from the tradition (see 4:12a). The idea of not loving the brother whom one *has seen* may be derived from the history of the Community, as illustrated in 3:17 which speaks about someone shutting out compassion toward his brother whom he *perceives* in need. I suggested there the possibility that the secessionists were the wealthier members of the Community whose departure had left their former confreres destitute. The secessionists may have refused to help these "brothers" in need and thus have indicated that they have no love for those whom they once saw regularly.[67] The author's challenge to the claim to love God (a perfectly possible claim in the Johannine tradition) may, then, be based on a practical situation. Of course, as I pointed out on p. 85, the author is no more loving toward the secessionists, *his* former brothers, than they are to him and his adherents.

Easily recognized in 4:20–21 are typical Johannine dualistic features: the lack of a middle territory between love and hate; the accusation that the person who hates (or does not love) is a liar and thus implicitly belongs to Satan; and the defining of the love commandment in terms of one's brother rather than of one's neighbor. But we should not overlook features shared with contemporary Jewish and Christian authors. Philo (*On the Decalogue* 23 ⌗120) describes one's father and mother as visible gods who copy the Uncreated and asks, "How can reverence be given to the invisible God by those who show irreverence to the gods who are near at hand and seen by the eyes?" In Matt 25:40, in the parable of judgment (a setting invoked in I John 4:17), the royal Son of Man says, "As you did to one of the least of these my brothers, you did to me." An agraphon (a saying attributed to Jesus but not recorded in the NT)[68] reads, "You have seen your brother; you have seen your God." Frequently the commandment in I John 4:21, "The person who loves God must love his brother as well," is described as the Johannine equivalent of Mark 12:28–31 (which combines Deut 6:4–5 and Lev 19:18): "The first commandment is . . . 'You shall love the Lord your God'. . . . The second is this: 'You shall love your neighbor as yourself.'" Yet the Johannine author does not speak of two commandments, nor does he give priority to love for God.[69] The one commandment involves both love for brother

[67] The past tense in 4:20d ("whom he has seen") *may* reflect the situation where, having gone out (2:19; II John 7), the secessionists do not see the author's adherents fraternally any more. In 3:17 the tense is pres., but perceiving the brother *in need* may represent a present situation produced by the secession. However, it is unwise to press too exactly the use of tenses.

[68] It is found in Clement of Alexandria, *Stromata* 1.19.94 and 2.15.70 (GCS 15, 60 and 150); and in Tertullian, *De oratione* 26, 1 (CC 1, 273). See J. Finegan, *Hidden Records of the Life of Jesus* (Philadelphia: Pilgrim, 1969) 131.

[69] The statement of Jesus in John 14:15, "If you love me and keep my commandments [i.e., the commandment to love one another] . . . ," is to be read as a simultaneous demand. The Johannine outlook is not precisely the same as that of Paul in

and love for God; and if there is practical priority, it is with love for brother.

Verse 1a of ch. 5 suddenly introduces the theme of believing; and as I mentioned on p. 544, many commentators regard this as a sign that a new unit begins here with faith as its main theme rather than the love that dominated in 4:7–21. However, since faith is mentioned only in this first line, and the love theme continues from 5:1b to 5:4a,[70] I consider the first verses of ch. 5 to be part of the same unit as the end of ch. 4. (Thus also Alexander, Bultmann, Marshall, Schnackenburg, THLJ.) The theme of commandment, absent since 3:23–24, has returned in 4:21 in reference to love; and so in the next verse (5:1a) the author mentions the other half of the twofold commandment from 3:23, namely the commandment to believe the name of Jesus Christ. Also 4:20 has described the person who hates his brother as a liar. In 2:22 the evil figure expected in the last hour was identified thus: "Who, then, is the Liar? None other than the person who denies that *Jesus* is the Christ." And so in 4:20 and 5:1 the author describes the opposite of the "Liar" as the person who loves his brother and believes that *Jesus* is the Christ. Still another way of connecting the end of ch. 4 and the beginning of ch. 5 is suggested by Schnackenburg (*Johannesbriefe* 250–51), who finds a sequence of three arguments for the love of brother, introduced in 4:20abc: the first argument (4:20de) involves the impossibility of loving the invisible God without loving the visible brother; the second (4:21) is that there is a positive commandment to love one's brother; the third (5:1) is that the love for the begotten flows from the love one has for the begetter.

Granted all this, I find the dominant unity in these verses to stem from polemics against the secessionists, who claim to love their brothers but in fact do not love the author's adherents who had been their brothers in the Johannine Community. Three times in 4:20–21 the author mentioned "brother," and his subsequent remarks clarify that concept. In 5:1a he resorts to a familiar Johannine creedal affirmation concerning God's children, similar to the statement in the GJohn Prologue (1:12–13): "Those who did accept him [the Word], he empowered to become God's children, that is, those who believe in his name." (The last phrase is clarified in John 20:31, which speaks of believing "that Jesus is the Christ, the Son of God.") The author does not intend to introduce a new theme of faith

---

Gal 5:14: "The whole law is fulfilled in one word: 'You shall love your neighbor as yourself.'" Nor is it the same as the Dead Sea Scroll simplification where Micah 6:8, "Walk humbly with your God," is changed to "Walk humbly with your neighbor" (1QS 8:2–3—see Boismard, "First Epistle" 160).

[70] Those who want to start a new unit with 5:1 will sometimes resort to alternating themes: faith in 5:1a; love in 5:1b–4; faith in 5:5–12 (thus, with variations, Brooke, Hort). Others contend that despite appearances faith dominates in 5:1–4, for love manifests faith and depends on it for existence (thus, Chaine, de la Potterie, Vellanickal).

in 5:1a; rather, belief "that Jesus is the Christ" is mentioned because it is part of the classical description of those begotten by God, one that cannot be denied by the secessionists.[71] The author's argument is that his own adherents, who continue the belief in the name of Jesus which has been traditional in Johannine circles, are truly begotten by God and therefore are the brothers that one must love if one is going to love God.[72] He supports this argument with the aphorism (5:1b): "Everyone who loves the parent loves the child begotten by him." This is not a simple *a minori ad maius* argument, any more than was 4:20de ("The person who has no love for the brother he has seen cannot love the God he has never seen"). It reminds the reader about the similarity to a parent that makes one a brother, so that loving one's brother is really a way of loving the parent.

Vellanickal (*Sonship* 320) argues that, since the author speaks here of believing (*pisteuein*) rather than of confessing (*homologein*), he wants to emphasize the interior aspect of faith. But surely the whole point is to identify the brother, and so the faith of 5:1a must be professed. Public confession is implicit in the author's appeal to a traditional Johannine creedal formula. As we move to the more obscure verses in 5:2ff., we must remember that a faith which is used to show who are brothers becomes a way of giving the lie to adversaries who claim to love their brothers. A chiasm in 5:2 applies the preceding aphorism thus:[73]

> 5:1b: Everyone who loves the *parent* loves the **child** begotten by him
>
> 5:2:   We love God's **children** whenever we love *God* and obey His commandments

To many this may seem circular reasoning: One tests love for God by love for brothers (4:20–21) and then tests love for brothers by love for God. But the author's chain of thought involves the inability of the secessionists to love God since they cannot love their brothers on either of two scores. First, by way of object, he thinks that, as we have seen above, the secessionists have in their group no "brothers" to love, since only those with a true christological faith are God's children and hence "brothers." Second, by way of agent, he thinks that the secessionists cannot love with that *agapē* which comes from God; for part of such *agapē* is to love God and keep His commandments. They may claim to love God, but they put

---

[71] They might deny the other descriptions the author offers as (his personal?) criteria for those begotten by God: "Everyone who acts justly" (2:29); "Everyone who loves" (4:7); One who does not act sinfully (3:9; 5:18).

[72] As interpreted by the author (belief in Jesus Christ come in the flesh) this criterion excludes the secessionists from being children begotten by God; and so, in his judgment, the author violates no commandment when he does not love them as brothers.

[73] I work here with what seems to me the most reasonable of many possible ways to read 5:2a (see NOTE).

no emphasis on keeping commandments;[74] and authentic love is obedient love (de la Potterie, "Le croyant" 392). They have neither God's children nor God's love among them.[75] It is noteworthy that in associating love for God and obeying the commandments the author is again reflecting a Jewish heritage. Wisdom 6:18 states: "Love [of Wisdom] means the keeping of her laws"; and *Midrash Sifre* 33 on Deut 6:6 relates loving God "with the whole heart" to taking His words (commandments) to heart.

Having attacked his adversaries on the issue of commandments, the author once more shows pastoral apprehension that his demands will discourage his own followers, making them more vulnerable to secessionist inroads. And so he ends his treatment of love on the encouraging note that for God's children the commandments are not burdensome (5:3). The very status of being begotten by God makes Christians share in Jesus' victory over the world (5:4a; see John 16:33), a world that now includes the secessionists (I John 4:5).[76] The author is reiterating his previous theme (4:4): "As for you, Little Children, you belong to God, and so you have conquered those people; for he who is in you is greater than he who is in the world." And in 2:17 he stressed: "The world is passing away . . . but the person who does the will of God remains forever."

BIBLIOGRAPHY PERTINENT TO I JOHN 4:7–5:4a

Bourgin, C., "L'Eglise, fraternité dans l'amour divin (1 Jn 4, 7–10)," AsSeign, 2d series, 27 (1972) 24–29.

———. "L'amour fraternel chrétien, expérience de Dieu (1 Jn 4, 11–16)," AsSeign, 2d series, 29 (1973) 31–37.

Charlier, C., "L'amour en Esprit (I Jean 4, 7–13)," BVC 10 (1955) 57–72.

de Jonge, M., "To Love as God Loves (I John 4:7)," *Jesus: Inspiring and Disturbing Presence* (Nashville: Abingdon, 1974) 110–27.

[74] If here the author implicitly rejects the claim to love God without obeying His commandments, in 2:4 he explicitly rejected the claim to know God without keeping His commandments.

[75] None of this constitutes convincing logic to the outsider; but the author is not offering proofs in the ordinary sense of the word—he is applying the maxims of Johannine theology in an inner Johannine debate.

[76] In the NOTE on 5:4a I indicated that it is not clear how conquering the world makes God's commandments less burdensome. We may be encountering standard Johannine rhetoric of encouragement. If here the author states that being begotten by God (and thus experiencing God's love) enables one to keep the commandments so that they are not burdensome, in John 14:23 we find the opposite order where keeping the commandments leads to divine presence: "If anyone loves me, he will keep my word; then my Father will love him, and we shall come to him."

de la Potterie, I., "Le croyant qui a vaincu le monde (1 Jn 5, 1–6)," AsSeign, 2d series, 23 (1971) 34–43.

Dideberg, D., "Esprit Saint et charité: L'exégèse augustinienne de 1 Jn 4,8 et 16," NRT 97 (1975) 97–109, 229–50.

Harrison, E. F., "A Key to the Understanding of First John," BibSac 111 (1954) 39–46, on 4:17.

Kittler, R., "Erweis der Bruderliebe an der Bruderliebe? Versuch der Auslegung eines 'fast unverständlichen' Satzes im 1. Johannesbrief," KD 16 (1970) 223–28, on 5:2.

Klein, G., "Quasimodogeniti, 1. Johannes 5, 1–5," GPM 22 (1967–68) 205–12.

Malatesta, E., ". . . *tēn agapēn hēn echei ho theos en hēmin:* A Note on 1 John 4:16a," to be published in the Bo Reicke Festschrift, ed. D. A. Brownell and W. C. Weinrich (Leiden: Brill).

Romaniuk, K., "'Die vollkommene Liebe treibt die Furcht aus.' Eine Auslegung von 1 Jo 4, 17–18," BibLeb 5 (1964) 80–84.

Schütz, R., *Die Vorgeschichte der johanneischen Formel* Ho Theos Agapē Estin (Göttingen: Hubert, 1917).

Schweizer, E., "Zum religionsgeschichtlichen Hintergrund der 'Sendungsformel': Gal 4,4f.; Rom 8,3f.; Joh 3,16f.; I Joh 4,9," ZNW 57 (1966) 199–210.

Segalla, G., "Il Dio" 118–20, on I John 4:12,20.

Spicq, C., "Notes d'exégèse johannique: La charité est amour manifeste," RB 65 (1958) 358–70, esp. 363–65 on 4:8,16; 365–70 on 4:10–11.

van der Horst, P. W., "A Wordplay in 1 Joh 4, 12?" ZNW 63 (1972) 280–82.

10. I John 5:4b–12: *Faith as Conqueror of the World and the Role of Testimony*

4b	4bNow this is the conquering power that has conquered the
4c	this faith of ours. <u>| world:</u>
5a	5Who then is the one who conquers the world?
5b	None other than the person who believes that *Jesus* is the Son of God:
6a	6Jesus Christ—this is the one who came by water and blood,
6b	not in water only,
6c	but in water and in blood.
6d	And the Spirit is the one who testifies,
6e	for the Spirit is the truth.
7	7Indeed, there are three who testify:
8a	8the Spirit and the water and the blood,
8b	and these three are of one accord.
9a	9If we accept human testimony,
9b	God's testimony is even greater;
9c	for this is God's testimony:
9d	that He has testified on behalf of His own Son.
10a	10The person who believes in the Son of God possesses that testimony within himself,
10b	while the person who does not believe God has made Him a
10c	by refusing to believe in the testimony <u>| liar</u>
10d	that God has testified on behalf of His own Son.
11a	11Now this is the testimony:
11b	that God gave us eternal life
11c	and this life is in His own Son.
12a	12The person who possesses the Son possesses life;
12b	while the person who does not possess the Son of God does not possess life.

NOTES

5:4b. *Now this is the conquering power that has conquered the world.* The *kai houtos estin* formula (NOTE on 1:5a), followed by a noun, gives a stronger affirmation about faith than if the author used an adjectival construction equivalent to "victorious." The normal English translation of the noun *nikē* is "victory," but that loses the connection with the verb *nikan,* "to conquer," which follows it. (*Nikē* occurs only here in the NT, and indeed in Hellenistic Greek was yielding in frequency to the related noun *nikos.*) I prefer "conquering power" to "conquest"; for here *nikē* is a metonymy for the means of victory, or the power that grants victory (BAG 541; BAGD 539).

For the verb *nikan,* see the NOTE on 2:13d. The aorist participle used here has been given different temporal values (Schnackenburg, *Johannesbriefe* 254), which affect the meaning of the passage. (Originally participles had no absolute time value but expressed states of action in relation to the main verb.) Three may be distinguished: (1) Present meaning: the Vulgate rendered it as *vincit,* "conquers," and that translation influenced Wycliffe, Luther, Tyndale, and the KJV (also NEB and Moffatt). *Nikan* was used in the present tense in the preceding line (5:4a), and the present participle will appear in the next verse. The present rendering, then, offers the least difficulty here as regards sense. Grammatically it is possible; for one can posit a comprehensive aorist (BDF 332) covering a victory still taking place (Vellanickal), although a perfect tense would be more normal for that. One would then conclude that the shift from an aorist participle in 5:4b to a present participle in 5:5 is just the Johannine predilection for variation without difference of meaning. Nevertheless, an aorist participle would normally indicate action before the main verb, and thus a relative past (BDF 339). (2) Past perfect meaning: it has conquered and continues to conquer—a translation that avoids a direct conflict with the surrounding present tenses of *nikan.* A perfect (finite) tense of this verb was used by the author in 4:4: "You belong to God, and so you have conquered those people; for he who is in you is greater than he who is in the world." However, the use of an aorist participle with a perfect sense would be more defensible if this were a narrative (BDF 340: GJohn shows a subtle use of the perfect). (3) True aorist meaning: a past conquest that has been completed before the present tense of the main verb. This is best grammatically but offers the greatest conflict in sense. How can "our faith" have conquered the world in the past when the author says both before and after this verse that Christians, as those begotten by God, are now conquering the world? The answers can again be divided into three groups: (a) It was Jesus who conquered the world in the past (John 16:33: "I have conquered [perf.] the world"); and while through faith Christians have a part in that victory, they must work out a continued conquest in their own lives. Support for this position (Bonsirven,

Bruce, Schnackenburg, etc.) is often sought in the use of different senses of *nikan* in Revelation. The aorist is used in Rev 5:5 for Jesus' victory: "The Lion of the tribe of Judah has conquered"; the aorist is also used in 12:11 for the Christians who share in Jesus' victory: "They have conquered him [the devil] by the blood of the Lamb"; but the pres. is used as an acknowledgment that Christians have not finished conquering: "I will give to him who conquers [pres.] to sit with me on my throne, as I myself conquered [aorist]" (3:21; also 2:26). See also I Cor 15:57: "Thanks be to God who gives us the conquest [*nikos*] through our Lord Jesus Christ." One cannot deny that such an interpretation of I John is possible and even probable; nevertheless, it does not do literal justice to the idea that *our faith* has conquered the world. (b) The conversion and baptism of I John's Christian readers constituted the past moment in which their faith conquered the world (Brooke? Stott?). This agrees with the next verse, which says that the conqueror of the world is he who believes that Jesus is the Son of God (5:5). "Jesus is the Son of God" is a creedal formula, perhaps associated with conversion or baptism; and so the author may be referring to the expression of faith used when his readers entered the Johannine Community. This interpretation also makes sense of 5:4a, "All that is begotten by God conquers the world"; for the Christian was begotten by God at the moment of baptism through water and Spirit (John 3:5). The idea would be that this past victory won by faith at conversion or baptism would continue to be worked out as the Christian victor lives and encounters manifestations of the world. For example, the rejection of secessionist blandishments would be a present victory. Continuing struggle and past victory were combined in I John 2:14: "Young People, I have been writing to you: you are strong, for the word of God abides in you, and you have conquered [perf.] the Evil One." (The reference to the word of God may relate the past victory to the moment when they first heard the word.) (c) The past victory was the expulsion of the secessionists. (This view, preferred by Stott and B. Weiss, is mentioned as possible by Brooke and Schnackenburg.) Since that struggle is still going on, the combination of past and present tenses would be quite intelligible. Clearly in 4:4 and perhaps in 2:14 the author uses the perfect tense of *nikan* to refer to a victory already won over the secessionists. In summary, although I favor the true aorist meaning of the verb, I see no way to be certain as to which past action I John means here.

4c. *this faith of ours.* The Byzantine tradition reads "yours," a reading that, if it were not so lacking in support among the great textual witnesses, could have a claim to be accepted as the more difficult reading (i.e., one that the scribes would be likely to change); for there is no second plural pronoun in the context, while there is a first plural in the preceding verse (5:3b). The verb *pisteuein*, "to believe, have faith," was discussed in the NOTE on 3:23b; but this is the only occurrence of the noun *pistis*, "faith, belief," in the Johannine corpus (it occurs 4 times in Revelation). As I have insisted before (see 5:1), the faith meant by the author is not a purely internal act, but involves the public profession of what one believes. Moreover, it is not only an act by which one commits oneself to Jesus but also has a christological content, specifying who Jesus is. This can be seen from the parallelism between 5:4bc and 5:5: First, the author says that our faith has conquered the world; then he says that the person who believes that Jesus is the Son of God conquers the world—"our faith" is a faith that Jesus is the Son of God. Miguens, "Testigos" 79, argues that *pistis*, akin to *pistos*, "faithful," has a sense of fidelity to Christ, and this fidelity helps one to conquer. In that case the present verse would be equivalent to Rev 2:26: "He who *conquers* and *keeps* my words *until the end*."

5a. *Who then is the one who conquers the world?* A *de*, "then," appears before the verb "is" in Codex Sinaiticus and after it in Vaticanus, while it is absent in Alexandrinus, the Byzantine tradition, the Vulgate, and the Sahidic. A "then" is implied by the style of the question, even as it was in 2:22, "Who then is the Liar?", where the textual evidence is more clearly against its explicit presence. (Here the Vaticanus positioning of the *de* is unusual and may have led scribes to transpose or omit it.) "The one who conquers" is the pres. ptcp. of *nikan*, by contrast with the aorist ptcp. in 4b. Some would translate it as "the one who can conquer"; but that might imply doubt about the conquest, whereas the author means that Christian conquest is inevitable, flowing from the fact that the world has already been conquered by Jesus. The seven letters of Revelation all end with a promise to "the one who conquers" (pres. ptcp. of *nikan*: 2:7,11,17,26; 3:5,12,21), and there it seems as if some in the various communities will not conquer. But that is not the idea here, for all within the Johannine Community share the same faith. Those who do not conquer have "gone out" because they lacked the true faith.

5b. *None other than the person who believes that* Jesus *is the Son of God.* Just as the question in 5a had the same phrasing as the question in 2:22, so in each case the answer begins with *ei mē*, "if not," which I translate as "None other." The Greek of the objective clause governed by "believes" is exactly the same as in 4:15 ("Whenever anyone confesses that *Jesus* is the Son of God"). As in 5:1a ("Everyone who believes that *Jesus* is the Christ"), the emphasis is that the holder of the divine title is the Jesus who lived and died.

6a. *Jesus Christ—this is the one who came.* Literally, "This is the one who came by water and blood—Jesus Christ." To reproduce the Greek emphasis, it seems best to shift "Jesus Christ" to the front. The use of "Christ" immediately after "*Jesus* is the Son of God," and the stress on his having come by water and blood confirm what was said at the end of the previous NOTE. In various modifications (*kai houtos estin; houtos* [*de*] *estin*) the formula "This is . . ." is popular among the Johannine writers (see NOTE on 1:5a); and the use of a definite article following it stresses the definite or well-known quality of the predicate (BDF 273; MGNTG 3, 183). In the present instance Brooke, *Epistles* 134, speaks of that quality thus: "He is the one whose office or work is rightly characterized by the description given." In the other I John instances the predicate is an abstract or impersonal noun. Here E. Norden, *Agnostos Theos* (Leipzig: Teubner, 1913) 183–88, would relate the personal predicate to the Johannine "I AM" formula (ABJ 29, 533–38) where a predicate was used by Jesus to describe himself, and the confessional formula "You are" where a predicate was used by others to describe Jesus (as Son of God, King of Israel [1:50]; prophet [4:19]; Holy One of God [6:69]; Christ, Son of God [11:27]—cf. Mark 1:11: "You are my beloved Son [also 3:11; 8:29; 14:61]). Examples of the "This is" formula used christologically include John 1:34 (God's chosen one or God's Son); 4:42 (Savior of the world); 7:40 (the Prophet); 7:41 (Messiah). Some Synoptic examples are Matt 3:17 ("This is my beloved Son") and 26:26 ("This is my body"). Particularly instructive for our purposes is the comparison between "This is the bread that comes/ came down from heaven" (John 6:50,58), and "I am the living bread that came down from heaven" (6:51). And so, even though the author of I John is phrasing this verse in a peculiarly polemic way, he is following a standard confessional pattern.

by water and blood. This is the reading of Codex Vaticanus, the Old Latin, Vulgate, Peshitta, and Tertullian. However, Codices Sinaiticus and Alexandrinus, the Coptic, Harclean Syriac, and Origen add "and [Holy] Spirit" to the phrase, a reading accepted by Dodd, Manson, Merk, Moffatt, Vogels, and von Soden. Other witnesses (Greek minuscules, Armenian, Ethiopic) insert "and Spirit" between "water" and "and blood," while still other Greek minuscules replace "blood" by "Spirit." Most likely the introduction of "Spirit" in these various readings was suggested to scribes by its occurrence as a third factor with "water and blood" in the next verse; also scribes would have been influenced by the mention of "water and Spirit" in John 3:5, and by the association of the Spirit with the baptism of Jesus (thought to be symbolized by "water").

The preposition here is *dia* and the two genitive nouns are anarthrous; this would normally mean that "water and blood" constitute a unit. Moule, IBNTG 57, suggests that *dia* here means attendant circumstances, while Chaine, *Epîtres* 213, denies that it refers to the means whereby Jesus came. However, BAG 178 (BAGD 179) argues that the primary meaning is not circumstance but a literal description of the way through which Jesus came. This would agree with taking the aorist ptcp. "the one who came" as a historical reference designed to attach "Son of God" and "Christ" to Jesus in specific circumstances of his earthly career. "The one who is coming" (pres. ptcp.) was a title attached to Jesus in GJohn (1:15,27; 12:13); it is applied here to that past.

6bc. *not in water only, but in water and in blood.* A pattern of "not . . . but" phrases or clauses occurs some dozen times in the Epistles; but the closest parallel to the present construction is in I John 2:2, "not only for our sins but also for the whole world," which also employs the neuter of *monos,* "alone, only," as an adverb. (In 5:6b Codex Vaticanus substitutes the adjectival *monō,* which modifies the noun "water"; see MGNTG 3, 226.) There are three differences between 6bc and 6a: *first,* the preposition here is *en* not *dia; second,* the preposition is repeated before each noun (thus three times), whereas previously the one *dia* covered two nouns; *third,* each noun has the definite article, which was lacking in 6a.

As for the first point, a few scholars would argue for a significant difference between the prepositions. *En,* "in," more easily represents accompanying circumstances, like a dative of manner (BDF 198[4], 219[4]). The circumstances of water and blood in 6bc would be those that accompanied Christ's own coming, and his coming would make the water and blood meaningful to others. Windisch sees the difference between *dia* and *en* as between coming "through" and coming "with." As a basis for the latter one can cite the LXX of Lev 16:3 where Aaron *comes* with (*en*) a calf; also I Cor 4:21, "Shall I *come* with [*en*] a rod or with [*en*] love?" Bonsirven and Wilder contend that *dia* refers to a historical manifestation in Jesus' lifetime, while *en* refers to the cause or instrument through which Jesus acts, namely, the sacraments (see below). Others speak of a shift in prepositions to the sphere in (*en*) which Jesus saves. Klöpper, "1 Joh" 383–84, thinks that *en* gives emphasis to the lasting nature of the coming. However, the majority of scholars see no significant difference in I John's variation between *dia* and *en* (Barth, Bruce, Büchsel, Bultmann, Chaine, Denney, Dodd, Schnackenburg, B. Weiss, Wengst). In the LXX both Greek prepositions can translate Hebrew *b^e*. In the NT both Heb 9:12 and 9:25 speak of the priest entering the Holy Place *with* blood, but the first uses *dia* while the second uses *en*. Romans 6:4 and Col 2:12 both speak of being buried with Christ *in* baptism, but the former uses *dia* while the latter uses *en*. The likelihood that we have in 5:6a and 5:6bc a meaningless variation of prepositions is of limited help, however, because the meaning of *dia* is not clear, as we saw.

The second difference between 6a and 6bc is of more importance; for the repetition of the preposition *en* in the latter suggests to many interpreters that "water" and "blood" are now being treated as separate entities or symbols, while they were joined in 6a. Such a conclusion is uncertain, however; for the author is denying a coming "in water only," and he may have repeated *en* to stress the importance rather than the separateness of the blood in the phrase "but in water and in blood."

The third difference (the use of the definite article in 6bc) is also unclear in its implication. Many insist that, like the repeated preposition, the definite article tends to make the water and the blood distinct; but THLJ 119 contends, "The use of the article serves to show that 'water' and 'blood' refer back to what has been said in the first part of v. 6."

Before we turn to the precise meaning of the symbolism in these first three lines of v. 6, some issues should be raised. The verb "came" covers both prepositions *dia* and *en*. The "came by/in water and blood" describes how Jesus Christ came, not how "Christ" came to Jesus. Some of the awkwardness of this description may stem from the use of "came by/in" by the adversaries whose language the author is bending to his own formula. Whether or not they originated the expression, evidently the secessionists can use "came in" with reference to "water"—that is why the author says that Jesus Christ is *not* one who came in water only. Did the adversaries deny altogether that he came in blood, or only that he came in water and in blood together? While we have not yet discussed the reference to "the Spirit" at the end of v. 6, somehow that notion fits into the picture of the coming by/in water and blood. Reflecting upon these points, let us now ask *what precise manifestation of Jesus Christ, Son of God, was involved when he "came by/in water and in blood."* I shall not bother discussing antiquated opinions, e.g., water and blood mean Jesus' innocence and sacrifice (Grotius).

(1) **"Came by/in water and blood" refers to the sacraments of baptism and the eucharist.** (In this case "the Spirit" mentioned in 5:6de might refer to a third sacrament, e.g., prebaptismal anointing—see NOTES on 2:20a; 5:8a.) In this theory *dia/en* means "with": Christ came bringing the sacraments. There are several variations of this theory. That the sacramental meaning is primary in all three lines (6abc) is suggested by church writers of the fourth and fifth centuries (Ambrose, Augustine, Chrysostom, Cyril of Alexandria) and was still popular in the last century (Bisping, Karl). Others think that the sacramental meaning is only secondary after a primary reference to some event(s) in the life of Jesus. Tertullian (*De baptismo* 16.1–2; CC 1, 290), for instance, thinks that "water" refers to Jesus' own baptism, and secondarily to the baptism of Christians. Westcott, *Epistles* 182, is one of several modern scholars (Bonsirven, Windisch) who think that 6a (*dia*) refers to the historical career of Jesus, but 6bc (*en*) refers to the sacraments. The change of preposition shows that "St. John is speaking of a continuation of the first coming under some new but analogous form." (The theory that, while the whole of v. 6 refers to the historical career of Jesus, the passage in vv. 7–8 refers to the sacraments will be discussed in the NOTES below on those verses.) The Johannine evidence used to support this symbolic understanding of "water" and "blood" includes the following: In John 3:5 "begotten of *water* and Spirit" is a reference to baptism; in 6:54–56, "My flesh is real food and my *blood* real drink," is a reference to the eucharist; moreover, there is a possible reference to the two sacraments in the blood and water that flowed from the side of Christ in 19:34.

The objections to this theory are serious. The author would be choosing a remarkably obscure way of referring to sacraments, so that one would have to posit that this was well-known inner-Community language. The preposition *dia* can mean accompanying circumstances when the context points in that direction, but there is nothing in the context here to encourage us to understand "came through or by water and blood" as bringing the sacraments. We have no evidence in I John that the secessionists denied the sacraments. In GJohn there may have been Jewish Christian adversaries who rejected an emphasis on Jesus' (eucharistic) blood (6:53–66), and disciples of John the Baptist who rejected Jesus' baptism in the Spirit (1:33, plus 3:22–26—see my *Community* 69–71,78–80). But the secessionists are former members of the Johannine Community who should have shared some of the implicit sacramental outlook of GJohn. It is true that Ignatius of Antioch criticizes an antieucharistic group (presumably Jewish Christians) by insisting on the blood (and flesh) of Jesus (*Smyrn.* 6–7); but I have argued in the INTRODUCTION (IV B3b) that these opponents of Ignatius are not necessarily the docetists attacked by him elsewhere, who have some affinities with the secessionist adversaries of I John. Thus the polemic tone of 5:6abc seems to exclude a sacramental interpretation of the symbolism of those lines (but not necessarily of 5:7–8).

(2) **"Came by/in water and blood" refers to the incarnation.** This thesis has been strongly defended by Richter, "Blut," whose arguments have been chal-

lenged by Wengst, *Häresie* 19–20. (Richter's arguments assume that GJohn is clear as to when the incarnation took place—at the conception or birth but not at the baptism of Jesus—but, in fact, GJohn is not specific about when the Word became flesh.) The Johannine evidence for this interpretation includes: the use of the verb "come" for the entrance of the Word into the world (John 1:11: "He came to [*eis*] his own"); see also 16:28 ("I have come into [*eis*] the world"), and 5:43 ("I have come in my Father's name"). Elsewhere in the Epistles the verb "come" is used only twice with the preposition *en* (I John 4:2; II John 7), both times in reference to Jesus Christ coming in the flesh. May not "came by/in water and blood" be another form of "come in flesh"? Richter's assumption is that the adversaries of I John were docetists who denied that Jesus was truly human, maintaining that he had only an apparent body, composed of water. He argues (p. 128) that in the physiology of the time the human embryo was thought to be composed of the woman's menstrual blood and the male seed (Wisdom 7:2), and that the author's insistence on "water and blood" was a statement about the reality of the body. (In ABJ 29A, 947 I pointed to the thesis that the gods did not have ordinary blood, but blood mixed with water.)

The objection to this theory centers on the implied thesis of the adversaries. We do not have evidence that they were true docetists denying the human body of Jesus. Moreover, none of the many later docetist documents states that Jesus' body was composed of water only, as opposed to blood. (It is true that the Mandaeans [*Ginza Right* 1.29.5; 2.53.3; Lidzbarski, pp. 29,48] held that the Enosh-Uthra or Savior came clothed with a garb [body] made of water, but they made no contrast with blood.) When Ignatius of Antioch stresses the blood of Jesus against his opponents (*Smyrn.* 1:1; 12:2), he is underlining the passion and the cross, not the incarnation. Could former members of the Johannine Community have denied that Jesus had blood when blood and water came from his dead body (John 19:34—not part of the redactor's addition in 19:35)? Of course, the secessionists might have allegorized the blood of the crucifixion account (e.g., the docetic *Acts of John* 101 [HSNTA 2, 234]: "Blood flowed from me; yet it did not flow"), but one would like some positive Johannine evidence for Richter's thesis. Moreover, that thesis does not really explain the invocation of the Spirit in the latter part of 5:6; for GJohn associates the Spirit with the Baptist's acknowledgment of Jesus and with Jesus' death, but never with the incarnation or coming into the world.

(3) **"Came by/in water and blood" refers to the baptism and the death of Jesus.** With variations this is the most common theory (Bengel, Bruce, Bultmann, Heitmüller, Holtzmann, Marshall, Michaelis, B. Weiss, Windisch, Winterbotham) and, at least in part (baptism), was already current by the time of Tertullian (A.D. 200). "Coming" in this theory is not simply entrance into the world but salvific mission—the sense in which Jesus was hailed as "the one who is coming" (*erchomenos*), not only in GJohn but also in works that show no knowledge of incarnation (Matt 11:3; Luke 7:20). Thus, the one who "came by/in water and blood" becomes a statement about how Jesus' life and death contributed to his identity as Son of God. There is little doubt that

"water" can be understood as a reference to the baptism by John the Baptist; for John 1:26,31,33 reiterates that John baptized with [*en*] *water*, an indication found also in Mark 1:8; Acts 1:5; 11:16. And "blood" can be a reference to the death of Jesus, not only because of John 19:34 where blood flows from the side of Jesus, but from general Christian usage where shedding blood refers to Jesus' violent demise (Matt 23:35; 27:4,6,8,24,25; Acts 5:28) or to the death of others (Acts 18:6; 20:26; Heb 12:4; Rev 6:10; 19:2; *I Clem.* 55:1). We saw that the references in I John 1:7; 2:2 to the blood of Jesus as an atoning victim cleansing us from sin are very close to the imagery of Hebrews which portrays the death of Christ as the Christian sacrifice on the Day of Atonement. Hebrews 4:14 and 6:19–20 describe Jesus' death in terms of movement—not as coming, but as passing through the heavens or as entering the inner shrine—and Heb 9:12 says, "He entered once for all into the Holy Place taking his own blood." Thus, the language of "water and blood" offers no difficulty for this interpretation of I John as baptism and death, and the image of two salvific comings does justice to 5:6c: "in (the) water and in (the) blood." Yet two comings do not fit 5:6a where the single preposition *dia* covers two anarthrous nouns, so that "came by water and blood" should mean one composite action.

A variant of this theory recognizes that grammatical point by interpreting the whole of 5:6abc as a reference to the baptism of Jesus, which really took place or was made effective at his death. Since the baptism of Jesus by John was only a baptism with water, one may argue that the baptism in the Spirit occurred when Jesus was glorified in death, a thesis supported by John 7:39: "For there was as yet no Spirit, since Jesus had not been glorified." This idea is reinforced by Mark 10:38 and Luke 12:50, where Jesus refers to his death as his baptism. Ignatius, *Eph.* 18:2, may have been moving in that direction when he said, "Jesus was born and baptized that by his suffering he might purify the water." Such a variant suggestion would meet another objection against the baptism *and* death theory, namely, the unlikelihood that a Johannine author would stress that Jesus "came" by his baptism in the Jordan. GJohn never describes the baptism of Jesus and never says that John the Baptist baptized him. (At most that is implied in 1:31–32.) However, there is no Johannine text that uses the term "baptism" in reference to the death of Jesus.

What theory of the adversaries would have been refuted by stressing a coming of Jesus Christ by baptism and by death? Frequently it has been assumed that this verse was written to refute Cerinthus, who maintained that Christ in the form of a dove descended upon Jesus after his baptism and departed from him before he died. However, I argued in the INTRODUCTION (IV B3d) that there is little to establish a relationship between I John and Cerinthus, and that at most the author's adversaries may have been pre-Cerinthian in emphasizing baptism over death.

(4) **"Came by/in water and blood" refers to the death of Jesus.** Just after Jesus died, blood and water flowed from his side (John 19:34); and this is the only other Johannine passage where the two elements are joined. Thus it is quite possible that "by water and blood" in 6a refers to Jesus' death. (Augus-

tine already made a connection between the two passages; but it has been denied by many, e.g., Düsterdieck, Ewald, B. Weiss.) But in what sense could his death be a *coming* of Jesus Christ, Son of God? Even without polemic thrust, this language would not have been inappropriate against the background of GJohn; for in speaking to Pontius Pilate just before being sentenced to death, Jesus speaks of what he is doing as "the reason why I have come into the world" (18:37). It is noteworthy that the only other mention of blood in I John (1:7) refers to death: "The blood of Jesus, His Son, cleanses us from all sin." If the epistolary author knew the tradition that "blood and water" flowed from the dead Jesus as he handed over the Spirit (John 19:30,34—a connection that would explain the sudden introduction of the Spirit in I John 5:6de), why does he change the word order to "water and blood"? (There is only minor evidence for the order "water and blood" in 19:34; see ABJ 29A, 936.) It may be because his adversaries are emphasizing a coming in water, and against them he wants to stress the blood. (In 19:34 the startling thing was water [symbolic of the Spirit in 7:39] flowing from a dead body, and that is why it was mentioned in the last and climactic position.) Accordingly the secessionists and not the author would be concentrating on the baptism of Jesus. (It is not easy to say which modern scholars hold the "death" interpretation of "water and blood," because most mention Jesus' baptism but without distinguishing whether it is the author or his adversaries who are advocating it.) Thus understood, the secessionist view need have nothing to do with that of Cerinthus or that of the docetists who thought Jesus did not have a human body. I theorized in the INTRODUCTION (V B2b) that they believed in a true incarnation but interpreted the Johannine Community hymn (the GJohn Prologue), with its references to John the Baptist in close proximity to "the Word became flesh" (1:6–9,14–15), to mean that this incarnation took place at the baptism. For them the full coming of Jesus Christ as Son of God (see John 1:49 where Jesus is hailed as Son of God immediately) took place in water, and that was when the Spirit descended (1:32)—nothing further was salvifically necessary. (Such a view may be related to the later Mandaean thesis: "When I came, the One sent by Light. . . . I came with the mark [of oil?] on me and baptism" [*Ginza Right* 2.64.10–14; Lidzbarski, pp. 57–58].) The author is denying the thesis that the coming at Jesus' baptism was sufficient, and he is insisting that Jesus Christ, the Son of God, fully came as Savior of the world (I John 4:14) only through his death when he served as an atonement for the whole world (2:2). It is not clear what the epistolary author would say affirmatively about the coming at the baptism, but he is certainly not interested in emphasizing it.

This last explanation of what the author meant by stating, "Jesus Christ—this is the one who came by water and blood, not in water only, but in water and in blood," is not without some obscurity; but it solves more problems than any other theory. And it puts emphasis on the one point the author clearly meant to emphasize: the salvific value of the death of Jesus.

6d. *And the Spirit is the one who testifies.* Some would start v. 7 with this clause. (For verse divisions, see the NOTE on 4:18ab above.) The versification of 5:6–8 is aggravated by the fact that versifiers based themselves on a Greek (and Latin) text that had the Johannine Comma (Appendix IV below). In 5:6–11 the verb *martyrein*, "to testify, bear witness," occurs 4 times; and the noun *martyria*, "testimony, witness," occurs 6 times, almost one-sixth of the total Johannine usage (NOTE on 1:2b). Modern translations tend to shift back and forth between "witness" and "testify/testimony" within these verses for the sake of English style, but I have thought it important to reflect the Greek usage of a verb and noun of the same root. A few scholars translate the initial *kai* in this line as "also," a translation which would equate "the Spirit" with "water and blood" as agents, or equate them with the Spirit as testifying (JB: "with the Spirit as another witness"). This is the wrong approach; for the author does not say that Jesus Christ came by/in the Spirit, nor in this verse does he describe the function of water and blood as testifying. If there is any parallelism in v. 6, it is between Jesus Christ who is "the one who came [aorist ptcp.] by water and blood" and the Spirit who is "the one who testifies [pres. ptcp.]." How and when does the Spirit testify? Plummer, *Epistles* 115, lists six specific agents of testimony in GJohn (Scripture, John the Baptist, the disciples, Jesus' own works, Jesus' words, the Father) besides the Spirit/Paraclete; and the Spirit/Paraclete is thought to testify through the disciples (John 15:26–27). Chaine, *Epîtres* 214, thinks that the author of I John means the general testimony borne by the Spirit in and through GJohn, while others (Preiss) think of an internal witness of the Spirit in the heart of the Christian. However, something less vague and more public seems to be demanded as a solemn refutation of the secessionists.

The context points to a connection between the Spirit's testifying and Jesus Christ's coming by/in water and blood. If the latter refers to Jesus' death on the cross (number 4 in the preceding NOTE), the role of the Spirit should be related to that death. As Jesus finished his life on the cross, with the Beloved Disciple and his Mother standing nearby (19:25–27), he handed over the Spirit (19:30). And when the blood and water flowed from Jesus' side (19:34), the Beloved Disciple testified to that; and his testimony was stated to be true (19:35), even as here the author will insist in the next line that the Spirit who testifies is the truth. It would make good sense of the present verse if the epistolary author was arguing that the Spirit gave testimony through the Beloved Disciple to the correct meaning of the blood and water flowing from Jesus' side, because the Spirit had been given to that Disciple before Jesus died. Many different interpretations of 19:34 have been proposed; and to the literature I cited in ABJ 29A, 961–62, may now be added the survey of views by E. Malatesta, "Blood and Water from the Pierced Side of Christ (Jn 19,34)," in *Segni e Sacramenti nel Vangelo di Giovanni*, ed. P.-R. Tragan (Studia Anselmiana 66; Sacramentum 3; Rome: San Anselmo, 1977) 165–81. As I argued in ABJ and shall stress in the COMMENT below, there are good reasons for thinking that the immediate flow of blood portrayed Jesus as a sacrificial victim, and the flow of water symbolized his gift of the Spirit to believers—the very meaning of death that the epistolary author wants to stress. The Spirit may have come upon Jesus in relation to his baptism and have marked the salvific revelation of God (as the secessionists held); but this Spirit became a reality for others (John 7:39) only through the sacrificial death of Jesus, and the Spirit himself testified to that by enabling the Beloved Disciple to penetrate the meaning of the death. By stating that the Spirit is the one who testifies (pres. tense), the author indicates that he does not think of the Spirit's testimony purely as a past phenomenon. It continues in the testimony of the "we" of the Johannine School (I John 1:2) who join themselves to and prolong the testimony of the Beloved Disciple. It is no accident that the closest passage in GJohn to "The Spirit is the one who testifies, for the Spirit is the truth" is the description of the Beloved Disciple in 21:24: "This is the disciple who testifies . . . and we know that his testimony is true." Probably that verse is redactional, but it shows a tendency among the Johannine writers (especially the later writers) to identify the testimony of the Spirit and that of the Beloved Disciple.

6e. *for the Spirit is the truth.* The predicate has the definite article. The three Johannine descriptions of God as "Spirit" (John 4:24), "light" (I John 1:5), and "love" (I John 4:8,16) have an anarthrous predicate, while the Johannine self-descriptions of Jesus tend to have an arthrous predicate, e.g., "I am the light" (John 8:12); "I am the way, and the truth, and the life" (14:6). Nevertheless, the anarthrous "I am light" (9:5) warns against theorizing about too precise a difference. For instance, some would argue that the God-formulas are more functional while the Jesus-formulas are more essential (as is this Spirit-formula). De la Potterie, *La vérité* 1, 323–26, argues that the issue in 5:6e is not a revelation of the divine essence (Cyril of Alexandria, Bultmann, Law, Schnackenburg, Swete, Westcott) but a function of teaching the truth manifested in Jesus; and he may well be correct (see ABJ 29, 499–501). However, as I have already insisted (p. 235), I find oversubtle his contention that the Johannine author could not say "God is truth" (a formula attested in Jewish thought: 1QH 4:40; *Midrash Rabbah* 38:1 on Exod 29:1), and that "truth" is predicated differently of Jesus than it is of the Spirit. As Jesus is the revelation of the truthfulness of God, the Spirit is the revelation of the truth that is Jesus. He is the Spirit of Truth.

Some commentators (Ebrard, Greiff) take the *hoti* introducing this clause as declarative ("that"), so that the clause represents the content of what the Spirit testifies. Even though *hoti* after *martyrein* normally does give the content of the testimony (John 1:34; 3:28; 4:39,44; etc.), it sometimes means "because, for" (John 8:14; 15:27); and that is more likely here. Self-testimony is not impossible on Jesus' part who states, "I am the truth" (14:6); but the role of the Paraclete/Spirit is to testify on behalf of Jesus (15:26) and not to speak on his own behalf (16:13). The Latin textual tradition and the Latin-influenced Greek minuscule 61 of the sixteenth century recognized that the Spirit could not testify "that the Spirit is the truth" and so read "that Christ is the truth." (I think a deliberate change is more plausible than Westcott's suggestion [*Epistles* 183] that scribes may have confused the abbreviations for "Christ" and the "Spirit," or T. W. Manson's contention [JTS 48 (1947) 27, n. 3] that originally there was no expressed subject and that scribes guessed, with different results.)

7. *Indeed, there are three who testify.* Literally, "Because three are they who testify." A *hoti* begins this clause, even as *hoti* began the last clause. It is awkward to have another "for, because," especially since this clause does not offer another reason but a further specification. (Despite the attempt of some to render the initial *kai* of 5:6d as "also" [see NOTE there], v. 7 introduces the new idea that the water and the blood can be counted as witnesses.) THLJ 120 suggests that *hoti* is either to be ignored in translation (RSV, TEV) or is to be rendered as "yes" or "actually"; see also BDF 456[1] for the frequent loose use of *hoti*. A partial concession to the causal sense is the meaning "because of all this" or "because, I repeat," so that it is equivalent to "thus." The Greek word order emphasizes the "three," and there can be little doubt that the author is consciously referring to the law of testimony in Deut 19:15 concerning the need for two or three witnesses, a law involved in GJohn (ABJ 29, 223 and 341). The Greek numeral is masculine, although all three witnesses specified in the next line are neuter. Plummer, *Epistles* 116 (also Bonsirven), presses the gender too far when he states, "The masculine points to the personality of the Spirit," unless one wishes to claim the personality of water and blood as well— something that Greiff, "Zeugen" 477–78, does not hesitate to do, for he sees the water as the baptized Christian, and the blood as the martyr! It is rather the personal character of the *witnessing* that is underlined by the masculine numeral, as well as by the use of the pres. ptcp. ("those who bear witness" rather than "witnesses"): the three go on testifying. In Jewish tradition personal testimony can be given by impersonal witnesses, e.g., by a heap of stones (Gen 31:45–48), by heaven and earth (Deut 31:28), by clouds and rain (*Enoch* 100:11). The Elkasaites (*ca.* A.D. 100), according to Hippolytus (*Refutatio* 9, 15; PG 16[3], 3391C), cited seven witnesses to their cleansing: heaven, water, Holy Spirit, angel of prayer, oil, salt, and earth.

8a. *the Spirit and the water and the blood.* The Latin additions to v. 8 are discussed in Appendix IV. According to 5:6 Jesus Christ came by/in water and blood, while the Spirit "is the one who testifies"; but now in vv. 7–8 all three testify. The numeral "three" (v. 7), the three uses of "and," and the three definite articles all suggest that there is no subordination in the witness. Nevertheless, since the time of Cyprian there have been scholars who argue that even in 7–8 the author means that the Spirit testifies through the water and blood, or that the water and blood voice their witness through the Spirit. On the other hand, the shift of function and relationship from 6 to 7–8 has led Bultmann to posit that 7–8 is the addition of an Ecclesiastical Redactor. A more popular and less drastic course is to posit that Spirit, water, and blood in 7–8 mean something different from what they mean in 6 (or at least water and blood have a different meaning). The shift has been diagnosed as a move from the historical setting of Jesus' ministry in 6 (indicated by "came") to a more symbolic thrust for the three witness-bearers in 7–8. Within that framework a fascinating variety of symbolisms has been proposed. The oldest attested (*ca.* 200) is in Clement of Alexandria (*Hypotypōseis* [*Adumbrationes*] *In Joh.* 5:6; GCS 17, 214): "There are three that give testimony: the Spirit which is *life*, the water which is regeneration and *faith*, and the blood which is *knowledge*"—an exegesis that, alas, has little inner Johannine support. More perceptive and destined to be more influential is the trinitarian interpretation, which ultimately gave rise in the Latin Church to the Johannine Comma (Appendix IV). It is attested in North Africa from the third century onward (Cyprian, Pseudo-Cyprian). The trinitarian interpretation of vv. 7–8 by Augustine, Facundus of Hermiane, and others is fortified with inner Johannine argumentation: John 4:24 identifies God the Father as "Spirit"; John 7:38–39 symbolizes the Holy Spirit by flowing "water"; and in John 19:34 from the side of the Son comes forth "blood." Also it may be observed that the Spirit, God, and the Son are mentioned in the immediate context (I John 5:8–9) of the three witnesses. Nevertheless, the trinitarian interpretation reflects doctrine that goes beyond the theological insights of the first century and is in part based on the Latin interpretations of v. 8b to mean "these three are one." Modern interpretations often shift the symbolism to the life of the Christian, e.g., Hoskyns, *Epistles* 668: "The water, the blood, and the Spirit of the evangelical narrative [John 19:30,34] are the sanctification, new life, and inspiration which God has poured out upon us through His Son." Others speak of the testimony of Christian blood in martyrdom, citing Ignatius, *Rom.* 3:2; 4:2, that one is truly a Christian disciple only when one suffers, so that blood plays the same role in the life of the Christian that it played in the historical career of Jesus. Obviously water is harder to fit into such a symbolism.

More simply one may argue that the Spirit, the water, and the blood represent Christ's continuing powers to vivify, cleanse, and atone—a view that finds support in John 6:63; 13:10; I John 1:7; 2:2. M. Barth, *Taufe* 405, who denies that vv. 6 and 7–8 have different meanings, interprets the author to mean that the actions of Jesus in his lifetime did not cease to have effects with his death. Johannine thought could have moved in this direction by reflection upon the OT. Already Zech 12:10, "They shall look upon him whom they have pierced," is cited in John 19:37; and the rest of the Zechariah context speaks of the pouring out of a spirit of compassion, and the opening of a fountain to cleanse from sin (Zech 12:10; 13:1). Even in this attractive thesis it is not clear how an understanding of water and blood as pure symbols would enable them to give testimony.

The most popular suggestion for the new symbolism of Spirit, water, and blood in vv. 7–8 (as distinct from that of v. 6) is to find there a reference to the sacraments of baptism and the eucharist. I mentioned above the arguments against seeing a sacramental reference in v. 6; but those do not apply here, for there is no reference now to a *coming* by/in water and blood and no longer a strong polemic against "water only." We saw above that "water" was prominent in the descriptions of Jesus' baptism by John the Baptist, and by analogy it is not surprising to find the term "water" in early descriptions of Christian baptism (Acts 8:36–39; I Pet 3:20–21; Eph 5:26; Heb 10:22; *Didache* 7:1–3; *Barnabas* 11:8,11). Although "blood" is very prominent in the eucharistic words of Jesus in John 6:53–56, it is not so certain that by itself "blood" would be readily intelligible as a description of the eucharist, comparable to "the breaking of the bread." (The closest one comes is the use of "the cup of the Lord" for the liquid eucharistic element in *The Gospel of the Hebrews* 7

[HSNTA 1, 165].) Perhaps one can meet this objection by assuming that the idiom in I John 5:7-8 would have been influenced in part by the historical reference to Jesus' death in 5:6 (and John 19:34). Naturally those scholars who have already posited a sacramental reference for 5:6 posit one for 5:7-8 as well, and so the number of those who support this interpretation of the three witnesses is large: Balz, F.-M. Braun, Bultmann, de la Potterie, Dodd, Goodenough, Holtzmann, Loisy, Schlatter, Schnackenburg, Schneider, Westcott, and Windisch. (There are exotic variations as well, e.g., Greiff's thesis that Spirit/flesh/water/blood represented a sequence in the Johannine baptismal eucharistic liturgy.) It is rejected altogether, however, by M. Barth, Brox, and Wendt, and found to be insufficiently demonstrated by others (Bruce, Marshall, etc.).

The real problem in the sacramental interpretation is how the Spirit fits into the picture. One approach, with many variations, is to have the Spirit play an overall role in relation to baptism (water) and the eucharist (blood). Preiss, *Témoignage* 36-39, speaks of the Spirit as an interior witness corresponding to the exterior witness of the two sacraments (similar to Calvin's notion that the Spirit works from within, corresponding to the exterior witness of the Scriptures). Dodd, *Epistles* 131, thinks of the living voice of prophecy (the Spirit) and the two evangelical sacraments. Schnackenburg, *Johannesbriefe* 261, states succinctly, "The Spirit is the principle of life from which these [two] sacraments acquire their supernatural power." In the ancient *Apostolic Constitutions* 3.17.2-4 (Funk 1, 211-13) we find the Spirit given at baptism to be the Paraclete who proclaims Christ. This overall approach to the Spirit, while attractive, does not do justice to the grammatical distinction and equality given to "the Spirit and the water and the blood," who should all testify in a somewhat similar way. For that reason some scholars seek to find a separate sacramental reference for "the Spirit" as well. In discussing the "anointing from the Holy One" (NOTE on 2:20a; also 2:27) we saw the possibility of an ancient initiatory anointing with oil before or after baptism, which would symbolize the gift of the Spirit. There would then be a perfect parallelism of three sacraments, anointing, baptism, and the eucharist, symbolized respectively by the Spirit, water, and blood. A prebaptismal anointing (defended by de la Potterie, Manson, Nauck) would even explain the order in which the three witnesses are mentioned. The following supporting evidence (of uneven value) is offered for the early existence of prebaptismal anointing or giving of the Spirit: in Acts 10:44-48 the Spirit is given before people are baptized (but see Acts 2:28; 8:15-16 for the contrary order); the *Testament of Levi* 8:4-5 describes a ceremony in which Levi becomes a priest: "The first man anointed me [but *aleiphein*, not *chriein/chrisma*] with holy oil . . . the second washed me with pure water and fed me with bread and wine"; the Pseudo-Clementine *Recognitions* 3.67.4 (GCS 51, 141) speaks of being anointed with oil before being baptized with water, a practice confirmed for the Syrian church by the *Didascalia Apostolorum* 16.3.12 (Connolly p. 146), the *Acts of Thomas* 10, 121 (HSNTA 2, 507), and the *Liturgical Homilies* of Narsai (Manson, "Entry" 26); an anointing or chrism of catechesis before baptism is mentioned by Origen, Pseudo-Chrysostom, and Cyril of Alexandria (de la Potterie, "Anointing" 119–21). As one seeks to evaluate this theory of a sacrament of the Spirit preceding baptism in I John 5:8, there are two major difficulties: the absence of positive proof for its existence in the Johannine Community, and the failure of the author to use the designation *chrisma,* employed in 2:20,27, which would have made the parallelism with water and blood even more perfect. (Cf. the use of "oil and water and bread" in *Acts of Thomas* 13, 152 [HSNTA 2, 523].) Once more this objection may be met by assuming that the terminology of 5:8 has been dictated in part by the terminology of 5:6 (and John 19:30,34). At most, however, one can allot possibility to the attractive theory that the three witnesses are three sacraments that give visible testimony to the salvific death of Jesus. Indeed, the same judgment, but with lesser uncertainty, would have to be passed on the theory of the Spirit and the two sacraments as the three witnesses.

Since I maintain that 5:6 refers to the death of Jesus when it speaks of his coming by/in water and blood and of the accompanying testimony of the Spirit, I would judge that 5:7–8 refers to the same subject in terms of the testimony of the three. The testimony, then, would not be even partially to the baptism of Jesus (*pace* Dodd, *Epistles* 131). Even farther from the mark would be the thesis of Nauck, *Tradition* 180–82, that the Spirit here is conceived as mediating divine childhood in imitation of the sonship of Jesus. Whether the three witnesses are sacraments or the ongoing power of Jesus to vivify, cleanse, and atone, they remain in the Community as a living testimony to the salvific power of Jesus' death. Do the secessionists deny the very existence of such witnesses, or would they claim that such witnesses bear testimony to something other than Jesus' death? In particular, if the sacramental theory has any value, how did the adversaries think of baptism and the eucharist? Following my general understanding that the secessionists accepted the kind of tradition found in GJohn and erred in terms of too high a christology, I would assume that the difference between them and the author would have been over the significance of the sacraments. If they accepted John 6:51–58, they may have acknowledged the eucharist as the flesh and blood of Jesus, but may have resembled the opponents of Ignatius in *Smyrn.* 7:1 who did not "confess that the eucharist is the flesh of our Savior Jesus Christ *who suffered for our sins.*" After all, in the GJohn passage, Jesus speaks of his eucharistic flesh in terms of bread come down from heaven (incarnational language), while there is nothing in GJohn about a Last Supper setting where the eucharist could commemorate his death. Johannine theology presents the eucharist as the food of life but has no echo of Paul's "Whenever you eat this bread and drink this cup, you proclaim the Lord's death until he comes" (I Cor 11:26). Still another possibility is that the secessionists held a water eucharist as did some of the later gnostics; for, as the Mandaean texts show, such a water eucharist could be a sacramental reference to baptism, i.e., the reception of a heavenly water of life. (See G. Bornkamm, "On the Understanding of Worship," in *Early Christian Experience* [New York: Harper & Row, 1969; German orig. 1952] 173–74.) If the secessionists thought of the descent of the Spirit upon Jesus at his baptism in water as the coming of salvation into the world, they may have related the testimony of the Spirit and the water (baptism) and the blood (eucharist) to that moment. (Remember that in John 1:29, in the context of baptism with water, Jesus is identified as "the Lamb of God who takes away the world's sin.") The epistolary author would be insisting that those three witnesses testify to the death of Jesus ("not in water only but in water and in blood"), for only through the shedding of blood did he atone for our sins, "and not only for our sins but also for the whole world" (I John 1:7; 2:2).

8b. *and these three are of one accord.* Literally, "are into [*eis*] the one," i.e., the cardinal number with the article. A pregnant use of "one" as the predicate of the verb "to be" is found in GJohn: "The Father and I are one" (10:30); "That they may be one just as we (are one)" (17:11,22). Even closer to the present usage is 11:52: "to gather even the dispersed children of God into [*eis*] one," and 17:23: "That they may be completed into [*eis*] one" (although neither of these GJohn "into one" examples has the definite article). In ABJ 29A, 777 I pointed out that such usage of "one" has some parallels among the Dead Sea Scrolls. Our I John instance, however ("to be into the one"), is a particular problem, and occurs nowhere else in the NT. Some seek to ameliorate it by the contention that *eis*, "into," and *en*, "in," are interchangeable in NT Greek (although BDF 205 mentions that this interchange is infrequent in John, especially the Epistles), but "in the one" is not much of an improvement. BDF 145[1] and ZBG 32 suggest a Semitism where *eis* with the accusative (imitating Hebrew *le*) replaces the predicate nominative after the verb "to be," so that the author would be saying "are one." (The exact Hebrew expression "to be a unity," employing the preposition *le*, occurs in 1QS 5:2.) That is the way the Latin tradition translated the expression and thus facilitated a trinitarian interpretation which produced the Johannine Comma (Appendix IV). As usual, de la Potterie insists on the literal force of the preposition in terms of convergence ("toward one," "for the same object") and here that is less strained than usual, for it would mean that three witnesses tend to give the same testimony. My own translation ("are of one accord") is meant to straddle "are one" and "toward one."

9ab. *If we accept human testimony, God's testimony is even greater.* This is the only epistolary instance of *lambanein*, "to receive, take," used with "testimony" in the sense of accepting as valid (4 times in GJohn [3:11,32,33; 5:34]). The condition is introduced by *ei* with the indicative, which could be translated, "Granting the fact that we accept. . . ." No doubt is cast on the fact of accepting human testimony (literally, "the testimony of men [*anthrōpoi*]"); rather, if that fact is operative, the consequence follows. One might have expected the author to say, "how much the more do we accept God's testimony." Rather he uses the comparative *meizōn*, "greater," to indicate something, not about our acceptance but about the divine testimony, which is more powerful and, therefore, more demanding of assent. Elsewhere in I John, *meizōn* is used in 3:20, "God is greater than our heart," and in 4:4, "He who is in you [the Spirit] is greater than he who is in the world." A close parallel to the idea and wording here may be found in John 5:33–36, which speaks of the testimony of John the Baptist as "human testimony" that Jesus does not accept (*lambanein*), and which contends that Jesus has even greater (*meizōn*) testimony from his Father.

To what *human testimony* does the epistolary author refer? There are three possibilities: (1) The testimony of the three witnesses just cited in vv. 6–8 (Bonsirven). While that may seem the most obvious reading, how could the author use "the testimony of men" to designate the testimony of the Spirit, or the testimony attached to the water and the blood through which Christ came? In Johannine thought both Christ and the Spirit come from above, i.e., from God. Greiff, "Zeugen" 479, argues that the Spirit/water/blood are the prophet/ baptized(Christian)/martyr who could be called human witnesses. Some would argue that "of men" does not mean "by/from men" (but the parallel in John 5:34 clearly means a testimony by John the Baptist). Another suggestion is that "of men" means "according to human standards," i.e., according to the Mosaic Law which requires two or three witnesses. None of these attempts to avoid the basic objection is very plausible. (2) Human testimony in general (Schnackenburg), since the conditional clause is a general one. In John 8:15–18 Jesus moves from judging according to human standards to the validity of his own judgment, which is based on the testimony of two persons (his Father and himself). The point there, however, is different, for he is insisting that the heavenly witnesses meet human requirements. (3) The testimony is that of John the Baptist invoked by the secessionists. Their claim that Christ "came in water" rests upon the tradition reflected in John 1:32: "John gave this testimony too, 'I have seen the Spirit descend like a dove from the sky, and it came to rest upon him.'" The author of I John would be characterizing this as human testimony (even as Jesus did in John 5:34) in comparison to which God's testimony (to the importance of Jesus' death) would be greater. This would echo John 5:36, "I have testimony even greater than John's, namely, the works the Father has given me to complete [*teleioun*]," interpreted by Jesus' dying words which affirmed that he had completed all things (John 19:28–30; see 17:4). In John 3:31–33 a contrast similar to the one in I John is found implicitly since John the Baptist is described as one who is of the earth and Jesus is the one who comes from heaven, but whose testimony is not accepted. (The following verse there, "Whoever does accept his testimony has certified that God is truthful," is remarkably like the following verse here [5:10].) I think this is the most plausible interpretation of the "human testimony" of I John 5:9a, even though it rests for its validity on the ability to reconstruct the theology of the secessionists in light of a GJohn tradition that both they and the author's readers would have had to know thoroughly.

To what *testimony of God* does the epistolary author refer? There are two possibilities: (1) A new testimony in addition to the three already described (Balz, Bonsirven, del Álamo, Hoskyns, Schnackenburg, Schneider). Obviously this interpretation would be popular among those who think that the three witnesses of 5:6–8 constitute human testimony, but it is a possible interpretation no matter what one thinks of the human testimony. If the three are thought to be of divine origin, how can a new witness of God be added? A parallel may be found in the list of witnesses in John 5:31–40, where God the Father's testimony is added to such divine witnesses as Jesus' own works. As for what this further divine testimony consists in, one may speculate that the author does not specify the content of the testimony (see Schnackenburg, *Johannesbriefe* 270), or that it is something from GJohn, like miracles and prophecies (Chaine), or that it is an interior testimony that makes the other three effective (Augustine [grace], Bonsirven, Bruce, de Jonge), or that it is the testimony of the faith experience which is introduced in v. 10 (Bultmann). As a proof for the newness of the divine testimony, one can note that in 5:9d God's testimony is described in the past (perf. tense), while in 5:7 the testimony of the three witnesses is in the present. (2) God's testimony is that of the three witnesses described in 5:6–8 (F.-M. Braun, de la Potterie, Dodd, Hauck, Houlden, Klöpper, Kohler, Marshall, Stott, Vrede, B. Weiss, Westcott). With remarkable liberty NEB translates the next line of this verse: "And this threefold testimony is indeed that of God himself." God may be mentioned in order to underline the true meaning of the three historical elements of 5:6, i.e., that they were means by which God testified to Jesus Christ as His Son (whence the past tense of 5:9d). If the three witnesses of vv. 7–8 are life-giving sacraments, the testimony of God is described in 5:11 in terms of His gift of life, which is in and through those sacraments. While not without difficulty, this theory is preferable to that form of the preceding interpretation which would classify the three witnesses as human testimony that the author is downplaying. But overall I think the parallelism with John 5:31–40 (where God's testimony is added) favors the form of the preceding interpretation which regards the testimony of God Himself as a fourth witness added to the three God-given witnesses of 5:7–8.

9c. *for this is God's testimony*. The initial *hoti* is causal. The formula "This is" plus a predicate noun (impersonal) was discussed in the NOTE on 1:5a, where I commented that generally the predicate, which has been introduced in the lines that precede, is explained in the lines that follow. A few scholars refer the "this" here back to vv. 7–8 (Hauck, B. Weiss, NEB). Even were the divine testimony of v. 9 the same as that of the three witnesses of vv. 7–8, however, one would be free to see "this" as pointing forward to a further explanation. Clearly the parallel expression in v. 11a ("Now this is the testimony") points forward.

9d. *that He has testified on behalf of His own Son*. The idea of testifying or testimony "on behalf of" (*peri*) occurs in the Epistles only in this verse and the next. It appears some 16 times in GJohn, but only rarely elsewhere in the NT (Acts 22:18; 23:11). The tense of the verb is perfect (and there will be three more perfect tenses in v. 10), so that God's testimony was clearly given at some time in the past, either in the ministry of Jesus (5:6) or in the conversion of the readers when they were begotten as God's children. The range of the perf. tense, however, leaves open the possibility that the testimony continues to have effect in the present (e.g., in the present testimony of 5:7–8).

The first word of this clause is *hoti*, so that 9c and 9d begin the same way. There are three possible ways of understanding how the *hoti* of 9d relates that line to 9c: (1) *hoti* epexegetical or declarative, introducing a noun clause that explains the predicate of the preceding line: "God's testimony, consisting in the fact that He has testified on behalf of His own Son" (Bisping, Brooke, Lücke, Plummer, Schnackenburg, Westcott). Such a construction is found in John 3:19. The only other epistolary instance of an epexegetical *hoti* coming *immediately* after the nominal predicate of a "This is" statement is I John 5:11 ("Now this is the testimony that . . ."), the parallel to this verse. But that very parallelism raises a problem: within three verses does the author give two different interpretations of God's testimony? (Are they really different, however, since v. 11 might be a further explanation of the way in which God has testified?) Moreover, if we concentrate on v. 9, is it not tautological to state that God's testimony is that God Himself has testified? Or can one find some newness in the fact that the testimony is now specified to be "on behalf of His own Son"? While grammatically this interpretation is the strongest, the logical difficulties have caused scholars like Keppler and Klöpper to reject it firmly. (2) *hoti* causal, introducing an adverbial clause explaining why it is God's testimony: "because He has testified on behalf of His own Son" (B. Weiss). In this interpretation we are not told in v. 9 what the testimony is, and so v. 11 does not represent a duplication when it defines the testimony. It is quite awkward to have two *hoti* causal clauses in a row (9c,9d), but the second could be resumptive: "because this is the testimony of God, because, I repeat, He has testified . . ." For another example of this, see 7b in the NOTE on 3:20b above. (3) *ho ti* relative, introducing an adjectival clause modifying "testimony": "that (which) He has testified on behalf of His own Son" (Hauck). In this interpretation once again we are not told in v. 9 what the testimony is, so that there is no conflict with v. 11. A few scholars theorize that *hoti* is an overliteral rendition of the Aramaic *dᵉ*, which should have been rendered into Greek as a relative. A more frequent grammatical justification is that the indefinite relative *hostis* (neuter *ho ti*) occasionally serves for the definite relative (BDF 293; see 7d in the NOTE on 3:20 above). The objection that a neuter relative should not have been used to modify the feminine noun *martyria*, "testimony," is only partially answered by occasional Johannine preference for the neuter and by the infrequency of certain declined forms of the indefinite relative. Over half the "This is" statements of I John are followed in the next line by a (definite) relative clause modifying the predicate (1:5a; 2:25; 3:11; 5:4,14), and at the end of the next verse (5:10cd) there is a (definite) relative clause with almost the same verbatim contents as the present clause: "the testimony that [*hēn*] God has testified on behalf of His own Son." (Clearly some scribes read the *hoti* in 9d as a relative, since they substituted for it the more correct definite relative *hēn* in imitation of 10d.) One may argue that the same writer is not likely to have modified *martyria* with a neuter indefinite relative (*ho ti*) in one verse and with a feminine definite relative (*hēn*) in the next, although the Johannine love for variety is not predictable in its range. While the grammatical basis is weak, this interpretation gives the smoothest translation.

My translation is phrased ambiguously so that it can be understood in either sense (1) or (3); for, in fact, there is not much difference of meaning between them.

9e. At the end of v. 9 an addition is attested in the Spanish tradition of the Latin text of I John (e.g., Heterius et Beatus *ad Elipandum* 26; PL 96, 909B) and in some Armenian MSS. dependent upon the Latin: "[Son] whom He sent upon earth as a Savior. And the Son gave testimony on earth fulfilling the Scriptures; and we offer testimony since we have seen him, and we proclaim to you that thus you may believe." For such Latin additions, see INTRODUCTION VI B. The composer of this addition perceived that the references to testifying that come near the end of I John form an inclusion with the theme of "we testify" in the epistolary Prologue (1:2), and he has reused some themes from that Prologue ("We have seen and testify, and we proclaim to you"), combining them with John 20:31 ("that you may believe that Jesus is the Christ, the Son of God").

10a. *The person who believes in the Son of God possesses that testimony within himself.* Literally, "the testimony," referring to the testimony of God in the preceding verse, as Codex Alexandrinus and the Vulgate have underlined by adding "of God" here. The phrase at the end of the line, *en autō*, uses a personal pronoun and would normally mean "in him," i.e., in the Son of God. Scribes and editors have correctly recognized that the context demands the meaning "in himself," i.e., in the believer. And so either they have substituted the reflexive form *en heautō* (Sinaiticus and some minuscules, followed by UBSGNT), or have accented *autō* with a rough breathing as *hautō* (Westcott-Hort margin), the contracted form of *heautō*, which is rare in the NT and the papyri (BDF 64[1]; ZBG 210). Rather one should recognize that in NT Greek reflexive pronouns are often replaced by personal pronouns, especially after prepositions, when the phrase is governed by a noun interposed between the verb and the phrase (BDF 283[2]; ZBG 211).

This is the first of 3 instances of *pisteuein eis*, "to believe in[to]" in I John (also 5:10c,13b), a construction that occurs 36 times in GJohn but only about 10 times in the rest of the NT. Scholars like Brooke, Büchsel, Chaine, de la Potterie, and Westcott regard it as an expression of full commitment to Jesus, when contrasted to *pisteuein* with the dative, which is regarded as ambiguous about commitment. (MGNTG 2, 463 would trace the two constructions to a Hebrew difference of the *hiphil* of *'mn* used with *b^e* and with *l^e*.) While there is some difference between the two uses of *pisteuein*, it is not absolute (ABJ 29, 513), as proved by the use of *pisteuein* with the dative in the very next line (5:10b), which is in parallelism with this line (Bultmann, THLJ). Attempts to see profound or subtle distinctions between kinds of belief in these two lines border upon eisegesis. (Similarly there is no difference between believing in [*eis*] the name of the Son of God in 5:13, and believing the name [dative] of His Son above in 3:23.) The difference between the believer in 5:10a and the nonbeliever in 10b is not a difference of commitment; it involves the acceptance vs. the refusal of a christological evaluation of the historical Jesus as the Son of God.

The phrase "to have/possess [*echein*] testimony," which occurs only here in the Epistles, has its sole GJohn use in 5:36: "I have testimony even greater than John's," a passage that has many parallels to these verses of I John. Three uses in Revelation (6:9; 12:17; 19:10) suggest that the idiom involves not only accepting testimony but making it a part of oneself by one's way of life. As Bultmann, Schnackenburg, and Schneider rightly recognize, such interiorized divine testimony is quite different from what B. Weiss and Wilder (?) describe as an inner witness speaking out of the depth of one's being. Generally the latter (see COMMENT) is understood as a human witness, not a divine one; and so B. Weiss is quite consistent (even if incorrect) in arguing that the testimony of v. 10 is not the divine testimony of v. 9. Klöpper, "I Joh" 397–98, advocates a compromise view whereby God's testimony strengthens the internal witness and enables the believer to bear witness.

10b. *while the person who does not believe God has made Him a liar*. As an opposite to 10a one might have expected: "the person who does not believe in the Son of God." That expectation has affected scribes; for in place of "God" Codex Alexandrinus and most Latin MSS. read "the Son," while other minor witnesses read "the Son of God" or "Jesus Christ." Plummer, *Epistles* 118, raises the possibility that in the original there may have been no object for the verb (see the second line of John 3:18); but such a proposal does not explain why the best textual witnesses would have supplied the unexpected "God." The fact that the author uses *mē* rather than *ou* as the negative with the participle suggests to some that the author is stressing the general character of nonbelief rather than the simple fact (Brooke, *Epistles* 139). However, *mē* is simply standard Johannine usage with a pres. ptcp. governed by an article (BDF 430[1]). In the phrase "believe God" *pisteuein* is followed by the dative; see the previous NOTE for the rejection of a sharp distinction between this construction and "believe in [*eis*]." The use of the perf. tense ("has made him a liar") is proleptic; the basic idea is future ("will make") but the result is so certain that it may be treated as past (ZGB 257). This is the first of three consecutive perfect tenses in three lines ("made, believe, testified"), which give a tone of enduring stance rather than of single action. Whether the divine testimony involves the Spirit of vv. 7–8 or is a new testimony centered on Christ as divine life (v. 11), that testimony is the truth; for both the Spirit and Jesus are called "truth" in Johannine theology. Therefore a denial of that testimony makes a liar of God, the source of truth, from whom both the Son and the Spirit have come forth (John 16:28; 15:26). The implicit logic of this statement is based on John 3:33: "Whoever does accept his [Jesus'] testimony has certified that God is truthful."

10c. *by refusing to believe in the testimony*. Literally, "because he has not believed [perf.]." The alternation continues: *pisteuein eis* in 10a; *pisteuein* with dative in 10b; *pisteuein eis* here. Evidently belief in the Son of God (10a) and belief in the testimony of God are much the same—a proof of the claim above that faith here is not primarily an issue of being committed to Jesus but of confessing who Jesus is. It is somewhat tautological to say that a person who does not believe has made God a liar by not believing, but this echoes almost verbatim John 3:18: "Whoever does not believe has already been condemned because he has not believed in the name of God's only Son." In each case the repetition and the use of the perf. tense gives the impression of deliberateness, whence my translation "refusing to believe." Perhaps the modal tone explains why the negative *mē* (normally used with the subjunctive) was employed in John 3:18, but here the more correct *ou* is employed.

10d. *that God has testified on behalf of His own Son.* The relative clause here is very clear, employing the feminine relative pronoun *hēn* in agreement with "testimony." We saw a (relative?) clause in v. 9d that would say the same thing. See the NOTE there for the Johannine use of "testify on behalf of [*peri*]." The tautological *"testimony* that God has *testified to"* lends emphasis with its cognate accusative, perhaps reflecting a Semitic speech pattern (BDF 153[1]).

11ab. *Now this is the testimony: that God gave us eternal life.* For the formula "Now this is," plus the (impersonal) predicate noun, see the NOTE on 1:5a above. There can be little doubt that here at last the author describes the testimony of God of which he has spoken in 9cd and 10cd, so that "this is" points forward to 11b, as I have indicated by the colon, which interprets the *hoti*, "that," as epexegetical, explaining the "testimony" of 11a (similar to a *hoti* declarative after a verb of saying [BDF 397[3]]). In what way does God's gift of eternal life constitute God's testimony (as Alexander, Belser, Brooke, Plummer, and others hold)? THLJ suggests that eternal life is the effect of the testimony; Schnackenburg and Schneider think that life makes the relevance of the testimony clear. In any case 11b ("that God gave us eternal life") is a more plausible definition of God's testimony (11a) than is 9d ("that He has testified on behalf of His Son"), which follows the reference to God's testimony in 9c. True, "eternal life" is not audible or visible; but neither the author nor his secessionist adversaries would be questioning the reality of eternal life —they would be debating only as to which side possessed it. I John began with a testimony that eternal life was revealed; it is not illogical that the reception of eternal life be seen as the final testimony.

The Greek word order in 11b (Codex Vaticanus) is worthy of attention: "eternal life [object] has given God [subject] to us." The order calls attention to "eternal life," but the fact that this life has been given "to us" is also underlined. The scribes of Codices Sinaiticus, Alexandrinus, and the Byzantine MSS. (followed by Aland) preferred to put "to us" in a more normal position, immediately after the verb; but the more difficult word order is to be preferred as original. We are not far from I John 4:10: "Not that we have loved God but that He loved us." "Eternal life" is anarthrous, as it will be in 5:13,20; see the NOTE on 1:2d for this frequent Johannine usage. The verb "gave" is aorist, a change after the sequence of perf. tenses in v. 10; but one should not press too sharply the unique force of the aorist as if the author were stressing only the punctiliar past action of the verb in the incarnation of Jesus. The testimony certainly includes the Christian appropriation of life through faith and baptism. For the tense usages of this verb and for the variety of objects given us by God, see the NOTE on 3:1a above.

11c. *and this life is in His own Son.* Although Plummer insists that this is an independent statement, there is no grammatical reason for thinking that it is not a clause governed by the *hoti* of 11b and thus part of the explanation of the testimony (Schnackenburg). Relating the eternal life to the Son gives an external or objective aspect to the divine testimony that has as its governing motif "that Jesus is the Son of God" (5:5b).

12a. *The person who possesses the Son possesses life.* The peculiar Johannine use of *echein*, "to have, possess," with a divine person as object was discussed in the NOTE on 2:23ab, which also treated the use of *echein* for possessing various divine realities (with "life" as one of the most frequently mentioned). This statement helps to show that the testimony of vv. 9–11 is an interiorized testimony coming from God, rather than an interior testimony coming from human beings.

12b. *while the person who does not possess the Son of God does not possess life.* Bultmann attributes this contrast to the pre-Johannine source. Here the antithesis is more exact than it was in 10ab: the only two changes from 12a being in the Greek word order (the object has been moved from after the verb to before it) and the addition of "of God" after "Son." The latter creates an inclusion with "the Son of God" in 5:5b; it also reminds us that, although life is in the Son (11c), ultimately it comes from God, even as does the Son.

COMMENT

I mentioned above (p. 543) that there is little agreement where the preceding unit should be terminated, with many ending it in 4:21 and starting the new unit in 5:1. But even those who push beyond 4:21 into ch. 5 do not agree whether the break between the last unit and the present unit should be placed between 5:4a and 5:4b (Alexander, Bonsirven), or between 5:4c and 5:5 (de Jonge, THLJ), or between 5:5b and 5:6 (Dodd, Hort, Stott, Wilder, Williams). Since I regard the main theme of the preceding unit to be love and commandments, while that of the present unit is faith and christology, I think it wiser to follow the first of the three views; for faith begins to be mentioned prominently in 5:4c, while the theme of love and commandment is last mentioned in the sentence contained in 5:3–4a. Indeed, if we begin the unit with 5:4b, 50% of the I John vocabulary of faith/belief occurs in this unit.[1] The two preceding units, 4:1–6 dealing with belief and confession, and 4:7–5:4a dealing with love and ending with commandment, were governed by the twofold commandment in 3:23 to believe in Jesus Christ and to love. The author is now returning to the motif of belief.[2]

[1] It contains 4 of 9 uses of *pisteuein*, "to believe," and the only Johannine use of the noun *pistis*, "belief, faith."

[2] Hauck and Schneider claim that this last unit of the body of I John is a harmony of all the main themes of the writing; but, unless one includes 5:1–5, there is no mention of love.

There is also a dispute about the precise ending of this unit, whether it should be 5:12, 5:13, or 5:17. I shall discuss that in more detail in the COMMENT which begins the next unit, but I regard the shift to the first person singular in 5:13 as an indication that another unit (the Conclusion) begins there.

If the most likely extent of the present unit is 5:4b–12, it breaks neatly into two subdivisions of equal length (twelve and thirteen lines in my translation), namely 5:4b–8 and 5:9–12. The first subdivision picks up the linking theme of conquest from the last line of the preceding unit (5:4a "All that is begotten by God conquers the world") as a transition to a faith that is "the conquering power that has conquered the world." Faith for I John involves content as well as commitment; and so the author now spells out the christological content in terms of a threefold imagery for Jesus' life and death—an imagery of water, blood, and Spirit taken from GJohn—for it is in his life and death that he was the Son of God. These three factors constitute an ongoing testimony against the world (the secessionists). The second subdivision (5:9–12) has a peculiar internal structure. Twice do we hear "This is God's testimony [namely] that . . ." (5:9cd, 11ab), and twice do we have a positive/negative antithesis describing the person who does and does not (5:10ab, 12ab). This internal structure makes it clear that the author has moved on from the threefold symbolic testimony of the first subdivision to the testimony of God Himself, and it is this testimony that divides the believer from the nonbeliever. This testimony has the power to give life—the same eternal life that belonged to Jesus as God's Son. The gift of life is another way of saying that we are begotten by God, so that the end of this unit in 5:12 has a theme similar to the end of the preceding unit in 5:4a.[8] In the present unit the reasoning is allusive; and, as we move from one line to another, the themes interlock like a chain. In the end it becomes clear, however, that the organization is not haphazard.

This is the last unit in the body of I John (the next unit is the Conclusion); and it has been influenced by two factors: by the last chapter of the body of GJohn (ch. 20),[4] and by inclusion with the Prologue of I John. The theme of testifying found in the Prologue (1:2) returns here to a prominent position.[5] The testimony in the Prologue concerned "life" (zōē), which occurred there 3 times; the theme of "life" occurs in the

[8] Keppler, "Geist" 4–5, argues that the opening lines of this unit are not particularly close to what has gone before because they do not tell us how faith is strong enough to conquer the world. By the end of the unit, however, we see that faith leads God to make us His children and that those who receive His life are the ones who conquer the world.

[4] Chapter 21 does not belong to the original GJohn but is the work of a redactor (ABJ 29A, 1077–82).

[5] This unit of I John contains 4 of its 6 uses of martyrein, "to testify," and all 6 uses of the noun martyria.

present unit 4 times, also in relation to testimony. The parallelism with the original final chapter of GJohn centers on John 20:31: "I have written these things to you so that you may believe that Jesus is the Christ, the Son of God, and that believing you may possess life in his name." That line is the original Conclusion of GJohn, and so it is not surprising to find part of it ("I have written these things to you so that") echoed in the next unit or Conclusion of I John (5:13). But the rest of John 20:31 is echoed in the present unit which begins by stressing belief in Jesus as the Son of God (5:5b) and ends on the theme of possessing eternal life which is given to us in God's Son (5:11–12).

A. *Testimony to Jesus Christ, Son of God, by Water, Blood, and Spirit* (5:4b–8)

The previous unit ended with a ringing victory cry: "All that is begotten by God conquers the world," although the author did not make clear how that present and ongoing victory is to be related to the past conquest of the world by Jesus at the end of his ministry (John 16:33), or to the past conquest of the Evil One by Christians at the time of conversion (I John 2:13–14). The present unit will contribute to a solution by stressing that our faith is the agency of conquest—a faith in what Jesus did in his ministry and death, and a faith that remains firm despite the present struggle caused by the secessionists who "belong to the world" (4:5), a world that is still being conquered.

Although the description of faith as "the conquering power that has conquered the world" (5:4bc)[6] and the believer as "the one who conquers the world" (5:5ab) is peculiarly Johannine, the basic ideas have solid biblical foundation. On pp. 279, 497 I pointed to passages which insisted that Israel's victories over enemies were not won purely by human agency but by God's help (also Ps 98:1–3; II Sam 23:10). In a dualistic context the same theme is echoed in the Dead Sea Scrolls (1QM 3:5,9): "The mighty deeds of God shall crush the enemy. . . . God has struck all the sons of darkness." If I John attributes the victory to "this faith of ours," it is because through faith we are children of God and share in His life (John 1:12–13). In choosing faith as the link to divine power, the Johannine writer joins other NT thought. In Matt 17:20 and Luke 17:6 Jesus says that faith as small as a mustard seed can move mountains and transplant trees. In Gal 5:6 Paul states that the only thing of avail is faith working through love.

---

[6] There is a rhetorical character in the statement in 5:4bc, perhaps because the author is imitating secular victory proclamations in war. Certainly Rev 19:11–16 describes Jesus in the panoply of an imperial conqueror.

What is different in the Johannine presentation of this victory is that here faith is not simply trust in God's power but a specific christological understanding of Jesus as God's Son. Only such a faith gives eternal life and makes us God's children with a share in Jesus' victory. The conqueror of the world is not simply the person who believes—the secessionists do that, in a sense—but "the person who believes that *Jesus* is the Son of God" (5:5b).

The language the author uses in 5:6–8 to describe his particular christology is an excellent example of the strengths and weaknesses of I John. The burning conviction of the author, the oratorical power of his short phrases, the vividness of the imagery of water, blood, and Spirit, and the probative force of three witnesses: These illustrate the flare and genius of the writer. The weakness, from our point of view at least, is the utter obscurity of what he is talking about. (I say "from our point of view" because one can hope that his readers who shared his linguistic world understood much better.) For a change the main problem is not the imprecise grammar that mars much of I John, but the imagery for which we have no certain key. If one counts the discussions of the Johannine Comma (Appendix IV), more ink has been applied to paper in discussing these verses than in discussing any other comparable section of I John. I have devoted long NOTES to the various theories with their pros and cons. Here I shall settle for one theory that makes the most sense to me and explain the passage accordingly.[7]

What the author has said thus far about Jesus was largely in reaction to secessionist propaganda on the subject, and that appears to be true here as well. The secessionists seem to have been employing a formula stating that the Christ, the Son of God, "came in water." Since I find in I John no convincing evidence that they were docetists in the classic sense, I do not think that such a formula refers to the composition of Jesus' body (not a real body of flesh and blood), or even to a temporary divine presence descending on Jesus at his baptism but leaving before his death (Cerinthus; see Appendix II). Rather the secessionists associated salvation with the incarnation of the divine Son, which they related in some way to the revelation of Jesus as the preexistent by John the Baptist.[8] The latter testified that this revelation was the reason for his baptizing *with water* (John 1:31), and spoke of the revelation in terms of the Spirit descending and

[7] Those who disagree have ample material in the NOTES for interpreting the passage in the light of another theory.

[8] In the INTRODUCTION (V B2b) I pointed out that all the incarnational verses of the GJohn Prologue are connected to John the Baptist (1:6–9, 14–15) and the Prologue itself is followed by the story of John baptizing with water. The secessionists need not have thought that the incarnation occurred at the baptism (although that is a possible interpretation of their thought) but that the baptism was the moment of its revelation.

resting on Jesus (1:32).[9] Thus, in the context of the Baptist's ministry, it is said of the Johannine Jesus: "The one whom God has sent speaks the words of God; truly boundless is His gift of the Spirit" (3:34).[10] Since immediately after the Baptist's testimony about the Spirit, Andrew can confess Jesus as the Christ (1:41) and Nathanael can confess him as "the Son of God" (1:48), the secessionist interpretation of Johannine tradition may have claimed that Jesus was the Christ, the Son of God, through his coming in water, as revealed by the Spirit.

While not necessarily denying a revelation through the Spirit to the Baptist, the author has a larger view of the salvific life-giving role of Jesus, signified by the designation "the Christ, the Son of God."[11] The Spirit came upon Jesus at the baptism; but for the disciples, "There was as yet no Spirit, since Jesus had not been glorified [in death]" (John 7:39). And so to refute the secessionists the author resorts to a crucifixion scene (19:34–35) that in the present form of GJohn[12] is underlined as having been the subject of testimony by the Beloved Disciple. The scene is that of the flow of blood and water from the side of the dead Jesus, a scene that provoked amazement because of the water, which was interpreted as a literal fulfillment of Jesus' promise about himself, "From within him shall flow rivers of living water" (7:38), with the Spirit symbolized by the living water (7:39). The flow of blood, while in itself not startling,[13] had a sign value as well; for it showed that Jesus died according to the law for the sacrificial victim where the blood could not be congealed but had to flow forth at the moment of death so that it could be sprinkled (ABJ 29A, 951). The epistolary author seizes upon these events which in

[9] Did the secessionists think that the Spirit was the preexistent divine principle? If one did not have the Prologue, one might interpret GJohn that way. However, if I am right in positing that the GJohn Prologue was a Community hymn (ABJ 29, 18–23), it would have been known to the secessionists. Later docetist or gnostic thought identified "the Christ" that came down upon Jesus with the Holy Spirit in the form of a dove at the Jordan (Epiphanius, *Panarion* 30.3 and 34.10; PG 41, 409B, 601C).

[10] In ABJ 29, 158–62, I pointed out that literally the speaker says, "Indeed not by measure does he give the Spirit." The "he" is ambiguous; and if the secessionists knew this tradition, they probably interpreted it in terms of God's giving the Spirit to Jesus.

[11] In Johannine theology such titles signify the life-giver as we see from John 20:31: "So that you may believe that Jesus is the Christ, the Son of God, and that believing you may possess life in his name."

[12] One cannot be sure whether John 19:35 was added to GJohn before or after I John was written (INTRODUCTION V D2b). But even if it was added after I John, it reflects the same tradition to which I John refers and is a response to the same issue.

[13] The order in GJohn is climactic: "blood and water." That Jesus had died was not an issue in the debate with "the Jews," and so the shedding of blood did not need special attesting. It is true that blood is not pumped forth from a corpse, but Jesus' body was hanged in a vertical position where a wound could drain the blood from part of it. The author of I John changes the order to "water and blood" because he has to emphasize the death of Jesus against the secessionists.

Johannine thought were true history with symbolic meaning.[14] He correctly insists that the symbolism of this scene shows that the death of Jesus was life-giving, so that, if one wishes to use the language of the secessionists,[15] one should not say, "Jesus is the Christ, the Son of God, who came by/in water," but "who came by/in water and blood." The true salvific coming in water was not John's baptizing with water, but water flowing from the side of Jesus. For the Christian the life-giving moment of the Spirit was not simply the descent of the Spirit upon Jesus in the form of a dove, but the Spirit flowing from within Jesus after his death. And the flowing blood, the sign of the sacrificial victim, showed that Jesus' death was an atoning sacrifice for sin, as the author has already affirmed in I John 1:7; 2:2. Indeed, the author would probably contend that if the secessionists had correctly understood the scene involving John the Baptist beyond the Jordan, they should have realized all this. By baptizing with water and by his vision of the descent of the Spirit, John the Baptist proclaimed Jesus as the preexistent who was to come, but he also identified Jesus as the Lamb of God who was to take away the world's sin and thus foreshadowed the death of Jesus as a sacrifice (ABJ 29, 61–63).

Even if the secessionists might disagree with the author's interpretation of these scenes, especially John 19:34, he has an answer to all objections. The Spirit that was handed over to the Beloved Disciple by the dying Jesus (19:30) could testify to the meaning of the blood and water (and thus to the salvific import of Jesus' death) through the Beloved Disciple. The latter's testimony had to be true (19:35) because the Spirit is the Spirit of Jesus who is the truth (14:6) and is thus the Spirit of Truth (14:17; 15:26; 16:13) who can know what the death of Jesus really meant. This testimony of the Spirit given through the Beloved Disciple has been preserved and continued in the tradition of the Johannine Community, so that the Spirit is still testifying.[16] In other words, at the end of I John the author is going back to the principle enunciated in the epistolary Prologue by joining himself to the Johannine School of tradition stemming from the Beloved Disciple: "What we have seen with our

[14] Holtzmann, "Problem" 710–11, accuses the author of I John of wrongly historicizing John 19:34; but one may ask if it is not Holtzmann who is wrong. The Johannine notion of a sign involves a symbolic interpretation of what is thought to have happened. GJohn implicitly criticizes interpreters of Jesus' deeds who stop at the level of what happened and fail to see the symbolic import of the deeds, but it would be foreign to Johannine method simply to have invented the flow of blood and water in John 19:34.

[15] It is not clear that the secessionists coined the language, and the author may have had to answer them in this language because it was traditional and could therefore be convincing.

[16] I John 5:6d uses the pres. tense, but it is important for the logic of the whole verse (where "came by water and blood" is aorist) that the pres. tense continues a past testimony given at the cross.

own eyes, what we looked at" (I John 1:1).[17] The author is trusting that the Spirit with whom all the members of the Community have been anointed (2:20,27) will enable them to recognize this testimony as true.[18] As he states in 4:2: "Everyone who confesses Jesus Christ come in the flesh reflects the Spirit which belongs to God" (also 3:24cd).

The above explanation accounts for the author's enigmatic statement in 5:6 that Jesus Christ "came" (past) by/in water and blood, while the Spirit "testifies" (pres.) to this. However, in 5:7–8 he says that all three "testify" (pres.) and that they are "of one accord" or testify to the same thing. In his emphasis on the unity to which the three tend (literally, "into one"), he is undoubtedly recalling the debates with "the Jews" described in GJohn. Deuteronomy 19:15 states, "Only on the evidence of two witnesses or three witnesses shall a charge be sustained"; and the Johannine Jesus, who was charged with blasphemous arrogance because of his "I AM" statements, invoked the Deuteronomy principle in proving his case (John 8:17). Consequently, on several occasions he listed witnesses, e.g., he and his Father are two witnesses (8:18), while John the Baptist, the miracles, the Father, and the Scriptures form a series of witnesses (5:31–40). This technique, which has been employed in the past debates of the Johannine Community with the synagogue over the divinity of Jesus,[19] is now invoked in the debate between the author and the secessionists over the humanity of Jesus. The secessionists wrongly think that they have the testimony of John the Baptist for the all-sufficiency of the incarnation; the author has a contrary set of three witnesses (the legal number) for the salvific importance of the death.

How does the author conceive the Spirit, the water, and the blood as three *ongoing* witnesses? If it were just the Spirit, the explanation offered above for 5:6 might be sufficient; but the introduction of the water and the blood as witnesses creates a problem. Various theories have been discussed in the NOTES. It is possible that the author is giving a purely symbolic description of the continuing power of Jesus who conquered the world through his glorious death (John 16:33)—a power to vivify through the Spirit (6:63), to cleanse as if by water (13:10), and to atone

[17] I have insisted that this need not mean that the author was himself an eyewitness, but only that he considered himself as part of the Johannine School, who were heirs to the tradition of the Beloved Disciple (INTRODUCTION V C2c).

[18] Bultmann, *Epistles* 80, says that the Spirit gives its testimony in the faith, knowledge, and confession of the congregation itself. This is true once it is recognized that the continuation of the testimony of the Beloved Disciple by the "we" of the Johannine School has a mediating role. In a chapter where Irenaeus (*Adv. haer.* 3.24.1) is stressing a continuation in the church of testimony from the prophets, apostles, and disciples, he seems to cite I John 5:6e: "Where the church is, there is the Spirit of God . . . the Spirit is truth."

[19] While GJohn reflects struggles with authorities that took place in Jesus' lifetime, it has been reshaped by debates that took place in Johannine Community history in the 70s and 80s. See ABJ 29, 223,227–28,341.

by his blood (I John 1:7; 2:2). But the thrust of 5:7–8 seems to imply a more objective or visible set of witnesses, and so most scholars think that the author has now shifted to sacramental actions[20] well-known to the Community. For instance, "the Spirit" may symbolize the anointing spoken of in I John 2:20,27; "the water" may symbolize baptism, which involves the divine begetting of the Christian as God's child (John 3:5); and "the blood" may symbolize the eucharist as food and drink to nourish the God-given life of the Christian (6:51–58).[21] Or else the Spirit in 5:7–8 may have the same meaning as in 5:6 where it was already described as testifying; only now it would be pictured as working through baptism and the eucharist.[22] In either case, the logic of the argument is that all Johannine Christians recognize the life-giving powers of the Spirit, of baptism, and of the eucharist; and they should reflect that all three were already symbolized in the outpouring of the Spirit, water, and blood on the cross (19:30–35). Thus the sacraments testify to the salvific character of the death of Jesus;[23] and by constituting people as children of God and feeding them with heavenly food and drink, the sacraments are ways in which true believers share in the action by which Christ conquered the world (16:33).

B. *Testimony to the Son of God by God Himself* (5:9–12)

After discussing the testimony of the three witnesses, the author turns to the testimony of God Himself. Here he is following the pattern of an ascending set of witnesses found in John 5:31–40.[24] There the first witness to Jesus was John the Baptist; but although the Baptist testified to the truth, Jesus said, "I myself do not accept such human testimony," and went on to list "greater" witnesses. So also here the secessionists have called upon the testimony of John the Baptist by presenting his baptism with water as the all-sufficient moment revealing the coming of the preexistent into the world. The author, however, argues that if his readers are influenced by such "human testimony," God's testimony is "greater." Among the "greater" witnesses of John 5:36–40 were Jesus' works given

[20] The term "sacrament" would not yet have been in use, but Johannine thought presents physical actions as the vehicle of divine action.

[21] A serious difficulty in this explanation is that logically the author should have used "anointing/unction" as a symbol for the Spirit, not vice versa.

[22] The Spirit is mentioned in the context of both baptismal and eucharistic passages in GJohn (3:5–8; 6:63). An objection to this explanation is that the author seems to put all three witnesses on the same plane.

[23] While the sacraments help to refute secessionist christology, the author's statements may or may not also be meant to refute the sacramental theory of the secessionists. I speculate upon this at the end of the NOTE on 5:8a.

[24] See also John 10:38, and the ascending relationship of the basis of faith in 4:42.

him by the Father, the Scriptures inspired by God, and the testimony of the Father Himself—in other words, all the greater witnesses were divine witnesses, but there was a special place for God Himself. So also here, while the three witnesses of 5:7–8 are of divine origin and God has testified through them, there is a special and more direct testimony by God Himself. After all, the issue from the beginning of the unit has been that of *Jesus* as the Son of God, and who should know more about the Son than the Father? It is no accident that vv. 9,10,11 all end on the note of "His own Son"; for while the other witnesses can attest to the salvific character of the death of Jesus, they cannot directly prove that Jesus was God's Son.

What is the additional testimony of God to His Son? Because I John 5:10 speaks of the believer possessing that testimony within himself, not infrequently scholars speak of an inner witness that would enable Christians to recognize the value of the three (exterior) witnesses.[25] They base themselves on GJohn passages positing a divinely given predisposition to accept Jesus, e.g., "No one can come to me unless the Father who sent me draws him" (6:44); "He calls by name those that belong to him and leads them out . . . and the sheep follow him because they recognize his voice" (10:3–4). But it is not clear that such a predisposition would be called a testimony or witness in the Johannine tradition.[26] The theory of inner witness becomes even more complicated when that witness is identified with the Spirit dwelling in Christians (14:16). It is true that the anointing (probably with the Spirit) in I John 2:20,27 enables Christians to recognize the truth, but the *witnessing* function of the Spirit is external, directed against the world and vocalized through the Christians in whom the Spirit dwells (15:26–27; 16:8–10). Moreover, the probable interpretation of I John 5:9–12 is that the testimony of God is different from and in addition to that of the three witnesses in 5:6–8, one of which is the Spirit.[27]

A better key to the nature of God's testimony is found in the two passages in 5:9–12 that begin: "This is God's testimony," namely 5:9d, "that He has testified on behalf of His own Son," and 11bc, "that God gave us eternal life and this life is in His own Son." The first of these makes it clear that the Father is involved (not the Spirit) and that more likely the testimony comes from the outside. The second defines the witness as eter-

[25] The idea may be influenced by Reformation theology of the Spirit within the Christian helping to interpret the Scriptures.

[26] Some cite John 5:37–38: "The Father who sent me has Himself given testimony on my behalf . . . but His word you do not have abiding in your hearts because you do not believe the one He sent." Yet it is unlikely that the *predisposition* to believe in Jesus is involved in that passage; and the parallel in 8:18 makes it clear that the testimony of God is contemporaneous with Jesus—indeed, is in and through Jesus.

[27] Schnackenburg, *Johannesbriefe* 267–71, gives an effective refutation of the theory of Klöpper, Häring, and Preiss that God's testimony is the Spirit.

nal life which is in God's own Son.[28] Here the author supposes a knowledge of the chain of life-giving that is a strong theme in GJohn. Jesus as the divine Son has life from the Father: "Just as the Father possesses life in Himself, so has He granted that the Son also possess life in himself" (5:26); "I have life because of the Father" (6:57); "That which came to be in him [the Word] was life" (1:4). Those who believe in Jesus receive life from him and possess it in him (3:36; 5:24; 20:31).[29] Thus, the eternal life of the Christians, which they had to get from Jesus who in turn as a Son had to get it from the Father, constitutes a proof that Jesus is God's Son. I John began with the "we" of the Johannine School giving testimony to the life that was revealed in Jesus; it draws to a close with God giving a testimony involving the life that is in Jesus (5:11).

It is standard Johannine theology that God's gift (whether called light, life, or love, all three of which are embodied in Jesus) provokes a dualistic division between those who accept and those who refuse (John 3:16–21 for light; I John 4:7–8 for love). In I John 5 the dualistic reaction to life is described in paired sets of antitheses:

10a: The person who believes in the Son of God possesses [God's] testimony within himself;

10b: the person who does not believe God has made Him a liar.

12a: The person who possesses the Son possesses life;

12b: the person who does not possess the Son of God does not possess life.

A comparison of the positive lines (10a, 12a) shows that believing in the Son is tantamount to possessing (having) the Son. Similarly possessing God's testimony within oneself is the same as possessing life—a parallelism confirming that 11ab is a definition: "Now this is [God's] testimony: that God gave us eternal life." A good parallel to the first of the two positive lines (10a) is John 3:16: "Whoever believes in him [the Son] . . . possesses eternal life."[30] As for the negative lines in the above antitheses, 10b is typically Johannine in leaving no room for ignorance or misconception. Just as the alternative to love is not indifference but

[28] In the NOTE on 5:11ab I mentioned that many refuse to see a definition here because they do not think that eternal life is visible enough to serve as a witness. While not visible, it is discernible; for the author's readers know that they possess it, and so he can appeal to it.

[29] This theme is continued in Ignatius, who calls Jesus Christ "our inseparable life" (*Eph.* 3:2), "our true [*alēthinos*] life" (*Smyrn.* 4:1).

[30] Reaction to Jesus has the same effect for the Christian that reaction to God has for the Jew. Philo, *On the Special Laws* 1.63 ≠345, says, "The Law tells us that 'all who cleave to God live'"; and in *On Flight* 15 ≠78 he asks, "Is not eternal life to take refuge with God, and death to flee away from Him?"

hatred (I John 2:10–11), and the alternative to light is not obscurity but darkness (1:5), so the alternative to truth is the lie. One is either on the side of God and His Son, or on the side of the devil and the Antichrist who are liars (John 8:44; I John 2:22). Early in I John (1:10) the author made a statement that is a good parallel to 10b: "If we boast, 'We have not sinned,' we make Him a liar." A wrong ethical stance and a wrong christological stance have the same effect because both impugn what God did in sending His Son.

It is sad to realize that the other negative line (12b) brings to an end the body of I John.[31] The body of GJohn ended on a more positive note. Although GJohn described the rejection of God's emissary by "his own" (John 1:11), the ultimate goal of that work was optimistic: ". . . that you may believe that Jesus is the Christ, the Son of God, and that believing you may possess life in his name" (20:31). But a decade has passed and the Johannine Community that received the gospel has not lived up to the evangelist's hope. It has divided and the majority has gone out into the world; and so the epistolary author ends his main message with a negative warning, paradoxically echoing the GJohn promise. The last line before the Conclusion of I John is a condemnation of former confreres who no longer possess (i.e., correctly believe in) the Son of God and, not believing, do not possess life in his name.

BIBLIOGRAPHY PERTINENT TO I JOHN 5:4b–12

Barth, M., *Die Taufe—ein Sakrament?* (Zollikon/Zurich: Evangelischer Verlag, 1951), esp. 395–407 on 5:6–8.

Braun, F.-M., "L'eau et l'Esprit," RevThom 49 (1949) 5–30, esp. 20–22 on 5:6.

Brooks, O. S., "The Johannine Eucharist. Another Interpretation," JBL 82 (1963) 293–300, on 5:6–8.

del Álamo, M., "Los 'Tres Testificantes' de la primera Epístola de San Juan, V. 7," *Cultura Bíblica* 4 (1947) 11–14.

de la Potterie, I., "La notion de témoignage dans Saint Jean," SP 2 (Paris: Gabalda, 1959) 193–208, esp. 202–8.

Denney, J., "He that Came by Water and Blood," *The Expositor,* seventh series, 5 (1908) 416–28.

Greiff, A., "Die drei Zeugen in 1 Joh 5,7f.," TQ 114 (1933) 465–80.

Jaubert, A., "O Espírito, e Agua e o Sangue (1 Jo 5,7–8)," in *Actualidades Bíblicas,* ed. S. Voigt and F. Vier (Festschrift J. J. Pedreira de Castro; Petrópolis, Brazil: Vozes, 1971) 616–20.

---

[31] Williams, *Epistles* 58, "Verse 12 is the real *finale* of the letter."

Keppler, P. W., "Geist, Wasser und Blut. Zur Erklärung von I. Joh. 5,6–13 (ev. Joh. 19,34)," TQ 68 (1886) 3–25.

Klöpper, A., "1 Joh. 5, 6–12," ZWT 43 (1900) 378–400.

Manson, T. W., "Entry into Membership of the Early Church," JTS 48 (1947) 25–32 on 5:6–8.

Miguens, M., "Tres testigos: Espiritu, agua, sangre," SBFLA 22 (1972) 74–94.

Nauck, W., Die Tradition, 147–82, excursus "Geist" on 5:6–8.

Richter, G., "Blut und Wasser aus der durchbohrten Seite Jesu (Joh 19,34b)," MTZ 21 (1970) 1–21. Reprinted in Studien zum Johannesevangelium, ed. J. Hainz (BU 13; Regensburg: Pustet, 1977) 120–42, esp. 122–34 on 5:6.

Winterbotham, R., "The Spirit and the Water and the Blood," The Expositor, eighth series, 2 (1911) 62–71.

The Conclusion
(I John 5:13–21)

The author states the purpose for his writing I John through reflections related to GJohn's statement of purpose: "I have written these things to you so that you may believe that Jesus is the Christ, the Son of God, and that believing you may possess life in his name" (John 20:31).

11. I John 5:13–21: *The Conclusion*

13 I have written this to you *b* so that you may know that you possess this eternal life—*c* you who believe in the name of the Son of God. 14 Now this is the confidence which we possess in the presence of God, *b* namely, that whenever we ask anything according to His will, He hears us. 15 And since we know that He hears us whenever we ask, *b* we know that what we have asked Him for is ours. 16 If anyone sees his brother sinning (so long as the sin is not deadly), *b* he should ask; and thus life will be given to the sinner. This is only for those whose sin is not deadly. *c* After all, there is such a thing as deadly sin, *d* and I do not say that one should pray about that. 17 All wrongdoing is sin, but not all sin is deadly.

18a	18 We know that no one who has been begotten by God commits
18b	rather, the one begotten by God is protected,　　　　⌊ sin;
18c	and so the Evil One cannot touch him.
19a	19 We know that it is to God we belong,
19b	while the whole world lies in the grasp of the Evil One.
20a	20 We know, finally, that the Son of God has come
20b	and has given us insight to know the One who is true.
20c	And we are in the One who is true,
20d	for we are in His Son, Jesus Christ.
20e	He is the true God and eternal life.

21 LITTLE CHILDREN, guard yourselves against idols.

NOTES

5:13a. *I have written this to you.* This aorist is clearly epistolary as it was previously in 2:21a,26a, and probably in 2:14 (pp. 296–97). The return to the first person singular for the first time since 2:26 is noteworthy, although it is almost stereotyped in these Epistles with the verb "to write" (17 times), the sole exception being I John 1:4a, "We are writing this." What is the reference here for "this," literally "these things"? Many scholars (Alexander, Brooke, Klöpper, Schnackenburg, Schneider) refer it to 5:1–12 or to the last verse of that unit. Their chief argument is that 5:5 spoke about "the person who believes that Jesus is the Son of God," and 5:12 states, "The person who possesses the Son possesses life." Those verses could explain why the author would now say, "I have written these things to you so that you may know that you possess this eternal life—you who believe in the name of the Son of God." Such an interpretation makes 5:13 a transition to what follows. However, others (Bultmann, Chaine, Haas, THLJ, Westcott) think that in 5:13 the author is referring back to the whole of I John. The parallel with the Conclusion of GJohn supports this; for there "I have written these things to you so that you may believe" (20:31) refers back to the whole Gospel. Also I John 5:13 constitutes an inclusion with the "We are writing this" of the epistolary Prologue (1:4) which looks ahead to all that follows. One wonders could the author in 5:13 consciously have confined himself to just the preceding verses.

13b. *so that you may know that you possess this eternal life.* In the Greek word order the adjective "eternal" comes at the end separated by the verb from the noun it modifies. (This is so awkward that Codex Sinaiticus and scribes of the Byzantine tradition shift it before the verb to a position adjacent to the noun.) The emphatic position means that the author is referring to the "eternal life" mentioned in the preceding verse as object of the same verb "to have, possess" (see NOTE on 2:23ab). Two parallel Johannine statements about writing (p. 594 above), namely, John 20:31 and I John 1:4, are followed by a *hina* purpose clause just as here. The verb "to know" (*eidenai, oida*) will occur 6 times in this Conclusion as a way of expressing confidence.

13c. *you who believe in the name of the Son of God.* Codices Vaticanus and Sinaiticus* have a dative ptcp. ("those believing") which is in apposition to the "to you" of the initial clause. As scribal improvements, Alexandrinus reads a nominative ptcp., while the Byzantine tradition shifts the word order and adds a clause: "I have written this to you who believe in the name of the Son of God so that you may know that you possess this eternal life and may believe in the name of the Son of God." However, a pres. ptcp. in apposition to and defining the somewhat distant pronoun of an earlier clause is not unusual in the Johannine writings (5:16 below; John 1:12–13). For "the name" see the NOTE on 2:12b above; and for the idea of believing in the name of God's Son, see the NOTE on 3:23b.

14a. *Now this is the confidence.* We encounter the third instance within six verses (5:9–14) of a "This is . . ." construction (NOTE on 1:5a) followed by a *hoti*, "that," clause; and here it is certain that the clause is epexegetical of the noun. Curiously, Bultmann, "Redaktion" 192, argues that this proves the hand of the Redactor, for he thinks (wrongly) that for the author the "this" always points to what precedes. See the NOTE on 2:28b for *parrēsia*, "confidence"; we saw there that confidence before God is connected both to judgment and to prayer. The passage in 3:21–22 illustrates the twofold thrust and offers a parallel for the present passage: "Beloved, if the heart knows nothing prejudicial, we can have confidence in the presence of God and can receive from Him whatever we ask."

which we possess in the presence of God. This repeats the language of the passage just quoted. *Echein,* "to have, possess," governs "life" twice in 5:12 and once in 5:13—the possession of confidence here flows from the possession of life, i.e., from being God's children who speak to their Father. "In the presence of God" is literally "toward [*pros*] him"; see the NOTE on 1:2e for the preposition. Although the last person mentioned was the Son of God, there is little doubt that the "him" is God, as "in the presence of the Father/God" in 1:2; 2:1; 3:21. The "His will" in the next clause points in the same direction.

14b. *namely, that whenever we ask anything according to His will.* Some (Bonsirven) would understand this conditional clause with *ean,* "if," and the subjunctive to be more hypothetical than *ean* with the indicative ("if we know") in 5:15a. More likely, however, the *ean* is expectative ("whenever"), leaving no doubt that the request will be made. The "we" combines the "I" and the "you" of the preceding verse. The frequent Johannine theme of asking (and receiving) is expressed in 5:14–16 thrice with the verb *aitein* (and once with *erōtan,* "pray"; NOTE on 5:16d below). In classical Greek the middle voice of *aitein* (used here) would differ from the active in that it would imply asking for oneself. (Westcott, *Epistles* 190, and ZBG 234 are inclined to see that shade of meaning here; contrast MGNTG 1, 160 and 3, 54–55.) However, the active in John 16:24 and the middle in 16:26 have no perceptible difference of meaning, and BAG (BAGD) 25 points out the loss of the classical distinction in the Greek of the NT period. Bultmann, "Redaktion" 192, sees the cautious condition placed upon the asking ("according to His will") as a reflection of the theology of the Ecclesiastical Redactor. However, as B. Weiss, *Briefe* 149–50, points out, even in GJohn it is assumed that believers shall do God's will in all things, including prayer. In GJohn passages about "asking" God, frequently there is a condition. For example, in 14:14–16; 15:16; and 16:23–26 the asking is to be done in the name of Jesus, which implies true faith; in 15:7 the petitioners must remain in Jesus and have Jesus' words remain in them; in I John 3:21–22 the basis for receiving whatever we ask is "because we are keeping His commandments and doing what is pleasing in His sight." Thus the "according to His will" in 5:14b is nothing novel. It may even be a Johannine echo of the Synoptic account of Jesus' own prayer: "Not what I will, but what You will" (Mark 14:36 and par.). Bonsirven, *Epîtres* 238–39, thinks that here God's will means His commandments specifying a life-style, and that the author is forbidding purely selfish prayers (James 4:3). More specifically, God's will is described in the verses that follow in terms of not praying about the deadly sin of the secessionists but only for one's Johannine brother.

He hears us. Westcott, *Epistles* 190, claims that this sense of "hear" is peculiar to John in the NT. In John 11:41–42 Jesus expresses assurance that the Father had heard him and always hears him, and in 9:31 it is affirmed that God "hears someone who is devout and obeys His will."

15a. *And since we know that He hears us.* Notice the chiastic arrangement in 14b and 15a ("ask . . . hear . . . hear . . . ask"), a touch of style in this laborious and prosaic section. This is a condition with *ean*, "if," and the indicative, which differs little from *ean* with the subjunctive in 14b (although MGNTG 3, 116, would regard it as somewhat more actual and less hypothetical). It is a general statement with no contingency involved. *Ean* can stand for *epei*, "since" (a usage deemed a vulgarism by BDF 372[1a]). The real reason for the indicative *oidamen*, "we know," in this protasis may be its occurrence in the apodosis (15b) and the author's desire to show the connection between the two.

whenever we ask. Literally, "about whatever we ask." The verb "to hear" takes two objects: the person heard ("us") and the object about which the person is heard. For "whatever" the author uses *ho ean* (short form of *ho ti* [e]an: BDF 107, 293) plus the subjunctive, as he returns to the *ean* construction of 14b. The phrase "according to His will" is not repeated from 14b but is certainly understood.

15b. *we know that what we have asked Him for is ours.* Literally, "we know that we possess the asked-for-things that we asked for from Him." The form of "we know" (*oidamen*) is repeated from earlier in the verse; and the use of the pres. tense, "we possess," rather than the future, increases the tone of certainty. (Notice how the theme of "possessing" [*echein*] is continued from vv. 12,13,14.) Bultmann, *Epistles* 86, states that the "we" here is not the Community as elsewhere, "but those who pray from time to time." This unproved assertion runs against the whole purpose of these verses to build up confidence among Community members that they possess life. Verse 15b seems to add little to 15a; and Bultmann, "Redaktion" 193, sees this tautology as a sign of the Redactor. However, the overall style of I John is quite repetitious, and in the preceding unit there is a similar tautology in the relation between 5:9c and 9d. What increases the tautology in 15b is the use of the cognate accusative (*aitēma*, "something asked for"—only Johannine usage) governed by the verb "ask for." (We saw a similar construction in 5:10cd, "the testimony God has testified.") Indeed, the threefold use of *aitein, aitēma, aitein* constitutes a type of paronomasia; see NOTES on 3:24b; 4:7a. Perhaps the author is saved from pure tautology by the prepositional phrase "from Him," whether that is governed by "we asked for" or by "we possess." (Special confidence would be inculcated if already we possess from God what we ask for, even if that does not become visible till later; cf. Mark 11:24: "All that you pray and ask for, believe that you received it, and it will be yours.") In Codices Vaticanus and Sinaiticus the "from" is *apo*, used some 19 times in I John (similarly in Matt 20:20 with *aitein*), while in Codex Alexandrinus and the Byzantine tradition it is *para* (never used in I John). Although the latter might be defended as the more difficult reading, it probably reflects the influence of GJohn (4:9) and other NT passages using *para* with *aitein* (Acts 3:2; 9:2; James 1:5; scribal variant in Matt 20:20).

16a. *If anyone sees his brother sinning (so long as the sin is not deadly).* Once again this is *ean* with the subjunctive, and here it introduces a condition describing what is expected under certain circumstances (BDF 371[4]). Although the *ean*, "if," governs "sees," the condition is more centered on the "sinning." There is help available to a Johannine Christian ("brother") who sins, but for that help the sin has to be known. The use of "sees" indicates that the author is not talking about a purely internal sinful state; but it is dubious that Cook, "Problems" 257–58, is correct in insisting that the sin must be physical. The last part of the line is literally: "sinning a sin *not* unto [*mē pros*] death." For Bultmann, *Epistles* 86, the use of "sinning a sin" (only here in Johannine usage) is a sign of the Redactor, for the author uses "doing a sin" (3:4,8,9). However, we have seen the author's love of variety, and here he is simply following the pattern of a cognate accusative from v. 15. The cognate accusative may be a type of Semitism (BDF 153[1]); and with the verb *hamartanein*, "to sin," the cognate accusative is good LXX style (Lev 5:6), especially in reference to dying in the sins that one sins (Ezek 18:24)—a theme that may have influenced the author here. The use of *mē* as a negative here and again in 16b is not classical; the *ou* of 17 is more correct. The explanation that the author used *mē* because of the proximity of *ean* plus the subjunctive (BDF 426) may help in 16a but not in 16b (unless by imitation). MGNTG 3, 281, says that there is no distinction between the negative particles in such a passage. The Greek phrase "unto death" does not in itself make clear whether the idea is that of a sin that *will* (or will not) lead to death or of a sin that *has* led to death. For theories about the nature of this sin, see the end of the NOTES on this verse (16).

16b. *he should ask; and thus life will be given to the sinner.* Literally, "he will ask and [he] will give life to him": two verbs in the future tense with a tone of the imperative (BDF 362). My deliberately impersonal translation of the second verb is meant to acknowledge the obscurity of the original, which is capable of at least three different interpretations. (1) The petitioner will give life to the sinner (Brooke, Büchsel, Bultmann, Chaine, Cook, Dodd, Goodspeed, Haas, Herkenrath, Moffatt, Plummer, Stott, Windisch). Grammatically this is the easiest, for it follows the obvious indication of the Greek that the two verbs have the same subject. However, would a Johannine writer say that a human being can give (eternal) life to another? Is that not a divine prerogative, since "flesh begets flesh, and Spirit begets spirit" (John 3:6)? The believer may possess life, but Jesus gives it. However, since this whole section is governed by 5:14, the author may mean that Christians give life in the sense that through their prayers God is moved to give life. Notice James 5:20 (unfortunately also uncertain): "The one who turns back a sinner from the error of his way will save his soul from death and will cover a multitude of sins"; and James 5:15: "The prayer of faith will save the sick man." Also *II Clem.* 19:1: "I ask [*aitein*] you to repent with all your heart, giving salvation and life to yourselves." (2) God will give life to the sinner (Alexander, Bonsirven, Bruce, Marshall, Schnackenburg, Scholer, Westcott, NEB, RSV). Theologically this is easier, but grammatically it is difficult to posit a shift of subject from the immediately preceding verb. Moreover, the following third-person verb ("one should pray") also has the petitioner as subject. (3) God will give life to the petitioner (as a reward for showing love for the brother by praying for him).

This has the same difficulties to overcome as (2), plus the difficulty that the next phrase (see below) seems to specify the "to him" in terms of sinners. This interpretation has little following. In summary, it is very difficult to choose between (1) and (2), and in any case (1) has to be so interpreted as to make God the ultimate source of life.

This is only for those whose sin is not deadly. Although for intelligibility I have translated this as an independent sentence, it is only a prepositional phrase dependent on "will give" in the preceding clause (literally, "to the sinners not unto death"). If one follows (3) above, one could understand this to mean: "will give life to him [the petitioner] for the sinners." However, despite the harshness of having a dative plural in apposition to a dative singular, most scholars read: "will give life to him, i.e., to the sinners." (The resumptive dative plural participle interpreting a dative *plural* pronoun in the main clause was seen in 5:13 and John 1:12.) The Vulgate corrects the Greek by reading a singular: "to the sinner." The negative in "not unto death" is again *mē;* see NOTE on 5:16a.

16c. *After all, there is such a thing as deadly sin.* Plummer, *Epistles* 123, argues that this could be a state of sin—he is probably wrong, but at least one should not translate *"a* deadly sin." Dodd, *Epistles* 135, plausibly contends that the author is thinking of an overt sinful action or course of actions that can be observed and known (just as for the sin that is not unto death). The emphasis, then, does not imply that the sin is hard to recognize, but that the readers must be convinced that it is unto death.

16d. *and I do not say that one should pray about that.* Literally, "Not about that do I say in order that one should pray." Only here in I John does the author use of himself the first person sing. form of a verb other than "write." It is possible to translate, "I am not speaking about that" (Schnackenburg, Scholer, Trudinger); but then logically one would have to repeat the prepositional phrase with the second verb: "so that one should pray (about that)." It is just as easy, then, to put the phrase with the verb "to pray." The author now switches from *aitein,* "to ask" (3 times in 5:14–16), to *erōtan,* "to question, ask, pray," used in the Epistles only here and in II John 5. In 27 uses of *erōtan* in GJohn, the verb covers both asking for information (1:19; 5:12; 9:2,15; 16:5) and making requests. However, the GJohn usage of *erōtan* for requests made of God (the Father) is confined to requests made by Jesus (14:16; 16:26; 17:9,15,20—see NOTE on 16:23 in ABJ 29A, 722–23). R. C. Trench, *Synonyms of the New Testament* (London: Clarke, 1961; reprint of 9th ed. of 1880) 134–37, argues that, while *aitein* implies supplication by an inferior, *erōtan* involves requests by one who is on a virtually equal or familiar basis. The attempt to invoke that distinction will be mentioned below; but it is scarcely valid even for GJohn, since *erōtan* covers requests made of superiors in 4:40,47; 19:31. It is probably only an accident of GJohn usage that *aitein* is employed for requests of God by the disciples, and *erōtan* for requests of God by Jesus. I John 5:14–16 shows the verbs as synonymous, interchanged for stylistic reasons.

THE DEADLY SIN OR "SIN UNTO DEATH." It is now appropriate to stop to consider what the author has been talking about in 5:16. With reference to the nature of the sin about which one should not pray, Bultmann, *Epistles* 87, says, "A decision can scarcely be taken, as the diverse efforts of exegetes indicate." Bultmann posits both an author and a redactor; and we may reflect with amusement that 5:6 and 5:16 would indicate respectively that the two were equally able to write obscurely and confuse interpreters. (As I have insisted, I see no reason to bifurcate this dubious achievement.) Before launching into the various proposals about this sin, let me note some points from the text that must be taken into account. While the "brother" (presumably the Johannine Christian) may be seen committing a sin that is not deadly, nothing is said about who commits the sin that is deadly, i.e., whether it is a brother or an outsider. The possibility of prayer "giving life" to someone is in relation to a brother who has committed a sin *not* unto death but who nevertheless has lost life or is in danger of losing life! We are not told, then, the presumably worse effects of the sin unto death. Although the readers are assumed to know that there is a sin unto death, in v. 17 they are told that not every sin is unto death. We shall return again to these points as we discuss the various proposals which for convenience I have grouped under four headings:

(1) Different Types of Petitions. A very simple solution has the author telling his readers that they have no obligation to pray about certain serious sins but can leave in God's hands those who commit such sins. Ambrose, *De poenitentia* 1.10.44–47 (PL 16, 500–1), thought that the author was assigning graver sins to the prayers of the just. The "I do not say that one should pray about that" is interpreted to mean "I do not command," so that the author is not *forbidding* prayers for those who commit deadly sins. While this suggestion is faithful to the literal wording, it does not do justice to the tone of the passage where the exclusion from prayer in 16a and 16d certainly means that the author does not want prayers for such sins. Since this verse follows the reference in 5:14 to asking "according to God's will," it is patent that he does not think that prayers in reference to deadly sin would be according to God's will. A variation of this attempt to distinguish types of petitions would insist on the use of *erōtan* in 16d as distinct from *aitein* in 14–16b (see Trench's distinction above; also Abbott, Westcott), so that supplication (*aitein*) for nondeadly sinners will be granted, but no assurance is given about prayer (*erōtan*) for deadly sins, i.e., prayer uttered by Christians in their exalted status as God's children, comparable to prayer uttered by Jesus as God's Son. In the NOTE on 5:16d I rejected such a distinctive use of the two verbs; and clearly the request in 5:16ab, expressed by *aitein*, is based on the petitioner's status as a child of God in relation to a fellow Christian ("brother"). Still another proposal in this vein is offered by Trudinger, "Concerning Sins" 541–42, who insists that *erōtan* means "to ask questions," not "to pray," so that v. 16d means: "I am not speaking about the sin unto death in order that one should ask questions or debate about that." While this meaning for the *intransitive* verb is attested in the LXX (Deut 13:15[14]), it is not familiar in the NT; and clearly in GJohn *erōtan* means "to ask, pray." All such efforts in relation to *erōtan* fail to do justice to the author's implicit exclusion of requests (*aitein*) about the deadly sin

(16a), so that, whether or not *aitein* and *erōtan* are synonyms, the author discourages *both* in reference to deadly sin. The same objection applies to the thesis of Bauernfeind, "Fürbitte" 51–54, who thinks that the author is not urging human prayer (*aitein*) for those who commit deadly sin, but is leaving open the possibility that the Spirit of God will give rise to prayer (*erōtan*) for deadly sin. (He cites the rabbinic example in Mishnah *Middoth* 2:2 where it is prayed that God will move people "to draw nigh" those who were put under the ban.) Still another variation is urged by Seeberg, "Sünden" 27–30, who thinks that the author is not urging *private* prayer (*erōtan*) for deadly sins that have not been publicly confessed—such sinners should come before the Community and be the subject of public prayer (I Tim 5:20).

Such theories really seek to explain away the offensiveness implied in the idea that the author of I John did not want prayers to be said for those who committed deadly sins. For instance, Wilder, "Introduction" 300, appeals to "the deeper NT view that God's love persists to the uttermost." But one must understand the world view in which the author writes. After all, Jeremiah was told by God, "Do not pray for the welfare of this [sinful] people" (Jer 14:11; also 7:16; 11:14); in Deut 3:26 the Lord tells Moses to intercede no more; and I Sam 3:14 insists that the sins of Eli's house shall not be expiated by any sacrifice and offering. The Lord of Hosts speaks to Jerusalem in Isa 22:14, "Surely this iniquity will not be forgiven you till you die." Indeed, the Johannine Jesus said, "I do not pray for the world"—a world of human beings that Jesus distinguished from those (Christians) whom the Father had given him (John 17:9). Whatever the deadly sin is (see below), the author is continuing the attitude of Jesus and is equating those who commit the deadly sin with "the world."

(2) **Different Types of Penalties.** Another approach to the problem of the sin unto death and the sin not unto death places emphasis on the presence or absence of a death penalty (or of death) as an inevitable consequence. The sin unto death may lead to *natural death,* whether inflicted by the Community or by divine visitation. In Num 18:22 the Lord forbids the ordinary Israelites from approaching the Tent of Meeting lest they incur the "death-bearing" sin. Deuteronomy 22:25–26 draws a distinction: While the rapist shall be slain, his victim "has not committed a sin worthy of death." In *Jubilees* 33:12–18 incest of a son with his father's wife is called "a sin unto death," for which there is a death penalty and no atonement. In the NT Ananias and Sapphira are struck dead by God and by apostolic judgment because of their sin against community rules (Acts 5:1–11), and Paul speaks of death as a punishment for sin (I Cor 5:5; 11:30). It may be remembered that the phrase "unto death" occurs in John 11:4 precisely in relation to physical death: "This sickness is not unto death." The idea would be that I John is discouraging prayer for those sins that bring death, or even prayers for those who died as a result of such sins. (See Bruce, *Epistles* 124–25; Reynolds, "Sins.") However, there is no reason to think that a *Johannine* audience would have been taught to fear sin on the basis of whether or not it would lead to physical death. The Johannine Jesus says, "If a person keeps my word, he shall never see death" (John 8:51); and

"Everyone who is alive and believes in me shall never die at all" (11:26). Indeed, in 12:24 Jesus speaks of physical death as fruit-bearing; and I John 3:14 treats death as something of the past: "That we have passed from death to life we know."

If the death theory has any plausibility, it must be based on *spiritual* death as a penalty. In Rev 3:1 a judgment is passed on the Christians of Sardis: "You have the name of being alive, but you are dead." In *Soṭah* 48a of the Babylonian Talmud the neglect of the "great *terumah*" offering is designated a deadly sin, i.e., one to be punished by God with death; but in a Judaism that came to believe in future life after physical death, such punishment might be understood as spiritual death. Cook, "Problems" 258, argues that in I John a warning against a sin unto spiritual death could apply only to nonbelievers, for a born-again believer cannot die spiritually. In fact, however, it is difficult to know how believers who committed serious sin would be treated in Johannine theology. On the one hand, it might be claimed that such people had never really believed—see I John 2:19 which denies that the secessionists ever really belonged to the Community. On the other hand, the statement about asking in 5:16 which says that "life will be given to the sinner" may mean that through sin a believer can lose eternal life but not irretrievably. The sin unto death would be one that leads to an irretrievable loss of life. Why then would the readers have to be told not to pray about such a sin (5:16d), since by definition it would be unforgivable?

(3) **Different Types of Sins.** The designation of sins as "unto death" and "not unto death" had led most commentators to place the crucial difference, not in the area of petition or penalty, but in terms of the gravity of the sins. A simple form of this theory is to distinguish between sins involving major matters and sins involving minor matters. Although in the teaching attributed to Jesus there is a reaction against casuistry (Matt 23:16–24), a distinction between the more and less grave is inevitable in any developed moral teaching. The Dead Sea Scroll Community Rule (1QS 7) lists various sins (some deliberate) with punishments proportionate to their gravity. Augustine thought of the sins not unto death as daily sins, while medieval theologians tended to identify the two kinds of sin in I John with mortal and venial sins (and one factor in a mortal sin is grave matter). However, it is doubtful that such a distinction was formally established in Christianity so early as the end of the first century. (It is more characteristic of the late second century, e.g., Tertullian, for which reason Baur, "Briefe" 321, dated the Johannine Epistles late.) *Didache,* from this same period, in its "Way of Death" (5:1–2) places side by side murder and impudence, adultery and foul speech. Moreover, a tolerance of minor sins would seem strange in the Johannine Community with its strong sense of perfectionism. The sin *not* unto death is connected in 5:16b with the loss of eternal life or the danger thereof, so that by later ethical standards it would be a grave sin. Herkenrath, "Sünde" 134, argues that the author would not have described light sins with such emphatic language as "sinning sin" (5:16a—see NOTE above).

Another form of distinction between sins is closer to NT times, namely, that both types of sin are grave, but one can be forgiven and the other cannot. Plummer, *Epistles* 122, explains "the sin unto death" in terms of closing "the heart against the influences of God's Spirit so obstinately and persistently that repentance becomes a moral impossibility." I Sam 2:25 warns, "If a man sins against another man, God will mediate for him; but if a man sins against the Lord, who can intercede for him?" Specifically, Williams, *Letters* 60, states in reference to I John: "Probably our writer meant by *deadly* sin a permanent and deliberate rejection of the true faith in favor of the old paganism or some new heresy" (also Dodd, B. Poschmann). As support for this thesis it is noted that in 5:21 the author warns against idols. Some scholars (Herkenrath, Windisch) mention other sins besides apostasy, e.g., murder; and Heb 12:16–17 mentions Esau who could not repent even though he sought repentance with tears. That such sinfulness could be termed deadly is seen in *Jubilees* 26:34 where Esau is warned that he will commit "a sin unto death" and his seed will be rooted out from under heaven. Murder was often regarded as unforgivable, and I John 3:15 states, "No murderer has eternal life abiding in him" (Lazure). It is also argued (by a dubious interpretation, however) that I John 2:16 condemns as opposed to the love of God concupiscence and avarice. In the mid-second century *Hermas* (*Similitudes* 6.2.1–4) distinguishes between "those destroyed to corruption" who have given themselves to luxury and deceit but for whom there is still hope of repentance in which they continue to live, and "those destroyed to death" who have given themselves to the lusts of this world and have blasphemed against the name of God and for whom there is no hope of repentance. At the end of the second century Tertullian, *De pudicitia* 2,14–16; 19,26–28 (CC 2, 1285–86, 1323), interpreted I John to be referring to murder, idolatry, injustice, apostasy, adultery, and fornication, for which there is no pardon: "If one commits them, he will not be a child of God." While one cannot disprove these suggestions, there is not enough internal evidence in I John to make them plausible. I John gives no attention to apostasy *to paganism;* the author's hostility is directed against secession from the Community. The epistolary statement against the murderer relates to the secessionist's hating his former brother whom he has left behind, for "Everyone who hates his brother is a murderer" (3:15). Highly questionable, then, is the argument of Bultmann, *Epistles* 86–87, who, interpreting "the sin unto death" as an example of early church penitential practice of not forgiving certain sins, concludes that the appearance of such a theme in 5:14–21 "clearly demonstrates the character of the appendix, i.e., that it is the work of an Ecclesiastical Redactor."

Still another form of the distinction between types of sin is based on the sayings of the Synoptic Jesus about an unforgivable sin (thus Augustine). In passages like Mark 8:38; Luke 9:26; Matt 10:33; and Luke 12:9 Jesus speaks of himself or of the Son of Man denying or being ashamed in the future (before the angels) of those who deny him or are ashamed of him on earth. This is close to refusing forgiveness at judgment, and presumably the reference is to those who deliberately do not believe. In Mark 3:29; Matt 12:32 Jesus says that everyone who blasphemes or speaks against the Holy Spirit will never be forgiven, a passage that Luke 12:10 joins to the preceding. In Mark and Matthew this saying occurs in the context of attributing to Beelzebul the healings of Jesus that are really the work of divine power. The mysterious character of the blasphemy against the Holy Spirit led to speculation, and indeed the text was used at times to justify the above-mentioned refusal of church forgiveness to certain sins. Eventually, while maintaining the saying of Jesus, the church tacitly acknowledged its inability to determine what Jesus meant, so that all sins were regarded as forgivable through repentance and the Sacrament of Penance. (This illustrated another saying of Jesus, "Anything is possible for God" [Mark 10:27].) To apply these Synoptic sayings to I John 5:16–17 is to define the unknown through the more unknown. Nevertheless, while they may not tell us what "the sin unto death" is, they do give us an early Christian context for regarding some sin as outside the pale of human intervention and even of divine forgiveness. I John 5:16 is not uniquely harsh in early Christianity.

A final variation on the theme of different kinds of sin is based on a distinction in Hebrew law between deliberate sins (committed "with a high hand") and indeliberate sins. (This was an interpretation of I John by Origen, *On Matthew* 13.30 [GCS 40, 264], and it plays an important role in Nauck's discussion.) Sacrifices could be offered for indeliberate sins at the Tabernacle or Temple (Lev 4:1–3; Num 15:22–29); but the perpetrator of a deliberate sin was more harshly treated: "Because he has despised the word of the Lord and has broken His commandment, that person shall be utterly cut off; his iniquity shall be upon him" (Num 15:30–31). See also Ps 19:13–14(12–13). The Rule of the Dead Sea Scroll community (1QS 8:21–9:2, a section missing from the oldest MSS.) allows one who has sinned inadvertently to be restored to the community after two years, but one "who deliberately transgressed even one word of the Law of Moses . . . shall never return." Indeed, the language of "deadly sin" seems to have been used in Jewish circles for deliberate sins. In one MS. tradition of *T. Issachar* 7:1 the patriarch says, "I am not conscious of committing any sin unto [*eis*] death." *Jubilees* 21:22 (Hebrew text in RB 73 [1966] 104) warns against walking in the ways of the children of men and sinning "a sin unto death before the Most High God; or He will hide His face from you . . . and root you out of the land and your seed from under heaven." There is nothing in I John, however, that would identify "the sin unto death" with deliberate sin, even though deliberateness would surely be a factor in "the sin unto death." In John 3:18–21 the judgment of all human beings is based on whether they believe in the name of God's only Son and come to the light, or refuse to believe and prefer the darkness.

(4) **Different Types of People.** The passage just cited brings us to what I would judge the best approach to the difference between the sin unto death and the sin not unto death. The text of I John 5:16 ascribes the sin not unto death to the "brother," i.e., the fellow Johannine Christian, for whose life one should pray. Since in Johannine dualism eternal life is possessed only by those who believe in the name of God's Son, the sin unto death is a sin by nonbrothers, i.e., those who do not believe in the name of God's Son. As Jesus states in John

16:9, the sin of which the Paraclete/Spirit shall convict the world is "that they refuse to believe in me"—the Johannine interpretation of the sin against the Holy Spirit. In John 8:19–21 Jesus says to those who do not recognize him, "You will die in your sin"; and in 15:22 he says of nonbelievers, "They have no excuse for their sin." Stott, *Epistles* 188–90, acknowledges that the sin unto death involves a refusal to believe, but he identifies the sinners as non-Christians. Yet non-Christians, whether pagans or Jews, are not the subject of I John; and so there is no reason to posit that the author is introducing such an extraneous topic in his Conclusion.

Throughout I John the nonbelievers have been the former brothers, the secessionists. While in their own self-estimation the secessionists may be Christians, in the author's estimation they do not have life (3:12–17); for they have abandoned the *koinōnia* with the Father and Son, which preserves eternal life (1:2–3). Here the author is close to Dead Sea Scroll mentality, attested by the Qumran psalmist: "I shall have no pity on those who depart from the Way" (1QS 10:20–21). Secessionists belong to the realm of darkness, the Lie, the Evil One, and death. It makes perfect sense, then, that the author discourages (and implicitly forbids) prayer for them. Jesus refused to pray for the world (John 17:9), and they belong to the world (I John 4:5). The Conclusion of I John is meant as an encouragement for the author's adherents, who possess life; they are being told that even sin cannot destroy all opportunity for life. But as he stresses this, the author always keeps an eye on his adversaries and insists that they should not be prayed for by his adherents, even as II John 10–11 insists that they should not be greeted or received into the house. By refusing to believe in *Jesus* as the Christ come in the flesh and as the Son of God (I John 2:22; 3:23; 4:2–3; 5:1,5,10), the secessionists have preferred darkness to light. Scholars, like Herkenrath, "Sünde" 135, who argue that the sin unto death is not a single action but an orientation of life, are partly right; for secessionist existence, with its hatred of former brothers, flows from the basic sinful act of refusing to believe in the Community's understanding of Jesus Christ. The secessionists are the living continuation of those whom in his lifetime Jesus condemned because they refused to believe (John 3:18–21). In speaking of the secessionist refusal to believe as "the sin unto death," the author is bringing to bear on them the Hebrew heritage of the deliberate sin that cannot be forgiven because it is against God's Law and it involves a blasphemy of God's name. He is also bringing to bear on them the Christian heritage of the unforgivable sin against the Holy Spirit, which attributes to the devil what belongs to Christ. I do not mean that the author is necessarily talking about the same sin to which those other passages refer, but only that they supply background and terminology for his judgment upon the secessionists. His readers know of this background, and he is telling them that it applies to the secessionists and that they must resist any misplaced affection by praying for them as former brothers. This interpretation of "the sin unto death" is in perfect harmony with the thrust of I John and Johannine dualism. As Scholer, "Sins" 238, points out, it has been missed by many because they made the mistake of thinking that I John attributed this sin to "brothers." Among modern scholars Klöpper was one of the forerunners of this interpretation; but in antiquity Augustine, *De sermone Domini* 1.22.73 (CC 35, 81–83), came close to it, for he diagnosed the object of I John as a former Christian brother who is now combatting the fraternity.

17a. *All wrongdoing is sin.* Some would see *adikia* as "wrongdoing" in the social order, e.g., Klöpper quotes a saying of Xenophon, *Cyropaedia* 8.8.7, that involves *asebeia* or "impiety" toward the gods, and *adikia* toward fellow human beings. However, the I John reference to God and Christ as *dikaios*, "just, good" (1:9; 2:2,29), a terminology also used for the person who does good actions (3:7) and for the good actions themselves (3:12), suggests that the opposite term *adikia* covers anything wrong. It is tempting to compare this statement to 3:5, "Sin is the Iniquity [*anomia*]"; but there the author was talking about acknowledged sins and insisting upon their almost apocalyptic evil. Here, after speaking about the possibility of sins not unto death and about the gift of life despite such sins, he wishes to be sure that his reaffirmation of forgiveness does not make wrongdoing seem less sinful.

17b. *but not all sin is deadly.* This clause is introduced by an adversative *kai* (BDF 442[1]): "and there is sin not unto death." The negative here, *ou*, is better grammatically than the *mē* used twice in 5:16 for "the sin not unto death." This shift of particle seems to have bothered scribes; for the negative is omitted altogether in some minuscule MSS., Tertullian, and the Vulgate, Coptic, Syriac, and Armenian translations. Büchsel and Harnack are among those who accept the omission as original, but that would have 17b simply repeat 16c. Moreover, if the addition of the negative came from scribes, one would expect them to have used the same negative as in v. 16.

18a. *We know that.* This is the first of three "We know" (*oidamen*) clauses opening vv. 18, 19, and 20, which reiterate what the author has said previously in I John. The "know" motif was inaugurated in v. 13, and there was a double "we know" in v. 15. Previously "we know" clauses appeared in 3:2,14, as did "you [pl.] know" in 2:20,21; 3:5,15—another indication that there is no stylistic need to posit a different hand for this Conclusion.

no one who has been begotten by God commits sin. Literally, "everyone who has been begotten/born [*gennan*, perf. pass. ptcp.] from God does not sin [*hamartanein*]." *Pas* plus the arthrous participle ("everyone who") is frequent in I John (NOTE on 2:23ab); and when a negative is used with the main verb, it really modifies the *pas*, changing it from "all" to "none" (NOTE on 2:19f). The peculiar Johannine use of *gennan* in the passive for the divine begetting of the Christian was treated in the NOTE on 2:29b. As for the connection between divine begetting and sinlessness, see the NOTE on 3:9cd, where four statements of sinlessness/impeccability (3:6a,9a,9c; 5:18a) were analyzed against the contrasting background of two statements that challenge a claim to sinlessness (1:8,10) and of three statements that take for granted that Christians do sin (1:9; 2:1–2; 5:16–17). The present statement varies only slightly from 3:9a, "No one who has been begotten by God acts sinfully [*hamartian poiein*]." At the end of the present line the Venerable Bede reads: "does not sin the sin unto death"; but that is a misinterpretation. The "sin unto death" is not in question here, since it is a sin of disbelief that is inapplicable to one begotten by God; rather, the author is excluding the sins *not* unto death. They can be forgiven through prayer, but no real Christian commits them.

18b. *rather, the one begotten by God is protected.* Here the passive participle of *gennan* is aorist, and the last part of the line is literally, "keeps or guards [*tērein*] him/himself." At least five interpretations of this line have been proposed by scholars.

(1) "The begetting by God guards him [the Christian who has been begotten]." Two Greek minuscule MSS., the Vulgate, Harclean Syriac, Chromatius of Aquilea (before A.D. 400), and Bede read *gennēsis*, "begetting," for *gennētheis*, "begotten." Harnack points out that the latter could easily be a scribal mistake for the former, which he and Dibelius take to be original. In "Text-kritik" 539, Harnack argues that, since 5:18a matches 3:9a (see preceding NOTE), 5:18b should match 3:9b ("because God's seed abides in him"), and that "the begetting from God" best matches "the seed of God." However, it seems more likely that *gennēsis* is a scribal attempt to clarify the much better attested *gennētheis*.

(2) "The one begotten by God [Jesus] guards him [the Christian who has been begotten]." This is the interpretation of Alexander, Boismard, Bonsirven, Brooke, Bruce, Büchsel, Bultmann, Chaine, Charue, Cook, de Ambroggi, Dodd, Hauck, Howard, Loisy, Marshall, Nauck, Plummer, Schlatter, Scholer, Stott, THLJ, Vellanickal, Westcott, Wohlenberg; NEB, RSV. It is startling to find Jesus introduced so abruptly here simply as "the one begotten by God," especially when virtually the same title has been used for the Christian in the preceding line. One would have expected "the Son of God" if Jesus were meant, and that is precisely what NEB has audaciously supplied. Yet it is argued (for instance, by Scholer, "Sins" 245) that Jesus is the logical opponent to the Evil One who will be mentioned in the next line. The shift from the perf. ptcp. of *gennan* to the aorist is thought to be a signal that Jesus is being introduced into the passage, for he was begotten once and for all by the Father (the punctiliar aspect of the aorist). Philo, *On the Confusion of Tongues* 14 ✕63, describes the *Logos* as begotten (*gennētheis*) by God. There are contrary arguments, however. In I John the Christian *children* of God are the opponents of the Evil One (2:13,14) and are contrasted with Cain who belonged to the Evil One (3:12). In the very next verse (5:19) the Christians who belong to God are opposed to the world, which belongs to the Evil One. Moreover, elsewhere in GJohn or I, II, and III John the verb *gennan* is never used in any tense to describe Jesus' origin from God, so that it is highly dubious that a Johannine writer would say that Jesus was begotten by God. The one clear Johannine use of *gennan* for Jesus (perf. tense) refers not to his divine origin but to his temporal birth (John 18:37). (*Gennan* is not used of Jesus by Paul; it is used of his conception in Mary and physical birth by Matt 1:16,20; 2:1,4 and Luke 1:35 [but may for that very reason be avoided by Johannine theology which did not have a conception christology]; and it became enshrined in Christian thought through the Nicene Creed.) No Greek MS. supports the third person singular reading in John 1:13, which would make Jesus the one

begotten by God (ABJ 29, 11–12). Finally, as we have seen throughout this commentary, interpretations based on exact Johannine distinction between the perf. and the aorist are very dubious. Perhaps the best argument for this interpretation is that the protection of the Christian is a task that GJohn assigns to Jesus: "I protected [*tērein*] them with Your name" (17:12; see Rev 3:10). Nevertheless, the task is not peculiar to Jesus, for he asks the Father "to keep them safe from the Evil One" (John 17:15). Vellanickal, *Sonship* 282, gives a structural argument for this interpretation of I John 5:18b; but he achieves his structure only by neglecting some of the lines.

(3) "The one begotten by God [the Christian] guards himself." This is the interpretation of many Greek church fathers, and of Belser, Holtzmann, Schmiedel, B. Weiss, and KJV. Sometimes it is predicated upon acceptance of the reflexive pronoun *heauton*, "himself," supported by Codex Sinaiticus, the corrector of Alexandrinus, the Byzantine tradition, the Peshitta, Sahidic, Armenian, and by Origen, Epiphanius, Didymus, Theophylact, and the critical versions of Merk, Vogels, and von Soden. However, the reading *auton* is better attested, so that the reflexive was probably introduced as a scribal clarification. Even less plausible is the attempt to accentuate *auton* as *hauton*, the contracted reflexive form that is rare in NT Greek (MGNTG 2, 180; IBNTG 119), although it is generally accepted in John 2:24. A simpler explanation is that the personal pronoun *auton*, "him," was often used as a reflexive (BDF 283). The main objection to this interpretation is that *tērein* never elsewhere in its frequent Johannine usage (25 times) governs a reflexive accusative, although that construction is attested in II Cor 11:9; I Tim 5:22; James 1:27; Jude 21 (but always with a further modifier, which is lacking here). The idea of self-protection against the Evil One (who is mentioned in the next line) matches the affirmation addressed to Johannine Christians in I John 2:13,14: "You have conquered the Evil One." One objection against this interpretation is that if the subject of "guards" is the Christian, there should have been no need to have the subject awkwardly repeated in this line; for one could simply have continued the previous line: "No one begotten by God commits sin; rather he guards himself." Nevertheless, repetition in a slightly variant form (aorist ptcp. replacing the perf.) is certainly not unJohannine. The objection that the nominative aorist ptcp. of *gennan* is never used by John for the Christian is not particularly persuasive, for that particular form is very rare in the NT (only Heb 11:23, of Moses). Other aorist passive forms of *gennan* are used of believers in John 1:13; 3:3,4,5,7.

(4) "The one begotten by God [the Christian] holds on to Him [God]." Schneider seems inclined to this interpretation. It is awkward, however, to have the *auton*, "him," in this line refer to God, while the *auton* in the next line (18c) refers to the Christian. Moreover, while *tērein* can mean "to hold on to, cling to" (BAG 822 [BAGD 815] 3, which cites this passage), as in Rev 3:3, it does not have that meaning elsewhere in Johannine usage. (The idea is most often "to keep/observe" commandments or words.) If the author wished to speak of holding on to God, he would more likely have used the verb *echein*, "to have" (I John 2:23; 5:12; II John 9).

(5) "The one begotten by God [the Christian], God guards him [the Christian]." This interpretation is defended by Balz, Beyer, Schnackenburg (3d ed.), and Segond. It supposes Semitic syntax with a *casus pendens* construction (BDF 466²) whereby a description that modifies a pronoun is moved out of the clause to an anticipatory position in front, e.g., John 17:2: ". . . so that everyone whom You have given him, he may give to them eternal life." For a grammatical defense of this interpretation of the present passage, see SSNT 1, 216ff. Like interpretation (1), this interpretation has the advantage of having God (or an action of God) protect the Christian.

In making a decision about these five interpretations, I judge (1) and (4) to be the weakest. The really crucial point is whether the one begotten is the Christian (3,5) or Jesus (2). I am inclined to favor the former; for I find it hard to believe that if the Johannine writers thought that Jesus had been begotten by God, they would never elsewhere have used that language in the many passages on the subject. As for the issue of whether the Christian guards himself or God guards him, my translation "is protected" leaves that undecided. It does not make much difference, for only the Christian's status as a child of God enables him to protect himself. The next line makes clear from what the Johannine Christian is protected.

18c. *and so the Evil One cannot touch him.* For the Johannine use of "the Evil One," see the NOTE on 2:13d. The verb *haptesthai,* "to touch, lay hands on," can be used benevolently (to bless) or hostilely (to harm). The latter sense, where it translates Hebrew *ng',* is seen in the LXX of Gen 26:11; Ps 105:15; Jer 4:10; and Zech 2:12(8). In particular, in Job 2:5 the Satan tries to persuade God "to touch" Job's bones and flesh, i.e., to strike him with illness. In rabbinic literature the verb *ng'* is used in Midrash *Siphre* 42 on Num 6:26: "Satan will not touch him." In *T. Judah* 3:10 we read, "An angel of power followed me everywhere so that I should not be touched"; and other passages in the *Testaments* (*Levi* 5:6; *Dan* 6:1–2; *Benj.* 3:4) show that such protection by the angel or by God is against the evil spirit or Beliar or Satan. That Christians will not be destroyed by the devil despite the fear he causes is a well-attested theme (I Pet 5:8–9; *Hermas Man.* 12.4.7). I John 2:13–14 assures the "Young People" that they have conquered the Evil One. During his lifetime Jesus protected his "sheep" so that no one could snatch them from him (John 10:28), and in fact none perished (17:12). As Jesus prepared to depart, he prayed to the Father to keep his followers safe from the Evil One (17:15). Compare Matt 6:13 where Jesus teaches his disciples to pray, "Deliver us from the Evil One."

19a. *We know that it is to God we belong.* This is the expression *einai ek,* "to be from," discussed in the NOTE on 2:16ef as implying not only origin but a sense of belonging. In the almost identical expression in 4:6, "We belong to God," the personal pronoun "we" was expressed. Its absence here is significant for Westcott, *Epistles* 194, who sees the present statement throwing all the emphasis on the divine source: "We know that it is from God that we draw our being." Johannine grammar is scarcely so precise, and any greater emphasis upon the divine source comes from the contrast with the Evil One in the next line.

19b. *while the whole world lies in the grasp of the Evil One*. The opening conjunction is *kai*, "and." The expression "the whole world" was encountered in I John 2:2: Jesus Christ "is an atonement for our sins, and not only for our sins but also for the whole world [*holos ho kosmos*]." The slightly different (chiastic?) word order here (*ho kosmos holos*) is used by Westcott and Brooke to solve the seeming contradiction between the two passages, for the order here is said to mean "the world as a whole." Again the grammatical base is too fragile; the alternating position of *holos*, "whole," hints at the inclusiveness of the phrase. While 2:2 describes the saving purpose of God, 5:19 reflects the standard Johannine understanding that those who believe in Jesus, unlike the secessionists, do not belong to the world (John 17:14: *einai ek*). (A Pauline equivalent is Gal 1:4 referring to Jesus Christ "who gave himself for our sins to deliver us from the present evil eon.") By contrast with "we belong to God" in 5:19a, one would have expected the author to say "the whole world belongs to the Evil One." That vocabulary would have been possible, for in 3:12 it was said that Cain belonged to the Evil One; but the author's contrasts are never perfect. The expression actually used, *keisthai en*, "to lie in [the Evil One]," occurs nowhere else in the NT, although it appears in the LXX meaning "to be in the state of" (II Macc 3:11; 4:31,34). Here the idea seems to be one of dependence upon the Evil One, as well as being in his realm. Compare the *Corpus Hermeticum* 6, 4: "The world is the pleroma of evil; God, of good." Some scholars would translate I John abstractly as "lies in evil condition," but the article before *poneros* and the clear reference to "the Evil One" in the preceding verse militate against this.

20a. *We know, finally, that the Son of God has come*. While *oidamen de* is read in Codices Vaticanus, Sinaiticus, and the Byzantine tradition, *kai oidamen* is read in Alexandrinus, the Vulgate, Sahidic, Syriac, and Armenian; and both particles are omitted in minor witnesses. Chaine, *Epîtres* 223, rejects the *de* as Alexandrian elegance. However, in this instance *de* would not be an adversative but mark the conclusion of a series; and so my translation can render either *kai* or *de*. The word "come" translates a form of *hēkein*, conveying the idea of having come in the past and still being present. Used 4 times in GJohn, the verb covered the coming of Jesus from Judea (4:47), the coming to Jesus of those whom the Father had given him (6:37), and more important: "From God I came forth and *am come*" (8:42). Closely parallel is Heb 10:7,9: "I have come to do Your will." BAG 345 (BAGD 344) 1d points to the pagan usage of the verb for the solemn appearance of a deity, and there is an element of that connotation here. Elsewhere I John (3:5,8) uses equivalently the passive form of *phaneroun*: Christ, the Son of God, "was revealed."

At the end of this clause several Vulgate MSS. add: "and put on flesh for our sake, and suffered, and rose from the dead; he took us up." This Latin addition is attested (sometimes with variants) by Julian of Toledo, Hilary of Poitiers, Pseudo-Augustine, and the trinitarian work attributed to Vigilius of Thapsus (see INTRODUCTION VI B for Latin additions). Harnack, "Textkritik" 570–71, admits that it is not original but argues that the variants point to a Greek original and that it reflects an old creedal formula shaped in the antignostic struggles of the third or even the second century.

20b. *and has given us insight to know the One who is true.* This is the only Johannine occurrence of *dianoia*, "understanding, intelligence, faculty of thinking," a word that sometimes renders the Hebrew for "heart," which was looked upon as the seat of thought and decision-making. (Bultmann, "Redaktion" 20, cites the use of *dianoia* and of *alēthinos*, "true," as a sign that a hand other than the author's wrote this verse.) Is the "insight in order to know [*ginōskein*]" a circumlocution to avoid the noun *gnōsis*, "knowledge," which the Johannine writers never use? (Cf. Ignatius, *Eph.* 17:2: "We have received knowledge [*gnōsis*] of God, that is, Jesus Christ.") If so, it might be an indication that the adversaries were using this word. As for the verb "to know," the textual witnesses are divided on whether to read the pres. indicative (Codices Sinaiticus, Alexandrinus, Vaticanus*) or the subjunctive (corrector of Vaticanus and the Byzantine tradition). After *hina*, "in order to," the subjunctive is normal; and wherever the indicative appears, the subjunctive is to be expected as a scribal variant (see John 17:3, and the list of instances in Brooke, *Epistles* 150–51). Despite that and despite the strength of the textual witnesses for the indicative here, BDF 396[6] describes the indicative as a corruption; and Westcott, *Epistles* 196, suggests that the seeming indicative form is a corrupt pronunciation of the subjunctive (an explanation scarcely applicable in all cases). Brooke is more persuasive in speaking of the indicative as a vulgarism, later corrected by scribes. The indicative might heighten the actuality of the knowledge: "insight so that we may (and in fact do) know." In any case the pres. tense underlines the endurance of the knowledge. Westcott's interpretation stresses this: God has given them a power of understanding so that they may know by a continuous and progressive apprehension.

"The One who is true" is an arthrous substantival form of *alēthinos*, an adjective used elsewhere in I John only of "light" (see NOTE on 2:8b). This adjective is used to describe God in Isa 65:16; *III Macc.* 6:18; Philo, *Gaius* 45 ※366; I Thess 1:9; John 17:3 (cf. 7:28). The adjective describes Jesus in Rev 3:7,14; 19:11; and is used in the "I am" statements of the Johannine Jesus as he identifies himself as the true/real bread, light, and vine (John 6:32; 15:1; cf. 1:9). Here "the One who is true" is God, not Jesus, as indicated by the OT background concerning the knowledge of God, and by the logic of the sentence where the Son of God has a role in giving insight to know the True One. It is not surprising then, to find scribes adding the word "God" after "the true" (Codex Alexandrinus, 33, and other Greek minuscules, the Vulgate Bohairic, and Ethiopic versions, and many church writers), especially since elsewhere in Johannine usage there is always a substantive with *alēthinos*. A few scholars would contend that "God" was in the original writing but fell out by haplography (since the ending of *alēthinon* would resemble *thn̄*, the abbreviation for "God"), but most accept as original the shorter text of Vaticanus and the Byzantine tradition. Frequently in GJohn *alēthinos* implies a contrast ("real" versus putative or counterfeit; ABJ 29, 500–1). While that is less clear in I John, some would see God as "the True One" being contrasted with the Evil One "in whom there is no truth" (John 8:44).

20cd. *And we are in the One who is true, for we are in His Son, Jesus*

Christ. The Latin reads a subjunctive, "and that we may be in . . . ," a rather gnostic reading, for it traces our being in God to insight. The Greek puts the gifts of insight and indwelling on the same level. For *einai en,* "to be in," see the NOTE on 1:5e. This is an example of the use of that phrase to express divine indwelling (group A), and the closest parallel is John 17:21: "Just as you Father in me and I in you, that *they also may be* [one] *in us.*" In the Greek here there is no connective between the two phrases: "in the true One, in His Son, Jesus Christ"; and inevitably there have been scribal attempts at improvement. A few minuscules and some church writers omit the second "in," so that "true" becomes an adjective: "in His true Son, Jesus Christ." However, as we saw in 5:20b, this reflects scribal uneasiness with *alēthinos,* "true," as a title. Codex Alexandrinus and the Vulgate omit "Jesus Christ," while the Coptic versions substitute "in life" for "in the true One." Nevertheless, a sequence of prepositional phrases dealing with the Father and His Son Jesus Christ is quite Johannine, even if elsewhere the connection is smoother: "The communion we have is with [*meta*] the Father and with His Son, Jesus Christ" (I John 1:3); "Peace from [*para*] God the Father and from Jesus Christ, the Father's Son" (II John 3). The pattern of describing the Father but naming the Son is attested in John 17:3: "That they know you, the one true [*alēthinos*] God, and Jesus Christ, the one whom you sent." By inserting the conjunction "for" in my translation, I indicate the probable relationship between the two prepositional phrases: We are in the God who is true by being in His Son who is the truth. This is suggested by John 14:6: "I am the way and the truth and the life: no one comes to the Father except through me." See also Ignatius, *Magn.* 8:2, "There is one God who manifested Himself through Jesus Christ, His Son."

20e. *He is the true God and eternal life.* The pronoun is *houtos,* "this (one)." I John, which began with an example of stunning grammatical obscurity in the Prologue, continues to the end to offer us examples of unclear grammar. Dodd, *Epistles* 140, pays the author the compliment of thinking that I John's final obscurity is deliberate: the "this" is all that the author has been saying about God-known-in-Christ and about the knowledge of God (also Vellanickal). But rather than opting for both a double personal meaning and a simultaneous impersonal meaning of "this," most scholars think that the author is referring either to the Father or to Jesus. A reference of *houtos* to the Father is defended by Alexander, Brooke, Chapman, Harnack, Moulton, Ross, Stott, and Westcott. A reference to Jesus Christ was held in earlier times by Athanasius, Cyril of Alexandria, Jerome, Bede, Calvin, and Luther, and is defended in modern times by Balz, Belser, Bengel, Bonsirven, Bruce, Büchsel, Bultmann, Chaine, Charue, Haas, Hauck, Hoskyns, Houlden, Marshall, Rivera, Rothe, Schackenburg, Schneider, THLJ, and B. Weiss.

The following factors enter into a decision: (1) The nearest antecedent is "Jesus Christ"; but sometimes when that is true, the pronoun can still refer to God, as in I John 2:3. (The *houtos* of II John 7, although it follows "Jesus Christ," refers to the secessionists.) Some would treat "in His Son, Jesus Christ," of the preceding line as a gloss, so that the nearest antecedent becomes "the One who is true" of 20c, but the well-attested Johannine pattern of sequential phrases referring to Father and Son militates against this. (2) The first predicate identifying *houtos* is "the true [*alēthinos*] God," which is clearly a title of the Father in John 17:3. Moreover, *alēthinos* has just been used of the Father in 5:20c, and within two verses it would be surprising to find the author switching the title to Jesus without some explicit indication. On the other hand, after a description of the Father as "the One who is true," it is somewhat tautological to say, "This [true One] is the true God," whereas the author would be saying something further if he said that this Jesus Christ is the true God. (3) There is an uneasiness (sometimes unexpressed) among scholars about NT texts that call Jesus "God"—an unwarranted uneasiness, especially for the Johannine writings where that description is solidly attested (John 1:1,18; 20:28). See my article "Does the New Testament Call Jesus God?" cited above in the INTRODUCTION, footnote 162. (4) The second predicate identifying *houtos* is "eternal life," which, since it lacks the definite article, is closely joined to the first predicate—the true God who is (for us) eternal life. (Moffatt and NEB, "This is the real [true] God, this is life eternal," are not helpful here.) This predicate fits Jesus better than it fits God. The Father possesses life in Himself (John 5:26; 6:57), even as there is life *in* Jesus (John 1:4; 6:57; I John 5:11); but "life" is not predicated of the Father as it is of Jesus (John 11:25; 14:6). If the reference here is to Jesus, then there is an inclusion with the I John Prologue (1:2): "This eternal life which was in the Father's presence . . . was revealed to us." Ignatius, who has many affinities to I John, describes Jesus as "God in man, true life in death" (*Eph.* 7:2), using all the predicates of I John 5:20e. In summary, I think the arguments clearly favor *houtos* as a reference to Jesus Christ.

21. *Little Children*. This is the seventh use of *teknion* (pl.) as an address in I John; see NOTE on 2:1a.

guard yourselves. Although some would press the once-for-all character of the aorist tense of this imperative of *phylassein*, the guarding has to be ongoing. The argument that the author thinks that it is the last hour (2:18) is partially offset by his distinction between "now" and "what shall be" (3:2) which implies some duration. MGNTG 3, 77 plausibly lists this among aorist imperatives used for precepts that will be in effect until the second coming of Christ. Does the instruction "guard [*phylassein*] yourselves" help to clarify 5:18b: "The one begotten by God protects [*tērein*] him/himself"? The difference of verb need not be significant, for in John 17:12 the verbs are virtually interchangeable: "I protected [*tērein*] them with your name which you have given to me; I kept guard [*phylassein*] and not one of them perished." However, a reflexive use in I John 5:21 does not necessarily imply a reflexive use in 5:18. Cf. Jude 21, "Protect [*tērein*] yourselves in the love of God," and Jude 24, "The One who is able to guard [*phylassein*] you from falling." The reflexive pronoun in the present verse is *heauta*, third person neuter. The use of the third person for all persons is well attested in Hellenistic Greek (BDF 64[1]), and the neuter is by way of agreement with "Little Children." Codex Alexandrinus and the Byzantine tradition "correct" by using the masculine. The use of a reflexive instead of the middle voice has been read as a sign of emphasis, but this may be oversubtle (BDF 310[2]).

against idols. Literally, "from the idols." MGNTG 2, 460 regards the use of *apo*, "from," instead of the classical accusative, after *phylassein* as a reflection of Semitic influence (*min*). These last words of I John present us with a final obscurity. The definite article implies that the writer was quite clear about which idols he meant, but interpreters are in complete disarray in reading his mind. The following suggestions have been made; but they are not necessarily exclusive of one another, and some commentators advocate several: **(1)** "Idols" is Plato's designation of the "unreal" objects of the senses when contrasted with the "real" world of ideas, the world of absolute truth and beauty. Those who identify the Johannine and the Platonic concepts of truth (the heavenly as opposed to the earthly) favor this interpretation and point to I John 2:15–17 as a warning against the things of this world. Such an interpretation of truth is very questionable for John (ABJ 29, 499–501; above, NOTE on 1:6d). **(2)** The images of the pagan deities are idols, e.g., the silver shrines of Artemis at Ephesus are dubbed "gods made with hands" (Acts 19:23–41, where, however, the term "idol" does not appear). This interpretation, held by many of the older commentators (e.g., Zahn) and also by Ross, is related to the theory that I John was written at Ephesus and might represent the same struggle some forty years later than the Artemis incident. They point to the polemic in Rev 9:20 (written in the Ephesus area, presumably in the 90s) against "idols of gold, silver, bronze, and stone." This represents the most literal understanding of *eidōlon* (attested in Acts 7:41; I Cor 12:2; II Cor 6:16; I Thess 1:9). **(3)** "Idols" is an abbreviated description for food dedicated to idols (Büchsel, Windisch). This was a widespread problem in the early church (Acts 15:29; I Cor 8:4,7; 10:19) and was still an issue in Rev 2:14,20. The usual word for such food, however, was *eidōlothytos*, and it would be strange to have *eidōlon* alone describe the food, without a clarifying context. **(4)** "Idols" represents a compromise with paganism (Dodd, Schneider). This would be the Christian equivalent of the warning to the Israelites as they entered Jericho, "Guard yourselves from [*phylassein apo*] the accursed thing," i.e., what was dedicated to God through destruction (Josh 6:18). In *T. Joseph* 6:5 the patriarch refuses the food the Egyptian seductress has put before him because it is filled with enchantments, and he does not wish "to come near to idols." Earlier (4:5) she had promised to leave her idols and to walk in the Law of the Lord, but she had not remained faithful to her promise. **(5)** "Idols" stands for the mystery religions and their practices. Where Rev 2:20 warns against food dedicated to idols, there is a reference to Jezebel, a prophetess who was teaching such things; and often she has been identified as the spokeswoman of a mystery cult or a sibyl. The passages in I John about knowing God (1:6a; 2:4a) and about seeing Him (3:2) have been thought by some to be aimed at the claims of the devotees of the mystery religions. **(6)** "Idols" refers to gnostic ideologies or philosophies, e.g., the theory of Cerinthus (Appendix II below). Often the proponents of this explanation would identify the secessionist adversaries of I John as gnostics; and they invoke Col 2:8, which speaks of deceptive philosophy and human tradition, involved with the elemental spirits of the universe. Colossae, we are reminded, was in the Ephesus region. **(7)** Jewish worship in the Jerusalem Temple might be considered idolatrous by Johannine Christians who thought that God was no longer worshiped either on Gerizim or in Jerusalem but in Spirit and truth (John 4:20–24). Hebrews, which has affinities with Johannine thought, proclaims that the cultic practices under the Law were but a shadow of the true realities and warns against backsliding (Heb 10). **(8)** Sins of various kinds could be "idols" (Böcher, Nauck, Schnackenburg). This would agree with the immediate context, since 5:18 warns against sin. In *T. Reuben* 4:5–6 we hear: "Guard [*phylassein*] all things that I have commanded you, and you shall not sin. For a pit to the soul is fornication, separating it from God and bringing it near to idols." The attractions of this world are cited in I John 2:15–17 as part of a wider campaign against sin and evil. **(9)** "Idols" may be a figurative expression describing anything that takes the place of God. Nunn, "First Epistle" 301–3, counterposes *eidōlon* to the *alēthinos*, "true," of 5:20b,20e, so that the "idols" are "unrealities" or "false appearances" and can cover religion, wealth, sex, power, etc. For some imaginative commentators the author is almost anticipating Francis Bacon, who spoke of the the Idols of the Tribe, the Idols of the Cave, the Idols of the Market Place, and the Idols of the Theater. Such an interpretation lends itself to polemic applications. Plummer, *Epistles* 129, asks disapprovingly, "Is it reasonable to suppose that S. John was warning his readers against 'systematising influences of scholastic theology; theories of self-vaunting orthodoxy' . . . or against superstitious honour paid to the 'Madonna, or saints, or pope, or priesthood'?" **(10)** Under idolatry there may be a reference to the secession from the Community, which has led former brothers to a different understanding of God reflected in Christ (Balz, Houlden, Ska, B. Weiss) and to underplaying the importance of moral behavior in their own lives—a secession that makes them children of the devil. In Philo, *Moses* 2, 32 ⅌171, Moses tells the Levites to slay those who have left "the true [*alēthēs*] God and made false gods." Similar language is used for those who have seceded from the Qumran community and who were not going over to Gentile ways but opting for another understanding of God's revelation to Israel. With polemic very close to that of I John, the Qumran psalmist denounces "the teachers of lies and false prophets" who, in speaking to God's people, substitute smooth things for the Law: "They walk in stubbornness of heart and seek You among idols" (1QH 4:9–11,15). The Damascus Rule (CD 20:8–10) speaks of "those who repudiate and set up idols in their hearts . . . they shall have no share in the House of the Law." The Community Rule (1QS 2:11–12, 16–17) proclaims: "Cursed be the person who enters this Covenant while walking among the idols of his heart and who sets up before himself the stumbling-block of sin so that he may backslide. . . . He shall be cut off from the midst of all the sons of light; and because he has turned aside from God on account of his idols and his stumbling-block of sin . . . his lot shall be among those who are cursed forever." (Indeed, as a deduction from such expressions D. N. Freedman suggests that "idols" came to designate the people who pursued such idolatry [Jer 2:5], i.e., the secessionists themselves.) Some scholars who hold (8) above cite these texts as showing that idols are the equivalent of sins, but the sins are idolatrous precisely because they lead the person out of the Community. The several references to a "stumbling-block" alongside "idols" are interesting in light of the use of the same term in I John 2:10 in the dualism between the Community and the secessionists, between those who love their brothers and those who do not. Elsewhere, a NT passage (II Cor 6:14–7:1), which has been regarded as a quotation from a (lost) Qumran writing, lines up on one side righteousness, light, Christ, and God; and on the other side iniquity, darkness, Beliar, and idols. The terms "iniquity," "darkness," and "Evil One [= Beliar]" are associated with the secessionists in I John, and so it is logical that the "idols" of 5:21 share this association.

Among the above interpretations some are based on guesses that the recipients of I John were largely Gentiles who would be tempted to return to paganism (※※2,3,4,5) or were Jews (7). Others are based on attempts to identify the adversaries of I John with known systems of thought (※※1,5,6). Interpretations (8) and (9) are the most general, so general, in fact, that one wonders why the author would have considered it important to end his work by such an emphasis. A fault in many of these interpretations is that they posit an abrupt change of topic from 5:18–20, which dealt with the theology of the secession —a change all the more difficult to justify when traditional Jewish usage would make "idols" a perfect antithesis to "the one true God" of 5:20. In my judgment interpretation (10) makes perfect sense of this antithesis, and it connects 5:21 tightly to the mention of sin, the Evil One, and the world in 5:18–19. Rather than demanding any extraneous guesses about the identity of the audience or the adversaries, this interpretation relies on information supplied by I John itself, namely, that there are false prophets and liars who have left the Community because they have a false notion of Jesus Christ, and who, because they do not possess Jesus Christ, do not know or possess God. They belong to the world and seek by their teaching to seduce the author's adherents. The warning "Guard yourselves against idols" resembles other I John warnings: "Have no love for the world" (2:15); "You have no need for anyone to teach you" (2:27); "Do not believe every Spirit; rather put these Spirits to a test to see which one belongs to God" (4:1). The examples cited under (10) make it clear that, in speaking of joining the secession and accepting its theology as "going after idols," the author would have been intelligible to a Christian Community whose language and thought had Jewish parallels—a background we have found in both GJohn and I John.

Some later Greek MSS., the Byzantine tradition, and the Clementine Vulgate read "Amen" at the end of 5:21, an addition that appears in various witnesses at the end of GJohn and II John as well. In the NT a concluding "Amen" is genuine as part of the blessing in Gal 6:18, and is debatable in II Pet 3:18. Elsewhere it is a liturgical addition, influenced by the custom of reading the Scriptures in church services.

COMMENT

In entitling this unit, "The Conclusion," the same title I gave to John 20:30–31 in ABJ 29A (1053), I have made a judgment about the nature of the last verses of I John.[1] The reason for and significance of that judgment can be seen by answering two questions.

SHOULD THIS UNIT BEGIN WITH V. 13 OR WITH V. 14?[2] Those who join v. 13 to what precedes and start this unit with v. 14 include Bonsirven, Bultmann, Chaine, and Dodd. Several arguments are offered for this view. (1) The theme of eternal life in v. 13 is related to what precedes in vv. 11–12, as is the theme of believing in the Son of God (vv. 5,10,12). However, the presence of a transitional verse that continues the theme of a preceding unit while introducing a new unit is characteristic of the Johannine writers (see p. 119 above). The real issue then is whether v. 13 is also related to what follows, for I have normally placed such a transitional passage as the opening of a unit. (2) From the pattern of GJohn where a Conclusion in 20:30–31 is followed by a separate Epilogue in ch. 21, it is argued that the similarity of I John 5:13 to John 20:30–31 implies that 5:14–21 is a separate Epilogue like John 21. This is an important argument, but it assumes that the author of I John knew and patterned himself on the final form of GJohn as it now stands with the added ch. 21.

Many more scholars think that v. 13 introduces the unit that follows, and that the whole of 5:13–21 serves as the Conclusion of the work (Alexander, Balz, Brooke, Bruce, Hauck, Houlden, Marshall, Plummer, Schnackenburg, Schneider, THLJ, B. Weiss, Westcott, Williams, Windisch, NEB, RSV). They too have arguments for their view. (1) A sharp change of style is inaugurated by v. 13. In the unit beginning there the first person is dominant, much more than in the preceding lines. In particular, the unexpected singular "I" of 5:13 (last used 2:26) serves notice that the author is speaking directly to the "you" of the audience, a feature that reappears by inclusion in 5:21. A remarkable combination of

---

[1] I am implicitly arguing that it is not an Epilogue comparable to John 21, composed by a redactor. Nor do I think that Postscript (Dodd) is appropriate, since I do not judge I John to be a letter. This Conclusion is a statement of the author's purpose.

[2] An occasional scholar, like Stott, agrees with Hort (see A. Westcott, "Divisions" 485) that the finale should begin with v. 18 where the pattern changes. I regard that change as indication of a subdivision.

pastoral concern and of confidence in the state of the true believer marks
vv. 13–21. Overall the style of 13–17 is much more prosaic than the
semipoetic style of the verses that precede.[8] Verses 18–20 may be close to
the poetic format and to the christological reflection encountered elsewhere in I John, but vv. 13–17 are not. (2) Themes from v. 13 are continued through 14–21. The author says in v. 13 that he has written "that
you may know." The "know" motif continues in 5:15,18,19,20. Verse 13
stresses eternal life, a theme found in 5:16,17,20. Verse 13 speaks of believing "in the name of the Son of God," and v. 20 mentions the Son (of
God) twice, again by way of inclusion. As for a counterargument against
(2) in the preceding paragraph, it is true that there is a parallelism between I John 5:13 and John 20:31, especially when the two verses are
translated literally:

5:13: These things I have written to you so that you may know that
you possess eternal life—you, the ones believing in the name of the
Son of God.

20:31: These things have been written so that you may believe that
Jesus is the Christ, the Son of God, and that believing you may possess life in his name.

Nevertheless, this parallelism does not necessarily mean that I John 5:
14–21 is an Epilogue, for there is virtually nothing in common between
this I John passage and John 21, which serves as the Epilogue for GJohn,
following 20:31. One can argue more plausibly that I John 5:13–21 is a
unified, expanded reflection related to the Conclusion of GJohn
(20:31–32), just as I John 1:1–4 is a reflection on the Prologue of
GJohn (1:1–18).[4]

Is 5:14–21 THE WORK OF A REDACTOR? One of Bultmann's main arguments for joining v. 13 to what precedes is that it was the original ending
of I John and that the Ecclesiastical Redactor subsequently added the following verses.[5] (Actually Bultmann has to admit that the style of

---

[8] Some authorities (JB, Malatesta) would set up these verses in a poetic format
similar to the one I have been using, but they differ radically from each other in assigning lines, showing that 14–17 do not easily lend themselves to such format (any
more than did John 20:30–31). For instance, Malatesta assigns 4 lines to v. 14, 5 to
v. 15, while JB assigns 3 lines (very differently divided) to v. 14 and 2 to v. 15.
Strangely, they agree on assigning 6 lines to v. 16, a verse that is prosaic by any
standards. In the long run, however, the assignment of poetic format in the Johannine writings is a most inexact science for all of us.

[4] See INTRODUCTION, footnote 210. Although a redactor may have added the Prologue to GJohn, in my judgment the Prologue existed as a hymn before the redactor's work.

[5] There is no MS. evidence that I John ever existed without 5:14–21; and both
Tertullian, De pudicitia 19,27 (CC 2, 1323), and Clement of Alexandria, Stromata
2, 15 (GCS 15, 148), know 5:16–18, which means that these verses belonged to I

5:14–21 is not uniform; for vv. 18–20 are a passable imitation of the Johannine style of the author, while 21 is quite unJohannine, in Bultmann's estimation.) Bultmann's arguments on small details were discussed and found wanting in the NOTES. In fact he has had little following in this part of his theory, and has been convincingly refuted by Noack, *Tradition* 133–46 (see INTRODUCTION V D2b). Bultmann's overall argument is that 5:14–21 does not fit the pattern of alternating christological and paraenetic patterns he finds elsewhere in I John; but that pattern is not nearly so regular as Bultmann would make it.

On the other side of the picture I John 5:14–21 shares many themes with the rest of I John.[6] The theme of asking with confidence and receiving (5:14–15) is found in 3:21–22. In the NOTES I have argued that the sin that is deadly (5:16–17) is a reference to the sin of secession condemned in 2:19; it is not a reflection of the second-century church practice that Bultmann advances as an indication of the Ecclesiastical Redactor's interest. The pattern of three "We know" sentences (5:18–20) is similar to the pattern of three "If we boast" sentences in 1:6,8,10, and the pattern of three "The person who claims" sentences in 2:4,6,9. The contents of the sentences in 5:18–20 are typical of the dualism of I John, e.g., between God and the Evil One (see 2:13–14; 3:10,12). The theme of perfectionist sinlessness (5:18a) echoes 3:6,9. Bultmann makes much of the warning against idols in 5:21 as being strange to I John. However, in the NOTE I showed that setting up idols and walking among them is Jewish language for secession from the people of God, and the imperative style of "Guard yourselves against idols" is not unlike "Have no love for the world" of 2:15.[7]

There is solid evidence, then, for treating 5:13–21 as a Conclusion written by the author himself to explain his motive for composing I John. He wishes to strengthen readers in their christology since only a faith that is correct christologically gives life. Throughout the work his attacks on the secessionists have been provoked by the danger they presented by proselytizing his adherents. He has struggled to prevent further erosion among those adherents, and he draws his work to an end by stressing the positive values of their Community faith.

As for the interior structure of 5:13–21, a symmetrical arrangement is sometimes proposed (Westcott, THLJ):

John even before the evidence of the oldest MSS. However, the same can be said of John 21, and there most scholars agree with Bultmann in detecting a redactor's hand.

[6] Bultmann would dismiss these similarities as imitation of the author by the Ecclesiastical Redactor.

[7] Of course, Bultmann, *Epistles* 32, thinks that 2:15–17 "has perhaps been inserted by the redactor."

13:   Aim (transitional verse)
14–17:   Confidence about spiritual action
18–20:   Confidence about spiritual knowledge
21:   Warning

Attractive as that is, it is not clear that v. 13 can be separated from vv. 14–17, since it introduces the theme of confidence that is expanded there. A glance at v. 15 will show that themes of knowing and possessing reappear from v. 13, as does the theme of asking from v. 14, and all of this serves to lead into vv. 16–17. The separate character of 18–20 is clear from the triple "We know" pattern, even though the theme of sin connects those verses to what precedes.[8] The pattern lends an oratorical touch to the assurance that "we" are on God's side both ethically and in the understanding of His Son. Despite all this assurance the author cannot refrain from a last word of warning to his "Little Children" (5:21) lest they lose all they possess by following the secessionists in their false understanding of the Son and thus of the Father, an understanding that is tantamount to idolatry. Recognizing that 5:13 leads into 5:14–17, while 5:21 concludes 5:18–20, we find two subsections.

A. Confidence in Possessing Life despite Sin (5:13–17)

The last unit ended by discussing the dualistic possibility of possessing the Son and possessing life or not possessing the Son and not possessing life—the same kind of covenant choice Moses offered in Deuteronomy 30. But then Moses turned to Israel and continued, "Be strong and of good courage, . . . for it is the Lord your God who goes with you" (31:6), and he gave the same encouragement to Joshua (31:8,23). Then we are told, "Moses finished writing all the words of the Law in a book" (31:24). And so it is not surprising to find the author of I John, after he has presented the choice of possessing or not possessing life, now offering words of encouragement as part of a statement as to why he has written this work.[9] Several times previously, after he has described dualistically the situation vis-à-vis the secessionists, his pastoral sense has led him to reassure his readers that they are on the right side and hence are not the object of his polemics.[10] (Nevertheless, if there were no danger that they

---

[8] The seeming contradiction between seeing one's brother sinning (v. 16) and the statement that no one begotten by God commits sin (v. 18) is no greater than the seeming contradiction between 1:8–9 and 3:6,9.

[9] I do not claim that the author is consciously copying Deuteronomy, but simply that his is a pattern illustrated and encouraged by Deuteronomy.

[10] See 2:12–14, after the two sets of debates against the secessionist-inspired positions in 1:5–2:2 and 2:3–11. Also 2:20–21, which comes after the warning about the secessionists as Antichrists in 2:18–19.

might slip over to the other side, he would not be writing.) Here, picking up the vocabulary from 5:11–12 about the choice of possessing life in God's Son, the author says that he has written this so that they may know that they possess this eternal life by believing in God's Son (5:13).[11]

The parallelism with John 20:31 cited a few pages back is instructive, for that Johannine passage too betrays the self-reflective desire to justify what has been written. There the evangelist said he was writing "so that you may believe . . . and that believing you may possess life in his name." While GJohn is not clear on whether the readers already believe (ABJ 29A, 1056), there is no doubt that I John is addressed to those who believe; and so the author expresses his purpose in terms of their *knowing* rather than in terms of believing. Several times previously he has stopped to reassure his readers about their knowing (2:3,13b,14d; 4:13), and this fits in with the thesis I have advocated throughout that he is appealing to them from what they experienced and learned at the time when they entered the Community. (I mentioned on pp. 279, 320 that the language of "knowing" was inherited from Jeremiah's and Ezekiel's promises about the New Covenant.) At the beginning of I John the author expressed his writing purpose in the language of joy (1:4), literally, "We are writing these things so that our joy may be fulfilled." I suggested in the NOTE there that a "joy" received at the believers' entrance into the Community was to grow and be fulfilled by living in *koinōnia* with God, Christ, and other members of the Johannine Community. Thus the beginning and ending of I John phrase the purpose of writing in only slightly different ways: if the readers remain loyal to what they were taught and received "from the beginning," they will continue to be God's children possessing His life. This context of entrance into the Community probably explains why the author defines his adherents as those "who believe in *the name* of the Son of God" (5:13; also John 20:31). As we have seen before, "Christ's name" is associated with "the beginning" (2:12–13) because at the time when they were baptized, Christians made a profession of faith in Jesus by giving him a name or title, e.g., "Jesus is the Christ, the Son of God" (see NOTE on 2:12b).

The atmosphere of confidence becomes explicit in 5:14 as the author shifts from "you" to "we" in order to argue from the status shared by Johannine Christians. He has said that they have eternal life; this means that they are God's children, and so they can stand in the presence of God and expect to be heard. Once again this may be a common Christian motif derived from baptismal catechesis; for Paul says in Rom 8:15, "You did not receive the spirit of slavery to fall back into fear, but you

---

[11] In the NOTE on 5:13a I have agreed with those scholars who contend that "I have written this" refers to the whole work and not exclusively to the preceding verses.

have received the spirit of sonship, in which we cry out, '*Abba*, Father.'"
Being able to address God confidently in prayer may have been the primitive Christian community's way of assuring itself that it was God's chosen people (see Acts 12:5). In I John 5:14 it is specified that the prayer be according to God's will. Some scholars think that this condition reflects people's experience that Jesus' promise, "Ask and you shall receive" (John 16:24), was not always fulfilled.[12] However, the author means that assurance in prayer flows from a union with God that is brought about by oneness of will between the petitioner and the petitioned. This is illustrated in Jesus' own prayer: He is one with the Father (John 10:30, and so he can say, "Father, I thank you because you heard me; of course, I knew that you always hear me" (11:41–42). The promise of Jesus in 15:7 also catches this nuance: "If you remain in me and my words remain in you, ask for whatever you want and it will be done for you."

Nevertheless, even if petitioning according to God's will is presupposed in all Johannine thought about prayer, why does the author choose to bring "according to His will" to the fore here? It is because his general assurance that prayers will be heard is only a preparation for the theme of praying about sin (5:16–17). The author has encouraged his readers by stating that they possess eternal life; he now goes farther by assuring them that even if they sin, that need not destroy their life, provided that they pray for one another.[13] He presupposes what he has already said in 2:1–2: "But if anyone does sin, we have a Paraclete in the Father's presence, Jesus Christ, the one who is just; and he himself is an atonement for our sins, and not only for our sins but also for the whole world." If Jesus can pray as a Paraclete in the Father's presence, the author now affirms that the other children of God can stand in His presence (5:14) and ask, and "life will be given to the sinner" (5:16). The readers know that they possess eternal life (5:13); so also must they know that they possess this power of asking (5:15) and thus giving life.[14] As Schnackenburg, *Johannesbriefe* 275–76, points out, it was well established in Judaism that the great saints could intercede for sinners, e.g., the patriarchs (Gen 18:23–32; 20:7), Moses (Exod 32:11–14; 34:8–9), the prophets (Amos 7:1–6; II Kings 19:4; Jer 42:2–4), and the martyrs (II Macc 7:37–38).

---

[12] As I pointed out in the NOTE on 5:14b, there are conditions in almost all the Johannine sayings on prayer; see also Mark's condition (11:23) of not doubting when one asks.

[13] The author does not go so far as to command the prayer; since sin is presented as an anomaly in Johannine Christian life, he may have felt that prayer for the sinning brother cannot be made mandatory upon those who might be repelled by it.

[14] The Greek text of 5:16b (see NOTE) is not clear as to whether God or the petitioner gives the life; in any case the petitioner would have the power only from and through God. Bultmann, *Epistles* 86, denies that intercessory prayer is mentioned elsewhere in I John or in John 16; but it is not clear how he can be so sure about the nature of prayer that is not specified in the texts.

But in the community of "saints" of the NT, ordinary Christians pray for one another with this effectiveness (see I Thess 5:25; Heb 13:18), especially in terms of the forgiveness of sins (James 5:15; also *I Clem.* 56:1: "Let us then also intercede for those who have fallen into any transgression").

The main purpose of 5:16–17, then, is positive: through prayer, sin need not be deadly for the believer. Against secessionist ethical indifference the author has had to stress the need for avoiding sin (3:6,9), and so his readers who had experience of sin might well be tempted to despair.[15] But amidst his reassurances the author mentions also a deadly sin or sin unto death (5:16) about which one should not pray.[16] In the NOTES I discussed at length various theories about this sin; for even though the author's reference to it is almost parenthetical, it has been the subject of endless discussion. The best solution by far is that it is the sin of the secessionists, i.e., refusing to believe that Jesus is the Christ come in the flesh. A refusal to believe kept people away from Jesus during his lifetime and kept people away from Christianity during the early mission; now it has led to a schism within the Johannine Community. The author's adherents have been encouraged to pray for brothers and sisters whom they know to be sinners, but the author adds in passing that he is not talking about former brothers and sisters who have opted to be children of the devil by going out to the world that prefers darkness to light. Since Jesus refused to pray for such a world (John 17:9), the author's adherents should not pray for those who belong to the world (I John 4:5). When his readers came to faith and joined the Johannine Community of "brothers," they passed from death to life (I John 3:14). By leaving the Community the secessionists have shown that they hate the "brothers" and have reversed the process by passing from life to death.[17] In that sense theirs is a sin that is unto death. By discouraging prayer for them[18] and by ordering that they not be greeted or received into the house (II John 10–11), the author is seeking to quarantine the secessionists so

[15] Drumwright, "Problem" 58: "There was a large question as to the genuineness of the experience of grace itself."

[16] I think it sheer casuistry to contend that the author is simply not encouraging prayers about the deadly sin; the whole tone is to discourage such prayer.

[17] As I indicated in the NOTES, it is not clear whether the author would admit that they ever had life, since he says that the secessionists never really belonged to the Community (2:19); but certainly he would use the language of death for their present condition.

[18] Since secession is a new experience in Johannine circles, the audience, which does not seem to need an explanation of what the author means by deadly sin, might still not know enough not to pray for the secessionists. In James 5:15,19–20, after the reference to the prayer of faith that will forgive a sick man's sins, the author says, "If anyone among you wanders from the truth and someone brings him back, let it be known that whoever brings back a sinner from the error of his way will save his soul from death and cover a multitude of sins."

that they cannot further contaminate his adherents. While this may strike us as bigoted and scarcely Christian, it stands in a lineage of OT references to sins too heinous to pray about and NT references to the sin against the Holy Spirit that will not be forgiven (pp. 616–17). It is a logical (even if unhappy) reflection of Johannine dualism in which "the world lies in the grasp of the Evil One," so that if one does not belong to God, one belongs to the devil by choice (I John 5:19).

B. *The Known Privileges of Christians and a Warning to Guard Them* (5:18–21)

Solemnly the author now proclaims three times, "We know."[19] Although he has insisted throughout on the need to confess one's belief (2:23; 4:2,15), he ends his missive with assurances based on knowledge. He exemplifies his own contention that the best defense against secessionist teaching is the principle: "All of you have knowledge . . . you do know the truth . . . you have no need for anyone to teach you" (2:20,21,27). In fact, everything he says in 5:18–20 has already been said earlier in I John.[20] Nevertheless, he does not mean "We know" simply in the sense of "we have already seen." Nor would I agree with Brooke, *Epistles* 148, that the knowledge is intuitive, flowing from the nature of God and of divine life. He is referring once again to what has been known from "the beginning" of Christian experience, what was part of the catechesis learned as the readers entered the Community, what was part of the teaching associated with having an anointing from the Holy One. Particularly noteworthy are the three privileges of Christian existence that "We know," namely, the privilege of having been begotten by God (v. 18), of belonging to God (19), and of knowing the true God (20). Early in I John the author challenged the secessionists on these very privileges (1:6; 2:4,6); he concludes by insisting that his own adherents can be sure of them and also of their respective effects: sinlessness, freedom from the Evil One, indwelling in God and His Son.

The first "We know" (v. 18) relates sinlessness to the status of the Christian as one begotten by God who is protected from the Evil One. It virtually repeats 3:9a, "No one who has been begotten by God acts sinfully," with an added touch from 4:4: "He who is in you is greater than

[19] The presence of a similar "We know" in John 21:24, which is the work of a redactor, is advanced as an argument for detecting the hand of a redactor in I John 5:14–21. At most it shows that the redactor of GJohn shared some ideas with I John and may even have known the ending of I John if he wrote after that work.

[20] For Bultmann, "Redaktion" 196, vv. 18–20 are the Ecclesiastical Redactor's summary of I John. It is more plausible that they are the author's own summary, and the minor variations of style fit within the range of Johannine fluctuation.

he who is in the world." Christian sinlessness is not that of a preexistent soul that has been trapped in a material world through accident of birth, but a status given to the Christian by God through Jesus. Some who argue for different writers in I John find confirmation in the contrast between vv. 16–17 which make provision for brothers who sin and v. 18 which says that a Christian brother does not commit sin. However, this is just more of the (single) author's complex view of Christian life that has continued throughout I John and was discussed in detail on pp. 430–32. Against the secessionists' form of once-for-all perfectionism (which logically causes them to deny sin) the author has insisted that Christians do sin but still have hope because the blood of Christ supplies forgiveness (1:8–2:2). But that pastoral assurance does not reflect his vision of what true Christian life is. In this eschatological period God is preparing a sinless generation of believers; and where the vitality of divine begetting is allowed to manifest himself, it rules out sin,[21] as affirmed in 3:6,8–9. In those passages sin was shown to be the realm of the devil, the final Iniquity of the last time, while sinlessness was the mark of being on God's side. And so it is quite logical that here the author associates freedom from sin with protection from the Evil One. In a sense, then, Christians have a twofold confidence: if they sin, the prayers of brothers and sisters will give them life; but the very fact of divine begetting should eventually lead them not to sin at all.[22]

The second "We know" (v. 19) distinguishes between the Johannine Christians who belong to God and the whole world, which lies in the grasp of the Evil One, thus rephrasing the distinction in 3:8–10 between God's children and the devil's children, and the distinction in 4:4–5 between those who belong to God and those who belong to the world. Some think that 5:19 says no more than 5:18;[23] but it makes clear that the

---

[21] Some would stress the force of the perfect in 5:18a ("No one who has been begotten"): The begetting took place in the past but is exercising its continuing force in keeping the Christian free from sin. But the aorist ("the one begotten") is used in 5:18b and may also refer to the Christian, and so the dependence on the exact connotation of tenses is dubious. Nevertheless, on the basis of 5:19 which refers to our belonging to God, it is clear that the sinlessness of the Christian is traced to continuing divine activity.

[22] In the NOTE on 5:18b I argued against the thesis that "the one begotten by God" is Christ; but those who opt for such an interpretation see a third reason for confidence: Christ himself protects the Christian. In my judgment the ongoing role of Christ is more that of a Paraclete for sinners than of a protector for the sinless. In John 17:12,15 Jesus has kept his own safe while he has been with them, but he turns the protective role over to God when he leaves the earth.

[23] There is a parallelism between 5:18 and 5:19, but it should be carefully analyzed, for it favors reading 18b as a reference to the Christian (rather than to Christ). Lines 18b and 19a refer to the protected status of the Christian as begotten by and belonging to God; lines 18c and 19b refer to the machinations of the Evil One.

efforts of the Evil One against the Johannine Christians[24] in 5:18 are not a matter of personal temptation. A dualism between the world and the realm of God is involved. The Evil One is the Prince of this world (John 12:31; 14:30; 16:11) who, although he was said to have no hold on Jesus, is now feared to be gaining a hold on members of the Community through the secession. In 5:19 it also becomes clearer that the sin in mind in 5:18a (also in 5:16c) is primarily that of the secessionist children of the devil with their doctrinal and moral faults: They have gone out into the world (4:1d) and belong to the world (4:5a). The true believers in Jesus do not belong to this world (John 17:16), for "the world" described in John 16:8–11 is one that refuses to believe in Jesus. The secessionists by denying that *Jesus* is the Christ (I John 2:22) have added themselves to it. In discussing the dualism in 4:1–6 (p. 487), we saw its proximity to the dualism of the Dead Sea Scroll community. Similarly 5:19 is reminiscent of 1QS 3:17–21, which places all human beings under the influence of the spirits of truth and iniquity: "All the sons of iniquity are under the rule of the angel of darkness."

The third "We know" (v. 20) reminds us of the role of the Son of God in all this: He is the one who has been able to give insight to know the one true God because he himself is true God. We are not in the grasp of the Evil One only because "we belong to God" (5:19a), but also because "we are in His Son, Jesus Christ" (5:20d). I John contrasts dependencies in terms of "belonging to" (being from) God and devil (3:8–10); it also contrasts spheres of activity in terms of "lying in the grasp of the Evil One" and "being in God and in His Son." The idea that the Son has "given us insight [*dianoia*] to know" is comparable to 2:27e: "His [Christ's] anointing teaches you about all things." There is an interesting mutuality expressed in ch. 5 of I John: God has testified on behalf of His Son (5:9), while the Son has given insight to know the Father (5:20). The author is quite far from a Platonic view where human beings must ascend to heaven to know the real or the true; rather we know because the Son of God has descended. The moment of the giving of the *dianoia* or revelatory insight is surely the moment when the author's readers became Christians,[25] and 5:20 echoes in several ways covenantal vocabulary and imagery. God is referred to as "the One who is true," even as *'ĕmet*, "truth, fidelity," is the primary attribute of the covenanting God of the

---

[24] Although the author's statements are applicable to Christians in general, he is speaking to his own adherents who constitute the Johannine Community and who are threatened by the Evil One through the secession.

[25] In I Pet 1:13, a passage often related to baptismal preaching, those who have received the good news foretold by the prophets are told "to gird up" their *dianoia;* and II Pet 3:1 says that the letter is written to rouse their sincere *dianoia*. This may mean that for Christians *dianoia* is the faculty of knowledge enlightened by revelation. Alfaro, "Cognitio Dei" 88–90, argues that *dianoia* is a faculty.

OT; but now in Johannine dualism the truth of God sets Him off against the Evil One who is a liar (John 8:44; I John 2:22). As we have seen before (pp. 279–80), knowing God is a motif fulfilling the promise of Jeremiah about a renewed covenant where "they shall all know me from the least to the greatest" (Jer 31:33–34). And this is not taught knowledge but flows from intimacy.[26] The word *dianoia* (which Bultmann regards as a sign that another writer is involved) reflects covenant background; for frequently in the LXX it translates *lēb,* "heart," e.g., in the Jeremiah passage: "I shall put my laws into their *dianoia.*"[27] In the covenant picture of the NT Jesus Christ plays a major role alongside God, to the point that I John 5:20e dares to call him "the true God and eternal life." Many commentators point out that surely the author does not yet mean what Nicaea means by "true God of true God," even though the reference in 5:20 to both Father and Son as "true" may have led to that formula (see p. 228 above). THLJ 130 states: "It does not mean to say that Christ and God are one and the same being, but that in Christ we have to do with God." That may be an insufficient evaluation of Johannine christology where the terms "God" and "true" are equally applicable to Father and Son, for we know God when we know Jesus Christ. The difference between Father and Son is that, while Jesus Christ is the life (John 1:4), he "has life because of the Father" (6:57)[28]—Jesus may be God but he is not the Father. The fact that both GJohn (20:28) and I John end by confessing Jesus as God shows how important this was in Johannine thought—and not simply in an abstract way, for in each case the confession of Jesus as God is followed by a mention of the (eternal) life that such belief brings to his followers.[29]

Verse 21 is the negative counterpart of the three positive affirmations in 5:18–20. The covenant background shows that there is a connection between "the true God" of 5:20 and the "idols" of 5:21 when the latter is

---

[26] Such covenant background makes intelligible why the epistolary author shifts from knowing the One who is true (20b) to being in the One who is true (20c). Both Jeremiah and Ezekiel (37:26–27) stress the indwelling of the divine gift (Law or spirit) in the renewed covenant.

[27] The demand for a new standard of moral behavior in the OT covenant passages suggests that the I John statement that the Son "has given us insight to know the One who is true" involves a way of life as well as an understanding of Jesus as the true God. It involves the ethical and christological elements that have been a key to the struggle between the author and the secessionists.

[28] As indicated in the NOTE on 5:18b, however, the Johannine writings never say clearly that the Son was begotten by the Father.

[29] Although the author has attacked the secessionists for an overly high christology, namely, the contention that Jesus Christ did not come in the flesh (4:2), he does not refute them by a low christology. For the author the Jesus Christ who has come in the flesh is true God. The final statements in I John 5:20 are almost a rearrangement of John 17:3: "Eternal life consists in this: that they know you, the one true God, and Jesus Christ, the one whom you sent."

understood in terms of the secession (see NOTE on 5:21, evaluating the many theories). The covenanted people of Israel were warned many times against leaving the one true God to go after idols, and against abandoning His commandments for the permissive life of the worshippers of the false gods of the surrounding nations. In the author's judgment, the secessionists are trying to seduce his adherents to leave the covenanted Community and its understanding of the God who was revealed in Jesus Christ come in the flesh, and to adopt a false life-style in which commandments are not important and sin is not a source of worry. This is the contemporary form of going after idols, for the secessionists have themselves become "idols."

BIBLIOGRAPHY PERTINENT TO I JOHN 5:13–21

Bauernfeind, O., "Die Fürbitte angesichts der 'Sünde zum Tode,'" in *Von der Antike zum Christentum* (V. Schultze Festgabe; Stettin: Fischer & Schmidt, 1931) 43–54.

Dammers, A. H., "Hard Sayings—II: I John 5. 16ff.," *Theology* 66 (1963) 370–72.

Francis, O., "Form."

Herkenrath, J., "Sünde zum Tode," in *Aus Theologie und Philosophie*, ed. T. Steinbüchel and T. Müncker (F. Tillmann Festschrift; Dusseldorf: Patmos, 1950) 119–38.

Kilpatrick, G. D., "Idioms," on 5:20.

Klöpper, A., "Zur Lehre von der Sünde im 1. Johannesbrief, Erläuterung von 5,16 fin.," ZWT 43 (1900) 585–602.

Nauck, W., "Das Problem der Redaktion," *Tradition*, esp. 133–46.

Reynolds, S. M., "The Sin unto Death and Prayers for the Dead," *Reformation Review* 20 (1973) 130–39.

Scholer, D. M., "Sins Within and Sins Without: An Interpretation of 1 John 5:16–17," in *Current Issues in Biblical Interpretation*, ed. G. F. Hawthorne (M. C. Tenney Festschrift; Grand Rapids: Eerdmans, 1975) 230–46.

Segond, A., "1re Epître de Jean, chap. 5:18–20," RHPR 45 (1965) 349–51.

Ska, J.-L., "'Petits enfants, prenez garde aux idoles' 1 Jn 5,21," NRT 101 (1979) 860–74.

Trudinger, P., "Concerning Sins, Mortal and Otherwise. A Note on 1 John 5,16–17," *Biblica* 52 (1971) 541–42.

The Second Epistle

of John

A letter from the Presbyter to a church warning against any reception of secessionist teachers who are spreading christological and moral errors (of the type described more fully in I John).

12. The Second Epistle of John

OPENING FORMULA:
Sender: 1 The Presbyter,
Addressee: To an Elect Lady and to her children:
   b In truth I love you—*c* and not only I but also those who have come to know the truth. 2 This love is based on the truth that abides in us *b* and will be with us forever.
Greeting: 3 With us there will be grace, mercy, and peace *b* from God the Father and from the Father's Son, Jesus Christ, *c* in truth and love.

BODY OF LETTER:
   4 It gave me much joy to find some of your children walking in truth, *b* just as we received a commandment from the Father.
   5 But now, my Lady, I would make a request of you—*b* it is not as if I were writing you some new commandment; *c* rather it is a commandment we have had from the beginning: *d Let us love one another.* 6 Now this is love: *b* that we walk according to His commandments. *c* That is the commandment. *d* As you heard it from the beginning, *e* so must you walk in it.
   7 For many deceivers have gone out into the world, *b* men who do not confess Jesus Christ coming in the flesh. *c* There is the Deceiver! There is the Antichrist! 8 Look out yourselves that you do not lose what we have worked for; *b* you must receive your reward in full. 9 Anyone who is so "progressive" that he does not remain rooted in the teaching of Christ *b* does not possess God, *c* while anyone who remains rooted in the teaching *d* possesses both the Father and the Son. 10 If anyone comes to you *b* who does not bring this teaching, *c* do not receive him into the house *d* and greet him; 11 for whoever greets him shares in his evil deeds.
   12 Though I have much more to write you, *b* I cannot be bothered

with paper and ink. °Instead, I hope to come to you ᵈand have a heart-to-heart talk, °so that our joy may be fulfilled.

CONCLUDING FORMULA:

13 The children of your Elect Sister send you greetings.

NOTES

Title: "The Second Epistle of John." This work, which was known already in the mid-second century, began to be treated as canonical Scripture toward the end of the second century when it was accepted as a writing of John, son of Zebedee (INTRODUCTION I B). This history explains the title "Second of John" found in the great Greek biblical codices. The attribution reflects the custom of crediting NT works to apostles or to "apostolic men" (i.e., to those like Mark and Luke who were thought to be companions of the apostles). In some later codices, e.g., K, "Catholic" is added to the title of II John (INTRODUCTION I A). A more exact title drawn from the contents of the Epistle would have been: "The Epistle of the Presbyter to an Elect Lady."

In the *Hypotypōseis* (*Adumbrationes;* GCS 17, 215) of Clement of Alexandria, written *ca* A.D. 200, we find: "The Second Epistle of John which was written to virgins" (*ad virgines,* presumably translating the Greek *pros parthenous*). Since Clement continues by speaking of "a certain Babylonian woman named 'Electa,'" the adscription "to virgins" may stem from reflection upon "the Elect Lady" of II John 1 and her "Elect Sister" of v. 13. The specific mention in II John of the children of both women does not preclude their designation as "virgins" if they were understood to represent churches (as Clement indicates), for already in the mid-second century *Hermas Vis.* 4.2.1–2 described the church as a virgin. In an imaginative interpretation, Chapman, "Historical Setting" 528–33, argues that the "Babylonian" reference by Clement indicates that the church addressed in II John is Rome, as in the "Babylon" references of I Pet 5:13 and Rev 14–18. (One could then explain the Presbyter's statement that the Elect Lady is loved "by all those who have come to know the truth" in harmony with Ignatius' statement [*Romans,* Preface] that the Roman church was "preeminent in love.") For Chapman, II John is warning Rome about the coming of Cerinthians! (See Appendix II.) A different explanation of the adscription "to virgins" has been proposed by Zahn who thinks that *pros parthenous* (presumably found in the lost Greek of Clement) was a misinterpretation of *pros Parthous* and thus represents ancient evidence for the later theory directing the Epistle(s) of John "to the Parthians" (Appendix III). Others would reverse the relationship, theorizing that the title "to the Parthians," attested in the fourth century, was a corruption of the mysterious *pros parthenous.* In this obscure issue it may be useful to the reader to have the Latin translation of Clement's remarks in the *Adumbrationes*, which I have been rendering in English above:

> Secunda Iohannis epistola, quae ad virgines scripta est, simplicissima est. Scripta vero est ad quandam Babyloniam, Eclectam nomine, significat autem electionem ecclesiae sanctae (see INTRODUCTION above, footnote 17).

1a. *The Presbyter.* In the format of Hellenistic letters (Appendix V below), the Opening Formula (*Praescriptio*) supplied the identity of the sender, which in ordinary letters consisted simply of a personal name. In public or official letters the name might be accompanied by an identifying title, e.g., "Jonathan the high priest" (I Macc 12:6); "Arius king of the Spartans" (12:20); "Lucius consul of the Romans" (15:16). This is a normal practice also in NT letters where of the 13 Pauline Epistles and 4 other Catholic Epistles only 2 (I and II Thessalonians) use the personal names of the senders without some identifying title. In the others we find "apostle" (8 epistles), "servant" (3), "servant and apostle" (3), and "prisoner" (Philemon). Moving beyond the NT to the "Apostolic Fathers," we find the simple personal name used by Polycarp and by Ignatius ("who is also called Theophorus"). II and III John are our only Christian examples from this period (A.D. 50–150) of a sender giving a title or designation and no personal name. Although a few (Schwartz, E. Meyer) have mentioned the possibility that an original personal name was lost in transmission, this is an unlikely hypothesis for *two* letters. Rather, one may suppose that in a close-knit body of Christians the recipients would have known the personal name of the sender, but that the designation "the Presbyter" was customary or preferred by him, by them, or by both. (One may wonder whether titles of reverence were not a Johannine trait, for in GJohn such symbolically important figures as the Beloved Disciple and the mother of Jesus are never identified by personal name.) The theory that the letters are fictional and that their creator prefixed this title to make readers think that they came from an important figure in Asia Minor (e.g., John the Presbyter mentioned by Papias; see below) has been proposed by Hirsch; but then one might wonder why the creator did not go farther in his fiction and supply the personal name "John" or imitate common NT style by supplying the more impressive title "the Apostle."

What does the author mean by the self-designation *ho presbyteros*? Before reporting on five different explanations, let me survey two types of information that cast light on the question. The first is internal. What does the author describe himself as doing in II (and III) John that might illuminate his role as "the Presbyter"? In II John he can judge when one is walking in the truth according to God's command (v. 4); he can reiterate the commandment that "we have had from the beginning" (v. 5); and he can diagnose a christological error proposed by those who have not remained rooted in the teaching of Christ (vv. 7–9). Thus he is one who can speak authoritatively about the tradition. He gives a practical directive for ostracizing false teachers (vv. 9–10), and he assumes that the members of the church to whom he is writing want to hear more from him when he comes to visit them (v. 12). He communicates to his readers greetings from Christians in the church in which he lives (v. 13). This role arching over several communities is confirmed by III John wherein he writes to Gaius who lives in another community and praises him for hospitality shown to "the brothers" who have come to him seemingly from the Presbyter (vv. 3,5–8,12). In so doing Gaius is acting as one of the Presbyter's "children" (v. 4). The clear paternalistic attitude makes intelligible the Presbyter's indignation about Diotrephes who is not so docile (vv. 9–10). Diotrephes' act of ignoring the Presbyter's previous letter is astounding, and the Presbyter plans to bring this up if he visits. In particular, the Presbyter gives his testimonial to Demetrius who apparently is coming to Gaius and says, "You know that our testimony is true" (v. 12). One gets the impression of prestige but not of juridical authority.

The second type of information is external to II and III John, being derived from an analysis of the term *presbyteros*. As a comparative of the adjective *presbys*, "old," the term means "older man." However, in the Greek of this period one may not always press the comparative force (BDF 244). As for age there were various ways of dividing the human lifespan current in the Greco-Roman world (F. Boll, *Die Lebensalter* [Leipzig: Teubner, 1913]), but a common schema differentiated five stages: infants, children, boys or adolescents, young people, elders (Irenaeus, *Adv. haer.* 2.22.4; Servius, *In Aeneida* 5.295). In such a schema old age would have begun about the fortieth year (van Unnik, "Authority" 251). However, "elder" has a usage that goes beyond an age bracket; for it was recognized among both Jews and Greeks that older, experienced men made good leaders, so that "elders" became a designation for officials. (The Roman *senator* derives from the adjective *senex*, "old.") In the Jewish sphere Ruth 4:2; Deut 19:12; Josh 20:4; and Ezra 10:14 show elders playing an important role in community life, certainly in the post-exilic period but probably earlier. Before A.D. 70 "elders" had become a title for officials of the Jewish synagogue. Mark 15:1 and Acts 6:12 describe the elders as a component in the Sanhedrin, a body with judiciary and some executive power in the Judaism of Jesus' time. In the Hellenistic sphere "elder" was a title used for magistrates with a religious function in Asia Minor and Egypt (H. Hauschildt, ZNW 4 [1903] 235–42), particularly in various temple associations.

Let me now report five different explanations that have been offered for *ho presbyteros* in II John 1 and III John 1: (1) An elderly man of dignity and importance. Advanced age has been detected not only in the basic meaning of the word but also in the paternal tone of III John 4 ("my children") and in the advisory tone of II John. Those who think the author was John son of Zebedee recall the legends that he lived to extreme age (ABJ 29, lxxxviii–lxxxix). "The Elder" might have been an affectionate but respectful nickname for the author, much as English "the Old Man" can be used for a person in authority. (Cf. also German "Der Alte" for Konrad Adenauer in his latter years.) Yet while others might call the author this, it seems unlikely that he would have so designated himself in a formal letter to a church, especially in III John where a leader in the area was unfriendly to him.

(2) One of the college of presbyters (elders) in charge of the community from which II John was sent. With variations (e.g., as to whether he was principal presbyter), this is held by Donfried, Haenchen, Käsemann, and Pastor. By the last third of the first century in widely spread Christian churches there were officials called "presbyters" (a designation often interchangeable with "bishops"), as attested in Jas 5:14; I Pet 5:1; I Tim 5:17; Titus 1:5; *I Clem.* 44:5, and in most of the Ignatian letters (where *one* of the presbyters served as bishop). The Book of Acts assumes that such organization existed in the 40s and 50s in Jerusalem (11:30; 15:2,23; 16:4) and in the communities founded in Asia Minor by Paul (14:23; 20:17). In favor of a similar situation in the Johannine church(es) Bonsirven, *Epîtres* 28, would cite the information of Clement of Alexandria (*Quis dives salvetur* 42.1–2; GCS 17, 188) that after the death of Domitian (98) John the Apostle left Patmos for Ephesus and established bishops in the churches he organized in that region. (Streeter, "Epistles" 88,97, proposes that John the apostle ordained John the presbyter as second bishop of Ephesus with precedence over the bishops of the province of Asia—thus, a contemporary of Clement of Rome and of Ignatius of Antioch.) If, however, the author of II and III John was one of a group of presbyters, how would the title "The Presbyter" distinguish him? Would he not have had to designate himself "A Presbyter of the church of X"? The suggestion that he was the principal presbyter and the administrative head of the Johannine Community has problems too. Such a supreme presbyter-bishop had emerged (recently) in the churches addressed by Ignatius *ca.* 110, but this ecclesiastical figure is not clearly attested in other NT books. James as head of the presbyters in Jerusalem is not a good parallel because he held his distinctive position as "the brother of the Lord" and probably was recognized as an apostle (although not one of the Twelve; confer Gal 1:19). Moreover, even when the single leader emerged, we find no evidence for the use of "the Presbyter" as his title. In III John 9–10 while one person (Diotrephes) is putting himself as first in a local church, the Presbyter who writes regards this as an act of pride to be resisted; and so one would not spontaneously think of the Presbyter in a similar role. Furthermore, if the Presbyter also wrote I John, as most think (INTRODUCTION II A2), he disclaims the role of teacher (2:27) that was a major function of the officials called presbyters in the Pastorals and Acts. Nor is it clear why, if he is a presbyter or even the leading presbyter in one church, he is taking upon himself the task of addressing other churches and telling them what to do, unless he is an archbishop or metropolitan for which office we have no evidence this early. Many of these objections would apply as well to Käsemann's variant of this theory whereby the writer of II and III John had been a presbyter and still used the title, even though he had been dismissed from office as an incipient gnostic heretic and was shunned by a presbyter like Diotrephes. In my judgment, Käsemann's thesis faces an insurmountable obstacle if the author of III John wrote II John, which in turn is related to I John; for certainly I John is not a gnostic tract.

(3) One of the apostles for whom *presbyteros* served as another designation. (This is often combined with theory that the author was John son of Zebedee.)

Sympresbyteros, "fellow presbyter [elder]," is used of Peter in I Pet 5:1. *Presbyteros* is applied to various members of the Twelve in a statement attributed to Papias who lived in Asia Minor *ca.* A.D. 130 (Eusebius, *Hist.* 3.39.4; see ABJ 29, xci): "If, then, anyone came who had been a follower of the *presbyteroi,* I inquired into the sayings of the *presbyteroi*—what Andrew or what Peter said, or what Philip or Thomas or James or JOHN or Matthew, or any of the other disciples of the Lord said; and the things which Aristion and the *presbyteros* JOHN, disciples of the Lord, were saying." This evidence is not as impressive as might seem at first. As a sympathy-winning gesture, Peter is represented in I Pet 5:1 addressing presbyters as a fellow presbyter; but that is only after he has identified himself as an apostle at the beginning of the letter (1:1; cf. II Pet 1:1). This is exactly what one would expect if the author of II and III John were an apostle, especially in III John where he should have invoked his full authority as he tried to put down Diotrephes "who likes to be first." The fact that in the Papias statement the term *presbyteros* seems to be used for both members of the Twelve (the first group) and nonmembers (the second John) suggests that without further specification it would not identify an apostle.

(4) A companion or disciple of Jesus who was not one of the Twelve Apostles. The Papias statement (which is not clear) speaks of "the presbyter John" as a disciple of the Lord but seemingly distinct from another John whose name is associated with members of the Twelve. Munck, "Presbyters" 235, is probably right in arguing that for Papias presbyters were men of the first generation who had seen Jesus, a generation that would be dying off at the end of the first century (Polhill, "Analysis" 463). If II and III John were written *ca.* A.D. 100, "the Presbyter" might have been an appropriate title for one of the last living disciples of Jesus who did not have the status of being an apostle. Some would find this first-generation status confirmed by I John 1:1: "What we have heard, what we have seen with our own eyes, what we looked at and felt with our own hands" (but see my NOTE on "we" in I John 1:1b). A specification of this theory is that "the Presbyter" is "the Beloved Disciple" of Jesus, so prominent in GJohn, who may not have been one of the Twelve. The most serious objection against this theory stems from the lack of authority in the Johannine Epistles: the author of I John does not seem effective against the secessionists, and the author of III John will have to plead his case against Diotrephes if he visits the church involved. Would not one who had been with Jesus have had more authority (*a fortiori,* if he were the Beloved Disciple)? Not all commentators distinguish between the interpretations I have numbered (3) and (4), but the supporters of these two theories would be numerous. Interpretation (4) is favored by those who argue that one of the Johannine writers was "the presbyter John" mentioned by Papias, and sometimes by those who think the Epistles had an author different from the fourth evangelist, or that II and III John had an author different from the writer of GJohn and I John.

(5) A disciple of the disciples of Jesus and thus a second-generation figure who served as a transmitter of the tradition that came down from the first generation. Among the commentators who hold this interpretation (with varia-

tions, including the suggestion that it is a fictional claim by the writer) are Bornkamm, Bultmann, Kümmel, and Schnackenburg. As support this theory invokes a second-century usage of *presbyteros* by Irenaeus, *Adv. haer.* 4.27.1 (who is clearer than Papias): "I heard it from a certain presbyter who had heard it from those who had seen the apostles and from those who had taught." Van Unnik, "Authority" 254, analyzes Irenaeus' chain of tradition as starting with Jesus, moving through the apostles and disciples who were eyewitnesses of his ministry, and then through the presbyters who had associated with the eyewitnesses. Irenaeus had contact with such presbyters, for elsewhere (*Adv. haer.* 3.3.4) he mentions Polycarp who was instructed by the apostles; and so Irenaeus was in a position to argue that the gnostics were innovators rather than preservers of the apostolic tradition. In this connection he specifically mentions presbyters who saw John (*Adv. haer.* 5.33.3). Apparently Eusebius had a similar understanding of *presbyteros,* for he cites Irenaeus as mentioning the memoirs of a certain "apostolic presbyter" (*Hist.* 5.8.8). Against this background "the Presbyter" of II and III John might have been a disciple of the Beloved Disciple of GJohn and an intermediary for the tradition that came down from him about Jesus. This would correspond with John 21:24: "It is he [the Beloved Disciple] who wrote; and his testimony, *we* know, is true"—a passage with parallels to III John 12: "We give our testimony as well, and you know that our testimony is true." The title "Presbyter" would have been the Johannine Community designation of honor for such tradition-bearers who had been associated with the Beloved Disciple. The writer of II and III John may have been such a tradition-bearer (perhaps elderly at the turn of the century) living in a large Johannine Community center and corresponding with smaller Johannine churches in somewhat distant towns (INTRODUCTION II C1b). His influence would have been that of a prophetic witness rather than that flowing from jurisdiction or structure (Bornkamm, *"Presbys"* 671). In harmony with my understanding of the Johannine School (INTRODUCTION V C2c), I find this interpretation (5) the most plausible.

To an Elect Lady (*and to her children*). Here again, in using a title rather than a name, II John is unique in the NT. Four of the Pauline Epistles have a named individual as the addressee (Philemon, I-II Timothy, Titus), as does III John. The rest of the Pauline Epistles are addressed to communities in named sites ("To the church[es of God] in/of . . ."; "To the saints in. . . ."), with the possible exception of Ephesians where there is a textual problem. The non-Johannine Catholic Epistles are addressed to Christian groups, with geographical sites specified only in I Peter. The seven letters of Revelation 2–3 follow the pattern: "To the angel of the church in. . . ." The letters among "the Apostolic Fathers" are all addressed to churches (usually "To the church of God in . . .") in named sites, with the exception of Ignatius *To Polycarp,* which is addressed to an individual "who is bishop of the church of the Smyrnaeans." Thus, on percentages alone one might guess that the symbolic designation used for the addressees of II John represents a community of Christians.

Whom or what does the author mean by the dative of *eklektē kyria?* As in the previous Note, before reporting on five different explanations, let me survey the internal information to be gained from the letter, and the external information from the vocabulary. No definite article is used in II John 1, but an article is used for "your Elect Sister" in v. 13. There are, then, two female "Elects," both with children; and it is to the children of the first that the author pays attention in v. 4. Indeed, the children of the "Elect Sister" send the greetings in v. 13, not the Sister herself. Verse 5, on the other hand, brings the *kyria*, "my Lady," back on the scene; and she is addressed in the second person plural in v. 6 ("you heard"), a usage that continues in 8,10, and 12. Suddenly, however, the second singular reappears in the "you" who are greeted in v. 13. The fluctuation is easier to understand if a collectivity is involved, e.g., in addressing the post-exilic Jewish community the prophet shifts from the second person plural in Isa 58:3 to the second singular in 58:8. One may object that the plurals of II John may reflect the Lady (an individual) *and her children;* however, it is curious that the Presbyter expects the false teachers to come to the house of this lady (II John 10), unless one wishes to suppose that her home served as the meeting place of the house-church. II John is much more general in tone and content than is III John, which was clearly sent to an individual. Bresky's detailed study of this issue (*Verhältnis*), although now dated in some details, is right in claiming that the internal evidence favors a collective interpretation of the "Elect Lady."

As for the vocabulary, the adjective *eklektos* (which may be used as a substantive) means "chosen, select, excellent." *Kyrios,* masculine, and *kyria,* feminine, can be adjectival ("strong, valid, essential, noble"); but more frequently they serve as nouns for "Lord" and "Lady, Mistress."

Let me now report five different explanations that have been offered for *eklektē kyria,* the first three of which assume that the addressee is an individual Christian. Even though, as I indicated above, I think the contents favor a collective interpretation, scholars like Deissmann, de Wette, Ebrard, Harris, Lücke, and Ramsay opt for an individual reference.

(1) The lady Electa. At the end of the Note on "Title" above, I cited the *Adumbrationes* or Latin translation of the *Hypotypōseis* of Clement of Alexandria who *ca.* 200 wrote that II John was directed "to a certain Babylonian woman named 'Electa,' which signifies the election of the holy church." His statement that II John was written "to virgins" also favors the thesis that II John was speaking of an individual woman. In modern times Harris, "Problem," points out that *kyria* can be a mark of affection in letters, meaning "My dear." (The Oxyrhynchus papyri examples of this [112, 123], however, tend to have the "my" expressed, and that is lacking here.) Accordingly, Harris uses the "Let us love one another" of v. 5 to construct a theory of II John as a love letter written to a Gentile proselyte widow (see also the Note on v. 8b below). Such a theory casts no light on why the lady is loved by all those who know the truth (v. 1c), or why the writer is worried about false teachers (rather than other suitors) coming to the house (v. 10). Verse 6, which is meant to interpret the "love" of v. 5, would make this one of the most chaste love letters of all time! Moreover, the translation "the lady Electa" faces a

grammatical difficulty, for in Greek as in English this construction would require the definite article, which is lacking here. Evidence is insufficient for *eklektē* as a personal name at this time, e.g., it is lacking in the examples of Greek usage in Egypt supplied by F. Preisigke, *Namenbuch* (Heidelberg, 1922). The use of *eklektē* with "your Sister" in v. 13 increases the likelihood that in v. 1 it is an adjective describing *kyria*, "lady." Clement was probably not a witness to a preserved historical tradition but reflected on II John 1 in light of I Pet 5:13, where he found the idea of a *syneklektē* in Babylon (actually a church).

(2) The noble Kyria. This explanation, proposed by Athanasius, and supported in times past by Alford, Bengel, de Wette, Ebrard, Lücke, and Neander, turns the previous suggestion around and understands *eklektē* as the modifier and *Kyria* as the personal name. It is an improvement on both scores. We have seen that *eklektē* is almost surely an adjective in II John, and the NT offers examples of this adjective applied to individuals: "Greet Rufus, the elect in the Lord" (Rom 16:13); also Ignatius, *Phld.* 11:1: "Rheus Agathopous, an elect man from Syria." There is attestation of *Kyria* as a personal name, e.g., 3 instances in Preisigke's *Namenbuch* 188. However, the lack of a definite article is still a problem. Moreover, scholars like Hug, Knauer, and Poggel have pointed out that the NT evidence for adjectival modifiers accompanying personal names would make us expect a Christian designation ("my beloved Kyria"; "my sister Kyria"; or "Kyria elect in the Lord"), rather than such a simple, neutral designation as "noble."

(3) Dear Lady. Ramsay, "Note," agrees with Harris that an individual woman is meant; but he thinks that no name is given, and that *kyria* like *domina* (Latin for "Lady") is a colorless term of courtesy. Plummer and Ross endorse this theory that II John was written to an unnamed lady of importance in one of the churches of Asia Minor, but the pattern of III John ("To the beloved Gaius") suggests that normally the Presbyter would name an individual recipient. Pure fantasy is involved in speculation that the woman might be Mary, the mother of Jesus, who was left in the care of the Beloved Disciple (John 19:27; see ABJ 29A, 923), and who could be further identified with the mother of the messianic child in Rev 12:5 and of other offspring in 12:17 (= "her children" in II John 1; see ABJ 29, 108–9). Not much better is the theory that she is Martha of John 11, the Semitic form of whose name (feminine of *mar*, "lord") is equivalent to *kyria*, feminine of *kyrios*, "lord."

(4) An Elect Lady (which is the church at large). The internal evidence of II John favors a collective symbol, as we saw; and the lack of an article might suggest that no particular locale was in mind. Clement of Alexandria spoke of "the holy church" (see under "Title" above), and II John has been classified as a Catholic Epistle addressed to the church universal. This theory has been supported by Jerome, Oecumenius, and Bede, and in modern times by Schmiedel. However, a greeting from "the children of your Elect Sister" to an Elect Lady who is the universal church is implausible. A modern modification of the theory removes some of the force of that objection and makes the lack of the definite article with "Elect Lady" more understandable, namely, that II

John was a circular letter meant to be read in several communities, whence the lack of direction to a specific church. Granted Johannine history, I would think this modification would need a further specification to have any real plausibility, i.e., that II John was meant to be read in several *Johannine* churches. As we shall see, vv. 5–7 are directed against a misinterpretation of GJohn's ethical and christological stress (as was I John), and the "all those who have come to know the truth" of v. 2 is a Johannine self-description.

(5) An Elect Lady and her children (a symbolic reference to a Johannine church in a town at some distance from the Johannine Community center in which the author is living). This theory, which is held by Gibbins, Houlden, Schnackenburg, and Williams, supposes that there is insufficient evidence for the "circular letter" modification of the preceding theory and no need to posit it. In the INTRODUCTION (II C1B) I explained that if the author of I John and the Presbyter of II and III John are the same man, his lack of title in the former work may be explained if I John was written by him to the Johannine Community (perhaps consisting of several or many house-churches) in which he lived. Verse 10 in II John seems to imply that there was only one house-church of the Johannine Community in the town to which that was sent. (The interplay between Gaius and Diotrephes suggests that there were two Johannine house-churches in adjacent towns or regions, which were the focus of III John.) As for the symbolism of II John, a female representing the/a church offers no difficulty. Nations in general and Israel in particular are addressed as women in the OT, e.g., "O Virgin Israel" (Jer 31:21) and "O Daughter [of] Zion" (6:23). In Rev 18–19 both Babylon, the enemy of Christians, and the church are described as women, and female imagery is used for Israel in John 3:29 (cf. 1:31). The objection that a woman addressed in II John cannot herself represent a church and still have children who are members of that church does not respect the plasticity of symbols; for children are mentioned in personified female descriptions of Israel and of Zion/Jerusalem in Isa 54:1,13; Lam 4:2–3; Baruch 4:30–32; 5:5; and also in Gal 4:25–26 in describing earthly and heavenly Jerusalem. As for treating one church as a sister of another (II John 13), Samaria (Israel) is the sister of Jerusalem (Judah) in Ezek 16:46; 23:4. When we turn more specifically to II John's *kyria*, evidence from the third century B.C. is given by BAG 459 (BAGD 458) for the figurative use of *kyria hē ekklēsia*, "the lady congregation." Dölger, "Domina," points to an early second-century A.D. Jerash inscription dedicated to *kyria patridi*, "the lady hometown." In the *Shepherd of Hermas* the old lady who is identified as the church (*Vis.* 2.4.1) is addressed as *kyria* (*Vis.* 3.1.3). Tertullian (*ca.* 200) supplies in Latin our first example of a particular church (at Carthage) called "Lady": *Domina mater ecclesia* ("Lady Mother Church"; *Ad martyras* 1.1 CC 1, 3), a usage that is scarcely his creation. Furthermore, there is no difficulty with applying to a local church the other II John term *eklektē*, for in the NT groups of believers are frequently designated as "chosen, elect" (Rom 8:33; Col 3:12; II Tim 2:10; Rev 17:14; also *I Clem.* 6:1; *Hermas Vis.* 1.3.4). In the Johannine background the related verb *eklegesthai* is used by Jesus of his disciples in John 15:16: "It was not you who chose me; it was I who chose you."

At the beginning of letters *eklektos* is used to describe both Christians (Titus 1:1; *I Clem.* 1:1) and the church (Ignatius, *Trall.* Opening Formula). The most important parallel to II John is supplied by the Opening in I Pet 1:1, "To the *elect* exiles of the diaspora in Pontus, Galatia . . . ," when that is joined to the reference in the Concluding Formula in I Pet 5:13: "The Co-elect Woman [*syneklektē*] in Babylon sends you greetings." (The latter passage supplies NT evidence that a local church can be *eklektē,* for most think that "Babylon" is a pejorative symbol for Rome.) In both II John and I Peter the article is lacking when *eklektos* is used at the beginning of the letter, but is present in the greetings from the other church at the end of the letter. Overall, then, the evidence clearly favors this fifth interpretation of the identity of the addressee in II John.

and to her children. In three verses (here, 4, 13) the Presbyter speaks of the children (pl. of *teknon*) of a local church, and in III John 4 he speaks of the local church members as *his* children. This is a different usage from I John (NOTE on 2:1a) where the author uses *teknion* and *paidion* to speak to members of the Community as (his) little children but reserves *teknon* for the children of God and of the devil. Elsewhere Paul calls Christians "children" (using *teknon*) in I Cor 4:14,17; II Cor 6:13; and in *Hermas Vis.* 3.9.1 the Lady who is the church uses this title for Christians.

1b. *In truth I love you.* Literally, "whom I love in truth," with a masc. pl. relative referring to both the lady (fem. sg.) and her children (neut. pl.). See BDF 134[2], as well as Gal 4:19 where the masc. pl. relative pronoun modifies the neut. pl. of *teknon.* The Presbyter loves the church collectively and its members individually. The "I" is expressed by the pronoun *egō,* which lends emphasis. Harnack, "Das Wir" 99, stresses that the usage of "I" in II and III John is not comparable to that of "we" in I John 1:1–4 where the author joined himself to other tradition-bearers. However, while it is true that the Presbyter tends to speak in the singular and in his own name, in III John 12 he resorts to *hēmeis,* "we," even as sometimes the author of I John writes as "I" (especially with the verb "to write"; NOTE on 2:1a).

The anarthrous phrase "in truth" (*en alētheia*) occurs here and in v. 3; the noun "truth" is an object in v. 1c; and the arthrous phrase "through [or based on; *dia* + accusative] the truth" appears in v. 2. A major discussion concerns whether "in truth" (also III John 1) is adverbial ("truthfully, authentically, sincerely") or is to be taken more literally and theologically as a sphere for the author's love. We saw a similar problem in the NOTE on I John 3:18ab and the compound phrase *"in* deed and *truth,"* where the statistics for the use of *en* with *alētheia* were given.

Among those who support the adverbial usage are Balz, Bultmann, Schnackenburg, Schneider, and THLJ. In its favor is cited the absence of the article, although de la Potterie, *La vérité* 2, 662, argues that the Johannine *en* phrase tends to be anarthrous. A proposed parallel is the adverbial use of *pros alētheian* and *ex alētheia* in final greetings in papyri letters. (B. P. Grenfell and A. S. Hunt, *Fayum Towns and their Papyri* [London: Egypt Exploration Fund, 1900] pp. 274–75: #118, 25–26; #119, 25–27, for the former phrase;

and *Papyri and Ostraca from Karanis*, ed. H. C. Youtie and J. G. Winter [Michigan Papyri 8; Ann Arbor: Univ. of Michigan, 1951] p. 59: 卅477, 39–41, for the latter phrase.) However, examples of the exact phrase with *en* are hard to find—a proposed example in Plato, *Laches* 183d, is of dubious authenticity—so de la Potterie, *La vérité* 2, 639–63, argues that it is a phrase quite unknown in secular Greek. He contends that it is a Semitism translating *be'ĕmet* or *bĕqŭštā'*; however, such Semitic phrases can also be used adverbially as in 1QGenAp 2:6,7,10: "to speak truthfully."

A theological use of "in truth" is supported by Alexander, Bonsirven, Brooke, Chaine, de Ambroggi, de la Potterie, Dodd, Houlden, Plummer, Polhill, Ross, Stott, and Williams. The LXX uses the phrase *en tē alētheia* (with the definite article) when it is accompanied by a possessive referring to God, e.g., Ps 89:50(49), "Your ancient mercies which you swore to David in your truth"; but it uses *en alētheia* anarthrously some 14 times, e.g., Tob 14:7: "All those who *love* the Lord God *in truth* and justice" (thus Vaticanus and Alexandrinus, while Sinaiticus reads the phrase adverbially [= "truthfully"] without the accompanying "and justice"). The anarthrous phrase is used 3 times in the *Psalms of Solomon* (6:9[6]; 10:3–4; 14:1) with *agapan*, e.g., "Faithful is the Lord to them that love Him in truth" (14:1). There it is hard to decide whether such a phrase is adverbial (= "truly love Him"), but the appearance in the context of other nouns governed by *en* suggests that sometimes at least "truth" is a sphere, e.g., "The mercy of the Lord is upon those who love Him in truth, and the Lord remembers His servants in mercy" (*Ps. Sol.* 10:3–4). In this connection 1QS 5:24–25 is interesting: "Let a man correct his neighbor in truth, in humility, and with merciful love." See also 1QSb 3:24 where there is parallelism between "establishing God's covenant in truth" and "watching over God's ordinances in righteousness [justice]." Well does Alexander (*Epistles* 147) state that in the Johannine view, "Truth is the sphere in which Christians live, act, and are related." And so "to love in truth" would involve a love based on a revelation of God in Jesus Christ who is the truth. *Pace* Bergmeier ("Verfasserproblem"), Johannine dualism is still at work here: the author writes only to those who share with him a faith that makes them the children of God—the love of "brother" ties him to them. (Bergmeier's observation that a notion of orthodox teaching is *introduced* in II John fails to recognize that christology in GJohn and I John also has an aspect of orthodoxy which excludes those who do not share the respective view of Jesus.) Indeed, Houlden (*Epistles* 151) may be right when he speculates that, since common participation in truth is what bound Johannine Christians together, "I love in truth" was a Community "catch-phrase." Although Schnackenburg (*Johannesbriefe* 307) argues that the three other uses of "truth" in vv. 1–3 mark a progression over the colorless, nontheological use of "in truth" in v. 1b, I contend that "truth" is a leitmotif in the Opening Formula of this letter and has the same meaning throughout (see Dodd, *Epistles* 145). "Walking in truth" in v. 4 also confirms the theological use of "in truth I love."

1c. *and not only I but also those who have come to know the truth.* Literally, "who have known," the perf. tense of *ginōskein*, for which see the NOTE on I John 4:16a. The future of this verb governs "truth" in John 8:32: "You will know the truth, and the truth will set you free." In I John 2:21bc we encountered the only Johannine use of *oida* [*eidenai*] "to know," with "truth": "I have not been writing, then, to tell you that you do not know the truth, but that you do know it." *Pace* de la Potterie, there is no detectably different import between the phrase there and the phrase here (see also ABJ 29, 514). In Johannine thought, knowing the truth is coextensive with being a Christian, for it involves knowing the one true God and Jesus Christ whom He sent (John 17:3; I John 5:20). Indeed, I John 2:3 and 3:19 present the living out of the commandments as a criterion respectively for knowing God and for belonging to the truth—a criterion for one state described in two different ways. In GJohn "know that I AM" (8:28) is parallel to "know the truth" (8:32). The author of I John 2:4 challenges any claim to know God made by those who have a secessionist indifference toward commandments; surely the Presbyter would not include among "those who have come to know the truth" the people whom he will soon characterize as "deceivers who have gone out into the world" (v. 7). Other Christian authors foresee the possibility of a lapse after knowledge of the truth (Heb 10:26; *Hermas Vis.* 3.6.2), but in Johannine thought not remaining is a sign of never having known the truth. When the Presbyter assures the addressees that they as a church are loved by all the Johannine Christians (and when he sends greetings in v. 13 from the church where he dwells), he may be hinting that such love would cease were the church addressed to join the secessionist cause from which missionaries are likely to come (vv. 9–10). That proper behavior would affect the way a church was regarded is already hinted at in I Thess 1:7, the earliest Christian writing.

Other NT works speak of "knowledge [*epignōsis*] of the truth" (I Tim 2:4; II Tim 2:25; 3:7; Tit 1:1; Heb 10:26), while I Tim 4:3 uses the verb *epiginō-skein* to govern "truth." De la Potterie, *La vérité* 2, 539–47, has studied the chronological and geographical spread of language associating "knowledge/knowing" and "truth." Despite Dodd's claim (*Interpretation of the Fourth Gospel* [Cambridge Univ., 1954] 159) that knowledge of the truth is a "characteristically Greek conception," the precise language is not found in the Greek philosophers, not even in Plato. However, it appears in the LXX where the truth that is known involves things of divine origin (Wis 3:9; Sinaiticus of Tob 5:14, when joined with 12:11). At Qumran the equivalent Hebrew expression is used for a knowledge of the interpretation of the Law that is equivalent to knowing God's mysteries (1QH 7:26–27; 11:9–10; 1QS 9:17–19). Understandably, knowledge of the truth was claimed by Christian gnostics (*Gospel of Thomas* #78 II 47:2; NHL 127; *Gospel of Philip* II 77:15–30; NHL 146; *Gospel of Truth* I 17:14–20; NHL 38).

2a. *This love is based on the truth that abides in us.* Literally, "on account of the truth abiding in us"—not a new sentence but a phrase continuing the previous sentence. (In place of *menein*, "to abide," Codex Alexandrinus has the verb *enoikein*, "to live, dwell," and minuscule 33 has *einai*, "to be.") It is not clear whether the continuation is from "I love you" in 1b or from "those who have come to know the truth" in 1c. However, since the love for the Lady in

1b stems from knowing the truth in 1c, it is safe to say that this participial phrase in 2a is related to the total action described in 1bc; we know the truth because divine truth abides within us (Johannine Christians) and that abiding truth leads us to love other Johannine Christians who share it, e.g., the church addressed. The use of "truth" as the subject of *menein en* (only here) is an example of the (B) usage discussed in the NOTE on I John 2:6a and is not far from the idea of Jesus' words or God's word abiding in the Christian (John 15:7; I John 2:14). "Truth" here is an active force moving its host to know and to love.

2b. *and will be with us forever.* While "abide" (*menein*) in 2a is a pres. ptcp., the verb in 2b is finite in a relative clause, literally, "and with us will be forever." For such irregular coordination see BDF 468[3] and ZBG 375; it may reflect a Hebrew pattern (BDF 442[6]; MGNTG 2, 428–29). The phrase *eis ton aiōna*, "forever," was discussed in the NOTE on I John 2:17d, its only other Johannine epistolary occurrence: "The person who does the will of God remains [*menein*] forever." Theoretically in the present instance the phrase could be read with the next verse: "Forever there will be with us grace . . ." However, in its frequent GJohn usage it is always a conclusion. The author could have condensed his thought in 2ab by writing: ". . . the truth that abides in us forever"; but by inserting "and will be with us," he highlights the enduring quality of the truth.

"To be with," expressed by *einai* followed by *meta* with the genitive, has its only Johannine epistolary occurrences here and in v. 3. (It is implied in I John 1:3d in reference to *koinōnia*, while I John 2:19d has *menein meta*.) It occurs 16 times in GJohn, always with a person as subject, and that statistic supports the almost personal force that "truth" has here. The closest parallel is John 14:16–17: "The Father will give you another Paraclete to be with you forever; he is the Spirit of Truth"—truth and the Spirit of Truth have almost the same function. Bultmann, *Epistles* 108, points out the existential import: The truth is not simply a possession but must always be grasped anew as a gift. In any case this passage refutes Bergmeier's thesis that in II John *alētheia* can be equated with doctrine (even though, I would agree, it has a doctrinal aspect). As for the exact connotation of *einai meta*, de la Potterie, *La vérité* 1, 358–61, contends that it means more than *einai en*, for it covers not only presence but assistance, as in John 17:12: "As long as I *was with* them, I kept them safe with Your name which You have given to me." While there is a connotation here of truth as a supporting factor, I do not agree that the Johannine writers always keep distinct the connotations of the various prepositions (*en, meta, para*) used with *einai*. Schnackenburg, *Johannesbriefe* 308, correctly underlines the factor of stylistic variation, as illustrated in John 14:16–17 where the three prepositions are interchangeable.

3a. *With us there will be.* The Pauline Epistles (except the Pastorals), I-II Peter, Jude, and *I Clement* extend their greetings (grace, peace, mercy, or love) "to you." The Pastorals and the Ignatian Letters use no personal pronoun. Only II John uses "with [*meta*] us" in the Greeting. (A scribal tendency to conform to the more general pattern is reflected in the "with you" reading of minor MSS. and versions.) The awkward result is two instances of "to be with us" (*einai meta*) in two lines (the second of which Codex Alexandrinus omits either by haplography or "improvement"). Both of them are in the future, a tense that is unique in the Greeting section of a letter, where normally there is no copulative verb, but only an implied optative (MGNTG 3, 304). A few scholars follow this norm by translating the future here as an optative, "Let there be" (BDF 362); but the indicative force is to be preferred in harmony with the preceding line, and with the author's desire to give assurance to the Elect Lady (see COMMENT).

grace, mercy, and peace. I have supplied the "and." Eleven Pauline letters, I-II Peter, and *I Clement* use two nouns in the Greeting: "grace" (*charis*) and "peace" (*eirēnē*). Where there are three nouns (Jude, I-II Timothy, here), the combination involves one or both of those plus "love" (*agapē*) and/or, more frequently, "mercy" (*eleos*). In the LXX the latter frequently renders *hesed*, "covenant mercy or graciousness." The combination of "mercy" and "peace" in Aaron's blessing (Num 6:25–26) may have led to frequent usage of that pair, e.g., in the Opening Formula of a letter in *II Bar.* 78:2, and in a Concluding Formula in Gal 6:16. This is the only Johannine instance of "mercy"; there are 4 other instances of "grace" (all in the GJohn Prologue: 1:14,16,17) and 6 other instances of "peace" (in the GJohn Last Supper and resurrection sections: 14:27; 16:33; 20:19,21,26). For the association of each of these three nouns with "truth," see respectively I John 1:14,17; Josh 2:14; Jer 14:13 (LXX).

3b. *from God the Father and the Father's Son, Jesus Christ.* In 11 Pauline letters; II Peter; *I Clement;* Ignatius, *Magnesians;* and Polycarp, *Philippians,* the Greeting is from (with variants) "God our/the Father and our/the Lord Jesus Christ." (Colossians has the Greeting only "from God our Father"; Ignatius, *Smyrnaeans,* has it "in the word of God.") Codex Sinaiticus, the Byzantine tradition, and some versional evidence would conform II John to the pattern by adding "Lord" to "Jesus Christ." In Paul the preposition "from" is always *apo;* in II John it is *para.* While *theos patēr,* "God [the] Father," is standard epistolary format, the expression occurs only here in Johannine writings, although John 6:27 has *ho patēr . . . ho theos.* This is the only NT instance of Jesus Christ being designated as "the Son of the Father," although the title is continued in the *Gloria in Excelsis,* a hymn with second-century origins, which has been influenced by the Johannine writings: "O Lord God, Lamb of God, Son of the Father."

3c. *in truth and love.* How are we to understand grammatically this phrase with two anarthrous nouns governed by one preposition? (a) Does it continue the "with us" phrase from the beginning of v. 3, so that "in truth and love" modifies the way in which grace, mercy, and peace indwell (Schnackenburg, THLJ)? In this case the preposition *en* is modal. (b) Or are truth and peace the condition for God's gift of grace, mercy, and peace (Schneider), so that, modifying "with us," they are the criteria of the true disciple (Chaine)? (c) Or are grace, mercy, and peace an exercise of truth and love (Bonsirven)? I see no way to resolve the issue and wonder whether the author's thought was that precise. More simply the phrase helps to underline that truth and love go together in governing the author's relation to the Elect Lady and her children. The phrase forms an inclusion with the opening words of the Presbyter's address to her in 1b, "In truth I love you," and thus serves to mark the end of the Opening Formula (*Praescriptio*). Some commentators (Chaine, de Ambroggi) suggest that "truth" and "love" constitute the main topics to be treated in the Body of the Letter (Message), which will now follow in vv. 4–11(12), with "love" being covered specifically in vv. 5–6, and doctrinal truth in v. 7. If that were the author's intent, one would have expected the inverted order, "in love and truth." Moreover, in Johannine thought "truth" would underlie both the command to love one another in vv. 5–6 and the confession that Jesus is the Christ coming in the flesh in v. 7. As for the yoking of "truth" with another noun in an *en* ("in") phrase, see the NOTE on 3:18ab. While this is an example (the first) of "truth" preceding the other noun, such combinations are best understood when both nouns are given equal force, and one is not reduced to a modifier of the other.

4a. *It gave me much joy.* Literally, "I rejoiced exceedingly," with the aorist of the verb *chairein*, which normally expresses the Greeting of a Hellenistic letter (Appendix V A). I shall reserve to the COMMENT the topic of the relation between the Presbyter's expression of his own joy and the more normal Hellenistic and Pauline pattern at this point in the letter of expressing thanks (*eucharistein/ charis*) to the deity. Virtually no modern commentator gives the strictest interpretation of the aorist, namely, that the Presbyter rejoiced in the past when he made his finding but his joy has now ceased. Some, like Schnackenburg and B. Weiss, think of an ingressive aorist (BDF 331), which reflects the beginning of an action that still continues: He rejoiced when he got the news, and his joy persists because the state of affairs is still true. Others, like Plummer, speak of an epistolary aorist (BDF 334) expressing time contemporary with the writing of the letter but past from the viewpoint of those who will have received it—an example is v. 12 where the author says "I did not wish" to write down many things with paper and ink, and this can mean only: "I do not wish at this moment." A simpler comment, backed by the use of the aorist of *chairein* in III John 3 and Polycarp, *Philip.* 1:1 (*synchairein*), is that the author was following an epistolary convention, and the aorist has no biographical import. Nor is the import of the adverb *lian,* "exceedingly, great," to be pressed; it has no more (and no less) meaning than the Pauline "I give thanks to God *always.*" Even the source of the author's joy (love for fellow Christians) may be conventional, as we see in a passage in the *Gospel of the Hebrews* ✳5 (HSNTA 1, 164): "Never be joyful except when you look upon your brother in love."

to find. Literally, "that I have found," with the perf. tense of *euriskein.* In English the perf. tense value would be shifted to the main verb: "I have rejoiced greatly in finding," a pattern closer to that of III John 3. The general impression is that the author is describing a past situation that continues. Older commentators tended to press the literal sense of "find" by surmising, for example, that the Presbyter had previously visited the congregation (even though one would then expect to find the word "again" in v. 12, when he says "I hope to come to you"), or that traveling brethren had come to the Presbyter's community after having visited the sister community now addressed and had reported to the Presbyter (a situation verified in III John, but made clear there), or that "some of your children" mentioned in v. 4 had visited the Presbyter to inform him of the situation in the church he now addresses (Schneider), or that the perf. tense refers to knowledge acquired over a period of time and in different ways. One cannot deny the *possibility* of such explanations, all of which suppose that the Presbyter had direct or indirect information about "some of your children," whom he mentions. But such precise information need not be posited, for the verb "to find" may be used loosely for a statement of fact, i.e., "It gave me great joy that some of your children *are* walking." Bultmann, *Epistles* 110, endorses as possible a meaning suggested by Schnackenburg: "It gave me great joy to think [imagine] that some . . . ." See the examples of usage in BAG (BAGD) 325, under #2.

some of your children. Literally, "from your children," an anarthrous, partitive *ek* phrase, which may be a Semitism (MGNTG 4, 137). In the NT it is an acceptable substitute for the more precise pronominal *tis*, "someone" (MGNTG, 208–9), and for the partitive genitive (ZBG 80). See John 16:17: "Some of his disciples said . . ." Most commentators understand the Presbyter to mean, "I have found some but not all," so that the statement indicates that all is not well with the church addressed. This is dubious on three grounds: (a) Theologically, would the author speak of those who were *not* walking in truth as "children" of the Elect Lady (as this interpretation implies)? Such a designation would be equivalent to saying that they are Johannine Christians. Rather, in the author's dualism, the failure to walk in the truth means that truth does not abide in the person as an active force. (b) From the viewpoint of Epistolary Format, this verse is the Johannine equivalent to a Thanksgiving over the status of the church addressed. Even though sometimes admonitions are found in the Pauline Thanksgiving (Appendix V B), the normal practice would be to laud all that is praiseworthy and to leave unmentioned at this early stage of the letter what cannot be praised and needs to be corrected. In Galatians, for example, where Paul is very angry, he does not give a halfhearted Thanksgiving but chooses to omit it altogether. (c) Grammatically, the partitive need not be taken literally, and the Presbyter may be saying no more than that he rejoiced because there were among the Lady's children those who were walking in truth, without the implication that he had also found some children who were not so walking (Schnackenburg, *Johannesbriefe* 310). This last interpretation is reinforced if one does not take "find" in a literal sense: The Presbyter would know, of course, that all was not perfect in the church addressed; but rather than hinting that here, he would turn his attention to improvement only in the next verse after the present *captatio benevolentiae*.

walking in truth. This is the third *en alētheia* in as many verses, but the first to be used with *peripatein*, "to walk," a usage found also in III John 3 and 4 (in the latter with a definite article before the noun—see de la Potterie, *La vérité* 2, 646–57). The Semitism whereby this verb is used for pursuing a way of life was discussed in the Note on I John 1:6b; but hitherto the dominant Johannine metaphorical use has been that of walking in darkness or light, which is less violent an image than walking in truth. The latter expression is found in the OT for living in fidelity to God's commands found in the Law (rendered by *peripatein* in II Kings 20:3, but also by *poreuesthai* ["to go in truth"] in I Kings 2:4; Isa 38:3). Psalm 86:11 illustrates such a meaning: "Teach me your way, O Lord, that I may walk in your truth." The Dead Sea Scroll group requires that all members "will walk according to the standard of truth" (1QS 8:4), and its life pattern is described as "the ways of truth" (4:17) with a warning against behaving treacherously "in departing from the truth" (7:18). Synonymous expressions include: "to live one's life in truth" (*Aristeas* 260); and "You shall be God's sons in truth and go in His commandments first and last" (*T. Judah* 24:3). In the NT, while "walk in truth" occurs only in II and III John, approximations include "the way of truth" (II Pet 2:2); "teach the way of God in truth" (Matt 22:16); and the warning in Jas 5:19 not to "wander [*planan*] from the truth." As for the meaning of *alētheia* in the present instance, the passage militates against Bergmeier's thesis that it is equatable with doctrine. Bultmann continues to argue for an adverbial usage ("truly") because it is anarthrous—a dubious argument as seen in the Note on v. 1b above. Granted the large Johannine range of interchangeability between light and truth, the parallel expression "walk in light" suggests that "walk in truth" may refer to a sphere of activity that flows from an internal principle of truth. "Those who have come to know the truth" (1c) and in whom the truth abides (2a) and are "in truth" (3c) act according to their God-given status when they walk in truth.

4b. *just as we received a commandment from the Father.* I have preferred a literal translation, rather than the smoother "we were commanded by," so that the reader may see the connection with other references to "commandment" in these verses. Codex Sinaiticus and minuscule MS. 33 read "I have received"; this is a scribal attempt to make the subject conform with the first person singular used in the surrounding verses by interpreting the first plural as editorial or "apostolic" (pp. 158–59 above). The "I" interpretation would give the author the role of an intermediary between the Father and the audience of the letter and would fit in with later interpretations of "The Presbyter" as a man of apostolic authority. (In fact, however, the commandment is not specified as coming from Jesus, and so the description is not meant to be a claim to eyewitness status.) The "we" reading, which has much better textual support, probably means "you and I," not the "we" distinct from "you" encountered in I John 1:1–5 (the "we" of the Johannine School). It is in harmony with the "us" of v. 3a, and with the parallel expression in 6cd: "That is the commandment—as you heard it from the beginning." Thus, there is no convincing reason to think that in II John the Presbyter is distinguishing between a "we group" that *received* a commandment from God (v. 4b) and a "you audience" that heard the commandment (v. 6d) from the "we group."

"Commandment," *entolē*, is one of the most frequent nouns in II John, occurring 4 times (comparable with *alētheia*, 5 times, and *agapē/agapan*, 4 times), which is almost half the usage in the whole of GJohn (NOTE on I John 2:3b). In II John *entolē* is singular 3 times and plural once, a variation that is characteristically Johannine. The expression "to receive [*lambanein*] a commandment from [*para*] the Father" occurs in John 10:18 where Jesus describes his own experience. In I John I interpreted the 8 uses of *"His* commandment(s)"* and 4:21, "the commandment we have had from *Him*," as references to God rather than to Christ; II John does not leave any doubt.

How are we to understand "walking in truth *just as* we received a commandment"? As we shall see under 5d below, the commandment is "Let us love one another," not simply "Walk in truth." The commandment is meant to lead to walking in truth; and the context that follows suggests that walking in truth involves both loving one another (vv. 5–6) and confessing Jesus Christ come in the flesh (v. 7). Walking in truth as we received a commandment makes sense, then, against the background of I John 3:23: "Now this is God's commandment: we are to believe the name of His Son, Jesus Christ; and we are to love one another just as He gave us the command." Although some scholars would press the II John aorist ("received") as having a punctiliar force ("received a commandment at the moment of coming to faith"), such as interpretation really depends upon confirmation from the next verse (5c): "a commandment we have had from the beginning." THLJ 143 states, "The writer may have had in mind an occasion like the one described in Jn 13:34, where God's commandment to love is given through the mouth of Jesus." That suggestion *for this verse* is less plausible if the "we" is inclusive of the audience.

5a. *But now.* The Greek *kai nyn* (NOTE on I John 2:18c) introduces a specification of the preceding general statement: a specific way of walking in truth. However, once more, the *nyn*, "now," may not have lost all temporal force. B. Weiss, *Briefe* 177, would see a shift from the past ("It *gave* me much joy to find") to the present ("I would make a request"). Or is "now" particularly significant for the Presbyter because of the impending onslaught of the false teachers (v. 10)? I have given the *kai* a mild adversative translation because I take v. 4 positively (your children are already walking in the truth); yet despite the good behavior described therein, the author has to stress some basics of Johannine Christianity because of danger on the horizon.

my Lady. The Greek has simply *kyria* (see NOTE on 1a); but in current English "Lady" cannot stand gracefully as an unaccompanied form of address (ABJ 29, 172), whence the tendency of translators to add "my" or "dear," or even to omit "Lady" (NEB). The reintroduction of this respectful form of address softens the way for the admonitions to follow. Clearly the Presbyter is speaking to the whole church and not just to the "some" of v. 4 (as might be concluded by those who stress that partitive). The literary conceit will be continued by the use of the second person singular in 5b, but in 6de the "you" will shift into the plural.

I would make a request of you. This is the second epistolary use of *erōtan*, "to question, ask, pray" (NOTE on I John 5:16d). Although I rejected Temple's contention that in Johannine usage this verb always involves a request among equals, one should not press in the other direction by translating it here as if the Presbyter were begging (RSV). Mullins, "Petition" 47, shows that such a request is part of the literary form of many letters (Appendix V C below), and *erōtan* is one of the four verbs regularly employed in the request.

5b. *it is not as if I were writing you some new commandment.* Literally, this is a participle ("not as writing"), which some minor textual witnesses have rewritten as a finite verb. The awkwardness of the construction also produced variant word orders in the textual witnesses. The implication is *not* that the Presbyter is requesting rather than commanding. The implication is that his request involves a basic Christian commandment, not something new asked in his own name.

5c. *rather it is a commandment we have had from the beginning.* Literally, "but which we were having [imperf.] from the beginning," with Codices Sinaiticus and Alexandrinus placing an aorist ending on an imperf. stem. The Peshitta introduces the idea of *old* commandment under the influence of I John 2:7: "no new commandment that I write you but an old commandment that you had from the beginning." The anarthrous phrase "from [the] beginning" (here and again in 6d) was discussed in the NOTE on I John 1:1a (see especially explanations E and F there). Here it refers to the moment when Johannine Christians first heard and believed the word transmitted by those who bore witness to Jesus, a meaning that presupposes "the beginning" of Jesus' revelation to his disciples during his lifetime. The "we were having from the beginning" is equivalent to "you heard from the beginning" in v. 6d.

5d. *Let us love one another.* Literally, "in order that [*hina*] we should love one another." Syntactically and logically this clause is to be related primarily to the governing verb that precedes the parenthetical remark about the commandment, thus, "I would make a request of you . . . that we should love one another." Secondarily the *hina* clause is epexegetical of the commandment, thus, "a commandment we have had from the beginning, namely, that we should love one another." (Compare I John 3:11: "This is the gospel you heard from the beginning [*hina:* namely that]: we should love one another.") B. Weiss, *Briefe* 176–77, would make the second interpretation primary, for he argues that if the clause continued the verb "I would make a request of you," it would have to read: "that *you* love one another." His reasoning is refuted by the parallel in I John 3:11, which changes person (you/we), just as here. Indeed, while the *second* person plural appears in GJohn when Jesus commands love (13:34; 15:12,17), elsewhere when someone in the chain of tradition reiterates the commandment in direct address, the *first* person plural seems to be standard (I John 3:23; 4:7,11,12).

6a. *Now this is love.* The formula *kai houtos estin* ("And this is") followed by an impersonal predicate noun occurs 5 times in I John (NOTE on 1:5a) but only here in II and III John. (The minor variant *houtos gar estin* ["For this is"] occurs in I John 5:3 with "love" as a predicate: "For the love of God consists in this: that we keep His commandments.") Frequently in the use of this phrase a concept that has just been mentioned is being explained, and in both I John 5:4 and 5:11 the concept (predicate noun) is derived from the preceding *verb*, even as it is here. As for the kind of love to which the Presbyter refers, see the end of the next Note.

6b. *that we walk according to His commandments*. As we saw in the Note on I John 1:5d, *kai houtos estin* is usually followed by either a *hoti* or *hina* (as here) introducing a clause that expounds the contents of the noun that has served as the predicate. In v. 4 the Presbyter spoke about "walking" (in truth), and that Semitic idiom occurs twice in this verse (see Note on I John 1:6b); but here with the preposition *kata*, "according to," an idiom not found elsewhere in John (cf. Mark 7:5: "walk according to the tradition of the elders"; Rom 14:15: "walk according to love"). The Presbyter will speak of "walking in it [the commandment]" in v. 5e, and that is the normal Johannine idiom, comparable to Prov 8:20: "I walk in the ways of righteousness." Most scholars take "His" here as a reference to God, because of the previous reference to the "commandment from the Father." Of the four instances of *entolē* in II John, this is the only plural, whereas half the I John uses (total 14) are plural. I discussed in the Note on I John 2:3b whether the variance has significance, e.g., all the commandments distinct from the commandment to love—thus Polhill, "Analysis" 464, who sees love as striving to realize in detail every separate aspect of the will of God. Or is the variance simply stylistic, so that the author is still speaking of the commandment to love mentioned in the previous verse? (See I John 3:22–23 and John 15:10–12 where "This is God's/my commandment" sums up the "commandments" [pl.] mentioned just before.) A decision here is complicated by the obscure logic of the whole section which must now be examined.

The normal Johannine pattern has been to define the special commandment of Jesus/God in terms of loving one another (John 13:34; 15:12,17; I John 3:23; 4:21), but here the Presbyter defines love in terms of keeping the commandments. Houlden, *Epistles* 145, sees this as another instance of the "writer's familiar reversals of previous formulations. He loves to combine his favorite words in all possible directions." But is it tautology to say: I am writing you a commandment to love one another, and this is *love:* to walk according to the commandments? Some scholars (Bonsirven, Camerlynck, Chaine, Vrede, and B. Weiss) avoid tautology by their contention that love (italicized above) is love for God. We did hear in I John 5:3: "For the love of [for] God consists in this: that we keep His commandments." However the natural flow of language in II John makes it likely that "love" in 6a means what it means in the preceding line (5d): "Let us love one another," as proposed by Brooke, Büchsel, Windisch. If a scholar like B. Weiss, *Briefe* 177, refuses to accept this, it is by invoking logic against syntax: Keeping God's commandments more obviously shows love for God than for one another. (In fact, though, beginning with "Thou shall not kill," many of the Ten Commandments deal with love for one another.) However, even this not-too-persuasive argument falters if "commandments" in II John 6b is only a stylistic variant of "commandment" in v. 5, for then the author is saying that the commandment to love consists in walking according to the commandment to love. Understandably Bultmann, *Epistles* 111, is annoyed: "The definition of love in v. 6a, by means of the *hina* clause, is strangely pedantic and unnecessary." Since he finds the second half of the verse (below) no less redundant, this verse exemplifies his thesis that II John was (poorly) formed in imitation of I John. Schnackenburg, *Johannesbriefe* 311, argues that the connection between love in v. 6 and the command to love one another in v. 5 is only external, and that in v. 6 the author is speaking about love in general, so that neither love for God nor for brother is being specified. In face of such unsatisfying explanations it is sometimes suggested that II John is saying awkwardly what I John 3:18 urged: "Let us not give lip service to our love with words but show its truth in deeds," or even what Paul stated in Rom 13:8: "Owe no one anything except to love one another, for one who loves the other person has fulfilled the Law." What is clear is something we have seen before (pp. 473–74): There is no opposition between love and commandments in Johannine thought, and the commandment to love is comprehensive, affecting one's whole behavior (commandments).

6cde. *That is the commandment. As you heard it from the beginning, so must you walk in it.* This appears to be just as tautological as what has preceded and is even more complicated grammatically. If for convenience it is divided into three lines, it may be translated literally thus:

6c This [*houtos*] is the commandment
6d that [*hina*] as [*kathōs*] you [pl.] heard from the beginning
6e that [*hina*] you walk in it [*autē*].

For the plural "you" in 6d and the phrase "from the beginning," see the NOTES above on 5a ("my Lady") and 5c respectively. Without undue stress on the punctiliar force of the aorist "heard," it is plausible that the author is thinking of the time when his audience became Christian. Beyond these points there are four main problems to be discussed.

(1) What is the reference of the *houtos* in 6c? Does it point back to 6ab so that it should be translated "that," as I have done? Or does it point forward to what follows, especially to 6e? The problem is similar to the one encountered in deciding the reference of *en toutō* (NOTE on I John 2:3a), a phrase employing the dative of *houtos*. To come to a decision here, one must first wrestle with the other problems described below.

(2) The *hina* that begins line 6d is missing in most textual witnesses (including Codex Vaticanus), but present in Codices Sinaiticus, Alexandrinus, minuscules 33 and 69, the Vulgate and the Coptic. It constitutes a very difficult reading (more so if one also accepts a *hina* at the beginning of 6e), and one can see why scribes might have omitted it. B. Weiss, *Briefe* 179, explains its presence in terms of a scribal feeling that *kathōs* belongs in the subordinate rather than in the main clause; and Chaine, *Epîtres* 245, holds a similar view when he says that scribes moved the *hina* up from 6e to 6d. In any case, if one reads a *hina* in 6d and 6e, the *houtos* of 6c must point forward, so that, for instance, 6d is incorporated into the explanatory remarks about the commandment, and the second *hina* (6e) is repetitive as an awkward resumptive: "This is the commandment: that as you heard it from the beginning, [that] you walk in it." On the other hand, if one does not read a *hina* in 6d, the *houtos* in 6c can point ei-

ther forward or backward. If *houtos* points forward, 6d becomes a modifying thought and the real sequence of 6c is 6e: "This is the commandment (as you heard it from the beginning) that you walk in it [love?]."

(3) What is the function of the *hina* that begins 6e? (A few MSS. omit it because they have the *hina* before 6d.) Is it epexegetical of "This is the commandment" in 6c? (Schnackenburg, *Johannesbriefe* 312, would relate it to 6c, but not as giving the contents of the commandment.) Or does it introduce a purpose clause dependent upon "heard" in 6d ("You heard the commandment so that you should walk in it")? Or does it correspond to *kathōs* in 6d ("As you heard it from the beginning, so must you walk in it"), so that both clauses are in only a loose syntactic connection to 6c? A parallel for the last suggestion, which I favor, is found in John 13:34: "I am giving you a new commandment that you should love one another—as [*kathōs*] I have loved you, so [*hina*] must you love one another."

(4) To what does *en autē*, "in it," in 6e refer? The pronoun is feminine, but there are three feminine nouns in the preceding context, any of which may serve as antecedent. (a) ENTOLĒ, "commandment," is the nearest plausible noun (6c) and so has an edge over the other candidates. This interpretation is found in the Latin translations, Oecumenius, Theophylact, Brooke, Büchsel, Charue, de Ambroggi, Houlden, B. Weiss, and Wilder. The objection that the Presbyter would not speak of walking *in* the commandment when he has just spoken of walking *according to* the commandments is convincing only to those who think that the Johannine writers are very precise about prepositions. The shift from *kata* to *en* can be a stylistic variant, as can be seen from comparing Rom 14:15 and Eph 5:2 in terms of walking according to or in love. The most serious objection to "commandment" as an antecedent is that it renders the statement tautological, especially if *houtos* points forward: "This is the commandment . . . that you should walk in the commandment." The objection is surmountable if *houtos* points backward, as in my translation. (b) AGAPĒ, "love," is the next possible antecedent (6a) and is supported by most modern commentators (Balz, Belser, Bonsirven, Bruce, Calmes, Camerlynck, Chaine, Dodd, Hauck, Marshall, Plummer, Polhill, Schnackenburg, Schneider, Stott, Vrede, Westcott—Windisch speaks of a reference to *entolē* which is *agapē*). This construction gives good sense; but syntactically it is awkward to have the pronoun refer to an antecedent from which it is separated by sixteen words and several clauses. One may argue for a chiasm, however (as D. N. Freedman has suggested to me), involving 6ab and 6ce: This is love that we walk according to His commandments; this is the commandment that you walk in love. (c) ALĒTHEIA, "truth," which was last mentioned in v. 4, is suggested as a possible antecedent by Brooke and defended by de la Potterie. Since the Presbyter has already spoken of walking in truth (and elsewhere no Johannine work speaks of walking in a commandment or walking in love—NOTE on I John 1:6b), Johannine usage favors this; and it would explain how the Presbyter easily turns to "deceivers" by way of contrast at the beginning of the next line. Nevertheless, separation of a pronoun from the proposed antecedent by forty-six words represents a formidable difficulty.

It is not possible to come to certitude on these points, and I am not sure the meaning is greatly affected whatever grammatical decisions are made. But overall I am inclined to think the *houtos* in 6c refers to what precedes in 5cd (i.e., the commandment is the one mentioned previously, to love one another). I think that probably there was a *hina* only in 6e, not in 6d. Lines 6de are a self-contained observation about the commandment (a *kathōs* . . . *hina* construction, "just as . . . so"), similar to the one found in John 13:34; and it emphasizes the manner in which the commandment must be observed. The "in it" in 6e refers to the nearest antecedent, "commandment," a commandment to love.

7a. *For.* This line begins with *hoti,* "because," and so is grammatically subordinate to the verb that terminates the previous verse—a complexity added to the complexities discussed above. On the one hand, too much should not be made of the subordination as if it would militate against a new paragraph here (see the same phenomenon discussed in the NOTE on I John 3:11ab where in my judgment *hoti* begins a new Part). Some break is required to do justice to the new christological discussion that will now be opened. On the other hand, the subordination suggests that the christology about to be discussed cannot be separated from the stress on the commandment to love.

many deceivers have gone out into the world. This is the only Johannine use of *planos,* "deceiver" (which occurs twice here); but the verb *planan,* "to deceive," is used 3 times in I John, and *planē,* "deceit," once (NOTE on 1:8b). In three passages (I John 2:26; 3:7; 4:6) the deceit or deceiving is related to the devil and/or the Antichrist who are at work in the secession from the Johannine Community. Deceit is a feature of Johannine dualism. The use of "many" may be stereotyped in expressing the seriousness of the secession: "Many Antichrists have made their appearance" (I John 2:18); "Many false prophets have gone out into the world" (4:1).

Bultmann, *Epistles* 112, takes the world "in the sense of the public sphere, in which they are active precisely as deceivers." This is not adequate. The expression "gone out into the world," employing the aorist of *exerchesthai,* is clearly parallel to the use of the aorist of that verb in I John 2:19, which is a reference to the Antichrists of 2:18 and to "those who deceive" of 2:26: "It was from our ranks that they went out." The going out is the secession from the Community and is comparable to the going out of Judas when Satan entered into him (John 13:27,30). Another parallel is the perfect tense of *exerchesthai* in I John 4:1: "Many false prophets have gone out into the world," manifesting the Spirit of the Antichrist, which is the Spirit of Deceit (4:6). Thus, opposed to the Johannine Community of the children of truth and light, the "world" is the realm of darkness and deceit ruled by the devil, its Prince. It is the realm of which I John 2:15 warns, "Have no love for the world, nor for the things that are in the world. If anyone loves the world, there is in him no love of the Father." Those who have gone out (*exerchesthai*) into the world are the devilish parody of Jesus who came into (*erchesthai eis*) the world (John 18:37—the Byzantine tradition reads *eiserchesthai* here in II John for going into the world).

7b. men who do not confess Jesus Christ coming in the flesh. Literally, "those not confessing," a pres. ptcp. with the definite article. A relative clause would have been better Greek, and MGNTG 3, 152–53 raises the possibility of Semitic influence. MGNTG 3, 80–81 cites this as a possible example of the pres. ptcp. indicating a time prior to that of the main verb, e.g., there went out deceivers who had not (or because they had not) confessed. More plausibly the ptcp. is equivalent to an imperf. tense, describing past continued action, e.g., there went out deceivers who were not confessing. But I see no difficulty in rendering it literally as a pres. tense since their failure to confess continues.

Homologein, "to confess," was discussed in the NOTE on I John 1:9a where we saw that, with one exception, the content of (public) confession in Johannine literature is christological. The closest parallel is I John 4:2–3, which criticizes those who do not make a proper christological confession. The literal wording of the two passages may be compared:

I John 4:2: Jesus Christ in the flesh having come [perf. ptcp.]
II John 7: Jesus Christ coming [pres. ptcp.] in the flesh

The NOTE on 4:2bc described three possible interpretations of that confession: (a) Jesus-Christ-come-in-the-flesh; (b) Jesus Christ as come in the flesh; (c) Jesus as the Christ come in the flesh. I opted for (a) as the most plausible, taking the whole phrase as one object. The same discussion applies here, but there is an added problem: Is II John's pres. ptcp. significantly different in meaning from I John's perf. ptcp.?

Two interpretations of the II John confession are possible: (a) The pres. ptcp. may refer to the second coming or parousia. Such an interpretation which gives a future meaning to the ptcp. (BDF 339²) is advocated by K. and S. Lake but rejected by IBNTG 101. I would observe that, while syntax favors the future meaning, it does not demand it. In a clear reference to the parousia of Jesus ("about to be manifested in the flesh") *Barnabas* 6:9 uses a future form rather than a present participle. If we accept a future meaning in II John, the adversaries may be denying the parousia, an error that has no exact parallel in GJohn and I John, although there are strains in the former work and in secessionist thought that would deemphasize the parousia. Or the adversaries may be accepting the parousia but denying that it will be "in the flesh," an error possibly related to the secessionist view attacked in I John whereby little stress is placed on what Jesus did in the flesh at his first coming. Westcott, *Epistles* 229, thinks that the error of the adversaries centers upon "the Lord's Manhood which *is* still, and is to be manifested, and not upon the past fact of His coming."

(b) The pres. ptcp. may refer to the first coming or incarnation. Although overwhelmingly favored by scholars, this interpretation depends primarily not on syntax but on parallelism with I John 4:2 which (more correctly) uses a past tense. Already Polycarp, *Philip.* 7:1, "Everyone who does not confess Jesus Christ to have come [perf. infin.] in the flesh is Antichrist," seems to have read II John 7 and I John 4:2 as saying the same thing (INTRODUCTION I B1). But in this interpretation why would the Presbyter who wrote (or, at least, knew) I John have shifted to a less exact pres. tense? Bultmann, *Epistles*

112, regards this as an indication of the secondary character of II John over against I John; yet why would a secondary copyist change a more correct past tense to a pres.? (Copyists usually seek to improve.) In another statement Bultmann seems to join other scholars (Alford, Balz, Brooke, Marshall, Schnackenburg, Stott, B. Weiss) who think the solution lies in the timeless character of Jesus' abiding in the flesh: Having come in the flesh (I John), he remains in the flesh. The secessionists, then, having denied Jesus Christ come in the flesh, deny the importance of his abiding in the flesh. While this explanation for the use of a pres. tense by II John is possible, there may be another factor. In I John *erchesthai*, "to come," is employed to describe both the Antichrist (2:18b; 4:3) and Christ (4:2; 5:6), a practice probably influenced by the GJohn description of Jesus as "the one [who is] to come" in three passages (1:15,27; 12:13) using the pres. ptcp. *erchomenos*. Thus the Presbyter may simply have been repeating a stereotyped formula when he uses *erchomenos* in insisting on confessing "Jesus Christ *coming* in the flesh." The "in the flesh" part of the confession (NOTE on I John 4:2b) would represent his corrective addition against his opponents.

7c. *There is the Deceiver! There is the Antichrist!* Literally, "This is," one phrase governing both predicates (although Bultmann, *Epistles* 112, speaks of the "This" as the predicate with the two nouns as subjects). The Presbyter switches from the plural "many deceivers" to the singular "the Deceiver," a sequence just the opposite to that in I John 2:18bc, which moved from "Antichrist" to "Antichrists." Probably the Presbyter does not mean that each deceitful person is the Deceiver or Antichrist, but that collectively they constitute the expected *well-known* apocalyptic evil figure (for this force of the article, see BDF 273). I discussed the Antichrist expectation in the NOTES on 2:18b and 4:3c. Parallel to the Antichrist, I John 4:22a spoke of the Liar, *pseustēs* (see NOTE there), while II John speaks of the Deceiver, *planos*. This is not a separate expectation but another aspect of the one personification as we see from I John 4:3,6 where the Spirit of the Antichrist and the Spirit of Deceit are titles for the opponent of the Spirit of God or the Spirit of Truth. In Rev 13:11–18 a parody of Christ with the number 666, the beast from the land, is described as one who "deceives those who dwell on earth." It is significant that in Matthew Jesus' opponents who deny that he is "the Christ" (26:62) condemn him as "the Deceiver" (27:63).

8a. *Look out yourselves.* The use of the reflexive does *not* mean: "Look out, not for those men, but for yourselves." Rather it shifts attention to what the addressees can do about the danger: "As for you, you are to look out." (Irenaeus, *Adv. haer.* 3.16.8, seems to have read the personal pronoun *autous* for the reflexive *heautous:* "Look out for them [i.e., the deceivers].") This is the only epistolary use of *blepein*, "to see, look," which occurs 17 times in GJohn. Nine of those are in John 9, the story of the man born blind; and since that story has baptismal symbolism (ABJ 29, 379–82) as a parable of coming to "see" Jesus with eyes of faith, it is possible that the Presbyter is using an expression that would remind the children of the Elect Lady of the moment when they became Christians. But any such hint would be secondary, for more important is the use of this expression in the apocalyptic context of being on the outlook for the last times. (The two meanings, seeing with faith and looking for judgment, are not so far apart in the use of *blepein* in John 9:39: "I came into the world for judgment: that those who do not see may be able to see, and that those who do see may become blind.") The second plural form *blepete* is found in apocalyptic contexts in Eph 5:15; Col 2:8; and Heb 10:25; and 4 times in the Marcan Apocalypse (13:5,9,23,33). Particularly interesting, granted the context in II John, is Mark 13:21–23, where the disciples are told to watch out for "false christs" and "false prophets." See also Mark 13:5–6(= Matt 24:4–5; Luke 21:8) where the watch is against "any one who would deceive [*planan*] you" (and Col 2:8 where there is other vocabulary for the deception).

that you do not lose what we have worked for. This will be followed in the second half of the verse by *"you* must receive"; and so one has an alternating sequence of plural subjects: "you, we, you." This awkward sequence, while found in relatively few major textual witnesses (Vaticanus, Sahidic), probably should be accepted as Hauck, Metzger, Nestle-Aland, B. Weiss, NEB, and JB recognize; for it explains the variants attested in other witnesses as scribal attempts at improvement, e.g., the "we, we, we" (favored by Byzantine MSS., Oecumenius, Theophylact, KJV), or "you, you, you" (Sinaiticus, Alexandrinus, Latin, Syriac; and Balz, Bultmann, Harnack, Schnackenburg, Schneider, Stott, Wilder, Windisch, RSV). The explanation of the textual problem is complicated by how various interpreters have understood the "we" in the "you, we, you" sequence. Many older interpreters understood it as the distinctive "we" discussed in relation to I John 1:1–5 (the Johannine School of tradition-bearers), with some citing it as proof that the Presbyter was an apostle (John son of Zebedee) who had evangelized the church he now addressed. (For *ergazesthai*, "to work," with the meaning of doing evangelical work, see I Cor 16:10 where Timothy and Paul "work the work of the Lord".) Metzger, TCGNT 721, speaks of the "we" as "apostles and teachers"; Schnackenburg, *Johannesbriefe* 314, thinks that a scribe changed the original "you have worked" into "we have worked" to favor the thesis that the author was a missionary in the community addressed. Some conservative scholars are troubled by the "we [apostles] have worked" because then to the addressees would be credited the power to bring to a loss what an apostle worked for. Even though I favor the "you, we, you" sequence, I deny that the "we" is distinctive in the I John 1:1–5 sense (which is not "apostolic" in any case). Rather it means "we Johannine Christians" and includes the "you" of the addressees. One finds a similar alternation between a "we" and a plural "you" a few verses earlier (II John 5c–6). There is nothing in II John to indicate that the Presbyter founded the church addressed or regards himself as its official "teacher" (a term rejected in I John 2:27). Indeed, such a preeminent role is challenged by the respectful address to the Elect Lady, by the failure to refer to the recipients as *his* children, and by the failure to modify "walking in truth" (v. 4) with something like "just as we directed you," instead of "just as *we* received a commandment from the Father."

The issue of losing (*apollynai*) what has been worked for (*ergazesthai*) makes some commentators uneasy because of their opposition to the suggestion of merit, an opposition heightened by Reformation disputes. They point to Rom 4:4–5, which makes a distinction between wages due to one who works (*ergazesthai*) and a gift given to one who believes. (One may make a case that the idea of merit is not foreign to Paul, and that in any event another NT author may have had a different outlook.) For instance, Schneider, *Briefe* 192, evaluates the present passage as unJohannine and reminiscent of Jewish formulations, while Stott, *Epistles* 210, insists that the Presbyter was not speaking of losing salvation, which is a free gift (rather than something worked for). Leaving aside such preconceptions, let us seek background in the Johannine writings. While this is the only epistolary use of *apollynai*, it occurs 10 times in GJohn, most frequently in the context of not losing those who belong to Jesus (3:16; 6:39; 10:28; 17:12; 18:9). Particularly interesting for the present passage is John 6:27, "You should not be working [*ergazesthai*] for the food which is subject to loss [*apollynai*] but for the food that lasts for eternal life." In 6:29 Jesus says, "This is the work [*ergon*] of God: have faith in [*pisteuein*] him whom He sent." Thus in Johannine thought correct christological belief is a "work" that opens the recipient to receive eternal life. To slip from this belief to the deceit of those who deny Jesus Christ coming in the flesh would be to lose what one has been working for (MGNTG 1, 116 argues that the aorist here means "we have been working").

8b. *you must receive your reward in full.* Literally, "but [that] you receive [*apolambanein*] a full reward [*misthos*]." The adjective *plērēs*, "full," is treated here as indeclinable, a vulgarism that became common from the second century B.C. on (ZBG 11; MGNTG 2, 162); but some scribes improved on this grammar by supplying the declined form. Recent commentators are more disturbed by the Presbyter's theology of merit than by his grammar (preceding NOTE). Bultmann, *Epistles* 113, finds v. 8b "surprising, because it is a typical Jewish expression . . . found neither in I John nor in John." Yet the word *misthos* appears in John 4:35–36 where Jesus speaks of the conversion of the Samaritans: "The fields are ripe for the harvest; the reaper is already receiving [*lambanein*] his reward [*misthos*]." In the realized eschatology of GJohn one could speak of receiving a reward when people are brought to eternal life through faith; but in the Epistles final eschatology is stronger (INTRODUCTION V C2d), and so the same expression is used in reference to the future reward of believers (when they see God as He is: I John 3:2). In speaking of the *misthos* or reward as still to come, the Presbyter is close to common NT usage: Matt 5:12 blesses the persecuted, "Rejoice and be glad for your reward is great in heaven"; Mark 9:41 promises, "Whoever gives you a cup of water to drink because you are in the name of Christ will by no means lose [*apollynai*] his reward"; in I Cor 3:8–9 Paul insists, "The one who plants and the one who waters are alike; and each shall receive [*lambanein*] his own reward according to his labor, for we are fellow-workers [*synergos*] of God" (also Rev 11:18; 22:12). Thus it is an oversimplification to characterize the thought of II John 8 as Jewish, distinct from Christian—it is one common form of Christian thought as distinct from certain aspects of Pauline thought. Nor is it unJohannine except for those who refuse to recognize that even in GJohn there runs a submerged stream of final eschatology that comes to the surface in the Epistles.

Nevertheless, a tension between realized and final eschatology is detectable here in the designation of the reward as "full" (*plērēs*). Elsewhere in the Johannine writings this adjective appears only in John 1:14, which describes the Word-become-flesh: "We have seen his glory, the glory of an only Son from the Father, full of enduring love." Using a cognate noun (*plērōma*) the Prologue hymn continues in 1:16: "And of his fullness we have all had a share." This same possibility of fullness here and now was indicated by I John 1:4 where the author, speaking as a member of the Johannine School, expressed his purpose in writing about the *koinōnia* of the Johannine Community as "thus filling out our joy." The Presbyter will echo that hope in II John 12e, the only other epistolary use of *plēroun*, "to fill." Despite different emphases, a fullness here and a fullness to be obtained hereafter are not irreconcilable, if one lays aside pure logic and recognizes that in ordinary parlance "full" allows degrees.

Some of the wording of II John 8 is found in Ruth 2:12, "May the Lord recompense your work [*ergasia*]; may a *full reward* be yours from the God of Israel." On the fragile basis of this parallelism J. Rendel Harris built his thesis (p. 652 above) that the Elect Lady addressed in this letter, like Ruth, was a proselyte widow.

9a. *Anyone who is so "progressive" that he does not remain.* Literally, "Everyone going ahead and not remaining"; see the NOTE on I John 2:23ab for the construction of *pas*, "all, every," followed by an articular ptcp. While this is the only instance of the construction in II and III John, it occurred 13 times in I John, reflecting the author's tendency to divide people into two groups, all of whom do one thing or its opposite. In my book *Community* I traced the roots of this dualistic mentality to a history wherein, having been cut off from Judaism through expulsion from the synagogue (John 9:22), some Johannine Christians had now been cut off from others through secession (I John 2:19)—such history exacerbates a "with us or against us" attitude. This is the only Johannine use of *proagein*, "to go ahead, advance, make progress," a verb that of itself has no negative connotation when describing progression in thought: "The wise man *advances* himself by his words" (Sir 20:26[27]). The negative tone here is derived from the other ptcp. ("and not remaining in the teaching of Christ"), for, since the one article governs the two ptcps., a compound activity is envisaged. Possibly (see COMMENT) the Presbyter is protesting against the secessionist appropriation and distortion of what had been a good term in Johannine usage, namely, "being progressive." The epistolary insistence on "walking" makes it logical that "going ahead" should not itself be objectionable, provided that one does not wander from the way (*planan*). Wendt, "Zum zweiten" 23, argues that, while *proagein* does not mean "to go too far," it does imply proceeding in a dictatorial manner, so that it is exemplified by Diotrephes of III John 9 who pays no attention to the tradition. However, besides the difficulty of demonstrating that Diotrephes is of the same mind as the secessionists, a different verb is used in the condemnation of Diotrephes: he "likes to be first" (*philoprōteuein*). Scribes, recognizing the neutral tone of *proagein* in II John 9, clarified the Presbyter's thought by substituting *parabainein*, "to go aside, deviate" (Byzantine tradition, Syriac, Clementine Vulgate).

remain rooted in the teaching of Christ. Here *menein en*, "to remain or abide in" (NOTE on I John 2:6a), is used with *didachē*, which in the Epistles occurs only in this verse and the next, but in GJohn 3 times for the teaching of Jesus (7:16,17; 18:19). Perhaps the infrequency of this noun explains why minuscule 33 reads *agapē* for *didachē*, imitating I John 4:16d which refers to abiding in love.

There is debate among scholars whether the genitive "of Christ" is objective, subjective, or both, a debate similar to that about the genitive in "the love of God" (NOTE on I John 2:5b). (a) AN OBJECTIVE GENITIVE, "teaching about Christ," is supported by Bultmann, Marshall, Rengstorff, B. Weiss, and the NEB. A genitive can have this meaning, although the use of *peri*, "about," would have been clearer. As an object, "teaching" becomes equivalent to "doctrine," and the substance of the doctrine is usually assumed to concern how Jesus is the Christ. Bergmeier uses this passage to argue that II John represents a Johannine thought hardened beyond I John (which denies the need of teachers) and thus increases the likelihood of different authors. As an argument for an objective genitive, we note that v. 7 contains a quasi-doctrinal formula about Jesus Christ. Moreover, the parallel statement in I John 2:23 ("No person who denies the Son possesses the Father either, while the person who confesses the Son possesses the Father as well") would seem to make the Son the *object* of attention. Interesting NT parallels are: "This is not the way you learned Christ, assuming indeed that you have heard about him and were indoctrinated [*didaskein*] in him, as truth is in Jesus" (Eph 4:20–21); "Let us leave behind the beginning word of [about] Christ and be taken on to maturity, not laying down again a foundation . . . with teaching [*didachē*] about ablutions" (Heb 6:1–2; see also 13:8–9). If one maintains this interpretation, it is not necessary or plausible to maintain that the Presbyter is referring to a whole body of thought, as in I Tim 1:10 with its reference to "sound doctrine" (*didaskalia;* see also I Tim 4:6; II Tim 4:3; Titus 2:1).

(b) A SUBJECTIVE GENITIVE, "Christ's teaching" or "teaching from Christ," is supported by Brooke, Bruce, Chaine, Luther, Polhill, Schnackenburg, Schneider, Stott, THLJ, Westcott. Distinctly favorable to this interpretation are the uses of *didachē* in GJohn ("my teaching" and "teaching from me" in 7:16,17; "his [Christ's] teaching" in 18:19). See also the patently subjective genitives with *didachē* in Rev 2:14,15: "the teaching of Balaam," "the teaching of the Nicolaitans." Since the Presbyter criticizes the secessionists for being too advanced and neglecting the "commandment we have had from the beginning" (v. 5), it would be quite logical for him to want people to remain rooted in teaching that comes from Jesus himself. This subjective interpretation of the genitive eliminates the need to posit a human teaching about Christ, and so eliminates any conflict with I John 2:27, which denies the need of teachers.

One objection against this theory, which has been offered by B. Weiss, *Briefe* 182, is that the author should have said "teaching of Jesus" not "teaching of Christ" if he meant a possessive. However, as we saw in I John 2:22; 5:1, it is important to stress against the secessionists that "Jesus is the Christ." Of the 14 epistolary instances of the name "Jesus," it is associated with "Christ" 10 times. (As for the other 4 instances, in I John 4:3 "Christ" is implied from 4:2; and in 1:7; 4:15; 5:5 "Son of God" takes its place.) Indeed, this is the only epistolary instance where "Christ" is found without "Jesus." In speaking of "the teaching of Christ," the Presbyter is probably using the set terminology of faith (Schnackenburg, *Johannesbriefe* 315).

(c) Both SUBJECTIVE AND OBJECTIVE GENITIVE, a "teaching from Christ which is now teaching about Christ," is proposed by Balz, Wilder (?), and Windisch. While this is an attractive explanation, in judging it one must distinguish between fact and the Johannine perception of fact. From the historian's viewpoint the christological formulations that we find in the Johannine Epistles go beyond what Jesus taught during his ministry (even as portrayed in GJohn), and so they constitute teaching about Christ. But in Johannine self-understanding, with its emphasis upon "what was from the beginning," this teaching about Christ may have been considered the teaching of Christ. After all the Paraclete speaks "only what he hears . . . it is from me that he will receive what he will declare to you" (John 16:14–15).

My own view is that there is no need to introduce the objective genitive into the interpretation. Indeed, the idea of anything other than Jesus' own teaching may have been anathema to the Johannine tradition. I shall develop in the COMMENT the role of the Paraclete in Christ's teaching.

9b. *does not possess God.* The verb is *echein*, "to have," encountered in a similar construction in I John 2:23 (cited under [a] in the preceding NOTE), namely, "to possess the Father." G.A.J. Ross, *The Expositor*, seventh series, 9 (1910) 187–92, would translate this as "does not retain his hold on God." However, in the NOTE on I John 2:23 we saw that "to have God" echoes covenantal language and involves a living relationship based on having God's own life, which is possible only through Jesus. We saw also that, while the claim to possess God may have been shared by the author and the secessionists, for the author not remaining in Jesus' teaching invalidates the secessionist claim. Heise, *Bleiben* 168–69, paradoxically uses the parallel passages, I John 2:23 and II John 9, as proof of a serious difference between the two works. In the context of the former (2:27) it is Jesus' anointing that teaches, and one must abide in him, while in II John 9 it is the teaching of Jesus in which one must abide. However, in I John there is already some localizing of truth in doctrine or teaching as can be seen from the christological formulas. I John 2:24 states, "If you have abiding in you what you heard from the beginning, then will you yourselves abide in the Son"—a passage that almost bridges what Heise sees in conflict.

9c. *while anyone who remains rooted in the teaching.* The Byzantine tradition and some MSS. of the Vulgate add "of Christ" (Augustine: "his"), thus making 9c agree with 9a.

9d. *possesses both the Father and the Son.* To remain in Jesus' teaching implies the indwelling of the Paraclete (see COMMENT), who is the ongoing presence of Jesus while Jesus is with the Father—thus the possession of "the Son." True understanding of Jesus enables one to recognize God (the term used in 9b) as "Father." Codex Alexandrinus, minuscule 33, and some Vulgate MSS. reverse the word order to "the Son and the Father," probably as an expression of the logic just mentioned.

10ab. *If anyone comes to you who does not bring this teaching.* The condition, expressed by *ei* and the indicative, is not merely hypothetical. The same type of condition occurs in II Cor 11:4: "If anyone comes proclaiming another Jesus whom we have not proclaimed . . . ," and there too the writer expects the event described to happen. (Have the secessionist teachers already set out from the area where the Presbyter lives so that they are on their way to the "Elect Lady"?) Yet II John is more precise than II Corinthians, for the Presbyter has identified the "another Jesus" whom the secessionists are proclaiming; it is a Jesus not coming in the flesh. The coordination of the two verbs for coming and bringing (teaching) suggests that those who come do so for the purpose of alien teaching.

10cd. *do not receive him into the house and greet him.* Literally, "and do not say to him, 'Greetings,'" employing the verb *chairein,* which is normally used at the beginning of a secular letter (Appendix V A). It is replaced in the "Greeting" of II John (v. 3) by *charis,* "grace," but its use here as the letter closes is not inappropriate for it serves both in receiving people ("Hello") and in dismissing them ("Goodbye"). Some would use that fact to argue that the two actions in 10cd are sequential: Neither receive such a person when he comes nor wish him well when he leaves. However, the rhythm of the verse where the two verbs in the protasis (10ab) constitute the one action of coming to teach suggests that the two verbs in the apodosis also constitute the one action of receiving and initial greeting. (The repeated negative, "do not," indicates emphasis, not distinction.) More may be involved than incivility at the door of a private home, for the anarthrous *oikia* may be the house used for Community meetings: the Johannine house-church in the area addressed. The Presbyter would then be forbidding the reception of the false teachers at the place and on the occasion where their teaching could be spread. (It is noteworthy, however, even if not decisive, that not *oikia* but *oikos* is used in the clear references to house-churches in Rom 16:5; I Cor 16:19; Col 4:15; Philem 2.) The import of refusing a greeting is heightened because Christians greeted one another, not simply as fellow human beings, but as brothers and sisters in the sense of being fellow children of God.

11. *for whoever greets him shares in his evil deeds.* A few minor witnesses omit the "him," making the statement even more universal. The Greek word order, "in his deeds, the evil ones," emphasizes the danger of contamination; for in Johannine dualism "the Evil One" is a title for Satan (I John 2:13–14), the Prince of this world. A close parallel is in I John 3:12: "Not like Cain who belonged to *the Evil One* and killed his brother. And why did he kill him? Because *his own deeds were evil,* while his brother's were just." "Evil" and

"deeds" (*erga*) are joined in John 3:19: "Now the judgment is this: the light has come into the world, but people have preferred darkness to light because their deeds were evil"; and in 7:7: "The world . . . hates me because of the evidence that I bring against it that its deeds are evil." The verb "to share, have communion with" is *koinōnein*, used only here in the Johannine writings, but related to the *koinōnia*, "communion," of I John 1:3–7 (NOTE on 1:3c). The fact that II John uses the verb while I John uses the noun 3 times with *echein*, "to have [communion]," is scarcely a proof of different authors, especially since here it is a case of sharing in deeds rather than having communion with people. Similar to II John in vocabulary and mindset is I Tim 5:22, "Do not share [*koinōnein*] in another man's sins."

11b. There is a Latin addition that appears with variants in some Vulgate MSS. (particularly in the Spanish tradition influenced by Isidore of Seville) and in the *Speculum* of Pseudo-Augustine: "Look! I have foretold [it] to you lest you be confused/condemned on the Day of the Lord." (Harnack, "Über" 15, argues that the condemn/confuse variant reflects a Greek original.) It is a negative counterpart to I John 4:17, which speaks of our having "confidence on Judgment Day." The addition brings out the implicit eschatological message of the preceding verses in II John.

12ab. *Though I have much more to write you, I cannot be bothered with paper and ink.* Literally, "Having [pres. ptcp.] many things to write [pres. infin.] to you [pl.], I did not desire [aorist *boulesthaī*] through paper and ink." One must supply the infinitive "to write" after "desire," even though that produces an illogical sentence, as if there were some other way of writing than by using paper and ink. The similar statement in III John is only slightly less unpolished: "I had [imperf.] many things to have written [aorist infin.] to you [sg.], but I do not wish [pres. *thelein*] to write [pres. infin.] through ink and pen." (Variants betray scribal attempts to improve the Greek of both passages and/or to conform one to the other.) Presumably the Presbyter means that he had many other things *to say* to the addressees, but he did not wish to write them. *Boulesthai*, "to wish, intend, desire," appears as an epistolary aorist (BDF 334) expressing the present mind of the author (cf. the present tense in III John), but one that will be a past intention by the time the letter is received. The preposition *dia*, "through," with the genitive is used for manner and means (MGNTG 3, 267; IBNTG 54–57). The word *chartēs*, translated as "paper," refers to a papyrus product, rather than to the more expensive parchment (*membrana*) mentioned in II Tim 4:13. The neuter of the adjective for "black" (*melas*) serves as a substantive for "ink," since that liquid often was made of lampblack (or black obtained by burning resin) mixed in a gum that had been thinned by water or vinegar, with the quality determined by the proportion of the components. The noun is used symbolically in II Cor 3:3, "You are an epistle of Christ . . . written not with ink but with the Spirit of the living God."

12cd. *Instead, I hope to come to you and have a heart-to-heart talk.* In place of "Instead" (*alla*, "but"), Codex Alexandrinus, minuscule 33, and some versional witnesses read "For" (*gar*). The last part is literally "to speak mouth-to-mouth." Cf. the similar statement in III John 14: "Rather [de] I hope to see you immediately, and we shall speak mouth-to-mouth." The use of the verb *ginesthai* (literally, "to become") with a preposition of motion to cover a change of location (metaphorical or actual), thus "to come," is well attested in the Johannine writings (John 6:19,21; 10:35). It is also found in the papyri, e.g., Tebtunis Papyri II 298: "As soon as you have received my letters, *come* to me." Bonsirven, *Epîtres* 259, cites such vulgar Greek as an indication of the author's mediocre culture; and later scribes improved by substituting *erchesthai*, "to come." The "mouth-to-mouth" expression, used in II and III John, occurs in both the MT and LXX of Num 12:8 (God to Moses) and Jer 32(39):4, but also in a Greek magical papyrus (Berlin Zenon I 39). An equivalent expression, "face-to-face," occurs in I Cor 13:12 (also Gen 32:31[30]; and of God to Moses in Deut 34:10).

12e. *so that our joy may be fulfilled.* The "our" reading is supported by Codex Sinaiticus, some Byzantine Greek and Syriac witnesses, while a "your [pl.]" reading is supported by Codices Vaticanus and Alexandrinus, and by the Vulgate, Coptic, and Ethiopic versions. (Minor scribal improvements caused by this division include the omission of the pronoun altogether and the substitution of "my.") Modern scholars are as divided as the textual witnesses, with Marshall, Metzger, Schnackenburg, and Wilder favoring "our," and Brooke, Chaine, and Harnack favoring "your." The "our" supporters argue that this pronoun was changed by scribes to "your" to match the two instances of "you [pl.]" that occur in 12a and 12c. The "your" supporters argue that this pronoun was changed by scribes to "our" to match the expression in I John 1:4, "so that our joy may be fulfilled" (where, however, the pronoun is also disputed). Even if one decides upon the "our" as the more difficult reading and therefore most likely to have been changed, it is unclear what the pronoun means. Is it simply an editorial or majestic first person plural (Houlden), meaning "my"? Is it the "we" of the Johannine School as in I John 1:1–5? Or is it simply "mine" *and* "yours" as the Presbyter includes the children of the Elect Lady in his joy (Metzger, THLJ)? See the NOTE on "we" in I John 1:1b for the details of the various possibilities. Since the Johannine School has not hitherto been in evidence in II John, and since there is no other instance of "we" for "I" in II John, I judge it most likely that "we" means "you and I," as in II John 3a,5c, and 6b. "Joy may be fulfilled" is a periphrastic construction found also in John 16:24 and I John 1:4b (see NOTE there).

13. *The children of your Elect Sister send you greetings.* The verb *aspazesthai*, "to send greetings," is normal epistolary style (Appendix V D). The Presbyter suddenly shifts from the second person plural to the second singular ("your," "you"), as he addresses the church as a collective person. (The theory that the Elect Lady is an individual woman breaks down here, for why would the Elect Sister's children, rather than the Elect Sister herself, send the greetings to the Elect Lady? Holders of that theory have to speculate that the Lady's Elect Sister was dead.) The neuter plural subject "children" (*tekna*) is followed by a singular verb, a rule of classical Greek not always observed in the NT (MGNTG 3, 313); and this nicety tends to give a collective sense to "chil-

dren." Some MSS. of the Latin Vulgate and some late Greek witnesses read "your Sister Church" in place of "your Elect Sister"—a correct scribal interpretation. (Indeed one eleventh-century Greek minuscule [465] identifies the church as Ephesus.) The scribes who made such specifications were not without NT analogies, e.g., "The churches of Asia send you greetings" (I Cor 16:19). The closest parallel is I Pet 5:13: "The Co-elect Woman in Babylon sends you greetings."

13b. Some Greek minuscules and minor versional witnesses add "Grace [be] with/to you," in imitation of the standard benediction in the Pauline Concluding Formula (Appendix V D). That such a benediction would not be foreign to Johannine style is shown by the benediction found authentically in III John 15: "Peace [be] to you." Another addition, "Amen," is found in the Byzantine tradition and the Syriac Peshitta, but is missing in the great majuscule Greek codices. It is of liturgical origin. See the end of the last NOTE on I John 5:21.

COMMENT

Unlike I John, which I do not regard as an epistle (INTRODUCTION V C1), II John and III John are letters of almost equal length (that of a single papyrus sheet). To understand some of the features, a modern reader needs to know how letters were written in antiquity. I have discussed Epistolary Format in Appendix V below, and many of my observations here assume acquaintance with that Appendix. For the similarity of II John to III John in length and structure, see INTRODUCTION II A1.

A. *Opening Formula* (vv. 1–3)

The Sender and the Addressee sections of the *Praescriptio* of II John are succinctly phrased: "The Presbyter to an Elect Lady and her children." In the NOTES I have discussed five theories about the Presbyter and five about the Lady, and here I follow the view I regard as most plausible. "Presbyter" was a current term for designating members of the second generation in the chain of witnesses to the tradition: those who were not eyewitnesses of Jesus themselves but were disciples of the eyewitness disciples (who constituted the first generation). In particular, this Presbyter is plausibly a disciple of the Beloved Disciple,[1] and so is one whose solidarity with the Johannine eyewitness par excellence enabled him to in-

---

[1] I do not find adequate reason for identifying him as John the Presbyter mentioned by Papias (pp. 12–14 above), although that is a possibility.

clude himself in the "we" of the Johannine School, echoed in I John 1:1–5. I regard him also as the author of I John, which was written to the Community in which he lived, perhaps the central Johannine Community. If he employs a title in writing II and III John,[2] it is because he is in a different relationship to the churches addressed or described therein, which are at a distance from him. The "Elect Lady" is a symbolic designation for one of the churches, a "sister" (v. 13) to the church of the author.

Why did the Presbyter not simply designate his addressee as "the church of God in/of [place]," as in the Pauline Epistles? Or why did he not use an address akin to the formula in Revelation's seven letters, "To the angel of the church in [place]"? He has no general aversion to the word "church," for he uses it in III John 9 precisely in reference to a letter that he wrote "to the church."[3] And if the author wanted to stress the notion of "elect" apparent in "Elect Lady," one may ask why he did not write, "To the elect in [place]," along the lines of I Pet 1:1? There are many suggestions that I would deem unconvincing, e.g., he used symbolic language to disguise his purpose from non-Christian readers (Why would they have any interest in such a letter?); or he wished to escape persecution by anti-Christians (Why then mention Jesus Christ so clearly in vv. 3,5?). Less unlikely is the contention by Dodd (*Epistles* 145) that such symbolism as "Elect Lady" was simply a "conceit conforming to the taste of the period." Yet even then does not such a designation betray a high understanding of the value of the group of disciples so addressed? This church is so related to the Lord (*kyrios*) that one can give to it a form of his name, "Lady" (*kyria*). Such closeness may reflect the Johannine imagery of Jesus as the vine and his followers as the branches (John 15). And the designation of the Lady as *eklekta*[4] may reflect John 15:16 where the Johannine Jesus says to his followers, "I chose you," using the related verb, *eklegesthai*. The collective thrust of the symbolic title "Elect Lady" is extended by the family imagery whereby the Christians in that church are designated as "her children." The language is different from that of *koinōnia*, "communion," in the opening of I John (1:3), but the import is the same.

After the designation of the Addressee but before the Greeting of the letter, the Presbyter with intensity states three times that his love for the

---

[2] Also in these letters he speaks most often as "I," whereas "we" is more common in I John (except with the verb of writing).

[3] One may theorize, however, that the network unifying the Johannine churches was so tightly woven that a house-church did not think of itself as "the church at [place]."

[4] Ignatius, *Trall.* Opening Formula, calls the church at Tralles "elect and worthy of God," a designation supportive of the reverential attitude I detect in the "Elect Lady" of II John.

church addressed is based on truth:[5] "In truth I love you"; "And not only I but also those who have come to know the truth"; "This love is based on the truth that abides in us" (vv. 1b,1c,2a). While NT letters tend to expand the Opening Formula by underlining the privileges of Christians (Appendix V A), such a preoccupation to relate love to truth needs an explanation, especially since the simple "In truth I love you" of III John is not intense. In my judgment the truth-love statements of II John 1–2 help to prove that in Johannine theology love of one another or love of brother means loving one's fellow Johannine Christians who share the truth that Jesus is the Christ, the Son of God—a truth that is not simply an abstract doctrine but a salvific principle.[6] The Presbyter loves the church he addresses in II John because its members are Johannine Christians and are his brothers and sisters inasmuch as they are God's children.[7] They have not "gone out" (I John 2:19) as have those whom he will condemn in the letter for not confessing Jesus properly (v. 7). Since the secessionists do not have the truth, one need not show love for them (vv. 10–11). Implicit in all this is the warning that if those addressed are seduced by the secessionists or even welcome the secessionist missionaries, they will no longer be in the truth and loved with a love that is based on the truth. "Those who have come to know the truth" (1c) is probably a self-description used by members of the Johannine Community,[8] and the Presbyter is reminding his addressees that such a designation imposes an obligation to keep walking in the truth (4). It is a truth that has to "be with us forever" (2b), because it is a manifestation of the presence of the Spirit of Truth, of whom Jesus said, "the Father will give you another Paraclete to be with you forever" (John 14:16).

The Greeting in v. 3 is unusual because it is not expressed as a wish but as a confident statement.[9] Truth already abides and will be with us forever, but now the Presbyter adds that it will be accompanied by "grace, mercy, and peace." This confidence represents an interesting blend of the realized eschatology dominant in GJohn and the final eschatology of I

[5] In the respective NOTES I argued that de la Potterie and others are correct in taking all the "in truth" phrases in II John 1–4 theologically (i.e., "truth" is the sphere from which the activity flows) and not simply adverbially ("sincerely," "truly").

[6] Those who believe in Jesus and thus know the truth receive eternal life (John 20:31; I John 5:20).

[7] The same term (plural of *teknon,* "child") is used 4 times in I John for children of God and 3 times in II John for children of a church (the Elect Lady and her Elect Sister).

[8] If the truth involved doctrine about Jesus (II John 7) and a commandment to love that was "had from the beginning" (v. 5), knowledge of the truth may have been associated with entrance into the Community.

[9] However, even in the usual Pauline Greeting, which is expressed in part as a wish, "Grace [be] to you and peace," one should not underestimate Paul's assurance that these gifts are being given by God.

John. An author faithful to the Johannine tradition might well be uncomfortable with the usual Christian epistolary wish that the addressee receive grace, mercy, and peace; for Johannine Christians should already possess these gifts. In the GJohn Prologue we heard, "Of his fullness we have all had a share, grace in place of grace" (1:16). At the Last Supper Jesus said to his disciples, "My 'peace' is my gift to you" (14:27) and the risen Jesus bestowed peace on those who encountered him (20:21,26). True, there is no mention of *eleos*, "mercy," in GJohn, but that word is a standard LXX translation of *ḥesed*, the covenant virtue for which *charis*, "grace," is another translation (ABJ 29, 14). Thus the combination "grace and mercy" represents the fruits of the New Covenant of which the prophets had spoken (see also Wis 3:9; 4:15), even as peace is a promised aspect of the reign of God (Isa 52:7). Such marks of divine favor, in Johannine thought, would have been received when believers became part of the Community. Nevertheless, it is important to the author in II John, even as it was in I John, to underline a future aspect of God's benevolence, as a check against those who would maintain that Christians need not worry about sin or about how they "walk." There are false teachers on the horizon who may come to the Elect Lady and her children in order to deny "the truth" (vv. 9–10) and thus to lead people out of the Johannine *koinōnia* (vv. 7,10). Consequently, the Presbyter speaks of "grace, mercy, and peace" as gifts that "will be with us forever" *in truth and love,* i.e., so long as "we" do not move away from the truth (v. 9) and lose the love of the Johannine brotherhood.

B. *Expression of Joy Transitional to the Body of the Letter* (v. 4)

In Epistolary Format a statement of joy is often transitional to the Body of the Letter. (As I shall report in Appendix V BC, what is not clear is whether in II and III John [and in Polycarp, *Philippians*] this is another form of the Thanksgiving, or is simply a feature of the Body-Opening.) The joy expressed by the Presbyter is not merely a statement of benevolence to win favor; it gives us an insight into the state of the church addressed. Joy at finding "some of your children walking in truth" indicates that the secession, while a danger, has not yet torn the church apart.[10] What is the author's precise thought in speaking of "walking in truth, just as we received a commandment from the Father"? Plausibly he

[10] As mentioned in the NOTE on 4a, many commentators take the partitive to mean that some but not all the children are walking in truth and that, therefore, in the church addressed there is a group of whom the Presbyter disapproves, a group not walking in truth. I see no such implication: the author is speaking of the "some" of whom he has knowledge.

is speaking of a general attitude, involving both belief and behavior, which shows that those who so walk have the truth abiding in them (see v. 2). Jesus' own ministry of preaching and healing was considered as a word or command given him by the Father (John 8:55; 10:18), i.e., a living out of the Father's will, which was his own will (10:30). Correspondingly the Christian child of God who has received Jesus' life and Spirit comes under the commandment or expressed will of the Father. Yet if this is the meaning of "walking in truth" and if the Presbyter has found the Christians addressed walking in truth, why in the verses that follow does he need to stress love for one another (vv. 5–6) and belief in Jesus Christ coming in the flesh (v. 7)? In the light of I John and II John 7 a plausible explanation is that they are the two points of established Johannine practice and belief that will be challenged by the secessionists when they arrive teaching false doctrine (v. 10). In all this the Presbyter shows the same sovereign confidence in judging Johannine truth and its proper manifestation that the author of I John demonstrated, a fact that supports identical authorship.[11]

C. *Request Concerning the Commandment to Love* (vv. 5–6)

In discussing Epistolary Format (Appendix V C) I point to the petition as a second feature of the Body-Opening, following the expression of joy. II John 5 announces the petition politely, "My Lady, I would make a request of you," and then gives the content of the request in terms of the commandment to love one another that "we have had from the beginning." The Presbyter's comments on this commandment are couched in obscure syntax, and in the NOTES I have explained the various attempts by scholars to avoid the seeming tautology of *walking according to a commandment to walk in it!* From the syntactical quagmire the following points emerge as significant.

First, the polite vocative, "my Lady," and the verb for requesting are established features of Epistolary Format; and so one must be careful in using them to diagnose the relationship between the Presbyter and the church addressed, e.g., in arguing that his making a request proves that he had no authority. In vv. 8 and 10 the Presbyter moves closer to a directive; and with all his formal politeness he expects cooperation.[12] The most

[11] If the authors are not thought to be the same, at least one must admit that they have similar pastoral roles vis-à-vis their addressees. And as becomes apparent in vv. 5–6, they have much the same vocabulary and lack of concern about syntax (to a degree that separates them from the evangelist of GJohn).

[12] In III John 9–10 he betrays indignation when a letter from him has been ignored. Yet all this falls short of the tone of apostolic authority we see in the Pauline Epistles.

one can argue is that the lack of such formal politeness in I John (which has a different literary format, however) may indicate that the writer's relationship to the recipients of I John is more familiar than his relationship to the recipients of II John. He addresses the latter as the children of the Elect Lady; he addresses the former as his children.

Second, in presenting his request about observing the commandment to love one another, the Presbyter stresses that it is a commandment received from the Father (v. 4b), a commandment that is not new (5b) but which we have had from the beginning (5c,6d). The traditional character of the Presbyter's demands is probably meant to contrast with novelties of the progressive teachers (9). By using the idiom of walking "according to His commandments" and walking "in it," the author thinks of the commanded love as expressing itself in a way of life. Presumably the Presbyter feels there is some challenge to the necessity of such "walking," but he does not explain what this will be. Since in the next verse (7) he mentions secessionists (those who have "gone out") who are guilty of a christological error similar to that condemned in I John, and since the language of keeping commandments, new commandment, "heard from the beginning," and loving one another is shared with I John, surely the Presbyter is worried by the ethical errors of the I John secessionists, namely, that the way one lives is of little salvific importance and that one need not show love for one's former Johannine "brothers."

Third, although he uses a traditional formula in the first person plural, "Let *us* love one another" (NOTE on 5d), his use of "we" in 5c and 6b makes it plausible that he is deliberately including himself in the exhortation. He may be worried that the challenge to come from the false teachers (vv. 9–10) will disrupt love not only among the children of the Elect Lady (by creating a secession in that church) but also between them and him (and his adherents). The teachers will seek to set the children of the Elect Lady against the Presbyter with whose christology and ethics they disagree.[13]

While these three points have a relatively firm basis in the text of II John, far less certain is the contention of Klein, "Licht" 506, that II John 5–6 betrays a loss of eschatological sense over against I John, and *a fortiori* over against GJohn. For Klein the reference in John 13:34 to "a new commandment" reflects "the hour" that transcends time and makes all things new. In I John 2:7–8 a historicizing process has set in (pp. 287–88 above); for the commandment is described as not new but old and thus has been fitted into a time sequence, so that it was given long ago. Yet the

---

[13] The Presbyter's attempt to exclude the teachers from the house(-church?) of the Christians addressed, whether or not successful, will certainly produce propaganda against the Presbyter by the teachers, if they are not already hostile to him from past conflict.

author of I John corrects himself ("On second thought, the commandment I write you is new"), indicating that he still has some eschatological sensitivity. But II John 5b states without qualification, "It is not as if I were writing you some new commandment." However, is Klein methodologically correct in pressing this argument from silence, based on the omission of a qualification, when he is comparing works of such different length as I John and II John? Even if we suppose that there were two authors, if the author of II John knew I John, did he omit the afterthought about the newness of the commandment because he had a different view, or was he being governed by the planned size of II John (determined by the length of one papyrus sheet) and so could mention only essentials? If the newness of the commandment were part of the Johannine tradition enshrined in John 13:34, there may have been no need to emphasize it. And certainly emphasis on newness was not the Presbyter's goal as he sought to alert the addressees against *progressive* teachers.

D. *Warning against the Antichrists and Their Teaching* (vv. 7–11)

The Presbyter moves on from the commandment about loving one another to the need for confessing Jesus Christ coming in the flesh. The grammatical connection between the two ("For") reinforces the impression that he is dealing with one set of opponents. (Compare the twofold commandment to believe and to love in I John 3:23.) The apocalyptic language he uses for those opponents ("the Deceiver . . . the Antichrist") calls sharply into question Klein's thesis that II John is the most deeschatologized of the Johannine writings, for it is the same language used for the secessionists in I John 2:18–27; 4:1–6.[14] Both works see "those who have gone out [into the world]" (II John 7; I John 2:19; 4:1,5) as a sign of the last times, for the secessionists are the embodiment of the Antichrist expectation (NOTE on I John 2:18a) and are the expected false prophets who will *deceive* even the elect.[15]

Their deception that moves against (*anti*) Christ is manifested in the refusal to confess "Jesus Christ coming in the flesh." (As seen many times before, the Johannine mentality does not attribute to ignorance a failure to confess "the truth"; the failure is always malicious and a manifestation

---

[14] So close is II John 7 to I John that Irenaeus, in citing the II John passage verbatim, speaks of it as belonging to the same epistle as I John 2:18–19 (INTRODUCTION I B2).

[15] Terms such as "the Deceiver" and "the Liar" (II John 7; I John 2:22; cf. 4:6) may be related to the eschatological expectations of the deceiving false christs and false prophets (Mark 13:21–22) and of the deceiving man of iniquity (II Thess 2:3,9–12).

of the diabolic.[16]) There is insufficient context in II John to enable us to surmise what the author means by this formula, and so most scholars interpret it through the similar formula in I John 4:2, "Jesus Christ come in the flesh," calling on the more ample context in that work (see NOTE on II John 7b). The past tense in I John is closer to the heart of the secessionist error than is the pres. tense of II John;[17] for seemingly that error consisted in giving no major salvific value to Jesus' earthly ministry (and not in a denial of the incarnation itself). The language of "coming" in relation to Jesus may have sprung from the insistence in Mal 3:1 that the angel of the covenant would *come*.[18] For Christians Jesus was this "one to come"; and I and II John are insisting that in Johannine theology the coming was not completed by the incarnation but continued in the kind of life Jesus lived ("in the flesh"). The use of the present tense ("the coming one") in II John 7 repeats the traditional language, but employs it as an eschatological contrast with the Antichrist. Both eschatological expectations have been realized, so that the person who denies that in his flesh Jesus is "the one to come" becomes the personification of the evil opponent of the one to come. And the appearance of the latter (the Antichrist, the Deceiver) is a sign that the last hour is at hand (I John 2:18). This means that the parousia is at hand, and the "one to come" will come again (cf. I John 2:28). Just as I John warned the readers to be ready for that ("so that, when he is revealed, we may have confidence and not draw back in shame from him at his coming"), so II John 8 warns, "Look out yourselves," a standard apocalyptic formula (see NOTE). We saw in I John that part of the secessionists' error was a lack of emphasis on the parousia; for them judgment had already taken place and there would be no second judgment passed by God on their lives, since the way one walked was not important. Thus with the one formula, "Jesus Christ coming in the flesh," the Presbyter may be striking at the whole range of secessionist deceit: they do not accept the full effects of the first coming and they neglect the second coming.

The implicit motif of the parousia (with accompanying judgment) explains the Presbyter's reference in v. 8 to reward and to loss of "what we have worked for."[19] John 17:12,16 shows that being lost from the companionship of Jesus leads to the realm of evil: Jesus keeps his own "safe

[16] In John 13:27,30 Satan entered into Judas and he "went out" from the company of Jesus.

[17] Yet an interchangeability of tense is suggested by comparing descriptions of Jesus with the past tense of "come" in John 3:19; 9:39; 12:46; and 18:37 and one with the pres. ptcp. in 11:27.

[18] Notice the title of the book on Jewish messianism by S. Mowinckel, *He that Cometh* (Nashville: Abingdon, 1954).

[19] The same context is found in Rev 22:12: "Behold, I am *coming* soon, and my *reward* is with me to give to each according to his *work*."

from the Evil One" so that "not one of them was lost except the son of perdition [loss]." The latter is a reference to Judas who had "gone out" (footnote 16). The idea of working for a reward must be understood in light of John 6:29, which illustrates the breadth of the term "work" by describing faith as a work. Those who are made children of God through faith in Jesus Christ shall see God as He is (I John 3:2). If the secessionists come and lead them astray by false teaching about Christ, they will lose the very basis for such a reward.

Verse 9 repeats this in another way: The addressees will not continue to possess God if they do not remain rooted in the teaching of Christ.[20] I have argued in the NOTE on 9a that "teaching of Christ" means primarily teaching that comes from Christ. Many comment on this passage in light of other late NT works that stress the themes of fidelity to original teaching and of dangerous new ideas. One finds in Jude 3 an appreciation for "the faith delivered once for all to the saints," and in II Tim 4:3–4 an apprehension that "the time will come when people will not put up with sound doctrine [*didaskalia*] but according to their own preferences will collect teachers who will tell them what they want to hear; and they will turn their ears away from the truth to myths." The Paul of Acts 20:30–31 warns, "From among you will arise men who speak perverted things in order to draw away the disciples after them, and so you must watch out." The Paul of the Pastorals warns Timothy in I Tim 1:3 to curb "certain people who teach other doctrines." Of such people he writes, "If anyone teaches differently and does not agree with the sound words of our Lord Jesus Christ and with pious teaching, he is conceited and understands nothing" (I Tim 6:3–4). Through the ages such passages have reinforced the Christian struggle against self-delusion; but they have also offered an oratorical quarry for those who judge that all new thoughts are bad thoughts. In judging II John's attack on progressives Dodd, *Epistles* 150, complains, "The writer has incautiously expressed himself in terms which might seem to stigmatize any kind of 'advance' as disloyalty to the faith, and so to condemn Christian theology to lasting sterility." While in this commentary I have not felt obliged to defend the many infelicities of the epistolary author, in this instance I think the subtlety of his thought is being overlooked. The only "progressive" the Presbyter criticizes is one who does not remain rooted in the teaching of Christ. The qualification suggests that in itself the idea of being a progressive was not anathema in the Johannine tradition. Of the four Gospels only GJohn betrays a reflex

---

[20] The attack in v. 9 on "Anyone who is so 'progressive' that he does not remain rooted in the teaching of Christ" refers primarily to the secessionist deceivers; but if the addressees join the ranks of the deceived, it applies to them as well. Moreover, it is the addressees, not the secessionist teachers, whom the Presbyter hopes to reach with this letter.

awareness that what Jesus says was not understood during Jesus' ministry but reflects postresurrectional insight (John 2:21–22; 7:39). That awareness probably came about defensively as the Johannine Community was criticized by other Christians because its traditions (crystallized in GJohn) had moved far beyond what we would call today "the historical Jesus."[21] The elaborate attention to the Paraclete as the legitimate inter- preter of Jesus is best explained if the Community had been challenged as to whether Jesus really said some of the things attributed to him in the Community's tradition. The Johannine Jesus deals with such an objection by announcing, "I have much more to tell you, but you cannot bear it now. When that Spirit of Truth comes, he will guide you along the way of all truth. For he will not speak on his own, but will speak only what he hears and will declare to you the things to come. . . . It is from me that he receives what he will declare to you" (John 16:12–15). This passage would explain why the Presbyter condemns teachers who do not remain rooted in the teaching of Christ—even the Paraclete remains rooted in what was "from the beginning." We are very close here to I John's insist- ence on the necessity of proclaiming what was heard, seen with the eyes, looked at, and felt with the hands (1:1).

The Presbyter's condemnation of progressives, then, is not the same as condemnations in other NT books coming from churches that had a fixed hierarchy of presbyters or an established body of apostolic teaching. The control in the Johannine situation is the Paraclete, and the chain of witnesses is the guide to what has been heard from the beginning. A pro- gressive attitude within those guidelines would not have been con- demned.[22] The dynamic relationship between the teaching of Jesus (the first Paraclete: John 14:16) and the Paraclete/Spirit of Truth who remains in the Christian as the ongoing teacher[23] may explain why the Presbyter can insist alternatively that the Christian must remain in the teaching of Christ and that the truth must remain/abide in the Christian (vv. 9 and 2). It may also explain why the Presbyter can say that the per- son who remains in the teaching possesses both the Father and the Son— the Paraclete who teaches the teaching of Christ is given or sent by the Father (John 14:16,26) and constitutes the continued presence of Jesus,

[21] I do not imagine that the modern question was raised in the first century, but by the end of the second century Clement of Alexandria recognized that the Fourth Gospel was different in degree from the others by calling it "a spiritual Gospel" (Eusebius, *Hist.* 6.14.7).

[22] In my view only in III John and with Diotrephes do we encounter Johannine Christians who, from bitter experience, may have come to believe that the correct al- ternative does exclude being a progressive.

[23] There is peril in explaining II John texts by appealing to the Paraclete figure of GJohn. But II John offers no context; and so one must either be satisfied with no ex- planation or resort to the most plausible Johannine parallel.

God's Son among us.[24] The "reward in full" for the Johannine Christians who already possess the Father and the Son will take place when Christ is revealed at his coming (I John 2:28); for then, although they are "God's children right now," they shall "be like Him" because they shall see Him as He is (3:2).

In vv. 7–9 the Presbyter has been giving a general warning to the addressees about progressives who constitute the Deceiver and the Antichrist, but in 10–11 he gets specific about the danger and thus provides us with an insight into the church situation. He expects that some people will come to the "Elect Lady" and deny his christological affirmation about Jesus Christ come in the flesh. The grammar (NOTES on v. 10) makes it unlikely that he is speaking of haphazard travelers or even of general missionaries. He is thinking of those who will come specifically to teach a contradictory interpretation of the coming of Christ. Harnack, "Über" 18, supposes that practice of visiting missionaries must be a relatively new one since proportionately there is so much instruction on it in II John. I think the opposite is more likely: Because the addressees are accustomed to having people come proclaiming the Johannine teaching of Christ,[25] the Presbyter must alert them that now there will come those who are bringing a teaching that is not of Christ, a teaching that betrays the tradition. (He is not rebuking the addressees about having been too hospitable in the past, for up to now there has been no reason not to be hospitable.) If so, this would mean that the various Johannine churches constituted a network, with emissaries customarily going from one to the other (a situation confirmed in III John). Only recently has a danger arisen because of former Johannine Christians (now "gone out") who have a diverse teaching. This picture would make sense if II John was written shortly after the schism described in I John 2:19. The secessionists would not have been in existence long enough for them automatically to be recognizable as different, and so the Presbyter is supplying a doctrinal criterion to an outlying church that secessionist missionaries have not reached but soon will.

One may raise an objection to this thesis from the customary letters of recommendation of which we know from other NT writings (NOTE on III John 12a below). These are letters written by a known Christian figure to vouch for prospective Christian travelers, encouraging churches in the places they would visit to receive and listen to them. How could the envi-

---

[24] In GJohn theology eternal life is given by divine begetting through the Spirit (3:5), and that life is the life of Jesus, the Son, who has it because of the Father (6:57).

[25] In III John the hospitable receiving of those who set out for the sake of the Name is the usual and desirable practice, and the Presbyter is upset that Diotrephes refuses to follow it.

sioned deceivers of II John hope to be received by the "Elect Lady" without such a letter, and would not its absence have been an easy way of detecting them? One might speculate that they would have letters of recommendation from *their* leaders and that a major danger in the secession lay in its being advanced by Johannine leaders of note.[26] There is no suggestion of that in I John, however, for the author seems confident that he speaks in the name of the "we" of the Johannine School. More plausibly one may speculate that the practice of letters of recommendation had not yet developed in the Johannine network of churches precisely because this Community was so close-knit. Perhaps the crisis of the present moment made it necessary to introduce that practice, and we shall see the beginnings of it in III John 12.

In any case it is clear that the Presbyter does not think he is facing a problem created by well-meaning Christians who are in error. He sees his opponents as dedicated propagandists who are going from one Johannine church to another spreading the secession through their false teaching. These teachers intend to do damage to the addressees whom the Presbyter loves "in truth," i.e., loves on the basis of the common Johannine faith about Christ (II John 1). They can do that only if they are received into the house-church so that they can speak to the assembled addressees and also receive from them the support to go to another church (III John 6b). Thus the "Do not receive him into the house and greet him" of v. 10 is not an invitation to petty harassment by the refusal of amenities; it is an attempt to keep the teachers away from the church[27] and to put obstacles in the way of their continued mission. If to receive the Presbyter's emissaries is to "become coworkers with the truth" (III John 8), to receive the secessionist teachers is to share in their evil deeds (II John 11) and to become coworkers with deceit. Since the verb "to share" in v. 11 is *koinōnein*, greeting the secessionist teachers as fellow Christians is to have *koinōnia* with them; but in the mind of the author of I John, in order to have eternal life one must have *koinōnia* with him and the other members of the Johannine School (I John 1:3) and precisely not with those who have gone out. *Koinōnia* with that author and his fellow witnesses involves *koinōnia* "with the Father and with His Son, Jesus Christ." *Koinōnia* with the secessionist teachers, says the Presbyter, involves *koinōnia* with the Evil One whose deeds they manifest (NOTE on 11). The

[26] Again, we must remember that from the viewpoint of the adversaries of I and II John the epistolary author was the one who had departed from the tradition (perhaps by not being progressive enough) and they may have spoken of his seceding from them.

[27] House-churches will be discussed at the beginning of the COMMENT on III John, and the fact that house-churches are almost certainly involved in that letter increases the possibility that "house" in II John 10 refers to the house where the "Elect Lady" is centered, i.e., the house where the church meets (NOTE on 10cd).

inhospitality urged by vv. 10–11 is part of the warfare between Christ and Antichrist, between the Spirit of Truth and the Spirit of Deceit (I John 4:6), between the people who belong to God and the people who belong to the world (I John 4:2,5; II John 7), between God's children and the devil's children (I John 3:10).[28]

In judging this inhospitable attitude we may begin by discussing its relation to other NT thought. There are NT passages that advocate kindness even toward those with whom one disagrees: "If you greet only your brothers, are you doing anything outstanding? Do not even pagans do that?" (Matt 5:47). Yet we do not find unlimited kindness toward former Christians or former members of a church: "If a person refuses to listen even to the church, let him be to you as a pagan and a tax collector" (Matt 18:17). Paul's judgment in I Cor 5:4–5 is severe on a fellow Christian with whom he disagrees: "When you are assembled . . . you are to deliver this man to Satan for the destruction of the flesh, so that the spirit may be saved on the Day of the Lord." The Pastoral Epistles continue this tradition: "As for a man who is divisive [hairetikos], after admonishing him once or twice, have nothing more to do with him" (Titus 3:10). In Rev 2:2 John the prophet has Christ praise the angel of the church of Ephesus: "I know that you cannot tolerate wicked men, and that you have tested those who claim to be apostles but are not, and that you have found them liars." In a story reported by Irenaeus (Adv. haer. 3.3.4), when John the disciple of the Lord encountered Cerinthus in the baths of Ephesus, he fled from any contact with this "enemy of truth," even as Polycarp bishop of Smyrna shunned Marcion, "I do not know you, first-born of Satan." Irenaeus comments, "Such was the horror of the apostles and their disciples against holding even verbal communication with any corrupters of the truth."

The attitude of avoiding contact with deviating brothers may have been heightened by the missionary situation. Hospitality to traveling coreligionists was an extremely important motif among early Christians.[29] To some extent the attitude was traceable to the demand placed by Jesus upon his disciples, "Whoever receives you receives me, and whoever receives me receives Him who sent me" (Matt 10:40; Mark 9:37). Those who used the expected hospitality to disseminate false doctrine became a

---

[28] Bonsirven, Epîtres 257, thinks that in vv. 10–11 the Presbyter is pronouncing an excommunication against the deceiving teachers. Rather, in the Johannine outlook the Presbyter is calling attention to their own choice to "go out" from the Community and thus to reveal what they already were. The Presbyter never hints that such resistance to the teachers will bring them to see their errors. Probably he would think that they have no more chance of conversion than has the Prince of this world who already has been condemned (John 16:11), for they have gone out to the world that is his.

[29] Rom 12:13; I Tim 5:10; Heb 13:2; I Pet 4:9; Matt 10:11–14.

problem in many places at the end of the first century. An anguish about how to differentiate among coreligionists is apparent in *Didache* 11:1–2: "Whenever someone comes and teaches you all these things we have talked about, receive him. But if the teacher himself has deviated by teaching another doctrine that contradicts these things, do not listen to him." Ignatius writes to the *Smyrnaeans* (4:1), "I guard you in advance against beasts in the form of men whom you must not only not receive but, if possible, not even meet—only pray for them."[30] In *Eph.* 7:1 Ignatius criticizes those "who make a practice of carrying about the Name with wicked guile and do certain other things unworthy of God; these you must shun as wild beasts."[31] He continues in 9:1: "I have learned that there have stayed with you some outsiders who had bad doctrine; but by stopping your ears you did not allow them to sow it among you." Of course, this was not a problem peculiar to Christianity. Trypho, the Jewish scholar of Justin's *Dialogue* (38:1), is portrayed as saying to Christians, "We should have obeyed our teachers when they made a law that we should not converse with you . . . for you say many blasphemous things." In the Mandaean *Ginza Right* 9.1 (Lidzbarski, p. 224) we read, "My disciple, do not offer the prophet any greeting or extend your hand."

A dualistic mentality produced the directive in I John 10–11, and it had many parallels in antiquity; but some comments are in order about its repetition through the ages. Irenaeus, *Adv. haer.* 1.16.3, made it contemporary when he applied it to gnostic opponents who separated from the church and gave heed to fables: "John the disciple of the Lord has intensified their condemnation when he desires us not even to address them with a greeting of 'good-speed.'" With Latin logic Tertullian (*De praescriptione haereticorum* 37:1–7; CC 1, 217–18) concludes that heretics have no rights in the church; and in later centuries Christians have concluded that the way to be certain that heretical ideas are not taught is to execute the heretics. And in our times II John 10–11 has been used as justification for slamming doors in the face of Jehovah's Witnesses and other door-to-door missionaries. Typical of one type of comment is Plummer, *Epistles* 139, who recognizes that "the severity of injunction [in II John] is almost without a parallel in the NT," but then goes on to say,

[30] In encouraging prayers Ignatius is more generous than the author of I John 5:16cd, who discourages prayer for the deadly sin (of the secessionists). In *Smyrn.* 7:1–2 Ignatius speaks of Christians who do not confess that the Eucharist is the flesh of Jesus Christ who suffered for our sins: "It is right to stay away from such people and not even to speak about them in private or in public." He is not far from the mentality of the Presbyter who wants his addressees to stay away from Christians who deny Jesus Christ coming *in the flesh,* or from the attack of I John upon those who do not give attention to Jesus' death as an atonement for sin (1:7; 2:2).

[31] In III John 7 those who "set out for the sake of *the Name*" is a description of missionaries.

"Charity has its limits: it must not be shewn to one man in such a way as to do grievous harm to others." To those who acknowledge the time-conditioned limitations in II John's injunction, Alford would reply: We are not "at liberty to set aside direct ethical injunctions of the Lord's Apostles in this manner." Dodd, *Epistles* 152, on the other hand, argues, "We may similarly decline to accept the Presbyter's ruling here as a sufficient guide to Christian conduct," for it is "incompatible with the general purport of the teaching of the New Testament." While the examples from the NT quoted above call the latter part of Dodd's statement into question, the first part is obvious. Fierce exclusiveness, even in the name of truth, usually backfires on its practitioners; and in III John we find the Presbyter angry when the very practice that he advocates toward the secessionist missionaries is put into effect against his own missionaries. In retrospect the Presbyter may have come to wonder whether it would not have been wiser to do unto his adversaries as he would have them do unto him. Stott, *Epistles* 213–14, tends to justify the Presbyter on the grounds that the disputed issue involved the essence of Christianity and that the Presbyter had the truth. The problem is that almost every dispute in church history has been judged by one of the parties as involving an essential question, and that almost every drastic action has been justified as done for the sake of the truth. Dodd's question touches a real issue: "Does truth prevail the more if we are not on speaking terms with those whose view of the truth differs from ours—however disastrous their error may be?"

E. *Promise of a Visit, Closing the Body of the Letter* (v. 12)

Among the standard features of the Body-Closing of the Greco-Roman letter (Appendix V C) were a statement about the *writing* of the letter and a proposal of further contact by a *visit*. The stereotyped character of such features must be kept in mind when we analyze how the Presbyter closes the Body of his letter.

Many commentators have interpreted "I have much more to write you" (12a) as if it contained a key to the origin of this letter and to the interrelationship of the Johannine correspondence. It has been asked: Why did the Presbyter not write more? If I John had been written earlier, why did he not attach a copy of it to II John, so that it could serve as the "much more" he wanted to write? Or had the audience already received I John, in which case it is puzzling what more could be said? Could it be that the Presbyter was not able to make the contemplated visit and was forced to write I John after II John,[32] so that I John became the "much more" he wanted to write? (See Houlden, *Epistles* 140.) Did the "much more" consist of confidential matters that he did not wish to mention in a public missive to a church, e.g., matters that would require the naming of names (see Schnackenburg, *Johannesbriefe* 318)? While granting that the Presbyter surely had more that he could write, I maintain that the clause about writing more in 12a is virtually meaningless; and its presence in III John 13 shows that it was simply the writer's way of finishing a letter as he came near the bottom of a papyrus sheet (INTRODUCTION II A1). Even today such a clause can serve as a ploy for bringing a letter to a quick conclusion. Thus v. 12a tells nothing about the relative order of the Johannine Epistles. It simply reinforces the information gained from v. 10 that the secessionist teachers have not yet arrived at the church addressed and it is not yet split, so that a cautionary word arriving in time may avert the need for major polemic. The "I have much more to write to you" is the Presbyter's own phrasing of the reflection on the reason for writing that terminates many Greco-Roman letters. The particular wording "much more" (*polla*) may have been influenced by the most authoritative document of the Johannine Community, for originally GJohn terminated with these words: "Jesus also performed many more [*polla*] signs in the presence of his disciples, signs not recorded in this book."

Commentators have speculated also on the information in v. 12bc: "I hope to come to you and have a heart-to-heart talk." Why was the Presbyter writing if he intended to visit? Was the danger of false teachers so imminent that he had to protect the recipients in the interval before he arrived? Was it that he did not wish to seem arrogant instructing them from a distance and so softened his missive by promising to come and "dialogue" with them? Since there is a similar promise in III John addressed to a different church situation, was the Presbyter planning to visit both places on the same journey, and were these Johannine churches in the same general region? While not dismissing such possibilities, I would insist again that one should not read too much into a phrase that is rather standard in the letters of the time (and ever since). The fact that it occurs at the end of both II and III John[33] suggests that it may have been normal style for the Presbyter writing to churches at a distance. This does not

---

[32] There is no promise of a visit in I John, and that is advanced as proof of this theory. Such theories rest on unproved assumptions, e.g., that I John is a letter, or that the same audience is involved.

[33] Bultmann, *Epistles* 115, suspects that II John 12 is copied from III John 13–14, so that imitation explains the similarity of the two Body-Closings. This theory does not explain minor differences (which subsequent scribes smoothed out, illustrating the instinct of the true copier), especially when the Greek of the II John sentence is even more awkward than that of the III John passage (see NOTES on v. 12).

mean that the Presbyter is insincere in his hope of visiting the addressees, any more than a modern letter writer is insincere by completing a letter with the remark, "I hope to see you soon." We may be dealing with a velleity rather than with a fixed plan about the when and how of a visit, just as in the preceding paragraph we saw that the Presbyter need not have had a fixed idea about what and how much more he wanted to write. One may protest that a projected visit cannot have been so indefinite; for in III John at least the Presbyter mentions even earlier in the Body of the letter (where it might not be simply a stereotyped feature of the format), "If I come, I shall bring up what Diotrephes is doing in spreading evil nonsense about us" (v. 10). But the conditional language in which that statement is cast reaffirms that the hope "to come to [or see] you" in II John 12 and III John 14 is not very definite. The contact by letter has been made lest the hope of visit not be realized at all.[34] Most commentators see nothing theological in the "I hope" phrase, which would then be unlike the hope to see God in I John 3:2–3 that was based on God Himself. Yet here the parallelism of other NT letters makes us cautious. In I Cor 16:7 Paul's hope to visit and remain is "if the Lord permits"; and in I Thess 2:17–18 Paul's desire to visit and see the church has been frustrated again and again because "Satan hindered us." In the dualistic Johannine worldview even the simplest hopes were probably seen as dependent on the struggle between the Spirit of Truth and the Spirit of Deceit.

In v. 12a the Presbyter speaks of the purpose of the hoped-for visit: "so that our joy may be fulfilled." The fulfillment of joy is a common Johannine theme (NOTE on I John 1:4b), but in II John as part of the Body-Closing it constitutes an inclusion with the Body-Opening in v. 4. There the Presbyter wrote, "It gave me much joy to find some of your children walking in truth." His aim in the Body of the letter (framed by the Opening and Closing) was to keep the addressees bound together in mutual love and in a correct confession of Jesus Christ—a love and a faith that will bring them to their full reward. If the Presbyter does visit them and is well received, it will be because the anticipated onslaught of the Antichrist teachers has not led them astray (deceived them) from the truth. That will truly be a fulfillment of the joy he has hitherto experienced in his relationship with the "Elect Lady and her children." The fulfillment of joy in I John 1:4 was based on the readers' being joined in *koinōnia* ("communion") with the Johannine School of witnesses ("we/us") and thus with the Father and the Son. In II John a friendly visit by the Pres-

---

[34] Highly problematic is speculation that the Presbyter was uncertain about his plans to visit because of the state of the Johannine church where he lived, already torn apart by the secession.

byter to the Elect Lady will come about if the *koinōnia* and love among "those who have come to know the truth" (v. 1c) have been preserved.

F. *Concluding Formula* (v. 13)

Among the three typical features that constituted the Concluding Formula of a letter in the Roman period (Appendix V D), an expression of greetings (*aspazesthai*) is the only one that appears regularly in NT letters. Frequently Paul joins to his own greetings those of named co-workers. In neither II nor III John does the Presbyter send his own greetings; he sends rather those of the Johannine Christians in the area where he dwells. (This may reflect the *koinōnia* that underlies his understanding of being one in Christ.) In the Opening Formula of II John the addressees are children of the Elect Lady, and in the Concluding Formula the greetings are from the children of her Elect Sister. This constitutes an inclusion that dramatizes the family relationship among believers, whose status as children ultimately flows from their having been begotten by God (John 1:12–13).

BIBLIOGRAPHY PERTINENT TO II JOHN

(See the *Bibliography* for Appendix V on Epistolary Format.)

Bacon, B. W., "Marcion, Papias, and 'The Elders,'" JTS 23 (1922) 134–60, pertinent to "The Presbyter" in II John 1 and III John 1.

Bartlet, V., "The Historical Setting of the Second and Third Epistles of St. John," JTS 6 (1905) 204–16.

Bergmeier, R., "Verfasserproblem."

Bornkamm, G., "*Presbys, presbyteros* . . . ," TDNT 6, 670–72, pertinent to "The Presbyter" in II John 1 and III John 1.

Bresky, Bennona, *Das Verhältnis des zweiten Johannesbriefes zum dritten* (Münster: Aschendorff, 1906).

Chapman, J., "The Historical Setting of the Second and Third Epistles of St John," JTS 5 (1904) 357–68, 517–34.

Dölger, F. J., "*Domina Mater Ecclesia* und die 'Herrin' im zweiten Johannesbrief," in *Antike und Christentum* (6 vols.; Münster: Aschendorff, 1929–50) 5 (1936) 211–17.

Donfried, K. P., "Ecclesiastical Authority in 2-3 John," in *L'Evangile de Jean*, ed. M. de Jonge (BETL 44; Gembloux: Duculot, 1977) 325–33.

Funk, R. W., "The Form and Structure of II and III John," JBL 86 (1967) 424–30.

Gibbins, H. J., "The Problem of the Second Epistle of St. John," *The Expositor*, sixth series, 12 (1905) 412–24.

————. "The Second Epistle of St. John," *The Expositor*, sixth series, 6 (1902) 228–36.

Harris, J. R., "The Problem of the Address in the Second Epistle of John," *The Expositor*, sixth series, 3 (1901) 194–203.

Käsemann, E., "Ketzer und Zeuge: Zum johanneischen Verfasserproblem," ZTK 48 (1951) 292–311. Cited as reprinted in his *Exegetische Versuche und Besinnungen* (2 vols.; Göttingen: Vandenhoeck und Ruprecht, 1960) 1, 168–87.

Marty, J., "Contribution à l'étude des problèmes johanniques: Les petites épîtres 'II et III Jean,'" *Revue de l'Histoire des Religions* 91 (1925) 200–11.

Munck, J., "Presbyters and Disciples of the Lord in Papias," HTR 52 (1959) 223–43, pertinent to "The Presbyter" in II John 1 and III John 1.

Polhill, J. B., "An Analysis of II and III John," RevExp 67 (1970) 461–71.

Ramsay, W. M., "Note on the Date of Second John," part of "Historical Commentary on the Epistles to the Corinthians," *The Expositor*, sixth series, 3 (1901) 354–56.

Schepens, P., "'Joannes in epistula sua' (Saint Cyprien, *passim*)," RSR 11 (1921) 87–89.

Schnackenburg, R. "Zum Begriff der 'Wahrheit' in den beiden kleinen Johannesbriefen," BZ 11 (1967) 253–58.

van Unnik, W. C., "The Authority of the Presbyters in Irenaeus' Works," in *God's Christ and His People*, ed. J. Jervell and W. A. Meeks (N. A. Dahl Festschrift; Oslo: Universitet, 1977) 248–60.

Wendt, H. H., "Beziehung."

————. "Zum zweiten und dritten Johannesbrief," ZNW 23 (1924) 18–27.

The Third Epistle

of John

A letter from the Presbyter to Gaius urging his continued hospitality to missionaries (and to Demetrius in particular)—a hospitality now all the more important because Diotrephes has refused it in the church in which he ranks first.

13. The Third Epistle of John

OPENING FORMULA:
Sender: 1 The Presbyter
Addressee: To the beloved Gaius:
  b In truth I love you.
Health Wish: 2 Beloved, I hope you are in good health and as well off
in every other way *b* as you are spiritually.

BODY OF LETTER:
3 For it gave me much joy to have the brothers coming and testifying to your truth, *b* as exemplified by the way you walk in truth.
4 Nothing gives me greater joy than to hear that my children are
walking in the truth.

5 Beloved, you demonstrate fidelity by all the work that you do for
the brothers, *b* even though they are strangers. 6 Indeed, they have
testified to your love before the church; *b* and you will do a good thing
by helping them to continue their journey in a way worthy of God.
7 For it was for the sake of "the Name" that they set out, *b* and they
have been accepting nothing from the pagans. 8 Therefore, for our
part we ought to support such men, *b* and thus become coworkers with
the truth.

9 I did write something to the church; *b* but Diotrephes, who likes
to be first among them, does not pay attention to us. 10 Therefore, if
I come, *b* I shall bring up what he is doing in spreading evil nonsense
about us. *c* And he is not content with that! *d* He refuses to welcome
the brothers himself, *e* and furthermore he hinders those who wish
to do so *f* and expels them from the church.

11 Beloved, do not imitate what is bad but what is good. *b* Whoever
does what is good belongs to God; *c* whoever does what is bad has
never seen God. 12 Demetrius gets a testimonial from all, *b* even from
the truth itself. *c* And we give our testimonial as well, *d* and you know
that our testimony is true.

13 I had much more that I should write you, *b* but I do not wish to

write it out with pen and ink. ¹⁴ Rather, I hope to see you soon, ᵇ and we can have a heart-to-heart talk.

CONCLUDING FORMULA:

¹⁵ Peace to you. ᵇ The beloved here send you greetings; ᶜ greet the beloved there, each by name.

NOTES

1a. *The Presbyter.* See NOTE on II John 1a.

To the beloved. The temptation to translate this as "To my dear [Gaius]" should be resisted, for the colorless "dear" of current epistolary English does not do justice to the significance of *agapētos* as a NT form of addressing fellow Christians. Comparable to the 6 instances of this address in I John are the 4 instances of it in III John. Here it is attached to a personal name (as in Rom 16:5,8,9,12), while in the 3 direct addresses of vv. 2,5,11 it stands by itself (see Jude 3; I Pet 2:11; 4:12). As we saw in the NOTE on I John 2:7a, Jesus is God's "beloved" par excellence, and through him Christians are God's beloved. The logic of why Christians use this address for one another is summed up in I John 4:11: "Beloved, if God so loved us, we in turn ought to love one another."

Gaius. It is not clear from the letter (see COMMENT) whether Gaius attended the house-church over which Diotrephes exercised leadership (v. 9), or belonged, either as leader or member, to another house-church in the same general region. We know nothing certain of him beside what can be reconstructed from this letter. Dubious is the tradition found in the *Apostolic Constitutions* (7.46.9; Funk 1, 454), dated *ca.* A.D. 370, that John ordained Gaius as bishop of Pergamum—dubious because it assumes that the Presbyter was John the Apostle, that in the late first century there was a regular practice of ordination to the episcopate, and indeed that the single-bishop model existed at this period in Johannine Christianity. (Findlay, *Fellowship* 306–7, uses this identification to argue that both II and III John were sent to Pergamum.) The name Gaius or Caius (the praenomen of Julius Caesar) was very common in the Roman Empire, and it was borne by two or three other Christians mentioned in the NT: (a) Gaius, inhabitant of Corinth, whom Paul baptized during his stay there in the early 50s (I Cor 1:14) and who in the year 58 served as host during Paul's visit to Corinth (Rom 16:23): "Gaius who is host to me and to the whole church." Origen, *Commentary on Romans* 10.41 (PG 14, 1289C) reports a tradition that he became the first bishop of Thessalonica. (b) A Macedonian Gaius who was a traveling companion of Paul and who in the year 56 was involved in a riot at Ephesus (Acts 19:29) over the statues of Artemis. (c) A companion of Paul during the return to Jerusalem from Corinth (Acts 20:4) at the end of "the third missionary journey" in the spring of 58. He is called Gaius Derbaios; and if the adjective means that he is from Derbe, he is to be kept distinct from the other two men of the same name. The likelihood that the Gaius addressed in III John is to be identified with any of these companions of Paul is very small.

1b. *In truth I love you*. Literally, "whom I love in truth," just as in II John 1b (see NOTE there), although III John does not expand upon this clause as II John does. It is likely that "in truth" (anarthrous) is theological here as it was there and thus is not equivalent simply to the adverb "truly." Belief in Christ who is the truth makes one a child of God and constitutes the basis of love. The similarity to II John makes it questionable that we should read into III John 1 a veiled reference to the Diotrephes of v. 9: "I love you even if Diotrephes does not" or "I love *you* rather than Diotrephes."

2a. *Beloved*. This address will be repeated in vv. 5,11; see NOTE on I John 2:7a.

I hope you are in good health and as well off in every other way. Literally, "Concerning [*peri*] all things I hope [*euchesthai*] you to be well off [*euodousthai*] and to be healthy [*hygiainein*]." Some wish to read *pro* for *peri* in the initial phrase, thus, "*above* all I hope," a very common expression in secular letters (MGNTG 3, 270; BDF 229²). However, there is no textual support for the *pro* reading, and the *peri* phrase cannot be interpreted as "above all." Accepting *peri*, Bresky, *Verhältnis* 26, suggests that *pantōn* is masculine, and the phrase means "on behalf of all." BAG 650 (BAGD 644), 1e, has greater following in interpreting *peri pantōn* as "in all respects," a phrase to be taken with the infinitive "to be well off," rather than with the main verb "I hope."

Euchesthai is a verb used in secular letters to express the writer's wish or hope for the welfare of the recipient (Appendix V A below). It can also mean "to pray" (although *proseuchesthai* is more common for that), but then it is normally followed by a clarifying phrase, e.g., "to God." Perhaps it is possible to compromise between "wish" and "pray," as does Chaine, *Epîtres* 252: "a wish that is at the same time one of politeness and religious inspiration." (The English translation "I pray" would be tantamount to "I wish.") B. Weiss, *Briefe* 185, is too strong when he compares *euchesthai* here to the *euchē* of James 5:15, "The prayer of faith will save the sick man." The use of the verb in secular letters as a polite wish for good health means that receivers of a NT letter would interpret it the same way unless there was a contextual indication of more profound intent, and that is lacking here.

Euodousthai, "to be well off, to prosper on one's way," is common in the LXX and the papyri. Elsewhere in the NT it is found at the beginning of Romans (1:10) and the end of I Corinthians (16:2). Bartlett, "Historical Setting" 215, makes the uncontrollable suggestion that the verb is a play on the name Euodius (masc. form of a name found in Philip 4:2), the name borne by the predecessor of Ignatius at Antioch, so that III John becomes the key for how Gaius Euodius became bishop of Antioch!

Hygiainein, "to be in good health, to be sound," is regularly employed toward the ending of the Opening Formula in epistolary format in reference to physical health. In the Pauline Pastorals (I Tim 1:10; 6:3; Titus 1:9,13; 2:1) it is used for "sound" teaching or words, or for being healthy in faith.

2b. *as you are spiritually*. Literally, "just as [*kathōs*] your *psychē* is well off [*euodousthai*]." Inevitably there is a tendency to interpret the Presbyter's hope or wish in 2a and 2b in terms of health for the body (*sōma*) and the soul (*psychē*) as the basic human components. Often a parallel is found in Philo, *Who is the Heir* 58 ✸285: If a man be "nourished with peace, he will depart, having gained a calm, unclouded life . . . welfare in the body, welfare in the soul [*psychē*] . . . health [*hygeia*] and strength . . . delight in virtues." Some NT passages mention soul and body, e.g., Matt 10:28, "Do not be afraid of those who kill the *sōma* but cannot kill the *psychē*"; also Rev 18:13.

However, 6 out of 10 GJohn uses of *psychē* and both I John uses (NOTE on 3:16b) refer not to "soul" but to "life"—a life that one can lay down, as differentiated from *zōē*, "eternal life," e.g., John 12:25: "The person who loves his *psychē* destroys it, while the person who hates his *psychē* in this world preserves it to eternal life [*zōē*]." (Cf. Mark 8:35: "Whoever wishes to save his *psychē* will lose it; but whoever loses his *psychē* for my sake and for the Gospel will save it.") The remaining two GJohn uses (10:24; 12:27) show the *psychē* as capable of feeling, i.e., being held in suspense or being disturbed. Thus we may say that for the Johannine writers *psychē* represents the sentient and most precious aspect of human existence, an aspect that remains human rather than divine. The fact that Gaius is "in truth" (v. 1b) speaks for his eternal life, but now the Presbyter is referring to well-being on another level. There are other members of the church who are "in truth"; but Gaius has distinguished himself, as we shall see, by his fidelity to the brothers even though they are strangers. Such generosity and decency are the marks of a *noble spirit*.

The joining of physical health and spiritual health in the Presbyter's wish in III John 2 is more than an imaginative conceit. For instance, James 5:13–16 assumes a relationship between sickness and sin, so that the saving of the sick man is connected to the forgiving of his sins, and I Cor 11:29–30 traces physical sickness to an unworthy reception of the eucharist. The Presbyter's employment of *kathōs* in this comparison is significant; for the conjunction has been used frequently in the Epistles to introduce as a basis of comparison either the behavior of Jesus or the revelation of God (III in the NOTE on 2:6bc).

3a. *For it gave me much joy*. This is the same Greek found in II John 4a with the addition here of a *gar*, "for." (Scribes made the parallelism perfect by dropping it, as in Codex Sinaiticus, and some Latin, Coptic, Ethiopic, and Armenian witnesses.) The Presbyter thus connects the spiritual welfare of Gaius (v. 2b) with the fact that he is solidly reported to be walking in the truth. I Peter 1:22 constitutes an interesting parallel in combining *psychē* and *alētheia*: "Having purified your souls by obedience to the truth unto the point of sincere love for the brothers." All three Johannine Epistles mention "joy" in the opening verses (NOTE on I John 1:4b).

to have the brothers coming and testifying. Literally, "while the brothers are coming . . . ," a genitive absolute construction. The pres. tense of the ptcp. may imply that more than one occasion is meant. The Presbyter, then, would be a person who was accustomed to receive traveling Christians and their reports about the journey. Gaius would have been showing hospitality over a period of time and not only in this emergency when Diotrephes has refused to show hospitality. The first verb suggests that the brothers have been traveling to the Presbyter from a church at a distance, i.e., the church in which Gaius lives. Who are these "brothers" who have been coming? I John frequently uses "brother" to describe a fellow Christian as distinct from a secessionist (see NOTE on I John 2:9b). Further identification depends on whether the brothers of this verse are to be identified with the brothers of v. 5 who are strangers to Gaius. (Harnack, "Über" 9, denies that they are necessarily the same; yet the probabilities favor identification in such a short letter.) That identification would mean that the "brothers" did not originate in Gaius' area which is the same as or close to the area in which Diotrephes exercised primacy. There are at least two possible explanations for this situation. *First*, the brothers may have consisted exclusively of Johannine Christians from the Presbyter's own area who went to Gaius' area and were received by him with hospitality and who have now returned to the Presbyter with their report. *Second*, the brothers may have consisted of Johannine Christians from various areas distant to Gaius (including the Presbyter's area). Such traveling Johannine Christians would have been received by Gaius and then have moved on to the Presbyter's church. The identification of the brothers of v. 3 with those of vv. 5–8 makes it likely that the brothers included missionaries who "set out for the sake of 'the Name.'" A further partial identification with the brothers of vv. 9–10 would indicate that they included missionaries who, having been sent by the Presbyter, went first to Diotrephes and were refused hospitality by him because of their connection with the Presbyter. In this case Gaius' hospitality rescued them from the inhospitality of Diotrephes, and they have served as forerunners of the Demetrius of v. 12 who now seemingly will go directly from the Presbyter to Gaius. Much guesswork is involved, but I regard this second interpretation as the most likely (see COMMENT).

3ab. *testifying to your truth, as exemplified by the way you walk in truth.* Literally, "testifying to the truth of you even as [*kathōs*] you walk in truth." MGNTG 3, 177–78 finds the use of the article before the first instance of "truth" inexplicable by the rules of anaphora (i.e., the article is not normally used when a topic is being introduced). However, "truth" was already mentioned without an article in v. 1b ("in truth"). In II John also there were 2 anarthrous instances of "in truth" in vv. 1,3 surrounding an arthrous use of "truth." More important is the question of what "your truth" means. B. Weiss, *Briefe* 186, suggests that the Presbyter previously had heard criticism of Gaius (perhaps by supporters of Diotrephes, mentioned in v. 9), but now he has found witnesses to testify to Gaius' truth (*"your"* truth) or orthodoxy. But a simpler counterpart to the "you" pronoun in v. 3 is the "I" pronoun in v. 1b (Schnackenburg), and there is no need to posit a sharp contrast to Diotrephes before he is mentioned. As for "truth," we have seen it used in the Epistles both for christology (I John 2:21–23; 4:2,6; 5:10,20; II John 7) and for a principle of behavior (I John 1:6; 2:4; 3:18–19; 4:20). While the Presbyter would not speak of Gaius' truth unless Gaius had a correct christology, we shall see that there is no evidence that Diotrephes had a false christology. Consequently, if there is any element of anticipated contrast to Diotrephes in the reference in v. 3 to Gaius who walks in truth, that element involves his behavior toward the brothers—he shows them love and Diotrephes does not. I share this view with Bultmann, Marshall, Schnackenburg, and Westcott, and thus disagree with Bergmeier, Bonsirven, Brooke, and Büchsel who think the primary issue is Gaius' doctrinal stance. Confirmation for this interpretation will be found in v. 5 where work done for the brothers illustrates "walking in truth" in v. 4.

If Gaius' truth (v. 3a) is illustrated by his hospitable behavior, what is the force of *kathōs* in v. 3b? Bultmann, *Epistles* 98, argues for the comparative force, "as indeed you walk in the truth." But it is not clear what is being compared since both main and subordinate clauses concern Gaius. Can Gaius' truth be compared to his walking in truth? (A *kathōs* comparative here is not so clear as the *kathōs* in I John 2:6: "The person . . . ought himself to walk just as Christ walked.") A simpler explanation is that, instead of being a comparative, *kathōs* here means "to the degree that" or "as exemplified by the fact that." (One must leave open the complementary possibility that this is an instance of *kathōs* introducing indirect discourse: THLJ 150; BDF 453[2]; BAG 392[5]; BAGD 391[5].) The words that follow *kathōs* would then be the Presbyter's own statement, "You are walking in truth," a reinforcement of the very words of the brothers, "He is walking in truth." BDF 396 points out that a particular aspect of *hōs*, a variant of *kathōs*, is that it tells us not only "that" but "how." Such an emphasis here would mean that the brothers told the Presbyter not only that Gaius was walking in truth but how he was doing this.

4. *Nothing gives me greater joy than to hear that my children are walking in the truth.* Literally, "Greater [*meizoteros*] than these I do not have joy [*chara*] that [*hina*] I hear. . . ." *Meizoteros* is a Hellenistic double comparative ("more greater"), a form developed when the normal comparative *meizōn* had lost its force (MGNTG 1, 236), so that the language formed a comparative of the comparative. As for connotation, the least one may say is that the Presbyter is being emphatic. A close syntactic parallel to this sentence is John 15:13 when rendered literally, "Greater [*meizōn*] than this no one has love that [*hina*] anyone lays down his life for his beloved." Parallel in vocabulary and idea is II John 4: "It gave me much joy to find some of your children walking in truth." In the present passage Codex Vaticanus, the Bohairic, and some Latin witnesses read *charis*, "grace," for *chara*, "joy"; and Chaine, *Epîtres* 253, opts for "no greater grace" as the less banal reading. However, "grace" may have been introduced by scribes who sought variety by avoiding two references to "joy" in a row (vv. 3,4) and were influenced by Paul's use of *charis* at the beginning of letters (Rom 1:5; Philip 1:2; I Cor 1:3; etc.). A mention of "joy" as the Body-Opening of a letter is standard format; it is found in II John 4 and seems the more plausible reading here.

The *hina* clause is epexegetical of the "these" in the main clause, but the pl. demonstrative antecedent is unusual—witness the sg. demonstrative antecedent in John 15:13 cited above. Some suggest that it reflects the plural reports implied in v. 3, or else that there may be an element of purpose in the *hina* (Harnack, "Über" 8; rejected by B. Weiss, *Briefe* 187) so that the clause is not totally epexegetical. More simply, we may be encountering the meaningless vagaries of Johannine grammar.

"My children" employs the plural of *teknon* (NOTE on I John 2:1a) with the possessive adjective. Some would find the latter emphatic, meaning "my *own*" (see MGNTG 3, 191) and used to distinguish the Presbyter's converts or special friends from others who are not (B. Weiss). However, one should not overtranslate the first person singular possessive adjective that is so frequent in Johannine style (over one half the total NT usage); it may be simply the ordinary Greek way of saying "my" in this region (BDF 285: "Koine of Asia Minor?"). While II John 1,4 (cf. II John 13) refers to the addressees as children of the Elect Lady (i.e., of the church), III John refers to the addressee as one of "my children." On the analogy of Paul's use of child/children in Gal 4:19; Philem 10, some have suggested that Gaius was one of the Presbyter's converts; but one gets the impression from v. 3 that the Presbyter has never met Gaius and is dependent upon second-hand information. Moreover, although Paul can write, "My children . . . I begot you through the gospel" (I Cor 4:14–15), in Johannine thought it is God who begets Christians as His children (John 1:13; 3:3,5) and not a human preacher. In all likelihood, in using the term "my children" (pl. of *teknon*), the Presbyter is referring to Christians with whom he is joined in *koinōnia* and from whom he expects respect as a Johannine tradition-bearer. It is uncertain why I John uses *teknion* ("little child") in the plural with exactly the same connotation as III John's *teknon*, especially if the two works had the same author. One suggestion is that he uses the diminutive in I John, which is addressed to those among whom he lives, and the more formal term in III John in reference to those at a distance. Again I judge it more likely that we encounter a meaningless variant of Johannine style.

The Presbyter hears "my children are *walking in the truth*," a participial construction similar to the one found in II John 4 ("joy to find some of your children walking in truth"). However, here by exception a definite article is used in the phrase "in truth," whereas it was absent in 5 previous epistolary instances (II John 1,3,4; III John 1,3) as well as in John 4:23,24; 17:19 (see IBNTG 112). Scribes recognized this problem, and so the article was omitted in Codex Sinaiticus and much of the Byzantine tradition. However, the article is sometimes found in Johannine instances of this phrase (John 8:44; 17:17); and the juxtaposition of the arthrous phrase in John 17:17 and the anarthrous phrase in 17:19 illustrates Johannine variation without difference of meaning (de la Potterie, *La vérité* 2, 648). For the Semitic idiom of "walking," see NOTES on I John 1:6b and II John 4a.

5a. *Beloved.* This address was used with Gaius' name in v. 1b, and then by itself in v. 2a; see NOTE on I John 2:7a. Funk, "Form" 429, points out that it can serve to indicate where a letter should be divided (marked in our convention by a paragraph), a feature I found verified in subdividing I John (4:1,7).

you demonstrate fidelity by all the work that you do. Literally, "you do [the] faithful/sure whatever you work [*ergazein*]." In the petition section of the

Body-Opening of a Greco-Roman letter (Appendix V C below), *kalōs poiein*, "to do well," often appears as a polite introductory formula; and that phrase will occur in III John 6b. The expression here *piston poiein*, "to do [the] faithful/sure," is a Christian equivalent which has several possible theological overtones. The interpretation that it means "to do something sure/worthy [of a reward]" underlies the reading in the sixth-century Codex 80, which has substituted *misthon*, "reward" (see II John 8b), for *piston*. In this exegesis Gaius' actions would be looked upon as trustworthy by God. An impressive list of scholars (Bultmann, de Jonge, Schnackenburg) interprets the phrase to mean "to act faithfully/loyally"; and although there are few parallels for this translation, it is possible (BAG 670, 1b; BAGD 665, 1b). Gaius would then be praised for being a "good and faithful [*pistos*] servant" (Matt 25:21).

But such interpretation still leaves us with the question of how this loyalty or fidelity is understood. Is it fidelity to previous instructions by the Presbyter about hospitality? That is unlikely since the Presbyter seems to be contacting Gaius for the first time on the subject of hospitality. More likely Gaius is praised for acting as a true believer, conformable to a faith (*pistis*) that is showing itself in works (Bernard, Bonsirven, de la Potterie, Estius, Oecumenius, Wilder, Zorell). In that sense *piston poiein* would be very close to "walking in truth." Confirmation that Gaius is being praised as a believer is found in the partly parallel expression *ginesthai pistos*, "to become/be faithful," used in John 20:27: "Do not persist in your disbelief, but *become a believer*." The interpretation makes especially good sense if, as I shall argue in the COMMENT, Gaius is being encouraged to offer hospitality to a group that includes missionaries employed by the Presbyter to combat the secessionists.

It is possible to give a future force to this phrase: "You will demonstrate fidelity" (see BDF 323 for the futuristic use of the pres.). The implication might be that the Presbyter is so confident of Gaius that he can use the pres. tense for a future activity as though it were already being exercised. But B. Weiss, *Briefe* 187–88, would press the future note more sharply by suggesting that the Presbyter is urging Gaius to do what he has not done before. Certainly some of the specific requests of the Presbyter involve new action, e.g., in v. 6b where he uses the future, and in 8 where he says, "We ought." Here in 5, however, as Bonsirven and Schnackenburg recognize, the pres. tense implies that Gaius is already observing what is being encouraged. Whether or not he has yet been attacked by Diotrephes (v. 9), Gaius is being shored up by the Presbyter to continue a course of action on which he has embarked but which will now become more difficult because of Diotrephes.

The subordinate phrase, "whatever you work/do," consists of an aorist subjunctive introduced by *ean*, serving in the place of *an* (BDF 107). As we shall see, the aorist offers difficulty in translating; and Codex Alexandrinus and some minuscules have substituted a pres. to match the tense of the main verb. B. Weiss would again argue for a future implication, pointing to *an* and the aorist subjunctive in John 1:33, "When you [will] see the Spirit descend and rest on someone." Accordingly, the rendition of v. 5 would be: "You will demonstrate fidelity by all that you will do." More plausibly in my judgment

MGNTG 1, 116 suggests a constative aorist (or complexive aorist: BDF 332) covering a group of actions taken as a whole. It includes, then, what Gaius has done, what he is doing, and what he will continue to do. While the range of the verb *ergazesthai* ("to work or do") is wide, it is found (along with *ergon*, the related noun for "work") in reference to pastoral activity in a Christian church, e.g., I Thess 5:12–13 where Paul urges Christians to hold in highest regard those who are over them in the Lord "because of their work." One cannot surmise, however, from this reference that Gaius had an official function as head of a house-church; for clearly the Presbyter is thinking of Gaius' work for the brothers as voluntary and charitable (Bultmann, Schnackenburg). It is interesting to note the use of *ergon* in Titus 3:13–14 where Paul urges Titus to "help on their way" two Christians: "Our people must learn good works in order that they may provide for necessary wants."

5ab. *for the brothers, even though they are strangers.* Literally, "for the brothers—and this [these] strangers"; see BDF 290⁵; 442⁹; also I Cor 6:6: "And brother goes to law against brother—and this before unbelievers." As I mentioned in the NOTE on 3a, Harnack thinks that the "brothers" who testified to Gaius in that verse are not the same as the "brothers" mentioned here. However, the statement in the next verse (6) that the "brothers" of 5 *have* testified to Gaius' love suggests that at least some of those who have already testified to Gaius' truth (3) are included, even though the present verse may be more general in scope, covering past, present, and future recipients of hospitality. Demetrius, whom the Presbyter introduces to Gaius in v. 12, is one of the "brothers" toward whom Gaius is urged to be faithful in his hospitable work.

6a. *Indeed, they have testified to your love.* The aorist here may refer to a single instance of testimony; or may be complexive (as discussed at the end of the NOTE on 5a), covering a series of testimonies. The pres. ptcpls. in v. 3 ("coming and testifying") would be in harmony with the latter interpretation. In v. 3 the testimony was to Gaius' truth; here it is to his love (although some minuscules read "truth and love" by way of harmonizing 6 with 3). Since "truth" for John has an element of christology, Gaius' truth involves his status as a child of God. "Love" involves obedience to the basic commandment given to God's children by Jesus, and so becomes an external manifestation of "truth" (de la Potterie, *La vérité* 2, 878).

before the church. This is an instance of *enōpion* (a neuter noun) serving as a preposition. This usage in the LXX was probably influenced by Hebrew *lipnê*, "in the visible presence of, to the face of" (MGNTG 4, 69; see John 20:30; I John 3:22). There is no definite article in the Greek, but the loss of the article after prepositions is not uncommon (BDF 255). The phrase "in the church" occurs anarthrously in I Cor 14:19,35. This is the first instance of *ekklēsia* in the Johannine writings, and it will appear twice in vv. 9,10. The fact that those two uses are in relation to the church of which Diotrephes likes to be leader has led some to speculate that Johannine theology is opposed to the idea of church and the failure to use *ekklēsia* (except in a pejorative context) is deliberate. I find this thesis quite implausible. The Book of Revelation, a distant cousin of the Johannine writings, employs *ekklēsia* 20 times, a possible indication that the term is not foreign to the Johannine tradition. The absence of *ekklēsia* from GJohn has no significance, since the term is missing also from Mark and Luke—probably it was not part of the tradition of Jesus' words, and its presence in Matthew is best explained as the retrojection of postresurrectional terminology. One might be tempted to give significance to the absence of *ekklēsia* from I John until one reflects that it is also absent from II Timothy and Titus (which together are about as long as I John). We know that in the latter case the absence is not ideological, since those two works were written by the author who wrote I Timothy, which uses *ekklēsia* 3 times (even as III John uses it 3 times). In short, it can be accidental that the author uses the word in one of his works and not in another. As for II John, we saw that "Elect Lady" is a symbolic name for a local church. Finally, the use of "church" in III John 6a is favorable and reflects the Presbyter's acceptance of the term.

Which church is involved here, the church of Gaius (which may or may not be the same as the church of Diotrephes) or the church of the Presbyter? Or is it some third church to whom the brothers reported the news about Gaius before they came to the Presbyter? Or finally is it the Church in a larger sense referring to the totality of the Johannine Christians? We should probably dismiss the last suggestion simply on the grounds that there is no evidence of any such use of *ekklēsia* in the Johannine writings, but with the cautious reiteration that, after all, the term occurs only 3 times and not outside III John. As for the first suggestion, if it was the church of Gaius that heard the testimony to Gaius' love, why does the Presbyter have to tell Gaius about it? There is no way to refute the possibility of a third church, but that seems an unnecessary complication. Thus it seems most likely that the Presbyter is referring to the church in which he himself lives, a suggestion agreeing with v. 3 where the brothers are *coming* to testify.

6b. *and you will do a good thing by helping them to continue their journey.* Literally, "whom you will do well having sent them forward." In the NOTE on 5a (and Appendix V C below) I call attention to *kalōs poiein*, "to do well [kindly do]," as a standard way in Epistolary Format for introducing the request that embodies the whole purpose of the letter. Two instances where it accompanies a theme similar to that of III John are James 2:8 ("If indeed you fulfill the royal law found in the Scripture, 'You shall love your neighbor as yourself,' you do well") and Ignatius, *Smyrn.* 10:1 ("You did well to receive as deacons of God Philo and Rheus Agathopous, who followed me in the cause [*logos*] of God; and they too are thankful to the Lord for you because you refreshed them in all ways"). The ancient versions recognized the grammatical awkwardness of this relative clause in III John, and some of them shifted to a new main clause as I have done. Other scribes noticed the complication of a future verb ("will do") followed by an aorist ptcp. ("having sent"), since the brothers cannot have testified in the past to what Gaius would do in the future. Consequently in Codex Ephraemi Rescriptus there is a shift so that the main verb is read as aorist and the ptcp. as a future. However, this neglects the subtlety of the Presbyter who is praising what Gaius has done in the past, and is doing so in order to invite Gaius to a future manifestation of love. Normally an aorist ptcp. would indicate action before the main verb, but at times it indicates the coincidence of the two actions (even if that is infrequent when the main verb is future: MGNTG 3, 79–80; also Brooke, *Epistles* 185, who offers papyri parallels). Here the aorist gives a tone of surety (the action is as good as done) as well as providing a basis for continuity with the future.

The verb *propempein*, "to send forward," in this context has almost a technical sense of providing missionaries with supplies that would enable them to journey to the next stop (Acts 15:3; I Cor 16:6,11; II Cor 1:16; Titus 3:13; Rom 15:24). Polycarp, *Philip.* 1:1, sees the action described by this verb as a manifestation of love: "I rejoice greatly with you in the Lord Jesus Christ that you have followed the pattern of true love and have sent forward on their way those who were bound in chains."

in a way worthy of God. It is not clear whether this adverbial expression modifies what Gaius is to do (outfit the journey), or what the missionaries are to do (make the journey), or both (most likely). In any case the journey must be worthy of its goal, which is about to be explained in v. 7. The language throughout this passage probably stems from Christian paraenesis. In I Thess 2:11–12, when he is exhorting and consoling as a father does his own children, Paul writes, "You are to walk worthily of God"—an impressive parallel since in III John 4 the Presbyter has rejoiced that his "children are walking in the truth" and now he is urging such a child to help others on their journey "in a way worthy of God." Similarly the author of Colossians (1:10) prays that "you may *walk worthily of the Lord* . . . bearing fruit in every good *work*," even as the Presbyter has praised the work of Gaius.

7a. *For it was for the sake of "the Name."* Early Christian writings often use "the Name" without explanatory clarification (*Barnabas* 16:8; Ignatius, *Phld.* 10:1); and in the NOTE on I John 2:12b I discussed the ambiguous "his name" in light of the Johannine thesis that God gave His name to Jesus. As interpretations of the phrase "for the sake of [*hyper*] the Name," the following three possibilities may be mentioned. (a) The "Name" is the name of God (Bengel, Bonsirven, Büchsel, B. Weiss), a thesis that is supported by the absolute tone of this expression, which employs the definite article. For the OT background, see ABJ 29A, 754–56. In Jewish usage "the Name" (*haššēm*) is a substitute to be read for the Tetragrammaton YHWH. First-century B.C. Pharisee thought is found in the address to God in the *Psalms of Solomon* 7:5(6): "While your name dwells in our midst, we shall find mercy." Christian usage at the end of the first century A.D. is found in *Didache* 10:2: "We thank you, Father most holy, for the sake of [*hyper*] your holy name which you made to dwell in our hearts." Ignatius, *Phld.* 10:2, speaks of sending emissaries to a church "for the sake of [*hyper*] the name of God." In III John such an interpretation establishes a good sequence from the phrase that has just preceded: ". . . in a way worthy of God—since it was for the sake of [His] name that they set out." (b) The "Name" is the name of the Johannine "brotherhood," or of the Christian cause (Houlden), or refers to the designation of believers in Jesus as "Christians" (Acts 11:26). Chapman, "Historical Setting" 358, hypothesizes that those mentioned in III John had set out from Rome during the Neronian persecution in the mid-60s when their lives were in danger because they were identified as Christians. (This fits in with his thesis that the "Elect Lady" of II John was the church of Rome, and that the Demetrius of III John was the Demas who deserted Paul in Rome—see NOTES on the title of II John above, and on III John 12a below.) His thesis is refuted by Bartlett, "Historical Setting" 205, who argues that *hyper* means "on behalf of" and not "because of" (which would require *dia* [John 15:21] or *en* [I Pet 4:14]). Nevertheless, the use of *hyper* in Acts 5:41 where the disciples suffer "because of the Name" warns against an argument based on precision in the use of prepositions. (c) The "Name" is the name borne by Jesus (a thesis favored by most scholars). In Rom 1:5 Paul speaks of an apostleship received through Jesus Christ "to bring about obedience of faith among all the nations for the sake of [*hyper*] his name." I John 2:12 writes encouragingly, "Little Children . . . your sins have been forgiven because of [*dia*] his [Christ's] name." We should probably relate this language to the custom of being baptized in(to) the name of Jesus (Acts 8:16; cf. I Cor 1:13,15) or to the partial Johannine equivalent of believing in(to) the name of Jesus (John 1:12; 3:18). In such phrases the writers may be thinking of a specific name given to Jesus or employed in proclaiming him, e.g., Lord, Son of Man, Son of God. The missionary custom is implied in Ignatius, *Eph.* 7:1: "There are some who make a practice of carrying about the Name with wicked deceit."

In summary one must recognize that the context in III John is not specific, but the strongest cases can be made for (a) and (c) above. Justice may be done to both if one recognizes that in the Johannine tradition the divine name is borne by Jesus who is one with the Father (ABJ 29A, 754–56). On the analogy of other NT texts, THLJ 153 suggests that the specific divine name used of Jesus may have been "Lord" (Rom 10:9; I Cor 12:3; Philip 2:9–11), but in Johannine tradition the name may have been "I AM" (ABJ 29, 533–38). By proclaiming the divine name given to Jesus, the missionary "brothers" of III John would have been proclaiming Jesus as God's presence in the flesh. Those who have the approval of the Presbyter would be underlining "in the flesh" over against the secessionist missionaries (II John 7,10).

that they set out. The verb *exerchesthai,* "to go out," was used previously of the secessionists in I John 2:19; 4:1; II John 7; but we cannot be sure that the Presbyter is making a deliberate contrast. Acts 14:20 uses the verb to describe the Pauline missionary travels from one town to another; indeed in 15:40 it describes the setting out on "the second missionary journey." Despite the use of the aorist (which normally is not used for repeated action), the Presbyter seems to be generalizing about the reason why Christian missionaries have left their homes. There is no necessary connotation that these missionaries "went out" from the church where the Presbyter is.

7b. *and they have been accepting nothing from the pagans.* This translates a pres. ptcp., which serves to confirm the general character of the aorist, "set out," as mentioned above. Chapman, "Historical Setting," implausibly rearranges the sentence so that these are refugees from persecution in Rome: They *set out from the pagans,* not taking along any possessions. The negative *mēden* (form of *ouden* with the non-indicative) often has modal force and may connote a *determination* to take nothing. There is no implication that the pagans have offered anything; rather the idea is that the proclamation of Jesus is made without either expecting or begging for support. Unlikely is the thesis of Horvath, "3 John 11[b]," that the settled communities of Johannine Christians were taxed for the support of missionaries. If that were the case, the Presbyter would have mentioned among the crimes of Diotrephes (vv. 9–10) his cutting off the tax. Rather, the Presbyter objects to Diotrephes' stopping those who *wish* to support the missionaries. The praise of Gaius' generosity suggests that support of missionaries was on a voluntary basis, with the hope that those who did not "set out" would be generous by way of support, even as those who set out were generous by way of activity. We are not far in spirit from the Essenes as Josephus describes them (*War* 2.8.4; ##124–25): "When any of the sectarians arrive from a distance, all the goods of the group are put at their disposal just as if they were their own. They enter the houses of people whom they have never seen before as though they were most intimate friends. Therefore they carry nothing [*ouden*] whatever with them on their journeys . . . . In every city there is one of their order expressly appointed to attend to strangers." Philo, *Every Good Man* 12 #85, says of the Essenes, "The door is open to visitors from elsewhere who share their convictions."

Ethnikos, "pagan, Gentile," appears only 3 times more in the NT, all in Matthew. Scribes of the Byzantine tradition read here *ethnos* (sg. "nation"; pl. "Gentiles") which is used 162 times in the NT. *Ethnikos* represents a sharper distinction from Jews (and a contemptuous one if we may judge from Matt 5:47; 6:7), for the sg. of *ethnos* can refer to Jews as well as to Gentiles. It is interesting that in III John, instead of referring to the non-Jew, *ethnikos* refers to the non-Christian Gentile (since there is no reason to think that the Presbyter is excluding support from Gentile *Christians* [recent converts]).

8a. *Therefore*. Textually, this is the only authentic use of *oun* in the Johannine Epistles as compared with 194 uses in GJohn! But see the cautious evaluation of this statistic on p. 23 above. The force here is paraenetic, as a suggested plan of action is predicated on what has been said.

for our part we ought. The first person pronoun is emphatic, meaning "we Johannine believers" in contrast to the pagans. (Clearly here it is not equivalent to "I.") The use of *opheilein*, "ought," is significant since its previous uses in GJohn and I John (most often in relation to loving) suggest that it refers to an obligation that springs from one's identity as a (Johannine) Christian; see NOTE on I John 2:6bc.

to support. Although the Byzantine tradition reads *apolambanein*, "to receive, welcome," the better attested reading *hypolambanein* makes excellent sense: "to receive amicably with support and protection" (see G. Delling, TDNT 4, 15). It picks up a theme from the *lambanein*, "accept," of the preceding sentence: Since the brothers are accepting (receiving) nothing, we ought to support (receive) them. A similar play on the two verbs is found in Acts 1:8–9 where the apostles receive (*lambanein*) power with the coming of the Spirit, as the clouds receive or take up (*hypolambanein*) Jesus.

such men. The NT use of *toioutos* is often colorless, meaning no more than *houtos*, "this" (BDF 304); but here it probably should be taken literally: "of such a kind," as in the other two Johannine uses (John 4:23; 9:16). The author is referring to the missionaries who are *so generous* as to set out for the sake of the Name without accepting anything.

8b. *and thus become.* Literally, "so that we may become." Although at times *ginesthai*, "to become," means little more than *einai*, "to be," de la Potterie, *La vérité* 2, 892–95, argues that in GJohn it has its literal force when accompanied by a predicate substantive or adjective. The use here may be compared to that in John 1:12 (becoming children of God) and 15:8 (becoming disciples). Yet one may not press such logic to the point of concluding that the Johannine Christians were not already in some way "coworkers with the truth." Paradoxically the Presbyter is telling his readers that an active support of the missionaries will make them even more what they already are. Bultmann and Schnackenburg are right in stressing that the idea involves proving oneself, as part of the general epistolary theme that internal Christian realities must find external expression. One must walk according to what one is.

coworkers with the truth. This pl. of *synergos*, "with-worker," governs a dative. (Codices Sinaiticus* and Alexandrinus read "church" in place of "truth," probably because "church" occurs in the next verse and because of the difficult image of coworking with an abstract concept like "truth.") Neither the LXX nor the NT uses the dative with this noun, which normally governs the genitive or *eis* with the accusative. However, the dative occurs with the cognate verb *synergesthai*, "to work with." How is the dative to be understood? (See Hall, "Fellow-Workers.") A *dativus commodi* ("of advantage": BDF 188), meaning "for, on behalf of, in the service of," is supported by Alexander, Bergmeier, Hauck, Loisy, Plummer, B. Weiss, JB, and TEV. The idea, then, would be to work with missionaries for the truth. A dative meaning "with," corresponding to the *syn* component in the noun, is supported by Brooke, Bruce, Chaine, Charue, de Ambroggi, de la Potterie, Hall, THLJ, Westcott, and Windisch. (RSV and others translate "in the truth" which is vague syntactically.) The idea, then, would be to work with the truth that is already at work in the missionaries. The objection that such a dative requires a personal object can be met if we recall that "truth" is sometimes personified in Johannine writing, e.g., "The truth will set you free" (John 8:32). Parallels for either type of dative are found in *syn-* word constructions. For the *dativus commodi*, see II Tim 1:8, which uses *synkakopathein* when Paul invites Timothy to "suffer together for the sake of the gospel"; and Philip 1:27: "striving together [*synathlein*] for the faith of the gospel." For the dative meaning "with," see James 2:22 which uses *synergesthai* describing Abraham: faith "worked with his works." By way of extra-NT evidence for *synergos* with this type of dative, see the second-century B.C. papyrus example in U. Wilcken, *Urkunden der Ptolemäerzeit* (2 vols.; Berlin: de Gruyter, 1927, 1957) 1, 632 ⚹146, and the Pseudo-Clementine *Homily* 17.19.7 (GCS 42, 240) where Peter proposes to Simon Magus to "work together [*synergesthai*] with the truth [dative]" and to "become coworkers with us." In summary, I think the evidence favors the connotation of "cooperation with" rather than "service of."

What is the sense of "truth" in "coworkers with the truth"? A common suggestion is that it is equivalent to the gospel of the Christian message proclaimed by the missionaries (thus, with variations: Bergmeier, Büchsel, Bruce, Chaine, Charue, Dodd, Hall). Not only does the context make this possible, but there are parallels in Paul, e.g., where the gospel is personified as a saving power (Rom 1:16), or where Christians are seen as sharing in Paul's ministry of preaching the gospel (Philip 4:14–16). By way of support John 17:17 is cited, "Your word is truth." The context there, however, indicates that the evangelist is not thinking of external preaching but of an interiorized truth ("Consecrate them in truth"). Indeed, the general Johannine usage points to the christological sense of "truth." Thus, Belser, Brooke, and Windisch think that in III John 8 the truth may be Jesus (John 14:6), or the Spirit (I John 5:6), while de la Potterie and Schnackenburg think of a revelation in and of Jesus that has been appropriated by faith and interiorized. Such facets of "truth" can be combined: Jesus is the truth; those who believe have dwelling within them the truth revealed in Jesus; it is not an inert principle; and there is a Spirit of Truth within the believer interpreting the truth: This Spirit bears witness on behalf of Jesus, and the Spirit does this in and through Christians (John 15:26–27). Missionaries who "set out for the sake of the Name" are allowing the truth that is within them to find a voice and are the instruments of the Spirit of Truth. By helping them as an act of love, Christians like Gaius are coworkers of the truth. The Presbyter is simply giving to his "Beloved" another form of the appeal in I John 3:18: "Little Children, let us not give lip service to our love with words but show its truth in deeds."

De la Potterie, *La vérité* 2, 868–73, points to helpful parallels in the *Testaments of the Twelve Patriarchs* (*T. Reuben* 3:6; *T. Dan* 1:7) where *synergein* is used with "spirit." Particularly helpful is *T. Gad* 4:7: "The spirit of love works together in patience with the Law [dative] of God unto the salvation of human beings," while the spirit of hatred works together with Satan for death. The Presbyter thinks that his missionaries who proclaim Jesus Christ coming in the flesh are coworkers with the Spirit of Truth, and surely he regards the secessionist missionaries as coworkers with the Spirit of Deceit (I John 4:6).

9a. *I did write something to the church.* No article appeared before "church" in the Greek of v. 6, but one does here. Although often the definite article indicates reference to a previously mentioned subject (BDF 252[1]), the church mentioned here to which the Presbyter may come (v. 10) is different from the church in v. 6, which is seemingly the church in which he lives. Instead, in 9a the article indicates that the church of which Diotrephes likes to be the leader is a church known to Gaius (to whom III John is addressed). The fact that the Presbyter speaks of having written to the church rather than to Diotrephes does not tell us anything about the structure of the church; for even when there are local authorities (I Thess 5:12), Paul writes to the church (I Thess), even as does Ignatius who is a great defender of the role of the single bishop. (Each of the seven letters of Revelation is addressed to "the angel of the church," but that probably means the guardian angel rather than [directly or solely] a local bishop.) The context implies that Diotrephes was able to ignore this letter written (aorist) in the past, an ability that suggests that the church addressed was already under his supervision. Such disrespect toward the Presbyter's letter bothered scribes who thought that III John was written by the Apostle John; and so some minor Greek witnesses have added the particle *an* introducing a subjunctive element: "I would have written" (also Latin and Syriac). Another scribal stratagem is reflected in the "You [Gaius] have written something" (Codex Bezae; Coptic). Some interpreters (Hoskyns, "Epistles" 673) move in the same direction by proposing the verb as an epistolary aorist: "I am writing" in this letter. Yet would the Presbyter have phrased a reference to III John itself in such an awkward way: "I have written something to the church"? I John 5:13 shows what he would have said: "I have written [aorist] these things." A variant theory is that v. 9 refers not to III John but to another letter that would accompany it, so that the messenger would have carried both III John to Gaius and a letter to the church even if the author anticipates rejection by Diotrephes of this other letter. One cannot disprove such a theory; but the letter reads smoothly if v. 9 describes a past action by the Presbyter, while v. 10 describes an option open to him now that the letter has failed.

If one takes the aorist as a genuine past action, what was the "something" he wrote? Very few scholars have contended that it was I John (which has no address to a church). Many scholars have argued that the "something" was II John addressed "To an Elect Lady" which is a church (Belser, Bresky, Calmes, Dibelius, Findlay, Hauck, Holtzmann, Jülicher, Loisy, McNeile, Meinertz, Moffatt, Strathmann, B. Weiss, Wendt, Zahn). An implication in this theory is that, since II John concerns secessionists, Diotrephes ignored the letter because he was a secessionist or a secessionist sympathizer. But then one would have expected III John to raise the issue of secession in order to convey the message that Diotrephes had ignored. (Moreover, one wonders whether the Presbyter would have referred to his urgent assault upon the secession in II John or, *a fortiori*, in I John as "something"?) The "something" written in the past has to be related to why III John is being sent to Gaius. It probably was looked upon by Diotrephes as an interference in the church of which he was leader. Accordingly, most scholars think that the reference in v. 9 is to no known Johannine work but to a lost letter which Diotrephes destroyed. Chapman and Windisch propose a testimonial letter for a missionary (see v. 12); Bonsirven thinks of a letter of advice and admonition for the church in which Diotrephes lives, somewhat similar to the letters in Rev 2–3; Streeter thinks it contained a request to address the church through missionaries. In any case, for the Presbyter to have been so upset by Diotrephes' ignoring the letter means that such a refusal constituted a major rupture of the Presbyter's previous relationship to the church.

9b. *Diotrephes*. The name ("God-nurtured") is not overly common, but not so rare as to justify Findlay's suggestion that he belonged to the aristocracy. BAG 198 (BAGD 199) points to occurrences in Thucydides and Diodorus of Sicily, and Greek inscriptions.

who likes to be first among them. The plural "them" after the singular "church" is an example of pronominal agreement according to sense

(MGNTG 3, 40); it cannot be used to argue that there were factions in the church or that it consisted of several house congregations. The third person pronoun makes it unlikely that Gaius (who is consistently addressed in the second person) is to be considered a member of the church. The verb form is a pres. ptcp.: "The-liking-to-be-first Diotrephes," a construction which implies that what follows ("does not pay attention to us") flows from his liking to be first. The verb *philoprōteuein* is found in Greek only in III John and in patristic writings dependent on III John, a fact that has led Bultmann, *Epistles* 100, to suggest that perhaps the author coined it to avoid the real title of Diotrephes (*episkopos*, "bishop"), which the Presbyter would disparage. However, the component parts (*philos*, "beloved," and *prōtos*, "first") are extremely common, and the corresponding noun *philoprōteia* and adjective *philoprōtos* are known in secular Greek. Some would press the verb to mean that Diotrephes had not yet become the recognized leader in the church but only *desired* or loved that position, e.g., "their would-be leader" (NEB). The actions that follow in v. 10, however, indicate an actual exercise of authority: Diotrephes can refuse to pay attention to the Presbyter; he can refuse to show hospitality (the practice of which is the duty of the presbyter-bishop of the Pauline Pastorals: I Tim 3:2; Titus 1:8); and he can have individuals expelled from the house-church (whether by direct order or by persuading the church to do so). Clearly the Presbyter does not approve of Diotrephes' ambition, but the need to write III John testifies to the independence of Diotrephes, who has succeeded in frustrating the Presbyter's goals. Diotrephes' primacy is a fact, then, not just a desire.

does not pay attention to us. In v. 8 the "we" referred to Johannine Christians in general; but this clause describes a reaction to "I did write," and so the meaning has to be more confined. A number of scholars speak of an editoral or majestic plural, so that "to us" is equivalent to "to me." Elsewhere in this letter, however, the Presbyter consistently writes in the first person singular when he means "I"; and certainly that is the situation in the immediate context (9a; "I did write"; 10a: "I come . . . I shall bring up"). Throughout this commentary I have recognized that Johannine style is replete with meaningless variants, a principle that Schnackenburg invokes here. Yet this is a context where the Presbyter would have wanted the seriousness of his grievance to be clear, and so more may be involved in the choice of the "us" than a stylistic variant. Is the pronoun here a genuine pl. distinguishing the Presbyter and some others (NOTE on "we" in I John 1:1b)? One possibility is the Presbyter and those who have sided with him in the secessionist struggle (Wendt). This explanation would place Diotrephes on the opposite side with the secessionists, but there is no other suggestion of that in III John. Another explanation is that the Presbyter is speaking as a member of the Johannine School (INTRODUCTION V C2c), so that the "we" here refers to the tradition-bearers mentioned in I John 1:1–5. (If this is true, the argument for common authorship is enhanced.) This last interpretation is strengthened in my judgment by v. 12: "We give our testimonial as well," for the primary function of the Johannine School is to bear witness (give testimony) to the tradition.

The present tense of the verb (*epidechesthai*) indicates that Diotrephes' action was not a solitary incident but part of an enduring attitude. This verb has two shades of meaning either of which could be applicable here. (a) The meaning "to receive or welcome" would indicate that Diotrephes was refusing hospitality to the Presbyter. The verb definitely has that sense in the next verse, which states that Diotrephes refuses to *welcome* the brothers. But III John gives no evidence that the Presbyter attempted a visit and was turned away; and so one would have to assume that he regarded his letter as a surrogate for his presence (B. Weiss). Refusal to receive his letter was a refusal to receive him (as a representative of the Johannine School). (b) The meaning "to acknowledge, accept, recognize" would indicate that Diotrephes had rejected the role of the Presbyter (and of the Johannine School) in being responsible for the tradition. Presumably Diotrephes arrogated that role to himself as leader of the local church. Too free is the NEB translation, "will have nothing to do with us," even though it leaves room for Käsemann's interpretation whereby Diotrephes is a bishop who will not enter into association with the heretical Presbyter. Verse 9b does not exclude Diotrephes' dealing with the Presbyter as a brother Johannine Christian; it excludes Diotrephes' acknowledging that the Presbyter has a right to intervene and be heard. Against this second meaning of *epidechesthai* is the objection that the verb would then have meaning (b) in v. 9b and meaning (a) in v. 10d; but that phenomenon is found in I Macc 10:1 ("welcome") and 10:46 ("accept"). In my view both meanings of *epidechesthai* are present in 9b: the letter was looked upon as an extension of the Presbyter's presence in his role as a member of the Johannine School; his missionaries would have had precisely the same function. The refusal to welcome the missionaries (10d) and to accept the letter (9b) are two sides of the one policy. Nevertheless, I find lacking in evidence the thesis that Diotrephes' refusal to accept the letter was based on the doctrine therein (W. Bauer, Käsemann, Wendt).

10a. *Therefore. Dia touto,* "on account of this, for this reason," was discussed in the NOTE on I John 3:1de. Here it is not followed by an epexegetical clause and so refers to what precedes (as also in I John 4:5). In the two I John instances it introduces hostile action by the world; here it introduces hostile action by the Presbyter against Diotrephes.

if I come. Ean followed by the subjunctive normally has an element of the hypothetical. Yet on the basis of v. 14 some interpreters argue that the Presbyter surely intends to come, and so they translate, "When I come." That is possible; for *ean* may mean "whenever" (NOTE on I John 2:28b), and any uncertainty may center on the time rather than on the eventuality. Nevertheless, I prefer "if" here for two reasons. First, by using a hypothetical construction the Presbyter indicates that he has no desire to come in such a hostile way and subtly expresses his hope that he will not have to do so. Second, since I do not think that Gaius was a member of Diotrephes' house-church (see COMMENT), it is not certain that the expressed hope to visit Gaius (v. 14) need involve a visit to Diotrephes' church.

10b. *I shall bring up what he is doing.* Literally, "the works [*erga*] he makes [*poiein*]." Words of the same root occur in the praise of Gaius in v. 5 ("You demonstrate [*poiein*] fidelity by all the work that you do [*ergazesthai*] for the brothers"), so that the Presbyter is contrasting Gaius and Diotrephes, both of whom "do works." "Bring up" translates *hypomimnēskein*, "to remind," of which the only other Johannine use is in John 14:26: "The Paraclete . . . will remind you of all that I told you." A reminder can be positive or negative; the verb is used in Wis 12:2; II Tim 2:14 to remind people of a past situation that requires chastisement. To whom will the Presbyter "bring up" what Diotrephes is doing? On the analogy of v. 6 where the brothers testify "before the church" to Gaius' loving deeds, it is likely that the charges in v. 10 will be made before the church mentioned in v. 9. The least the Presbyter would hope to gain from such a confrontation is a change of Diotrephes' behavior. Does he also want Diotrephes removed from his position of primacy? Seemingly that power rested with the local church, as we see in *I Clem.* 44:6. Thus, Chaine, *Epîtres* 256, exaggerates when he states that the Presbyter felt assured that he could reestablish things as they should be. Rather, uncertainty about the outcome of an appeal to the church may have contributed to the hypothetical character of the author's "if I come."

in spreading evil nonsense about us. The grammar in 10b and 10c is as follows: two ptcps. illustrate "the works" that Diotrephes is doing, namely, (10b) "spreading nonsense"; (10c) "not being content." Then the second ptcp. is expanded by three verbs (10def) that illustrate further actions by which Diotrephes shows his not being content ("refuses to welcome . . . hinders . . . expels"). The verb *phlyarein*, "to gossip, chatter, talk nonsense," occurs only here in the NT (but the related adjective *phlyaros* is used to describe idle widows in I Tim 5:13). The hostile tone of the verb comes from the accompanying phrase "with evil [*ponēros*] words," an expression comparable to the "evil deeds" of I John 3:12; II John 11. Such evil belongs to the realm of the Evil One (NOTE on I John 2:13d). If the "us" of v. 9b means that the Presbyter is a representative of the Johannine School, the evil nonsense refers not to his personal character but to his role as an authoritative witness to the tradition.

10c. *And he is not content with that.* Literally, "and not being satisfied with these things," a ptcp. parallel to the ptcp. in the preceding clause. The actions that follow are governed by this second ptcp.

10d. *He refuses to welcome the brothers himself.* Literally, "he does not welcome," an instance of *epidechesthai* discussed in the last NOTE on 9b above. This is the first of three finite clauses that illustrate how Diotrephes has expressed his discontent with the Presbyter. The three clauses (10def) are coordinated in a negative, positive, positive pattern of conjunctions (*oute . . . kai . . . kai;* see BDF 444, 445[3]; also the two-clause *oute . . . kai* pattern in John 4:11). All the verbs are in the pres. tense, indicating a continuing policy.

10e. *and furthermore he hinders those who wish to do so.* This is the only instance of *kōlyein*, "to hinder, forbid," in the Johannine writings. Some interpreters who think that Gaius is a member of Diotrephes' congregation cannot believe that in vv. 5–8 the Presbyter is asking Gaius to do something that will ultimately lead to his expulsion from the church (v. 10f). Hence they translate v. 10ef not as two actions already in effect but as two conative pres. tenses: "trying to hinder . . . trying to expel" (BDF 319). However, the coordination of three clauses mentioned in the previous NOTE militates against such a translation: the three actions are on the same level, and the first is already in effect. "Wish to do so" involves the verb *boulein*, although minor witnesses, influenced by the context where *epidechesthai* occurs twice (9b, 10d), use that verb here as well in place of *boulein* ("hinders those who receive them").

10f. *and expels them from the church.* The verb *ekballein*, "to throw out," used for expulsion from the Essene order by Josephus (*War* 2.8.8.; ℵ143), was also used by John 9:34–35 for expulsion from the synagogue. (Despite the *ek* component in the verb, an additional *ek* appears here before the noun; Codex Sinaiticus omits the latter in order to achieve more elegant Greek.) Some, like Bresky and Käsemann, who think that Diotrephes was a bishop, find in this verse an indication of his power to excommunicate by personal decree. (The closest one comes to the idea of excommunication in GJohn is 9:22, but there the verb *ekballein* is not used; see ABJ 29, 374.) However, I Cor 5:2 shows Paul appealing to a church to remove (*airein*) from their midst one who has done evil; and Matt 18:17 places in the church the final power of decision against a recalcitrant. From these parallels one might guess that, although the Presbyter speaks of Diotrephes' expelling people from the church, the action may have involved Diotrephes' instigating community action against them and not necessarily expelling by personal fiat.

11a. *Beloved. Agapētos* modified the name Gaius in 1b and was used as an address in vv. 2, 5, marking a structural progression in the letter. (See NOTE on I John 2:7a.) That pattern tips the scale in favor of joining the content of v. 11 with v. 12 rather than with v. 10. The Presbyter, after his criticism of Diotrephes, is returning to the theme of vv. 5–8 by asking Gaius not to imitate Diotrephes but to extend hospitality to missionaries, especially to Demetrius.

do not imitate what is bad but what is good. This is the only Johannine use of the verb *mimeisthai* (4 NT occurrences). The order of the "bad/good" contrast may have been dictated by the mention of the bad example (Diotrephes) in the preceding verses and a good example (Demetrius) in what follows. The "bad" is not the normal *ponēros*, "evil," but *kakos* opposed to *agathos*. This contrast occurs nowhere else in the Johannine writings, for the only other instance of *kakos* used in contrast (John 18:23) is opposed adverbially to a form of *kalos* ("wrong" versus "right"). In John 5:29 *agathos* is contrasted to *phaulos* ("good" versus "wicked"). Nevertheless, the *kakos/agathos* pattern is attested in the Greek Bible (Ps 37:27; I Pet 3:17). Is III John 11a, then, a general non-Johannine maxim that the Presbyter cites and comments upon in Johannine language in 11bc? This is possible, for v. 11a is grammatically independent of 11bc (and indeed, by exception in II and III John, the whole verse could be set in the semipoetic format I have used for I John).

11bc. *Whoever does what is good belongs to God; whoever does what is bad has never seen God.* The parallelism (good/bad) is in a chiastic relationship to v. 11a (bad/good); and the construction is an asyndeton, all the more notable by contrast with the correlative *oute . . . kai . . . kai* in v. 10def. The substantival adjectives from 11a, *kakos* and *agathos,* have been compounded with the verb *poiein,* "to do, act," partially echoing the dualistic phraseology in I John, e.g., "Everyone who loves has been begotten by God" (4:7); "Everyone who does not act justly [do justice] does not belong to God" (3:10); "The person who has no love for his brother . . . cannot love the God he has never seen" (4:20). In a sense the judgment of III John upon those who do what is bad could apply to all human beings, for in Johannine thought *no one* has ever seen God (John 1:18; 5:37; 6:46; I John 4:12). That is why THLJ 156 argues that one cannot reverse the statements and say, "Whoever does what is good has seen God." Nevertheless, the Presbyter probably means that those who believe have seen the Father in seeing Jesus (John 14:9) and that evildoers are denied this privilege since they prefer darkness to light (John 3:19; 9:39). The clause in 11c is a logical application of I John 3:6: "Everyone who commits sin has never seen him [Jesus] or come to know him." The dualism of good/bad in I John, however phrased, most often centers on love/hate for brothers; and the hospitality/inhospitality motif in III John is simply an application of the love commandment. If Diotrephes clearly illustrates the bad and inhospitable, is it Gaius or Demetrius (v. 12) who illustrates the good? Gaius as a person who extends hospitality and does good work (v. 5) would be a more obvious contrast to Diotrephes than is Demetrius who is to receive hospitality; but the Presbyter would regard both of them as doing good since the host to the missionary is a coworker (v. 8).

Horvath, "3 Jn 11b," has reflected on the broadness of "Whoever does what is good belongs to God," asking whether it could not serve as an ecumenical creed, defining belonging to God (*einai ek:* NOTE on I John 2:16ef) in terms of good behavior rather than of christological confession. He asks further whether the Presbyter means to reverse the normal Johannine pattern of tracing good deeds to having been begotten by God and belonging to the truth (I John 3:19). I doubt this, for I suspect that the Presbyter's "Whoever" refers to *believers* (even as doing good in this context refers to hospitality). If the Presbyter who wrote III John 11b also wrote II John 9, he could scarcely be as cavalier about christology as Horvath would make him: "Anyone who . . . does not remain rooted in the teaching of Christ does not possess God."

12a. *Demetrius.* The fourth-century *Apostolic Constitutions* (7.46.9; Funk 1, 454) reports that the Apostle John ultimately made him bishop of Philadelphia in Asia Minor (NOTE on Gaius in 1a above); but this information is of dubious historical value, exemplifying as it does a tendency to invent successful careers for NT worthies. Although this common name is frequent in Greek inscriptions, there has been the usual attempt to identify Demetrius with Christians of the same name in the NT. (a) Since tradition associates the Johannine writings with Ephesus, it has been suggested imaginatively that here we have in later life and as a Christian convert the Demetrius of Acts 19:24 who made silver shrines of Artemis/Diana of Ephesus. (b) Chapman, "Historical Setting" 364ff., proposes identification with Demas (perhaps a shortened form of Demetrius), a fellow-worker of Paul who is known to the church at

Colossae, near Ephesus (Philem 24; Col 4:14), and who is later mentioned as being at Thessalonica after he had deserted Paul (II Tim 4:10). Obviously both identifications are pure conjecture.

What follows may be surmised reasonably from III John. Demetrius' name but not his person is known to Gaius, and certainly he is not one of those mentioned in v. 3 as having already enjoyed Gaius' hospitality. He is mentioned in the letter because he is going to come to Gaius' area and will need hospitality. (B. Weiss thinks Demetrius may already be in place in the church of Diotrephes as a rival to that unworthy, and that the Presbyter is asking Gaius to throw his support to Demetrius; but this would make III John's concentration on hospitality to missionaries strange.) The Presbyter may be anticipating that the coming of Demetrius will encounter opposition, whence the very strong testimonial in 12, backed by three witnesses. As Bartlett, "Historical Setting" 207, remarks, the recommendation "doth protest too much."

This leaves many questions. From where will Demetrius come to Gaius? Is Demetrius with the Presbyter and thus a missionary "brother" similar to those to whom Diotrephes is now refusing hospitality? (Indeed, one may wonder whether Demetrius was not the subject of the earlier letter [of recommendation] described in v. 9 as written by the Presbyter but ignored by Diotrephes.) Or is he a member of Diotrephes' church who has been expelled (for showing hospitality to "the brothers"?) and who is now seeking another house-church that he may join? The suggestion that he was formerly from Gaius' own church (Camerlynck, Harnack, Vrede) and that he has had an unfortunate past does not fit the tone of the testimonial in 12 which implies that he is not well known to Gaius. The possibility that Demetrius comes from a church or area in which none of the principals of III John lived is lessened by the fact that the Presbyter knows him well enough to recommend him strongly.

Why is Demetrius singled out for special testimonial? Both the (a) and (b) attempts above to identify him as another NT Demetrius posit in his personal life faults that would create a demand among Christians for reassurance as to his character and purpose. More often the explanation is sought in the difficult task he is about to undertake: Is he to be head of the missionary expedition about to set out? Is he to reestablish the Presbyter's influence in the church against Diotrephes? Is he to replace Diotrephes as "first" in the local church? (That seems unlikely in light of the Presbyter's negative attitude in 9b toward seeking primacy.) Is he going to carry the letter to Gaius? Again we are lost in conjecture.

gets a testimonial. Literally, "has been testified to," a perfect passive tense, suggesting that such testimony has been given over a period of time. In vv. 3 and 6 we heard of testimony that was given to the truth and the love of Gaius; and so presumably it is to the truth and love of Demetrius that this testimony refers, namely, that he is a true Johannine Christian in belief and practice. If Demetrius is going to carry this letter, or if eventually Demetrius is going to come to Gaius' house, this letter constitutes a recommendation for Demetrius. In the NT, especially in the Pauline churches, we find a practice of letters to and fro recommending Christians to be received, supported, and listened to

(Acts 18:27; Rom 16:1–2; I Cor 16:3; II Cor 3:1; Philip 2:25–30; Col 4:7–9). The struggles of Paul with the Judaizers and other opponents made it necessary for his churches to have a way of knowing whether strangers who came preaching Christ were on Paul's side or not. But we have no way of ascertaining whether the practice of letters of commendation was in vogue early in all Christian communities. Would the Johannine Community with its distinctiveness and its stress on love within the brotherhood have required a letter commending Johannine Christians as they moved from one Johannine church to another? The secession described in I John 2:19 may well have been the Johannine occasion for introducing letters of recommendation since it would no longer have been easy to detect immediately on which side of the dispute a Christian of the Johannine heritage stood. Indeed this problem may have led Diotrephes to close his church to all visiting missionaries (see COMMENT). For his part the Presbyter may have been meeting the problem by sending just such a recommendation as we find in III John 12.

from all. Presumably this means from all (true) Johannine Christians, i.e., those who are in *koinōnia* with the Presbyter and the Johannine School (I John 1:3)—the "not only I but also those who have come to know the truth" of II John 1c. In fact, the "all" is hyperbolic, for it can cover only the Johannine Christians who know Demetrius. If he has been a missioner, it would include those affected by his mission. If he is with the Presbyter in the central Johannine city, it would include the largest body of Johannine Christians.

12b. *from the truth itself.* In a list of three testimonials, this comes between the witness "from all" and the witness from the Presbyter, but what does it mean? Dodd, *Epistles* 167, prosaically suggests that it may mean no more than "that the common opinion of Demetrius is the plain truth"; but he admits that general Johannine usage would suggest that "truth" has to have a deeper meaning. Bultmann, *Epistles* 102, speaks of personified divine revelation, while others think of truth as doctrine and of a testimony borne through Demetrius' conformity with that doctrine. Grammar, however, would suggest that testimony "from [*hypo*, 'by'] truth" and testimony "from all" have the same kind of agency, so that truth is personified. A possible early reference to this passage by Papias (INTRODUCTION I B1, footnote 12) speaks of "commandments given by the Lord to faith and reaching [us] from truth himself [itself]." Hoskyns, "Epistles" 673, speaks of Demetrius being "approved by God (the Truth itself)," even though the Johannine writers never call God "truth." Harnack thinks that Jesus is meant (John 14:6: "I am the truth"); Belser thinks that the Spirit is meant (I John 5:6: "The Spirit is the truth"), while de Ambroggi and Windisch suggest that it may be one or both. In the Johannine thought pattern, however, the Spirit testifies about Jesus (John 15:26; I John 5:7–8), and Jesus testifies about God or the divine plan that is being revealed (John 3:32; 4:44; 7:7; 13:21); but neither testifies about people. Moreover, it would be odd to "sandwich" a purely divine testimony by God, Jesus, or the Spirit between a testimony from all and a testimony from the Presbyter. Without eliminating the divine element in the testimony by the truth, it seems best here to think of the truth that abides in the Christian (II John 2) and to which the

Christian belongs (I John 3:19), namely, a truth about Jesus that has been appropriated through faith and that expresses itself in the way one walks (III John 3) and manifests itself in love (III John 6; I John 3:18). In Demetrius' case the truth that abides in him finds expression in the holiness of his life and the soundness of his preaching, and so constitutes a powerful witness on his behalf. Others have been testifying to him, and his own life confirms their testimony. See Schnackenburg, "Begriff" 256.

12c. *And we give our testimonial as well.* Literally, "and we too testify." Brooke, *Epistles* 194, contends that in this instance "there is nothing to suggest that he means more than 'we who are personally acquainted with Demetrius'"; but if that were the case, how would the "we" differ from the "all" just mentioned? Harnack, "Über" 13, thinks it means "I." More likely, the "we" has the same sense as the "us" in vv. 9–10, namely, the Presbyter speaking as a member of the Johannine School (NOTE on 9b). That would explain why "our testimonial" is reserved to the last and most solemn place, even after testimony from the truth; for the Johannine School preserves the tradition that interprets the truth. In I John 1:2 this "we" testified to the truth of the life revealed in Jesus; here the "we" testifies that Demetrius walks in the way of truth.

12d. *and you know that our testimony is true.* Some MSS. of the Byzantine tradition read a pl. "you," even though the Presbyter is addressing Gaius. The scribes behind such a pl. reading may have been influenced by the pls. in GJohn passages concerning the Beloved Disciple: "This testimony has been given by an eyewitness, and his testimony is true. He is telling what he knows to be true that you too [pl.] may have faith" (John 19:35); also "It is this same disciple who gives testimony about these things . . . and his testimony, we know, is true" (21:24). The Johannine School is built around the Beloved Disciple and his witness, and the last-cited passage is the classic proof text for the School's existence. III John 12d shows that the School of disciples related to the Beloved Disciple applied to themselves the claim of truth originally made for him. Chapman, "Historical Setting" 363, interprets the "you [sg.] know" to mean that Gaius knew Demetrius well, and thus knew that the Presbyter was speaking the truth in praising him. Rather, the text of v. 12d indicates that Gaius knows the truth of the Presbyter's testimony because the Presbyter is part of the Johannine School—the quality of the testifier and not the object of the testimony is what Gaius knows.

13a. *I had much more that I should write you.* Literally, "I had [imperf.] many things to have written [aorist infin.] to you [sg.]." This varies slightly from II John 12a, "Having [pres. ptcp.] many things to write [pres. infin.] to you [pl.]"; and as I mentioned in the NOTE there, the MS. tradition betrays scribal attempts to harmonize the two formulas. The differences reflect a letter writer who has a general pattern but who shifts details unconsciously and without significance within that pattern. In the sequence of III John the change from the "we" of v. 12 to the "I" of v. 13 is notable and may have been motivated by the stereotypic character of the Body-Closing where the writer normally referred to himself/herself as "I." Or else one may speculate that the Presbyter has now laid aside the mantle of the Johannine School to conclude on a more personal tone. Schnackenburg and THLJ find a sense of obligation in III John's use of the imperfect (BDF 358); and my translation tries to catch that sense by the way it renders the accompanying verb. The aorist of that verb is epistolary, looking at the present letter from the recipient's point of view: upon receiving it Gaius may say, "He should *have* written me more." The stereotyped character of the "much more to write" formula as a Body-Closing makes unlikely various psychological hypotheses as to why the Presbyter did not write more, e.g., he was afraid Diotrephes would intercept the letter and learn the strategy based on Demetrius.

13b. *but I do not wish to write it out with pen and ink.* This is somewhat more elegant than II John 12b: "I did not desire [aorist *boulesthai*] through paper and ink," where one had to supply the infinitive "to write." The verb in II John was an epistolary aorist, equivalent to the pres. tense of *thelein* here. There is no difference between "pen and ink" and "paper and ink," and both phrases taken literally leave the illogical impression that he might write in some other way. For the nature of the ink, see the NOTE on II John 12b; normally a reed pen would have been employed. Synesius, *Epistolae* 157, uses all three nouns ("pen, paper, and ink"), while Papyrus Oxyrhynchus 326 mentions "pen and ink," as does III John.

14a. *Rather, I hope to see you soon.* This is comparable to II John 12c, "Instead, I hope to come to you." Again III John may be more elegant in its choice of vocabulary. Much attention has been paid to III John's "soon" (*eutheōs*, "immediately"), for interpreters argue whether 12c describes the same visit planned in II John. Was III John written somewhat later than II John, so that now the time for the visit was more immediate? If the same visit was involved, would the Presbyter reach the church of Gaius sooner than he would reach the church he designates as "Elect Lady"? Had the situation provoked by Diotrephes' refusal of hospitality to missionaries favorable to the Presbyter caused the Presbyter to move up his timetable and arrive sooner? All this speculation is useless, for the promise to visit soon need have been no more than a common ploy for concluding a letter and thus have involved no definite plans for a visit.

14b. *and we can have a heart-to-heart talk.* With the exception of using a finite verb rather than an infinitive, this is identical with II John 12d: "and have a heart-to-heart talk." As mentioned in the NOTE there, both Epistles refer literally to speaking "mouth-to-mouth."

15a. *Peace to you.* "Peace" occurs, not in the Concluding Formula, but in the Opening Formula of II John (v. 3): "With us there will be grace, mercy, and *peace* from God." That is the normal position for the wish of peace in Jewish and Pauline Epistles, although as I shall point out in Appendix V D, a benediction including "peace" is found in I Peter, Galatians, and Ephesians. The normal benediction closing a Pauline Epistle is a longer or shorter form of "Grace [is/be] with you" (employing the preposition *meta*, "with"). The form in III John consists simply of the anarthrous noun *eirēnē* plus the dative. For the reason why this should be translated as a declaration rather than as a wish ("Peace *be* to you"), see ABJ 29A, 1021. Such a conclusion reflects the Jewish custom of using *"Shalom"* both as introductory greeting and farewell. Even more influential on III John is the greeting of the risen Jesus to his disciples, "Peace to you," in John 20:19,26, which was the fulfillment of Jesus' promise to give peace in John 14:27.

15bc. *The beloved here send you greetings; greet the beloved there.* Literally, "The *philoi* greet you; greet the *philoi*," with the context supplying the "here" and "there." (The imperative in the second clause is in the pres. tense; Codex Sinaiticus reads the aorist, which would be more customary for a single action.) The greetings may be compared to II John 13: "The children of your Elect Sister send you greetings," symbolically designating the agents as Johannine Christians at the church where the Presbyter is. In III John Codex Alexandrinus, some minuscules, and part of the Syriac tradition read "brothers" (*adelphoi*) for *philoi*, thus substituting the standard Johannine term for fellow Christians whom one must love. Clearly, then, we are dealing with more than the wishes from "friends" (*philoi*) found in secular letters. Just as the Opening Formula of NT letters shows in its "Greeting" a spiritualization of the standard Greeting of the secular letter, so also the Concluding Formula—not the human love of friendship, but the divine love of Christ (binding together those who are God's children in his image) is the primary relationship. The absolute *philoi* (notice, not "my *philoi*," equivalent to "my friends") resembles the usage in Acts 27:3 where Paul visits "the *philoi*" at Sidon, presumably the Christian group there, some of whom would have been known to him but all of whom were *philoi*. In discussing the Johannine use of *philos* in John 15:13–15 (ABJ 29A, 664, 682–83), I argued that it should not be translated as "friend" but as "beloved"; for just as *agapein* and *philein* are interchangeable as Johannine verbs "to love" (ABJ 29, 497–99), so also the nouns *agapētos* and *philos* designating the Christian believer as the recipient of God's love—the "beloved" for whom Jesus had laid down his life. (Especially significant is the interchangeability of forms of *agapan* and *philein* in describing "the Disciple whom Jesus *loved*.") Gaius the *agapētos* is hailed at the beginning of III John; the *philoi* of his church are greeted at the end. Thus the greetings sent at the end of III John are just as general as those sent at the end of II John, not from special people at the Presbyter's church to select friends at Gaius' church, but from the Christians of one section of the Johannine Community to the Christians of another section.

each by name. This phrase has been regarded as proof that the Presbyter was referring to specific friends whose names he knew rather than more generally to the Johannine Christians in Gaius' region. Yet the phrase *kat' onoma*, "by name," is not unusual in letters (Papyrus Oxyrhynchus 123; Papyrus Tebtunis 299; LFAE 193), and it can mean no more than "individually" (BAG 574 [BAGD 571] I 3). In Ignatius, *Smyrn.* 13:2, it appears after Ignatius has greeted those whose names he knows; by implication the greeting *kat' onoma* is for those whose names Ignatius does not know or recall but wants saluted individually. The Presbyter may want the Johannine Christians of Gaius' region to be greeted individually in order to avoid any who would not be on his side in the secession or in the dispute with Diotrephes. The latter would not be "beloved" and should not be greeted—see the attitude in II John 10–11. Thus it is far from clear that the Presbyter knows the names of those he wants greeted "by name"; Gaius would know their names. (We should remember that the reference is to small house-churches where Gaius would know well all those who came.) It is important to reflect upon the only other NT use of *kat' onoma* (John 10:3): "The sheep hear his voice as he calls *by name* those that belong to him and leads them out." The Presbyter sends greeting "by name" only to those who are in *koinōnia* with him.

COMMENT

III John is the shortest book in the NT.[1] It has the shortest Opening Formula (*Praescriptio*) of any NT Epistle and the one that most resembles the Opening of secular Greco-Roman letters.[2] Funk, "Formula" 203, calls this letter to Gaius "the most secularized in the NT," and indeed it is the only NT book totally devoid of the names "Jesus" and "Christ" (separately or joined).[3] Within the Johannine corpus it alone supplies the personal names of Johannine Christians, all three (Gaius, Diotrephes, Demetrius) being Greco-Roman rather than Hebrew, suggesting the presence of Gentiles (INTRODUCTION II C2b, footnote 81). Some have conjectured that this personal character of the work explains the slow acceptance of it into the canon of Scripture.[4] The Gaius letter has been said to be to the rest of the Johannine corpus as the Philemon letter is to the Pauline corpus; but III John is much more concerned with a situation directly affecting a church or churches than is Philemon. In fact, it supplies the only instances of the Johannine use of *ekklēsia*, "church"; and it may be the NT key to a major development in Christian church structure, i.e., the emergence of a local-church leader over against the influence of the second-generation disciples (the disciples of the disciples of Jesus). All the more

---

[1] In the 21st edition of the Nestle Greek NT it has 219 words, as compared with 245 words in II John, 355 in Philemon, and 457 in Jude.

[2] Compare the second/third-century A.D. papyrus letter in NTBD ⅀22: "Irenaeus to his dearest brother Apollinarius, many greetings. I pray continually for your health, and I myself am well." Also the letter of Serapion cited in Appendix V A below.

[3] Notice, however, that in v. 7 the missionaries set out "for the sake of 'the Name,'" which some take to be the name borne by Jesus.

[4] See above, INTRODUCTION I B2. In the first references we possess to the minor Johannine Epistles the fact that II and III John are *not* joined is significant. It challenges not only those who insist that II John must be the previous writing to the church mentioned in III John 9, but also those who think one letter is a forgery based on the other. From either of those theories one might have expected the two letters to have been kept together.

frustrating, then, is the discovery that there is little agreement among scholars and no possibility of certitude about the basic situation that has called forth this letter. The roles of the persons named and the issues over which they are in contention remain very obscure. This obscurity stems from no deliberate attempt by the Presbyter to be mysterious. The letter is simply too brief and does not give details about what must have been quite obvious to those involved. But let us review the information available, covering some of the theories proposed to explain why the Presbyter is writing to Gaius and what the dispute is between the Presbyter and Diotrephes. In this commentary I have spared the general reader the brunt of scholarly dispute by confining the long debates to the NOTES and by working in the COMMENT only with the position I deem most tenable. But the dispute here is so germane to the whole point of III John that all readers need to understand the issues involved.

A. *General Observations on Gaius and Diotrephes*

1. The Position of Gaius

III John is quite clear about certain aspects of this question. The Presbyter is pleased that Gaius has shown hospitality to the Johannine "brothers," even though they (or some of them) were strangers to him; and the Presbyter wants him to go on doing so. The reason he is writing to Gaius is that Diotrephes refuses to show such hospitality. Indeed, the letter lists the hostile actions of Diotrephes toward the Presbyter, on the presumption that Gaius will be sympathetic.[5] All of this implies that Gaius is one whose means, home, and social position enable him to serve a hospitable role once played by the house-church now dominated by Diotrephes.

A move beyond these surface facts and impressions finds a situation that is enigmatic on several scores. For instance, what is the time relationship between Gaius' hospitality and Diotrephes' refusal of hospitality, which are somehow related? Does Gaius offer hospitality to those who have recently been rejected by Diotrephes, or is it to those whom Gaius was helping that Diotrephes refuses welcome? The latter view is espoused by Shepherd, "Letters," and it would explain why Gaius has to be informed of Diotrephes' subsequent actions. Most scholars, however, opt for the former view since the praise of Gaius' hospitality is more understandable if some of the "brothers" who give voice to that praise have previously been turned away by Diotrephes. But if Gaius already knows

[5] Bacon, *Fourth Gospel* 186, remarks that Gaius has a function for Presbyter similar to that of Theophilus for Luke (Acts 1:1).

by personal experience that Diotrephes has been turning people away, why does the Presbyter report to him what Diotrephes is doing? A possible answer, but not a totally satisfactory one, is that he is repeating the charges for emphasis.

Another question is whether Gaius belongs to the church of which Diotrephes likes to be a leader or is attached to another church? The first of these possibilities is the more common assumption, sometimes with the implication that, while Diotrephes is a bishop, Gaius is a layman (or a presbyter) who has the courage to disobey the bishop's wicked commands against hospitality. The Presbyter, then, would be encouraging Gaius in this disobedience. Yet this picture of bishop, clergy, and laity is of dubious accuracy both for this time period and for the Johannine Community; and so let us lay it aside from our considerations for the moment. If one chooses to interpret Gaius as rebellious against Diotrephes, a less anachronistic picture is offered by Büchsel who thinks of Gaius as the head of one party or division within the church of Diotrephes, even as a division of parties was present in the church of Corinth some fifty years earlier.[6] In particular, it is supposed that he heads the party of those who accept the Presbyter's guidance. Nevertheless, there is little in the letter pitting Gaius against Diotrephes—the "brothers" have had dealings with both men, but nothing is said of their dealings with each other. The only reasons for assuming that Gaius and Diotrephes belong to the same house-church are the use of "the church" in vv. 9–10 as if there were only one, and the mention *to Gaius* in v. 10 of a possible visit to Diotrephes' church.[7]

But there are many objections to the thesis of the same church. In referring to the church in v. 9, why does the Presbyter tell Gaius that Diotrephes likes to be first "among *them*," as if Gaius were not involved? Why does the Presbyter have to tell Gaius about the letter written to the church? If one responds that Diotrephes destroyed the letter and did not tell others in the church about it, one still must ask why the Presbyter tells Gaius in v. 10 about actions of which everyone in the church would be aware. Büchsel suggests that Gaius had been absent during these occurrences; but surely when he came back, he would have heard of the expulsion order. Moreover, how has Gaius been able to extend hospitality

[6] However, according to I Cor 1–3 the parties were aligned behind churchwide figures like Paul, Apollos, and Cephas, while here we would have parties aligned behind local leaders. But one can respond that the Gaius party would have said, "We are for the Presbyter."

[7] Some strengthen this argument for one church by identifying the hoped-for visit to Gaius (v. 14) with the possible visit to the church of Diotrephes in v. 10. But this argument backfires, for the Presbyter seems less hypothetical about the visit to Gaius than about the visit to Diotrephes' church.

(v. 5), which is quite public (v. 6),[8] without being expelled by Diotrephes? And how does the Presbyter expect Gaius to avoid expulsion in
the future if he follows the advice in the letter (v. 8) to offer the very
support that Diotrephes has forbidden? The suggestion that the Presbyter
hopes that Gaius can overthrow Diotrephes or frustrate his policy in the
church is not justified by the letter, for the only hope the Presbyter seems
to have against Diotrephes is in terms of a visit and a public accusation
before the church (v. 10). If Demetrius is a missionary who is going to
come to Gaius (as seems probable), how does he hope to be received by
or receive support from a church where Diotrephes holds sway?

Because of these difficulties a few scholars have opted for the other possibility, namely, that Gaius is associated with another house-church near
the house-church where Diotrephes "likes to be first." That would explain
why he has not been expelled by Diotrephes and how he can be expected
to follow the Presbyter's encouragement toward continued hospitality, especially for Demetrius. The Presbyter's reference to "the church" in v. 9
need mean no more than that it was a church known to Gaius. Gaius may
have heard of some procedures adopted by Diotrephes in a neighboring
house-church but may not know the extent and thoroughness of Diotrephes' campaign against missionaries. Thus vv. 9–10 may have been
meant to reassure Gaius that the brothers rejected by Diotrephes and received by him truly were faultless and have the approval of the Presbyter
(whereas hitherto Gaius has been dependent on their word). These verses
would locate for Gaius the real problem: not simply the inhospitality of
Diotrephes but his rejection of the Presbyter. Certainly the information
given by the Presbyter is less of a problem if Gaius is not a member of the
same church as Diotrephes.

A particular form of this theory has been advocated by Malherbe
("Inhospitality" 226–29), namely, that Gaius and Diotrephes are the
heads of different house-congregations in the same area, each having a
house that serves as a Christian meeting place. The letter mentioned in
v. 9 was written by the Presbyter to all the house-congregations that together
constitute "the church" in this region. Gaius knows its contents, having
accepted it while Diotrephes rejected it. Since Diotrephes is now refusing
hospitality in his house to any more of "the brothers" associated with the
Presbyter, Demetrius will be sent with a testimonial letter of explanation
(III John) to Gaius whose home is still open to the Presbyter's confreres.[9] Malherbe's attractive hypothesis faces several minor objections. I
do not interpret III John 9 to mean that Gaius knows the previous letter

---

[8] In the NOTE on 6a I argue that "the church" in that verse is the church of the
Presbyter, not the church of Diotrephes mentioned in vv. 9–10. But granting the
strained relationship between the Presbyter and Diotrephes, it would be surprising if
Diotrephes did not keep himself informed both about Gaius and about the Presbyter.

[9] See the second-century *Martyrium S. Iustini* 3 for Christians visiting a strange
city being made welcome.

sent by the Presbyter or its contents.[10] Indeed, the fact that the Presbyter has to tell Gaius that previously he wrote "something to the church" of Diotrephes is an argument supporting the thesis that the two men do not belong to the same congregation. More importantly, I doubt Malherbe's contention that "the church" means a larger entity, overarching several house-congregations. I think that in v. 9, as in v. 6, "the church" means the local congregation or house-church. In the Pauline Epistles "church" is used for each house-congregation, e.g., "the church at the house of Prisca and Aquila" (Rom 16:4–5; I Cor 16:19), and "the church at the house of Nympha" (Col 4:15). Accordingly, were Malherbe's theory about the roles of Gaius and Diotrephes correct, one might expect v. 9 to read, "I did write something to the churches." Another objection to Malherbe's thesis is that III John does not give the impression that Gaius and Diotrephes are on an equal level. One can respond that, although both are leaders of house-churches, Diotrephes has become arrogant in the power he claims, while Gaius remains properly modest. However, the difference of level does not flow simply from the attitudes of the two men, but from the attitude of the Presbyter toward each. For instance, why did the Presbyter write to (the church of) Diotrephes previously but seemingly not to Gaius?

In light of these problems I wish to propose a possible variation of Malherbe's thesis. Gaius is not a member of Diotrephes' house-church, but neither is he fully the host or head of another house-church. Notice that while the Presbyter wrote to "the church" of which Diotrephes likes to be first, now he writes directly to Gaius as if a church were not so directly involved. Gaius may be a wealthy Johannine Christian in an area not far from Diotrephes where there are adherents (and perhaps even friends) of the Presbyter—those whom he wishes greeted by name or individually in v. 15. The Presbyter may not know Gaius personally since he is not the host of a church; but in the emergency created by Diotrephes' refusal of hospitality, "the brothers" on several occasions have gone to Gaius' home and he has given them hospitality.[11] Their report of this to the Presbyter (vv. 3,6a) may have suggested to him a plan for the future.

[10] It is true that the Presbyter does not go on to tell Gaius of the contents of what he sent to the church, but that may be because the contents are not what now concern the Presbyter. The issue has now become the nonacceptance of the letter (and all that implies), not its contents.

[11] Much of III John makes sense only if Diotrephes has recently changed church policy (after the Presbyter wrote to the church the letter mentioned in v. 9) and if Gaius has recently been burdened with guests to whom he has shown hospitality. The double mention of testimony to Gaius in vv. 3,6 implies something noteworthy and recent. It is possible that those rejected by Diotrephes did not tell Gaius all the details when they came to him, lest they appear dubious to him as possible troublemakers. Only reassurance from the Presbyter would convince Gaius that a church-host like Diotrephes is at fault.

Not only does he ask Gaius to continue the hospitality (vv. 6b,8); but by explaining Diotrephes' situation,[12] he may be suggesting implicitly that Gaius should set up his house as a church meeting place. In other words the situation Malherbe envisages may be future rather than present. If Gaius eventually became the host of a Johannine church, the letter addressed to him was preserved by that church as part of the heritage of the Johannine Community (unless one assumes that the Presbyter kept a copy that has come down to us). At least Diotrephes, who had destroyed a previous letter, was not successful in blocking this one or in consigning it to the waste basket.

2. The Stance of Diotrephes

The church position of Diotrephes is clearer than that of Gaius. What is not clear is the motivation and nuance of his attitude toward the missionaries and the Presbyter. He has the first position in a church;[13] correspondence from the Presbyter to the church reaches him, and he can ignore it and the Presbyter as well (v. 9); the most the Presbyter can do by reprisal is to come and bring up before the church what Diotrephes is doing. The range of that "doing" affects the Presbyter (spreading evil nonsense against him), "the brothers" (refusing to welcome them), and members of Diotrephes' church (hindering them from welcoming the brothers; expelling those who do). Presumably all the actions are related: spreading evil nonsense against the Presbyter continues the opposition previously expressed in the rejection of the letter; and "the brothers" are missionaries who help the Presbyter, so that refusal of them is a refusal of him.

Why the hostility between Diotrephes and the Presbyter? Proposed answers may be classified under several headings. An *ecclesiastical disagreement,* concerning the form of church governance or the amount of authority or the manner of its exercise, is suggested as the source of hostility by Bornkamm, F.-M. Braun, Bruce, Donfried, Haenchen, Harnack, Krüger, Marshall, Pastor, Schnackenburg, Schneider, and von Campenhausen. This interpretation is based on statements in 9b–10. A *doctrinal disagreement,* concerning christology or ethics or both, is proposed by W. Bauer, Bresky, Käsemann,[14] and Wendt. This interpretation is based on the secessionist theme of I and II John, with the assumption that the se-

[12] If Gaius is not the head of a rival house-church, then the only existing church that concerns the Presbyter in III John is *the* church of Diotrephes, whence the definite article in v. 9a.

[13] See the NOTE on 9b: the clause "who likes to be first among them" expresses the Presbyter's unfavorable opinion of an existing primacy. The Presbyter's challenge suggests that Diotrephes did not enter an office that already had the powers he exercises; rather he shaped the office.

[14] His approach is rejected by Bornkamm, TDNT 6, 671; Haenchen, "Literatur" 277–81; Schnackenburg, *Johannesbriefe* 299.

cession has affected the church described in III John also. The use of "truth" in III John 1,3,4,8,12 is offered as a proof that doctrine must be in question; yet it is never said that Diotrephes does not belong to the truth, only that Gaius and the Presbyter do. A *combined ecclesiastical and doctrinal disagreement* has been proposed by Hilgenfeld, Houlden,[15] and Wilder.

Within such general classifications there are many variations. For instance, among those who propose a doctrinal disagreement there is disagreement about which figure represents "orthodoxy." And so it is necessary to investigate some prominent theories in more detail. Six suggestions will be discussed, the first three of which involve ecclesiastical disagreement, while the second three involve doctrinal disagreement. Combinations of these suggestions are possible.

(1) Diotrephes is an example of the emerging presbyter-bishop,[16] the sole supreme figure in the local church, as described with enthusiasm a few years later by Ignatius of Antioch. Harnack's claim ("Über" 21) has become famous: Diotrephes is the first monarchical bishop whose name we know. Minor variations of this theory concern how Diotrephes acquired his position. For Michaelis he is an upstart of the presbyterial college, a suggestion that supposes the development of the single bishop through the enterprise of a dominant personality among the hitherto equal presbyters. Others assume that he is a bishop who has come from a non-Johannine church, thus introducing a new system of governance that was foreign to Johannine tradition. Still another suggestion is that Johannine secessionists in the church of III John opted for episcopal governance because of their preference for authoritative teachers (I John 2:27). Major variations of this theory concern the status of the Presbyter who can be pictured as equal, superior, or inferior to Diotrephes. (a) The Presbyter may be Diotrephes' equal, in the sense that he too is a presbyter-bishop. But he would be a representative of a style of governance by a group of presbyter-bishops (the "we"), while Diotrephes would have become a single bishop claiming primacy over the other presbyters. That a presbyter might write to another church giving advice on church government is confirmed by the *First Epistle of Clement* (of Rome to the Corinthian church).[17] (b)

---

[15] Houlden, *Epistles* 8: "A point where a congregation wishes to emancipate itself from dependence on those individuals and groups to whom, perhaps, it owed its foundation and both its possession and its formulation of the Christian faith."

[16] Hitherto the Johannine house-churches may have had hosts who exercised no ruling or teaching function. Filson, "Significance" 112, however, is right that inevitably hosting a church would become a training ground for those who emerged as official leaders after the death of the great first-generation figures.

[17] Yet Clement uses no title or even personal name; his letter comes from "The Church of God which dwells in Rome." It is an intelligent guess that Clement was a (prominent) presbyter of the Roman Church but scarcely the single bishop.

The Presbyter may have been superior in status to Diotrephes (Donfried, Harnack, Pastor, Schneider, Zahn). Often the Apostle Paul is held up as a parallel to the Presbyter, since Paul considered himself to be above local church administrators and expected to be obeyed by them. The comparison to Paul seems natural to those who identify the Presbyter as the Apostle John.[18] Harnack speaks of a model whereby the Presbyter (John but not the Apostle) controls a group of churches through a network of missionaries. Donfried, "Ecclesiastical" 328, thinks of the Presbyter as *the* most important presbyter in a regional network of churches." Streeter, *Primitive Church* 91–92, thinks his importance is related to his being situated at the apostolic see of Ephesus, which made him a type of metropolitan or archbishop in relation to (bishop) Diotrephes; thus, the Presbyter is "president of the mother church of Asia." (c) The Presbyter may have been inferior in structural status to Diotrephes (Bornkamm, Käsemann, Schweizer, von Campenhausen). For von Campenhausen, *Ecclesiastical Authority* 121–23, the Presbyter is "a prophet or teacher of the earlier type." (It is unfortunate that von Campenhausen, Dodd, Donfried, and others introduce "teacher" into this discussion, since, if the Presbyter wrote I John 2:27, he was certainly not a teacher.) Such a status based on personal charism would count for little in the eyes of bishops (like Diotrephes) representing a formally structured church. Indeed, Diotrephes may have been purging his church of uncontrollable charismatics such as those whom the Presbyter calls "brothers." Käsemann, "Ketzer" 173–74, characterizes Diotrephes as "a monarchical bishop who considers himself to be confronting a false bishop and acts accordingly."

(2) Diotrephes represents a charismatic form of church leadership where guidance is supplied by the Spirit rather than by office holder. In this theory it is the Presbyter who represents a more structured church authority (an apostle, or companion of the apostles, or a bishop, or one of the presbyters). Accordingly Diotrephes would preserve an older form of leadership while the Presbyter becomes the spokesman of an emerging Early Catholicism which tolerates neither uncontrollable charisms nor incipiently gnostic attitudes. Diotrephes would be resisting such innovation and, because of an inner light or guidance by the Spirit, would expel people. The church, impressed by his charisms, is allowing him to do this.

(3) Diotrephes places his house at the disposal of Johannine Christians in the area, and he has now begun to use his role as host to run the affairs of the church and to control what is taught. This exercise of privileges

---

[18] The Muratorian Fragment, Jerome, and Augustine all imagined John presiding over a group of bishops in Asia Minor, attributing to the first century a church situation of their own times. Baur ("Briefe" 334), who thought that I John was written well into the second century, compared Diotrephes to the Roman bishop Victor (d. 199), considered as "bishop of bishops."

resembles in some ways the functioning of the (emerging) bishop whom Ignatius will describe. However, we know no title for Diotrephes (Schnackenburg), nor need we posit a previous history of governance by groups of presbyters. Diotrephes is not claiming a new office or adopting a new title; otherwise there would be a strong charge of innovation placed against him in III John. Diotrephes may be a wealthy man if he has a house large enough to host a whole Johannine Christian group, whereas the presbyter-bishops described by the Pauline Pastorals are paid wages (I Tim 5:17–18). Over against Diotrephes the Presbyter represents the Johannine School of tradition-bearers and the principle that Jesus (or the Paraclete who takes his place) is the only teacher (John 14:26; 16:13). If one may judge from I John, the Presbyter thinks that love, not authority, marks the Christian and, *a fortiori,* the host of the Christian church.

(4) Diotrephes is one of the Deceivers, Antichrists, or secessionists attacked in I John, and one of the progressives attacked in II John (W. Bauer, Bresky, Wendt)—this is the most common view among those who posit a doctrinal disagreement. Diotrephes is a teacher who has won over a Johannine house-church to which he came as a missionary (cf. II John 9–10). Indeed, III John may be written to the same "Elect Lady" congregation addressed in II John if that congregation did not obey the Presbyter and allowed Diotrephes to enter and proselytize. When the Presbyter says in III John 9, "I did write something to the church," he may be referring to II John, a letter that was not successful in its goal of stopping the secession from spreading to the Elect Lady.

(5) Diotrephes is doctrinally a representative of the Great Church (INTRODUCTION V D, footnote 242), as well as being a monarchical bishop. The Presbyter, on the other hand, is a former member of the college of presbyters who has been expelled for heresy, even as his "brothers" are now being ejected by Diotrephes. This thesis advocated by Käsemann is related to the view that GJohn is a gnostic work either in itself or through its sources. One may recall Bultmann's view that GJohn could be accepted by the Great Church only after the Ecclesiastical Redactor (censor) had edited it. A variant of this theory is that Diotrephes, both in his episcopate and theology, represents a Jewish Christianity, akin to that of James or "the brothers of the Lord" (who are criticized as nonbelievers in John 7:5)—a Christianity critical of the Hellenizing and gnosticizing tendencies of the Johannine thought.[19] Another variant was proposed by Hilgenfeld, namely, that Diotrephes represents an older Johannine strain associated with Judaism and Judea (and sometimes with the Book of Revelation), while the Presbyter represents a

[19] GJohn hostility toward a certain group of Jewish Christians is suggested in my *Community* 73–81. See also J. L. Martyn, *Gospel* 83–84.

new Johannine strain associated with one of the Gentile centers (and GJohn).[20]

(6) Diotrephes and the Presbyter share the same opposition to the secessionists. In most forms of this view it is assumed that doctrine plays no role in the hostile situation described in III John. It is possible, however, that Diotrephes and the Presbyter are quarreling over the most effective means of combatting the secessionists. In favor of this is the fact that II John (10–11) and III John (12) share a practice of refusing hospitality to traveling teachers coming from the outside. II John raises the issue because of the danger that missionary teachers will spread secessionist doctrine. May that also have been Diotrephes' motive? One may object that, since the Presbyter promotes the missionaries in III John, they must be anti-secessionist. But when travelers come and ask to address a local house-church, how is the host to know what they will say until they have actually spoken and perhaps done harm?[21] The inability to tell the difference between acceptable and unacceptable traveling teachers and prophets is a major problem according to *Didache* 11, a work written about the same time as III John. Faced with such a dilemma, Diotrephes may have decided that the only safe remedy was to refuse all missionaries. By this step, which affects the Presbyter's missionaries as well, Diotrephes may be hoping to keep the whole dispute out of his church and thus to preserve peace by quarantine.

When we evaluate these six suggestions, it is a question of which proves to be the least unlikely. Certitude is not possible, nor perhaps is high probability. If below I cite arguments against some of the suggestions, I do not pretend the arguments are conclusive, only dissuasive. First, let me evaluate together suggestions 1, 2, and 3, which concern ecclesiastical differences, and then 4, 5, and 6, which concern doctrinal differences.

Suggestions 1 and 2 face the same objection, namely, that in the Johannine writings we have no evidence for the existence of bishops (presupposed in 1) nor any stress on charisms (2) as important factors in the life of the Community. These suggestions draw their support from analogies to Pauline community history (respectively the Pastorals and I Corinthians) and from the writings of the Apostolic Fathers. In suggestion 1, I find quite implausible the theory that "bishop" Diotrephes was an outsider from a non-Johannine church who settled in the church of which he is now head. In his polemic the Presbyter would not have omitted a charge of alien influence were that the case. Surely Diotrephes belongs to the church addressed and has a basis of support in that church, which makes

[20] One might naturally think of Ephesus, but Hilgenfeld thinks also of Rome because of the struggle between Jerusalem and Rome over the Quartodeciman issue, which involved the Johannine dating of the day of Jesus' death (ABJ 29A, 555–56).

[21] Especially would this be true if a pattern of letters of recommendation did not exist. As we shall see, the testimonial given to Demetrius in III John 12 may be the Presbyter's attempt to remedy what has become a problem.

it difficult for the Presbyter to correct him. (The idea that the Presbyter has the power to remove Diotrephes but does not choose to use it fits neither the tone of his hostility to Diotrephes nor his readiness to take strong steps evidenced in I and II John.) One must do justice to two facts: First, the Presbyter who writes I, II, and III John expects to be heard and is hurt when he is not; second, his is not a status that enables him to remove Diotrephes by simple fiat. Thus he does not seem to be a church officer superior in the structure to Diotrephes (not an apostle, nor a metropolitan, nor a monarchical bishop). Neither does his joining himself to a "we" who are witnesses, with arguments based on a tradition held from the beginning, suggest charismatic authority. Of the first three suggestions, then, 3 makes the best sense against the known Johannine background.

The last three suggestions concern doctrinal issues, with 4 and 5 assuming that the Presbyter and Diotrephes are on different sides in the secessionist movement discussed in I and II John. The arguments for that assumption are weak. I and II John are almost monomaniacal in attacking secessionist christology and ethics, but in III John there is not a single word about Jesus as the Christ, nor is the love commandment explicitly mentioned. If Diotrephes holds the secessionist views, it is virtually inconceivable that the Presbyter would fail to mention this in his attack.[22] Käsemann's thesis that the Presbyter is a (semi-)gnostic heretic is equally indefensible in my opinion. Something can be said for finding proto-gnostic tendencies in GJohn; indeed, it has been my contention throughout this volume that the secessionists are interpreting GJohn in a way that would lead to gnosticism. But I and II John constitute a strong refutation of some gnostic possibilities in Johannine thought; and if the Presbyter of III John wrote II John, it is inconceivable that Diotrephes[23] could have regarded him as a secessionist progressive. Moreover, unless one assumes that the previous letter to the church (v. 9) was written before Diotrephes assumed any primacy, the Presbyter wrote that letter assuming that the church of Diotrephes would provide hospitality for missionary brothers of the Presbyter's persuasion—an assumption scarcely possible if the two men were doctrinally divided. (The network of sister churches implied in the Concluding Formulas of II and III John makes it likely in my opinion

[22] Occasionally III John 11 is cited as an implied doctrinal charge against Diotrephes ("Whoever does what is good belongs to God; whoever does what is bad has never seen God"), for it has parallels to the anti-secessionist dualism of I John (e.g., 3:6, "Everyone who commits sin has never seen him [Christ]"). I would concede that the Presbyter sees Diotrephes' refusal of hospitality as an offense against the commandment to love one's brother, against which the secessionists also offend. But that is scarcely proof that Diotrephes shares the christological and ethical aberrations of the secessionists.

[23] For Käsemann's thesis to make sense Diotrephes has to be a non-Johannine outsider for whom all Johannine Christians would be progressives, even a moderate like the Presbyter. I have argued above that III John's polemic would likely have included the charge of alien thought or influence if Diotrephes were not a Johannine Christian.

that the Presbyter is informed of what is happening in other Johannine churches.) And so I judge 6 to be the most plausible among the last three suggestions.

In summary I propose that 3 combined with a form of 6 yields an intelligible reconstruction of the situation in III John. Diotrephes has been the host of a Johannine house-church for a while and hitherto has not been in conflict with the Presbyter, who lives in the city of the main Johannine Community and who is a member of the Johannine School of witnesses to the tradition. Thus the two men have different roles and one is not structurally inferior to the other. The host of a house-church in the Johannine tradition offers hospitality for meetings and for visitors but he is not an authoritative teacher,[24] as would be the presbyter-bishop in house-churches of the Pauline (Pastorals) tradition. Now the secession and secessionist missionaries have complicated the Johannine scene. The Presbyter thinks it can be shown who is on the right side by testing the Spirits (I John 4:1) and by asking for professions of christological faith (4:2; II John 7), but such appeals may not have been enough to halt the secessionist movement (I John 4:5). Indeed, in II John 10–11 the Presbyter becomes practical by telling those faithful to him to refuse hospitality to secessionist missionaries by not even talking to them. Diotrephes seems to have pursued that policy farther by refusing hospitality to *all* would-be missionaries, thus saving the church from possible contamination by having to listen to missionaries and discovering only too late their dangerous teaching. In doing this Diotrephes is (implicitly, at least) making himself the teacher of the church and moving away from the pure Johannine tradition of the sole Paraclete-teacher so dear to the Presbyter. It is not surprising then that the Presbyter criticizes him for liking "to be first among them"—Diotrephes is on his way to become a presbyter-bishop in the style of the Pastorals, or even the sole bishop in the style of Ignatius. In his brutal practicality Diotrephes may have been more effective than the Presbyter in preserving the Johannine tradition against secessionist contamination.[25] My INTRODUCTION V D2b has suggested that in ecclesiology Diotrephes would be closer than the Presbyter to the redactor of GJohn, a redactor who in 21:15–17 shows Jesus appointing Simon Peter as a human shepherd of Jesus' sheep. And in terms of ultimate union between part of the Johannine Community and the Great Church, the shep-

---

[24] I John 2:27: "You have no need for anyone to teach you." Notice that the Presbyter asks Gaius to supply hospitality but he does not ask him to teach.

[25] In my view three groups of Johannine Christians emerge from the situations described in the Epistles: the secessionists; the Presbyter and his anti-secessionist followers; Diotrephes and his anti-secessionist, anti-Presbyter supporters. Later history knows of gnostic interpreters of GJohn (who may be related to the secessionist movement). It knows of orthodox bishops who used GJohn to refute the gnostics (an authoritative attitude not unlike that of Diotrephes). One is left with the suspicion that the anti-secessionists who followed the ecclesiology of the Presbyter left no discernible traces in the second century, perhaps because they did not survive.

herd bishops of the latter would understand the authoritative attitude of Diotrephes[26] more easily than the Presbyter's rejection of any need for human teachers.

Having theorized about the general situation that provoked III John, I now turn to the individual sections of the letter. I remind the reader that Appendix V on Epistolary Format covers III John as well as II John, and I shall not repeat what is said there.

B. *Opening Formula* (vv. 1–2)

Both Bultmann and Schnackenburg confine the Opening (*Praescriptio*) to v. 1. Yet, as I point out in Appendix V A, a health wish is part of the Opening Formula of many Greco-Roman letters; and so I include v. 2 as well. In interpreting the information provided by the Opening, we must remember the stylized language of letters. "Beloved" is a set Johannine and Christian designation. "In truth I love you" (1b), found also in II John 1b, is evidently a set expression that can be addressed even to a church. Since "truth" involves a correct christology and "love" is the Johannine commandment, all that we learn from v. 1 is that Gaius is a fellow Johannine Christian who lives up to the expectations of the Presbyter. We cannot assume from v. 1 that the Presbyter has ever met Gaius or has long-standing knowledge of him.

Because the hope or wish for good health in v. 2 is a standard epistolary feature, it constitutes no indication that Gaius has been sick (*pace* Camerlynck, Vrede), or that he has suffered from persecution by Diotrephes (*pace* Bresky). The affirmation that Gaius is well off spiritually is related to what follows in vv. 3–6 where we are told that the brothers have testified to Gaius' hospitable works. Far from illustrating intimate knowledge of Gaius, such information implies that the Presbyter has heard of him only recently and that, consequently, Gaius has not had a prominent ecclesiastical role up to now.

C. *Expression of Joy Transitional to the Body of the Letter* (vv. 3–4)

Once again (see Appendix V BC) it is not clear whether this expression of joy is equivalent to the Pauline Thanksgiving or is a feature of the

---

[26] Although Harnack ("Über" 24) may have exaggerated in making Diotrephes a monarchical bishop, he is right in connecting the two roles. The memory of bishops associated with John the Apostle (footnote 18 above) means that ultimately bishops were not seen as a contradiction of Johannine thought.

Body-Opening.[27] In II John the Presbyter's joy over the fact that children of the Elect Lady were walking in truth indicated that the christological error of the secessionists (attacked in II John 7–11) had not yet made serious inroads. Here the Presbyter's joy over Gaius' truth and walking in truth is associated entirely with the love he has manifested in showing hospitality to the brothers (III John 5–8). (Thus we are dealing with a stereotyped feature of "joy" that takes on its coloring from the contents of the letter.) While "love" is easier to associate with hospitality than is "truth" (3 times in vv. 3–4),[28] part of the truth for John is the Christian's status as child of God through belief in Jesus as God's Son. Hospitality to the "brothers" is a manifestation of that status and thus of truth. In I John 2:4 we read that a person who does not keep the commandments "is a liar, and there is no truth in such a person"; and 4:20–21 makes clear that the author is thinking of love of brother as the commandment par excellence. In I John 3:18–19 it is said that showing love in deeds is a sign of belonging to the truth.

Verse 4 is repetitious of v. 3—a stylistic repetition that indicates the depth of the joy felt by the Presbyter. The church that meets under Diotrephes' leadership (and probably in Diotrephes' house) has been closed to the Presbyter; and so Gaius has rendered him a signal service in showing hospitality (as the Presbyter will go on to explain in vv. 5–8). This service leads him to refer to Gaius as one of "my children," a designation that need not mean that Gaius had been converted by him (NOTE on v. 4). Like the "my Little Children" of I John, the address means only that Gaius is a Johannine Christian in *koinōnia* or communion with the Presbyter and the Johannine School of tradition-bearers.[29] In I John it is an address implicitly contrasting the hearers to the secessionists who "went out from our ranks." Here the designation of Gaius is by way of contrast to Diotrephes who is not willing to show hospitality to the brothers.

D. *Request for Hospitality and Support* (vv. 5–8)

All that we know of Epistolary Format would lead us to expect that now the writer would come to the main purpose for which he is writing the let-

---

[27] Funk, "Form" 429, lists III John 3–4 as a "thanksgiving."

[28] III John is not far in implication from the combination "truth and love" in II John 3. In John 5:33, however, the expression "testify to the truth" has christological import, for it is used of the Baptist's testimony to Jesus.

[29] When he is writing simply as a fellow Johannine Christian, others in the Community are the author's "Beloved" or "Brothers"; but when he is implicitly calling attention to his position in the School, the author tends toward paternal language. If Jesus addresses his disciples as "Little Children" (John 13:33), it is not surprising to find those disciples (e.g., the Beloved Disciple) and others intimately associated with them using that language for the next generation, i.e., for those who have become believers through the preaching of the first generation (17:20).

ter. We are not disappointed, for the petition in these verses involves the main concern of the Presbyter. The vocative address "Beloved" in v. 5 helps to mark off the shift to the request but also continues to stress Gaius' status as child of God bound to other Johannine Christians in love —the status that is the basis of the petition. The petition itself is clear: Gaius is being asked to extend hospitality and support to the Johannine brothers who will visit him. The difficulty is how to relate this request to the role Gaius has hitherto had and why the request is now so urgent. I have argued in the NOTES[30] that the petition is not for a totally new course of action but for a continuation under a new rubric of the work that Gaius has already been doing for the brothers. But why then is the Presbyter writing to Gaius to do what he is already doing? The answer involves an analysis of the situation that has precipitated the letter. The pres. ptcp. in v. 3 and the whole tone of vv. 5-6 ("all that you do"; "your love") imply that Gaius has had a reputation for hospitality to fellow Johannine Christians. It is that very reputation that has caused the brothers who were refused house-church hospitality by Diotrephes (v. 10) to turn to Gaius and to be received by him. Over a period of time Johannine brothers have been coming to the Presbyter's church and testifying to Gaius' generous behavior, but now the brothers include those rejected by Diotrephes; and that is the new situation which causes the Presbyter to write so urgently. Up to now the regular stopping place has been the house-church of Diotrephes. With that closed it is crucial that a new stopping place be found.[31] Instinctively Gaius has offered hospitality in the emergency, but the Presbyter must be certain that this will continue on *a regular basis,* especially when he knows that pressure may be put on Gaius to discontinue—pressure from Diotrephes, and the neighboring house-church. The Presbyter must assure Gaius that he is doing the right thing in extending hospitality, for wrong is exemplified by Diotrephes and not by those rejected by him. Indeed, the hospitality requested is so important that it constitutes a testimony of love and truth and thus a manifestation of Gaius' status as a true Christian. It is a question, then, of obligation on Gaius, although diplomatically the Presbyter generalizes the obligation, *"We* ought" (8a). The root of that obligation becomes clear when one studies this verb *opheilein* in the works of the Johannine tradition demanding brotherly love: "You too ought to wash one another's feet" (John 13:14); "For us Christ laid down his life; so ought we in turn to lay down our lives for the brothers" (I John 3:16); "If He so loved us, we in turn ought to love one another" (I John 4:11).

[30] For instance I have resisted the attempt of B. Weiss and others to translate the verbs in v. 5 as future tenses.

[31] I argued under A above that most sense can be made of the Gaius/Diotrephes relationship if we posit that Gaius is not a member of the church of Diotrephes but owns a large house not too distant from Diotrephes' house-church.

The urgency of the demand is unintelligible if the "brothers" are no more than general Johannine Christians or even simply those on the Presbyter's side in the dispute over the secession. The "such men" (8) who "set out for the sake of 'the Name'" (7) are missionaries proclaiming the Christian message.[32] More specifically they are proclaiming "the gospel" (*angelia:* I John 1:5; 3:11) as the Presbyter understands it, in terms of Jesus Christ come in the flesh[33] and of keeping the commandments. Thus they are the Presbyter's indispensable weapons against the spread of the secession. No wonder he is concerned that they be supported so that they can continue their travels! If we may judge from the Pauline churches, Christians quickly developed a custom of receiving missionaries and of helping them on with money and supplies to their next destination (I Cor 16:6,11; Rom 15:24). While the commonsense attitude would have been to start out with enough money for the whole journey, apparently Christian missionaries were guided by Jesus' own style: "Jesus ordered them to take nothing for the journey except a staff: no bread, no wallet, no money in their belts" (Mark 6:8). The willingness of those along the way to help them was looked on as openness to Christ: "The one who receives you receives me" (Matt 10:40); "Whoever welcomes anyone I shall send welcomes me" (John 13:20). Obviously at first the welcome had to be extended by nonbelievers; but when convert groups came into existence, such generosity was looked on as their part in evangelization: "You received freely, give freely" (Matt 10:8). By the end of the first century, then, it was probably an increasingly fixed principle not to take money from pagans.[34] I John 3:17 suggests that the secessionists constitute the wealthier segment of the divided Johannine Community, and they may well have had the means to equip their missionaries so that they did not have to beg. The Presbyter cannot do this; and without the hospitality of the churches to be visited, his proclamation of the truth to outlying areas

[32] In *Community* 55–58 I suggest that after the Johannine Community was expelled from the synagogue, it turned to the Gentile mission in a serious way, as the Greco-Roman names of the Johannine Christians mentioned in III John suggest. But we do not know if Harnack was right in comparing the Johannine situation to Paul's very structured missionary network where he sent Timothy, Titus, and others to convey his advice and demands to the churches converted in the Pauline travels.

[33] In the NOTE I have argued that "the Name" for which the missionaries set out is a reference to the divine name borne by Jesus who is one with the Father (John 17:12) and thus reflects traditional Johannine theology. Of course, the Presbyter may now have given to this traditional terminology his own anti-secessionist thrust: the Name borne by Jesus Christ come in the flesh.

[34] Certainly a factor was the desire to avoid the scandal of making money from the new religion. Ignatius, *Trall.* 8:2, warns, "Give the Gentiles no occasion because of a few fools to blaspheme the multitude gathered in God." LFAE 108ff. calls attention to the profitable career of the begging adherents of the goddess Syria, and *Didache* cautions against Christian prophets who ask for money (11:4–6) and the one who "comes in the Name of the Lord" but is really making a business of Christ (12:2–5).

will be silenced. It is not oratory, then, when the Presbyter writes that receiving the missionary brothers and giving them the means to pursue their journey makes Gaius a "coworker with the truth" (8b). The truth that is Christ (John 14:6) is appropriated internally by the Christian (I John 1:8c; 2:4d; etc.) so that the Spirit of Truth abides in the anointed believer (John 14:17; I John 2:27). That truth and that Spirit must be given voice by bearing witness (John 15:26–27; I John 5:6de), and Gaius' support of the anti-secessionist missionaries constitutes his witness. It is his way of confessing Jesus Christ come in the flesh and thus reflecting the Spirit, which belongs to God (I John 4:2). In a personal way the Presbyter is presenting to Gaius the challenge of I John 4:6: "We belong to God and anyone who has knowledge of God listens to us, while anyone who does not belong to God refuses to listen to us. That is how we can know the Spirit of Truth from the Spirit of Deceit."

E. *The Hostility of Diotrephes* (vv. 9–10)

In vv. 11–12 the Presbyter will resume urging upon Gaius the need for good work by way of hospitality toward a "brother" of special importance (Demetrius). But now he interrupts his petition in order to comment on the hostile actions of Diotrephes toward himself and the brothers. A logical conclusion is that the hospitality requested of Gaius is meant to replace that being denied by the church of Diotrephes. I devoted the first section of this COMMENT on III John (A2) to discussing the many suggestions of scholars about the position of Diotrephes and the reasons for his hostility toward the Presbyter. Let me turn here to what the text tells us about Diotrephes and the five actions that he has taken.

THE DESCRIPTION OF DIOTREPHES (v. 9b). He is a figure who likes to be first among those who constitute a particular church. I argued in the NOTE that this does not mean simply that he wishes to be first; rather he has achieved that position and the Presbyter does not like it. The contempt suggests that this is a recent occurrence which is still debatable and that he does not hold an office which of itself carries primacy, e.g., that of the monarchical bishop described by Ignatius.[35] Thus, one gets the impression that Diotrephes has emerged as leader through his own enterprise. In analyzing the Presbyter's dislike, commentators often cite passages that warn Christians in general or presbyter-bishops in particular not to lord it over others (Matt 20:25–27; II Cor 1:24; I Pet 5:3). However, the issue here seems to be more radical: not the criticism of the

---

[35] It makes less sense if the Presbyter is criticizing Diotrephes for doing what his office demanded and what he was appointed to do.

abuse of a necessary position of primacy, but the challenge to any human primacy.[36] Such resistance to authoritative church positions would be unusual at the end of the first century; for the evidence of Acts, the Pastorals, Matthew, I Peter, *I Clement,* and Ignatius shows that various types of structured authority, particularly for teaching and community supervision, had been developed. Yet GJohn's insistence on the Paraclete as the teacher and on Jesus as the Good Shepherd, and I John's rejection of the need of any human teachers must be coupled with the complete silence in GJohn and the Epistles about apostles. If it is argued that John 21:15–17 shows Peter being appointed as a shepherd, I would respond that ch. 21, written by the redactor, represents the ultimate Johannine concession to the ecclesiology of the Great Church and its structure, a concession conceivably made after the Epistles were written. Nevertheless, if it is primacy and not simply the style of primacy that the Presbyter is attacking, clearly the use of that primacy against the Presbyter's interests is what has provoked this letter to Gaius. Five actions of Diotrephes are described, two of which affect the Presbyter directly, while three affect Johannine Christians directly (and the Presbyter indirectly).

DIOTREPHES' TWO ACTIONS AFFECTING THE PRESBYTER DIRECTLY. The Presbyter had written "something" previously to the church of Diotrephes (v. 9a). This vague description suggests that the fact of the writing (and its nonreception), rather than the contents, has become the issue; and it does nothing to encourage the theories that the previous writing was I John, II John, or a major statement of christology. If one must guess about the contents, the context of III John would favor the thesis that the previous writing concerned the reception of missionaries in general or of Demetrius in particular. Evidently Diotrephes regarded the previous writing or letter as objectionable and perhaps even as a threat to his own position. That may have been because of what it said or even because the Presbyter felt free to write *to the church* and thus to interfere in Diotrephes' area. Diotrephes' position enabled him to ignore or reject that writing, even though it was directed to the church—proof that he had real authority. His destruction of it would be the easiest explanation of why it has been lost to us. In any case the Presbyter regards Diotrephes' treatment of his letter as part of a larger practice of "not paying attention to us" (v. 9b). In the NOTE I have argued that the first person pl. resembles the usage of I John 1:1–5 where the author writes as a representative of the Johannine School of tradition-bearers, so that rejection of the writing

---

[36] This challenge may be part of the dualistic mentality of the Johannine writers if they regard human primacy as a contamination by the Prince of this world. One of the marks of the anti-God figure in II Thess 2:4 is that he exalts himself, while *Hermas, Man.* 11:12, criticizes as marked by the false spirit the person who "exalts himself and wishes to have the first seat." See above, pp. 334–35.

is more than a personal affront. It threatens the *koinōnia* "with us" demanded in I John 1:3 as essential to *koinōnia* with the Father and the Son. The Presbyter's sensitivity about his rejected letter will not seem exaggerated if one understands early Christian procedures. In Appendix V C there is a reference to the thesis of Funk that finds an "apostolic parousia" in the Pauline letter in general and especially in the promise of a visit by Paul which is part of the Body-Closing of his letter. A letter from Paul was an extension of apostolic care for a church and a surrogate for the apostle's presence; the promise of a visit to encourage or chastise was a further indication of this concern. Even granted the differences between Pauline and Johannine attitudes, the Presbyter clearly regards the rejection of his previous writing as a rejection of his influence[37] in the area where Diotrephes has assumed primacy. And on the other side, Diotrephes' rejection of the Presbyter's previous writing or letter was an aspect of his own care for the church. He is the teacher of the church, and he does not need interference from the Presbyter. If the secessionists have developed a system of human teachers and prophets (as implied by the criticism in I John 2:27; 4:1), and if the (seemingly ineffective) answer of the Presbyter is to reject the need for any human teachers and prophets (an answer that gives preeminence to his role as a Spirit-guided witness to the tradition), Diotrephes seems to have chosen a third position, namely, that of the non-secessionist teacher. The Presbyter claims attention as a disciple of the Beloved Disciple in a chain of witnesses; Diotrephes claims pastoral authority as a local church leader.

The Presbyter complains in v. 10b about a second procedure of Diotrephes against him: "He is spreading evil nonsense against us." Again the first person pl. of the Johannine School indicates that more than personal criticism or calumny is involved. Diotrephes is challenging the right of the Johannine tradition-bearers to supervise gospel-proclamation in churches in which they do not live. He may be propagandizing against the Presbyter's letter(s) and missionaries by attributing such efforts to arrogance and presumption (*"evil* nonsense"), just as the Presbyter attributes arrogance to Diotrephes. The resolution of the impasse is foreseen by the Presbyter in terms of a possible visit (10ab: "If I come, I shall bring up what he is doing"). In II Cor 13:2 Paul threatens a hostile visit to a church: "If I come again, I shall not spare you." But that very statement illustrates the difference between an apostle and the Presbyter, and between the Pauline and Johannine outlook. The "if" used by both the Presbyter and Paul reflects the sensitive desire to avoid a hostile confrontation. But if Paul comes, he has the authority to do something by his own

---

[37] That the Presbyter regards his writing as an extension of his person is seen in his statement about Diotrephes at the end of v. 9; literally, "He does not receive us."

power. The most the Presbyter can do is convince the church to take
some action against Diotrephes.[38] (I have argued against the contention
that the Presbyter has the power to remove Diotrephes but charitably refuses to use it; the other letters show a man who uses all the power he has
for the sake of the gospel.) The fact that Diotrephes is effective in all the
steps described in vv. 9–10 indicates that he has already persuaded the
majority in the church to his course of action, and the Presbyter only
hopes to persuade the church in the opposite direction. Administratively
Diotrephes has more ecclesiastical power than the Presbyter. Thus the
Presbyter's "if," making the visit only possible, may reflect more than sensitivity. It may reflect a fear of failure.[39]

DIOTREPHES' THREE ACTIONS AFFECTING THE JOHANNINE CHRISTIANS
DIRECTLY. Diotrephes is not content with action directly against the Presbyter (v. 10c); in addition he takes three steps: He refuses to welcome
the missionary brothers (10d); he hinders those who wish to do so (10f);
and he expels them from the church (10f). The first of these steps is the
logical continuation of the refusal to receive the Presbyter's letter, provided we understand that the missionaries came from the Presbyter and
were sent to accomplish his purpose.[40] Once again Funk's theory of the
"apostolic parousia" casts light on the Presbyter's attitude. In the Pauline
situation emissaries whom he mentions in his letters carried both the word
and the delegated authority of the apostle. The refusal to treat them well
was an affront to Paul and hindered his relationship to a church. So also
here, "the brothers," like the letter the Presbyter wrote, are the extension
of his presence and the instruments of his influence. We may assume that
they serve in the Presbyter's anti-secessionist campaign. That is why in
v. 11 he is so severe in characterizing Diotrephes' refusal of them: "Whoever does what is bad has never seen God." He never indicates that Diotrephes is guilty personally of a secessionist distortion of the gospel, but
de facto Diotrephes' obstructionism is helping the secessionist movement.

The fourth and fifth steps taken by Diotrephes illustrate the
thoroughness of his rejection of the Presbyter's influence. He hinders any

---

[38] The Presbyter does not specify the audience before whom he will bring up Diotrephes' behavior, but surely it is the "them" constituting the church of the preceding
verse. This means that, even though Diotrephes can keep out missionaries, the Presbyter expects to gain admittance to the house-church and the privilege of speaking.
Seemingly even Diotrephes cannot keep out a distinguished member of the Johannine School when he comes in person.

[39] Paul may not have been certain of success either, but one suspects that his
apostolic role would not have allowed him to omit the visit if his letter was unsuccessful. The Presbyter does not seem to have such apostolic responsibility.

[40] Probably the rejected letter concerned missionary enterprise, but we need not
posit that in order to assume a connection between the Presbyter and the "brothers"
rejected by Diotrephes—v. 10c makes that connection. That the brothers are missionaries is shown by vv. 5–7, and that the Presbyter is involved in a missionary enterprise is seen in his testimonial to Demetrius who presumably is coming to Gaius.

who wish to welcome the brothers and expels from the church those who
do so. To love one another or one's brother (cf. I John 3:10c and 11c) is
the Johannine commandment par excellence. The fact that the members
of this Johannine church can be forced to reverse their custom of hospitality to visiting brothers and thus move against the impetus of the commandment shows Diotrephes' power. That is further illustrated by Diotrephes' ability to expel from the church those who do not observe his
antihospitality policy; for, by comparison, the Presbyter does not seem
able to expel Diotrephes from the church.[41] Clearly the issue between
Diotrephes and the Presbyter is more than personal if Diotrephes is
willing to have people separated from koinōnia over it. It must have concerned the very survival of the church. Because of the Presbyter's anger,
most commentators assume that Diotrephes had bad or misguided mo-
tives; and so Windisch, Briefe 142, is refreshing in suggesting that Diotrephes may have been a sincere pastor of the church trying to protect his
community against false teachers such as the secessionists. As seen under
A above, I have opted for this as the most plausible solution. His action
against the brothers is no more brutal than the action the Presbyter en-
courages against secessionist missionaries in II John 10–11. (That the
Presbyter cannot see this paradox is not surprising, for neither can he see
that his attitude toward the secessionists exemplifies that lack of love for
which he condemns them—in a dualistic mentality all actions of opponents are wrong in themselves and cannot be compared to similar actions
on the good side.)

A more subtle way of dealing with visiting teachers is found in Didache
11:1–5:[42]

> Whenever someone comes and teaches you all these things we have
> talked about, receive him. But if the teacher himself has deviated by
> teaching another doctrine that contradicts these things, do not listen
> to him. . . . Let every emissary [apostle] who comes to you be re-
> ceived as the Lord; but let him not stay more than one day (or two if
> absolutely necessary). If he stays three days, he is a false prophet.

Diotrephes seems to have agreed with those Christians who thought that
two and a half days of troublemaking were too much. Paul in Acts 20:29
warns the authorities of Ephesus that "savage wolves will come in among

[41] As explained in the NOTE on 10f, Diotrephes is not necessarily able to expel
people by fiat; he may have had to convince the church to take this action. Nevertheless, he has succeeded in doing that, whereas the Presbyter is not certain he can
persuade the church to take action against Diotrephes.

[42] The following passage in Didache (11:7) speaks of testing the prophet speaking
in a spirit; compare I John 4:1 on putting the Spirits to a test (above, p. 506).
Clearly Didache 11 has parallels to the ambience or mentality of the Johannine
Epistles.

you and not spare the flock." Titus 1:10–11 seems suspicious of all teachers not authorized by the presbyters: "It is necessary to stop their mouth." By not allowing outside missionaries even to enter the house-church Diotrephes was stopping their mouths in a most effective way.

F. An Appeal to Do Good and a Testimonial for Demetrius (vv. 11–12)

To some extent the information about Diotrephes in vv. 9–10 is parenthetical to the Presbyter's main stream of thought, namely, the petition (made in vv. 5–8 and continued in 11) for Gaius to offer regular hospitality to the missionaries, now that Diotrephes has closed their previous stopping place. Even though Gaius has already been offering hospitality in the emergency, some hesitation on his part seems to be anticipated; and that is more understandable if Diotrephes was not only the leader of a neighboring house-church but acting in the name of orthodoxy. The Presbyter, however, is also acting in the name of orthodoxy; and by his threat to challenge Diotrephes by a visit, he is indicating how serious is the need for finding means to keep the missionary enterprise going. He is not allowing Gaius the opportunity to remain neutral, for in v. 11 he presents a choice between good and bad. If Gaius does not continue the hospitality, he is imitating Diotrephes whose bad action is tantamount to a denial of the truth and alienation from God. The mindset is again that of I John 1:3: *koinōnia* with "us" is necessary for *koinōnia* with God, and this *koinōnia* or communion is expressed by love manifested toward the brothers: "The person who has no love for the brother whom he has seen cannot love the God he has never seen" (4:20). The implication in such reasoning is that Gaius must decide that the Presbyter and his adherents are "brothers," while Diotrephes and his are not.

The appeal finishes with a testimonial to Demetrius, an enigmatic figure (see the long NOTE on v. 12) who is plausibly a prominent missionary coming to Gaius with or shortly after this letter. If he is one of those previously rejected by Diotrephes, the need for a testimonial to reassure Gaius becomes apparent. Indeed, I have suggested that we may have here the *beginning* of a practice of testimonial letters for Johannine missionaries, so that (in very different ways) both the Presbyter and Diotrephes would be reacting to the need for greater clarity about missionaries, now that secessionist missionaries are also circulating. The strength of the testimonial is based on three witnesses: (12a) the witness of all the Johannine Christians (of the Presbyter's persuasion) who know him; (12b) the witness of his own way of life, which flows from the truth in which he abides;[43] (12c) and the witness of the Presbyter speaking on behalf of the "we" of the Johannine School. In the last instance Gaius is being asked to "pay attention to us," the very thing Diotrephes refuses to do (v. 9). The seriousness of this testimonial shows once more that the issue of hospitality must be related in the Presbyter's mind to the proclamation of his form of the gospel. Many scholars take this seriousness as an indication that Diotrephes is a secessionist; but it is just as intelligible if Diotrephes, although not a secessionist, is endangering the missionary battle against the spread of the secession. And the latter thesis makes better sense of the fact that the Presbyter does not seem concerned about the doctrine of Diotrephes' church, but only about finding a substitute for the hospitality and missionary help it formerly provided. That Gaius acceded to the Presbyter's request is suggested by the survival of III John,[44] a fate unlike that of the previous letter sent to the church of Diotrephes.

G. *Promise of a Visit, Closing the Body of the Letter* (vv. 13–14)

The Body-Closing of III John is almost identical with the Body-Closing of II John (12); and the cautions given in the COMMENT there should be remembered lest we seek precise information from stereotyped formulas. The statement that the Presbyter has much more to write (v. 13) is simply a ploy to finish the letter and cannot be pressed for details about the friendship or history of the persons involved. Nor from the hope to visit soon (v. 14) can much be determined about the definiteness of the Presbyter's plans. It is tempting to argue that the hope to visit Gaius is more definite than the "if I come" (v. 10) of the visit to Diotrephes' church, and that therefore the two men are not in the same house-church. But from the two references one can say with certainty that the Presbyter has a stature that makes it appropriate for him to visit churches in difficulty, both to encourage and to challenge. (Even then we have no proof that visits have been a long-standing practice.) II John 12e contains the clause "so that our joy may be fulfilled"; and the absence of a parallel in III John has been thought to indicate that the Presbyter is more deeply disturbed about the situation described in III John than he was about the

---

[43] The testimony "from the truth itself" is not clearly defined, but of the views discussed in the NOTE on v. 12b this is the most likely.

[44] Implicitly, then, he would have become the host of a house-church—a destiny that could be confirmed by the later tradition that he served as bishop (NOTE on 1a), were that reliable.

"Elect Lady" and her children. But the argument from silence based on such a minor clause is risky.

H. *Concluding Formula* (v. 15)

The presence in III John of the phrase "Peace to you" (lacking in II John) has been thought to confirm the suspicion mentioned immediately above. Yet the presence of "Peace" in other NT epistolary Concluding Formulas (NOTE on 15a; also Appendix V D) cautions us against giving to it much specific content. One can say that the Presbyter stands in a tradition where peace is an eschatological gift realized in the present, according to Jesus' promise, "My peace is my gift to you" (John 14:27). If Gaius is troubled by the decision being forced on him because of the action of Diotrephes, he may be reminded by the Presbyter's wish of peace that the Johannine Jesus in the Last Discourse associated that peace with the commandment to love one another (13:34–35; 15:12,17)—the very commandment that is the basis for the Presbyter's appeal for hospitality toward the "brothers."

In commenting upon the Concluding Formula of II John, I stressed that the Presbyter's sending greetings from other Johannine Christians (in II John "the children of your Elect Sister"; in III John "the beloved here"[45]) constitutes his reminder that *koinōnia* is an essential part of Johannine life (I John 1:3). Diotrephes has done more than cut himself off from the Presbyter; he has endangered the relationship of one Johannine church to another. Gaius' good works for the brothers, on the other hand, "testified to before the church" (6a), build up the *koinōnia* between branches of the Johannine Community. The members of that Community are a group of "beloved," loved by God and one another; and only those who show that love (in this case, by hospitality) belong to the confraternity. The extension of greetings to "each by name" (see NOTE on 15c) makes possible the refusal of greetings in Gaius' area to any adherents of Diotrephes' position (whom Gaius would be expected to know). The Presbyter remains consistent in considering as "brothers" and "beloved" only those who "listen to us" (I John 4:6).

*   *   *

The interpretation of III John presented here relates its main concern, the necessity of hospitality toward missionary brothers, to the Presbyter's campaign against the secessionists, the main theme of I and II John. I John has been interpreted as a loose commentary on the Johannine gos-

---

[45] For the translation of *philos* as "beloved" rather than "friend," see NOTE on 15bc.

pel, expounded for the main center of the Johannine Community where a secession has already taken place over a contrary interpretation of the gospel. Secessionist propaganda disturbs the remnant that has stayed loyal to the traditional interpretation of the gospel (*angelia*) advocated by the Presbyter and the Johannine School of tradition-bearers, whence the need for the reassuring counterpropaganda that constitutes I John. II and III John have been interpreted as part of the Presbyter's campaign for protecting outlying Johannine churches against being decimated by secessionist emissaries. II John warns a church against admitting them; III John attempts to get help for the Presbyter's countermissionaries who move about spreading the warning. There is no necessity then to posit a considerable time interval separating the three works. All seem to stem from the same crucial moment in the history of the Johannine Community.

BIBLIOGRAPHY PERTINENT TO III JOHN

(See the *Bibliography* pertinent to II John, for many entries there deal with both Epistles; also the *Bibliography* for Appendix V on Epistolary Format; and the *Bibliography* on House-Churches in the INTRODUCTION VII F2.)

Bartina, S., "Un papiro copto de 3 Jn 1–2 (PPalau Rib. inv. 20)," *Studia Papyrologica* 6 (1967) 95–97.

Hall, D. R., "Fellow-Workers with the Gospel," ExpT 85 (1973–74) 119–20.

Harnack, A. von, "Über den dritten Johannesbrief," TU 15³ (1897) 3–27.

Hilgenfeld, A., review of the preceding entry, ZWT 41 (1898) 316–20.

Horvath, T., "3 Jn 11ᵇ: An Early Ecumenical Creed?" ExpT 85 (1973–74) 339–40.

Krüger, G., "Zu Harnack's Hypothese über den dritten Johannesbrief," ZWT 41 (1898) 307–11.

Malherbe, A. J., "The Inhospitality of Diotrephes," in *God's Christ and His People*, ed. J. Jervell and W. A. Meeks (N. A. Dahl Festschrift; Oslo: Universitet, 1977) 222–32.

Schnackenburg, R., "Der Streit zwischen dem Verfasser von 3Joh und Diotrephes und seine verfassungsgeschichtliche Bedeutung," MTZ 4 (1953) 18–26.

Appendixes

Appendix I: Charts

Chart One: Similarities between II-III John and the Other Johannine Writings*

III JOHN AND GJOHN/I JOHN

III John 3: walk in truth
I John 1:7: walk in the light
I John 3:18: (love) in deed and truth

III John 4: Nothing gives me greater joy than . . . .
John 15:13: No man has greater love than . . . .

III John 11: (people who) belong to God
I John 3:10; 4:6: (people who do not) belong to God

III John 11: Whoever does what is bad has never seen God
I John 3:6: Everyone who does commit sin has never seen him

III John 12: You know that our testimony is true
John 8:14: My testimony is true

III John 13: I had much more to write you
John 16:12: I have much more to tell you

II JOHN AND GJOHN/I JOHN

II John 1: know (*ginōskein*) the truth
John 8:32: know (*ginōskein*) the truth
I John 2:21: know (*eidenai* [*oida*]) the truth

II John 2: the truth that abides in us and will be with us forever
John 14:16–17: Another Paraclete to be with you forever; he is the Spirit of truth . . . he abides with you and is in you

II John 4: walk in truth (see III John 3)

II John 4: We received a commandment from the Father
John 10:18: I received this commandment from my Father

II John 5: It is not as if I were writing you some new commandment
I John 2:7: This is no new commandment that I write you

II John 5: A commandment . . . Let us love one another
John 15:12,17; 13:34: This I command you: Love one another
I John 3:23: This is God's commandment: . . . we are to love one another

II John 6: This is love: that we walk according to His commandments
I John 5:3: The love of God is this: that we keep His commandments

II John 6: The commandment, as you heard it from the beginning
I John 3:11: This is the gospel that you heard from the beginning

---

* The similarities presuppose the Greek text and are sometimes less apparent in English translation.

II John 7: Many deceivers have gone out into the world . . . . There is the Deceiver; there is the Antichrist

    I John 2:18,22: Many Antichrists have made their appearance . . . . Who, then, is the Liar? . . . . Such is the Antichrist

    I John 2:26: I have been writing this to you about those who deceive you (see also 3:7)

    I John 4:1,3,6: Many false prophets have gone out into the world . . . reflecting a Spirit of the Antichrist . . . . That is how we can know . . . the Spirit of Deceit

II John 7: confess Jesus Christ coming in the flesh

    I John 4:2: confess Jesus Christ come in the flesh

II John 8: You must receive your reward in full

    John 4:36: The reaper is receiving his reward

II John 9: remain in the teaching of Christ

    John 8:31: If you remain in my word

II John 9: Anyone who does not remain in the teaching of Christ does not possess God

    John 15:23: To hate me is to hate my Father

    I John 2:23: No person who denies the Son possesses the Father

II John 12: I have much more to write you (see III John 13 above)

II John 12: so that our joy may be fulfilled

    John 15:11: so that your joy may be fulfilled (also 16:24)

    John 17:13: so that they may have my joy fulfilled in themselves

Chart Two: Similarities between I John and GJohn

I John	GJohn	Similarity
1:1–3	1:1,2,4,14	was, beginning, word, life, revealed/made flesh, in the Father's (God's) presence
1:2	3:11	we have seen and testify
1:4	15:11; 16:24; 17:13	joy fulfilled
1:5	8:12; 9:5 (12:35)	God is light; I am the light
1:6	3:21	act in (do) truth
1:6–7; 2:10–11	8:12; 11:9–10; 12:35,40	walking (abiding) in darkness/light; not knowing where one is going
1:8	9:41	free from the guilt of sin
1:8; 2:4	8:44	truth being in a person
2:1,12,28; 3:7, 18; 4:4; 5:21	13:33	"Little Children" (pl. *teknion*) address
2:1	14:16	Jesus Christ a Paraclete
2:1 (see 1:1–3)		in the Father's presence
2:2	1:29 (11:51–52)	for our sins, also for the whole world
2:3,4; 3:22,24; 5:3	14:15,21; 15:10	keeping (God's, Jesus') commandments
2:4 (see 1:8)		truth in a person
2:5	8:51,52,55; 14:23–24; 15:20; 17:6	keeping (God's, Jesus') word(s)
2:6,27,28; 3:6	15:4,6,7	abide (remain: *menein*) in God/Christ
2:7–8	13:34	new commandment
2:8	1:5	darkness passing and light shining
2:10–11 (see 1:6–7)		walking (abiding) in darkness/light
2:12 (see 2:1)		"Little Children" (pl. *teknion*)
2:13,14	16:11	conquered Evil One (Prince of world)
2:14,18	21:5	"Children" (pl. *paidion*) address
2:14	5:38	word of God abiding in you
2:15	(15:18)	have no love for the world
2:15	5:42	no love of God (Father) in a person
2:16; 4:5	8:23; 15:19; 17:16	belong to (be of) the world
2:17	8:35; 12:34	a person remaining forever
2:18 (see 2:14)		"Children" (pl. *paidion*) address
2:21	8:32	know (*eidenai, ginōskein*) the truth
2:21; 3:19	18:37	belong to (be of) the truth
2:23	(15:23)	denying Son; not possessing Father
2:24	(15:7)	what you heard abiding in you
2:27	2:25; 16:30	no need for anyone to . . .
2:27	(14:26; 16:13)	anointing teaches you about all things
2:27,28 (see 2:6)		abide in Christ
2:28 (see 2:1)		"Little Children" (pl. *teknion*)
2:29; 3:9; 5:1,4,18	1:13	begotten by (from: *ek*) God
3:1,2,10	1:12; 11:52	children (pl. *teknon*) of God

1 John	GJohn	Similarity
3:1	17:25	world did not know (*ginōskein*) God
3:3	11:55	making oneself pure
3:4	8:34	everyone who acts sinfully (*poiein hamartian*)
3:5	(1:29,31)	Christ was revealed to take away sins
3:5	(8:46)	nothing sinful in Christ
3:6 (see 2:6)		abide in Christ
3:6	14:9	seeing (*horan*) Christ
3:7 (see 2:1)		"Little Children" (pl. *teknion*)
3:8 (3:12)	8:44	belonging to the devil, a sinner (murderer) from the beginning
3:9 (see 2:29)		begotten by God
3:10 (see 3:1)		children of God
3:10	(8:44)	children of the devil
3:10; 4:1,2,3,4, 6; 5:19	8:47	belong to (be from) God
3:11,23; 4:7,11	13:34; 15:12,17	we should love one another
3:12	6:58	not like Cain (ancestors)
3:12 (see 3:8)		belonged to the Evil One
3:12–13	(7:7)	evil deeds . . . hatred
3:13	3:7; 5:28	do not be surprised
3:13	7:7; 15:18	the world hates you
3:14	5:24	passed from death to life
3:16	10:11,15(17,18); 13:37	lay down one's life for others
3:16	13:14–15	so ought we in turn (imitating Christ)
3:18 (see 2:1)		"Little Children" (pl. *teknion*)
3:19 (see 2:21)		belong to the truth
3:20 (4:4)	10:29; 14:28	God/Father is greater
3:22; 5:14	14:13,14; 15:7; 16:23	receive (from God) whatever we ask
3:22 (see 2:3)		keeping God's commandments
3:22	8:29	doing what pleases God
3:23 (5:10)	3:18	believe (in) the name of God's Son
3:23 (see 3:11)		we should love one another
3:23	14:31 (12:49)	God gave a command to us/me
3:24 (see 2:3)		keeping God's commandments
3:24; 4:13,15,16	6:56; 15:5	mutual indwelling (abiding) between God/Christ and the Christian
3:24	14:17	divine indwelling (abiding) and Spirit
4:1 (see 3:10)		belong to God
4:2	9:22	confess Jesus Christ
4:2	1:14	come in the flesh; became flesh
4:2,3,4 (see 3:10)		belong to God
4:4 (see 2:1)		"Little Children" (pl. *teknion*)
4:4 (see 3:20)		he who is in you is greater
4:5 (see 2:16)		belong to the world
4:5	3:31	speaks from the world/earth
4:6	8:47	refuse to listen = not belong to God
4:6 (see 3:10)		belong to God

4:6	14:17; 15:26; 16:13	Spirit of Truth
4:7 (see 3:11)		let us love one another
4:7	(7:17)	love (doctrine) is from God
4:9,10	3:16–17	God's love in sending His only Son
4:11 (see 3:11)		we ought to love one another
4:12(20)	1:18 (5:37); 6:46	no one has ever seen God
4:12	6:56	God/Christ abiding in Christian
4:13 (see 3:24)		mutual indwelling
4:13	3:34	God has given us *of* the Spirit
4:14	3:17 (4:42)	Father sent Son as Savior of world
4:15,16 (see 3:24)		mutual indwelling
4:16	6:69	known (*ginōskein*) and believed
4:16	15:10	abide/remain (*menein*) in love
4:20 (see 4:12)		never seen God
5:1	20:31	believe Jesus is Messiah/Christ
5:1	1:12–13	believer begotten by God
5:3 (see 2:3)		keeping God's commandments
5:4 (see 2:27)		begotten by God
5:4–5 (cf. 2:13)	16:33	conquered the world
5:6	19:30,34 (7:38–39)	water, blood, Spirit
5:6–8	15:26	Spirit testifies (bears witness)
5:9–10	5:34,32,37; 8:18	human testimony and God's testimony on behalf of Christ
5:10 (see 3:23)		belief in God's Son
5:12–13	3:15,36; 20:31	possess (believe in) Son = possess life
5:13	20:31	purpose of writing
5:14,15 (see 3:22)		whenever we ask, He hears us
5:16	(17:9)	not praying for deadly sin (world)
5:18 (see 2:29)		begotten by God
5:18	(14:30)	Evil One cannot touch (Prince of this world has no hold)
5:19 (see 3:10)		belong to God
5:20	17:3	to know (*ginōskein*) the True One. Jesus Christ is true God and eternal life—eternal life is to know the one true God and Jesus Christ
5:21 (see 2:1)		"Little Children" (pl. *teknion*)

Chart Three: Bultmann's Reconstructed Source for I John*

A. 1:5?   God is light
            and in him is no darkness at all.
    1:6   If we say we have fellowship with him
            while we walk in darkness,
            we lie and do not live according to the truth.
    1:7   But if we walk in the light,
            as he is in the light,
            we have fellowship with him.

    1:8   If we say we have no sin,
            we deceive ourselves,
            and the truth is not in us.
    1:10   If we say we have not sinned,
            we make him a liar,
            and his word is not in us.

    2:4   He who says, "I know him,"
            but disobeys his commandments
            is a liar and the truth is not in him.
    2:5   But whoever keeps his word,
            in him truly love for God is perfected.

    2:9   He who says he is in the light
            and hates his brother
            is in the darkness [? still].
    2:10   He who loves his brother
            abides in the light,
            and in him there is no cause for stumbling.
    2:11   But he who hates his brother
            is in the darkness
            and walks in the darkness.

B. 2:29b Every one who does right is born of him,
    3:4   Every one who commits sin is guilty of lawlessness.
    3:6   No one who abides in him sins.
            No one who sins has either seen him or known him.
    3:7   He does right [? is born of God].
    3:8   He who commits sin is of the devil.
    3:9   No one born of God commits sin,
            for his seed abides in him.
            And he cannot sin
            because he is born of God.

* Cf. Bultmann, *Epistles* 16, 18, 45, 39, 54[45], 57[04], 65, 68[10], 76, 83; also see footnote 89
in my INTRODUCTION III A2 above. The English (with slight punctuation modifications) is
that of Bultmann's *Epistles;* a question mark indicates an expression of uncertainty by Bultmann.

C. 2:23   No one denying the Son has the Father.
           He who confesses the Son has the Father also.

   3:15   Everyone who hates is a murderer
           and does not have eternal life.

   3:19?   Before him we shall reassure our hearts,
           if our hearts condemn us.

   4:7b   He who loves is born of God.
   4:8a   He who does not love does not know God.

   4:12?   If we love one another, God abides in us
           and his love is perfected in us.

   5:1   Everyone who loves his brother is born of God,
   5:4a   and whatever is born of God overcomes the world.

   5:12   He who has the Son has life.
           He who has not the Son of God has not life.

Chart Four: Epistolary Statements Pertinent
to the Adversaries' Views*

A. *General description; attitude toward Jesus:*

1 II John 9:   Anyone who is so "progressive" that he does not remain
                 rooted in the teaching of Christ does not possess God, while
                 anyone who remains rooted in the teaching possesses both the
                 Father and the Son.

2 4:6:   We belong to God and anyone who has knowledge of God
                 listens to us, while anyone who does not belong to God refuses
                 to listen to us. That is how we can know the Spirit of Truth
                 from the Spirit of Deceit.

3 2:18–19:   Now many Antichrists have made their appearance. . . . It
                 was from our ranks that they went out—not that they really
                 belonged to us; for if they had belonged to us, they would have
                 remained with us.

4 5:5–6:   Who then is the one who conquers the world? None other than
                 the person who believes that *Jesus* is the Son of God: Jesus
                 Christ—this is the one who came by water and blood, not in
                 water only, but in water and in blood. And the Spirit is the one
                 who testifies, for the Spirit is the truth.

5 2:22–23:   Who, then, is the Liar? None other than the person who
                 denies that *Jesus* is the Christ. Such is the Antichrist: the
                 person who denies the Father and the Son. No person who
                 denies the Son possesses the Father either.

6 II John 7:   Many deceivers have gone out into the world, men who do not
                 confess Jesus Christ coming in the flesh. There is the Deceiver!
                 There is the Antichrist!

7 4:1–3:   Do not believe every Spirit; rather, put these Spirits to a test
                 to see which belongs to God, because many false prophets
                 have gone out into the world. . . . Everyone who confesses
                 Jesus Christ come in the flesh reflects the Spirit which belongs
                 to God, while everyone who negates the importance of Jesus
                 reflects a Spirit which does not belong to God. It is rather of
                 the Antichrist . . . here it is in the world already.

8 4:5:   Those people belong to the world; that is why they speak the
                 language of the world and why the world listens to them.

9 2:15–16:   If anyone loves the world, there is in him no love of the
                 Father. For all that is in the world . . . does not belong to
                 the Father.

B. *Moral behavior; attitude toward sin; failure to love the brothers:*

1 1:8:   If we boast, "We are free from the guilt of sin," we deceive
                 ourselves.

2 1:10:   If we boast, "We have not sinned," we make God a liar.

3 1:6:   If we boast, "We are in communion with God," while
                 continuing to walk in darkness, we are liars.

4 2:4:   The person who claims, "I know God," without keeping His
                 commandments, is a liar.

* Citations are from I John unless otherwise indicated.

5 2:6:   The person who claims to abide in God ought himself to walk just as Christ walked.

6 3:3–6:   Everyone who has this hope based on God makes himself pure even as Christ is pure. Everyone who acts sinfully is really doing iniquity, for sin is the Iniquity. . . . Everyone who abides in Christ does not commit sin. Everyone who does commit sin has never seen him nor come to know him.

7 3:7–8:   The person who acts justly is truly just even as Christ is just. The person who acts sinfully belongs to the devil.

8 5:18:   We know that no one who has been begotten by God commits sin.

9 3:9–10:   Everyone who has been begotten by God does not act sinfully. . . . That is how God's children and the devil's children are revealed. Everyone who does not act justly does not belong to God, nor does anyone who does not love his brother.

10 3:11–12:   We should love one another—not like Cain who belonged to the Evil One and killed his brother.

11 3:14–15:   The person who does not love remains in the abode of death. Everyone who hates his brother is a murderer; and, as you know, no murderer has eternal life abiding in him.

12 3:17–18:   When someone has enough of this world's livelihood and perceives his brother to have need, yet shuts out any compassion toward him—how can the love of God abide in such a person? Let us not give lip service to our love with words but show its truth in deeds.

13 4:8–10:   One who does not love has known nothing of God, for God is love. . . . In this, then, does love consist: not that we have loved God but that He loved us and sent His Son as an atonement for our sins.

14 4:20:   If anyone boasts, "I love God," while continuing to hate his brother, he is a liar.

15 2:9:   The person who claims to be in the light, all the while hating his brother, is still in the darkness even now.

C. *How the readers should react toward the adversaries:*

1 2:27:   As for you, the anointing that you received from him abides in you; and so you have no need for anyone to teach you.

2 II John 10–11: If anyone comes to you who does not bring this teaching, do not receive him into the house and greet him; for whoever greets him shares in his evil deeds.

3 5:16:   If anyone sees his brother sinning (so long as the sin is not deadly), he should ask; and thus life will be given to the sinner. This is only for those whose sin is not deadly. After all, there is such a thing as deadly sin, and I do not say that one should pray about that.

Chart Five: Sample Proposed Divisions of I John[1]

Division into Two Parts:[2]
1:5–2:28	2:29–5:13	Chaine, Vrede, Tomoi
1:5–2:29	3:1–5:12	Feuillet, Francis

Division into Three Parts:[3]
1:1–2:17	2:18–3:24	4:1–5:21	Thüsing (*npe*)
1:1–2:17	2:18–4:6	4:7–5:21	Ewald (*npe*)
1:1–2:26	2:27–4:6	4:7–5:21	Smit Sibinga (*npe*)
1:5–2:14	2:15–3:18	3:19–5:12	Erdmann
1:5–2:17	2:18–3:24	4:1–5:12	Hort, Hauck, Nestle, Prat, Schnackenburg, Schneider, THLJ, Vogel, NEB
1:5–2:17	2:18–3:24	4:1–5:21	Gaugler (*ne*)
1:5–2:17	2:18–4:6	4:7–5:21	Westcott (*ne*)
1:5–2:27	2:28–3:24b	3:24c–5:21	Luthardt (*ne*)
1:5–2:27	2:28–3:24	4:1–5:12	Balz
1:5–2:27	2:28–4:6	4:7–5:12	Häring, Brooke, Jones
1:5–2:27	2:28–4:6	4:7–5:17	Schwertschlager (½ *ne*)
1:5–2:27 (28–29)	3:1–24	4:1–5:20 (5:21)	de Ambroggi (½ *ne*)
1:5–2:28	2:29–3:22	3:23–5:17	Huther (½ *ne*)
1:5–2:28	2:29–4:6	4:7–5:12	F.-M. Braun, de la Potterie, Škrinjar, SBJ
1:5–2:28	2:29–4:6	4:7–5:13	Malatesta
1:5–2:28	2:29–4:6	4:7–5:19	Nagl (½ *ne*)
1:5–2:28	2:29–4:6	4:7–5:21	Law (*ne*)
1:5–2:28	2:29–4:12	4:13–5:13	Dodd
1:5–2:29	3:1–4:6	4:7–5:13	JB
1:5–2:29	3:1–5:4a	5:4b–21	Bonsirven (*ne*)
2:3–28	2:29–4:6	4:7–5:21	Oke (*ne*)

Division into Seven Parts:[4]
1:1–4	1:5–2:6	2:7–17	2:18–3:24	4:1–21	5:1–12	5:13–21	Lohmeyer (*npe*)
1:1–4	1:5–2:17	2:18–27	2:28–3:24	4:1–6	4:7–5:12	5:13–21	Wilder (*npe*)
1:5–2:6	2:7–17	2:18–28	2:29–3:10	3:11–22	3:23–5:4	5:5–17	Giurisato (½*ne*)
1:5–2:11	2:12–17	2:18–27	2:28–3:24	4:1–6	4:7–21	5:1–12	Houlden

[1] See footnote 269 in the INTRODUCTION (VI A) for other divisions. At times, as indicated by parentheses, scholars do not make a precise decision. In speaking of "Parts" I am not counting the Prologue (1:1–4) and the Epilogue (5:[12]13–21) in the instance of those scholars who acknowledge such features as separate. Thus, for instance, Balz holds for three "Parts" plus a Prologue and an Epilogue. For those scholars who do not acknowledge either or both features as separate, the respective verses are counted as belonging to one of the "Parts." In such instances, *np* = no Prologue; *npe* = neither Prologue nor Epilogue; *ne* = no Epilogue; ½ *ne* = partial Epilogue.

[2] Alford, Braune, Camerlynck, Fillion, Hilgenfeld, Knopf, Lusseau, and Roesch are among others listed as opting for two Parts.

[3] Bengel, Bisping, Brückner, Cornely, de Wette, and Sand are among others listed as opting for three Parts.

[4] Estius and Oecumenius are among others listed as opting for seven Parts.

Chart Six: Outline of I John

Appendix II: Cerinthus

In the INTRODUCTION (IV B3d) I discussed briefly the possibility that the christological views opposed by I and II John were those of Cerinthus, supposedly an adversary of John (the son of Zebedee) at Ephesus in the Apostle's old age. What do we really know of the views held by Cerinthus? Our knowledge of him, as of most early heretics, comes not from his own writings but from descriptions by his adversaries among the church writers, in particular, from the compilations of heretical positions by the heresiologists who wrote many years later. Their works betray an ever more damning accumulation of accusations. Let me first survey[1] these ancient accusations against Cerinthus and then seek to analyze briefly the main thrust of his position.

1. Ancient Information about Cerinthus

The first known reference[2] to Cerinthus is in the *Epistula Apostolorum* or *Dialogues of Jesus with His Disciples after the Resurrection*, a work composed in Greek in mid-second century, but now extant only in Ethiopic and (partially) in Coptic and Latin. It refers to Simon Magus and Cerinthus as "the false apostles concerning whom it is written that no man shall cleave unto them, for there is in them deceit whereby they bring men to destruction."[3] This reference is important, for one later strain of opinion about Cerinthus makes him a gnostic; and for the church fathers Simon Magus was the father of gnosticism.

The most important information about Cerinthus is gleaned from the great anti-gnostic treatise of Irenaeus, *Adversus haereses* (*ca.* A.D. 180). In 1.23–28 he lists the gnostic schools in this order: Simon Magus, Menander, Saturninus (Satornil), Basilides, Carpocrates, Cerinthus, Ebionites, Nicolaitans, Cerdo(n), Marcion, Tatian, and the Encratites. Since Acts 8:9–24 describes Simon Magus as a contemporary of Peter, some scholars have guessed that Cerinthus lived halfway between Simon in the 30s and Marcion *ca.* 140, thus about 90. (However, Irenaeus probably drew upon an earlier catalogus of heresies to which he made additions,[4] and we are far from certain that he is giving us exact chronological sequence.) They find confirmation for this in Irenaeus' story about

---

[1] An invaluable guide here is Bardy, "Cérinthe."

[2] It seems unlikely that the *Apocryphon of James*, addressed to ". . . thos" (I 1:1; NHL 29), was written to Cerin*thos;* see Wengst, *Häresie* 35. If it were, one could argue that the *Apocryphon's* statement, "None will be saved unless they believe in my cross" (I 6:3–4; NHL 31), was a correction of Cerinthus.

[3] J. Quasten, *Patrology* (3 vols.; Utrecht: Spectrum, 1966) 1, 152.

[4] A careful discussion of this is found in F. Wisse, "The Nag Hammadi Library and the Heresiologists," VC 25 (1971) 205–23, esp. 213–15.

Cerinthus supposedly gleaned from Polycarp (*Adv. haer.* 3.3.4), namely, that John the disciple fled from a public bath at Ephesus, crying out, "Let us save ourselves; the bath house may fall down, for inside is Cerinthus, the enemy of truth."[5] The fact that Irenaeus relates this information so vaguely ("There are still some people around who heard Polycarp relate . . .") makes it extremely unlikely that Irenaeus himself heard this from Polycarp; and it may well be that we have here an etiological tale personifying in the figures of Cerinthus and John a dispute between Cerinthians and a branch of the Johannine Community.

As for Cerinthus' theology, in 1.26.1 Irenaeus records: "In Asia a certain[6] Cerinthus taught that the world was not made by the First (Supreme) God but by a power that is quite separate and distinct from that Power which is above all. He thought that Jesus was not born of a virgin, for that seemed impossible to him; rather Jesus was the son of Mary and Joseph (conceived) like other men. Jesus is thought to have outdistanced all others in righteousness, prudence and wisdom; and after his baptism, Christ descended upon him in the form of a dove from the Supreme Ruler. Then he proclaimed the unknown Father and performed miracles. In the end, however, Christ withdrew again from Jesus— Jesus suffered and rose again, while Christ remained impassible, inasmuch as he was a spiritual being." Despite this wealth of detail, the vague description of "a certain Cerinthus" raises the possibility that Irenaeus did not know much about him and that some of the doctrines attributed to Cerinthus were the essential traits of the gnostic systems that had developed in the second century and which were under attack. For instance, in 1.26.2 Irenaeus associates Cerinthus with errors of Carpocrates; and in 3.11.1 Irenaeus associates him with errors of the Nicolaitans against whom GJohn was written[7] (see INTRODUCTION IV B3a).

The next source chronologically for information about Cerinthus is the *Philosophoumena* or the *Refutatio omnium haeresium*, once attributed to Origen but now recognized to have been written by Hippolytus, a presbyter originally from the East who lived in Rome at the beginning of the third century. This work, drawing heavily on Irenaeus, was written some time after A.D. 222. In 7.33 and 10.21 (PG 16[3], 3342A, 3438CD) Hippolytus writes of Cerinthus, adding little new to the information supplied by Irenaeus, save that now Cerinthus is located in Egypt rather than in Asia and is said to have derived his system from Egyptian ideas. This localization may reflect a generalization that Egypt was the fatherland of (gnostic) heresies. Theodoret, bishop of the small town of Cyr (Cyrus) near Antioch in the years 423–466, combined the information from Irenaeus and Hippolytus. In his *Haereticarum*

[5] The story of this encounter is told twice by Eusebius (*Hist.* 3.28.6; 4.14.6).

[6] The words "a certain" are in the Latin translation of Irenaeus and in one passage that Hippolytus drew from Irenaeus (*Refutatio* 7.33; PG 16[3], 3342A) but are missing in another passage (10.21; PG 16[3], 3438C).

[7] In fact, however, the only definite NT reference to Nicolaitans is in Rev 2:6,15, which tells us nothing about what they held. It is dubious that the attack on immorality in Rev 2:14 is directed against Nicolaitans; but if it is, the lack of any such charge against Cerinthus does nothing to promote the thesis of his relation to the Nicolaitans.

fabularum compendium (2.3; PG 83, 389) he says that Cerinthus, having had his philosophical training in Egypt, went to Asia to spread his doctrine.

The next source is the *Adversus omnes haereses* of Pseudo-Tertullian, written *ca.* A.D. 210–20 and attached to Tertullian's *De praescriptione haereticorum* as chs. 46–53. It draws on the *Syntagma* of Hippolytus (a smaller, lost collection of heresies, earlier than the *Refutatio*) but adds some new details. In ch. 48 (or 3), 2–3 (CC 2, 1405) we find that Cerinthus taught that the world was created by angels (instead of by a demiurge) who also were responsible for the giving of the Law. Pseudo-Tertullian also reports that the Ebionites (a Jewish Christian movement) were the successors of Cerinthus in some of their ideas—perhaps a development of the earlier tradition of Irenaeus and Hippolytus that associated Ebion with Cerinthus and Carpocrates.

The Jewish Christian connections of Cerinthus are attested elsewhere. Dionysius Bar Salibi (d. 1171) had available material from Hippolytus now lost to us.[8] In his commentary on Revelation (CSEO, Syri, Series II, tome 101, p. 1, lines 30ff.) Dionysius tells us that Gaius (or Caius), a learned ecclesiastic of Rome at the end of the second century (see p. 114 above), is supposed to have denied that John wrote either Revelation or GJohn, works really composed by Cerinthus. Hippolytus, we are told, disproved this claim of Gaius on the principle that the doctrine of Cerinthus was quite unlike that of GJohn, e.g., Cerinthus taught the necessity of circumcision, that the creator was an angel, that Jesus was not born of a virgin, and that eating and drinking certain things were forbidden.[9]

The relation of Gaius to Cerinthus is also discussed by Eusebius (*Hist.* 2.25.6). He cites Gaius (whom he designates as an "ecclesiastic" and thus perhaps as orthodox) to this effect: "Through revelations purported to have been written by a great apostle, Cerinthus presents us in a fraudulent way with narratives of wonderful things supposedly shown him by angels. He says that after the resurrection the kingdom of Christ will be on this earth, that flesh will have life again at Jerusalem and will serve passions and desires . . . and there will be a thousand years of nuptial festivities" (3.28.1–2). Gaius thus makes Cerinthus a millenarian and connects Cerinthus' thought with Rev 20:5–6, a work that Gaius rejected. Cerinthus has become "an enemy of God's Scriptures."

Ca. A.D. 260 Dionysius of Alexandria wrote *Peri Epangeliōn*, a work preserved only in quotations in Eusebius' *History*. The fact that Dionysius is the first Egyptian writer to mention Cerinthus is an indication that Cerinthus was not active in Egypt. Like Gaius,[10] Dionysius makes Cerinthus a millenarian, attributing to his followers the notion that the kingdom of Christ would be on earth and would involve carnal pleasures (7.25.1–3).

Epiphanius of Salamis, the greatest of the heresiologists, devoted a chapter

---

[8] These were the *Kephaleia kata Gaiou* and the *Syntagma* (early third century). Irenaeus was Hippolytus' main source, but he may have had additional material.

[9] According to Dionysius Bar Salibi, Hippolytus referred to a letter written by Cerinthus, a unique indication that Cerinthus committed his ideas to writing.

[10] Dionysius of Alexandria may have drawn upon Gaius, or both may have had a common source.

(28) to Cerinthus in his *Panarion* (*ca.* 375). One must be careful in evaluating information from Epiphanius; for when his sources were deficient, he was not above using informed imagination to fill in the lacunae. He speaks of a Merinthus and the Merinthians; and while he admits that Merinthus may be another form of Cerinthus (28.8; PG 41, 388A), he also portrays Merinthus as second in command in the Cerinthian heresy. He notes a possible doctrinal resemblance between the Cerinthians/Merinthians and the (Jewish Christian) Nazoraeans (29.7.6; PG 41, 401D) and the Ebionites (30.3.7; PG 41, 409B); and he reports that both Cerinthus and Merinthus were denounced by Luke in the Prologue to his Gospel for having tried in vain to write gospels (51.7; PG 41, 900C). It was a common practice among gnostics to write gospels, but only Epiphanius mentions a *Gospel according to Cerinthus.* He also places Cerinthus and Merinthus among the opponents of John (51.6; PG 41, 897C). Epiphanius implies that the Cerinthian heresy was still active in Asia Minor and Galatia in the late fourth century, and that the Cerinthians had a custom of baptism for the dead (28.6.4–5; PG 41, 384CD)—this probably reflects a confusion of the Cerinthians with the Marcionites attacked by Tertullian. If Irenaeus reported that Cerinthus thought that Christ descended upon Jesus after the baptism in the form of a dove, Epiphanius has Cerinthus identifying Christ with the Holy Spirit, a teaching similar to that of the Ebionites (30.14; PG 41, 429BC). Epiphanius also makes Cerinthus one of the troublemakers of Acts 15:24 and reports that Cerinthus was at Jerusalem when Paul returned there with Titus in Acts 21:28 (28.2.3–6; 28.4.1). Thus Cerinthus, the Jewish Christian, becomes a Judaizer of early NT times.[11] Cerinthus is said to have rejected all the Gospels except that of Matthew (28.5.1; PG 41, 384A), a charge that Irenaeus had made against Ebionites. Here we have an example of Epiphanius' tendency to confuse Cerinthus and Ebion (an eponymous figure who probably never existed). He has Ebion preaching in Asia and has John writing to refute him (30.18.1; 51.6.9; 69.23; PG 41, 436A, 897B; 42, 237B). All of this would be explained if Epiphanius knew contemporary Jewish Christian heretics, connected their origins with Ebion whom he confused with Cerinthus, and so imagined a contemporary Cerinthian sect.[12] Cerinthus thus serves as the founder of a Jewish Christian sect that remained faithful to circumcision and other observances of the Law; for them Jesus was the Messiah but human and not to be worshiped.

2. Analysis of Cerinthus' Position

The *Epistula Apostolorum* and Irenaeus give to Cerinthus a decidedly *gnostic* coloring (and in this they are followed by Theodoret and Pseudo-Tertullian). Cerinthus is related to Simon Magus and other gnostics; he proclaims the unknown God and has a semidocetic christology.[13] However, in the infor-

---

[11] In this Epiphanius was followed by Filaster of Brescia, *ca.* 390, another heresiologist.

[12] Confusion about this sect may be represented by the information that Cerinthus taught that "Christ suffered and was crucified but has not yet been raised; he will rise at the general resurrection of the dead," when that information is combined with the claim that there were Cerinthians who denied that there would be a resurrection (28.6.1,6).

[13] See ※ ※1–4 in the list of Cerinthian doctrines on p. 66 above.

mation preserved from Hippolytus by Pseudo-Tertullian and Dionysius Bar
Salibi, Cerinthus emerges as a *Jewish Christian,* related to the Ebionites and
stressing circumcision and forbidden food. In the information from Gaius
(preserved in Eusebius) and from Dionysius of Alexandria, Cerinthus is portrayed as the *millenarian* author of Revelation, dreaming of a kingdom to be
established on earth. Thus before 250 there were two or three different evaluations of Cerinthus in circulation, the number depending on whether the
millenarian portrayal was an aspect of the larger Jewish Christian portrayal.
Similarly there were two theories of his origins: Asia and Egypt. By the time
of Epiphanius these evaluations had been combined and enlarged with imaginative additions. Schwartz, "Kerinthos," points out that Epiphanius presents almost two different figures named Cerinthus; and the discrepancy is harmonized
by positing a development in Cerinthus' heretical thought, even as earlier the
geography was harmonized by supposing that Cerinthus came from Egypt to
Asia.

In modern scholarship, A. Hilgenfeld[14] proposed the thesis that Cerinthus
embodied the meeting of gnosticism and Jewish Christianity; but such a harmonization (shades of Epiphanius!) has generally been rejected by opting for
one or the other of the ancient evaluations of Cerinthus as more authentic.
Harnack was a supporter of the gnostic evaluation, and certainly that has the
earliest attestation. However, we have seen that there are weaknesses in the historical chain of evidence that leads Irenaeus to this evaluation, and it is complicated by Irenaeus' tendency to let his anti-gnostic interests color his reports of
other early groups.[15] Consequently, Bardy argues for the originality of
Cerinthus as a Jewish Christian (also Wurm). The millenarian Cerinthus is intimately related to the thesis of his authorship of Revelation, which seems most
unlikely in light of the book's own claim that it was written by a prophet
named John. (If we recognize that this John was an unknown figure and not
one of the Twelve, there is little reason to doubt the claim.) Moreover, early
antimillenarians like Papias and Irenaeus show no awareness of Cerinthus' having a part in that movement.

I agree with Wengst, *Häresie* 35–36, that there is good reason to take
seriously Irenaeus' portrayal of Cerinthus as akin to gnosticism. We now have
more evidence of gnostic acceptance of the kind of christology that Irenaeus
attributes to Cerinthus. In the gnostic *Second Treatise of Seth* we read: "I
visited a bodily dwelling. I cast out the one who was in it first, and I went in.
. . . He was an earthly man, but I, I am from above the heavens" (VII
51:20–52.3; NHL 330). Also, "They struck me with the reed; it was another,
Simon, who bore the cross on his shoulder" (VII 56:8–11; NHL 332). Moreover, the contrary traditions, one opposing Cerinthus to John and the other attributing GJohn to Cerinthus, could make sense if Cerinthus interpreted GJohn
in a gnostic manner opposed by orthodox Johannine followers. In the INTRO-

14 *Die Ketzergeschichte des Urchristentums* (Leipzig: Fues, 1884) 411–21.
15 See Bardy, "Cérinthe" 346, who points to Irenaeus' handling of the Ebionites. Yet
Wengst, *Häresie* 26, argues that Irenaeus did not really state that such groups were gnostics
and meant only to point out similarities to gnostic positions.

DUCTION (V D1) I have suggested that Cerinthian thought may represent a development of the interpretation of GJohn advocated by the secessionists described in I John—a development as they moved down the path toward gnosticism.[16]

[16] This is similar to the position of Wengst, *Häresie* 61, who thinks that Cerinthus carried the secessionist position farther by drawing out the consequences for cosmogony and by speculations about the pleroma. On p. 29 he judges it possible that Cerinthus used GJohn in defending his christology and that anti-gnostic opponents made him its author.

Appendix III: The Epistle(s) to the Parthians

Above in the first NOTE on I John there is a discussion of the standard titles given to that work in Greek MSS. However, in the Latin tradition there is another title for I John that deserves attention for what it may tell us about the recipients. Augustine's commentary, written in A.D. 415, is entitled: "On the Epistle of John to the Parthians [*ad Parthos*]" (SC 75, 105), a title that portrays the recipients as inhabitants of Parthia on the eastern frontiers of the Roman Empire. Toward the end of the first century, especially under Trajan (A.D. 98–117, the approximate date of I John), Rome was on the move eastward, bringing under its control Mesopotamia and Babylon, which had been subject to the Parthians. Afterward these territories were lost back to the Parthians. This means that a letter could have been sent to Babylon while it was within the Roman Empire, but from the viewpoint of later generations that letter would have gone to Parthia.

It is important to trace the Latin use of this title beyond Augustine. "To the Parthians" appears again, with the innuendo that it is a well-known designation, in the *Contra Varimadum* 1.5 (CC 90, 20). The authorship of this trinitarian work is unknown although it has been attributed to Augustine (by Cassiodorus), Athanasius (by Bede), Vigilius Thapsus, and Idacius Clarus—a battery of fourth-century or fifth-century authors. The latest theory (CC 90, vii) is that it was written *ca.* 450 by a North African author, perhaps in exile in Naples. If so, the influence of Augustine, a North African bishop, would have been strong. It is generally agreed that there was African influence as well on Cassiodorus, who *ca.* 560 spoke not only of I John as an "Epistle to the Parthians" (PL 70, 1369–70) but also of the Johannine Epistles as "those of John to the Parthians" (PL 70, 1125). From the ninth century on, I John was entitled "To the Parthians" in many copies of the Vulgate, e.g., Codex Vallicellianus.

Is there Greek evidence for this title? *Ca.* 730 Venerable Bede in the prologue to his exposition of the Catholic Epistles (PL 93, 9–10) says that among the many church writers who testify to I John having been written to the Parthians was the fourth-century Greek writer, Athanasius, bishop of Alexandria. In terms of Greek Bible MS. evidence, the eleventh-century *minuscule 89* (= Gregory 459) in the Laurentian collection (IV 32) at Florence contains on folio 99r the inscription: "The Second Epistle of John to the Parthians [*pros Parthous*]." The same designation is found in the inscription of a thirteenth-century supplement to the *minuscule 30* (= Gregory 325) in the Bodleian collection at Oxford on folio 56r. The fourteenth-century *minuscule 62* (= Von Soden α 453) in the Paris National Library collection (Gr. 60) contains on folio 38ʳ this designation in a subscription. All of these MSS. have the normal (non-Parthian) titles for the other Johannine Epistles.[1] P. Sabatier[2] reports at second hand the existence in Geneva of a Vulgate MS. referring to I John as an epistle "Ad Sparthos." This corruption may represent a misreading of *pros Parthous* as *pros Spartous* and thus ultimately reflect a Greek title.

This sparse and scattered textual evidence is scarcely compelling in relation to the original destination of I John. However, one must wonder, even if the title is secondary, what gave rise to it. There are two main explanations, one in terms of actual history, the other in terms of a misread original.[3]

HISTORICAL EXPLANATION. The basic thesis here is that the Epistle(s) really addressed Christians in Parthia or Babylon. Acts 2:9 mentions Parthians and the residents of Mesopotamia among those who heard the preaching at Pentecost; but if there were Christians in those areas, would they have been *Johannine* Christians, as supposed in I John? The possible, warlike symbolic references to Parthians in Rev 6:2; 9:17; and 16:12 offer no indication. In the (untrustworthy) traditions that localize the missionary activities of the Twelve, it is generally Thomas (sometimes Matthew) who is said to have labored in Parthia, while John is pictured as preaching in Asia Minor (Eusebius, *Hist.* 3.1). An exception, albeit not a convincing one, is the fourth-century *Acts of Philip* 32 which places Peter and John in the Parthian regions. Another solution, offered by older writers like Grotius and Estius, posits that merchants from John's community in Ephesus brought Christianity to Mesopotamia, making converts among Babylonian Jews to whom the author was now addressing himself. J. D. Michaelis (1788) found in the references to light and darkness in I John 1:5–7 evidence of a community affected by Parthian/Persian dualism, and Grotius and Paulus make similar observations. Nevertheless, as the destination of I John, Parthia finds no scholarly support today.

MISREAD ORIGINAL. The Latin *ad Parthos* may represent a misreading or corrupted transliteration of an earlier Greek title indicating the recipients or even the author. Several ingenious suggestions have been offered for the underlying title. (a) In a minor MS. of Revelation (Apocalypse) the writer John is entitled "the Virgin [Celibate]";[4] and it is theorized (Lücke, Plummer) that there may have been a MS. which designated I John as "The Epistle of John the Virgin" (*Iōannou tou parthenou*). The last phrase might have been corrupted into *tous Parthous*. The tradition that John remained celibate was known in the late second century (Tertullian, *De monogamia* 17.1; CC 2, 1252) and was subsequently espoused by Augustine who is the chief support for the Parthian destination of I John. This suggestion is possible but is completely speculative, without MS. support. (b) Another hypothetical title, "The

---

[1] I am indebted to Professors K. Aland and B. M. Metzger for their help in acquiring some of this information.

[2] *Bibliorum Sacrorum Latinae versiones antiquae* (Rheims: Reginald Florentain, 1743) 3, 965.

[3] Most helpful in all this is A. Bludau, "Die 'Epistola ad Parthos,'" TG 11 (1919) 223–36.

[4] See Metzger, *Text* 205; also TCGNT 731; the MS. is Gregory 1775, and the title was copied in A.D. 1847.

Epistle of John to (the) Virgins" (*pros parthenous*), would be even more likely to be corrupted to *pros Parthous,* to yield in turn *ad Parthos.* Variations of this suggestion have been proposed by Baur, Bertholdt, Cornely, Hilgenfeld, Hug, Reuss, and Zahn. Support is sought in the indication in the *Adumbrationes* of Clement of Alexandria (pp. 10, 646 above) that II John was "written to virgins," and to a certain Babylonian woman! Zahn proposed that the confusion may have moved in the opposite direction: The lost Greek of Clement read "The Epistle of John *pros Parthous*"; but the Latin translator could make no sense of this and so assumed that *Parthous* was an abbreviation of *parthenous,* which he translated as *vírgines.* (Zahn's theory would move the Parthian title back to the second century and to Greek—but for *II* John!—and it might lend support to Bede's contention that a century later Athanasius of Alexandria knew the title.) In either case (Greek original or Latin mistranslation), who would the "virgins" be? II John is addressed to an "Elect Lady" (a church), but she has children and is with difficulty to be symbolized as a virgin.[5] Thinking I John was of later date, Baur wondered if the virgins might not be the women prophets so influential in the Montanist movement. Overall one must judge that the explanation of the title *ad Parthos* through a hypothetical *pros parthenous* is *obscurum per obscurius.* (c) Another misreading possibility posits influence from I Peter and/or James. Just as II John is addressed to an "Elect Lady" (church), so I Peter 1:1 is addressed to "elect sojourners of the diaspora [*diasporas*]"; and just as II John ends with a greeting from an "Elect Sister" (church), so I Peter 5:13 ends with a greeting from "the Co-elect Woman [church] in Babylon." The audiences of the two Catholic Epistles may have been judged by scribes to have been the same, and the Greek *diasporas* may have been rendered in Latin as *ad sparsos* ("to the scattered") which then was corrupted or interpreted into *ad Parthos* (under the catalyst of I Peter's mention of Babylon?). Variations of this complicated theory have been proposed by Eichhorn, Holtzmann, and Schott. Holtzmann ("Problem IV") sees the possibility that the Greek original was *pros tous diasparsamenous* which he relates to a Latin tradition that James was written *ad dispersos* (derived from Jas 1:1: "to the Twelve Tribes in the diaspora").

The hypothesis that a misreading gave rise to the title "To the Parthians" seems more likely than the historical hypothesis, and so the title gives us no real information about those to whom the Johannine Epistles were earlier thought to be addressed. The exact sequence of misreading, however, lies beyond reliable reconstruction.

[5] *Hermas, Vis.* 4.2.1–2, describes the church as a virgin.

Appendix IV: The Johannine Comma

The standard Greek text of I John 5:7–8 may be rendered literally:
    Because there are three who testify,
    the Spirit and the water and the blood;
    and these three are unto one.
The symbolism in the passage is obscure, as we have seen in the Commentary; and so it is no surprise that there have been attempts to clarify and that these have left marks upon the text in the course of transmission. The most famous, which refers to three heavenly witnesses, is known as the Johannine Comma and consists of the words italicized below:[1]
    Because there are three who testify *in heaven:*
    Father, Word, and Holy Spirit;
    and these three are one;
    and there are three who testify on earth:
    the Spirit and the water and the blood;
    and these three are unto one.
The Comma offers some explanation for the Spirit, the water, and the blood (footnote 31 below) but leaves unexplained the exact witness that is borne. It is not surprising then that in the late eighth century, Heterius and Beatus in their response to the Archbishop of Toledo[2] glossed the Comma by supplying information about the contents of the witness. But with or without further explanation the Comma is not pellucid. Isaac Newton, who was interested in the Bible as well as in mathematics, remarked of the Comma, "Let them make good sense of it who are able; for my part I can make none." Without yielding to such despair, one may recognize that, even were the textual evidence for the Comma stronger, one could be suspicious on several scores that the Comma did not belong to I John. The terms "Holy Spirit" and personified "Word" are not found elsewhere in I John. Even in the GJohn Prologue the personified Word is not joined with the "Father" as in the Comma—the GJohn Prologue says, "The Word was with *God.*" The Comma awkwardly has the Spirit as

---

[1] The word "comma" in this usage means part of a book or sentence. The Latin witnesses show variance as to the exact text of the Comma, e.g., most read the heavenly witnesses before the earthly ones, but early instances such as Priscillian, *Contra Varimadum,* Cassiodorus, and the Palimpsest of León have the opposite order. (Information about these authors and works will be given below under A2 and C.) Künstle, *Comma* 48, argues for a variant line 3 of the Comma as stated by Priscillian and the Palimpsest of León: "and these three are one *in Christ Jesus"*—a variant that appears in the genuine text of I John 5:7–8 as well (footnote 9 below). Occasionally "Son" is read for "Word" in the Comma (e.g., Cassiodorus).

[2] *Ad Elipandum epistolam* 1.26; PL 96, 909B.

both an earthly and a heavenly witness, and the latter idea is foreign to the Johannine picture where the Spirit/Paraclete bears witness on earth and within the Christian. No other passage in the NT betrays the trinitarian sophistication of the Comma, which mentions not only three divine entities (as does Matt 28:19) but also that they are one. And while such a statement of unity among the three divine figures would have been helpful in the trinitarian debates of the fourth century, it is awkward in the first-century context of I John where a plurality of witnesses was needed to give force to the argument. (In the undisputed Greek text of I John the three witnesses are "unto one," i.e., of one accord; but they are not one witness.) Today scholars are virtually unanimous that the Comma arose well after the first century as a trinitarian reflection upon the original text of I John and was added to the biblical MSS. hundreds of years after I John was written. Nevertheless, the Comma has had such an important place in the history of textual criticism and in theology that it must be discussed in a serious commentary on the Johannine Epistles. This will be done under three headings: A. The Textual Evidence before A.D. 1500; B. Important Discussions since 1500; and C. The Origins of the Comma.

A. The Textual Evidence before 1500

The key to the Comma lies in the history of the Latin Bible in Spain, but first let us discuss the non-Latin evidence (or lack thereof) pertinent to the Comma.

1. The Non-Latin Evidence

The italicized words above that constitute the Comma appear in only eight among some five thousand known Greek biblical MSS. and lectionaries; and in none of the eight can they be dated before A.D. 1400. In four of the eight the Comma appears in the text; in the other four it is a marginal addition serving as an alternative or variant reading. The eight are as follows according to the Gregory enumeration:[3]

- 61: the Codex Montfortianus (Britannicus), an early-sixteenth-century MS. at Trinity College, Dublin.[4] This codex was copied from an earlier Lincoln (Oxford) Codex (326) that did not have the Comma. Insertions elsewhere in Montfortianus have been retroverted from the Latin.
- 629: the Codex Ottobonianus at the Vatican. It is of the fourteenth or fifteenth century and has a Latin text alongside the Greek, which has been revised according to the Vulgate.

[3] I am indebted to Professor B. M. Metzger for information about these MSS. (see also his TCGNT 716–18), all of which are listed in the apparatus of the 26th edition of the Nestle-Aland Greek NT (1979). I have omitted Codex Ravianus (Tischendorf ω110), preserved in the Royal Library of Berlin. It is of the sixteenth century and has merely copied from the *printed* Complutensian Polyglot of 1514.

[4] Seemingly the scribe was a Franciscan monk named Froy(e) or Frater Roy (d. 1531). As we shall see, this was the codex that forced Erasmus to change his Greek text of the NT, and perhaps the Comma was translated from Latin to Greek and inserted into a Greek codex in order to bring about that change.

- 918: an Escorial (Spain) MS. of the sixteenth century.
- 2318: a Bucharest (Rumania) MS. of the eighteenth century influenced by the Clementine Vulgate.
- 88vl: a variant reading of the sixteenth century added to the twelfth-century Codex Regius at Naples.
- 221vl: a variant reading added to a tenth-century MS. in the Bodleian Library at Oxford.
- 429vl: a variant reading added to a sixteenth-century MS. at Wolfenbüttel.
- 636vl: a variant reading added to a fifteenth-century MS. at Naples.

It is quite clear from a survey of this evidence that the Comma in a form probably translated from the Latin was added very late to a few Greek MSS. by scribes influenced by its presence in Latin MSS. Within the uncontaminated Greek tradition the Comma is never quoted by a Greek author of the first Christian millennium. This silence cannot be dismissed as accidental; for the genuine Greek text of I John 5:7 is quoted (e.g., three times by Cyril of Alexandria) without the Comma. And there is no reference to the Comma by the Greeks even in the midst of the trinitarian debates when it would have been of help were it known. Indeed, the first instance of the appearance of the Comma in Greek seems to have been in a translation of the Latin *Acts of the IV Lateran Council* (1215). Later Manuel Kalekas (d. 1410), who was heavily influenced by Latin thought, translated the Comma into Greek from the Vulgate.

If we turn from the Greek to ancient versions other than the Latin, we note that the Comma is absent from all pre-1500 copies of the Syriac, Coptic, Armenian,[5] Ethiopic, Arabic, and Slavonic translations of the NT—an incredible situation if it were once part of the original Greek text of I John. The Oriental church writers do not seem to know the Comma before the thirteenth century. Let us be more specific, however, about the Aramaic/Syriac tradition. There were no Catholic Epistles in the Palestinian Syriac version. By the mid-fourth century three of the seven Catholic Epistles (I Peter, James, I John) began to be accepted in the Syriac-speaking churches. Nevertheless, all the old copies of I John in the Peshitta and Harclean Syriac lack the Comma. Where it appears in the later Syriac MSS., it has been translated from the Latin Vulgate. While absent from the first 1555 edition of the Syriac NT by Widmanstadt, it is found in the margin of the 1569 Tremellius edition; and by the next century it is incorporated into the body of the text with the supposition that it was original but had been excised by the Arians.[6] No clear knowledge of the Comma appears among the great church writers in Syriac, although a debate has arisen about Jaqub of Edessa (d. 708). In the Borgia collection of the Vatican Li-

5 While the Comma is totally absent from Coptic and Ethiopic NT MSS., it appears in a few late Armenian witnesses under Latin influence. In the Armenian edition of Oskan (1662), which he conformed to the Latin Vulgate, the Comma appears marked with an asterisk. The Comma (with variants known in the Latin) entered into debates of the thirteenth and fourteenth centuries between the Armenian and Roman churches over unification and the use of water in the chalice at Mass. See Bludau, "Orientalischen Übersetzungen" 132–37.

6 Bludau, *Ibid.*, 126–32.

brary there are two copies (133, 159) of a commentary "On the Holy [Eucharistic] Mysteries" attributed to Jaqub, albeit written in a style very different from his other works. In them there is a reference to: "The soul and the body and the mind which are sanctified through three holy things: through water and blood and Spirit, and through the Father and the Son and the Spirit." Baumstark, "Citat" 440–41, discusses the possibility that Jaqub knew a Latin or Greek (from Latin?) MS. that had the Comma. Yet a reference to Father, Son (note: not Word), and Spirit need not reflect a knowledge of the Comma —the mention of *three* witnesses in the standard text of I John 5:7–8 led many Western church writers to think of the Father, Son, and Spirit in Matt 28:19. Indeed, as we shall see below, the Comma probably arose through allegorical reflection on what the three witnesses (Spirit, water, blood) of I John 5:7 might symbolize in relation to the Trinity, especially on the basis of texts in GJohn. Thus we are far from certain that Jaqub was an exception to the Syriac ignorance of the Comma.

2. The Latin Textual Tradition

The two great textual traditions of the Bible in Latin are the Old Latin (OL) and Jerome's Vulgate (Vg). In the instance of the Catholic Epistles, Jerome did not revise the OL; and although eventually a revision appeared in the Vg, we are not certain of the date of origin. In both the OL and the Vg, before the appearance of the Comma, the translation of the Greek of I John 5:7–8 was almost literal.[7] However, in the course of Latin textual transmission, independently of the Comma, variants appeared that show that the passage was the subject of reflection and "improvement" by scribes. (Some of these would be retained when the Comma was introduced.) For instance, Facundus of Hermiane (*ca.* 550) reads I John as saying, "There are three who give testimony *on earth*" (*Pro Defensione Trium Capitulorum ad Iustinianum* 1.3.9; CC 90A, 12; also inferior MSS. of Bede). If that addition was an older tradition, it may have facilitated the creation of the Comma with its corresponding witnesses in heaven. Instead of the masc./fem. numeral for "three" (*tres*) corresponding to the mixed masc. and fem. genders of the Latin nouns for "Spirit, water, and blood," the neuter *tria* appears. This neuter may reflect trinitarian reflection.[8] Still another variant occurs at the end of the passage, after "these three are one," when a phrase is added, whether it be "in Christ Jesus"[9] or "in us."[10]

---

[7] *Quoniam (quia) tres sunt qui testimonium dant, Spiritus (et) aqua et sanguis, et tres unum sunt.* The *quoniam* ("that, because") and *quia* ("because") are alternative translations of *hoti.* The "three are one," for the awkward Greek "are unto [into] one," is a change that ultimately facilitated trinitarian reflection.

[8] See below how Tertullian makes a point of the neuter "one." Some early Latin NT MSS. must have had *tres* and some must have had *tria* in the opinion of Riggenbach, "Comma" 384–85. The neuter appears in Priscillian, who is the first clear witness to the Comma.

[9] Cassiodorus (?), *Speculum,* and the Palimpsest of León. We can see the roots of this addition in the *Adumbrationes* of Clement of Alexandria: after citing "these three are one," he says, "For *in the Savior* are those saving virtues."

[10] In *Contra Varimadum.* Another variant is Priscillian's "water, *flesh,* and blood." The replacement of "Spirit" with "flesh" may have had sacramental overtones, e.g., "water" is baptism, and "flesh and blood" is the eucharist.

As for the Comma itself, in the MSS. known to us it does not appear in the OL until after A.D. 600, nor in the Vg until after 750, although obviously these MSS. reflect an already existing tradition. Even then its appearance is geographically limited, for until near the end of the first millennium the Comma appears only in Latin NT MSS. of Spanish origin or influence.[11] These include:

- Palimpsest of León Cathedral: OL-Vg, seventh century, Spanish origin.
- Fragment of Freising: OL-Vg, seventh century, Spanish.
- Codex Cavensis: Vg, ninth century, Spanish.
- Codex Complutensis: Vg, tenth century, Spanish.
- Codex Toletanus: Vg, tenth century, Spanish.
- Codex Theodulphianus: Vg, eighth or ninth century, Franco-Spanish.
- Some Sangallense MSS.: Vg, eighth or ninth century, Franco-Spanish.

If we try to go back beyond the evidence of our extant MSS.,[12] it is not clear that the Comma was included in the text of I John when St. Peregrinus edited the Vulgate in Spain in the fifth century. After a stage when the Comma was written in the margin, it was brought into the Latin text in or before the time of Isidore of Seville (early seventh century). In the period of the Spaniard Theodulf (d. 821), who served in France as bishop of Orleans, the Comma was brought from Spain and made its way into some of the copies of the Vg written in the Carolingian era. Nevertheless, in a survey of some 258 MSS. of the Vg in the National Library of Paris, among those predating the twelfth century more lacked the Comma than had it.[13]

B. *Important Discussions since 1500*

Granted the poor textual attestation of the Comma, it would merit a historical footnote, not an appendix, were it not for some curious events related to it that have occurred since 1500. It was absent from Erasmus' first Greek NT edition (1516) and from his second edition (1519). D. Lopez de Zuñiga (Stunica), the editor of the Complutensian Polyglot Bible of Cardinal Ximenes (NT printed 1514, published 1522), criticized Erasmus for omitting it and included it in his own work (wherein the Greek form of the Comma was translated from the Latin!). Another critic of Erasmus was the Englishman E. Lee in 1520, and Erasmus replied to Lee that he would have inserted the Comma in his editions of the Greek NT if he had found a Greek MS. that had it.[13a] Between May 1520 and June 1521 it was pointed out to Erasmus that the

---

[11] However, it is still absent in some tenth-century Spanish MSS. (Legionensis and Valvanera), and in a Catalan witness (Farfensis) which is a recension based on earlier witnesses. The Comma is not attested before the tenth century in Latin biblical MSS. with a pure Italian, French, or British lineage. It is absent, for instance, in the following Latin codices: Fuldensis (A.D. 546, Italian origin); Amiatinus (early eighth century, Northumbrian); Vallicellianus* (ninth century, Alcuin tradition); Sangermanensis (ninth century, French); and in the Lectionary of Luxeuil (sixth–seventh century, French).

[12] For a list of post-tenth-century MSS. containing the Comma, see Brooke, *Epistles* 156–58.

[13] See Ayuso Marazuela, "Nuevo estudio" 220–21.

[13a] Usually this is referred to as a promise by Erasmus, but see H. de Jonge, "Erasmus and the Comma Johanneum," ETL 56 (1980) 381–89.

Comma existed in Greek in the Codex Montfortianus (in which, almost surely, the Comma had been translated into Greek from the Vulgate in order to embarrass Erasmus). Reluctantly and not believing that it was original, Erasmus inserted the Comma into the third edition of his Greek NT (1522); and it remained in the fourth (1527) and fifth (1535) editions. Erasmus' reputation for scholarship lent support to the contention that the Comma must be genuine; and the Parisian printer Robert Estienne the Elder (Stephanus) included the Comma (conformed to the form in the Complutensian Polyglot) in his third Paris edition (1550) of the Greek NT. Finally the Comma found its way into the Textus Receptus (Elzevir, 1633) which served for centuries as the standard Greek NT. On both sides of the Reformation it won acceptance. Although it was absent at first from Luther's NT,[14] it was inserted by editors at Frankfurt after 1582. Although Zwingli rejected the Comma, Calvin accepted it with hesitation. On the Catholic side, the Comma appeared in both the Sixtine (1590) and the Clementine (1592) editions of the Vulgate, the latter of which became the official Bible of the Roman Catholic Church.[15] Although Tyndale placed the Comma in brackets in the English NT, ultimately it was accepted by both the KJV and Rheims translations. Even if the Comma had won the battle for acceptance in the sixteenth and seventeenth centuries, the war was not over; for in 1764 J. S. Semler challenged it, thus opening a new campaign of rejection. Doubts increased, and since the nineteenth century no recognized authority upon the Greek text of the NT has accepted the authenticity of the Comma.[16]

In Roman Catholicism still another battle remained to be fought over the Comma. On January 13, 1897, the Sacred Congregation of the Inquisition in Rome issued a declaration (confirmed by Pope Leo XIII on January 15) that one could not safely deny or call into doubt the authenticity of the Comma. Such an extraordinary intervention of church authority on a matter of textual criticism produced consternation; and very quickly Cardinal Vaughan wrote to Wilfrid Ward[17] with the assurance (which he said was officially sanctioned) that the declaration was not meant to end discussion or discourage biblical criticism. This was confirmed by H. Janssens (who was to become Secretary of the Roman Pontifical Biblical Commission) writing in 1900, as well as by the absence of hostile Roman reaction to Künstle's *Comma* published in Freiburg in 1905 (with the Archbishop's *imprimatur*), which attributed the origin of the

14 Luther commented on I John 5:7–8 in the years 1522–24 and again in 1543–45. In his earlier remarks he stated that the Comma had been inserted secondarily into the Greek Bible; in his later remarks he commented upon the meaning of the Comma without raising the critical question of its origin. See Abbot, "I John V. 7." Before the Comma was introduced into Luther's NT, the 1541 edition added "on earth" (a Latin addition mentioned above) after "there are three who testify." I am grateful to Prof. J. Reumann for help on this point.

15 Ayuso Marazuela, "Nuevo estudio" 99, traces the roots of the Clementine form of the Comma to the usage in a Parisian family of thirteen Vg MSS.

16 For the history of the Comma in the printed Greek NT, see Bludau, "Im 16. Jahrhundert" 280–86.

17 The *Guardian* of June 9, 1897, and RB 15 (1898) 149.

Comma to the Spanish heretic Priscillian in the fourth century. How could one reconcile such freedom with the declaration of the Inquisition? One explanation was that the declaration was disciplinary, not doctrinal. A more popular explanation was that the Inquisition was not speaking about the *genuineness* of the Comma (i.e., that it was written by the author of I John) but about its *authenticity* as Scripture.[18] The latter would have to be judged by the norms of the Council of Trent, which declared (DBS 1504) to be holy and canonical those books or parts of books that were customarily used in church over the centuries and belonged to the Latin Vulgate.[19] However, the authenticity of the Comma could scarcely meet such criteria: It was totally ignored for the whole first millennium of Christianity by all but a small section of the Latin Church, and it was not part of Jerome's original Vg. *De facto* the nonauthenticity of the Comma for Roman Catholics may now be regarded as settled; for Rome has permitted church translations of the NT from the Greek rather than from the Latin, and naturally such recent Catholic translations, including those approved for use in the liturgy (NAB, JB), omit the Comma. All recent Roman Catholic scholarly discussion has recognized that the Comma is neither genuine nor authentic.[20]

C. *The Origins of the Comma*

Granted that the Comma was not written by the author of I John, when, where, and how did it originate? The first clear appearance of the Comma is in the *Liber apologeticus* 1.4 (CSEL 18, 6) of Priscillian who died in 385.[21] Priscillian seems to have been a Sabellian or modalist for whom the three figures in the Trinity were not distinct persons but only modes of the one divine person. Seemingly he read the Comma ("Father, Word, and Holy Spirit; and these three are one [in Christ Jesus]") in that sense; and because the Comma fits Priscillian's theology many have surmised that he created it. Before commenting on that, let me survey the subsequent history of the Comma

[18] This interpretation was confirmed on June 2, 1927, by a declaration of the Holy Office (the renamed successor to the Congregation of the Inquisition) stating that, while scholars were free to discuss and deny the genuineness of the Comma, only the Church could decide whether it was authentically a part of Scripture. A good example of the distinction is supplied by the story of the adulteress in John 7:53–8:11. Like other scholars, Roman Catholic exegetes recognize that it was not written by the evangelist but added to GJohn by scribes (thus, not genuine). However, they would also recognize that it is authentic Scripture according to the norms of the Council of Trent, which did *not* make authorship a criterion of canonicity.

[19] There was discussion at Trent of certain disputed scriptural passages the authenticity of which participants wanted affirmed. However, the Comma was not one of these.

[20] See Rivière, "Authenticité" 303–9.

[21] Occasionally it has been attributed to his follower Instantius. Priscillian founded a sect with ascetic (Manichean? gnostic?) leanings in southern Spain *ca.* 375. He was consecrated bishop of Avila but aroused the strong opposition of Ithacius of Ossonoba. In 385 Priscillian was executed in Trier for heresy and magic by the usurper Emperor Maximus, despite the intervention of St. Martin of Tours. The persecution of his followers continued after his death.

among Latin writers before its appearance two hundred or three hundred years later in the extant MSS. of the NT, as discussed above.

1. The Comma in Writers after Priscillian (A.D. 400–650)

Whether or not modalist in origin, the Comma could be read in an orthodox trinitarian manner. For instance, it was invoked at Carthage in 484 when the Catholic (anti-Arian) bishops of North Africa confessed their faith before Huneric the Vandal (Victor of Vita, *Historia persecutionis Africanae Prov.* 2.82 [3.11]; CSEL 7, 60). Indeed, in the century following Priscillian, the chief appearance of the Comma is in tractates defending the Trinity. In PL 62, 237–334 there is a work *De Trinitate* consisting of twelve books. Formerly it was attributed to the North African bishop Vigilius of Thapsus who was present at the Carthage meeting; it has also been designated Pseudo-Athanasius; but other guesses credit it to a Spanish scholar such as Gregory of Elvira (d. 392) or Syagrius of Galicia (*ca.* 450).[22] Recently the first seven books have been published (CC 9, 3–99) as the work of Eusebius of Vercelli (d. 371), but not without debate (see CPL ※105). In any case, the work is probably of North African or Spanish origin; and its parts may have been composed at different times, e.g., Books 1–7 written just before 400, and 8–12 at a period within the next 150 years. In Books 1 and 10 (PL 62, 243D, 246B, 297B) the Comma is cited three times. Another work on the Trinity consisting of three books *Contra Varimadum* has also been the subject of speculation about authorship and dating,[23] but North African origin *ca.* 450 seems probable. The Comma is cited in 1.5 (CC 90, 20–21). Victor, the bishop of Vita in North Africa toward the end of the Vandal crisis (*ca.* 485), wrote the *Historia persecutionis Africanae Provinciae* in the course of which he cited the Comma as representing the testimony of John the evangelist (2.82 in CSEL 7, 60; 3.11 in PL 58, 227C). Early in the next century the Comma was known as the work of John the apostle as we hear from Fulgentius, the bishop of Ruspe in North Africa (d. 527), in his *Responsio contra Arianos* (*Ad* 10; CC 91, 93), and in his *De Trinitate* (1.4.1; CC 91A, 636). The Vandal movements in the fifth century brought North Africa and Spain into close relationship, and the evidence listed above shows clearly that the Comma was known in those two regions between 380 and 550. How and when was it known elsewhere?

To the period before 550 belongs a *Prologue to the Catholic Epistles*, falsely attributed to Jerome, which is preserved in the Codex Fuldensis (PL 29, 827–31). Although the Codex itself does not contain the Comma, the *Prologue* states that the Comma is genuine but has been omitted by unfaithful translators. The *Prologue* has been attributed to Vincent of Lerins (d. 450) and to Peregrinus (Künstle, Ayuso Marazuela), the fifth-century Spanish editor of the

[22] Ayuso Marazuela, "Nuevo estudio" 69.

[23] Implausible are the attributions to Augustine (by Cassiodorus), to Athanasius (by Bede), to Vigilius of Thapsus, to Idacius of Clarus (or Hydatius, a Spanish bishop *ca.* 400). The editor of CC 90 (p. vii) thinks that the unknown North African author may have gone into exile in Naples whence came the later knowledge of the Comma in Italy by Cassiodorus.

Vg. In any case, Jerome's authority was such that this statement, spuriously attributed to him, helped to win acceptance for the Comma.

In Italy Cassiodorus (d. *ca.* 583) cited the Comma in his commentary *In Epistolam S. Joannis ad Parthos* (10.5.1; PL 70, 1373A), although it is not clear that he thought it belonged to the Bible and was written by John. The work of Cassiodorus was a channel through which knowledge of the Comma came also to France. As for England, no MS. of the commentary on the Catholic Epistles by Venerable Bede (d. 735) was thought to show knowledge of the Comma, although two inferior MSS. had the phrase "on earth" after "testify" in the standard text of I John 5:7–8. C. Jenkins has now found a late-twelfth-century MS. (177 at Balliol, Oxford) that does contain the Comma, but by that date it may well have been read into Bede from the Latin Bible.

Overall, then, the evidence from the writers of the period 400–650 fits in with the evidence of the Latin Bible where the Comma begins to appear after 600 in the MSS. known to us. (Isidore of Seville, d. 636, who shows knowledge of the Comma in his *Testimonia divinae Scripturae* 2 [PL 83, 1203C], if the work is genuinely his, may have served as a bridge to the biblical MSS., for his name is connected with editorial work on the Latin Bible.) The Comma was known in North Africa and Spain, and knowledge of it elsewhere was probably derivative from North African and Spanish influence.

2. The Comma in Writers before Priscillian (A.D. 200–375)

Let us now look in the other direction to see if there was pre-Priscillian knowledge of the Comma. On the one hand, del Álamo ("Comma" 88–89) gives evidence to show that Priscillian was quite free with biblical texts and might well have shaped the Comma himself by combining the original I John passage with the reflections of the North African church writers (e.g., Cyprian) on the Trinity. On the other hand, as we saw in A2 above and also in the INTRODUCTION (VI B), there were early Latin additions to I John for which there is little or no support in Greek MSS.; and one may wonder if the origins of the Comma are to be divorced from such earlier Latin textual expansions.[24] Moreover, Riggenbach (*Comma* 382–86) argues on the basis of variants[25] that Priscillian's was only one form of the Comma which, therefore, must have antedated him. (However, Lemmonyer, "Comma" 71–72, points out that variants would have arisen when the Comma was still a meditation on I John 5:7–8 and before it became part of the Latin biblical text.) One way to control these theoretical observations is to check through the church writers before Priscillian for knowledge of the Comma; and because of subsequent history, particular attention must be paid to North Africa.

In Tertullian's *Adversus Praxean* (25.1; CC 2, 1195), written *ca.* 215, he comments on John 16:14 in terms of the connection among the Father, the

[24] Thiele, "Beobachtungen" 72–73, argues that since some Latin additions to I John may have been translated from lost Greek originals, we cannot deny the possibility of a Greek original for the Comma. I judge this quite implausible—see A1 above.

[25] These may be seen from comparing the Comma in Priscillian's *Liber apologeticus*, in *Contra Varimadum*, and in the Palimpsest of León.

Son, and the Paraclete: "These three are one thing [*unum*], not one person [*unus*], as it is said, 'My Father and I are one' [John 10:30]." This is scarcely a reference to the Comma, but it should be kept in mind as we turn to Cyprian (d. 258), another North African.[26] In *De ecclesiae catholicae unitate* 6 (CC 3, 254) Cyprian states, "The Lord says, 'The Father and I are one [John 10:30],' and again of the Father, Son, and Holy Spirit it is written, 'And three are one.' "[27] There is a good chance that Cyprian's second citation, like the first, is Johannine and comes from the OL text of I John 5:8, which says, "And these three are one," in reference to the Spirit, the water, and the blood. His application of it to the divine trinitarian figures need not represent a knowledge of the Comma,[28] but rather a continuance of the reflections of Tertullian combined with a general patristic tendency to invoke any scriptural group of three as symbolic of or applicable to the Trinity. In other words, Cyprian may exemplify the thought process that gave rise to the Comma. That Cyprian did not know the Comma is suggested by its absence in the early Pseudo-Cyprian work *De rebaptismate* which twice (15 and 19; CSEL 3³, 88, 92) cites the standard text of I John 5:7–8.[29] Similarly other church writers, even in North Africa, who knew Cyprian's work show no knowledge of the Comma. In particular, the mid-sixth-century African, Facundus of Hermiane, in his *Pro Defensione Trium Capitulorum ad Iustinianum* (1.3.9–14; CC 90A, 12–14), cites I John 5:7–8 without the Comma (which he does not seem to know) as proof for the Trinity—the trinitarian references are derived from the significance of the Spirit, the water, and the blood. Facundus then goes on to quote Cyprian in the same vein, thus understanding Cyprian to have given a trinitarian interpretation of the *standard* I John text.

Augustine (d. 430) was a North African bishop a generation after the time when Priscillian was a bishop in Spain. A serious debate centers on whether or not Augustine knew the Comma. He never cites it;[30] but in his *De civitate Dei* (5. 11; CC 47, 141) he speaks of Father, Word, and Spirit and says "the three [neuter] are one." To jump from that to a knowledge of the Comma is hasty, for all that it shows is that Augustine meditated in a trinitarian way on

---

[26] It has been argued seriously by Thiele and others that Cyprian knew the Comma, a knowledge which would make second- or third-century North Africa the most probable area of origin. I would rather speak of area of formation.

[27] See also Cyprian's *Epistula* 73.12 (CSEL 3², 787) where the same "three are one" statement is applied to God, Christ, and the Spirit without a reference to Scripture.

[28] Somewhat favorable to Cyprian's knowledge of the Comma is that he knew other Latin additions to the Greek text of I John, e.g., the addition to 2:17 (NOTE on 2:17e). Unfavorable to knowledge of the Comma is his use of "Son" instead of "Word," although that is an occasional variant in the text of the Comma, e.g., Fulgentius, *Contra Fabianum* (Frag. 21.4; CC 91A, 797), applies the "three are one" to the Divine Persons, and speaks of the "Son," while in his *Responsio contra Arianos* (cited above) he speaks of the "Word."

[29] The Pseudo-Cyprianic *Sermo de Centesima*, published by R. Reitzenstein, ZNW 15 (1914) 60–90, is attributed by H. Koch, ZNW 31 (1932) 248, to fourth-century Africa and (possibly) to a follower of Priscillian, drawing upon Cyprian's works. It speaks of Father, Son, and Holy Spirit as "three witnesses" without any reference to I John (PL Supp 1, 65; Reitzenstein, 87).

[30] His commentary on I John does not reach beyond 5:3.

the "three" of I John. We see this clearly in *Contra Maximinum* 2.22.3 (PL 42, 794–95) where he says that I John 5:7–8 (standard text without the Comma) brings the Trinity to mind; for the "Spirit" is the Father (John 4:24), the "blood" is the Son (see John 19:34–35), and the "water" is the Spirit (John 7:38–39). Such reflection on the symbols of I John in light of other Johannine symbolic usage may have been exactly what gave rise to the wording of the Comma.[31] Fickermann, "Augustinus," has recently raised the possibility that in fact he did know the Comma but rejected it (and for that reason never quoted it). Fickermann points to a hitherto unpublished eleventh-century text which says that Jerome considered the Comma to be a genuine part of I John—clearly a memory of the Pseudo-Jerome *Prologue* mentioned above. But the text goes on to make this claim: "St. Augustine, on the basis of apostolic thought and on the authority of the Greek text, ordered it to be left out." No known text of Augustine substantiates this, and yet it is strange that a medieval writer would dare to invent a testimony of Augustine against what was being widely accepted as a text of Scripture and which seemingly had Jerome's approval.[32] Could the Comma have come from Spain to North Africa and have been rejected by him? Such an explanation would mean that the Comma was not part of the Latin Bible known to Augustine[33] and would make it most unlikely that the Comma was known to have had Cyprian's approval.

Without seeking to be exhaustive, I should mention that, besides never being quoted in Jerome's writings, the Comma is absent from the writings of the following major Latin theologians: Hilary of Poitiers (d. 367) who wrote on the Trinity; Ambrose (d. 397) who cited I John 5:7–8 four times; Leo the Great (d. 461); and Gregory the Great (d. 604).

*   *   *

The following picture emerges from the information drawn from the church writers. In North Africa in the third and fourth centuries (a period stretching from Tertullian to Augustine), the threefold witness of the Spirit, the water, and the blood in I John 5:7–8 was the subject of trinitarian reflection, since the OL translation affirmed that "these three *are one*." Woven into this reflection

---

[31] In PG 5, 1300 Claudius Apollinaris of Hierapolis (late second century) interprets the "blood" and "water" of John 19:34–35 as Word and Spirit. Eucherius of Lyons (d. 450), living just after Augustine, makes no reference to the Comma but interprets the water, blood, and Spirit in John 19:30–35 as references to Father, Son, and Spirit who testify (*Instructionum I: De Epistula Iohannis;* CSEL 31, 137–38). A century later Facundus of Hermiane was applying the three elements of I John to Father, Son, and Holy Spirit without clearly indicating he knew the Comma.

[32] Invention would have been all the more difficult because there were then in circulation spurious works of Augustine (thought to be genuine) that cited the Comma, e.g., *Liber de divinis Scripturis sive Speculum* (CSEL 12, 314—a work from fifth-century Africa?).

[33] Thiele, "Beobachtungen" 71–72, would argue that Augustine's silence in reference to the Comma (which is not as serious as his rejection of it) does not necessarily tell us whether the Comma was already present in the OL text of North Africa, for Augustine used a Latin text more closely revised according to the Greek. However, Augustine seems to know some Latin readings of I John not found in the Greek, and the history of Latin MSS. narrated in A2 above does nothing to support the thesis of such an early presence of the Comma in the OL.

were statements in GJohn offering symbolic identifications of each of the three elements, plus John 10:30, "The Father and I are one." Eventually, in the continued debates over the Trinity, the modalist Priscillian or some predecessor[34] took the Johannine equivalents of Spirit, water, and blood, namely, Father, Spirit, and Word, and shaped from them a matching statement about another threefold witness that was also one. If the phrase "on earth" had already appeared in the OL reference to the Spirit, the water, and the blood, the counterpart "in heaven" was obvious for the added threefold witness of the divine figures. At first this added witness was introduced into biblical MSS. as a marginal comment on I John 5:7–8, explaining it; later it was moved into the text itself. Some who knew the Comma may have resisted it as an innovation, but the possibility of invoking the authority of John the Apostle on behalf of trinitarian doctrine won the day in the fifth-century debates against the Arians and their Vandal allies. The close connection of Spain to North Africa explains that the Comma appeared first in Latin biblical texts of Spanish origin. In summary, Greeven[85] phrases it well: "The Johannine Comma must be evaluated as a dogmatic expansion of the scriptural text stemming from the third century at the earliest in North Africa or Spain."

BIBLIOGRAPHY PERTINENT TO THE JOHANNINE COMMA

Abbot, E., "I John V. 7 and Luther's German Bible," in *The Authorship of the Fourth Gospel and Other Critical Essays* (Boston: Ellis, 1888) 458–63.

Ayuso Marazuela, T., "Nuevo estudio sobre el 'Comma Ioanneum,'" *Biblica* 28 (1947) 83–112, 216–35; 29 (1948) 52–76.

Baumstark, A., "Ein syrisches Citat des 'Comma Johanneum,'" *Oriens Christianus* 2 (1902) 438–41.

Bludau, A., "Das Comma Johanneum (I Joh. 5, 7) in den orientalischen Übersetzungen und Bibeldruchen," *Oriens Christianus* 3 (1903) 126–47.

———. "Das Comma Johanneum (1 Io 5, 7) im 16. Jahrhundert," BZ 1 (1903) 280–302, 378–407.

———. "Das Comma Johanneum (1 Io 5, 7) in den Schriften der Antitrinitarier und Socinianer des 16. und 17. Jahrhunderts," BZ 2 (1904) 275–300.

———. "Richard Simon und das Comma Johanneum," *Der Katholik* 84 (1904) 29–42, 114–22.

---

[34] Harnack, "Textkritik" 572–73, argues that the trinitarian modalism of the Comma is close to that of the so-called Symbol of Sardica (343) sometimes attributed to the Western bishops under the leadership of Hosius of Cordoba; and he and Jülicher and Thiele would move the formation of the Comma back into the third century. The evidence, in my judgment, shows the formative process at work in the third century, but we do not know that the Comma existed before the fourth century; and we remain uncertain how soon after its formation it found its way into biblical texts.

[85] "Comma Johanneum" RGG 1, 1854.

——. "Das Comma Johanneum bei den Griechen," BZ 13 (1915) 26–50, 130–62, 222–43.

——. "Das Comma Ioanneum (I Joh 5,7) in den Glaubensbekenntnis von Karthago vom Jahre 484," TG 11 (1919) 9–15.

——. "Der hl. Augustinus und I Joh 5, 7–8," TG 11 (1919) 379–86.

——. "Das 'Comma Johanneum' bei Tertullian und Cyprian," TQ 101 (1920) 1–28.

——. "Der Prolog des Pseudo-Hieronymus zu den katholischen Briefen," BZ 15 (1918–1921) 15–34, 125–38.

——. "The Comma Johanneum in the Writings of English Critics of the Eighteenth Century," ITQ 17 (1922) 66–67.

del Álamo, M., "El 'Comma Joaneo,'" EstBib 2 (1943) 75–105.

Fickermann, N., "St. Augustinus gegen das 'Comma Johanneum'?" BZ 22 (1934) 350–58.

Fischer, B., "Der Bibeltext in den pseudo-augustinischen 'Solutiones diversarium quaestionum ab haereticis obiectarum," Biblica 23 (1942) 139–64, 241–67, esp. 263–64.

Jenkins, C., "A Newly Discovered Reference to the 'Heavenly Witnesses' (I John v., 7,8) in a Manuscript of Bede," JTS 43 (1942) 42–45.

Künstle, K., Das Comma Joanneum auf seine Herkunft untersucht (Freiburg: Herder, 1905).

Lemmonyer, A., "Comma Johannique," DBSup 2 (1934) 67–73.

Martin, J. P., Introduction à la critique textuelle du Nouveau Testament: Partie Pratique (5 vols.; Paris: Maisonneuve, 1884–86) vol. 5.

Metzger, B. M., The Text of the New Testament (New York: Oxford, 1964) 101–2.

Riggenbach, E., Das Comma Johanneum (Beiträge zur Forderung christlicher Theologie 31[4]; Gütersloh: Bertelsmann, 1928) 367–405 (or 5–43).

Rivière, J., "Sur 'l'authenticité' du verset des trois témoins," Revue Apologétique 46 (1928) 303–9.

Thiele, W., "Beobachtungen zum Comma Johanneum (I Joh 5, 7f.)," ZNW 50 (1959) 61–73.

Appendix V: General Observations on Epistolary Format

Letters tend to follow a set format, and one who lacks knowledge of that format can seriously misinterpret a letter. (For example, in a modern English letter one might draw the wrong inference about a relationship between a man and a woman if one gave "Dear" in the opening its normal value and did not realize that it is stereotyped and meaningless in a letter.) This Appendix, then, is meant to aid the intelligibility of II and III John, which, unlike I John, are truly letters and follow set epistolary format.

Our knowledge of letter format at the end of the first century A.D. (the approximate time of the Johannine Epistles) is drawn from several sources: letters contained in Greco-Roman literature;[1] thousands of private and business letters recovered since 1880 in papyri finds, chiefly in Egypt; Jewish letters preserved in the OT, especially in I–II Maccabees, and in the Dead Sea region; the NT letter corpus, especially the Pauline Epistles.[2] Generally, four parts of a letter are distinguished: (A) Opening Formula; (B) Thanksgiving; (C) Body or Message; (D) Concluding Formula. Of course, the habitual distinction of parts does not mean that writers necessarily so divided their thoughts. But having been shaped by the conventions of their times, they would normally follow this progression.

A. *Opening Formula* (Praescriptio)

Occasionally one finds the term "Address" used for this part of the letter; but it is wiser to keep that designation for what was written on the *outside* of the folded papyrus (on the inside of which the letter was written)—the equivalent of our envelope address. The Opening Formula of the Greco-Roman letter consisted of three basic elements (Sender, Addressee, Greeting), although

---

[1] The letters of Isocrates (*ca.* 350 B.C.) seem to be the first public letters preserved for us. Doty, *Letters* 2–3, points to the unique impact of over nine hundred letters of Cicero, made public after his death in 43 B.C., in establishing the pattern of what a letter should be. The letters of Apollonius of Tyana (first century A.D.) show how, contemporaneously with the NT, this genre was used as a vehicle of religious or philosophical teaching. Handbooks of letter style were also developed, e.g., under the name of the writing stylist, Demetrius.

[2] Of the 27 NT books only 6 are not identified in our Bibles as epistles (and 2 of those 6 contain letters: Acts 15:23–29; 23:26–30; Rev 2–3). Of the 21 identified as epistles (correctly or incorrectly), 13 bear the name of Paul. A glance at the *Bibliography* of this Appendix will show that the study of the Pauline letter has been a key factor in analyzing letter format. Some would even argue that by adapting the Greco-Roman letter for his missionary work, Paul became the creator of a literary subgenre: the Christian epistle.

sometimes another element is found,[3] e.g., one in which the writer says he remembers (*mnēmoneuein*) the addressee, or one in which he wishes good health to the addressee and reports on his own (good) health. An example of an Opening Formula is: "Serapion, to his brothers Ptolemaeus and Apollonius, greetings. If you are well, it would be excellent; I myself am well."[4] The Jewish letter of the period uses "peace" for "greetings," and tends to be more expansive in its description of the persons involved, e.g., "Baruch, the son of Neriah, to the brothers carried into captivity, mercy and peace" (*II Baruch* 78:2). Let us examine each of these elements in early Christian letters, paying special attention to parallels in II and III John (but also noting features in which II John is atypical[5]).

SENDER (*Superscriptio*). This involves the personal name of the author,[6] sometimes further identified with a title to establish his authority, and sometimes accompanied by the name of a cosender. Pauline examples identify Paul as "an apostle of Christ Jesus"[7] or as "a servant of Christ Jesus."[8] In over half his letters, companions of Paul are included. In this epistolary feature II and III John are anomalous in using a title for the sender without a personal name (whence the need for such a long NOTE on "the Presbyter" in II John 1, as I tried to determine what was meant by the title and why the author used it).

ADDRESSEE (*Adscriptio*). The simplest form is a personal name; but in the few NT and sub-apostolic letters written to individuals, further identification is supplied (e.g., "To Polycarp who is bishop") and/or an expression of affection. Thus III John's "To the beloved Gaius" is normal Christian style. Most NT and sub-apostolic letters are to communities ("the church" or "the saints") in stated regions. The addressee of II John, *eklektē kyria*, "an Elect Lady," is probably a symbolic designation for a church (rather than a person, "the lady *Eklekta*" or "the noble *Kyria*"), but II John remains atypical in not stating where that community is. Thus, in terms of both sender and addressee, II John conveys little information to those who do not already know the people involved.

GREETING (*Salutatio*). While Jewish letters use "peace" as a greeting, some NT examples have the regular Greek *chairein* (= Latin *ave*), e.g., Jas 1:1, "James . . . to the twelve tribes in the diaspora, greetings."[9] However, neither

---

[3] It is precarious to call this a fourth element, for it may replace an aspect of the third element (the Greeting).

[4] Papyrus Paris 43, from 154 B.C., cited in Doty, *Letters* 13.

[5] I offered detail in the NOTES on II John 1–3 and III John 1–2; here I stress general format.

[6] The custom of using scribes means that the sender or author may not be the actual writer. From the viewpoint of length, a scribe would scarcely have been needed for II or III John; but the sender's level of literacy was also a factor in employing a scribe.

[7] I–II Corinthians, Galatians, Ephesians, Colossians, Pastorals.

[8] Romans, Philippians; cf. "servant of God" in Titus. Among the Catholic Epistles, "apostle'" appears in II Peter and I Peter, while "servant" appears in II Peter, James, and Jude—the last mentioned also speaks as "brother of James." In the Ignatian letters we find "Ignatius who is also called Theophorus [God-bearer]."

[9] Also Acts 15:23, and a secular example in 23:26. Compare the pagan example offered by Wilder, "Introduction" 308: "Ammon to Kallinika, my lady mother, greetings."

the Jewish "peace" nor the Greek "greetings" is typical of NT letters,[10] but a combination of two or three nouns like "grace, peace, mercy, love," characterized as coming from God the Father (and Jesus Christ). III John has none of these and really lacks a greeting. II John has "grace, mercy, and peace" but, quite unusually, as a statement of existing Christian fact rather than as a wish. In the Greco-Roman personal letter, still within the Opening Formula, the greeting was often expanded by a health wish (see below), as the sender prayed for the health of the addressee and gave assurance of his own health.[11] While lacking this, most NT letters expand the Opening Formula by describing the status and privileges of Christians. In Romans, Titus, and II Timothy this expands the designation of the sender; in I Corinthians and I–II Peter this expands the description of the addressee; in Galatians it expands the greeting. Perhaps comparable to this is the expansion of the addressee in III John ("In truth I love you") and the even longer expansion of the addressee in II John.

REMEMBRANCE OR HEALTH WISH. While either of these features is common in a secular letter, III John gives the best and only clear example of an opening health wish in a NT letter. In I Thessalonians the remembrance is part of the Thanksgiving rather than part of the Opening Formula; for after "we give thanks" in 1:2, the letter continues in 1:3, *"remembering* before our God and Father your work of faith."

B. *Thanksgiving*

In Hellenistic letters the Opening Formula is often followed by a statement wherein the sender gives thanks (*eucharistein*) to the gods for specified reasons, e.g., deliverance from a calamity. A good Jewish example is the letter in II Macc 1:11, "Having been saved by God from grave dangers, we thank Him greatly for taking our side against the king." Sometimes there is another prayer that such care will be continued. A different pattern appears in the Pauline Thanksgiving (which is lacking in Galatians and Titus).[12] The introductory wording is usually, "I/we give thanks to [my] God because . . ." The specified reason for the thanks is not deliverance from disaster but the faithfulness of the congregation addressed, and the supplication is for the continuance of such fidelity. Often some of the main themes of the Body of the letter are briefly anticipated in the Thanksgiving. Thus admonitions can appear

---

10 Paul's favorite, "grace [*charis*] and peace [*eirēnē*, probably implying salvation]," is often thought to combine a noun resembling the Greco-Roman *chairein* with the Jewish "peace" greeting.

11 When the letter was to be interpreted by a carrier, another feature of the greeting might be a statement establishing the credibility and credentials of the carrier by clarifying his relationship to the sender.

12 One must speak in generalities, for the Pauline Thanksgiving is not so neatly regular as the Opening Formula. It can consist of a few lines or over 50% of the letter (I Thessalonians). In Eph 1:3–16 and II Cor 1:3–11 an extended blessing precedes the Thanksgiving.

in this section, or a specific paraenetic tone.[13] In II and III John there is no expression of thanks after the Opening Formula, although the issue of health raised in III John 2 is frequently part of the Thanksgiving in ordinary letters. I shall discuss below the expression of joy over the spiritual state of those addressed, which appears in II John 4 and III John 3–4 and which may be seen as transitional to the Body of these letters. The Johannine expression of joy serves much the same function as the Thanksgiving of other NT letters, i.e., that of a compliment which puts the readers in a benevolent mood to receive a message which may contain a demand or even a warning.

C. Body or Message

The Body of a letter is sometimes defined as what comes between the Opening Formula (+ Thanksgiving) and the Concluding Formula—a description that reflects two factors: First, the Body until recently has been the least studied epistolary element from the viewpoint of form; second, it has been thought that there is little by way of set form in the Body.[14] Increasingly, however, thanks to scholars like Funk, Koskenniemi, Mullins, and White, it is being recognized that there are discrete sections in the Body with definite formal characteristics, especially in the transitional sentences at the beginning (Body-Opening) and the end (Body-Closing). In between there is the Body-Middle (for want of a better term), which is more difficult to analyze from a formal viewpoint. Greco-Roman letters offer limited help for studying the formal characteristics of the Body of most NT letters, because the Body of NT letters, especially those of Paul and I–II Peter, is considerably longer than the Body of ordinary letters. II and III John, on the other hand, with their brevity determined by the length of a papyrus sheet, would have been closer in length to ordinary expectation and rules.

BODY-OPENING. Since this element introduces the occasion for writing the letter, tactically it tends to proceed from a hint about what is common in the relationship between the writer and the addressee.[15] And so there is a rather narrow range of opening sentences in the Body of secular letters: "I know [or want that] you should know . . ."; "Do not think that . . ."; "Please do [not] . . ."; "I regretted [or was astonished, or rejoiced] when I heard that you . . ."; "I/you wrote previously about . . ."; "I appeal to you . . ." Equivalent formulas are found in the Body-Opening of the Pauline letters.

[13] It has been suggested that Paul began his oral preaching with a thanksgiving to God and that this practice left its mark on his use of the Thanksgiving in letters. Others, especially J. M. Robinson, stress a background in Jewish liturgical life with its blessings, including the Dead Sea *Thanksgiving Hymns* (1QH).

[14] Many speak of two parts in the Body of the Pauline letter: first, a doctrinal exposé (the Pauline indicative), and then an ethical, paraenetic exhortation (the Pauline imperative). As valid as that analysis may be, it is based on content rather than on form, and ignores the stereotyped features at the opening and closing of the Body.

[15] See White, *Body* 18–19, 69.

Of particular interest for our purposes is the opening expression of joy, chiefly over news of the addressees' welfare. Among the Pauline letters, in Philip 1:4 there is joy in praying for the addressees; in II Tim 1:4 the sender longs to see the addressees so that he may be filled with joy; in Philemon 7 joy has already been derived by the sender from the love of the addressees. In Jas 1:2–3 the author tells the addressees to count meeting trials as a joy, since testing produces steadfastness. It is not without parallel, then, that in II John 4 and III John 3–4 the Presbyter expresses joy. However, since that joy is over the blessed status of the addressees (walking in truth)—the same subject involved in the Thanksgiving of the Pauline letters—and since there is no Thanksgiving in II and III John, one may legitimately ask, as I did above, whether these verses should not be considered as the Johannine functional equivalent to the Thanksgiving and so be treated somewhat separately from the Body.[16] Indeed, one finds the same format in the letter of Polycarp *To the Philippians* (1:1–2); and perhaps one should speak of a step in Christian epistolary format wherein the blessed state of the addressee was acknowledged by using either *eucharistein*, "to give thanks," or *chairein*, "to rejoice."[17]

Another feature of the Body-Opening, transitional to the main message, is a petition or request. In his study of this feature of epistolary format, Mullins points out that characteristically it comes near the beginning of the Body of the letter and has the following features: (a) a background for the petition is usually given first, often in terms of joy over the state of the addressee, as a prelude to asking something more; (b) the petition itself is expressed in terms of one of four verbs of asking, which include *erōtan;* (c) the addressee is written to directly in the vocative; (d) there is some expression of courtesy; (e) the desirable action is described. As one reflects upon II John in the light of these characteristics, one finds the background for the petition in the expression of joy in v. 4, while v. 5 contains other features of the petition: the verb of requesting (*erōtan*), the courteous direct address "my Lady," and the action desired, "Let us love one another."

III John also contains a petition, albeit an indirect one. The formula *kalōs poiein*, "to do well, do a kindness," is found in letters preparatory to a request: "You would do well to . . ."[18] or "You did well to do so and so [please keep it up]."[19] In III John 5 we find *piston poiein*, "to do something faithful," which I have translated as "You demonstrate fidelity"; and this is a Christian variant of the secular formula,[20] preparing for a request to continue the behavior. That request, which comes in v. 6 and which is phrased indirectly, begins with *kalōs*

16 Funk, "Form" 426, makes this suggestion, but then in a footnote seems to regard the suggestion as equivalent to saying that the expression of joy is an opening formula of the Body of the letter.

17 There is little reason, then, to accept the thesis that the Presbyter of III John avoided a Thanksgiving because there was heresy in the church addressed.

18 Funk, "Format" 427–28, discusses this, citing the third-century B.C. Papyrus Michigan I 35: "Would you do the kindness of writing Panakestor?" See also MGNTG 1, 228, who says that is a way of saying "Please."

19 Ignatius, *Smyrn.* 10:11: "You did well to receive as deacons [servants] of God Philo and Rheus Agathopous."

20 The theological overtone of the variant was discussed in the NOTE on III John 5a.

poiein: "You will do a good thing by helping them to continue their journey." Thus both II and III John hew closely to what would be expected in a Body-Opening.

BODY-CLOSING. The other segment of the Body of a Greco-Roman letter, besides the Opening, that has predictable characteristics is the Closing. Here the writer solidifies or recapitulates what has been written in the Body, creating a bridge to further correspondence or communication.[21] In both the papyri and the Pauline letters features of this portion include: (a) a statement why the letter was written—the motivation; (b) an indication of how the addressees should respond to it—either a reminder of responsibility (as often in the papyri) or an expression of confidence (as often in Paul); (c) a proposal of further contact by a visit, or by an emissary, or by continuing correspondence. As Funk has pointed out, this last feature serves an eschatological function for Paul, since through it Paul promises to make present to the addressees the judging or the consoling presence of apostolic authority. Aspects of the "apostolic parousia," as Funk has dubbed it, involve the hope of being able to visit (granted the possibility of a hindrance that will delay) and a reference to the mutual benefits and joy that will result therefrom.

A few Pauline formulas illustrate clearly such features: "We endeavored eagerly and with great desire to see your face because we wanted to come to you . . . for you are our glory and joy" (I Thess 2:17–20). "I myself am satisfied about you, my brothers. . . . But I wrote to you quite boldly on some points as a reminder . . . that by God's will I may come to you in joy and be refreshed in your company" (Rom 15:14,15,32). "Trusting in your obedience I wrote to you, knowing that you will do more than I say. At the same time prepare for me a guest room, for I hope that through your prayers I shall be given back to you" (Philemon 21–22). While scholars treat the promised visit as part of the Body-Closing, normally in Paul it is not the very last feature of the Body (before the Concluding Formula) but occurs earlier. In letters where there is a dispute in the community addressed, the promise of an apostolic visit may be followed by some verses of paraenesis and exhortation. For example, "I shall visit you after passing through Macedonia. . . . Be watchful, stand firm in your faith, and be courageous" (I Cor 16:5,13); and "I write this while I am away from you, so that when I come, I may not have to be severe. . . . Mend your ways; heed my appeal" (II Cor 13:10–11).

II John 12 and III John 13–14 have several distinguishable features of the Body-Closing. In both the Presbyter says he has much more to write, a statement that corresponds partially to Paul's explanation of what has been written and why. In II and III John the Presbyter promises a personal visit that will enable him to see the addressees. In II John the goal of such a visit is spelled out: "so that our joy may be fulfilled"—a clause that matches the reference to "joy" in Paul's Body-Closings. Besides the mention of a visit in the Body-Closing, III John resembles Pauline format in having a previous mention of a visit earlier in the Body of the letter (v. 10), followed by paraenesis in vv. 11–12 as the Presbyter urges Gaius not to imitate Diotrephes whose inhospitality makes

---

[21] White, *Body* 25–30, 59–68, 97–99.

a threatening visit necessary. Indeed, v. 10 raises implicitly the issues of the response of the addressees, for the Presbyter plans to challenge his adversary, Diotrephes, before the community.

D. Concluding Formula

Two conventional expressions marked the end of a Greco-Roman letter, namely, a wish for good health[22] and a word of farewell (*errōso*). An example of how brief this can be comes from the last two lines of Papyrus Oxyrhynchus 746, "For the rest take care of yourself that you may remain in good health. Farewell" (Doty, *Letters* 10–11). In the Roman period an expression of greetings (*aspazesthai*) became customary as a third feature. In this area of epistolary format the Pauline letters do not follow the normal conventions, for Paul never has either the health wish or *errōso*.[23] He does have greetings (*aspazesthai*), however, coming from the coworkers who are with him and addressed to people whom he knows at the community to whom he is writing.[24] Brief examples are: "Greet every saint in Christ Jesus; the brothers who are with me send greetings. All the saints send greetings, especially those who are of the household of Caesar" (Philip 4:21–22); and "Everyone who is with me sends you greetings; greet those who love us in the faith" (Titus 3:15). Besides greetings, Paul's Concluding Formula sometimes contains a doxology of God (Rom 16:25–27; Philip 4:20) and a benediction of the recipients. In eight of the Pauline letters the benediction is a slight variant of this general form: "The grace of our Lord Jesus Christ [be] with you"; but five letters have a shorter form: "Grace [be] with you." These Pauline features are found in the Concluding Formulas of other NT letters as well; for Hebrews and I Peter have both greetings and a benediction, while a doxology is found in Hebrews, I–II Peter, and Jude.[25]

Both II and III John have greetings sent from the community where the letter originates to the addressee, and III John wants the beloved who are being addressed to be greeted "each by name." (This resembles the Pauline custom of listing by name those to be greeted.) A secular parallel[26] reads, "Many salutations to your wife and to Serenus and to all who love you, each by name." In addition III John has the benediction, "Peace be with you," joining I Peter in preferring "peace" to the Pauline "grace."[27] The combination of "peace" and

---

22 This sometimes duplicated an acknowledgment of good health earlier in the letter (Thanksgiving). See Doty, *Letters* 39–40.

23 A form of *errōso*, "farewell," was a regular feature of the letters of Ignatius of Antioch; also Polycarp, *Philippians*.

24 Rom 16:3–23; I Cor 16:19–20; Philip 4:21–22; Col 4:10–15; I Thess 5:26; II Tim 4:19–21; Titus 3:15; Philem 23–24.

25 Greetings (*aspazesthai*) are normal in the Ignatian letters; a benediction appears in *I Clement* and in Ignatius, *To Polycarp;* a doxology appears in *I–II Clement*.

26 From the second century A.D.; this is quoted by Barrett, NTBD 29 (¥22).

27 Imitating Pauline style, scribes added to II John (see last Note on II John 13), "Grace be with you."

"grace" in Eph 6:23–24, and of "peace" and "mercy" in Gal 6:16 confirms the practice of using "peace" as an alternative benediction in Concluding Formulas of Christian letters.

Bibliography Pertinent to Epistolary Format

Doty, W. G., *Letters in Primitive Christianity* (Philadelphia: Fortress, 1973).

Fitzmyer, J. A., "Some Notes on Aramaic Epistolography," JBL 93 (1974) 201–25. Reprinted in his *A Wandering Aramean* (SBLMS 25; Missoula: Scholars Press, 1979) 183–204.

Funk, R. W., "The Apostolic Parousia: Form and Significance," in *Christian History and Interpretation: Studies Presented to John Knox*, ed. W. R. Farmer *et al.* (Cambridge Univ., 1967) 249–68.

Koskenniemi, H., *Studien zur Idee und Phraseologie des griechischen Briefes bis 400 n. Chr.* (Annales Academiae Scientiarum Fennicae, Sarja-Ser. B, Nide-Tom. 102, 2; Helsinki, 1956).

Mullins, T. Y., "Greeting as a New Testament Form," JBL 87 (1968) 418–26.

———. "Petition as a Literary Form," NovT 5 (1962) 46–54.

Robinson, J. M., "Die Hodajot-Formel in Gebet und Hymnus des Frühchristentums," in *Apophoreta*, ed. W. Eltester (E. Haenchen Festschrift; Berlin: Töpelmann, 1964) 194–235.

Sanders, J. T., "The Transition from Opening Epistolary Thanksgiving to Body in the Letters of the Pauline Corpus," JBL 81 (1962) 348–62.

Schubert, P., *Form and Function of the Pauline Thanksgivings* (BZNW 20; Berlin: Töpelmann, 1939).

White, J. L., *The Body of the Greek Letter* (SBLDS 2; Missoula: Scholars Press, 1972).

Bibliographic Index of Authors

This is not a frequency index reporting each reference to an author. The goal is to indicate which footnote or bibliography contains the publishing information pertinent to an author's work. When in the various *bibliographies* several works of the same author have been listed, this index includes a key word from each title in order to differentiate. (References to those works in the course of this volume have employed the same key word.) My general policy with names containing the preposition *de, du, van,* and *von* is to list them under "d" and "v" respectively.

* All Westcott references are to B. Westcott unless the initial A. is given specifically.

Subject Index

In this index, the indication *"see GI"* means *"see* Greek Index" (the index that immediately follows the Subject Index) under the word indicated.

INDEX OF GREEK WORDS

Greek words are discussed in the NOTES on passages where they occur, so there is no need for an index that would cover the whole Greek vocabulary of the Epistles, including rare words that occur only once. This index supplies references for the *principal* discussion of significant words and phrases. As a help to those who rely on transcription, the order of the Greek alphabet followed below (which ignores initial "h") is: a, b, g, d, e, z, ē, th, i, k, l, m, n, x, o, p, r, s, t, y, ph, ch, ps, ō.